14th Annual Meeting of the Special Interest Group on Discourse and Dialogue

(SIGDIAL 2013)

Metz, France
22 – 24 August 2013

ISBN: 978-1-62748-987-4

Printed from e-media with permission by:

Curran Associates, Inc.
57 Morehouse Lane
Red Hook, NY 12571

Some format issues inherent in the e-media version may also appear in this print version.

Printed by Curran Associates, Inc. (2013)

Association for Computational Linguistics
209 N. Eighth Street
Stroudsburg, Pennsylvania 18360

Phone: 1-570-476-8006
Fax: 1-570-476-0860

acl@aclweb.org

Additional copies of this publication are available from:

Curran Associates, Inc.
57 Morehouse Lane
Red Hook, NY 12571 USA
Phone: 845-758-0400
Fax: 845-758-2634
Email: curran@proceedings.com
Web: www.proceedings.com

SIGDIAL 2013

14th Annual Meeting of the Special Interest Group on Discourse and Dialogue

Proceedings of the Conference

22-24 August 2013
SUPELEC
Metz, France

In cooperation with:

Association for Computational Linguistics (ACL)
International Speech Communication Association (ISCA)
Association for the Advancement of Artificial Intelligence (AAAI)

We thank our sponsors:

Amazon Apple AT&T
Heidelberg Institute for Theoretical Studies (HITS) Honda Research Institute (HRI)
La Région Lorraine Microsoft Nuance Samsung SUPELEC

This page intentionally left blank.

Introduction

Welcome to the SIGDIAL 2013 Conference, the 14th Annual Meeting of the Special Interest Group on Discourse and Dialogue. The conference is held in Metz, France, August 22-24, 2013, and is co-located with the 14th Annual Conference of the International Speech Communication Association (INTERSPEECH).

We received a record 115 submissions. Submissions were received from 24 different countries around the world, including countries in Asia (24 submissions), Australia/New Zealand (2), Europe (49), North America (37), and South America (3). Of the 115 submissions, 63 were long paper submissions, 35 short paper submissions, and 17 demonstration submissions.

All papers received 3 reviews, and demonstrations 2 reviews. The members of the Program Committee did a superb job in reviewing the submitted papers. We thank them for their advice in selecting the accepted papers and for helping to maintain the high quality of the program. In line with the SIGDIAL tradition, our aim has been to create a balanced program that could accommodate as many favorably rated papers as possible. Of the 63 long paper submissions, 40 were accepted: 26 were accepted as long papers for oral presentation, 5 were accepted as long papers for poster presentation, and 9 were accepted as short papers for poster presentation. Of the 35 short paper submissions, 17 were accepted for poster presentation, for a total of 31 posters. Of the 17 demonstration submissions, 14 were accepted. In light of the record number of papers and demonstrations, this year SIGDIAL runs 2.5 days, rather than 2 days as had been the convention for the past few meetings.

SIGDIAL continues to serve as a publication venue for research that spans many aspects of discourse and dialogue. This year, the program contained oral presentation sessions and poster papers on discourse, semantics, generation, situated and multi-modal dialogue, dialogue system control and evaluation, models of dialogue and spoken discourse, speech processing technology in dialogue, and dialogue state tracking, as well as on the SIGDIAL 2013 special theme on "Discourse and Dialogue in Social Media". SIGDIAL 2013 also hosted results from the "Dialogue State Tracking Challenge", organized by Jason D. Williams, Antoine Raux, Deepak Ramachandran, and Alan Black. Papers related to this challenge were submitted and reviewed as normal SIGDIAL papers, with 9 being accepted.

We particularly thank the two keynote speakers for their contributions to research on discourse and dialog systems: Bonnie Webber (University of Edinburgh) and Jerome Bellegarda (Apple Inc).

We thank Kallirroi Georgila, Mentoring Chair for SIGDIAL 2013. The goal of mentoring is to assist authors of papers that contain innovative ideas to improve their quality regarding English language usage or paper organization. This year, 7 of the accepted papers were mentored. We thank the Program Committee members who volunteered to serve as mentors: Ron Artstein, Heriberto Cuayáhuitl, Kallirroi Georgila, Andrei Popescu-Belis, Matthew Purver, Carolyn Penstein Rosé, and Amanda Stent.

We extend special thanks to Olivier Pietquin, the local arrangements chair, and his local arrangements team of Calogero Bomba, Danièle Cebe, Jérémy Fix, Thérèse Fressengeas, Matthieu Geist, Sébastien Van Luchène, Claudine Mercier, Nathalie Ruch, and Chantal Sabbagh. SIGDIAL 2013 would not have been possible without Olivier, who worked tirelessly to handle a seemingly unending stream of details for the local arrangements, from organizing the venue, handling registration, arranging student accommodation, planning video recording, helping individual participants navigate public transport in France, and more. We also thank the student volunteers for on-site assistance. Thanks to Casey Kennington for preparing the USB drives with the proceedings.

We thank Amanda Stent, Sponsorships Chair, for recruiting and liaising with our conference sponsors. The sponsorship program enables valuable aspects of the program, such as the invited speakers, conference reception and dinner, and best paper awards. We gratefully acknowledge the support of our sponsors, including Amazon, Apple, AT&T, Heidelberg Institute for Theoretical Studies (HITS), Honda Research Institute (HRI), La Région Lorraine, Microsoft, Nuance, Samsung, and SUPELEC. We also thank Priscilla Rasmussen at the ACL for handling the financial aspects of sponsorship for SIGDIAL 2013.

We gratefully acknowledge SoftConf for use of the START conference management system.

We also thank the SIGdial board, especially officers Tim Paek, Amanda Stent, and Kristiina Jokinen, for their advice and support. In particular we thank Amanda Stent for providing continuity, as a program chair for SIGDIAL 2012.

Finally, we thank all the authors of the papers in this volume, and all the conference participants for making this event such a great opportunity for new research in dialogue and discourse.

Maxine Eskenazi and Michael Strube
General Co-Chairs

Barbara Di Eugenio and Jason D. Williams
Technical Program Co-Chairs

SIGDIAL 2012

General Co-Chairs:

Maxine Eskénazi, Carnegie Mellon University, USA
Michael Strube, Heidelberg Institute for Theoretical Studies, Germany

Program Co-Chairs:

Barbara Di Eugenio, University of Illinois at Chicago, USA
Jason D. Williams, Microsoft Research, USA

Local Chair:

Olivier Pietquin, SUPELEC, France

Mentoring Chair:

Kallirroi Georgila, University of Southern California Institute for Creative Technologies (ICT), USA

Sponsorship Chair:

Amanda Stent, AT&T Labs - Research, USA

SIGdial Officers:

President: Amanda Stent, AT&T Labs - Research, USA
Vice President: Jason D. Williams, Microsoft Research, USA
Secretary/Treasurer: Kristiina Jokinen, University of Helsinki, Finland

Program Committee:

Hua Ai, 360i, USA
Jan Alexandersson, German Research Institute for Artificial Intelligence (DFKI GmbH), Germany
Ron Artstein, University of Southern California Institute for Creative Technologies (ICT), USA
Srinivas Bangalore, AT&T Labs - Research, USA
Timo Baumann, University of Hamburg, Germany
Luciana Benotti, Universidad Nacional de Cordoba, Argentina
Nate Blaylock, Nuance Communications, USA
Dan Bohus, Microsoft Research, USA
Johan Boye, KTH Royal Institute of Technology, Sweden
Kristy Boyer, North Carolina State University, USA
Harry Bunt, Tilburg University, The Netherlands
Sandra Carberry, University of Delaware, USA
Giuseppe Carenini, University of British Columbia, Canada
Christophe Cerisara, Loria, France
Joyce Chai, Michigan State University, USA
Jennifer Chu-Carroll, IBM T. J. Watson Research Center, USA
Mark Core, University of Southern California Institute for Creative Technologies (ICT), USA
Paul A. Crook, Microsoft, USA
Heriberto Cuayáhuitl, Heriot-Watt University, UK
David DeVault, University of Southern California Institute for Creative Technologies (ICT), USA
Giuseppe Di Fabbrizio, Amazon Research, USA

Myroslava Dzikovksa, University of Edinburgh, UK
Raquel Fernández, University of Amsterdam, The Netherlands
Claire Gardent, CNRS/Loria, Nancy, France
Kallirroi Georgila, University of Southern California Institute for Creative Technologies (ICT), USA
Gary Geunbae Lee, POSTECH, Korea
Jonathan Ginzburg, Université Paris Diderot, France
Agustin Gravano, University of Buenos Aires, Argentina
Nancy Green, University of North Carolina at Greensboro, USA
Alexander Gruenstein, Google, USA
Curry Guinn, University of North Carolina at Wilmington, USA
Joakim Gustafson, KTH Royal Institute of Technology, Sweden
Peter Heeman, Oregon Health and Sciences University, USA
Michael Johnston, AT&T Labs - Research, USA
Kristiina Jokinen, University of Helsinki, Finland
Arne Jönsson, Linköping University, Sweden
Pamela Jordan, University of Pittsburgh, USA
Tatsuya Kawahara, Kyoto University, Japan
Simon Keizer, Heriot-Watt University, UK
Alistair Knott, University of Otago, New Zealand
Kazunori Komatani, Nagoya University, Japan
Stefan Kopp, Bielefeld University, Germany
Ian Lane, Carnegie Mellon University, USA
Alex Lascarides, University of Endinburgh, Scotland
Sungjin Lee, Carnegie Mellon University, USA
Oliver Lemon, Heriot-Watt University, UK
Anton Leuski, University of Southern California Institute for Creative Technologies (ICT), USA
Diane Litman, University of Pittsburgh, USA
Ramón López-Cózar, University of Granada, Spain
Wolfgang Minker, University of Ulm, Germany
Teruhisa Misu, Honda Research Institute, USA
Sebastian Möller, Telekom Innovation Laboratories, TU Berlin, Germany
Mikio Nakano, Honda Research Institute, Japan
Ani Nenkova, University of Pennsylvania, USA
Vincent Ng, University of Texas at Dallas, USA
Tim Paek, Microsoft Research, USA
Olivier Pietquin, SUPELEC IMS-MaLIS research group - UMI 2958 (GeorgiaTech – CNRS), France
Paul Piwek, Open University, UK
Andrei Popescu-Belis, Idiap Research Institute, Switzerland
Matthew Purver, Queen Mary University of London, UK
Antoine Raux, Lenovo, USA
Norbert Reithinger, German Research Institute for Artificial Intelligence (DFKI GmbH), Germany
Hannes Rieser, Bielefeld University, Germany
Carolyn Penstein Rosé, Carnegie Mellon University, USA
David Schlangen, Bielefeld University, Germany
Elizabeth Shriberg, Microsoft Research, USA
Candace Sidner, Worcester Polytechnic Institute, USA
Gabriel Skantze, KTH Royal Institute of Technology, Sweden
Manfred Stede, University of Potsdam, Germany
Amanda Stent, AT&T Labs - Research, USA

Matthew Stone, Rutgers University, USA
Svetlana Stoyanchev, Columbia University, USA
Kristina Striegnitz, Union College, USA
Marc Swerts, Tilburg University, The Netherlands
Takenobu Tokunaga, Tokyo Institute of Technology, Japan
Thora Tenbrink, Bangor University, UK
Joel Tetreault, Nuance Communications, USA
Blaise Thomson, University of Cambridge, UK
Gokhan Tur, Microsoft Research, USA
Renata Vieira, PUCRS, Brazil
Marilyn Walker, University of California at Santa Cruz, USA
Nigel Ward, University of Texas at El Paso, USA
Kai Yu, Shanghai Jiao Tong University, China
Ingrid Zukerman, Monash University, Australia

Additional Reviewers:

Hendrik Buschmeier, Bielefeld University, Germany
Lin Chen, University of Illinois at Chicago, USA
Nina Dethlefs, Heriot-Watt University, UK
Klaus-Peter Engelbrecht, TU-Berlin, Germany
Roger Granada, IRIT, France
Stefan Hillmann, TU-Berlin, Germany
Ethan O. Selfridge, Oregon Health and Sciences University, USA

Invited Speakers:

Jerome Bellegarda, Apple Inc, USA
Bonnie Webber, University of Edinburgh, UK

Table of Contents

Conference Program

Thursday, August 22, 2013

9:00 Welcome and conference overview

Keynote I

9:10 *Discourse Relations, Discourse Structure, Discourse Semantics*
Bonnie Webber

10:10 Break

Oral session: Discourse, semantics, and generation

10:35 *Expressivity and comparison of models of discourse structure*
Antoine Venant, Nicholas Asher, Philippe Muller, Pascal Denis and Stergos Afantenos

10:55 *Unsupervised structured semantic inference for spoken dialog reservation tasks*
Alejandra Lorenzo, Lina Rojas-Barahona and Christophe Cerisara

11:15 *Toward a Better Understanding of Causality between Verbal Events: Extraction and Analysis of the Causal Power of Verb-Verb Associations*
Mehwish Riaz and Roxana Girju

11:35 *Training an integrated sentence planner on user dialogue*
Brian McMahan and Matthew Stone

11:55 Lunch

Oral session: Dialog and Discourse in social media and interpersonal relationships

13:00 *Topic Independent Identification of Agreement and Disagreement in Social Media Dialogue*
Amita Misra and Marilyn Walker

13:20 *Automatic Prediction of Friendship via Multi-model Dyadic Features*
Zhou Yu, David Gerritsen, Amy Ogan, Alan Black and Justine Cassell

13:40 *Stance Classification in Online Debates by Recognizing Users' Intentions*
Sarvesh Ranade, Rajeev Sangal and Radhika Mamidi

Thursday, August 22, 2013 (continued)

Poster and demonstration session

14:00 Poster "madness" (short presentations of each poster)

14:25 Poster session (with coffee)

Generating More Specific Questions for Acquiring Attributes of Unknown Concepts from Users
Tsugumi Otsuka, Kazunori Komatani, Satoshi Sato and Mikio Nakano

Modeling Collaborative Referring for Situated Referential Grounding
Changsong Liu, Rui Fang, Lanbo She and Joyce Chai

A quantitative view of feedback lexical markers in conversational French
Laurent Prévot, Brigitte Bigi and Roxane Bertrand

On the contribution of discourse structure to topic segmentation
Paula Cardoso, Maite Taboada and Thiago Pardo

Will my Spoken Dialogue System be a Slow Learner ?
Layla El Asri and Romain Laroche

Model-free POMDP optimisation of tutoring systems with echo-state networks
Lucie Daubigney, Matthieu Geist and Olivier Pietquin

Patterns of Importance Variation in Spoken Dialog
Nigel Ward and Karen Richart-Ruiz

Reinforcement Learning of Two-Issue Negotiation Dialogue Policies
Kallirroi Georgila

Dialogue Act Recognition in Synchronous and Asynchronous Conversations
Maryam Tavafi, Yashar Mehdad, Shafiq Joty, Giuseppe Carenini and Raymond Ng

Improving Interaction Quality Recognition Using Error Correction
Stefan Ultes and Wolfgang Minker

Thursday, August 22, 2013 (continued)

Oral session: Situated and multi-modal dialog

16:30 *Exploring the effects of gaze and pauses in situated human-robot interaction*
Gabriel Skantze, Anna Hjalmarsson and Catharine Oertel

16:50 *Interpreting Situated Dialogue Utterances: an Update Model that Uses Speech, Gaze, and Gesture Information*
Casey Kennington, Spyros Kousidis and David Schlangen

17:10 *Multimodality and Dialogue Act Classification in the RoboHelper Project*
Lin Chen and Barbara Di Eugenio

17:30 *Verbal indicators of psychological distress in interactive dialogue with a virtual human*
David DeVault, Kallirroi Georgila, Ron Artstein, Fabrizio Morbini, David Traum, Stefan Scherer, Albert (Skip) Rizzo and Louis-Philippe Morency

Day 1 conclusion and banquet

17:50 Informational announcements

19:00 Buses depart venue for banquet

Friday, August 23, 2013

9:00 Day overview and informational announcements

Keynote II

9:05 *Spoken Language Understanding for Natural Interaction: the Siri Experience*
Jerome Bellegarda

10:05 Break

Oral session: Dialog system control and evaluation

10:30 *Learning Dialogue Management Models for Task-Oriented Dialogue with Parallel Dialogue and Task Streams*
Eun Ha, Christopher Mitchell, Kristy Boyer and James Lester

10:50 *POMDP-based dialogue manager adaptation to extended domains*
Milica Gasic, Catherine Breslin, Matthew Henderson, Dongho Kim, Martin Szummer, Blaise Thomson, Pirros Tsiakoulis and Steve Young

11:10 *Training and evaluation of an MDP model for social multi-user human-robot interaction*
Simon Keizer, Mary Ellen Foster, Oliver Lemon, Andre Gaschler and Manuel Giuliani

11:30 *Evaluation of Speech Dialog Strategies for Internet Applications in the Car*
Hansjörg Hofmann, Ute Ehrlich, André Berton, Angela Mahr, Rafael Math and Christian Müller

11:50 Lunch, business meeting, and sponsor talks

Oral session: Models of dialog and spoken discourse

13:30 *Predicting Tasks in Goal-Oriented Spoken Dialog Systems using Semantic Knowledge Bases*
Aasish Pappu and Alexander Rudnicky

13:50 *Surface Text based Dialogue Models for Virtual Humans*
Sudeep Gandhe and David Traum

14:10 *Speech Reduction, Intensity, and F0 Shape are Cues to Turn-Taking*
Oliver Niebuhr, Karin Görs and Evelin Graupe

Poster and demonstration session

14:30 Poster "madness" (short presentations of each poster)

14:55 Poster session (with coffee)

Gesture Semantics Reconstruction Based on Motion Capturing and Complex Event Processing: a Circular Shape Example
Thies Pfeiffer, Florian Hofmann, Florian Hahn, Hannes Rieser and Insa Röpke

Open-ended, Extensible System Utterances Are Preferred, Even If They Require Filled Pauses
Timo Baumann and David Schlangen

A Four-Participant Group Facilitation Framework for Conversational Robots
Yoichi Matsuyama, Iwao Akiba, Akihiro Saito and Tetsunori Kobayashi

Tacit Social Contracts for Wheelchairs
Daniel Couto Vale and Vivien Mast

Laugher and Topic Transition in Multiparty Conversation
Emer Gilmartin, Francesca Bonin, Carl Vogel and Nick Campbell

IMHO: An Exploratory Study of Hedging in Web Forums
Liliana Mamani Sanchez and Carl Vogel

Impact of ASR N-Best Information on Bayesian Dialogue Act Recognition
Heriberto Cuayáhuitl, Nina Dethlefs, Helen Hastie and Oliver Lemon

Investigating speaker gaze and pointing behaviour in human-computer interaction with the mint.tools collection
Spyros Kousidis, Casey Kennington and David Schlangen

In-Context Evaluation of Unsupervised Dialogue Act Models for Tutorial Dialogue
Aysu Ezen-Can and Kristy Boyer

Spoken Dialog Systems for Automated Survey Interviewing
Michael Johnston, Patrick Ehlen, Frederick G. Conrad, Michael F. Schober, Christopher Antoun, Stefanie Fail, Andrew Hupp, Lucas Vickers, Huiying Yan and Chan Zhang

Friday, August 23, 2013 (continued)

Oral session: Speech processing technology in dialog

16:55 *A Data-driven Model for Timing Feedback in a Map Task Dialogue System*
Raveesh Meena, Gabriel Skantze and Joakim Gustafson

17:15 *Continuously Predicting and Processing Barge-in During a Live Spoken Dialogue Task*
Ethan Selfridge, Iker Arizmendi, Peter Heeman and Jason Williams

17:35 *Which ASR should I choose for my dialogue system?*
Fabrizio Morbini, Kartik Audhkhasi, Kenji Sagae, Ron Artstein, Dogan Can, Panayiotis Georgiou, Shri Narayanan, Anton Leuski and David Traum

Day 2 conclusion

17:55 Informational announcements

Saturday, August 24, 2013

	Oral session: Dialog state tracking
9:00	Session introduction
9:05	*The Dialog State Tracking Challenge* Jason Williams, Antoine Raux, Deepak Ramachandran and Alan Black
9:25	*Recipe For Building Robust Spoken Dialog State Trackers: Dialog State Tracking Challenge System Description* Sungjin Lee and Maxine Eskenazi
9:40	*A Simple and Generic Belief Tracking Mechanism for the Dialog State Tracking Challenge: On the believability of observed information* Zhuoran Wang and Oliver Lemon
9:55	*Multi-domain learning and generalization in dialog state tracking* Jason Williams
10:10	*Structured Discriminative Model For Dialog State Tracking* Sungjin Lee
	Poster session: Dialog state tracking
10:25	Poster "madness" (short presentations of each poster)
10:35	Poster session (with coffee)
	Comparison of Bayesian Discriminative and Generative Models for Dialogue State Tracking Lukáš Žilka, David Marek, Matěj Korvas and Filip Jurčíček
	Dialog State Tracking using Conditional Random Fields Hang Ren, Weiqun Xu, Yan Zhang and Yonghong Yan
	Engineering Statistical Dialog State Trackers: A Case Study on DSTC Daejoong Kim, Jaedeug Choi Choi, Kee-Eung Kim, Jungsu Lee and Jinho Sohn
	Deep Neural Network Approach for the Dialog State Tracking Challenge Matthew Henderson, Blaise Thomson and Steve Young
	Future challenge task information sessions
11:50	Dialog state tracking challenge 2
12:05	The REAL dialog challenge
	Conference closing
12:20	Best paper award ceremony and closing

Discourse Relations, Discourse Structure, Discourse Semantics

Bonnie Webber
Institute for Language, Cognition and Computation
School of Informatics, University of Edinburgh
10 Crichton Street, Edinburgh EH8 9AB, Scotland, UK
bonnie@inf.ed.ac.uk

It is generally accepted that a discourse connective expresses a semantic and/or pragmatic relation between its matrix sentence or clause and something in the previous discourse. Usually the sense of this relation is expressed as a label, often within a hierarchy of sense labels. But the meaning of these labels may vary from system to system, and the same connective may be assigned different labels in different systems. Given this, we might learn more and make better predictions if (i) sense labels were associated with (some of) their entailments and (ii) connectives were characterized in terms of both their formal properties and their use conditions. I'll give examples of both.

The above-mentioned predictions tie in with an interesting property of Penn Discourse TreeBank annotation. Annotators were allowed to assign multiple sense labels to a single connective, to imply that all the senses held simultaneously. For those cases where adjacent sentences lacked an intervening connective, annotators were instructed to try to insert one or more connectives that (together) expressed the relation(s) between the sentences. Here too, in many cases, annotators inserted a single connective to which they assigned multiple meanings, Other times they inserted multiple connectives to convey the relation(s) they took as being expressed. Some of this will be shown to make more sense in terms of the entailments and formal properties of the connectives than in terms of any sense labels.

I'll close by trying to distinguish discourse connectives that are associated with coordinating or subordinating relations between sentences or clauses, which is an feature of discourse structure, from those connectives that simply convey additional relevant semantic or pragmatic content.

Expressivity and comparison of models of discourse structure

Antoine Venant[1] **Nicholas Asher**[2] **Philippe Muller**[1] **Pascal Denis**[3] **Stergos Afantenos**[1]
(1) IRIT, Toulouse University, France, (2) IRIT, CNRS, France (3) Mostrare, INRIA, France *

Abstract

Several discourse annotated corpora now exist for NLP. But they use different, not easily comparable annotation schemes: are the structures these schemes describe incompatible, incomparable, or do they share interpretations? In this paper, we relate three types of discourse annotation used in corpora or discourse parsing: (i) RST, (ii) SDRT, and (iii) dependency tree structures. We offer a common language in which their structures can be defined and furnished a range of interpretations. We define translations between RST and DT preserving these interpretations, and introduce a similarity measure for discourse representations in these frameworks. This will enable researchers to exploit different types of discourse annotated data for automated tasks.

1 Introduction

Computer scientists and linguists now largely agree that representing discourse structure as a hierarchical relational structure over discourse units linked by discourse relations is appropriate to account for a variety of interpretative tasks. There is also some agreement over the taxonomy of discourse relations —almost all current theories include expressions that refer to relations like *Elaboration, Explanation, Result, Narration, Contrast, Attribution*. Sanders, Spooren, and Noordman 1992; Bateman and Rondhuis 1997 discuss correspondences between different taxonomies.

Different theories, however, assume different sets of constraints that govern these representations; some advocate trees: RST Mann and Thompson 1987, DLTAG Webber et al. 1999; others, graphs of different sorts: SDRT Asher and Lascarides 2003, Graphbank Wolf and Gibson 2005. Consider:

(1) ["he was a very aggressive firefighter.]$_{C_1}$ [he loved the work he was in,"]$_{C_2}$ [said acting fire chief Lary Garcia.]$_{C_3}$. ["He couldn't be bested in terms of his willingness and his ability to do something to help you survive."]$_{C_4}$ (from Egg and Redeker 2010)

Using RST, Egg and Redeker 2010 provide the tree annotated with nuclearity features for this example (given by the linear encoding in (s_1)), while SDRT provides a different kind of structure (s_2). Dependency trees (DTs), similar to syntactic dependency trees and used in Muller et al. 2012 for automated parsing, give yet another representation (s_3). Elab stands for elaboration, Attr for attribution, and Cont for continuation.

$$Elab_1(Attr(Elab_2(C_{1N}, C_{2S})_N, C_{3S})_N, C_{4S}) \quad (s_1)$$

$$Attr(\pi, C_3) \wedge \pi : \mathrm{Elab}(C_1, \pi_1) \wedge \pi_1 : \mathrm{Cont}(C_2, C_4) \quad (s_2)$$

$$Elab_1(C_1, C_2) \wedge \mathrm{Attr}(C_1, C_3) \wedge \mathrm{Elab}(C_1, C_4) \quad (s_3)$$

Several corpora now exist annotated with such structures: RSTTB Carlson, Marcu, and Okurowski 2002, Discor Baldridge, Asher, and Hunter 2007, GraphBank[1]. But how exactly do these annotations compare? In the illustrative example chosen and for the relation types they agree on (Elaboration and Attribution), different annotation models and theoretical frameworks invoke different numbers of instances of these relations and assign the instances different arguments or different scopes, at least on the surface. In this paper we develop a method of comparing the scopes of relations in different types of structures by developing a notion of *interpretation* shared between different structures. This interpretation specifies the set of *possible scopes of relations* compatible with a given structure. This theoretical work is important for furthering empirical research on discourse. Discourse annotations are expensive. It behooves researchers to use as much data as they can, annotated in several formalisms, while pursuing prediction or evaluation in their chosen theory. This paper provides a theoretical basis to do this.

What a given structure expresses exactly is often not clear; some discourse theories are not completely formalized or lack a worked out semantics. Nevertheless, in all of them rhetorical relations have semantic consequences bearing on tasks like text summarization, textual entailment, anaphora resolution, as well as the temporal, spatial and thematic organization of a text Hobbs, Stickel, and Martin 1993; Kehler 2002; Asher 1993; Lascarides and Asher 1993; Hobbs, Stickel, and Martin 1993; Hitzeman, Moens, and Grover 1995, *inter alia*. Theories like SDRT or Polanyi et al. 2004 adopt a conception of discourse structure as logical form. Discourse structures are like logical formulae and relations

*This research was supported by ERC grant 269427.

[1]The Penn Discourse Treebank Prasad et al. 2008 could also be considered as a corpus with partial dependency structures.

function like logical operators on the meaning of their arguments. Hence their exact scope has great semantic impact on the phenomena we have mentioned, in exactly the way the relative scope of quantifiers make a great semantic difference in first order logic. By concentrating on exact meaning representations, however, the syntax-semantics interface becomes quite complex: as happens with quantifiers at the intra sentential level, discourse relations might semantically require a scope that is, at least a priori, not determined by syntactic considerations alone and violates surface order (see s_2).

Other theories like Polanyi's Linguistic Discourse Model (LDM) of Polanyi 1985; Polanyi and Scha 1984, and DLTAG Webber et al. 1999 explicitly adopt a syntactic point of view, and RST with strongly constrained (tree-shaped) structures is subject to parsing approaches duVerle and Prendinger 2009; Sagae 2009; Subba and Di Eugenio 2009 that adhere to the syntactic approach in adopting decoding strategies of syntactic parsing. In such theories, discourse structure representations, subject to syntactic constraints (*e.g.* dominance of spans of text one over another) respect surface order but do not always and unproblematically yield a semantic interpretation that fits intuitions. According to Marcu 1996, an RST tree is not by itself sufficient to generate desired predictions; he employs the *nuclearity principle*, NP, as an additional interpretation principle on scopes of relations.

We focus on two theories: RST, which offers the model for the annotations of the RST treebank Carlson, Marcu, and Okurowski 2002 and the Potsdam commentary corpus Stede 2004, and on SDRT, which counts several small corpora annotated with semantic scopes, Discor Baldridge, Asher, and Hunter 2007 and Annodis Afantenos et al. 2012. We describe these theories in section 2. We will also compare these two theories to dependency tree representations of discourse Muller et al. 2012. Section 3 introduces a language for describing semantics scopes of relations that is powerful enough to: i) compare the expressiveness (in terms of what different scopes can be expressed) of the different formalisms considered; ii) give a formal target language that will provide comparable interpretations of the different structures at stake. Section 4 discusses Marcu's nuclearity principle and proposes an alternative way to interpret an RST tree as a set of different possible scopes expressed in our language. Section 5 provides intertranslability results between the different formalisms. Section 6 defines a measure of similarity over discourse structures in different formalisms.

2 Discourse formalisms

These formalisms we introduce here all require the input text to be segmented into elementary units (EDUs). The definition of what an EDU is varies slightly with the formalism, but roughly corresponds to the clause level in RST, SDRT and other theories. We assume a segmentation common to the different formalisms and use examples with a non controversial and intuitive segmentation.

Rhetorical Structure Theory (RST), the theory underlying the RST-Treebank is the most used corpus for discourse parsing, cf. duVerle and Prendinger 2009, Subba and Di Eugenio 2009, *inter alia*.

In its Mann and Thompson 1987 formulation, RST builds a descriptive tree for the discourse by the recursive application of *schemata* in a bottom-up procedure. Each schema application ideally reflects the most plausible relation the writer intended between two contiguous spans of text, as well as hierarchical information about the arguments of the relation, distinguishing between *nuclei* as essential arguments of a relation and *satellites* as more contingent parts. The set of RS Trees is inductively defined as follows:

1- An EDU is a RS Tree.

2- if R is a nucleus-statellite relation symbol, s_1 and s_2 are both RS Trees with contiguous spans (the leftmost leaf in s_2 is textually located right after the rightmost one in s_1), and $\langle a_1, a_2\rangle \in \{\langle N, S\rangle; \langle S, N\rangle\}$ then $R(t_1\_a_1, t_2\_a_2)$ is an RS Tree.

3- if R is a multinuclear relation symbol and $\langle s_1, \ldots, s_n\rangle$ are n RS Trees with contiguous spans then $R(s_1\_N, \ldots, s_n\_N)$ is an RS Tree.

Following Mann and Thompson 1987 a complete RS tree makes explicit the content the author intended to communicate. RS Trees are graphically represented Marcu 1996 with intermediate nodes labelled with relation names, leaves with symbols referring to EDUs, and edges with nucleus/satellite distinctions.

Segmented Discourse Representation Theory (SDRT), our second case-study theory, inherits a framework from dynamic semantics and enriches it with rhetorical relations. The set of SDRSs is inductively defined as follows:

Assume a set of rhetorical relations $\mathcal{R}$, distinguished between coordinating and subordinating relations.

- Any EDU is an SDRS.
- Any Complex Discourse Unit (CDU) is a SDRS.
- a CDU is an acyclic labelled graph (A, E) where every node is a discourse unit (DU) or SDRS and each labelled edge is a discourse relation such that:

(i) every node is connected to some other node;

(ii) no two nodes are linked by subordinating and coordinating relations,

(iii) given EDUs $a_1, \ldots, a_{n+1}$ in their textual order that yield a CDU $(A, E) = G$, each EDU a_{j+1} $j < n$ is linked either: (a) to nodes on the right frontier of the CDU $G*$ a subgraph of G constructed from $a_1, \ldots, a_j$; or (b) to one or more nodes in $G' = (A', G')$, a subgraph of G, which linked to one or more nodes on the right frontier of the graph $G*$, and where G' is constructed from a subset of $a_{j+2}, \ldots a_n$.

The right frontier of a graph G consists of the nodes a that are not the left arguments to any coordinating relation and for which if any node b is linked to some node dominating a, then there is a path of subordinating relations from b to a.

A Segmented Discourse Representation Structure (SDRS), is assigned a recursively computed meaning in terms of context-change potential (relation between pairs of $\langle$ world, assignation function $\rangle$) in the tradition of dynamic semantics. The semantics of a complex constituent is compositionally defined from the semantics of rhetorical relations and the interpretation of its subconstituents. In the base case of an EDU, the semantics is given in dynamic semantics.

We also consider dependency trees (DTs). Muller et al. 2012 derive DTs from the SDRSs of the ANNODIS corpus to get a reduced search space, simplifying automated discourse parsing. A DT is an SDRS in which there are no CDUs and there is a unique arc between any two nodes. Muller et al. 2012 provide a procedure from SDRSs to DTs, which we slightly modify to respect the Frontier Contraint that they use. ζ works in a bottom-up fashion replacing every CDU X that is an argument of a rhetorical relation in γ by their top-most immediate sub-constituent which do not appear on the right of any relation in X, or distributing the top relation when necessary to preserve projectivity. To give a simple example: $\zeta(R([R'(a,[R''(b,c)])],d)) = \zeta(R([R'(a,b) \wedge R''(b,c)],d)) = R(a,d) \wedge R'(a,b) \wedge R''(b,c)$. (1) provides a more complicated example we discuss in Section 6).

3 Describing the scope of relations

We provide here a language expressive and general enough to express the structures of the 3 theories. All our case-study theories involve structures described by a list of rhetorical relations and their arguments. Two things may vary: first, the nature of the arguments. SDRT for instance, introduces *complex constituents* as arguments of relations (*e.g.* $\begin{cases} \pi : R_{subord}(b,c) \\ R_{subord}(a,\pi) \end{cases}$), which finds a counterpart within RS Trees, where a relation may directly appear as argument of another ($R(a_N, R(b_N, c_S)_S)$) but not within dependency trees. Second, the set of constraints that restrict the possible lists of such relations can vary across theories (e.g. right frontier, or requirement for a tree structure).

To deal with the first point above, we remark that it suffices to list, for each instance of a discourse relation, the set of *elementary* constituents that belong to its left and right scope in order to express the three kinds of structures. We do this in a way that an isomorphic structure can always be recovered. Models of our common language will be a list of relation instances and elementary constituents, together with a set of predicates stating what is in the scope of what. As for the second point, we axiomatize each constraint in our common language, thereby describing each of the 3 types of discourse structures as a theory in our language.

Our language contains only binary relations. Among discourse formalisms, only RST makes serious (and empirical) use of n−ary discourse relations. Nevertheless, such RST structures are expressible in our framework, if we assume certain semantic equivalences. RST allows for two cases of non-binary trees: (i) nucleus with n satellites, each one linked to the nucleus by some relation R_n. Such a structure is semantically equivalent to the conjunction of n-binary relations R_n between the nucleus and the nth satellite, which is expressible in our framework. (ii) RST also allows for n-ary multinuclear relations such as *List* and *Sequence*. In our understanding, multinuclear relations $R(a_1, \ldots a_n)$, essentially serve a purpose of expressiveness, and such an n-ary tree is an equivalent to the split non-tree shaped structure $R(a_1,a_2) \wedge R(a_2,a_3) \ldots R(a_{(n-1)}, a_n)$. This seems clear for the *Sequence* relation, which states that $a_1 \ldots a_n$ are in temporal sequence and can be equivalently formulated as "each a_i precedes a_{i+1}". This might appear less obvious for the *List* relation. The semantics (as it appears on the RST website `http://www.sfu.ca/rst/`) of this relation requires the a_i to be "comparable", and as far as this is a transitive property, we can split the relation into a set of binary ones.

Formally, our scope language L_{scopes} is a fragment of that of monadic second order logic with two sorts of individuals: relation instances (i), and elementary constituants (l). Below, we assume $\mathcal{R}$ is the set of all relation names (elaboration, narration, justification, ...).

Definition 1 (Scoping language)**.** Let S be the set $\{i, l\}$. The set of primitive, disjoint types of L_{scopes} consists of i, l and t (type of formulae). For each of the types in S, we have a countable set of variable symbols V_i (V_l). Two additional countable sets of variable symbols $V_{\langle i,t\rangle}$ and $V_{\langle l,t\rangle}$ range over sets of individuals. These four sets of variable symbols are pairwise disjoint.

The alphabet of our language is constituted by V_i, V_s, a set of predicates, equality, connector and quantifier symbols. The set of predicate symbols is as follows:

1) For each relation symbol r in $\mathcal{R}$, L_R is a unary predicate of type $\langle i,t\rangle$—i.e., $L_R : \langle i,t\rangle$.

2) unary predicates, *sub*, *coord* and $sub^{-1} : \langle i,t\rangle$.

3) binary predicates $\in_l$ and $\in_r : \langle i,l,t\rangle$.

4) two equality relations, $=_s : \langle s,s,t\rangle$ for $s \in \{i,l\}$.

Logical connectors, and quantifiers are as usual. The sets of terms Γ_i, Γ_l and Γ_t are recursively defined: 1. $V_i \subseteq \Gamma_i$, $Var_l \subseteq \Gamma_l$. 2. For $v \in V_{s,t}, v : \langle s,t\rangle$. 3. For each symbol σ of type $\langle u_1,\ldots,u_n\rangle$ in the alphabet, for all $(t_1,\ldots,t_{n-1}) \in \Gamma_{u_1} \times \cdots \times \Gamma_{un-1}$, $\sigma[t_1,\ldots,t_{n-1}] \in \Gamma_{u_n}$. Γ_t is the set of well formed formulae of the scope language.

The predicates $\in_l$ and $\in_r$ take a relation instance r of type i and a elementary constituent x of type l as arguments. Intuitively, they mean that x has to be included in the left (for $\in_l$) or right (for $\in_r$) scope of r. For each relation symbol R such as *justification* or *elaboration*, the predicate L_R takes a relation instance r has argument and states that r is an instance of the rhetorical relation R. Predicates *sub*, *coord* and sub^{-1} apply to a relation instance r, respectively specifying that r's left argument hierarchically dominate its right argument, that both are of equal hierarchical importance, or that the left one is subordinate to the right one.

Definition 2 (Scope structure and Interpretation). A *scope structure* is an L_{scopes}-structure $\mathcal{M} = \langle D_i, D_l, |.|^{\mathcal{M}}\rangle$. D_i and D_l are disjoint sets of individuals for the sorts i and l respectively, and $|.|^{\mathcal{M}}$ assigns to each predicate symbol P of type $\langle u_1, \ldots, u_n, t\rangle$ a function $|.|^P : D_{u_1} \times \cdots \times D_{u_n} \mapsto \{0, 1\}$. Variables of type $\langle i, t\rangle$ are assigned subsets of D_i and similarly for variables of type $\langle l, t\rangle$. The predicates $=_i$ and $=_s$ are interpreted as equality over D_i and D_l respectively.

The interpretation $[\![\cdot]\!]_v^{\mathcal{M}}$ of a formula $\phi \in \Phi_S$ is the standard interpretation of a monadic second order formula w.r.t to a model and a valuation (interpretation of first order quantifiers and connectors is as usual, quantification over sets is over all sets of individuals). Validity $\models$ also follows the standard definition.

These scope structures offer a common framework for different discourse formalisms. Given one of the three formalisms, we say that two structures S_1 and S_2 are equivalent iff there is an encoding from one structure into a scoped structure or set of scoped structures and a decoding back from the scoped structure or set of scoped structures into S_2

Fact 1. One can define two algorithms I and E such that:

- from a given structure s which is a RS Tree, a SDRS or a DT, I computes a scope structure $I(s)$.
- given such a computed structure, E allow to retrieve the original structure s $(E(I(s)) = s)$.

RST Encoding and Decoding To flesh out I and E for RST, we need to define dominance. Set $lArgs(r) = \{e \in D^l \mid (r, e) \in |\in_l|^{\mathcal{M}}\}$; $rArgs(r)$ is defined analogously (where $\in_r$ replaces $\in_l$). The left and right dominance relations $\sqsubseteq_l$ and $\sqsubseteq_r$ are defined as follows: $r \sqsubseteq_l r'$ iff $(Args(r) \subseteq lArgs(r'))$.
- $r \sqsubseteq_l r' \leftrightarrow \forall z{:}l((z \in_l r) \vee z \in_r r)) \rightarrow z \in_l r')$ with $r \sqsubseteq_r r'$ defined analogously.
Dominance $\sqsubseteq$ is: $\sqsubseteq = \sqsubseteq_l \cup \sqsubseteq_r$.
- $lArgs(r, X) \leftrightarrow \forall z{:}l(z \in_l r) \leftrightarrow z \in X)$, with $rArgs(r, X)$ similar and
-$Args(r, X) \leftrightarrow \forall z{:}l((z \in_l r) \vee z \in_r r)) \leftrightarrow z \in X)$.

The NS, NN and NS schemes of RST will be respectively encoded by the predicates *sub*, *coord* and sub^{-1}. We proceed recursively. If t is an EDU e, return $M_t = \langle D_i = \emptyset, D_l = \{e\}, \epsilon\rangle$ where ϵ is the interpretation that assigns the empty set to each predicate symbol. If the root of t is a binary node instantiating a relation $R(t_{1a_1}, t_{2a_2})$, let $T_r \in \{sub, coord, sub^{-1}\}$ be the predicate that encodes the schema a_1a_2, let $M_{t_1} = \langle D_i^1, D_l^1, |.|^1\rangle$ and $M_{t_2} = \langle D_i^2, D_l^2, |.|^2\rangle$. The algorithm returns $M_t = \langle D_i^1 \cup D_i^2 \cup \{r\}, D_l^1 \cup D_l^2, |.|^{M_t}\rangle$ where r is a 'fresh' relation instance variable not in D_i^1 or D_i^2, and $|.|^{M_t}$ is updated in the appropriate fashion to reflect the left and right arguments of r. Finally, if the root of t is an n-ary node, split it into a sequence of binary relation $R_1(t_1, t_2), R_2(t_2, t_3), \ldots,$ proceed to recursively compute the scope-structures M_i for each of the relations using 2 (take care to introduce a 'fresh' relation instance individual for each relation of the sequence), then return the union of the models M_i.

RST Decoding Given a **finite** scope structure $\mathcal{M} = \langle D^i, D^l, |.|^{\mathcal{M}}\rangle$, for each relation instance r compute the left arguments of r and its right arguments. We then identify $L(r)$, the unique relation symbol R such that $r \in |L_R|^{\mathcal{M}}$. If that fails, the algorithm fails. Similarly retrieve the right nuclearity schema from the adequate predicate that applies to r. Then compute the dominance relations for r. If the input structure $\mathcal{M} = I(t)$ for some RS Tree t then there is at least one maximal relation instance for the dominance relation. If t the root node of t is a binary relation, there is exactly one maximal element in the dominance relation. If there is none, then we return fail. If there is exactly one, recursively compute the two RS Trees obtained from the models computed from the left and right arguments and descendants of r. If there is more than one, the root node of the encoded RS Tree was a n-ary relation and one has to reconstruct the n-ary node if that is possible; if not the algorithm fails (but that means the input structure was not obtained from a valid RS Tree).

SDRT Encoding and Decoding: This is similar to the RST encoding and decoding; for the encoding algorithm, we proceed recursively top down. A SDRS s is a complex constituent that contents a graph $g = \langle V, E\rangle$ whose edges are relations holding between sub-constituents, simple or complex as well. First come up with an encoding of the set E of all edges that hold between two sub-constituents of s, *i.e.* a structure $\mathcal{M} = \langle D_i = E_i, D_l = V, \{L_R\}, \in_l, \in_r\rangle$, where, for each edge $e \in E_i$, L_R encodes its relation type, and ${\in_l}^1$ and ${\in_r}^1$ consists of all the pairs (x, e) of left and right nodes x of the edges $e \in E$. Finally, for each complex immediate sub-constituent of s in D_l, update $\mathcal{M}$ as follows: for c such a subconsituent, recursively compute its encoding M_c, then add everything of M_c to M, finally remove c from M but add instead for each relation r scoping over c to the right (left), all the pairs $\{(r, x) \mid x \text{ is a constituent in } M^c\}$. The decoding works again similarly to the one for RST, top-down once again: one recursively retrieves immediate content of the current complex constituent at each level then moves to inner constituents.

DT: Dependency trees are syntactically a special case of SDRSs; there is only one CDU whose domain is only EDUs.

The scope language allows us to axiomatize three classes of scope structures corresponding to RS Trees, SDRSs and DTs. Not every scope structure will yield a RS Tree when fed to the RST decoding algorithm, only those obtainable from encoding an RS tree. As not all scope structures obey these axioms, our language is strictly more expressive than any of these discourse formalisms.

As an example of an axiom, the following formula expresses that a relation cannot have both left and right scope over the same elementary constituent:

Strong Irreflexivity:

$$\forall r{:}i\forall x{:}l\neg(x \in_l r \ \wedge \ x \in_r r)) \qquad (A_0)$$

Strong irreflexivity entails irreflexivity; a given relation instance cannot have the same (complete) left and right scopes. All discourse theories validate A_0.

In the Appendix, we define left and right strong dominance relations $\sqsubseteq_{l(r)}$ as well as n-ary RS trees and CDUs of SDRT. We exploit these facts in the Appendix to express axioms (A1-A9) that axiomatize the structures corresponding to RST, SDRT and DTs. Axiom A_1 says that every discourse unit is linked via some discourse relation instance. Axiom A_2 insures that all our relation instances have the right number of arguments; Axioms A_3 and A_4 ensure acyclicity and no crossing dependencies. A_5a and A_5b restrict structures to a tree-like dominance relation with a maximal dominating element, while A_6 defines the Right Frontier constraint for SDRT, and A_7 fixes the domain for SDRT constraints on CDUs. A_8 ensures that no coordinating and subordinating relations have the same left and right arguments, while A_9 provide the restrictions needed to define the set of DTs. We use the encoding and decoding maps to show:

Fact 2.

1. The theory T_{RST}={$A_0, A_1, A_2, A_3, A_4, A_5a, A_5b, A_8$} characterizes RST structures in the sense that:

   - E applied to any structure M such that $M \models T_{RST}$ yield an RST Tree.

   - for any RST Tree t, $I(t) \models T_{RST}$.

2. The theory T_{SDRT}={$A_0, A_1, A_2, A_3, A_6, A_7, A_8$} similarly characterizes SDRSs.

3. The theory $T_{DT}=T_{SDRT} \cup \{A_9a, A_9b\}$ similarly characterizes Dependency Trees structures.

4 Different Interpretations of Scope

The previous section defined the set of scope structures as well as the means to import, and then retrieve, RS trees, DTs, or SDRs into, and from, this set. Some of these scope structures export both into RST and SDRT, yielding a $1-1$ correspondence between a subset of SDRT and RST structures. But what does this correspondence actually tell us about these two structures? In mathematics, the existence of an isomorphism relies on a bijection that *preserves* structure. Our correspondence preserves the *immediate interpretation* of the semantic scopes of relations.

Immediate Interpretation Consider a scope structure $\mathcal{M}$ (validating A_0, A_1, A_2). The predicates $lArgs(r)$ and $rArgs(r)$ are the sets of all units in the left or right scope of a relation instance r. Whether r, labelled by relation name R holds of two discourse units or not in $\mathcal{M}$, depends on the semantic content of its left and right arguments, recursively described by $lArgs(r)$ and all relations r' such that $r' \sqsubset_l r$, and $rArgs(r)$ and all relations r' such that $r' \sqsubset_r r$. Algorithm I computes what we call the *immediate* interpretation of an input structure. Intuitively, in this interpretation the semantic scope of relations is directly read from the structures themselves; a node $R(t_1, t_2)$ in a RS Tree expresses that R holds between contents expressed by the whole substructures t_1 and t_2. Similarly, for SDRT and DTs, immediate interpretation of an edge $\pi_1 \rightarrow_R \pi_2$ is that R holds between the whole content of π_1 and π_2.

While this immediate interpretation is standard in SDRT, it is not in RST. Consider again (1) from the introduction or:

(2) [In 1988, Kidder eked out a \$ 46 million profit,]$_{31}$ [mainly because of severe cost cutting.]$_{32}$ [Its 1,400-member brokerage operation reported an estimated \$ 5 million loss last year,]$_{33}$ [although Kidder expects to turn a profit this year]$_{34}$ (RST Treebank, wsj_0604).

(3) [Suzanne Sequin passed away Saturday at the communal hospital of Bar-le-Duc,]$_3$ [where she had been admitted a month ago.]$_4$ [...] [Her funeral will be held today at 10h30 at the church of Saint-Etienne of Bar-le-Duc.]$_5$ (annodis corpus).

These examples involve what are called *long distance attachments*. (2) involves a relation of contrast, or comparison between 31 and 33, but which does not involve the contribution of 32 (the costs cutting of 1988). (3) displays something comparable. A causal relation like result, or at least a temporal narration holds between 3 and 5, but it should not scope over 4 if one does not wish to make Sequin's admission to the hospital a month ago a consequence of her death last Saturday. Finally in (1) C_4 elaborates on C_1, but not on the fact that C_1 is attributed to chief Garcia, so the corresponding elaboration relation should not scope over C_3.

It is impossible however, to account for long distance attachment using the immediate interpretation of RST trees. (2), for instance, also involves an explanation relation between 31 and 32, which should include none of 33 or 34 in its scope. Since 31 is in the scope of both the explanation and the contrast relation, Axiom A_5a of the previous section entails than an RST tree involving the two relations has to make one of the two relations dominates the other.

Marcu's Nuclearity Principle (NP) Marcu 1996 provides an alternative to the immediate interpretation and captures some long distance attachments Danlos 2008; Egg and Redeker 2010. According to the NP, a relation between two spans of text, expressed at a node of a RS Tree should hold between the most salient parts of these spans. *Most salient part* is recursively defined: the most salient part of an elementary constituent is itself, for a multinuclear relation $R(t_{1N}, \ldots, t_{kN})$ its most salient part is the union of the most salient parts of the t_i[2]. Following Egg and Redeker 2010, the NP, or *weak* NP is a constraint on which RST trees may correctly characterize an input text; it is not a mechanism for computing scopes. Given their analysis of (1) given in the introduction, NP entails that $Elab_1$ holds between C_1 and C_4, accounting for the long distance attachment, and that Attribution holds between C_1 and C_4 which meets intuition in this case. There is however no requirement that *Attribution* do *not* hold between the wider span $[C_1, C_2]$ and C_3, as there is no requirement that $Elab_1$ does not hold between $[C_1, C_2, C_3]$ and C_4. In order to accurately account for (1), the former must be true and the latter false.

However, this interpretation of NP together with an RST tree does not determine the semantic scope of all relations. Danlos 2008 reformulates NP as a *Mixed* Nuclearity Principle (MNP) that outputs determinate scopes for a given structure. The MNP requires for a given node, that the most salient parts of his daughters furnish the **exact** semantic scope for the relation at that node. The MNP transforms an RST tree t into a scope structure $\mathcal{M}_t$, which validates $A_0 - A_3$ but also A_6.[3], A_7 and A_8. Hence $\mathcal{M}$ could be exported back to SDRT and the MNP would yield a translation from RST-trees to SDRSs.

But when applied to the RST Treebank, the MNP yields wrong, or at least incomplete, semantic scopes for intuitively correct RS Trees. The mixed principle applied to the tree of s_1 gives the Attribution scope over C_1 only, but not C_2, which is incorrect. Focusing on the attribution relation which is the second most frequent in the RST Treebank, we find out that, regardless of whether we assign Attribution's arguments S and N or N and S, this principle makes wrong predictions 86% of the time in a random sampling of 50 cases in which we have attributions with multi-clause second argument spans. Consider the following example from the RST Treebank:

(4) [Interprovincial Pipe Line Co. said]$_1$ [it will delay a proposed two-step, 830 million Canadian-dollar [(US$705.6 million)]$_3$ expansion of its system]$_2$ [because Canada's output of crude oil is shrinking.]$_4$

Applied to the annotated RS Tree for this example (figure 1), the MNP yields an incorrect scope of the attribution relation over 2 only, regardless of whether the attribution is annotated *N-S* or *S-N*. The idea behind the weak NP provides a better fit with intuitions. The principle gives *minimal* semantic requirements for scoping relations; everything beyond those requirements is left *underspecified.* We formalize this as the *relaxed* Nuclearity Principle (RNP), which does not compute one structure where each relation is given its exact scope, but **a set** of such structures.

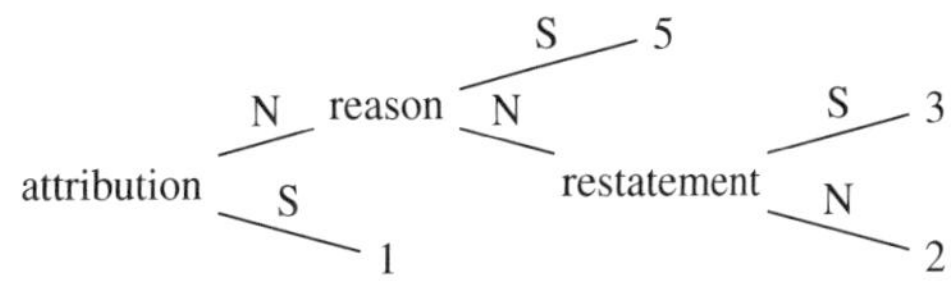

Figure 1: Annotated RST Tree for example (4).

The target structures are not trees any more, but we want them to still reflect the dominance information present in the RS Tree. We therefore define a notion of *weak dominance* over structures of the scoping language: for two sets of constituents, $X \leq Y$ iff $X \subseteq Y$ or there is a subordinating relation whose left argument is X and right one Y. Weak dominance is given by transitive closure $\leq^*$ of $\leq$. For two relations, $r \leq_l^* r'$ iff the left argument of r weakly dominates both arguments of r'. $\leq_r^*$ is symmetrically defined. Finally, structures computed by the RNP have to validate the weakened version of A_5: if two relations scope over the same elementary constituent one has to weakly dominates the other. Let A_5^W denote this axiom.

Definition 3 (Relaxed Nuclearity Principle)**.** One can assign to an RS Tree t a formula of the scoping language $\phi_t = \exists\bar{x}\exists\bar{r}\psi_t \cup \Gamma_t$ such that:

1– ψ_t is a formula specifying that all individuals quantified in $\bar{x}$ and $\bar{r}$ are pairwise distinct, and that there is no other individuals that the ones just mentioned. ψ_t also specifies for each intermediate node n that the corresponding relation instance r_n is labelled with the adequate relation symbol R and relation type (subordinating if *N-S* ...).

2– Γ_t encodes the nuclearity principle applied to t: for all intermediate nodes n_i and n_j in t such that n_l is the left (resp. right) daughter of n_i, Γ_t specifies that n_i must scope to the left (resp. right) over the nucleus of n_j.

The interpretation $[\![t]\!]$ is defined as the set of structures $\mathcal{M}$ that validate ϕ_t and $A_0, A_1, A_2, A_3, A_5^W$ (they all have $|t|$ individuals, as fixed by ψ_t). Moreover, it can be shown that each model of this set validates T_{SDRT}; so we have a interpretation of an RS-Tree into a set of SDRSs.

5 Intertranslability between RST/DTs

DTs are a restriction of SDRSs to structures without complex constituents. So the ζ function of section 2

[2]Except for Sequence which only retains the most salient part of t_k

[3]That A_6 is valid in the resulting model is not immediate. Assume a multinuclear (coordinating) relation instance r has scope over x_n and x_{n+k} later in the textual order. Then it is impossible to attach with r' a later found constituent x_{n+k+l} to x_n alone, for it would require that x_{n+1} escapes the scope of r' from the MNP which it will not do by multinuclearity of r.

can transform distinct SDRSs transform into the same DT with a consequent loss of information.

$$\begin{array}{c} a \rightarrow_{R_1} \pi \\ \pi : b \rightarrow_{R_2} c \end{array} \mid a \rightarrow_{R_1} b \rightarrow_{R_2} c \mid \begin{array}{c} \pi \rightarrow_{R_2} b \\ \pi : a \rightarrow_{R_1} b \end{array} \quad (1)$$

Each of the SDRSs above yields the same DT after simplification, namely the second one $a \rightarrow_{R_1} b \rightarrow_{R_2} c$.

The natural interpretation of a DT g describes the set of fully scoped SDRS structures that are compatible with these minimal requirements, *i.e* that would yield g by simplification. To get this set, every edge $r(x, y)$ in g, r, must be assigned left scope among the *descendants* of x in g (and right scope among those of y); this is a consequence of i) x and y being *heads* of the left and right arguments of r and ii) the SDRSs that are compatible with g do not admit relations with a right argument in one constituent and a left one outside of it.

Definition 4. Assume that we map each node[4] x of g into a unique variable $v_x \in V_l$ and each edge e into a unique variable symbol $r_e \in V_i$. Define $\bar{x}$ and $\bar{r}$ in an analogous way as in definition 3.

For a given dependency tree g, we compute a formula $\phi_g = \exists\bar{x}\exists\bar{r}\ \psi_g \cup \Gamma_g$ such that

- ψ_g is defined analogously as in definition 3, defining the set of relation instances and EDUs.
- Γ_g is the formula stating the minimal scopes for each relation instance: for all edge in $e = R(x, y)$ in g, Γ_g entails i) r_e has v_x in its left scope and v_y in its right scope and ii) let $Des(x)$ be the set of variable symbols for all the descendants of x in g, Γ_g entails that if r_e has left scope over some v_z then v_z is in $Des(x)$ (symmetrically for y and right scope).

The interpretation $[\![g]\!]$ of a DT is: $\{\mathcal{M} \mid \mathcal{M} \models \phi_g, A_0\text{-}A_3, A_6, A_7\}$. The DT $a \rightarrow_{R_1} b \rightarrow_{R_2} c$ for instance, is interpreted as a set of three structures isomorphic to the ones in (1) above.

We now relate DTs to RS Trees interpreted with the RNP. To this aim, we focus on a restricted class of DTs, those who involve i) coordinating chains of 3 edus or more only if they involve a single coordinating relation: $x_1 \rightarrow_{R_1} x_2 \rightarrow_{R_2} \cdots \rightarrow_{R_{n-1}} x_n$ may appear only for $n > 2$ if all the R_i are the same coordinating relation, and ii) subordinating nests of 3 edus or more only if they involve a single subordinating relation:

$$x \;\; (R_1 \swarrow \; \downarrow \; \searrow R_n) \;\; y_1 \cdots y_n$$

is allowed for $n > 1$ only if all R_i are labelled with the same subordinating relation.

This restricted class of DTs corresponds exactly with the set of RS-Trees interpreted with the RNP, provided that we restrict the interpretation of a DT in the following way: a principle called *Continuing Discourse Pattern*, CDP Asher and Lascarides 2003 must apply, who states that whenever a sequence of coordinating relation R_c^i originates as a node which appear to be also in the right scope of a subordinating relation R_s, R_s must totally include all the R_c^i in its right scope. A second principle is required, who states that whenever two subordinating relations $R0_s$ and R'_s originate at the same node in the DT, and the right argument of R'_s is located after the right argument of R_s, any structure in the interpretation of the DT must verify $R'_s \preceq_l R_s$. The translation needs these requirements to work, because: i) with the NP a relation scoping over a multinuclear one must includes all the nucleus in RST, and ii)a node in a RS Tree cannot scope over something that is not its descendant). Let CDP$^+$ denote these requirements.

Using the restricted interpretation of a DT g; $[\![g]\!]^{CDP} = \{\mathcal{M} \mid \mathcal{M} \models A_0\text{-}A_3, A_6, A_7, \text{CDP}^+\}$, we transform an RS Tree t into a dependency graph $\mathcal{G}(t)$ such that $[\![t]\!] = [\![\mathcal{G}(t)]\!]^{CDP}$:

Definition 5 (RS Trees to dependency graphs)**.** The translation $\mathcal{G}$ takes a RS Tree t as input and outputs a pair $\langle G, n\rangle$, where $G = \langle Nodes, Edges\rangle$ is the corresponding dependency graph, and n an attachment point used along the recursive definition of $\mathcal{G}$.

- If t is an EDU x then $(G)(t) = \langle(\{x\}, \{\}), x\rangle$.
- If $t = R(t_{1N}, t_{2S})$ then let $\langle G_1, n_1\rangle = \mathcal{G}(t_1)$ and $\langle G_2, n_2\rangle = \mathcal{G}(t_2)$.

  $$\mathcal{G}(t) = \langle(G_1 \cup G_2 \cup \{R_{subord}(n_1, n_2)\}; n_1\rangle$$
- If $t = R(t_{1S}, t_{2N})$ then $\mathcal{G}(t) = \mathcal{G}(R(t_{2N}, t_{1S}))$
- If $t = R(t_{1N}, \ldots, t_{kN})$ (multinuclear), let $\langle G_i, n_i\rangle = \mathcal{G}(t_i)$, let G be the result of adding a chain $n_1 \rightarrow_{R_{coord}} \cdots \rightarrow_{R_{coord}} n_k$ to the union of the G_i,

  $$\mathcal{G}(t) = \langle G; n_1\rangle$$
- If t is a nuclear satellite relation with several satellites $R(t_{1S}, \ldots t_{jN}, \ldots t_{kS})$, compute the G_i has in the previous case, then add to the union of the G_i the nest of $k-1$ subordinating relations R linking n_j to each of the n_i, $i \neq j$.

Recall RS Tree (s_1). Applying $\mathcal{G}$ to this tree yields the dependency tree (s_3): $Elab_1(C_1, C_2) \wedge \text{Attr}(C_1, C_3) \wedge Elab_2(C_1, C_4)$. $[\![s_3]\!]$ supports any reading of (s_1) provided by RNP, but also an additional one where *Attr* scopes over $[C_1, C_2, C_4]$. This is however forbidden by CDP+ for C_4 is after C_3 in the textual order but $Elab(C_1, C_4) \not\preceq_l Attr(C_1, C_3)$.

6 Similarities and distances

The framework we have presented yields a notion of similarity that applies to structures of different formalisms. To motivate our idea, recall example (1); the structure in (s_3) in which Attribution just scopes over C_1 differs from the intuitively correct interpretation only in that Attribution should also scope over C_2

[4] Recall that unlike RS Trees, DTs have EDUs as nodes and relations as edges.

as in (s_2), while a structure that does this but in which C_3 is in the scope of the Elaboration relation is intuitively further away from the correct interpretation.

Our similarity measure *Sim* over structures $\mathcal{M}_1$ and $\mathcal{M}_2$ assumes a common set of elementary constituents and a correspondence between relation types in the structures. We measure similarity in terms of the scopes given to the relations. The intuition, is that given a map f from elements of relation instances in $\mathcal{M}_1$ relation instances in $\mathcal{M}_2$, we achieve a similarity score by counting for each relation instance r the number of EDUs that are both in the left scope of one element of r and in $f(r)$, then divide this number by the total number of diffrents constituents in the left scope of r_1 and r_2, and do the same for right scopes as well. The global similarity is given by the correspondence which yields the best score.

Given a relation $r_1 \in \mathcal{M}_1$ and a relation $r_2 \in \mathcal{M}_2$, let $\delta(r_1, r_2) = \begin{cases} 1 \text{ if } r_1 \text{ and } r_2 \text{ have the same label} \\ 0 \text{ otherwise} \end{cases}$. Define $C_l(r_1, r_2) = |\{x : l \mid \mathcal{M}_1 \models x \in_l r_1 \wedge \mathcal{M}_2 \models x \in_l r_2\}|$, the number of constituents over which r_1 and r_2 scope and $D_l(r_1, r_2) = |\{x : l \mid \mathcal{M}_1 \models x \in_l r_1 \vee \mathcal{M}_2 \models x \in_l r_2\}|$. Define C_r and D_r analogously and assume that $\mathcal{M}_1$ has less relation instances than $\mathcal{M}_2$. Let $Inj(D_i^1, D_i^2)$ be the set of injections of relations instances of $\mathcal{M}_1$ to those of $\mathcal{M}_2$.

$$Sim(\mathcal{M}_1, \mathcal{M}_2) = \frac{1}{2Max(|\mathcal{M}_1|, |\mathcal{M}_2|)} \times$$
$$\underset{f \in Inj(D_i^1, D_i^2)}{Max} \sum_{r:i} \delta(r, f(r)) \times \left(\frac{C_l(r, f(r))}{D_l(r, f(r))} + \frac{C_r(r, f(r))}{D_r(r, f(r))}\right)$$

If M_2 has more relation instances, Invert arguments and use the definition above. If they have same number of instances, both directions coincide.

$$d(\mathcal{M}_1, \mathcal{M}_2) = 1 - Sim(\mathcal{M}_1, \mathcal{M}_2)$$

For a discourse structure $\mathcal{M}$, $Sim(\mathcal{M}, \mathcal{M}) = 1$; Sim ranges between 1 and 0. d is a Jaccard-like metric obeying symmetry, $d(x, x) = 0$ $d(x, y) \neq 0$ for $x \neq y$, and the triangle equality. One can further define the maximal or average similarity between any pair of structures of two sets S_1 and S_2. This gives an idea of the similarity between two underspecified interpretations, such as the ones provided by RNP of section 4. For example, the maximal similarity between (s_2) interpreted as itself (immediate interpretation) and a possible scope structure for the DT (s_3), interpreted with the underspecified $[\![]\!]$ of section 5, is 7/12. It is provided by the interpretation of (s_3) where Attr is given left scope over C_1, C_2, C_4, $Elab_1$ holds between C_1 and C_2, and the second *Elab* fails to match the continuation of (s_3). $sim([\![s_2]\!], [\![\zeta(s_2)]\!]) = 7/12$ also, because ζ must distribute $[2, 4]$ in s_2 to avoid crossing dependencies; so $[\![\zeta(s_2)]\!] \cong [\![s_3]\!]$. The maximal similarity between the RS tree in (s_1) with RNP (or equivalently, (3) with $[\![]\!]^{CDP+}$) and (s_2) is 19/36, achieved when both C_1 and C_2 are left argument of Attr (though not C_4). With MNP, the similarity is 17/36.

Given our results in sections 4 and 5, we have:

Fact 3. (i) For any DT g without a > 3 length flat sequence and interpreted using CDP+, there an RS tree t interpreted with RNP such that $Sim(g, t) = 1$. (ii) For any RS tree with RNP there is a DT g such that $Sim(t, g) = 1$.

To prove (i) construct a model using Definition 4 and then use RST decoding. To prove (ii) construct a model given Definition 3 and use DT encoding. Our similarity measure provides general results for SDRSs and DTTs (and *a fortiori* SDRSs and RS trees) (See Appendix).

7 Related Work

Our work shares a motivation with Blackburn, Gardent, and Meyer-Viol 1993: Blackburn, Gardent, and Meyer-Viol 1993 provides a modal logic framework for formalizing syntactic structures; we have used MSO and our scope language to formalize discourse structures. While many concepts of discourse structure admit of a modal formalization, the fact that discourse relations can have scope over multiple elementary nodes either in their first or second argument makes an MSO treatment more natural. Danlos 2008 compares RST, SDRT and Directed Acyclic Graphs (DAGs) in terms of their *strong generative capacity* in a study of structures and examples involving 3 EDUS. We do not consider generative capacity, but we have given a generic and general axiomatization of RST, SDRT and DT in a formal interpreted language. We can translate any structure of these theories into this language, independent of their linguistic realization. We agree with Danlos that the NP does not yield an accurate semantic representation of some discourses. We agree with Egg and Redeker 2010 that the NP is rather a constraint on structures, and we formalize this with the relaxed principle and show how it furnishes a translation from RS trees to sets of scoped structures. Danlos's interesting correspondence between restricted sets of RST trees, SDRSs and DAGs assumes an already fixed scope-interpretation for each kind of structure: SDRSs and DAGs are naturally interpreted as themselves, and RS Trees are interpreted with the mixed NP Our formalism allows us **both** to describe the structures themselves and various ways of computing alternate scopes for relations.

With regard to the discussion in Egg and Redeker 2008; Wolf and Gibson 2005 of tree vs. graph structures, we show exactly how tree based structures like RST with or without the NP compare to graph based formalisms like SDRT. We have not investigated Graphbank here, but the scope language can axiomatize Graphbank (with A_0-A_3, A_8).

8 Conclusions

We have investigated how to determine the semantic scopes of discourse relations in various formalisms by developing a canonical formalism that encodes scopes of relations regardless of particular assumptions about discourse structure. This provides a *lingua franca* for comparing discourse formalisms and a way to measure similarity between structures, which can help to compare different annotations of a same text.

References

Afantenos, S. et al. (2012). "An empirical resource for discovering cognitive principles of discourse organisation: the ANNODIS corpus". In: *Proceedings of LREC 2012*. ELRA.

Asher, N. and A. Lascarides (2003). *Logics of Conversation*. Cambridge University Press.

Asher, N. (1993). *Reference to Abstract Objects in Discourse*. Studies in Linguistics and Philosophy 50. Dordrecht: Kluwer.

Baldridge, J., N. Asher, and J. Hunter (2007). "Annotation for and Robust Parsing of Discourse Structure on Unrestricted Texts". In: *Zeitschrift fr Sprachwissenschaft* 26, pp. 213–239.

Bateman, J. and K. J. Rondhuis (1997). "Coherence relations : Towards a general specification". In: *Discourse Processes* 24.1, pp. 3–49.

Blackburn, P., C. Gardent, and W. Meyer-Viol (1993). "Talking about Trees". In: *EACL 6*, pp. 21–29.

Carlson, L., D. Marcu, and M. E. Okurowski (2002). *RST Discourse Treebank*. Linguistic Data Consortium, Philadelphia.

Danlos, L. (2008). "Strong generative capacity of RST, SDRT and discourse dependency DAGSs". English. In: *Constraints in Discourse*. Ed. by A. Benz and P. Kuhnlein. Benjamins, pp. 69–95.

duVerle, D. and H. Prendinger (2009). "A Novel Discourse Parser Based on Support Vector Machine Classification". In: *Proceedings of ACL-IJCNLP 2009*. ACL, pp. 665–673.

Egg, M. and G. Redeker (2008). "Underspecified discourse representation". In: *PRAGMATICS AND BEYOND NEW SERIES* 172, p. 117.

– (2010). "How Complex is Discourse Structure?" In: *Proceedings of LREC'10*. Ed. by N. Calzolari et al. ELRA.

Hitzeman, J., M. Moens, and C. Grover (1995). "Algorithms for Analyzing the Temporal Structure of Discourse". In: *Proceedings of the 7th Meeting of the European Chapter of the Association for Computational Linguistics*, pp. 253–260.

Hobbs, J. R., M. Stickel, and P. Martin (1993). "Interpretation as Abduction". In: *Artificial Intelligence* 63, pp. 69–142.

Kehler, A. (2002). *Coherence, Reference and the Theory of Grammar*. CSLI Publications.

Lascarides, A. and N. Asher (1993). "Temporal Interpretation, Discourse Relations and Commonsense Entailment". In: *Linguistics and Philosophy* 16, pp. 437–493.

Mann, W. C. and S. A. Thompson (1987). "Rhetorical Structure Theory: A Framework for the Analysis of Texts". In: *International Pragmatics Association Papers in Pragmatics* 1, pp. 79–105.

Marcu, D. (1996). "Building up rhetorical structure trees". In: *Proceedings of the thirteenth national conference on Artificial intelligence - Volume 2*. AAAI'96. Portland, Oregon: AAAI Press, pp. 1069–1074. ISBN: 0-262-51091-X.

Muller, P. et al. (2012). "Constrained decoding for text-level discourse parsing". Anglais. In: *COLING - 24th International Conference on Computational Linguistics*. Mumbai, Inde.

Polanyi, L. (1985). "A Theory of Discourse Structure and Discourse Coherence". In: *Papers from the General Session at the 21st Regional Meeting of the Chicago Linguistics Society*. Ed. by P. D. K. W. H. Eilfort and K. L. Peterson.

Polanyi, L. and R. Scha (1984). "A Syntactic Approach to Discourse Semantics". In: *Proceedings of the 10th International Conference on Computational Linguistics (COLING84)*. Stanford, pp. 413–419.

Polanyi, L. et al. (2004). "A Rule Based Approach to Discourse Parsing". In: *Proceedings of the 5th SIGDIAL Workshop in Discourse and Dialogue*, pp. 108–117.

Prasad, R. et al. (2008). "The penn discourse treebank 2.0". In: *Proceedings of the 6th International Conference on Language Resources and Evaluation (LREC 2008)*, p. 2961.

Sagae, K. (2009). "Analysis of Discourse Structure with Syntactic Dependencies and Data-Driven Shift-Reduce Parsing". In: *Proceedings of IWPT'09*. ACL, pp. 81–84.

Sanders, T., W. Spooren, and L. Noordman (1992). "Toward a taxonomy of coherence relations". In: *Discourse processes* 15.1, pp. 1–35.

Stede, M. (2004). "The Potsdam Commentary Corpus". In: *ACL 2004 Workshop on Discourse Annotation*. Ed. by B. Webber and D. K. Byron. Barcelona, Spain: Association for Computational Linguistics, pp. 96–102.

Subba, R. and B. Di Eugenio (2009). "An effective Discourse Parser that uses Rich Linguistic Information". In: *Proceedings of HLT-NAACL*. ACL, pp. 566–574.

Webber, B. et al. (1999). "Discourse Relations: A Structural and Presuppositional Account Using Lexicalised TAG". In: *Proceedings of the 37th ACL Conference*. College Park, Maryland, USA: Association for Computational Linguistics, pp. 41–48. DOI: 10.3115/1034678.1034695.

Wolf, F. and E. Gibson (2005). "Representing Discourse Coherence: A Corpus Based Study". In: *Computational Linguistics* 31.2, pp. 249–287.

Appendix

In what follows, let $\sqsubset$ denotes the irreflexive part of $\sqsubseteq$ We assume that we have access to the textual order of EDUs as a function $f : \text{EDUs} \to N$ with an associated strict linear ordering $<$ over EDUs. We also appeal to the notion of a chain over EDUs $\{x_1, x_2, \dots x_n\}$ with a set of relation instances $r_1, \dots, r_n\}$ *all of which are instances of an n-ary relation type*, of the form $x_1 \to^{r_1} x_2 \to^{r_2} \dots \to^{r_n} x_n$ which can be defined in MSO. To handle RST relations with multiple satellites, we define a *nest*: $Nest(X, R)$ iff all $r \in R$ have the same left argument in X but take different right arguments in X. Finally, we define CDUs:

$$cdu(X,R) \leftrightarrow \exists r Args(r,X) \wedge$$
$$\forall r' \, (\forall x \, x \in_r r' \to x \in X) \to r' \in R$$

Axiomatization

$$\forall x{:}l \; \exists r{:}i \quad (x \in_l r) \vee (x \in_r r)$$
(A_1:Weak Connectedness)

$$\forall r \exists x, y (x \in_r r) \wedge y \in_l r))$$
(A_2 :Properness of the relation)

$$\forall X{:}(l,t)(X \neq 0 \to \exists y{\in}X \; \forall n \neg y \in_l n$$
(A_3 :Acyclicity or Well Foundedness)

No crossing dependencies using the textual order $<$ of EDUs:

$$\forall x, y, z, w((x < y < z < w) \to \forall m, n \neg(x \in_l n \wedge z \in_r n \wedge y \in_l m \wedge w \in_r m)) \qquad (A_4)$$

Tree Structures. Define $scopes(r, x) := x \in_l r \vee x \in_r r$.

$$\forall r, r' \, ((\neg(\exists X, R \; r, r' \in R \wedge \text{chain}(X,R) \wedge \text{nest}(X,R)) \wedge (\exists x \; scopes(r,x) \wedge scopes(r',x))) \to (r \sqsubseteq r' \vee r' \sqsubseteq r))$$
(A_5a)

$$\forall R{:}(i,t) \exists ! r{:}i \; \forall r' \in R \;\; r' \sqsubseteq r \qquad (A_5b)$$

Right Frontier:
$\forall n, x_n, x_{n+1} \forall r \; ((x_{n+1} \in_r r) \to (x_n \in_l r) \vee (\neg x_n \in_l r$
$\to \exists X, R(\text{chain}(X,R) \wedge \forall r'(r' \in R \to sub(r'))$
$\wedge \; \exists y \in X \exists z \exists k \; \exists m, j \in R \; (scopes(j,y) \wedge acc(z,y)$
$\wedge \; scopes(m, x_n) \wedge z \in_l k \wedge k < *x_{n+1}))))$ $\qquad (A_6)$
(The definition of SDRS accessibility *acc* is easy)
CDUs or EDUs and no overlapping CDUs:

$$\exists ! x{:}l \vee \exists X, R \; cdu(X,R) \wedge \forall X, Y, R, R' \;\; (cdu(X,R) \wedge cdu(Y,R') \to (R \cap R' \neq 0 \to (R \subseteq R' \vee R' \subseteq R)) \qquad (A_7)$$

The same arguments cannot be linked by subordinating and coordinating relations. The formal axiom is evident.

Finally, two axioms for restricting SDRSs to dependency trees:

$$\forall r \forall x, y((x \in_l r) \wedge y \in_l r)) \vee (x \in_r r) \wedge y \in_r r))) \to x = y$$
$(A_9a : NoCDUs.)$

$$\forall r \forall r' \forall X, Y(lArgs(r,X) \wedge rArgs(r,Y) \wedge lArgs(r',X) \wedge rArgs(r',Y)) \to r = r'$$
$(A_9b$:unique arc)

We note that as a consequence of A_5a and A_5b we have no danglers or contiguous spans:

$$\forall x, y, n \; (x \in_l n \wedge y \in_l n \wedge x \neq y) \to \neg \exists m \exists z \; (x \in_l m \wedge z \in_r m \wedge \neg(z \in_l n \vee z \in_r n))$$

We also note that A_5a and A_5b entail A_7, A_8 and A_9b, though not vice-versa.

Fact 4. Where γ is any SDRS and $\zeta{:}SDRS \to DT$ as in section 2, set $R_1 = \{r{:}i \; : \; |\{x{:}M_\gamma \models x \in_l r)\}| > 1\}$, $R_2 = \{r{:}i \; : \; |\{x{:}M_\gamma \models x \in_r r)\}| > 1\}$, and $R_{\{x,y\}} = \{r | \exists r' : i(x \in_l r' \wedge y \in_r r' \wedge r' \neq r\}$. Assume the **immediate interpretation** of γ and $\zeta(\gamma)$:

$$Sim(\gamma, \zeta(\gamma)) = \frac{2|I| - |(R_1 \cup R_2) \cup \bigcup_{x,y \in D_l^2} X_{\{x,y\}}|}{2|I|} + \frac{1}{2|I|}\{\Sigma_{r \in R_1} \frac{1}{|x{:}M_\gamma \models x \in_l r)\}|} + \Sigma_{r \in R_2} \frac{1}{|x{:}M_\gamma \models x \in_r r)\}|}\}$$

Explanation: We suppose that I is the number of relation instances in the SDRS. ζ removes CDUs in an SDRS and attaches all incoming arcs to the CDUs to the head of the CDU. It also removes multiple arcs into any given node. So for any node m such that $|\{r : m \in_r r\}| = a > 1$, then the information contained in the $a - 1$ arcs will be lost. In addition ζ will restrict that one incoming arc that in the SDRS has in its scope all the elements in the CDU to just the head. So the scope information concerning all the other elements in the CDU will be lost.

Unsupervised structured semantic inference for spoken dialog reservation tasks

Alejandra Lorenzo
Université de Lorraine
LORIA, UMR 7503
Nancy, France
alejandra.lorenzo@loria.fr

Lina M. Rojas-Barahona
LORIA, UMR 7503
Nancy, France
lina.rojas@loria.fr

Christophe Cerisara
LORIA, UMR 7503
Nancy, France
cerisara@loria.fr

Abstract

This work proposes a generative model to infer latent semantic structures on top of manual speech transcriptions in a spoken dialog reservation task. The proposed model is akin to a standard semantic role labeling system, except that it is unsupervised, it does not rely on any syntactic information and it exploits concepts derived from a domain-specific ontology. The semantic structure is obtained with unsupervised Bayesian inference, using the Metropolis-Hastings sampling algorithm. It is evaluated both in terms of attachment accuracy and purity-collocation for clustering, and compared with strong baselines on the French MEDIA spoken-dialog corpus.

1 Introduction

Many concrete applications that involve human-machine spoken dialogues exploit some hand-crafted ontology that defines and relates the concepts that are useful for the application. The main challenge for the dialog manager used in the application is then to interpret the user's spoken input in order to correctly answer the user's expectations and conduct a dialogue that shall be satisfactory for the user. This whole process may be decomposed into the following stages:

- Automatic speech recognition, to transform the acoustic signal into a sequence of words (or sequences of word hypotheses);
- Spoken language understanding, to segment and map these sequences of words into concepts of the ontology;
- Semantic analysis, to relate these concepts together and interpret the semantic of the user input at the level of the utterance, or of the speaker turn;
- Dialogue act recognition
- Dialogue planning
- Text generation
- ...

Note that the process sketched here often further involves several other important steps that are used internally within one or several of these broad stages, for instance named entity recognition, co-reference resolution, syntactic parsing, marcov decision process, reinforcement learning, etc.

This work focuses mainly on the second and third stages, since we assume that segmentation is given and we want to discover the underlying concepts and relations in the data. The third stage is very important because it exhibits the latent semantic structure hidden in the user utterance: what is the object affected by a given predicate ? What are the modifiers that may alter the meaning of a predicate ? Without such a structure, the system can hardly push understanding beyond lexical semantics and reach fine-grained semantic representations, which are thus often limited to well-formed inputs and cannot handle spontaneous speech as considered here. But still, despite its importance, most spoken dialog systems do not make use of such structure.

We propose an approach here to address this issue by directly inferring the semantic structure from the flat sequence of concepts using the unsupervised Bayesian learning framework. Hence, the proposed model does not rely on any predefined corpus annotated with semantic structure, which makes it much more robust to spoken inputs and adaptable to new domains than traditional supervised approaches.

2 Related work

In recent years, an increasing number of works have addressed robustness and adaptability issues in most of standard Natural Language Processing tasks with unsupervised or semi-supervised machine learning approaches. Unsupervised learning attempts to induce the annotations from large amounts of unlabeled data. Several approaches have recently been proposed in this context for the semantic role labeling task. (Swier and Stevenson, 2004) were the first to introduce an unsupervised semantic parser, followed by (Grenager and Manning, 2006), (Lang and Lapata, 2010), (Lang and Lapata, 2011b) and (Lang and Lapata, 2011a). Finally, (Titov and Klementiev, 2012), introduced two new Bayesian models that achieve the best current state-of-the-art results. However, all these works use some kind of supervision (namely a verb lexicon or a supervised syntactic system, which is the case in most of the approaches). (Abend et al., 2009) proposed an unsupervised algorithm for argument identification that uses a fully unsupervised syntactic parser and where the only supervised annotation is part-of-speech (POS) tagging.

Semi-supervised learning attempts to improve the performance of unsupervised algorithms by using both labeled and unlabeled data for training, where typically the amount of labeled data is smaller. A variety of algorithms have been proposed for semi-supervised learning[1]. In the context of semantic role labeling, (He and Gildea, 2006) and (Lee et al., 2007) hence tested self-training and co-training, while (Fürstenau and Lapata, 2009) used a graph-alignment method to semantic role labeling (SRL). Finally, in (Deschacht and Moens, 2009) the authors present a semi-supervised Latent Words Language Model, which outperforms a state-of-the-art supervised baseline. Although semi-supervised learning approaches minimize the manual effort involved, they still require some amount of annotation. This annotation is not always available, sometimes expensive to create and often domain specific. Moreover, these systems assume a specific role labeling (e.g. PropBank, FrameNet or VerbNet) and are not generally portable from one framework to another.

A number of works related to semantic inference have already been realized on the French MEDIA corpus. Hence, dynamic Bayesian networks were proposed for semantic composition in (Meurs et al., 2009), however their model relies on manual semantic annotation (i.e. concept-value pairs) and supervised training through the definition of 70 rules. In (Huet and Lefèvre, 2011; Camelin et al., 2011) unsupervised models were proposed that use stochastic alignment and Latent Dirichlet Allocation respectively, but these models infer a flat concept-value semantic representation. Compared to these works, we rather propose a purely unsupervised approach for structured semantic Metropolis-Hastings inference with a generative model specifically designed for this task.

[1] We refer the reader to (Zhu, 2005) or (Pise and Kulkarni, 2008) for an overview on semi-supervised learning methods.

3 Proposed model

3.1 Principle

We consider a human-machine dialog, with the objective of automatically building a semantic structure on top of the user's spoken utterances that shall help the dialog system to interpret the user inputs. This work focuses on inferring the semantic structure, and it assumes that a segmentation of users' utterances into concepts is given. More precisely, we exploit as input a manual segmentation of each utterance into word segments, where each segment represents a single concept that belongs to MEDIA ontology (Denis et al., 2006) (see Figure 1).

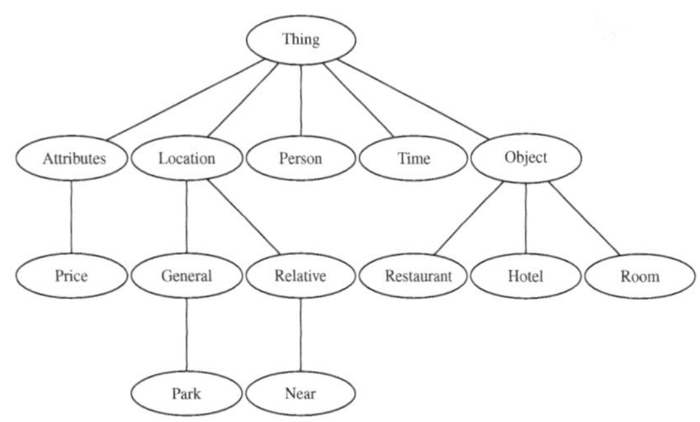

Figure 1: Excerpt of MEDIA ontology

This ontology identifies the concepts that can have arguments, and we thus use this information to further distinguish between *head* segments that can have arguments (noted W_h[2] in Figure 3) and *argument* segments that cannot govern another concept (noted W_a). From these two classes of

[2] W_h actually represents one word in a segment composed of N_h words, but by extension, we implicitly refer here to the full segment.

segments and the words' inflected forms that compose each segment we infer:

- A semantic structure composed of triplets (W_a, W_h, A) where A is the type of argument, or, in other words, the type of semantic relation between both segments;
- A semantic class C_t for the head segment

An example of the target structure we want to obtain is shown in Figure 2.

Inference of these structure and classes is realized with an unsupervised Bayesian model, i.e., without training the model on any corpus annotated with such relations. Instead, the model is trained on an unlabeled dialog corpus composed of raw manual speech transcriptions, which have also been manually segmented into utterances and words' segments as described above. Training is actually realized on this corpus using an approximate Bayesian inference algorithm that computes the posterior distribution of the model's parameters given the dataset. We have used for this purpose the Metropolis-Hastings Markov Chain Monte Carlo algorithm.

3.2 Bayesian model

Figure 3 shows the plate diagram of the proposed model. The plate N_h (respectively N_w) that surrounds a shaded node represents a single words' segment of length N_h (respectively N_w). The outer plate N_u indicates that the graphical model shall be repeated for each of the N_u utterances in the corpus.

Variable	Description
C_t	latent semantic type assigned to predicate t
W_h	observed words in each head segment. $P(W_h\|C_t)$ encodes lexical preferences for the semantic inference
A_i	latent semantic type assigned to the ith argument of predicate t
Rp_i	latent relative position assigned to the ith argument of predicate t
W_a	observed words in each argument segment. $P(W_a\|A_i)$ encodes lexical preferences for the semantic inference

Table 1: Variables of the model

Each *head* word segment has a latent semantic type C_t, and governs N_a arguments. Each argument is represented by an *argument* words' segment, which has a latent semantic type A. Each argument is further characterized by its relative position Rp with respect to its *head* segment. Rp

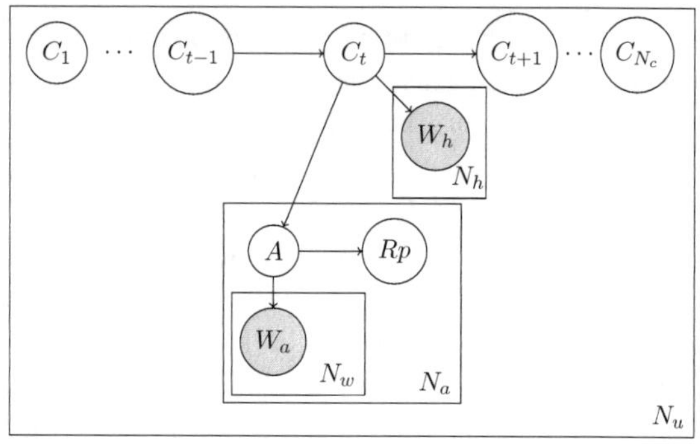

Figure 3: Plate diagram of the proposed model. N_u represents the number of utterances; N_h, the number of words in a head segment; N_w, the number of words in an argument segment; and N_a the number of arguments assigned to predicate t.

can have 4 values, depending on whether the argument is linked to the closest (1) or another (2) verbal[3] head, or the closest (3) or another (4) nominal head. Rp is derived from the argument-to-head assignment, which is latent. So, Rp is also latent. The sequence of N_c *head* segments in utterance u is captured by the HMM shown on top of the plate diagram, which models the temporal dependency between successive "semantic actions" of the user.

The variables of the model are explained in Table 1.

The most important property of this model is that the number of arguments N_a is not known beforehand. In fact, every *argument* segment can be governed by any of the N_c *head* segments in the utterance, and it is the role of the inference process to actually decide with which head it should be linked. This is why the model performs *structured* inference.

Concretely, at any time during training, every argument is governed by a single head. Then, inference explores a new possible head attachment for an argument W_a, which impacts the model as follows:

- The number of arguments N_a of the previous head is decreased by one;
- The number of arguments N_a of the new head is increased by one;

[3]Morphosyntactic classes are obtained with the Treetagger

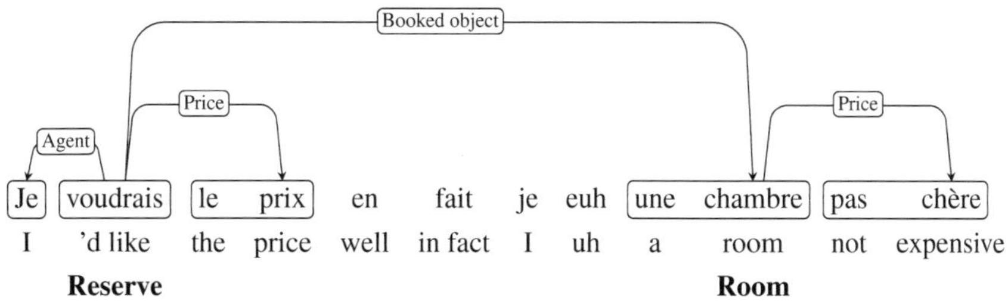

Figure 2: Example of inferred semantic structure for a sentence in the MEDIA corpus. Traditional dependency notations are used: the head segment points to the argument segment, where segments are shown with boxes (arrows link segments, not words !). The semantic class assigned to each head segment is shown in bold below the translated text.

- The relative position Rp of the argument is recomputed based on its new head position;
- The argument type A is also re sampled given the new head type C_t.

This reassignment process, which is at the heart of our inference algorithm, is illustrated in Figure 4.

3.3 Metropolis inference

Bayesian inference aims at computing the posterior distribution of the model's parameters, given the observed data. We assume that all distributions in our model are multinomial with uniform priors. The parameters are thus:

$P(W_h \mid C_t) \sim \mathcal{M}(\theta^H_{C_t})$	Distribution of the words for a given head semantic class
$P(C_t \mid C_{t-1}) \sim \mathcal{M}(\theta^C_{C_{t-1}})$	Transition probabilities between semantic classes
$P(W_a \mid A) \sim \mathcal{M}(\theta^W_A)$	Distribution of the words for a given argument type
$P(Rp \mid A) \sim \mathcal{M}(\theta^R_A)$	Distrib. of the relative position of a given argument to its head given the argument type
$P(A \mid C_t) \sim \mathcal{M}(\theta^A_{C_t})$	Distrib. of the argument types given a head semantic class

3.3.1 Inference algorithm

To perform inference, we have chosen a Markov Chain Monte Carlo algorithm. As our model is finite, parametric and identifiable, Doob's theorem guarantees the consistency of its posterior, and thus the convergence of MCMC algorithms towards the true posterior. Because changing the head of one argument affects several variables simultaneously in the model, it is problematic to use the basic Gibbs sampling algorithm. A block-Gibbs sampling would have been possible, but this would have increased the computational complexity and we also wanted to keep as much flexibility as possible in the jumps that could be realized in the search space, in order to prevent slow-mixing and avoid (nearly) non-ergodic Markov chains, which are likely to occur in such structured inference problems.

We have thus chosen a Metropolis-Hastings sampling algorithm, which allows us to design an efficient proposal distribution that is adapted to our task. The algorithm proceeds by first initializing the variables with a random assignment of arguments to one of the heads in the utterance, and a uniform sampling of the class variables. Then, it iterates through the following steps:

1. Sample uniformly one utterance u
2. Sample one jump following the proposal distribution detailed in Section 3.3.2.
3. Because the proposal is uniform, compute the acceptance ratio between the model's joint probability at the proposed (noted with a $'$) and current states:

$$r = \frac{P(C', W'_h, W'_a, Rp', A')}{P(C, W_h, W_a, Rp, A)}$$

4. Accept the new sample with probability $\min(1, r)$; while the sample is not accepted, iterate from step 2.

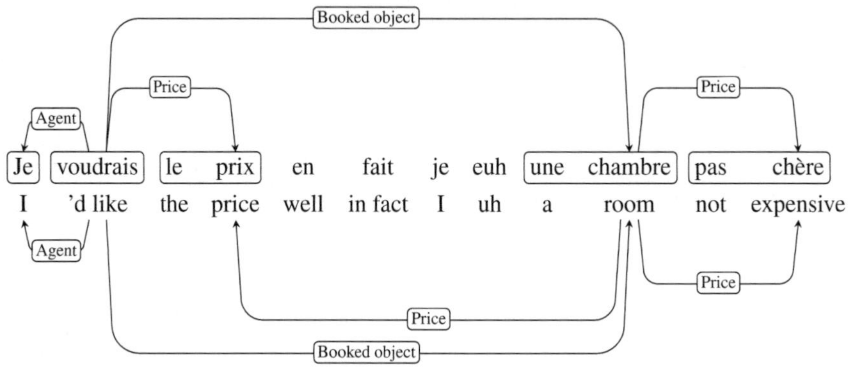

Figure 4: Illustration of the reassignment process following the expample presented in Figure 2. This example illustrates the third Metropolis proposed move, which changes the head of argument "le prix": arcs above the text represent the initial state, while arcs below the text represent the new proposed state.

5. When the sample is accepted, update the multinomials accordingly and iterate from step 1 until convergence.

This process is actually repeated for 2,000,000 iterations, and the sample that gives the largest joint probability is chosen.

3.3.2 Metropolis proposal distribution

The proposal distribution is used to explore the search space in an efficient way for the target application. Each state in the search space is uniquely defined by a value assignment to every variable in the model, for every utterance in the corpus. It corresponds to one possible *sample* of all variables, or in other words, to the choice of one possible semantic structure and class assignment to all utterances in the corpus.

Given a current state in this search space, the proposal distribution "proposes" to jump to a new state, which will then be evaluated by the Metropolis algorithm. Our proposal samples a new state in the following successive steps:

1. Sample uniformly one of the three possible moves:

Move1: Change the semantic class of a head;

Move2: Change the argument type of an argument segment;

Move3: Change the assignment of an argument to a new head;

2. If Move1 is chosen, sample uniformly one head segment and one target semantic class;

3. If Move2 is chosen, sample uniformly one argument segment and one target argument type;

4. If Move3 is chosen, sample uniformly one argument segment W_a and "detach" it from its current head. Then, sample uniformly one target head segment W'_h, and reattach W_a to its new head W'_h. Because the distribution of argument types differ from one head class to another, it would be interesting at this stage to resample the argument type of W_a from the new head class distribution. But in this work, we resample the argument type from the uniform distribution.

This proposal distribution $Q(x \rightarrow x')$ is reversible, i.e., $Q(x \rightarrow x') > 0 \Rightarrow Q(x' \rightarrow x) > 0$. We can show that it is further symmetric, i.e., $Q(x \rightarrow x') = Q(x' \rightarrow x)$, because the same move is sampled to jump from x to x' than to jump from x' to x, and because the proposal distribution within each move is uniform.

4 Experimental validation

4.1 Experimental setup

The French MEDIA corpus collects about 70 hours of spontaneous speech (1258 dialogues, 46k utterances, 494.048 words and 4068 distinct words) for the task of hotel reservation and tourist information (Bonneau-Maynard et al., 2005). Calls from 250 speakers to a simulated reservation system (i.e. the Wizard-of-Oz) were recorded and transcribed. Dialogues are full of disfluencies, hesitations, false starts, truncations or fillers words (e.g., euh or ben).

Gold Standard Annotation	
Semantic Relation	Frequency
Agent	320
Booked object	298
Location	285
Time	209
Coordination	134
Beneficiary	117
Price	108
Reference Location	66

Table 2: Most frequent semantic relations in the gold annotation.

This corpus has been semantically annotated as part of the French ANR project PORT-MEDIA (Rojas-Barahona et al., 2011). We are using a set of 330 utterances manually annotated with gold semantic relations (i.e. High-Level Semantics). This gold corpus gathers 653 head segments and 1555 argument segments, from which around 20% are both arguments and heads, such as *une chambre* in Figure 4. Table 2 shows the semantic relations frequencies in the gold annotation. 12 head segment types and 19 different argument segment types are defined in the gold annotations. In the evaluation, we assume the number of both classes is given. A possible extension of the approach to automatically infer the number of classes would be to use a non-parametric model, but this is left for future work.

4.2 Evaluation metrics

The proposed method infers three types of semantic information:

- The semantic relation between an argument and its head;
- The argument type A
- The semantic class of the head C_t.

The three outcomes are evaluated as follows.

- The output structure is a forest of trees that is similar to a partial syntactic dependency structure. We thus use a classical unsupervised dependency parsing metric, the Unlabeled Attachment Score (UAS), which is simply the accuracy of argument attachment: an argument is correctly attached if and only if its inferred head matches the gold head.
- Both argument and head classes correspond to the outcome of a clustering process into semantic classes, akin to the semantic classes obtained in unsupervised semantic role labeling tasks. We then evaluate them with a classical metric used to evaluate these classes in unsupervised SRL (as done for instance in (Lang and Lapata, 2011a) and (Titov and Klementiev, 2012)): purity and collocation.

Purity measures the degree to which each cluster contains instances that share the same gold class, while collocation measures the degree to which instances with the same gold class are assigned to a single cluster.

More formally, the purity of argument segments' (head segment') clusters for the whole corpus is computed as follows:

$$PU = \frac{1}{N}\sum_i \max_j |G_j \cap C_i|$$

where C_i is the set of argument (head) segments in the ith cluster found, G_j is the set of argument (head) segments in the jth gold class, and N is the number of gold argument (head) segment instances. In a similar way, the collocation of argument segments' (head segment') clusters is computed as follows:

$$CO = \frac{1}{N}\sum_j \max_i |G_j \cap C_i|$$

Finally the F1 measure is the harmonic mean of the purity and collocation:

$$F1 = \frac{2 * CO * PU}{CO + PU}$$

4.3 Experimental results

We compare the proposed approach against two baselines:

- An argument-head "attachment" baseline, which attaches each argument to the closest head segment.
- A strong clustering baseline, which respectively clusters the head and argument segments using a very effective topic model: the Latent Dirichlet Allocation (LDA) approach (Blei et al., 2003).

Table 3 shows the UAS obtained for the proposed model on the MEDIA corpus, while Table 4 shows the obtained Purity, Collocation and F1-measure. In both cases, we compare the performances of the proposed model with the respective baseline. Our system outperforms both baselines by a large margin.

System	UAS
Closest attachment	68% ($\pm 2\%$)
Proposed - UAS	**74%** ($\pm 2\%$)

Table 3: Experimental results for UAS on the MEDIA database. The statistical confidence interval at 95% with Gaussian approximation is reported.

System	Purity	Col.	F-mes
LDA - Heads	51.7%	25.5%	34.2%
LDA - Args	31.7%	22.2%	26.1%
Proposed - Heads	78.7%	50.8%	**61.8%**
Proposed - Args	61.8%	53.3%	**59.3%**

Table 4: Experimental results on the MEDIA database for purity, collocation and F1-measure.

4.3.1 Qualitative Evaluation

We further carried out a qualitative evaluation, where we inspected the inferred clusters and compared them with the baseline. Figures 7 and 8 show, for every head class C_t in each stacked column, the distribution of instances from all gold clusters. Each column can also be viewed as a graphical representation of the intersection of one inferred class with all gold clusters. Figure 7 illustrates this for our model, and Figure 8 for LDA. The same comparison for the argument types is shown, respectively, in Figure 5 and Figure 6.

For head segment clusters, we can observe that most inferred clusters contain many instances of the Reservation type (in dark blue), both in the LDA baseline and in the proposed system. The main reason for that is that the corpus is very unbalanced in favor of the Reservation class, while we do not assume any prior knowledge about the data and thus use a uniform prior. Still, every other gold type that occurs with a reasonnably high enough frequency, apart from two special types that are discussed next, is well captured by one of

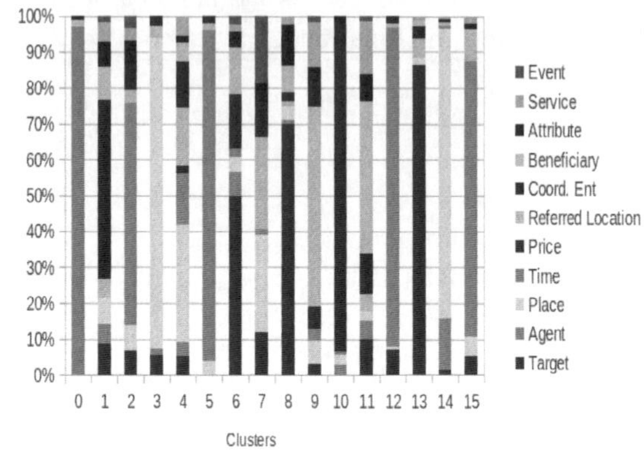

Figure 5: Distribution of the gold types (one per color) into the clusters inferred by our system (shown on the X-axis) for argument segments.

our inferred class: this is the case for "Room" that mainly intersects with our class 1, "Place" with our class 2 and "Hotel" with our class 9.

Some examples of instances for each case are:

- Reservation: *"voudrais réserver", "aimerais partir", "voudrais une *réservation une réservation", "prends", "recherche" , "*désire désire", "il me faudrait", "opte", "aimerais s' il vous plaît si c' est possible avoir prendre".*
- Room: *"deux chambres pour un coup(le) avec trois enfants avec bon standing", "trois singles", "deux chambres de bon standing à peu près niveau trois étoiles", "trois doubles".*
- Place: *"Paris", "à Saintes", "à Charleville", "dans le dix huitième arrondissement de Paris".*
- Hotel: *"un hôtel deux étoiles", "dans un hôtel beau standing", "un hôtel formule un", "l' hôt(el) le l' hôtel", "un autre hôtel dans les mêmes conditions", "le Beaugency", "l' autre", "au Novotel", "le premier".*

Two "special" head segment types that are neither nicely captured by our system nor LDA are Coordination and Inform, which are instead assigned to the clusters corresponding to the gold segments that they coordinate or inform about.

For argument segments we also observed that the inferred clusters are semantically related to the gold types. We found, for instance, four clusters

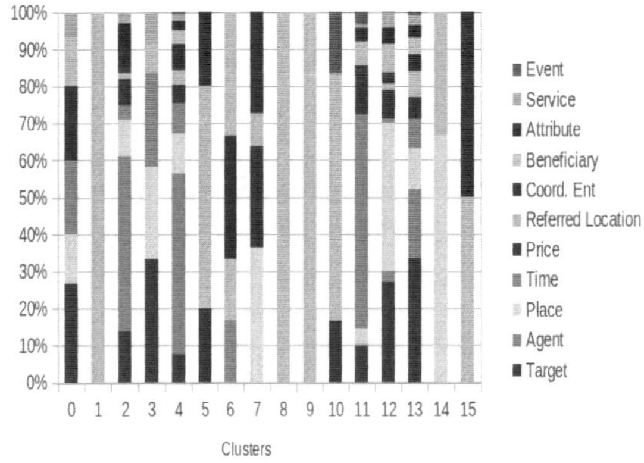

Figure 6: Distribution of the gold types (one per color) into the clusters inferred by the LDA baseline (shown on the X-axis) for argument segments.

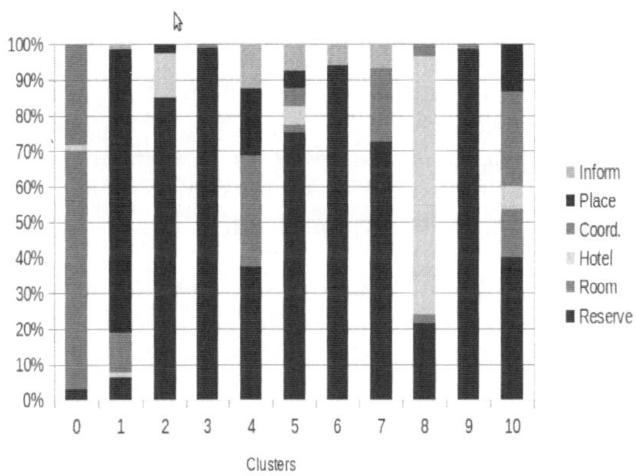

Figure 7: Distribution of the gold types (one per color) into the clusters inferred by our system (shown on the X-axis) for head segments.

(2, 5, 12 and 15) containing mainly "Time" arguments (*"du premier au trois Novembre", "dix nuit", "le festival du film", "au seize Novembre"*, etc.), two (3 and 14) dedicated to "Location" arguments (*"à Menton", "au festival lyrique de belle euh Belle Ile En mer", "bastille", "sur le ville de Paris", "parking privé"*), one (10) for "Price" arguments (*"pas plus de cent euros par personne", "un tarif inférieur à quatre vingts euros", "pas trop chère", "à cent vingt euros", "moins de cent* cent euros"*) etc.

Finally, as noted for the head segments, we can observe that the most frequent gold types largely intersect with several inferred clusters, for the same reason: data is very unbalanced and we do not assume any prior knowledge about the data

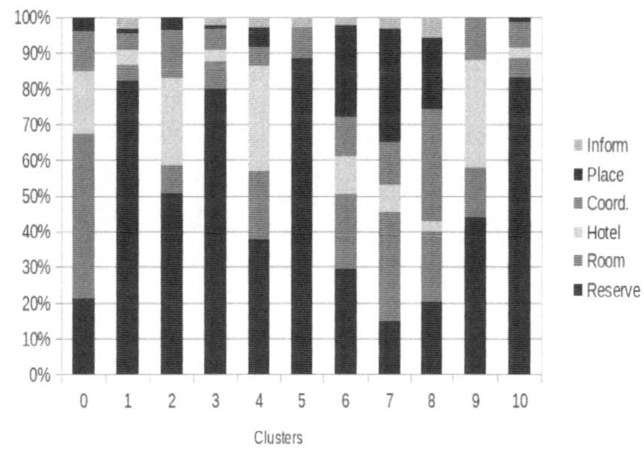

Figure 8: Distribution of the gold types (one per color) into the clusters inferred by the LDA baseline (shown on the X-axis) for head segments.

and thus use an uniform prior. Nevertheless, several other important classes such as Event, Price and Agent are well captured by our system.

5 Conclusions

This work proposes an unsupervised generative model to infer latent semantic structures on top of user spontaneous utterances. It relies on the Metropolis-Hastings sampling algorithm to jointly infer both the structure and semantic classes. It is evaluated in the context of the French MEDIA corpus for the hotel reservation task. Although the system proposed in this work is evaluated on a specific spoken dialog reservation task, it actually relies on a generic unsupervised structured inference model and can thus be applied to many other structured inference tasks, as long as observed word segments are given.

An interesting future direction of research would be to modify this model so that it jointly infers both the latent syntactic and semantic structures, which are known to be closely related but still carry complementary information. We of course also plan to evaluate the proposed model with automatic speech transcriptions and concepts decoding. Another advantage of the proposed model is the possibility to build better Metropolis-Hastings proposals, which may greatly improve the convergence rate of the algorithm. In particular, we would like to investigate the use of some non-uniform proposal distributions when reattaching an argument to a new head, which shall improve mixing.

References

Omri Abend, Roi Reichart, and Ari Rappoport. 2009. Unsupervised argument identification for semantic role labeling. In *Proceedings of the Joint Conference of the 47th Annual Meeting of the ACL and the 4th International Joint Conference on Natural Language Processing of the AFNLP*, ACL '09, pages 28–36, Stroudsburg, PA, USA. Association for Computational Linguistics.

D.M. Blei, A.Y. Ng, and M.I. Jordan. 2003. Latent dirichlet allocation. *the Journal of machine Learning research*, 3:993–1022.

Helene Bonneau-Maynard, Sophie Rosset, Christelle Ayache, Anne Kuhn, and Djamel Mostefa. 2005. Semantic annotation of the french MEDIA dialog corpus. In *INTERSPEECH-2005, 3457-3460.*

N. Camelin, B. Detienne, S. Huet, D. Quadri, and F. Lefèvre. 2011. Unsupervised concept annotation using latent dirichlet allocation and segmental methods. In *EMNLP 1st Workshop on Unsupervised Learning in NLP*, Edinburgh (UK).

Alexandre Denis, Matthieu Quignard, and Guillaume Pitel. 2006. A Deep-Parsing Approach to Natural Language Understanding in Dialogue System: Results of a Corpus-Based Evaluation. In *Proceedings of the 5th international Conference on Language Resources and Evaluation (LREC 2006) Proceedings of Language Resources and Evaluation Conference*, pages 339–344, Genoa Italie.

Koen Deschacht and Marie-Francine Moens. 2009. Semi-supervised semantic role labeling using the latent words language model. In *Proc. EMNLP*, pages 21–29.

Hagen Fürstenau and Mirella Lapata. 2009. Graph alignment for semi-supervised semantic role labeling. In *Proc. EMNLP*, pages 11–20.

Trond Grenager and Christopher D. Manning. 2006. Unsupervised discovery of a statistical verb lexicon. In *Proceedings of the 2006 Conference on Empirical Methods in Natural Language Processing*, EMNLP '06, pages 1–8, Stroudsburg, PA, USA. Association for Computational Linguistics.

S. He and H. Gildea. 2006. Self-training and Cotraining for Semantic Role Labeling: Primary Report. Technical report, TR 891, University of Colorado at Boulder.

Stéphane Huet and Fabrice Lefèvre. 2011. Unsupervised alignment for segmental-based language understanding. In *Proceedings of the First Workshop on Unsupervised Learning in NLP*, EMNLP '11, pages 97–104, Stroudsburg, PA, USA. Association for Computational Linguistics.

Joel Lang and Mirella Lapata. 2010. Unsupervised induction of semantic roles. In *Human Language Technologies: The 2010 Annual Conference of the North American Chapter of the Association for Computational Linguistics*, HLT '10, pages 939–947, Stroudsburg, PA, USA. Association for Computational Linguistics.

Joel Lang and Mirella Lapata. 2011a. Unsupervised semantic role induction via split-merge clustering. In *Proc. ACL*, pages 1117–1126.

Joel Lang and Mirella Lapata. 2011b. Unsupervised semantic role induction with graph partitioning. In *EMNLP*, pages 1320–1331. Association for Computer Linguistics.

Joo-Young Lee, Young-In Song, and Hae-Chang Rim. 2007. Investigation of weakly supervised learning for semantic role labeling. In *ALPIT*, pages 165–170. IEEE Computer Society.

Marie-Jean Meurs, Fabrice Lefèvre, and Renato de Mori. 2009. Spoken language interpretation: On the use of dynamic bayesian networks for semantic composition. In *Proc. ICASSP*, pages 4773–4776.

Nitin Namdeo Pise and Parag Kulkarni. 2008. A survey of semi-supervised learning methods. In *Proceedings of the 2008 International Conference on Computational Intelligence and Security - Volume 02*, CIS '08, pages 30–34, Washington, DC, USA. IEEE Computer Society.

Lina Maria Rojas-Barahona, Thierry Bazillon, Matthieu Quignard, and Fabrice Lefevre. 2011. Using MMIL for the high level semantic annotation of the french MEDIA dialogue corpus. In *Proceedings of the Ninth International Conference on Computational Semantics (IWCS 2011).*

Robert S. Swier and Suzanne Stevenson. 2004. Unsupervised Semantic Role Labelling. In *EMNLP*, pages 95–102. Association for Computational Linguistics.

Ivan Titov and Alexandre Klementiev. 2012. A bayesian approach to unsupervised semantic role induction. In *Proceedings of the Conference of the European Chapter of the Association for Computational Linguistics*, Avignon, France, April.

Xiaojin Zhu. 2005. Semi-Supervised Learning Literature Survey. Technical report, Computer Sciences, University of Wisconsin-Madison.

Toward a Better Understanding of Causality between Verbal Events: Extraction and Analysis of the Causal Power of Verb-Verb Associations

Mehwish Riaz and Roxana Girju
Department of Computer Science and Beckman Institute
University of Illinois at Urbana-Champaign
Urbana, IL 61801, USA
{mriaz2, girju}@illinois.edu

Abstract

The identification of causal relations between verbal events is important for achieving natural language understanding. However, the problem has proven notoriously difficult since it is not clear which types of knowledge are necessary to solve this challenging problem close to human level performance. Instead of employing a large set of features proved useful in other NLP tasks, we split the problem in smaller sub problems. Since verbs play a very important role in causal relations, in this paper we harness, explore, and evaluate the predictive power of causal associations of verb-verb pairs. More specifically, we propose a set of knowledge-rich metrics to learn the likelihood of causal relations between verbs. Employing these metrics, we automatically generate a knowledge base (KB_c) which identifies three categories of verb pairs: Strongly Causal, Ambiguous, and Strongly Non-causal. The knowledge base is evaluated empirically. The results show that our metrics perform significantly better than the state-of-the-art on the task of detecting causal verbal events.

1 Introduction

The identification of semantic relations between events is a mandatory component of natural language understanding. In this paper, we focus on the identification of causal relations between events represented by verbs. Following Riaz and Girju (2010), we define a verbal event e_{v_i} as "[subject$_{v_i}$] v_i [object$_{v_i}$]", where the subject and object of the verb may or may not be explicitly present in an instance. Consider the following examples:

1. Yoga **builds** stamina because you **maintain** your poses for a certain period of time. (CAUSE ($e_{maintain}, e_{build}$))
2. The monster storm Katrina **raged** ashore along the Gulf Coast Monday morning. There were early reports of buildings **collapsing** along the coast. (CAUSE ($e_{rage}, e_{collapse}$))

In example 1, the two bold events are causally connected by an explicit and unambiguous discourse marker (*because*). However, in English, not all discourse markers unambiguously identify causality (Prasad et al., 2008) - for example, Bethard and Martin (2008) proposed a corpus of 1000 causal and non-causal event pairs conjoined by the marker *and*. Even more, causal relations can be encoded by implicit contexts - i.e., those where no discourse marker is present (example 2). Despite the recent achievements obtained in discourse processing, it is still unclear what types of knowledge can contribute most towards detecting causality in both explicit and implicit contexts (Sporleder and Lascarides, 2008). The complexity of the task of detecting causality between events stems from the fact that there are many factors involved, such as contextual features of an instance (e.g., lexical items, tenses of verbs, arguments of verbs, etc.), semantic and pragmatic features of events, background knowledge, world knowledge, common sense, etc. Prior approaches have employed contextual features of an instance to identify causality between events or discourse segments (Bethard and Martin, 2008; Pitler and Nenkova, 2009; Pitler et al., 2009). Although contextual features provide important knowledge about sentence(s) in which events appear, humans also make use of other information such as background knowledge to comprehend causality. For instance, in example 2 we use knowledge about the causal association between verbal entities **rage** and **collapse** to label it with causality.

This research is motivated by the need to extract and analyze other type of knowledge necessary for the identification of causal relations between verbal events. We start from the fact that verbs are the main components of language to express events and semantic relations between events. Thus, in order to identify and extract causal relations between events (denoted by (e_{v_i}, e_{v_j})), it is critical for a model to employ knowledge about the tendency of a verb pair (v_i, v_j) to encode causation. For example, the pair (kill, arrest) has a high tendency to encode a cause relation irrespective of the context in which it is used, thereby a good indicator of causality. The state-of-the-art resources on verb semantics, such as WordNet, VerbNet, PropBank, FrameNet, etc. (Miller, 1990; Kipper et al., 2000; Kingsbury et al., 2002; Baker et al., 1998), provide information about the semantic classes, thematic roles and selectional restrictions of verbs. Among these, WordNet is the only resource which provides information about the cause relation between verbs, but it has very limited coverage. For VerbOcean, a semi-automatically generated resource, Chklovski and Pantel (2004) have used explicit lexical patterns (e.g., "verb * by verb") as means of mining enablement (cause-effect) relations between verbs. Such approaches help detecting causality with high precision but suffer from limited coverage due to the highly implicit nature of language. Moreover, such resources do not provide any information about the likelihood of a causal relation in verb pairs - e.g., (kill, arrest) has a high tendency to encode cause relation as compared with the pair (build, maintain). The pair (build, maintain) seems ambiguous because it can encode both cause and non-cause relations depending on the context, as shown by examples 1 and 3. Thus, causality detection models should employ knowledge about which verb pairs are strongly causal (non-causal) in nature and for which pairs the context plays an important role to signal causality.

3. Republicans had not cut the funds for **maintaining** the levee and **building** up the ecological protections. (NON-CAUSE)

We propose a fully automated procedure to learn the likelihood of causal relations in verb pairs. In this process, we create three categories of verb pairs: Strongly Causal (S_c), Ambiguous (A_c) and Strongly Non-causal ($S_{\neg c}$). The result is a knowledge base (KB_c) of causal associations of verbs. In KB_c, the category S_c ($S_{\neg c}$) contains the verb pairs which have the greatest (least) likelihood to encode a causal relation, respectively. However, the category A_c contains ambiguous verb pairs which have the likelihood to encode both causal and non-causal relations. The information about such causal associations provides a rich knowledge source to causality detection models.

The main contributions of our research are as follows:

- We propose a set of novel metrics (i.e., Explicit Causal Association (ECA), Implicit Causal Association (ICA) and Boosted Causal Association (BCA)) to identify the likelihood of verb pairs to encode causality. Our metrics exploit the information available from a large number of unlabeled explicit and implicit instances of verb pairs for this purpose.
- We introduce an automated procedure to build a training corpus of causal and non-causal event pairs. This prevents us from the trouble of annotating a large number of event pairs for cause and non-cause relations. Our metrics make use of supervision from the training corpus to identify causality in verb pairs. We also provide a mechanism to determine causal verb pairs which remain undiscovered due to the issue of training data sparseness.
- We revisit recent approaches employing distributional similarity methods to predict causality between events (Riaz and Girju, 2010; Do et al., 2011). The state-of-the-art metric Cause-Effect Association (CEA) (Do et al., 2011) identifies causality mainly based on probabilities of verb-verb, verb-argument, and argument-argument pairs. In comparison with CEA, our metrics perform significantly better by improving the prior knowledge about the causal associations from CEA's components.

After a brief review of related work in next section, we describe our approach for acquisition of training corpus in section 3. The model for the extraction of causal associations is presented in section 4, followed by the evaluation and discussion in section 5 and conclusion in section 6.

2 Related Work

Causality has long been studied from various perspectives by philosophers, data-mining researchers and computer scientists (Menzies, 2008; Woodward, 2008; Suppes, 1970; Silverstein et al., 2000; Pearl, 2000).

In NLP, the problem of detecting causality between events is a very challenging but less researched topic. Previously, researchers have studied this task by focusing on supervised classification models for both verbal and nominal events (Girju, 2003; Bethard and Martin, 2008). Bethard and Martin (2008), for example, have focused mainly on the contextual features available in test instances of verbal event pairs to predict causality. They have relied on a small scale dataset of 1000 instances (697 training and 303 test) for this task. Unlike above models, recently some researchers have employed unsupervised causality detection metrics and minimal supervision for this task. For example, Riaz and Girju (2010) have proposed an unsupervised metric Effect-Control Dependency (ECD) to determine causality between events in news scenarios. Following their model, Do et al. (2011) introduced an improved metric CEA which uses PMI and some components of ECD to predict the causal relation in verbal and nominal event pairs in a text document. They also proposed a minimally supervised method using explicit discourse markers. For example, they used ILP framework to assign a non-causal relation to all the event pairs appearing in two discourse segments connected by a non-causal marker. They evaluated their model on a set of 20 documents, a highly skewed evaluation set with around 2-3% causal instances and 58% human inter-annotator agreement on cause-effect relations. On verbal events, they reported 38.3% F-score with CEA and 1-2% improvement using minimally supervised method. As compared with above mentioned metrics, we introduce knowledge rich association measures which employ supervision from the automatically generated training corpus to learn causality.

Several other NLP researchers have studied related topics e.g., identifying events, building of temporal chain of events sharing a common protagonist (participant), predicting future events and identifying hidden links in news articles to build a coherent chain (Chambers and Jurafsky, 2008; Chambers and Jurafsky, 2009; Radinsky and Horvitz, 2013; Shahaf and Guestrin, 2010). Unlike these tasks, our focus is on identifying causality between events.

3 Acquisition of Training Corpus

In this section, we propose a fully automated procedure to build a training corpus of event pairs which encode cause and non-cause relations. This training corpus is used in our model to identify the likelihood of cause relations in verb pairs. As discussed earlier, previous researchers have worked with a small scale dataset of annotated event pairs. The current task requires us to use a large training corpus to learn the pervasive relation of causality and the manual generation of such corpus is a laborious task. Therefore, we decided to depend on the unambiguous discourse markers *because* and *but* to automatically collect training instances of cause and non-cause event pairs, respectively. For example, the marker *because* in the instance 1 of section 1 encodes a cause relation between the events e_{build} and $e_{maintain}$. Some researchers have utilized unambiguous discourse markers to acquire training instances of semantic relations between discourse segments (Marcu and Echihabi, 2001; Sporleder and Lascarides, 2008). However, the process is not simple for the current problem since it is not always clear how to create a causal instance of an event pair. Consider the following meta instance I:

I : <s>/$m_1 \ldots v_1 \ldots v_2 \ldots v_k \ldots$ *because* $\ldots v_{k+1} \ldots v_{k+2}, \ldots, v_r, \ldots m_2$/</s>.

It is composed of main verbs (v_1, v_2, ..., v_r), discourse markers (m_1, m_2), and sentence boundaries (<s>, </s>). Here, we assume that the discourse markers or the sentence boundaries whichever appear first in I represent the boundaries of discourse segments for the marker *because* (appendix A contains a table of notations used in this paper). In I, there are k and $r-k$ main verbs appearing before and after *because*, respectively. The problem here is to determine the event pair encoding causality out of $k \times (r-k)$ choices. Here, we consider that the most dependent pair among all choices in I is the best candidate to encode causality.

In this work, we propose the following function $f(I)$ to pick the most dependent pair:

$$f(I) = \underset{(v_i \prec m_c, v_j \succ m_c)}{\arg\max} \; CD(v_i, v_j) \times PS_I(v_i, v_j) \quad (1)$$

Here, i (j) refers to all verbs that appear before (after) the causal marker (i.e., m_c) *because* in I. CD (equation 2) is a component of predicate-predicate association of CEA (Do et al., 2011) to determine causal dependency of a pair (v_i, v_j). Do et al. (2011) used the score CD to determine causality in an unsupervised fashion but here we employ this to build a training corpus of causal event pairs.

$$CD(v_i, v_j) = PMI(v_i, v_j) \times max(v_i, v_j) \times IDF(v_i, v_j) \quad (2)$$

The functions PMI, max and IDF depend on co-occurrence probabilities and idf scores to determine causal dependency. Due to space limitations, for details we refer the reader to Do et al. (2011).

Next, we define a novel penalization factor PS_I for the verbs of a pair appearing at greater distance from the causal marker *because*. For example, this assumes the verbs in the pair (v_2, v_{k+2}) are less likely to be in a cause relation as compared with (v_k, v_{k+1}) in I. We came up with this idea because our initial experiments revealed that the causal instances obtained by penalizing CD with PS_I provide better training for our model as compared to using only CD for this purpose. The similar behavior of reduction in the likelihood of causality with respect to increase in distance between two events was observed by Riaz and Girju (2010).

$$PS_I(v_i, v_j) = -\log \frac{pos(v_i) + pos(v_j)}{2.0 \times (C(v_p) + C(v_q))} \quad (3)$$

Here, $\text{C}(v_p)$ $(\text{C}(v_q))$ is the count of the main verbs appearing before (after) *because*, respectively. The distance of the verb is measured in terms of its position (i.e., $\text{pos}(v_i)$) with respect to *because*. The position is 1 for the verb closest to *because* and 2 for the verb next to the closest verb. PS_I has maximum value for (v_k, v_{k+1}) and it reduces for other pairs with verbs at greater distance from *because* in instance I.

In order to extract non-causal event pairs, we utilized instances with two discourse segments conjoined by the marker *but* which represents comparison (non-causal) relation. Any event pair collected from the two discourse segments in non-causal relation encodes non-causality. Therefore, we depend on selecting the closest verb pair from the instances of form I with marker *but* instead of *because*.

In this paper, we present the results produced using a training corpus of 240K instances (50% for each class) from the English Gigaword Corpus. In order to prepare this corpus, we identified discourse markers (i.e., m_1, m_2), if available, before and after *because/but* in each instance I and assumed that only those markers which have discourse usage in I define boundaries of discourse segments of *because/but*. We used the list of 100 explicit discourse markers provided by Prasad et al. (2008) and the supervised approach of Pitler and Nenkova (2009) to detect markers and the discourse versus non-discourse usage of these markers. We use this training corpus to identify causation for both explicit and implicit instances of event pairs. Using this training corpus, a model tends to give higher causal weights to those instances in which events are connected by the explicit causal marker *because* as compared to implicit instances of causation. Thus, to provide fair supervision to both explicit and implicit instances of event pairs, we remove the cue words *because* and *but* which were used to automatically label the training instances.

4 Causal Associations of Verb Pairs

In this section, we explain our approach to learn the likelihood of causal relations in verb pairs by exploiting information available from both explicit and implicit instances of these pairs. We extracted around $12,000$ documents from the English Gigaword corpus to collect instances of verb pairs from single sentences (intra-sentential) and adjacent sentences (inter-sentential) of text. In this set, we added instances from $3,000$ articles on news stories "Hurricane Katrina" and the "Iraq war". These articles were collected and used to identify causal relations in news scenarios by Riaz and Girju (2010). We used these collections because natural disaster and war-related news articles are rich in causal events and chains of such events. In order to identify the causal associations with high confidence, we decided to apply our model on those verb pairs which have at least 30 instances in the above mentioned documents. We acquired $10,455$ such verb pairs. The set of intra- and inter-sentential instances of these verb pairs is referred to as the development set for our model.

4.1 Explicit Causal Association (ECA)

In order to find the likelihood of a verb pair to encode causal relations, we define our novel metric Explicit Causal Association (ECA) as follows:

$$ECA(v_i, v_j) = \frac{1}{|\,VP\,|} \sum_{I_{(v_i, v_j)} \in VP} (CD(v_i, v_j) \times C_I) \quad (4)$$

where VP is the set of intra- and inter-sentential instances (denoted by $I(v_i, v_j)$) of the verb pair (v_i, v_j), CD determines the causal dependency of the verb pair in unsupervised fashion (equation 2), and C_I finds the tendency of instance I of (v_i, v_j) to belong to the cause class as compared to the non-cause class using training corpus of event pairs. The goal of ECA is to combine the unsupervised causal dependency (i.e., CD) with the supervised score of instance I of belonging to cause class than the non-cause one (i.e., C_I). Here, CD represents the prior knowledge about the causal association based on co-occurrence probabilities and idf scores (equation 2). It can discover lots of false positives because the co-occurrence probabilities can fail to differentiate causality from any other type of correlation. Therefore, we improve this prior knowledge with the help of supervision from the training corpus containing instances of both cause and non-cause relations. The global decision of the causal association is made by taking the average of scores on all the instances containing that verb pair. Notice that CD can also be moved out from the summation function in equation 4.

We define the function C_I as follows:

$$C_I = \sum_{k=1}^{n} log(\frac{P(f_k \mid c)}{P(f_k \mid \neg c)}) \quad (5)$$

Here, the notations c and ¬ c represent cause and non-cause class, respectively. The notation f_k represents the feature of an instance I. In this work, we use some language features of events and context of an instance I which are defined later in this section. P(f_k | c) and P(f_k | $\neg c$) are the smoothed probabilities of feature f_k given the cause and non-cause training instances. The value of C_I is positive only when the instance I has more tendency to encode a cause relation than a non-cause one. To avoid negative values, we map C_I scores to the range $[0, 1]$ using $\frac{C_I - C_{min}}{C_{max} - C_{min}}$ where C_{min} (C_{max}) is the minimum (maximum) value of C_I obtained on our development set, respectively. Also, we add a small value ϵ to C_I to avoid 0 value. Similarly, to avoid negative scores of PMI in equation 2 we can map it to the range [0,1].

We present below the features for the calculation of C_I . We use lexical, syntatic and semantic features on verbs and verb phrases of both events of a pair. These features include words, lemmas, part-of-speech tags, all senses from WordNet for the verbs and the lexical items of verb phrases. These features were introduced by Bethard and Martin (2008) (for an in-depth description of these features see Bethard and Martin (2008)). Next, we describe the set of features which are the contributions of this research.

1. **Verbs Arguments:** Words, lemma, part-of-speech tags and all senses from WordNet for subject and object of verbs of both events.
2. **Verbs and Arguments Pairs:** For this feature, we take the cross product of both events of a pair (e_{v_i},e_{v_j}) where e_{v_i} = [subject$_{v_i}$] v_i [object$_{v_i}$] and e_{v_j} = [subject$_{v_j}$] v_j [object$_{v_j}$]. Some examples of this feature are (subject$_{v_i}$,subject$_{v_j}$), (subject$_{v_i}$,v_j), (subject$_{v_i}$,object$_{v_j}$), etc. In this work, we use unordered pairs as features (i.e., (v_i,v_j)) is same as (v_j,v_i)) because the temporal order of events is unknown for the unlabeled development set instances. In future, this feature can be improved by adding temporal information.

The next three features are taken from the minimum relevant context ($min_{context}$) of a verb pair which we define as follows. $min_{context}$ of a pair (v_i, v_j) in an intra-sentential instance is <s>/$m_1 \ldots v_i \ldots v_j \ldots m_2$/</s> – i.e., words between the discourse markers (i.e., m_1, m_2) or sentence boundaries (i.e., <s>, </s>) whichever appear first in the sentence. The $min_{context}$ for the pair (v_i, v_j) in an inter-sentential is given below:

<s> / $m_1 \ldots v_i \ldots m_2$ / </s>
<s> / $m_1 \ldots v_j \ldots m_2$ / </s>

3. **Context Words:** Lemmas of all words from $min_{context}$. This feature captures words other than two events.
4. **Context Main Verbs:** All main verbs and their lemmas from $min_{context}$. It collects information about all verbs that appear with the causal and non-causal event pair.
5. **Context Main Verb Pairs:** The pairs of main verbs from $min_{context}$. The lemmas are taken from the feature "Context Main Verbs" and then the pairs on these lemmas are used as this feature. For example, for lemmas of verbs (i.e., $v_1, v_2, \ldots, v_k$), pairs (i.e., (v_1, v_2), (v_1, v_k), etc.) are used for this feature. This feature is used to get information about the interesting causal chains of verbs that may appear in causal instances.

We propose next a novel metric ICA to avoid the problem of training data sparsity.

4.2 Implicit Causal Association (ICA)

In order to determine the causal associations using ECA, we depend on explicit cause and non-cause training instances for supervision. However, it is possible that some strongly causal verb pairs may frequently appear in implicit causal contexts. Therefore, the causality of such pairs can remain uncaptured by ECA which merely relies on explicit training instances. For example, a pair (fall, break) seems strongly causal, but it does not appear often in our explicit training corpus due to training data sparsity. Thus, in order to handle this problem, we propose a new metric called ICA. This metric makes use of functions for the identification of roles of events in a cause relation. After briefly describing the roles of events in causal relations below, we continue with the description of ICA.

4.2.1 Roles of Events in Cause Relation

Each of the two events in a cause relation can be assigned either cause or effect role. For example for the following training instance, the verb appearing after *because* represents cause event and the verb before *because* represents effect event.

1. Yoga *builds* stamina because you **maintain** your poses for a certain period of time. (**Role:** r_C)
2. Yoga **builds** stamina because you *maintain* your poses for a certain period of time. (**Role:** r_E)

The notation r_C and r_E represents the classes of cause and effect role of events, respectively. We use core features of events to determine the likelihood of their roles in causation. These features include lemma, part-of-speech tag, all senses from WordNet of both verbs and their arguments (i.e., subject and object). Next, we use these features to handle training data sparseness.

4.2.2 Handling of Training Data Sparsity

To deal with the problem of training data sparsity, we define the metric ICA as follows:

$$ICA(v_i, v_j) = \frac{1}{|VP|} \sum_{I_{(v_i,v_j)} \in VP} (CD(v_i, v_j) \times C_I \times ERM_{(e_{v_i}, e_{v_j})}) \quad (6)$$

where CD and C_I are defined earlier and ERM determines the likelihood of roles of the events in the cause relation. We remind the reader that CD is the unsupervised causal dependency of verb pair and C_I is the likelihood of instance I of the verb pair to belong to the cause class than the non-cause one using full set of features from section 4.1.

Events Roles Matching (ERM$_{(e_{v_i}, e_{v_j})}$) (equations 7 and 8) is the negative log-likelihood of events e_{v_i} and e_{v_j} appearing as cause or effect role determined using the explicit causal instances of the training corpus and the core features of events defined in section 4.2.1.

$$ERM_{(e_{v_i}, e_{v_j})} = -1.0 \times \max(S(e_{v_i}, r_C) + S(e_{v_j}, r_E), S(e_{v_i}, r_E) + S(e_{v_j}, r_C)) \quad (7)$$

$$S(e_{v_i}, r_C) = \sum_{k=1}^{n} log(P(f_k \mid r_C)) \quad (8)$$

$$S(e_{v_j}, r_E) = \sum_{k=1}^{n} log(P(f_k \mid r_E))$$

Here, S(e_{v_i}, r_C) is the score of e_{v_i} being the cause event and S(e_{v_j}, r_E) is the score of e_{v_j} being the effect event. These scores are computed using smoothed probabilities – i.e., P($f_k \mid r_C$) and P($f_k \mid r_E$). Similarly, S(e_{v_i}, r_E) and S(e_{v_j}, r_C) are calculated and max is taken. The high value of ERM represents low matching of an event pair (verbs and their arguments) in the explicit causal instances of the training corpus. The high value of ERM of an event pair can have one of the following two interpretations: (A) it is a non-causal event pair, or (B) it is a causal event pair but this pair and the pairs which are semantically closer to it hardly appear in explicit causal contexts. In the metric ICA, $C_I \times$ CD(v_i, v_j) is used as a guiding score to interpret ERM as follows:

1. If $C_I \times$ CD(v_i, v_j) has high score then the value of ERM is not penalized by this guiding score because ERM's value can be interpreted using (B) above.
2. If $C_I \times$ CD(v_i, v_j) has low score then the value of ERM is penalized by this guiding score because (e_{v_i}, e_{v_j}) can be a non-causal pair according to the interpretation (A) above.

ICA is a boosting factor to determine causal verb pairs which remain undiscovered because of training data sparseness. We also define a Boosted Causal Association (BCA) metric by adding ICA to original ECA metric as follows:

$$BCA(v_i, v_j) = \frac{1}{|VP|} \sum_{I_{(v_i,v_j)} \in VP} (CD(v_i, v_j) \times C_I + CD(v_i, v_j) \times C_I \times ERM_{(e_{v_i}, e_{v_j})}) \quad (9)$$

To build the knowledge base of causal associations (KB_c), we generate a ranked list of all verb pairs based on the likelihood of causality encoded by these pairs. Here, we assume that verb pairs are uniformally distributed across three categories - i.e., top one-third and bottom one-third ranked verb pairs belong to Strongly Causal (S_c) and Strongly Non-Causal ($S_{\neg c}$) categories and rest of the pairs are considered Ambiguous (A_c). Following our assumption, we evaluate this categorization in next section, but in future researchers can perform empirical study of how to automatically cluster verb pairs into three or more categories with respect to causation.

5 Evaluation and Discussion

In this section, we present our evaluation of knowledge base to identify causality between verbal events. Specifically we performed experiments to evaluate (1) the ranking of verb pairs based on their likelihood of encoding causality, and (2) the quality of the three categories of verb pairs in KB_c (i.e., S_c, A_c and $S_{\neg c}$). For this purpose, we collected two test sets. For each test set, we randomly selected 50 verb pairs from the list of $10,455$ verb pairs in KB_c. For each verb pair, we selected randomly 3 intra- and 3 inter-sentential instances from the English Gigaword corpus and the "Hurricane Katrina" and "Iraq war" articles. In order to keep the development set different from the test sets, we automatically traversed the development set to determine if any test instance is available in it. In case of finding any such test instance, we removed it from the development set to perform evaluation on unseen test instances. Two annotators were asked to provide Cause or Non-Cause labels for each instance. They were provided with annotation guidelines from the manipulation theory of causality (Woodward, 2008). Given these guidelines have been successfully used by Riaz and Girju (2010), we use them here as well. For ease of annotation, we randomly selected inter-sentential instances such that the length of each sentence is at most 40 words.

The human inter-annotator agreement achieved on Test-set$_1$ (Test-set$_2$) is 90% (88.3%) and the agreement on the cause class is 70% (62.7%), respectively. The kappa score on Test-set$_1$ (Test-set$_2$) is 0.75 (0.69), respectively. The Test-set$_1$ (Test-set$_2$) contains 25% (22%) causal instances, respectively.

We employed Spearman's rank correlation coefficient (equation 10) to compare the ranked list of verb pairs based on the scores of our metrics and the rank given by the human annotators. The score P ranges from $+1$ to -1 where $+1$ and -1 show strong and negative correlation, respectively.

$$P = \frac{n(\sum x_i y_i) - (\sum x_i)(\sum y_i)}{\sqrt{n(\sum x_i^2) - (\sum x_i)^2}\sqrt{n(\sum y_i^2) - (\sum y_i)^2} \qquad (10)$$

Here, n is the total number of verb pairs in the test set, x_i is the human annotation rank and y_i is the metric's rank of verb pair i of the test set. The values of x_i and y_i are determined as follows. For each verb pair, C_h is calculated which is the number of cause labels given by both human annotators out of 6 instances of a verb pair. The pairs are ranked in descending order according to the score C_h s.t. the top scored pair(s) gets rank 50 and the next to the top pair(s) gets rank 49 and so on. Similarly, ranks are given to the verb pairs according to the metric's scores. This way of evaluation was also used by Beamer and Girju (2009) for temporally ordered adjacent verb pairs. But here, we are working with verb pairs appearing in any temporal order in both intra- and inter-sentential instances.

Metric	CEA	ECA	ICA	BCA
Test-set$_1$	-0.077	0.144	0.427	0.435
Test-set$_2$	0.167	0.217	0.353	0.338

Table 1: The Spearman's rank correlation coefficient for the metrics CEA, ECA, ICA and BCA.

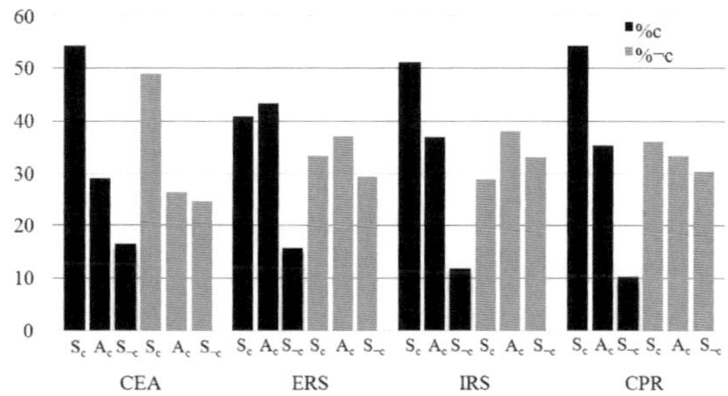

Figure 1: The percentage of causal ($\%c$) and non-causal ($\%\neg c$) test instances in S_c, A_c and $S_{\neg c}$ generated by the metrics CEA, ECA, ICA and BCA.

We used ECA, ICA and BCA scores to generate the ranked list of all verb pairs. In this work, we also used the state-of-the-art causality identifier CEA (Do et al., 2011) as baseline metric. For each verb pair, we computed the likelihood of causality by taking the average of CEA scores on all instances of that pair in the development set.

The results with Spearman's rank correlation coefficient in Table 1 show that CEA is not very capable of matching the human ranked list of pairs as compared with our metrics (i.e., ECA, ICA and BCA). Specifically, the difference is significant for Test-set$_1$ where the correlation coefficient with CEA goes below 0. This behavior of CEA makes sense because it is unsupervised and requires more knowledge to perform well. As compared with ECA, both ICA and BCA perform significantly better to match human ranking. The Spearman's score gain by BCA on Test-set$_1$ is of about 30 (52) points over ECA (CEA) and the gain by ICA on Test-set$_2$ is of about 13 (18) points over ECA (CEA), respectively.

In order to explain the behavior of our metrics

more clearly, we performed an evaluation of three categories of verb pairs as follows. We generated three categories of verb pairs using our metrics and CEA. We combined two test sets to show the percentage of total causal and non-causal instances of verb pairs that lie in S_c, A_c and $S_{\neg c}$ using following procedure. If a verb pair belongs to S_c and has 3 causal and 2 non-causal instances after human agreement, then these 5 instances are considered members of S_c. This step is performed for all verb pairs in the test set. After this the percentage of total causal and non-causal test instances are calculated for each category (see Figure 1).

Figure 1 reveals that ICA, BCA and CEA are successful in pulling more causal instances in S_c as compared to ECA. But, CEA has a hard time distinguishing cause from non-cause instances because it also brings the highest percentage of non-causal instances in S_c. The reason is the dependence of CEA on PMI scores of pairs of verbs and arguments to make decision for causality where PMI is not good enough to distinguish a simple correlation from an asymmetric relation of causality. However, ICA and BCA work better by placing less non-causal instances in S_c as compared with CEA. ICA and BCA also work better because by pulling more causal instances in S_c and A_c, these metrics are keeping least percentage of causal instances in $S_{\neg c}$. Also, ICA and BCA bring more causal instances in S_c as compared with ECA by handling training data sparseness.

Another important line of research is the construction of a classifier on top of the component of knowledge base for the classes of cause and non-cause relations. This allows us to evaluate our model in terms of standard evaluation measures - i.e., precision, recall and F-score. These measures can also be used to compare our model with supervised classifier depending merely on shallow contextual features with no information from the knowledge base. Due to space limitations, we plan to present such classifiers and evaluation in the future.

5.1 Analysis

In this work, we have focused on determining the predictive power of knowledge of causal associations of verb pairs to identify causality between events. Our results reveal that our best metrics (i.e., ICA and BCA) bring desired behavior of keeping least percentage of total causal instances in category $S_{\neg c}$. However, there is need to build a classifier on top of knowledge base which can help detection of non-causal instances for verb pairs lie in S_c and A_c. Here, we state some brief details of our test set which can help building such classifier in future. An important aspect to consider is the highly skewed nature of real distribution of test set. There are only 23.69% causal instances in the test set and majority of these instances (i.e., 56.7%) are intra-sentential instances. Therefore, a classifier should have mechanism to decide why inter-sentential instances of event pair are non-causal most of the time. For example, some inter-sentential events may not even be directly relevant at first place because they appear in different sentences. Another critical point to consider is the encoding of non-causal instances by strongly causal verb pairs. For example, we asked one of the annotators to identify strongly causal verb pairs out of 100 verb pairs of the test set. There are 22 such verb pairs determined by our annotator and each of these pairs contain 43% causal instances on the average. There are many factors (e.g., temporal information, arguments of verbs) which can make an instance of strongly causal verb pair non-causal. For example, (call, respond) may encode causality only if e_{call} temporally precedes $e_{respond}$ as demonstrated by the following instances.

1. Deputies spotted the truck parked at the home of the suspect's father and **called** for assistance. The Border Patrol agents and others **responded**. (CAUSE)
2. Prime Minister of Israel promptly **responded** to the widespread unrest in the West Bank and Gaza, saying that he would **call** a timeout to rethink Israel's commitment to peace talks. (NON-CAUSE)

In future, the above issues need to be addressed to improve performance for the current task.

6 Conclusion

In this research, we have developed a knowledge base (KB_c[1]) of causal associations of verb pairs to detect causality. This resource provides the causal associations in terms of three categories of verb pairs (i.e., Strongly Causal, Ambiguous and Strongly Non-Causal). We have proposed a set of knowledge rich metrics to learn these associations. Our analysis of results reveals the biases of different metrics and brings important insights into the future research directions to address the challenge of detecting causality between verbal events.

[1] We will make the resource available.

References

Collin F. Baker, Charles J. Fillmore and John B. Lowe. 1998. The Berkeley FrameNet project. *In proceedings of COLING-ACL. Montreal, Canada.*

Brandon Beamer and Roxana Girju. 2009. Using a Bigram Event Model to Predict Causal Potential. *In proceedings of Computational Linguistics and intelligent Text Processing (CICLING), 2009.*

Steven Bethard and James H. Martin. 2008. Learning Semantic Links from a Corpus of Parallel Temporal and Causal Relations. *In proceedings of ACL-08: HLT.*

Nathanael Chambers and Dan Jurafsky. 2008. Unsupervised learning of narrative event chains. *In proceedings of ACL-HLT 2008.*

Nathanael Chambers and Dan Jurafsky. 2009. Unsupervised learning of narrative schemas and their participants. *In proceedings of ACL 2009.*

Timothy Chklovski and Patrick Pantel. 2004. VerbOcean: Mining the Web for Fine-Grained Semantic Verb Relations. *In proceedings of Conference on Empirical Methods in Natural Language Processing (EMNLP-04). Barcelona, Spain.*

Quang X. Do, Yee S. Chen and Dan Roth. 2011. Minimally Supervised Event Causality Identication. *In proceedings of EMNLP-2011.*

Roxana Girju. 2003. Automatic detection of causal relations for Question Answering. *Association for Computational Linguistics ACL, Workshop on Multilingual Summarization and Question Answering Machine Learning and Beyond 2003.*

Paul Kingsbury, Martha Palmer and Mitch Marcus. 2002. Adding semantic annotation to the Penn Tree-Bank. *In proceedings of HLT-2002. San Diego, California.*

Karin Kipper, Hoa T. Dang, and Martha Palmer. 2000. Class-based construction of a verb lexicon. *In proceedings of AAAI-2000. Austin, TX.*

Daniel Marcu and Abdessamad Echihabi. 2001. An unsupervised approach to recognizing discourse relations. *In proceedings of the 40th Annual Meeting on Association for Computational Linguistics (ACL).*

Peter Menzies. 2008. Counterfactual theories of causation. *Online Encyclopedia of Philosophy, 2008.*

George A. Miller. 1990. WordNet: An online lexical database. *International Journal of Lexicography, 3(4).*

Judea Pearl. 2000. *Causality.* Cambridge University Press.

Emily Pitler, Annie Louis and Ani Nenkova. 2009. Automatic Sense Prediction for Implicit Discourse Relations in Text. *In proceedings of ACL-IJCNLP, 2009.*

Emily Pitler and Ani Nenkova. 2009. Using Syntax to Disambiguate Explicit Discourse Connectives in Text. *In proceedings of ACL-IJCNLP, 2009.*

Rashmi Prasad, Nikhil Dinesh, Alan Lee, Eleni Miltsakaki, Livio Robaldo, Aravind Joshi, Bonnie Webber. 2010. The penn discourse treebank 2.0. *In proceedings of LREC 2008.*

Kira Radinsky and Eric Horvitz. 2013. Mining the Web to Predict Future Events. *In proceedings of sixth ACM international conference on Web search and data mining, WSDM '13.*

Mehwish Riaz and Roxana Girju. 2010. Another Look at Causality: Discovering Scenario-Specific Contingency Relationships with No Supervision. *In proceedings of the IEEE 4th International Conference on Semantic Computing (ICSC).*

Dafna Shahaf and Carlos Guestrin. 2010. Connecting the Dots Between News Articles. *In proceedings of Knowledge Discovery and Data Mining KDD 2010.*

Craig Silverstein, Sergey Brin, Rajeev Motwani and Jeff Ullman. 2000. Scalable Techniques for Mining Causal Structures. *Data Mining and Knowledge Discovery, 2000, 4(2–3):163–192.*

Caroline Sporleder and Alex Lascarides. 2008. Using automatically labelled examples to classify rhetorical relations: An assessment. *Journal of Natural Language Engineering Volume 14 Issue 3, July 2008 Pages 369–416.*

Patrick Suppes. 1970. *A Probabilistic Theory of Causality.* Amsterdam: North-Holland Publishing Company, 1970.

James Woodward. 2008. Causation and Manipulation. *Online Encyclopedia of Philosophy, 2008.*

Appendix A. Notations

This appendix presents the details of important notations used in this paper.

Notation	Equation(s)	Explanation
e_{v_i}	6, 7, 8, 9	Verbal event represented by the verb v_i
KB_c	–	Knowledge base of causal associations of verb pairs
S_c	–	Strongly Causal category of verb pairs
A_c	–	Ambiguous category of verb pairs
$S_{\neg c}$	–	Strongly Non-Causal category of verb pairs
m_i	–	Discourse marker
m_c	1	Causal marker (e.g., *because*)
$f(I)$	1	Function to select the most dependent pair from two discourse segments conjoined with causal marker
$CD(v_i, v_j)$	1, 2, 4, 6, 9	Causal dependency of the verb pair (v_i, v_j)
$PS_I(v_i, v_j)$	1, 3	Penalization factor for the verbs of the pair (v_i, v_j) with respect to their distance from the causal marker
$pos(v_i)$	3	Distance of verb in terms of its position with respect to causal marker
$C(v_p)$	3	Count of main verbs appearing before causal marker
$C(v_q)$	3	Count of main verbs appearing after causal marker
$ECA(v_i, v_j)$	4	Explicit Causal Association of the verb pair (v_i, v_j)
VP	4, 6, 9	Set of intra- and inter-sentential instances of a verb pair
$I(v_i, v_j)$	4, 6, 9	Instance of the verb pair (v_i, v_j)
C_I	4, 5, 6, 9	Tendency of the instance I to belong to cause class than the non-cause one
c	5	Cause class
$\neg c$	5	Non-cause class
C_{min}	–	Minimum value of C_I obtained on the development set
C_{max}	–	Maximum value of C_I obtained on the development set
r_C	7, 8	Class of cause role
r_E	7, 8	Class of effect role
$ICA(v_i, v_j)$	6	Implicit Causal Association of the verb pair (v_i, v_j)
$ERM(e_{v_i}, e_{v_j})$	6, 7	Events Roles Matching (ERM) determines the negative log-likelihood of events to belong to class of cause or effect role
$S(e_{v_i}, r_C)$	8	Score of e_{v_i} to belong to the class of cause role
$S(e_{v_j}, r_E)$	8	Score of e_{v_j} to belong to the class of effect role
$P(f_k\|.)$	5, 8	Probability of feature f_k given some class
$BCA(v_i, v_j)$	9	Boosted Causal Association of the verb pair (v_i, v_j)

Table 2: Details of notations.

Training an Integrated Sentence Planner on User Dialogue

Brian McMahan
Computer Science
Rutgers University
brian.mcmahan@rutgers.edu

Matthew Stone
Computer Science
Rutgers University
matthew.stone@rutgers.edu

Abstract

An appealing methodology for natural language generation in dialogue systems is to train the system to match a target corpus. We show how users can provide such a corpus as a natural side effect of interacting with a prototype system, when the system uses mixed-initiative interaction and a reversible architecture to cover a domain familiar to users. We experiment with integrated problems of sentence planning and realization in a referential communication task. Our model learns general and context-sensitive patterns to choose descriptive content, vocabulary, syntax and function words, and improves string match with user utterances to 85.8% from a handcrafted baseline of 54.4%.

1 Introduction

Natural language generation (NLG) in dialogue involves a complex array of choices. It's appealing to scale up NLG by training systems to make these choices with models derived from empirical data. Sometimes, these choices have a measurable effect on the flow of the interaction. Systems can plan such choices with a model of dialogue dynamics that predicts which utterances will fulfill communicative goals successfully and efficiently (Lemon, 2011; Janarthanam et al., 2011; Garoufi and Koller, 2011).

Other times, a wide variety of utterances work well (Belz and Gatt, 2008). In these cases, systems can instead be designed simply to choose those utterances that most closely resemble specified target behavior. This paper describes and evaluates a new data-driven methodology for training sentence planning and realization in interactive dialogue systems this way. Our work is particularly inspired by Walker et al. (2002), who train a dialogue sentence planner by annotating its possible outputs for quality; and Jordan and Walker (2005), who train a referring expression generator to match annotated human–human dialogue.

In text generation, researchers have been able to exploit automatic analysis of existing resources on such tasks as ordering words more naturally (Langkilde and Knight, 1998) and identifying named entities in line with attested mentions (Siddharthan and Copestake, 2004). However, previous work on training dialogue generation has involved the acquisition or annotation of relevant data *ad hoc*, for example by collecting human–human dialogue, running Wizard of Oz experiments, or rating system outputs. Our work is different: we use a bootstrapping approach that automatically mines interactions with a running prototype to adapt NLG to match users.

As described in Section 2, our work builds on the COREF system of DeVault and Stone (2009). COREF and its users chat together to identify simple objects in a visual scene. COREF is designed with reversible models of language and dialogue—it tracks users' utterances and its own utterances with the same data structures and represents them as updating the conversational state in parallel ways. Because of this symmetry, COREF's understanding of each user utterance determines an input–output pair that the system could take as a target for NLG. We explain the significance of learning from such data in Section 3. However, we argue in Sections 4 and 5 that this learning will yield significant results only if system and user do in fact turn out to make similar contributions to dialogue.

Our main experiment therefore uses data collected with a new version of COREF with more flexible strategies for taking initiative, as described in Section 6. We use the system's understanding of user utterances in the experiment, along with its productive capacity to generate alternative paraphrases of those utterances, to build an automatically labeled training set of good and bad NLG examples. We learn a model of the difference and evaluate its use in choosing novel utterances. As documented in Section 7, the learned model leads to improvements in naturalness over COREF's handcrafted baseline generator; our experiments document these improvements qualitatively and quantitatively.

Our work suggests new ways to design dialogue systems to adhere to formal models with guaranteed behavior (Paek and Pieraccini, 2008) while reaping the benefits of data-driven approaches (Rieser and Lemon, 2011) by improving themselves through ongoing interactions with users. Our experiments suggest that engaging with user expertise is a key factor in enabling such new design strategies. Our technique crucially exploits synergies in our domain between the architecture of the dialogue system, the specific dialogue policy that the system implements, and users' abilities to contribute to domain problem solving.

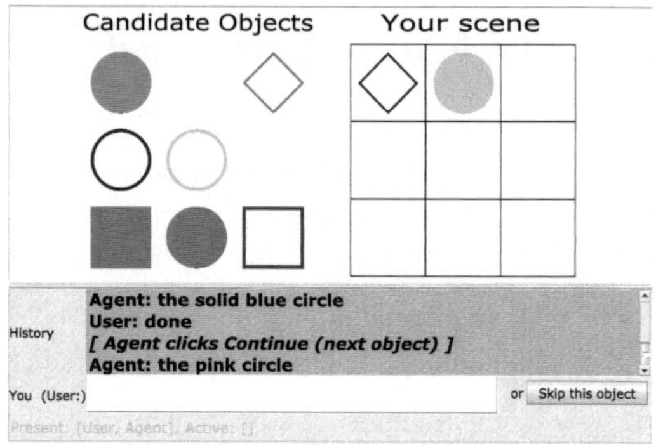

Figure 1: User's view of the chat interface in an interaction with COREF acting as director.

2 Background

COREF, short for "collaborative reference", communicates with users through a text-chat window for human–computer dialogue. A graphical interface provides task context and realizes domain actions; it orchestrates a basic referential communication task like those studied by Clark and Wilkes-Gibbs (1986) or Brennan and Clark (1996). In each round of interaction, the participants in the conversation are presented with a set of simple geometric shapes that they must talk about; the shapes are displayed on screen to human users and described as a knowledge base to the COREF agent. As the dialogue proceeds, one participant, assigned to work as the director, gets an indication of which object to describe next. The other participant, assigned to work as the matcher, must move this target object to its final disposition. Figure 1 is a snapshot of the interface in a session where the user works as matcher. Experimental sessions normally involve multiple rounds where participants alternate serving as director and as matcher.

COREF's architecture factors its reasoning into three integrative problem-solving modules, as shown in Figure 2. The modules use different algorithms and control flow, but are linked together by common representations and knowledge bases. One shared resource is COREF's probabilistic context model, which tracks the likely state of ongoing activity, maintains a linguistic context describing what has probably been said and what should be salient as a result, and represents the information available through the interface as grounded in interlocutors' perception. Another shared resource is COREF's tree-adjoining grammar (TAG; Joshi and Schabes (1997)), which assigns syntactic structures and semantic representations to utterances, and predicts what utterances will refer to in context and what dialogue moves they will contribute. Finally, both understanding and generation use a common representation of the interpretation of utterances, *utterance plans*, which associate specific strings of words with the updates that they are predicted to achieve via grammar and context.

The dialogue manager handles interaction with the user, coordinates understanding and generation, tracks updates to the context, and selects updates that COREF should contribute to the conversation. In case of ambiguity, the dialogue manager propagates uncertainty forward in time and works to resolve it through interaction. (COREF has general mechanisms for engaging in clarification subdialogues.) In fact, by the time each object has been identified, COREF has committed retrospectively, in light of what has happened, to a single most likely interpretation for everything the user has said about it. COREF has evidence that other interpretations it originally entertained were not what the user intended. This links each user utterance with a corresponding utterance plan that can be used for subsequent learning (DeVault and Stone, 2009).

The understanding module parses utterances using the grammar and resolves them using the con-

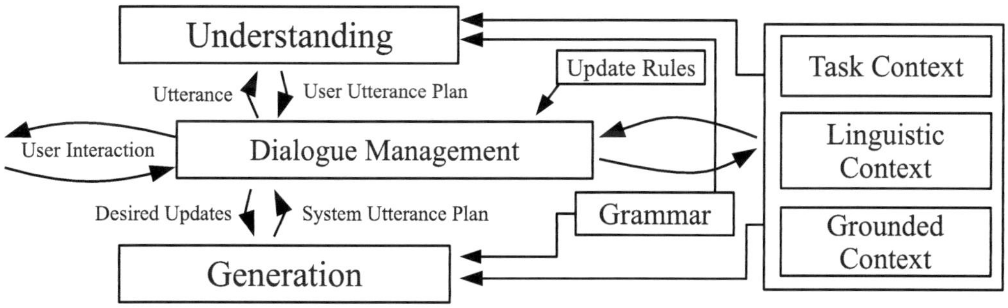

Figure 2: COREF system architecture, showing representations and knowledge shared across modules: utterance plans show how each agent's contributions follow from the system's representations of grammar and context; update rules map out consistent contextual effects for each agent's contributions.

text model to recognize the possible utterance plans behind them. The generator, meanwhile, uses the grammar and the context model to synthesize an utterance plan for a grammatical expression that is predicted to achieve some desired updates unambiguously, as in SPUD (Stone et al., 2003). A range of choices are folded together by this integrated problem-solving process. For example, the grammar specifies alternative realizations involving different syntactic frames and functional items, as in the paraphrases *'the target is a square'*, *'a square'* and *'square'*. The grammar also specifies lexical paraphrases, as in the equivalents *'dark blue'* and *'navy blue'* or *'beige'* and *'tan'*. SPUD's problem solving also creates choices about how much descriptive content to include in a reference, as *'the square'* versus *'the blue square'*, and what kind of descriptive content to include, as in *'the blue square'* versus *'the solid square'*. Full utterances involve all these choices, potentially in overlapping combinations, as in *'the target is the light brown object'* versus *'the solid square'*. See the Appendix for examples of NLG search, and DeVault (2008) for full details about COREF's design and implementation.

COREF's handcrafted NLG search heuristics draw on ideas from Stone et al. (2003) and Dale and Reiter (1995) to prioritize efficient, specific utterances which use preferred descriptive attributes and respect built-in preferences for certain words and constructions. When we implemented these heuristics, we had no intention of revising the model using learning. However, COREF's strategy never generates human-like overspecification, its lexical and syntactic choices are determined by hand-coded logical constraints, and it offers few tools to discriminate among comparable paraphrases. In principle, a system like COREF ought to be able to find out how people tend to make such choices in interacting with it, and learn to speak the same way. This is the central problem we address in this paper.

3 Related Work

Our key contribution is demonstrating that a dialogue system can bootstrap an integrated NLG strategy from interactions with a prototype system by training a model to imitate user utterances. This complements DeVault and Stone (2009), who train an interpretation model in a similar way. Bootstrapping NLG for dialogue requires new insights, and require us to synthesize of a number of trends in dialogue, in NLG and in social learning.

A number of researchers have trained generators for dialogue based on human specifications of desired output. For example, Walker et al. (2002) and Stent et al. (2004) optimize sentence plans based on expert ratings of candidate output utterances. Jordan and Walker (2005) learn rules for predicting the content of referring expressions to match patterns found in corpora of human descriptions in context. Garoufi and Koller (2011) tune the referential strategies of a general-purpose sentence planner based on metrics of utterance effectiveness mined from human–human interactions. Our work involves a new domain and for the first time involves integrated training of all these dimensions of NLG, but we draw closely on the architectures, features and learning techniques developed by these researchers. The key difference that they use data collected, and to some degree hand-annotated, specifically to train NLG.

At the same time, a range of research has explored the way existing data sets can improve NLG results. For example, Langkilde and Knight (1998) *n*-gram statistics to bias a non-deterministic realization system towards frequent utterances. Siddharthan and Copestake (2004) use references in corpora to bootstrap a generator for named entities in text. Such methods, however, have generally focused on offline text generation applications. Our research shows that specific infrastructure must be in place to tune NLG to a dialogue system's own experience.

In addition, our work finds echoes in work across AI on learning by imitation. Interactive robots can learn in new ways by modeling their behavior on competent humans (Breazeal et al., 2005). Other domains require agents to develop cooperative relationships and elicit meaningful behavior from one another before they can learn to act effectively together (Zinkevich et al., 2011). Our work helps to establish the connections of these ideas to dialogue.

Finally, we note that our work is orthogonal to a range of other research that aims to extend and improve NLG in dialogue through learning. Given specified target utterances, knowledge acquisition techniques can be used to induce new resources that describe those utterances for NLG as well as to optimize the use of those resources to match the corpus (Higashinaka et al., 2006; DeVault et al., 2008). Moreover, given a model of the differential effects of utterances on the conversation, reinforcement learning can be used to identify utterances with the best outcomes (Lemon, 2011; Janarthanam et al., 2011). We see no reason not to combine these techniques with imitation learning in the development of future systems.

4 Training COREF

Our method for mining COREF's dialogue experience involves three steps. First, we compile training data: positive instances are derived from user utterances and negative instances are derived from the generator's alternative realizations of communicative goals inferred from user utterances. Next, we build a machine learning model to distinguish positive from negative instances, using features describing the utterance itself, the current state of the conversation and relevant facts from the dialogue history. Finally, we apply the learned model on new NLG problems by collecting candidate paraphrases and finding the one rated most likely to be natural by the learned model.

4.1 Data Analysis

Each user utterance in COREF's interaction logs is associated with a particular state of the dialogue and with the utterance plan ultimately identified as its best interpretation. Our method extracts the task moves in the utterance plan as candidate communicative goals for the utterance. It swaps the role of the user and the system, so as to realize an NLG problem instance to plan a contribution with the utterance's inferred communicative goals, given the user's role in the dialogue and their reconstructed dialogue state. It then calls a revised version of the generator that's non-deterministic and accumulates a range of plausible solutions.[1]

This process automatically creates a representation of the NLG problem faced by the user and the set of possible solutions to that problem implicitly determined by COREF's models of language in context. Our method partitions the training instances based on how the user chose to solve the NLG problem. If the NLG output string matches what the user actually said here, it becomes a positive training example. If it differs from what the user actually said, it becomes a negative one.

4.2 Machine Learning

We can now build a machine learning model of this data set. Given an unlabeled candidate solution to an NLG problem, we want to build a model of the probability that the solution is representative of human behavior in our transcripts. We train a maximum entropy model (Berger et al., 1996) to make the prediction, using the MALLET software package (McCallum, 2002). Given that the generator ultimately wants to choose the best utterance, we could explore approaches to learn rankings directly, such as RankBoost (Freund et al., 2003).

Formally, the machine learning model characterizes an input–output pair for NLG with a set of features that would be available to a generator in assessing a candidate output. Each training example pairs an inventory of features with an observed value indicating whether the instance does or does not match the utterance produced by the human user. Given a training set, MALLET selects a set

[1] Our specific approach was to capture all the successful utterances that differ from the preferred NLG path by any three derivation steps of the lexicalized generation grammar. This heuristic was easy to implement with COREF's existing infrastructure for look-ahead search, and we found empirically that more comprehensive search was expensive to carry out and tended primarily to add unnaturally verbose and redundant utterances. See the Appendix for examples.

of features to use and fits numerical weights for the features for logistic regression by maximum entropy. That is, the features determine the predicted probability that candidate output j for problem t (utterance $u_{t,j}$) is good (a match with a hypothetical user utterance), as a logistic function of the sum of the feature weights describing the instance—formally,

$$P(u_{t,j} = Good \mid features(u_{t,j})) = 1/(1 + \exp(-w_0 - \sum_i features(u_{t,j})_i * w_i))$$

This model can then be applied to unlabeled instances with features derived from novel NLG problem instances and candidate outputs.

The features we use in our experiments are described in full in Tables 4 and 5 in the Appendix. Most are from DeVault and Stone (2009). We have features describing the form of the output utterance: what phrase structure it has and what lexical items are used. We have features describing what task moves are achieved by the utterance and what links the utterance has to context. For completeness, we also add DeVault and Stone's features describing the context itself, including the conversational tasks underway, the facts on the conversational record, and the properties relevant to ongoing problem solving.[2]

In designing features for learning, we also draw on the experience of Jordan and Walker (2005) in predicting the form of referring expressions. Many of their features closely align with those we inherit from DeVault and Stone (2009). One kind that doesn't is Jordan and Walker's conceptual pacts feature set. These features are designed to capture utterance choices that are contingent on other participants' previous choices in interaction—entrainment (Brennan and Clark, 1996). We make it possible for the learner to detect entrainment by introducing a new set of *history features*, which list the presuppositions of recent utterances.

We do not need Jordan and Walker's distractor features, however. Unlike them, we do not try to learn the difference between distinguishing descriptions and ambiguous ones. Our architecture, like that of Garoufi and Koller (2011), doesn't even consider a candidate utterance unless it's unambiguous on a standard reference model (Dale and Reiter, 1995). Garoufi and Koller (2011) provide evidence for the effectiveness of this kind of factorization of modeling and learning.

4.3 Assessing the Model

To use the trained model, we start from the NLG problem of generating an utterance to achieve specified communicative goals in context. Our NLG model constructs its space of candidate utterances. Each candidate input–output pair is analyzed in terms of its features, and then the learned model assigns it a probability score. We pick our output via the candidate with the highest score.

In evaluating how well this works, we are interested in how well the learned model predicts the utterances of new subjects given data from other subjects. We assess this by reporting cross-validation results, predicting the choices of one, held-out subject given a model trained on the data from all other users in an experiment. We report an exact match error measure. In a more complex generation task, we could measure error based on edit distance to give partial credit to NLG results that are closer to user utterances. As a baseline, we report comparable measures for COREF's original NLG implementation.

5 Pilot: The Need for Reciprocity

We applied our NLG training methodology to the data set reported by DeVault and Stone (2009) with 20 subjects interacting with COREF. The results were not compelling.

Analysis of this data set transforms human subjects' utterances into 889 problem instances for NLG. In 247 of these instances, the user's utterance is not in the NLG search space, usually because it is interpreted by robust methods rather than COREF's grammar. Of the remaining 642 utterances, our baseline generator already matches the user utterance 308 times (48%); it differs on the other 334 instances (52%). After learning, a model-based generator trained on the other 19 users' data now matches the utterance of a held-out user on 546 instances (85%) across cross-validation runs. This sounds promising, but in fact almost all of the model successes (534 instances) are due to just five utterance types that fulfill simple dialogue-management functions: *'yes'*, *'no'*,

[2] If these context features were shared across all outputs for a given input, they would not affect what option for NLG was best. But this is not always the case in COREF, because contexts can be uncertain and because COREF can trigger accommodation that changes the context as part of NLG. Moreover, including these features might allow us to capture possible variability in NLG, since the model can then predict that otherwise marked utterances work naturally in some contexts.

'click continue', *'done'* and *'ok'*.

There is in fact quite little evidence in this data about how COREF should make its typical generation decisions. Looking under the hood, the problem is that COREF's dialogue management policy did not exploit the symmetry and reciprocity of its dialogue models and NL representations. COREF took the initiative in object-identification dialogues when it was the director, offering descriptions of the target object, but it also took the initiative when it was the matcher, asking the user to confirm or reject its suggestions about the identity and properties of the target objects.

System builders often make such design choices to foster task success. Giving the system the initiative generally means that user utterances are understood more reliably, which helps keep the dialogue on track. However, in settings where the system can potentially improve its behavior, we may have to design the system to take more risks so it can acquire the data it needs; we may even want to sacrifice short-term task success to enable long-term improvement. Such trade-offs of exploration and exploitation are endemic in reinforcement learning, but learning by imitation gives the problem a distinctively social dimension: getting the right data may mean not only trying new actions in new situations, but actively creating the right relationship with the user.

6 Collecting Mixed-initiative Data

We revised COREF's dialogue strategy to better reflect users' interactive competence using simple statistics about dialogue outcomes. For each class of dialogue move by the agent in DeVault and Stone's evaluation data, we tabulated the number of subsequent utterances required to identify the object. These measures give COREF's planned utterance an empirical score quantifying its anticipated effect in dialogue. For example, after asking if a particular object was the target, the subdialogue finished in 6.0 more turns on average. Analogous measures give a comparable score to the most effective kind of contribution that's potentially available to the user at each point in the dialogue. For example, after saying that a particular object was the target, the subdialogue finished in 3.2 more turns on average. Our new dialogue policy compares COREF's planned move with the user's best option. COREF proceeds with its utterance if its score is better but waits for the user if its score is worse. This analysis gives our revised version of COREF an empirical threshold for taking initiative in the dialogue based on the strengths of the contributions COREF and the user could make next in context. In practice, the revised strategy lets user directors drive the dialogue much more often than DeVault and Stone's original handcrafted policy. For example, COREF now waits for the user to propose a description rather than asking about a candidate object.

We had 42 subjects interact with the revised COREF in a protocol of 29 object identification tasks, grouped in blocks of 4, 9 and 16 as in DeVault and Stone (2009). Subjects were recruited by advertisement and word of mouth from our institution and were paid for their participation. The data was collected as part of an independently-motivated assessment of COREF's trade-offs between asking for clarification and proceeding under uncertainty with its best interpretation, so COREF varied these choices across the dialogues.

Analysis of our new data set induces 2006 NLG problem instances corresponding to human utterances, including 1382 cases where the user's utterance is (1) completely described by COREF's grammar, (2) found in the NLG search space, and (3) represented as unambiguous by the underlying NLG model. To confirm the diversity of utterances in this set, we automatically partitioned the utterances into four classes based on surface form and communicative goals achieved: acknowledgments that coordinate on the current state of the dialogue (569 instances), task instructions (23 instances), yes/no answers (434 instances) and other dialogue contributions with explicit descriptive content (356 instances). Thus, this data set contains substantial evidence about human strategies in COREF's domain. We continue to perform analyses of utterances by category to document the results of our learning experiment.

7 Results

Table 1 compares the aggregate performance of the learned NLG module in comparison to COREF's baseline generator across all cross-validation runs (training on 41 users and testing on data from one held-out user). Except in the small category of task instructions, where the baseline is already good, the learned model offers a substantial improvement in rate of exact match to user utterance across all categories. These differences in

Table 1: Comparison of learned model and baseline generator.

System	Descriptive	Acknowledgments	Yes/No	Instructions	Total
Baseline	$\frac{170}{356} = 47.8\%$	$\frac{349}{569} = 61.3\%$	$\frac{210}{434} = 48.4\%$	$\frac{23}{23} = 100\%$	$\frac{752}{1382} = 54.4\%$
Model	$\frac{259}{356} = 72.8\%$	$\frac{477}{569} = 83.8\%$	$\frac{427}{434} = 98.4\%$	$\frac{23}{23} = 100\%$	$\frac{1186}{1382} = 85.8\%$

Evaluation of exact match to user utterances across hold-one-user-out cross-validation runs. We report number of matching instances out of number of instances with the user utterance in the NLG search space, along with percentage match, broken down by form and communicative goal of the utterance.

Table 2: Comparison of accuracy by item.

		Baseline	
		Match	Mismatch
Model	Match	720	466
	Mismatch	32	164

(a) Counts of NLG problem instances of all types, comparing matches in the baseline generator against matches in the learned model.

		Baseline	
		Match	Mismatch
Model	Match	152	107
	Mismatch	18	79

(b) Counts of NLG problem instances with substantive contributions and explicit descriptive material, comparing matches in the baseline generator against matches in the learned model.

rates are all statistically significant ($p < .005$ by Fisher's exact test).

Table 2 breaks down overall results (Table 2a) and results on descriptive utterances (Table 2b), to explore associations between the performance of the baseline generator and the performance of the learned model on individual items. We find a clear link between the two methods: when the model gets an utterance wrong, the baseline method is much more likely to have gotten the utterance wrong as well ($p < .001$ by Fisher's exact test). We conclude that the model is not just improving on the baseline generator in aggregate, but has learned to correct specific choices in the baseline system that are not representative of user behavior.

The breakdown in Table 1 gives a sense of the range of cases covered by the learned model. The 'yes/no' cases mostly involve training COREF to say *'yes'* rather than *'yeah'*. The acknowledgment cases involve understanding the subtle ways that people trade off alternatives such as *'ok'*, *'done'* and *'I added it'*—a difficult problem but one where we have little choice but to trust machine learning results.

Descriptive utterances are more substantial. To understand these cases better, we built an overall model with data from all 42 users and looked at the features selected by MALLET and the weights fit for them in the maximum entropy model. Table 3 shows a sample of the MALLET output. We think of these features as establishing a network of prioritized defaults; lower-weighted features must conspire together to override higher-weighted ones. Syntax is the strongest effect; for example, the contrast between $[_S$ DET N$]$ and $[_S$ NP IS DET N$]$ gives a preference of 1.27 to the simpler structure. Lexical features encode more natural items (*'brown'* versus *'beige'*) but also implicitly encode natural descriptive patterns (as with the color modifier *'light'*). Presupposition features, meanwhile, help ensure that words have their most natural meanings. On this analysis, the model contents corroborate our hypothesis that user data gives evidence to refine a wide variety of NLG choices.

8 Discussion

In this paper, we show how users' utterances can give a dialogue system consistent and reliable indicators not only of how to solve its NLU problems, as in DeVault and Stone (2009), but also how to solve its NLG problems. Thus, we can now design dialogue systems to learn to imitate their human users in certain cases. To do so, the system needs to work in a domain where users are prepared to offer the same kind of contributions

Table 3: Sample features used to identify user tuples and their weights in an overall model.

Syntax Features:	
Fits $[_S$ DET N$]$	2.29
Fits $[_S$ COLOR N$]$	2.09
Fits $[_S$ DET COLOR N$]$	1.86
Fits $[_S$ NP IS DET N$]$	1.12
Lexical Features:	
Includes word *light*	0.87
Includes word *dark*	0.60
Includes word *brown*	0.22
Includes word *beige*	0.005
Presupposition Features:	
Uses *square* for square object	2.05
Uses *diamond* for rhombus	2.09
Uses *pink* for pale red-purple	1.70
Describes light blue as *light*	0.92

as the system, the system needs to represent those contributions symmetrically, and the system needs to be able to actually elicit, analyze and learn from relevant user utterances.

Our approach, like that of Garoufi and Koller (2011), is to combine a symbolic account of utterance interpretation with a learned model of utterance quality. Thus, on our approach, system utterances always come with formal guarantees that they fulfill specified communicative goals and have a unique interpretation in context. That may help underwrite the guarantees that Paek and Pieraccini (2008) emphasize, that data-driven systems must respect the coherence of dialogue and must continue to do so even as they learn to improve dialogue efficiency and naturalness.

Our work suggests some natural followups. It would be interesting to refine the NLG model based on the disambiguation strategy learned in DeVault and Stone (2009). If the system discovers that utterances are not as ambiguous as the initial model suggests, it opens up new possibilities for tuning NLG to match what users say. Scaling up the ideas, meanwhile, invites us to build factored models that describe NLG decisions in a more compositional way, as well as finding more powerful and generalizable features.

Further work is also required to use these techniques in a broader range of settings. Our technique requires the system to give users the opportunity to say the same kinds of things it says, so it is most appropriate for collaborative problem solving. Further research is required to use the methodology for asymmetric situations such as information seeking. Use in spoken dialogue systems, meanwhile, would challenge the limits of mixed-initiative interaction and would require techniques to discount users' errors and disfluencies. Although these limitations make our techniques difficult to use in many current applications, we are optimistic that our methods will apply quite naturally to emerging open-domain settings such as human–robot interaction, where users and systems meet on a more equal footing.

Acknowledgments

This authors were supported by NSF DGE 0549115 (IGERT) and IIS 1017811. Thanks to the reviewers, and to David DeVault and Lara Martin for discussion and assistance.

References

Anja Belz and Albert Gatt. 2008. Intrinsic vs. extrinsic evaluation measures for referring expression generation. In *Proceedings of ACL*, pages 197–200.

Adam L. Berger, Stephen Della Pietra, and Vincent J. Della Pietra. 1996. A maximum entropy approach to natural language processing. *Computational Linguistics*, 22(1):39–71.

Cynthia Breazeal, Daphna Buchsbaum, Jesse Gray, and Bruce Blumberg. 2005. Learning from and about others: Towards using imitation to bootstrap the social understanding of others by robots. *Artificial Life*, 11(1–2):1–32.

Susan E. Brennan and Herbert H. Clark. 1996. Conceptual pacts and lexical choice in conversation. *J. Experimental Psychology*, 22(6):1482–1493.

Herbert H. Clark and Deanna Wilkes-Gibbs. 1986. Referring as a collaborative process. *Cognition*, 22(1):1–39.

Robert Dale and Ehud Reiter. 1995. Computational interpretations of the Gricean maxims in the generation of referring expressions. *Cognitive Science*, 18:233–263.

David DeVault and Matthew Stone. 2009. Learning to interpret utterances using dialogue history. In *Proceedings of EACL*, pages 184–192.

David DeVault, David Traum, and Ron Artstein. 2008. Practical grammar-based NLG from examples. In *Proceedings of INLG*, pages 78–85.

David DeVault. 2008. *Contribution Tracking: Participating in Task-Oriented Dialogue under Uncertainty*. Ph.D. thesis, Rutgers.

Yoav Freund, Raj Iyer, Robert E. Schapire, and Yoram Singer. 2003. An efficient boosting algorithm for combining preferences. *J. Machine Learning Research*, 4:933–969.

Konstantina Garoufi and Alexander Koller. 2011. Combining symbolic and corpus-based approaches for the generation of successful referring expressions. In *Proceedings of EWNLG*, pages 121–131.

Ryuichiro Higashinaka, Rashmi Prasad, and Marilyn A. Walker. 2006. Learning to generate naturalistic utterances using reviews in spoken dialogue systems. In *Proceedings of ICCL–ACL*, pages 265–272.

Srinivasan Janarthanam, Helen Hastie, Oliver Lemon, and Xingkun Liu. 2011. "The day after the day after tomorrow?" a machine learning approach to adaptive temporal expression generation: training and evaluation with real users. In *Proceedings of SIGDIAL*, pages 142–151.

Pamela W. Jordan and Marilyn A. Walker. 2005. Learning content selection rules for generating object descriptions in dialogue. *J. Artif. Intell. Res. (JAIR)*, 24:157–194.

Aravind K. Joshi and Yves Schabes. 1997. Tree-adjoining grammars. In Grzegorz Rozenberg and Arto Salomaa, editors, *Handbook of Formal Languages*, pages 69–123. Springer.

Irene Langkilde and Kevin Knight. 1998. Generation that exploits corpus-based statistical knowledge. In *Proceedings of COLING–ACL*, pages 704–710.

Oliver Lemon. 2011. Learning what to say and how to say it: Joint optimisation of spoken dialogue management and natural language generation. *Computer Speech & Language*, 25(2):210–221.

Andrew McCallum. 2002. MALLET: A MAchine learning for LanguagE toolkit. http://mallet.cs.umass.edu.

Tim Paek and Roberto Pieraccini. 2008. Automating spoken dialogue management design using machine learning: An industry perspective. *Speech Communication*, 50(8–9):716–729.

Verena Rieser and Oliver Lemon. 2011. *Reinforcement Learning for Adaptive Dialogue Systems: A Data-driven Methodology for Dialogue Management and Natural Language Generation*. Springer.

Advaith Siddharthan and Ann A. Copestake. 2004. Generating referring expressions in open domains. In *Proceedings of ACL*, pages 407–414.

Amanda Stent, Rashmi Prasad, and Marilyn A. Walker. 2004. Trainable sentence planning for complex information presentations in spoken dialog systems. In *Proceedings of ACL*, pages 79–86.

Matthew Stone, Christine Doran, Bonnie Webber, Tonia Bleam, and Martha Palmer. 2003. Microplanning with communicative intentions: the SPUD system. *Computational Intelligence*, 19(4):314–381.

Marilyn A. Walker, Owen Rambow, and Monica Rogati. 2002. Training a sentence planner for spoken dialogue using boosting. *Computer Speech & Language*, 16(3–4):409–433.

Martin Zinkevich, Michael H. Bowling, and Michael Wunder. 2011. The lemonade stand game competition: solving unsolvable games. *SIGecom Exchanges*, 10(1):35–38.

Appendix: NLG Search and Features

User utterance	*pink square*
Goal(s) found	1. Target is pink 2. Target is square, *or* 3. Target is both pink and square
Baseline	1. the target is pink 2. the target is square 3. pink square
Model	1. pink square 2. square 3. pink square
Candidates	a box, a fuschia box, a fuschia fuschia box, a fuschia fuschia square, a fuschia pink box, a fuschia pink square, a fuschia purple box, a fuschia purple square, a fuschia square, a like fuschia box, a like fuschia square, a like pink box, a like pink square, a like purple box, a like purple square, a pink box, a pink fuschia box, a pink fuschia square, a pink pink box, a pink pink square, a pink purple box, a pink purple square, a pink square, a purple box, a purple fuschia box, a purple fuschia square, a purple pink box, a purple pink square, a purple purple box, a purple purple square, a purple square, a square, box, fuschia box, fuschia square, pink box, pink square, purple box, purple square, square, the target is fuschia, the target is pink, the target is purple, the target is square

Model confirms baseline vocabulary, learns to overspecify color goal (1) for more natural syntax. COREF can't spell 'fuchsia'.

Table 4: Features derived from the current state of the dialogue (s_t).

feature set	**description**
NumTasksUnderway	The number of tasks underway in the state s_t.
TasksUnderway	For any task that is underway in state s_t, a feature includes its name, its depth on the task stack, and its current status in its formal task network.
NumRemainingReferents	The number of targets that remain to be identified in state s_t.
TabulatedFacts	For any fact on the conversational record at state s_t there is a corresponding string feature—a formula with any unique reference symbols anonymized (e.g. *X34* becomes *some-object*).
CurrentTargetConstraints	For any positive or negative constraint on the current target in state s_t, there is a corresponding string feature.
UsefulProperties	For any property instantiated in the display in state s_t there is a corresponding feature.
History	Each assertion and presupposition on the conversational record in state s_t is represented as a string feature.

Table 5: Features derived from the proposed utterance ($u_{t,j}$).

feature set	**description**
Presuppositions	Each of the atomic presuppositions of the utterance $u_{t,j}$ is represented as a string feature. The string captures predicate–argument structure but anonymizes references to individuals (e.g. *target12* becomes *sometarget*).
Assertions	Each of the dialogue moves that the utterance contributes corresponds to a feature. This string also captures predicate–argument structure but anonymizes references to individuals.
Syntax	A string representation of the bracketed phrase structure, including non-terminal categories, of the utterance.
Words	We represent each word that occurs in the utterance as a feature.

User utterance	*the light blue diamond*
Goal(s) found	Target is specified object
Baseline	the blue object
Model	the light blue diamond
Candidates	the blue blue diamond, the blue blue object, the blue blue rhombus, the blue diamond, the blue diamond outline, the blue object, the blue object outline, the blue rhombus, the blue rhombus outline, the empty blue diamond, the empty blue object, the empty blue rhombus, the hollow blue diamond, the hollow blue object, the hollow blue rhombus, (continued)
Candidates	the light blue diamond, the light blue object, the light blue rhombus, the lighter blue diamond, the lighter blue object, the lighter blue rhombus, the like blue diamond, the like blue object, the like blue rhombus, the outline blue diamond, the outline blue object, the outline blue rhombus, the sky blue diamond, the sky blue object, the sky blue rhombus

Model confirms baseline pattern of color and type reference but learns to overspecify color as *light blue* and to use basic type *diamond*.

Topic Independent Identification of Agreement and Disagreement in Social Media Dialogue

Amita Misra & Marilyn A. Walker
Natural Language and Dialogue Systems Lab
Computer Science Department
University of California, Santa Cruz
maw|amitamisra@soe.ucsc.edu

Abstract

Research on the structure of dialogue has been hampered for years because large dialogue corpora have not been available. This has impacted the dialogue research community's ability to develop better theories, as well as good off-the-shelf tools for dialogue processing. Happily, an increasing amount of information and opinion exchange occur in natural dialogue in online forums, where people share their opinions about a vast range of topics. In particular we are interested in rejection in dialogue, also called disagreement and denial, where the size of available dialogue corpora, for the first time, offers an opportunity to empirically test theoretical accounts of the expression and inference of rejection in dialogue. In this paper, we test whether topic-independent features motivated by theoretical predictions can be used to recognize rejection in online forums in a topic-independent way. Our results show that our theoretically motivated features achieve 66% accuracy, an improvement over a unigram baseline of an absolute 6%.

1 Introduction

Research on the structure of dialogue has been hampered for years because large dialogue corpora have not been publicly available. This has impacted the dialogue research community's ability to develop better theories, as well as good off-the-shelf tools for dialogue processing that account for the richness of human dialogue. Happily, an increasing amount of information and opinion exchange occurs in natural dialogue in online forums, where people can express their opinion on a vast range of topics from *Should there be more stringent gun laws?* to *Are school uniforms a good idea?* (Walker et al., 2012a). For example, consider the dialogic exchange in Fig. 1.

Post **P**, Response **R**
P1: **Can the** government force abortion clinics to carry anti-abortion articles and papers? Or maybe force them provide a sonogram? Force them to have a psychologist on staff? Force them to have 3x3 foot posters of aborted babies on the wall? **Seems like** it makes more sense for a state to restrict something from the people rather than force the people to have something. No?
R1: **I don't see** why this matters. **Could you** please elaborate a little more, and in that elaboration, could you address why the government may require a private company to provide this commonly recommended medical remedy (plan b) **when it does not** do so with countless other common medically recommended remedies?

Figure 1: Disagreement from `4forums.com`. Possible features in **bold**.

In particular we are interested in the phenomenon of REJECTION in dialogue (Horn, 1989; Walker, 1996a), also called disagreement and denial. Our data show that the amount of disagreement in online ideological dialogues ranges from 80% to 90% across topic. Such data provides a rich resource for testing theoretical accounts of rejection, as well as for developing computational models of how to recognize rejection in dialogue. To date, rejection has received relatively little attention in computational models of discourse because of its rareness in task-oriented, tutorial or SwitchBoard style dialogue. Computational models of argumentative discourse do not typically attempt to account for rejection in dialogue, focusing instead on monologic sources displaying legal reasoning, logical accounts of rejection, or how to produce good arguments using natural language generation (Zukerman et al., 2000; Carenini and Moore, 2000; Wiley, 2005; Sadock, 1977).

Moreover, the theoretical literature strongly suggests that there should be topic-independent indicators of rejection. In work on politeness theory, rejection is a dispreferred response, predicting that rejection should be associated with markers of dispreferred responses such as disfluencies and hedging (Brown and Levinson, 1987). Work on negation specifies markers of negation and contrast such as *but* or *only* for different types of rejection, and work on discourse relations and their

Type	Context	Rejection
DENIAL	Pigs can fly.	**No**, you idiot, pigs **can't** fly! (Horn's 29)
LOGICAL CONTRADICTION	Kim and Lee have been partners since 1989.	But Lee said they met in 1990.
IMPLICIT DENIAL	Julia's daughter is a genius.	Julia **doesn't have** any children.
REFUSAL	Come and play ball with me.	**No**, I don't want to. (Horn's 33)
IMPLICATURE REJECTION	There's a man in the garage.	There's something in the garage. (Walker's 6)
DENYING BELIEF TRANSFER	B: Well ah *he uh ... he belongs to a money market fund now and uh they will do that for him.* H: The money market fund will invest it in government securities as part of their individual retirement account – is that what you're saying? B: Right.	H: **I'm not so sure of that.** (Walker's 31)
INCONSISTENT PAST BELIEF	H: Then they are remiss in not sending it to you because that money is taxable sir.	M: I know it's taxable, **but I thought** they would wait until the end of the 30 months.
CITING CONTRADICTORY AUTHORITY	H: No sir....	R: That's what **they told me**.

Figure 2: Classification and Examples of the Types of Rejections.

markers suggests that DENIAL is a type of COMPARISON relation (Horn, 1989; Groen et al., 2010; Webber and Prasad, 2008). These observations, among others, suggest a range of theoretically motivated features for the classification of rejection in online dialogue, e.g. phrases such as *I think*, *but*, *I don't see*, and *Can you*. See Fig. 1.

Our aim is to test whether theoretical predictions and topic-independent features motivated by them can be used to recognize rejection in online forums. We generalize our topic independent features using a development set on the topic *Evolution*. We then test a rejection (disagreement) classifier trained on *Evolution* on 1757 posts covering a collection of other topics, and compare our results to a ngram model trained on *Evolution* and tested on the same test set. See Table 1.

We first describe our corpus in Sec. 2, and then review previous work characterizing the theoretical basis of rejection in dialogue in Sec. 3. Sec. 4 describes our method for classifying rejections and Sec. 5 presents our results, showing that our theoretically motivated rejection cues are reliable across topic. We show that cue words, polarity, punctuation, denial and claim features motivated by the theoretical literature provide a significant improvement over a 50% baseline, and that all of the theoretically motivated features combined achieve 66% accuracy as compared to a unigram accuracy of 60%. We delay reviewing previous computational work rejection to Sec. 6 when we can compare it with our own work.

Topic	Agr	DisAgr	Total
Evolution	460	460	920
Abortion	250	280	530
Climate Change	17	10	27
Communism vs. Capitalism	10	13	23
Death Penalty	15	19	34
Existence Of God	53	48	101
Gay Marriage	173	134	307
Gun Control	334	331	665
HealthCare	21	37	58
Marijuana Legalization	6	6	12
All Topics (test set)	879	878	1757

Table 1: Distribution of (Dis)Agreement by Topic. The Evolution topic is for development and training. The test set of other topics is balanced overall, but not by topic.

2 Corpus

We utilize the publicly available Internet Argument Corpus (IAC), an annotated collection of 109,553 forum posts (11,216 discussion threads)(Walker et al., 2012a). We use the portion of the IAC containing dialogues from `http://4forums.com`. On 4forums, a person starts a discussion by posting a topic or a question in a particular category, such as society, politics, or religion. Forum participants can then post their opinions, choosing whether to respond directly to a previous post or to the top level topic (start a new thread). Conversants may simply agree or disagree with a previous post or they may provide a reasoned argument.

The corpus contains posts on topics such as *Abortion, Evolution, Existence of God, Gay Marriage* and *Gun control* along with a range of useful annotations. First, there are annotations that collapse different discussions into a single topic for 14 topics. For example, the *Evolution* and *Gun Control* topics include discussions initiated with the range of titles in Table 2, which guaran-

First Post (P), Response (R)
Disagreements
P1: No I didn't miss it, I was hoping you'd actually put forward an argument against what I said, not what you think I said. See what I actually said was the tautology. Then make your argument. Note Post 30 He said evolution is a tautology. I said that Darwin preferred a tautology to "Natural Selection" You may have mixed up who it is you're arguing against. **R1: I'm wondering**. What do we call someone who debates feverishly on scientific theories, yet admittedly **does not** understand the concepts they are arguing against? Is it productive to debate something that **you don't understand** the concepts of when it's a fairly involved theory based on scientific evidence? What **if you** convinced someone NOT to believe in it, **but** you did so using falsifiable reasons, **since** you aren't an expert and might not know any better**?** Irresponsible, is one such word, that comes to mind.
P2: What in Vishnu's name does this have ANYTHING to do with evolution vs creation??? **R2: Well**, many have argued that **if you don't** except a literal Genesis, you're damned. **Perhaps** not in this particular thread, **but** the arguments are **essentially** the same. **I believe that** the theological implications of that position are fair game for discussing the validity of creationism.
P4: You have this backwards. The word theory was originally a scientific word, and then it was adapted into common speech to mean a range of things not originally designated to that word. Words like evolve, gravity and congruent have different meanings within the realm of science than they have outside. If you can't appreciate the difference between the definition of a word in the context of science as opposed to the context of common speech, then maybe you have no business in science. **R4:** When it comes to all the examples that Behe had provided in both his first book, and his second book , **it has been shown** to be able to evolve naturally. That means, in principle, IC systems can evolve. **If you don't** believe so, bring forth the I.C. system of your choice. To say '**you don't know** all the answers' is just the logical fallacy known as 'argument from ignorance'. Behe brings a system up that he claims is IC. the pathway for evolution is discovered, and Behe trys another one. How dishonest **can you** get? The concept is falsified.
P5: Well, Genesis has God making all the animals "and their kind", and then when he's done with that he makes humans. So I would assume that humans don't fit into the "kind" schema, or perhaps are a kind unto themselves........ **R5:** : **So we can't** base our definition of "kind" on mere appearances? **I mean** if we are going to put things into categories and call the category "kind", **we should** do this by common appearances. A penguin is in the same kind as a hummingbird, **but** is a lobster in the same kind as an oyster? ....
Agreements
P6: I think its nonsense interpretation developed by people who were afraid that if they fought for guns as valiantly as they did for free speech, they wouldn't receive any donations. **R6**: I think you are entirely correct. From the page VOR linked: There is no evidence ANYWHERE that the second amendment is a collective right. We have been over this multiple times, and the evidence simply does not exist, and an organization like the ACLU should be well aware of this.
P7: Correction: If one isn't a fundementalist, literal christian, jew or muslim, then marc considers them a atheist. He's never going to deal with the fact that he's quite wrong on that subject. It's obvious to everyone that he's constantly avoiding it even when asked point blank several times. A sign of argumental failure is constant avoidance of a simple question. **R7:** Quite **right**. My mistake. Once again, quite **right**...
P8: thats pretty neat. Did they finish up the feeder? **R8: yeah**, this is clearly the best thread on these forums in probably the past year....give us some more pics length)
P9: This is probably the most rational site in all of the creationist's online arguments. Arguments we think creationists should NOT use **R9: Thanks**, DuoMax, for this link. How delightful to see here mention of this solid gesture, on the part of a major creationist organization, in the direction of intellectual integrity..... ....Each time a Christian stands in the pulpit and pours out poor argument, s/he loses ground for the faith. **Thanks** again.

Figure 3: Disagreements and Agreements from `4forums.com`. Theoretically motivated features are in **bold**.

Evolution	Evolution in school, Dinosaurs and Human Footprints, Can Evolution & Religion Coexist, Did Charles Darwin Recant, Shrinking Sun, Bombardier beetle, Moon Dust, Second Law of Thermodynamics, Magnetic Field, Nebraska Man
Gun Control	Gun Control, Trigger Locks, Guns in the Home, Right to Carry, Assault Weapons, One gun a month, Gun Buy Back, Gun-Seizure Laws, Plastic Guns, Does gun ownership deter crime, Second Amendment, Enforced Gun Control Laws?, Gun Registration, Armor piercing bullets, Background Checks at Gun Shows

Table 2: Discussions Mapped to the Evolution and Gun Control Topics.

tees variation in the focus of the discussion even within topic. The topics we use are in Table 1. Each discussion is threaded so that we can identify direct responses. Discussions may have a tree-like structure, so a post may have multiple direct responses. In addition to the adjacency pairs yielded by threading, `4forums` also provides a quote/response **Q/R** mechanism where a post may include a quote of part or all of a previous post. We do not use the Q/R pairs here.

The IAC also includes annotations collected via Mechanical Turk on these dialogue pairs. There are 20,000 pairs from threads of 3 posts P1,P2,P3 with annotations for (dis)agreement for pairs (P1, P2) and (P2, P3). Agreement was a scalar judgment on an 11 point scale [-5,5] implemented with a slider. The annotators were also able to signal uncertainty with a CAN'T TELL option. Each of the pairs was annotated by 5-7 annotators, in response to the annotation question *Does the respondent agree or disagree with the prior post?*. Annotators achieved high agreement on dis(agreement) annotation with an α of 0.62. We used thresholds of 1 and -1 on the mean agreement judgment to determine agreement and disagreement respectively. We omitted dialogue adjacency pairs with mean annotator judgment in the (-1,1) range. Table 1 provides the distribution of topics for the 1757 posts in the test set.

3 Theories of Rejection in Dialogue

A common view of dialogue is that the conversational record is part of the COMMON GROUND of the conversants. As conversants A and B participate in a dialogue, A and B communicate through dialogue speech acts such as PROPOSALS, ASSERTIONS, ACCEPTANCES and REJECTIONS. If A asserts a proposition ϕ and B accepts A's assertion, the ϕ becomes a mutual belief in the common ground. If B rejects A's assertion or proposal, the common ground remains as it was (Stalnaker, 1978). For conversants to remain coordinated (Thomason, 1990), they must monitor whether their utterances are accepted or rejected by their conversational partners.

Computational models of dialogue also must track what is in the common ground (Traum, 1994; Stent, 2002). This would be simple if conversants always explicitly indicated rejection with forms such as *I reject your assertion*. However recognizing rejection typically relies on making inferences. Horn categorizes rejections into: DENIAL a straightforward negation of the other's assertion; LOGICAL CONTRADICTION following from logical inference; IMPLICIT DENIAL where B denies a presupposition of A's; and REFUSAL, also called REJECTION where B refuses an offer or proposal of A's (Horn, 1989). See Fig. 2. All of Horn's forms can be identified as rejections by recognizing logical inconsistency either directly from what was said, or via an inferential chain.

However subsequent work by Walker on the *Harry Gross Corpus* (henceforth **HGC**) of advice-giving dialogues (Pollack et al., 1982) demonstrated that REJECTION IMPLICATURES as seen in the 5th row of Fig. 2, are common in natural dialogue (Walker, 1996a). A number of similar examples can also be found in (Hirschberg, 1985). Here, the proposition realized by the response follows from the original assertion as an entailment via existential generalization. Thus the REJECTION IMPLICATURE is logically consistent with the original assertion.

Walker argues that the fact that an implicature can function as a rejection clearly indicates that inference rules about what gets added to the common ground must have the same logical status as implicatures, i.e. they must be default rules of inference that can be defeated by context. She then goes on to identify additional types of rejections in **HGC** that rely on detecting conflicts in the default inferences triggered by the epistemic inference rules used in speech act theory. Walker uses a compressed version of rules from (Perrault, 1990; Appelt and Konolige, 1988), assuming that conflicting defaults can arise between these inferences and implicature inferences (Hirschberg, 1985). The first rule is given in 1:

(1) BELIEF TRANSFER RULE:
Say(A,B,p) $\rightarrow$ Bel (B,p)

The Belief Transfer Rule states that if one agent A makes an assertion that p then by default another agent B will come to believe that p. The second rule is in 2:

(2) BELIEF PERSISTENCE RULE:
Bel (B,p,t_0) $\rightarrow$ Bel (B,p,t_1)

The Belief Persistence Rule states that if an agent B believes p at time t_0 then by default agent B still believes p at a later time t_1. These rules provide the basis for inferring three additional types of rejections:

- DENYING BELIEF TRANSFER: Agent B can deny the consequent of the Belief Transfer Rule by negatively evaluating A's assertion or expressing doubt as to its truth.
- INCONSISTENT PAST BELIEF: Inferring that B's expression of an inconsistent past belief is a type of rejection relies on detecting conflicting defaults with the Belief Transfer Rule and the Belief Persistence Rule. The two beliefs may directly conflict, or the conflict may arise via an inferential chain.
- CITING CONTRADICTORY AUTHORITY: Inferring that citing a contradictory authority is a type of rejection relies on recognizing two inconsistent instantiations of the Belief Transfer rule. For example, agent A1 asserted p and agent A2 asserted $\neg$p, leaving B in an inconsistent belief state caused by the conflicting defaults generated by the alternate instantiations of the Belief Transfer Rule.

Fig. 2 provides Walker's examples of these new types of rejection and Fig. 3 illustrates disagreements and agreements in the IAC corpus.[1] While we see many instances of the rejection types in Fig. 2 in IAC, especially CITING CONTRADICTORY AUTHORITY and DENYING BELIEF TRANSFER, we also find new types such as adhominem attacks on the other speaker as the source of particular propositions (e.g. **R1** in Fig. 3, which would not have occurred in **HGC** talk show context. Other cases that we have noted are a different type of DENYING BELIEF TRANSFER, which occurs when a previous speaker's asserted proposition is marked by the hearer as hypothetical using a conditional, e.g. *If capital punishment is a deterrent, then .....* In future work we aim to expand the taxonomy of rejections using IAC.

4 Empirical Method

Our primary hypothesis is that certain expressions and phrases are reliable cues to the automatic identification of the speech acts of REJECTION and ACCEPTANCE, i.e. (dis)agreement, independently of the topic. We assume that it will not always be possible to get annotated data for a particular topic, given the ever-burgeoning range of topics discussed online. We use the *Evolution* topic as our development set, and ask: given (dis)agreement annotations for only one topic, is it possible to develop features that perform well on another arbitrary topic?

There is limited previous research on disagreement, thus it is an open issue what types of features might be useful. One line of previous work suggests that various pragmatic features might help (Galley et al., 2004). Another line suggests that disagreement is subtype of the COMPARISON (CONTRAST) discourse relation, in the Penn Discourse TreeBank taxonomy, suggesting that features for identifying COMPARISON, such as polarity and discourse cues might also be useful (Hahn et al., 2006; Prasad et al., 2010; Louis et al., 2010).

We began by selecting and manually inspecting 460 agreements and 460 disagreements from the *Evolution* topic, and extracting their most frequent unigrams, bigrams and trigrams. This showed that features suggested by theoretical work on rejection were indeed highly frequent: our aim was to generalize what we observed in the *Evolution* dataset and then test whether the generalized features can distinguish agreements from disagreements. We first observed that very few unigrams were useful for disagreements, e.g. *liar, no, don't,* while bigrams such as *I don't, How can, If I, how could, show me* seemed to be better indicators. Furthermore, trigrams such as *I don't agree, how can you, point is that,* and *I do not understand* are even stronger indicators of disagreement, but of course these higher order ngrams are less frequent and are more likely to contain topic-specific words. In order to provide better generalization, we generalized the ngrams that we observed, e.g. an instance such as *how can you* would also result in *how can we* and *how can they* being added to the same feature set. We also generalized over hedges and other categories of features on the basis of the theoretical literature. The total set of features we developed are grouped into the sets in Table 3 discussed in detail below.

Feature	Description	Examples
Agreement	Ngrams indicative of accepting others claim.	*right, yes, yeah, correct, accepted, thanks, good, agree, acknowledge*
Cue Words	Cues as Ngrams and their LIWC CogMech generalizations	*oh, so, uh, yes, no, dont, cogmech, claim, i, yeah, because, well, just, and, you, you mean, i see, i COGMECH*
Denial	Ngrams indicative of denying another's claim	*You don't know, That does not, I don't think, what is, This has nothing, I don't see, You do not, do you mean, I don't know, we don't have, Problem with that, I do not, Does not, why do, But I don't, how can*
Hedges	Unigrams, bigrams, and trigrams that include hedge terms.	*Im wondering, I am wondering, whatever, somewhat, may be, possibly, anyway, it seems to me, my view, actually, my opinion, essentially, somewhat, my perspective, rather, although, really, I suppose, perhaps*
Duration	Sentence, word and post lengths	
Polarity	Means of positive and negative polarity terms.	
Punctuation	Counts of question marks and exclamation points.	

Table 3: Feature Sets, Descriptions, and Examples. The unigrams features are our baseline case; these features are not theoretically motivated.

Unigrams. Results of previous work on stance identification in argumentative discourse suggest that a unigram baseline can be difficult to beat (Thomas et al., 2006; Somasundaran and Wiebe, 2010). Thus we test our theoretically motivated features against unfiltered unigrams and un-

[1]Since participants are not generally making plans together in these dialogues, we leave aside Walker's classification of rejections of proposals.

igrams+bigrams as baselines.

Agreement and Denial. As described above we used *Evolution* to manually develop generalizations of the observed unigrams, bigrams and trigrams that were consistent with theoretical predictions. We split the indicator features into two categories Agreement and Denial. See Table 3. Our manual analysis suggested that agreements have few topic independent markers. Unigrams such as *agree correct* and *right* were also present in disagreements, and trigrams such as *I agree but, You may be correct however I do not agree, I don't agree* were better indicators of disagreement. Our agreement markers are thus a small category where we check that the keywords *agree, correct* and *right* are not preceded by a negation marker and not followed by discourse markers such as *but*, *yet*, or *however*. However, the denial category at present has more than 300 ngrams extracted and generalized from the *Evolution* topic. Pitler et al, (2009) also used ngrams consisting of the first and last three words for recognition of the PDTB COMPARISON relation. Other work on the PDTB also suggests that DENIAL can be indicated by contrast (Webber and Prasad, 2008).

Cue Words. Both psychological research on discourse processes (Fox Tree and Schrock, 1999; Groen et al., 2010) and computational work on agreement and discourse markers (Galley et al., 2004; Louis et al., 2010) indicate that discourse markers are strongly associated with particular pragmatic functions such as stating a personal opinion (Asher et al., 2008; Webber and Prasad, 2008). Based on manual inspection of the *Evolution* devset we selected 18 items for the CUE WORDS feature set, as in Table 3. Examples are *well* in **R2** and *so* and *but* in **R5**.

Durational Features. Brown and Levinson's theory of politeness would suggest that disagreements are dispreferred responses and thus that the length of the post could indicate disagreement; it predicts that people will elaborate more and provide reasons and justifications for disagreement (Brown and Levinson, 1987). Our durational features measure the length of the utterance in terms of characters, words and sentences.

Hedges. In Brown and Levinson's theory of politeness, hedges are one of many possible strategies for mitigating a face-threatening act (Brown and Levinson, 1987; Lakoff, 1973). Hedges can be used to be deliberately vague or simply to soften a claim. We see many examples of hedges in online dialogue, e.g. the speaker of **R2** in Fig. 3 uses the hedges *Perhaps* and *essentially*, and *I mean* in **R5**. Thus hedges are hypothesized to be useful feature for distinguishing (dis)agreement, yielding the hedge features in Table 3.

Polarity. Work on discourse relations in the PDTB also suggests that differences in polarity across adjacent utterances might be an indicator of the COMPARISON relation. In addition, Horn's classes of REJECTIONS shown in Fig. 2 all include markers of negation. Thus to capture the overall sentiment of the post we used the MPQA subjectivity lexicon (Wiebe et al., 2003; Wilson et al., 2005). Each word is POS tagged and then categorized as strongly or weakly subjective. The positive polarity feature is the sum of the strongly subjective words of positive polarity, and the negative polarity feature represents the sum of strongly subjective words of negative polarity.

Punctuation. Another indication of DENYING BELIEF TRANSFER rejections are the question marks and exclamation marks that conversants frequently use to express their disbelief and doubt about another conversant's claim. For example, **R1** and **R5** in Fig. 3 have a high frequency of question marks.

5 Results

Our aim was to test how well we can distinguish agreements and disagreements in IAC using classifiers trained with theoretically motivated features. As described above, we developed our features by manual inspection of (dis)agreements in 920 posts on the topic *Evolution*. We do not train on a mixture of topics for any feature set, including unigrams, because we assume that in general, new topics are always arising so there will not be annotated data for every topic. We evaluate the performance of all types of features on classifying (dis)agreements on other topics combined. We do not report per-topic results because our test set baseline accuracies vary a great deal by topic as do the size of the topic sets. See Table 1.

Features	Random Forest	J 48
ALL-TM	63.1	66.0
Unigram	56.6	59.8
Bigram	59.3	60.1

Table 4: Accuracies for Theoretically Motivated Features (**ALL-TM**), Unigrams and Bigrams with Random Forest and J48 Trees over a 50% baseline. No interesting differences observed in precision and recall.

Table 3 summarizes our theoretically-motivaed topic-independent features, and Table 4 compares the accuracies of classifiers using these features to unigrams and bigrams when we train on *Evolu-*

tion and then test on our mixed-topic test set, using the Weka learners for Random forest and J48 Tree. Although unigrams and unigram+bigram achieves approximately 60% accuracy over a 50% baseline, paired t-tests on the result vectors show that the differences in accuracies are statistically significant when we compare ALL-TM features with unigrams and unigram+bigrams: Random Forest (p = .004) and J48 Trees (p < .0001).

Ngram	N Feats	Acc	Feats Selected
Uni	2K	62.5	*understand, fail, never, nothing,* **catholic**, **gene**, *irrelevant, acceptable, show, didn't,* **geologist**, **creationist**
Bigram	4k	62.7	*? you, do we, understand that, ? just, really?, is based, well said, ? did, can the, the nature,* **the church**, *failed to, then what*

Table 5: Accuracy when fitting to test set for number of features selected for ngrams, with sample features.

Moreover even if we optimize on the test set by examining the variations in performance as a function of the number of features selected, ALL-TM still beats both unigram and unigram+bigram, when features are selected according to ranking by Gain Ratio. ALL-TM is significantly more accurate when compared to unigrams (p = .003) best accuracy of 62.5 with 2000 features, and better than unigram+bigram best accuracy of 62.7 for 4000 features (p = .007). See Table 5.

More interestingly though, if we look at what features get selected (Table 5), we see many features reminiscent of our theoretically motivated features. Features highly ranked by the Gain Ratio were topic-independent cues for disagreement such as *understand, fail, nothing, never* and Bigrams such as *? how, perhaps you, would you, never said.* However there were few high ranked unigrams and bigrams for agreement. Also note that topic specific cues such as *gene, catholic, creationist, geologist* and *the church* are selected over any topic-independent cues for agreement. This corroborates our manual construction of a combined denial category with more than 300 words and a very limited agreement category.

To test which features make the most difference, we also conducted ablation experiments (Table 6), as well as tests with individual features (Table 7). Table 6 shows that the CUE WORDS (p = .0008) and PUNCTUATION features (p = .01) have the biggest impact on performance. The decrease in performance when ablating agreement features is

Ablated Feature	Random Forest	J48
No Agreement	62.2	65.0
No Cue Words	59.1	62.1
No Denial	63.3	66.0
No Duration	63.6	66.3
No Hedges	64.2	66.5
No Polarity	64.4	66.8
No Punctuation	60.3	61.6

Table 6: Accuracy when Ablating each Theoretically Motivated Feature with Random Forest and J48 Trees over a 50% baseline .

not statistically significant (p = .20).

Feature	Acc	Prec	Recall
Agreement	54.4	.55	.54
Cue words	62.5	.63	.62
Denial	52.0	.54	.52
Duration	53.6	.54	.53
Hedges	50.4	.51	.50
Polarity	53.4	.53	.53
Punctuation	65.3	.65	.65

Table 7: Results for Individual Features for J48 Trees over a 50% baseline .

Since the J48 learner performs consistently better, we restrict our comparison of individual features in Table 7 to that learner. Table 7 shows that PUNCTUATION and CUE WORDS features by themselves provide significant performance improvements over the unigram baseline, and that the POLARITY, AGREEMENT, DENIAL and DURATION feature sets provide significant improvements on their own over the majority class baseline of 50%. A paired t-test shows these differences are significant at p =.02. To our surprise, the HEDGE feature was not effective, and we plan further refinements of it. These results support the hypothesis that there are clearly markers for agreement and disagreement that are suggested by the theoretical literature and which are not topic specific.

6 Discussion and Future Work

We develop topic-independent features for classifying (dis)agreement in online dialogue, and show that we can beat an unfiltered unigram baseline by 6%, and even beat the best feature-selection ngram-based classifers fitted to the test set.

Features we didn't use from previous work include word pairs as introduced by (Marcu and Echihabi, 2002), and used subsequently by (Pitler et al., 2009) and (Biran and Rambow, 2011). The issue of whether word pairs are topic-dependent has never been addressed, but the examples given in previous work suggest that they may indicate topic-specific comparisons. Previous work also suggests that context might be helpful in recognizing disagreement (Walker et al., 2012b), but we did not test the effect of context.

The most similar work to our own trains a disagreement classifier for **Q/R** response pairs in online forums (Abbott et al., 2011). Their work used ngrams, MPQA opinion words (Stoyanov et al., 2005), LIWC (Pennebaker et al., 2001), and a different dataset (**Q/R** instead of **P1,P2** datasets), and does not aim to develop a classifier that works well independently of topic. Their best accuracy is about 68% for a feature set called BothLocal for the JRip classifier using χ^2 feature selection. BothLocal includes unigrams, bigrams, trigrams, LIWC, punctuation, cue words, dependency features, generalized dependency features and utterance length measures, and it is unclear whether these features are specific to topic. It is also difficult to directly compare the results because they do not report accuracies for individual feature sets or ablated feature experiments. For example, their unigram accuracy of 63% includes cue words, and is reported for training and testing on a mixture of topics without any held-out topics.

Other work on disagreement recognition includes that of (Wang et al., 2011) who describe conditional random field model for detecting (dis)agreement between speakers in English broadcast conversations. They use sampling and prosodic features such as pause, duration and speech rate on an unbalanced dataset. They report an increase in F-measure of 4.5% for agreement and 4.7% for disagreement over a baseline of lexical, structural, and durational features. (Hahn et al., 2006) show that a contrast classifier improves the accuracy of dis(agreement) classification in the ICSI meetings corpus, and that their results are less affected by imbalanced data. They improve the F-measure to .755 over a baseline SVM with F-measure .726. (Yin et al., 2012) use sentiment, emotion and durational features for (dis)agreement classification in online forums, and they show that aggregating local positions over posts yields 3 to 4% better performance than non-aggregating baselines.

While recognizing (dis)agreement can be useful in its own right, it has also been shown to be useful for the identification of stance (Gawron et al., 2012; Hassan et al., 2010; Thomas et al., 2006; Bansal et al., 2008; Murakami and Raymond, 2010; Agrawal et al., 2003). Work that focuses on the social network structure of online forums as a way to improve stance classification has either assumed that adjacent posts always disagree, or used simple rules for identifying agreement based on patterns in the reply post (Murakami and Raymond, 2010; Agrawal et al., 2003). Previous work by Somasundaran & Wiebe (2009, 2010) develops positive and negative arguing features for the classification of stance, that at least in motivation, resemble our denial features . They show that arguing features are helpful in stance classification. Work by (Galley et al., 2004) on detecting disagreement in meetings corpora similarly shows that pragmatic features are useful for detecting disagreement using models based on Bayesian Networks. (Walker et al., 2012b) use a number of linguistic features such as unigrams, bigrams, and repeated punctuation and proposed a supervised model for stance classification in online debates. Related work by (Hassan et al., 2010) focuses on identifying the attitude of the participants towards one another in online debates. They relate the polarity of words to the second person pronoun for classification, while related work by (Abu-Jbara et al., 2012) uses the polarity of expressions and named entity recognition to identify a subgroup of participants, where participants within a subgroup are inclined to agree with one another. Methods for stance classification in congressional debates do not separately evaluate the accuracy of (dis)agreement classification (Thomas et al., 2006; Bansal et al., 2008; Awadallah et al., 2010; Burfoot, 2008).

In future work, we plan to develop more detailed patterns based on LIWC categories and syntactic parses (Thelen and Riloff, 2002). For example, an error analysis suggests that sometimes two people mutually reject the proposal or claim of a third person, e.g. *How can* **they** *say that....* In such cases our classifier finds the disagreement marker *how can* and classifies it as disagreement. More detailed syntactic processing would allow us to refine our patterns to identify particular classes of targets such as third person vs. first person. Similarly, here we extended patterns by hand, e.g. generalizations over pronouns such as *I can't, we can't, can you, can we*. In future we aim to generalize such patterns automatically using tagsets. We expect that more general patterns should improve the accuracy of the topic-independent feature sets. We also plan to carry out further annotation of the IAC corpus using the classes of rejections summarized in Fig. 2 to determine whether there are forms for indicating each type that are not represented by our features, and to determine the frequency across a sample of our corpus of the different types.

References

R. Abbott, M. A. Walker, J. E. Fox Tree, P. Anand, R. Bowmani, and J. King. 2011. How can you say such things?!?: Recognizing Disagreement in Informal Political Argument. In *Proc. of the ACL Workshop on Language in Social Media*.

A. Abu-Jbara, M. Diab, P. Dasigi, and D. Radev. 2012. Subgroup detection in ideological discussions. In *Proc. of the 50th Annual Meeting of the Association for Computational Linguistics*, ACL '12, p. 399–409.ACL.

R. Agrawal, S. Rajagopalan, R. Srikant, and Y. Xu. 2003. Mining newsgroups using networks arising from social behavior. In *Proc. of the 12th international conference on World Wide Web*, p. 529–535. ACM.

D. Appelt and K. Konolige. 1988. A practical nonmonotonic theory for reasoning about speech acts. In *Proc. of the 26th Annual Meeting of the Association for Computational Linguistics*.

N. Asher, F. Benamara, and Y. Yannick Mathieu. 2008. Distilling opinion in discourse: A preliminary study. In *COLING 2008*, p. 7–10.

R. Awadallah, M. Ramanath, and G. Weikum. 2010. Language-model-based pro/con classification of political text. In *Proc. of the 33rd international ACM SIGIR conference on Research and development in information retrieval*, p. 747–748. ACM.

M. Bansal, C. Cardie, and L. Lee. 2008. The power of negative thinking: Exploiting label disagreement in the min-cut classification framework. *Proc. of COLING: Companion volume: Posters*, p. 13–16.

O. Biran and O. Rambow. 2011. Identifying justifications in written dialogs. In *2011 Fifth IEEE International Conference on Semantic Computing (ICSC)*, p. 162–168. IEEE.

Penelope Brown and Steve Levinson. 1987. *Politeness: Some universals in language usage.* Cambridge University Press.

C. Burfoot. 2008. Using multiple sources of agreement information for sentiment classification of political transcripts. In *Australasian Language Technology Association Workshop 2008*, v.6, p. 11–18.

G. Carenini and J. Moore. 2000. A strategy for generating evaluative arguments. In *Proc. of the 1st International Conference on Natural Language Generation (INLG-00)*.

J.E. Fox Tree and J.C. Schrock. 1999. Discourse Markers in Spontaneous Speech: Oh What a Difference an Oh Makes. *Journal of Memory and Language*, 40(2):280–295.

M. Galley, K. McKeown, J. Hirschberg, and E. Shriberg. 2004. Identifying agreement and disagreement in conversational speech: Use of bayesian networks to model pragmatic dependencies. In *Proc. of the 42nd Annual Meeting on Association for Computational Linguistics*, p. 669. ACL.

J.M. Gawron, D. Gupta, K. Stephens, M.H. Tsou, B. Spitzberg, and L. An. 2012. Using group membership markers for group identification in web logs. In *The 6th International AAAI Conference on Weblogs and Social Media (ICWSM 2012)*.

M. Groen, J. Noyes, and F. Verstraten. 2010. The Effect of Substituting Discourse Markers on Their Role in Dialogue. *Discourse Processes: A Multidisciplinary Journal*, 47(5):33.

S. Hahn, R. Ladner, and M. Ostendorf. 2006. Agreement/disagreement classification: exploiting unlabeled data using contrast classifiers. In *Proc. of the Human Language Technology Conference of the NAACL*, NAACL06, p. 53–56. ACL.

A. Hassan, V. Qazvinian, and D. Radev. 2010. What's with the attitude?: identifying sentences with attitude in online discussions. In *Proc. of the 2010 Conference on Empirical Methods in Natural Language Processing*, p 1245–1255. ACL.

J.B. Hirschberg. 1985. *A Theory of Scalar Implicature*. Ph.D. thesis, University of Pennsylvania, Computer and Information Science.

L. R. Horn. 1989. *A natural history of negation*. Chicago University Press.

G. Lakoff. 1973. Hedges: A study in meaning criteria and the logic of fuzzy concepts. *Journal of Philosophical Logic*, 2(4):458–508.

A. Louis, A. Joshi, R. Prasad, and A. Nenkova. 2010. Using entity features to classify implicit relations. In *Proc. of the 11th Annual SIGdial Meeting on Discourse and Dialogue*, Tokyo, Japan.

D. Marcu and A. Echihabi. 2002. An unsupervised approach to recognizing discourse relations. In *Proc. of the 40th Annual Meeting on Association for Computational Linguistics*, p. 368–375. ACL.

A. Murakami and R. Raymond. 2010. Support or Oppose? Classifying Positions in Online Debates from Reply Activities and Opinion Expressions. In *Proc. of the 23rd International Conference on Computational Linguistics: Posters*, p. 869–875. ACL.

B. Pang and L. Lee. 2008. Opinion mining and sentiment analysis. *Foundations and Trends in Information Retrieval*, 2(1-2):1–135.

J. W. Pennebaker, L. E. Francis, and R. J. Booth, 2001. *LIWC: Linguistic Inquiry and Word Count.*

R. Perrault. 1990. An application of default logic to speech-act theory. In Philip Cohen, Jerry Morgan, and Martha Pollack, editors, *Intentions in Communication*, p. 161–187. MIT Press.

E. Pitler, A. Louis, and A. Nenkova. 2009. Automatic sense prediction for implicit discourse relations in text. In *Proc. of the Joint Conference of the 47th Annual Meeting of the ACL: Vol. 2*, p. 683–691. ACL.

M. Pollack, J. Hirschberg, and B. Webber. 1982. User participation in the reasoning process of expert systems. In *Proc. First National Conference on Artificial Intelligence*, pages pp. 358–361.

R. Prasad, A. Joshi, and B. Webber. 2010. Exploiting scope for shallow discourse parsing. In *Language Resources and Evaluation Conference*.

E. Riloff and J. Wiebe. 2003. Learning extraction patterns for subjective expressions. In *Proc. of the 2003 conference on Empirical methods in Natural Language Processing-Vol.10*, p. 105–112. ACL.

J. M. Sadock. 1977. Modus brevis: The truncated argument. In *Papers from the 13th meeting of the CLS*. Chicago Linguistic Society.

S. Somasundaran and J. Wiebe. 2009. Recognizing stances in online debates. In *Proc. of the Joint Conference of the 47th Annual Meeting of the ACL*, p. 226–234. ACL.

S. Somasundaran and J. Wiebe. 2010. Recognizing stances in ideological on-line debates. In *Proc. of the NAACL HLT 2010 Workshop on Computational Approaches to Analysis and Generation of Emotion in Text*, p. 116–124. ACL.

R. C. Stalnaker. 1978. Assertion. In Peter Cole, editor, *Syntax and Semantics, Vol. 9: Pragmatics*, p. 315–332. Academic Press.

A. Stent. 2002. A conversation acts model for generating spoken dialogue contributions. *Computer Speech and Language: Special Issue on Spoken Language Generation*.

V. Stoyanov, C. Cardie, and J. Wiebe. 2005. Multi-perspective question answering using the MPQA corpus. In *Proc. of the conference on Human Language Technology and Empirical Methods in Natural Language Processing*, HLT '05, p. 923–930, ACL.

M. Thelen and E. Riloff. 2002. A bootstrapping method for learning semantic lexicons using extraction pattern contexts. In *Proc. of the ACL-02 conference on Empirical methods in Natural Language Processing. Vol. 10*, p. 214–221. ACL.

M. Thomas, B. Pang, and L. Lee. 2006. Get out the vote: Determining support or opposition from Congressional floor-debate transcripts. In *Proc. of the 2006 conference on empirical methods in natural language processing*, p. 327–335. ACL.

R. Thomason. 1990. Propagating epistemic coordination through mutual defaults i. In R. Parikh, editor, *Proc. of the Third Conference on Theoretical Aspects of Reasoning about Knowledge*, p. 29–39.

D. Traum. 1994. *A Computational Model of Grounding in Natural Language Conversation*. Ph.D. thesis, University of Rochester.

M. Walker, P. Anand, R. Abbott, and J. E. Fox Tree. 2012a. A corpus for research on deliberation and debate. In *Language Resources and Evaluation Conference, LREC2012*.

M.A. Walker, P. Anand, R. Abbott, and R. Grant. 2012b. Stance classification using dialogic properties of persuasion. In *Meeting of the North American Association for Computational Linguistics. NAACL-HLT12*.

M. A. Walker. 1996a. Inferring acceptance and rejection in dialogue by default rules of inference. *Language and Speech*, 39-2:265–304.

W. Wang, S. Yaman, K. Precoda, C. Richey, and G. Raymond. 2011. Detection of agreement and disagreement in broadcast conversations. In *The 49th Annual Meeting of the Association for Computational Linguistics*, p. 374–378. ACL.

B. Webber and R. Prasad. 2008. Sentence-initial discourse connectives, discourse structure and semantics. In *Proc. of the Workshop on Formal and Experimental Approaches to Discourse Particles and Modal Adverbs, Hamburg, Germany*.

J. Wiebe, E. Breck, C. Buckley, C. Cardie, P. Davis, B. Fraser, D. Litman, D. Pierce, E. Riloff, T. Wilson, et al. 2003. Recognizing and organizing opinions expressed in the world press. In *Working Notes-New Directions in Question Answering (AAAI Spring Symposium Series)*.

J. Wiley. 2005. A fair and balanced look at the news: What affects memory for controversial arguments? *Journal of Memory and Language*, 53(1):95–109.

T. Wilson, P. Hoffmann, S. Somasundaran, J. Kessler, J. Wiebe, Y. Choi, C. Cardie, E. Riloff, and S. Patwardhan. 2005. Opinionfinder: A system for subjectivity analysis. In *Proc. of HLT/EMNLP on Interactive Demonstrations*, p. 34–35. ACL.

J. Yin, P. Thomas, N. Narang, and C. Paris. 2012. Unifying local and global agreement and disagreement classification in online debates. In *Proc. of the 3rd Workshop in Computational Approaches to Subjectivity and Sentiment Analysis*, WASSA '12, p. 61–69, ACL.

I. Zukerman, R. McConachy, and K. Korb. 2000. Using argumentation strategies in automated argument generation. In *Proc. of the 1st International Natural Language Generation Conference*, p. 55–62.

Automatic Prediction of Friendship via Multi-model Dyadic Features

Zhou Yu, David Gerritsen, Amy Ogan, Alan W Black, Justine Cassell
School of Computer Science, Carnegie Mellon University
{zhouyu, dgerrits, aeo, awb, justine }@cs.cmu.edu

Abstract

In this paper we focus on modeling friendships between humans as a way of working towards technology that can initiate and sustain a lifelong relationship with users. We do this by predicting friendship status in a dyad using a set of automatically harvested verbal and nonverbal features from videos of the interaction of students in a peer tutoring study. We propose a new computational model used to model friendship status in our data, based on a group sparse model (GSM) with L2,1 norm which is designed to accommodate the sparse and noisy properties of the multi-channel features. Our GSM model achieved the best overall performance compared to a non-sparse linear model (NLM) and a regular sparse linear model (SLM), as well as outperforming human raters. Dyadic features, such as number and length of conversational turns and mutual gaze, in addition to low level features such as F0 and gaze at task, were found to be good predictors of friendship status.

1 Introduction and Related Work

While significant advances have been made in detecting the speech and nonverbal social signals emitted by individuals (see Vinciarelli, Pantic & Bourlard, 2009, for a review), and research has addressed the social roles and states of individuals in groups (see Gatica-Perez, 2009, for a review), considerably less computational work has focused on the automatic detection of speech or nonverbal correlates of specifically dyadic states, such as rapport. And yet rapport has been shown to have important effects on interactions as diverse as survey interviewing (Berg, 1989), sales (Brooks, 1989), and health (Harrigan et al., 1985). If we are to build interactive systems that are successful, then, we believe that the ability to build rapport with a human user will be essential.

Rapport can be instantaneous and can also build over time. Granovetter (1973) describes the strength of an interpersonal "tie" as a function of the time, emotional intensity, and reciprocity that accumulates between people. These ties mediate effects in myriad domains such as learning (Azmitia & Montgomery, 1993) and healthcare (Harrigan & Rosenthal, 1983).

Accordingly, analysis of initial exchanges and those after many years of interaction suggests that the behavioral signals that indicate rapport change over time. For example, in Tickle-Degnen and Rosenthal's highly cited model (1990), rapport consists of mutual attention, positivity, and coordination. High levels of positivity between conversational partners are common in the initial phases of a relationship, but positivity has been shown to decline, without a loss in rapport, as the number of interactions increases. In fact, Ogan et al. (2012) gave evidence that the use of playful rudeness between friends during peer tutoring correlates to greater learning. This leads to an associated challenge of spoken dialogue system development: creating systems that can develop social ties, and increase rapport with the user over repeated interactions to maximize beneficial outcomes.

While little work has addressed automatic detection, some prior work has addressed the problem of emitting signals to build rapport in dialogue and agent systems (Stronks et al., 2002; Bickmore & Picard, 2005; Gratch et al., 2006; Cassell et al., 2007; Bickmore et al., 2011), and we turn to this research for what cues might be important in rapport. The majority of this prior work, however, has addressed harmony – or instant rapport – rather than rapport over time. For those systems that have addressed friendship or the growth of rapport, most commonly the *number of interactions* has been used as a meter of relationship progression, instigating changes in the dialogue system as the social odometer scrolls onward (Cassell & Bickmore, 2003; Vardoulakis et al., 2012). Counting the times a dyad has interacted is a crude approximation of a relationship state, however; being able to detect the behavioral signals that people actually use to indicate relationship status would be superior.

In our own prior work (Cassell et al.,2007) we looked at particular hand-annotated nonverbal signals (such as nodding and mutual gaze) as operationalizations of rapport, and found that friends and non-friends indeed show differing distributions of each signal as a function of relationship state. In the current study, we move to the next step and automatically harvest a set of multimodal dyadic and time contingent features to identify those features that play a significant role in predicting friendship state. A major challenge for predicting relational states such as these is to construct a compact feature space that captures only reliable rapport signals and also generalizes across different users. To provide strength to our model (as well as to fit the multimodal nature of embodied conversational agents), we look at both acoustic and visual features. Such an approach takes advantage of the fact that multimodal aspects of communication are not redundant, but often complementary (Cassell, 2000).

However, dyadic behaviors such as conversational turns, mutual/non-mutual smile, mutual/non-mutual gaze, and mutual/non-mutual lean forward provide an additional challenge in modeling; no matter how important, they appear relatively rarely in conversational data. Thus standard non-sparse linear models, normally trained on high frequency factors, might assign too much weight to low frequency (i.e., sparse) features. In order to address issues of this sort Yuan and Lin (2007) introduced the group lasso. To address the sparse nature of our features in real-world data and the noise that occurs from different production sources, we propose an extension to this genre of technique in the form of a Group Sparse Model (GSM) which enforces sparsity with a L2,1 norm instead of the group lasso penalty (Chen, et al., 2011), due to the relatively efficient optimization process of L2,1 norms (Liu, et al., 2009). Unlike a straightforward sparse linear model (SLM) (Yang et al., 2010), which treats each feature independently, GSMs group features which share the same production source in the optimization process. In the GSM linear model, the removal of the assumption of independence between features means that the penalty is on group rather than individual features. Thus the model has general robustness to noise, since grouping features from the same production source can increase the overall confidence of the feature group.

Our contributions in this work, then, are three-fold: we (1) designed and implemented a method for automatic dyadic feature extraction which is based on low level features, and which yields strong predictive power of friendship status, (2) propose a new Group Sparse Model (GSM) with L2,1 norm, that deals with the noisy and sparse nature of the feature sets, and (3) illuminate, from this model, the nature of verbal and nonverbal behavior between friends and non-friends in a peer tutoring setting.

The remainder of the paper is organized as follows. We first describe the data set and introduce the features used in our experiments. We then describe the performance of the three computational models we evaluated. Finally, we discuss the contributions of different features to friendship prediction and provide an error analysis of our proposed model.

2 The Data Set

Figure 1: Camera View 1 and Camera View 2

We collected data from dyads of students engaged in a reciprocal peer tutoring task. We chose peer tutoring as it is a domain in which friendship has been shown to have a positive effect on student learning (see e.g. Ogan et al, 2012). In addition, tutoring systems that rely on dialogue are common, and peer tutoring dialogue systems are increasingly common. Thus, being able to assess friendship state in this domain is a useful step on the path to creating a peer tutoring agent that can use rapport to increase learning gains.

Each dyad consisted of two American English speakers with a mean age of 13.3 years (range = 12 – 15). We collected data from 12 dyads, of which 6 dyads were already friends. Dyads were either both girls or both boys, and each condition contained 3 boy dyads and 3 girl dyads.

Each dyad came to the lab for 3 sessions, with an average interval between visits of 4.6 days (*SD* = 3.1), totaling 36 sessions across all dyads. Each session consisted of about 90 minutes of interaction recorded from three camera views (a frontal view of each participant and a side view of the two participants). With close talk microphones, we also recorded the participants' speech in separate audio channels for the purpose of automatic dyadic acoustic feature extraction. The setting is shown in Figure 1.

Each session began with a short period of time for participants to become acquainted. After that, using a standard reciprocal tutoring procedure (see Fantuzzo et al., 1989), participants tutored each other on procedural and conceptual aspects of an algebra topic in which both participants were relatively novice. Order of seating and assignment of tutoring roles (tutor or tutee) was determined in the first session by alphabetical order of participant name. Tutoring roles alternated from that point on, such that both participants had the opportunity to take on the role of "expert" during each session. After a period of individual study time to familiarize themselves with the material, the first tutoring period began and lasted approximately 25 minutes. This was followed by a 5 minute break, after which students' tutoring roles were reversed for a second tutoring period of 25 minutes. Finally, each student answered a survey about the interaction.

The current study examines only the tutoring sections of each session, which were divided into 30-second clips or "thin slices" (Ambady et al., 2006). In total, the data points used for modeling comprise 2259 clips from the 12 dyads.

3 Multimodal Information

In our analyses, low-level audio and visual features were automatically extracted using three off-the-shelf toolkits. Dyadic features, which are a second order derivative of the low level features, and which capture the interaction of two participants, are also automatically produced. Taken together, analysis of these features allows us to determine if the verbal and nonverbal behaviors of the participants index their friendship status in any significant way.

3.1 Low Level Audio Features (LA)

Type	# of Features
Prosodic Features	
F0	72
Energy	38
Duration	154
Voice Quality Features	
Jitter	68
Shimmer	34
Voicing	38
Spectral Features	
MFCC	570
Total	**974**

Table 1: Acoustic Feature Groups

For acoustic feature extraction, a large set of acoustic low-level descriptors (LLD) and derivatives of LLDs combined with appropriate statistical functionals, i.e., **maxPos** (the absolute position of the maximum value in frames), **minPos** (the absolute position of the minimum value in frames), **amean** (The arithmetic mean of the contour), etc., were extracted for each of the split channel recordings. The "INTERSPEECH 2010 Paralinguistic Challenge Feature Set" in the openSMILE toolkit (Schuller et al., 2012) was used as our basic acoustic feature set. For spectral features, Mel Spectrum and LSP were excluded due to the possible overlap with MFCC. The set contained 974 features which resulted from a base of 32 low-level descriptors (LLD) with 32 corresponding delta coefficients, and 21 functionals applied to each of these 68 LLD contours. In addition, 19 functionals were applied to the 4 pitch-based LLD and their four delta coefficient contours. Finally the number of pitch onsets (pseudo syllables) and the total duration of the input were included. The dimension of each feature group is shown in Table 1.

3.2 Low Level Vision Features (LV)

Type	# of Features
Face Position Feature	10
38 Face Interest Points	114
Gaze Features	3
Face Direction Features	4
Mouth and Eye Openness	6
Smile Intensity	1
Discretized Smile	1
Total	**139**

Table 2: Vision Feature Groups

Since participants were facing the camera directly most of the time, as seen in Fig 1, current technology for facial tracking can efficiently be applied to our dataset. OMRON's OKAO Vision System was used in face detection, facial feature extraction, and basic face related features extrapolation. For each frame, the vision software returns a smile intensity (0-100) and the gaze direction, using both horizontal and vertical angles expressed in degrees. Apart from gaze direction, the software also provides information about head orientation: horizontal, vertical, and roll (in or out). 38 additional face interest points, position and confidence, were also extracted. These were normalized to pixel coordinates, which turned out to lead to quite noisy data, and hence to diminished utility of these 38 points (in the future we will consider normalizing to face coordinates). We also calculated the openness of the left eye, right eye, mouth, and the location of the face. Details are shown in Table 2. Similar to our audio feature extraction method, one static feature vector per 30 second video clip was produced. All the features were computed at the same rate as the original videos: 30 Hz. Altogether, 139 dimensions were extracted in each frame from each camera view.

3.3 Dyadic Features (DF)

All of the features discussed above are low-level acoustic and visual features, extracted with respect to individual participants. While individual behavior may index friendship state, we posit that patterns of interaction will be more effective. For example, prior research (Baker et al., 2008) suggests that the number and length of conversational turns (Cassell et al., 2007), presence of mutual smiles and non-mutual smiles (Prepin et al., 2012), mutual gaze and non-mutual gaze (Nakano et al., 2010), as well as posture shifting (Cassell, et al., 2001; Tickle-Degnen & Rosenthal, 1990), are important features to investigate in dyadic data. While other features such as gestures and mutual pitch shift may also play a role in indexing relationship state, these are not yet a part of the dyadic features we address here.

3.3.1 Number and Average Length of Conversational Turns

We recorded individual audio channels for each participant, which makes the automatic extraction of conversational turns possible. First, we extracted intervals of silence with toolbox SoX which produced speech chunks, and then identified the speaker by comparing the speech energy (loudness) in each audio channel, as speech from each speaker is carried by the other's microphone. After that we combined the speech chunks and speaker ID to approximate conversational turns. The approximation quality is not perfect, given the variability of the audio recording, but noise can be mediated during model building.

3.3.2 Mutual Smile and Non Mutual Smile

Prepin et al. (2012) describe the role of mutual smiles (smiles that occur during the same time period) in "stance alignment" and make the point that interactional alignment of this behavior reflects synchronization of internal states. Such synchrony predicts mutual understanding and increased quality of interaction, and as such is a fundamental quality in the formation of adolescent friendships (Youniss, 1982). Cappella & Pelachaud (2002) likewise describe "mutuality" as the precondition for how smiles function in contingent ways in a dyad. Smiles are clearly therefore important to assess in data such as ours. We defined a maximum window of 500 milliseconds between the end of one participant's smile and the beginning of the next for smiles to be considered mutual.

3.3.3 Mutual Gaze and Non-mutual Gaze

Nakano & Ishii (2010) describe eye gaze as a clue to engagement, and integrate mutual gaze into their conversational agents. There is no feature for direct gaze at partner provided in the OKAO vision toolkit. Mutual gaze was therefore approximated by annotating a gaze "in front," achieved by combining the information from three directions of gaze: vertical, horizontal, and depth. Gaze "in front", or at the partner, was recorded only if the participant gaze had less than a 15 degree angle from straight forward in all of these three directions. A maximum window of 500 milliseconds for gaze to be considered mutual was also employed here.

3.3.4 Mutual Lean Forward and Non-Mutual Lean Forward

Forward leaning has been shown to be a significant predictor of the ability to establish rapport in a dyad (Harrigan et al., 1985). In fact, friends who lean in are seen as more socially competent, while strangers are seen as less socially competent when they lean in (Burgoon & Hale, 1988). For our study, lean forward was approximated by detecting the smooth trend of face enlargement within the video frame. In order to improve precision of the feature, the segments with high confidence in face detection were processed. Furthermore, posture shifting, i.e., forward leaning, is not as quickly executed as changes in gaze or smile. We therefore used a 1 second sample window for lean forward, rather than a 500 millisecond window.

3.3.5 Mutual Gaze followed by Mutual Smile

Mutual gaze followed by mutual smile is also approximated using a similar approach as above. It is a relatively dense feature compared to all the other possible combinations of nonverbal behaviors, thus it is the only combination that is included in the feature set in this paper. The window within which mutual gaze is considered to be followed by mutual smile is set to be within 2 seconds.

4 Computational Model

We formulate friendship prediction as a set of binary classifications. In order to have the least variance and make sure no participant appeared in both the training and testing set, a leave-one-out cross-validation setting was adopted in all of our experiments. Each session had approximately 180 30-second video clips, totaling 2259 data points. Z-score normalization by dyad was used to scale all the features into the same range. Early fusion, which is simple concatenation of feature vectors, was adopted throughout our experiments to combine different features. We evaluated our group sparse model (GSM), along with a non-sparse linear model (NLM) and sparse linear model (SLM).

4.1 Non-sparse Linear Model (NLM)

We began with a standard non-sparse linear model (NLM), which is a Support Vector Machine (SVM) (Cortes & Vapnik, 1995) with a linear kernel. The libsvm (Fan et al., 2008) package was used in our experiment, and the parameter, the slack value of SVM that controls the scale of the soft margin, was obtained by cross validation.

4.2 Sparse Linear Model (SLM)

In order to prevent over-fitting on rare dyadic features, a sparse sensitive model SLM was introduced. As well as preventing over-fitting, through weight shrinkage the sparse model can also exclude redundant features. In our experiment, an L2,1 norm sparse model with linear kernel (Yang et al., 2012) was selected as our baseline sparse model.

4.3 Group Sparse Model (GSM)

Based on the SLM, we propose a group-sparse model (GSM) with the novel use of an L2,1 norm. Instead of assuming every feature is uncorrelated to other features, the GSM groups some of the features together and utilizes their correlated information to mediate the noise of the data. For an arbitrary matrix $A \in R^{r \times p}$, its $L_{2,1-\text{norm}}$ is defined as

$$||A||_{2,1} = \sum_{i=1}^{r} \sqrt{\sum_{j=1}^{p} A_{ij}^2}$$

Suppose that we have n training data indicated by $x_1, x_2, \ldots x_n$ and sampled from c classes. In our setting, c = 2, friends or non-friends. $y_i \in \{0,1\}$ $(1 \leq i \leq n)$ is the corresponding label. The total scatter matrix S_t and between class scatter matrix S_b are defined as follows.

$$S_t = \sum_{i=1}^{n} (x_i - \mu)(x_i - \mu)^T = XX^T$$

$$S_b = \sum_{i=1}^{n} n_i(\mu_i - \mu)(\mu_i - \mu)^T = XGG^TX^T$$

where μ is the mean of all samples, μ_i is the mean of samples in the i-th class. n_i is the number of samples in the i-th class, $Y = [y_1, y_2, \ldots, y_n]$.

$$G = [G_1, \ldots, G_n]^T = Y(Y^TY)^{-1/2}$$

G is the scaled label matrix. A well-known method to utilize discriminate information is to find a low dimensional subspace in which S_b is maximized while S_t is minimized (Fukunaga et al., 1990). So the object function could be easily written as follows

$$\min_W \left(W^T(S_t S_b{}^{-1})W\right) + \gamma ||W||_{2,1}$$

$$s.t. W^TW = 1$$

The optimization of the above object function was introduced in Yang et al. (2012). It is an adaptation of iterative singular value decomposition. In GSM, a block-wise constraint is imposed on the diagonal matrix (D) which is the intermediate result of the iterative single value decomposition.

$$D = diag\left(\frac{1}{||w^1||_2} I_1, \ldots, \frac{1}{||w^G||_2} I_G\right)$$

W in the equation is the weight function, w^i is the ith feature group in W, and there are a total number of G sub diagonal matrices corresponding to G groups of features.

For acoustic features, Steidl et al., (2012) designed a grouping schema which consists of Prosodic Features, Voice Quality Features and Spectral features which we adopted. For visual features, based on our observation of the highly unstable performance of the 38 feature points of the face, we introduced group bondage for the entire group to prevent single face features over-fitting the classifier. Detailed group information is shown in Table 1 and Table 2.

5 Human Baseline

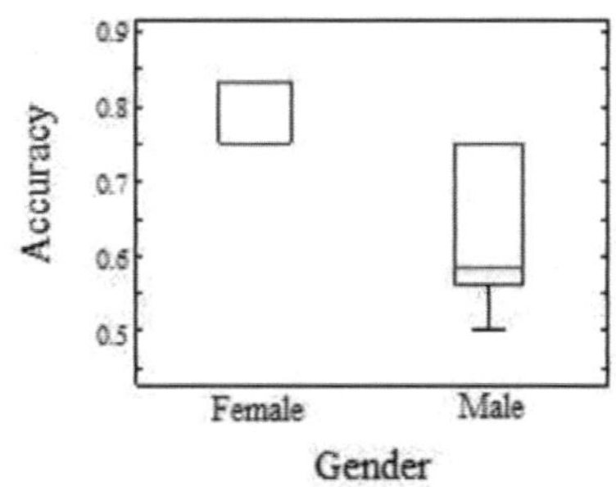

Figure 2: Boxplot of human rating accuracy with respect to gender.

In order to establish a baseline of the difficulty of predicting friendship, we conducted an experiment with humans, rating whether two people in a video were friends or not, after watching a 30-second video/audio clip taken from the first session of tutoring (in which the behaviors of strangers are most likely to be distinct from friends). We recruited 14 people and screened out participants with prior theoretical knowledge of nonverbal behavior, gesture, friendship, and rapport, or who rated all 12 clips in under 8 minutes, leaving 10 participants, half male, with an average age of 23 (*SD* 4.8). Each participant was asked to watch one 30-second clip per dyad, taken from 3 minutes after tutoring began. The mean accuracy of their friendship prediction was 0.717 (*SD* 0.119), which is significantly lower than our best GSM model (trained on all three sessions) applied to those same 12 clips, with a performance of 0.837 ($t(11) = -2.1381$ $p.<.05$). When we split the ratings by gender, we found females on average were more accurate than males (see Figure 2). According to Hall et al., (1979) females are generally better decoders of nonverbal behaviors, which may lead to better judgment of friendship.

6 Results: Models

	Human	NLM	SLM	GSM
LV		0.743	0.768	0.792*
LA		0.674	0.664	0.682*
LV+DF		0.752	0.769	0.801*
LA+DF		0.679	0.681	0.683
LV+LA		0.744	0.780	0.803*
LV+LA+DF	0.717	0.749	0.782	0.814#

Table 3: The classification accuracy of the three algorithms on different features sets. Feature sets were combined with early fusion (+). Values marked * are significantly better ($p<.05$, pairwise t-test) than other results in the same row. Values marked # are significantly better ($p<.001$, pairwise t-test) than other results in the same column.

Our group sparse model (GSM) along with the non-sparse linear model (NLM) and sparse linear model (SLM) were evaluated on different combinations of three sets of features: low-level vision features (LV), low-level audio features (LA) and dyadic features (DF), and their performance is presented in Table 3. We did not evaluate dyadic features (DF) alone due to their sparse nature.

In particular, we found that adding the automatically extracted DF to LV and LA with early fusion improved the performance ($t(2258)= -3.12, p<.001$) of the GSM model. When using fewer modalities, our newly proposed GSM outperformed NLM and SLM ($t(2258)=-1.65$, $p<0.05$). However, when the number of feature sets increased, there was no statistical difference in performance between GSM and the other two models. We suspect that when features are abundant, the information that the features provide reaches a ceiling. The advantage of the GSM was gained by mediating the noise and sparseness of the data, which resulted in better weight assignment for each feature. Alternatively, when features are abundant, even NLM can have a comparative weight assignment by performing a greedy high dimensional feature space search. Thus there is limited room for further improvement by better weight assignment among the group features which GSM assumes.

When we looked at the top features selected by NLM using the vision modality alone, two (out of 38) face features, which had an unstable nature, appeared high in rank, which suggests the possibility of NLM over-fitting the noise of these features. Surprisingly, when more modalities are added, NLM stops picking single face features as top informative features. In GSM, none of the 38 face features are listed in the top ranked features for any of the modalities, which demonstrates its ability in noise mediation.

In real world applications, data sets which produce ideal, abundant, and accurate features are rarely encountered. We often end up with data that are poor in video quality, e.g. with no split channels for each participant or no frontal face view. Our newly proposed GSM may therefore be more robust when features are noisy or certain modalities are not available.

7 Results: Contributions of Features

Feature Name	Weight
Number of Conversational Turns & Average Length of Turns	0.041
Gaze Down	-0.036
Mutual Gaze	0.014
F0	0.013
Non-mutual Gaze	-0.013
Voicing	0.014
MFCC	-0.007
Non-mutual Smile	0.004
Non-mutual Lean Forward	0.004
Mutual Gaze followed by Mutual Smile	0.001

Table 4: The top 10 informative features and their weights as trained by GSM. Positive weight is associated with friends while negative weight is associated with non-friends.

After building the model and ranking the features, we looked into the weights learned for each feature. This weight comprises not only the magnitude, which tells us if the feature is important, but also the polarity. A detailed list of the most informative features and their weights is shown in Table 4.

The strongest feature is number and length of **conversational turns** which is grouped in the table and should be interpreted as meaning that friends have more and shorter conversational turns. This is consistent with previous research on direction giving (Cassell et al., 2007), and mirrors the fact that friends are more likely to interrupt one another.

We expected that unfamiliar participants, seated about two feet across from one another, would maintain a low level of eye contact (Argyle & Dean, 1965). In fact we found that non-friends tend to **gaze down** more often. In this context, non-friends spend more time looking down at their study materials. In turn, **mutual gaze** is higher among friends.

Among the audio features, **F0**, which captures pitch related information such as range and mean, has been shown to differ between conversational and non-conversational speech (Bolinger, 1986). Here, friends show that more conversational style in their speech, despite the tutoring nature of the interaction.

In order to further examine the lessons to be learned from this GSM model about verbal and nonverbal behavior in friends and strangers, we also ran a repeated measures ANOVA, including both gender and friendship status as factors. There were no significant effects for gender, however, and so that factor was collapsed for further analysis. The four features described above were all significantly different between friends and strangers (although gaze down was simply a trend, at $p<.08$).

The following features were also important to the model, but did not show significance in the ANOVA, perhaps because of their sparse nature in our data. **MFCC** (Mel-Frequency Cepstral Coefficients) was associated with strangers and the similar audio feature of **voicing** was associated with friends. Both of these features have been described as approximating speech style – voicing, for example, may indicate more backchannels, such as "uh huh" and "hmm" (Ward, 2006).

In Nakano et al. (2003), listener gaze at the speaker is interpreted as evidence of non-understanding. We found similar results whereby non-friends were more likely to engage in **non-mutual** gaze – looking at one another when the other person was not looking back. Mutual smile did not distinguish between friends and non-friends, while **non-mutual smile**, on the other hand, provided indicative strength, in spite of its sparse nature, for friendship. This may relate to our prior work (Ogan et al., 2012) which found significant teasing and other behavior whereby friends appear comfortable enjoying themselves at the expense of the other.

Mutual lean forward lacked predictive power in our model, while **non-mutual lean forward** was more salient between friends. We often found, for example, that friends maintained very different postures, with a tutor leaning back much of the time, leaning forward only to answer a direct question from the tutee. Non-friends, on the other hand, tended to remain fixed on the study material. This may have been a display of formality, where a casual attitude would have been perceived as either impolite or inappropriate. In either relationship state, the tutee tended to sit hunched over the worksheet, and since we did not enter tutor state into the model, this may have washed out some tutor-specific results.

For the time contingent feature**, mutual gaze followed by mutual smile** is informative and predictive of friends.

8 Error Analysis and Discussion

Dyad ID	LA+DF	LV+DF	LA+LV+DF
1	0.732	0.809	0.819
2*	0.703	0.793	0.804
3*	0.574	0.771	0.778
4*	0.713	0.708	0.762
5	0.653	0.879	0.880
6	0.728	0.827	0.835
7	0.624	0.873	0.882
8*	0.712	0.861	0.852
9*	0.698	0.820	0.830
10	0.606	0.834	0.854
11*	0.700	0.682	0.743
12	0.749	0.780	0.785

Table 5: The average accuracy of classification in each dyad using the group sparse model (GSM) with different combination of feature sets. Dyads marked with * are friends

We performed an error analysis to understand the contexts under which our model failed to accurately predict friendship states, and here we discuss the implications of these examples for our work. Table 5 shows the average accuracy of each dyad using audio, visual, and dyadic features to predict friendship. Dyads 2, 3, 4, 8, 9 and 11 are friend dyads, and the rest are strangers.

Dyad 3 (friends) showed very low accuracy in audio and dyadic features alone, which might be explained by the fact that in one early session for this dyad, most of the 30-second clips contain very sparse numbers of low-level audio features (LA). An examination of the audio recording reveals that one of the participants was more aggressive than in the other sessions. The student told his friend, *"Just be quiet—I am trying to work,"* and *"Shh, you don't understand, so I basically have to teach you how to work that, but I'm trying to work."* At this point in the interaction, his partner stopped participating in the task and said virtually nothing for the rest of the session. This lack of speech led to a lower number of turns – a pattern with a closer resemblance to strangers than friends.

It seems that such rude behavior would be more likely between friends than strangers, meaning that ultimately our model will need to be sensitive to this kind of variance. With more pairs of friends, different styles of friendship can be further distinguished. However, this specific phenomenon signals that in the future, lexical information which could be obtained by automatic speech recognition could further improve performance.

Dyad 11 also showed low relative accuracy in predication, particularly when the model used vision features. We found that one of the participants often tilted her head, which partially blocked the frontal camera view of the other participant, thus resulting in less confidence in automatically extracted visual features. In the future we will set our cameras in a better position in order to reach higher feature extraction accuracy.

When we combined all our features, the prediction accuracy of Dyad 3 and 11 improved, further demonstrating that multimodal information improves friendship modeling.

9 Conclusion and Future Work

As a first step towards predicting the state of friendship between two interlocutors, we analyzed a set of automatically harvested low-level and dyadic features from dialogues in a peer-tutoring task. Both low level features and dyadic features were shown to be useful in discriminating between those who are friends and those who are not.

To perform the analysis, we introduced a new computational group sparse model (GSM) in order to accommodate the sparse and noisy properties of multi-channel features. GSM outperformed a baseline of human raters who make these types of social judgments in everyday interactions. GSM also statistically outperformed a non-sparse linear model (NLM) and a sparse linear model (SLM) when the analysis used only a single set of low level features or single set of low level features combined with dyadic features. When all features were used, the distinctions between models decreased, since in a huge multimodal feature space, even a naïve model could greedy search for a good weight assignment. Thus our newly proposed model did not significantly outperform the others in this scenario. And in general, more features produced more accurate prediction.

Based on the outcomes of the GSM model, we investigated differences between verbal and nonverbal behavior cues as a function of different friendship states. While much research on rapport detection and building in ECAs has focused on low level features, we found that dyadic features provided some of the most distinguishing differences between friends and non-friends. For example, mutual gaze and non-mutual gaze were both indicative, as friends are comfortable looking directly at one another while non-friends may have used direct gaze only to signal non-understanding. This comfort between friends was also notable in other salient dyadic features; i.e., while non-friends often work in concert looking down at the task, friends were relaxed such that one partner could lean back, interrupt to take more conversational turns, and smile at the other without needing to reciprocate the smile each time.

In future work we will look at temporal contingency more closely, examining whether participants' actions are contingent on the behavior of their partner. We will also examine whether the behavior of friends and strangers changes over multiple sessions. In this context, we include one suggestive graph, which shows that strangers increase their mutual gaze over sessions but friends decrease it. We are currently collecting further sessions for each dyad so as to be able to further analyze the nature of these relationships over time.

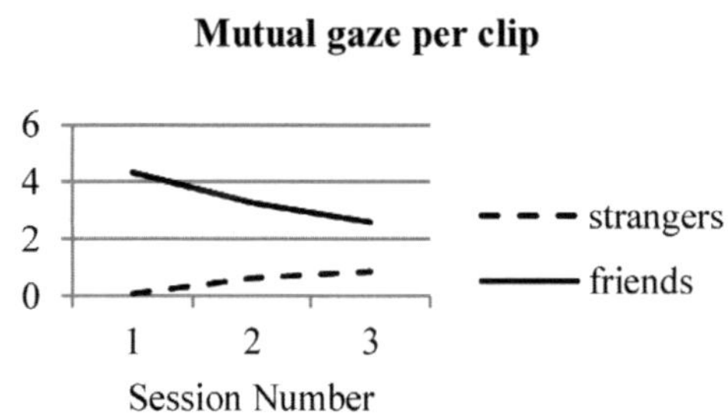

Figure 3: Weight of the mutual gaze in each session, by friendship status

To date we have found that the inclusion of automatically extracted dyadic features can lead to better prediction of friendship state. Both verbal and nonverbal behaviors were discovered that distinguish between different friendship status and that suggest how to design embodied dialogue systems that intend to spend a lifetime on the job.

Acknowledgements

Thanks to Angela Ng, Rachel Marino and Marissa Cross for data collection, Giota Stratou for visual feature extraction, Yi Yang, Louis-Philippe Morency, Shoou-I Yu, William Wang, and Eric Xing for valuable discussions, and the NSF IIS for generous funding.

References

Ambady, N., Krabbenhoft, M. A. & Hogan, D. (2006). The 30-sec sale: Using thin-slice judgments to evaluate sales effectiveness. *Journal of Consumer Psychology*, *16*(1), 4–13.

Argyle, M. & Dean, J. (1965). Eye-contact, distance and affiliation. *Sociometry*, *28*(3), 289–304.

Azmitia, M. & Montgomery, R. (1993). Friendship, transactive dialogues, and the development of scientific reasoning. *Social Development*, *2*(3), 202–221.

Baker, R. E., Gill, A. J., & Cassell, J. (2008). Reactive redundancy and listener comprehension in direction-giving. In *Proceedings of the 9th SIGdial Workshop on Discourse and Dialogue* (pp. 37–45).

Brooks, M. (1989). *Instant rapport* (p. 205). New York: Warner Books.

Berg, B. L. (1989). *Qualitative research methods for the social sciences*. Boston: Allyn and Bacon.

Bernieri, F. J. (1988). Coordinated movement and rapport in teacher-student interactions. *Journal of Nonverbal Behavior*, *12*(2), 120–138.

Bickmore, T. W. & Picard, R. W. (2005). Establishing and maintaining long-term human-computer relationships. *ACM Transactions on Computer-Human Interaction*, *12*(2), 293–327.

Bickmore, T. W., Pfeifer, L., & Schuman, D. (2011). Relational agents improve engagement and learning in science museum visitors. In *Intelligent Virtual Agents* (pp. 55–67). Reykjavik.

Bolinger, D. (1986). *Intonation and its parts: Melody in spoken English*. Stanford, CA: Stanford University Press.

Burgoon, J. K. & Hale, J. L. (1988). Nonverbal expectancy violations: Model elaboration and application to immediacy behaviors. *Communications Monographs*, (May 2013), 37–41.

Cappella, J. N. & Pelachaud, C. (2002). Rules for responsive robots: Using human interactions to build virtual interactions. In Reis, Firzpatrick, & Vangelisti (Eds.), *Stability and change in relationships*. New York, NY: Cambridge University Press.

Cassell, J. (2000). Nudge nudge wink wink: Elements of face-to-face conversation for embodied conversational agents. In J. Cassell, J. Sullivan, S. Prevost, & E. Churchill (Eds.), *Embodied conversational agents* (pp. 1–27). MIT Press.

Cassell, J., Gill, A. J., & Tepper, P. A. (2007). Coordination in conversation and rapport. *Proceedings of the ACL Workshop on Embodied Natural Language*, 40 –50.

Cassell, J., Bickmore, T. W., Campbell, L., Vilhjálmsson, H. H., & Yan, H. (2001). More than just a pretty face: Conversational protocols and the affordances of embodiment. *Knowledge-Based Systems*, *14*(1-2), 55–64.

Cassell, J. & Bickmore, T. W. (2003). Negotiated collusion: Modeling social language and its relationship effects in intelligent agents. *User Modeling and User-Adapted Interaction*, *13*(1), 89–132.

Chen, X., Lin, Q., Kim, S., Carbonell, J. G., & Xing, E. P. (2012). Smoothing proximal gradient method for general structured sparse regression. *The Annals of Applied Statistics*, *6*(2), 719–752.

Cortes, C. & Vapnik, V. (1995). Support-vector networks. *Machine Learning*, *20*(3), 273–297.

Fan, R., Chang, K., Hsieh, C., Wang, X., & Lin, C. (2008). LIBLINEAR: A library for large linear classification. *The Journal of Machine Learning Research*, *9*, 1871–1874.

Fantuzzo, J., Riggio, R., Connelly, S., & Dimeff, L. (1989). Effects of reciprocal peer tutoring on academic achievement and psychological adjustment: A component analysis. *Journal of Educational Psychology, 81(2),* 173-177.

Fukunaga, K. (1990). *Introduction to Statistical Pattern Recognition, Second Edition* (2nd ed., p. 592). San Diego, CA: Academic Press.

Gatica-Perez, D. (2009). Automatic nonverbal analysis of social interaction in small groups: A review. *Image and Vision Computing, 27*(12), 1775–1787.

Granovetter, M. S. (1973). The strength of weak ties. *American Journal of Sociology*, *78*(6), 1360–1380.

Gratch, J., Okhmatovskaia, A., Lamothe, F., Marsella, S., Morales, M., van der Werf, R. J., & Morency, L.-P. (2006). Virtual rapport. In *Intelligent Virtual Agents* (pp. 14–27). Springer Berlin/Heidelberg.

Hall, J. A., DiMatteo, M. R., Rogers, P. L., & Archer, D. (1979). *Sensitivity to nonverbal communication: The PONS test.* Baltimore, MD: Johns Hopkins University Press.

Harrigan, J. A., Oxman, T. E., & Rosenthal, R. (1985). Rapport expressed through nonverbal behavior. *Journal of Nonverbal Behavior*, *9*, 95–110.

Harrigan, J. A. & Rosenthal, R. (1983). Physicians' head and body positions as determinants of perceived rapport. *Applied Social Psychology*, *13*(6), 496–509.

Liu, J., Ji, S., & Ye, J. (2009). Multi-task feature learning via efficient l2, 1-norm minimization. In *Proceedings of the Twenty-Fifth Conference on Uncertainty in Artificial Intelligence* (pp. 339–348). AUAI Press.

Nakano, Y. I., Reinstein, G., Stocky, T., & Cassell, J. (2003). Towards a model of face-to-face grounding. In *Proceedings of the 41st Annual Meeting on Association for Computational Linguistics. ACL'03* (Vol. 1, pp. 553–561). Sapporo: Association for Computational Linguistics.

Nakano, Y. I. & Ishii, R. (2010). Estimating user's engagement from eye-gaze behaviors in human-agent conversations. In *Proceedings of the 15th international conference on Intelligent user interfaces. IUI'10* (pp. 139–148). Hong Kong: ACM Press.

Ogan, A., Finkelstein, S., Walker, E., Carlson, R., & Cassell, J. (2012). Rudeness and rapport: Insults and learning gains in peer tutoring. In *Proceedings of the 11 International Conference on Intelligence Tutoring Systems (ITS 2012).*

Prepin, K., Ochs, M., & Pelachaud, C. (2012). Mutual stance building in dyad of virtual agents: Smile alignment and synchronisation. In *Privacy, Security, Risk and Trust (PASSAT), 2012 International Conference on Social Computing (SocialCom)* (pp. 938–943).

Schuller, B., Steidl, S., Batliner, A., Nöth, E., Vinciarelli, A., Burkhardt, F., … Weiss, B. (2012). The INTERSPEECH 2012 speaker trait challenge. In *Proceedings of the 13th Annual Conference of the International Speech Communication Association (INTERSPEECH 2012).* Portland, OR: ISCA.

Steidl, S., Polzehl, T., Bunnell, H. T., Dou, Y., Muthukumar, P. K., Perry, … Metze, F. (2012). Emotion identification for evaluation of synthesized emotional speech. In *Proceedings of the 6th International Conference on Speech Prosody 2012* (pp. 4–7). Shanghai: Tongji University Press.

Stronks, B., Nijholt, A., van Der Vet, P., Heylen, D., & Machado, A. (2002). Designing for friendship: Becoming friends with your ECA. In A. Marriott, C. Pelachaud, T. Rist, Z. M. Ruttkay, & H. Vilhjalmsson (Eds.), *Workshop on Embodied Conversational Agents - Let's specify and evaluate them!, AMAAS 2002* (pp. 91–96). Bologna: AMAAS.

Tickle-Degnen, L. & Rosenthal, R. (1990). The nature of rapport and its nonverbal correlates. *Psychological Inquiry, 1*(4), 285–293.

Vardoulakis, L. P., Ring, L., Barry, B., Sidner, C. L., & Bickmore, T. W. (2012). Designing relational agents as long term social companions for older adults. In Y. Nakano, M. Neff, A. Paiva, & M. Walker (Eds.), *Intelligent Virtual Agents* (pp. 289–302). Santa Cruz, CA: Springer Berlin Heidelberg.

Vinciarelli, A., Pantic, A., Bourlard, H. (2009) Social signal processing: Survey of an emerging domain. *Image and Vision Computing, (27)*12, 1743-1759.

Ward, N. (2006). Non-Lexical Conversational Sounds in American English. *Pragmatics and Cognition, (14)*1, 113-184.

Wang, W. Y., Finkelstein, S., Ogan, A., Black, A. W., & Cassell, J. (2012). "Love ya, jerkface": Using sparse log-linear models to build positive (and impolite) relationships with teens. In *Proceedings of the 13th Annual SIGDIAL Meeting on Discourse and Dialogue* (pp. 20–29). Seoul, South Korea.

Yang, Y., Shen, H. T., Ma, Z., Huang, Z., & Zhou, X. (2010). l2,1-regularized discriminative feature selection for unsupervised learning. In *Proceedings of the Twenty-Second International Joint Conference on Artificial Intelligence* (pp. 1589–1594). AAAI Press.

Youniss, J. (1982). *Parents and peers in social development: A Sullivan-Piaget perspective.* University of Chicago Press.

Yuan, M. & Lin, Y. (2007), Model selection and estimation in regression with grouped variables. *Journal of the Royal Statistical Society, Series B* 68(1), 49-67.

Stance Classification in Online Debates by Recognizing Users' Intentions

Sarvesh Ranade, Rajeev Sangal, Radhika Mamidi
Language Technologies Research Centre
International Institute of Information Technology
Hyderabad, India
sarvesh.ranade@research.iiit.ac.in, {sangal, radhika.mamidi}@iiit.ac.in

Abstract

Online debate forums provide a rich collection of differing opinions on various topics. In dual-sided debates, users present their opinions or judge other's opinions to support their stance. In this paper, we examine the use of users' intentions and debate structure for stance classification of the debate posts. We propose a domain independent approach to capture users' intent at sentence level using its dependency parse and sentiWordNet and to build the intention structure of the post to identify its stance. To aid the task of classification, we define the health of the debate structure and show that maximizing its value leads to better stance classification accuracies.

1 Introduction

Online debate forums provide Internet users a platform to discuss popular ideological debates. Debate in essence is a method of interactive and representational arguments. In an online debate, users make assertions with superior content to support their stance. Factual accuracy and emotional appeal are important features used to persuade the readers. It is easy to observe that personal opinions are important in ideological stance taking (Somasundaran and Wiebe, 2009). Because of the availability of Internet resources and time, people intelligently use the factual data to support their opinions.

Online debates differ from public debates in terms of logical consistency. In online debates, users assert their opinion towards either side, sometimes ignoring discourse coherence required for logical soundness of the post. Generally they use strong degree of sentiment words including insulting or sarcastic remarks for greater emphasis of their point. Apart from supporting/opposing a side, users make factual statements such as "Stan lee once said Superman is superior than batman in all areas." to strengthen their stance.

We collected debate posts from an online site called *'convinceme.net'* which allows users to instantiate debates on questions of their choice. The debates are held between two topics. To generalize the debate scenarios, we refer to these topics as Topic A and B. When users participate in the debate, they support their stance by posting on the appropriate side, thus self-labeling their stance. Users' *stance* is determined by the debate topic they are supporting and we refer to each instance of users' opinion as a *post*. Each *post* can have multiple *utterances* which are the smallest discourse units. This site has an option to rebut another post, thus enabling users to comment on others' opinion.

A post with most of its utterances supporting a debate topic most likely supports that topic. This shows that users' intentions play an important role in supporting their stance. In this paper, we employ topic directed sentiment analysis based approach to capture utterance level intentions. We have designed debate specific utterance level intentions which denote users' attitude of supporting/opposing a specific debate topic or stating a known fact.

Message level intention is denoted by the stance users are taking in the debate. We build posts' intention structure and calculate posts' debate topics related sentiment scores to classify their stance in ideological debates. Intuitively, posts by same author support same stance and rebutting posts have opposite stances. This inter-post information presented by debates' structure is also used to revise posts' stance. As mentioned earlier, we use the debate data collected from *'convinceme.net'* to evaluate our approach on stance classification task and it beats baseline systems and a previous approach by significant margin and achieves overall accuracy of 74.4%.

The rest of the paper is organized as follows: Section 2 presents previous approaches to stance classification and sentiment analysis. Section 3 highlights the importance of users' intentions in ideological debates and presents our algorithm to capture utterance intentions using topic directed sentiment analysis. In Section 4, we describe the use the utterance level intentions to capture intention of the entire post. We explain our stance classification method using post content features and post intention structure in this section. Section 5 describes the use of the dialogue structure of the debate and presents a gradient ascent method for re-evaluating posts' stance. We present experiments and results on capturing users' intentions and stance classification in Section 6. This is followed by conclusions in Section 7.

2 Related Work

To classify posts' stance in dual-sided debates, previous approaches have used probabilistic (Somasundaran and Wiebe, 2009) as well as machine learning techniques (Anand et al., 2011; Somasundaran and Wiebe, 2010). Some approaches extensively used the dialogue structure to identify posts' stance (Walker et al., 2012) whereas others considered opinion expressions and their targets essential to capture sentiment in the posts towards debate topics (Somasundaran and Wiebe, 2009; Somasundaran and Wiebe, 2010).

Pure machine learning approaches (Anand et al., 2011) have extracted lexical and contextual features of debate posts to classify their stance. Walker et al. (2012) partitioned the debate posts based on the dialogue structure of the debate and assigned stance to a partition using lexical features of candidate posts. This approach has a disadvantage that it loses post's individuality because it assigns stance based on the entire partitions whereas our approach treats each post individually.

To extract opinion expressions, Somasundaran and Wiebe (2009) used the Subjectivity lexicon and Somasundaran and Wiebe (2010) used the MPQA opinion corpus (Wiebe et al., 2005). These opinion expressions were attached to the target words using different techniques. Somasundaran and Wiebe (2009) attached opinion expressions to all plausible sentence words whereas Somasundaran and Wiebe (2010) attached opinion expressions to the debate topic closest to them. Probabilistic association learning of target-opinion pair and the debate topic was used by Somasundaran and Wiebe (2010) as an integer linear programming problem to classify posts' stance. Even though opinions might not be directed towards debate topics, these approaches attach the opinions to debate topics based only on their context co-occurrence. Our approach finds the target word for an opinion expression by analyzing the full dependency parse of the utterance.

There has also been a lot of work done in social media on target directed sentiment analysis (Agarwal et al., 2011; O'Hare et al., 2009; Mukherjee and Bhattacharyya, 2012) which we incorporate for capturing users' intentions. Agarwal et al. (2011) used syntactic features as target dependent features to differentiate sentiment's effect on different targets in a tweet. O'Hare et al. (2009) employed a word-based approach to determine sentiments directed towards companies and their stocks from financial blogs. Mukherjee and Bhattacharyya (2012) applied clustering to extract feature specific opinions and calculated the overall feature sentiment using subjectivity lexicon.

Discourse markers cues were used by Sood (2013) to prioritize the conversational sentences and by Yelati and Sangal (2011) to identify users' intentions in help desk emails. Most of the discourse analysis theories defined their own discourse segment tagging schema to understand the meaning of each utterance. Yelati and Sangal (2011) devised a help desk specific tagging schema to capture the queries and build email structure in help desk emails. Lampert et al. (2006) used verbal response modes to understand the client/therapist conversations. We incorporate target directed sentiment analysis to capture utterance level intentions using a sentiment lexicon and dependency parses as described in the following section.

3 Capturing User Intentions

Users' intention at the utterance level plays a vital role in overall stance taking. We define a set of intentions each utterance can hold. The proposed topic directed sentiment analysis based approach will automatically identify users' intention behind each utterance.

Because of the unstructured and noisy nature of social media, we need to pre-process the debate data before analyzing it further for users' intentions.

3.1 Preprocessing

The posts data is split into utterances, i.e. smallest discourse units, based on sentence ending markers and a few specific Penn Discourse Tree Bank (PDTB) (Prasad et al., 2008) discourse markers listed in Table 2. Merged words like 'mindboggling', 'super-awesome', etc. are split based on the default Unix dictionary and special character delimiters. Once the debate posts are broken into utterances, we identify the intention behind each utterance in the post to compute entire post's stance.

Table 1 presents the statistics of the debate data collected from *'convinceme.net'*.

Debates	Posts	Author	P/A	Utterances
28	2040	1333	1.53	12438

Table 1: Debate Data Statistics

3.2 Debate Intention Tagging Schema

Based on the intent each utterance can have, we have devised a debate specific intention tagging schema. In debates, users either express their opinion or state a known fact.

For a dual-sided debate between topic A and topic B, our tagging schema includes the following intention tags:

1. $A+$ and $B+$: These tags capture users' intent to support topic A or B. For example, in utterance "Superman is very nearly indestructible." the user is supporting Superman's indestructibility in the debate between Superman and Batman.

2. $A-$ and $B-$: These tags capture users' intent to oppose topic A or B. For example, "Superman is a stupid person who has an obvious weakness, like cyclops." the user is opposing Superman by pointing out his weakness.

3. NI: This category includes utterances which hold no sentiment towards the debate topics or can utter about non-debate topic entities, In utterance "We are voting for who will win in a battle between these two." is neither praising nor opposing either of the sides.

Type	Discourse Connectives
Contrast	but, by comparison, by contrast, conversely, even though, in contrast, in fact, instead, nevertheless, on the contrary, on the other hand, rather, whereas, even if, however, because, as
Reason	because, as
Result	as a result, so, thus, therefore, thereby
Elaboration	for instance, in particular, indeed
Conjunction	and, also, further, furthermore, in addition, in fact, similarly, indeed, meanwhile, more ever, while

Table 2: PDTB Discourse Markers List

Evaluation data was created by five linguists who were provided with a complete set of instructions along with the sample annotated data. Each utterance was annotated with its intention tag by 2 linguists and the inter-annotator agreement for the evaluation data was 81.4%.

Table 3 gives a quantitative overview of the annotations in the corpus. There are total 12438 utterances spread over 2420 debate posts.

Tag	$A+$	$A-$	$B+$	$B-$	NI
Corpus%	20.8	18.4	16.7	21.8	22.3

Table 3: Utterance Annotation Statistics

3.3 Topic Directed Sentiment Analysis

To identify intetion behind each utterance, we calculate debate topic directed sentiment. In topic directed sentiment analysis, the sentiment score is calculated using dependency parses of utterances and the sentiment lexicon sentiWordNet (Baccianella et al., 2010). *sentiWordNet* is a lexical corpus used for opinion mining. It stores positive and negative sentiment scores for every sense of the word present in the wordNet (Fellbaum, 2010).

First, pronoun referencing is resolved using the Stanford co-reference resolution system (Lee et al., 2011). Using the Stanford dependency parser (De Marneffe et al., 2006), utterances are represented in a tree format where each node represents an utterance word storing its sentiment score and the edges represents dependency relations. Each

$$parentScore = sign(parentScore) \times (|parentScore| + updateScore(childScore)) \quad (1)$$

utterance word is looked in the *sentiWordNet* and the sentiment score calculated using Algorithm 1 is stored in the word's tree node. For words missing from sentiWordNet, average of sentiment scores of its synset member words is stored in the word's tree node, otherwise a zero sentiment score is stored. If words are modified by negation words like {'never','not','nonetheless',etc.}, their sentiment scores are negated.

Algorithm 1 Word Sentiment Score

1: $S \leftarrow Senses\ of\ word\ W$
2: $wordScore \leftarrow 0$
3: **for all** $s \in S$ **do**
4: $\quad s_{score} = s_{posScore} - s_{negscore}$
5: $\quad wordScore = wordScore + s_{score}$
6: **end for**
7: $wordScore = \frac{wordScore}{|S|}$

In noun phrases such as 'great warrior', 'cruel person', etc., the first word being the adjective of the latter, it influences its sentiment score. Thus, based on the semantic significance of the dependency relation each edge holds, sentiment score of parent nodes are updated with that of child nodes using Equation 1. Tree structure and recursive nature of Equation 1 ensures that sentiment scores of child nodes are updated before updating their parents' sentiment scores. Table 4 lists the semantically significant dependency relations used to update parent node scores.

Type	Dependency Relations
Noun Modifying	nn, amod, appos, abbrev, infmod, poss, rcmod, rel, prep
Verb Modifying	advmod, acomp, advcl, ccomp, prt, purpcl, xcomp, parataxis, prep

Table 4: List of Dependency Relations

In a sentence, "Batman killed a bad guy.", sentiment score of word 'Batman' is affected by action 'kill' and thus for verb-predicate relations like 'nsubj','dobj','cobj','iobj',etc., predicate sentiment scores are updated with that of verb scores using Equation 1.

Extended targets (extendedTargets) are the entities closely related to debate topics. For example, 'Joker','Clarke Kent' are related to 'Batman' and 'Darth Vader', 'Yoda' to 'Star Wars'. To extract the extended targets, we capture named entities (NE) from the Wikipedia page of the debate topic (fetched using jsoup java library) using the Stanford Named Entity Recognizer (Finkel et al., 2005) and sort them based on their page occurrence count. Out of *top-k* ($k = 20$) NEs, some can belong to both of the debate topics. For example, 'DC Comics' is common between 'Superman' and 'Batman'. We remove these NEs from individual lists and the remaining NEs are treated as extended targets (extendedTargets) of the debate topics.

Debate topic directed sentiment scores are calculated by adding the sentiment scores of the utterance words which belong to the extended targets list of each debate topic. We refer to these scores as *AScore* and *BScore* representing scores directed towards topics A and B. We also count the occurrences of each debate topic in the utterance by checking word with topics' extended targets.

We use these topic sentiment scores along with utterance lexical features mentioned in Table 5 to classify utterance intentions into one of the proposed 5 intention tags.

Set	Description/Example
Unigrams, Bigrams	Word and word pair frequencies
Cue Words	Sentece beginning unigrams and bigrams
Verb Frame	Opinion, action or statement verb
Sentiment Count	count of subjective adjectives and adverbs
topic Count	count of words representing debate topics

Table 5: Lexical Features for Intention Capturing

We analyze the experiments and results on capturing user intention in Subsection 6.1. User intentions are used in building the intention structure, thus to calculate the sentiment score of the entire post.

$$Post\ Sentiment\ Score = \sum_{A}(A\ Score)\ where\ A\ \in\ Argument\ Structure \qquad (2)$$

4 Argument Structure and Post Sentiment Score

Arguments are the basis of persuasive communication. An argument is a set of statements of which one (conclusion) is supported by others (premises). In our debate data, the implicit conclusion is to support/oppose the debate topics and premises are users' opinion/knowledge about the topics. Thus, neighboring utterances with same intentions are merged into single argument forming the argument structure for debate posts. *Argument structure*, also referred to as *'Intention Structure'*, may contain multiple arguments with different intentions. But to identify the intention behind the entire post, we need to consider sentiment strength and correlation of each argument.

Sentiment Strength: Sentiment strength of arguments with different intentions are compared to compute intention behind entire post. Algorithm 2 the computes sentiment strength of an argument from its constituent utterances.

Algorithm 2 Argument Sentiment Score

```
U ← Argument Utterances
for all u ∈ U do
    u_score = u_AScore − u_Bscore
end for
Argument Score = Σ_{u ∈ U}(u_score)
```

First example in Table 6 shows two utterances one of which praising 'Superman' and other praising 'Batman'. Our argument structure has two arguments containing an utterance each. Comparing the sentiment strength of the 2 arguments, we can conclude that author supports 'Batman' in this example.

	Debate Post	Score
A1	Superman is a good person.	0.34
A2	Batman is the best hero ever.	0.62
A1	Superman has high speed, agility and awesome strength.	1.23
A2	**But**, Batman is a better hero.	0.42

Table 6: Argument Structure Examples

Correlation Between Arguments: The Second example in Table 6 shows that though the first argument has a higher sentiment strength, the contrasting discourse marker 'but' nullifies it, resulting in an overall stance supporting 'Batman'. Discourse markers listed in the first row of Table 2 are used to identify 'contrast' between two utterances out of which sentiment strength of the former utterance is nullified.

Algorithm 3 Utterance Level Sentiment Score

```
1: U ← Post Utterances
2: postScore ← 0
3: for u ∈ U do
4:     u_score = u_AScore − u_Bscore
5:     u_weight = | |U|/2 − u_position |
6:     postScore = postScore + u_score * u_weight
7: end for
```

4.1 Calculating Post Sentiment Score

To calculate sentiment score of the entire post, three different approaches mentioned below are tried out:

1. *uttrScore* (Utterance Level): Given two utterances connected by a contrasting discourse markers from Table 2, sentiment score of the former is nullified. The posts' sentiment scores are calculated using Algorithm 3. In this algorithm, the utterance score is multiplied by function of its position (line 5) which gives more importance to the initial and ending utterances than to those in the middle.

2. *argScore* (Argument Level): First, the sentiment score of each argument is calculated using Algorithm 2. As in the above method, sentiment score of the former argument connected with contrast discourse marker is nullified and then posts' sentiment scores are calculated using Equation 2.

3. *argSpanScore* (Argument Level with Span): For each argument in the posts, argument score is multiplied by its span i.e., the number of utterances in an argument. We use Equation 2 to calculate posts' sentiment score.

Count of each debate topic entities in the posts and of each intention type are used as post features along with the posts' sentiment scores to classify their stance, the results of which are discussed in Subsection 6.2.

5 Gradient Ascent Method

In the previous section, sentiment score and intention of the utterances were used to calculate the posts' sentiment scores. In this section, we focus on the use of the dialogue structure of the debate to improve stance classification. *convinceme.net* stores user information for posts and also provides an option to rebut another posts. Intuitively, the rebutting posts should have opposite stances and same author posts should support the same stance. Walker et al. (2012) uses the same intuition to split the debate posts in two partitions using a max-cut algorithm. This approach loses the post's individuality because it assigns the same stance to all posts belonging to a partition. Our approach described below uses the debate structure to refine posts sentiment scores, calculated in the previous section, thus maintaining post individuality.

If two posts by same author $P1$ and $P2$ have sentiment scores -0.1 and 0.7, the previous approach would classify post $P1$ as supporting topic B and $P2$ as supporting A, even if they are by same author and supporting the same stance. What if an error crept in while calculating post sentiment or utterance sentiment score? Can we use the debate structure to refine posts' sentiment scores such that same author posts support same stance and rebuttal author posts support opposite stance? We use a gradient ascent method to accomplish this task.

Gradient ascent is a greedy, hill-climbing approach used to find the local maxima of a function. It maximizes a health/cost function by taking steps proportional to gradient of the health function at a given point. In our case, the dialogue structure of the debate is represented by a Graph $G(V, E)$ using rebuttal and same author links. Nodes ($v \in V$) of graph represents debate posts with their sentiment score, and edges ($e \in E$) represent the dialogue information between two posts with value '1' denoting same author posts and '-1' rebutting participant posts.

We formulate the health function $H(G)$ which measures the health of the given graph $G(V, E)$ in Algorithm 4. This health function signifies the health or correctness of each edge in the debate structure.

Algorithm 4 Debate Health Function

Require: Debate Graph G(V,E)

1: $H(G) \leftarrow 0$
2: **for all** $e_{ij} \in E$ **do**
3:   **if** $e_{ij} = 1$ **then**
4:     **if** $V_i * V_j > 0$ **then**
5:       $H(G) = H(G) + 1$
6:     **else**
7:       $H(G) = H(G) + (1 - \frac{|V_i - V_j|}{2})$
8:     **end if**
9:   **else**
10:     **if** $V_i * V_j < 0$ **then**
11:       $H(G) = H(G) + 1$
12:     **else**
13:       $H(G) = H(G) + |V_i - V_j|$
14:     **end if**
15:   **end if**
16: **end for**
    Return H(G)

It calculates health of each edge based on dialogue information it holds and participating nodes' scores. A perfect score of 1 is assigned to each edge if participating nodes satisfy edge criteria (line 4–5, 10–11). If not, difference of nodes' sentiment scores are used to calculate edges' health. (line 6–7, 12–13)

For an imperfect edge, updating sentiment scores of its connecting nodes will increase its health thus improving health of the graph. Thus we aim to increase the health of the graph by gradually modifying posts' sentiment scores.

Gradient Ascent algorithm (Algorithm 5) is fed with parameters set to ($EPOCH = 1000$, $\delta = 0.01$ and $\alpha = 0.05$). For each iteration, let $G(V, E)$ represent the current state of the graph and H its health. For each node, the sentiment score is updated by adding partial derivative of health function with respect to given node at the current state (line 9). Partial derivative of the Health function with respect to current node is defined in line 8. This continues (line $1 - 15$) untill there is no such node which improves the graph's health or till the number of iterations reach epoch.

These refined post sentiment scores along with post features (topic Count and intention type count) are used to classify posts' stance. We discuss the results in Subsection 6.2.

Algorithm 5 Gradient Ascent Approach

Require: Debate Graph G(V,E) and H(G) Health Function

for $iteraton = 1 \rightarrow EPOCH$ **do**
  $H \leftarrow Health(G(V, E))$
  $newH \leftarrow H$
  for all $v_i \in V$ **do**
    $V' \leftarrow V$
    $v_i' \leftarrow v_i' + \delta$
    $H' \leftarrow Health(G'(V', E))$
    $PD_i \leftarrow \frac{(H'-H)}{\delta}$
    $v_i \leftarrow v_i + \alpha * PD_i$
    $newH = \max(newH, H')$
  end for
  if $newH = H$ **then**
    Break
  end if
end for

Figure 1 gives a working example of our approach. It clearly shows improving health of the graph using the gradient ascent method helps in rectifying post $P1$'s stance.

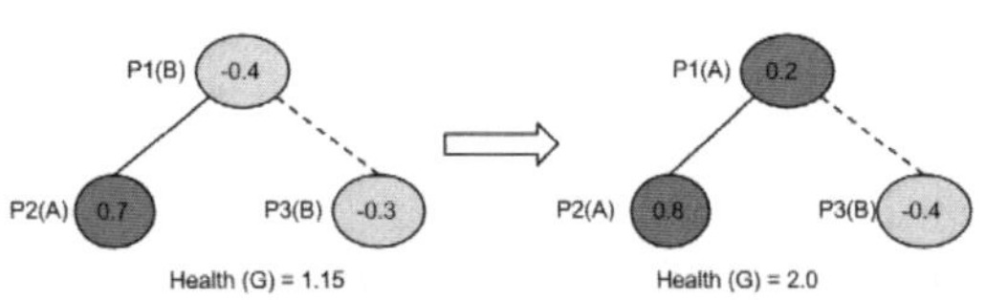

Figure 1: Working Example of Gradient Ascent

6 Experiments and Results

This section highlights experiments, results, advantages and shortcomings of our approach on intention capturing and posts' stance classification tasks.

6.1 Capturing User Intentions

Experiments on debate posts from following debates are carried out: Superman vs Batman, Firefox vs Internet Explorer, Cats vs Dogs, Ninja vs Pirates and Star Wars vs Lord Of The Rings. Our experimental data for utterances' intention capturing includes 1928 posts and 9015 utterances from 5 debates with equal intention class distribution for each domain. Thus our data has 1803 correctly annotated utterances belonging to each intention class. The first task focuses on classifying each utterance into one of the proposed intention tags.

Our first baseline is a *Unigram* system which uses unigram content information of the utterances. Unigram systems are proved reliable in sentiment analysis (Mullen and Collier, 2004; Pang and Lee, 2004). The second baseline system *LexFeatures* uses the lexical features (Table 5). This baseline system is a strong baseline for the evaluation because it captures sentiment as well as pragmatic information of the utterances. We construct two systems to capture intentions: a *TopicScore* system which uses the topic directed sentiment scores (described in Subsection 3.3) and topic occurrence counts to capture utterance intentions, and a *TopicScore+LexFeatures* system which uses topic sentiment scores (described in Subsection 3.3) along with lexical features in Table 5. All systems are implemented using the Weka toolkit with its standard SVM implementation. Table 7 shows the accuracies of classifying utterance intentions for each of described baseline and proposed systems.

Accuracy	Total	$A+$	$A-$	$B+$	$B-$	NI
Unigram	64.2	63.2	65.4	60.3	66.5	65.6
LexFeatures	62.7	64.3	60.7	64.2	61.9	62.4
TopicScore	68.4	68.1	68.7	67.2	68.7	69.3
TopicScore+ LexFeatures	74.3	73.9	74.8	75.1	73.6	74.1

Table 7: Accuracy of Utterance Intention Classification

Overall we notice that the proposed approaches perform better than baseline systems, with *TopicScore+LexFeatures* outperforming all systems. This shows that topic directed sentiment score helps in capturing users' intentions better than the word level sentiment analysis. We can also conclude that the *Unigram* system achieves higher accuracies than the *lexFeatures* system, showing that what the user says is a better indicator of user's intentions than his sentiments and thus confirming previous research results (Somasundaran and Wiebe, 2010; Pang and Lee, 2008). *TopicScore* performs lower in capturing 'NI' tag than the baseline systems, denoting that *TopicScore* is not capturing debate topics and their sentiments correctly. Thus it assigns non-NI tagged utterances an 'NI' tag, lowering its accuracy.

We run the same approach but comparing utterance words only with the debate topics in calculating topic directed sentiment score and not with the lists of extended targets. This produces an accuracy of 70.8% clearly highlighting the importance of extended targets in calculating debate topic directed sentiment analysis.

6.2 Post Stance Classification

Experiment data covers 2040 posts with equal topic stance distribution from each of the following domains: Superman vs Batman, Firefox vs Internet Explorer, Cats vs Dogs, Ninja vs Pirates and Star Wars vs Lord Of The Rings. Two baseline systems are designed for this task of debate post's stance classification. The first baseline, *sentVicinity*, assigns each word's sentiment score to the closest debate topic entity. Then, the sentiment score of the debate topics over an entire post is compared to classify post stance. The second baseline, *subjTopic*, counts the number of subjective words in each utterance of the post and assigns them to debate topic related entity if present in the utterance. It compares overall subjective positivity of debate topics to assign post stance. We also compared our approach with the (Arg+Sent) method proposed by Somasundaran and Wiebe (2010).

Three systems described in Subsection 4.1 are used to compute post's sentiment score by analyzing its content namely, *uttrScore*, *argScore* and *argSpanScore*. Post sentiment scores from these three techniques along with post features (topic Count and intention type count) are used to classify post stance and results are compared in Table 8. Table 8 shows that the second approach of calculating posts' sentiment scores using their argument structure outperforms the other approaches.

System	**Accuracy**
sentVicinity	61.6%
subjTopic	58.1%
Arg+Sent	63.9%
uttrScore	67.4%
argScore	**70.3%**
argSpanScore	69.2%

Table 8: Stance Classification Using Post Content

Our approach perform better than Somasundaran and Wiebe (2010)'s approach signifying the importance of identifying target-opinion dependency relation as opposed to assigning the opinion words to each content word in the sentence. It is important to notice that the *argSpanScore* method which multiplies argument score by its span doesn't perform as well as *argScore* alone. This shows the utterance sentiment strength matters more than neighboring same intention utterance. This supports our hypothesis that online debate posts focus more on sentiments rather than discourse coherence.

We experiment with gradient ascent approach and study how refining posts' sentiment scores based on the dialogue structure of the debate helps improving stance classification. Table 9 gives the classification accuracies between *argScore* technique and gradient ascent method.

System	**Accuracy**		
	Total	Dialogue	Non-dialogue
argScore	70.3%	70.5%	70.1%
argScore + gradientAscent	**74.4%**	**80.1%**	70.1%

Table 9: Stance Classification: Dialogue Structure

The dialogue column in Table 9 shows accuracies for posts participating in dialogue structure i.e., those linked to other post with same author or rebutting links. It shows a remarkable improvement (10% gain) which clearly signifies importance of the dialogue structure. The non-dialogue column shows the accuracies for posts not involved in dialogue structure. As health function for debate graph is a function of dialogue participating posts, it does not affect stance classification accuracy for non-dialogue participating posts. Dialogue participating posts cover 41% of the experiment data giving 4% accuracy improvement over *argScore* system on complete dataset.

7 Conclusions

In this paper, We designed debate specific utterance level intention tags and described a topic directed sentiment analysis approach to capture these intentions. We proposed a novel approach to capture the posts' intention structure. Our results validate our hypothesis that capturing user intentions and post intention structure helps in classifying posts' stance. It also emphasizes the importance of building the intention structure rather than just aggregating utterances' sentiment scores.

This is the first application of Gradient Ascent method for stance classification. Results show re-modifying the posts' sentiment scores by taking the debates' structure into account highly improves stance classification accuracies over intention based method. We aim to apply topic directed sentiment scores along with lexical features for debate summarization in our future work.

References

Apoorv Agarwal, Boyi Xie, Ilia Vovsha, Owen Rambow, and Rebecca Passonneau. 2011. Sentiment analysis of twitter data. In *Proceedings of the Workshop on Languages in Social Media*, pages 30–38. Association for Computational Linguistics.

P. Anand, M. Walker, R. Abbott, J.E.F. Tree, R. Bowmani, and M. Minor. 2011. Cats rule and dogs drool!: Classifying stance in online debate. In *Proceedings of the 2nd Workshop on Computational Approaches to Subjectivity and Sentiment Analysis (WASSA 2.011)*, pages 1–9.

S. Baccianella, A. Esuli, and F. Sebastiani. 2010. Sentiwordnet 3.0: An enhanced lexical resource for sentiment analysis and opinion mining. In *Proceedings of the Seventh conference on International Language Resources and Evaluation (LREC10), Valletta, Malta, May. European Language Resources Association (ELRA)*.

M.C. De Marneffe, B. MacCartney, and C.D. Manning. 2006. Generating typed dependency parses from phrase structure parses. In *Proceedings of LREC*, volume 6, pages 449–454.

Christiane Fellbaum. 2010. *WordNet*. Springer.

Jenny Rose Finkel, Trond Grenager, and Christopher Manning. 2005. Incorporating non-local information into information extraction systems by gibbs sampling. In *Proceedings of the 43rd Annual Meeting on Association for Computational Linguistics*, pages 363–370. Association for Computational Linguistics.

A. Lampert, R. Dale, and C. Paris. 2006. Classifying speech acts using verbal response modes. In *Australasian Language Technology Workshop*, page 34.

Heeyoung Lee, Yves Peirsman, Angel Chang, Nathanael Chambers, Mihai Surdeanu, and Dan Jurafsky. 2011. Stanford's multi-pass sieve coreference resolution system at the conll-2011 shared task. In *Proceedings of the Fifteenth Conference on Computational Natural Language Learning: Shared Task*, pages 28–34. Association for Computational Linguistics.

Subhabrata Mukherjee and Pushpak Bhattacharyya. 2012. Feature specific sentiment analysis for product reviews. In *Computational Linguistics and Intelligent Text Processing*, pages 475–487. Springer.

Tony Mullen and Nigel Collier. 2004. Sentiment analysis using support vector machines with diverse information sources. In *Proceedings of EMNLP*, volume 4, pages 412–418.

Neil O'Hare, Michael Davy, Adam Bermingham, Paul Ferguson, Páraic Sheridan, Cathal Gurrin, and Alan F Smeaton. 2009. Topic-dependent sentiment analysis of financial blogs. In *Proceedings of the 1st international CIKM workshop on Topic-sentiment analysis for mass opinion*, pages 9–16. ACM.

Bo Pang and Lillian Lee. 2004. A sentimental education: Sentiment analysis using subjectivity summarization based on minimum cuts. In *Proceedings of the 42nd annual meeting on Association for Computational Linguistics*, page 271. Association for Computational Linguistics.

Bo Pang and Lillian Lee. 2008. Opinion mining and sentiment analysis. *Foundations and trends in information retrieval*, 2(1-2):1–135.

Rashmi Prasad, Nikhil Dinesh, Alan Lee, Eleni Miltsakaki, Livio Robaldo, Aravind K Joshi, and Bonnie L Webber. 2008. The penn discourse treebank 2.0. In *LREC*. Citeseer.

S. Somasundaran and J. Wiebe. 2009. Recognizing stances in online debates. In *Proceedings of the Joint Conference of the 47th Annual Meeting of the ACL and the 4th International Joint Conference on Natural Language Processing of the AFNLP: Volume 1-Volume 1*, pages 226–234. Association for Computational Linguistics.

S. Somasundaran and J. Wiebe. 2010. Recognizing stances in ideological on-line debates. In *Proceedings of the NAACL HLT 2010 Workshop on Computational Approaches to Analysis and Generation of Emotion in Text*, pages 116–124. Association for Computational Linguistics.

Arpit Sood, Thanvir P Mohamed, and Vasudeva Varma. 2013. Topic-focused summarization of chat conversations. In *Advances in Information Retrieval*, pages 800–803. Springer.

M.A. Walker, P. Anand, R. Abbott, and R. Grant. 2012. Stance classification using dialogic properties of persuasion. *Proceedings of the 2012 Conference of the North American Chapter of the Associaotion for Computational Linguistics: Human Language Technologies*, pages 592–596.

J. Wiebe, T. Wilson, and C. Cardie. 2005. Annotating expressions of opinions and emotions in language. *Language Resources and Evaluation*, 39(2):165–210.

S. Yelati and R. Sangal. 2011. Novel approach for tagging of discourse segments in help-desk e-mails. In *Proceedings of the 2011 IEEE/WIC/ACM International Conferences on Web Intelligence and Intelligent Agent Technology-Volume 03*, pages 369–372. IEEE Computer Society.

Generating More Specific Questions for Acquiring Attributes of Unknown Concepts from Users

Tsugumi Otsuka[†], **Kazunori Komatani**[†], **Satoshi Sato**[†], **Mikio Nakano**[‡]

† Graduate School of Engineering, Nagoya University, Nagoya, Aichi 464–8603, Japan
‡ Honda Research Institute Japan Co., Ltd., Wako, Saitama 351–0114, Japan
{t_ootuka,komatani,ssato}@nuee.nagoya-u.ac.jp, nakano@jp.honda-ri.com

Abstract

Our aim is to acquire the attributes of concepts denoted by unknown words from users during dialogues. A word unknown to spoken dialogue systems can appear in user utterances, and systems should be capable of acquiring information on it from the conversation partner as a kind of self-learning process. As a first step, we propose a method for generating more specific questions than simple wh-questions to acquire the attributes, as such questions can narrow down the variation of the following user response and accordingly avoid possible speech recognition errors. Specifically, we obtain an appropriately distributed confidence measure (CM) on the attributes to generate more specific questions. Two basic CMs are defined using (1) character and word distributions in the target database and (2) frequency of occurrence of restaurant attributes on Web pages. These are integrated to complement each other and used as the final CM. We evaluated distributions of the CMs by average errors from the reference. Results showed that the integrated CM outperformed the two basic CMs.

1 Introduction

In most spoken dialogue systems, knowledge bases for the systems are constructed off-line. In other words, they are not updated during dialogues. On the other hand, humans update their knowledge not only by reading books but also through interaction with other people. When they encounter an unknown word during conversations, humans notice that it is new to them and acquire knowledge about it by asking their conversational partner. This self-learning process is one of the

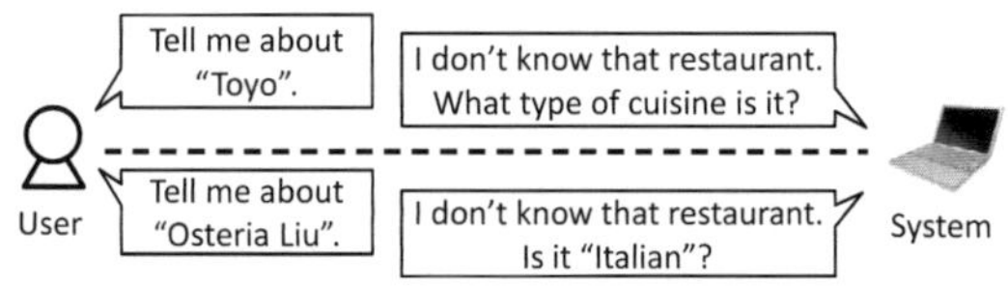

Figure 1: Example of simple and specific questions.

most intelligent features of humans. We think that applying this intelligent feature to spoken dialogue systems will make them more usable.

We present a method that generates appropriate questions in order to acquire the attributes of a concept that an unknown word denotes when it appears in a user utterance. Here, we define unknown words as those whose attributes necessary for generating responses were not defined by the system developer; that is, unknown to the response generation module in the spoken dialogue system. The system cannot reply to user utterances including such words even if they are correctly recognized by its automatic speech recognition (ASR) module.

Questions to the user to acquire the attribute should be specific. In spoken dialogue systems, specific questions are far preferable to wh-questions because they can narrow down variations of the following user response. Such questions lead to a better ASR performance of the response and reduce the risk that it includes new other unknown words.

Two example dialogues are shown in Figure 1. Since our target task is restaurant database retrieval, we set the unknown words as restaurant names and the attribute as their cuisine in our restaurant database. In the examples shown, the system uses a simple wh-question (the upper part) and a specific Yes-No question (the lower part) to obtain cuisine types. Here, "Toyo" and "Osteria Liu" are restaurant names. We assume that the

Table 1: Question types according to the number of cuisines (num).

num	Question form	Example
1	Yes-No question	Is it cuisine c_1?
2	Alternative question	Which cuisine is it, c_1 or c_2?
3	3-choice question	Which cuisine is it, c_1, c_2, or c_3?
$\geq$4	Wh-question	What cuisine is it?

system already knows these are restaurant names but does not know its attributes such as its cuisine type. The system uses a wh-question for "Toyo" since no clue is obtained for it. In contrast, since "Osteria Liu" contains information on cuisines in the name itself, a concrete Yes-No question is used to ask whether the cuisine is "Italian".

We propose a method for providing a well-distributed confidence measure (CM) to generate more specific questions. For this purpose, we estimate the cuisine type of a restaurant from its name, which is assumed to be unknown to the system. There have been many previous studies that estimate word and character attributes using Web information (Pasca et al., 2006; Yoshinaga and Torisawa, 2007). Our two estimation methods are relatively simpler than these studies, since our main focus is to generate more concrete questions on the basis of appropriate CMs. That is, the CMs should be high when the system seems to correctly estimate a cuisine type and low when the estimation seems difficult.

We assume a restaurant name as the input; that is, we suppose that the system can recognize the restaurant name in the user's utterance correctly by its ASR module and understand it is a restaurant name by its LU module. Nevertheless, it still remains unknown to its response generation module. This is a feasible problem when using a large vocabulary continuous speech recognition (LVCSR) engine containing over several million words (Jyothi et al., 2012) and a statistical named entity (NE) tagger (Tjong Kim Sang and Meulder, 2003; Zhou and Su, 2002; Ratinov and Roth, 2009).

The problem we tackle in this paper is different from trying to estimate the NE class of an unknown word (Takahashi et al., 2002; Meng et al., 2004). We assume the system already knows that it is a restaurant name. Rather, we try to acquire the attribute (e.g., cuisine type) of the concept of the unknown word, which is required for generating responses about the restaurant in subsequent dialogues.

2 Generating Questions Based on CM

The system determines a question type on the basis of CM. The CM is estimated for each cuisine type c_j in the target database. In this paper, the number of cuisine types is 16, all of which are in our restaurant database; that is, $c_j \in C$ and $|C| = 16$.

Table 1 shows the four question types and their examples. These are determined by parameter num, which is the number of cuisine types that should be included in the question. If the system obtains one cuisine type that it is very confident about and thus has a high CM, it should generate the most specific question, i.e., a Yes-No question; in this case, the number should be 1. In contrast, if unreliable cuisine types are obtained, which means lower CMs, the system generates questions including several cuisine types.

The num can be determined by Equation (1):

$$num = min(n) \text{ s.t. } \sum_{j=1}^{n} CM(c_j) > \theta, \quad (1)$$

where $CM(c_j)$ is a confidence measure for cuisine type c_j in its descending order. θ is a constant and can be manually decided considering the distribution of $CM(c_j)$. This equation means that if only the $CM(c_1)$ is greater than θ (i.e., $n = 1$), the system generates a specific question including only cuisine type c_1, while if the total from $CM(c_1)$ to $CM(c_4)$ is smaller than θ (i.e., $n = 4$), the system does not use estimated cuisine types and instead generates a wh-question.

If the CM on the cuisine type is well-distributed, the system can generate appropriate questions. In the following section, methods to obtain such CMs are explained.

3 Estimating Cuisine Types and Calculating CM

The final CM is obtained by integrating two basic CMs. The system then uses this final CM to

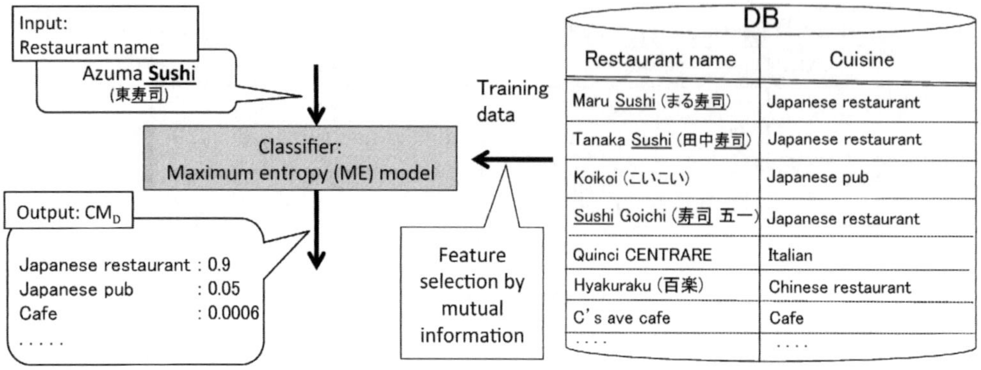

Figure 3: Overview of CM_D calculation.

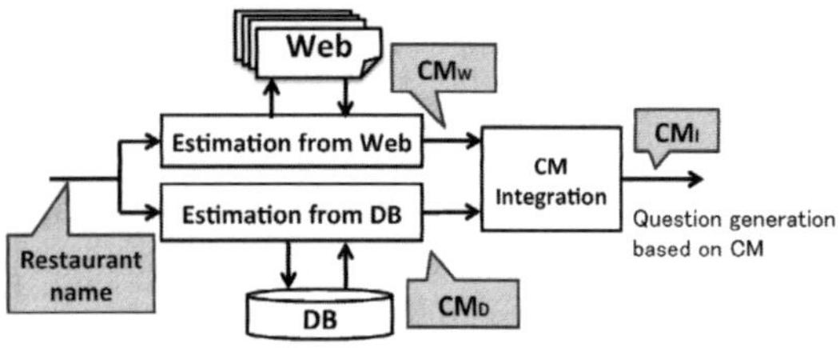

Figure 2: Process overview.

generate questions. The two basic CM estimation methods are:

1. Using word and character distribution in the target database
2. Using frequency of the restaurant attributes on the Web

A process overview of the proposed method is shown in Figure 2. Its input to the system is an unknown restaurant name and its output is the estimated CMs. The system generates questions on the basis of the estimated CMs, which are calculated for each cuisine type.

3.1 Attribute Estimation Using Word and Character Distribution in Database

We estimate the cuisine types of an unknown restaurant by using the word and character distribution in the target database. The target database contains many pairs of restaurant names and cuisine types. The estimation is performed by using supervised machine learning trained with the pairs. The overview of calculating CM_D is shown in Figure 3. This approach is based on our intuition that some cuisine types can be estimated from restaurant names on the basis of their character types or typical character sequences they contain. For example, a restaurant name composed of only katakana[1] is probably a French or Italian restaurant because words imported from other countries to Japan are called "katakana loanwords" and are written in katakana characters (Kay, 1995).

We use the maximum entropy (ME) model (Berger et al., 1996) as a classifier. Its posterior probability $p(c_j|s_i)$ is used as a CM_D denoting the CM estimated using a database. CM_D is calculated as

$$CM_D(s_i, c_j) = p(c_j|s_i) = \frac{1}{Z}\exp\left[\vec{\lambda}(c_j)\cdot\vec{\phi}(s_i)\right], \quad (2)$$

where s_i is a restaurant name, c_j ($\in C$) is a cuisine type, $\vec{\phi}(s_i)$ is a feature vector obtained from a restaurant name, $\vec{\lambda}(c_j)$ is a weight vector, and Z is a normalization coefficient that ensures $\sum_{c_j} CM_D(s_i, c_j) = 1$.

We use three types of feature vectors obtained from each restaurant name:

- Character n-grams (n = 1, 2, 3)
- Words
- Character types

The feature values of the character n-gram and the word are scored as 1 if such features are contained in the restaurant name. The Japanese morphological analyzer Mecab (Kudo et al., 2004) with the IPADIC dictionary is used to segment restaurant names into word sequences. The character type

[1] Katakana is a Japanese syllabary. There are three kinds of characters in Japanese. Kanji (Chinese character) are logograms and hiragana and katakana are syllabaries. Katakana is mainly used for writing imported words and hiragana is used for writing original Japanese words.

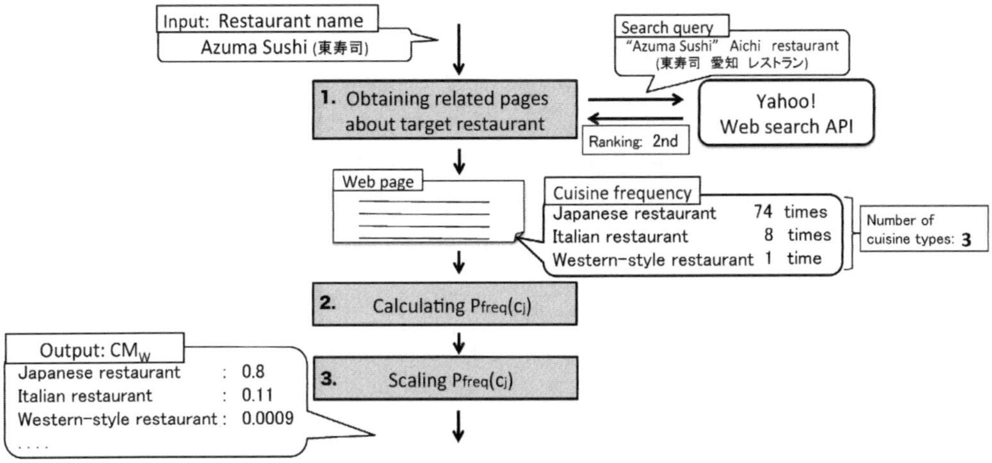

Figure 4: Overview of CM_W calculation.

is represented by the four character types used in the Japanese writing system: hiragana, katakana, kanji (Chinese characters), and romaji (Roman letters). For example, the restaurant name "Maru Sushi (まる寿司)" includes two character types: "Maru (まる)" is written in hiragana and "Sushi (寿司)" is written in kanji. Therefore, the feature values for hiragana and kanji are both 1, while those for katakana and romaji are 0. Another example is shown using the restaurant "IB cafe (IB カフェ)", in which the "IB" part is romaji and the "cafe (カフェ)" part is katakana. Therefore, in this case, the feature values of katakana and romaji are 1 and those of hiragana and kanji are 0.

We perform feature selection for the obtained features set (Guyon and Elisseeff, 2003). The classifier needs to be built without overfitting because we assume that a restaurant name as the input to this module is unknown and does not exist in the database. We use the mutual information (Peng et al., 2005; Yang and Pedersen, 1997) between each feature and the set of cuisine types as its criterion. This represents how effective each feature is for the classification. For example, in the features obtained from the restaurant name "まる寿司", which is a Japanese restaurant, the 2-gram feature "寿司" frequently co-occurs with the cuisine type "Japanese restaurant". This is an effective feature for the cuisine type estimation. In contrast, the 2-gram feature "まる" is not effective because its co-occurrence with cuisine types is infrequent. Mutual information is calculated as

$$I(f_k; C) = \sum_{c_j \in C} p(f_k, c_j) \log \frac{p(f_k, c_j)}{p(f_k)p(c_j)}, \quad (3)$$

where $p(f_k)$ is an occurrence probability of feature f_k in the database, $p(c_j)$ is an occurrence probability of cuisine type c_j ($\in C$), and $p(f_k, c_j)$ is a joint probability of the feature and the cuisine type.

Features having lower mutual information values are removed until we deem that overfitting has been avoided, specifically, when the estimation accuracies become almost the same between the closed and open tests. We confirm this by cross-validations (CV) instead of open tests.

3.2 Estimation Using the Web

We estimate a restaurant's cuisine type and calculate CMs by using its frequency on the Web as CM_W. This is based on an assumption that a restaurant's name appears with its cuisine type on Web pages. CM_W is calculated in the following steps, as shown in Figure 4.

1. Obtaining related Web pages:
   Twenty pages per search query were obtained, as this was the limit of the number of pages when this experiment was performed. We used the Yahoo! Web search API[2]. The query is formed with the target restaurant name and the following two words: "Aichi (愛知)" and "restaurant (レストラン)". The two are added to narrow down the search result since our domain is a restaurant search in Aichi prefecture. For example, the query is "<rest> 愛知 レストラン" for the target restaurant name <rest>.

[2]http://developer.yahoo.co.jp/webapi/search/websearch/v2/web search.html

2. Calculating $P_{freq}(c_j)$:
We count the frequency of each cuisine type c_j in the i-th Web pages, which are ranked by the Web search API. We then sum up the frequency through all the obtained pages and calculate its posterior probability.

$$P_{freq}(c_j) = \frac{\sum_i w_i \cdot freq_i(c_j)}{\sum_{c_j} \sum_i w_i \cdot freq_i(c_j)} \quad (4)$$

Here, $freq_i(c_j)$ is the frequency of c_j in the i-th page. Weight w_i is calculated using two factors, $rank(i)$ and $cuisine(i)$:

$$w_i = \frac{1}{rank(i) \cdot cuisine(i)} \quad (5)$$

(a) $rank(i)$: The ranking of pages in the Web search API
We assume that a Web page is more related to the target restaurant if the Web search API ranks it higher.

(b) $cuisine(i)$: The number of cuisine types in the i-th Web page
We assume that a Web page containing many different cuisine types does not indicate one particular cuisine. For example, a page on which only "Chinese restaurant" appears is more reliable than that on which more cuisine types ("Chinese restaurant", "Japanese restaurant", "Japanese pub", and "Western-style restaurant", for example) appear, as a page indicating a "Chinese restaurant".

3. Scaling $P_{freq}(c_j)$:
CM_W is calculated by scaling each $P_{freq}(c_j)$ with the corresponding α_j. α_j is a scaling coefficient that emphasizes the differences among CM_W: α_j is equal to or smaller than 1 and becomes smaller as j increases.

$$CM_W(c_j) = \frac{\alpha_j P_{freq}(c_j)}{\sum_{c_j} \alpha_j P_{freq}(c_j)} \quad (6)$$

$$\alpha_j = P_{freq}(c_j)/P_{freq}(c_1) \quad (7)$$

3.3 Integration of CMs

We define CM_I by integrating the two basic CMs: CM_D and CM_W. Specifically, we integrate them by the logistic regression (Hosmer Jr. et al., 2013) shown in Equation (8). The optimal parameters, i.e., weights for the CMs, are determined using a data set with reference labels. The teacher signal is 1 if the estimated cuisine type is correct and 0 otherwise.

$$CM_I(c_j) = \frac{1}{1 + \exp(-f(c_j))} \quad (8)$$

$$f(c_j) = w_D CM_D(c_j) + w_W CM_W(c_j) + w_0$$

Here, w_D and w_W are the weights for CM_D and CM_W, and w_0 is a constant.

4 Experiment

We evaluate our method to obtain the CMs from three aspects. First, we evaluate the effect of feature selection based on mutual information. Second, we evaluate how the CMs were distributed and whether they were appropriate measures for question generation. Third, we determine the effectiveness of integrating the two basic CMs. In this paper, we used a restaurant database in Aichi prefecture containing 2,398 restaurants with 16 cuisine types.

4.1 Effect of Feature Selection Based on Mutual Information

We determined whether overfitting could be avoided by feature selection based on mutual information in the estimation using a database. We regard overfitting to be avoided when estimation accuracies become almost the same between the closed and open tests. For the closed test, estimation accuracy was calculated for all 2,398 restaurants in the database by using a classifier that was trained with the same 2,398 restaurants. For the open test, it was calculated by 10-fold CV for the 2,398 restaurants. This experiment is not for determining a feature set but rather for determining a feature selection ratio. That is, the feature selection result is kept not as a feature set but as a ratio. The resulting ratio is applied to the number of features appearing in another training data (e.g., that in Section 4.2) and then the feature set is determined.

Figure 5 shows the estimation accuracy of the closed test and the 10-fold CV when the feature selection was applied. The horizontal axis denotes ratios of features used to train the classifier out of 20,679 features in total. They were selected in descending order of mutual information. The vertical axis denotes the estimation accuracy of the

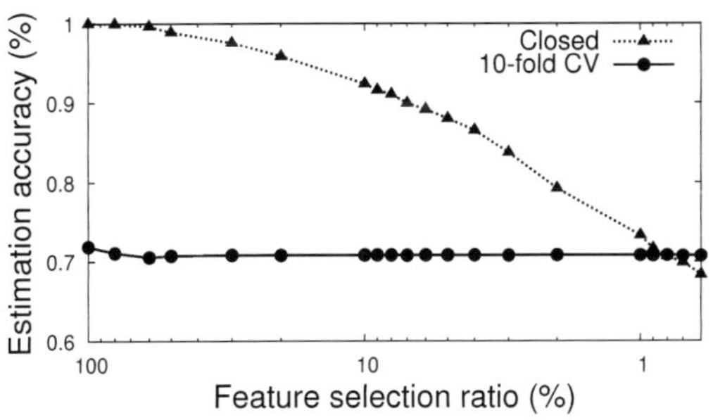

Figure 5: Estimation accuracies of closed test and 10-fold CV.

cuisine types. Figure 5 shows that, at first, over-fitting occurs if all features were used for training; that is, the feature selection ratio = 100%. This can be seen by the difference in estimation accuracies, which was 28.1% between the closed test and the 10-fold CV. The difference decreased as the number of used features decreased, and almost disappeared at feature selection ratio = 0.8%. In these selected features, as an example, the 2-gram "gyoza (餃子)", which seems intuitively effective for cuisine type estimation is, included[3].

4.2 Evaluation for Distribution of CMs

We evaluate the distribution of CMs obtained with the estimation results. Specifically, we evaluated three types of distributions: CM_D, CM_W, and CM_I. We extracted 400 restaurants from the database and used them as evaluation data. The remaining 1,998 restaurants were used as training data for the classifier to calculate CM_D. In all features obtained from these 1,998 restaurants, the ME classifier uses 0.8% of them, which is the feature selection ratio based on the mutual information determined in Section 4.1. That is, the feature set itself obtained in the feature selection is not delivered into the evaluation in this section.

We used average distances between each CM score and its reference as the criterion to evaluate the distribution of the CMs. Generally, CMs should be as highly scored as possible when the estimation is correct and as lowly scored as possible otherwise. We calculate the distances over the 400 estimation results.

$$eval(CM_x) = \frac{\sum_i^N |CM_x^i - \phi_x^i|}{N} \quad (9)$$

Here, N is the total number of the estimation result, so $N = 400$ in this paper. ϕ_x^i for CM_x^i is defined as

$$\phi_x^i = \begin{cases} 1, & \text{If estimation result } i \text{ is correct} \\ 0, & \text{Otherwise} \end{cases} \quad (10)$$

Note that ϕ_x depends on CM_x because estimation results differ depending on the CM_x used.

We also set the majority baseline as Equation (11). Here, all CMs are regarded as 0 or 1 in Equation (9). Because there were more correct estimation results than incorrect ones, as shown in Table 2, we used 1 for the majority baseline, as

$$MB(CM_x) = \frac{\sum_i^N |1 - \phi_x^i|}{N}. \quad (11)$$

Table 3: Evaluation against each CM.

	$eval(CM_x)$	$MB(CM_x)$
CM_D	0.31	0.37
CM_W	0.28	0.32
CM_I	0.25	0.28

The results are shown in Table 3. A comparison of the three $eval(CM_x)$ demonstrates that the integrated CM_I is the most appropriate in our evaluation criterion because it is the lowest of the three. The relative error reduction rates from CM_I against CM_D and CM_W were 16% and 37%, respectively. Each $eval(CM_x)$ outperformed the corresponding majority baseline.

4.3 Effectiveness of Integrated CM

We verify the effectiveness of the CM integration from another viewpoint. Specifically, we confirm whether the number of correct estimation results increases by integration.

First, we show the distribution of the three CMs and whether they were correct or not in Table 2. The bottom row of the table shows that CM_I obtained correct estimation results for 297 restaurants, which is the highest of the three CMs.

More specifically, we investigated how many estimation results changed by using the three CMs. Here, an estimation result means the cuisine type that is given the highest confidence. This result is shown in Table 4, where C denotes a case

[3]"Gyoza (餃子)" is a kind of dumplings and one of the most popular Chinese foods. It often appears in Chinese restaurant names in Japan.

Table 2: Distribution of estimation results by CM values.

	CM_D		CM_W		CM_I	
CM range	Correct	Incorrect	Correct	Incorrect	Correct	Incorrect
0.0 – 0.1	0	0	0	32	2	10
0.1 – 0.2	0	0	0	11	9	15
0.2 – 0.3	1	16	14	22	15	18
0.3 – 0.4	6	19	28	19	10	8
0.4 – 0.5	11	25	29	21	13	12
0.5 – 0.6	21	29	56	9	13	12
0.6 – 0.7	22	28	85	7	15	7
0.7 – 0.8	41	16	42	3	17	6
0.8 – 0.9	21	9	19	1	19	9
0.9 – 1.0	131	4	1	1	184	10
Total	254	146	274	124	297	103

Table 4: Estimation results by three CMs.

		CM_D / CM_W			
		I / I	I / C	C / I	C / C
CM_I	C	0	51	33	213
	I	85	10	8	0

C: correct, I: incorrect

when a cuisine type was correctly estimated and I denotes that it was not. The four columns with '/' denote the numbers of estimation results for CM_D and CM_W. For example, the C/I column denotes that estimation results based on the database were correct and those using the Web were incorrect, that is, the I/C and C/I columns mean that the two estimation results differed. The table shows that 102 of 400 restaurants corresponded to these cases, that is, either of the two estimation results was incorrect. It also shows that estimation results for 84 of the 102 (82%) restaurants became correct by the integration.

Two examples are shown for which the estimation results became correct by the integration. First, "Kaya (加屋)" is a restaurant name whose cuisine type is "Japanese-style pancake". Its cuisine type was correctly estimated by CM_W while it was incorrectly estimated as "Japanese pub" by CM_D. This was because, in Japanese, "Kaya (加屋)" has no special meaning associated with specific cuisine types. Thus, it is natural that its cuisine type was incorrectly estimated from the word and character distribution of the name. On the other hand, when Web pages about it were found, "Japanese-style pancake" co-occurs frequently in the obtained pages, and thus it was correctly estimated by CM_W. Second, "Tama-Sushi Imaike (玉寿司 今池)" is a restaurant name whose cuisine type is "Japanese restaurant". Its cuisine type was estimated correctly by CM_D while it was incorrectly estimated as "Japanese pub" by CM_W. CM_D was effective in this case because the part of "Sushi (寿司)" indicates a Japanese cuisine. No Web pages for it were found indicating its cuisine type correctly, and thus CM_W failed to estimate it.

5 Conclusion

Our aim is to acquire the attributes of an unknown word's concept from the user through dialogue. Specifically, we set restaurant cuisine type as the attribute to obtain and showed how to generate specific questions based on the estimated CM. We use two estimation methods: one based on the target database and the other on the Web. A more appropriate CM was generated in terms of its distribution and estimation accuracy by integrating these two CMs.

There is little prior research on obtaining and updating system knowledge through dialogues, with the notable exception of the knowledge authoring system of (Knott and Wright, 2003). Their system also uses the user's text input for constructing the system knowledge from scratch, which is used to generate simple stories. Our study is different in two points: (1) we focus on generating several kinds of questions because we use ASR, and (2) we try to handle unknown words, which will be stored in the target database to be used in future dialogues.

We should point out that these kinds of questions can be generated only when the types of unknown concepts are given. We assume the type of unknown concepts is already known and thus the attributes to be asked are also known. More specifically, we assume that the concept denoted by an unknown word is a restaurant name and its attributes are also known. The cuisine type has been estimated as one of the attributes. However, when the type is unknown, the system first needs to identify its attributes to ask. That is, the system first needs to ask about its supertype and then to ask about attributes that are typical for objects of this type. This issue needs to be addressed in order for the system to acquire arbitrary new concepts. This paper has shown the first step for obtaining concepts through dialogues by generating questions. Many issues remain in this field for future work.

References

Adam L. Berger, Vincent J. Della Pietra, and Stephen A. Della Pietra. 1996. A maximum entropy approach to natural language processing. *Computational Linguistics*, 22(1):39–71.

Isabelle Guyon and André Elisseeff. 2003. An introduction to variable and feature selection. *The Journal of Machine Learning Research*, 3:1157–1182.

David W. Hosmer Jr., Stanley Lemeshow, and Rodney X. Sturdivant. 2013. *Applied logistic regression*. Wiley. com.

Preethi Jyothi, Leif Johnson, Ciprian Chelba, and Brian Strope. 2012. Large-scale discriminative language model reranking for voice search. In *Proceedings of the NAACL-HLT 2012 Workshop: Will We Ever Really Replace the N-gram Model? On the Future of Language Modeling for HLT*, pages 41–49.

Gillian Kay. 1995. English loanwords in Japanese. *World Englishes*, 14(1):67–76.

Alistair Knott and Nick Wright. 2003. A dialogue-based knowledge authoring system for text generation. In *AAAI Spring Symposium on Natural Language Generation in Spoken and Written Dialogue, Stanford, CA*, pages 71–78.

Taku Kudo, Kaoru Yamamoto, and Yuji Matsumoto. 2004. Applying conditional random fields to Japanese morphological analysis. In *Proceedings of Conference on Empirical Methods in Natural Language Processing (EMNLP-2004)*, pages 230–237.

Helen Meng, P. C. Ching, Shuk Fong Chan, Yee Fong Wong, and Cheong Chat Chan. 2004. ISIS: An adaptive, trilingual conversational system with interleaving interaction and delegation dialogs. *ACM Transactions on Computer-Human Interaction*, 11(3):268–299.

Marius Pasca, Dekang Lin, Jeffrey Bigham, Andrei Lifchits, and Alpa Jain. 2006. Organizing and searching the World Wide Web of facts - step one: the one-million fact extraction challenge. In *Proceedings of the 21st National Conference on Artificial intelligence - Volume 2*, AAAI '06, pages 1400–1405. AAAI Press.

Hanchuan Peng, Fuhui Long, and Chris Ding. 2005. Feature selection based on mutual information criteria of max-dependency, max-relevance, and min-redundancy. *IEEE Transactions on Pattern Analysis and Machine Intelligence*, 27(8):1226–1238.

Lev Ratinov and Dan Roth. 2009. Design challenges and misconceptions in named entity recognition. In *Proceedings of the Thirteenth Conference on Computational Natural Language Learning*, pages 147–155.

Yasuhiro Takahashi, Kohji Dohsaka, and Kiyoaki Aikawa. 2002. An efficient dialogue control method using decision tree-based estimation of out-of-vocabulary word attributes. In *Proc. Int'l Conf. Spoken Language Processing (ICSLP)*, pages 813–816.

Erik F. Tjong Kim Sang and Fien De Meulder. 2003. Introduction to the CoNLL-2003 shared task: Language-independent named entity recognition. In *Proceedings of the seventh conference on Natural language learning at HLT-NAACL 2003-Volume 4*, pages 142–147.

Yiming Yang and Jan O Pedersen. 1997. A comparative study on feature selection in text categorization. In *ICML*, volume 97, pages 412–420.

Naoki Yoshinaga and Kentaro Torisawa. 2007. Open-domain attribute-value acquisition from semi-structured texts. In *Proceedings of the Workshop of OntoLex07 - From Text to Knowledge: The Lexicon/Ontology Interface*, pages 55–66.

Guo Dong Zhou and Jian Su. 2002. Named entity recognition using an HMM-based chunk tagger. In *Proceedings of the 40th Annual Meeting of the Association for Computational Linguistics*, pages 473–480.

Modeling Collaborative Referring for Situated Referential Grounding

Changsong Liu, Rui Fang, Lanbo She, Joyce Y. Chai
Department of Computer Science and Engineering
Michigan State University
East Lansing, MI 48824
{cliu, fangrui, shelanbo, jchai}@cse.msu.edu

Abstract

In situated dialogue, because humans and agents have mismatched capabilities of perceiving the shared physical world, referential grounding becomes difficult. Humans and agents will need to make extra efforts by collaborating with each other to mediate a shared perceptual basis and to come to a mutual understanding of intended referents in the environment. In this paper, we have extended our previous graph-matching based approach to explicitly incorporate collaborative referring behaviors into the referential grounding algorithm. In addition, hypergraph-based representations have been used to account for group descriptions that are likely to occur in spatial communications. Our empirical results have shown that incorporating the most prevalent pattern of collaboration with our hypergraph-based approach significantly improves reference resolution in situated dialogue by an absolute gain of over 18%.

1 Introduction

As more and more applications require humans to interact with robots, techniques to support situated dialogue have become increasingly important. In situated dialogue, humans and artificial agents (e.g., robots) are co-present in a shared environment to achieve joint tasks. Their dialogues often involve making references to the environment. To ensure the conversation proceeds smoothly, it is important to establish a mutual understanding of these references, a process called *referential grounding* (Clark and Brennan, 1991): the agent needs to identify what the human refers to in the environment and the human needs to know whether the agent's understanding is correct; and vice versa.

Although reference resolution (Heeman and Hirst, 1995; Gorniak and Roy, 2004; Siebert and Schlangen, 2008) and referential grounding (Traum, 1994; DeVault et al., 2005) have been studied in previous work, the unique characteristics of situated dialogue post bigger challenges to this problem. In situated dialogue, although humans and agents are co-present in a shared world, they have different capabilities in perceiving the environment (a human can perceive and reason about the environment much better than an agent). The shared perceptual basis, which plays an important role in facilitating referential grounding between the human and the agent, thus is missing. Communication between the human and the agent then becomes difficult, and they will need to make extra efforts to jointly mediate a shared basis and reach a mutual understanding (Clark, 1996). The goal of this paper is to investigate what kinds of collaborative efforts may happen under mismatched perceptual capabilities and how such collaborations can be incorporated into our referential grounding algorithm.

Previous psycholinguistic studies have indicated that grounding references is a collaborative process (i.e., *collaborative referring*) (Clark and Wilkes-Gibbs, 1986; Clark and Brennan, 1991): The process begins with one participant presenting an initial referring expression. The other participant would then either accept it, reject it, or postpone the decision. If a presentation is not accepted, then either one participant or the other needs to refashion it. This new presentation (i.e., the refashioned expression) is then judged again, and the process continues until the current presentation is accepted. To understand the implication of collaborative referring under the situation of mismatched perceptual capabilities, we have conducted experiments on human-human conversation using a novel experimental setup. Our collected data demonstrate an overwhelming use of collaborative referring to mediate a shared perceptual basis.

Motivated by these observations, we have developed an approach that explicitly incorporates collaborative referring into a graph-matching algorithm for referential grounding. As the conversation unfolds, our approach incrementally builds a dialogue graph by keeping track of the contributions (i.e., presentation and acceptance) from both the human and the robot. This dialogue graph is then matched against the perceived environment (i.e., a vision graph representing what are perceived by the robot from the environment) in order to resolve referring expressions from the human. In addition, in contrast to our previous graph-based approach (Liu et al., 2012), the new approach applies hypergraphs: a more general and flexible representation that can capture group-based (n-ary) relations (whereas a regular graph can only model binary relations between two entities). Our empirical results have shown that, incorporating the most prevalent pattern of collaboration (i.e., *agent-present-human-accept*, discussed later) with the hypergraph-based approach significantly improves reference resolution in situated dialogue by an absolute gain of over 18%.

In the following sections, we first give a brief discussion about the related work. We then describe our experiment setting and the patterns of collaboration observed in the collected data. We then illustrate how to build a dialogue graph as the conversation unfolds, followed by the formal definition of the hypergraph representation and the referential grounding procedure. Finally we demonstrate the advantage of using hypergraphs and incorporating a prevalent collaborative behavior into the graph-matching approach for reference resolution.

2 Related Work

In an early work, Mellish (Mellish, 1985) used a constraint satisfaction approach to identify referents that could be only partially specified. This work illustrated the theoretical idea of how to resolve referring expressions based on an internal model of a world. Heeman and Hirst (Heeman and Hirst, 1995) presented a planning-based approach to cast Clark's collaborative referring idea into a computational model. They used plan construction and plan inference to capture the processes of building referring expressions and identifying their referents. Previous work in situated settings (Dhande, 2003; Gorniak and Roy, 2004; Funakoshi et al., 2005; Siebert and Schlangen, 2008) mainly focused on developing/learning computational models that map words to visual features of objects in the environment. These "visual semantics" of words were then integrated into semantic composition procedures to resolve referring expressions.

These previous work has provided valuable insights in computational approaches for reference resolution. However, they mostly dealt with a single expression or a single referent. In this paper, our goal is to resolve complex referring dialogues that involve multiple objects in a shared environment. In our previous work (Liu et al., 2012), we developed a graph-matching based approach to address this problem. However, the previous approach can not handle group-based relations among multiple objects. Furthermore, it did not look into incorporating collaborative behaviors, which is a particularly important characteristic in situated dialogue. This paper aims to address these limitations.

3 Experiments and Observations

To investigate collaborative referring under mismatched perceptual capabilities, we conducted experiments on human-human interaction (details of the experimental setup can be found in (Liu et al., 2012)). In these experiments, we have two human subjects play a set of naming games. One subject (referred to as the *human-player*) is provided with an original image containing over ten objects (Figure 1(a)). Several of these objects have secret names. The other subject (referred to as the *robot-player*) only has access to an impoverished image of the same scene (Figure 1(b)) to mimic the lower perceptual capability of a robot. The human-player's goal is to communicate the names of target objects to the robot-player so that the robot-player knows which object in his view has what name. The impoverished image was automatically created by applying standard computer vision algorithms and thus may contain different types of processing errors (e.g., mis-segmentation and/or mis-recognition).

Using this setup, we have collected a set of dialogues. The following shows an example dialogue segment (collected using the images shown in Figure 1):

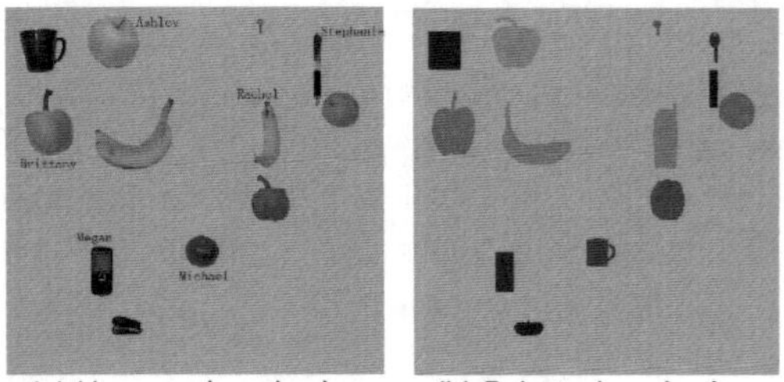

(a) Human-player's view (b) Robot-player's view

Figure 1: An example of different images used in our experiments.

H[1]: there is basically a cluster of four objects in the upper left, do you see that
R[2]: yes
H: ok, so the one in the corner is a blue cup
R: I see there is a square, but fine, it is blue
H: alright, I will just go with that, so and then right under that is a yellow pepper
R: ok, I see apple but orangish yellow
H: ok, so that yellow pepper is named Brittany
R: uh, the bottom left of those four? Because I do see a yellow pepper in the upper right
H: the upper right of the four of them?
R: yes
H: ok, so that is basically the one to the right of the blue cup
R: yeah
H: that is actually an apple, it is green, I guess it has some amount of yellow on it, but that is a green apple and it is named Ashley
... ...

This example demonstrates two important characteristics regarding referential communication under mismatched perceptual capabilities. First, conversation partners rely on both object-specific properties (e.g., object class, color) and spatial relations to describe objects in the environment. Spatial expressions include not only the binary relations (e.g., "the one to the left of the blue cup"), but also the *group-based* references (Tenbrink and Moratz, 2003; Funakoshi et al., 2005) (e.g., "the upper right of the four of them").

Second, because the shared perceptual basis is missing here, the partners make extra efforts to refer and ground references. For example, the human-player go through step-by-step *installments* (Clark and Wilkes-Gibbs, 1986) to come to the targeted object. The robot-player often proactively provides what he perceives from the environment. The human-player and the robot-player collaborate with each other through iterative *presentation-acceptance* phases as described in the *Contribution Model* proposed in (Clark and Schaefer, 1989; Clark and Brennan, 1991).

[1] *H* stands for the human-player.

[2] *R* stands for the robot-player.

These observations indicate that, the approach to referential grounding in situated dialogue should capture not only binary relations but also group-based relations. Furthermore, it should go beyond traditional approaches that purely rely on semantic constraints from single utterances. It should incorporate the step-by-step collaborative dynamics from the discourse as the conversation proceeds.

4 Modeling Collaboration

In this section, we first give a brief description of collaboration patterns observed in our data, and then discuss one prevalent pattern and illustrate how it may be taken into consideration by our computational approach for referential grounding.

4.1 Patterns of Collaboration

Consistent with Clark's Contribution Model, the interactions between the human-player and the robot-player in general fall into two phases: a *presentation* phase and an *acceptance* phase. In our data, a presentation phase mainly consists of the following three forms:

- A complete description: the speaker issues a complete description in a single turn. For example, "there is a red apple on the top right".
- An installment: a description is divided into several parts/installments, each of which needs to be confirmed before continuing to the rest. For example,

  A: under the big green cup we just talked about,
  B: yes
  A: there are two apples,
  B: OK
  A: one is red and one is yellow.
- A trial: a description (either completed or incomplete) with a try marker. For example, "Is there a red apple on the top right?"

In an acceptance phase, the addressee can either accept or reject the current presentation. Two major forms of accepting a presentation are observed in our data:

- Acknowledgement: the addressee explicitly shows his/her understanding, using assertions (e.g., "Yes","Right", "I see") or continuers (e.g., "uh huh", "ok").
- Relevant next turn: the addressee proceeds to the next contribution that is relevant to the current presentation. For example: A says "I see a red apple" and directly following that B says "there is also a green apple to the right of that red one".

In addition, there are also two forms of rejecting a presentation:

- Rejection: the addressee explicitly rejects the current presentation, for example, "I don't see any apple".
- Alternative description: the addressee presents an alternative description. For example, A says "there is a red apple on the top left," and immediately following that B says "I only see a red apple on the right".

In general, referential grounding dialogues in our data emerge as hierarchical structures of recursive presentation-acceptance phases. The acceptance to a previous presentation often represents a new presentation itself, which triggers further acceptance. In particular, our data shows that when mediating their shared perceptual basis, the human-player often takes into consideration what the robot-player sees and uses that to gradually lead to his intended referents. This is demonstrated in the following example[3], where the human-player accepts (Turn 3) the robot-player's presentation (Turn 2) through a *relevant next turn*.

(Turn 1) *H*: There is a kiwi fruit.
(Turn 2) *R*: I don't see any kiwi fruit. I see an apple.
(Turn 3) *H*: Do you see a mug to the right of that apple?
(Turn 4) *R*: Yes.
(Turn 5) *H*: OK, then the kiwi fruit is to the left of that apple.

As shown later in Section 5, this is one prominent collaborative strategy observed in our data. We give this pattern a special name: **agent-present-human-accept** collaboration. Next we continue to use this example to show how the agent-present-human-accept pattern can be incorporated to potentially improve reference resolution.

4.2 An Illustrating Example

In this example, the human and the robot face a shared physical environment. The robot perceives the environment through computer vision (CV) algorithms and generates a graph representation (i.e., a *vision graph*), which captures the perceived objects and their spatial relations[4]. As shown in Figure 2(a), the kiwi is represented as an unknown object in the vision graph due to insufficient object recognition. Besides the vision graph, the robot also maintains a *dialogue graph* that captures the linguistic discourse between the human and the robot.

At Turn 1 in Figure 2(b), the human says "there is a kiwi fruit". Upon receiving this utterance, through semantic processing, a node representing "a kiwi" is generated (i.e., x_1). The dialogue graph at this point only contains this single node. Identifying the referent of the expression "a kiwi fruit" is essentially a process that matches the dialogue graph to the vision graph. Because the vision graph does not have a node representing a kiwi object, no high confidence match is returned at this point. Therefore, the robot responds with a rejection as in Turn 2 (Figure 2(c)) "I don't see any kiwi fruit" [5]. In addition, the robot takes an extra effort to proactively describe what is being confidently perceived (i.e., "I see an apple"). Now an additional node y_1 is added to the dialogue graph to represent the term "an apple" [6]. Note that when the robot generates the term "an apple", it knows precisely which object in the vision graph this term refers to. Therefore, as shown in Figure 2(c), y_1 is mapped to v_2 in the vision graph.

In Turn 3 (Figure 2(d)), through semantic processing on the human's utterance "a mug to the right of that apple", two new nodes (x_2 and x_3) and their relation ($RightOf$) are added to the dialogue graph. In addition, since "that apple"(i.e., x_2) corefers with "an apple" (i.e., y_1) presented by the robot in the previous turn, a coreference link is created from x_2 to y_1. Importantly, in this turn human displays his acceptance of the robot's previous presentation ("an apple") by coreferring to it and building further reference based on it. This is exactly the *agent-present-human-accept* strategy described earlier. Since y_1 maps to object v_2 and x_2 now links to y_1, it becomes equivalent to consider x_2 also maps to v_2. We name a node such as x_2 a **grounded node**, since from the robot's point of view this node has been "grounded" to a perceived object (i.e., a vision graph node) via the agent-present-human-accept pattern.

At this point, the robot matches the updated dialogue graph with the vision graph again and can

[3]This is a clean-up version of the original example to demonstrate the key ideas.

[4]The spatial relations between objects are represented as their relative coordinates in the vision graph.

[5]Note that, since in this paper we are working with a dataset of human-human (i.e., the human-player and the robot-player) dialogues, decisions from the robot-player are assumed known. We leave robot's decision making (i.e., response generation) into our future work.

[6]We use x_i to denote nodes that represent expressions from the human's utterances and y_i to represent nodes from the robot's utterances.

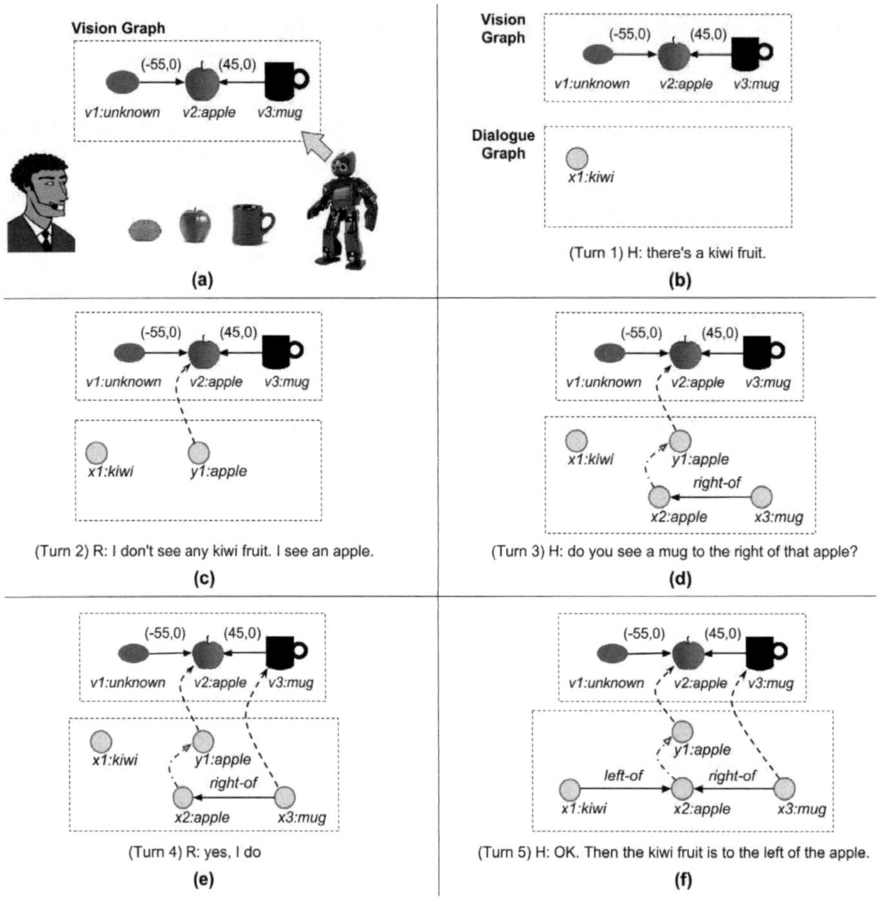

Figure 2: An example of incorporating collaborative efforts in an unfolding dialogue into graph representations.

successfully match x_3 to v_3. Note that, the matching occurs here is considered *constrained graph-matching* in the sense that some nodes in the dialogue graph (i.e., x_2) are already grounded, and the only node needs to be matched against the vision graph is x_3. Different from previous approaches that do not take dialogue dynamics into consideration, the constrained matching utilizes additional constraints from the collaboration patterns in a dialogue and thus can improve both the efficiency and accuracy of the matching algorithm. This is one innovation of our approach here.

Based on such matching result, the robot responds with a confirmation as in Turn 4 Figure 2(e)). The human further elaborates in Turn 5 "the kiwi is to the left of the apple". Again semantic processing and linguistic coreference resolution will allow the robot to update the dialogue graph as shown in Figure 2(f). Given this dialogue graph, based on the context of the larger dialogue graph and through constrained matching, it will be possible to match x_1 to v_1 although the object class of v_1 is unknown.

This example demonstrates how the dialogue graph can be created to incorporate the collaborative referring behaviors as the conversation unfolds and how such accumulated dialogue graph can help referential resolution through constrained matching. Next, we give a detailed account on how to create a dialogue graph and briefly discuss graph-matching for reference resolution.

4.3 Dialogue Graph

To account for different types of referring expressions (i.e., object-properties, binary relations and group-based relations), we use hypergraphs to represent dialogue graphs.

4.3.1 Hypergraph Representation

A directed hypergraph (Gallo et al., 1993) is a 2-tuple in the form of $G = (X, A)$, in which

$$X = \{x_m\}$$
$$A = \{a_i = (t_i, h_i) \mid t_i \subseteq X, h_i \subseteq X\}$$

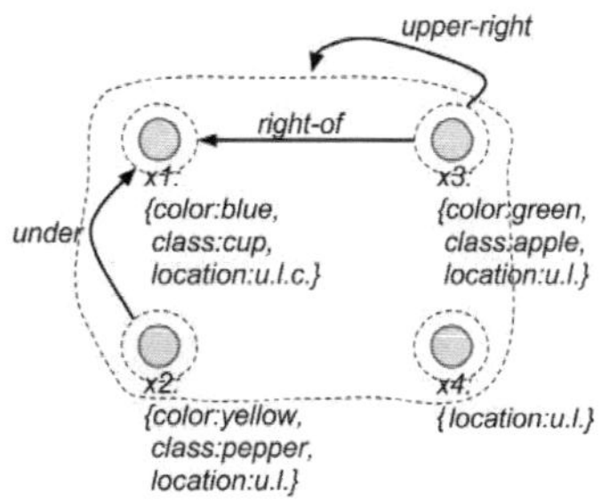

(a) Dialogue Graph

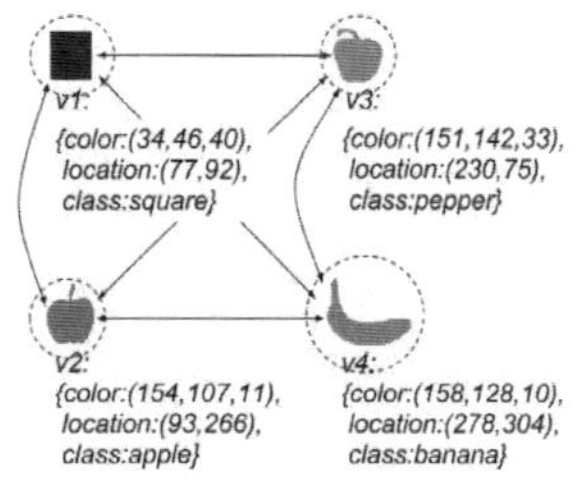

(b) Vision Graph

Figure 3: Example hypergraph representations

X is a set of nodes, and A is a set of "hyperarcs". Similar to an arc in a regular directed graph, each hyperarc a_i in a hypergraph also has two "ends", i.e., a tail (t_i) and a head (h_i). The tail and head of a hyperarc are both subsets of X, thus they can contain any number of nodes in X. Hypergraph is a more general representation than regular graph. It can represent not only binary relations between two nodes, but also group-based relations among multiple nodes.

For example, suppose the language input issued by the human includes the following utterances:

1. There is a cluster of four objects in the upper left.
2. The one in the corner is a blue cup.
3. Under the blue cup is a yellow pepper.
4. To the right of the blue cup, which is also in the upper right of the four objects, is a green apple.

The corresponding dialogue graph $G_d = (X_d, A_d)$ is shown in Figure 3(a), where $X_d = \{x_1, x_2, x_3, x_4\}$ and $A_d = \{a_1, a_2, a_3\}$. In A_d, for example, $a_1 = (\{x_1\}, \{x_3\})$ represents the relation "right of" between the tail $\{x_3\}$ and the head $\{x_1\}$, and $a_3 = (\{x_3\}, \{x_1, x_2, x_3, x_4\})$ represents the group-based relation "upper right" between one node and a group of nodes.

As also illustrated in Figure 3(a), we can attach a set of labels (or attributes) $\{attr_k\}$ to a node/hyperarc, and use them to store specific information about this node/hyperarc. The perceived visual world can be represented by a hypergraph in a similar way (i.e., a vision graph), as shown in Figure 3(b) [7].

4.3.2 Building Dialogue Graphs

Given the hypergraph representation, a set of operations can be applied to build a dialogue graph as the conversation unfolds. It mainly consists of three components:

[7]Hyperarcs of the vision graph are not shown in the figure. A hyperarc may exist between any two subsets of objects.

Semantic Constraints. Apply a semantic parser to extract information from human utterances. For example, the utterance "*The kiwi is to the left of the apple*" can be parsed into a formal meaning representation as

$$[x1, x2], [Kiwi(x1), Apple(x2), LeftOf(x1, x2)]$$

This representation contains a list of discourse entities introduced by the utterance, and a list of FOL predicates specifying the properties and relations of these entities. For each discourse entity, a node is added to the graph. Unary predicates become the labels for nodes, and binary predicates become arcs in the graph. Group-based relations are incorporated into the graphs as hyperarcs.

Discourse Coreference. For each discourse entity in a referring expression, identify whether it is a new discourse entity or it corefers to a discourse entity mentioned earlier. In our previous example in Figure 2(d), x_2 corefers with y_1, thus a coreference link is added to link the coreferring nodes. Coreferring nodes are merged before matching.

Dialogue Dynamics. Different types of dialogue dynamics can be modeled. In this paper, we only focus on a particularly prevalent type of dynamics as observed from our data, i.e. the agent-present-human-accept pattern as we described in Section 4.1. When such a pattern is identified, the associated nodes (e.g., x_2 in the previous example) will be marked as *grounded nodes* and the mappings to their grounded visual entities (i.e., vision graph nodes) will be added into the dialogue graph.

Based on the above three types of operations, the dialogue graph is updated at each turn of the conversation.

4.3.3 Constrained Matching

Given a dialogue graph $G = (X, A)$ and a vision graph $G' = (X', A')$, reference resolution becomes a graph matching problem which is to find a one-to-one mapping between the nodes in X and in X'. Due to the insufficiencies of the NLP and the CV components, both the dialogue graph and the vision graph are likely to contain errors. Therefore, we do not require every node in the dialog graph to be mapped to a node in the vision graph, but follow the inexact graph matching criterion (Conte et al., 2004) to find the best match even if they are only partial.

The matching algorithm is similar to the one used in our previous work for regular graphs (Liu et al., 2012), which uses a state-space search approach (Zhang, 1999). The key difference here is to incorporate the agent-present-human-accept collaboration pattern. The search procedure can now start from the state that already represents the known matching of grounded nodes (as illustrated in Section 4.2), instead of starting from the root. Thus it is constrained in a smaller and more promising subspace to improve both efficiency and accuracy.

5 Evaluation

A total of 32 dialogues collected from our experiments (as described in Section 3) are used in the evaluation. For each of these dialogues, we have manually annotated (turn-by-turn) the formal semantics, discourse coreferences and grounded nodes as described in Section 4.3.2. Since the focus of this paper is on incorporating collaboration into graph matching for referential grounding, we use these annotations to build the dialogue graphs in our evaluation. Vision graphs are automatically generated by CV algorithms from the original images used in the experiments. The CV algorithms' object recognition performance is rather low: only 5% of the objects in those images are correctly recognized. Thus reference resolution will need to rely on relations and collaborative strategies.

The 32 dialogue graphs have a total of 384 nodes[8] that are generated from human-players' utterances (12 per dialogue on average), and a total of 307 nodes generated from robot-players' utterances (10 per dialogue on average). Among the 307 robot-player generated nodes, 187 (61%) are initially presented by the robot-player and then coreferred by human-players' following utterances (i.e., relevant next turns). This indicates that the agent-present-human-accept strategy is a prevalent way to collaborate in our experiment. As mentioned earlier, those human-player generated nodes which corefer to nodes initiated by robot-players are marked as grounded nodes. In total, 187 out of the 384 human-player generated nodes are in fact grounded nodes.

To evaluate our approach, we apply the graph-matching algorithm on each pair of dialogue graph and vision graph. The matching results are compared with the annotated ground-truth to calculate the accuracy of our approach in grounding human-players' referring descriptions to visual objects. For each dialogue, we have produced matching results under four different settings: with/without modeling collaborative referring (i.e., the agent-present-human-accept collaboration) and with/without using hypergraphs. When collaborative referring is modeled, the graph-matching algorithm uses the grounded nodes to constrain its search space to match the remaining ungrounded nodes. When collaborative referring is not modeled, all the human-player generated nodes need to be matched.

The results of four different settings (averaged accuracies on the 32 dialogues) are shown in Table 1. Modeling collaborative referring improves the matching accuracies for both regular graphs and hypergraphs. When regular graphs are used, it improves overall matching accuracy by 11.6% ($p = 0.05$, paired Wilcoxon T-test). The improvement is even higher as 18.3% when hypergraphs are used ($p = 0.012$, paired Wilcoxon T-test). The results indicate that proactively describing what the robot sees to the human to facilitate communication is an important collaborative strategy in referential grounding dialogues. Humans can often ground the robot presented object via the agent-present-human-accept strategy and use the grounded object as a reference point to further describe other intended object(s), and our graph-matching approach is able to capture and utilize such collaboration pattern to improve the referential grounding accuracy.

The improvement is more significant when hypergraphs are used. A potential explanation is that those group-based relations captured by hypergraphs always involve multiple (more than 2) objects (nodes). If one node in a group-based relation is grounded, all other involved nodes can have a better chance to be correctly matched.

[8] As mentioned in Section 4.3.2, multiple expressions that are coreferential with each other and describing the same entity are merged into a single node.

	Regular graph	Hypergraph
Not modeling collaborative referring	44.1%	47.9%
Modeling collaborative referring	55.7%	66.2%
Improvement	11.6%	18.3%

Table 1: Averaged matching accuracies under four different settings.

	Group 1	Group 2	Group 3
Number of dialogues	9	11	12
% of grounded nodes	<30%	30%~60%	>60%
Average number of object properties [a]	20	21	12
Average number of relations [b]	11	13	8
Not modeling collaborative referring	49.7%	49.4%	45.3%
Modeling collaborative referring	57.0%	76.6%	63.6%
Improvement	7.3%	27.2%	18.3%

[a]Specified by human-players.

[b]Specified by human-players. The number includes both binary and group-based relations.

Table 2: Matching accuracies of three groups of dialogues (all the matching results here are produced using hypergraphs).

Whereas in regular graphs one grounded node can only improve the chance of one other node, since only one-to-one (binary) relations are captured by regular graphs.

To further investigate the effect of modeling collaborative referring, we divide the 32 dialogues into three groups according to how often the agent-present-human-accept collaboration pattern happens (measured by the percentage of the grounded nodes among all the human-player generated nodes in a dialogue). As shown at the top part of Table 2, the agent-present-human-accept pattern happened less often in the dialogues in group 1 (i.e., less than 30% of human-player generated nodes are grounded nodes). In the dialogues in group 2, robot-players more frequently provided proactive descriptions which led to more grounded nodes. Robot-players were the most proactive in the dialogues in group 3, thus this group contains the highest percentage of grounded nodes. Note that, although the dialogues in group 3 contain more proactive contributions from robot-players, human-players tend to specify less number of properties and relations describing intended objects (as shown in the middle part of Table 2).

The matching accuracies for each of the three groups are shown at the bottom part of Table 2. Since the agent-present-human-accept pattern appears less often in group 1, modeling collaborative referring only improves matching accuracy by 7.3%. The improvements for group 2 and group 3 are more significant compared to group 1. However, group 3's improvement is less than group 2, although the dialogues in group 3 contain more proactive contributions from robot-players. This indicates that in some cases even with modeling collaborative referring, underspecified information from human speakers (human-players in our case) may still be insufficient to identify the intended referents. Therefore, incorporating a broader range of dialogue strategies to elicit adequate information from humans is also important for successful human-robot communication.

6 Conclusion

In situated dialogue, conversation partners make extra collaborative efforts to mediate a shared perceptual basis for referential grounding. It is important to model such collaborations in order to build situated conversational agents. As a first step, we developed an approach for referential grounding that takes a particular type of collaborative referring behavior, i.e. *agent-present-human-accept*, into account. By incorporating this pattern into the graph-matching process, our approach has shown an absolute gain of over 18% in subsequent reference resolution. Extending the results in this paper, our future work will address explicitly modeling the collaborative dynamics with a richer representation. The dialogue graph presented in this paper represents all the mentioned entities and their relations that are currently available at any given dialogue status. But we have not modeled the collaborative dynamics at the illocutionary level. Our next step is to explicitly represent those dynamics, not only for grounding human references to the physical world, but also generating the collaborative behaviors for the agent.

Acknowledgments

This work was supported by N00014-11-1-0410 from the Office of Naval Research and IIS-1208390 from the National Science Foundation.

References

Herbert H Clark and Susan E Brennan. 1991. Grounding in communication. *Perspectives on socially shared cognition*, 13(1991):127–149.

Herbert H Clark and Edward F Schaefer. 1989. Contributing to discourse. *Cognitive science*, 13(2):259–294.

Herbert H Clark and Deanna Wilkes-Gibbs. 1986. Referring as a collaborative process. *Cognition*, 22(1):1–39.

Herbert H Clark. 1996. *Using language*, volume 4. Cambridge University Press Cambridge.

Donatello Conte, Pasquale Foggia, Carlo Sansone, and Mario Vento. 2004. Thirty years of graph matching in pattern recognition. *International journal of pattern recognition and artificial intelligence*, 18(03):265–298.

David DeVault, Natalia Kariaeva, Anubha Kothari, Iris Oved, and Matthew Stone. 2005. An information-state approach to collaborative reference. In *Proceedings of the ACL 2005 on Interactive poster and demonstration sessions*, pages 1–4. Association for Computational Linguistics.

Sheel Sanjay Dhande. 2003. A computational model to connect gestalt perception and natural language. Master's thesis, Massachusetts Institute of Technology.

Kotaro Funakoshi, Satoru Watanabe, Takenobu Tokunaga, and Naoko Kuriyama. 2005. Understanding referring expressions involving perceptual grouping. In *4th International Conference on Cyberworlds*, pages 413–420.

Giorgio Gallo, Giustino Longo, Stefano Pallottino, and Sang Nguyen. 1993. Directed hypergraphs and applications. *Discrete applied mathematics*, 42(2):177–201.

Peter Gorniak and Deb Roy. 2004. Grounded semantic composition for visual scenes. *J. Artif. Intell. Res.(JAIR)*, 21:429–470.

Peter A Heeman and Graeme Hirst. 1995. Collaborating on referring expressions. *Computational Linguistics*, 21(3):351–382.

Changsong Liu, Rui Fang, and Joyce Y Chai. 2012. Towards mediating shared perceptual basis in situated dialogue. In *Proceedings of the 13th Annual Meeting of the Special Interest Group on Discourse and Dialogue*, pages 140–149. Association for Computational Linguistics.

Christopher S Mellish. 1985. *Computer interpretation of natural language descriptions*. John Wiley and Sons, New York, NY.

Alexander Siebert and David Schlangen. 2008. A simple method for resolution of definite reference in a shared visual context. In *Proceedings of the 9th SIGdial Workshop on Discourse and Dialogue*, pages 84–87. Association for Computational Linguistics.

Thora Tenbrink and Reinhard Moratz. 2003. Group-based spatial reference in linguistic human-robot interaction. In *Proceedings of EuroCogSci*, volume 3, pages 325–330.

David R Traum. 1994. *A Computational Theory of Grounding in Natural Language Conversation*. Ph.D. thesis, University of Rochester.

Weixiong Zhang. 1999. *State Space Search: Algorithms, Complexity, Extensions, and Applications*. Springer.

A quantitative view of feedback lexical markers in conversational French

Laurent Prévot **Brigitte Bigi** **Roxane Bertrand**
Aix Marseille Université & CNRS
Laboratoire Parole et Langage
Aix-en-Provence (France)
`firstname.lastname@lpl-aix.fr`

Abstract

This paper presents a quantitative description of the lexical items used for linguistic feedback in the Corpus of Interactional Data (CID). The paper includes the raw figures for feedback lexical item as well as more detailed figures concerning inter-individual variability. This effort is a first step before a broader analysis including more discourse situations and featuring communicative function annotation.

Index Terms: Feedback, Backchannel, Corpus, French Language

1 Objectives

Conversational feedback is mostly performed through short utterances such as *yeah, mh, okay* not produced by the main speaker but by one of the other participants of a conversation. Such utterances are among the most frequent in conversational data (Stolcke et al., 2000). They also have been described in psycho-linguistic models of communication as a crucial communicative tool for achieving coordination or alignment in dialogue (Clark, 1996).

The general objective of the project (ANR CoFee: Conversational Feedback)[1](Prévot and Bertrand, 2012) in which this work takes place is to propose a fine grained model of the form/function relationship concerning feedback behaviors in conversation. The present study is first exploration aiming at knowing better the distribution of these items in one of our corpus. More precisely, we would to verify how much inter-individual variability we will face in further study and whether we can identify a structure in this variability (e.g speaker profiles). Second, we tried to check there some strong trends in terms of evolution of use of these items in the course of the conversation. This later point was not conclusive and is not developed in this paper.

Some data-intensive works exist for English (Gravano et al., 2012), Japanese (Kamiya et al., 2010; Misu et al., 2011) or Swedish (Allwood et al., 1992; Cerrato, 2007; Neiberg et al., 2013) but not on many other languages such as French for example. On French, the work of (Muller and Prévot, 2003; Muller and Prévot, 2009) concerned a smaller scale (A hour corpus) and very specific task. (Bertrand et al., 2007) was focussed on the feedback inviting cues and also on a smaller scale (2 × 15 minutes). They showed that particular pitch contours and discursive markers play a systematic role as inviting-cues both for vocal and gestural back-channels.

The paper is structured as follow. Section 2 presents the conversational corpus used for this study, then section 3 presents how this corpus has been processed. Section 4 is related to general figures for the feedback lexical items, followed by more detailed information about inter-individual variability (section 5).

2 The corpus

The Corpus of Interactional Data (CID) (Bertrand et al., 2008; Blache et al., 2009)[2] is an audio-video recording of 8 hours of spontaneous French dialogues, 1 hour of recording per session. Each dialogue involved two participants of the same gender. One of the following two topics of conversation was suggested to participants: conflicts in their professional environment or unusual situations in which participants may have found themselves. It features a nearly free conversational style with only a single theme proposed to the participants at the beginning of the experiment. This

[1]See the project website: http://cofee.hypotheses.org

[2]`http://www.sldr.org/sldr000027/en`

corpus is fully transcribed and forced-aligned at phone level. Moreover, it has been annotated with various linguistic information (Prosodic Phrasing, Discourse units, Syntactic tags, ...) (Blache et al., 2010) which will allow us later to take advantage of these levels of analysis.

Numerous studies have been carried out in prepared speech. However, conversational speech refers to a more informal activity, in which participants have constantly to manage and negotiate turn-taking, topic changes (among other things) without any preparation. As a consequence, numerous phenomena appear such as hesitations, repeats, backchannels, etc. Phonetic phenomena such as non-standard elision, reduction phenomena, truncated words, and more generally, non-standard pronunciations are also very frequent. All these phenomena can impact on the phonetization, then on alignment.

3 Processing the corpus

The transcription process is done following specific conventions derived from that of the GARS (Blanche-Benveniste and Jeanjean, 1987). The result is what we call an enriched orthographic transcription (EOT), from which two derived transcriptions are generated automatically : the standard orthographic transcription (the list of orthographic tokens) and a specific transcription from which the phonetic tokens are obtained to be used by the grapheme-phoneme converter. From the phoneme sequence and the audio signal, the aligner outputs for each phoneme its time localization. This corpus has been processed with several aligners. The first and main one (Brun et al., 2004) is HMM-based, it uses a set of 10 macro-classes of vowel (7 oral and 3 nasal), 2 semi-vowels and 15 consonants. Finally, from the time aligned phoneme sequence plus the EOT, the orthographic tokens is time-aligned.

The alignment for this paper is another version that has been carried out using SPPAS[3] (Bigi, 2012). SPPAS is a tool to produce automatic annotations which include utterance, word, syllabic and phonemic segmentations from a recorded speech sound and its transcription.

Alignment of items of the list given in (1) were then manually verified. Largest errors were corrected to obtain reliable alignments.

DM prononciations are the standard ones except for a few cases. There are only two items with non standard cases that are over 2 occurrences: sampa: `m.w.e.`) that is an hybrid between *mh* and *ouais*, and sampa `w.a.l.a`, a reduction of `v.w.a.l.a` *voilà*.

The extraction themselves have been realized by the authors with a Python script and all the statistical analyses and plots have been produced with R statistical analysis tool.

4 Descriptive statistics for the lexical markers used in feedback

All the lexical items of the list given in (1) were automatically extracted and categorized into two categories: (i) *Isolated* items are items or sequence of items surrounded by pauses of at least 200 ms and not including any extra material than the items of this list ; (ii) *Initial* items (or sequence items) are located in front of some other items (but there is no other material within the sequence). Most of these items also occur in final or even *surrounded* positions but we did not consider these cases since they do are not clearly related to feedback. More precisely *surrounded* items are mostly consisting in breaks of disfluencies or genuinely integrated construction (e.g *j'étais d'accord avec lui / I agreed with him*). Final ones can play a role in eliciting feedback or sometimes bring some kind of closure at the end of the utterance (what has been described as Pivot Ending in (Gravano et al., 2012)).

(1) ah (ah), bon (well), ben (well), euh (err, uh), mh (mh), ouais (yeah), oui (yes), non (no), d'accord (agreed), OK (okay), voilà (that's it, right)

Strictly speaking, the list (1) is not exhaustive. However, other items are already in the thin part of the distribution's tail. Moreover, some of the items such as *euh / err* are not necessarily related to feedback. However, by crossing lexical values with position we expect to get close enough the full set of tokens involved in feedback. For example, initial *euh* not followed by a feedback related item will not be included in the final dataset. This is also an objective of the present work to identify these situations.

The different markers exhibit very different figures with regard to their location as it can be seen in 1. While some are specialized in isolated feedback such as the continuer *mh* which is most of the

[3]http://www.lpl-aix.fr/~bigi/sppas/

time backchanneled, others are found at the beginning of utterances such as *euh, ah*. The later makes sense since *euh* is also a filled pause.

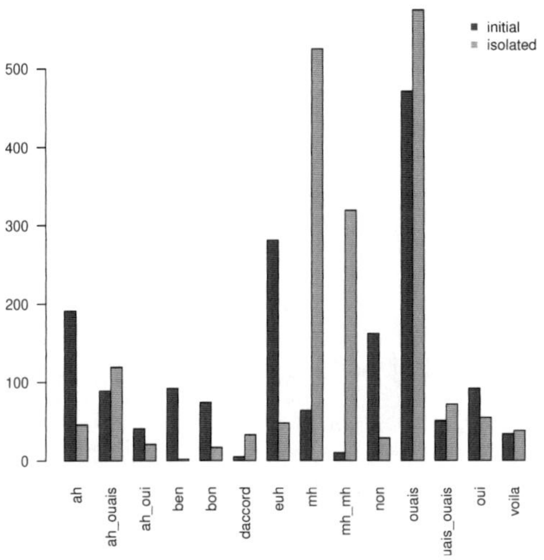

Figure 1: Distribution of isolated vs. initial position for the most frequent lexical items

In total 197 different combinations of the basic markers were identified. The most frequent are the simple repetitions of items such as *ouais* (up to nine times) or *mh*. There are also more complex structures as exhibited in (2) that seem to mix two kinds of items: base ones and *modifiers (ah, euh)*. The base ones seem by default to carry general purpose communicative functions as described in (Bunt, 2009; Bunt, 2012) while the others can also be produced alone but are generally dealing specific dimension such as turn-taking, attitude expression or time management.

(2) a. ah ouais d'accord ok *(ah yeah right okay)*
 b. voilà oui non *(that's it yes no)*

With regard to duration, the data is rather messy concerning the very long items. There are extreme lengthening on these units. Aside that and the filler *uh* that exhibit a wide spread, the other items are not produced with huge variations. Monosyllabic remain well centered around 150-250 ms while disyllabic and repeated items are distributed in the 250-500 ms range. This is important for our next step in which automatic acoustic analysis of these items will be performed.

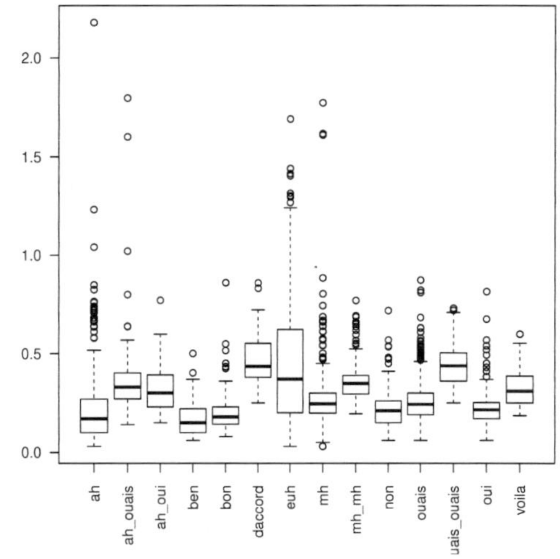

Figure 2: Duration (in seconds) of each lexical type

5 Inter-individual variability

Inter-individual variation is a big issue on the way to the generalizability. We would like to understand some of the feedback producing profiles. Our intuitions coming from familiarity of the data is that there are strong variation but they correspond to a few different speaking styles. In future work, we would like to see in a second step whether we can identify and characterize these styles.

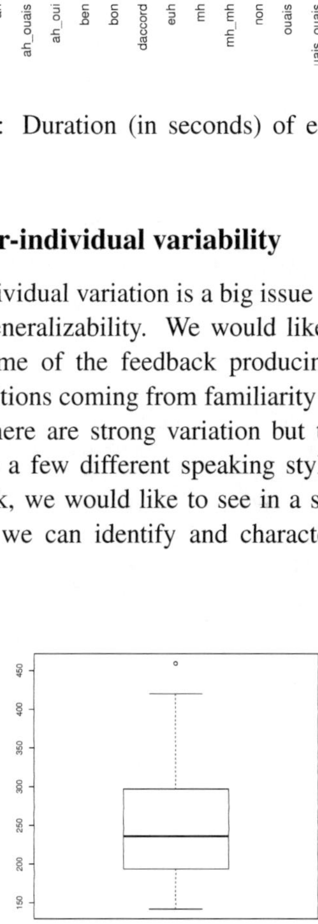

Figure 3: Number of feedback items per speaker

Figure 3 illustrates the total figures of feedback per speaker. As expected variation is huge, from 132 to 425 but with in fact with few outliers with a nice batch of speaker in the $200 - 300$ range. The wider spread of the distribution in the high range comes from two factors. First of all, there are participants producing a high quantity of feedback items. They produce a massive amount of light backchannels (*mh, ouais)* compared to low-quantity feedback producers. The later also produce feedback during the long pauses of the main speaker but they produce much less overlapping backchannels. This should be double checked with a specific measure (adding overlapping as a factor). However, a second effect seems important for at least one speaker (the outlier): the amount to time holding the floor. In fact the speaker producing the most feedback did so because she was rarely the main speaker.

In order to get a global idea of the different uses of these items, Figure 5 represents the proportion of each item per speaker. As expected, the variation is important but one can spot some tendencies. For examples for the most frequent items, the rank seems to preserved across speakers.

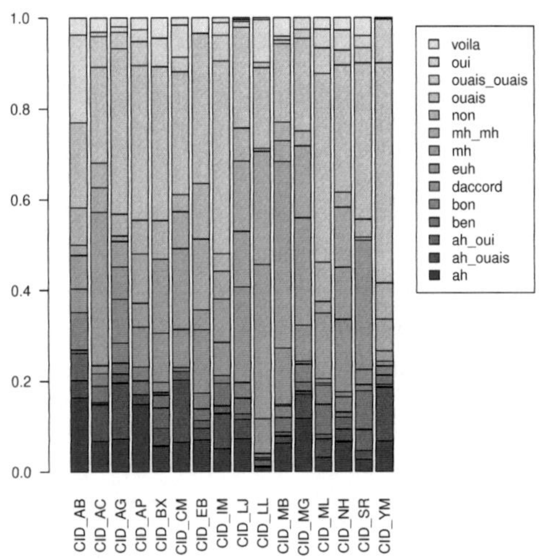

Figure 4: Distribution of the lexical items

Based on their feedback profile (proportion of use of each items as illustrated in Figure 5), we attempted to cluster the participants as showed in 5. While the lower parts of the dendrogram are hard to interpret the higher part matches well with the impression acquired by listening to the corpus (no backchannels and rather formal feedback vs. lots of backchannels and very colloquial style).

6 Current and Future Work

About this first batch of analyses, we will complete the analysis of the evolution during the conversation. More precisely, we will go at the individual level looking for time-based changes

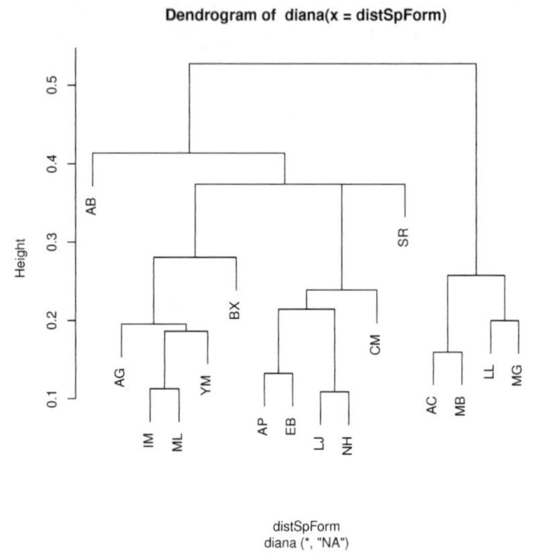

Figure 5: Dendrogram of the participants cluster based on their feedback profile

in their profiles as well as looking at the pairs for tracking potential convergence effect either in terms of distribution of lexical marker types or in their duration.

In parallel to this work, we are launching independent prosodic and kinesic analyses of the forms, as well as a discourse analysis of the functions. Moreover the work is being extended by adding two corpora in the study in order to allow for a better situation generalisability: A French MapTask; and a third corpus consisting in a less cooperative situation. The idea is later to bring together the observations from the different levels in order to propose a multidimensional model for feedback in French dialogues.

Those are steps toward more extensive studies in the spirit of (Gravano et al., 2012) or (Neiberg et al., 2013) on French language and in which we hope to address more directly the issue of discourse situation generalisability.

Acknowledgment

This work has been realized with the support of the ANR (Grant Number: ANR-12-JCJC-JSH2-006-01) and exploited aligned data produced in the framework of the ANR project (Grant Number ANR-08-BLAN-0239). We would like to thank all the members of these two projects.

References

J. Allwood, J. Nivre, and E. Ahlsen. 1992. On the semantics and pragmatics of linguistic feedback. *Journal of Semantics*, 9.

R. Bertrand, G. Ferré, P. Blache, R. Espesser, and S. Rauzy. 2007. Backchannels revisited from a multimodal perspective. In *Proceedings of Auditory-visual Speech Processing*. Citeseer.

R. Bertrand, P. Blache, R. Espesser, G. Ferré, C. Meunier, B. Priego-Valverde, and S. Rauzy. 2008. Le cid-corpus of interactional data-annotation et exploitation multimodale de parole conversationnelle. *Traitement Automatique des Langues*, 49(3):1–30.

B. Bigi. 2012. SPPAS: a tool for the phonetic segmentation of speech. In *Language Resource and Evaluation Conference*, pages 1748–1755, ISBN 978–2–9517408–7–7, Istanbul (Turkey).

P. Blache, R. Bertrand, and G. Ferré. 2009. Creating and exploiting multimodal annotated corpora: the toma project. *Multimodal corpora*, pages 38–53.

P. Blache, R. Bertrand, B. Bigi, E. Bruno, E. Cela, R. Espesser, G. Ferré, M. Guardiola, D. Hirst, E. Muriasco, J.-C. Martin, C. Meunier, M.-A. Morel, I. Nesterenko, P. Nocera, B. Palaud, L. Prévot, B. Priego-Valverde, J. Seinturier, N. Tan, M. Tellier, and S. Rauzy. 2010. Multimodal annotation of conversational data. In *Proceedings of Linguistic Annotation Workshop*.

C. Blanche-Benveniste and C. Jeanjean. 1987. *Le français parlé. Edition et transcription*. Paris, Didier Erudition.

A. Brun, C. Cerisara, D. Fohr, I. Illina, D. Langlois, O. Mella, and K. Smaïli. 2004. Ants: le système de transcription automatique du loria. In *Actes des XXV Journées d'Etudes sur la Parole*, Fès, Morocco.

H. Bunt. 2009. Multifunctionality and multidimensional dialogue act annotation. In *Proceedings of DiaHolmia*, SEMDIAL.

H. Bunt. 2012. The semantics of feedback. In *16th Workshop on the Semantics and Pragmatics of Dialogue (SEMDIAL 2012)*, pages 118–127, Paris (France).

L. Cerrato. 2007. *Investigating Communicative Feedback Phenomena across Languages and Modalities*. Ph.D. thesis.

H.H. Clark. 1996. *Using language*. Cambridge: Cambridge University Press.

A. Gravano, J. Hirschberg, and Š. Beňuš. 2012. Affirmative cue words in task-oriented dialogue. *Computational Linguistics*, 38(1):1–39.

Y. Kamiya, T. Ohno, and S. Matsubara. 2010. Coherent back-channel feedback tagging of in-car spoken dialogue corpus. In *Proceedings of the 11th Annual Meeting of the Special Interest Group on Discourse and Dialogue*, pages 205–208. Association for Computational Linguistics.

T. Misu, E. Mizukami, Y. Shiga, S. Kawamoto, H. Kawai, and S. Nakamura. 2011. Toward construction of spoken dialogue system that evokes users' spontaneous backchannels. In *Proceedings of the SIGDIAL 2011 Conference*, pages 259–265. Association for Computational Linguistics.

P. Muller and L. Prévot. 2003. An empirical study of acknowledgement structures. In *Proceedings od Diabruck, 7th workshop on semantics and pragmatics of dialogue, Saarbrucken*.

P. Muller and L. Prévot. 2009. Grounding information in route explanation dialogues. In *Spatial Language and Dialogue*. Oxford University Press.

D. Neiberg, G. Salvi, and J. Gustafson. 2013. Semi-supervised methods for exploring the acoustics of simple productive feedback. *Speech Communication*.

L. Prévot and R. Bertrand. 2012. Cofee-toward a multidimensional analysis of conversational feedback, the case of french language. In *Proceedings of the Workshop on Feedback Behaviors*. (poster).

A. Stolcke, K. Ries, N. Coccaro, E. Shriberg, R. Bates, D. Jurafsky, P. Taylor, R. Martin, C.V. Ess-Dykema, and M. Meteer. 2000. Dialogue act modeling for automatic tagging and recognition of conversational speech. *Computational linguistics*, 26(3):339–373.

On the contribution of discourse structure to topic segmentation

Paula C. F. Cardoso[1], Maite Taboada[2], Thiago A. S. Pardo[1]

[1]Núcleo Interinstitucional de Linguística Computacional (NILC)
Instituto de Ciências Matemáticas e de Computação, Universidade de São Paulo
Av. Trabalhador São-carlense, 400 - Centro
Caixa Postal: 668 – CEP: 13566-970 – São Carlos/SP

[2]Department of Linguistics – Simon Fraser University
8888 University Dr., Burnaby, B.C., V5A 1S6 - Canada

pcardoso@icmc.usp.br, mtaboada@sfu.ca, taspardo@icmc.usp.br

Abstract

In this paper, we describe novel methods for topic segmentation based on patterns of discourse organization. Using a corpus of news texts, our results show that it is possible to use discourse features (based on Rhetorical Structure Theory) for topic segmentation and that we outperform some well-known methods.

1 Introduction

Topic segmentation aims at finding the boundaries among topic blocks in a text (Chang and Lee, 2003). This task is useful for a number of important applications such as information retrieval (Prince and Labadié, 2007), automatic summarization (Wan, 2008) and question-answering systems (Oh et al., 2007).

In this paper, following Hearst (1997), we assume that a text or a set of texts develop a main topic, exposing several subtopics as well. We also assume that a topic is a particular subject that we write about or discuss (Hovy, 2009), and subtopics are represented in pieces of text that cover different aspects of the main topic (Hearst, 1997; Hennig, 2009). Therefore, the task of topic segmentation aims at dividing a text into topically coherent segments, or subtopics. The granularity of a subtopic is not defined, as a subtopic may contain one or more sentences or paragraphs.

Several methods have been tested for topic segmentation. There are, however, no studies on how discourse structure directly mirrors topic boundaries in texts and how they may contribute to such task, although such possible correlation has been suggested (e.g., Hovy and Lin, 1998).

In this paper, we follow this research line, aiming at exploring the relationship of discourse and subtopics. In particular, our interest is mainly on the potential of Rhetorical Structure Theory (RST) (Mann and Thompson, 1987) for this task. We propose and evaluate automatic topic segmentation strategies based on the rhetorical structure of a text. We also compare our results to some well-known algorithms in the area, showing that we outperform these algorithms. Our experiments were performed using a corpus of news texts manually annotated with RST and subtopics.

The remainder of this paper is organized as follows. Section 2 gives a brief background on text segmentation. Section 3 describes our automatic strategies to find the subtopics. The corpus that we use is described in Section 4. Section 5 presents some results and Section 6 contains the conclusions and future work.

2 Related work

Several approaches have tried to measure the similarity across sentences and to estimate where topic boundaries occur. One well-known approach, that is heavily used for topic segmentation, is TextTiling (Hearst, 1997), which is based on lexical cohesion. For this strategy, it is assumed that a set of lexical items is used during the development of a subtopic in a text and, when that subtopic changes, a significant proportion of vocabulary also changes.

Passoneau and Litman (1997), in turn, have combined multiple linguistic features for topic segmentation of spoken text, such as pause, cue words, and referential noun phrases. Hovy and Lin (1998) have used various complementary techniques for topic segmentation, including those based on text structure, cue words and high-frequency indicative phrases for topic identification in a summarization system. Although the authors do not mention an evaluation of these features, they suggested that discourse structure might help topic identification. For this, they suggested using RST.

RST represents relations among propositions in a text and discriminates nuclear and satellite information. In order to present the differences among relations, they are organized in two groups: subject matter and presentational relations. In the former, the text producer intends that the reader recognizes the relation itself and the information conveyed, while in the latter the intended effect is to increase some inclination on the part of the reader (Taboada and Mann, 2006). The relationships are traditionally structured in a tree-like form (where larger units – composed of more than one proposition – are also related in the higher levels of the tree).

To the best of our knowledge, we have not found any proposal that has directly employed RST for topic segmentation purposes. Following the suggestion of the above authors, we investigated how discourse structure mirrors topic shifts in texts. Next section describes our approach to the problem.

3 Strategies for topic segmentation

For identifying and partitioning the subtopics of a text, we developed four baseline algorithms and six other algorithms that are based on discourse features.

The four baseline algorithms segment at paragraphs, sentences, random boundaries (randomly selecting any number of boundaries and where they are in a text) or are based on word reiteration. The word reiteration strategy is an adaptation of TextTiling[1] (Hearst, 1997) for the characteristics of the corpus that we used (introduced latter in this paper).

The algorithms based on discourse consider the discourse structure itself and the RST relations in the discourse tree. The first algorithm (which we refer to as Simple Cosine) is based on Marcu's idea (2000) for measuring the "goodness" of a discourse tree. He assumes that a discourse tree is "better" if it exhibits a high-level structure that matches as much as possible the topic boundaries of the text for which that structure was built. Marcu associates a clustering score to each node of a tree. For the leaves, this score is 0; for the internal nodes, the score is given by the lexical similarity between the immediate children. The hypothesis underlying such measurements is that better trees show higher similarity among their nodes. We have adopted the same idea using the cosine measure. We have proposed that text segments with similar vocabulary are likely to be part of the same topic segment. In our case, nodes with scores below the average score are supposed to indicate possible topic boundaries.

The second algorithm (referred to as Cosine Nuclei) is also a proposal by Marcu (2000). It is assumed that whenever a discourse relation holds between two textual spans, that relation also holds between the most salient units (nuclei) associated with those spans. We have used this formalization and measured the similarity between the salient units associated with two spans (instead of measuring among all the text spans of the relation, as in the previous algorithm).

The third (Cosine Depth) and fourth (Nuclei Depth) algorithms are variations of Simple Cosine and Cosine Nuclei. For these new strategies, the similarity for each node is divided by the depth where it occurs, traversing the tree in a bottom-up way. These should guarantee that higher nodes are weaker and might better represent topic boundaries. Therefore, we have the assumption that topic boundaries are more likely to be mirrored at the higher levels of the discourse structure. We also have used the average score to find out less similar nodes. Figure 1 shows a sample RST tree. The symbols N and S indicate the nucleus and satellite of each rhetorical relation. For this tree, the score between nodes 3 and 4 is divided by 1 (since we are at the leaf level); the score between Elaboration and node 5 is divided by 2 (since we are in a higher level, 1 above the leaves on the left); and the score between Sequence and Volitional-result is divided by 3 (1 above the leaves on the right).

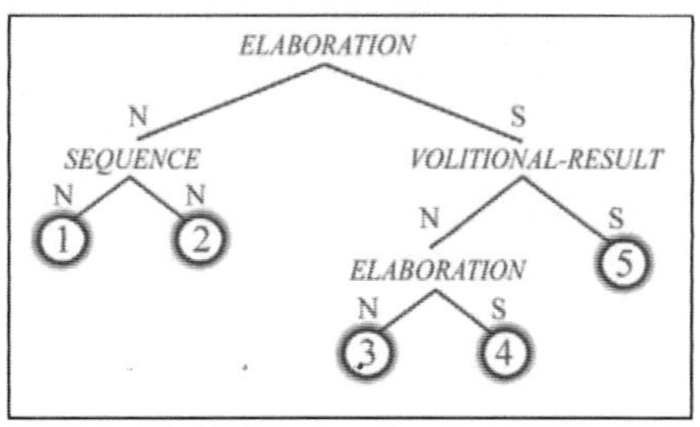

Figure 1. Example of an RST structure

[1] We have specifically used the block comparison method with block size=2.

The next algorithms are based on the idea that some relations are more likely to represent topic shifts. For estimating this, we have used the CSTNews (described in next section), which is manually annotated with subtopics and RST.

In this corpus, there are 29 different types of RST relations that may connect textual spans. In an attempt to characterize topic segmentation based on rhetorical relations, we recorded the frequency of those relations in topic boundaries. We realized that some relations were more frequent on topic boundaries, whereas others never occurred at the boundaries of topics. Out of the 29 relations, 16 appeared in the reference annotation. In topic boundaries, Elaboration was the most frequent relation (appearing in 60% of the boundaries), followed by List (20%) and Non-Volitional Result (5%). Sequence and Evidence appeared in 2% of the topic boundaries, and Background, Circumstance, Comparison, Concession, Contrast, Explanation, Interpretation, Justify, and Non-Volitional Cause in 1% of the boundaries.

We used this knowledge about the relations' frequency and attributed a weight associated with the possibility that a relation indicates a boundary, in accordance with its frequency on topic boundaries in the reference corpus. Figure 2 shows how the 29 relations were distributed. One relation is weak if it usually indicates a boundary; in this case, its weight is 0.4. One relation is medium because it may indicate a boundary or not; therefore, its weight is 0.6. On the other hand, a strong relation almost never indicates a topic boundary; therefore, its weight is 0.8. Such values were empirically determined. Another factor that may be observed is that all presentational relations are classified as strong, with the exception of Antithesis. This is related to the definition of presentational relations, and Antithesis was found in the reference segmentation with a low frequency.

Class	Relations
Weak (0.4)	Elaboration, Contrast, Joint, List
Medium (0.6)	Antithesis, Comparison, Evaluation Means, Non-Volitional Cause, Non-Volitional Result, Solutionhood, Volitional Cause, Volitional Result, Sequence
Strong (0.8)	Background, Circumstance, Concession, Conclusion, Condition, Enablement, Evidence, Explanation, Interpretation, Justify, Motivation, Otherwise, Purpose, Restatement, Summary

Figure 2. Classification of RST relations

From this classification we created two more strategies: Relation_Depth and Nuclei_Depth_Relation. Relation_Depth associates a score to the nodes by dividing the relations weight by the depth where it occurs, in a bottom-up way of traversing the tree. We also have used the average score to find out nodes that are less similar. As we have observed that some improvement might be achieved every time nuclei information was used, we have tried to combine this configuration with the relations' weight. Hence, we computed the scores of the Nuclei Depth strategy times the proposed relations weight. This was the algorithm that we called Nuclei_Depth_Relation. Therefore, these two last algorithms enrich the original Cosine Depth and Nuclei Depth strategies with the relation strength information.

The next section presents the data set we have used for our evaluation.

4 Overview of the corpus

We used the CSTNews corpus[2] that is composed of 50 clusters of news articles written in Brazilian Portuguese, collected from several sections of mainstream news agencies: Politics, Sports, World, Daily News, Money, and Science. The corpus contains 140 texts altogether, amounting to 2,088 sentences and 47,240 words. On average, the corpus conveys in each cluster 2.8 texts, 41.76 sentences and 944.8 words. All the texts in the corpus were manually annotated with RST structures and topic boundaries in a systematic way, with satisfactory annotation agreement values (more details may be found in Cardoso et al., 2011; Cardoso et al., 2012). Specifically for topic boundaries, groups of trained annotators indicated possible boundaries and the ones indicated by the majority of the annotators were assumed to be actual boundaries.

5 Evaluation

This section presents comparisons of the results of the algorithms over the reference corpus.

The performance of topic segmentation is usually measured using Recall (R), Precision (P), and F-measure (F) scores. These scores quantify how closely the system subtopics correspond to the ones produced by humans. Those measures compare the boundary correspondences without considering whether these are close to each other: if they are not the same (regardless of wheth-

[2] www2.icmc.usp.br/~taspardo/sucinto/cstnews.html

er they are closer or farther from one another), they score zero. However, it is also important to know how close the identified boundaries are to the expected ones, since this may help to determine how serious the errors made by the algorithms are. We propose a simple measure to this, which we call Deviation (D) from the reference annotations. Considering two algorithms that propose the same amount of boundaries for a text and make one single mistake each (having, therefore, the same P, R, and F scores), the best one will be the one that deviates the least from the reference. The best algorithm should be the one with the best balance among P, R, F, and D scores.

The results achieved for the investigated methods are reported in Table 1. The first 4 rows show the results for the baselines. The algorithms based on RST are in the last 6 rows. The last row represents the human performance, which we refer by topline. It is interesting to have a topline because it possibly indicates the limits that automatic methods may achieve in the task. To find the topline, a human annotator of the corpus was randomly selected for each text and his annotation was compared with the reference one.

As expected, the paragraph baseline was very good, having the best F values of the baseline set. This shows that, in most of the texts, the subtopics are organized in paragraphs. Although the sentence baseline has the best R, it has the worst D. This is due to the fact that not every sentence is a subtopic, and to segment all of them becomes a problem when we are looking for major groups of subtopics. TextTiling is the algorithm that deviates the least from the reference segmentation. This happens because it is very conservative and detects only a few segments, sometimes only one (the end of the text), causing it to have a good deviation score, but penalizing R.

Algorithm	R	P	F	D
TextTiling	0.405	0.773	0.497	0.042
Paragraph	0.989	0.471	0.613	0.453
Sentence	1.000	0.270	0.415	1.000
Randomly	0.674	0.340	0.416	0.539
Simple Cosine	0.549	0.271	0.345	0.545
Cosine Nuclei	0.631	0.290	0.379	0.556
Cosine Depth	0.873	0.364	0.489	0.577
Nuclei Depth	0.899	0.370	0.495	0.586
Relation_Depth	0.901	0.507	0.616	0.335
Nuclei_Depth Relation	0.908	0.353	0.484	0.626
Topline	0.807	0.799	0.767	0.304

Table 1. Evaluation of algorithms

In the case of the algorithms based on RST, we may notice that they produced the best results in terms of R, P, and F, with acceptable D values. We note too that every time the salient units were used, R and P increase, except for Nuclei_Depth_Relation. Examining the measures, we notice that the best algorithm was Relation_Depth. Although its F is close to the one of the Paragraph baseline, the Relation_Depth algorithm shows a much better D value. One may see that the traditional TextTiling was also outperformed by Relation_Depth.

As expected, the Topline (the human, therefore) has the best F with acceptable D. Its F value is probably the best that an automatic method may expect to achieve. It is 25% better than our best method (Relation_Depth). There is, therefore, room for improvements, possibly using other discourse features.

We have run t-tests for pairs of algorithms for which we wanted to check the statistical difference. As expected, the F difference is not significant for Relation_Depth and the Paragraph algorithms, but it was significant with 95% confidence for the comparison of Relation_Depth with Nuclei_Depth and TextTiling (also regarding the F values). Finally, the difference between Relation_Depth and the Topline was also significant.

6 Conclusions and future work

In this paper we show that discourse structures mirror, in some level, the topic boundaries in the text. Our results demonstrate that discourse knowledge may significantly help to find boundaries in a text. In particular, the relation type and the level of the discourse structure in which the relation happens are important features. To the best of our knowledge, this is the first attempt to correlate RST structures with topic boundaries, which we believe is an important theoretical advance.

At this stage, we opted for a manually annotated corpus, because we believe an automatic RST analysis would surely decrease the correspondence that was found. However, better discourse parsers have arisen and this may not be a problem anymore in the future.

Acknowledgments

The authors are grateful to FAPESP, CAPES, CNPq and Natural Sciences and Engineering Research Council of Canada (Discovery Grant 261104-2008) for supporting this work.

References

Paula C.F. Cardoso, Erick G. Maziero, Maria L.R. Castro Jorge, Eloize M.R. Seno, Ariani Di Fellipo, Lúcia H.M. Rino, Maria G.V. Nunes, Thiago A.S. Pardo. 2011. CSTNews – A discourse-annotated corpus for single and multidocument summarization of texts in Brazilian Portuguese. In: *Proceedings of the 3rd RST Brazilian Meeting*, pp. 88-105.

Paula C.F. Cardoso, Maite Taboada, Thiago A.S. Pardo. 2013. Subtopics annotation in a corpus of news texts: steps towards automatic subtopic segmentation. In: *Proceedings of the Brazilian Symposium in Information and Human Language Technology*.

T-H Chang and C-H Lee. 2003. Topic segmentation for short texts. In: *Proceedings of the 17th Pacific Asia Conference Language*, pp. 159-165.

Marti Hearst. 1997. TextTiling: Segmenting Text into Multi-Paragraph Subtopic Passages. *Computational Linguistics* 23(1), pp. 33-64.

Leonhard Hennig. 2009. Topic-based multi-document summarization with probabilistic latent semantic analysis. In: *Recent Advances in Natural Language Processing*, pp. 144-149.

Eduard Hovy and C-Y Lin. 1998. Automated Text Summarization and the SUMMARIST system. In: *Proceedings of TIPSTER*, pp. 197-214.

Eduard Hovy. 2009. Text Summarization. In: Ruslan Mitkov. *The Oxford Handbook of Computational Linguistics*, pp. 583-598. United States: Oxford University.

Anna Kazantseva and Stan Szpakowicz. 2012. Topical Segmentation: a study of human performance and a new measure of quality. In: *Proceedings of the 2012 Conference of the North American Chapter of the Association for Computational Linguistics: Human Language Technologies*, pp. 211-220.

Willian C. Mann and Sandra A. Thompson. 1987. *Rhetorical Structure Theory: A Theory of Text Organization*. Technical Report ISI/RS-87-190.

Daniel Marcu. 2000. *The Theory and Practice of Discourse Parsing and Summarization*. The MIT Press. Cambridge, Massachusetts.

Hyo-Jung Oh, Sung Hyon Myaeng and Myung-Gil Jang. 2007. Semantic passage on sentence topics for question answering. *Information Sciences* 177(18), pp. 3696-3717.

Rebecca J. Passonneau and Diane J. Litman. 1997. Discourse segmentation by human and automated means. *Computational Linguistics* 23(1), pp. 103-109.

Violaine Prince and Alexandre Labadié. 2007. Text segmentation based on document understanding for information retrieval. In: *Proceedings of the 12th International Conference on Applications of Natural Language to Information Systems*, pp. 295-304.

Maite Taboada and William C. Mann. 2006. Rhetorical Structure Theory: Looking back and moving ahead. *Discourse Studies* 8(3), pp.423-459.

Xiaojun Wan. 2008. An exploration of document impact on graph-based multi-document summarization. In: *Proceedings of the Conference on Empirical Methods in Natural Language Processing*, pp. 755-762.

Will my Spoken Dialogue System be a Slow Learner ?

Layla El Asri
Orange Labs / UMI 2958 (IMS-MaLIS)
Issy-les-Moulineaux (France) / Metz (France)
layla.elasri@orange.com

Romain Laroche
Orange Labs
Issy-les-Moulineaux (France)
romain.laroche@orange.com

Abstract

This paper presents a practical methodology for the integration of reinforcement learning during the design of a Spoken Dialogue System (SDS). It proposes a method that enables SDS designers to know, in advance, the number of dialogues that their system will need in order to learn the value of each state-action couple. We ask the designer to provide a user model in a simple way. Then, we run simulations with this model and we compute confidence intervals for the mean of the expected return of the state-action couples.

1 Introduction

The Dialogue Manager (DM) of a Spoken Dialogue System (SDS) selects actions according to its current beliefs concerning the state of the dialogue. Reinforcement Learning (RL) has been more and more used for the optimisation of dialogue management, freeing designers from having to fully implement the strategy of the DM.

A framework known as Module-Variable Decision Process (MVDP) was proposed by Laroche et al. (2009) who integrated RL into an automaton-based DM. This led to the deployment of the first commercial SDS implementing RL (Putois et al., 2010).

Our work intends to continue this effort in bridging the gap between research advances on RL-based SDS and industrial release. One important issue concerning the design of an RL-based SDS is that it is difficult to evaluate the number of training dialogues that will be necessary for the system to learn an optimal behaviour. The underlying mathematical problem is the estimation of the training sample size needed by the RL algorithm for convergence. Yet, designers are often not experts in RL. Therefore, this paper presents a simple methodology for evaluating the necessary sample size for an RL algorithm embedded into an SDS. This methodology does not require any RL expertise from designers. The latter are asked to provide a model of user behaviour in a simple way. According to this model, numerous simulations are run and the sample size for each module-state-action triple of the DM is estimated. This methodology was tested on an SDS designed during the CLASSiC European project[1] (Laroche et al., 2011) and we show that these computations are robust to varying models of user behaviour.

2 Dialogue Management as a Module-Variable Decision Process

Module-Variable Decision Processes (MVDP) factorise learning into modules, each module having its own state and action spaces. Formally, an MVDP is a tuple (M, V_M, A_M, T) where M is the module space, V_M is the space of *local contexts*, for each module m, $V_m \subset V_M$ is the set of variables which are relevant for m's decision making. $A_m \subset A_M$ is the set of possible actions, an action beeing a transition in the automaton. $T \subset \mathbb{R}$ is the time scale. In the following, time is measured in number of dialogue turns, a turn being the time elapsed between two ASR results.

[1]Computational Learning in Adaptive Systems for Spoken Conversation, http://www.classic-project.org/

2.1 The Compliance Based Reinforcement Learning Algorithm

The *Compliance-Based Reinforcement Learning* algorithm (CBRL, Laroche et al., 2009) is an adaptation of the Monte Carlo algorithm to online off-policy learning. Each evaluation phase in the Monte Carlo procedure requires numerous new episodes. CBRL enables to accelerate this process by adjusting the current policy not after a set of many new episodes but right after each episode and using all the previous episodes to evaluate the policy. Each dialogue is modelled as a sequence of decisions $d_t = (m_t, s_t, a_t, t)$ where m_t is the module encountered at time t, s_t is the current local context of m_t and a_t is the action chosen by m_t. Each decision d_t leads to an immediate reward R_t. With γ a discount factor, the return for a decision d_t is $r_t = \sum_{t_i=t}^{t_f} \gamma^{t_i - t} R_{t_i}$, t_f being the final turn of the dialogue. For a given module m, the value of any state-action couple (s, a) is the expected return starting from (s, a) and then choosing actions according to π, the policy of the system: $Q_m^\pi(s, a) = E[r_t \mid m_t = m, s_t = s, a_t = a, \pi]$. π is the set of all the policies of the modules: $\pi = \{\pi_{m_1}, ..., \pi_{m_{|M|}}\}$. After a dialogue is taken under policy π, the value of any triple (m, s, a) is updated as in Equation 1.

$$Q_m^\pi(s,a) = \frac{\sum\limits_{\Theta_m(s,a)} \omega_t r_t}{\Omega_m(s,a)} \quad (1)$$

$$\text{where } \Omega_m(s,a) = \sum_{\Theta_m(s,a)} \omega_t,$$

$$\text{and } \Theta_m(s,a) = \{d_t\}_{m_t=m; s_t=s; a_t=a} \quad (2)$$

For any module m, the algorithm evaluates the value of each couple (s, a) according to all the decisions in which this tuple has been involved from the beginning of learning (the set of decisions $\Theta_m(s, a)$). After each evaluation of the Q-function, the policy π is updated following an exploratory strategy based on the *Upper Confidence Bound 1 - Tuned* approach (Auer et al., 2002). The weights ω_t in Equation 1 are there to take into account the fact that π is evaluated according to all the rewards observed since the beginning of learning, rewards that were obtained following other policies. A local compliance $c_\pi(d_t)$ is associated with each decision d_t: it is the expected regret induced by a_t not being the optimal action according to the system's current policy π, $c_\pi(d_t) = Q_{m_t}^\pi(s_t, a_t) - max_{a \in A_{m_t}} Q_{m_t}^\pi(s_t, a)$. The global compliance with π of the decisions following d_t is a discounted sum of the local compliances. The weight w_t is then an increasing function of the global compliance.

3 Problem Resolution

3.1 Approach

The problem to be solved is the following. Let an MVDP (M, V_M, A_M, T). For each triple (m, s, a), we want to compute the error made on the estimate $Q_m(s, a)$ of $E[r \mid m, s, a]$ according to the number of observations $\Theta_m(s, a)$. Let $r_1, ..., r_{|\Theta_m(s,a)|}$ be the returns corresponding to the decisions in $\Theta_m(s, a)$ and $\sigma_{m(s,a)}$ the variance of these returns. We build a confidence interval for $E[r \mid m, s, a]$, centered in the estimate $Q_m(s, a)$ from user simulations with a bi-gram model specified by the designer.

3.2 User Simulations

User simulation has been an active line of research as it is often costly to gather real data (Scheffler and Young, 2002; Georgila et al., 2006; Yang and Heeman, 2007; Pietquin and Hastie, 2010). Task-oriented systems such as commercial ones aim to respond to a specific need. They are often conceived as slot-filling systems (Raux et al., 2003; Chandramohan et al., 2011). The dialogue is relatively well-guided by the system so there is no need to take into account complex conversational groundings to simulate user behaviour. Therefore, we choose here to ask the designer to provide a bi-gram model (Eckert et al., 1997): a probability distribution of user behaviour only conditioned on the latest system action. For each possible response, the designer provides a lower and an upper bound for its probability of occurring. Eckert et al. (1997) showed that slight modifications of user behaviour in the bi-gram model did not entail great differences of system performance. We support this claim in Section 4 where we show that the confidence intervals computation is robust to varying user behaviour.

3.3 Confidence Intervals

According to the Lyapunov central limit theorem, $Q_m(s,a)$ converges in law to the normal distribution of mean $E[Q_m(s,a)] = E[r \mid m,s,a]$ and variance $\texttt{var}(Q_m(s,a)) = \frac{\sum_{\Theta_m(s,a)} w_k^2}{\Omega_m^2(s,a)}\sigma_m^2(s,a)$. However, since $\sigma_m^2(s,a)$ is unknown and the observations are not necessarily distributed according to a normal law, we can only rely on an asymptotic result according to which, for a sufficiently large number of samples, the previous convergence result holds with the unbiased estimate of the returns variance $\tilde{\sigma}_m(s,a)$. A confidence interval of probability $1-\alpha$ for $E[r \mid m,s,a]$ is then:

$$[Q_m(s,a) - \epsilon_{m,s,a}, Q_m(s,a) + \epsilon_{m,s,a}] \quad (3)$$

We note $u_\alpha = \Phi^{-1}_{N(0,1)}(1-\frac{\alpha}{2})$, with $\Phi_{N(0,1)}$ the cumulative distribution function of $N(0,1)$:

$$\epsilon_{m,s,a} = \frac{\sqrt{\sum_{\Theta_m(s,a)} \omega_k^2}}{\Omega_m(s,a)}\tilde{\sigma}_m(s,a)u_\alpha \quad (4)$$

In the non-weighted case, the previous asymptotic result is generally considered to hold for a number of samples greater than 30. We thus consider the confidence intervals to be valid for $\overline{\Omega}_m(s,a) = \frac{\Omega_m^2(s,a)}{\sum_{\Theta_m(s,a)} \omega_k^2} > 30$.

3.4 β-Convergence Definition

A confidence interval can be computed for each (m,s,a) triple of the system. From this computation, we deduce the number of dialogues necessary for convergence *i.e.* for the width of the confidence interval to be under a given threshold. The confidence interval radius of a triple (m,s,a) depends on the variance of observed returns (see equation 4) so we define the normalised confidence interval radius:

$$\overline{\epsilon}_{m,s,a} = \frac{\epsilon_{m,s,a}}{\tilde{\sigma}_m(s,a)} = \frac{u_\alpha}{\sqrt{\overline{\Omega}_m(s,a) - 1}} \quad (5)$$

We will consider that a triple (m,s,a) will have β-converged once the normalised confidence interval radius will have come under β.

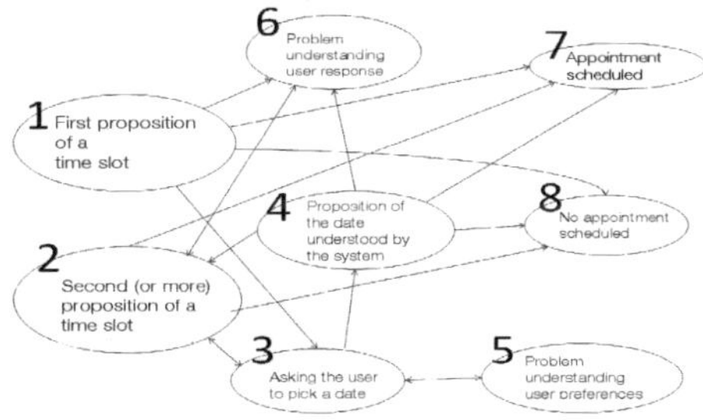

Figure 1: A schematic view of the system.

4 Experiments

4.1 System Description

The negotiation strategy of the system is hard-coded (see Figure 1). The system starts each dialogue proposing to the user its first availability (module 1). Then, if the user rejects the proposition, the system asks them to give their first availability (module 3). If the first two steps have not resulted in success, the system proposes its next availabilities (module 2) until an appointment is booked (module 7) or the system has no more propositions to make (module 8). When a user proposes a date, the system asks for a confirmation through module 4. Two error-repair modules (modules 6 and 5) notify the user that they have not been understood or heard (in case of a time out). More details can be found in (Laroche et al., 2011). Each module has to choose between three actions: uttering with a calm (action 1), neutral (action 2) or dynamic (action 3) tone. In our experiments, user simulation was modelled so that the first two alternatives were artificially disadvantaged: the number of failures was slightly increased whenever one of them was chosen. We modelled here the fact that users would always prefer the dynamic intonation.

We ran 2000 simulations, one simulation consisting of a complete dialogue ending with an update of the state-action value function for each of the system's modules. The following results are averages on 100 runs.

We set the hanging-up rate to 10%. α was set to 0.05 and β to 0.1. In the following section, we use the notation (i,j,k) to refer to (m_i, s_j, a_k).[2]

[2] s_j is always equal to 1 because the local contexts space is equal to the module space

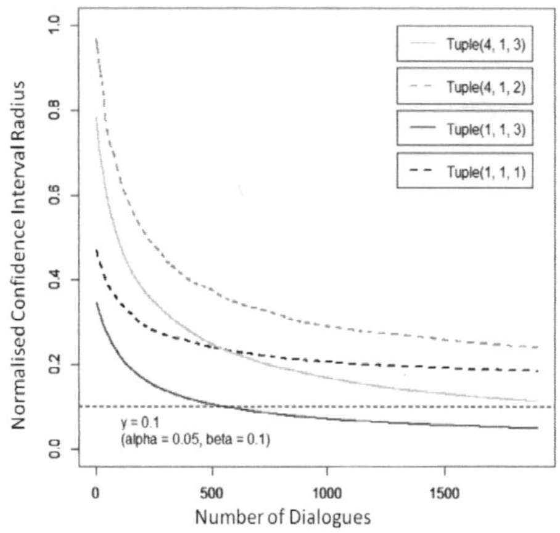

Figure 2: Evolution of $\bar{\epsilon}_{m,s,a}$ for triples (1, 1, 1), (1, 1, 3), (4, 1, 2) and (4, 1, 3) according to the total number of dialogues. Users prefer action 3.

4.2 Results

By the end of our experiments, modules 4, 5 and 8 had not $\beta_{0.1}$-converged. Module 5 was not likely to be visited quite often according to our specification of user behaviour. The same happened for module 4, only accessible from module 3 (see Figure 1), which was not itself often visited. Module 1 is, with module 8, a starting module of the system. At the beginning of a dialogue, module 1 had a 95% probability of being visited whereas this probability was of 5% for module 8 (this only happened when all available appointments had already been booked). Therefore, module 1 was visited once during almost every dialogue. We will now focus on modules 1 and 4 for clarity of presentation.

We can conclude from Figure 2 that triple (1, 1, 3) $\beta_{0.1}$-converged after about 640 dialogues, corresponding to about 425 visits whereas neither triple (1, 1, 1) nor (4, 1, 2) nor (4, 1, 3) $\beta_{0.1}$-converged, even after 2000 dialogues. Indeed, these triples did not receive enough visits during the simulations. Triple (1, 1, 3) $\beta_{0.1}$-converged whereas (1, 1, 1) did not because, at one point, the growth of the number of visits to (1, 1, 1) slowed down as module 1 favoured action 3 and reduced its exploration of other actions. The fact is that the RL algorithm did not need such a precise estimation for (1, 1, 1) to understand action 1 (the neutral tone) was suboptimal.

The variance over the 100 runs of the final estimation of $\bar{\epsilon}_{m,s,a}$ was below 0.01. For all triples of the system, the variance was very low after about 500 dialogues only (from 10^{-5} to 0.02). This means that the approximate user behaviour, defined with probability windows, only had a limited impact on the reliability of the computed confidence intervals. The probability windows used in the experiments were narrow (of an average size of 10%) so user behaviour did not change drastically from a run to another. With a behaviour much more erratic (larger probability windows), the variance over 10 runs was higher but did not exceed 0.02.

5 Related Work

Suendermann et al. (2010) tackled the issue of reducing the risk induced by on-line learning for commercial SDS with contender-based dialogue management. Our study relates to this work but within the more complex learning structure of RL.

Closer to our study, Tetreault et al. (2007) compared confidence intervals for the expected return for different MDPs, all modelling the same SDS but with a different state space. They showed how the intervals bounds as well as the expected cumulative returns estimations could be used in order to select an appropriate state space. More recently, Daubigney et al. (2011) as well as Gasic et al. (2011) developed an efficient exploration strategy for an MDP-based DM based on the uncertainties on the expected returns estimations. The difference between these two approaches and ours is that they compute the confidence intervals for a known policy whereas we compute the expected confidence intervals for an unknown policy that will be learnt on-line.

6 Conclusion

To help the development of SDS embedding on-line RL, we have designed and implemented an algorithm which computes the normalised confidence interval radius for the value of a state-action couple. We have illustrated this algorithm on an appointment scheduling SDS. We believe our method can be transferred to any system implementing an RL episodic task, as long as the environment can be simulated.

References

Senthilkumar Chandramohan, Matthieu Geist, Fabrice Lefèvre, and Olivier Pietquin. 2011. User simulation in dialogue systems using inverse reinforcement learning. In *Proceedings of Interspeech*.

Lucie Daubigney, Milica Gasic, Senthilkumar Chandramohan, Matthieu Geist, Olivier Pietquin, and Steve Young. 2011. Uncertainty management for on-line optimisation of a pomdp-based large-scale spoken dialogue system. In *Proceedings of Interspeech*, pages 1301–1304.

Wieland Eckert, Esther Levin, and Roberto Pieraccini. 1997. User modeling for spoken dialogue system evaluation. In *Proceedings of IEEE ASRU*, pages 80–87.

Milica Gasic, Filip Jurcicek, Blaise Thomson, Kai Yu, and Steve Young. 2011. On-line policy optimisation of spoken dialogue systems via live interaction with human subjects. In *Proceedings of IEEE ASRU*.

Kallirroi Georgila, James Henderson, and Oliver Lemon. 2006. User simulation for spoken dialogue systems: Learning and evaluation. In *Proceedings of Interspeech*.

Romain Laroche, Ghislain Putois, Philippe Bretier, and Bernadette Bouchon-Meunier. 2009. Hybridisation of expertise and reinforcement learning in dialogue systems. In *Proceedings of Interspeech*.

Romain Laroche, Ghislain Putois, Philippe Bretier, Martin Aranguren, Julia Velkovska, Helen Hastie, Simon Keizer, Kai Yu, Filip Jurcicek, Oliver Lemon, and Steve Young. 2011. D6.4: Final evaluation of classic towninfo and appointment scheduling systems. Technical report, CLASSIC Project.

Olivier Pietquin and Helen Hastie. 2010. Metrics for the evaluation of user simulations. Technical Report Deliverable 3.5, CLASSIC Project.

Ghislain Putois, Romain Laroche, and Philippe Bretier. 2010. Enhanced monitoring tools and on-line dialogue optimisation merged into a new spoken dialogue system design experience. In *Proceedings of SIGdial Workshop on Discourse and Dialogue*, pages 185–192.

Antoine Raux, Brian Langner, Allan Black, and Maxine Eskenazi. 2003. LET'S GO: Improving Spoken Dialog Systems for the Elderly and Non-natives. In *Proceedings of Eurospeech*.

Konrad Scheffler and Steve Young. 2002. Automatic learning of dialogue strategy using dialogue simulation and reinforcement learning. In *Proceedings of HLT*, pages 12–18.

David Suendermann, John Liscombe, and Roberto Pieraccini. 2010. Contender. In *Proceedings of IEEE SLT*, pages 330–335.

Joel R. Tetreault, Dan Bohus, and Diane J. Litman. 2007. Estimating the reliability of mdp policies: A confidence interval approach. In *Proceedings of HLT-NAACL*, pages 276–283.

Fan Yang and Peter A. Heeman. 2007. Exploring initiative strategies using computer simulation. In *Proceedings of Interspeech*, pages 106–109.

Model-free POMDP optimisation of tutoring systems with echo-state networks

Lucie Daubigney[1,3] **Matthieu Geist**[1] **Olivier Pietquin**[1,2]
[1]IMS-MaLIS – Supélec (Metz, France), [2]UMI2958 – GeorgiaTech/CNRS (Metz, France)
[3]Team project MaIA – Loria (Nancy, France)

Abstract

Intelligent Tutoring Systems (ITSs) are now recognised as an interesting alternative for providing learning opportunities in various domains. The Reinforcement Learning (RL) approach has been shown reliable for finding efficient teaching strategies. However, similarly to other human-machine interaction systems such as spoken dialogue systems, ITSs suffer from a partial knowledge of the interlocutor's intentions. In the dialogue case, engineering work can infer a precise state of the user by taking into account the uncertainty provided by the spoken understanding language module. A model-free approach based on RL and Echo State Newtorks (ESNs), which retrieves similar information, is proposed here for tutoring.

1 Introduction

For the last decades, Intelligent Tutoring Systems (ITSs) have become powerful tools in various domains such as mathematics (Koedinger et al., 1997), physics (Vanlehn et al., 2005; Litman and Silliman, 2004; Graesser et al., 2005), computer sciences (Corbett et al., 1995), reading (Mostow and Aist, 2001), or foreign languages (Heift and Schulze, 2007; Amaral and Meurers, 2011). Their appeal relies on the fact that each student does not have to follow an average teaching strategy, especially as the one-to-one tutoring has been proven the most efficent (Bloom, 1968). The expertise of a teacher relies on his capacity to advice at the right time the student to acquire new skills. To do so, the teacher is able to choose iteratively pedagogical activities. From this perspective, teaching is a sequential decision-making problem. To solve it, the reinforcement learning (Sutton and Barto, 1998) approach and the Markov Decision Process (MDP) paradigm have been successfully used (Iglesias et al., 2009). Given a situation, each teacher's decision is locally quantified by a *reward*. However, the consequences of the teacher's actions on the student's cognition cannot be exactly determined, which introduce uncertainty.

To find a solution, one can notice that spoken dialogue management and tutoring are closely related. Both are humain-computer interactions in which the human user's intentions are not perfectly known. In the spoken dialogue case, the partial observability is due to the recognition errors introduced by the speech understanding module. They are taken into account by using some hypotheses about how the language is constructed. Thus, accurate models to link observations from the user's recognised utterances to the underlying intentions can be set up. For example, the Hidden Information State paradigm (Young et al., 2006; Young et al., 2010) builds a state which is a summary of the dialogue history (Gašić et al., 2010; Daubigney et al., 2011; Daubigney et al., 2012). However, in the ITS case, such a state is harder to develop since the cognition cannot be determined by analysing a physical signal. Thus, a model-free approach is preferred here.

To do so, a memory of the past observations and actions is built by means of a Recurrent Neural Network (RNN) and more precisely an Echo State Network (ESN) (Jaeger, 2001). The internal state of the network can be shown (under some resonable conditions) to meet the Markov property (Szita et al., 2006). This internal state is then used with a standard RL algorithm to estimate the optimal solution. It has already been applied to RL in (Szita et al., 2006) in limited toy applications and it is, to our knowledge, the first attempt to use it in an interaction framework. The proof of concept presented in Szita's article uses the common SARSA algorithm which is an *on-line* and *on-policy* algorithm. Each improvement of the strategy is directly tested. In the case of teaching, testing poor decisions can be problematic. Here, we thus propose the combination of an ESN with an *off-line* and *off-policy* algorithm, namely the Least Square Policy Algorithm (LSPI) (Lagoudakis and Parr, 2003), which is another original contribution of this paper. Indeed, learning the solution with Partially Observable MDPs in a batch and off-policy manner is not common in the literature.

2 Markov Decision Process and Reinforcement Learning

Formally, an MDP is a tuple $\{S, A, T, R, \gamma\}$ set up to describe the tutor environment. The set S is the *state space* which represents the information about the student, A is the *action space* which contains the tutor's actions, T is a set of *transition probabilities* defined such that $T = \{p(s'|s,a), \forall(s',s,a) \in S \times S \times A\}$, R is the *reward function*, given according to the student progression for example, and $\gamma \in [0,1]$ is the *discount factor* which weights the future rewards. The set of transitions probabilities in the ITS case is unknown: the evolution of the student intentions cannot be determined. Solving the MPD consists in finding the optimal strategy, called the optimal policy which brings the highest expected cumulative reward.

However, in the ITS case, information about the student's knowledge, represented by s, can only be known through observations. Let $O = \{o_i\}$ be the set of possible observations. Yet, if only observations are available, a memory of what happened during previous interactions (the history) is necessary, because the process of observations does not meet the Markov property. The history is the sequence of observation-action pairs encountered during a whole teaching phase. Let $H = \{h_i\}$ be the set of all possible histories with $h_i = \{o_0, a_0, o_1, a_1, ..., o_{i-1}, a_{i-1}, o_i\}$.

When the POMDP framework is used, the underlying state s_i is inferred from the history by means of a model of probabilities linking s_i to h_i. In the case of human-machine interactions, this model is not available. It can be approximated but the considered solutions are *ad-hoc* to a particular problem, thus difficult to reuse. Here, we propose an approach with as few assumptions as possible about the student cognitive model by using Echo States Networks (ESNs). This approach builds a compact representation of the history space H.

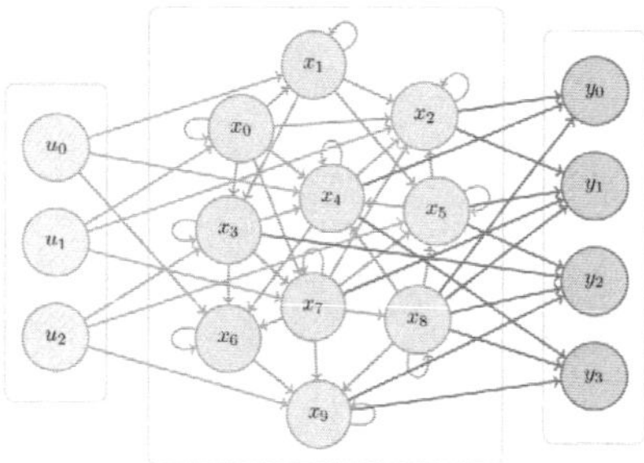

Figure 1: RNN structure (for sake of readability, all the connections do not appear).

3 Echo State Networks

An Echo State Network is represented by three layers of neurons (Fig. 1): an input, a hidden and an output. The number of neurons in the hidden layer is supposed to be large and each of them can be connected to itself. These recurrent connections are responsible for reusing the value of the neurons at a previous time step. Consequently, a memory is built in the reservoir and trajectories can be encoded. Only the connections from the hidden layer to the output one are learnt since all the other connections are randomly and sparsely set. The recurrent connections are defined so that the echo state property is met (Jaeger, 2001): if after a given number of updates of the input neurons, two internal states are exactly the same, then the input sequences which led to these two internal states are identical.

The connections of the ESN are presented in Fig. 2, with $u_k \in \mathbb{R}^{N_i}$, $x_k \in \mathbb{R}^{N_h}$ and $y_k \in \mathbb{R}^{N_o}$, respectively representing the values of the input, hidden and output layers, N_i, N_h and N_o being the respective number of neurons and $W^{in} \in \mathbb{M}_{N_h \times N_i}$, $W^{hid} \in \mathbb{M}_{N_h \times N_h}$ and $W^{out} \in \mathbb{M}_{N_o \times N_h}$, matrix containing the synaptic weights. After a training, the output y_k returns a linear approximation of the internal state of the reservoir. This output depends on the sequence of inputs $u_0, \cdots, u_k$ and not only u_k, through x_k.

Combining ESNs and RL is of interest. By means of the echo state property, a summary of the observations and decisions encountered during the tutoring phase is provided through the internal state x. In (Szita et al., 2006), it has been proven to meet the Markov property with high probability. It thus can be used as a state for standard RL algorithms. Here, more precisely, it represents the basis function of an approximation of the Q-

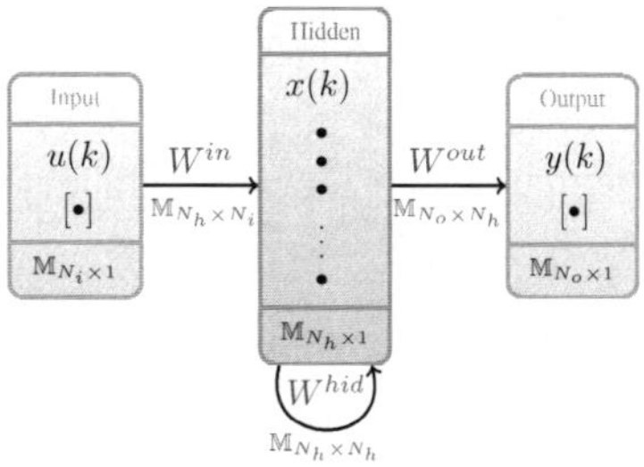

Figure 2: Structure of an ESN. For the example, $N_i = 1$ and $N_o = 1$.

function. This function is associated with a policy π, defined for each couple $(s, a) \in S \times A$ such that $Q^\pi(s, a) = E\left[\sum_i \gamma^i r_i | s_0 = s, a_0 = a\right]$ and quantifies the policy. ESNs are used in the following way to solve RL problems. The network is responsible for giving, from an observations o_k and an action a_k at time step k, a linear estimation of the value of the Q-function $\hat{Q}_\theta(h_k, a_k)$ (with $h_k = \{o_0, a_0, ..., o_{k-1}, a_{k-1}, o_k\}$). The state s is not used in the estimation of the Q-function since it is unknown. Instead, it is replaced by the history h_k. The input of the ESN, u_k, is thus the concatenation of the observation o_k and the action a_k: $u_k = (o_k, a_k)$. The internal state x_k which component are in $[-1, 1]$, is a summary of the history h_k and the action a_k. Thus, the estimation of the Q-function is $\hat{Q}_\theta(h_k, a_k) = \theta^\top x_k$. The values of the output connections are learnt by means of the LSPI algorithm. With this algorithm, the optimal policy is learnt from a fixed set of data.

4 Experimental settings

For the experiments, we assume that the teaching can be done by means of three actions. First, a lesson can be presented to make the knowledge of the student increase. The second and third actions are evaluations. They can either be a simple question or a final exam. The final exam consists in asking a hundred yes/no questions of equal complexity and on the same topic. The student does not have a feedback. Once it is proposed, a new teaching episode starts. Three observations are returned to the ITS. If a lesson is proposed to the user, the observation is neutral: no feedback comes from the student since the direct influence of the lesson remains unknown. The two other observations appear when a question is asked (yes or no). Consequently, one observation is not enough to choose the next action since no clue is given about how many lessons have led to this result. A non-null reward is only given when a final exam is proposed. In this case, it is proportional to the rate of correct answers among all the answers given during the exam. Thus, each improvement is taken into account. The γ factor is set to 0.97.

In this proof of concept, the results have been obtained with simulated students from (Chang et al., 2006) to ensure the reproducibility of the experiments. The simulation implements two abilities: answering a question and learning with a lesson. Three groups of students have been set up. The first one, $T1$, is supposed to be able to learn very efficiently, the second, $T2$, needs a few more lessons to provide good answers, and the third, $T3$, needs a lot of lessons to answer correctly.

5 Results

Several teaching strategies have been compared. As a lower bound baseline, a random strategy has been tested. With a probability (w.p.) of 0.6, a lesson is proposed, w.p. of 0.2 a question is chosen, and w.p. of 0.2 a final exam is proposed. The data generated with this random strategy have been used by the LSPI algorithm and an informed state space. The second baseline proposed is the reactive policy learnt by LSPI (called *reactive-LSPI*), only from obervations. Neither the information about the number of lessons proposed nor the internal state of the ESN is used. The third strategy is learnt by using the observations and a counter of lessons already given (called *informed-LSPI*). Thus, this state supposedly contains sufficient information to take the decision. For this case, since the numbers of observations and lessons are discrete thus countable, a tabular representation is chosen for the Q-function. The fourth strategy uses the internal state of the ESN as basis function for the Q-function (called *ESN-LSPI*). There are 50 hidden neurons. Different sizes of training data sets are tested. Among the data, the three types of students are represented in equal proportions. One hundred policies are learnt for each of the methods presented, except for the ESN-LSPI. For this one, 10 ESNs are generated and 10 training sessions are performed with each one of them. The mean over the average results of each of the 10 learnings is presented in the results. Each of the policies have been tested 1000 times.

Fig. 3 shows a comparison of the learnt strategies. The three types of students are used for the training and test phases. One can notice that

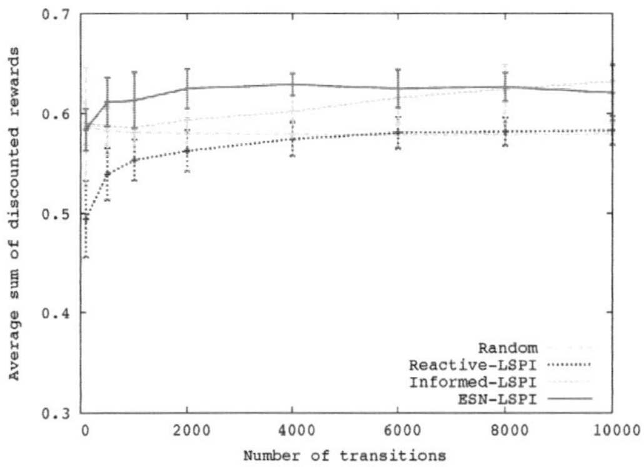

Figure 3: Comparison of the different strategies.

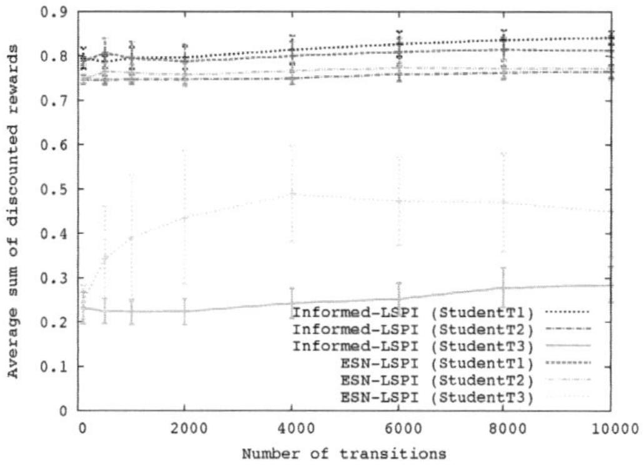

Figure 4: Results of the learnt policies for each group of students.

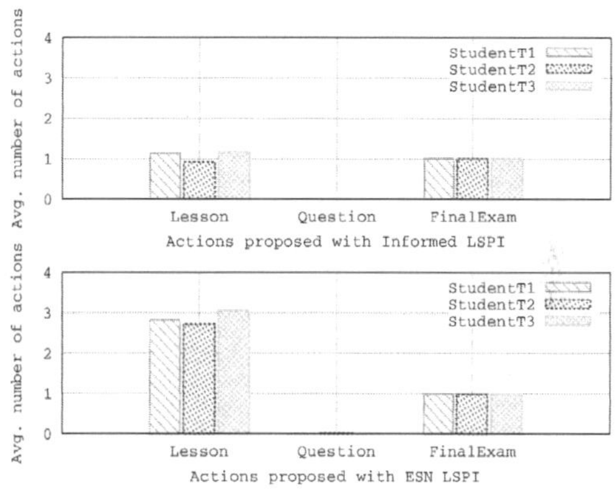

Figure 5: Distribution of the actions (the size of the training dataset is 10000).

the standard deviation is larger when the ESN are used because uncertainty is added when generating the ESN since the connections are randomly set. The random and the reactive policies give the poorest results. Yet, the average reward increases because of the data in the training set. For small sets, long sequences of lessons only have not been encountered. Thus, larger rewards have not been encountered either. For the two other curves, with a reasonable number of interactions (around 8000), a good strategy is learnt by using informed-LSPI. The strategies learnt with the ESN require fewer transitions and allow a faster learning. In this case, the optimum is reached with 2000 transitions while 8000 ones are needed to reach the same quality with the informed-LSPI strategy. Around 10000 samples, both policies give the same results. However, less information is given in the ESN approach (only observations). Thus, this approach is more generic. The counter information may not be sufficient for more complex problems.

To compare the efficiency of the learnt policies, the informed-LSPI and ESN-LSPI are plotted for each group of students in Fig. 4. All the strategies are learnt with the same data sets than previously, but only one type of students is tested at a time. For the $T2$ and $T3$ types, the average results are better with ESN-LSPI (especially for the $T3$ type). For the $T1$ group, informed-LSPI returns slighlty better results. A better insight of the behaviour of each policy is given in Fig. 5 by plotting the distribution of the actions used during the test phase. A comparison reveals that the number of lessons is higher in the ESN-LSPI case (around 3) whereas only one lesson is given in average with informed-LSPI. This is of benefit to students of the third group and thus implicitly to those of the first and second groups. The number of lessons is even larger for the third group than for the two others (0.5 more in average). However, in the informed-LSPI case, the learnt policy is only profitable for those of the first group, who are already skilled (this conclusion is consistent with the Fig. 4). Questions are very rarely asked because once the number of lessons has been learnt, they bring no more information.

6 Conclusion

We proposed a model-free approach which uses only observations to find optimal teaching stategies. A summary of the history encountered is implemented by means of an ESN. This summary has been proven to be Markovian by (Szita et al., 2006). A standard RL algorithm which can learn from already collected data, is then used to perform the learning. Preliminary experiments have been presented on simulated data. In future works, we plan to apply this method to SDSs.

Acknowledgments

Results have been computed with the InterCell cluster funded by the Région Lorraine.

References

L. Amaral and D. Meurers. 2011. On using intelligent computer-assisted language learning in real-life foreign language teaching and learning. *ReCALL*, 23(1):4–24.

B. Bloom. 1968. Learning for mastery. *Evaluation comment*, 1(2):1–5.

K. Chang, J. Beck, J. Mostow, and A. Corbett. 2006. A bayes net toolkit for student modeling in intelligent tutoring systems. In *Intelligent Tutoring Systems*, pages 104–113. Springer.

A. Corbett, J. Anderson, and A. OBrien. 1995. Student modeling in the act programming tutor. *Cognitively diagnostic assessment*, pages 19–41.

L. Daubigney, M. Gašić, S. Chandramohan, M. Geist, O. Pietquin, and S. Young. 2011. Uncertainty management for on-line optimisation of a POMDP-based large-scale spoken dialogue system. In *Proceedings of Interspeech'11*.

L. Daubigney, M. Geist, S. Chandramohan, and O. Pietquin. 2012. A Comprehensive Reinforcement Learning Framework for Dialogue Management Optimisation. *IEEE Journal of Selected Topics in Signal Processing*, 6(8):891–902.

M. Gašić, F. Jurčíček, S. Keizer, F. Mairesse, B. Thomson, K. Yu, and S. Young. 2010. Gaussian processes for fast policy optimisation of POMDP-based dialogue managers. In *Proceedings of SIGdial'10*.

A. Graesser, P. Chipman, B. Haynes, and A. Olney. 2005. Autotutor: An intelligent tutoring system with mixed-initiative dialogue. *Education, IEEE Transactions on*, 48(4):612–618.

T. Heift and M. Schulze. 2007. *Errors and intelligence in computer-assisted language learning: Parsers and pedagogues*, volume 2. Psychology Press.

Ana Iglesias, Paloma Martínez, Ricardo Aler, and Fernando Fernández. 2009. Learning teaching strategies in an adaptive and intelligent educational system through reinforcement learning. *Applied Intelligence*, 31(1):89–106.

H. Jaeger. 2001. The "echo state" approach to analysing and training recurrent neural networks. Technical report, Technical Report GMD Report 148, German National Research Center for Information Technology.

K. Koedinger, J. Anderson, W. Hadley, M. Mark, et al. 1997. Intelligent tutoring goes to school in the big city. *International Journal of Artificial Intelligence in Education (IJAIED)*, 8:30–43.

M. Lagoudakis and R. Parr. 2003. Least-squares policy iteration. *The Journal of Machine Learning Research*, 4:1107–1149.

D. Litman and S. Silliman. 2004. Itspoke: An intelligent tutoring spoken dialogue system. In *Demonstration Papers at HLT-NAACL 2004*, pages 5–8. Association for Computational Linguistics.

J. Mostow and G. Aist. 2001. Evaluating tutors that listen: an overview of project listen. In *Smart machines in education*, pages 169–234. MIT Press.

R. Sutton and A. Barto. 1998. *Reinforcement learning: An introduction*. The MIT press.

I. Szita, V. Gyenes, and A. Lőrincz. 2006. Reinforcement learning with echo state networks. *Artificial Neural Networks–ICANN 2006*, pages 830–839.

K. Vanlehn, C. Lynch, K. Schulze, J. Shapiro, R. Shelby, L. Taylor, D. Treacy, A. Weinstein, and M. Wintersgill. 2005. The andes physics tutoring system: Lessons learned. *International Journal of Artificial Intelligence in Education*, 15(3):147–204.

S. Young, J. Schatzmann, B. Thomson, H. Ye, and K. Weilhammer. 2006. The HIS dialogue manager. In *Proceedings of IEEE/ACL Workshop on Spoken Language Technology (SLT'06)*.

S. Young, M. Gasic, S. Keizer, F. Mairesse, J. Schatzmann, B. Thomson, and K. Yu. 2010. The hidden information state model: A practical framework for POMDP-based spoken dialogue management. *Computer Speech & Language*, 24(2):150–174.

Patterns of Importance Variation in Spoken Dialog

Nigel G. Ward
University of Texas at El Paso
El Paso, Texas, 79968 USA
nigelward@acm.org

Karen A. Richart-Ruiz
University of Texas at El Paso
El Paso, Texas, 79968 USA
karichart@miners.utep.edu

Abstract

Some things people say are more important, and some less so. Importance varies from moment to moment in spoken dialog, and contextual prosodic features and patterns signal this. A simple linear regression model over such features gave estimates that correlated well, 0.83, with human importance judgments.

1 Importance in Language and Dialog

Not everything people say to each other is equally important, for example many *ums* and *uhs* have almost no significance, in comparison to those content words or nuances that are critical in one way or another.

Many language processing applications need to detect what is important in the input stream, including dialog systems and systems for summarization, information retrieval, information extraction, and so on. Today this is primarily done using task-specific heuristics, such as discarding stopwords, giving more weight to low frequency words, or favoring utterances with high average pitch. In this paper, however, we explore a general, task-independent notion of importance, taking a dialog perspective.

Section 2 explains our empirical approach. Sections 3 and 4 explore the individual prosodic features and longer prosodic patterns that dialog participants use to signal to each other what is important and unimportant. Section 5 describes predictive models that use this information to automatically estimate importance and Section 6 summarizes the significance and future work needed.

2 Annotating Importance

No standard definition of importance is useful for describing what happens, moment-by-moment, in spoken dialog. The closest contender would be entropy, as defined in information theory. For text we can measure the difficulty of guessing letters or words, as a measure of their unpredictability and thus informativeness (Shannon, 1951), but this is indirect, time-consuming, and impossible to apply to non-symbolic aspects of language. We can also measure the value of certain information, such as prosody, for improving the accuracy of predictions, but again this is indirect and time-consuming (Ward and Walker, 2009).

We therefore chose to do an empirical study. We hired a student to annotate importance. Wanting to capture her naive judgments, atheoretically, we did not precisely define importance for her. Instead we discussed the concept briefly, noting that importance may be judged: not just by content but also by value for directing the future course of the dialog, not just from the speaker's perspective but also from the listener's, and not just from the words said but also from how they were said.

The labeling tool used enabled the annotator to navigate back and forth in the dialogs, listen to the speakers together in stereo or independently, delimit regions of any desired size including words and word fragments, and ascribe to each region an importance value. While importance is continuous, for convenience we used the whole numbers from 0 to 5, with 5 indicating highest importance, 4 typical importance, 3 somewhat less importance, 2 and 1 even less, and 0 silence. To have a variety of speakers, topics, and speaking styles, the material was from the Switchboard corpus (Godfrey et al., 1992).

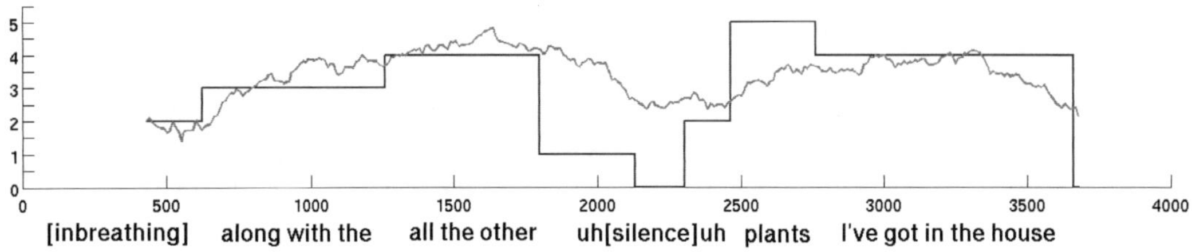

Figure 1: Importance versus Time, in milliseconds. Rectangular line: Annotator judgments; Jagged line: Predictions (discussed below). The words are all by one speaker, horizontally positioned by approximate occurrence.

In total, she labeled both tracks of just over 100 minutes of dialog. There was diversity in labels, supporting our belief that importance is not monotone: the largest fraction of non-zero-labeled regions, covering 38% of the total time, was at level 4, but there were also 20% at level 3 and 37% at level 5. In general importance was variable, on average staying at the same level for only 1.5 seconds. Figure 1 illustrates.

In parallel, the second author labeled 17 minutes of the same dialogs[1]. The agreement in terms of Kappa was .80 ("very good") across all categories, and .67 ("good") excluding the zero-level labels, which were mostly for silent regions and thus easy to agree on. In terms of Weighted Kappa, appropriate here since the labels are ordered (and thus, for example, a 1-point difference matters much less than a 5-point difference), the agreement levels were .92 and .71, for all and for the zero-excluding sets, respectively. The differences were mainly due to minor variations in boundary placement, missing labels for small quiet sounds such as inbreaths and quiet overlapping backchannels, and different ratings of repeated words, and of backchannels (Ward and Richart-Ruiz, 2013).

3 Correlating Prosodic Factors

First we briefly examined lexical correlates of importance, by examining the average importance of words in this corpus (Ward and Richart-Ruiz, 2013). To summarize some key findings: Less frequent words tend to have higher average per-word importance, however ratings vary widely, depending on context. Some words have effects at a distance, for example, *because* tends to indicate that whatever is said one second later will be important. The interlocutor's words can also be informative, for example *oh* and *uh-huh* tend to indicate that whatever the interlocutor said one second ago was important. The "words" with the most extreme average importance — notably *uh-huh*, *um-hum*, *um* and laughter — are fillers, backchannels and other vocalizations of types which can be detected well from the prosodic and interactional contexts (Neiberg and Gustafson, 2011; Truong and van Leeuwen, 2007). Thus a word-based model of importance would be challenging to build and might not have much value. We therefore turned our attention to prosody.

While prosody-importance connections have not been considered directly, several studies have found correlations between prosodic features and various importance-related constructs, such as predictability, involvement, engagement, activation, newness, and interest (Bell et al., 2009; Yu et al., 2004; Batliner et al., 2011; Roehr and Baumann, 2010; Oertel et al., 2011; Hsiao et al., 2012; Kahn and Arnold, 2012; Kawahara et al., 2010). However these studies have all been limited to specific features, functions, or hypotheses. Our aims being instead exploratory, we looked for features, from among a broad inventory, which correlate with importance, as it occurs in a broad variety of contexts.

Our feature inventory included features of 8 classes: four basic types — volume, pitch height, pitch range, and speaking-rate — each computed for both participants: the speaker and the interlocutor. Within each class, features were computed over windows of various widths and at various offsets, for a total of 78 features (Ward and Richart-Ruiz, 2013).

[1] All labels are freely available at http://www.cs.utep.edu/nigel/importance/

The speaker features correlating most strongly with importance were volume and speaking rate. Although the very strongest correlations were with volume slightly in the past, volume both before and after the current moment was strongly correlated over all windows, with one exception. Speaker pitch height, in contrast, correlated negatively with importance across all windows, contrary to what is often seen in monolog data.

The interlocutor features correlating most strongly with importance were again volume and speaking rate, but only over windows close to the point of interest, perhaps due to co-construction or supportive back-channeling; over more distant windows, both past and future, these correlate negatively. Interlocutor pitch range correlated negatively over all windows.

4 Correlating Dialog-Activity Patterns

Thus we find that some prosodic features have different effects depending on their offset from the frame of interest. Perhaps prosody is not just marking importance vaguely somewhere in the area, but more precisely indicating important and unimportant moments.

To explore this we used Principal Components Analysis (PCA), as described in detail in (Ward and Vega, 2012). In short, this method finds patterns of prosodic features which co-occur frequently in the data, and so provides an unsupervised way to discover the latent structure underlying the observed regularities. We correlated the dimensions resulting with PCA with the importance values. Many dimensions had significant correlations, indicating that importance relates to many prosodic structures and contexts. Each dimension had two characteristic patterns, one corresponding to high values on that dimension and one to low values. We were able to interpret most of these in terms of dialog activities (Ward and Vega, 2012).

Tending to be more important was: speech in the middle of other speech (dimension 1), rather than words snuck in while the other has the floor; simultaneous speech (dimension 2), understandably as such times tended to be high in involvement and/or backchannels; times of encountering and resolving turn conflicts (dimension 7), more than places where the participants were supportively interleaving turns, which in this corpus were generally more phatic than contentful; crisp turn ends (dimension 8), rather than slow repetitious wind-downs; "upgraded assessments," in which a speaker agrees emphatically with an assessment made by the other (dimension 6); and times when speakers were solicitous, rather than controlling (dimension 19). Dimension 6 is interesting in that it matches an interaction pattern described as an exemplar of prosodic co-construction (Ogden, 2012). Dimension 19 was one of those underlying the exception noted above: the negative correlation between importance and speaker volume over the window from 0–50 milliseconds after the point of prediction. Upon examination, low volume at this offset often occurred when seeking agreement and during quiet filled pauses in the vicinity of high-content words.

model	correlation	m.a.e.
m5pTree decision tree	.38	1.21
neural network	.66	1.20
simple linear regression	.79	.89
linear regression	.83	.75
ditto, past-only features	.83	.79

Table 1: Prediction Quality in terms of correlation and mean absolute error, for various learning algorithms.

5 Predictive Models

We next set out to build predictive models, for two reasons: to judge whether the features discussed above are adequate for building useful models, and to determine what additional factors would be required in a more complete model.

The task is, given a timepoint in a track in a dialog, to predict the importance of what the speaker is saying at that moment. Our performance metrics were the mean absolute error and the correlation coefficient, computed over all frames; thus a predictor is better to the extent that its predictions are close to and correlate highly with the annotator's labels, including the implicit zero labels in regions of silence or noise.

We built models using four algorithms in Weka. All models performed poorly on dialogs for which there was cross-track bleeding or other noise. As these are artifacts of this corpus and would not be relevant for most applications, our main evaluation used only the five tracks with good audio quality. These all had different speakers. We did five-fold cross-validation on this; Table 1 gives the results. Linear regression was best, by both measures and

		past		future	all
	−400	−200	0		
speaker	.55	.64	.66	.59	.70
interloc.	.37	.43	.43	.37	.47
both	.62	.70	.71	.65	.74

Table 2: Model Quality, in terms of R^2, as a function of the features used.

across every fold, and this was consistent for all the other training and test sets tried.

To compare the performance of this predictor to human performance, we also trained a model using 5 tracks to predict performance over two test tracks, a total of 224495 test datapoints, which the second judge also had annotated. Over these the predictor did almost as well as second judge in correlation (.88 versus .92), but not so well in terms of mean absolute error (.75 versus .31).

Analyzing the errors, we noted several types of cause (Ward and Richart-Ruiz, 2013). First, performance varied widely across tracks, with mean absolute errors from .55 to .97, even though all the features were speaker-normalized. The high value was for a speaker who was an outlier in two respects: the only female among four males, and the only East-Coast speaker among four Texans. Thus results might be improved by separately modeling different genders and dialects. Second, predictions were often off in situations like those where the two human judges disagreed. Third, most of the errors were due to feature-set issues: robustness, poor loudness features, and not enough fine-grained features. Fourth, our prosodic-feature-only model did very poorly at distinguishing between the highest importance levels, 4 and 5, but was otherwise generally good.

Table 2 shows how performance varies with the features used; here quality is measured using simply the R^2 of a linear regression over all the data. Performance is lower with only the left-context features, as would be required for real-time applications, but not drastically so; as seen also in the last line of Table 1. Performance is only slightly lower when predicting slightly in advance, without using any features closere than 200 ms prior to the prediction point, but notably worse 400 ms before. Features of the interlocutor's behavior are helpful, partially why explaining dialog can be easier to understand than monolog (Branigan et al., 2011).

6 Broader Significance and Future Work

Sperber and Wilson argue that "attention and thought processes . . . automatically turn toward information that seems relevant: that is, capable of yielding cognitive effects" (Sperber and Wilson, 1987). This paper has identified some of the cues that systems can use to "automatically turn toward" the most important parts of the input stream. Overall, these findings show that task-independent importance can be identified fairly reliably, and that it can be predicted fairly well using simple prosodic features and a simple model. Significantly, we find that importance is frequently not signaled or determined by one participant alone, but is often truly a dialog phenomenon. We see three main directions for future work:

First, there is ample scope to build better models of importance, not only by pursuing the prosodic-feature improvements noted above, but in examining lexical, semantic, rhetorical-structure and dialog-structure correlates of importance.

Second, one could work to put our pretheoretical notion of importance on a firmer footing, perhaps by relating it to entropy, or to the time course of the psychological processes involved in retrieving, creating, managing, and packaging information into speech; or to the design and timing of dialog contributions so as not to overload the listener's processing capacity.

Third, there are applications. For example, a dialog system needing to definitely convey some information to the user could use an appropriate prosodic lead-in to signal it properly, doing an interactional dance (Gratch et al., 2007; Brennan et al., 2010) to prepare the recipient to be maximally receptive at the moment when the critical word is said. Another potential application is in voice codecs, as used in telecommunications. Today's codecs treat all speech as equally valuable. Instead we would like to transmit more important words and sounds at higher quality, and less important ones at lower quality, thereby increasing perceived call quality without increasing the average datarate, of course while properly considering all perceptual factors (Voran and Catellier, 2013).

Acknowledgments

This work was supported in part by the NSF under projects IIS-0914868 and CNS-0837556. We thank Timo Baumann, Alejandro Vega, Shreyas Karkhedkar, Gabriela Almeida and David Novick.

References

Anton Batliner, Stefan Steidl, Bjorn Schuller, et al. 2011. Whodunnit: Searching for the most important feature types signalling emotion-related user states in speech. *Computer Speech and Language*, 25:4–28.

Alan Bell, Jason M. Brenier, Michelle Gregory, Cynthia Girand, and Dan Jurafsky. 2009. Predictability effects on durations of content and function words in conversational English. *Journal of Memory and Language*, 60:92–111.

Holly P. Branigan, C.M. Catchpole, and M.J. Pickering. 2011. What makes dialogues easy to understand? *Language and Cognitive Processes*, 26:1667–1686.

Susan E. Brennan, Alexia Galati, and Anna K. Kuhlen. 2010. Two minds, one dialog: Coordinating speaking and understanding. In Brian H. Ross, editor, *The Psychology of Learning and Motivation, volume 53*, pages 301–344. Elsevier.

John J. Godfrey, Edward C. Holliman, and Jane McDaniel. 1992. Switchboard: Telephone speech corpus for research and development. In *Proceedings of ICASSP*, pages 517–520.

Jonathan Gratch, Ning Wang, Jillian Gerten, Edward Fast, and Robin Duffy. 2007. Creating rapport with virtual agents. In *Intelligent Virtual Agents*, pages 125–138. Springer.

Joey Chiao-yin Hsiao, Wan-rong Jih, and Jane Yung-jen Hsu. 2012. Recognizing continuous social engagement level in dyadic conversation by using turn-taking and speech emotion patterns. In *Activity Context Representation Workshop at AAAI*.

Jason M. Kahn and Jennifer E. Arnold. 2012. A processing-centered look at the contribution of givenness to durational reduction. *Journal of Memory and Language*, 67:311–325.

Tatsuya Kawahara, K.Sumi, Z.Q. Chang, and K.Takanashi. 2010. Detection of hot spots in poster conversations based on reactive tokens of audience. In *Interspeech*, pages 3042–3045.

Daniel Neiberg and Joakim Gustafson. 2011. A dual channel coupled decoder for fillers and feedback. In *Interspeech 2011*, pages 3097–3100.

Catharine Oertel, Stefan Scherer, and Nick Campbell. 2011. On the use of multimodal cues for the prediction of degrees of involvment in spontaneous conversation. In *Interspeech*.

Richard Ogden. 2012. Prosodies in conversation. In Oliver Niebuhr, editor, *Understanding Prosody: The role of context, function, and communication*, pages 201–217. De Gruyter.

Christine Tanja Roehr and Stefan Baumann. 2010. Prosodic marking of information status in German. In *Speech Prosody Conference*.

Claude E. Shannon. 1951. Prediction and entropy of printed English. *Bell System Technical Journal*, 30:50–64.

Dan Sperber and Deirdre Wilson. 1987. Précis of Relevance: Communication and cognition. *Behavioral and Brain Sciences*, 10(04):697–710.

Khiet P. Truong and David A. van Leeuwen. 2007. Automatic discrimination between laughter and speech. *Speech Communication*, 49:144–158.

Stephen D. Voran and Andrew A. Catellier. 2013. When should a speech coding quality increase be allowed within a talk-spurt? In *IEEE ICASSP*.

Nigel G. Ward and Karen A. Richart-Ruiz. 2013. Lexical and prosodic indicators of importance in spoken dialog. Technical Report UTEP-CS-13-41, University of Texas at El Paso, Department of Computer Science.

Nigel G. Ward and Alejandro Vega. 2012. A bottom-up exploration of the dimensions of dialog state in spoken interaction. In *13th Annual SIGdial Meeting on Discourse and Dialogue*.

Nigel G. Ward and Benjamin H. Walker. 2009. Estimating the potential of signal and interlocutor-track information for language modeling. In *Interspeech*, pages 160–163.

Chen Yu, Paul M. Aoki, and Alison Woodruff. 2004. Detecting user engagement in everyday conversations. In *Interspeech*, pages 1329–1332.

Reinforcement Learning of Two-Issue Negotiation Dialogue Policies

Kallirroi Georgila
Institute for Creative Technologies, University of Southern California
12015 Waterfront Drive, Playa Vista, CA 90094, USA
kgeorgila@ict.usc.edu

Abstract

We use hand-crafted simulated negotiators (SNs) to train and evaluate dialogue policies for two-issue negotiation between two agents. These SNs differ in their goals and in the use of strong and weak arguments to persuade their counterparts. They may also make irrational moves, i.e., moves not consistent with their goals, to generate a variety of negotiation patterns. Different versions of these SNs interact with each other to generate corpora for Reinforcement Learning (RL) of argumentation dialogue policies for each of the two agents. We evaluate the learned policies against hand-crafted SNs similar to the ones used for training but with the modification that these SNs no longer make irrational moves and thus are harder to beat. The learned policies generally do as well as, or better than the hand-crafted SNs showing that RL can be successfully used for learning argumentation dialogue policies in two-issue negotiation scenarios.

1 Introduction

The *dialogue policy* of a dialogue system decides on what dialogue move (also called *action*) the system should make given the dialogue context (also called *dialogue state*). Building hand-crafted policies is a hard task, and there is no guarantee that the resulting policies will be optimal. This issue has motivated the dialogue community to use statistical methods for automatically learning dialogue policies, the most popular of which is Reinforcement Learning (RL) (Szepesvári, 2010).

To date, RL has been used mainly for learning dialogue policies for slot-filling applications such as restaurant recommendations (Williams and Young, 2007; Chandramohan et al., 2010; Jurčíček et al., 2012; Gašić et al., 2012), flight reservations (Henderson et al., 2008), sightseeing recommendations (Misu et al., 2010), appointment scheduling (Georgila et al., 2010), technical support (Janarthanam and Lemon, 2010), etc., largely ignoring other types of dialogue. RL has also been applied to question-answering (Misu et al., 2012) and tutoring domains (Tetreault and Litman, 2008; Chi et al., 2011). There has also been some work on applying RL to the more difficult problem of learning negotiation policies (Heeman, 2009; Paruchuri et al., 2009; Georgila and Traum, 2011a; Georgila and Traum, 2011b; Nouri et al., 2012), which is the topic of this paper.

In negotiation dialogue the system and the user have opinions about the optimal outcomes and try to reach a joint decision. Dialogue policy decisions are typically whether to present, accept, or reject a proposal, whether to compromise, etc. Rewards may depend on the type of policy that we want to learn. For example, a cooperative policy should be rewarded for accepting proposals.

Recently, Georgila and Traum (2011a; 2011b) learned argumentation dialogue policies for negotiation against users of different cultural norms in a one-issue negotiation scenario. We extend this work by learning argumentation policies in a two-issue negotiation setting. We aim to learn system (or agent) policies that will persuade their interlocutor (a human user or another agent) to agree on the system's preferences.

Our research contribution is two-fold: First, to our knowledge this is the first study that uses RL for learning argumentation policies in a two-issue negotiation scenario and one of the few studies on using RL for negotiation. Second, for the first time, we learn policies for agents with different degrees of persuasion skills, i.e., agents that provide strong or weak arguments.

Section 2 introduces RL, and section 3 describes our two-issue negotiation domain and our learning methodology. Section 4 presents our evaluation results and section 5 concludes.

2 Reinforcement Learning

Reinforcement Learning (RL) is a machine learning technique used to learn the policy of an agent (Szepesvári, 2010). RL is used in the framework of Markov Decision Processes (MDPs) (Szepesvári, 2010) or Partially Observable Markov Decision Processes (Williams and Young, 2007). In this paper we use MDPs.

An MDP is defined as a tuple (S, A, P, R, γ) where S is the set of states that the agent may be in, A is the set of actions of the agent, $P : S \times A \rightarrow P(S, A)$ is the set of transition probabilities between states after taking an action, $R : S \times A \rightarrow \Re$ is the reward function, and $\gamma \in [0, 1]$ a discount factor weighting long-term rewards. At any given time step i the agent is in a state $s_i \in S$. When the agent performs an action $\alpha_i \in A$ following a policy $\pi : S \rightarrow A$, it receives a reward $r_i(s_i, \alpha_i) \in \Re$ and transitions to state $s_i^{'}$ according to $P(s_i^{'}|s_i, \alpha_i) \in P$. The quality of the policy π followed by the agent is measured by the *expected future reward* also called Q-function, $Q^{\pi} : S \times A \rightarrow \Re$.

To estimate the Q-function we use Least-Squares Policy Iteration (LSPI) (Lagoudakis and Parr, 2003; Li et al., 2009). LSPI can learn directly from a corpus of dialogues and is sample efficient. We use linear function approximation of the Q-function. Thus $Q(s, \alpha) = \sum_{i=1}^{k} w_i \phi_i(s, \alpha)$ where s is the state that the agent is in and α the action that it performs in this state, and $\hat{w}$ is a vector of weights w_i for the feature functions $\phi_i(s, \alpha)$. The magnitude of a weight w_i shows the contribution of the feature $\phi_i(s, \alpha)$ to the $Q(s, \alpha)$ value.

3 Learning Argumentation Policies

In our experiments, two agents negotiate on two issues that are independent of each other. Each issue may have three possible outcomes. Our approach can be applied to any such issues. For the sake of readability, from now on we will use a negotiation scenario in which Agents 1 and 2 are having a party and need to agree on the type of food that will be served (Thai, Italian, Mexican) and the day of the week that the party will be held (Friday, Saturday, Sunday). Agents 1 and 2 have different goals. Table 1 shows the points that Agents 1 and 2 earn for each negotiation outcome.

We build hand-crafted simulated negotiators (SNs) for the two agents that interact with each other to generate simulated corpora. The SNs differ not only in their goals but also in whether they use strong or weak arguments to persuade

	Agent 1	**Agent 2**
Food type		
Thai	200	0
Italian	100	40
Mexican	0	80
Day of the week		
Friday	80	0
Saturday	40	100
Sunday	0	200

Table 1: Rewards for Agents 1 and 2.

their counterparts, and sometimes make irrational moves, i.e., moves not consistent with their goals. For example, Agent 1 may reject an offer for "Thai" food, and Agent 2 may offer or accept "Friday". This is to generate a variety of negotiation patterns. There is also some randomness regarding whether the SN will start the conversation by a direct offer or by providing an argument.

The SNs for Agents 1 and 2 can choose among 13 actions: "offer-Thai", "offer-Italian", "offer-Mexican", "offer-Friday", "offer-Saturday", "offer-Sunday", "provide-argument-Thai", "provide-argument-Mexican", "provide-argument-Friday", "provide-argument-Sunday", "accept", "reject", "release-turn". In our setup Agents 1 and 2 do not provide arguments for "Italian" or "Saturday" since these are acceptable options for both agents. Because Agent 1 cares more about the food type and Agent 2 cares more about the day there is potential for trade-offs, i.e., "I'll give you the food type that you want if you agree on the day that I want". So we have one more action "trade-off" which is basically a combined action "offer-Thai, offer-Sunday". The two agents have to agree on both issues for the dialogue to end. If there is no agreement in 40 turns then the dialogue stops.

Note that for testing our learned policies (see section 4) we use a rationalized version of these SNs. For example, Agent 1 never offers "Sunday" and never accepts "Mexican". We will refer to the SNs that exhibit some degree of randomness and irrationality as "semi-rational" and the SNs that always behave rationally as "rational".

For training, 4 corpora are generated (50,000 dialogues each) using different SNs, each of which is limited to using either strong or weak arguments: SN for Agent 1 with strong arguments vs. SN for Agent 2 with strong arguments, SN for Agent 1 with strong arguments vs. SN for Agent 2 with weak arguments, SN for Agent 1 with weak arguments vs. SN for Agent 2 with strong arguments, and SN for Agent 1 with weak arguments vs. SN for Agent 2 with weak arguments.

We use LSPI to learn policies directly from the 4 corpora. Each agent is rewarded only at the end of the dialogue based on the agreement. So if the outcome is "Thai" and "Saturday" Agent 1 will earn 240 points and Agent 2 100 points. We set a small reward +1 point for each policy action taken. Table 2 shows our state representation.

The first 10 state variables are self-explanatory. Below we explain how the "counter" variables work. Initially the counter for "Thai" arguments is set to 0 and Agent 2 supports food type "Mexican". Every time the policy of Agent 1 provides an argument in favor of "Thai", the counter for "Thai" arguments is increased by 1 and the counter for "Mexican" arguments is decreased by 1 (like a penalty). Every time the policy of Agent 1 argues in favor of "Mexican" the counter for "Thai" arguments is decreased by 1 and the counter for "Mexican" arguments is increased by 1. When the counter for "Thai" arguments becomes 3, then the state variable "Thai-argument-counter-reached-threshold" becomes "yes" and Agent 2 is ready to yield to the demands of Agent 1. This threshold of 3 was set empirically after experimentation. Likewise for the rest of the "counter" variables. We also account for both strong and weak arguments. When the arguments of an agent are weak, even if the corresponding counters exceed the predefined threshold and the associated state variables change from "no" to "yes", the behavior of their interlocutor will not change. This is to simulate the fact that weak arguments cannot be persuasive. The release action counter works similarly. Initially it is 0 but after 4 consecutive actions of the same speaker it is set to 1 to ensure that the turns are not very long.

There are 786,432 possible states and 11,010,048 possible Q-values (state-action pairs). We use linear function approximation with 1,680 manually selected features. The rationale for selecting these features is as follows: We associate the action "offer-Thai" with the state variables "current-day-accepted", "Thai-rejected", "Italian-rejected", "Mexican-rejected", "Thai-argument-counter-reached-threshold", and "Mexican-argument-counter-reached-threshold". Thus we assume that the values of the other state variables are irrelevant. This is an approximation (to keep the number of features manageable) that has drawbacks, e.g., we may have an "offer-Thai" action even though the food type agreed so far is "Thai" (because there is no feature to associate the currently accepted food type value with a "Thai" offer). With this configuration we end up having $4 \times 2^5 = 128$ binary features just for the action "offer-Thai". Similarly, features are selected for the rest of the actions.

Current offer on the table (null/Thai/Italian/ Mexican/Friday/Saturday/Sunday/trade-off)
By whom is the current offer on the table (null/Agent1/Agent2)
Currently accepted food type (null/Thai/Italian/Mexican)
Currently accepted day (null/Friday/ Saturday/Sunday)
Has food type Thai been rejected? (no/yes)
Has food type Italian been rejected? (no/yes)
Has food type Mexican been rejected? (no/yes)
Has day Friday been rejected? (no/yes)
Has day Saturday been rejected? (no/yes)
Has day Sunday been rejected? (no/yes)
Has counter for food type Thai arguments reached threshold? (no/yes)
Has counter for food type Mexican arguments reached threshold? (no/yes)
Has counter for day Friday arguments reached threshold? (no/yes)
Has counter for day Sunday arguments reached threshold? (no/yes)
Has release action counter reached threshold (no/yes)

Table 2: State variables that we keep track of and all the possible values they can take.

We partition each one of our 4 simulated corpora into 5 subsets of 10,000 dialogues each. Each partition is processed independently and will be referred to as trial. We train policies for each trial of each corpus type (20 policies for each agent). Thus we end up with the following 4 types of policies for Agent 1 (and likewise for the policies of Agent 2): Agent 1 with strong arguments trained against Agent 2 with strong arguments (Agent 1 S(S)); Agent 1 with strong arguments trained against Agent 2 with weak arguments (Agent 1 S(W)); Agent 1 with weak arguments trained against Agent 2 with strong arguments (Agent 1 W(S)); and Agent 1 with weak arguments trained against Agent 2 with weak arguments (Agent 1 W(W)).

	Policy Score	Opponent Score	Policy #Actions	Opponent #Actions	Policy #Turns	Opponent #Turns
Agent 1 S(S) vs. Agent 2 S	214.3	164.3	7.6	6.2	2.0	1.6
Agent 1 S(S) vs. Agent 2 W	214.1	164.5	7.4	6.1	2.0	1.6
Agent 1 S(W) vs. Agent 2 S	213.9	165.1	7.6	6.2	2.0	1.6
Agent 1 S(W) vs. Agent 2 W	214.1	164.7	7.4	6.1	2.0	1.6
Agent 1 W(S) vs. Agent 2 S	192.4	196.5	9.1	8.5	2.5	2.4
Agent 1 W(S) vs. Agent 2 W	197.9	198.9	7.6	7.0	2.1	1.9
Agent 1 W(W) vs. Agent 2 S	195.0	197.9	8.8	8.5	2.5	2.4
Agent 1 W(W) vs. Agent 2 W	198.1	199.0	7.7	7.0	2.2	2.0

Table 3: Results of different training and testing combinations for learned policies of Agent 1 and rational SNs for Agent 2.

4 Evaluation

Each policy of Agent 1 resulting from a trial is evaluated against two hand-crafted SNs for Agent 2, one where Agent 2 provides strong arguments (Agent 2 S) and one where Agent 2 provides weak arguments (Agent 2 W). So for the condition "Agent 1 with strong arguments trained against Agent 2 with strong arguments (Agent 1 S(S))" we have 5 policies, each of which interacts with "Agent 2 S" (or "Agent 2 W"). We calculate the averages of the earned points for each of the agents, of the number of actions per dialogue of each agent, and of the number of turns per dialogue of each agent, over 10,000 dialogues per policy. Likewise for the policies of Agent 2. Note that the SNs used in the evaluation do not behave irrationally like the ones used for training, and thus are harder to beat.

In Table 3 we can see the results for the policy of Agent 1. Results for the policy of Agent 2 are similar given that the goals of Agent 2 mirror the goals of Agent 1. As we can see, the policy of Agent 1 with strong arguments learned to provide the appropriate arguments and make Agent 2 agree on "Thai" and "Friday" or "Saturday". When the policy of Agent 1 provides only weak arguments it cannot get day "Friday" but it can secure a trade-off. This is because both the learned policies and the SNs usually accept trade-off offers (due to the way the hand-crafted SNs were constructed). We also performed tests with SNs that did not propose or accept as many trade-offs. This arrangement favored the policy of Agent 1 with strong arguments, and hurt the performance of the policy of Agent 1 with weak arguments playing against Agent 2 with strong arguments. This shows that trade-offs help the weaker negotiators.

Furthermore, we experimented with testing on semi-rational SNs similar to the ones used for training and the results were better for the policy of Agent 1 with weak arguments and worse for the policy of Agent 1 with strong arguments. So like trade-offs a semi-rational SN favors the weaker negotiators.

5 Conclusion

We learned argumentation dialogue policies for two-issue negotiation, using simulated corpora generated from the interaction of two hand-crafted SNs that differed in their goals and in the use of strong and weak arguments to persuade their counterparts. These SNs sometimes made random or irrational moves to generate a variety of negotiation patterns.

We used these simulated corpora and RL to learn argumentation dialogue policies for each of the two agents. Each of the learned policies was evaluated against hand-crafted SNs similar to the ones used for training but with the modification that these SNs no longer made irrational moves and thus were harder to beat. The policies generally did as well as, or better than the hand-crafted SNs showing that RL can be successfully used for learning argumentation dialogue policies in two-issue negotiation scenarios.

For future work we would like to use automatic feature selection (Li et al., 2009; Misu and Kashioka, 2012) and learn policies for more than two issues and more than three outcomes per issue. Selecting features manually is a difficult process that requires a lot of experimentation and trial-and-error.

Acknowledgments

This work was funded by the NSF grant #1117313.

References

Senthilkumar Chandramohan, Matthieu Geist, and Olivier Pietquin. 2010. Sparse approximate dynamic programming for dialog management. In *Proc. of the Annual SIGdial Meeting on Discourse and Dialogue*, pages 107–115, Tokyo, Japan.

Min Chi, Kurt VanLehn, Diane Litman, and Pamela Jordan. 2011. Empirically evaluating the application of reinforcement learning to the induction of effective and adaptive pedagogical strategies. *User Modeling and User-Adapted Interaction*, 21(1-2):137–180.

Milica Gašić, Matthew Henderson, Blaise Thomson, Pirros Tsiakoulis, and Steve Young. 2012. Policy optimisation of POMDP-based dialogue systems without state space compression. In *Proc. of the IEEE Workshop on Spoken Language Technology (SLT)*, pages 31–36, Miami, FL, USA.

Kallirroi Georgila and David Traum. 2011a. Learning culture-specific dialogue models from non culture-specific data. In *Proc. of HCI International, Lecture Notes in Computer Science Vol. 6766*, pages 440–449, Orlando, FL, USA.

Kallirroi Georgila and David Traum. 2011b. Reinforcement learning of argumentation dialogue policies in negotiation. In *Proc. of Interspeech*, pages 2073–2076, Florence, Italy.

Kallirroi Georgila, Maria K. Wolters, and Johanna D. Moore. 2010. Learning dialogue strategies from older and younger simulated users. In *Proc. of the Annual SIGdial Meeting on Discourse and Dialogue*, pages 103–106, Tokyo, Japan.

Peter A. Heeman. 2009. Representing the reinforcement learning state in a negotiation dialogue. In *Proc. of the IEEE Automatic Speech Recognition and Understanding Workshop (ASRU)*, Merano, Italy.

James Henderson, Oliver Lemon, and Kallirroi Georgila. 2008. Hybrid reinforcement/supervised learning of dialogue policies from fixed datasets. *Computational Linguistics*, 34(4):487–511.

S. Janarthanam and O. Lemon. 2010. Adaptive referring expression generation in spoken dialogue systems: Evaluation with real users. In *Proc. of the Annual SIGdial Meeting on Discourse and Dialogue*, pages 124–131, Tokyo, Japan.

Filip Jurčíček, Blaise Thomson, and Steve Young. 2012. Reinforcement learning for parameter estimation in statistical spoken dialogue systems. *Computer Speech and Language*, 26(3):168–192.

Michail G. Lagoudakis and Ronald Parr. 2003. Least-squares policy iteration. *Journal of Machine Learning Research*, 4:1107–1149.

Lihong Li, Jason D. Williams, and Suhrid Balakrishnan. 2009. Reinforcement learning for dialog management using least-squares policy iteration and fast feature selection. In *Proc. of Interspeech*, pages 2475–2478, Brighton, United Kingdom.

Teruhisa Misu and Hideki Kashioka. 2012. Simultaneous feature selection and parameter optimization for training of dialogue policy by reinforcement learning. In *Proc. of the IEEE Workshop on Spoken Language Technology (SLT)*, pages 1–6, Miami, FL, USA.

Teruhisa Misu, Komei Sugiura, Kiyonori Ohtake, Chiori Hori, Hideki Kashioka, Hisashi Kawai, and Satoshi Nakamura. 2010. Modeling spoken decision making dialogue and optimization of its dialogue strategy. In *Proc. of the Annual SIGdial Meeting on Discourse and Dialogue*, pages 221–224, Tokyo, Japan.

Teruhisa Misu, Kallirroi Georgila, Anton Leuski, and David Traum. 2012. Reinforcement learning of question-answering dialogue policies for virtual museum guides. In *Proc. of the Annual SIGdial Meeting on Discourse and Dialogue*, pages 84–93, Seoul, South Korea.

Elnaz Nouri, Kallirroi Georgila, and David Traum. 2012. A cultural decision-making model for negotiation based on inverse reinforcement learning. In *Proc. of the Annual Meeting of the Cognitive Science Society (CogSci)*, pages 2097–2102, Sapporo, Japan.

P. Paruchuri, N. Chakraborty, R. Zivan, K. Sycara, M. Dudik, and G. Gordon. 2009. POMDP based negotiation modeling. In *Proc. of the IJCAI Workshop on Modeling Intercultural Collaboration and Negotiation (MICON)*.

Csaba Szepesvári. 2010. *Algorithms for Reinforcement Learning*. Morgan & Claypool Publishers.

Joel R. Tetreault and Diane J. Litman. 2008. A reinforcement learning approach to evaluating state representations in spoken dialogue systems. *Speech Communication*, 50(8-9):683–696.

Jason D. Williams and Steve Young. 2007. Scaling POMDPs for spoken dialog management. *IEEE Trans. on Audio, Speech, and Language Processing*, 15(7):2116–2129.

Dialogue Act Recognition in Synchronous and Asynchronous Conversations

Maryam Tavafi†, Yashar Mehdad†, Shafiq Joty‡, Giuseppe Carenini†, Raymond Ng†
†Department of Computer Science, University of British Columbia, Vancouver, Canada
‡Qatar Computing Research Institute, Qatar Foundation, Doha, Qatar
†{tavafi, mehdad, carenini, rng}@cs.ubc.ca ‡sjoty@qf.org.qa

Abstract

In this work, we study the effectiveness of state-of-the-art, sophisticated supervised learning algorithms for dialogue act modeling across a comprehensive set of different spoken and written conversations including: emails, forums, meetings, and phone conversations. To this aim, we compare the results of SVM-multiclass and two structured predictors namely SVM-hmm and CRF algorithms. Extensive empirical results, across different conversational modalities, demonstrate the effectiveness of our SVM-hmm model for dialogue act recognition in conversations.

1 Introduction

Revealing the underlying conversational structure in dialogues is important for detecting the human social intentions in spoken conversations and in many applications including summarization (Murray, 2010), dialogue systems and dialogue games (Carlson, 1983) and flirt detection (Ranganath, 2009). As an additional example, Ravi and Kim (2007) show that dialogue acts can be used for analyzing the interaction of students in educational forums.

Recently, there have been increasing interests for dialogue act (DA) recognition in spoken and written conversations, which include meetings, phone conversations, emails and blogs. However, most of the previous works are specific to one of these domains. There are potentially useful features and algorithms for each of these domains, but due to the underlying similarities between these types of conversations, we aim to identify a domain-independent DA modeling approach that can achieve good results across all types of conversations. Such a domain-independent dialogue act recognizer makes it possible to automatically recognize dialogue acts in a wide variety of conversational data, as well as in conversations spanning multiple domains/modalities; for instance a conversation that starts in a meeting and then continues via email.

While previous work in DA modeling has focused on studying only one (Carvalho, 2005; Shrestha, 2004; Ravi, 2007; Ferschke, 2012; Kim, 2010a; Sun, 2012) or, in a few cases, a couple of conversational domains (Jeong, 2009; Joty, 2011), in this paper, we analyze the performance of supervised DA modeling on a comprehensive set of different spoken and written conversations that includes: emails, forums, meetings, and phone conversations. More specifically, we compare the performance of three state-of-the-art, sophisticated machine learning algorithms, which include SVM-multiclass and two structured predictors SVM-hmm and Conditional Random Fields (CRF) for DA modeling. We present an extensive set of experiments studying the effectiveness of DA modeling on different types of conversations such as emails, forums, meeting, and phone discussions. The experimental results show that the SVM-hmm algorithm outperforms other supervised algorithms across all datasets.

2 Related Work

There have been several studies on supervised dialogue act (DA) modeling. To the best of our knowledge, none of them compare the performance of DA recognition on different synchronous (e.g., meeting and phone) and asynchronous (e.g., email and forum) conversations. Most of the works analyze DA modeling in a specific domain. Carvalho and Cohen (2005) propose classifying emails into their dialogue acts according to two ontologies for nouns and verbs. The ontologies are used for determining the speech acts of each single email with verb-noun pairs. Shrestha and McKeown (2004) also study the problem of DA modeling in email conversations considering the two dialogue acts of *question* and *answer*. Likewise, Ravi and Kin (2007) present a DA recognition method for detecting questions and answers in educational discussions. Ferschke et al. (2012) apply DA modeling to Wikipedia discussions to analyze the collaborative process of editing Wikipedia pages. Kim et al. (2010a) study the task of supervised classification of dialogue acts in one-to-one online chats in the shopping domain.

All these previous studies focus on DA recognition in one or two domains, and do not systematically analyze the performance of different dialog act modeling approaches on a comprehensive set of conversation domains. As far as we know, the present work is the first that proposes domain-independent supervised DA modeling techniques, and analyzes their effectiveness on different modalities of conversations.

3 Dialogue Act Recognition

3.1 Conversational structure

Adjacent utterances in a conversation have a strong correlation in terms of their dialogue acts. As an example, if speaker 1 asks a question to speaker 2, it is a high probability that the next utterance of the conversation would be an answer from speaker 2. Therefore, the conversational structure is a paramount factor that should be taken into account for automatic DA modeling. The conversational structure differs in spoken and written discussions. In spoken conversations, the discussion between the speakers is synchronized. The speakers hear each other's ideas and then state their opinions. So the temporal order of the utterances can be considered as the conversational structure in these types of conversations. However, in written conversations such as email and forum, authors contribute to the discussion in different order, and sometimes they do not pay attention to the content of previous posts. Therefore, the temporal order of the conversation cannot be used as the conversational structure in these domains, and appropriate techniques should be used to extract the underlying structure in these conversations.

To this aim, when reply links are available in the dataset, we use them to capture the conversation structure. To obtain a conversational structure that is often even more refined than the reply links, we build the Fragment Quotation Graph. To this end, we follow the procedure proposed by Joty et al. (2011) to extract the graph structure of a thread.

3.2 Features

In defining the feature set, we have two primary criteria, being domain independent and effectiveness in previous works. Lexical features such as unigrams and bigrams have been shown to be useful for the task of DA modeling in previous studies (Sun, 2012; Ferschke, 2012; Kim, 2010a; Ravi, 2007; Carvalho, 2005). In addition, unigrams have been shown to be the most effective among the two. So, as the lexical feature, we include the frequency of unigrams in our feature set.

Moreover, length of the utterance is another beneficial feature for DA recognition (Ferschke, 2012; Shrestha, 2004; Joty, 2011), which we add to our feature set. The speaker of an utterance has shown its utility for recognizing speech acts (Sun, 2012; Kim, 2010a; Joty, 2011). Sun and Morency (2012) specifically employ a speaker-adaptation technique to demonstrate the effectiveness of this feature for DA modeling. We also include the relative position of a sentence in a post for DA modeling since most of previous studies (Ferschke, 2012; Kim, 2010a; Joty, 2011) prove the efficiency of this feature.

3.3 Algorithms

Since most top performing DA models use supervised approaches (Carvalho, 2005; Shrestha, 2004; Ravi, 2007; Ferschke, 2012; Kim, 2010a), to analyze the performance of DA modeling on a comprehensive set of different spoken and written conversations, we compare the state-of-the-art supervised algorithms.

We employ three state-of-the-art, sophisticated supervised learning algorithms:

SVM-hmm predicts labels for the examples in a sequence (Tsochantaridis, 2004). This approach uses the Viterbi algorithm to find the highest scoring tag sequence for a given observation sequence. Being a Hidden Markov Model (HMM), the model makes the Markov assumption, which means that the label of a particular example is assigned only by considering the label of the previous example. This approach is considered an SVM because the parameters of the model are trained discriminatively to separate the label of sequences by a large margin.

CRF is a probabilistic framework to label and segment sequence data (Lafferty, 2001). The main advantage of CRF over HMM is that it relaxes the assumption of conditional independence of observed data. HMM is a generative model that assigns a joint distribution over label and observation sequences. Whereas, CRF defines the conditional probability distribution over label sequences given a particular observation sequence.

SVM-multiclass is a generalization of binary SVM to a multiclass predictor (Crammer, 2001). The SVM-multiclass does not consider the sequential dependency between the examples.

4 Corpora

Gathering conversational corpora for DA modeling is an expensive and time-consuming task. Due to the privacy issues, there are few available conversational datasets.

For asynchronous conversations, we use available corpora for email and forum discussions. For synchronous domains we employ available corpora in multi-party meeting and phone conversations.

BC3 (Email): As the labeled dataset for email conversations, we use BC3 (Ulrich, 2008), which contains 40 threads from W3C corpus. The BC3 corpus is annotated with twelve domain-independent dialogue acts, which are mainly adopted from the MRDA tagset, and it has been used in several previous works (e.g., (Joty, 2011)).

CNET (Forum): As the labeled forum dataset, we use the available CNET corpus, which is annotated with eleven domain-independent dialogue acts in a post-level (Kim et al, 2010b). This corpus consists of 320 threads and a total of 1332 posts, which are mostly from technical forums.

MRDA (Meeting): ICSI-MRDA dataset is used as labeled data for meeting conversation, which contains 75 meetings with 53 unique speakers (Shriberg, 2004). The ICSI-MRDA dataset requires one general tag per sentence followed by variable number of specific tags. There are 11 general tags and 39 specific tags in the annotation scheme. We reduce their tagset to the eleven general tags to be consistent with the other datasets.

SWBD (Phone): In addition to multi-party meeting conversations, we also report our experimental results on Switchboard-DAMSL (SWBD), which is a large-scale corpus containing telephone speech (Jurafsky, 1997). This corpus is annotated with the SWBD-DAMSL tagset, which consists of 220 tags. We use the mapping table presented by Jeong (2009) to reduce the tagset to 16 domain-independent dialogue acts.

All the available corpora are annotated with dialogue acts at the sentence-level. The only exception is the CNET forum dataset, on which we apply DA classification at the post-level.

5 Experiments and Results

5.1 Experimental settings

In our experiments, we use the SVM-hmm[1] and SVM-multiclass[2] packages developed with the SVM-light software. We use the Mallet package[3] for the CRF algorithm. The results of supervised classifications are compared to the baseline, which is the majority class of each dataset. We apply 5-fold cross-validation for the supervised learning methods to each dataset, and compare the results of different methods using micro-averaged and macro-averaged accuracies.

5.2 Results

Table 1 shows the results of supervised classification on different conversation modalities. We observe that SVM-hmm and CRF classifiers outperform SVM-multiclass classifier in all conversational domains. Both SVM-hmm and CRF classifiers consider the sequential structure of conversations, while this is ignored in the SVM-multiclass classifier. This shows that the sequential structure of the conversation is beneficial independently of the conversational modality. We can also observe that the SVM-hmm algorithm results in the highest performance in all datasets. As shown in (Altun, 2003), generalization performace of SVM-hmm is superior to CRF. This superiority also applies to the DA modeling task across all the conversational modalities. However, as it was investigated by Keerthi and Sundararajan (2007), the discrepancy in the performance of these methods may arise from different feature functions that these two methods use, and they might perform similarly when they use the same feature functions.

Comparing the results across different datasets, we can also note that the largest improvement of SVM-hmm and CRF is on the SWBD, the

[1]http://www.cs.cornell.edu/people/tj/svm_light/svm_hmm.html
[2]http://svmlight.joachims.org/svm_multiclass.html
[3]http://mallet.cs.umass.edu

Corpus	Baseline		SVM-multiclass		SVM-hmm		CRF	
	Micro	Macro	Micro	Macro	Micro	Macro	Micro	Macro
BC3	69.56	8.34	73.57 (4.01)	8.34 (0)	**77.75 (8.19)**	**18.20 (9.86)**	72.18 (2.62)	14.9 (6.56)
CNET	36.75	9.09	34.8 (-1.95)	9.3 (0.21)	**58.7 (21.95)**	**17.1 (8.01)**	40.3 (3.55)	11.5 (2.41)
MRDA	66.47	9.09	66.47 (0)	9.09 (0)	**80.5 (14.03)**	**32.4 (23.31)**	77.8 (11.33)	22.9 (13.81)
SWBD	46.44	6.25	46.5 (0.06)	6.25 (0)	**74.32 (27.88)**	**30.13 (23.88)**	73.04 (26.6)	24.05 (17.8)

Table 1: Results of supervised DA modeling; columns are micro-averaged and macro-averaged accuracies with difference with baseline in parentheses.

phone conversation dataset. Moreover, supervised DA recognition on synchronous conversations achieves a better performance than on asynchronous conversations. We can argue that this is due to the less complex sequential structure of synchronous conversations. A lower macro-averaged accuracy in asynchronous conversations (i.e., forums and emails) can be justified in the same way.

By looking at the results in asynchronous conversations, we observe a larger improvement of micro-averaged accuracy over the CNET corpus. This might be due to two reasons: *i)* the DA tagsets in both corpora are different (i.e., no overlap in tagsets); and *ii)* the conversational structure in forums and emails is different.

5.3 Discussion

We analyze the strengths and weakness of supervised DA modeling with SVM-hmm in different conversations individually.

BC3: SVM-hmm succeeds in classifying most of the *statement* and *yes-no question* speech acts in the BC3 corpus. However, it does not show a high accuracy for classifying *polite mechanisms* such as 'thanks' and 'regards'. Through the error analysis, we observed that in most of these cases the error arose from the voting algorithm. Moreover, the improvement of supervised DA modeling on the BC3 corpus is smaller than the other datasets. This may suggest that email conversation is a challenging domain for DA recognition.

CNET: The inventory of dialogue acts in the CNET dataset can be considered as two groups of *question* and *answer* dialogue acts, and we would need more sophisticated features in order to classify the posts into the fine-grained dialogue acts. The SVM-hmm succeeds in predicting the labels of *question-question* and *answer-answer* dialogue acts, but it performs poorly for the other labels. The improvement of DA modeling over the baseline is significant for this dataset. To further improve the performance, a hierarchical DA classification can be applied. In this way, the posts would be classified into *question* and *non-question* dialogue acts in the first level.

MRDA: SVM-hmm performs well for predicting the classes of *statement*, *floor holder*, *backchannel*, and *wh-question*. *Floor holders* and *backchannels* are mostly the short utterances such as 'ok', 'um', and 'so', and we believe the length and unigrams features are very effective for predicting these dialogue acts. On the other hand, SVM-hmm fails in predicting the other types of questions such as *rhetorical questions* and *open-ended questions* by classifying them as *statements*. Arguably by adding more sophisticated features such as POS tags, SVM-hmm would perform better for classifying these speech acts.

SWBD: The improvement of supervised DA recognition on the SWBD is higher than the other domains. Supervised DA classification correctly predicts most of the classes of *statement*, *reject response*, *wh-question*, and *backchannel*. However, SVM-hmm cannot predict some specific dialogue acts of phone conversations such as *self-talk* and *signal-non-understanding*. There are a few utterances in the corpus with these dialogue acts, and most of them are classified as *statements*.

6 Conclusion and Future Work

We have studied the effectiveness of sophisticated supervised learning algorithms for DA modeling across a comprehensive set of different spoken and written conversations. Through an extensive experiment, we have shown that our proposed SVM-hmm algorithm with the domain-independent feature set can achieve high results on different synchronous and asynchronous conversations.

In future, we will incorporate other lexical and syntactic features in our supervised framework. We also plan to augment our feature set with domain-specific features like prosodic features for spoken conversations. We will also investigate the performance of our domain-independent approach in a semi-supervised framework.

References

Congkai Sun and Louise-Philippe Morency. 2012. *Dialogue Act Recognition using Reweighted Speaker Adaptation.* 13th Annual SIGdial Meeting on Discourse and Dialogue.

Dan Jurafsky, Elizabeth Shriberg, and Debra Biasca. 1997. *Switchboard SWBD-DAMSL labeling project coder's manual, draft 13.* Technical report, Univ. of Colorado Institute of Cognitive Science.

Elizabeth Shriberg, Raj Dhillon, Sonali Bhagat, Jeremy Ang, and Hannah Carvey. 2004. *The ICSI Meeting Recorder Dialog Act (MRDA) Corpus.* HLT-NAACL SIGDIAL Workshop.

Gabriel Murray, Giuseppe Carenini, and Raymond T. Ng. 2010. *Generating and validating abstracts of meeting conversations: a user study.* INLG'10.

Ioannis Tsochantaridis, Thomas Hofmann, Thorsten Joachims, and Yasemin Altun. 2004. *Support vector machine learning for interdependent and structured output spaces.* Proceedings of the 21st International Conference on Machine Learning (ICML).

Jan Ulrich, Gabriel Murray, and Giuseppe Carenini. 2008. *A publicly available annotated corpus for supervised email summarization.* EMAIL'08 Workshop. AAAI.

John Lafferty, Andrew McCallum, and Fernando Pereira. 2001. *Conditional random fields: Probabilistic models for segmenting and labeling sequence data.* Intl. Conf. on Machine Learning.

Koby Crammer and Yoram Singer. 2001. *On the algorithmic implementation of multiclass kernel-based vector machines.* Journal of Machine Learning Research.

Lari Carlson. 1983. *Dialogue Games: An Approach to Discourse Analysis.* D. Reidel.

Lokesh Shrestha and Kathleen McKeown. 2004. *Detection of question-answer pairs in email conversations.* Proceedings of the 20th Biennial Int. Conf. on Computational Linguistics.

Minwoo Jeong, Chin-Yew Lin, and Gary G. Lee. 2009. *The Semi-supervised speech act recognition in emails and forums.* Proceedings of the 2009 Conf. Empirical Methods in Natural Language Processing.

Oliver Ferschke, Iryna Gurevych, and Yevgen Chebotar. 2012. *Behind the Article: Recognizing Dialog Acts in Wikipedia Talk Pages.* Proceedings of the 13th Conference of the European Chapter of the ACL.

Rajesh Ranganath, Dan Jurafsky, and Dan Mcfarland. 2009. *Its not you, its me: Detecting flirting and its misperception in speed-dates.* EMNLP-09.

S. S. Keerthi and S. Sundararajan. 2007. *CRF versus SVM-Struct for sequence labeling.* Technical report, Yahoo Research.

Shafiq R. Joty, Giuseppe Carenini, and Chin-Yew Lin. 2011. *Unsupervised modeling of dialog acts in asynchronous conversations.* IJCAI.

Su N. Kim, Lawrence Cavedon, and Timothy Baldwin. 2010a. *Classifying dialogue acts in one-on-one live chats.* EMNLP'10.

Su N. Kim, Li Wang, and Timothy Baldwin. 2010b. *Tagging and linking web forum posts.* Proceedings of the Fourteenth Conference on Computational Natural Language Learning, CoNLL '10.

Sujith Ravi and Jihie Kim. 2007. *Profiling student interactions in threaded discussions with speech act classifiers.* AIED'07, LA, USA.

Vitor R. Carvalho and William W. Cohen. 2005. *On the collective classification of email "speech acts".* Proceedings of the 31st Annual Int. ACM SIGIR Conf. on Research and Development in Information Retrieval.

Yasemin Altun and Ioannis Tsochantaridis and Thomas Hofmann. 2003. *Hidden Markov Support Vector Machines.* Proceedings of the 20th International Conference on Machine Learning.

7 Appendix A. Frequency of Dialogue Acts in the Corpora

Tag	Dialogue Acts	Email (BC3)	Forum (CNET)	Meeting (MRDA)	Phone (SWBD)
A	Accept response	2.07%	–	–	6.96%
AA	Acknowledge and appreciate	1.24%	–	–	2.12%
AC	Action motivator	6.09%	–	–	0.38%
P	Polite mechanism	6.97%	–	–	0.12%
QH	Rhetorical question	0.75%	–	0.34%	0.25%
QO	Open-ended question	1.32%	–	0.17%	0.3%
QR	Or/or-clause question	1.10%	–	–	0.2%
QW	Wh-question	2.29%	–	1.63%	0.95%
QY	Yes-no question	6.75%	–	4.75%	2.62%
R	Reject response	1.06%	–	–	1.03%
S	Statement	**69.56%**	–	**66.47%**	**46.44%**
U	Uncertain response	0.79%	–	–	0.15%
Z	Hedge	–	–	–	11.55%
B	Backchannel	–	–	14.44%	26.62%
D	Self-talk	–	–	–	0.1%
C	Signal-non-understanding	–	–	–	0.14%
FH	Floor holder	–	–	7.96%	–
FG	Floor grabber	–	–	2.96%	–
H	Hold	–	–	0.76%	–
QRR	Or clause after yes-no question	–	–	0.38%	–
QR	Or question	–	–	0.2%	–
QQ	Question-question	–	27.92%	–	–
QA	Question-add	–	11.67%	–	–
QCN	Question-confirmation	–	3.89%	–	–
QCC	Question-correction	–	0.36%	–	–
AA	Answer-answer	–	**36.75%**	–	–
AD	Answer-add	–	8.84%	–	–
AC	Answer-confirmation	–	0.36%	–	–
RP	Reproduction	–	0.71%	–	–
AO	Answer-objection	–	1.07%	–	–
RS	Resolution	–	7.78%	–	–
O	Other	–	0.71%	–	–

Table 2: Dialogue act categories and their relative frequency.

Table 2 indicates the dialogue acts of each corpus and their relative frequencies in that dataset. The table shows that the distribution of dialogue acts in the datasets are not balanced. Most of the utterances in the datasets are labeled as *statements*. Consequently, during the classification step, most of the utterances are labeled as the *statement* dialogue act. This always affects the performance of a classifier in dealing with low frequency classes. A possible approach to tackle this problem is to cluster the correlative dialogue acts into the same group and apply a DA modeling approach in a hierarchical manner.

Improving Interaction Quality Recognition Using Error Correction

Stefan Ultes
Ulm University
Albert-Einstein-Allee 43
89081 Ulm, Germany
stefan.ultes@uni-ulm.de

Wolfgang Minker
Ulm University
Albert-Einstein-Allee 43
89081 Ulm, Germany
wolfgang.minker@uni-ulm.de

Abstract

Determining the quality of an ongoing interaction in the field of Spoken Dialogue Systems is a hard task. While existing methods employing automatic estimation already achieve reasonable results, still there is a lot of room for improvement. Hence, we aim at tackling the task by estimating the error of the applied statistical classification algorithms in a two-stage approach. Correcting the hypotheses using the estimated model error increases performance by up to 4.1 % relative improvement in Unweighted Average Recall.

1 Introduction

Evaluating the quality of Spoken Dialogue Systems (SDSs) has long since been a challenging task. While objective metrics like *task completion* and *dialogue duration* are not human-centered, subjective measures compensate for this by modeling the user's subjective experience. This information may be used to increase the dialogue system's performance (cf. (Ultes et al., 2012b)).

In human-machine dialogues, however, there is no easy way of deriving the user's satisfaction level. Moreover, asking real users for answering questions about the system performance requires them to spend more time talking to the machine than necessary. It can be assumed that a regular user does not want to do this as human-machine dialogues usually have no conversational character but are task oriented. Hence, automatic approaches are the preferred choice.

Famous work on determining the satisfaction level automatically is the PARADISE framework by Walker et al. (1997). Assuming a linear dependency between objective measures and User Satisfaction (US), a linear regression model is applied to determine US on the *dialogue level*. This is not only very costly, as dialogues must be performed with real users, but also inadequate if quality on a finer level is of interest, e.g., on the *exchange level*.

To overcome this issue, work by Schmitt et al. (2011) introduced a new metric for measuring the performance of an SDS on the *exchange level* called Interaction Quality (IQ). They used statistical classification methods to automatically derive the quality based on interaction parameters. Quality labels were applied by expert raters *after* the dialogue on the exchange level, i.e., for each system-user-exchange. Automatically derived parameters were then used as features for creating a statistical classification model using static feature vectors. Based on the same data, Ultes et al. (2012a) put an emphasis on the sequential character of the IQ measure by applying temporal statistical classification using Hidden Markov Models (HMMs) and Continuous Hidden Markov Models (CHMMs).

However, statistical classifiers usually do not achieve perfect performance, i.e., there will always be misclassification. While most work focuses on applying different statistical models and improving them (Section 2), learning the error to correct the result afterwards represents a different approach. Therefore, we present our approach on estimating the error of IQ recognition models to correct their hypothesis in order to eventually yield better recognition rates (Section 4). The definition of IQ and data used for the evaluation of our approach (Section 5) is presented in Section 3. Our approach is also compared to a simple hierarchical approach also discussed in Section 5.

2 Related Work on Dialogue Quality

Besides Schmitt et al., other research groups have performed numerous work on predicting subjective quality measures on an exchange level, all not incorporating any form of error correction.

Engelbrecht et al. (2009) presented an approach using Hidden Markov Models (HMMs) to model

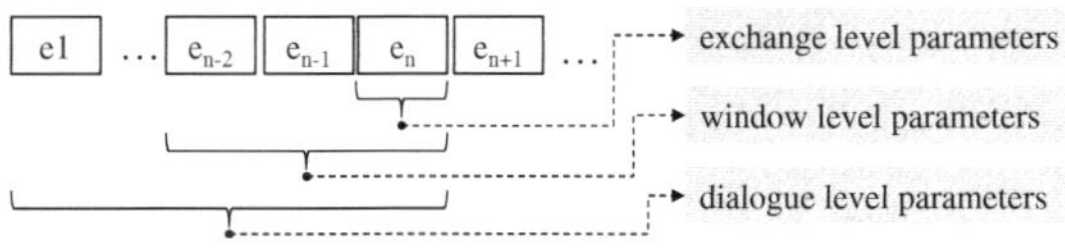

Figure 1: The three different modeling levels representing the interaction at exchange e_n.

the SDS as a process evolving over time. Performance ratings on a 5 point scale ("bad", "poor", "fair", "good", "excellent") have been applied by the users during the dialogue.

Higashinaka et al. (2010) proposed a model for predicting turn-wise ratings for human-human dialogues analyzed on a transcribed conversation and human-machine dialogues with text from a chat system. Ratings ranging from 1 to 7 were applied by two expert raters labeling for smoothness, closeness, and willingness.

Hara et al. (2010) derived turn level ratings from overall ratings of the dialogue which were applied by the users *afterwards* on a five point scale. Using n-grams to model the dialogue, results for distinguishing between six classes at any point in the dialogue showed to be hardly above chance.

3 The LEGO Corpus

For estimating the Interaction Quality (IQ), the LEGO corpus published by Schmitt et al. (2012) is used. IQ is defined similarly to user satisfaction: While the latter represents the true disposition of the user, IQ is the disposition of the user assumed by an expert rater. The LEGO corpus contains 200 calls (4,885 system-user-exchanges) to a bus information system (cf. (Raux et al., 2006)). Labels for IQ on a scale from 1 (extremely unsatisfied) to 5 (satisfied) have been assigned by three expert raters with an inter-rater agreement of $\kappa = 0.54$. In order to ensure consistent labeling, the expert raters had to follow labeling guidelines (cf. (Schmitt et al., 2012)).

Parameters used as input variables for the IQ model have been derived from the dialogue system modules automatically for each exchange on three levels: the *exchange level*, the *dialogue level*, and the *window level* (see Figure 1). As parameters like the confidence of the speech recognizer can directly be acquired from the dialogue modules, they constitute the *exchange level*. Based on this, counts, sums, means, and frequencies of exchange level parameters from multiple exchanges are computed to constitute the *dialogue level* (all exchanges up to the current one) and the *window level* (the three previous exchanges). A complete list of parameters is listed in (Schmitt et al., 2012).

Schmitt et al. (2011) performed IQ recognition on this data using linear SVMs. They achieved an Unweighted Average Recall (UAR) of 0.58 based on 10-fold cross-validation. Ultes et al. (2012a) applied HMMs and CHMMs using 6-fold cross validation and a reduced feature set achieving an UAR of 0.44 for HMMs and 0.39 for CHMMs.

4 Error Estimation Model

Error correction may be incorporated into the statistical classification process by a two-stage approach, which is depicted in Figure 2.

At the first stage, a statistical classification model is created using interaction parameters as input and IQ as target variable. For this work, a Support Vector Machine (SVM) and a Rule Learner are applied. At the second stage, the error e_r of the hypothesis h_0 is calculated by

$$e_r = h_0 - r \;, \tag{1}$$

where the reference r denotes the true IQ value. In order to limit the number of error classes, the signum function is applied. It is defined as

$$\operatorname{sgn}(x) := \begin{cases} -1 & \text{if } x < 0 \;, \\ 0 & \text{if } x = 0 \;, \\ 1 & \text{if } x > 0 \;. \end{cases} \tag{2}$$

Therefore, the error is redefined as

$$e_r = \operatorname{sgn}(h_0 - r) \;. \tag{3}$$

Next, a statistical model is created similarly to stage one but targeting the error e_r. The difference is that the input parameter set is extended by the IQ hypothesis h_0 of stage one. Here, two approaches are applied: Creating one model which estimates all error classes $(-1,0,1)$ and creating two models where each estimates positive $(0,1)$ or negative error $(-1,0)$. For the latter variant, the error of the class which is not estimated by the respective model is mapped to 0. By this, the final error hypothesis h_e may be calculated by simple addition of both estimated error values:

$$h_e = h_{e_{-1}} + h_{e_{+1}} \;. \tag{4}$$

Combining the hypothesis of the error estimation h_e with the hypothesis of the IQ estimation h_0

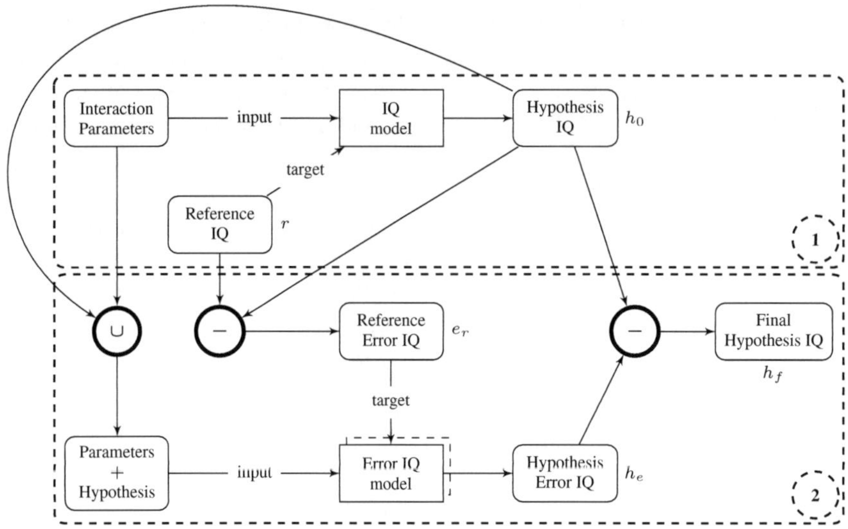

Figure 2: The complete IQ estimation process including error correction. After estimating IQ in Stage 1 (upper frame), the error is estimated and the initial hypothesis is corrected in Stage 2 (lower frame).

at stage one produces the final hypothesis h_f denoting the Interaction Quality estimation corrected by the estimated error of the statistical model:

$$h_f = h_0 - h_e \ . \quad (5)$$

As the error estimation will not work perfectly, it might recognize an error where there is none or – even worse – it might recognize an error contrary to the real error, e.g., -1 instead of $+1$. Therefore, the corrected hypothesis might be out of range. To keep h_f within the defined bounds of IQ, a limiting functions is added to the computation of the final hypothesis resulting in

$$h_f = \max(\min(h_0 - h_e), b_u), b_l) \ , \quad (6)$$

where b_u denotes the upper bound of the IQ labels and b_l the lower bound.

5 Experiments and Results

All experiments are conducted using the LEGO corpus presented in Section 3. By applying 5-fold cross validation, hypotheses for each system-user-exchange which is contained in the LEGO corpus are estimated. Please note that some textual interaction parameters are discarded due to their task-dependent nature leaving 45 parameters[1].

For evaluation, we rely on two measures: The unweighted average recall (UAR) and the root mean squared error (RMSE). UAR represents the accuracy corrected by the effects of unbalanced data and is also used by cited literature. RMSE is used since the error correction method is limited to correcting the results only by one. For bigger errors, the true value cannot be reached.

The performances of two different statistical classification methods are compared, both applied for stage one and stage two: Support Vector Machine (SVM) (Vapnik, 1995) using a linear kernel, which is also used by Schmitt et al. (2011), and Rule Induction (RI) based on Cohen (1995). Furthermore, a normalization component is added performing a range normalization of the input parameters in both stages. This is necessary for using the implementation of the statistical classification algorithms at hand.

For error estimation, two variants are explored: using one combined model for all three error classes (-1,0,$+1$) and using two separate models, one for distinguishing between -1 and 0 and one for distinguishing between $+1$ and 0 with combining their results afterwards. While using RI for error estimation yields reasonable performance results for the combined model, it is not suitable for error estimation using two separate models as all input vectors are mapped to 0. Hence, for the two model approach, only the SVM is applied .

Results for applying error correction (EC) are presented in Table 1. Having an SVM at stage one (column *SVM*), recognition performance is relatively improved by up to 4.6 % using EC. With RI

[1] Removed parameters: Activity, LoopName, Prompt, RoleName, SemanticParse, SystemDialogueAct, UserDialogueAct, Utterance

Table 1: Results for IQ recognition: UAR and RMSE for IQ recognition without stage two, with error correction at stage two, and with a simple hierarchical approach.

	UAR		**RMSE**	
stage two	*SVM*	*RI*	*SVM*	*RI*
none	51.1%	60.3%	0.97	0.88
error correction				
SVM	50.7%	59.6%	0.97	0.83
RI	52.5%	58.1%	0.88	0.85
2xSVM	53.2%	60.6%	0.88	0.85
simple hierarchical approach				
SVM	50.2%	57.6%	0.97	0.85
RI	58.9%	58.7%	0.88	0.88

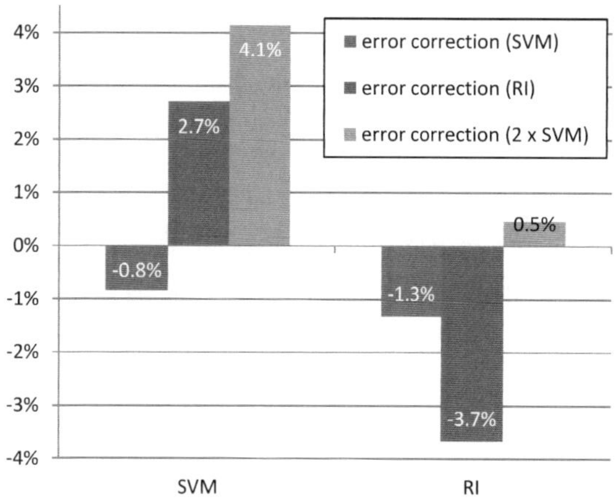

Figure 3: The relative improvement of EC in UAR grouped by stage one classifiers SVM and RI.

at stage one, performance is only increased by up to 0.5 % which has shown to be not significant using the Wilcoxon test. The relative improvements in UAR are depicted in Figure 3.

Furthermore, these results are compared to a simple hierarchical approach (SH) where the hypothesis h_0 of the stage one classifier is used as an additional feature for the stage two classifier targeting IQ directly. Here, the performance of the stage two classifier is of most interest since this approach can be viewed as one stage classification with an additional feature. The results in Table 1 show that RI does not benefit from additional information (comparison of last row with one stage RI recognition). SVM recognition at stage two, though, shows better results. While its performance is reduced using the SVM hypothesis as additional feature, adding the RI hypothesis improved UAR up to 12.6 % relatively. However, there is no reasonable scenario where one would not use the better performing RI in favor of using its results as additional input for SVM recognition.

The question remains why SVM benefits from Error Correction as well as from adding additional input parameters while RI does not. It remains unclear if this is an effect of the task characteristics combined with the characteristics of the classification method. It may as well be caused by low classification performance. A classifier with low performance might be more likely to improve its performance by additional information or EC.

6 Conclusion

In this work, we presented an approach for improving the recognition of Interaction Quality by estimating the error of the classifier in order to correct the hypothesis. For the resulting two-staged approach, two different statistical classification algorithm were applied for both stages, i.e., SVM and Rule Learner. Performance could be improved for both stage one classifiers using separate error models relatively improving IQ recognition by up to 4.1 %. The proposed error correction approach has been compared to a simple hierarchical approach where the hypohtesis of stage one is used as additional feature of stage two classification. This apprach relatively improved SVM recognition by up to 12.6 % using a Rule Learner hypothesis as additional feature. However, as one-stage Rule Learner classification already provides better results than this hierarchical approach, is does not seem reasonable to employ this configuration. Nonethelesse, why only the SVM could benefit from additional information (error correction or simple hierarchical appraach) remains unclear and should be investigated in future work.

Moreover, some aspects of the error correction approach have to be discussed controversially, e.g., applying the signum function for calculating the error. While the obvious advantage is to limit the number of error classes a statistical classification algorithm has to estimate, it also prohibits of being able to correct all errors. If the absolute error is bigger than one it can never be corrected.

Acknowledgments

This work was supported by the Transregional Collaborative Research Centre SFB/TRR 62 "Companion-Technology for Cognitive Technical Systems" which is funded by the German Research Foundation (DFG).

References

William W. Cohen. 1995. Fast effective rule induction. In *Proceedings of the 12th International Conference on Machine Learning*, pages 115–123. Morgan Kaufmann, July.

Klaus-Peter Engelbrecht, Florian Gödde, Felix Hartard, Hamed Ketabdar, and Sebastian Möller. 2009. Modeling user satisfaction with hidden markov model. In *SIGDIAL '09: Proceedings of the SIGDIAL 2009 Conference*, pages 170–177, Morristown, NJ, USA. Association for Computational Linguistics.

Sunao Hara, Norihide Kitaoka, and Kazuya Takeda. 2010. Estimation method of user satisfaction using n-gram-based dialog history model for spoken dialog system. In Nicoletta Calzolari (Conference Chair), Khalid Choukri, Bente Maegaard, Joseph Mariani, Jan Odijk, Stelios Piperidis, Mike Rosner, and Daniel Tapias, editors, *Proceedings of the Seventh conference on International Language Resources and Evaluation (LREC'10)*, Valletta, Malta, May. European Language Resources Association (ELRA).

Ryuichiro Higashinaka, Yasuhiro Minami, Kohji Dohsaka, and Toyomi Meguro. 2010. Issues in predicting user satisfaction transitions in dialogues: Individual differences, evaluation criteria, and prediction models. In Gary Lee, Joseph Mariani, Wolfgang Minker, and Satoshi Nakamura, editors, *Spoken Dialogue Systems for Ambient Environments*, volume 6392 of *Lecture Notes in Computer Science*, pages 48–60. Springer Berlin / Heidelberg. 10.1007/978-3-642-16202-2_5.

Antoine Raux, Dan Bohus, Brian Langner, Alan W. Black, and Maxine Eskenazi. 2006. Doing research on a deployed spoken dialogue system: One year of lets go! experience. In *Proc. of the International Conference on Speech and Language Processing (ICSLP)*, September.

Alexander Schmitt, Benjamin Schatz, and Wolfgang Minker. 2011. Modeling and predicting quality in spoken human-computer interaction. In *Proceedings of the SIGDIAL 2011 Conference*, Portland, Oregon, USA, June. Association for Computational Linguistics.

Alexander Schmitt, Stefan Ultes, and Wolfgang Minker. 2012. A parameterized and annotated corpus of the cmu let's go bus information system. In *International Conference on Language Resources and Evaluation (LREC)*.

Stefan Ultes, Robert ElChabb, and Wolfgang Minker. 2012a. Application and evaluation of a conditioned hidden markov model for estimating interaction quality of spoken dialogue systems. In Joseph Mariani, Laurence Devillers, Martine Garnier-Rizet, and Sophie Rosset, editors, *Proceedings of the 4th International Workshop on Spoken Language Dialog System (IWSDS)*, pages 141–150. Springer, November.

Stefan Ultes, Alexander Schmitt, and Wolfgang Minker. 2012b. Towards quality-adaptive spoken dialogue management. In *NAACL-HLT Workshop on Future directions and needs in the Spoken Dialog Community: Tools and Data (SDCTD 2012)*, pages 49–52, Montréal, Canada, June. Association for Computational Linguistics.

Vladimir N. Vapnik. 1995. *The nature of statistical learning theory*. Springer-Verlag New York, Inc., New York, NY, USA.

Marilyn Walker, Diane Litman, Candace A. Kamm, and Alicia Abella. 1997. Paradise: a framework for evaluating spoken dialogue agents. In *Proceedings of the eighth conference on European chapter of the Association for Computational Linguistics*, pages 271–280, Morristown, NJ, USA. Association for Computational Linguistics.

A Prolog Datamodel for State Chart XML

Stefan Radomski
TU Darmstadt
Telekooperation Group
Hochschulstrasse 10
radomski@tk.informatik.tu-darmstadt.de

Dirk Schnelle-Walka
TU Darmstadt
Telekooperation Group
Hochschulstrasse 10
dirk@tk.informatik.tu-darmstadt.de

Stephan Radeck-Arneth
TU Darmstadt
Telekooperation Group
Hochschulstrasse 10
arneth@rbg.informatik.tu-darmstadt.de

Abstract

SCXML was proposed as one description language for dialog control in the W3C Multimodal Architecture but lacks the facilities required for grounding and reasoning. This prohibits the application of many dialog modeling techniques for multimodal applications following this W3C standard. By extending SCXML with a Prolog datamodel and scripting language, we enable those techniques to be employed again. Thereby bridging the gap between respective dialog modeling research and a standardized architecture to access and coordinate modalities.

1 Introduction

Deploying multimodal applications has long been an activity of custom solutions, each with their own access to modalities, approaches to sensor fusion and fission and techniques for dialog modeling. With the advent of the W3C MMI architecture (Bondell et al., 2012), the W3C proposed a standardized approach to ensure interoperability among its constituting components (Schnelle-Walka et al., 2013; Dahl, 2013).

The architecture proposed by the W3C decomposes a multimodal application into a nested structure of *interaction managers* for dialog control and *modality components* for in- and output. An application is conceived as a set of control documents expressed in SCXML (Barnett et al., 2012) or CCXML (Auburn et al., 2011) for the interaction managers and a set of presentation documents with modality-specific markup for the modality components. A topmost root controller document describes the global dialog and instantiates modality components as required. Each modality component can, in turn, again be an interaction manager, handling more fine granular concerns of dialog control, such as error correction or even sensor fusion/fission.

As one proposed XML dialect for control documents, State Chart XML (SCXML) is given the responsibility to model an applications dialog behavior. SCXML as such is a markup language to express Harel state charts (Harel and Politi, 1998) with nested and parallel machine configurations. The transitions between configurations are triggered by events delivered into the interpreter either from external components or raised by the interpreter itself. Whenever an event arrives, the SCXML interpreter can perform actions described as *executable content*. This includes invoking or sending events to external components, processing data or updating the datamodel via an embedded scripting language.

SCXML has been proven to be suitable to decouple the control flow and presentation layer in dialog management (Wilcock, 2007). It has been used in several applications to express dialog states (Brusk et al., 2007) or to easily incorporate external information (Sigüenza Izquierdo et al., 2011). However, SCXML seems to be suited *only* to implement finite state or frame-based/form-filling dialogue management approaches. Applications using theses dialog techniques are oftentimes inflexible as they lack grounding and reasoning. In this regard, Fodor and Huerta (2006) demand that dialog managers should feature: (i) a formal logic foundation, (ii) an interference engine, (iii) general purpose planners and (iv) knowledge representation and expressiveness.

Most of these requirements are addressed by employing Prolog. Embedding it as a scripting language into SCXML allows multimodal applications in the W3C MMI Architecture to employ the more elaborate dialog management techniques, resulting in more natural and flexible interaction. In this paper we describe our integration of Prolog as an embedded scripting language in an SCXML datamodel. All of the work described here is implemented as part of our uSCXML interpreter[1] by embedding the SWI Prolog implementation.

2 The Prolog Datamodel

Datamodels in SCXML are more than simple repositories for storing data. With the exception of the `null` datamodel, they provide access to embedded scripting languages. The datamodels already specified by the SCXML draft are the `null`, the `xpath` and the `ecmascript` datamodel. Prolog itself is a declarative language for logic programming in which facts and rules are used to answer queries. The result of a query is either a boolean value or the set of valid assignments for the queries variables.

In the following sections, we will describe our integration of Prolog as a datamodel in SCXML. The structure of the description loosely follows the existing descriptions for datamodels already found in the SCXML draft.

2.1 Assignments

In an SCXML document, there are two elements which will assign values to variables in the datamodel. These are `<data>` for initial assignments and `<assign>` itself. In Prolog, variable assignment is only available in the scope of a query. To realize variable assignment nevertheless, we introduce the variables as predicates, with their assigned data as facts. Listing 1 exemplifies some assignments followed by their resulting Prolog facts.

```
<data id="father">
  bob, jim.
  bob, john.
</data>
% father(bob, jim).
% father(bob, john).

<data id="">
  mother(martha, jim).
  mother(martha, john).
</data>
% mother(martha, jim).
% mother(martha, john).

<assign location="">
  retract(father(bob, jim)).
  assert(father(steve, jim)).
</assign>
% father(bob, john).
% father(steve, jim).

<data id="childs">
  <child name="john" father="bob" />
  <child name="jim" father="bob" />
</data>
% childs([
%  element(child,
%    [father=bob, name=john], []),
%  element(child,
%    [father=bob, name=jim], [])]).

<data id="household">
  {
    name: "The Bobsons",
    members: ['bob', 'martha', 'jim', 'john']
  }
</data>
% household({
%   name:'The Bobsons',
%   members:[bob, martha, jim, john]}).
```

Listing 1: Assignments and their results in Prolog.

If given, the `id` or `location` attribute identifies the predicate for which the content is to be asserted as fact, otherwise the content is assumed to be a dot-separated list of prolog queries or expressions. The content might also be loaded per URL in the element's `src` attribute. In the context of SCXML, it is important to support XML and JSON data as shown in the last two examples. Not only enables this an application developer to load data from existing XML and JSON files, it is also important to support these representations for incoming events as we will see in the next section.

There is no standardized representation for XML DOMs or JSON data in Prolog. We pragmatically settled upon the structure returned by the SWI-Prolog SGML parser and the JSON converter as de-facto standards respectively.

With the Prolog datamodel, having an `id` or `location` attribute at assignment elements seems superfluous. We do keep them as the SCXML draft specifies these as required attributes.

2.2 Structure of Events

Whenever an event is received by the SCXML interpreter, it has to be transformed into a suitable representation in order to operate on its various fields and content as defined by the SCXML draft. We choose to represent an event as the single predicate `event/1` with its facts as compound terms reflecting the event's fields as shown in listing 2.

```
event(name('foo')).
event(type('external')).
event(sendid('s1.bar')).
event(origin('http://host/path/basichttp')).
event(origintype('http://www.w3.org/TR/scxml
    /#BasicHTTPEventProcessor')).
event(invokeid('')).
event(data(...)).
event(param(...)).
event(raw(...)).
```

Listing 2: Example facts for event/1.

This representation enables access to the events individual fields by simple queries such as `event(name(X))`, which will resolve X to the

[1] https://github.com/tklab-tud/uscxml

event's name `foo`. Whenever the interpreter is about to process a new event, all old facts about `event/1` are retracted and reasserted with regard to the new event.

The event's data field may contain a space normalized string as an atomic term, an XML DOM or, optionally, data from a JSON structure. The structure of JSON and XML DOMs is the same as with assignments in listing 1.

2.3 Scripting

The `<script>` element either contains Prolog expressions as they would be written in a Prolog file or references such a file directly via its `src` attribute. Together with `<assign>` and `<data>`, this element is the third available to load Prolog files into the SCXML interpreter. This is somewhat undesirable and we would propose to use (i) `<data>` to establish initial a-priori knowledge as facts, (ii) `<assign>` for subsequent changes and additions to facts and (iii) `<script>` to introduce new rules or load Prolog files containing primarily rules.

It is important to note that we do provide a full ISO-Prolog implementation at runtime. This enables an application developer to load arbitrary Prolog files with all their facts and rules.

2.4 System Variables

The SCXML draft requires the datamodel to expose various platform specific values to the datamodel. These are the identifier of the current session, the name of the document and the available I/O processors to send and receive events. Following the approach of defining predicates to provide access to information in the datamodel, we introduced predicates as given in listing 3.

```
% name/1:
name("foo").

% sessionid/1:
sessionid("bar").

% ioprocessors/1:
ioprocessors(
  basichttp(
    location('http://host/path/basichttp'))).
ioprocessors(
  scxml(location('http://host/path/scxml'))).

% ioprocessors/2:
ioprocessors(
  name(basichttp),
  location('http://host/path1')).
ioprocessors(
  name('http://www.w3.org/TR/scxml/#
      BasicHTTPEventProcessor'),
  location('http://host/path1')).
...
```

Listing 3: Predicates for system variables.

Defining two predicates for ioprocessors is simply a matter of convenience as their short names (e.g. basichttp or scxml) are suited as functors for compound terms, where their canonic names are not. Therefore `ioprocessors/1` will only contain the short names, and `ioprocessors/2` contains both. This allows us to send events, e.g with the basichttp ioprocessor via:

```
<send type="basichttp"
      targetexpr="ioprocessors(basichttp(
          location(X)))"
      event="foo">
```

Listing 4: Sending ourself an event via basichttp.

2.5 Conditional Expressions

Conditional expressions in SCXML are used to guard transitions and as part of `<if>` and `<elseif>` elements in executable content. They consist of a single, datamodel specific expression that ought to evaluate to a boolean value. In the case of our Prolog datamodel, these expressions can take the form of an arbitrary query (see listing 5). If there exists at least one solution to the query, the conditional expression will be evaluated to *true*, and *false* otherwise.

```
% Is there someone who is not the father
% of Jim and older than bob?
<if cond="not(father(X, jim)),
          older(X, bob).">

% Was the current event received from an
% external component?
<transition
  target="s3"
  cond="event(type(X)), X='external'"/>

% Does the JSON structure in the event's
% data contain a  household whose name
% is 'The Bobsons'?
<transition
  target="s5"
  cond="event(data(household(name:X))),
        X='The Bobsons'"/>
```

Listing 5: Boolean expressions in `cond` attribute.

2.6 Evaluating as String

There are several situations in the SCXML draft, where an element from the datamodel needs to be represented as a string. These are usually attributes of elements that equal or end in `expr`, e.g. `log.expr` or `send.targetexpr`.

In these contexts, the interpreter will allow for queries with a single free variable that has to resolve to an atomic term. The actual value of the expression is then the string representation of the variable from the last solution to the query (see listing 6).

```
% This query only has a single solution
<log label="Event Name"
     expr="event(name(X))" />

% This query has multiple solutions, only the
% last is used when evaluating as string
<log label="Bob's youngest son"
     expr="father(bob, X)" />
```

Listing 6: Evaluating an expression as string.

2.7 Foreach

The `<foreach>` element in SCXML allows to iterate over values as part of executable content. Its attributes are `array` as an iterable expression, `item` as the current element in the array and `index` as the current iteration index.

In our Prolog datamodel, this element is available to iterate over all solutions of a query as shown in listing 7.

```
<foreach array="father(bob, X)"
         item="child"
         index="index">
  <log label="child" expr="child(X)" />
  <log label="index" expr="index(X)" />
</foreach>

% results in the following log output
child: jim
index: 0
child: john
index: 1
child: jack
index: 2
```

Listing 7: Foreach expressions.

3 Example

Listing 8 exemplifies some of the language features of the Prolog datamodel. We start by introducing two predicates with the `<data>` element, the first defined as dot seperated facts, the second one as inline Prolog expressions. In the first state `s1`, we iterate all children of bob and log their names. Transitioning to the next state is performed if bob and martha have a common child. In `s2`, we send ourself an event containing a XML snippet using the basichttp I/O processor. Then we transition to the final state if there is an element with a tagname of `p` in the received XML document. In the final state we print all facts we established via Prolog's `listing/1` predicate and the interpreter stops.

```
<scxml datamodel="prolog">
  <datamodel>
    <data id="father">
      bob, jim.
      bob, john.
    </data>
    <data id="">
      mother(martha, jim).
      mother(martha, john).
    </data>
  </datamodel>
  <state id="s1">
    <onentry>
      <foreach array="father(bob, X)"
               item="child"
               index="index">
        <log label="index" expr="index(X)" />
        <log label="child" expr="child(X)" />
      </foreach>
    </onentry>
    <transition target="s2"
                cond="mother(martha, X),
                      father(bob, X)"/>
  </state>
  <state id="s2">
    <onentry>
      <send type="basichttp"
            targetexpr="ioprocessors(
                basichttp(location(X)))"
            event="foo">
        <content>
          <p>Snippet of XML</p>
        </content>
      </send>
    </onentry>
    <transition
      cond="member(element('p',_,_), X),
            event(data(X))" />
  </state>
  <state final="true">
    <log label="Listing" expr="listing." />
  </state>
</scxml>
```

Listing 8: Example SCXML document.

4 Conclusion

Providing a Prolog datamodel for SCXML enables applications in the W3C MMI architecture to employ grounding and reasoning for facts established during a prior to a dialog. It even enables developers to load complete, existing Prolog programs to to be used during event processing. This extends SCXML to fulfill the requirements for dialog management as defined by Fodor and Huerta (2006).

There are multiple variations to the integration of Prolog and more experience is needed still to determine whether the approach presented here is optimal.

References

RJ Auburn, Paolo Baggia, and Mark Scott. 2011. Voice browser call control (CCXML). W3C recommendation, W3C, July. http://www.w3.org/TR/2011/REC-ccxml-20110705/.

Jim Barnett, Rahul Akolkar, RJ Auburn, Michael Bodell, Daniel C. Burnett, Jerry Carter, Scott McGlashan, Torbjörn Lager, Mark Helbing, Rafah Hosn, T.V. Raman, Klaus Reifenrath, and No'am Rosenthal. 2012. State chart XML (SCXML): State machine notation for control abstraction. W3C working draft, W3C, February. http://www.w3.org/TR/2012/WD-scxml-20120216/.

Michale Bondell, Deborah Dahl, Ingmar Kliche, Jim Larson, Brad Porter, Dave Raggett, T.V. Raman, Bertha Helena Rodriguez, Muthuselvam Selvari, Raj Tumuluri, Andrew Wahbe, Piotr Wiechno, and Moshe Yudkowsky. 2012. Multimodal Architecture and Interfaces. W3C recommendation, W3C, October. http://www.w3.org/TR/2012/REC-mmi-arch-20121025/.

Jenny Brusk, Torbjörn Lager, Anna Hjalmarsson, and Preben Wik. 2007. Deal: dialogue management in scxml for believable game characters. In *Proceedings of the 2007 conference on Future Play*, pages 137–144. ACM.

Deboraha Dahl. 2013. The w3c multimodal architecture and interfaces standard. *Journal on Multimodal User Interfaces*, pages 1–12.

Paul Fodor and Juan M Huerta. 2006. Planning and logic programming for dialog management. In *Spoken Language Technology Workshop, 2006. IEEE*, pages 214–217. IEEE.

David Harel and Michal Politi. 1998. *Modeling Reactive Systems with Statecharts: The Statemate Approach*. McGraw-Hill, Inc., August.

Dirk Schnelle-Walka, Stefan Radomski, and Max Mühlhäuser. 2013. Jvoicexml as a modality component in the w3c multimodal architecture. *Journal on Multimodal User Interfaces*, pages 1–12.

Álvaro Sigüenza Izquierdo, José Luis Blanco Murillo, Jesús Bernat Vercher, and Luis Alfonso Hernández Gómez. 2011. Using scxml to integrate semantic sensor information into context-aware user interfaces.

Graham Wilcock. 2007. SCXML and voice interfaces. In *3rd Baltic Conference on Human Language Technologies, Kaunas, Lithuania*. Citeseer.

Exploring Features For Localized Detection of Speech Recognition Errors

Eli Pincus and **Svetlana Stoyanchev** and **Julia Hirschberg**
Department of Computer Science, Columbia University, USA
elipincus@gmail.com & sstoyanchev@cs.columbia.edu
& julia@cs.columbia.edu

Abstract

We address the problem of *localized error detection* in Automatic Speech Recognition (ASR) output to support the generation of *targeted clarifications* in *spoken dialogue systems*. Localized error detection finds specific mis-recognized words in a user utterance. Targeted clarifications, in contrast with generic 'please repeat/rephrase' clarifications, target a specific mis-recognized word in an utterance (Stoyanchev et al., 2012a) and require accurate detection of such words. We extend and modify work presented in (Stoyanchev et al., 2012b) by experimenting with a new set of features for predicting the likelihood of a local error in an ASR hypothesis on an unsifted version of the original dataset. We improve over baseline results, where only ASR-generated features are used, by constructing optimal feature sets for utterance and word mis-recognition prediction. The f-measure for identifying incorrect utterances improves by 2.2% and by 3.9% for identifiying incorrect words.

1 Introduction

Spoken Dialogue Systems typically indicate their lack of understanding of user input by simple requests for repetition or rephrasing – "I'm sorry, I didn't understand you.", or "Can you please repeat?". However human conversational partners generally provide more targeted clarification requests. Corpus analysis of human conversations have shown that people are more likely to indicate what they have understood and what they have *not* understood by producing *reprise clarification questions* (Purver, 2004; Stoyanchev et al., 2012a), as illustrated in the following exchange where XXX indicates a word misunderstood by speaker B:

A: Do you have any XXX in your bag?
B: Do I have any what in my bag?

A reprise clarification question targets a specific mis-recognized word and incorporates recognized context into a clarification question.

We investigate replacing generic *please repeat* clarifications with more natural targeted clarifications in automatic spoken systems. Targeted clarifications allow users to provide a concise response to a clarification question which is beneficial for spoken systems accepting broad vocabulary and flexible syntax. Examples of such systems include tutoring systems, intelligent assistants, and spoken translation systems (Litman and Silliman, 2004; Dzikovska et al., 2009; Akbacak et al., 2009).

To enable Spoken Dialogue Systems (SDS) to generate targeted clarification questions, we must first be able to identify mis-recognized words with high accuracy. We term such mis-recognition detection *localized error detection*. Accurate distinction between correctly and incorrectly recognized words is essential to the creation of appropriate targeted clarification questions.

In previous research on recognition error detection in dialogue systems, researchers have addressed error detection at the utterance level (Hirschberg et al., 2004; Komatani and Okuno, 2010). In this paper we present results of classification experiments designed to detect localized errors within the utterance. Our baseline results are obtained from a classifier trained only on word posterior probabilities generated by an Automatic Speech Recognition (ASR) engine. ASR confidence score computation is an active research area, relying upon acoustic and lexical collocation information to compute confidence scores. We determine whether improvement over baseline can be achieved by training a classifier for utterance and word mis-recognition prediction on an expanded feature set that includes lexical, positional, prosodic, semantic, syntactic as well as additional ASR score features. All of the features we experiment with can be computed from an ASR hypothesis without affecting the performance of a SDS materially. After determining optimal feature sets we experiment with one- and two-stage approaches for localized error detection. The first simply identifies whether a word is correctly recognized or not. The second first classifies an utterance as incorrect or correct and then classifies errors only on utterances labeled incorrect.

This work extends earlier work in which we evaluated a smaller set of syntactic and prosodic features (Stoyanchev et al., 2012b). In addition to improvements implemented in the ASR engine that we use to produce ASR hypotheses, our current work reports results on a larger dataset which includes commands to the system and utterances containing disfluencies. Here, we propose a framework for localized error detection that does not rely upon pre-filtering of the dataset.

In Section 2 we describe our corpus. In Section 3 we discuss our classification experiments. In Section 4 we discuss our results. In Section 5 we present our conclusions and discuss future research.

2 Data

We conduct our machine learning experiments on the DARPA TRANSTAC corpus (Weiss et al., 2008). The TRANSTAC corpus is comprised of staged conversations between American military personnel and Arabic interviewees utilizing IraqComm speech-to-speech translation system (Akbacak et al., 2009). This data was collected by NIST between 2005 and 2008 in evaluation exercises. The dataset contains audio recordings and manual transcript of English and Arabic utterances. We used SRI's DynaSpeak (Franco et al., 2002) speech recognition system to recognize the English utterances and use posterior probabilities from DynaSpeak as our baseline feature. We create a corpus from this dataset that contains over 99% of the English utterances. 38 utterances were removed from the dataset either for lack of actual speech data or errors in reference transcription. 26.2% of our cleaned corpus consist of mis-recognized instances and 6.4% of the total words in it are incorrectly recognized by DynaSpeak (see Table 1). We are using an unsifted version of the corpus used in our previous work (Stoyanchev et al., 2012b) whose hypotheses were produced with a new version of the DynaSpeak ASR system. In our previous work utterances containing disfluencies and commands to the system were excluded. We seek to avoid the cascading errors that would follow from implementing a 2-step framework for localized error detection where the first step is command and disfluency detection and the second step is localized error detection. The 1-step framework also has the advantage of working for all utterances including ones that contain commands or disfluencies. Due to these differences, our current results are not directly comparable with our previous results.

Table 1: *Corpus statistics*

	Overall	Correct ASR	Incorr ASR
All utts.	3,952	2,914 (73.7%)	1,038 (26.2%)
All wrds.	25,333	23,705 (93.6%)	1,628 (6.4%)
wrds in err utts	7,888	6,260 (79.4%)	1,628 (20.6%)

3 Method

We analyze how the performance of predicting mis-recognized utterances and words is affected by the use of lexical, positional, prosodic, semantic, and syntactic features in addition to ASR confidence scores. We perform machine learning experiments using the Weka Machine Learning Library to construct a J48 decision tree classifier boosted with MultiBoostAB method (Witten and Eibe, 2005).

Baseline confidence features We use ASR posterior scores extracted from the log files output by Dynaspeak as a baseline feature set in our experiments. In the utterance mis-recognition prediction experiment, we calculate the average of the logarithm of the ASR posterior scores over all words in the hypothesis. In the word mis-recognition prediction experiment we use the logarithm of the posterior score of a given word.

Feature selection We run a heuristic feature exploration experiment to identify optimal feature sets for predicting mis-recognized utterances and mis-recognized words. We first use a greedy approach adding one feature at a time to the baseline ASR feature set and only keep a feature in the set if it improves F-measure predicting mis-recognition. We then use an alternate greedy approach in which we begin with a feature set composed of all extracted features and proceed to remove one feature at a time and only leave it out of the set if incorrect F-measure improved or remained the same with its absence. The second approach yields the optimal feature sets for both utterance and word mis-recognition prediction. Table 2 lists the features that make up these optimal sets. For incorrect utterance prediction, we run a 10-fold cross validation on all utterances. For incorrect word prediction, we run a 10-fold cross validation on all words in mis-recognized utterances.[1] We next describe the features we found to be useful in prediction and those that did not improve performance.

3.1 Useful Features

ASR context features We use the logarithm of the posterior score of a given word and the average of the logarithm of the posterior scores for both a given word and its surrounding context. We use one word context before and after the given word. We also use the average of the logarithm of the posterior scores for all words in the utterance.

Lexical features We hypothesize that properties of words such as length and frequency are predictive of whether a word is correctly recognized. In particular, noting that words of greater length are often better recognized by an ASR engine, we examine the length, frequency, and posterior score of the maximum and min-

[1]Because of the size limitations of our dataset feature selection and evaluation are performed on the same dataset.

imum words in an utterance. For mis-recognized utterance prediction, we find that the average length of a word in the utterance are useful features for predicting both mis-recognized utterances and words. For mis-recognized word prediction, we find the word length of the surrounding words, the current word, and the frequency of the longest word in an utterance are useful. We also find that *utterance length* calculated in words is a useful feature for predicting both utterance and word mis-recognition.

Positional features Motivated by the use of dialogue history features in Lopes et al (2011), we find that the location of the hypothesis relative to the speaker's first utterance in the dialogue (*utterance location*) is a useful feature. Similarly, we obtain improvement from the *word index* feature, the distance of the word from the first word in the utterance.

Syntactic POS tags were shown to be helpful in our previous work and we find that these tags improve the current results as well. We obtain these from the Stanford POS tagger (et al., 2003). In mis-recognized utterance prediction, we use unigram and bigram counts of POS tags as a feature. For mis-recognized word prediction, we use the word's POS tag as well as the POS tag for the surrounding one or two words.

We obtain a binary *Func/Content* feature using a function word list to distinguish function from content words. The list includes certain adverbs, conjunctions, determiners, modal verbs, primary verbs such as *be*, prepositions, pronouns, and WP-pronouns. These tags also boost our ability to identify mis-recognized words. The feature *Func/Tot ratio* is the fraction of function words to total words in an ASR hypothesis. We hypothesize that an extreme value of the *Func/Tot ratio* may indicate a potential mis-recognition, and it does improve both utterance and word mis-recognition prediction.

3.2 Less Useful Features

Features we do not find helpful include information associated with the minimum length word in the utterance, the fraction of words in an utterance that possess greater length than the average length word in the corpus, as well as syntactic features such as a dependency tag assigned to the word. Additional unhelpful features include prosodic features, such as shimmer and jitter identified by PRAAT (Boersma and Weenink, 2013) and pitch and phrase information extracted from AuToBI(Rosenberg, 2010) software. Performing a semantic role label of our hypotheses with the software SENNA (Collobert et al., 2011) also did not provide helpful semantic features.

System Performance To evaluate performance of our mis-recognized word classifier, we use the selected features in 1-stage and 2-stage approaches. First, we train models for utterance and word classification sep-

Table 2: *Features*

Cat	Specific	In Optimal Utt Feature Set	In Optimal Wrd Feature Set
ASR	Log Post Score	Yes (avg of all wrds in utt)	Yes (curr wrd)
ASR-CTX	Log Post Score	No	Yes (avg of curr wrd, curr wrd context, avg of all wrds in utt)
Lex	Wrd length	Yes (avg wrd length in utt)	Yes (curr,prev,next)
	Max Wrd freq	No	Yes
	Utt length	Yes	Yes
POS	Utt location	Yes	Yes
	Word Index	No	Yes (curr)
Syn	POS Tag	Yes (unigram and bigram count)	Yes (curr,prev,next)
	Func/Cont tag	No	Yes (curr, prev, next)
	Func/Tot ratio	Yes	Yes

arately on 80% of the dataset with up-sampling (35%)[2] of the incorrect instances as well as with the actual distribution of incorrect instances in the corpus (20.6% utterances, 6.4% words). We then test these models on the remaining 20% of the dataset using the 1-stage and 2-stage approach. In the 1-stage approach we test on 20% of the total words in the corpus. In the 2-stage approach we first test on 20% of the total utterances in the corpus and then only test on the words in the utterances labeled as mis-recognized.

4 Results

New Feature Experiments Using our newly constructed utterance feature set we are able to boost incorrect utterance classification F-measure by 2.2% from .597 to .610 (see Table 3). The increase in F-measure for incorrect utterance mis-recognition is due to an increase in incorrect utterance recall from .531 to .555. There is a slight decrease in incorrect utterance precision from .682 to .678. Overall classification accuracy improves by 2.1% points (absolute) from 81.2% to 83.3%. Using our newly constructed word feature set we are able to improve incorrect word classification F-measure by 3.9% from .620 to .644 (see Table 4). For incorrect word classification there is an increase in both mis-recognized word precision and recall; the former increasing from .678 to .719 and the latter increasing from .571 to .584. The results for incorrect word classification represent a statistically significant improve-

[2]This percentage was derived empirically.

Table 3: *Utterance new feature experiment results*

Feature	Correct P — R — F	Incorrect P — R — F	% F-Measure Incorr Imp over ASR Only	Accuracy
ASR	.845 — .912 — .877	.682 — .531 — .597	-	81.2%
ASR+LEX+POS+SYN	.851 — .906 — .878	.678 — .555 — .610	2.2%	83.3%

Table 4: *Word new feature experiment results*

Feature	Correct P — R — F	Incorrect P — R — F	% F-Measure Incorr Imp over ASR only	Accuracy
ASR	.893 — .930 — .911	.678 — .571 — .620	-	85.5%
ASR+LEX+POS+SYN	.897 — .941 — .918	.719 — .584 — .644	3.9%	86.7%

Table 5: *1-stage and 2-stage approach results*

Experiment	Correct P — R — F	Incorrect P — R — F	Accuracy
Maj. Baseline	.94 — 1.00 — .97	- — 0 — -	94%
1-stage original	.97 — .94 — .96	.39 — .57 — .46	86.7%
1-stage (35% upsample)	.98 — .90 — .94	.31 — .72 — .44	92%
2-stage original	.96 — .98 — .97	.51 — .34 — .41	94%
2-stage (35% upsample)	.96 — .96 — .96	.41 — .46 — .43	89%

ment[3]. Overall classification accuracy improves by 1.2% points (absolute) from 85.5% to 86.7%.

1-stage and 2-stage experiments To estimate how well a dialogue system could perform incorrect word classification we run our 1-stage and 2-stage approaches. The 1-stage approaches (with and without up-sampling) are able to achieve higher recall; while the 2-stage approaches (with and without up-sampling) are able to achieve higher precision. The 2-stage result's higher precision is not surprising given that this approach has two chances to filter out correct words — first with utterance classification and then with word classification. In our 1-stage approach with up-sampling we are able to identify almost 3/4 (72%) of the incorrect words in the corpus (see Table 5). In our 2-stage approach without up-sampling we are able to accurately label just over 1/2 (51%) of the total instances we identify as incorrect. In future work we will experiment with additional features in order to boost precision for incorrect word classification to a level suitable for use in the construction of reprise clarification questions.

5 Conclusions

We have presented results of machine learning experiments that utilize new features to improve localized detection of ASR errors to assist spoken dialogue system's production of reprise clarification questions. We conducted feature selection experiments to find optimal feature sets to train classifiers for utterance and word mis-recognition prediction. We find that certain lexical, positional, and syntactic features improve classification results over a baseline feature set containing only ASR posterior score features. We improve incorrect F-measure for utterance mis-recognition prediction by 2.2% by adding utterance length, location, fraction of function words to total words, average word length, and unigram and bigram count to the baseline feature set. By removing average word length as well as unigram and bigram count from this optimal set for utterances and adding the current word's ASR-context features, length, distance from first word, POS tag, Content/Function tag as well as the length of the current's words surrounding 1 or 2 word contexts, we improve incorrect F-measure for word mis-recognition prediction by 3.9% . We then employ these feature sets in 1-stage and 2-stage approached to obtain our final results. The 2-stage (no up-sampling) approach yields the highest precision for detection of word mis-recognition at 51% while the 1-stage (with 35% up-sampling) approach yields the highest recall for detection of word mis-recognition at 72%.

In order to implement this approach in a working dialog system we would need to increase our word mis-recognition precision. The presence of false positives in mis-recognition prediction (correctly recognized words classified as mis-recognized) could lead to unnecessary clarification requests — potentially derailing the dialogue.

In future work we will experiment with additional corpora as well as with an even more fine-grained approach to local error detection, looking for deletions, insertions, and substitutions. Potentially, optimal classifiers could be found for each of these types of misrecognition. If we are able to identify the type of ASR error as well as its location, we should be able to improve our construction of clarifications questions.

We will also continue our investigation of how to use reprise clarification questions in SDS. Once we have detected localized ASR errors we must still refine our strategies for constructing clarification questions using this information. We are also studying how appropriate and inappropriate reprise clarification questions are handled by SDS users.

[3] $\chi^2 test(p < .01)$

References

M. Akbacak, H. Franco, M. Frandsen, S. Hasan, H. Jameel, A. Kathol, S. Khadivi, X. Lei, A. Mandal, S. Mansour, K. Precoda, C. Richey, D. Vergyri, W. Wang, M. Yang, and J. Zheng. 2009. Recent advances in sri's iraqcomm; iraqi arabic-english speech-to-speech translation system. In *Acoustics, Speech and Signal Processing, 2009. ICASSP 2009. IEEE International Conference on*, pages 4809–4812.

P. Boersma and D. Weenink. 2013. Praat: doing phonetics by computer [computer program]. http://www.fon.hum.uva.nl/praat/.

R. Collobert, J. Weston, L. Bottou, M. Karlen, K. Kavukcuoglu, and P. Kuksa. 2011. Natural language processing (almost) from scratch.

M. O. Dzikovska, C. B. Callaway, E. Farrow, J. D. Moore, N. Steinhauser, and G. Campbell. 2009. Dealing with interpretation errors in tutorial dialogue. In *Proceedings of the SIGDIAL 2009 Conference: The 10th Annual Meeting of the Special Interest Group on Discourse and Dialogue*, SIGDIAL '09, pages 38–45, Stroudsburg, PA, USA. Association for Computational Linguistics.

K. Toutanova et al. 2003. Feature-rich part-of-speech tagging with a cyclic dependency network. In *Proceedings of the 2003 Conference of the North American Chapter of the Association for Computational Linguistics on Human Language Technology - Volume 1*.

H. Franco, J. Zheng, J. Butzberger, F. Cesari, M. Fr, J. Arnold, V. Ramana, A. Stolcke R. Gadde, and V. Abrash. 2002. Dynaspeak: Sri's scalable speech recognizer for embedded and mobile systems. In *Proceedings of the second international conference on Human Language Technology Research*, HLT '02, pages 25–30, San Francisco, CA, USA. Morgan Kaufmann Publishers Inc.

J. Hirschberg, D. J. Litman, and M. Swerts. 2004. Prosodic and other cues to speech recognition failures. *Speech Communication*, 43(1-2):155–175.

K. Komatani and H. G. Okuno. 2010. Online error detection of barge-in utterances by using individual users utterance histories in spoken dialogue system.

D. J. Litman and S. Silliman. 2004. Itspoke: an intelligent tutoring spoken dialogue system. In *Demonstration Papers at HLT-NAACL 2004*, HLT-NAACL–Demonstrations '04, pages 5–8, Stroudsburg, PA, USA.

J. Lopes, M. Eskenazi, and I. Trancoso. 2011. Towards choosing better primes for spoken dialog systems. In *Proceedings of the IEEE Workshop on Automatic Speech Recognition and Understanding (ASRU)*, Keystone, CO.

M. Purver. 2004. *The Theory and Use of Clarification Requests in Dialogue*. Ph.D. thesis, King's College, University of London.

A. Rosenberg. 2010. Autobi - a tool for automatic tobi annotation. In Takao Kobayashi, Keikichi Hirose, and Satoshi Nakamura, editors, *INTERSPEECH*, pages 146–149. ISCA.

S. Stoyanchev, A. Liu, and J. Hirschberg. 2012a. Clarification questions with feedback 2012. In *Interdisciplinary Workshop on Feedback Behaviors in Dialog*.

S. Stoyanchev, P. Salletmayr, J. Yang, and J. Hirschberg. 2012b. Localized detection of speech recognition errors. In *Spoken Language Technology Workshop (SLT), 2012 IEEE*, pages 25–30.

B. Weiss, C. Schlenoff, G. Sanders, M. Steves, S. Condon, J. Phillips, and D. Parvaz. 2008. Performance evaluation of speech translation systems. In Nicoletta Calzolari (Conference Chair) et al., editor, *Proceedings of the Sixth International Conference on Language Resources and Evaluation (LREC'08)*, Marrakech, Morocco, may. European Language Resources Association (ELRA). http://www.lrec-conf.org/proceedings/lrec2008/.

I. Witten and F. Eibe. 2005. *Data Mining: Practical machine learning tools and techniques*. Morgan Kaufmann, San Francisco, 2nd edition.

Modelling Human Clarification Strategies

Svetlana Stoyanchev, Alex Liu, Julia Hirschberg
Columbia University, New York NY 10027
sstoyanchev, al3037, julia @cs.columbia.edu

Abstract

We model human responses to speech recognition errors from a corpus of human clarification strategies. We employ learning techniques to study 1) the decision to either stop and ask a clarification question or to continue the dialogue without clarification, and 2) the decision to ask a targeted clarification question or a more generic question. Targeted clarification questions focus specifically on the part of an utterance that is misrecognized, in contrast with generic requests to 'please repeat' or 'please rephrase'. Our goal is to generate targeted clarification strategies for handling errors in spoken dialogue systems, when appropriate. Our experiments show that linguistic features, in particular the inferred part-of-speech of a misrecognized word are predictive of human clarification decisions. A combination of linguistic features predicts a user's decision to continue or stop a dialogue with accuracy of 72.8% over a majority baseline accuracy of 59.1%. The same set of features predict the decision to ask a targeted question with accuracy of 74.6% compared with the majority baseline of 71.8%.[1]

1 Introduction

Clarification questions are common in human-human dialogue. They help dialogue participants maintain dialogue flow and resolve misunderstandings. Purver (2004) finds that in human-human dialogue speakers most frequently use *reprise* clarification questions to resolve recognition errors. Reprise clarification questions use portions of the misunderstood utterance which are thought to be correctly recognized to *target* the part of an utterance that was misheard or misunderstood. In the following example from (Purver, 2004), Speaker B has failed to hear the word *toast* and so constructs a clarification question using a portion of the correctly understood utterance — the word *some* — to query the portion of the utterance B has failed to understand:

A: Can I have **some** *toast* please?
B: Some?
A: Toast.

Unlike human conversational partners, most dialogue systems today employ generic 'please repeat/rephrase' questions asking a speaker to repeat or rephrase an entire utterance. Our goal is to introduce reprise, or targeted, clarifications into an automatic spoken system. Targeted clarifications can be especially useful for systems accepting unrestricted speech, such as tutoring systems, intelligent agents, and speech translation systems. Using a reprise question, a user can correct an error by repeating only a portion of an utterance. Targeted questions also provide natural grounding and implicit confirmation by signalling to the conversation partner which parts of an utterance have been recognized.

In order to handle a misrecognition, the system must first identify misrecognized words (Stoyanchev et al., 2012), determine the type of question to ask, and construct the question. In this work, we address two points necessary for determining the type of question to ask:

- Is it appropriate for a system to ask a clarification question when a misrecognized word is detected?
- Is it possible to ask a targeted clarification question for a given sentence and an error segment?

To answer these questions, we analyze a corpus of human responses to transcribed utterances with missing information which we collected using Amazon Mechanical Turk (2012). Although the data collection was text-based, we asked annotators to respond as they would in a dialogue. In Section 2, we describe related work on error recovery strategies in dialogue systems. In Section 3, we describe the corpus used in this experiment. In Section 4, we describe our experiments on human clarification strategy modelling. We conclude in Section 5 with our plan for applying our models in spoken systems.

2 Related work

To handle errors in speech recognition, slot-filling dialogue systems typically use simple rejection ("I'm sorry. I didn't understand you.") when they have low confidence in a recognition hypothesis and explicit or implicit confirmation when confidence scores

[1]This work was partially funded by DARPA HR0011-12-C-0016 as a Columbia University subcontract to SRI International.

are higher. Machine learning approaches have been successfully employed to determine dialogue strategies (Bohus and Rudnicky, 2005; Bohus et al., 2006; Rieser and Lemon, 2006), such as when to provide help, repeat a previous prompt, or move on to the next prompt. Reiser and Lemon (2006) use machine learning to determine an optimal clarification strategy in multimodal dialogue. Komatani et al. (2006) propose a method to generate a help message based on perceived user expertise. Corpus studies on human clarifications in dialogue indicate that users ask task-related questions and provide feedback confirming their hypothesis instead of giving direct indication of their misunderstanding (Skantze, 2005; Williams and Young, 2004; Koulouri and Lauria, 2009). In our work, we model human strategies with the goal of building a dialogue system which can generate targeted clarification questions for recognition errors that require additional user input but which can also recover from other errors automatically, as humans do.

3 Data

In our experiments, we use a dataset of human responses to missing information, which we collected with Amazon Mechanical Turk (AMT). Each AMT annotator was given a set of Automatic Speech Recognition (ASR) transcriptions of an English utterance with a single misrecognized segment. 925 such utterances were taken from acted dialogues between English and Arabic speakers conversing through SRI's *IraqComm* speech-to-speech translation system (Akbacak et al., 2009). Misrecognized segments were replaced by *"XXX"* to indicate the missing information, simulating a dialogue system's automatic detection of misrecognized words (Stoyanchev et al., 2012). For each sentence, AMT workers were asked to 1) indicate whether other information in the sentence made its meaning clear despite the error, 2) guess the missing word if possible, 3) guess the missing word's part-of-speech (POS) if possible, and 4) create a targeted clarification question if possible. Three annotators annotated each sentence. Table 1 summarizes the results. In 668 (72%) of the sentences an error segment corresponds to a single word while in 276 (28%) of them, an error segment corresponds to multiple words. For multiple word error segments, subjects had the option of guessing multiple words and POS tags. We scored their guess correct if any of their guesses matched the syntactic head word of an error segment determined from an automatically assigned dependency parse structure.

We manually corrected annotators' POS tags if the hypothesized word was itself correct. After this post-processing, we see that AMT workers hypothesized POS correctly in 57.7% of single-word and 60.2% of multi-word error cases. They guessed words correctly in 34.9% and 19.3% of single- and multi-word error cases. They choose to ask a clarification question in 38.3% /47.9% of cases and 76.1%/62.3% of these questions were targeted clarification questions. These results indicate that people are often able to guess a POS tag and sometimes an actual word. We observe that 1) in a single-word error segment, subjects are better at guessing an actual word than they are in a multi-word error segment; and 2) in a multi-word error segment, subjects are more likely to ask a clarification question and less likely to ask a targeted question. All three annotators agree on POS tags in 62% of cases and on hypothesized words in 25%. Annotators' agreement on response type is low — not surprising since there is more than one appropriate and natural way to respond in dialogue. In 39% of cases, all three annotators agree on the decision to stop/continue and in only 25% of cases all three annotators agree on asking a targeted clarification question. Figure 1 shows the annotator distribution for asking a clarification question vs. continuing the dialogue based on hypothesized POS tag. It indicates that annotators are more likely to ask a question than continue without a question when they hypothesize a missing word to be a content word (noun or adjective) or when they are unsure of the POS of the missing word. They are more likely to continue when they believe a missing word is a function word. However, when they believe a missing word is a verb, they are more likely to continue, and they are also likely to identify the missing verb correctly.

	Single-word error	**Agree**	**Multi-word error**
Total sent	668 (72%)	-	276 (28%)
Correct POS	57.7%	62%	60.2%
Correct word	34.9%	25%	19.3%
Ask a question	38.3%	39%	47.9%
Targeted question	76.1%	25%	62.3%

Table 1: *Annotation summary for single-word and multi-word error cases. Absolute annotator agreement is shown for single-word error cases.*

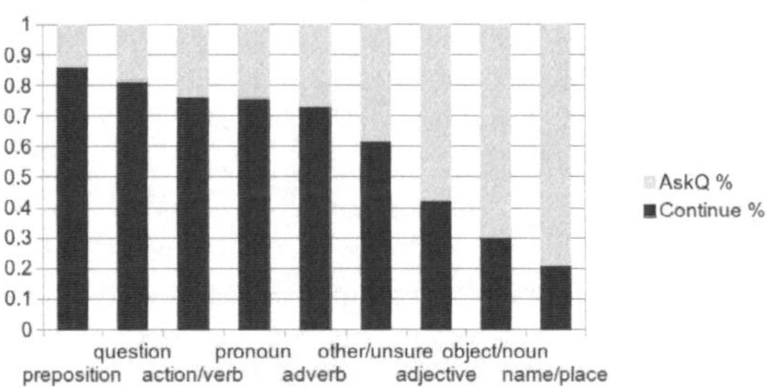

Figure 1: *Distribution of decisions to ask a question or continue dialogue without a question.*

Figure 2 shows a distribution of annotator decisions as to the type of question they would ask. The proportion of *targeted* question types varies with hypothesized POS. It is more prevalent than *confirm* and *generic* questions combined for all POS tags except preposition and question word, indicating that annotators are generally able to construct a targeted clarification question based on their analysis of the error segment.

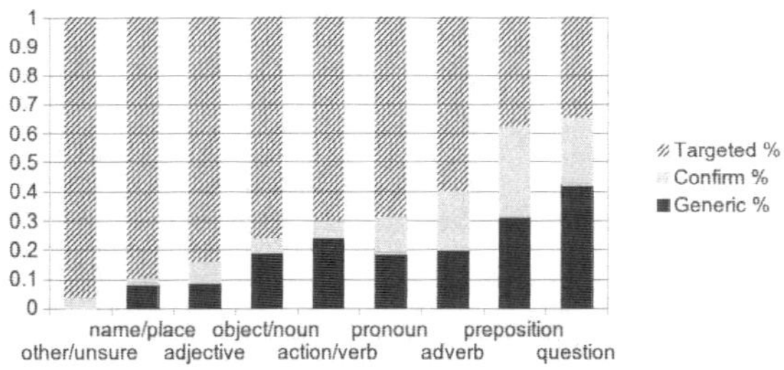

Figure 2: *Distribution of decisions for targeted, confirmation, and generic question types.*

4 Experiment

We use our AMT annotations to build classifiers for 1) choice of action: *stop* and engage in clarification vs. *continue* dialogue; and 2) type of clarification question (*targeted* vs. *non-targeted*) to ask. For the *continue/stop* experiment, we aim to determine whether a system should stop and ask a clarification question. For the *targeted vs. non-targeted* experiment, we aim to determine whether it is possible to ask a targeted clarification question.[2]

Using the Weka (Witten and Eibe, 2005) machine learning framework, we build classifiers to predict AMT decisions. We automatically assign POS tags to transcripts using the Stanford tagger (Toutanova and others, 2003). We compare models built with an automatically tagged POS for an error word (*POS-auto*) with one built with POS guessed by a user (*POS-guess*). Although a dialogue manager may not have access to a correct POS, it may simulate this by predicting POS of the error. We assign dependency tags using the AMU dependency parser (Nasr et al., 2011) which has been optimized on the Transtac dataset.

We hypothesize that a user's dialogue move depends on the syntactic structure of a sentence as well as on syntactic and semantic information about the error word and its syntactic parent. To capture sentence structure, we use features associated with the whole sentence: POS ngram, all pairs of parent-child dependency tags in a sentence (*Dep-pair*), and all semantic roles (*Sem-presence*) in a sentence. To capture the syntactic and semantic role of a misrecognized word, we use features associated with this word: POS tag, dependency tag (*Dep-tag*), POS of the parent word (*Parent-POS*), and semantic role of an error word (*Sem-role*).

We first model individual annotators' decisions for each of the three annotation instances. We measure the value that each feature adds to a model, using annotators' POS guess (*POS-guess*). Next, we model a joint annotators' decision using the automatically assigned *POS-auto* feature. This model simulates a system behaviour in a dialogue with a user where a system chooses a single dialogue move for each situation. We run 10-fold cross validation using the Weka J48 Decision Tree algorithm.

[2]If any annotators asked a targeted question, we assign a positive label to this instance, and negative otherwise.

Feature	Description
	Count
Word-position	*beginning* if a misrecognized word is the first word in the sentence, *end* if it is the last word, *middle* otherwise.
Utterance-length	number of words in the sentence
	Part-of-speech (compare)
POS-auto	POS tag of the misrecognized word automatically assigned on a transcript
POS-guess	POS tag of the misrecognized word guessed by a user
	POS ngrams
POS ngrams	all bigrams and trigrams of POS tags in a sentence
	Syntactic Dependency
Dep-tag	dependency tag of the misrecognized word automatically assigned on a transcript
Dep-pair	dependency tags of all (parent, child) pairs in the sentence
Parent-POS	POS tag of the syntactic parent of the misrecognized word
	Semantic
Sem-role	semantic role of the misrecognized word
Sem-presence	all semantic roles present in a sentence

Table 2: Features

4.1 Stop/Continue Experiment

In this experiment, we classify each instance in the dataset into a binary *continue* or *stop* decision. Since each instance is annotated by three annotators, we first predict individual annotators' decisions. The absolute agreement on continue/stop is 39% which means that 61% of sentences are classified into both classes. We explore the role of each feature in predicting these decisions. All features used in this experiment, except for the *POS-guess* feature, are extracted from the sentences automatically. Variation in the *POS-guess* feature may explain some of the difference between annotator decisions.

Features	Acc	F-measure	%Diff
Majority baseline	59.1%		
All features	**72.8%** †	**0.726**	0.0%
less utt length	72.9% †	0.727	+0.1%
less POS ngrams	72.8% †	0.727	+0.1%
less Semantic	72.6% †	0.724	-0.3%
less Syn. Depend.	71.5% †	0.712	-1.9%
less Position	71.2% †	0.711	-2.0%
less POS	67.9% †	0.677	-6.7%
POS only	70.1% †	0.690	-5.0%

Table 3: Stop/Continue experiment predicting individual annotator's decision with *POS-guess*. Accuracy, F-measure and Difference of f-measure from *All feature*. †indicates statistically significant difference from the majority baseline ($p<.01$)

Table 3 shows the results of continue/stop classification. A majority baseline method predicts the most frequent class *continue* and has 59.1% accuracy. In comparison, our classifier, built with all features, achieves 72.8% accuracy.

Next, we evaluate the utility of each feature by removing it from the feature set and comparing the model built without it with a model built on all features. POS is the most useful feature, as we expected: when it is removed from the feature set, the f-measure decreases by 6.7%. A model trained on the *POS-guess* feature alone outperforms a model trained on all other features. Word *position* in the sentence is the next most salient feature, contributing 2% to the f-measure. The syntactic dependency features *Syn-Dep, Dep-pair,* and *Parent POS* together contribute 1.9%.[3]

Next, we predict a majority decision for each sentence. Table 4 shows the accuracy of this prediction. A majority baseline has an accuracy of 59.9%. When we use a model trained on the *POS-auto* feature alone, accuracy rises to 66.1%, while a combination of all features further increases it to 69.2%.

Features	Acc	F-measure
Majority baseline	59.9%	
POS	66.1% †	0.655
All features	69.2% †	0.687

Table 4: Stop/Continue experiment predicting majority decision, using *POS-auto*. †indicates statistically significant difference from the majority baseline (p<.01).

4.2 Targeted Clarification Experiment

In this experiment, we classify each instance into *targeted* or *not targeted* categories. The *targeted* category comprises the cases in which an annotator chooses to stop and ask a targeted question. We are interested in identifying these cases in order to determine whether a system should try to ask a targeted clarification question. Table 5 shows the results of this experiment. The majority baseline predicts *not targeted* and has a 71.8% accuracy because in most cases, no question is asked. A model trained on all features increases accuracy to 74.6%. POS is the most salient feature, contributing 3.8% to the f-measure. All models that use POS feature are significantly different from the baseline. The next most salient features are POS ngram and a combination of syntactic dependency features contributing 1% and .5% to the f-measure respectively.

Table 6 shows system performance in predicting a joint annotators' decision of whether a targeted question can be asked. A joint decision in this experiment is considered *not targeted* when none of the annotators chooses to ask a targeted question. We aim at identifying the cases where position of an error word makes it difficult to ask a clarification question, such as for a sentence *XXX somebody steal these supplies.* Using the automatically assigned POS (*POS-auto*) feature alone achieves an accuracy of 62.2%, which is almost 10% above the baseline. A combination of all features, surprisingly, lowers the accuracy to 59.4%. Interestingly, a combination of all features *less POS* increases accuracy above the baseline by 7.6% points to 60.1% accuracy.

[3]All trained models are significantly different from the baseline. None of the trained models are significantly different from each other.

Features	Acc	F-measure	%Diff
Majority baseline	71.8%		
All features	74.6% †	**0.734**	0.0%
All feature (POS guess)			
less Utt length	74.8% †	0.736	+0.3%
less Position	74.9% †	0.731	-0.4%
less Semantic	74.8% †	0.737	+0.4%
less Syn. Depend.	74.2% †	0.730	-0.5%
less POS ngram	74.2% †	0.727	-1.0%
less POS	74.0%	0.706	-3.8%
POS	74.1% †	0.731	-0.4%

Table 5: Targeted/not experiment predicting individual annotator's decision with *POS-guess*. Accuracy, F-measure and Difference of f-measure from *All feature*. †indicates statistically significant difference from the majority baseline (p<.05)

Features	Acc	F-measure
Majority baseline	52.5%	
POS only	62.2% †	0.622
All features	59.4% †	0.594
All features *less POS*	60.1% †	0.600

Table 6: Targeted/not experiment predicting majority decision, using POS tag feature *POS-auto*. †indicates statistically significant difference from the majority baseline.

5 Conclusions and Future Work

In this paper we have described experiments modelling human strategies in response to ASR errors. We have used machine learning techniques on a corpus annotated by AMT workers asked to respond to missing information in an utterance. Although annotation agreement in this task is low, we aim to learn natural strategies for a dialogue system by combining the judgements of several annotators. In a dialogue, as in other natural language tasks, there is more than one appropriate response in each situation. A user does not judge the system (or another speaker) by a single response. Over a dialogue session, appropriateness, or lack of it in system actions, becomes evident. We have shown that by using linguistic features we can predict the decision to either ask a clarification question or continue dialogue with an accuracy of 72.8% in comparison with the 59.1% baseline. The same linguistic features predict a targeted clarification question with an accuracy of 74.6% compared to the baseline of 71.8%.

In future work, we will apply modelling of a clarification choice strategy in a speech-to-speech translation task. In our related work, we have addressed the problem of automatic correction of some ASR errors for cases when humans believe a dialogue can continue without clarification In other work, we have addressed the creation of targeted clarification questions for handling the cases when such questions are appropriate. Combining these research directions, we are developing a clarification component for a speech-to-speech translation system that responds naturally to speech recognition errors.

References

M. Akbacak, Franco, H., M. Frandsen, S. Hasan, H. Jameel, A. Kathol, S. Khadivi, X. Lei, A. Mandal, S. Mansour, K. Precoda, C. Richey, D. Vergyri, W. Wang, M. Yang, and J. Zheng. 2009. Recent advances in SRI's IraqComm^{tm} Iraqi Arabic-English speech-to-speech translation system. In *ICASSP*, pages 4809–4812.

Amazon Mechanical Turk. 2012. http://aws.amazon.com/mturk/, accessed on 28 may, 2012.

D. Bohus and A. I. Rudnicky. 2005. A principled approach for rejection threshold optimization in spoken dialog systems. In *INTERSPEECH*, pages 2781–2784.

D. Bohus, B. Langner, A. Raux, A. Black, M. Eskenazi, and A. Rudnicky. 2006. Online supervised learning of non-understanding recovery policies. In *Proceedings of SLT*.

Y. Fukubayashi, K. Komatani, T. Ogata, and H. Okuno. 2006. Dynamic help generation by estimating user's mental model in spoken dialogue systems. In *Proceedings of the International Conference on Spoken Language Processing (ICSLP)*.

T. Koulouri and S. Lauria. 2009. Exploring miscommunication and collaborative behaviour in human-robot interaction. In *SIGDIAL Conference*, pages 111–119.

A. Nasr, F. Béchet, J.F. Rey, B. Favre, and J. Le Roux. 2011. Macaon: an nlp tool suite for processing word lattices. In *Proceedings of the 49th Annual Meeting of the Association for Computational Linguistics: Human Language Technologies: Systems Demonstrations*, pages 86–91. Association for Computational Linguistics.

M. Purver. 2004. *The Theory and Use of Clarification Requests in Dialogue*. Ph.D. thesis, King's College, University of London.

V. Rieser and O. Lemon. 2006. Using machine learning to explore human multimodal clarification strategies. In *ACL*.

G. Skantze. 2005. Exploring human error recovery strategies: Implications for spoken dialogue systems. *Speech Communication*, 45(2-3):325–341.

Svetlana Stoyanchev, Philipp Salletmayr, Jingbo Yang, and Julia Hirschberg. 2012. Localized detection of speech recognition errors. In *SLT*, pages 25–30. IEEE.

K. Toutanova et al. 2003. Feature-rich part-of-speech tagging with a cyclic dependency network. In *Proceedings of the 2003 Conference of the North American Chapter of the Association for Computational Linguistics on Human Language Technology - Volume 1*. Association for Computational Linguistics.

J. D. Williams and S. Young. 2004. Characterizing task-oriented dialog using a simulated ASR channel. In *Proceedings of the ICSLP, Jeju, South Korea*.

I. Witten and F. Eibe. 2005. *Data Mining: Practical machine learning tools and techniques*. Morgan Kaufmann, San Francisco, 2nd edition.

Interactive Error Resolution Strategies for Speech-to-Speech Translation Systems

Rohit Kumar, Matthew Roy, Sankaranarayanan Ananthakrishnan, Sanjika Hewavitharana, Frederick Choi
Speech, Language and Multimedia Business Unit
Raytheon BBN Technologies
Cambridge, MA, USA
{rkumar, mroy, sanantha, shewavit, fchoi}@bbn.com

Abstract[1]

In this demonstration, we will showcase BBN's Speech-to-Speech (S2S) translation system that employs novel interaction strategies to resolve errors through *user-friendly* dialog with the speaker. The system performs a series of analysis on input utterances to detect out-of-vocabulary (OOV) named-entities and terms, sense ambiguities, homophones, idioms and ill-formed inputs. This analysis is used to identify potential errors and select an appropriate resolution strategy. Our evaluation shows a 34% (absolute) improvement in cross-lingual transfer of erroneous concepts in our English to Iraqi-Arabic S2S system.

1 Introduction

Great strides have been made in Speech-to-Speech (S2S) translation systems that facilitate cross-lingual spoken communication (Stallard et. al., 2011). However, in order to achieve broad domain coverage and unrestricted dialog capability, S2S systems need to be transformed from passive conduits of information to active participants in cross-lingual dialogs. These active participants must detect key causes of communication failures and recover from them in an efficient, user-friendly manner.

Disclaimer: This paper is based upon work supported by the DARPA BOLT Program. The views expressed are those of the authors and do not reflect the official policy or position of the Department of Defense or the U.S. Government.

Distribution Statement A (Approved for Public Release, Distribution Unlimited)

Our ongoing work on *eyes-free* S2S systems is focused on detecting three types of errors that affect S2S systems. First, out-of-vocabulary (OOV) words are misrecognized as phonetically similar words that do not convey the intended concept. Second, ambiguous words such as homophones and homographs often lead to recognition and translation errors. Also, unseen idioms produce erroneous literal translations. Third, user errors such as mispronunciations and incomplete utterances lead to ASR errors. We will demonstrate our interactive error resolution strategies to recover from each of these error types.

Section 2 presents our system architecture. Section 3 describes nine interactive error resolution strategies that are the focus of this demonstration. An evaluation of our English to Iraqi-Arabic S2S system is summarized in Section 4.

2 System Architecture

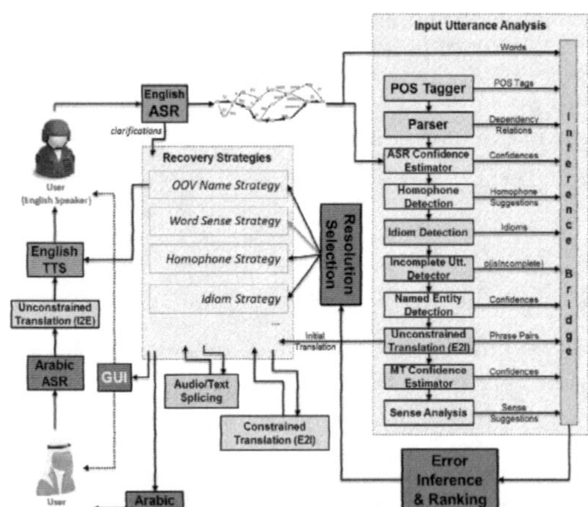

Figure 1: BBN S2S System with Error Recovery in English to Iraqi-Arabic direction

Figure 1 shows the architecture of our two-way

English to Iraqi-Arabic S2S translation system. In the English to Iraqi direction, the initial English ASR hypothesis and its corresponding translation are processed through a series of analysis (e.g. parsing, sense disambiguation) and error detection (e.g. ASR/MT confidence, Homophone/Idiom/Named-Entity detection) modules. A detailed discussion on the various error detection modules can be found in Prasad et. al. (2012). A novel *Inference Bridge* data structure supports storage of these analyses in an interconnected and retraceable manner. The potential erroneous spans are identified and ranked in an order of severity using this data structure.

Based on the top ranked error, one of nine error resolution strategies (discussed in Section 3), is selected and executed. Each strategy is composed of a sequence of steps which include actions such as TTS output, user input processing, translation (unconstrained or constrained) and other error type specific operations. This sequence is hand-crafted to efficiently recover from an error. Following a multi-expert design (Turunen and Hakulinen, 2003), each strategy represents an error-specific expert.

3 Error Resolution Strategies

Figure 2 illustrates the sequence of steps for the nine interaction strategies used by our system.

The *OOV Name* and *ASR Error* strategies are designed to interactively resolve errors caused by OOV words (names and non-names) as well as other generic ASR and MT errors. When a span of words is identified as an OOV named-entity, the user is asked to confirm whether the audio segment corresponding to those words is a name. Upon user confirmation, the audio segment is spliced into the output target language utterance. This is based on the principle that audio segments containing names are understandable across languages.

In the case where a generic erroneous span is detected, the user is asked to rephrase the utterance. This strategy is suitable for handling multiple error types including OOVs, mispronunciations, and generic ASR/MT errors. Additionally, the *ASR Errors* strategy has been designed to

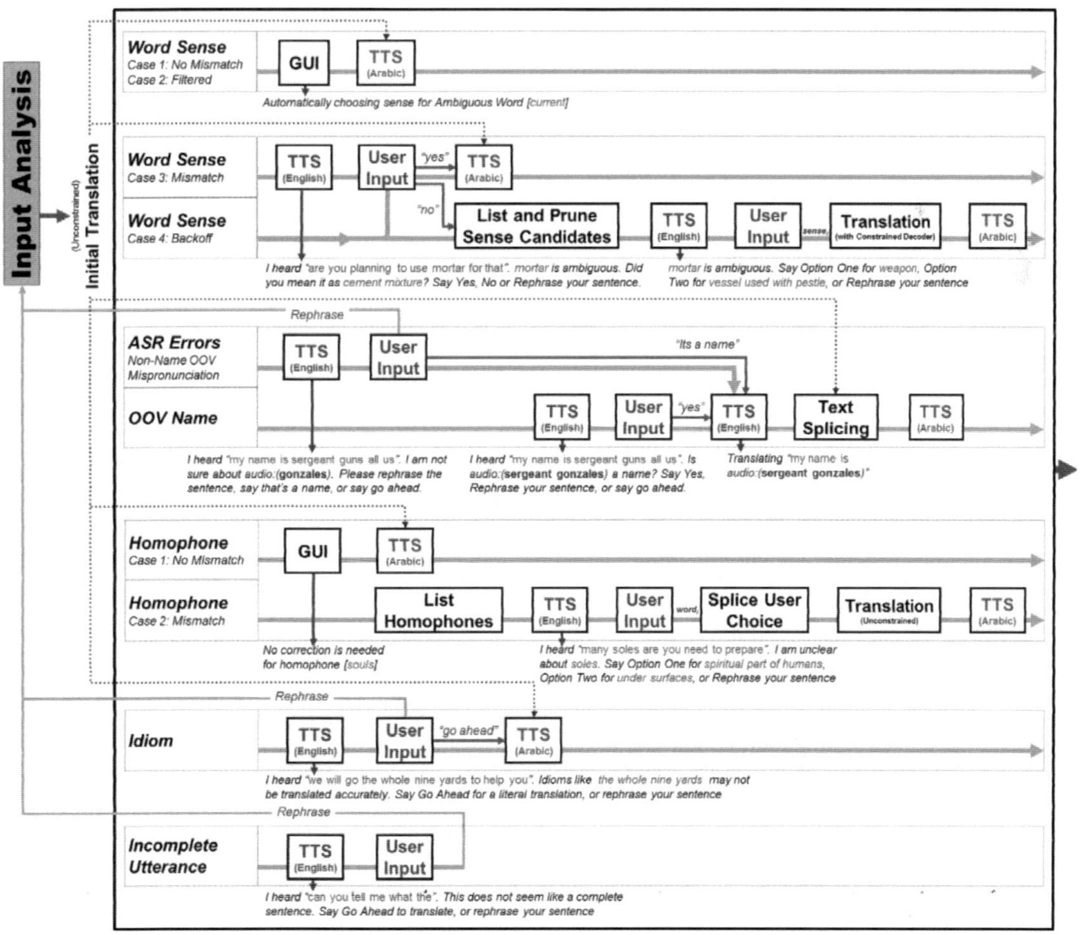

Figure 2. Interaction Strategies for Error Resolution

capture a large fraction of the OOV name false negatives (i.e. missed detections) by allowing the user to indicate if the identified erroneous span is a name. Because of the confusability between the errors handled by these two strategies, we have found it beneficial to maintain reciprocity between them to recover from all the errors handled by each of these strategies.

The four *Word Sense* (WS) disambiguation strategies resolve sense ambiguity errors. The underlying principle behind these strategies is that the sense of an ambiguous word must be confirmed by at least two of four possible independent sources of evidence. These four sources include (a) the translation system (sense lookup corresponding to phrase pair associated with the ambiguous word), (b) a list of source-language contextual keywords that disambiguate a word, (c) the sense predicted by a sense-disambiguation model and (d) sense specified by the user. Besides the objective to minimize user effort, these multiple sources are necessary because not all of them may be available for every ambiguous word. *Case 1: No Mismatch* strategy corresponds to the case where sources (a) and (c) agree. *Case 2: Filtered* strategy corresponds to the case where (a) and (b) agree. In both of these cases, the system proceeds to present the translation to the Arabic speaker without performing any error resolution. If these three sources are unable to resolve the sense of a word, the user is asked to confirm the sense identified by source (a) as illustrated in *Case 3: Mismatch* strategy. If the user rejects that sense, a list of senses is presented to the user (*Case 4: Backoff* strategy). The user-specified sense then drives constrained decoding to obtain an accurate translation.

Albeit simpler, the two homophone resolution strategies mimic the word sense disambiguation strategies in principle and design. The observed homophone variant produced by the ASR must be confirmed either by a homophone disambiguation model (*Case 1: No Mismatch*) or by the user (*Case 2: Mismatch*). The input utterance is modified (if needed) by substituting the resolved homophone variant in the ASR output which is then translated and presented to the Arabic speaker.

Strategies for resolving errors associated with idioms and incomplete utterances primarily rely on informing the user about these errors and eliciting a rephrasal. For idioms, the user is also given the choice to force a literal translation when appropriate.

Following a mixed-initiative design, at all times, the user has the ability to rephrase their utterance as well as to force the system to proceed with the current translation. This allows the user to override system false alarms whenever suitable. The interface also allows the user to repeat the last system message which is helpful for comprehension of some of the synthesized system prompts for unfamiliar users.

4 Summary of Evaluation

Our S2S system equipped with the error resolution strategies discussed in the previous section was evaluated on 103 English utterances (25 unique utterances repeated by multiple speakers). Each utterance was designed to elicit one of the error types listed in Section 1.

The ASR word error rate for these utterances was 23%. The error detection components were able to identify 59% of these errors and the corresponding error resolution strategies were correctly triggered.

The erroneous concepts in 13 of the 103 utterances (12.6%) were translated without any error. Using the error resolution strategies, an additional 34% of the erroneous concepts were accurately translated. This increased precision is achieved at the cost of user effort. On average, the strategies needed 1.4 clarifications turns per utterance.

Besides focusing on improving the error detection and resolution capabilities, we are currently working on extending these capabilities to two-way S2S systems. Specifically, we are designing interactive strategies that engage both users in eyes-free cross-lingual communication.

References

David Stallard, Rohit Prasad, Prem Natarajan, Fred Choi, Shirin Saleem, Ralf Meermeier, Kriste Krstovski, Shankar Ananthakrishnan, and Jacob Devlin. 2011. *The BBN TransTalk Speech-to-Speech Translation System.* Speech and Language Technologies, InTech, 31-52

Rohit Prasad, Rohit Kumar, Sankaranarayanan Ananthakrishnan, Wei Chen, Sanjika Hewavitharana, Matthew Roy, Frederick Choi, Aaron Challenner, Enoch Kan, Arvind Neelakantan, and Premkumar Natarajan. 2012. *Active Error Detection and Resolution for Speech-to-Speech Translation.* Intl. Workshop on Spoken Language Translation (IWSLT), Hong Kong

Markku Turunen, and Jaakko Hakulinen, 2003. *Jaspis - An Architecture for Supporting Distributed Spoken Dialogues.* Proc. of Eurospeech, Geneva, Switzerland

AIDA: Artificial Intelligent Dialogue Agent

Rafael E. Banchs, Ridong Jiang, Seokhwan Kim, Arthur Niswar, Kheng Hui Yeo
Natural Language Understanding Lab, Human Language Technology Department
Institute for Infocomm Research, Singapore 138632
{rembanchs,rjiang,kims,aniswar,yeokh}@i2r.a-star.edu.sg

Abstract

This demo paper describes our Artificial Intelligent Dialogue Agent (AIDA), a dialogue management and orchestration platform under development at the Institute for Infocomm Research. Among other features, it integrates different human-computer interaction engines across multiple domains and communication styles such as command, question answering, task-oriented dialogue and chat-oriented dialogue. The platform accepts both speech and text as input modalities by either direct microphone/keyboard connections or by means of mobile device wireless connection. The output interface, which is supported by a talking avatar, integrates speech and text along with other visual aids.

1 Introduction

Some recent efforts towards the development of a more comprehensive framework for dialogue supported applications include research on multi-domain or multi-task dialogue agents (Komatani et. al 2006, Lee et. al 2009, Nakano et. al 2011, Lee et. al 2012). With this direction in mind, our Artificial Intelligent Dialogue Agent (AIDA) has been created aiming the following two objectives: (1) serving as a demonstrator platform for showcasing different dialogue systems and related technologies, and (2) providing an experimental framework for conducting research in the area of dialogue management and orchestration.

The main objective of this paper is to present and describe the main characteristics of AIDA. The rest of the paper is structured as follows. First, in section 2, a description of APOLLO, the software integration platform supporting AIDA is presented. Then, in section 3, the main features of AIDA as a dialogue management and orchestration platform are described, and a real example of human interaction with AIDA is reported. Finally, in section 4, our conclusions and future work plans are presented.

2 The APOLLO Integration Platform

APOLLO (Jiang et al. 2012) is a component pluggable dialogue framework, which allows for the interconnection and control of the different components required for the implementation of dialogue systems. This framework allows for the interoperability of four different classes of components: dialogue (ASR, NLU, NLG, TTS, etc.), managers (vertical domain-dependent task managers), input/output (speech, text, image and video devices), and backend (databases, web crawlers and indexes, rules and inference engines).

The different components can be connected to APOLLO either by means of specifically created plug-ins or by using TCP-IP based socket communications. All component interactions are controlled by using XML scripts. Figure 1 presents a general overview of the APOLLO framework.

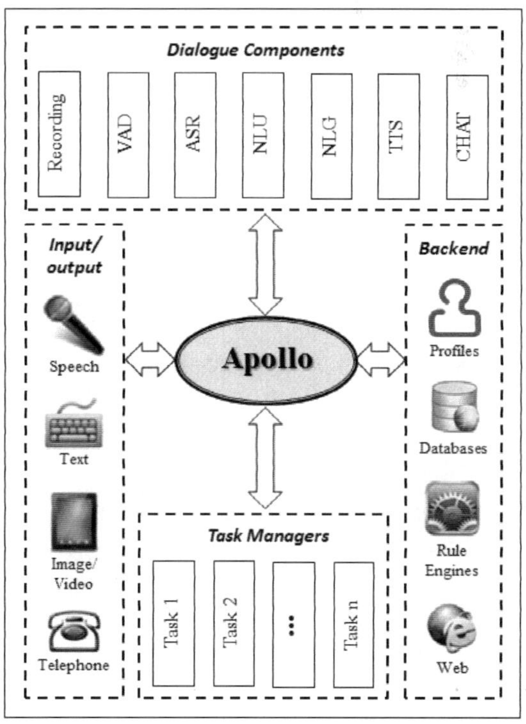

Figure 1: The APOLLO framework

3 Main Features of AIDA

AIDA (Artificial Intelligent Dialogue Agent) is a dialogue management and orchestration platform, which is implemented over the APOLLO framework. In AIDA, different communication task styles (command, question answering, task-oriented dialogue and chatting) are hierarchically organized according to their atomicity; i.e. more atomic (less interruptible) tasks are given preference over less atomic (more interruptible) tasks.

In the case of the chatting engine, as it is the least atomic task of all, it is located in the bottom of the hierarchy. This engine also behaves as a back-off system, which is responsible for taking care of all the user interactions that other engines fail to resolve properly.

In AIDA, a dialogue orchestration mechanism is used to simultaneously address the problems of domain switching and task selection. One of the main components of this mechanism is the user intention inference module, which makes informed decisions for selecting and assigning turns across the different individual engines in the platform.

Domain and task selection decisions are made based on three different sources of information: the current user utterance, which includes standard semantic and pragmatic features extracted from the user utterance; engine information states, which takes into account individual information states from all active engines in the platform; and system expectations, which is constructed based on the most recent history of user-system interactions, the task hierarchy previously described and the archived profile of the current user interacting with the system.

Our current implementation of AIDA integrates six different dialogue engines: (**BC**) a basic command application, which is responsible for serving basic requests such as accessing calendar and clock applications, interfacing with search engines, displaying maps, etc.; (**RA**) a receptionist application, which consists of a question answering system for providing information about the Fusionopolis Complex; (**IR**) I^2R information system, which implements as question answering system about our institute; (**FR**) a flight reservation system, which consists of a frame-based dialogue engine that uses statistical natural language understanding; (**RR**) a restaurant recommendation system, which implements a three-stage frame-based dialogue system that uses rule-base natural language understanding, and (**CH**) our IRIS chatting agent (Banchs and Li, 2012).

Regarding input/output modalities, speech and text can be used as input channels for user utterances. Direct connections via microphone and keyboard are supported, as well as remote connections via mobile devices.

Additionally, audio and video inputs are used to provide AIDA with user identification and tracking capabilities. In the first case, speaker identification techniques are used to compare the voice profile of the current speaker with a set of users already known by the system. In the second case, face detection and tracking are used in combination with sound localization to determine what the current speaker's location is when dealing with multi-party dialogue scenarios.

The main output of AIDA is composed of a browser interface in which several frames, including different visual elements, are presented along with a talking avatar. The different visual elements include a banner, a text display and a general purpose frame for displaying different html files, images or URL's as required.

For avatar and text-to-speech, AIDA relies on the SitePal API (SitePal 2013). This API allows for controlling both the avatar speech and gaze. Speech functionalities are used for generating a spoken form of the system's output (which is also displayed as text in one of the frames of the interface) and gaze functionalities are used in combination with face tracking to direct the avatar attention to the user who is speaking.

Figure 2 illustrates the main output interface of AIDA.

Figure 2: AIDA's output interface.

Finally, an actual example of a user interaction with the AIDA platform is presented in Table 1. In the table, the following information is provided for each of the turns composing the dialogue: the user utterance, the corresponding system response, the engine that was responsible for generating the response, and the action taken by the system (if any action was taken).

Turn	Speaker	Utterance/Action
1	USER	Good morning, how are you?
	AIDA-CH	How can I help you?
2	USER	Can you help me to book a flight?
	AIDA-FR	Flight reservation, how can I help you?
	(action)	*Displays flight reservation main screen*
3	USER	I want to fly from Singapore to Tokyo
	AIDA-FR	What day do you want to leave?
4	USER	Next Monday in the evening
	AIDA-FR	What day do you want to return?
5	USER	The second of April in the morning
	AIDA-FR	Here is your itinerary
	(action)	*Displays flight schedule on the screen*
6	USER	Is there any coffee shop nearby?
	AIDA-RA	There are three coffee shops in this building: Jass Café, Starbucks and Ya Kun
	(action)	*Shows logos of retrieved coffee shops*
7	USER	Do you drink coffee?
	AIDA-CH	Coffee?
8	USER	Yes, coffee
	AIDA-CH	No
9	USER	Why not?
	AIDA-CH	Well, for one thing you can't spell.
10	USER	Please suggest a good Italian restaurant
	AIDA-RR	What area of the city do you want me to search for?
	(action)	*Displays restaurant system main screen*
11	USER	Near Sentosa
	AIDA-RR	Ok, I have found one restaurant for you: Alkaff Mansion Ristorante. Do you want more information or do you want to make a reservation?
	(action)	*Displays http://www.alkaff.com.sg/*
12	USER	Yes please
	AIDA-RR	Ok, I will do a reservation for you! And, how many guests is this reservation for?
13	USER	Only two persons
	AIDA-RR	And, will you be interested in dinner or lunch?
14	USER	Please make it for tonight
	AIDA-RR	Your reservation has been made.
	(action)	*Displays reservation details*
15	USER	Great, thank you
	AIDA-CH	You are welcome

Table 2: Example of a user interaction with AIDA

4 Conclusions and Future Work

In this demo paper we have presented AIDA (Artificial Intelligent Dialogue Agent), the dialogue management and orchestration platform currently under development at the Institute for Infocomm Research in Singapore.

AIDA integrates different communication task styles (command, question answering, dialogue and chat) into a single conversational agent. It also combines speech recognition and synthesis, image processing and avatar technologies to improve the user-system interaction experience.

Our future plans include the incorporation of more vertical applications into the platform, as well as the integration of machine translation engines to develop multilingual capabilities.

Demonstration Plan

During the SIGDIAL demo presentation, the following functionalities will be demonstrated: text and speech input; dialogue orchestration among receptionist, flight reservation, I^2R information system, restaurant booking and chatting agent; and avatar-supported speech and visual output interface. For the case of speech input and avatar-supported output, the use of these technologies is subject to the availability of internet connection at the location of the demo.

References

R. E. Banchs and H. Li. 2012. IRIS: a chat-oriented dialogue system based on the vector space model, in Demo Session of Association of Computational Linguistics, pp. 37–42.

R. Jiang, Y. K. Tan, D. K. Limbu and H. Li. 2012. Component pluggable dialogue framework and its application to social robots. In *Proc. Int'l Workshop on Spoken Language Dialog Systems.*

K. Komatani, N. Kanda, M. Nakano, K. Nakadai, H. Tsujino, T. Ogata and H. G. Okuno. 2006. Multi-domain spoken dialogue system with extensibility and robustness against speech recognition errors. In *Proc. SIGdial Workshop on Discourse and Dialogue*, pp. 9–17.

C. Lee, S. Jung, S. Kim and G. G. Lee. 2009. Example-based dialog modeling for practical multi-domain dialog system. *Speech Communication*, 51, pp. 466–484.

I. Lee, S. Kim, K. Kim, D. Lee, J. Choi, S. Ryu and G. G. Lee. 2012. A two step approach for efficient domain selection in multi-domain dialog systems. In *Proc. Int'l Workshop on Spoken Dialogue Systems.*

M. Nakano, S. Sato, K. Komatani, K. Matsutama, K. Funakoshi and H. G. Okuno. 2011. A two stage domain selection framework for extensible multi-domain spoken dialogue systems. In *Proc. SIGdial Workshop on Discourse and Dialogue.*

SitePal API & Programmer Information, accessed on June 27th, 2013 http://www.sitepal.com/support/

Demonstration of an Always-On Companion for Isolated Older Adults

Candace Sidner
Worcester Polytechnic Institute
Worcester, MA, USA
sidner@wpi.edu

Timothy Bickmore
Northeastern University
Boston, MA, USA
bickmore@ccs.neu.edu

Charles Rich
Worcester Polytechnic Institute
Worcester, MA, USA

Barbara Barry, Lazlo Ring
Northeastern University
Boston, MA, USA

Morteza Behrooz, Mohammad Shayganfar
Worcester Polytechnic Institute
Worcester, MA, USA

Abstract

We summarize the status of an ongoing project to develop and evaluate a companion for isolated older adults. Four key scientific issues in the project are: embodiment, interaction paradigm, engagement and relationship. The system architecture is extensible and handles real-time behaviors. The system supports multiple activities, including discussing the weather, playing cards, telling stories, exercise coaching and video conferencing. A live, working demo system will be presented at the meeting.

1 Introduction

The Always-On project[1] is a four-year effort, currently in its third year, supported by the U.S. National Science Foundation at Worcester Polytechnic Institute and Northeastern University. The goal of the project is to create a relational agent that will provide social support to reduce the isolation of healthy, but isolated older adults. The agent is "always on," which is to say that it is continuously available and aware (using a camera and infrared motion sensor) when the user is in its presence and can initiate interaction with the user, rather than, for example requiring the user login to begin interaction. Our goal is for the agent to be a natural, human-like presence that "resides" in the user's dwelling for an extended period of time. Beginning in the fall of 2013, we will be placing our agents with about a number of users for a month-long, 4 arm, evaluation/comparison study.

[1] http://www.cs.wpi.edu/~rich/always

Figure 1: Virtual agent interface — "Karen"

Our project focuses on four key scientific issues:

- the embodiment of the agent,
- the interaction paradigm,
- the engagement between the user and the agent, and
- the nature of the social relationship between the user and the agent.

1.1 Embodiment

We are experimenting with two forms of agent embodiment. Our main study will employ the virtual agent Karen, shown in Figure 1, that comes from the work of Bickmore et al. (Bickmore et al., 2005). Karen is a human-like agent animated from a cartoon-shaded 3D model. She is shown in Figure 1 playing a social game of cards with user. Notice that user input is via a touch-screen menu. Also, the speech bubble does not appear in the actual interface, which uses text-to-speech generation.

We are also planning an exploratory study substituting the Reeti[2] robot, shown in Figure 2, for Karen, but otherwise keeping the rest of the system (i.e., the menus, text-to-speech and other screen graphics) as much the same as possible. One big difference we expect is that the effect of face tracking with the robotic agent will be much stronger than with Karen. On the other hand, because Reeti is not as human-like as Karen, it is possible that it will not be as well accepted overall as Karen.

1.2 Interaction Paradigm

The main interaction paradigm in our system is conversation, and in particular, dialog. The agent makes its contributions to the dialog using speech, and the user chooses his/her contribution from a menu of utterances provided on the touch screen. Dialogs evolve around various activities and can extend for quite a long time (up to five or ten minutes) if the user chooses to continue the conversation. Dialog models can be created using whatever system that the system designer chooses. In our work, we use models that are scripting formats, a Java state machine model based on adjacency pairs or created with the dialog tool Disco (Rich and Sidner, 2012). This variety of models makes our system more flexible for system designers.

The agent is not designed to accept speech input for several reasons:

- lack of voice models for older adults;
- no reliable means to circumscribe the collection of utterances that the system could understand;
- the wide range of activities to talk about with the agent results in a huge number of utterance structures, semantic structures and possible intentions. We doubt there are existing speech-to-utterance semantics systems available to support such a plethora of choices with high reliability. As our project is *not* about spoken language understanding, we opted not to take on this burden.

Some of the activities between user and agent involve additional on-screen graphics, such as the card game shown in Figure 1, or a Week-At-A-Glance™ style planning calendar. When playing cards together, the user is allowed to directly manipulate the cards on-screen. For the calendar, the user may only do deictic gestures. All other information is handled through dialog. We have thus eschewed other traditional GUI methods using icons, pull-down lists, etc., in favor of using speech and menu dialog interaction whenever possible. The other exception, like direct manipulation of cards on-screen, is a virtual keyboard to allow typing in of proper names of people and places. Our motivation for this design choice is to reinforce the relationship between the user and the agent, and to simplify the interaction in comparison to standard GUIs.

1.3 Engagement

Figure 2: Robotic interface — "Reeti"

Our system continuously maintains a model of the state of engagement (Sidner et al., 2005) between the user and the agent. For example, when the agent senses nearby motion (via infrared) followed by the appearance of a face in its vision system, it decides that the user is initiating engagement. Disengagement can come about at the natural conclusion of the conversation or when the user leaves for an unexpected reason, e.g., to answer a ringing door bell. Because our agent cannot understand sounds in the environment, it may not know why the user has disengaged, but it does have simple strategies for dealing with unexpected interruptions. Generally, the agent does not initiate disengagement, although it may attempt to hurry the conclusion of a session if some event in the user's calendar is about to start.

Since the user and agent have conversations over an extended period of time, it is natural to consider that they have some kind of social relationship (Bickmore and Schulman, 2012; Kidd and Breazeal, 2007). To reason about this relationship, we have implemented a planning system (Coon et al., 2013) that decides which activities are appropriate to suggest to the user each time they interact (in what we call a *session*). This planning system uses a relationship model based on

[2]http://www.reeti.fr

the *closeness* between the agent and user. Their closeness increases as they do activities together. Closeness decreases when the user and agent do not interact for a period of time, such as a few days.

Each available activity has a *required* closeness in order to be undertaken. Only those activities whose required closeness is less than or equal to the current closeness between the user and agent will be suggested for the current session. Activities that, although suggested, do not actually occur (due to user choice or other reasons) are reported to the relationship planning system for planning the next session.

2 Activities for User and Agent

We will demonstrate our operational system with a several of the activities that the user and agent can do together. In total, we will have more than ten different activities including: discuss the weather, learn about the activities to do with the agent, play a social game of cards, talk about family/friends, tell a life story to the agent, promote exercise, promote nutrition, hear a humorous tale from the agent, get health tips from the agent, speak with a friend/family member via Skype™ (with all the details of SKYPE managed by the agent), and manage a personal calendar for the user.

A typical interaction with the agent might start with some greetings (specific to the time of day) and then some discussion of the weather. The weather discussion can be as short as today's weather forecast or extend to the next day, weather in other cities, and weather where friends or family live. At the user's choice, weather might be followed by a social game of cards where the agent's and user's hands in the game and the way the game is played out are commented upon. If the user and agent are somewhat well acquainted, thereafter might follow discussion of the user's family and friends. For each person that agent has learned about, the agent might ask:

Figure 3 shows an excerpt from a menu-based interaction in our currently running system. Following ths discussion of family and friends the user might opt to end the conversation or continue with other activities such as the calendaring system, hearing some health tips from the agent, and so on.

Agent: So how is Mary doing?

- I don't want to talk about her today.
- I'm done talking about my family and friends.
- Overall pretty good.
- Not so great. ⇐*User*

Agent: Oh, what's wrong?

- She is ill.
- She had an accident.
- She lost a family member. ⇐*User*
- She is pretty lonely.
- She is postponing a visit to me.

Agent: That's very sad.

Figure 3: Example menu-based interaction.

Acknowledgments

This work is supported in part by the National Science Foundation under award IIS-1012083. Any opinions, findings, and conclusions or recommendations expressed in this material are those of the authors and do not necessarily reflect the views of the National Science Foundation.

References

T. Bickmore and D. Schulman. 2012. Empirical validation of an accomodation theory-based model of user-agent relationship. In *Proc. Int. Conf. on Intelligent Virtual Agents*, Santa Cruz, CA.

T. Bickmore, L. Caruso, K. Clough-Gorr, and T. Heeren. 2005. "It's just like you talk to a friend"– Relational agents for older adults. *Interacting with Computers*, 17(6):711–735.

W. Coon, C. Rich, and C. Sidner. 2013. Activity planning for long-term relationships. In *Proc. Int. Conf. on Intelligent Virtual Agents*, Edinburgh, UK.

C.D. Kidd and C. Breazeal. 2007. A robotic weight loss coach. In *Proc. 22nd National Conference on Artificial Intelligence*, Vancouver, Canada.

C. Rich and C. L. Sidner. 2012. Using collaborative discourse theory to partially automate dialogue tree authoring. In *Proc. Int. Conf. on Intelligent Virtual Agents*, Santa Cruz, CA, September.

C. L. Sidner, C. Lee, C. Kidd, N. Lesh, and C. Rich. 2005. Explorations in engagement for humans and robots. *Artificial Intelligence*, 166(1-2):104–164.

A Multithreaded Conversational Interface for Pedestrian Navigation and Question Answering

Srinivasan Janarthanam[1], Oliver Lemon[1], Xingkun Liu[1], Phil Bartie[2], William Mackaness[2], Tiphaine Dalmas[3]
[1]Interaction Lab, Heriot-Watt University, Edinburgh
[2] School of GeoSciences, University of Edinburgh
[3]School of Informatics, University of Edinburgh
sc445,o.lemon,x.liu@hw.ac.uk, philbartie@gmail.com,
william.mackaness@ed.ac.uk, tiphaine.dalmas@aethys.com

Abstract

We demonstrate a conversational interface that assists pedestrian users in navigating within urban environments and acquiring tourist information by combining spoken dialogue system, question-answering (QA), and geographic information system (GIS) technologies. In contrast to existing mobile applications which treat these problems independently, our Android agent addresses the problem of navigation and touristic question-answering in an integrated fashion using a shared dialogue context with multiple interleaved dialogue threads. In this paper, we present the architecture and features of our latest system, extended from an earlier version which was built and evaluated with real users (Janarthanam et al., 2013). The new features include navigation based on visible landmarks, navigation adapted to the user's previous route knowledge, and tourist information pushing based on visible and proximal points-of-interest. The system also uses social media to infer "popularity" of geographical entities.

1 Introduction

We demonstrate a conversational interface that addresses the problems of pedestrian navigation and Question Answering (QA) in urban environments, which is an extended version of the system evaluated in (Janarthanam et al., 2013). Our system brings together Spoken Dialogue Systems (SDS) and Question Answering (QA) with Geographic Information Systems (GIS) for user positioning and tracking, city modelling and urban visibility modelling. There has been little prior work that addresses these problems - navigation, visibility, and tourist information provision - in an integrated way. By *navigation*, we refer to the problem of finding appropriate destinations to go to and the task of wayfinding to reach them (Golledge, 1992; Raubal and Winter, 2002) and by *tourist information provision* we refer to the problem of meeting the informational needs of a user about entities such as museums, statues, famous personalities, etc. With the proliferation of smartphones, there has been a number of mobile apps developed to address these problems. However, these apps have the following problems: first, they demand the user's visual attention because they predominantly present information on a mobile screen. This can be dangerous in urban environments, as well as being distracting. Second, these apps address the problems of navigation and tourist information independently and do not employ a shared interaction context. This means that users cannot switch between tourist information and navigation tasks in a natural and fluid manner.

User1: Take me to the National Museum.
System2: The National Museum is about 300 meters away ...
System3: At the KFC, turn left on to South Bridge ...
System4 : Near you is the statue of David Hume.
User2: Who is David Hume.
System5: David Hume was a Scottish philosopher....
User3: Tell me more about David Hume.
System6: He was one of the most important figures in.. ...
System7: You should be able to see the museum in front of you.
User4: Tell me more about the museum.
System8: The National Museum of Scotland is a....

Table 1: An example interaction with SpaceBook

In contrast to existing mobile apps, we present a system that has a speech-only interface and addresses navigation and QA in an integrated way.

Table 1 presents an example interaction with our system showing the integrated use of navigation and question-answering capabilities. Utterance *System4-8* shows the system's capability to push information from the QA system about nearby points-of-interest (PoI) during a navigation task, which the user can then follow-up on (in utterances *User2* and *User3*). The final 3 utterances show a natural switch between navigation to an entity and QA about that entity.

2 Related work

Mobile applications such as Siri, Google Maps Navigation, Sygic, etc. address the problem of navigation while applications like Triposo, Guidepal, Wikihood, etc. address the problem of tourist information by presenting the user with descriptive information about various points of interest (PoI) in the city. While some exploratory applications present snippets of information about a precompiled list of PoI, others applications dynamically generate a list of PoI arranged based on their proximity to the users. Users can also obtain specific information about PoI using Search applications. Also, since these navigation and exploratory/search applications do not address both problems in an integrated way, users need to switch between them and therefore lose interaction context.

While most applications address these two problems independently, some like Google Now, Google Field Trip, etc, mix navigation with exploration. However, such applications present information primarily visually on the screen for the user to read. In contrast, our system has the objective of keeping the user's cognitive load low and preventing users from being distracted (perhaps dangerously so) from walking in the city (Kray et al., 2003). Also, our system allows users to interleave the two sub-tasks seamlessly and can keep entities discussed in both tasks in shared context (as shown in Table 1).

Several systems have addressed the issue of pedestrian navigation (Malaka and Zipf, 2000; Dale et al., 2003; Heinroth and Buhler, 2008). Some dialogue systems deal with presenting information concerning points of interest (Ko et al., 2005; Misu and Kawahara, 2007; Kashioka et al., 2011). In contrast to all these earlier work, we demonstrate a system that deals with both navigation and tourist information issues in an integrated fashion.

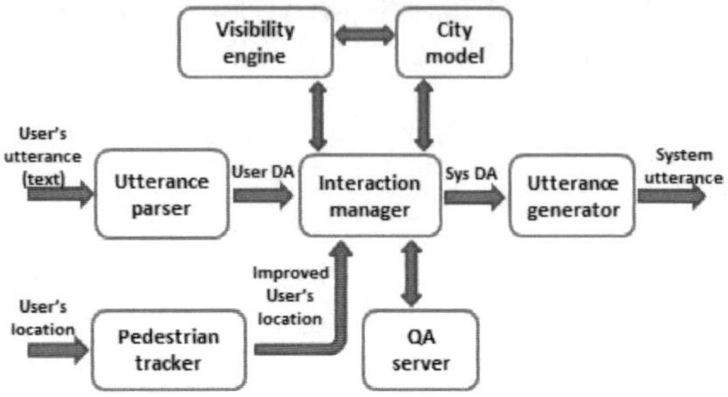

Figure 1: System Architecture

3 Multithreaded dialogue management

The architecture of the current system is shown in figure 1. The Interaction Manager (IM) is the central component of this architecture, which provides the user with navigational instructions, pushes PoI information and manages QA questions. It receives the user's input in the form of a dialogue act (DA) from the ASR module and the user's location (latitude and longitude), orientation and speed from the Pedestrian Tracker module. Based on these inputs and the dialogue context, the IM responds with a system output dialogue act. The Interaction Manager manages the conversation using five coversational threads: dialogue control, response, navigation, question answering, and PoI pushing. These different threads represent the state of different dimensions of the user-system conversation that interleave with each other. Each of these threads generates a dialogue action based on a dialogue policy. A dialogue policy is a mapping between dialogue states and dialogue actions, which are semantic representations of what the system wants to say next. Dialogue actions from the five threads are stored in five separate queues.

The queues are assigned priorities that decide the order in which items from the queues will be popped. For instance, informing the user of a PoI could be delayed if the user needs to be given an instruction to turn at the junction he is approaching. For this reason, priority is assigned to dialogue threads as follows.

Priority 1. Dialogue control (calibration phase, repeat request, clarifications etc)
Priority 2. Responding to user requests
Priority 3. System initiated navigation task actions
Priority 4. Responses to User initiated QA actions
Priority 5. PoI Push actions

Dialogue control The IM initiates the conversation with a calibration phase where the user's initial location and orientation are obtained. In this phase, the IM requests the user to walk a few yards so that the pedestrian tracker can sense the user's location and orientation. During the course of the coversation, the IM uses this thread to manage repeat requests, issues with unparsed user utterances, utterances that have low ASR confidence, and so on. The dialogue control thread is used to manage reference resolution in cases where referring expressions are underspecified.

Navigation The IM identifies the location of the destination entity and queries the City Model for a route plan. The plan provides information such as numbers of exits at junctions, the exit number the user should take, turn angle, popularity index of the street, and the slope of the road. In an attempt to adapt the route instructions to user route knowledge, the IM first picks the most popular street in the plan and asks the users if they can get to the street on their own. Also, the IM queries the Visibility Engine (VE) for highly salient visible landmarks (computed using Flickr tags) that can used to direct the user. Instructions based on visible landmarks are given whenever possible.

Question Answering The system also answers ad hoc questions from the user (e.g. "Who is David Hume?", "What is the Old College?", etc). These are sent to the QA server and answered based on responses from the QA server. The dialogue policy here is to answer the user's question with the first snippet available and ask the user to request for more if interested.

Pushing PoI Information When the user is mobile, the IM identifies points of interest on the route based on two factors: proximity and visibility. Proximity push is done by checking for PoIs near the user using high-scoring ones when there are many, based on tourist popularity ratings in the City Model. Visibility push is done by querying the VE for salient entities visible to the user that may be worth pushing. The dialogue policy is to introduce the PoI entity along with visual descriptors if available. The IM queries the QA server for snippets on entity and if available, pushes them the first snippet to the user. The user is encouraged to ask for more if interested.

4 Conclusion

We demonstrate a mobile conversational system to support pedestrian users in navigation and question-answering tasks in urban environments. The system is a speech-only interface and interleaves navigation and tourist information in an integrated way, using a shared dialogue context. For example, using the navigational context, our system can push point-of-interest information which can then initiate touristic exploration tasks using the QA module. An evaluation of an earlier version was reported in (Janarthanam et al., 2013).

Acknowledgments

The research leading to these results was funded by the European Commission's Framework 7 programme under grant agreement no. 270019 (SPACEBOOK project).

References

R. Dale, S. Geldof, and J. Prost. 2003. CORAL : Using Natural Language Generation for Navigational Assistance. In *Proceedings of ACSC2003, South Australia.*

R. G. Golledge. 1992. Place recognition and wayfinding: Making sense of space. *Geoforum*, 23.

T. Heinroth and D. Buhler. 2008. Arrigator: evaluation of a speech-based pedestrian navigation system. In *Proceedings of 4th International Conference on Intelligent Environments, 2008.*

S. Janarthanam, O. Lemon, P. Bartie, T. Dalmas, A. Dickinson, X. Liu, W. Mackaness, and B. Webber. 2013. Evaluating a city exploration dialogue system combining question-answering and pedestrian navigation. In *Proc. ACL 2013.*

H. Kashioka, T. Misu, E. Mizukami, Y. Shiga, K. Kayama, C. Hori, and H. Kawai. 2011. Multimodal Dialog System for Kyoto Sightseeing Guide. In *Asia-Pacific Signal and Information Processing Association Conference.*

J. Ko, F. Murase, T. Mitamura, E. Nyberg, M. Tateishi, I. Akahori, and N. Hataoka. 2005. CAMMIA: A Context-Aware Spoken Dialog System for Mobile Environments. In *IEEE Automatic Speech Recognition and Understanding Workshop.*

C. Kray, K. Laakso, C. Elting, and V. Coors. 2003. Presenting route instructions on mobile devices. In *Proceedings of IUI 03, Florida.*

R. Malaka and A. Zipf. 2000. Deep Map - challenging IT research in the framework of a tourist information system. In *Information and Communication Technologies in Tourism 2000*, pages 15–27. Springer.

T. Misu and T. Kawahara. 2007. An Interactive Framework for Document Retrieval and Presentation with Question-Answering Function in Restricted Domain. In *Proc. of the 26th IEA/AIE conference*, pages 126–134.

M. Raubal and S. Winter. 2002. Enriching wayfinding instructions with local landmarks. In *Second International Conference GIScience. Springer, Boulder, USA.*

Demonstration of the PARLANCE system: a data-driven, incremental, spoken dialogue system for interactive search

Helen Hastie, Marie-Aude Aufaure*, Panos Alexopoulos, Heriberto Cuayáhuitl, Nina Dethlefs, Milica Gasic, James Henderson, Oliver Lemon, Xingkun Liu, Peter Mika, Nesrine Ben Mustapha, Verena Rieser, Blaise Thomson, Pirros Tsiakoulis, Yves Vanrompay, Boris Villazon-Terrazas, Steve Young

email: h.hastie@hw.ac.uk. See `http://parlance-project.eu` for full list of affiliations

Abstract

The PARLANCE system for interactive search processes dialogue at a micro-turn level, displaying dialogue phenomena that play a vital role in human spoken conversation. These dialogue phenomena include more natural turn-taking through rapid system responses, generation of backchannels, and user barge-ins. The PARLANCE demonstration system differentiates from other incremental systems in that it is data-driven with an infrastructure that scales well.

1 Introduction

The PARLANCE system provides interactive search through a Spoken Dialogue System (SDS). This SDS aims to be *incremental* to allow for more natural spoken interaction. Traditionally, the smallest unit of speech processing for interactive systems has been a full utterance with strict, rigid turn-taking. The PARLANCE architecture, however, is an incremental framework that allows for processing of smaller 'chunks' of user input, which enables one to model dialogue phenomena such as barge-ins and backchannels. This work is carried out under the FP7 EC project PARLANCE [1], the goal of which is to develop interactive search through speech in multiple languages. The domain for the demonstration system is interactive search for restaurants in San Francisco. An example dialogue is given in Table 1.

SYS	Thank you for calling the Parlance Restaurant system. You may ask for information by cuisine type, price range or area. How may I help you?
USR	I want to find an Afghan restaurant.........which is in the cheap price range.
SYS	....[uhuhh]........
	The Helmand Palace is a cheerful setting for authentic Afghan cuisine.
USR	What is the address and phone number?
SYS	The address 2424 Van Ness Ave ....

Table 1: Example dialogue excerpt for restaurant information in San Francisco

2 Background

Previous work includes systems that can deal with 'micro-turns' (i.e. sub-utterance processing units), resulting in dialogues that are more fluid and responsive. This has been backed up by a large body of psycholinguistic literature that indicates that human-human interaction is in fact incremental (Levelt, 1989).

It has been shown that incremental dialogue behaviour can improve the user experience (Skantze and Schlangen, 2009; Baumann et al., 2011; Selfridge et al., 2011) and enable the system designer to model several dialogue phenomena that play a vital role in human discourse (Levelt, 1989) but have so far been absent from systems. These dialogue phenomena that will be demonstrated by the PARLANCE system include more natural turn-taking through rapid system responses, generation of backchannels and user barge-ins. The system differentiates from other incremental systems in that it is entirely data-driven with an infrastructure that potentially scales well.

3 System Architecture

Figure 1 gives an overview of the PARLANCE system architecture, which maintains

*Authors are in alphabetical order

[1] http://www.parlance-project.eu

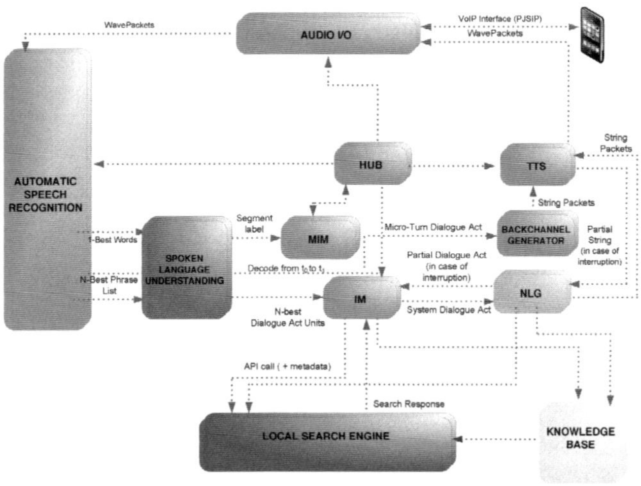

Figure 1: Overview of the PARLANCE system architecture

the modularity of a traditional SDS while at the same time allowing for complex interaction at the micro-turn level between components.

Each component described below makes use of the PINC (Parlance INCremental) dialogue act schema. In this scheme, a *complete* dialogue act is made up of a set of *primitive* dialogue acts which are defined as *acttype-item* pairs. The PINC dialogue act scheme supports incrementality by allowing SLU to incrementally output primitive dialogue acts whenever a complete *acttype-item* pair is recognised with sufficient confidence. The complete dialogue act is then the set of these primitive acts output during the utterance.

3.1 Recognition and Understanding

The Automatic Speech Recogniser (ASR) and Spoken Language Understanding (SLU) components operate in two passes. The audio input is segmented by a Voice Activity Detector and then coded into feature vectors. For the first pass of the ASR[2], a fast bigram decoder performs continuous traceback generating word by word output. During this pass, while the user is speaking, an SLU module called the "segment decoder" is called incrementally as words or phrases are recognised. This module incrementally outputs the set of primitive dialogue acts that can be detected based on each utterance prefix. Here, the ASR only provides the single best hypothesis, and SLU only outputs a single set of primitive dialogue acts, without an associated probability.

On request from the Micro-turn Interaction Manager (MIM), a second pass can be performed to restore the current utterance using a trigram language model, and return a full distribution over the complete phrase as a confusion network. This is then passed to the SLU module which outputs the set of alternative complete interpretations, each with its associated probability, thus reflecting the uncertainty in the ASR-SLU understanding process.

3.2 Interaction Management

Figure 1 illustrates the role of the Micro-turn Interaction Manager (MIM) component in the overall PARLANCE architecture. In order to allow for natural interaction, the MIM is responsible for taking actions such as listening to the user, taking the floor, and generating back-channels at the micro-turn level. Given various features from different components, the MIM selects a micro-turn action and sends it to the IM and back-channel generator component to generate a system response.

Micro-turn Interaction Manager A baseline hand-crafted MIM was developed using predefined rules. It receives turn-taking information from the TTS, the audio-output component, the ASR and a timer, and updates turn-taking features. Based on the current features and predefined rules, it generates control signals and sends them to the TTS, ASR, timer and HUB. In terms of micro-turn taking, for example, if the user interrupts the system utterance, the system will stop speaking and listen to the user. The system also outputs a short back-channel and stays in user turn state if the user utterance provides limited information.

Interaction Manager Once the MIM has decided when the system should take the floor, it is the task of the IM to decide what to say. The IM is based on the partially observable

[2]http://mi.eng.cam.ac.uk/research/dialogue/ATK_Manual.pdf

Markov decision process (POMDP) framework, where the system's decisions can be optimised via reinforcement learning. The model adopted for PARLANCE is the Bayesian Update of Dialogue State (BUDS) manager (Thomson and Young, 2010). This POMDP-based IM factors the dialogue state into conditionally dependent elements. Dependencies between these elements can be derived directly from the dialogue ontology. These elements are arranged into a dynamic Bayesian network which allows for their marginal probabilities to be updated during the dialogue, comprising the *belief state*. The belief state is then mapped into a smaller-scale summary space and the decisions are optimised using the natural actor critic algorithm.

HUB The HUB manages the high level flow of information. It receives turn change information from the MIM and sends commands to the SLU/IM/NLG to 'take the floor' in the conversation and generate a response.

3.3 Generation and TTS

We aim to automatically generate language, trained from data, that is (1) grammatically well formed, (2) natural, (3) cohesive and (4) rapidly produced at runtime. Whilst the first two requirements are important in any dialogue system, the latter two are key requirements for systems with incremental processing, in order to be more responsive. This includes generating back-channels, dynamic content reordering (Dethlefs et al., 2012), and surface generation that models coherent discourse phenomena, such as pronominalisation and co-reference (Dethlefs et al., 2013). Incremental surfacce generation requires rich context awareness in order to keep track of all that has been generated so far. We therefore treat surface realisation as a sequence labelling task and use Conditional Random Fields (CRFs), which take semantically annotated phrase structure trees as input, in order to represent long distance linguistic dependencies. This approach has been compared with a number of competitive state-of-the art surface realisers (Dethlefs et al., 2013), and can be trained from minimally labelled data to reduce development time and facilitate its application to new domains.

The TTS component uses a trainable HMM-based speech synthesizer. As it is a parametric model, HMM-TTS has more flexibility than traditional unit-selection approaches and is especially useful for producing expressive speech.

3.4 Local Search and Knowledge Base

The domain ontology is populated by the local search component and contains restaurants in 5 regional areas of San Francisco. Restaurant search results are returned based on their longitude and latitude for 3 price ranges and 52 cuisine types.

4 Future Work

We intend to perform a task-based evaluation using crowd-sourced users. Future versions will use a dynamic Knowledge Base and User Model for adapting to evolving domains and personalised interaction respectively.

Acknowledgements

The research leading to this work was funded by the EC FP7 programme FP7/2011-14 under grant agreement no. 287615 (PARLANCE).

References

T. Baumann, O. Buss, and D. Schlangen. 2011. Evaluation and Optimisation of Incremental Processors. *Dialogue and Discourse*, 2(1).

Nina Dethlefs, Helen Hastie, Verena Rieser, and Oliver Lemon. 2012. Optimising Incremental Generation for Spoken Dialogue Systems: Reducing the Need for Fillers. In *Proceedings of INLG*, Chicago, USA.

N. Dethlefs, H. Hastie, H. Cuayáhuitl, and O. Lemon. 2013. Conditional Random Fields for Responsive Surface Realisation Using Global Features. In *Proceedings of ACL*, Sofia, Bulgaria.

W. Levelt. 1989. *Speaking: From Intenion to Articulation.* MIT Press.

E. Selfridge, I. Arizmendi, P. Heeman, and J. Williams. 2011. Stability and Accuracy in Incremental Speech Recognition. In *Proceedings of SIGDIAL*, Portland, Oregon.

G. Skantze and D. Schlangen. 2009. Incremental Dialogue Processing in a Micro-Domain. In *Proceedings of EACL*, Athens, Greece.

B Thomson and S Young. 2010. Bayesian update of dialogue state: A POMDP framework for spoken dialogue systems. *Computer Speech and Language*, 24(4):562–588.

Multi-step Natural Language Understanding

Pierrick Milhorat, Stephan Schlögl, Gérard Chollet
Institut Mines-Télécom
Télécom ParisTech, CNRS LTCI
Paris, France
{lastname}@enst.fr

Jérôme Boudy
Institut Mines-Télécom
Télécom SudParis
Paris, France
boudy@telecom-sudparis.eu

Abstract

While natural language as an interaction modality is increasingly being accepted by users, remaining technological challenges still hinder its widespread employment. Tools that better support the design, development and improvement of these types of applications are required. This demo presents a prototyping framework for Spoken Dialog System (SDS) design which combines existing language technology components for Automatic Speech Recognition (ASR), Dialog Management (DM), and Text-to-Speech Synthesis (TTS) with a multi-step component for Natural Language Understanding (NLU).

1 Introduction

Recently speech and other types of natural language are experiencing an increased acceptance when being used for interacting with 'intelligent' computing systems. This trend is particularly reflected by products such as Apple's *Siri*[1], Google's *Now*[2] and Nuance's *Dragon Solutions*[3]. While these applications demonstrate the industry's vision of how we should be interacting with our current and future devices, they also highlight some of the great challenges that still exist. One of these challenges may be seen in the fact that Automatic Speech Recognition (ASR) remains a highly error-prone technology which influences subsequent natural language processing components such as Natural Language Understanding (NLU) and Dialog Management (DM) and leads to often unsatisfying user experiences. Hence we require appropriate tools that better support the testing and studying of language as an interaction modality and consequently allow us to build better, more user-centered applications.

[1] http://www.apple.com/ios/siri/

[2] http://www.google.com/landing/now/

[3] http://www.nuance.com/dragon/

This demo presents our approach of developing a prototyping tool for Spoken Dialog Systems (SDS). Our solution is particularly focusing on the natural language understanding aspect of SDS design. The overall framework is composed of a set of existing open-source technology components (i.e. ASR, DM, TTS) which are expanded by several additional NLP modules responsible for natural language understanding as well as generation. The following sections first provide a general overview of the entire framework and then focus particularly on the NLU part of our solution and the different sub-modules it integrates.

2 Spoken Dialog System Design

A state-of-the-art SDS usually consists of a set of technology components that are integrated to form a consecutive processing chain. Starting on the input side the ASR module produces a hypothesis about the orthographic content of a spoken utterance. The NLU takes this recognized utterance and converts it into a machine readable command or input Dialog Act (DA). The DM processes this input DA and sends the relevant output DA to the Natural Language Generation (NLG) component. The NLG is then responsible for converting the output DA into appropriate natural language text. Finally, the Text-to-Speech (TTS) synthesis component takes the text transmitted by the NLG and speaks it to a user.

According to this general architecture different open-source language components have been integrated to form a loosely coupled SDS framework. The framework includes ASR performed by the Julius Large Vocabulary Continuous Speech Recognition engine[4], dialog management based on the Disco DM library (Rich, 2009; Rich

[4] http://julius.sourceforge.jp/en_index.php

and Sidner, 2012) and TTS achieved through the MARY Text-to-Speech Synthesis Platform[5]. Additionally, we have integrated the WebWOZ Wizard of Oz Prototyping Platform[6] (Schlögl et al., 2010) in order to allow for the simulation of (flawless) natural language understanding. Expanding these existing components we have then developed as a set of modules responsible for actual system-based natural language processing. The following section describes these modules in more detail and highlights the types of challenges they try to overcome.

3 Natural Language Understanding

Within the processing chain of a spoken/text-based dialog system, the NLU component is the link between the wide and informal communication space of a user's input and the formal and rather restrictive semantic space that can be processed by the DM (Mori et al., 2007). Trying to bridge these two spaces we have connected several modules to form an NLU processing segment whose different modules are described below.

3.1 Semantic Parsing

First we use a Semantic Parsing (SP) module to convert the transcribed speech provided by the ASR into so-called Semantic Frames (SFs). To achieve this mapping Jurčíček et al. (2009) designed a Transformation-Based Learning Semantic Parser (Brill, 1995) which we adapted to integrate it with our framework. The algorithm applies an ordered set of rules to hypothetical [*utterance, SF*] pairs in order to find the closest matching SF.

3.2 Semantic Unification

Next we use what we call the Semantic Unifier and Reference Resolver (SURR) module to convert input SFs into SFs that can be processed by the DM input interface. To do this we implemented a bottom-up search algorithm for rewriting trees whose nodes contain lists of valued slots. The algorithm looks for a group of root nodes that can be reached in the forest (i.e. the existing number of trees) by transforming an input SF's set of slots according to the given rewriting rules. It succeeds when all slots can be rewritten into a root list of slots. This module is supported by external knowledge sources such as for example the context in which an utterance has been produced (i.e. it receives input from the Context Catcher module described below). Furthermore it could call operating system functions, sensor readings [7] or other knowledge sources capable of providing relevant data, in order to resolve and disambiguate input. For instance, special-valued slots like 'date=today' are dynamically resolved to the correct data type and value, making the NLU more sensitive to its surrounding environment.

3.3 Context Inclusion

In order to optimize information exchange Human-Human interactions usually build up a common knowledge between dialog participants. This inherent grounding process can be compared to the dialog history recorded in an SDS's DM. Using these recordings we have introduced a so-called Context Catcher (CC) module. The way this module is currently working is as follows: The DM requests information from the user to progress through the task-oriented dialog. The user replies without specifying the type of data he/she is providing, the overall intent of the utterance or the relation to any dialog slot. The CC evaluates the request expressed by the DM and consequently updates various parameters of the SURR component. Consequently the SURR is able to provide a better, more context-specific mapping between raw SFs provided by the SP module and the expected slots to be filled by the DM component.

3.4 Dialog Act Conversion

An SDS's DM expects formal meaning representations to be converted to actual dialog moves or Dialog Acts (DA); similar to parametrized dialog commands. A DA is the smallest unit of deterministic action to support the dialogue flow. The number of DAs that are available at any given point is finite, dynamic and depends on the current state of the dialog (Note: Here a state does not refer to a 'real' state, such as the ones used in Markov Decision Processes or Partially Observable Markov Decision Processes, but rather to a general status of the dialog). In other words, two input utterances carrying the same meaning may lead to different consequences depending on a given dialog state. The right action, i.e. the accurate DA, is to be determined by the NLU component. As there

[5]http://mary.dfki.de/

[6]https://github.com/stephanschloegl/WebWOZ

[7]Note: At the moment sensor readings are not implemented as they are currently not available in the developing environment

is usually a many-to-many matching between SFs and actual DAs we integrated an additional Dialog Act Converter (DAC) module. This module uses the context to generate a list of expected slots for which a user may provide a value (i.e. it converts possible DAs to SFs). Then a matching between the actual inputs and the expectations is applied in order to find the most probable DA.

4 Supporting Mixed Initiatives

SDS dialog designs usually run along an initiative scale that ranges from user-driven to strictly machine-driven interaction. In the case of a machine-driven dialog a user has to follow the requests of the system. Interactions that lie out of the scope of this dialog design are not understood and may either be discarded or, in the worst case, lead to a system failure. Despite this potential for failure, machine-driven designs make the dialog easier to control and thus less prone to errors, yet, due to the lack of adaptability exposed by the system, also less human-like. On the other hand, pure user-driven dialog designs minimize the functional range of a system as they only react to commands without assuring their functional integrity.

The above described modular approach to NLU aims to support a mixed initiative design where a system's integrity and its goals are sufficiently defined; the user, however, is not restricted by the type and amount of spoken input he/she can use to interact. To offer this type of interaction the system needs to handle three kinds of potential mis-usages: (1) out-of-application cases, (2) out-of-dialog cases and (3) out-of-turn cases. To address the first one our training corpus has been augmented so that it includes examples of garbage SFs. As a result an out-of-application utterance triggers a generic reply from the system, notifying the user that he/she is outside the scope of the application. In the case where a user stays within the scope of the application but tries to initiate a new unrelated dialog (i.e. out-of-dialog case), the DM's stack of tasks is incremented with the new dialog. The system will lead the user back to the previous topic once the newly added one is completed. Finally, as for the out-of-turn cases i.e. the cases where a user would answer a system request with a non-expected utterance such as an over-complete one, the NLU process, retrieving the DM's expectations, discards unrelated or over-complete information.

5 Demo Description

Focusing on the NLU aspect of the SDS pipeline this demo will demonstrate how the different modules described above (i.e. SP, SURR, CC, and DAC) work together. An application scenario from the ambient assisted living domain (i.e. the operation of a 'Pillbox' application) will serve as an example use case. It will be shown how the natural language input potentially recognized by an ASR component is further interpreted by our NLU processing segment. All the steps discussed in Section 3 will be visible.

6 Conclusion

In this paper we described a set of NLU components that were integrated as part of a loosely coupled SDS. Separate modules for semantic parsing, semantic unification and reference resolution, context inclusion as well as dialog act conversion have been described. Furthermore we have highlighted how our system offers support for mixed-initiative dialog interactions. A first test of this NLU processing chain showed that the use of our multi-component approach is feasible, and we believe that this solution can be seen as a valuable test and development framework for natural language processing research.

References

E. Brill. 1995. Transformation-based error-driven learning and natural language processing: A case study in part-of-speech tagging. *Computational linguistics*.

F. Jurčíček, F. Mairesse, M. Gašić, S. Keizer, B. Thomson, K. Yu, and S. Young. 2009. Transformation-based Learning for semantic parsing. *Proceedings of INTERSPEECH*, pages 2719–2722.

R. De Mori, F. Béchet, D. Hakkani-Tur, M. McTear, G. Riccardi, and G. Tur. 2007. Spoken language understanding: A survey. *Proceedings of ASRU*.

C. Rich and C. L. Sidner. 2012. Using collaborative discourse theory to partially automate dialogue tree authoring. *Intelligent Virtual Agents*, pages 327–340.

C. Rich. 2009. Building task-based user interfaces with ANSI/CEA-2018. *Computer*.

S. Schlögl, G. Doherty, S. Luz, and N. Karamanis. 2010. WebWOZ: A Wizard of Oz Prototyping Framework. In *Proceedings of ACM EICS*, pages 109–114.

WebWOZ: A Platform for Designing and Conducting Web-based Wizard of Oz Experiments

Stephan Schlögl
Institut Mines-Télécom
Télécom ParisTech, CNRS LTCI
Paris, France
schlogl@enst.fr

Saturnino Luz, Gavin Doherty
Trinity College
University of Dublin
Dublin, Ireland
{firstname.lastname}@scss.tcd.ie

Abstract

The Wizard of Oz (WOZ) method has been used for a variety of purposes in early-stage development of dialogue systems and language technology applications, from data collection, to experimentation, prototyping and evaluation. However, software to support WOZ experimentation is often developed ad hoc for specific application scenarios. In this demo we present WebWOZ, a web-based WOZ prototyping platform that aims at supporting a variety of experimental settings and combinations of different language technology components. We argue that a generic and distributed platform such as WebWOZ can increase the usefulness of the WOZ method.

1 Introduction

The use of language technologies such as Automatic Speech Recognition (ASR), Machine Translation (MT) and Text-to-Speech Synthesis (TTS) has significantly increased in recent years. Drivers of adoption have been enhanced quality and increasingly ubiquitous access to products and services. However, the technology is still far from perfect and typically substantial engineering effort is needed before prototypes can deliver a user experience robust enough to allow potential applications to be evaluated with real users. For graphical interfaces, well-known prototyping methods like sketching and wire-framing support the designer in obtaining early impressions and initial user feedback. These low-fidelity prototyping techniques do, however, not map well onto systems based around speech and natural language. Wizard of Oz (WOZ) tries to fill this gap by using a human 'wizard' to mimic some of the functionality of a system, which allows for evaluating potential user experiences and interaction strategies without the need for building a fully functional product first (Gould et al., 1983).

2 The WebWOZ Platform

WebWOZ is an entirely web-based, open-source Wizard of Oz prototyping platform[1]. It allows for testing interaction scenarios that employ one or more Language Technology Components (LTC). The integration of these LTCs is done via web services. Currently we have integrated ASR from Google using HTML-based Speech Input[2], on-the-fly MT from Microsoft[3] and TTS provided by the Muse Speech Technology Research Platform[4]. In addition we support pre-recorded audio and video files that are accessible through a web server. Table 1 shows the different components currently integrated into WebWOZ. Depending on the application scenario those components can be turned on and off as well as be used in combination (Schlögl et al., 2010; Schlögl et al., 2011).

2.1 Software Requirements

WebWOZ is written in Java and therefore can be hosted on a typical application server (e.g. Apache Tomcat). In addition a relational database (e.g. MySQL) is needed. In order to run experiments we further recommend the use of an up-to-date web browser that is able to adequately interpret recent HTML5 commands. For the moment, the Chrome browser is probably the best choice, since it supports speech input without the need for installing an additional plug-in. However, we are convinced that soon most web browsers will support the majority of HTML5 features required by WebWOZ.

[1] https://github.com/stephanschloegl/WebWOZ/
[2] http://lists.w3.org/Archives/Public/public-xg-htmlspeech/2011Feb/att-0020/api-draft.html
[3] http://msdn.microsoft.com/en-us/library/ff512419.aspx
[4] http://muster.ucd.ie/content/muse-speech-technology-research-platform

Table 1: WebWOZ Component List

ASR	HTML Speech Input
MT	Microsoft Translate
TTS	Muse Speech Technology
	Pre-recorded Audio Files

2.2 Supported Scenarios

One of the main features of WebWOZ is its integrated CMS-like editing functionality. This permits researchers/designers to create their own WOZ experiments without requiring from them any programming skills. They can add, edit, and delete utterances and organize them in different tabs (dialogue stages) using the wizard interface (cf. demo video[5]). Corresponding client (i.e. non-wizard) user/password combinations can be added and distinct interaction modes for the experiment can be set (e.g. ASR on/off, TTS on/off, MT on/off, etc.). The client interface itself runs in a separate browser window, which allows for an easy integration into already existing web applications.

Following this architecture WebWOZ supports the design of a variety of experimental settings. Different scenarios from classic monolingual text-to-text to multi-lingual speech-to-speech interactions are possible. From a wizard's perspective, tasks can reach from pure dialogue management to augmenting LTC output. That is, in WebWOZ a wizard can act as the substitute for a working dialogue manager, linking a test persons' input with an appropriate response by choosing from a set of pre-defined answer possibilities. Alternatively, however, one could be focusing on enhancing the quality of a single LTC by augmenting its output. Examples might include choosing from an n-best list of recognition results or the post-editing of output produced by an MT service.

3 Why a Web-based Solution?

The WOZ technique is usually used for four main purposes related to the design and implementation of dialogue systems: (1) it is used for dialogue data collection, (2) for controlled experimentation (including system evaluation), (3) for exploration of design alternatives and (4) for teaching of system design. Given this context, why should one build a web-based WOZ platform? What are the benefits of such a solution? As it turns out, one can identify benefits to each of the above mentioned main uses of the WOZ method.

[5]http://youtu.be/VPqHfXHq4X0

In terms of data collection, the gathering of multimodal dialogue corpora is often a complex and time consuming enterprise. It requires standardization and uniformity with respect to data format, timing and encoding, as well as collection settings and procedures. WOZ techniques have been increasingly used for this purpose, particularly in the gathering of data for studying multimodal information presentation and interaction e.g. (Rieser et al., 2011). A Web-based platform such as WebWOZ can facilitate data collection by geographically distributed groups while guaranteeing adherence to the requisite standards.

As regards experiments, a crucial requirement from the perspective of scientific methodology is reproducibility. Different research groups need to be able to replicate experiments according to precisely prescribed procedures and settings. Wizard of OZ experiments, however, are usually conducted using purpose built, ad hoc tools and software. This makes replication difficult, if not impossible. WebWOZ provides a widely available, standardized environment in which experimental protocols can be precisely specified and shared with interested research groups, thus supporting reproducibility. These features are similarly important for extrinsic system components evaluation e.g. (Schneider and Luz, 2011) where the overall system functionality should be kept constant while a specific component to be tested (say, an MT module) is varied.

WOZ techniques are also employed for exploration (through prototyping) of design ideas and alternatives, particularly at the early design stages of interactive systems that involve diverse language technology components. In this case, reproducibility and controlled conditions are less important. However, as distributed system development becomes a common practice WebWOZ can be used in such scenarios as a shared design artifact to support the activities of geographically distributed design teams as well as the communication among them.

Finally, WebWOZ can be (and has been) used in support of teaching the development of dialogue systems. While students are usually introduced to WOZ (i.e. written on a lecture slide) only a small portion of them receives actual hands-on experience. One reason for this lack of practical usage might be that in order to be applicable in a teaching context, any approach would have to have a low logistical and technical overhead to enable students to quickly design and carry out evaluations. Our experience with WebWOZ has shown that the web-based approach significantly lowers this barrier. To date more than 50 students were able to design experiments and hence improve their understanding of the complexity of dialogue systems.

4 Uses of WebWOZ in Research

WebWOZ has already been employed in two different research studies. The first study explored the effects of MT when it is used in combination with TTS (Schneider et al., 2010). The second study aimed at building and evaluating a corpus of feedback utterances sent to language learners who try to improve their pronunciation (Cabral et al., 2012).

The experimental set-up of these two studies differed greatly, highlighting the flexibility of WebWOZ. The first study tested the scenario of an intelligent computer system recommending appropriate Internet connection bundles to German speaking customers. To support this scenario a set of pre-defined dialogue utterances as well as the relevant domain utterances (i.e. examples of Internet connection bundles) were collected, automatically translated and then added to WebWOZ. On-the-fly translation was not used as the experimenters wanted to control for any possible inconsistencies. The TTS part of the experiment did not utilize a synthesis directly, but rather used the possibility of WebWOZ handling pre-synthesized audio files. ASR was simulated by the wizard. Voice-over-IP was used to transmit the participant's voice to the wizard, who then selected an appropriate response.

The second study was less restrictive. Here the researcher's goal was to built up and evaluate a corpus of feedback utterances, for which the wizard could be more open in terms of responses. Similarly to the first study a set of pre-defined responses was added to WebWOZ. However, in cases were those utterances were not sufficient, the wizard could use a free-text field to reply. Again Voice-over-IP was used to transfer speech input from a test user to the wizard and TTS was turned off, as the experiment design used textual feedback only.

5 Conclusion and Future Work

We presented WebWOZ a Wizard of Oz prototyping platform that is developed in our research group. WebWOZ differs from existing WOZ tools by being entirely web-based and through its goal of supporting various types of application scenarios. The different features of WebWOZ were highlighted and it was described how two independent studies already made use of them. Future work aims to optimize WebWOZ, to generalise it to further experimental settings and to extend it by integrating additional modalities. To do so the system has been installed in our partner institutions where it has currently been adapted to support additional settings in at least two other research projects. Although we are aware of the fact that the great difference between the interests of individual researchers pose challenges to the design of a truly generic WOZ tool, we believe that our platform can be a helpful starting point for a variety of researchers and designers who may wish to use the WOZ method.

References

J. P. Cabral, M. Kane, Z. Ahmed, M. Abou-Zleikha, É. Székely, A. Zahra, K. U. Ogbureke, P. Cahill, J. Carson-Berndsen, and S. Schlögl. 2012. Rapidly Testing the Interaction Model of a Pronunciation Training System via Wizard-of-Oz. In *Proceedings of LREC*.

J. D. Gould, J. Conti, and T. Hovanyecz. 1983. Composing letters with a simulated listening typewriter. *Communications of the ACM*, 26:295–308.

V. Rieser, S. Keizer, X. Liu, and O. Lemon. 2011. Adaptive Information Presentation for Spoken Dialogue Systems: Evaluation with human subjects. In *Proceedings of ENLG*, pages 102–109.

S. Schlögl, G. Doherty, N. Karamanis, A. H. Schneider, and S. Luz. 2010. Observing the wizard: In search of a generic interface for wizard of oz studies. In *Proceedings of Irish HCI*, pages 43–50.

S. Schlögl, A. H. Schneider, S. Luz, and G. Doherty. 2011. Supporting the wizard: Interface improvements in wizard of oz studies. In *Proceedings of BCS HCI*.

A. H. Schneider and S. Luz. 2011. Speaker alignment in synthesised, machine translated communication. In *Proceedings of IWSLT*, pages 254–260.

A. H. Schneider, I. Van der Sluis, and S. Luz. 2010. Comparing intrinsic and extrinsic evaluation of mt output in a dialogue system. In *Proceedings of the IWSLT*, pages 329–336.

Exploring the effects of gaze and pauses in situated human-robot interaction

Gabriel Skantze, Anna Hjalmarsson, Catharine Oertel
KTH Speech, Music and Hearing
Stockholm, Sweden
gabriel@speech.kth.se, annah@speech.kth.se, catha@kth.se

Abstract

In this paper, we present a user study where a robot instructs a human on how to draw a route on a map, similar to a Map Task. This setup has allowed us to study user reactions to the robot's conversational behaviour in order to get a better understanding of how to generate utterances in incremental dialogue systems. We have analysed the participants' subjective rating, task completion, verbal responses, gaze behaviour, drawing activity, and cognitive load. The results show that users utilise the robot's gaze in order to disambiguate referring expressions and manage the flow of the interaction. Furthermore, we show that the user's behaviour is affected by how pauses are realised in the robot's speech.

1 Introduction

Dialogue systems have traditionally relied on several simplifying assumptions. When it comes to temporal resolution, the interaction has been assumed to take place with a strict turn-taking protocol, where each speaker takes discrete turns with noticeable gaps in between. While this assumption simplifies processing, it fails to model many aspects of human-human interaction such as turn-taking with very short gaps or brief overlaps and backchannels in the middle of utterances (Heldner & Edlund, 2010). Recently, researchers have turned to more incremental models, where the dialogue is processed in smaller units (Schlangen & Skantze, 2011). On the output side, this allows dialogue systems to start speaking before processing is complete, generating and synthesizing the response segment by segment, until the complete response is realised. If a segment is delayed, there will be a pause in the middle of the system's speech. While previous studies have clearly shown the potential benefits of incremental speech generation (Skantze & Hjalmarsson, 2012; Dethlefs et al., 2012; Buschmeier et al., 2012), there are few studies on how users react to pauses in the middle of the system's speech.

Apart from the real-time nature of spoken interaction, spoken dialog technology has for a long time also neglected the physical space in which the interaction takes place. In application scenarios which involve *situated interaction*, such as human-robot interaction, there might be several users talking to the system at the same time (Bohus & Horvitz, 2010), and there might be physical objects in the surroundings that the user and the system refer to during the interaction (Boucher et al., 2012). In such settings, gaze plays a very important role in the coordination of joint attention and turn-taking. However, it is not clear to what extent humans are able to utilize the gaze of a robot and respond to these cues.

Here, we present a user study where a robot instructs a human on how to draw a route on a map, similar to a Map Task. The nature of this setting allows us to study the two phenomena outlined above. First, we want to understand how a face-to-face setting facilitates coordination of actions between a robot and a user, and how well humans can utilize the robot's gaze to disambiguate referring expressions in situated interaction. The second purpose of this study is to investigate how the system can either inhibit or encourage different types of user reactions while pausing by using filled pauses, gaze and syntactic completeness.

2 Background

2.1 Gaze in situated interaction

Gaze is one of the most studied visual cues in face-to-face interaction, and it has been associated with a variety of functions, such as managing attention (Vertegaal et al., 2001), expressing intimacy and exercising social control (Kleinke,

1986), highlighting the information structure of the propositional content of speech (Cassell, 1999) as well as coordinating turn-taking (Duncan, 1972). One of the most influential publications on this subject (Kendon, 1967) shows that speakers gaze away when initiating a new turn. At the end of a turn, in contrast, speakers shift their gaze towards their interlocutors as to indicate that the conversational floor is about to become available. Furthermore, it has been shown that gaze plays an important role in collaborative tasks. In a map task study by Boyle et al. (1994), it was shown that speakers in a face-to-face setting interrupt each other less and use fewer turns, words, and backchannels per dialogue than speakers who can not see each other.

A lot of research has also been done on how gaze can be used to facilitate turn-taking with robots (Mutlu et al., 2006; Al Moubayed et al., 2013) and embodied conversational agents (Torres et al., 1997). Several studies have also explored situated human-robot interaction, where the interlocutors sit around a table with objects that can be referred to, thus constituting a shared space of attention (Yoshikawa et al., 2006; Johnson-Roberson et al., 2011). However, there are very few studies on how the robot's gaze at objects in the shared visual scene may improve task completion in an interactive setting. One exception is a controlled experiment presented by Boucher et al. (2012), where the iCub robot interacted with human subjects. While the study showed that humans could utilize the robot's gaze, the interaction was not that of a free continuous dialogue.

Similarly to the study presented here, Nakano et al. (2003) presented a system that describes a route to a user in a face-to-face setting. Based on studies of human-human interaction, they implemented a model of face-to-face grounding. However, they did not provide a detailed analysis of the users' behaviour when interacting with this system.

Even if we successfully manage to model human-like behaviour in a system, it is not certain to what extent humans react to these signals when interacting with a robot. In the current work, we investigate to what extent the robot's gaze can be used to: (1) help the user disambiguate referring expressions to objects in the shared visual scene, and (2) to either inhibit or encourage different types of user reactions while the system pauses or at turn endings.

2.2 Pauses in the system's speech

Speakers in dialogue produce speech piece by piece as the dialogue progresses. When starting to speak, dialogue participants typically do not have a complete plan of how to say something or even what to say. Yet, they manage to rapidly integrate information from different sources in parallel and simultaneously plan and realize new dialogue contributions (Levelt, 1989). Still, pauses occur frequently within utterances and it has been shown that these play a significant role in human-human dialogue (for an overview, see Rochester, 1973). For example, the timing and duration of pauses have important structural functions (Goldman-Eisler, 1972), pauses (filled and silent) are associated with high cognitive load and planning difficulties (Brennan & Williams, 1995), and whether a pause is detected or not does not only depend on duration but also on its linguistic context (Boomer & Dittmann, 1962).

Recently, several studies have looked into the possibilities of replicating the incremental behaviour of humans in human-machine interaction. Work on incremental speech generation has focused on the underlying system architecture (Schlangen & Skantze, 2011), how to incrementally react to events that occur while realizing an utterance (Dohsaka & Shimazu, 1997, Buschmeier et al., 2012), and how to make the incremental processes more efficient in order to reduce the system's response time (e.g. Dethlefs et al., 2012). In a recent study, we implemented a model of incremental speech generation in a dialogue system (Skantze & Hjalmarsson, 2012). By allowing the system to generate and synthesize the response segment by segment, the system could start to speak before the processing of the input was complete. However, if a system segment was delayed for some reason, the system generated a response based on the information obtained so far or by generating a pause (filled or unfilled). The system also employed self-repairs when the system needed to revise an already realised speech segment. Despite these disfluencies (filled pauses and self-repairs), an evaluation of the system showed that in comparison to a non-incremental version, the incremental version had a shorter response time and was perceived as more efficient by the users.

However, pauses do not only have to be a side-effect of processing delays. Pauses could also be used wisely to chunk longer instructions into shorter segments, giving the user enough time to process the information. In this case, the system should instead invite user reactions during the course of its utterance. In the current work, we investigate to what extent the system can use filled pauses, syntactic completeness and gaze as cues to either inhibit or encourage the user to react when the system pauses.

3 Human-robot Map Task data

Map Task is a well establish experimental paradigm for collecting data on human-human dialogue [30]. Typically, an *instruction-giver* has a map with landmarks and a route, and is given the task of describing this route to an *instruction-follower*, who has a similar map but without the route drawn on it. In a previous study, (Skantze, 2012) we used this paradigm for collecting data on how humans elicit feedback in human-computer dialogue. In that study, the human was the instruction-giver. In the current study, we use the same paradigm for a human-robot dialogue, but here the robot is the instruction-giver and the human is the instruction-follower. This has resulted in a rich multi-modal corpus of various types of user reactions to the robot's instructions, which vary across conditions.

Figure 1: The experimental setup.

3.1 A Map Task dialogue system

The experimental setup is shown in Figure 1. The user is seated opposite to the robot head Furhat (Al Moubayed et al., 2013), developed at KTH. Furhat uses a facial animation model that is back-projected on a static mask. The head is mounted on a neck (with 3 degrees of freedom), which allows the robot to direct its gaze using both eye and head movements. The dialogue system was implemented using the IrisTK framework developed at KTH (Skantze & Al Moubayed, 2012), which provides a set of modules for input and output, including control of Furhat (facial gestures, eye and head movements), as well as a statechart-based authoring language for controlling the flow of the interaction. For speech synthesis, we used the CereVoice unit selection synthesizer developed by CereProc (www.cereproc.com).

Between the user and the robot lies a large map printed on paper. In addition, the user has a digital version of the map presented on a screen and is given the task to draw the route that the robot describes with a digital pen. However, the landmarks on the user's screen are blurred and therefore the user also needs to look at the large map in order to identify the landmarks. This map thereby constitutes a target for joint attention. While the robot is describing the route, its gaze is directed at the landmarks under discussion (on the large map), which should help the user to disambiguate between landmarks. In a previous study, we have shown that human subjects can identify the target of Furhat's gaze with an accuracy that is very close to that of observing a human (Al Moubayed et al., 2013). At certain places in the route descriptions, the robot also looks up at the user. A typical interaction between the robot and a user is shown in Table 1. As the example illustrates, each instruction is divided into two parts with a pause in between, which results in four phases per instruction: *Part I*, *Pause*, *Part II* and *Release*. Whereas user responses are not mandatory in the *Pause* phase (the system will continue anyway after a short silence threshold, as in U.2), the *Release* requires a verbal response, after which the system will continue. We have explored three different realisations of pauses, which were systematically varied in the experiment:

COMPLETE: Pauses preceded by a syntactically complete phrase (R.5).

INCOMPLETE: Pauses preceded by a syntactically incomplete phrase (R.9).

FILLED: Pauses preceded by a filled pause (R.1). The phrase before the filled pause was sometimes incomplete and sometimes complete.

To make the conditions comparable, the amount of information given before the pauses was balanced between conditions. Thus, the incomplete phrases still contained an important piece of information and the pause was inserted in the beginning of the following phrase (as in R.9).

Table 1: An example interaction.

Turn	Activity	Phase
R.1	[gazing at map] continue towards the lights, ehm...	Part I
U.2	*[drawing]*	Pause
R.3	until you stand south of the stop lights [gazing at user]	Part II
U.4	*[drawing] alright [gazing at robot]*	Release
R.5	[gaze at map] continue and pass east of the lights...	Part I
U.6	*okay [drawing]*	Pause
R.7	...on your way towards the tower [gaze at user]	Part II
U.8	*Could you take that again?*	Release
R.9	[gaze at map] Continue to the large tower, you pass...	Part I
U.10	*[drawing]*	Pause
R.11	...east of the stop lights [gaze at user]	Part II
U.12	*[drawing] okay, I am at the tower*	Release

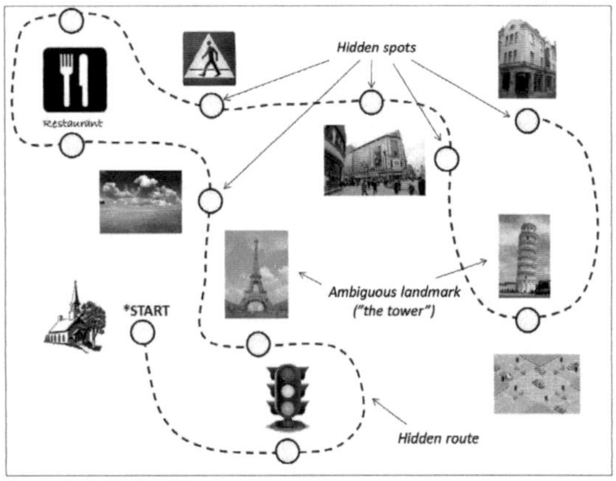

Figure 2: An example map.

Given the current limitations of conversational speech recognition, and lack of data relevant for this task, we needed to employ some trick to be able to build a system that could engage in this task in a convincing way in order to evoke natural reactions from the user. One possibility would be to use a Wizard-of-Oz setup, but that was deemed to be infeasible for the time-critical behaviour that is under investigation here. Instead, we employed a trick similar to the one used in (Skantze, 2012). Although the users are told that the robot cannot see their drawing behaviour, the drawing on the digital map, together with a voice activity detector that detects the user's verbal responses, is actually used by the system to select the next action. An example of a map can be seen in Figure 2. On the intended route (which obviously is not shown on the user's screen), a number of hidden "spots" were defined – positions relative to some landmark (e.g. "east of the field"). Each instruction from the system was intended to guide the user to the next hidden spot. Each map also contained an ambiguous landmark reference (as "the tower" in the example).

Pilot studies showed that there were three basic kinds of verbal reactions from the user: (1) an acknowledgement of some sort, encouraging the system to continue, (2) a request for repetition, or (3) a statement that some misunderstanding had occurred. By combining the length of the utterance with the information about the progression of the drawing, these could be distinguished in a fairly robust manner. How this was done is shown in Table 2. Notice that this scheme allows for both short and long acknowledgements (U.4, U.6 and U.12 in the example above), as well as clarification requests (U.8). It also allows us to explore misunderstandings, i.e. cases where the user thinks that she is at the right location and makes a short acknowledgement, while she is in fact moving in the wrong direction. Such problems are usually detected and repaired in the following turns, when the system continues with the instruction from the intended spot and the user objects with a longer response. This triggers the system to either RESTART the instruction from a previous spot where the user is known to have been *("I think that we lost each other, could we start again from where you were at the bus stop?")*, or to explicitly CHECK whether the user is at the intended location *("Are you at the bus stop?")*, which helps the user to correct the path.

Table 2: The system's action selection based on the user's voice activity and drawing.

User response	Drawing	Action
Short/Long	Continues to the next spot	CONTINUE
Short/Long	Still at the same spot	REPHRASE
Short (<1s.)	At the wrong spot	CONTINUE (with misunderstanding)
Long (>1s.)	At the wrong spot	RESTART or CHECK
No resp.	Any	CHECK

3.2 Experimental conditions

In addition to the utterance-level conditions (concerning completeness) described above, three dialogue-level conditions were implemented:

CONSISTENT gaze (**FACE**): The robot gazes at the landmark that is currently being described during the phases Part I, Pause and Part II. In accordance with the findings in for example Kendon (1967), the robot looks up at the end of phase Part II, seeking mutual gaze with the user during the Release phase.

RANDOM gaze (**FACE**): A random gaze behaviour, where the robot randomly shifts between looking at the map (at no particular landmark) and looking at the user, with an interval of 5-10 seconds.

NOFACE: The robot head was hidden behind a paper board so that the user could not see it, only hear the voice.

3.3 Data collection and analysis

We collected a corpus of 24 subjects interacting with the system, 20 males and 4 females between the ages of 21-47. Although none of them were native speakers, all of them had a high proficiency in English. First, each subject completed a training dialogue and then six dialogues that were used for the analysis. For each dialogue, different maps were used. The subjects were divided into three groups with 8 subjects in each:

Group A: Three maps with the CONSISTENT (FACE) version and three maps with the NOFACE version. All pauses were 1.5 s. long.

Group B: Three maps with the RANDOM (FACE) version and three maps with the NOFACE version. All pauses were 1.5 s. long.

Group C: Three maps with the CONSISTENT version and three maps with the NOFACE version. All pauses were 2-4 s. long (varied randomly with a uniform distribution).

For all groups, the order between the FACE and the NOFACE condition was varied and balanced. Group A and Group B allow us to explore differences between the CONSISTENT and RANDOM versions. This is important, since it is not evident to what extent the mere presence of a face affects the interaction and to what extent differences are due to a consistent gazing behaviour. Group C was added to the data collection since we wanted to be able to study users' behaviour during pauses in more detail. Thus, Group C will only be used to study within-group effects of different pause types and will not be compared against the other groups.

After the subjects had interacted with the system, they filled out a questionnaire. First, they were requested to rate with which version (FACE or NOFACE) it was easier to complete the task. Second, the participants were requested to rate whether the robot's gaze was helpful or confusing when it came to task completion, landmark identification and the timing of feedback. All ratings were done on a continuous horizontal line with either FACE or "the gaze was helpful" on the left end and NOFACE or "the gaze was confusing" on the right end. The centre of the line was labelled with "no difference".

During the experiments, the users' speech and face were recorded and all events in the system and the drawing activity were automatically logged. Afterwards, the users' voice activity that had been automatically detected online was manually corrected and transcribed. Using the video recordings, the users' gaze was also manually annotated, depending on whether the user was looking at the map, the screen or at the robot.

In this study, we also wanted to explore the possibility of measuring cognitive load in human-robot interaction using EDA (electrodermal activity). Hence, in an explorative manner, we investigated how the realisation of the system's pauses and the presence of the face affected the cognitive costs of processing the system's instructions. For measuring this, we used a wearable EDA device, which exerts a direct current on the skin of the subject in order to measure skin conductance responses. For these measurements as well as the logging of the data the Q-Sensor developed by Affectiva[1] was used. The measurements were taken from the fingertips of the subjects. The sampling rate was 8 Hz. All post processing was carried out in Ledalab[2]. We first applied the Butterworth filter and then carried out a Continuous Decomposition Analysis. All skin conductance responses (SCR) with a minimum amplitude of 0.01 muS and a minimal distance of 700ms were used for further analysis. Due to problems with the EDA device, we only have data for six subjects in Group A, six in Group B and none in Group C.

4 Results

Analyses of the different measures used here revealed that they were not normally distributed. We have therefore consistently used non-parametric tests. All tests of significance are done using two-tailed tests at the .05 level.

[1] http://www.affectiva.com/
[2] http://www.ledalab.de/

4.1 Subjective ratings

The questionnaire was used to analyse differences in subjective ratings between Group A and B. The marks on the horizontal continuous lines in the questionnaire were measured with a ruler based on their distance from the midpoint (labelled with "no difference") and normalized to a scale between 0 and 1. A Wilcoxon Signed Ranks Test was carried out, using these rankings as differences. The results show that the Consistent version differed significantly from the midpoint ("no difference") in four dimensions whereas there were no significant differences from the midpoint for RANDOM version. More specifically, Group A (CONSISTENT) (n=8) found it easier to complete the task in the face condition than in the no face condition (Mdn=0.88, Z=-2.54, p=.012). The same group thought that the robot's gaze was helpful rather than confusing when it came to task completion (Mdn=0.84, Z=-2.38, p=.017), landmark identification (Mdn=0.83, Z=-2.52, p=.012) and to decide when to give feedback (Mdn=0.66, Z=-1.99, p=.046). The results of the questionnaire are presented in Figure 3.

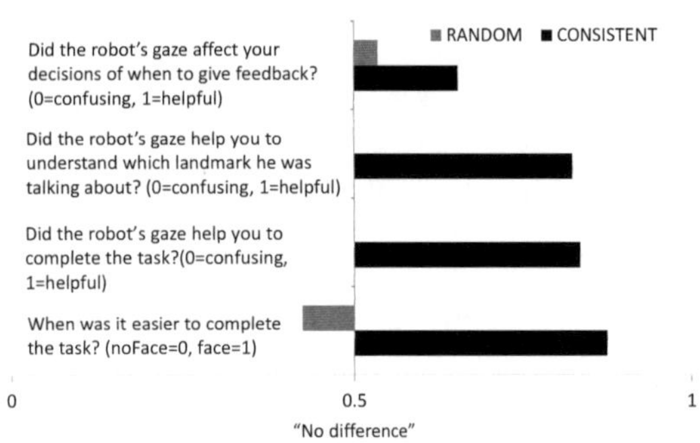

Figure 3: The results from the questionnaire. The bars show the median rating for Group A (consistent) and Group B (random).

4.2 Task completion

Apart from the subjective ratings, we also wanted to see whether the face-to-face setting affected task completion. In order to explore this, we analysed the time and number of utterances it took for the users to complete the maps. On average, the dialogues in Group A (CONSISTENT) were 2.5 system utterances shorter and 8.9 seconds faster in the FACE condition than in the NOFACE condition. For Group B (RANDOM), the dialogues were instead 2.3 system utterances and 17.3 seconds longer in the FACE condition (Mann-Whitney U-test, $p<.05$). Thus, it seems like the face facilitates the solving of the task, and that this is not just due to the mere presence of a face, but that the intelligent gaze behaviour actually contributes. In fact, the RANDOM gaze worsens the performance, possibly because subjects spent time on trying to make sense of signals that did not provide any useful information.

Looking at more local phenomena, it seems like there was also a noticeable difference when it comes to miscommunication. The dialogues in the RANDOM/FACE condition had a total of 18 system utterances of the type RESTART (vs. 7 in CONSISTENT), and a total of 33 CHECK utterances (vs. 15 in CONSISTENT). A chi-square test shows that the differences are statistically significant ($\chi^2(1, N=25) = 4.8$, p =.028; $\chi^2(1, N=48) = 6.75$, p=.009). This indicates that the users that did not get the CONSISTENT gaze to a larger extent did not manage to follow the system's instructions, most likely because they did not get guidance from the robot's gaze in disambiguating referring expressions.

4.3 Gaze behaviour

In order to analyse the users' direction of attention during the dialogues, the manual annotation of the participants' gaze was analysed. First, we explored how the completion type of the robot's utterance affected the users' gaze. In this analysis, FILLED and INCOMPLETE have been merged (since there was no difference in the users' gaze between these conditions). The percentage of gaze at the robot over the four different utterance phases for complete and incomplete utterances is plotted in Figure A in the Appendix. Note that the different phases actually are of different lengths depending on the actual content of the utterance and the length of the pause. However, these lengths have been normalized in order to make it possible to analyse the average user behaviour. For each phase, a Mann-Whitney U-test was conducted. The results show that the percentage of gaze at Furhat during the mid-utterance pause is higher when the first part of the utterance is incomplete than when it is complete (U=7573.0, $p<.001$). There were, however, no significant differences in gaze direction between complete and incomplete utterance during the other three phases ($p>.05$). This indicates that users gaze at the robot to elicit a continuation of the instruction when it is incomplete.

Second, we wanted to explore if gaze direction can be used as a cue of whether the user will provide a verbal response in the pause or not. The percentage of gaze at the robot over the four utterance phases for system utterances with and without user response in the pause is plotted in Figure B in the Appendix. For each phase, a Mann-Whitney U-test was conducted. The results show that the percentage of gaze at Furhat during the mid-utterance pause (U=1945.5, p=.008) and Part II (U=2090.0, p=.008) of the utterance is lower when the user gives a verbal response compared to when there is no response. There were however no significant differences in gaze direction between complete and incomplete utterance during the other two phases (p>.05).

4.4 Verbal feedback behaviour

Apart from the user's gaze behaviour, we also wanted to see whether syntactic completeness before pauses had an effect on whether the users gave verbal responses in the pause. Figure 4 shows the extent to which users gave feedback within pauses, depending on pause type and FACE/NOFACE condition. As can be seen, COMPLETE triggers more feedback, FILLED less feedback and INCOMPLETE even less. Interestingly, this difference is more distinct in the FACE condition ($\chi^2(2, N=157) = 10.32$, p<.01). In fact, the difference is not significant in the NOFACE condition (p >.05).

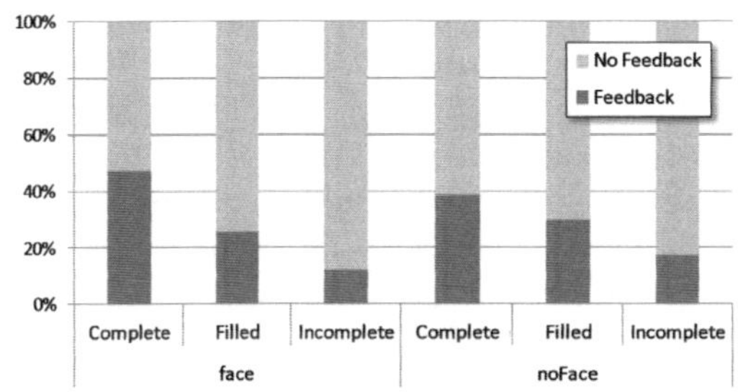

Figure 4: Presence of feedback depending on pause type (Group C).

In Skantze et al. (2013), we have also done a more thorough analysis of the verbal acknowledgements from the users. The analysis shows that the prosody and lexical choice in these acknowledgements ("okay", "yes", "yeah", "mm", "mhm", "ah", "alright" and "oh") to some extent signal whether the drawing activity is about to be initiated or has been completed. The analysis also shows how these parameters are correlated to the perception of uncertainty.

4.5 Drawing behaviour

Whereas gaze and verbal responses can be regarded as communicative signals, the users were told that the robot could not observe their drawing activity. However, the drawing of the route can be regarded as the purpose of the interaction and it is therefore important to understand how this is affected by the system's behaviour under different conditions. First, we wanted to see how the completeness of the robot's utterance in combination with the presence of the face affected the drawing activity. In this analysis, FILLED and INCOMPLETE have been merged (since there was no clear difference). The mean drawing activity over the four phases of the descriptions is plotted in Figure C in the Appendix. For each phase, a Kruskal-Wallis test was conducted showing that there is a significant difference between the conditions in the Pause phase (H(3) = 28.8, p<.001). Post-hoc tests showed that FACE/INCOMPLETE has a lower drawing activity than the other conditions, and that NOFACE/INCOMPLETE has a lower drawing activity than the COMPLETE condition. Thus, INCOMPLETE phrases before pauses seem to have an inhibiting effect on the user's drawing activity in general, but this effect appears to be much larger in the FACE condition.

Second, we aimed to investigate to what extent the robot's gaze at landmarks during ambiguous references helps users to discriminate between landmarks. The mean drawing activity over the four phases of the descriptions of ambiguous landmarks is plotted in Figure D in the Appendix. For each phase, a Kruskal-Wallis test was conducted showing that there is a significant difference between the conditions in the Part II phase (H(2)=10.2, p=.006). Post-hoc tests showed that CONSISTENT has a higher drawing activity than the RANDOM and NOFACE conditions. However, there is no such difference when looking at non-ambiguous descriptions. This shows that robot's gaze at the target landmark during ambiguous references makes it possible for the subjects to start to draw quicker.

4.6 Cognitive load

As mentioned above, we also wanted to study the cognitive costs of processing the system's instructions, as measured with a wearable EDA device. For each system utterance part (Part I and Part II), we calculated the sum of the amplitudes of the skin conductance responses (SoSCR) during the following three seconds. The SoSCR during the pause, depending on pause type are shown in Figure 5. A Kruskal-Wallis test revealed that there is an overall effect (H(2)=8.7, p=.13), and post-hoc tests showed that there is a significant difference between utterances which are incomplete and those with filled pauses, indicating that the syntactic incompleteness without a filled pause leads to a higher cognitive load. We have no good explanation for this, and we do not know whether this is due to how the syntactically incomplete segments were realised by the synthesizer, or whether the same effect would appear in human-human interaction.

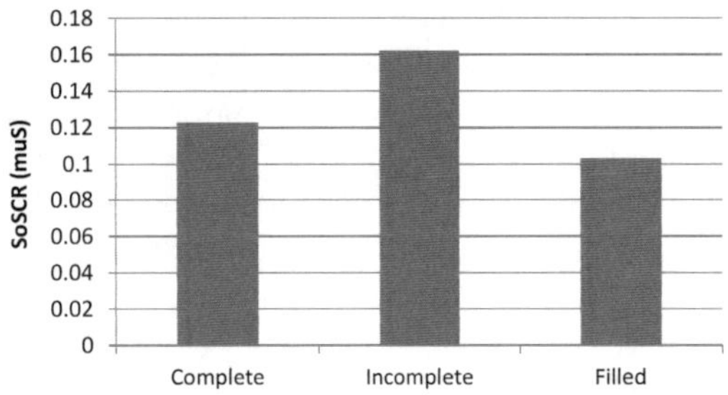

Figure 5: EDA at different pause types (Group A and B).

A similar analysis was done after both Part I and Part II to see if there is any difference in SoSCR between ambiguous and non-ambiguous references in the different conditions, as shown in in Figure 6. No such differences were found for Group B, but for Group A, ambiguous references were followed by a higher SoSCR in the NoFace condition, indicating that the robot's gaze helps in disambiguating the referring expressions and reduces cognitive load (Mann-Whitney U-test; $U = 6585$, $p = .001$).

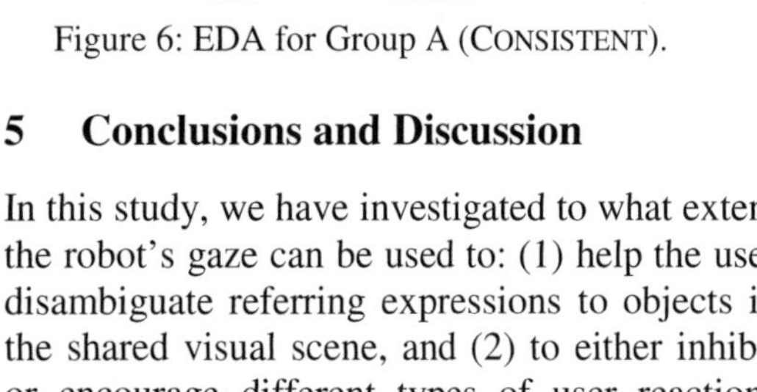

Figure 6: EDA for Group A (CONSISTENT).

5 Conclusions and Discussion

In this study, we have investigated to what extent the robot's gaze can be used to: (1) help the user disambiguate referring expressions to objects in the shared visual scene, and (2) to either inhibit or encourage different types of user reactions while the system pauses. The results show that the robot's gaze behaviour was rated as helpful rather than confusing for task completion, landmark identification and feedback timing. These effects were not present when the robot used a random gaze behaviour. The efficiency of the gaze was further supported by the time it took to complete the task and the number of misunderstandings. These results in combination with a faster drawing activity and lower cognitive load when system's reference was ambiguous, suggest that the users indeed utilized the system's gaze to discriminate between landmarks.

The second purpose of this study was to investigate to what extent filled pauses, syntactic completeness and gaze can be used as cues to either inhibit or encourage the user to react in pauses. First, the results show that pauses preceded by incomplete syntactic segments or filled pauses appear to inhibit user activity. Thus, our analyses of gaze and drawing activity show that users give less feedback, draw less and look at the robot to a larger extent when the preceding system utterance segment is incomplete than when it is complete. An interesting observation is that the inhibiting effect on drawing activity appears to be more pronounced in the face-to-face condition, which indicates that gaze also plays an important role here (since the robot looked down at the map during the pauses). Additionally, there is less cognitive load when the silence is preceded by a filled pause. These results suggest that incomplete system utterances prevent further user processing; instead the user waits for more input from the system before starting to carry out the system's instruction. After complete utterance segments, however, there is more drawing activity and the user looks less at the robot, suggesting that the user has already started to carry out the system's instruction.

The results presented in this study have implications for generating multimodal behaviours incrementally in dialogue systems for human-robot interaction. Such a system should be able to generate speech and gaze intelligently in order to inhibit or encourage the user to act, depending on the state of the system's processing. In future studies, we plan to extend our previous model of incremental speech generation (Skantze & Hjalmarsson, 2012) with such capabilities.

Acknowledgments

Gabriel Skantze is supported by the Swedish research council (VR) project *Incremental processing in multimodal conversational systems* (2011-6237). Anna Hjalmarsson is supported by the Swedish Research Council (VR) project *Classifying and deploying pauses for flow control in conversational systems* (2011-6152). Catharine Oertel is supported by *GetHomeSafe* (EU 7th Framework STREP 288667).

References

Al Moubayed, S., Skantze, G., & Beskow, J. (2013). The Furhat Back-Projected Humanoid Head - Lip reading, Gaze and Multiparty Interaction. International Journal of Humanoid Robotics, 10(1).

Anderson, A., Bader, M., Bard, E., Boyle, E., Doherty, G., Garrod, *S., Isard,* S., Kowtko, J., McAllister, J., Miller, J., Sotillo, C., Thompson, H., & Weinert, R. (1991). The HCRC Map Task corpus. *Language and Speech, 34*(4), 351-366.

Bohus, D., & Horvitz, E. (2010). Facilitating multiparty dialog with gaze, gesture, and speech. In *Proc ICMI'*10. Beijing, China.

Boomer, D. S., & Dittmann, A. T. (1962). Hesitation pauses and juncture pauses in speech. *Language and Speech, 5*, 215-222.

Boucher, J. D., Pattacini, U., Lelong, A., Bailly, G., Elisei, F., Fagel, S., Dominey, P. F., & Ventre-Dominey, J. (2012). I reach faster when I see you look: gaze effects in human-human and human-robot face-to-face cooperation. *Frontiers in neurorobotics, 6.*

Boyle, E., Anderson, A., & Newlands, A. (1994). The effects of visibility on dialogue and performance in a cooperative problem solving task. *Language and speech, 37*(1), 1-20.

Brennan, S., & Williams, M. (1995). The Feeling of Another's knowing: Prosody and Filled Pauses as Cues to Listeners about the Metacognitive States of Speakers. *Journal of Memory and Language, 34*, 383-398.

Buschmeier, H., Baumann, T., Dosch, B., Kopp, S., & Schlangen, D. (2012). Combining incremental language generation and incremental speech synthesis for adaptive information presentation. In *Proceedings of SigDial* (pp. 295–303). Seoul, South Korea.

Cassell, J. (1999). Nudge, nudge, wink, wink: Elements of face-toface conversation for embodied conversational agents. In Cassell, J., Suillivan, J., Prevost, S., & Churchill, E. (Eds.), *Embodied Conversational Agents*. Cambridge, MA: MIT Press.

Dethlefs, N., Hastie, H., Rieser, V., & Lemon, O. (2012). Optimising Incremental Dialogue Decisions Using Information Density for Interactive Systems. In *Proceedings of the Conference on Empirical Methods in Natural Language Processing (EMNLP)* (pp. 82-93). Jeju, South Korea.

Dohsaka, K., & Shimazu, A. (1997). System architecture for spoken utterance production in collaborative dialogue. In *Working Notes of IJCAI 1997 Workshop on Collaboration, Cooperation and Conflict in Dialogue Systems.*

Duncan, S. (1972). Some Signals and Rules for Taking Speaking Turns in Conversations. *Journal of Personality and Social Psychology, 23*(2), 283-292.

Goldman-Eisler, F. (1972). Pauses, clauses, sentences. *Language and Speech, 15*, 103-113.

Heldner, M., & Edlund, J. (2010). Pauses, gaps and overlaps in conversations. *Journal of Phonetics, 38*, 555-568.

Johnson-Roberson, M., Bohg, J., Skantze, G., Gustafson, J., Carlson, R., Rasolzadeh, B., & Kragic, D. (2011). Enhanced Visual Scene Understanding through Human-Robot Dialog. In *IEEE/RSJ International Conference on Intelligent Robots and Systems.*

Kendon, A. (1967). Some functions of gaze direction in social interaction. *Acta Psychologica, 26*, 22-63.

Kleinke, C. L. (1986). Gaze and eye contact: a research review. *Psychological Bulletin, 100*, 78-100.

Mutlu, B., Forlizzi, J., & Hodgins, J. (2006). A storytelling robot: Modeling and evaluation of human-like gaze behavior. In *Proceedings of 6th IEEE-RAS International Conference on Humanoid Robots* (pp. 518-523).

Nakano, Y., Reinstein, G., Stocky, T., & Cassell, J. (2003). Towards a model of face-to-face grounding. In *Proceedings of the Annual Meeting of the Association for Computational Linguistics (ACL 2003)* (pp. 553-561).

Rochester, S. R. (1973). The significance of Pauses in Spontaneous Speech. *Journal of Psycholinguistic Research, 2*(1).

Schlangen, D., & Skantze, G. (2011). A General, Abstract Model of Incremental Dialogue Processing. *Dialogue & Discourse, 2*(1), 83-111.

Skantze, G., & Al Moubayed, S. (2012). IrisTK: a statechart-based toolkit for multi-party face-to-face interaction. In *Proceedings of ICMI.* Santa Monica, CA.

Skantze, G., & Hjalmarsson, A. (2012). Towards Incremental Speech Generation in Conversational Systems. *Computer Speech & Language, 27*(1), 243-262.

Skantze, G., Oertel, C., & Hjalmarsson, A. (2013). User feedback in human-robot interaction: Prosody, gaze and timing. In *Proceedings of Interspeech.*

Skantze, G. (2012). A Testbed for Examining the Timing of Feedback using a Map Task. In *Proceedings of the Interdisciplinary Workshop on Feedback Behaviors in Dialog.* Portland, OR.

Torres, O., Cassell, J., & prevost, S. (1997). Modeling gaze behavior as a function of discourse structure. *Proc. of the First International Workshop on Human-Computer Conversation.*

Vertegaal, R., Slagter, R., van der Veer, G., & Nijholt, A. (2001). Eye gaze patterns in conversations: there is more to conversational agents than meets the eyes. In *Proceedings of ACM Conf. on Human Factors in Computing Systems.*

Yoshikawa, Y., Shinozawa, K., Ishiguro, H., Hagita, N., & Miyamoto, T. (2006). Responsive robot gaze to interaction partner. In *Proceedings of robotics: Science and systems.*

Appendix

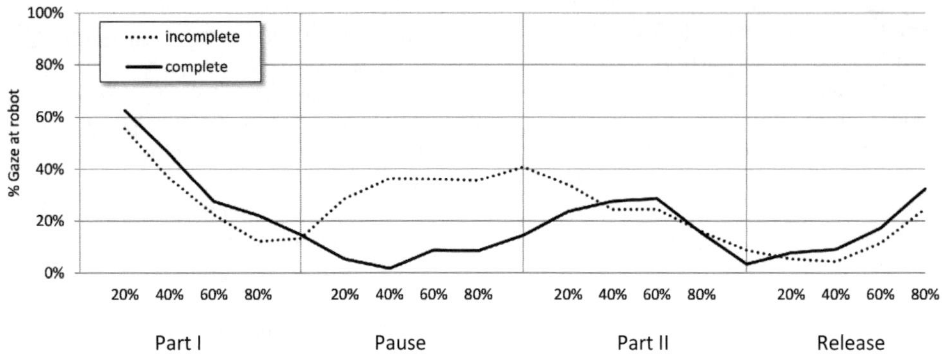

Figure A: Average user gaze depending on pause type (Group C).

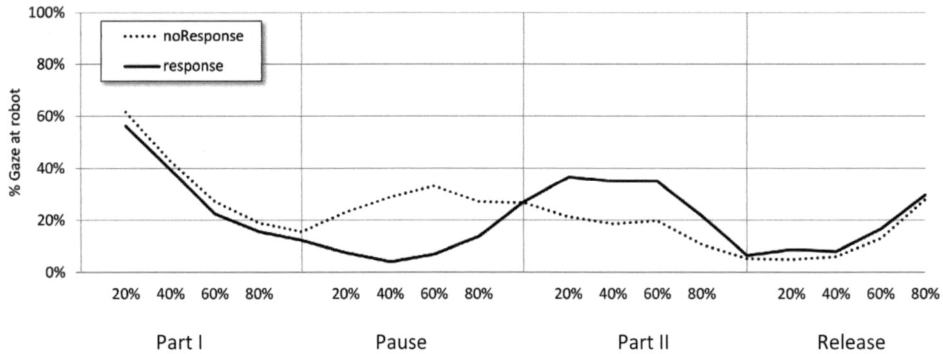

Figure B: Average user gaze depending whether the user responds in the pause (Group A and B).

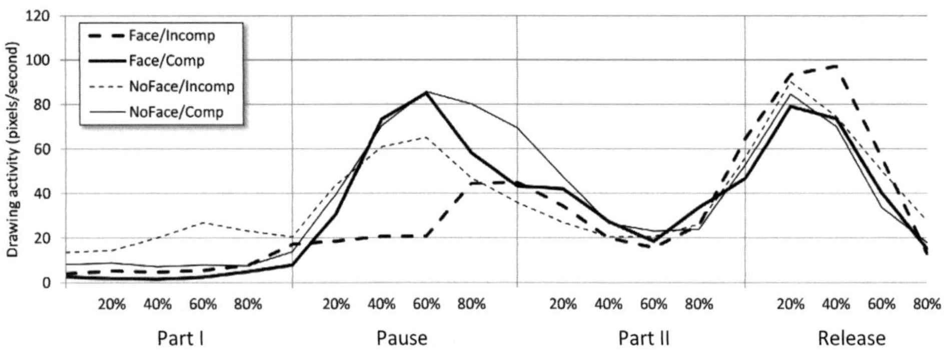

Figure C: Average drawing activity depending on pause type and the presence of the face (Group C).

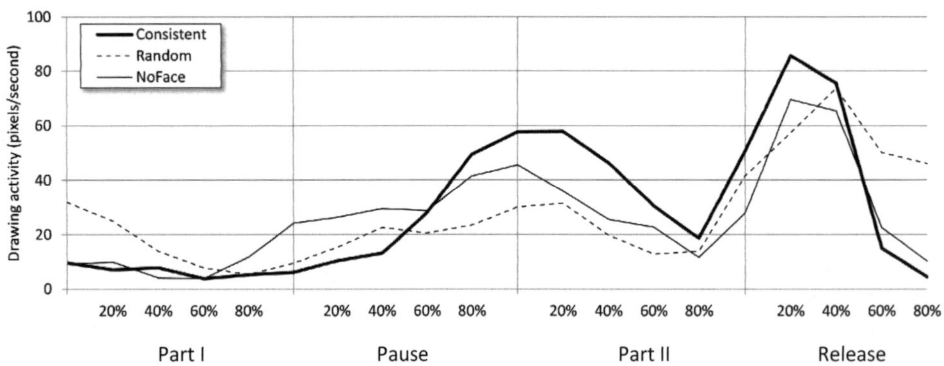

Figure D: Average drawing activity during ambiguous references depending on condition (Group A and B).

Interpreting Situated Dialogue Utterances: an Update Model that Uses Speech, Gaze, and Gesture Information

Casey Kennington
CITEC, Bielefeld University
ckennington[1]

Spyros Kousidis
Bielefeld University
spyros.kousidis[2]

David Schlangen
Bielefeld University
david.schlangen[2]

[1]@cit-ec.uni-bielefeld.de
[2]@uni-bielefeld.de

Abstract

In situated dialogue, speakers share time and space. We present a statistical model for understanding natural language that works incrementally (i.e., in real, shared time) and is grounded (i.e., links to entities in the shared space). We describe our model with an example, then establish that our model works well on non-situated, telephony application-type utterances, show that it is effective in grounding language in a situated environment, and further show that it can make good use of embodied cues such as gaze and pointing in a fully multi-modal setting.

1 Introduction

Speech by necessity unfolds over time, and in spoken conversation, this time is shared between the participants. Speakers are also by necessity located, and in face-to-face conversation, they share their (wider) location (that is, they are *co*-located). The constraints that arise from this set of facts are often ignored in computational research on spoken dialogue, and where they are addressed, typically only one of the two is addressed.

Here, we present a model that computes in an incremental fashion an intention representation for dialogue acts that may comprise both spoken language and embodied cues such as gestures and gaze, where these representations are grounded in representations of the shared visual context. The model is trained on conversational data and can be used as an understanding module in an incremental, situated dialogue system.

Our paper begins with related work and background and then specifies in an abstract way the task of the model. We describe our model formally in Section 4, followed by three experiments with the model, the first establishing it with a traditional spoken language understanding (SLU) setting, the second to show that our model works well under situated conditions, and the third shows that our model can make use of embodied cues. We finish the paper with a general discussion and future work.

2 Related Work and Background

The work presented in this paper connects and extends several areas of research: *grounded semantics* (Roy, 2005; Hsiao et al., 2008; Liu et al., 2012), which aims to connect language with the world, but typically does not work incrementally; *semantic parsing / statistical natural language understanding* (NLU), which aims to map an utterance to its meaning representation (using various routes and approaches, such as logical forms (Zettlemoyer and Collins, 2007; Zettlemoyer and Collins, 2009), dependency-based compositional semantics (Liang et al., 2011), neural networks (Huang and Er, 2010), Markov Logic Networks (MLN) (Meurs et al., 2008; Meza-Ruiz et al., 2008), and dynamic Bayesian networks (Meurs et al., 2009); see also overviews in (De Mori et al., 2008; Wang et al., 2011)), but typically neither provides situated interpretations nor incremental specifications of the representations; *incremental* NLU (DeVault et al., 2009; DeVault et al., 2011; Aist et al., 2007; Schlangen and Skantze, 2009), which focuses on incrementality, but not on situational grounding; integration of *gaze* into language understanding (Prasov and Chai, 2010), which was not incremental.

We move beyond this work in that we present a model that is incremental, uses a form of grounded semantics, can easily incorporate multi-modal information sources, and finally on which inference can be performed quickly, satisfying the demands of real-time dialogue. The model brings together aspects we've previously looked into separately: grounded semantics in (Siebert and Schlangen,

2008); incremental interpretation (reference resolution) in (Schlangen et al., 2009); incremental general NLU in (Heintze et al., 2010); and a more sophisticated approach that handled all of these using markov logic networks, but did not work in real-time or with multi-modal input (Kennington and Schlangen, 2012).

3 The Task

The task for our model is as follows: to compute at any moment a distribution over possible intentions (expressed as semantic frames), given the unfolding utterance and possibly information about the state of the world in which the utterance is happening. The slots of these frames are to be filled with semantic constants, that is, they are uniquely resolved; if appropriate, to objects in the shared environment.

This is illustrated in Figure 1, where for three successive *incremental units* (Schlangen and Skantze, 2009) (that is, successively available bits of information pertaining to the same act, such as words of an utterance, or information about speech accompanying gesture) three distributions over intentions are shown.[1]

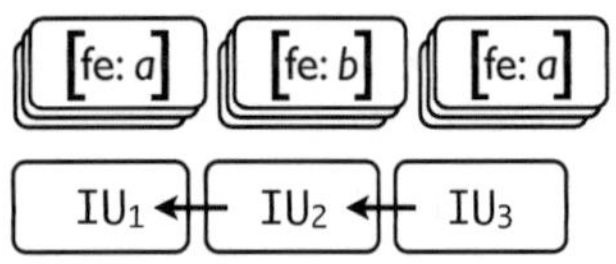

Figure 1: Schematic Illustration of Task

4 Our Model

More formally, the goal of the model is to recover I, the intention of the speaker behind her utterance, in an incremental fashion, that is, word by word. We make the assumption that the set of possible intentions is finite, and that they consist of (combinations of) entities (where however even actions like *taking* are considered 'entities'; more on this below). We observe U, the current word that the speaker uttered as part of their utterance (and features derived from that). We also assume that there is an unobserved mediating variable R, which represents the (visual or abstract) properties of the (visually present, or abstract) object of the intention. So, what we need to calculate is $P(I|U,R)$, even though ultimately we're interested only in $P(I|U)$. By definition of conditional probability, $P(I|U,R) = P(I,U,R)*P(U,R)^{-1}$. We factorise $P(I,U,R)$ as indicated in the following:

$$P(I|R,U) = \frac{P(R|I)P(I)P(U|R)}{P(U,R)} \quad (1)$$

That is, we make the assumption that R is conditional only on I, and U is conditional only on R. Marginalizing over R gets us the model we're interested in (and it amounts to a not uncommon tagging model with a hidden layer):

$$P(I|U) = P(I)\sum_{r \in R} \frac{P(U|R=r)P(R=r|I)}{P(U,R=r)} \quad (2)$$

Where we can move $P(I)$ out of the summation, as it is not dependent on R. Hence, we need three models, $P(I)$, $P(U|R)$ and $P(R|I)$, to compute $P(I|U)$. Figure 2 shows how these three models interact over time.

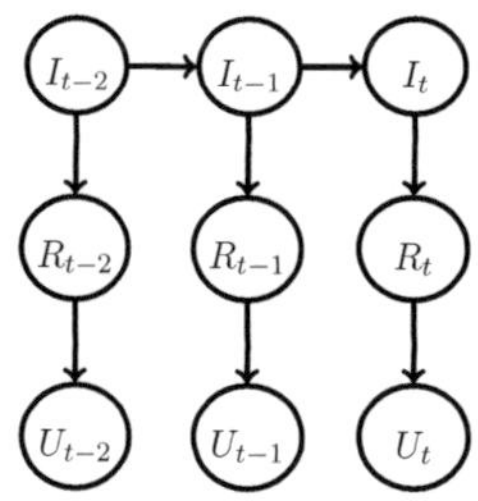

Figure 2: Our model represented as an unrolled DBN over three words.

Each sub-model will now be explained.

P(I) At the beginning of the computation for an incoming sentence, we set the prior $P(I)$ to a uniform distribution (or, if there is reason to do so, a different distribution to encode initial expectations about intentions; i.e., prior gaze information). For later words, it is set to the *posteriori* of the previous step, and so this constitutes a Bayesian updating of belief (with a trivial, constant transition model that equates $P(I_{t-1})$ and $P(I_t)$).[2]

[1]Here, no links between these intention representations are shown. The model we present in the next section is an *update* model, that is, it builds the representation at step t_n based on that at t_{n-1}; other possibilities are explored in (Heintze et al., 2010) and (Kennington and Schlangen, 2012).

[2]In that sense, our incremental understanding could be called "intra-sentential belief tracking," in analogy to the current effort to track system belief about user intentions across turns (Ma et al., 2012; Williams, 2010).

The other models represent knowledge about links between intentions and object properties, $P(R|I)$, and knowledge about language use, $P(U|R)$. We now explain how this knowledge is acquired.

P(R|I) The model $P(R|I)$ provides the link between objects (as occurring in the intentions) and their properties. Here we follow, to our knowledge, a novel approach, by deriving this distribution directly from the scene representation. This is best explained by looking at the overall model in a generative way. First, the intention is generated, $P(I)$, then based on that a property, $P(R|I)$. We assume that with equal probability one of the properties that the intended object actually has is picked to be verbalised, leaving zero probability for the ones that it does not have. This in a way is a rationality assumption: a rational speaker will, if at all, mention properties that are realised and not others (at least in non-negative contexts).

P(U|R), learned directly The other model, $P(U|R)$, can be learned directly from data by (smoothed) Maximum Likelihood estimation. For training, we assume that the property R that is picked out for verbalisation is actually observable. In our data, we know which properties the referent actually has, and so we can simply count how often a word (and its derived features) co-ocurred with a given property, out of all cases where that property was present.

P(U|R), via P(R|U) Instead of directly learning a model of the data, we can learn a discriminative model that connects words and properties.

In Equation 2, we can rewrite $P(U|R)$ using Bayes' Rule:

$$P(I|U) = P(I) \sum_{r \in R} \frac{P(U)P(R=r|U)P(R=r|I)}{P(R=r)P(U,R=r)} \quad (3)$$

$P(U)$ is a constant when computing $P(I|U)$ for all possible values of I whose actual value does not change the rank of each intention, and so can be dropped. $P(R)$ can be approximated with a uniform distribution, and can also be dropped, yielding:

$$P(I|U) = P(I) \sum_{r \in R} \frac{P(R=r|U)P(R=r|I)}{P(U,R=r)} \quad (4)$$

Other models could also be learned here; we chose a discriminative model to show that our model works under varied circumstances.

word	**red**	**round**	**square**	**green**
the	0.03	0.02	0.02	0.02
red	0.82	0.009	0.09	0.01
ball	0.02	0.9	0.02	0.07

Table 1: $P(U|R)$ for our toy domain for some values of U and R; we assume that this model is learned from data (columns are excerpted from a distribution over a larger vocabulary).

int.	**red**	**round**	**square**	**green**
`obj1`	0.5	0.5	0	0
`obj2`	0.5	0	0.5	0

Table 2: $P(R|I)$, for our example domain.

Properties An important part of our model is the set of properties. Properties can be visual properties such as color or shape or spatial properties (left-of, below, etc.). Though not the focus of this paper, they could also be conceptual properties (the verb *run* can have the properties of `movement`, `use_of_legs`, and `quick`). Another example, *New York* has the property of being `New_York`. (That is generally sufficient enough to denote New York, but note that descriptive properties (e.g., "location of the *Empire State Building*") could be used as well.) The purpose of the properties is to ground intentions with language in a more fine-grained way than the words alone.

We will now give an example of the generative approach as in Equation 2 (it is straight-forward to do the same for the discriminative model).

4.1 Example

The task is reference resolution in a shared visual context: there is an intention to refer to a visible object. For this example, there are two objects `obj1` and `obj2`, and four properties to describe those objects, `red`, `round`, `square` and `green`. The utterance for which we want to track a distribution over possible referents, going word-by-word, is *the red ball*. `obj1` happens to be a red ball, with properties `red` and `round`; `obj2` is a red cube, with the properties `red` and `square`.

We now need the models $P(U|R)$ and $P(R|I)$. We assume the former is learned from data, and for the four properties and three words gives us results as shown in Table 1 (that is, $P(U = \textit{the}|R = \texttt{red}) = 0.03$). The model $P(R|I)$ can be read off the representation of the scene: if you intend to refer to object obj1 (I = obj1), you can either pick the property red or the property round, so both get a probability of 0.5 and all others 0; similar for obj2 and red and square (Table 2).

Table 3 now shows an application of the full model to our example utterance. The cells in the columns labeled with properties show $P(U|R)P(R|I)$ for the appropriate properties and intentions (objects), the column Σ shows results after marginalizing over R. The final column then factors in $P(I)$ with a uniform prior for the first word, and the respectively previous distribution for all others, and normalises.

I	U	red	rnd.	sq.	Σ	$P(I\|U)$
obj1	*the*	.015	.01	0	.025	.5
obj2		.015	0	.01	.025	.5
obj1	*red*	.41	.0045	0	.41	.47
obj2		.41	0	.045	.46	.53
obj1	*ball*	.01	.45	0	.46	.96
obj2		.01	0	.01	.02	.04

Table 3: Application of utterance *the red ball*, where obj1 is the referred object

As these numbers show, the model behaves as expected: up until *ball*, the utterance does not give enough information to decide for either object probabilities are roughly equal, once *ball* is uttered obj1 is the clear winner.

This illustrated how the model works in principle and showed that it yields the expected results in a simple toy domain. In the next section we will show that this works in more realistic domains.

5 Experiments

Our model's task is to predict a semantic frame, where the required slots of the frame are known beforehand and each slot value is predicted using a separate model $P(I|U)$. We realise $P(U|R)$ as a Naive Bayes classifier (NB) which counts co-occurrences of utterance features (words, bigrams, trigrams; so U is actually a tuple, not a single variable) and properties (but naively treats features as independent), and which is smoothed using add-one smoothing. As explained earlier, $P(I)$ represents a uniform distribution at the beginning of an utterance, and the posteriori of the previous step, for later words. We also train a discriminative model, $P(R|U)$, using a maximum entropy classifier (ME) using the same features as NB to classify properties.[3]

[3]http://opennlp.apache.org/

5.1 A Non-Situated Baseline using ATIS

We performed an initial test of our model using a corpus in traditional NLU: the air travel information system (ATIS) corpus (Dahl et al., 1994) using the pre-processed corpus as in (Meza-Ruiz et al., 2008). In ATIS, the main task is to predict the slot attributes (the values were simply words from the utterance); however, the GOAL slot (representing the overall utterance intent) was was always present, the value of which required a prediction. We tested our model's ability to predict the GOAL slot (using very simple properties; the property of a GOAL intention is itself, i.e., the property of *flight* is flight) and found encouraging results (the GOAL slot baseline is 71.6%, see (Tur et al., 2010); our NB and ME models obtained scores of 77% and 77.9% slot value prediction accuracies, respectively). How our model works under more complicated settings will now be explained.

5.2 Puzzle Domain: Speech-Only

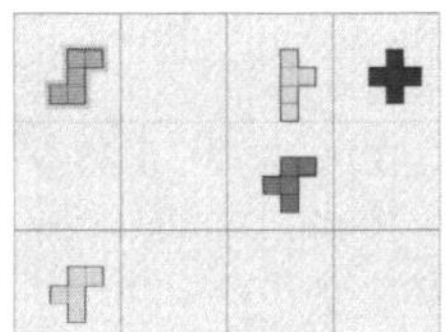

Figure 3: Example Pentomino Board

ACTION	rotate
OBJECT	object-4
RESULT	clockwise

Figure 4: Pento frame example

Data and Task The *Pentomino* domain (Fernández et al., 2007) contains task-oriented conversational data; more specifically, we worked with the corpus also used recently in (Heintze et al., 2010; Peldszus et al., 2012; Kennington and Schlangen, 2012). This corpus was collected in a Wizard-of-Oz study, where the user goal was to instruct the computer to pick up, delete, rotate or mirror puzzle tiles on a rectangular board (as in Figure 3), and place them onto another one. For each utterance, the corpus records the state of the game board before the utterance, the immediately preceding system action, and the intended interpretation of the utterance (as understood by the Wizard) in the form of a semantic frame specifying action-type and arguments, where those arguments are objects occurring in the description of the state of the board. The language of the corpus is German. An example frame is given in Figure 4.

The task that we want our model to perform is as follows: given information about the state of the world (i.e., game board), previous system action, and the ongoing utterance, predict the values of the frame. To this end, three slot values need to be predicted, one of which links to the visual scene. Each slot value will be predicted by an individual instantiation of our model (i.e., each has a different I to predict). Generally, we want our model to learn how language connects to the world (given discourse context, visual context, domain context, etc.). We used a combination of visual properties (color, shape, and board position), and simple properties to ground the utterance with I.

Our model gives probability distributions over all possible slot values, but as we are interested in single best candidates (or the special value `unknown` if no guess can be made yet), we applied an additional decision rule to the output of our model. If the probability of the highest candidate is below a threshold, `unknown` is returned, otherwise that candidate is returned. Ties are broken by random selection. The thresholds for each slot value were determined empirically on held-out data so that a satisfactory trade-off between letting through wrong predictions and changing correct results to `unknown` was achieved.

Procedure All results were obtained by averaging the results of a 10-fold validation on 1489 Pento boards (i.e., utterances+context, as in (Kennington and Schlangen, 2012)). We used a separate set of 168 boards for small-scale, held-out experiments. As this data set has been used in previous work, we use previous results as baselines/comparisons. For incremental processing, we used InproTK (Baumann and Schlangen, 2012).[4]

On the incremental level, we followed (Schlangen et al., 2009) and (Kennington and Schlangen, 2012) for evaluation, but use a subset of their incremental metrics, with a modification on the edit overhead:

first correct: how deep into the utterance do we make the first correct guess?

first final: how deep into the utterance do we make the correct guess, and don't subsequently change our minds?

edit overhead: what is the ratio of unnecessary edits / sentence length, where the only *necessary* edit is that going from `unknown` to the final, correct result anywhere in the sentence)?

[4]http://sourceforge.net/projects/inprotk/

Results The results for full utterances are given in Table 4. Both of our model types work better than (Heintze et al., 2010) which used support vector machines and conditional random fields, and (Peldszus et al., 2012) which was rule-based (but did not include utterances with pronouns like we do here). The NB version did not work well in comparison to (Kennington and Schlangen, 2012) which used MLN, but the ME version did in most metrics. Overall these are nice results as they are achieved using a more straightforward model with rather simple features (with room for extensions). Another welcome result is performance from noisy data (trained and evaluated on automatically transcribed speech; ASR); the ME version of our model is robust and performs well in comparison to previous work.

	NB	ME	K	H	P
fscore	81.16	**92.26**	92.18	76.9	
	(74.5)	**(89.4)**	(86.8)		
slot	73.62	**88.91**	88.88		
	(66.4)	**(85.1)**	(81.6)		
frame	42.57	74.08	**74.76**		
	(34.2)	**(67.2)**	(61.2)		
action	80.05	**93.62**	92.62		
object	76.27	**90.79**	84.71		64.3
result	64.4	82.34	**86.65**		

Table 4: Comparison of results from Pento: Naive Bayes **NB**, Maximum Entropy **ME**, (Kennington and Schlangen, 2012) **K**, (Heintze et al., 2010) **H**, (Peldszus et al., 2012) **P**; values in parentheses denote results from automatically transcribed speech.

A big difference between our current model and MLN is the way incrementality is realised: MLN was *restart incremental* in that at each increment, features from the full utterance prefix were used, not just the latest word; the present model is fully incremental in that a prior belief is updated based only on the new information. This, however, seems to lead our model to perform with less accuracy for the `result` slot, which usually occurs at the end of the sentence.

Incremental Table 5 shows the incremental results in the same way as (Kennington and Schlangen, 2012). Utterances are binned into short, normal, and long utterance lengths (1-6, 7-8, 9-17 words, respectively) as determined by looking at the distribution of utterance lengths, which appeared as a normal distribution with 7 and

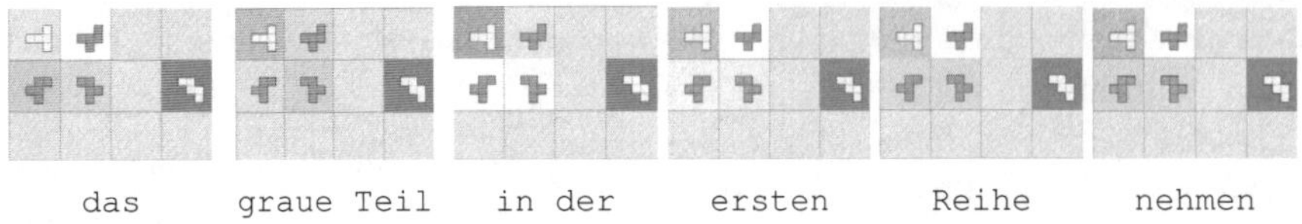

Figure 5: Example of reference resolution for the utterance: *das graue Teil in der ersten Reihe nehmen / the gray piece in the first row take*; lighter cell background means higher probability assigned to piece.

8-word utterances having highest representation. In comparison with (Kennington and Schlangen, 2012), our model generally takes longer to come to a *first correct* for `action`, but is earlier for the other two slots. For *first final*, our model always takes longer, albeit with lower *edit overhead*. This tells us that our model is more careful than the MLN one; it waits longer before making a final decision and it doesn't change its mind as much in the process, which arguably is desired behaviour for incremental systems.

action	**1-6**	**7-8**	**9-14**
first correct (% into utt.)	5.78	2.56	3.64
first final (% into utt.)	38.26	36.10	30.84
edit overhead	2.37		
object	**1-6**	**7-8**	**9-14**
first correct (% into utt.)	7.39	7.5	10.11
first final (% into utt.)	44.7	44.18	35.55
edit overhead	4.6		
result	**1-6**	**7-8**	**9-14**
first correct (% into utt.)	15.16	23.23	20.88
first final (% into utt.)	42.55	40.57	35.21
edit overhead	10.19		

Table 5: Incremental Results for Pento slots with varying sentence lengths.

Figure 5 illustrates incremental performance by showing the distribution over the pieces (using the ME model; lighter means higher probability) for the utterance *das graue Teil in der ersten Reihe nehmen* (*the gray piece in the first row take* / take the gray piece in the first row) for each word in the utterance. When the first word, *das* is uttered, it already assigns probabilities to the pieces with some degree of confidence (note that in German, *das* (the) denotes the neuter gender, and the piece on the right with the lowest probability is often referred to by a noun (Treppe) other than neuter). Once *graue* (gray) is uttered, the distribution is now more even upon the three gray pieces, which remains largely the same when *Teil* (piece) is uttered. The next two words, *in der* (in the) give more probability to the left gray piece, but once *ersten Reihe* (first row) is uttered, the most probable piece becomes the correct one, the second piece from the left on the top.

5.3 Puzzle Domain: Speech, Gaze and Deixis

Data and Task Our final experiment uses newly collected data (Kousidis et al., 2013), again from the Pentomino domain. In this Wizard-of-Oz study, the participant was confronted with a Pento game board containing 15 pieces in random colors, shapes, and positions, where the pieces were grouped in the four corners of the screen (example in Figure 6). The users were seated at a table in front of the screen. Their gaze was then calibrated with an eye tracker (*Seeingmachines FaceLab*) placed above the screen and their arm movements (captured by a *Microsoft Kinect*, also above the screen) were calibrated by pointing to each corner of the screen, then the middle of the screen. They were then given task instructions: (silently) choose a Pento tile on the screen and then instruct the computer game system to select this piece by describing and pointing to it. When a piece was selected (by the wizard), the participant had to utter a confirmation (or give negative feedback) and a new board was generated and the process repeated (each instance is denoted as an *episode*). The utterances, board states, arm movements, and gaze information were recorded, as in (Kousidis et al., 2012). The wizard was instructed to elicit pointing gestures by waiting to select the participant-referred piece by several seconds, unless a pointing action by the participant had already occurred. When the wizard misunderstood, or a technical problem arose, the wizard had an option to flag the episode. In total, 1214 episodes were recorded from 8 participants (all university students). All but one were native speakers; the non-native spoke proficient German (see Appendix for a set of random example utterances).

The task in this experiment was reference resolution (i.e., filling a single-slot frame). The information available to our model for these data include the utterance (ASR-transcribed and represented as words, bigrams, and trigrams), the vi-

Figure 6: Example Pento board for gaze and deixis experiment; yellow piece in the top-right quadrant has been "selected" by the wizard after the participant utterance.

sual context (game board), gaze information, and deixis (pointing) information, where a rule-based classifier predicted from the motion capture data the quadrant of the screen at which the participant was pointing. These data were very noisy (and hence, realistic) despite the constrained conditions of the task: the participants were not required to say things a certain way (as long as it was understood by the wizard); their hand movements potentially covered their faces which interfered with the eye tracker; each participant had a different way of pointing (each had their own gesture space, handedness, distance of hand from body when pointing, alignment of hand with face, etc.). Also, the episodes were not split into individual utterances, but rather interpreted as one; this indicates that the model can deal with belief tracking over whole interactions (here, if the wizard did not respond, the participant had to clarify her intent in some way, producing a new utterance).

Procedure Removing the flagged utterances and the utterances of one of the participants (who had misunderstood the task) left us with a total of 1051 utterances. We used 951 for development (fine-tuning of parameters, see below), and 100 for evaluation. Evaluation was leave-one-out (i.e., 100 fold cross validation) where the training data were all other 1050 utterances. For this experiment, we only used the ME model as it performed much better in the previous experiment. We give results as resolution accuracy. We incorporate gaze and deixis information in two ways: (1) We computed the distribution over tiles gazed at, and quadrant of the screen pointed at during the interval before and during an utterance. The distributions were then combined at the end of the utterance with the NLU distribution (denoted as *Gaze* and *Point*); that is, *Gaze* and *Point* had their own $P(I)$ which were evenly interpolated with the INLU $P(I|U)$, and (2) we incrementally computed properties to be provided to our INLU model; i.e., a tile has a property in R of being `looked_at` if it is gazed at for some interval of time, or tiles in a quadrant of the screen have the property of being `pointed_at`. These models are denoted as *Gaze-F* and *Point-F*. As an example, Figure 7 shows an example utterance, gaze, and gesture activity over time and how they are reflected in the model (the utterance is the observed U, where the gaze and gesture become properties in R for the tiles that they affect). Our baseline model is the NLU without using gaze or deixis information; random accuracy is 7%.

We also include the percentage of the time the gold tile is in the top 2 and top 4 rankings (out of 15); situations in which a dialogue system could at least provide alternatives in a clarification request (if it could detect that it should have low confidence in the best prediction; which we didn't investigate here). Importantly, these results are achieved with automatically transcribed utterances; hand transcriptions do not yet exist for these data. For gaze, we also make the naive assumption that over the utterance the participant (who in this case is the speaker) will gaze at his chosen intended tile most of the time.

speech	nimm	...	das	gelbe	Teil
gesture			< arm raise >	<point to top right>	
gaze	<scan of scene>		<gaze at target piece>		
U	nimm	...	das	gelbe	Teil
R			gazed_at	pointed_at	

Figure 7: Human activity (top) aligned with how modalities are reflected in the model for Gaze-F and Point-F (bottom) over time for example utterance: *take the yellow tile*.

Results See Table 6 for results. The models that have access to gaze and pointing gestures can resolve better than those that do not. Our findings are consistent in that referential success with gaze alone approaches 20% (a rate found by (Pfeiffer, 2010) in a different setting). Another interesting result is that the Gaze-F and Point-F variants, that continuously integrate multi-modal information, perform the same as or better than their non-incremental counterparts (where the distributions are weighted once at the end of the utterance).

Version	Acc	Top 2	Top 4
Gaze	18%		
(baseline) NLU	50%	59%	77%
NLU + Gaze	53%	62%	80%
NLU + Point	52%	65%	90%
NLU + Gaze + Point	53%	**70%**	**91%**
NLU + Gaze-F	53%	65%	78%
NLU + Point-F	**57%**	68%	88%
NLU+Gaze-F+Point-F	56%	69%	85%

Table 6: Accuracies for reference resolution task when considering NLU, gaze and pointing information before and during the utterance (Gaze and Point), and gaze and pointing information when considered as properties to the NLU model (Gaze-F and Point-F).

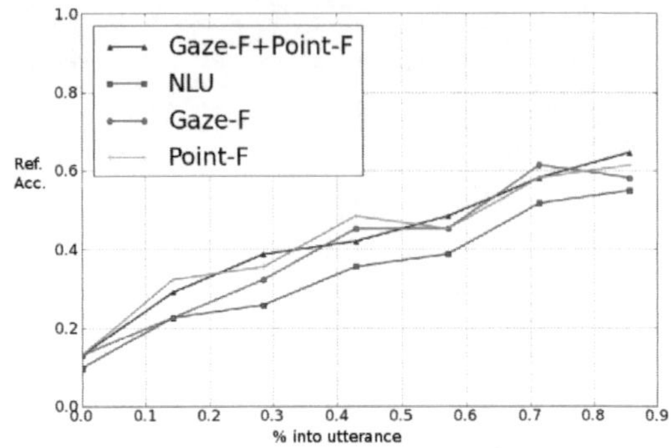

Figure 8: Incremental process for referential accuracy; comparing NLU, Gaze-F, Point-F, and Gaze-F + Point-F for utterances of length 7-8.

Incremental We also include incremental results when using gaze and deixis. We binned the sentences in the same way as in the previous experiment (the distribution of sentence lengths was similar). Figure 8 shows how the NLU model baseline, the (NLU+) Gaze-F, Point-F, and Gaze-F + Point-F models perform incrementally for utterances of lengths 7-8. All models increase monotonically, except for Point-F at one point in the utterance and Gaze-F at the end. It would appear that the gaze as an information source is a good early indicator of speaker intent, but should be trusted less as the utterance progresses. Deixis is more trustworthy overall, and the two taken together offer a more stable model. Table 7 shows the results using the previously explained incremental metrics. All models have little edit overhead, but don't make the correct final decision until well into the utterances. This was expected due to the noisy data. A consumer of the output of these models would need to wait longer to trust the results given by the models (though the number of words of the utterance can never be known beforehand).

NLU	1-6	7-8	9-14
first correct (% into utt.)	22.2	37.2	30
first final (% into utt.)	82.4	82.4	74.8
edit overhead	2.95		
Gaze-F	**1-6**	**7-8**	**9-14**
first correct (% into utt.)	23	32	31.1
first final (% into utt.)	84.1	81.5	75.4
edit overhead	2.89		
Point-F	**1-6**	**7-8**	**9-14**
first correct (% into utt.)	21.4	30	23.3
first final (% into utt.)	83.5	80	72.3
edit overhead	2.59		
Gaze-F + Point-F	**1-6**	**7-8**	**9-14**
first correct (% into utt.)	16.7	31	28
first final (% into utt.)	81.5	81	73.9
edit overhead	2.67		

Table 7: Incremental results for Pento slots with varying sentence lengths.

6 Discussion and Conclusions

We presented a model for the interpretation of utterances in situated dialogue that a) works incrementally and b) can ground meanings in the shared context. Taken together, the three experiments we've reported give good evidence that our model has the potential to be used as a successful NLU component of an interactive dialogue system. Our model can process at a speed which is faster than the ongoing utterance, which will allow it to be useful in real-time, interactive experiments. And, crucially, our model is able to integrate information from various sources, including gaze and deixis. We expect the model to scale to larger domains; the number of computations that are required grows with $|I| \times |R|$.

Our model makes use of *properties* which are used to connect an utterance to an intention. Knowing which properties to use requires empirical testing to determine which ones are useful. We are working on developing principled methods for selecting such properties and their contribution (i.e., properties should not be uniform). Future work also includes better use of linguistics (instead of just n-grams), building a more sophisticated DBN model that has fewer independence assumptions, e.g. tracking properties as well by making R_t depended on R_{t-1}. We are also in the process of using the model interactively; as a proof-of-concept, we were trivially able to plug it into an existing dialogue manager for Pento domains (see (Buß et al., 2010)).

Acknowledgements: Thanks to the anonymous reviewers for their useful comments and feedback. This work was partially funded through a DFG Emmy Noether grant.

Appendix A: Example Utterances (Pento Speech)

1. nimm die Brücke in der oberen Reihe
2. nimm das Teil in der mittleren Reihe das zweite Teil in der mittleren Reihe
3. und setz ihn in die Mitte links
4. dreh das nach links
5. ähm und setz ihn oben links in die Ecke
6. nimm bitte den gelben Winkel oben
7. bewege das Kästchen die Treppe unten links
8. lösche das Teil in der Mitte
9. nimm die gelbe Krücke aus der zweiten Reihe oben
10. und verschiebe es in die erste Zeile dritte Spalte

Appendix B: Example Utterances (Speech, Gaze and Deixis)

(as recognised by the ASR)
1. dieses teil genau st es oben links t
2. das t mit vier rechts oben ist d es direkt hier rechts
3. grüne von rechts uh fläche
4. das obere grüne zähl hm so es obersten hohles e rechts oben ecke
5. ähm das hintere kreuz unten links rechts rechts
6. äh das einzige blaue symbol oben rechts
7. das einzige grün okay oben rechts
8. hm innerhalb diesem blauen striche vorne hm so genau in die genau rechts
9. und das sind dann nehmen diese fünf zeichen oben nämlich genau das in der mitte so
10. oben links is die untere

References

Gregory Aist, James Allen, Ellen Campana, Carlos Gomez Gallo, Scott Stoness, Mary Swift, and Michael K Tanenhaus. 2007. Incremental understanding in human-computer dialogue and experimental evidence for advantages over nonincremental methods. In *Proceedings of Decalog (Semdial 2007)*, Trento, Italy.

Timo Baumann and David Schlangen. 2012. The InproTK 2012 Release. In *NAACL*.

Okko Buß Timo Baumann, and David Schlangen. 2010. Collaborating on Utterances with a Spoken Dialogue System Using an ISU-based Approach to Incremental Dialogue Management. In *Proceedings of SIGdial*, pages 233–236.

Deborah A Dahl, Madeleine Bates, Michael Brown, William Fisher, Kate Hunicke-Smith, David Pallett, Christine Pao, Alexander Rudnicky, and Elizabeth Shriberg. 1994. Expanding the scope of the ATIS task: the ATIS-3 corpus. In *Proceedings of the workshop on Human Language Technology*, HLT '94, pages 43–48, Stroudsburg, PA, USA. Association for Computational Linguistics.

Renato De Mori, Frederic Béchet, Dilek Hakkani-tür, Michael Mctear, Giuseppe Riccardi, and Gokhan Tur. 2008. Spoken Language Understanding. *IEEE Signal Processing Magazine*, pages 50–58, May.

David DeVault, Kenji Sagae, and David Traum. 2009. Can I finish?: learning when to respond to incremental interpretation results in interactive dialogue. In *Proceedings of the 10th SIGdial*, pages 11–20. Association for Computational Linguistics.

David DeVault, Kenji Sagae, and David Traum. 2011. Incremental Interpretation and Prediction of Utterance Meaning for Interactive Dialogue. *Dialogue & Discourse*, 2(1):143–170.

Raquel Fernández, Tatjana Lucht, and David Schlangen. 2007. Referring under restricted interactivity conditions. In *Proceedings of the 8th SIGdial*, pages 136–139.

Silvan Heintze, Timo Baumann, and David Schlangen. 2010. Comparing local and sequential models for statistical incremental natural language understanding. In *Proceedings of the 11th SIGdial*, pages 9–16. Association for Computational Linguistics.

Kai-yuh Hsiao, Soroush Vosoughi, Stefanie Tellex, Rony Kubat, and Deb Roy. 2008. Object schemas for grounding language in a responsive robot. *Connection Science2*, 20(4):253–276.

Guangpu Huang and Meng Joo Er. 2010. A Hybrid Computational Model for Spoken Language Understanding. In *11th International Conference on Control, Automation, Robotics, and Vision*, pages 7–10, Singapore. IEEE.

Casey Kennington and David Schlangen. 2012. Markov Logic Networks for Situated Incremental Natural Language Understanding. In *Proceedings of the 13th SIGdial*, pages 314–323, Seoul, South Korea, July. Association for Computational Linguistics.

Spyros Kousidis, Thies Pfeiffer, Zofia Malisz, Petra Wagner, and David Schlangen. 2012. Evaluating a minimally invasive laboratory architecture for recording multimodal conversational data. In *Proc. of the Interdisciplinary Workshop on Feedback Behaviours in Dialogue*.

Spyros Kousidis, Casey Kennington, and David Schlangen. 2013. Investigating speaker gaze and pointing behaviour in human-computer interaction with the mint.tools collection. In *Proceedings of the 14th SIGdial*.

Percy Liang, Michael Jordan, and Dan Klein. 2011. Learning Dependency-Based Compositional Semantics. In *Proceedings of the 49th ACLHLT*, pages 590–599, Portland, Oregon. Association for Computational Linguistics.

Changsong Liu, Rui Fang, and Joyce Chai. 2012. Towards Mediating Shared Perceptual Basis in Situated Dialogue. In *Proceedings of the 13th SIGdial*, pages 140–149, Seoul, South Korea, July. Association for Computational Linguistics.

Yi Ma, Antoine Raux, Deepak Ramachandran, and Rakesh Gupta. 2012. Landmark-Based Location Belief Tracking in a Spoken Dialog System. In *Proceedings of the 13th SIGdial*, pages 169–178, Seoul, South Korea, July. Association for Computational Linguistics.

Marie-Jean Meurs, Frederic Duvert, Fabrice Lefevre, and Renato De Mori. 2008. Markov Logic Networks for Spoken Language Interpretation. *Information Systems Journal*, pages 535–544.

Marie-Jean Meurs, Fabrice Lefèvre, and Renato De Mori. 2009. Spoken Language Interpretation: On the Use of Dynamic Bayesian Networks for Semantic Composition. In *IEEE International Conference on Acoustics, Speech, and Signal Processing*, pages 4773–4776.

Ivan Meza-Ruiz, Sebastian Riedel, and Oliver Lemon. 2008. Accurate Statistical Spoken Language Understanding from Limited Development Resources. In *IEEE International Conference on Acoustics, Speech, and Signal Processing*, pages 5021–5024. IEEE.

Andreas Peldszus, Okko Buß, Timo Baumann, and David Schlangen. 2012. Joint Satisfaction of Syntactic and Pragmatic Constraints Improves Incremental Spoken Language Understanding. In *Proceedings of the 13th EACL*, pages 514–523, Avignon, France, April. Association for Computational Linguistics.

Thies Pfeiffer. 2010. *Understanding multimodal deixis with gaze and gesture in conversational interfaces*. Ph.D. thesis, Bielefeld University.

Zahar Prasov and Joyce Y Chai. 2010. Fusing Eye Gaze with Speech Recognition Hypotheses to Resolve Exophoric References in Situated Dialogue. In *EMNLP 2010*, number October, pages 471–481.

Deb Roy. 2005. Grounding words in perception and action: computational insights. *Trends in Cognitive Sciences*, 9(8):389–396, August.

David Schlangen and Gabriel Skantze. 2009. A General, Abstract Model of Incremental Dialogue Processing. In *Proceedings of the 10th EACL*, pages 710–718, Athens, Greece. Association for Computational Linguistics.

David Schlangen, Timo Baumann, and Michaela Atterer. 2009. Incremental Reference Resolution: The Task, Metrics for Evaluation, and a Bayesian Filtering Model that is Sensitive to Disfluencies. In *Proceedings of the 10th SIGdial*, pages 30–37, London, UK. Association for Computational Linguistics.

Alexander Siebert and David Schlangen. 2008. A Simple Method for Resolution of Definite Reference in a Shared Visual Context. In *Proceedings of the 9th SIGdial*, pages 84–87, Columbus, Ohio. Association for Computational Linguistics.

Gokhan Tur, Dilek Hakkani-tür, and Larry Heck. 2010. What Is Left to Be Understood by ATIS? In *IEEE Workshop on Spoken Language Technologies*, pages 19–24, Berkeley, California. IEEE.

Ye-Yi Wang, Li Deng, and Alex Acero. 2011. *Semantic Frame-based Spoken Language Understanding*. Wiley.

Jason D Williams. 2010. Incremental partition recombination for efficient tracking of multiple dialog states. *Acoustics Speech and Signal Processing ICASSP 2010*, pages 5382–5385.

Luke S Zettlemoyer and Michael Collins. 2007. Online Learning of Relaxed CCG Grammars for Parsing to Logical Form. *Computational Linguistics*, pages 678–687.

Luke S Zettlemoyer and Michael Collins. 2009. Learning context-dependent mappings from sentences to logical form. *Proceedings of the Joint Conference of the 47th ACL and the 4th AFNLP: Volume 2 - ACL-IJCNLP '09*, 2:976.

Multimodality and Dialogue Act Classification in the RoboHelper Project

Lin Chen
Department of Computer Science
University of Illinois at Chicago
851 S Morgan ST, Chicago, IL 60607
lchen43@uic.edu

Barbara Di Eugenio
Department of Computer Science
University of Illinois at Chicago
851 S Morgan ST, Chicago, IL 60607
bdieugen@uic.edu

Abstract

We describe the annotation of a multimodal corpus that includes pointing gestures and haptic actions (force exchanges). Haptic actions are rarely analyzed as full-fledged components of dialogue, but our data shows haptic actions are used to advance the state of the interaction. We report our experiments on recognizing Dialogue Acts in both offline and online modes. Our results show that multimodal features and the dialogue game aid in DA classification.

1 Introduction

When people collaborate on physical or virtual tasks that involve manipulation of objects, dialogues become rich in gestures of different kinds; the actions themselves that collaborators engage in also perform a communicative function. Collaborators gesture while speaking, e.g. saying "Try there?" while pointing to a faraway location; they perform actions to reply to their partner's utterances, e.g. opening a cabinet to comply with "please check cabinet number two". Conversely, they use utterances to reply to their partner's gestures and actions, e.g. saying "not there, try the other one" after their partner opens a cabinet. Gestures and actions are an important part of such dialogues; while the role of pointing gestures has been explored, the role that haptic actions (force exchanges) play in an interaction has not.

In this paper, we present our corpus of multimodal dialogues in a home care setting: a helper is helping an elderly person perform activities of daily living (ADLs) such as preparing dinner. We investigate how to apply Dialogue Act (DA) classification to these multimodal dialogues. Many challenges arise. First, an utterance may not directly follow a spoken utterance, but a gesture or a haptic action. Likewise, the next move is not necessarily an utterance, it can be a gesture (pointing or haptics) only, or a multimodal utterance. Third, when people use gestures and actions together with utterances, the utterances become shorter, hence the textual context that has been used to advantage in many previous models is impoverished. Our contributions concern: exploring the dialogue functions of what we call *Haptic-Ostensive (H-O)* actions (Foster et al., 2008), namely haptics actions that often perform a referential function; experimenting with both offline and online DA classification, whereas most previous work only focuses on offline classification (Stolcke et al., 2000; Hastie et al., 2002; Di Eugenio et al., 2010a); highlighting the role played by multimodal features and dialogue structure (in the form of dialogue games) as concerns DA classification.

Our work is part of the RoboHelper project (Di Eugenio et al., 2010b) whose ultimate goal is to deploy robotic assistants for the elderly so that they can safely remain living in their home. The models we derive from our experiments are the building blocks of a multimodal information-state based dialogue manager, whose architecture is shown in Figure 1. The dialogue manager performs reference resolution, specifically resolving third person pronouns and deictics in utterances; classifies utterances to DAs; infers the dialogue games for utterances; updates the dialogue state, and finally decides what the next step is in the interaction. We have discussed our approach to multimodal reference resolution in (Chen et al., 2011; Chen and Di Eugenio, 2012). In this paper, we focus on the Dialogue Act classification component. We will also touch on Dialogue Game inference. Our collaborators are developing the speech processing, vision and haptic recognition components (Franzini and Ben-Arie, 2012; Ma and Ben-Arie, 2012; Javaid and Žefran, 2012), that, when integrated with the dialogue manager we are building,

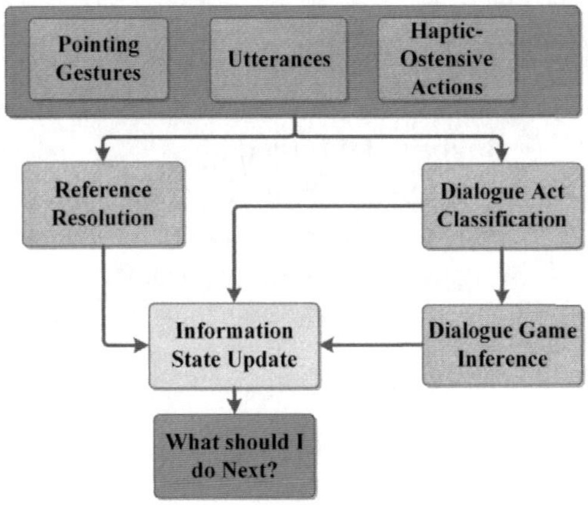

Figure 1: System Architecture

will make the interface situated in and able to deal with a real environment.

After discussing related work in Section 2, we present our multimodal corpus and the multidimensional annotation scheme we devised in Section 3. In Section 4 we discuss all the features we used to build machine learning models to classify DAs. Sections 5 is devoted to our experiments and the results we obtained. We conclude and discuss future work in Section 6.

2 Related Work

Due to its importance in dialogue research, DA classification has been the focus of a large body of research (Stolcke et al., 2000; Sridhar et al., 2009; Di Eugenio et al., 2010a; Boyer et al., 2011). Some of this work has been made possible by several available corpora tagged with DAs, including HCRC Map Task (Anderson et al., 1991), CallHome (Levin et al., 1998), Switchboard (Graff et al., 1998), ICSI Meeting Recorder (MRDA) (Shriberg et al., 2004), and the AMI multimodal corpus (Carletta, 2007).

Researchers have applied various approaches to this task. Initially only simple textual features were used, e.g. n-grams were used to model the constraints for DA sequences in an HMM model (Stolcke et al., 2000). Zimmermann et al. (2006) investigated the joint segmentation and classification of DAs using prosodic features. Sridhar et al. (2009) showed that prosodic cues can improve DA classification for a Maximum Entropy based model. Di Eugenio et al. (2010a) extended Latent Semantic Analysis with linguistic features, including dialogue game information. Boyer et al. (2011) integrates facial expressions to significantly improve the recognition of several DAs, whereas Ha et al. (2012) shows that automatically recognized postural features may help to disambiguate DAs.

It should be pointed out that most of this work focuses on offline DA classification – namely, DA classification is performed on the corpus using the gold-standard classification for the previous DA(s). Since some sort of history of previous DAs is used by all systems, using online classification for the previous DAs will unavoidably impact performance (Sridhar et al., 2009; Kim et al., 2012). Additionally, for models such as HMMs and CRF that approach the problem as sequence labeling, online processing means that only a partial sequence is available.

3 The ELDERLY-AT-HOME Corpus

This work is based on the ELDERLY-AT-HOME corpus, a multimodal corpus in the domain of elderly care (Chen and Di Eugenio, 2012). The corpus contains 20 human-human dialogues. In each dialogue, a helper (HEL) and an elderly person (ELD) perform *Activities of Daily Living* (ADL) (Krapp, 2002), such as getting up from chairs, finding pots, cooking pasta. The setting is a fully equipped studio apartment used for teaching and research in a partner university (see Figure 2). The corpus contains 482 minutes of recorded videos, which comprise 301 minutes of what we call *effective video*, obtained by eliminating irrelevant content such as explanations of the tasks and interruptions by the person who accompanied the elderly subject (who is not playing the part of the helper). This 301 minutes contain 4782 spoken turns. The corpus includes video and audio data in .avi and .wav format, haptics data collected via instrumented gloves in .csv format, and the transcribed utterances in xml format.

The *Find* subcorpus of our corpus comprises only *Find* tasks, where subjects look for and retrieve various kitchen objects such as pots, silverware, pasta, etc. from various locations in the apartment. We define a *Find* task as a continuous time span during which the two subjects are collaborating on finding objects. *Find* tasks naturally arise while performing an ADL such as preparing dinner. Figure 3 shows a *Find* task example.

Figure 2: Data Collection Experiment

1	ELD	And there is a spoon down there, in the second drawer? *[Point(ELD,Drawer1)]*
2	HEL	Down there?*[Point(HEL,Drawer1)]*
3	ELD	Yes.
4	HEL	This? *[Touch(HEL,Drawer1)]*
5	ELD	Uh-huh.
6	HEL	*[Open(HEL,Drawer1)]*
7	ELD	A spoon.
8	HEL	Is this the spoon? *[Takeout(HEL,spoon1)]*
9	ELD	No, the second drawer.
10	HEL	*[Close(HEL,Drawer1),Open(HEL,Drawer2)]*
11	ELD	Yes, there it is.
12	HEL	This one?*[Takeout(HEL,spoon2)]*
13	ELD	Yes, uh-huh.
14	HEL	OK.

Figure 3: Find Task Example

3.1 Annotation

We devised a multidimensional annotation scheme since we are interested in investigating the role played in the interaction by modalities different from speech. Our annotation scheme comprises three main components: the multimodal event annotation, which includes annotating for pointing gestures, haptic-ostensive actions, their features, and their relationships to utterances; the dialogue act annotation; and the referential expression annotations already described in (Chen et al., 2011; Chen and Di Eugenio, 2012).

3.1.1 Multimodal Event Annotation

To study the roles played by different sorts of multimodal actions, and how they contribute to the flow of the dialogue, pointing gestures, Haptic-Ostensive (H-O) actions, and the relations among them have been annotated on the *Find* subcorpus. The *Find* subcorpus contains 137 *Find* tasks, collected from the dialogues of 19 pairs of subjects from the larger corpus. [1] The multimodal annotation tool Anvil (Kipp, 2001) was used to transcribe all the utterances, and to annotate for all categories described in this paper. Each annotation category is an annotation group in Anvil. For each subject, one track is defined for each annotation group, for a total of 4 tracks per subject in Anvil.

Pointing gestures are used naturally when people refer to a far away object. We define a pointing gesture as a hand gesture without physical contact with the target. Our definition of pointing gesture does not include head or other body part movements used to indicate targets. Our corpus includes very few occurrences of those; additionally, our collaborators in the RoboHelper project focus on recognizing hand gestures. We have identified two types of pointing gestures. The first is, pointing gestures with an identifiable target, which is usually indicated by a short time stable hand pointing. The other type is without a fixed target. It usually happens when the subject points to several targets in a short time, or the subject just points to a large space area.

For a pointing gesture, we mark two attributes: the time span and the target. The time span of a pointing gesture starts when the subject initiates the hand movement, ends when the subject starts to draw the hand back. We have devised a Referring Index System (Chen and Di Eugenio, 2012) to mark the different types of targets: single identifiable target, multiple identifiable targets and unidentifiable target.

During *Find* tasks, subjects need to physically interact with the objects, e.g. they need to open cabinets to get plates, to put a pot on the stove etc. Those physical contact actions often perform a referring function as well, either adding new entities to the discourse model, or referring to an already established referent. For example, in Figure 3, the action [Touch(Hel,Drawer1)] that accompanies Utt_4 disambiguates *This* by referring to Drawer1, tantamount to a pointing gesture; conversely, the action [Takeout(HEL,spoon1)] associated with Utt_8 establishes a referent for spoon1. Following (Foster et al., 2008), we label Haptic-Ostensive (H-O) those actions that involve physical contact with an object, and that can at the same time perform a referring function. Note that target objects here exclude the partner's body parts, as when HEL helps ELD get up from a chair.

No existing work that we know of identifies

[1]One pair of subjects was excluded, because ELD appeared confused. Our goal was to recruit elderly subjects with intact cognitive functions, but this subject was an exception.

types of H-O actions. Hence, we had to define our own categories, based on the following two principles: (1) The H-O types must be grounded in our data, namely, the definitions are empirically based: these H-O actions are frequently observed in the corpus. (2) They are within the scope of what our collaborators can recognize from the haptic signals. The five H-O action types we defined are:

- **Touch**: when the subject only touches the targets, no immediate further actions are performed
- **MANIP-HOLD**: when the subject takes out or picks up an object and holds it stably for a short period of time
- **MANIP-NO-HOLD**: when the subject takes out or picks up an object, but without explicitly showing it to the other subject
- **Open**: starts when the subject has physical contact with the handle of the fridge, a cabinet or a drawer, and starts to pull; ends when the physical contact is off
- **Close**: when the subject has physical contact with the handle of the fridge, a cabinet or a drawer, and starts to push; ends when the physical contact is off

For H-O action annotation, three attributes are marked: time span, target and action type. The "Target" attribute is similar to the "Target" attribute in pointing gesture annotation. Since H-O actions are more accurate than pointing gestures (Foster et al., 2008), the targets are all identifiable.

Table 1 provides distributions of the length in seconds for different types of events in the *Find* corpus. Table 2 shows the counts of different events divided by type of participant. From these two tables, it is apparent that:

- Pointing gestures and H-O actions were frequently used: their total corresponds to 61% of the number of utterances
- Utterances are short: only 1.7", and 4.2 words on average
- ELD performed 66% of pointing gestures, and HEL 97.5% of H-O actions

Multimodal Event Relation Annotation. Pointing gestures and H-O actions can accompany an utterance, e.g. see move 2 in Figure 3: HEL asks "Down there" while pointing to a drawer; or can be used independently, e.g. see move 6 in Figure 3: HEL does not utter any words, but opens the drawer after ELD confirms that is the right drawer with "Uh-huh". In the latter case, HEL used an action to respond to ELD. Pointing gestures and H-O actions are followed by utterances as well, e.g. move 11 in Figure 3: after HEL opens a drawer, ELD says "Yes, there it is".

Utterances	Pointing	H-O Actions	Total
2555"	571"	1088"	4377"

Table 1: Find Subcorpus: Length in seconds

	ELD	HEL	Total
Utterances	756	760	1516
Words	3612	2981	6593
Pointing	219	113	332
H-O Actions	15	582	597

Table 2: Find Subcorpus: Counts

To understand how pointing gestures and H-O actions participate in the dialogues and how they interact with utterances, we further annotated the relationship between utterances, pointing gestures and H-O actions. Just using timespans is not sufficient. It is not necessarily the case that utterance U is associated with gesture / H-O action G if their timespans overlap. This type of annotation is purely local: the fact that turns 2-5 in Figure 3 confirm which drawer to open, would be captured at the dialogue game level.

First, we assign to each utterance, pointing gesture and H-O action a unique event index, so that we can refer to these events with their indices. For pointing gestures and H-O actions, we define two more attributes: "associates" and "follows". If a pointing gesture or H-O action is associated with an utterance, the "associates" value will be the index of that utterance; by default, the "associates" value is empty. If a pointing gesture or H-O action independently follows an utterance, the "follows" value will be that utterance's index. E.g., for move 6 in Figure 3, we mark the H-O action "Open" with "follows [5]".

For utterances, we only mark the "follows" attribute. If an utterance directly follows a pointing gesture or H-O action, we use the index of the pointing gesture or H-O action as the "follows" value. By default, the "follows" attribute of an utterance is empty. It means that an utterance follows its immediate previous utterance.

We define a *move* as any combination of related utterances, pointing gestures and H-O actions, performed by the same subject. On the basis of the event relation annotations, we can compute the dialogue's move flow using the following algorithm.

1. Order all the utterances in a *Find* task session by the utterance start time
2. Until all the utterances are processed, for each unprocessed utterance u_i:
   (a) If u_i *follows* a pointing gesture or H-O action, that pointing gesture or H-O action forms a new *move* m_k; add m_k to the sequence before u_i
   (b) Find all the pointing gestures and H-O actions labelled as *associates* of u_i. These events form the *move* m_i together with u_i
   (c) Recursively find the events which follow the last generated *move*, together with all their associated events to form another *move*

This algorithm computes 1791 *moves*, as shown in Table 3. More than 90% of pointing gestures are used with utterances. Only 377 out of 596 H-O actions are included in the *moves*, mostly because the H-O action "Close" frequently follows an "Open" action (these cases are not detected by the algorithm, because they don't advance the dialogue).

	ELD	HEL	Total
Utterances	545	507	1052
Pointing	9	11	20
H-O	5	213	218
Utterance&Pointing	209	100	309
Utterance&H-O	2	153	155
Total	770	984	1754

Table 3: Moves Statistics in Find Corpus

3.1.2 Dialogue Act Annotation

Since the *Find* corpus is task-oriented in nature, we built on the dialogue act inventory of HCRC MapTask, a well-known task oriented corpus (Anderson et al., 1991). The MapTask tag set contains 11 moves:[2] *instruct, explain, check, align, query-w, query-yn; acknowledge, reply-y, reply-n, reply-w, clarify*. However, this inventory of DAs does not cover utterances that are used to respond to gestures and actions, such as Utt.$_{11}$ in Figure 3. The semantics of the *reply-{y/n/w}* tags does not cover these situations. Hence, we devised three more tags, which apply **only** to statements that follow a move composed exclusively of a gesture or an action (in the sense of "follow" just discussed):

- **state-y**: a statement which conveys "yes", such as Utt.$_{11}$ in Figure 3.
- **state-n**: a statement which conveys "no", e.g. if Utt.$_{11}$ had been *Wait, try the third drawer.*
- **state**: still a statement , but not conveying acceptance or rejection, e.g. *So we got the soup.*

Hence, the DAs in {*state-y, state-n, state*} are used to tag responses to actions, and the DAs in {*reply-y, reply-n, reply-w*} are used to tag responses to utterances. Table 4 shows the distribution of DAs by subject.

Dialogue Act	ELD	HEL	Total	Ratio
Instruct	295	19	314	20.7%
Acknowledge	22	186	208	13.7%
Reply-y	179	3	182	12.0%
Check	1	155	156	10.3%
Query-yn	23	133	156	10.3%
Query-w	3	144	147	9.7%
Reply-w	132	4	136	9.0%
State-y	40	36	76	5.0%
State-n	16	50	66	4.4%
Reply-n	27	9	36	2.4%
State	7	15	22	1.5%
Explain	10	4	14	0.9%
Align	1	2	3	0.3%
Total	756	760	1516	100%

Table 4: Dialogue Act Counts in Find Corpus

Intercoder Agreement. In order to verify the reliability of our annotations, we double coded 15% of the data for pointing gestures, H-O actions and DAs. These are the dialogues from 3 pairs of subjects, and contain 22 *Find* tasks. Because the pointing gestures and H-O actions are time span based, when we calculate agreement, we use an overlap based approach. If the two annotations from the two coders overlap by more than 50% of the event length, and the other attributes are the same, we count this as a match. We used κ to measure the reliability of the annotation (Cohen, 1960). We obtained reasonable values: for pointing gestures, κ=0.751, for H-O actions, κ=0.703, and for DAs, κ=0.789.

[2] A twelfth move, *Ready*, does not appear in our corpus.

4 Experimental Setup

We ran experiments classifying the DA tag for the current utterance. We employ supervised learning approaches, specifically: Conditional Random Field (CRF) (Lafferty et al., 2001), Maximum Entropy (MaxEnt), Naive Bayes (NB), and Decision Tree (DT). These algorithms are widely used for DA classification (Sridhar et al., 2009; Ivanovic, 2008; Ha et al., 2012; Kim et al., 2012). We used Mallet (McCallum, 2002) to build CRF models. MaxEnt models were built using the MaxEnt [3] package from the Apache OpenNLP package. Naive Bayes and Decision Tree models were built with the Weka (Hall et al., 2009) package (for decision trees, we used the J48 implementation). All the results we will show below were obtained using 10 fold cross validation.

4.1 Features

Among our goals were not only to obtain effective classifiers, but also to investigate which kind of features are most effective for our tasks. As a consequence, beyond textual features and dialogue history features, we experimented with multimodal features extracted from other modalities, utterance features, and automatically inferred dialogue game features.

Textual features (TX) are the most widely used features for DA classification (Stolcke et al., 2000; Bangalore et al., 2008; Sridhar et al., 2009; Di Eugenio et al., 2010a; Kim et al., 2010; Boyer et al., 2011; Ha et al., 2012; Kim et al., 2012). The textual features we use include lexical, syntactic, and heuristic features.

- Lexical features: Unigrams of the words and part-of-speech tags in the current utterance. The words used in the features are processed using the morphology tool from the Stanford parser (De Marneffe and Manning, 2008).
- Syntactic features: The top node and its first two child nodes from the sentence parse tree. If an utterance contains multiple sentences, we use the last sentence. Sentences are parsed using the Stanford parser.
- Number of sentences and number of words in the utterance. We use Apache OpenNLP library [4] to detect sentences and tokenize them.
- Heuristic features: whether an utterance contains WH words (e.g. *what, where*), whether an utterance contains yes/no words (e.g. *yes, no, yeah, nope*).

Utterance features (UT) are extracted from the current utterance's meta information. Previous research showed that utterance meta information such as the utterance speaker can help classify DAs (Ivanovic, 2008; Kim et al., 2010).

- The actor of the utterance
- The time length of the utterance
- The distance of the current utterance from the beginning of the dialogue

The **pointing gesture feature (PT)** indicates whether the actor of the current utterance u_i is making a pointing gesture G, i.e., whether G is associated with u_i, and hence, part of move m_i.

Haptic-Ostensive features (H-O) indicate whether the actor of the current utterance u_i is performing any H-O action G i.e., whether G is associated with u_i, and hence, part of move m_i; and the type of that action, if yes.

Location features (LO) include the locations of the two actors, whether they are in the same location, whether the actor of the current utterance changes the location during the utterance. Since we do not have precise measurement of subjects' locations, we annotate approximate locations by dividing the apartment into four large areas: kitchen, table, lounge and bed.

The **dialogue game feature (DG)** models hierarchical dialogue structure. Some previous research on DA classification has shown that hierarchical dialogue structure encoded via the notion of conversational games (Carlson, 1983) significantly improves DA classification (Hastie et al., 2002; Sridhar et al., 2009; Di Eugenio et al., 2010a). In MapTask, a game is defined as a sequence of moves starting with an initiation (instruct, explain, check, align, query-yn, query-w) and encompassing all utterances up until the purpose of the game has been fulfilled, or abandoned. In the *Find* corpus, dialogue games have not been annotated. In order to use the DG feature, we use a just-in-time approach to infer dialogue games. For each dialogue, we maintain a stack for dialogue games. When an utterance is classified as an initiating DA tag, we assume the dialogue has

[3] http://maxent.sourceforge.net

[4] http://opennlp.apache.org/

entered a new dialogue game, and push the DA label as the dialog game to the top of the stack. The DG feature value is the top element of the stack. The dialogue game feature is always inferred at run time during classification process, just before an utterance is being processed. Hence, when we classify the DA for the current utterance u_i, the DG value that we use is the closest preceding initiating DA.

Dialogue history features (DH) model what happened before the current utterance (Sridhar et al., 2009; Di Eugenio et al., 2010a). We encode:

- The previous move's actor
- Whether the previous move has the same actor as the current move
- The type of the previous move; if it is an utterance, its DA tag; if it is an H-O action, the type of H-O action

5 DA Classification Experiments

We ran the DA classification experiments with three goals. First, we wanted to assess the effectiveness of different types of features, especially, the effectiveness of gesture, H-O action, location and dialogue game features. Second, we wanted to compare the performances of different machine learning algorithms on such a multimodal dialogue dataset. Third, we wanted to investigate the performances of different algorithms in the online and offline experiment settings. The DA classification task could be treated as a sequence labeling problem (Stolcke et al., 2000). However, different from other sequence labeling problems such as part-of-speech tagging, a dialogue system cannot wait until the whole dialogue ends to classify the current DA. A dialogue system needs online DA classification models to classify the DAs when a new utterance is processed by the system. There are two differences between online and offline DA classification modes. First, when we generate the dialogue history and dialogue game features, we use the previously classified DA tag results for online mode, while we use the gold-standard DA tags for offline mode. Second, MaxEnt (using beam search) and CRF evaluate and classify all the utterances in a dialogue at the same time in offline mode; however in online mode, MaxEnt and CRF can only work on the partial sequence up to the utterance to classify. Whereas this may sound obvious, it explains why the performance of these classifiers may be even more negatively affected in online mode with respect to their offline performance, as compared to other classifiers. We will see that indeed this will happen for CRF, but not for MaxEnt.

To evaluate feature effectiveness, we group the features into seven groups: textual features (TX), utterance features (UT), pointing gesture feature (PT), H-O action features (H-O), location features (LO), dialogue game feature (DG), dialogue history features (DH). Then we generate all the combinations of feature groups to run experiments. For each classification algorithm, we ran 10-fold cross-validation experiments, for each feature group combination, in both online and offline mode. It would be impossible to report all our results. Similarly to (Ha et al., 2012), we report our results with single feature groups and incremental feature group combinations, as shown in Table 5. Whereas all combinations were tried, the omitted results do not shed any additional light on the problem. The majority baseline, which always assigns the most frequent tag to every utterance, has an accuracy of 20.3%.

The CRF offline model performs best, which confirms the results of (Kim et al., 2010; Kim et al., 2012). This is due to the strong correlation between dialogue history features (DH) and the states of the CRF. In online mode, when there is noise in the previous DA tags, the CRF's performance drops significantly ($p \leq .005$, using χ^2). A significant drop in performance from offline to online mode also happens to NB ($p \leq .005$) and DT ($p < .025$). MaxEnt performs very stably, the best online model performs only .015 worse than the best offline model. The best MaxEnt offline model beats the other algorithms' best models except CRF, while the MaxEnt online model outperforms all the other algorithms' online models. Our results thus demonstrate that MaxEnt works best for online DA classification on our data.

As concerns features, for online models, textual features (TX) are the most predictive as a feature type used by itself. When we add pointing gesture (PT), H-O features (H-O) and location features (LO) together to textual features, we notice a significant performance improvement for most models (except CRF models). For MaxEnt, which gives the best results for online models, none of the gesture, H-O action and location features alone significantly improve the results, but all three to-

Features	CRF		MaxEnt		NB		DT	
	Offline	Online	Offline	Online	Offline	Online	Offline	Online
1. TX (Textual)	.654	.641	.630	.630	.449	.453	.450	.450
2. UT (Utterance)	.506	.376	.353	.353	.417	.417	.392	.392
3. PT (Pointing)	.225	.155	.210	.210	.212	.212	.212	.212
4. H-O (Haptic-Ostensive)	.187	.147	.237	.237	.243	.243	.212	.212
5. LO (Location)	.259	.176	.264	.264	.259	.259	.265	.265
6. DG (Dialogue Game)	.737	.136	.305	.189	.212	.212	.212	.212
7. DH (Dialogue History)	**.895**	.119	.480	.302	.478	.284	.471	.294
8. TX+PT	.654	.651	.639	.639	.453	.453	.450	.450
9. TX+PT+H-O	.670	**.649**	.637	.637	.456	.456	.449	.449
10. TX+PT+H-O+LO	.648	.645	.657*	.657*	.523*	.523*	.536*	.536*
11. TX+PT+H-O+LO+UT	.668	.612	.685	.685	.563	.563	.568	.568
12. TX+PT+H-O+LO+UT+DG	.770**	.528	.722**	.709**	.566	.591**	.576	.607**
13. TX+PT+H-O+LO+UT+DG+DH	.847†	.475	**.757†**	**.742†**	**.635†**	**.606**	**.671†**	**.627**

Table 5: Dialogue Act Classification Accuracy: * indicates significant improvement after adding PT+H-O+LO to TX (cf. lines 1 and 10); ** indicates significant improvement after adding DG to TX+PT+H-O+LO+UT (cf. lines 11 and 12); †indicates significant improvement after adding DH to TX+PT+H-O+LO+UT+DG (cf. lines 12 and 13); bold font indicates the feature group set giving best performance for each column.

gether do. This confirms the finding of (Ha et al., 2012) that non-verbal features help DA classification. To assess which feature is the most important among those three non-verbal features, we examined the experiment results with a leave-one-out strategy, that is for each classifier in offline and online modes, we leave one of the gesture, H-O and location features out from the full experiment feature set (TX+PT+H-O+LO+UT+DG+DH). No significant difference was discovered.

When the dialogue game features (DG) are added to the models, performance increases significantly for CRF offline model ($p<.005$), MaxEnt offline ($p<.005$) and online ($p<.05$) models, NB online model ($p<.05$) and DT online model ($p<.005$). It confirms previous findings, including by our group (Di Eugenio et al., 2010a), that dialogue game features (DG) play a very important role in DA classification, even via the simple approximation we used. When the dialogue history features (DH) are added to the models, performance increased significantly for all the offline models and the MaxEnt online model, with $p<.005$. This confirms previous findings that dialogue history helps with DA classification.

6 Conclusions and Future Work

In this paper we described our multimodal corpus which is annotated with multimodal information (pointing gestures and H-O actions) and dialogue acts. Our corpus analysis shows that people actively use pointing gestures and H-O actions alongside utterances in dialogues. The function of H-O actions in dialogue had hardly been studied before. Our experiments show that MaxEnt performs best for the online DA classification task. Multimodal and dialogue game features both improve DA classification.

Short-term future work includes manual annotation for dialogue games, in the hope that more accurate dialogue game features may further improve DA classification. Longer term future work includes prediction of the specific next move – the specific DA and/or the specific gesture, pointing or H-O action. We have now developed some of the building blocks of an information-state based multimodal dialogue manager. The major aspects we still need to address are defining the information-state for the *Find* task, and developing rules to update the information-state with multimodal information, the classified DAs, and the co-reference resolution models we already built (Chen et al., 2011; Chen and Di Eugenio, 2012). Once the information-state component is in place, we can expect better and more detailed predictions.

Acknowledgments

This work is supported by award IIS 0905593 from the National Science Foundation. Thanks to the other members of the RoboHelper project, for their many contributions, especially to the data collection effort.

References

Anne H. Anderson, Miles Bader, Ellen Gurman Bard, Elizabeth Boyle, Gwyneth Doherty, Simon Garrod, Stephen Isard, Jacqueline Kowtko, Jan McAllister, Jim Miller, Catherine Sotillo, and Henry S. 1991. The HCRC Map Task corpus. *Language and Speech*, 34(4):351.

Srinivas Bangalore, Giuseppe Di Fabbrizio, and Amanda Stent. 2008. Learning the structure of task-driven human–human dialogs. *IEEE Transactions on Audio, Speech, and Language Processing*, 16(7):1249–1259.

K.E. Boyer, J.F. Grafsgaard, E.Y. Ha, R. Phillips, and J.C. Lester. 2011. An affect-enriched dialogue act classification model for task-oriented dialogue. In *Proceedings of the 49th Annual Meeting of the Association for Computational Linguistics: Human Language Technologies-Volume 1*, pages 1190–1199. Association for Computational Linguistics.

Jean Carletta. 2007. Unleashing the killer corpus: experiences in creating the multi-everything AMI meeting corpus. *Language Resources and Evaluation*, 41(2):181–190.

Lauri Carlson. 1983. *Dialogue games: An approach to discourse analysis*. D. Reidel Publishing Company.

Lin Chen and Barbara Di Eugenio. 2012. Co-reference via pointing and haptics in multi-modal dialogues. In *The 2012 Conference of the North American Chapter of the Association for Computational Linguistics: Human Language Technologies*. The Association for Computational Linguistics.

Lin Chen, Anruo Wang, and Barbara Di Eugenio. 2011. Improving pronominal and deictic coreference resolution with multi-modal features. In *Proceedings of SIGdial 2011, the 12th Annual Meeting of the Special Interest Group on Discourse and Dialogue*, pages 307–311, Portland, Oregon, June. Association for Computational Linguistics.

J. Cohen. 1960. A coefficient of agreement for nominal scales. *Educational and psychological measurement*, 20(1):37–46.

Marie-Catherine De Marneffe and Christopher D. Manning. 2008. The Stanford typed dependencies representation. In *Coling 2008: Proceedings of the workshop on Cross-Framework and Cross-Domain Parser Evaluation*, pages 1–8. Association for Computational Linguistics.

Barbara Di Eugenio, Zhuli Xie, and Riccardo Serafin. 2010a. Dialogue act classification, higher order dialogue structure, and instance-based learning. *Dialogue & Discourse*, 1(2):1–24.

Barbara Di Eugenio, Miloš Žefran, Jezekiel Ben-Arie, Mark Foreman, Lin Chen, Simone Franzini, Shankaranand Jagadeesan, Maria Javaid, and Kai Ma. 2010b. Towards Effective Communication with Robotic Assistants for the Elderly: Integrating Speech, Vision and Haptics. In *Dialog with Robots, AAAI 2010 Fall Symposium*, Arlington, VA, USA, November.

M.E. Foster, E.G. Bard, M. Guhe, R.L. Hill, J. Oberlander, and A. Knoll. 2008. The roles of haptic-ostensive referring expressions in cooperative, task-based human-robot dialogue. In *Proceedings of the 3rd ACM/IEEE International Conference on Human Robot Interaction*, pages 295–302. ACM.

Simone Franzini and Jezekiel Ben-Arie. 2012. Speech recognition by indexing and sequencing. *International Journal of Computer Information Systems and Industrial Management Applications*, 4:358–365.

David Graff, Alexandra Canavan, and George Zipperlen. 1998. Switchboard-2 Phase I.

Eun Young Ha, Joseph F. Grafsgaard, Christopher Mitchell, Kristy Elizabeth Boyer, and James C. Lester. 2012. Combining verbal and nonverbal features to overcome the "information gap" in task-oriented dialogue. In *Proceedings of SIGdial 2012, the 13th Annual Meeting of the Special Interest Group on Discourse and Dialogue*, pages 247–256, Seoul, South Korea, July. Association for Computational Linguistics.

Mark Hall, Eibe Frank, Geoffrey Holmes, Bernhard Pfahringer, Peter Reutemann, and Ian H. Witten. 2009. The WEKA data mining software: An update. *SIGKDD Explorations*, 11(1).

Helen Wright Hastie, Massimo Poesio, and Stephen Isard. 2002. Automatically predicting dialogue structure using prosodic features. *Speech Communication*, 36(1–2):63–79.

Edward Ivanovic. 2008. Automatic instant messaging dialogue using statistical models and dialogue acts. Master's thesis, University of Melbourne.

Maria Javaid and Miloš Žefran. 2012. Interpreting communication through physical interaction during collaborative manipulation. Draft, October.

Su Nam Kim, Lawrence Cavedon, and Timothy Baldwin. 2010. Classifying dialogue acts in one-on-one live chats. In *Proceedings of EMNLP 2010, the Conference on Empirical Methods in Natural Language Processing*, pages 862–871. Association for Computational Linguistics.

Su Nam Kim, Lawrence Cavedon, and Timothy Baldwin. 2012. Classifying dialogue acts in multi-party live chats. In *Proceedings of the 26th Pacific Asia Conference on Language, Information, and Computation*, pages 463–472, Bali, Indonesia, November. Faculty of Computer Science, Universitas Indonesia.

Michael Kipp. 2001. Anvil-a generic annotation tool for multimodal dialogue. In *Proceedings of the 7th European Conference on Speech Communication and Technology*, pages 1367–1370.

Kristine M. Krapp. 2002. *The Gale Encyclopedia of Nursing & Allied Health*. Gale Group, Inc. Chapter Activities of Daily Living Evaluation.

John D. Lafferty, Andrew McCallum, and Fernando C.N. Pereira. 2001. Conditional Random Fields: Probabilistic Models for Segmenting and Labeling Sequence Data. In *Proceedings of the Eighteenth International Conference on Machine Learning*, pages 282–289. Morgan Kaufmann Publishers Inc.

L. Levin, A. Thymé-Gobbel, A. Lavie, K. Ries, and K. Zechner. 1998. A discourse coding scheme for conversational Spanish. In *Fifth International Conference on Spoken Language Processing*.

K. Ma and J. Ben-Arie. 2012. Multi-view multi-class object detection via exemplar compounding. In *IEEE-IAPR 21st International Conference on Pattern Recognition (ICPR 2012)*, Tsukuba, Japan, November.

Andrew Kachites McCallum. 2002. MALLET: A Machine Learning for Language Toolkit.

E. Shriberg, R. Dhillon, S.V. Bhagat, J. Ang, and H. Carvey. 2004. The ICSI Meeting Recorder Dialog Act (MRDA) Corpus. In *Proceedings of 5th SIGdial Workshop on Discourse and Dialogue*, pages 97–100, Cambridge, MA, April 30-May 1.

V.K.R. Sridhar, S. Bangalore, and S. Narayanan. 2009. Combining lexical, syntactic and prosodic cues for improved online dialog act tagging. *Computer Speech & Language*, 23(4):407–422.

A. Stolcke, K. Ries, N. Coccaro, E. Shriberg, R. Bates, D. Jurafsky, P. Taylor, R. Martin, C.V. Ess-Dykema, and M. Meteer. 2000. Dialogue act modeling for automatic tagging and recognition of conversational speech. *Computational linguistics*, 26(3):339–373.

Matthias Zimmermann, Andreas Stolcke, and Elizabeth Shriberg. 2006. Joint segmentation and classification of dialog acts in multiparty meetings. In *ICASSP 2006, the IEEE International Conference on Acoustics, Speech and Signal Processing*, volume 1. IEEE.

Verbal indicators of psychological distress in interactive dialogue with a virtual human

David DeVault, Kallirroi Georgila, Ron Artstein, Fabrizio Morbini, David Traum, Stefan Scherer, Albert (Skip) Rizzo, Louis-Philippe Morency
University of Southern California, Institute for Creative Technologies
Playa Vista, CA
devault@ict.usc.edu

Abstract

We explore the presence of indicators of psychological distress in the linguistic behavior of subjects in a corpus of semi-structured virtual human interviews. At the level of aggregate dialogue-level features, we identify several significant differences between subjects with depression and PTSD when compared to non-distressed subjects. At a more fine-grained level, we show that significant differences can also be found among features that represent subject behavior during specific moments in the dialogues. Finally, we present statistical classification results that suggest the potential for automatic assessment of psychological distress in individual interactions with a virtual human dialogue system.

1 Introduction

One of the first steps toward dealing with psychological disorders such as depression and PTSD is diagnosing the problem. However, there is often a shortage of trained health care professionals, or of access to those professionals, especially for certain segments of the population such as military personnel and veterans (Johnson et al., 2007). One possible partial remedy is to use virtual human characters to do a preliminary triage screening, so that mental healthcare providers can focus their attention on those who are most likely to need help. The virtual human would engage an individual in an interview and analyze some of their behavioral characteristics. In addition to serving a triage function, this automated interview could produce valuable information to help the healthcare provider make their expert diagnosis.

In this paper, we investigate whether features in the linguistic behavior of participants in a conversation with a virtual human could be used for recognizing psychological distress. We focus specifically on indicators of depression and post-traumatic stress disorder (PTSD) in the verbal behavior of participants in a Wizard-of-Oz corpus.

The results and analysis presented here are part of a broader effort to create an automated, interactive virtual human dialogue system that can detect indicators of psychological distress in the multimodal communicative behavior of its users. Realizing this vision requires a careful and strategic design of the virtual human's dialogue behavior, and in concert with the system's behavior, the identification of robust "indicator" features in the verbal and nonverbal responses of human interviewees. These indicators should be specific behavior patterns that are empirically correlated with specific psychological disorders, and that can inform a triage screening process or facilitate the diagnosis or treatment performed by a clinician.

In this paper, we report on several kinds of such indicators we have observed in a corpus of 43 Wizard-of-Oz interactions collected with our prototype virtual human, Ellie, pictured in Figure 1. We begin in Section 2 with a brief discussion of background and related work on the communicative behavior associated with psychological distress. In Section 3, we describe our Wizard-of-Oz data set. Section 4 presents an analysis of indicator features we have explored in this data set, identifying several significant differences between subjects with depression and PTSD when compared to non-distressed subjects. In Section 5 we present statistical classification results that suggest the potential for automatic assessment of psychological distress based on individual interactions with a virtual human dialogue system. We conclude in Section 6.

2 Background and Related Work

There has been a range of psychological and clinical research that has identified differences in the

Figure 1: Ellie.

communicative behavior of patients with specific psychological disorders such as depression. In this section, we briefly summarize some closely related work.

Most work has observed the behavior of patients in human-human interactions, such as clinical interviews and doctor-patient interactions. PTSD is generally less well studied than depression.

Examples of the kinds of differences that have been observed in non-verbal behavior include differences in rates of mutual gaze and other gaze patterns, downward angling of the head, mouth movements, frowns, amount of gesturing, fidgeting, emotional expressivity, and voice quality; see Scherer et al. (2013) for a recent review.

In terms of verbal behavior, our exploration of features here is guided by several previous observations in the literature. Cohn and colleagues have identified increased speaker-switch durations and decreased variability of vocal fundamental frequency as indicators of depression, and have explored the use of these features for classification (Cohn et al., 2009). That work studied these features in human-human clinical interviews, rather than in virtual human interactions as reported here. In clinical studies, acute depression has been associated with decreased speech, slow speech, delays in delivery, and long silent pauses (Hall et al., 1995). Aggregate differences in lexical frequencies have also been observed. For example, in written essays, Rude et al. (2004) observed that depressed participants used more negatively valenced words and used the first-person pronoun "I" more frequently than never-depressed individuals. Heeman et al. (2010) observed differences in children with autism in how long they pause before speaking and in their use of fillers, acknowledgments, and discourse markers. Some of these features are similar to those studied here, but looked at children communicating with clinicians rather than a virtual human dialogue system.

Recent work on machine classification has demonstrated the ability to discriminate between schizophrenic patients and healthy controls based on transcriptions of spoken narratives (Hong et al., 2012), and to predict patient adherence to medical treatment from word-level features of dialogue transcripts (Howes et al., 2012). Automatic speech recognition and word alignment has also been shown to give good results in scoring narrative recall tests for identification of cognitive impairment (Prud'hommeaux and Roark, 2011; Lehr et al., 2012).

3 Data Set

In this section, we introduce the Wizard-of-Oz data set that forms the basis for this paper. In this virtual human dialogue system, the character Ellie depicted in Figure 1 carries out a semi-structured interview with a single user. The system was designed after a careful analysis of a set of face-to-face interviews in the same domain. The face-to-face interviews make up the large human-human Distress Assessment Interview Corpus (DAIC) that is described in Scherer et al. (2013). Drawing on observations of interviewer behavior in the face-to-face dialogues, Ellie was designed to serve as an interviewer who is also a good listener, providing empathetic responses, backchannels, and continuation prompts to elicit more extended replies to specific questions. The data set used in this paper is the result of a set of 43 Wizard-of-Oz interactions where the virtual human interacts verbally and nonverbally in a semi-structured manner with a participant. Excerpts from the transcripts of two interactions in this Wizard-of-Oz data set are provided in the appendix in Figure 5.[1]

3.1 Procedure

The participants were recruited via Craigslist and were recorded at the USC Institute for Creative

[1]A sample demonstration video of an interaction between the virtual agent and a human actor can be seen here: http://www.youtube.com/watch?v=ejczMs6b1Q4

Technologies. In total 64 participants interacted with the virtual human. All participants who met requirements (i.e. age greater than 18, and adequate eyesight) were accepted. In this paper, we focus on a subset of 43 of these participants who were told that they would be interacting with an automated system. (The other participants, which we exclude from our analysis, were aware that they were interacting with a human-controlled system.) The mean age of the 43 participants in our data set was 36.6 years, with 23 males and 20 females.

We adhered to the following procedure for data collection: After a short explanation of the study and giving consent, participants completed a series of questionnaires. These questionnaires included the PTSD Checklist-Civilian version (PCL-C) and the Patient Health Questionnaire, depression module (PHQ-9) (Scherer et al., 2013) along with other questions. Then participants engage in an interview with the virtual human, Ellie. After the dialogue concludes, participants are then debriefed (i.e. the wizard control is revealed), paid \$25 to \$35, and escorted out.

The interaction between the participants and Ellie was designed as follows: Ellie explains the purpose of the interaction and that she will ask a series of questions. She then tries to build rapport with the participant in the beginning of the interaction with a series of casual questions about Los Angeles. Then the main interview begins, including a range of questions such as:

What would you say are some of your best qualities?

What are some things that usually put you in a good mood?

Do you have disturbing thoughts?

What are some things that make you really mad?

How old were you when you enlisted?

What did you study at school?

Ellie's behavior was controlled by two human "wizards" in a separate room, who used a graphical user interface to select Ellie's nonverbal behavior (e.g. head nods, smiles, back-channels) and verbal utterances (including the interview questions, verbal back-channels, and empathy responses). This Wizard-of-Oz setup allows us to prove the utility of the protocol and collect training data for the eventual fully automatic interaction. The speech for each question was pre-recorded using an amateur voice actress (who was also one of the wizards). The virtual human's performance of these utterances is animated using the SmartBody animation system (Thiebaux et al., 2008).

3.2 Condition Assessment

The PHQ-9 and PCL-C scales provide researchers with guidelines on how to assess the participants' conditions based on the responses. Among the 43 participants, 13 scored above 10 on the PHQ-9, which corresponds to moderate depression and above (Kroenke et al., 2001). We consider these 13 participants as positive for depression in this study. 20 participants scored positive for PTSD, following the PCL-C classification. The two positive conditions overlap strongly, as the evaluated measurements PHQ-9 and PCL-C correlate strongly (Pearson's r > 0.8, as reported in Scherer et al. (2013)).

4 Feature Analysis

4.1 Transcription and timing of speech

We have a set $D = \{d_1, ..., d_{43}\}$ of 43 dialogues. The user utterances in each dialogue were transcribed using ELAN (Wittenburg et al., 2006), with start and end timestamps for each utterance.[2] At each pause of 300ms or longer in the user's speech, a new transcription segment was started. The resulting speech segments were subsequently reviewed and corrected for accuracy.

For each dialogue $d_i \in D$, this process resulted in a sequence of user speech segments. We represent each segment as a tuple $\langle s, e, t \rangle$, where s and e are the starting and ending timestamps in seconds, and t is the manual text transcription of the corresponding audio segment. The system speech segments, including their starting and ending timestamps and verbatim transcripts of system utterances, were recovered from the system log files.

To explore aggregate statistical features based on user turn-taking behavior in the dialogues, we employ a simple approach to identifying turns within the dialogues. First, all user and system speech segments are sorted in increasing order of

[2]ELAN is a tool that supports annotation of video and audio, from the Max Planck Institute for Psycholinguistics, The Language Archive, Nijmegen, The Netherlands. It is available at `http://tla.mpi.nl/tools/tla-tools/elan/`.

Segment level features
(a) mean speaking rate of each user segment
(b) mean onset time of first segment in each user turn
(c) mean onset time of non-first segments in user turns
(d) mean length of user segments
(e) mean minimum valence in user segments
(f) mean mean valence in user segments
(g) mean maximum valence in user segments
(h) mean number of filled pauses in user segments
(i) mean filled pause rate in user segments
Dialogue level features
(j) total number of user segments
(k) total length of all user segments

Figure 2: List of context-independent features.

their starting timestamps. All consecutive segments with the same speaker are then designated as constituting a single turn. While this simple scheme does not provide a detailed treatment of relevant phenomena such as overlapping speech, backchannels, and the interactive process of negotiating the turn in dialogue (Yang and Heeman, 2010), it provides a conceptually simple model for the definition of features for aggregate statistical analysis.

4.2 Context-independent feature analysis

We begin by analyzing a set of shallow features which we describe as *context-independent*, as they apply to user speech segments independently of what the system has recently said. Most of these are features that apply to many or all user speech segments. We describe our context-independent features in Section 4.2.1, and present our results for these features in Section 4.2.2.

4.2.1 Context-independent features

We summarize our context-independent features in Figure 2.

Speaking rate and onset times Based on previous clinical observations related to slowed speech and increased onset time for depressed individuals (Section 2), we defined features for speaking rate and onset time of user speech segments.

We quantify the speaking rate of a user speech segment $\langle s, e, t \rangle$, where $t = \langle w_1, ..., w_N \rangle$, as $N/(e - s)$. Feature (a) is the mean value of this feature across all user speech segments within each dialogue.

Onset time is calculated using the notion of user turns. For each user turn, we extracted the first user speech segment in the turn $f_u = \langle s_u, e_u, t_u \rangle$, and the most recent system speech segment $l_s = \langle s_s, e_s, t_s \rangle$. We define the onset time of such a first user segment as $s_u - e_s$, and for each dialogue, feature (b) is the intra-dialogue mean of these onset times.

In order to also quantify pause length between user speech segments within a turn, we define feature (c), a similar feature that measures the mean onset time between non-first user speech segments within a user turn in relation to the preceding user speech segment.

Length of user segments As one way to quantify the amount of speech, feature (d) reports the mean length of all user speech segments within a dialogue (measured in words).

Valence features for user speech Features (e)-(g) are meant to explore the idea that distressed users might use more negative or less positive vocabulary than non-distressed subjects. As an exploratory approach to this topic, we used SentiWordNet 3.0 (Baccianella and Sebastiani, 2010), a lexical sentiment dictionary, to assign valence to individual words spoken by users in our study. The dictionary contains approximately 117,000 entries. In general, each word w may appear in multiple entries, corresponding to different parts of speech and word senses. To assign a single valence score $v(w)$ to each word in the dictionary, in our features we compute the average score across all parts of speech and word senses:

$$v(w) = \frac{\sum_{e \in E(w)} \text{PosScore}_e(w) - \text{NegScore}_e(w)}{|E(w)|}$$

where $E(w)$ is the set of entries for the word w, $\text{PosScore}_e(w)$ is the positive score for w in entry e, and $\text{NegScore}_e(w)$ is the negative score for w in entry e. This is similar to the "averaging across senses" method described in Taboada et al. (2011).

We use several different measures of the valence of each speech segment with transcript $t = \langle w_1, ..., w_n \rangle$. We compute the min, mean, and max valence of each transcript:

$$\begin{aligned} \text{minimum valence of } t &= \min_{w_i \in t} v(w_i) \\ \text{mean valence of } t &= \tfrac{1}{n} \textstyle\sum_{w_i \in t} v(w_i) \\ \text{maximum valence of } t &= \max_{w_i \in t} v(w_i) \end{aligned}$$

Features (e)-(f) then are intra-dialogue mean

values for these three segment-level valence measures.

Filled pauses Another feature that we explored is the presence of filled pauses in user speech segments. To do so, we counted the number of times any of the tokens *uh*, *um*, *uhh*, *umm*, *mm*, or *mmm* appeared in each speech segment. For each dialogue, feature (h) is the mean number of these tokens per user speech segment. In order to account for the varying length of speech segments, we also normalize the raw token counts in each segment by dividing them by the length of the segment, to produce a *filled pause rate* for the segment. Feature (i) is the mean value of the filled pause rate for all speech segments in the dialogue.

Dialogue level features We also included two dialogue level measures of how "talkative" the user is. Feature (j) is the total number of user speech segments throughout the dialogue. Feature (k) is the total length (in words) of all speech segments throughout the dialogue.

Standard deviation features For the classification experiments reported in Section 5, we also included a standard deviation variant of each of the features (a)-(i) in Figure 2. These variants are defined as the intra-dialogue standard deviation of the underlying value, rather than the mean. We discuss examples of standard deviation features further in Section 5.

4.2.2 Results for context-independent features

We summarize the observed significant effects in our Wizard-of-Oz corpus in Table 1.

Onset time We report our findings for individuals with and without depression and PTSD for feature (b) in Table 1 and in Figure 3. The units are seconds. While an increase in onset time for individuals with depression has previously been observed in human-human interaction (Cohn et al., 2009; Hall et al., 1995), here we show that this effect transfers to interactions between individuals with depression and virtual humans. We find that mean onset time is significantly increased for individuals with depression in their interactions with our virtual human Ellie ($p = 0.018$, Wilcoxon rank sum test).

Additionally, while to our knowledge onset time for individuals with PTSD has not been reported, we also found a significant increase in onset time

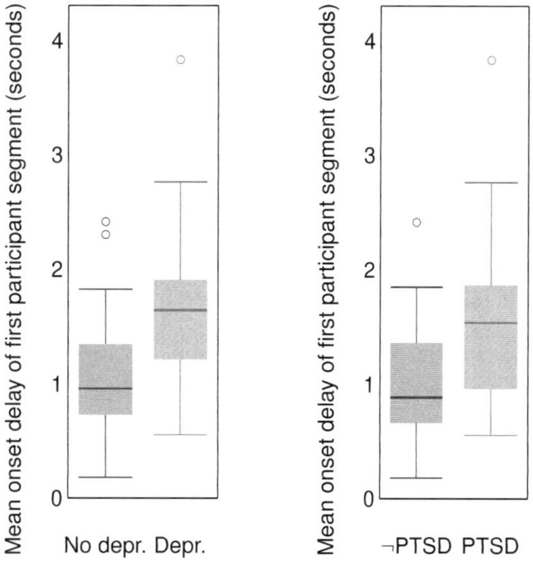

Figure 3: Onset time.

for individuals with PTSD ($p = 0.019$, Wilcoxon rank sum test).

Filled pauses We report our findings for individuals with and without depression and PTSD under feature (h) in Table 1 and in Figure 4. We observed a significant reduction in this feature for both individuals with depression ($p = 0.012$, Wilcoxon rank sum test) and PTSD ($p = 0.014$, Wilcoxon rank sum test). We believe this may be related to the trend we observed toward shorter speech segments from distressed individuals (though this trend did not reach significance). There is a positive correlation, $\rho = 0.55$ ($p = 0.0001$), between mean segment length (d) and mean number of filled pauses in segments (h).

Other features We did not observe significant differences in the values of the other context-independent features in Figure 2.

4.3 Context-dependent features

Our data set allows us to zoom in and look at specific contextual moments in the dialogues, and observe how users respond to specific Ellie questions. As an example, one of Ellie's utterances, which has system ID happy_lasttime, is:

> happy_lasttime = *Tell me about the last time you felt really happy.*

In our data set of 43 dialogues, this question was asked in 42 dialogues, including 12 users positive for depression and 19 users positive for PTSD.

Feature	Depression (13 yes, 30 no)			PTSD (20 yes, 23 no)		
(b) *mean onset time of first segment in each user turn*	↑	Depr.:	1.72 (0.89)	↑	PTSD.:	1.56 (0.80)
		No Depr.:	1.08 (0.56)		No PTSD.:	1.03 (0.57)
		$p =$	0.018		$p =$	0.019
(h) *mean number of filled pauses in user segments*	↓	Depr.:	0.32 (0.19)	↓	PTSD:	0.36 (0.24)
		No Depr.:	0.48 (0.23)		No PTSD:	0.49 (0.21)
		$p =$	0.012		$p =$	0.014

Table 1: Results for context-independent features. For each feature and condition, we provide the mean (standard deviation) for individuals with and without the condition. P-values for individual Wilcoxon rank sum tests are provided. An up arrow (↑) indicates a significant trend toward increased feature values for positive individuals. A down arrow (↓) indicates a significant trend toward decreased feature values for positive individuals.

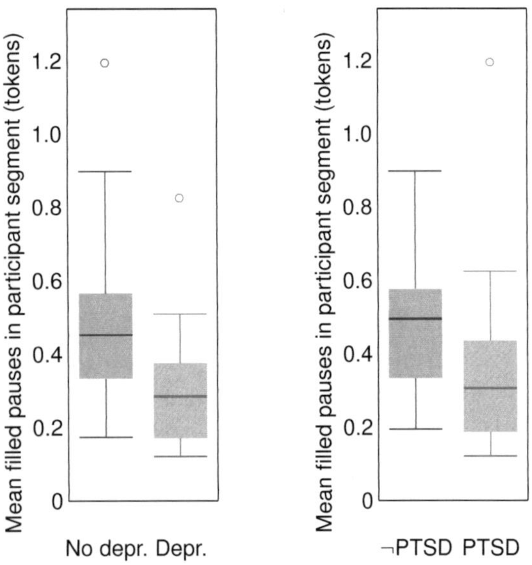

Figure 4: Number of filled pauses per speech segment.

This question is one of 95 *topic setting utterances* in Ellie's repertoire. (Ellie has additional utterances that serve as continuation prompts, backchannels, and empathy responses, which can be used as a topic is discussed.)

To define context-dependent features, we associate with each user segment the most recent of Ellie's topic setting utterances that has occurred in the dialogue. We then focus our analysis on those user segments and turns that follow specific topic setting utterances. In Table 2, we present some examples of our findings for context-dependent features for happy_lasttime.[3]

The contextual feature labeled (g′) in Table 2 is the mean of the maximum valence feature across all segments for which happy_lasttime is the most recent topic setting system utterance. We provide a full example of this feature calculation in Figure 5 in the appendix.

As the figure shows, we find that users with both PTSD and depression show a sharp reduction in the mean maximum valence in their speech segments that respond to this question. This suggests that in these virtual human interactions, this question plays a useful role in eliciting differential responses from subjects with these psychological disorders. We observed three additional questions which showed a significant difference in the mean maximum valence feature. One example is the question, *How would your best friend describe you?*.

With feature (b′) in Table 2, we find an increased onset time in responses to this question for subjects with depression.[4] Feature (d′) shows that subjects with PTSD exhibit shorter speech segments in their responses to this question.

We observed a range of findings of this sort for various combinations of Ellie's topic setting utterances and specific context-dependent features. In future work, we would like to study the optimal combinations of context-dependent questions that yield the most information about the user's distress status.

[3]While we provide significance test results here at the $p < 0.05$ level, it should be noted that because of the large number of context-dependent features that may be defined in a small corpus such as ours, we report these merely as observations in our corpus. We do not claim that these results transfer beyond this data set.

[4]In comparing Table 2 with Table 1, this question seems to induce a higher mean onset time for distressed users than the average system utterance does. This does not seem to be the case for non-distressed users.

Feature	Depression (12 yes, 30 no)			PTSD (19 yes, 23 no)		
(g′) *mean maximum valence in user segments following happy_lasttime*	↓	Depr.: No Depr.: $p =$	0.15 (0.07) 0.26 (0.12) 0.003	↓	PTSD: No PTSD: $p =$	0.16 (0.08) 0.28 (0.11) 0.0003
(b′) *mean onset time of first segments in user turns following happy_lasttime*	↑	Depr.: No Depr.: $p =$	2.64 (2.70) 0.94 (1.80) 0.030	n.s.	PTSD: No PTSD: $p =$	2.18 (2.48) 0.80 (1.76) 0.077
(d′) *mean length of user segments following happy_lasttime*	n.s.	Depr.: No Depr.: $p =$	5.95 (1.80) 10.03 (6.99) 0.077	↓	PTSD: No PTSD: $p =$	6.82 (5.12) 10.55 (6.68) 0.012

Table 2: Example results for context-dependent features. For each feature and condition, we provide the mean (standard deviation) for individuals with and without the condition. P-values for individual Wilcoxon rank sum tests are provided. An up arrow (↑) indicates a significant trend toward increased feature values for positive individuals. A down arrow (↓) indicates a significant trend toward decreased feature values for positive individuals.

5 Classification Results

In this section, we present some suggestive classification results for our data set. We construct three binary classifiers that use the kinds of features described in Section 4 to predict the presence of three conditions: PTSD, depression, and distress. For the third condition, we define distress to be present if and only if PTSD, depression, or both are present. Such a notion of distress that collapses distinctions between disorders may be the most appropriate type of classification for a potential application in which distressed users of any type are prioritized for access to health care professionals (who will make a more informed assessment of specific conditions).

For each individual dialogue, each of the three classifiers emits a single binary label. We train and evaluate the classifiers in a 10-fold cross-validation using Weka (Hall et al., 2009).

While our data set of 43 dialogues is perhaps of a typical size for a study of a research prototype dialogue system, it remains very small from a machine learning perspective. We report here two kinds of results that help provide perspective on the prospects for classification of these conditions. The first kind looks at classification based on all the context-independent features described in Section 4.2.1. The second looks at classification based on individual features from this set.

In the first set of experiments, we trained a Naïve Bayes classifier for each condition using all the context-independent features. We present our results in Table 3, comparing each classifier to a baseline that always predicts the majority class (i.e. no condition for PTSD, no condition for depression, and with condition for distress).

We note first that the trained classifiers all outperform the baseline in terms of weighted F-score, weighted precision, weighted recall, and accuracy. The accuracy improvement over baseline is substantial for PTSD (20.9% absolute improvement) and distress (23.2% absolute improvement). The accuracy improvement over baseline is more modest for depression (2.3% absolute). We believe one factor in the relative difficulty of classifying depression more accurately is the relatively small number of depressed participants in our study (13).

While it has been shown in prior work (Cohn et al., 2009) that depression can be classified above baseline performance using features observed in clinical human-human interactions, here we have shown that classification above baseline performance is possible in interactions between human participants and a virtual human dialogue system. Further, we have shown classification results for PTSD and distress as well as depression.

We tried incorporating context-dependent features, and also unigram features, but found that neither improved performance. We believe our data set is too small for effective training with these very large extended feature sets.

Disorder	Model	Weighted F-score	Weighted Precision	Weighted Recall	Accuracy
PTSD	Naïve Bayes	0.738	0.754	0.744	74.4%
	Majority Baseline	0.373	0.286	0.535	53.5%
Depression	Naïve Bayes	0.721	0.721	0.721	72.1%
	Majority Baseline	0.574	0.487	0.698	69.8%
Distress	Naïve Bayes	0.743	0.750	0.744	74.4%
	Majority Baseline	0.347	0.262	0.512	51.2%

Table 3: Classification results.

In our second set of experiments, we sought to gain understanding of which features were providing the greatest value to classification performance. We therefore retrained Naïve Bayes classifiers using only one feature at a time. We summarize here some of the highest performing features.

For depression, we found that the feature *standard deviation in onset time of first segment in each user turn* yielded very strong performance by itself. In our corpus, we observed that depressed individuals show a greater standard deviation in the onset time of their responses to Ellie's questions ($p = 0.024$, Wilcoxon rank sum test). The value of this feature in classification complements the clinical finding that depressed individuals show greater onset times in their responses to interview questions (Cohn et al., 2009).

For distress, we found that the feature *mean maximum valence in user segments* was the most valuable. We discussed findings for a context-dependent version of this feature in Section 4.3. This finding for distress can be related to previous observations that individuals with depression use more negatively valenced words (Rude et al., 2004).

For PTSD, we found that the feature *mean number of filled pauses in user segments* was among the most informative.

Based on our observation of classification performance using individual features, we believe there remains much room for improvement in feature selection and training. A larger data set would enable feature selection approaches that use held out data, and would likely result in both increased performance and deeper insights into the most valuable combination of features for classification.

6 Conclusion

In this paper, we have explored the presence of indicators of psychological distress in the linguistic behavior of subjects in a corpus of semi-structured virtual human interviews. In our data set, we have identified several significant differences between subjects with depression and PTSD when compared to non-distressed subjects. Drawing on these features, we have presented statistical classification results that suggest the potential for automatic assessment of psychological distress in individual interactions with a virtual human dialogue system.

Acknowledgments

This work is supported by DARPA under contract (W911NF-04-D-0005) and the U.S. Army Research, Development, and Engineering Command. The content does not necessarily reflect the position or the policy of the Government, and no official endorsement should be inferred.

References

Andrea Esuli Stefano Baccianella and Fabrizio Sebastiani. 2010. Sentiwordnet 3.0: An enhanced lexical resource for sentiment analysis and opinion mining. In *Proceedings of the Seventh conference on International Language Resources and Evaluation (LREC'10)*, Valletta, Malta, May. European Language Resources Association (ELRA).

Jeffery F. Cohn, Tomas Simon Kruez, Iain Matthews, Ying Yang, Minh Hoai Nguyen, Margara Tejera Padilla, Feng Zhou, and Fernando De la Torre. 2009. Detecting depression from facial actions and vocal prosody. In *Affective Computing and Intelligent Interaction (ACII)*, September.

Judith A. Hall, Jinni A. Harrigan, and Robert Rosenthal. 1995. Nonverbal behavior in clinician-patient interaction. *Applied and Preventive Psychology*, 4(1):21 – 37.

Mark Hall, Eibe Frank, Geoffrey Holmes, Bernhard Pfahringer, Peter Reutemann, and Ian H. Witten. 2009. The weka data mining software: an update. *SIGKDD Explor. Newsl.*, 11(1):10–18, November.

Peter A Heeman, Rebecca Lunsford, Ethan Selfridge, Lois Black, and Jan Van Santen. 2010. Autism and interactional aspects of dialogue. In *Proceedings of the 11th Annual Meeting of the Special Interest Group on Discourse and Dialogue*, pages 249–252. Association for Computational Linguistics.

Kai Hong, Christian G. Kohler, Mary E. March, Amber A. Parker, and Ani Nenkova. 2012. Lexical differences in autobiographical narratives from schizophrenic patients and healthy controls. In *Proceedings of the 2012 Joint Conference on Empirical Methods in Natural Language Processing and Computational Natural Language Learning*, pages 37–47, Jeju Island, Korea, July. Association for Computational Linguistics.

Christine Howes, Matthew Purver, Rose McCabe, Patrick G. T. Healey, and Mary Lavelle. 2012. Predicting adherence to treatment for schizophrenia from dialogue transcripts. In *Proceedings of the 13th Annual Meeting of the Special Interest Group on Discourse and Dialogue*, pages 79–83, Seoul, South Korea, July. Association for Computational Linguistics.

Shannon J Johnson, Michelle D Sherman, Jeanne S Hoffman, Larry C James, Patti L Johnson, John E Lochman, Thomas N Magee, David Riggs, Jessica Henderson Daniel, Ronald S Palomares, et al. 2007. *The psychological needs of US military service members and their families: A preliminary report.* American Psychological Association Presidential Task Force on Military Deployment Services for Youth, Families and Service Members.

Kurt Kroenke, Robert L. Spitzer, and Janet B. W. Williams. 2001. The phq-9. *Journal of General Internal Medicine*, 16(9):606–613.

Maider Lehr, Emily Prud'hommeaux, Izhak Shafran, and Brian Roark. 2012. Fully automated neuropsychological assessment for detecting mild cognitive impairment. In *Interspeech 2012: 13th Annual Conference of the International Speech Communication Association*, Portland, Oregon, September.

Emily Prud'hommeaux and Brian Roark. 2011. Extraction of narrative recall patterns for neuropsychological assessment. In *Interspeech 2011: 12th Annual Conference of the International Speech Communication Association*, pages 3021–3024, Florence, Italy, August.

Stephanie Rude, Eva-Maria Gortner, and James Pennebaker. 2004. Language use of depressed and depression-vulnerable college students. *Cognition & Emotion*, 18(8):1121–1133.

S. Scherer, G. Stratou, M. Mahmoud, J. Boberg, J. Gratch, A. Rizzo, and L.-P. Morency. 2013. Automatic behavior descriptors for psychological disorder analysis. In *IEEE Conference on Automatic Face and Gesture Recognition.*

Maite Taboada, Julian Brooke, Milan Tofiloski, Kimberly Voll, and Manfred Stede. 2011. Lexicon-based methods for sentiment analysis. *Computational Linguistics*, 37(2):267–307, June.

Marcus Thiebaux, Stacy Marsella, Andrew N. Marshall, and Marcelo Kallmann. 2008. Smartbody: behavior realization for embodied conversational agents. In *Proceedings of the 7th international joint conference on Autonomous agents and multiagent systems - Volume 1*, AAMAS '08, pages 151–158, Richland, SC. International Foundation for Autonomous Agents and Multiagent Systems.

Peter Wittenburg, Hennie Brugman, Albert Russel, Alex Klassmann, and Han Sloetjes. 2006. Elan: a professional framework for multimodality research. In *Proceedings of LREC 2006, Fifth International Conference on Language Resources and Evaluation.*

Fan Yang and Peter A. Heeman. 2010. Initiative conflicts in task-oriented dialogue. *Computer Speech & Language*, 24(2):175 – 189.

Appendix A. Wizard-of-Oz Dialogue Excerpts

Example user with PTSD and depression

	max valence	transcript
Ellie		(happy_lasttime) tell me about the last time you felt really happy
User	0.014	when i play with my dog
Ellie		when was the last time that happened?
User	0.000	this morning
Ellie		aw
Ellie		tell me more about that
User	0.312	i don't know i just
User	0.010	whenever i get
User	0.312	super bored or i just need some time to
User	0.312	for myself i just play with the dog
Ellie		that's good
User	0.000	yeah
		0.1371 = mean maximum valence in user segments following happy_lasttime
Ellie		(ideal_weekendC) tell me how you spend your ideal weekend

Example non-distressed user

	max valence	transcript
Ellie		(happy_lasttime) tell me about the last time you felt really happy
User	0.562	um the last time i felt really happy was
User	0.000	hm
User	0.000	today
Ellie		tell me more about that
User	0.688	uh just from the moment i woke up it was a beautiful sunny day
User	-0.062	i
User	0.565	went to see some friends we had a good time went to school
User	0.565	had some good grades on some papers um wrote a good essay
User	0.292	feel pretty accomplished and
User	0.312	i feel like my day is just
User	0.565	a good day
Ellie		that's so good to hear
		0.3487 = mean maximum valence in user segments following happy_lasttime
Ellie		(BF_describe) how would your best friend describe you?

Figure 5: Examples of maximum valence feature.

Spoken Language Understanding for Natural Interaction: the Siri Experience

Jerome Bellegarda

Apple, Inc
1 Infinite Loop, Cupertino, CA 95014, USA
jerome@apple.com

Natural language interaction has the potential to considerably enhance user experience, especially in mobile devices like smartphones and electronic tablets. Recent advances in software integration and efforts toward more personalization and context awareness have brought closer the long-standing vision of the ubiquitous intelligent personal assistant. Multiple voice-driven initiatives, such as Apple's Siri, have now reached commercial deployment. In this talk, I will review the two major semantic interpretation frameworks underpinning virtual personal assistance, and reflect on the inherent complementarity in their respective advantages and drawbacks. I will then discuss some of the attendant choices made in Siri, and speculate on their likely evolution going forward.

Learning Dialogue Management Models for Task-Oriented Dialogue with Parallel Dialogue and Task Streams

Eun Young Ha, Christopher M. Mitchell, Kristy Elizabeth Boyer, and James C. Lester
Department of Computer Science
North Carolina State University
Raleigh, NC 27695, USA
{eha,cmmitch2,keboyer,lester}@ncsu.edu

Abstract

Learning dialogue management models poses significant challenges. In a complex task-oriented domain in which information is exchanged via parallel, interleaved dialogue and task streams, effective dialogue management models should be able to make dialogue moves based on both the dialogue and the task context. This paper presents a data-driven approach to learning dialogue management models that determine when to make dialogue moves to assist users' task completion activities, as well as the type of dialogue move that should be selected for a given user interaction context. Combining features automatically extracted from the dialogue and the task, we compare two alternate modeling approaches. The results of an evaluation indicate the learned models are effective in predicting both the timing and the type of system dialogue moves.

1 Introduction

Automated dialogue systems allow users to interact with information systems in a natural and intuitive manner. With the growth of speech-enabled applications for mobile devices, the demands for practical dialogue systems have been increasing at an accelerating pace. The core tasks of automated dialogue systems include dialogue management, which is concerned with selecting system actions in response to a given user input. Traditionally, dialogue managers have been manually constructed. However, manually crafting dialogue managers is labor-intensive and yields systems that are brittle with respect to unexpected user behaviors. For rapid creation of robust and adaptive dialogue systems, data-driven approaches to dialogue management hold much appeal. Recent work on dialogue systems has explored machine learning techniques to automatically learn dialogue managers from corpora (Scheffler and Young, 2002; Hardy et al., 2006; Williams and Young, 2007; Bangalore et al., 2008; Sridhar et al., 2009).

To support more natural human-computer dialogue, earlier work on dialogue systems envisioned rich interaction environments that take into account observed user actions for selecting optimal dialogue strategies (Carberry, 1990; Rich and Sidner, 1998; Allen et al., 2001). However, recent data-driven approaches have primarily focused on application domains in which information between the user and the system are communicated solely by dialogue, such as telephone-based systems (Hardy et al., 2006; Bangalore et al., 2008) and online chat dialogues (Ivanovic, 2008; Kim et al., 2010). With increasing demands for natural human-computer interaction beyond these restricted application domains, dialogue systems are required to support more complex types of interaction, in which users perform tasks in parallel to exchanging dialogue. For instance, dialogue interfaces for task-assistance systems, such as intelligent tutoring systems, should be able to monitor users' task completion activities and incorporate the observed activities into dialogue management decisions such that the systems can provide users with spontaneous assistance (e.g., providing hints) even without an explicit request from the user.

We have been exploring data-driven approaches for a complex task-oriented application domain in which information is delivered both by exchanging dialogue with users and by observing users' task completion activities. Our previous work has focused on the automatic interpretation of user dialogue input (Boyer et al.,

2010; Ha et al., 2012). Findings suggest that identifying an effective representation to combine information from dialogue and users' task completion activities is key to effective dialogue processing in a domain consisting of parallel dialogue and task streams.

As the next step in this line of investigation on complex task-oriented domains with parallel dialogue and task streams, this work proposes an approach to automatically learning dialogue management models from a human dialogue corpus. The proposed approach combines information from a dialogue stream and a task stream in order to create spontaneous dialogue interventions for users based on monitoring users' activities. Two subtasks of dialogue management are addressed: the first is to determine when to provide dialogue feedback (*timing*), and the second is to determine what kind of dialogue feedback to provide (*type*). Dialogue managers in conventional domains have primarily focused on the selection of feedback type. However, determining the appropriate timing of system moves is critical for dialogue systems that support parallel dialogue and task streams.

The work presented here makes three contributions. First, it endeavors to expand data-driven dialogue management by addressing more complex task-oriented domains consisting of parallel dialogue and task streams. Second, it proposes a timing intervention model that determines the correct time to make spontaneous system interventions. Third, it presents a maximum entropy dialogue management model and compares alternate approaches. It also compares the predictive power of the dialogue and task streams on the targeted dialogue management tasks.

2 Related Work

Data-driven approaches to dialogue management continue to be the subject of increasing attention within the dialogue community. Prominent among these are reinforcement learning approaches for learning dialogue policies from corpora (Henderson et al., 2008; Levin et al., 2000; Lewis and Di Fabbrizio, 2006; Roy et al., 2000; Scheffler and Young, 2002; Singh et al., 2002; Williams and Young, 2007; Young, 2002). These approaches model dialogue as Markov decision processes, either fully observable (MDPs) or partially observable (POMDPs), in which the transitions of dialogue states are associated with system actions and rewards. The goal of reinforcement learning is to learn optimal policies that maximize aggregate expected rewards, such as user satisfaction (Walker et al., 1997). Learned policies that result from RL exploration do not, by design, necessarily reflect the patterns in the bootstrap dialogue corpus. Additionally, to cover all possible state spaces, reinforcement learning typically requires a very large set of training data, which limits the complexity of the dialogue system in its representation of the dialogue states and the system actions (Young et al., 2013).

A second body of related work focuses on dialogue act classification. Classification-based approaches aim at learning the patterns of dialogue that are present in the corpus. A variety of machine learning frameworks have been exploited, including hidden Markov models (Stolcke et al., 2000; Boyer et al., 2010), maximum entropy models (Bangalore et al., 2008; Sridhar et al., 2009; Ha et al., 2012), support vector machines (Ivanovic, 2008), conditional random fields (Kim et al., 2010), and memory-based classifiers in combination with latent semantic analysis (Di Eugenio et al., 2010). Classification-based approaches incorporate rich sets of features, including not only lexical information, syntactic features, and dialogue structure, but also prosodic features in the case of spoken dialogue (Stolcke et al., 2000; Sridhar et al., 2009) and non-verbal features such as facial expressions (Boyer et al., 2011) and shifts in posture (Ha et al., 2012).

While most work on dialogue act classification has focused on either offline analysis of dialogue (Stolcke et al., 2000; Ivanovic, 2008; Kim et al., 2010; Di Eugenio et al., 2010) or interpretation of user dialogue (Boyer et al., 2010; Ha et al., 2012), Bangalore et al. (2008) utilized dialogue act classification as a mechanism for determining system dialogue moves. They proposed a unified dialogue act classification approach for both the interpretation of user utterances and selection of system dialogue moves.

Our work is similar to Bangalore et al. (2008) in that it takes a dialogue act classification approach to the task of selecting system dialogue moves. However, it addresses the problems posed by complex task-oriented application domains in which information is communicated not only by dialogue exchanges but also by monitoring users' task performance. In such domains, a user's task activities constitute a full communicative stream in its own right, separate from the dialogue stream. The challenges of parallel dialogue and task streams are addressed by exploiting automatically obtained task features combined with dialogue features. In contrast to previous work (Bangalore et al. 2008, Boyer et al., 2010), in which task information was derived from manual annotation, our work utilizes automatically computed task features.

Our work also focuses on a growing application area of dialogue systems: intelligent tutoring. In support of student learning, recent work in this area utilized human tutorial dialogue corpora to learn effective tutorial strategies using MDPs (Chi et al., 2010; Mitchell et al., 2013), to develop tutorial dialogue models that adapt to students' affective states (Forbes-Riley and Litman, 2011), and to improve robustness of a symbolic tutorial dialogue system (Dzikovska et al., 2013).

3 Task-Oriented Dialogue Corpus

To learn dialogue management models from naturally occurring human-to-human dialogue we utilize a human tutorial dialogue corpus we collected in the domain of introductory programming in Java. The corpus consists of textual dialogue exchanges between students and tutors in a web-based remote-tutoring interface, aligned with task context logs (Appendix A). A subset of the corpus was annotated with dialogue acts, which was used to train and test the dialogue management models described in this paper.

3.1 Human tutoring study

The data collection study involved forty-two undergraduate students who were paired with one of four tutors. The students were enrolled in a first-year engineering course and were pre-screened to filter out those with significant programming experience. The students were compensated for their participation with partial course credit. The tutors were graduate students with previous tutoring or teaching experience in Java programming, and the students worked with the same tutor for the entire study. Each lesson consisted of between four and thirteen distinct subtasks.

The students completed six forty-minute tutoring lessons, covering progressive topics in introductory computer science over four weeks. Each lesson consisted of four to thirteen subtasks, in which later subtasks built upon earlier ones. During each tutoring session, the paired student and tutor interacted remotely using a web-based tutoring interface. With this tutoring interface, the student and the tutor were able to exchange textual dialogue and share a synchronized view of the task.

For each lesson, students completed a pre-test and a post-test before and after the main tutoring session. The pre- and post-test consisted of the same set of questions to assess students' knowledge related to the lesson's objectives. Compared to students' pre-test results, significant learning gains were observed on the post-test, which indicates that the tutorial dialogue was effective for student learning (Mitchell et al., 2012).

3.2 Dialogue annotation

A subset of the collected data was manually annotated with dialogue acts using an annotation scheme consisting of 13 dialogue act tags for task-oriented tutorial dialogue (Table 1). The annotated corpus consists of the first of the six tutoring lessons from 21 students, which contains 2564 utterances (1777 tutor, 787 student). The average number of utterances per tutoring session was 122 (min = 74; max = 201). The average number of tutor utterances per session was 84.6 (min = 51; max = 137), and the average number of student utterances per session was 37.4 (min = 22; max = 64).

Three human annotators were trained to apply the scheme. The training consisted of an iterative process involving collaborative and independent tagging, followed by refinements of the tagging protocol. At the initial phase of training, the annotators tagged the corpus collaboratively. In later phases annotators tagged independently. To compute agreement between different annotators, 24% (5 of the 21 sessions) of the corpus were doubly annotated by two annotators. All possible pairs of the annotators participated in double annotation. The aggregate agreement was 0.80 in Cohen's Kappa (Cohen, 1960).

4 Dialogue Management Models

To support a task-oriented dialogue system capable of not only responding to users' dialogue input but also providing spontaneous system intervention during users' task activities, a dialogue manager should provide two functionalities. The first is to determine the *timing* of a system dialogue move (i.e., whether or not to provide a tutorial dialogue move at a given context). The second is to determine the *type* of dialogue move (i.e., selecting from available system dialogue acts). In this work, the problem of determining the system's next dialogue move is cast as a classification task. In previous work we found a maximum entropy approach was effective for

Tag	Description	Agreement
H	**Hint:** The tutor gives advice to help the student proceed with the task	.50
DIR	**Directive:** The tutor explicitly tells the student the next step to take	.63
ACK	**Acknowledgement:** Either the tutor or the student acknowledges previous utterance; conversational grounding	.73
RC	**Request for Confirmation:** Either the tutor or the student requests confirmation from the other participant (e.g., *"Make sense?"*)	Insufficient data
RF	**Request for Feedback:** The student requests an assessment of his performance or his work from the tutor	1.0
PF	**Positive Feedback:** The tutor provides a positive assessment of the student's performance	.90
LF	**Lukewarm Feedback:** The tutor provides an assessment that has both positive and negative elements	.80
NF	**Negative Feedback:** The tutor provides a negative assessment of the student's performance	.40
Q	**Question:** A question which does not fit into any of the above categories	.95
A	**Answer:** An answer to an utterance marked Q	.94
C	**Correction:** Correction of a typo in a previous utterance	.54
S	**Statement:** A statement which does not fit into any of the above categories	.71
O	**Other:** Other utterances, usually containing only affective content	.69

Table 1. Dialogue act annotation scheme and inter-rater agreement

classifying user dialogue acts for task-oriented dialogue with parallel dialogue and task streams (Ha, 2012). Maximum entropy outperformed both Naive Bayes and conditional random fields. Building on these results, we employ a maximum entropy classifier to learn dialogue management models that predict both the timing and the type of the system dialogue move. The following sections describe two alternate approaches to dialogue management that can both determine the timing and determine the type of system dialogue interventions.

4.1 One-step dialogue management model

In the first model, the two dialogue management tasks are framed as a single classification problem by treating the decision of *not to make a tutorial dialogue move* as a special dialogue act. Thus, a finite set of dialogue moves allowed for the system is defined as $M = \{m_1, m_2, \cdots, m_n\}$, in which $M = DA \cup \{NoMove\}$ and $DA = \{da_1, da_2, \cdots, da_t\}$ is the set of dialogue acts available for the system. Given M and the ith step in a given user interaction history $H_i^{i-k} = h_{i-k}, h_{i-k+1}, \cdots, h_i$, the goal of the dialogue management model is to predict system's dialogue move m_{i+1} for the next step, which is determined by the following equation.

$$m_{i+1} = argmax_{m \in M} P\left(m \middle| H_i^{i-k}\right) \quad (1)$$

The task-oriented dialogue considered in this work includes two parallel and interleaved data streams: an explicit dialogue stream, consisting of textual exchanges between a student and a tutor, and an implicit task stream, consisting of the student's problem-solving activities. Thus, a given interaction history can be decomposed into a dialogue history and a task history, rewriting equation (1) as follows,

$$m_{i+1} = argmax_{m \in M} P\left(m \middle| D_i^{i-k}, T_i^{i-k}\right) \quad (2)$$

in which $D_i^{i-k} = d_{i-k}, d_{i-k+1}, \cdots, d_i$ and $T_i^{i-k} = t_{i-k}, t_{i-k+1}, \cdots, t_i$ represent the history of dialogue utterances and the history of student task activities, respectively.

In this work, the conditional probability distribution in Equation (2) is estimated using the maximum entropy framework (Berger et al., 1996). The maximum entropy framework selects a probability distribution that results in the highest entropy among all possible solutions. Given a vector π of feature set, the conditional probability distribution is estimated by the following equation,

$$P(X = m_i|\pi) = \frac{1}{Z(\pi)} e^{\lambda m_i \cdot \pi} \quad (3)$$

in which λ represents weights and Z is a normalizing factor. This work used MALLET

(McCallum, 2002) to estimate this conditional distribution.

4.2 Two-step dialogue management model

A potential shortcoming of the one-step model is that the probability distribution over dialogue acts is prone to distortion depending on the portion of *NoMove* in the training data. To avoid this, the second model takes a two-step approach, treating each dialogue management task as an independent classification task. The two-step model first determines whether or not to make a dialogue move. If a decision is made to provide a dialogue move, the second classifier is called for a selection of the type of dialogue move.

In this model, system's dialogue move m_{i+1} for the next interaction step is determined by a function $f(H_i^{i-k})$, such that

$$f(H_i^{i-k}) = NoMove, \quad (4)$$
$$\text{when } P(NoMove|H_i^{i-k}) > P(Move|H_i^{i-k})$$

$$f(H_i^{i-k}) = argmax_{da \in DA} P(da|H_i^{i-k}) \quad (5)$$
otherwise.

Similar to the one-step model, Equation (5) can be written as

$$f(H_i^{i-k}) = argmax_{da \in DA} P(da|D_i^{i-k}, T_i^{i-k}) \quad (6)$$

This conditional probability distribution is also estimated by the maximum entropy framework.

5 Features

To learn high-performing dialogue management models for task-oriented dialogue with parallel dialogue and task streams, it is crucial to have an effective representation of user interaction state that captures information from all available data streams. The dialogue management models described in the previous section determine the system's next dialogue move based on user interaction state specified by the features extracted from the dialogue and the task streams. In contrast to previous work on task-oriented dialogue, in which task information is incorporated into dialogue utterances by manual tagging (Bangalore et al., 2008; Boyer et al., 2010), our work does not require manual effort to obtain the relevant task information. Instead, we rely on task context logs generated during students' interactions with the tutoring interface, as well as a notion of students' task progress automatically estimated by a task analysis algorithm. The same set of features is used for the prediction of both the timing and the type of system move.

5.1 Automatic task analysis

In order to provide a measure of students' task progress through each of the tutoring sessions, an edit distance metric was implemented. This metric computes the minimum edit distance between a student's program at a particular time *t* and a representative solution for a given programming task, in order to estimate how far away the student is from completing the task. Because our tutors were experienced in the subject matter and were familiar with the lesson structures, we can safely assume that they knew what this final state of the code would be and thus had an intuitive metric of student progress, which is analogous to our edit distance metric. As this value changes over a session, one can observe how the student's progress is affected by tutor dialogue acts.

Because a character-based edit distance would not capture the relative functional importance of each part of the student's program, our edit distance metric is based on tokenized versions of the program, as generated by the Java compiler, and the output is the number of tokens that differ from the solution for that task. In this way, comments, variable names, or string literals with many characters are all treated as single tokens and do not artificially inflate the edit distance. This tokenization also allows for abstraction of these comments, variable names, and string literals into generalized tokens so that they can be more easily compared between students.

5.2 Dialogue features

Previous work on dialogue act classification has shown that lexical features extracted from dialogue utterances are good predictors of dialogue acts (Bangalore et al., 2008; Boyer et al., 2010a; Kim et al., 2010). However, this finding does not apply when the goal of dialogue act classification is to learn dialogue management models because determining system moves precedes system utterance generation. Instead, this work exploits features that represent local interaction structure within dialogue streams, which includes *current student dialogue act*, *current tutor dialogue act*, *previous tutor dialogue act*, and *tutor utterance count*.

- **Current student dialogue act** represents the interpreted dialogue act for the previous user dialogue input. Student dialogue act interpretation is not addressed in this paper, assuming the existence of an external module that carries out user dialogue interpretation (e.g., Ha et al., 2012).

- **Current tutor dialogue act** represents the type of system dialogue act at the current interaction step. In our tutorial dialogue corpus, we observed tutors often made several dialogue utterances in succession, such as a feedback (*"Great Job."*) followed by a question (*"Do you have any questions?"*). Thus, the value of the current tutor dialogue act impacts the probability distribution over the tutor's next dialogue move. This feature captures such temporal patterns present in tutor dialogue moves as observed in the corpus.
- **Previous tutor dialogue act** represents the type of system dialogue act generated for the previous interaction step. This is similar to the *current tutor dialogue act* feature, but models longer temporal patterns by extending the size of interaction history.
- **Tutor utterance count** represents the number of system dialogue acts generated in succession without interruption until the current interaction step. In our corpus, it was observed that the tutor dialogue turns often consist of multiple utterances. This feature is included to model system dialogue turns consisting of multiple utterances.

5.3 Task features

To create a rich representation of task context, a number of features were automatically extracted from task streams. Three groups of task information were considered, including types of task activity taken by user, the amount of time taken between certain activities, and the user's task progress estimated by the task analysis algorithm (Section 5.1). Alternate representations of these features were empirically compared, resulting in the following task features incorporated in current dialogue management models.

- **Current log type** represents the type of activity taken at the current interaction step either by the user or the system. A complete list of log types is shown in Appendix B.
- **Previous log type** represents the type of activity taken at the previous interaction step. Analogous to *previous tutor dialogue act* in dialogue stream, this feature models temporal patterns among task activities.
- **Same log type** is a binary feature indicating the type of activities at the current and previous interaction step is identical.
- **Previous and current log type** is a feature that combines the current and previous log types (i.e., a bigram of log types).
- **Elapsed time** is the amount of time since the last logged activity, which represents the duration of the user's inactivity. This feature is included to enable the learned dialogue management model to make spontaneous dialogue interventions when a user has been detected to be inactive for an excessive period of time.
- **Elapsed coding time** specifies the amount of time the user has taken since the beginning of current coding task.

6 Evaluation

The dialogue act models were trained and tested using the manually annotated portion of the task-oriented tutorial dialogue corpus described in Section 3. The textual dialogue exchanges in the corpus were aligned with the logged task-completion activities based on the timestamp, resulting in 6919 total interaction logs. Table 2 shows the distribution of different types of activities in the resulting interaction logs. It was observed that tutors made a dialogue move in 26.5% of the total logged interactions (Table 3).

Interaction Type	Frequency (%)
Programming	38.2
Compiling the Program	10.8
Running the Program	12.2
Progressing to Next Task	4.2
Exchanging Dialogue	34.6

Table 2. Distribution of interaction types

Tutor Dialogue Move	Frequency (%)
Move	26.5
NoMove	73.5

Table 3. Distribution of system dialogue move

Among the thirteen dialogue acts in the original annotation scheme (Section 3.2), four rarely occurring dialogue acts were combined into other categories, which include LF (*lukewarm feedback*) merged with NF (*negative feedback*) and RC (*request for confirmation*), RF (*request for feedback*), and C (*correction*) merged to O (*other*). A new category, GREET (*greetings*) was added to distinguish conventional expressions for greetings and thanks from more general statements and questions. Table 4 shows the resulting distribution of tutor dialogue acts in the corpus.

Dialogue Act	Frequency (%)
S (Statement)	35.4
PF (Positive Feedback)	19.8
Q (Question)	16.0
H (Hint)	8.0
DIR (Directive)	6.6
A (Answer)	5.7
GREET (Greetings)	3.1
ACK (Acknowledgement)	2.3
NF (Negative Feedback)	1.5
O (Other)	1.6

Table 4. Distribution of tutor dialogue acts

The performance of the dialogue act models were evaluated in a ten-fold cross validation. In the cross validation, the corpus was partitioned to ten non-overlapping sets and each set was used as testing data exactly once, while models were trained using the remaining nine sets.

6.1 Results

The first study compared the accuracies of the dialogue management models on predicting the timing and the type of tutor dialogue moves. The accuracy of the timing prediction was calculated for all user interaction logs in the data, including both dialogue exchanges and task-completion activities. The accuracy of the type prediction was calculated for dialogue activities by tutors only. The results are shown in Table 5.

Model	Timing	Type
Baseline	73.5	35.4
One-step	79.2*	40.5*
Two-step	**80.3*§**	**49.7*§**

Table 5. Model accuracy (%) on dialogue management tasks (*statistical significance over baseline, §statistical significance over one-step model)

Both the one-step ($t(9) = 4.14, p = 0.0013$) and the two-step ($t(9) = 6.26, p < .0001$) models performed significantly better than the majority baseline in predicting the timing of tutorial dialogue moves. The two-step model achieved higher accuracy than the one-step model. The difference between the two models was statistically significant ($t(9) = 2.17, p = 0.0291$).

The one-step ($t(9) = 2.68, p = 0.0126$) and the two-step ($t(9) = 10.93, p < 0.0001$) models achieved significantly higher accuracies over the baseline for the task of predicting the type of tutorial dialogue moves, as well. Again, the two-step model performed significantly better than the one-step model ($t(9) = 4.22, p = .0011$).

6.2 Comparing dialogue and task streams

The second study compared the predictive power of the dialogue stream and the task stream on the given two dialogue management tasks. In this study, the accuracy of the two-step model was compared in three conditions: using the dialogue features only (*Dialogue*), using the task features only (*Task*), and using all features (*All*). Table 6 reports the results.

Features	Timing	Type
Dialogue	79.6	45.0
Task	80.1	44.9
All	**80.3***	**49.7*§**

Table 6. Comparison of features on dialogue management tasks (*statistical significance over *Dialogue*, §statistical significance over *Task*)

For determining when to intervene, the dialogue and the task features exhibited similar predictive power. No statistical significance was found for the difference between the dialogue and the task conditions. The highest accuracy was achieved by the *All* condition. Compared to the *All* condition, the *Dialogue* condition showed statistically significant decrease in accuracy ($t(9) = 2.21$, $p = 0.0272$), which implies the task stream provided important features for the dialogue management model in determining the timing of tutorial dialogue moves.

A similar trend was observed for determining what type of dialogue move to make. The *Dialogue* and the *Task* conditions achieved similar accuracies, with the highest accuracy achieved by the *All* condition. The drops in accuracy compared to the *All* condition were statistically significant for both the *Dialogue* ($t(9) = 3.38$, $p = 0.0040$) and the *Task* conditions. ($t(9) = 4.36$, $p = 0.0009$). The results imply that the prediction of the type of tutorial dialogue moves required information from both the dialogue and the task streams.

7 Discussion

The experiments presented in Section 6 compared two alternate approaches to learning dialogue management models for two given subtasks: determining when to provide the user with a dialogue move, and determining which type of dialogue move to choose. The results suggest that the two-step approach, which models the two subtasks as separate classifiers, was more effective than the alternate one-step approach, which combined the two subtasks into a single classification problem. The two-step model achieved higher performance than the one-step model in both the timing and the type prediction. However, the difference in the performance of the two models was more apparent in the type prediction, with the two-step model achieving over 22% higher accuracy than the one-step model. One possible explanation for the superiority of the two step-model over the one-step model is that the corpus used to train the models was highly skewed. For more than 73% of the total interaction logs in the corpus, the tutors did not provide any dialogue feedback. Since the one-step model treated *NoMove* as a special dialogue act, the skewed distribution over *NoMove* and *Move* impacted the learned distribution over dialogue acts.

Two previous investigations reported the accuracies of dialogue act classification on system utterances. Bangalore et al. (2008) reported a prediction accuracy of 55% for system dialogue acts when a flat task model was used in a catalogue-ordering domain. When a hierarchical task structure was used in the same domain, the achieved prediction accuracy for system dialogue acts was 35.6% (Bangalore and Stent, 2009). Boyer (2010) achieved accuracy of 57% for system dialogue acts in a task-oriented tutorial dialogue. While both of these lines of investigation employed task structure features that were manually annotated, our best-performing two-step dialogue management model resulted in comparable performance utilizing only automatic features, achieving an accuracy of 49.7%.

A crucial distinction between user and system dialogue act classification is that lexical features for a given dialogue turn are not available for system dialogue act classification because a system utterance is generated after a system dialogue act is selected. The absence of lexical features poses a significant challenge to system dialogue act classification, given that lexical features have been among the most predictive features for this task. To address this challenge, future research should continue exploring larger spaces of features to improve prediction accuracies of learned models.

8 Conclusions and Future Work

Automatically learning dialogue management models for complex task-oriented domains with separate dialogue and task streams poses significant challenges. Effective dialogue management models in such domains should be able to proactively intervene by making spontaneous dialogue moves based on the observed history of both the dialogue and the user's task activities. With the overarching goal of creating a data-driven automated dialogue system that incorporates parallel dialogue and task streams, this paper has presented classification-based dialogue management models that integrate a rich set of features automatically extracted from parallel dialogue and task streams. Two subtasks of dialogue management were considered: *when* the system should provide user with a dialogue move and what *type* of system dialogue act the system should select for a given user interaction context. An evaluation found that a two-step approach that modeled the two subtasks as separate classifiers were effective, achieving significantly higher performance than an alternate approach that modeled the two subtasks with a single classifier.

The results suggest several promising directions for future work. First, incorporating richer features may improve the accuracies of learned models, such as more global interaction histories and deeper dialogue structures. Second, developing more sophisticated task analyses will inform the learned models with a representation of the user task context, guiding the models to make more context-appropriate decisions. Finally, it will be important to evaluate the learned models by incorporating them into a dialogue management system and validating their effectiveness in interactions with users in rich task-oriented dialogue.

Acknowledgments

This research was supported by the National Science Foundation under Grant DRL-1007962. Any opinions, findings, and conclusions expressed in this material are those of the authors and do not necessarily reflect the views of the National Science Foundation.

References

Allen, J., Ferguson, G., & Stent, A. (2001). An architecture for more realistic conversational systems. *Proceedings of Intelligent User Interfaces* (pp. 1–8). Santa Fe, NM.

Bangalore, S., Di Fabbrizio, G., & Stent, A. (2008). Learning the structure of task-driven human-human dialogs. *IEEE Transactions on Audio, Speech, and Language Processing*, *16*(7), 1249–1259.

Bangalore, S., & Stent, A. J. (2009). Incremental parsing models for dialog task structure. *Proceedings of the 12th Conference of the European Chapter of the Association for Computational Linguistics* (pp. 94–102). Athens, Greece.

Berger, A. L., Della Pietra, V. J., & Della Pietra, S. A. (1996). A maximum entropy approach to natural language processing. *Computational Linguistics*, *22*(1), 39–71.

Boyer, K. E. (2010). Structural and Dialogue Act Modeling in Task-Oriented Tutorial Dialogue. Ph.D. Dissertation. Department of Computer Science, North Carolina State University.

Boyer, K. E., Grafsgaard, J. F., Ha, E. Y., Phillips, R., & Lester, J. C. (2011). An affect-enriched dialogue act classification model for task-oriented dialogue. *Proceedings of the 49th Annual Meeting of the Association for Computational Linguistics: Human Language Technologies* (pp. 1190–1199). Portland, OR.

Boyer, K. E., Ha, E. Y., Phillips, R., Wallis, M. D., Vouk, M. A., & Lester, J. C. (2010). Dialogue Act Modeling in a Complex Task-Oriented Domain. *Proceedings of the 11th Annual SIGDIAL Meeting on Discourse and Dialogue* (pp. 297–305). Tokyo, Japan.

Carberry, S. (1991). *Plan Recognition in Natural Language Dialogue.* MIT Press.

Cavicchio, F. (2009). The modulation of cooperation and emotion in dialogue: The REC corpus. *Proceedings of the ACL-IJCNLP 2009 Student Research Workshop* (pp. 81–87). Suntec, Singapore.

Chi, M., VanLehn, K., Litman, D., & Jordan, P. (2010). Inducing Effective Pedagogical Strategies Using Learning Context Features. *Proceedings of the Eighteenth International Conference on User Modeling, Adaptation, and Personalization* (pp 147-158). Big Island, HI.

Cohen, J. (1960). A coefficient of agreement for nominal scales. *Educational and Psychological Measurement*, *20*(1), 37 – 46.

Di Eugenio, B., Xie, Z., & Serafin, R. (2010). Dialogue act classification, instance-based learning, and higher order dialogue structure. *Dialogue and Discourse*, *1*(2), 81 – 104.

Dzikovska, M.O., Farrow, E, & Moore, J.D. (2013). Combining deep parsing and classification for improved explanation processing in a tutorial dialogue system. *Proceedings of the 16th International Conference on Artificial Intelligence in Education* (pp. 279 - 288). Memphis, TN.

Forbes-Riley, K. & Litman, D. (2011). Designing and evaluating a wizarded uncertainty-adaptive spoken dialogue tutoring system. *Computer Speech and Language*, 25(1), 105-126.

Ha, E. Y., Grafsgaard, J. F., & Mitchell, C. M. (2012). Combining Verbal and Nonverbal Features to Overcome the "Information Gap" in Task-Oriented Dialogue. *Proceedings of the 13th Annual Meeting of the Special Interest Group on Discourse and Dialogue* (pp. 247–256). Seoul, South Korea.

Hardy, H., Biermann, A., Inouye, R. B., McKenzie, A., Strzalkowski, T., Ursu, C., Webb, N., et al. (2006). The Amitiés system: Data-driven techniques for automated dialogue. *Speech Communication*, *48*(3-4), 354–373.

Henderson, J., Lemon, O., & Georgila, K. (2008). Hybrid reinforcement/supervised learning of dialogue policies from fixed data sets. *Computational Linguistics*, *34*(4), 487–511.

Ivanovic, E. (2008). *Automatic instant messaging dialogue using statistical models and dialogue acts*. The University of Melbourne.

Kim, S. N., Cavedon, L., & Baldwin, T. (2010). Classifying dialogue acts in one-on-one live chats. *Proceedings of the 2010 Conference on Empirical Methods in Natural Language Processing* (pp. 862–871). Cambridge, MA, USA: Association for Computational Linguistics.

Levin, E., Pieraccini, R., & Eckert, W. (2000). A Stochastic Model of Human-Machine Interaction for Learning Dialog Strategies. *IEEE Transactions on Speech and Audio Processing*, *8*(1), 11–23.

Lewis, C., & Di Fabbrizio, G. (2006). Prompt selection with reinforcement learning in an AT&T call routing application. *Proceedings of the Ninth International Conference on Spoken Language Processing* (pp. 96–103).

Mitchell, C.M., Boyer, K.E., & Lester, J.C. (2013). A Markov Decision Process Model of Tutorial Intervention in Task-Oriented Dialogue. *Proceedings of the International Conference on Artificial Intelligence in Education* (pp. 828-831), Memphis, TN.

Mitchell, C. M., Ha, E. Y., Boyer, K. E., & Lester, J. C. (2012). Recognizing effective and student-adaptive tutor moves in task-oriented tutorial dialogue. *Proceedings of the Intelligent Tutoring Systems Track of the 25th International Conference of the Florida Artificial Intelligence Research Society* (pp. 450–455).

Rich, C., & Sidner, C. (1998). COLLAGEN: A collaboration manager for software interface agents. *User Modeling and User-Adapted Inter-action*, 8(3-4), 315–350.

Roy, N., Pineau, J., & Thrun, S. (2000). Spoken dialogue management using probabilistic reasoning. *Proceedings of the 38th Annual Meeting on Association for Computational Linguistics* (pp. 93–100). Wanchai, Hong Kong.

Scheffler, K., & Young, S. (2002). Automatic learning of dialogue strategy using dialogue simulation and reinforcement learning.

Proceedings of the second international conference on Human Language Technology Research (pp. 12–19). San Diego, CA.
Singh, S., Litman, D. J., Kearns, M., & Walker, M. (2002). Optimizing Dialogue Management with Reinforcement Learning: Experiments with the NJFun System. *Journal of Artificial Intelligence Research*, *16*, 105–133.
Sridhar, R., Bangalore, S., & Narayanan, S. (2009). Combining lexical, syntactic and prosodic cues for improved online dialog act tagging. *Computer Speech and Language*, *23*(4), 407 – 422.
Stolcke, A., Ries, K., Coccaro, N., Shriberg, E., Bates, R., Jurafsky, D., Taylor, P., et al. (2000). Dialogue act modeling for automatic tagging and recognition of conversational speech. *Computational Linguistics*, *26*(3), 339–373.
Walker, M., Litman, D., Kamm, C., & Abella, A. (1997). Paradise: A framework for evaluating spoken dialogue agents. *Proceedings of ACL* (pp. 271–280). Madrid, Spain.
Williams, J., & Young, S. (2007). Partially Observable Markov Decision Processes for Spoken Dialog Systems. *Computer Speech and Language*, *21*(2), 393–422.
Young, S. (2002). Talking to machines (statistically speaking). *Proceedings of ICSLP* (pp. 32–41). Denver, CO.
Young, S., Gasic, M., Thomson, B., & Williams, J. (2013). POMDP-Based Statistical Spoken Dialog Systems: A Review. *Proceedings of the IEEE*, *101*(5), 1160–1179.

Appendix A. An Excerpt from the Task-Oriented Dialogue Corpus

Lesson ID	Task ID	Role	Type	Text	Timestamp
1	4	STUDENT	CODING	`System.out.printIn("Hello World"`	2011-09-21 08:17:17.737
1	4	STUDENT	CODING	`System.out.printIn("Hello World")`	2011-09-21 08:17:19.407
1	4	STUDENT	CODING	`System.out.printIn("Hello World");`	2011-09-21 08:17:19.812
1	4	TUTOR	MESSAGE	good.	2011-09-21 08:17:24.913
1	4	TUTOR	MESSAGE	also you can try to compile at anytime.	2011-09-21 08:17:33.805
1	4	STUDENT	COMPILE_BEGIN	studentCode\jt101\JavaTutor3.java	2011-09-21 08:17:38.080
1	4	STUDENT	COMPILE_ERROR	line 1 : cannot find symbol symbol : method printIn(java.lang.String) location: class java.io.PrintStream System.out.printIn("Hello World"); ^ 1 error	2011-09-21 08:17:38.220
1	4	TUTOR	MESSAGE	carefully compare your line with the example	2011-09-21 08:17:57.330

Appendix B. Types of Activity Logs in Corpus

Log Type	Description	Action Initiator
MESSAGE	Either student or tutor has sent a chat message.	Student, Tutor
SESSION_PROGRESS	Tutor has allowed student to progress to next task.	Tutor
CODING	Student has written programming code.	Student
COMPILE_BEGIN	Student has begun compiling code.	Student
COMPILE_SUCCESS	Recent code compilation has ended successfully.	N/A
COMPILE_ERROR	Recent code compilation has failed with errors.	N/A
RUN_BEGIN	Student has begun running code.	Student
INPUT_SENT	Student has sent an input to a running code.	Student
RUN_SUCCESS	Recent code running has ended successfully.	N/A
RUN_STOP	Tutor has stopped running student's code because of errors in the code.	Tutor

POMDP-based dialogue manager adaptation to extended domains

M. Gašić, C. Breslin, M. Henderson, D. Kim, M. Szummer, B. Thomson, P. Tsiakoulis and S. Young
Cambridge University Engineering Department
{mg436,cb404,mh521,dk449,mos25,brmt2,pt344,sjy}@eng.cam.ac.uk

Abstract

Existing spoken dialogue systems are typically designed to operate in a static and well-defined domain, and are not well suited to tasks in which the concepts and values change dynamically. To handle dynamically changing domains, techniques will be needed to transfer and reuse existing dialogue policies and rapidly adapt them using a small number of dialogues in the new domain. As a first step in this direction, this paper addresses the problem of automatically extending a dialogue system to include a new previously unseen concept (or slot) which can be then used as a search constraint in an information query. The paper shows that in the context of Gaussian process POMDP optimisation, a domain can be extended through a simple expansion of the kernel and then rapidly adapted. As well as being much quicker, adaptation rather than retraining from scratch is shown to avoid subjecting users to unacceptably poor performance during the learning stage.

1 Introduction

Existing spoken dialogue systems are typically designed to operate in a static and well-defined domain, and are not well suited to tasks in which the concepts and values change dynamically. For example, consider a spoken dialogue system installed in a car, which is designed to provide information about nearby hotels and restaurants. In this case, not only will the data change as the car moves around, but the concepts (or slots) that a user might wish to use to frame a query will also change. For example, a restaurant system designed to be used within cities might not have the concept of 'al fresco' dining and could not therefore handle a query such as "Find me a French restaurant where I can eat outside". In order to make this possible, techniques will be needed to extend and adapt existing dialogue policies.

Adaptation can be viewed as a process of improving action selection in a different condition to the one in which the policy was originally trained. While adaptation has been extensively studied in speech recognition (see an overview in (Gales and Young, 2007)), in spoken dialogue systems it is still relatively novel and covers a wide range of possible research topics (Litman and Pan, 1999; Litman and Pan, 2002; Georgila and Lemon, 2004; Janarthanam and Lemon, 2010).

A recent trend in statistical dialogue modelling has been to model dialogue as a partially observable Markov decision process (POMDP). This provides increased robustness to errors in speech understanding and automatic dialogue policy optimisation via reinforcement learning (Roy et al., 2000; Zhang et al., 2001; Williams and Young, 2007; Young et al., 2010; Thomson and Young, 2010). A POMDP-based dialogue manager maintains a distribution over every possible dialogue state at every dialogue turn. This is called the *belief state*. Based on that distribution the system chooses the action that gives the highest expected reward, measured by the Q-function. The Q-function for a belief state and an action is the expected cumulative reward that can be obtained if that action is taken in that belief state. The optimisation typically requires $\mathcal{O}(10^5)$ to $\mathcal{O}(10^6)$ dialogues, so is normally done in interaction with a simulated user (Jurčíček et al., 2011b).

In reinforcement learning, policy adaptation has been addressed in the context of *transfer learning* (Taylor and Stone, 2009). The core idea is to exploit expertise gained in one domain (source domain) to improve learning in another domain (target domain). A number of techniques have been developed but they have not been previously applied to dialogue management.

Gaussian process (GP) based reinforcement learning (Engel, 2005) has been recently applied to POMDP dialogue policy optimisation in order to exploit the correlations between different belief states and thus reduce the number of dialogues needed for the learning process (Gašić et al., 2010).

An important feature of a Gaussian process is that it can incorporate a prior mean and variance for the function it estimates, in this case the Q-function. Setting these appropriately can significantly speed up the process of learning. If the mean or the variance are estimated in one environment, for example a particular user type or a particular domain, they can be used as a prior for adaptation in a different environment, i.e. another user type or another domain. A Gaussian process does not depend on the belief state but on the correlation between two belief states encoded by the *kernel function*. Therefore, if one defines a kernel function for two belief states in one domain, the policy can be used in a different domain, provided that the correlations between belief states follow a similar pattern.

This paper explores the problem of extending an existing domain by introducing a previously unseen slot. Specifically, a simple restaurant system is considered which allows a user to search for restaurants based on *food-type* and *area*. This domain is then extended by introducing an additional *price-range* slot. The policy is trained for the basic two-slot domain and then reused in the extended domain by defining a modified kernel function and using adaptation. This strategy not only allows for the knowledge of a previously trained policy to be reused but it also guards against poor performance in the early stages of learning. This is particularly useful in a real-world situation where the adaptation is performed in direct interaction with users. In addition, a potential application of this technique to reduce the number of training dialogues is examined. The domain is decomposed into a series of simple domains and the policy is gradually adapted to the final domain with a smaller number of dialogues than are normally needed for training.

The rest of the paper is organised as follows. In Section 2 the background on Gaussian processes in POMDP optimisation is given. Then Section 3 gives a description of the Bayesian Update of Dialogue State dialogue manager, which is used as a test-bed for the experiments. In Section 4, a simple method of kernel modification is described which allows a policy trained in the basic domain to be used in an extended domain. Methods of fast adaptation are investigated in Section 5 and this adaptation strategy is then tested via interaction with humans using the Amazon Mechanical Turk service in Section 6. Finally, the use of repeated adaptation to speed up the process of policy optimisation by learning gradually from simple to more complex domains is explored in Section 7, before presenting conclusions in Section 8.

2 Gaussian processes in POMDPs

The role of a dialogue policy π is to map each belief state $\mathbf{b} \in \mathcal{B}$ into an action $a \in \mathcal{A}$ so as to maximise the expected cumulative reward, a measure of how good the dialogue is.

The expected cumulative reward is defined by the Q-function as:

$$Q(\mathbf{b}, a) = E_{\pi}\left(\sum_{\tau=t+1}^{T} \gamma^{\tau-t-1} r_{\tau} | b_t = \mathbf{b}, a_t = a\right), \tag{1}$$

where r_τ is the reward obtained at time τ, T is the dialogue length and γ is the discount factor, $0 < \gamma \leq 1$. Optimising the Q-function is then equivalent to optimising the policy π.

A Gaussian process (GP) is a non-parametric Bayesian probabilistic model that can be used for function regression (Rasmussen and Williams, 2005). It is fully defined by a mean and a kernel function which defines prior function correlations.

GP-Sarsa is an on-line RL algorithm that models the Q-function as a Gaussian process (Engel et al., 2005), $Q(\mathbf{b}, a) \sim \mathcal{GP}\left(0, k((\mathbf{b}, a), (\mathbf{b}, a))\right)$ where the kernel $k(\cdot, \cdot)$ is factored into separate kernels over the belief state and action spaces $k_{\mathcal{C}}(\mathbf{b}, \mathbf{b}')k_{\mathcal{A}}(a, a')$. For a sequence of belief state-action pairs $\mathbf{B}_t = [(\mathbf{b}^0, a^0), \ldots, (\mathbf{b}^t, a^t)]^{\mathsf{T}}$ visited in a dialogue and the corresponding observed immediate rewards $\mathbf{r}_t = [r^1, \ldots, r^t]^{\mathsf{T}}$, the posterior of the Q-function for any belief state-action pair $(\mathbf{b}, a)$ is defined by the following:

$$
\begin{aligned}
&Q(\mathbf{b},a)|\mathbf{r}_t,\mathbf{B}_t \sim \mathcal{N}(\overline{Q}(\mathbf{b},a), cov((\mathbf{b},a),(\mathbf{b},a))),\\
&\overline{Q}(\mathbf{b},a) = \mathbf{k}_t(\mathbf{b},a)^\mathsf{T}\mathbf{H}_t^\mathsf{T}(\mathbf{H}_t\mathbf{K}_t\mathbf{H}_t^\mathsf{T} + \sigma^2\mathbf{H}_t\mathbf{H}_t^\mathsf{T})^{-1}\mathbf{r}_t,\\
&cov((\mathbf{b},a),(\mathbf{b},a)) = k((\mathbf{b},a),(\mathbf{b},a)) - \mathbf{k}_t(\mathbf{b},a)^\mathsf{T}\mathbf{H}_t^\mathsf{T}(\mathbf{H}_t\mathbf{K}_t\mathbf{H}_t^\mathsf{T} + \sigma^2\mathbf{H}_t\mathbf{H}_t^\mathsf{T})^{-1}\mathbf{H}_t\mathbf{k}_t(\mathbf{b},a)\\
&\mathbf{H}_t = \begin{bmatrix} 1 & -\gamma & \cdots & 0 & 0\\ 0 & 1 & \cdots & 0 & 0\\ \vdots & \ddots & \ddots & \vdots & \vdots\\ 0 & \cdots & 0 & 1 & -\gamma \end{bmatrix},\\
&\mathbf{k}_t(\mathbf{b},a) = [k((\mathbf{b}^0,a^0),(\mathbf{b},a)),\ldots,k((\mathbf{b}^t,a^t),(\mathbf{b},a))]^\mathsf{T},\\
&\mathbf{K}_t = [\mathbf{k}_t((\mathbf{b}^0,a^0)),\ldots,\mathbf{k}_t((\mathbf{b}^t,a^t))]
\end{aligned}
\tag{2}
$$

where $\mathbf{K}_t$ is the Gram matrix – the matrix of the kernel function values for visited points $\mathbf{B}_t$, $\mathbf{H}_t$ is a linear operator that captures the reward lookahead from the Q-function (see Eq. 1) and σ^2 is an additive noise parameter which controls how much variability in the Q-function estimate we expect during the process of learning.

If we assume that the Gaussian process places a prior mean on the Q-function, $Q(\mathbf{b},a) \sim \mathcal{GP}\left(m(\mathbf{b},a), k((\mathbf{b},a),(\mathbf{b},a))\right)$ then the posterior mean $\overline{Q}(\mathbf{b},a)$ is given by (Rasmussen and Williams, 2005):

$$
\overline{Q}(\mathbf{b},a) = m(\mathbf{b},a) + \mathbf{k}_t(\mathbf{b},a)^\mathsf{T}\mathbf{H}_t^\mathsf{T}(\mathbf{H}_t\mathbf{K}_t\mathbf{H}_t^\mathsf{T} + \sigma^2\mathbf{H}_t\mathbf{H}_t^\mathsf{T})^{-1}(\mathbf{r}_t - \mathbf{m}_t), \tag{3}
$$

where $\mathbf{m}_t = [m(\mathbf{b}^0,a^0),\ldots,m(\mathbf{b}^t,a^t)]^\mathsf{T}$. The estimate of the variance is same as in Eq. 2.

The Q-function posterior in Eqs. 2 and 3 defines a Gaussian distribution for every belief state-action pair. Thus, when a new belief state $\mathbf{b}$ is encountered, for each action $a \in \mathcal{A}$, there is a Gaussian distribution $Q(\mathbf{b},a) \sim \mathcal{N}(\overline{Q}(\mathbf{b},a), cov((\mathbf{b},a),(\mathbf{b},a))))$. Sampling from these Gaussian distributions gives a set of Q-values for each action $\{Q(\mathbf{b},a) : a \in \mathcal{A}\}$ from which the action with the highest sampled Q-value can be selected:

$$
\pi(\mathbf{b}) = \arg\max_a \{Q(\mathbf{b},a) : a \in \mathcal{A}\}. \tag{4}
$$

In this way, the stochastic model of the Q-function is effectively transformed into a stochastic policy model, which can be optimised to maximise the reward (Geist and Pietquin, 2011; Gašić et al., 2011; Gašić et al., 2012).

Due to the matrix inversion in Eq. 2, the computational complexity of calculating the Q-function posterior is $O(t^3)$, where t is the number of data points in $\mathbf{B}_t$, and this poses a serious computational problem. The algorithm used here to approximate the Gaussian process is the kernel span sparsification method described in (Engel, 2005). In this case, only a set of representative data points is retained – called the *dictionary* of visited points.

3 BUDS dialogue manager

The Bayesian Update of Dialogue State (BUDS) dialogue manager is a POMDP-based dialogue manager (Thomson and Young, 2010) which factorises the dialogue state into conditionally dependent elements. These elements are arranged into a dynamic Bayesian network, which allows for their marginal probability distributions to be updated during the dialogue. Thus, the belief state of the BUDS dialogue manager consists of the marginal posterior probability distribution over hidden nodes in the Bayesian network. The hidden nodes in the BUDS system consist of the history nodes and the goal nodes for each concept in the dialogue. For instance in a restaurant information domain these include *area*, *food-type*, *address*. The history nodes define possible dialogue histories for a particular concept, eg. *system-informed*, *user-requested*. The goal nodes define possible values for a particular concept, eg. *Chinese*, *Indian*. The role of the policy π is then to map each belief state into a summary action a from the summary action space $\mathcal{A}$. Once a summary action is found it is heuristically mapped into the master action that the system finally takes (Gašić et al., 2012). The master actions are composed of dialogue act type and list of slot value pairs. There are 15 dialogue act types in the BUDS system that facilitate not only simple information providing scenarios but also more complex dialogues where the user can change their mind and ask for alternatives.

To apply GP policy optimisation, a kernel function must be defined on both the belief state space $\mathcal{B}$ and the action space $\mathcal{A}$. The kernel function over the belief state $\mathbf{b}$ is constructed from the sum of individual kernels over the hidden node distributions, such that the kernel function of two corresponding nodes is based on the expected likelihood kernel (Jebara et al., 2004), which is also a simple linear inner product:

$$k_{\mathcal{B}}(\mathbf{b}, \mathbf{b}') = \sum_h \langle \mathbf{b}_h, \mathbf{b}'_h \rangle, \quad (5)$$

where $\mathbf{b}_h$ is the probability distribution encoded in the hth hidden node. This kernel gives the expectation of one belief state distribution under the other.

For history nodes, the kernel is a simple inner product between the corresponding node distributions. While it is possible to calculate the kernel function for the goal nodes in the same way as for the history nodes, in this case, the choice of system action, such as *confirm* or *inform*, does not depend on the actual values. It rather depends on the shape of the distribution and, in particular, it depends on the probability of the most likely value compared to the rest. Therefore, to exploit the correlations further, the kernel over two goal nodes is calculated as the dot product of vectors, where each vector represents the corresponding distribution sorted into order of probability. The only exceptions are the goal for the *method* node and the *discourse act* node. The former defines whether the user is searching for a venue *by name* or *by constraints* and the latter defines which discourse act the user used, eg. *acknowledgement*, *thank you*. Their kernels are calculated in the same way as for the history nodes.

For the action space kernel, the δ-kernel is used defined by:

$$k_{\mathcal{A}}(a, a') = \delta_a(a'). \quad (6)$$

where $\delta_a(a') = 1$ iff $a = a'$.

3.1 TopTable domain

The TopTable domain consists of restaurants in Cambridge, UK automatically extracted from the TopTable web service (TopTable, 2012). There are about 150 restaurants and each restaurant has 7 attributes – slots. This results in a belief space that consists of 25 concepts where each concept takes from 3 to 150 values and each value has a probability in $[0, 1]$. The summary action space consists of 16 summary actions.

3.2 The agenda-based simulated user

In training and testing a simulated user was used. The agenda-based user simulator (Schatzmann, 2008; Keizer et al., 2010) factorises the user state into an *agenda* and a *goal*. The goal ensures that the user simulator exhibits consistent, goal-directed behaviour. The role of the agenda is to elicit the dialogue acts that are needed for the user simulator to fulfil the goal. In addition, an error model adds confusions to the simulated user input such that it resembles those found in real data (Thomson et al., 2012). The length of the N-best list was set to 10 and the confusion rate was set to 15% during training and testing.[1] This error rate means that 15% of time the true hypothesis is not in the N-best list. Intermediate experimentation showed that these confusion rates are typical of real data.

The reward function was set to give a reward of 20 for successful dialogues, zero otherwise. In addition, 1 is deducted for each dialogue turn to encourage shorter dialogues. The discount factor γ is set to 1 and the dialogue length is limited to 30 turns.

4 Extended domains

Transfer learning is a reinforcement learning technique which address three problems:

- given a target domain, how to select the most appropriate source domain from a set of source domains,
- given a target and a source domain how to find the relationship between them, and
- given a target and a source domain and the relationship between them, how to effectively transfer knowledge between them.

[1]Except of course where the system is explicitly tested on varying noise levels.

Here we assume that we are given a source and a target domain and that the relationship between them is defined by mapping the kernel function. Knowledge transfer is then effected by adapting the source domain policy for use in the target domain. For the latter, two forms of adaptation are investigated: one simply continues to update the set of source data dictionary points with new dictionary points, the second uses the source domain posterior as a prior for the new target domain.

In this case, the source is a basic restaurant domain with slots *name*, *area*, *food-type*, *phone*, *address*, and *postcode*. The extended target domain has an additional *price-range* slot. We are interested primarily in training the policy on the basic domain and testing it on the extended domain. However, since real applications may also require a slot to be *forgotten*, we also investigate the reverse where the policy is trained in the extended domain and tested on the basic domain.

In order to enable the required cross domain portability, a kernel function defining the correlation between belief states from differing domains is needed. Since the extended domain has an extra slot and thus extra hidden nodes, we need to define the correlations between the extra hidden nodes and the hidden nodes in the belief state of the basic domain. This can be performed in various ways, but the simplest approach is to specify which slot from the basic domain is most similar to the new slot in the extended domain and then match their corresponding hidden nodes. In that way the belief state kernel function between two belief states $\mathbf{b}^{\mathsf{B}}$, $\mathbf{b}^{\mathsf{E}}$ for the basic B and the extended E domain becomes:

$$k_{\mathcal{B}}(\mathbf{b}^{\mathsf{B}}, \mathbf{b}^{\mathsf{E}}) = \sum_{h \in \mathsf{B}} \langle \mathbf{b}_h^{\mathsf{B}}, \mathbf{b}_h^{\mathsf{E}} \rangle + \sum_{e \notin \mathsf{B}} \langle \mathbf{b}_{l(e)}^{\mathsf{B}}, \mathbf{b}_e^{\mathsf{E}} \rangle, \quad (7)$$

where h are the hidden nodes in the basic domain, e are the hidden nodes in the extended domain and function $l : \mathsf{E} \rightarrow \mathsf{B}$ for each hidden node that does not exist in the basic domain finds its appropriate replacement. In the particular case studied here, the slot *area* is most similar to the new *price-range* slot since they both have a relatively small number of values, about 5. Hence, l(*price-range*) $\rightarrow$ *area*. If the cardinality of the mapped slots differ, the shorter is padded with zeros though other forms of normalisation are clearly possible.

The (summary) action space for the extended domain has more actions than the basic domain. For example, one action that exists in the extended domain and does not exist in the basic domain is *request(price-range)*. To define the kernel function between these sets of actions, one can specify for each extra action in the extended domain its most similar action in the basic domain:

$$k_{\mathcal{A}}(a^{\mathsf{B}}, a^{\mathsf{E}}) = \begin{cases} \delta_{a^{\mathsf{B}}}(a^{\mathsf{E}}) & a^{\mathsf{E}} \in \mathcal{A}^{\mathsf{B}}, \\ \delta_{a^{\mathsf{B}}}(L(a^{\mathsf{E}})) & a^{\mathsf{E}} \notin \mathcal{A}^{\mathsf{B}}, \end{cases} \quad (8)$$

where function $L : \mathcal{A}^{\mathsf{E}} \rightarrow \mathcal{A}^{\mathsf{B}}$ for each action that does not exist in the basic domain finds its replacement action.

Functions L and l are here defined manually. However, a simple but effective heuristic would be to find for each new slot in the extended domain, a slot in the basic domain with similar cardinality.

Porting in the reverse direction from the extended to the basic domain is easier since one can simply disregard the extra hidden nodes and actions in the kernel calculation.

To experimentally examine the extent to which this method supports cross domain portability, we trained policies for both domains until convergence, using 10^5 dialogues on the simulated user. We then cross tested them on the mismatching domains at varying user input error rates. The results are given in Fig. 1.

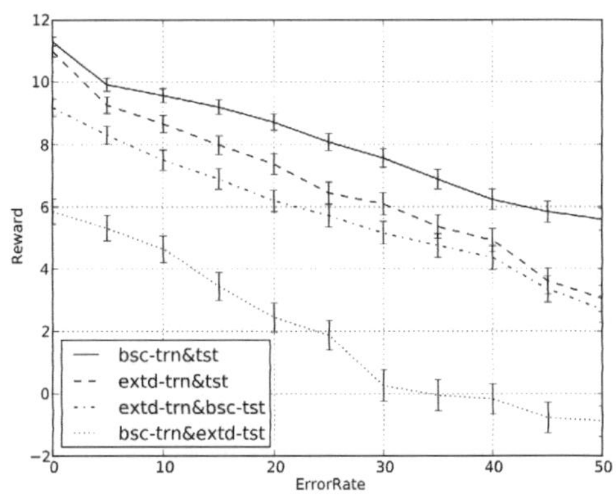

Figure 1: Cross testing policies trained on different domains. bsc refers to the basic domain, extd is the extended domain, trn is training and tst is testing.

From the results it can be seen that the policy trained for the basic domain has a better performance than the policy trained on the extended domain, when tested on the matching domain (compare bsc-trn&tst with extd-trn&tst). The extended domain has more slots so it is more difficult for the system to fulfil the user request, especially in noisy conditions. Secondly, the performance of the policy trained on the extended domain and tested on the basic domain is close to optimal (compare bsc-trn&tst with extd-trn&bsc-tst). However, the policy trained on the basic domain and tested on the extended domain has much worse performance (compare bsc-trn&extd-tst with extd-trn&tst). It is hard for the policy to adequately extrapolate from the basic to the extended domain. This difference in performance, however, motivates the need for adaptation and this is investigated in the next section.

5 Adaptation

Adaptation of a policy trained on one domain to another can be performed in several ways. Here we examine two adaptation strategies similar to the method described in (Taylor et al., 2007), where every action-value for each state in the target domain is initialised with learned source domain values.

The first strategy is to take the policy trained in the source domain and simply continue training it in the target domain until convergence. In Gaussian process reinforcement learning, this means that we assume a zero-mean prior on the Gaussian process for the Q-function and let the dictionary of visited points $\mathbf{B}_t$ from Eq. 2 consist of both points visited in the source domain and the extended target domain, making sure that the Gram matrix $\mathbf{K}_t$ uses extended domain kernel function where necessary. However, the estimate of the variance decreases with the number of visited points (see Eq. 2). The danger therefore when performing adaptation in this way is that the estimate of variances obtained in the source domain will be very small since the policy has already been trained until convergence with a large number of dialogues. As a consequence, the rate of exploration defined by sampling in Eq. 4 will be reduced and thus lead to the subsequent optimisation in the new target domain falling prematurely into a local optimum.

As an alternative, we propose another adaptation strategy. The estimate of the posterior of the mean for the Q-function, $\overline{Q}$ in Eq. 2, from the policy trained on the basic domain can be taken to be the prior of the mean when the policy is trained on the extended domain as in Eq. 3. More precisely, if $\overline{Q}_{\text{bsc}}$ is the posterior mean of the policy trained on the basic domain then $m_{\text{extd}} = \overline{Q}_{\text{bsc}}$. In this case it is also important to make sure that the kernel function used to calculate $\overline{Q}_{\text{bsc}}$ is redefined for the extended domain where necessary. The prior on the variance is the original kernel function renormalised:

$$k((\mathbf{b},a),(\mathbf{b}',a')) \leftarrow \frac{k((\mathbf{b},a),(\mathbf{b}',a'))}{\sqrt{k((\mathbf{b},a),(\mathbf{b},a))k((\mathbf{b}',a'),(\mathbf{b}',a'))}}. \quad (9)$$

Given that the estimate of the mean provides reasonable performance, it is not necessary to place a flat prior on the variance of the Q-function and therefore the kernel is normalised as in Eq. 9.

When comparing adaptation strategies, we are interested in two aspects of performance. The first is the performance of the policy during training. The second is how quickly the policy reaches the optimal performance. For that reason we adopt the following evaluation scheme. After every 100 adaptation dialogues we test the partially optimised policy with 1000 simulated dialogues, different to the ones used in adaptation. These 1000 dialogues are the same for every test point on the graph. The results are given in Fig. 2.

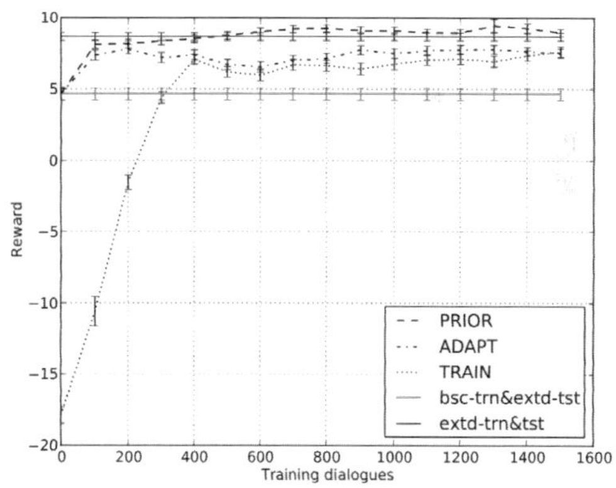

Figure 2: Different adaptation strategies

The lower horizontal line represents the performance of the policy trained on the basic source domain and tested on the extended target domain. This is the baseline. The upper horizontal line represents the policy trained until convergence on the extended domain and also tested on the extended domain. This provides the gold standard. The adaptation strategy that takes both the mean and variance of the policy trained on the basic domain and retrains the policy on the extended domain is denoted as ADAPT in Fig. 2. The adaptation strategy that uses the posterior mean of the policy trained on the source domain as the prior mean for adaptation is denoted as PRIOR in Fig. 2. Finally, for comparison purposes we show the performance of the policy that is trained from scratch on the extended domain. This is denoted as TRAIN on the graph. It can be seen that both adaptation strategies significantly reduce the number of training dialogues and, more importantly, maintain the level of performance during adaptation. The adaptation strategy that places the prior on the mean has slightly worse performance in the beginning but provides the best performance after 1500 dialogues. As already noted, this could be due to overly confident variances in the ADAPT case leading to a local optimum.

6 Human experiments

In order to adapt and evaluate policies with humans, we used crowd-sourcing via the Amazon Mechanical Turk service in a set-up similar to (Jurčíček et al., 2011a; Gašić et al., 2013). The BUDS dialogue manager was incorporated in a live telephone-based spoken dialogue system. The Mechanical Turk users were assigned specific tasks in the extended TopTable domain. They were asked to find restaurants that have particular features as defined by the given task. To elicit more complex dialogues, the users were sometimes asked to find more than one restaurant, and in cases where such a restaurant did not exist they were required to seek an alternative, for example find a Chinese restaurant instead of a Vietnamese one. After each dialogue the users filled in a feedback form indicating whether they judged the dialogue to be successful or not. Based on that binary rating, the subjective success was calculated as well as the average reward. An objective rating can also be obtained by comparing the system outputs with the predefined task.

During policy adaptation, at the end of each call, users were asked to press 1 if they were satisfied (i.e. believed that they had been successful in fulfilling the assigned task) and 0 otherwise. The objective success was also calculated. The dialogue was then only used for adaptation if the user rating agreed with the objective measure of success as in (Gašić et al., 2013). The performance based on user ratings during adaptation for both adaptation strategies is given in Table 1.

Table 1: Policy performance during adaptation

	#Diags	Reward	Success (%)
ADAPT	251	11.7 ± 0.5	92.0 ± 1.7
PRIOR	329	12.1 ± 0.4	96.7 ± 1.0

We then evaluated four policies with real users: the policy trained on the basic domain, the policy trained on the extended domain and the policy adapted to the extended domain using the prior and the policy adapted to the extended domain via interaction with real users using retraining. The results are given in Table 2.

Table 2: Human evaluation of four systems in the extended domain: trained in the basic domain, trained in the extended domain, trained in the basic and adapted in the extended domain using both ADAPT and PRIOR methods.

Training	#Diags	Reward	Success(%)
Basic	246	11.0 ± 0.5	91.9 ± 1.7
Extended	250	12.1 ± 0.4	94.4 ± 1.5
ADAPT	268	12.6 ± 0.4	94.4 ± 1.4
PRIOR	252	12.4 ± 0.4	95.6 ± 1.3

The results show two important features of these adaptation strategies. The first is that it is possible to adapt the policy from one domain to another with a small number of dialogues. Both adaptation techniques achieve results statistically indistinguishable from the matched case where the policy was trained directly in the extended domain. The second important feature is that both adaptation strategies guarantee a minimum level of performance during training, which is better than the performance of the basic policy tested on the extended domain. This is particularly important when training with real users so that they are not exposed to poor performance at any time during training.

7 Application to fast learning

The above results show that transfer learning through policy adaptation can be relatively fast. Since complex domains can be decomposed into a series of domains with gradually increasing complexity, an alternative to training a system to convergence starting from an uninformative prior is to train a system in stages iteratively adapting to successively more complex domains (Taylor and Stone, 2009).

We explored this idea by training the extended system in three stages. The first has only one slot that the user can specify: *food-type* and additional slots *phone*, *address* and *postcode* that can be requested (initial in Fig. 3). The second has an additional *area* slot (intermediate in Fig. 3) and the final domain has a the *price-range* slot added (final on the graph).

A policy for each of these domains was trained until convergence and the average rewards of these policies are the horizontal lines on Fig. 3. In addition, the following adaptation schedule was implemented. An initial policy was trained from scratch for the one-slot initial system using only 1500 dialogues. The resulting policy was then retrained for the intermediate two-slot system using again just 1500 dialogues. Finally, the required three-slot system was trained using 1500 dialogues. At each stage the policy was tested every 100 training dialogues, and the resulting performances are shown by the three graphs initial-train, intermediate-adapt and final-adapt in Fig. 3. The policies were tested on the domains they are trained on or adapted to.

It can be seen that after just 500 dialogues of the third stage (i.e. after just 3500 dialogues in total) the policy reaches optimal performance. It has been shown previously that Gaussian process reinforcement learning for this task normally takes 10^4 dialogues (Gašić et al., 2012) so this schedule halves the number of dialogues needed for training. Also it is important to note that when training from scratch the average reward is less than 5 for 300 dialogues (see TRAIN in Fig. 2), in this case that only happens for about 100 dialogues (see initial-train in Fig. 3).

8 Conclusions

This paper has investigated the problem of extending a dialogue system to handle new previously unseen concepts (i.e. slots) using adaptation based transfer learning. It has been shown that a GP kernel can be mapped to establish a relationship between a basic and an extended domain and that GP-based adaptation can restore a system to optimal performance within 200 to 300 adaptation dialogues. A major advantage of this technique is that it allows a minimum level of performance to be guaranteed and hence guards against subjecting the user to poor performance during the early stages of adaptation.

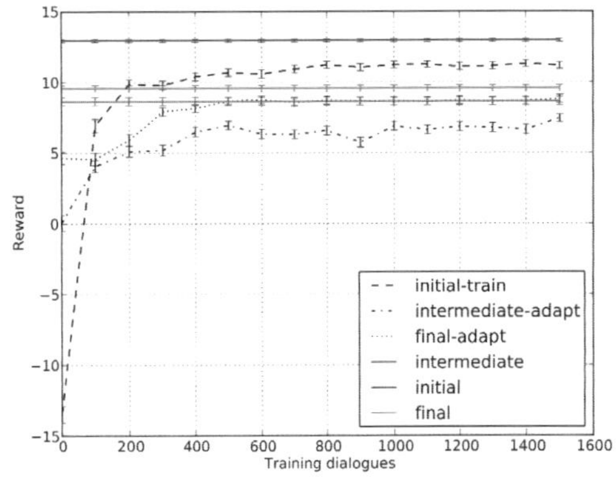

Figure 3: Application of transfer learning to fast training. The target is to achieve the performance of the fully trained 3 slot system as shown by the lower horizontal line final. This is achieved in three stages, with the target being achieved part way through the 3rd stage using just 3500 dialogues in total.

Two methods of adaptation have been studied – one based on augmenting the training points from the source domain with new points from the target domain, and a second which treats the source policy as a prior for the target policy. Results using the prior method were consistently better. In a further experiment, it was also shown that starting with a simple system and successively extending and adapting it slot by slot, can achieve optimal performance faster than one trained directly from scratch.

These results suggest that it should be feasible to construct dialogue systems which can dynamically update and extend their domains of discourse automatically during direct conversations with users. However, further investigation of methods for learning the relationship between the new and the old domains is needed. Also, the scalability of these results to large-scale domain expansion remains a topic for future work.

Acknowledgments

This work was partly supported by PARLANCE (www.parlance-project.eu), an EU Seventh Framework Programme project (grant number 287615).

References

Y Engel, S Mannor, and R Meir. 2005. Reinforcement learning with Gaussian processes. In *Proceedings of ICML*.

Y Engel. 2005. *Algorithms and Representations for Reinforcement Learning*. PhD thesis, Hebrew University.

M Gales and S Young. 2007. The application of hidden Markov models in speech recognition. *Found. Trends Signal Process.*, 1:195–304.

M Gašić, F Jurčíček, S Keizer, F Mairesse, J Schatzmann, B Thomson, K Yu, and S Young. 2010. Gaussian Processes for Fast Policy Optimisation of POMDP-based Dialogue Managers. In *Proceedings of SIGDIAL*.

M Gašić, F Jurčíček, B Thomson, K Yu, and S Young. 2011. On-line policy optimisation of spoken dialogue systems via live interaction with human subjects. In *Proceedings of ASRU*.

M Gašić, M Henderson, B Thomson, P Tsiakoulis, and S Young. 2012. Policy optimisation of POMDP-based dialogue systems without state space compression. In *Proceedings of SLT*.

M Gašić, C. Breslin, M. Henderson, Szummer M., B Thomson, P. Tsiakoulis, and S Young. 2013. On-line policy optimisation of Bayesian Dialogue Systems by human interaction. In *Proceedings of ICASSP*.

M Geist and O Pietquin. 2011. Managing Uncertainty within the KTD Framework. In *Proceedings of the Workshop on Active Learning and Experimental Design*, Sardinia (Italy).

K Georgila and O Lemon. 2004. Adaptive multimodal dialogue management based on the information state update approach. In *W3C Workshop on Multimodal Interaction*.

S Janarthanam and O Lemon. 2010. Adaptive Referring Expression Generation in Spoken Dialogue Systems: Evaluation with Real Users. In *Proceedings of SIGDIAL*.

T Jebara, R Kondor, and A Howard. 2004. Probability product kernels. *J. Mach. Learn. Res.*, 5:819–844, December.

F Jurčíček, S Keizer, M Gašić, F Mairesse, B Thomson, K Yu, and S Young. 2011a. Real user evaluation of spoken dialogue systems using Amazon Mechanical Turk. In *Proceedings of Interspeech*.

F Jurčíček, B Thomson, and S Young. 2011b. Natural actor and belief critic: Reinforcement algorithm for learning parameters of dialogue systems modelled as POMDPs. *ACM Transactions on Speech and Language Processing*.

S Keizer, M Gašić, F Jurčíček, F Mairesse, B Thomson, K Yu, and S Young. 2010. Parameter estimation for agenda-based user simulation. In *Proceedings of SIGDIAL*.

DJ Litman and S Pan. 1999. Empirically evaluating an adaptable spoken dialogue system. In *Proceedings of the seventh international conference on User modelling*.

DJ Litman and S Pan. 2002. Designing and evaluating an adaptive spoken dialogue system. *User Modelling and User-Adapted Interaction*, 12:111–137.

CE Rasmussen and CKI Williams. 2005. *Gaussian Processes for Machine Learning*. MIT Press, Cambridge, Massachusetts.

N Roy, J Pineau, and S Thrun. 2000. Spoken dialogue management using probabilistic reasoning. In *Proceedings of ACL*.

J Schatzmann. 2008. *Statistical User and Error Modelling for Spoken Dialogue Systems*. Ph.D. thesis, University of Cambridge.

ME Taylor and P Stone. 2009. Transfer learning for reinforcement learning domains: A survey. *J. Mach. Learn. Res.*, 10:1633–1685, December.

ME Taylor, P Stone, and Y Liu. 2007. Transfer learning via inter-task mappings for temporal difference learning. *J. Mach. Learn. Res.*, 8:2125–2167, December.

B Thomson and S Young. 2010. Bayesian update of dialogue state: A POMDP framework for spoken dialogue systems. *Computer Speech and Language*, 24(4):562–588.

B Thomson, M Gašić, M Henderson, P Tsiakoulis, and S Young. 2012. N-Best error simulation for training spoken dialogue systems. In *Proceedings of SLT*.

TopTable. 2012. TopTable. `https://www.toptable.com`.

JD Williams and SJ Young. 2007. Partially Observable Markov Decision Processes for Spoken Dialog Systems. *Computer Speech and Language*, 21(2):393–422.

S Young, M Gašić, S Keizer, F Mairesse, J Schatzmann, B Thomson, and K Yu. 2010. The Hidden Information State model: A practical framework for POMDP-based spoken dialogue management. *Computer Speech and Language*, 24(2):150–174.

B Zhang, Q Cai, J Mao, E Chang, and B Guo. 2001. Spoken Dialogue Management as Planning and Acting under Uncertainty. In *Proceedings of Eurospeech*.

Training and evaluation of an MDP model for social multi-user human-robot interaction

Simon Keizer, Mary Ellen Foster, Oliver Lemon
Interaction Lab
Heriot-Watt University
Edinburgh (UK)
{s.keizer,m.e.foster,o.lemon}@hw.ac.uk

Andre Gaschler, Manuel Giuliani
fortiss GmbH
Munich (Germany)
{gaschler,giuliani}@fortiss.org

Abstract

This paper describes a new approach to automatic learning of strategies for social multi-user human-robot interaction. Using the example of a robot bartender that tracks multiple customers, takes their orders, and serves drinks, we propose a model consisting of a Social State Recogniser (SSR) which processes audio-visual input and maintains a model of the social state, together with a Social Skills Executor (SSE) which takes social state updates from the SSR as input and generates robot responses as output. The SSE is modelled as two connected Markov Decision Processes (MDPs) with action selection policies that are jointly optimised in interaction with a Multi-User Simulation Environment (MUSE). The SSR and SSE have been integrated in the robot bartender system and evaluated with human users in hand-coded and trained SSE policy variants. The results indicate that the trained policy outperformed the hand-coded policy in terms of both subjective (+18%) and objective (+10.5%) task success.

1 Introduction

As the use of robot technology in the home as well as in public spaces is increasingly gaining attention, the need for effective and robust models for natural and social human robot interaction becomes more important. Whether it involves robot companions (Vardoulakis et al., 2012), game-playing robots (Klotz et al., 2011; Brooks et al., 2012; Cuayáhuitl and Kruijff-Korbayová, 2012), or robots that help people with exercising (Fasola and Mataric, 2013), human users should be able to interact with such service robots in an effective and natural way, using speech as well as other modalities of communication. Furthermore, with the emergence of new application domains there is a particular need for methods that enable rapid development of models for such new domains. In this respect, data-driven approaches are appealing for their capability to automatically exploit empirical data to arrive at realistic and effective models for interpreting user behaviour, as well as to learn strategies for effective system behaviour.

In spoken dialogue systems research, statistical methods for spoken language understanding, dialogue management, and natural language generation have proven to be feasible for effective and robust interactive systems (Rieser and Lemon, 2011; Lemon and Pietquin, 2012; Young et al., 2010; Young et al., 2013). Although such methods have recently also been applied to (multi-modal) human-robot interaction (Stiefelhagen et al., 2007; Cuayáhuitl et al., 2012), work on *multi-user* human-robot interaction has been limited to non-statistical, hand-coded models (Klotz et al., 2011).

On the other hand, substantial work has been done in the field of situated multi-party interaction in general, including data-driven approaches. In particular, Bohus & Horvitz (2009) have addressed the task of recognising engagement intentions using online learning in the setting of a screen-based embodied virtual receptionist, and have also worked on multi-party turn-taking in this context (Bohus and Horvitz, 2011).

In this paper we describe a statistical approach to automatic learning of strategies for selecting effective as well as socially appropriate robot actions in a multi-user context. The approach has been developed using the example of a robot bartender (see Figure 1) that tracks multiple customers, takes their orders, and serves drinks. We propose a model consisting of a Social State Recogniser (SSR) which processes audio-visual input and maintains a model of the social state, and a Social Skills Executor (SSE) which takes social state updates from the SSR as input and generates robot responses as output. The SSE is modelled as a hierarchy of two connected Markov Decision Processes (MDPs) with action selection policies that are jointly optimised in interaction with a Multi-User Simulation Environment (MUSE).

Figure 1: The robot bartender with two customers

In the remainder of this paper we will describe the robot system in more detail (Section 2), followed by descriptions of the SSR (Section 3), the SSE (Section 4), and MUSE (Section 5). In Section 6 we then discuss in more detail the MDP model for the SSE and the process of jointly optimising the policies, and present evaluation results on simulated data. Next, we present results of the first evaluation of the integrated SSE-MDP component with human users (Section 7). The paper is concluded in Section 8.

2 Robot bartender system

The robot system we used for evaluating the models is equipped with vision and speech input processing modules, as well as modules controlling two robot arms and a talking head. Based on observations about the users in the scene and their behaviour, the system must maintain a model of the social context, and decide on effective and socially appropriate responses in that context. Such a system must be able to engage in, maintain, and close interactions with users, take a user's order by means of a spoken conversation, and serve their drinks. The overall aim is to generate interactive behaviour that is both task- effective and socially appropriate: in addition to efficiently taking orders and serving drinks, the system should, e.g., deal with customers on a first-come, first-served basis, and should manage the customers' patience by asking them politely to wait until the robot is done serving another customer.

As shown in Figure 1, the robot hardware consists of a pair of manipulator arms with grippers, mounted to resemble human arms, along with an animatronic talking head capable of producing facial expressions, rigid head motion, and lip-synchronised synthesised speech. The input sensors include a vision system which tracks the location, facial expressions, gaze behaviour, and body language of all people in the scene in real time (Pateraki et al., 2013), along with a linguistic processing system (Petrick et al., 2012) combining a speech recogniser with a natural-language parser to create symbolic representations of the speech produced by all users. More details of the architecture and components are provided in (Foster et al., 2012). An alternative embodiment of the system is also available on the NAO platform.

3 Social State Recogniser

The primary role of the Social State Recogniser (SSR) is to turn the continuous stream of messages produced by the low-level input and output components of the system into a discrete representation of the world, the robot, and all entities in the scene, integrating social, interaction-based, and task-based properties. The state is modelled as a set of *relations* such as `facePos(A)=(x,y,z)` or `closeToBar(A)`; see (Petrick and Foster, 2013) for details on the representation used.

In addition to storing all of the low-level sensor information, the SSR also infers additional relations that are not directly reported by the sensors. For example, it fuses information from vision and speech to determine which user should be assigned to a recognised spoken contribution. It also provides a constant estimate of whether each customer is currently seeking attention from the bartender (`seeksAttention(A)`): the initial version of this estimator used a hand-coded rule based on the observation of human behaviour in real bars (Huth et al., 2012), while a later version (Foster, 2013) makes use of a supervised learning classifier trained on labelled recordings of humans interacting with the first version of the robot bartender.

The SSR provides a query interface to allow other system components access to the relations stored in the state, and also publishes an updated state to the SSE every time there is a change which might require a system action in response (e.g., a customer appears, begins seeking attention, or makes a drink order).

4 Social Skills Executor

The Social Skills Executor (SSE) controls the behaviour of the robot system, based on the social state updates it receives from the SSR. The output of the SSE consists of a combination of non-communicative robot actions and/or communicative actions with descriptions of their multi-modal realisations. In the bartender domain, the non-communicative actions typically involve serving a specific drink to a specific user, whereas the communicative actions have the form of dialogue acts (Bunt et al., 2010), directed at a specific user, e.g. `setQuestion(drink)` ("What would you like to drink?") or `initialGreeting()` ("Hello").

In our design of the SSE, the decision making process resulting in such outputs (including the 'no action' output) consists of three stages: 1) ***social multi-user coordination***: managing the system's engagement with the users present in the scene (e.g., accept a user's bid for attention, or proceed with an engaged user), 2) ***single-user interaction***: if proceeding with an engaged user, generating a high-level response to that user, in the form of a communicative act or physical action (e.g., greeting the user or serving him a drink), and 3) ***multi-modal fission***: selecting a combination of modalities for realising a chosen response (e.g., a greeting can be realised through speech and/or a nodding gesture). One advantage of such a hierarchical design is that strategies for the different stages can be developed independently. Another is that it makes automatic policy optimisation more scalable.

5 Multi-User Simulated Environment

In order to test and evaluate the SSE, as well as to train SSE action selection policies, we developed a Multi-User Simulated Environment (MUSE). MUSE allows for rapidly exploring the large space of possible states in which the SSE must select actions. A reward function that incorporates individual rewards from all simulated users in the environment is used to encode preferred system behaviour in a principled way. A simulated user assigns a reward if they are served the correct drink, and gives penalties associated with their waiting time and various other forms of undesired system responses (see Section 6.1 for more details about the reward function). All of this provides a practical platform for evaluating different strategies for effective and socially appropriate behaviour. It also paves the way for automatic optimisation of policies, for example by using reinforcement learning techniques, as we will discuss in Section 6.1.

The simulated environment replaces the vision and speech processing modules in the actual robot bartender system, which means that it generates 1) vision signals in every time-frame, and 2) speech processing results, corresponding to sequences of time-frames where a user spoke. The vision observations contain information about users that have been detected, where they are in the scene, whether they are speaking, and where their attention is directed to. Speech processing results are represented semantically, in the form of dialogue acts (e.g., `inform(drink=coke)`, "I would like a coke"). As described in Section 3, the SSR fuses the vision and speech input, for example to associate an incoming dialogue act with a particular user.

The simulated signals are the result of combining the output from the simulated users in the environment. Each simulated user is initialised with a random goal (in our domain a type of drink they want to order), enters the scene at some point, and starts bidding for attention at some point. Each simulated user also maintains a state and generates responses given that state. These responses include communicative actions directed at the bartender, which are translated into a multi-channel vision input stream processed by the SSR, and, in case the user realises the action through speech, a speech processing event after the user has finished speaking. Additionally, the simulated users start with a given *patience level*, which is reduced in every frame that the user is bidding for attention or being served by the system. If a user's patience has reduced to zero, s/he gives up and leaves the bar. However, it is increased by a given fixed amount when the system politely asks the user to wait, encoded as a `pausing` dialogue act. The behaviour of the simulated users is partly controlled by a set of probability distributions that allow for a certain degree of variation. These distributions have been informed by statistics derived from a corpus of human-human customer-bartender interactions (Huth et al., 2012).

In addition to information about the simulated users, MUSE also provides feedback about the execution of robot actions to the SSR, in particular the start and end of all robot speech and non-communicative robot actions. This type of information simulates the feedback that is also provided in the actual bartender system by the components that directly control the robot head and arms. Figure 2

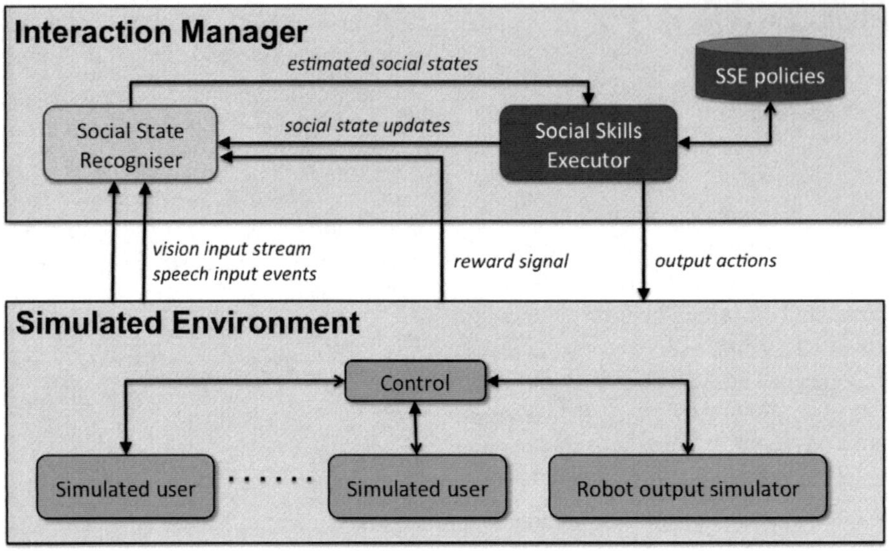

Figure 2: Social state recognition and social skills execution in a multi-user simulated environment.

shows the architecture of the system interacting with the simulated environment.

6 MDP model for multi-user interaction

To enable automatic optimisation of strategies for multi-user social interaction, the SSE model as described in Section 4 was cast as a hierarchy of two Markov Decision Processes (MDPs), corresponding to the *social multi-user coordination* and *single-user interaction* stages of decision making. Both MDPs have their own state spaces $\mathcal{S}_1$ and $\mathcal{S}_2$, each defined by a set of state features, extracted from the estimated social state made available by the SSR—see Tables 1 and 3. They also have their own action sets $\mathcal{A}_1$ and $\mathcal{A}_2$, corresponding to the range of decisions that can be made at the two stages (Tables 2 and 4), and two policies $\pi_1 : \mathcal{S}_1 \rightarrow \mathcal{A}_1$ and $\pi_2 : \mathcal{S}_2 \rightarrow \mathcal{A}_2$, mapping states to actions.

6.1 Policy optimisation

Using the MDP model as described above, we jointly optimise the two policies, based on the rewards received through the SSR from the simulated environment MUSE. Since MUSE gives rewards on a frame-by-frame basis, they are accumulated in the social state until the SSR publishes a state update. The SSE stores the accumulated reward together with the last state encountered and action taken in that state, after which that reward is reset in the social state. After each session (involving interactions with two users in our case), the set of encountered state-action pairs and associated rewards is used to update the policies.

The reward provided by MUSE in each frame is the sum of rewards R_i given by each individual simulated user i, and a number of general penalties arising from the environment as a whole. User rewards consist of a fixed reward in case their goal is satisfied (i.e., when they have been served the drink they wanted and ordered), a penalty in case they are still waiting to be served, a penalty in case they are engaged with the system but have not been served their drink yet, and additional penalties, for example when the system turns his attention to another user when the user is still talking to it, or when the system serves a drink before the user has ordered, or when the system serves another drink when the user already has been served their drink. General penalties are given for example when the system is talking while no users are present.

The policies are encoded as functions that assign a value to each state-action pair; these so-called *Q-values* are estimates of the long-term discounted cumulative reward. Given the current state, the policy selects the action with the highest Q-value:

$$\pi(s) = \arg\max_a \; Q(s, a) \tag{1}$$

Using a Monte-Carlo Control algorithm (Sutton and Barto, 1998), the policies are optimised by running the SSR and SSE against MUSE and using the received reward signal to update the Q-values after each interaction sequence. During training, the SSE uses an ϵ-greedy policy, i.e., it takes a random exploration action with probability $\epsilon = 0.2$.

Index	Feature	Values
$4 \cdot i$	Interaction status for user $i+1$	nonEngaged/seeksAttention/engaged
$4 \cdot i+1$	Location of user $i+1$	notPresent/!closeToBar/closeToBar
$4 \cdot i+2$	User $i+1$ was served a drink	no/yes
$4 \cdot i+3$	User $i+1$ asked to wait	no/yes

Table 1: State features for the *social multi-user coordination* policy. For each user, 4 features are included in the state space, resulting in $3^2 \cdot 2^2 = 36$ states for interactions with up to 1 user, increasing to 1296 states for interactions with up to 2 users and $46,656$ states for up to 3 users.

Index	Action
0	No action
$3 \cdot i+1$	Ask user $i+1$ to wait
$3 \cdot i+2$	Accept bid for attention from user $i+1$
$3 \cdot i+3$	Proceed interaction with (engaged) user $i+1$

Table 2: Actions for the *social multi-user coordination* policy.

In the policy update step, a discount factor $\gamma = 0.95$ is used, which controls the impact that rewards received later in a session have on the value of state-action pairs encountered earlier in that session.

Figure 3 shows the learning curve of a joint policy optimisation, showing average rewards obtained after running the SSE with trained policies for 500 runs, at several stages of the optimisation process (after every 2500 sessions/runs/iterations, the trained policy was saved for evaluation). In this particular setup, simulated users gave a reward of 550 upon goal completion but in the total score this is reduced considerably due to waiting time (-2 per frame), task completion time (-1 per frame) and various other potential penalties. Also indicated are the performance levels of two hand-coded SSE policies, one of which uses a strategy of asking a user to wait when already engaged with another user (labelled HDC), and one in which that second user is ignored until it is done with the engaged user (labelled HDCnp). The settings for user patience as discussed in Section 5 determine which of these policies works best; ideally these settings should be derived from data if available. Nevertheless, even with the hand-coded patience settings, the learning curve indicates that both policies are outperformed in simulation after 10k iterations, suggesting that the best strategy for managing user patience can be found automatically.

7 Human user evaluation

The SSE described above has been integrated in the full robot bartender system and evaluated for the first time with human users. In the experiment, both a hand-coded version and a trained version of the SSE component were tested; see Table 6 in Appendix A for the trajectory of state-action pairs of an example session. The hand-coded version uses the policy labelled HDC, not HDCnp (see Section 6.1). In each of the sessions carried out, one recruited subject and one confederate (one of the experimenters) approached the bartender together as clients and both tried to order a drink (coke or lemonade). After each interaction, the subject filled out the short questionnaire shown in Figure 4.

Q1: Did you successfully order a drink from the bartender? [Y/N]

Please state your opinion on the following statements:
[1:strongly disagree; 2:disagree; 3:slightly disagree; 4:slightly agree; 5:agree; 6:strongly agree]

Q2: It was easy to attract the bartender's attention [1–6]

Q3: The bartender understood me well [1–6]

Q4: The interaction with the bartender felt natural [1–6]

Q5: Overall, I was happy about the interaction [1–6]

Figure 4: Questionnaire from the user study.

37 subjects took part in this study, resulting in a total of 58 recorded drink-ordering interactions: 29 that used the hand-coded SSE for interaction management, and 29 that used the trained SSE.

The results from the experiment are summarised in Table 5. We analysed the results using a linear mixed model, treating the SSE policy as a fixed factor and the subject ID as a random factor. Overall, the pattern of the subjective scores suggests a slight preference for the trained SSE version, although

Index	Feature	Values
0	Reactive pressure	none/thanking/greeting/goodbye/apology
1	Status of user goal	unknown/usrInf/sysExpConf/sysImpConf/ grounded/drinkServed/sysAsked
2	Own proc. state	none/badASR

Table 3: State features for the *single-user interaction* policy. In this case, there are $5 \cdot 7 \cdot 2 = 70$ states.

Index	Action	Example
0	No action	
1	returnGreeting()	"Hello"
2	autoPositive()	"Okay"
3	acceptThanking()	"You're welcome"
4	autoNegative()	"What did you say?"
5	setQuestion(drink)	"What drink would you like?"
6	acceptRequest(drink=x) + serveDrink(x)	"Here's your coke"

Table 4: Actions for the *single-user interaction* policy, which correspond to possible dialogue acts, except for 'no action' and serving a drink. The specific drink types required for two of the actions are extracted from the fully specified user goal in the social state maintained by the SSR.

only the difference in perceived success was statistically significant at the $p < 0.05$ level. The actual success rate of the trained policy was also somewhat higher, although not significantly so. Also, the interactions with the trained SSE took slightly longer than the ones with the hand-coded SSE in terms of the number of system turns (i.e., the number of times the SSE receives a state update and selects a response action, excluding the times when it selects a non-action); however, this did not have any overall effect on the users' subjective ratings.

The higher success rate for the trained SSE could be partly explained by the fact that fewer ASR problems were encountered when using this version; however, since the SSE was not triggered when a turn was discarded due to low-confidence ASR, this would not have had an effect on the number of system turns. There was another difference between the hand-coded and trained policies that could have affected both the success rate and the number of system turns: for interactions in which a user has not ordered yet, nor been asked for their order, the hand-coded strategy randomly chooses between asking the user for their order and doing nothing, letting the user take the initiative to place the order, whereas the trained policy always asks the user for their order (this action has the highest Q-value, although in fact the value for doing nothing in such cases is also relatively high).

We also carried out a stepwise multiple linear regression on the data from the user experiment to determine which of the objective measures had the largest effect, as suggested by the PARADISE evaluation framework (Walker et al., 2000). The resulting regression functions are shown in Figure 5. In summary, all of the subjective responses were significantly affected by the objective task success (i.e., the number of drinks served); the number of low-ASR turns also affected most of the responses, while various measures of dialogue efficiency (such as the system response time and the time taken to serve drinks) also had a significant impact. In general, these regression functions explain between 15–25% of the variance in the subjective measures.

As an initial analysis of the validity of the simulated environment, we compared the state distribution of the simulated data accumulated during policy optimisation with that of the human user evaluation data. In terms of coverage, we found that only 46% of all states encountered in the real data were also encountered during training. However, many of these states do not occur very often and many of them do not require any action by the robot (a trained policy can easily be set to take no-action for unseen states). If we only include states that have been encountered at least 20 times, the coverage increases to over 70%. For states encountered at least 58 times, the coverage is 100%, though admittedly this covers only the 10 most frequently encountered states. The similarity of the two distributions can be quantified by computing the KL-divergence, but since such a number is

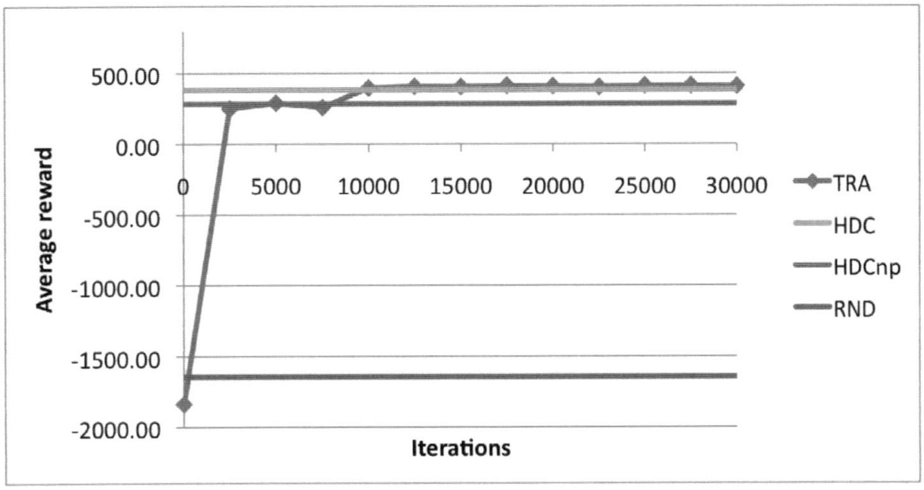

Figure 3: Learning curve for joint optimisation of SSE-MDP policies.

System	NS	PSucc*	PAtt	PUnd	PNat	POv	NDSrvd	NST	NBAsr
SSE-TRA	29	97%	4.10	4.21	3.00	3.83	1.97 (98.5%)	7.38	3.14
SSE-HDC	29	79%	4.14	3.83	2.93	3.83	1.76 (88.0%)	6.86	3.82
TOTAL	58	88%	4.12	4.02	2.97	3.83	1.86 (93.0%)	7.12	3.48

Table 5: Overview of system performance results from the experiment. In the leftmost column SSE-TRA and SSE-HDC refer to the trained and hand-coded SSE versions; the column NS indicates the number of sessions; the columns PSucc (perceived success), PAtt (perceived attention recognition), PUnd (perceived understanding), PNat (perceived naturalness), and POv (perceived overall performance) give average scores resulting from the 5 respective questionnaire questions; NDSrvd indicates the average number of drinks served per session (out of 2 maximum – the percentage is given in brackets); NST indicates the average number of system turns per session; while NBAsr indicates the average number of cases where the user speech was ignored because the ASR confidence was below a predefined threshold. The marked column indicates that the difference between the two SSE versions was significant at the $p < 0.05$ level.

hard to interpret in itself, this will only be useful if there were a state distribution from an alternative simulator or an improved version of MUSE for comparison.

8 Conclusion

In this paper we presented a new approach to automatic learning of strategies for social multi-user human-robot interaction, demonstrated using the example of a robot bartender that tracks multiple customers, takes their orders, and serves drinks. We presented a model consisting of a Social State Recogniser (SSR) which processes audio-visual input and maintains a model of the social state, and a Social Skills Executor (SSE) which takes social state updates from the SSR as input and generates robot responses as output. The main contribution of this work has been a new MDP-based model for the SSE, incorporating two connected MDPs with action selection policies that are jointly optimised in interaction with a Multi-User Simulation Environment (MUSE). In addition to showing promising evaluation results with simulated data, we also presented results from a first evaluation of the SSE component with human users. The experiments showed that the integrated SSE component worked quite well, and that the trained SSE-MDP achieved higher subjective and objective success rates (+18% and +10.5% respectively).

Our model currently only utilises two policies, but in more complex scenarios the task could be further modularised and extended by introducing more MDPs, for example for multimodal fission and natural language generation. The approach of using a hierarchy of MDPs has some similarity with the Hierarchical Reinforcement Learning (HRL) approach which uses a hierarchy of Semi-Markov Decision Processes (SMDPs). In (Cuayáhuitl et al.,

$$\text{PSucc} = 0.88 + 0.14 * \mathcal{N}(\text{NDSrvd}) - 0.07 * \mathcal{N}(\text{NBAsr}) \quad (r^2 = 0.21)$$

$$\text{PAtt} = 4.12 + 0.76 * \mathcal{N}(\text{NDSrvd}) - 0.46 * \mathcal{N}(\text{RTm}) - 0.38 * \mathcal{N}(\text{FDTm}) \quad (r^2 = 0.22)$$

$$\text{PUnd} = 4.02 + 0.41 * \mathcal{N}(\text{NDSrvd}) - 0.36 * \mathcal{N}(\text{NBAsr}) - 0.40 * \mathcal{N}(\text{NST}) - 0.41 * \mathcal{N}(\text{RTm}) - 0.39 * \mathcal{N}(\text{STm}) \quad (r^2 = 0.24)$$

$$\text{PNat} = 2.97 + 0.36 * \mathcal{N}(\text{NDSrvd}) - 0.29 * \mathcal{N}(\text{NBAsr}) - 0.31 * \mathcal{N}(\text{NST}) - 0.44 * \mathcal{N}(\text{RTm}) \quad (r^2 = 0.16)$$

$$\text{POv} = 3.83 + 0.65 * \mathcal{N}(\text{NDSrvd}) - 0.38 * \mathcal{N}(\text{NBAsr}) - 0.52 * \mathcal{N}(\text{RTm}) \quad (r^2 = 0.24)$$

Figure 5: PARADISE regression functions from the user study. The labels are the same as those in Table 5, with the following additions: RTm is the mean system response time per user, STm is the mean serving time per user, and FDTm is the mean time to serve the first drink; all times are measured in milliseconds. $\mathcal{N}$ represents a Z score normalisation function (Cohen, 1995).

2012) for example, this hierarchy is motivated by the identification of multiple tasks that the robot can carry out and for which multiple SMDP agents are defined. In every step of the interaction, control lies with a single SMDP agent somewhere in the hierarchy; once it arrives at its final state it returns control to its parent SMDP. An additional transition model is introduced to permit switching from an incomplete SMDP to another SMDP at the same level, making interactions more flexible. In our approach, control always starts at the top level MDP and lower level MDPs are triggered depending on the action taken by their parent MDP. For social interaction with multiple users, flexible switching between interactions with different users is important, so an arguably more sophisticated HRL approach to multi-user interaction will rely heavily on the transition model. Another approach to modularising the task domain through multiple policies is described in (Lison, 2011), where 'meta-control' of the policies relies on an activation vector. As in the HRL SMDP approach, this approach has not been applied in the context of multi-user interaction. In any case, a more thorough and possibly experimental analysis comparing our approach with these other approaches would be worth investigating.

In the future, we plan to extend our MDP model to a POMDP (Partially Observable MDP) model, taking uncertainty about both speech and visual input into account in the optimisation of SSE policies by incorporating alternative hypotheses and confidence scores provided by the input modules into the social state. Since hand-coding strategies becomes more challenging in the face of increased uncertainty due to noisy input, the appeal of automatic strategy learning in a POMDP framework becomes even stronger. In a previous offline version of our combined SSR and SSE, we have shown in preliminary simulation experiments that even in an MDP setting, an automatically trained SSE policy outperforms a hand-coded policy when noise is added to the speech channel (Keizer et al., 2013).

Another direction of research is to annotate the data collected in the described experiment for further analysis and use it to improve the features of the simulated environment. The improved models should lead to trained policies that perform better when evaluated again with human users. We will also make use of the findings of the PARADISE regression to fine-tune the reward function used for policy optimisation: note that two of the main features indicated by the PARADISE procedure—task success and dialogue efficiency—are already those included in the current reward function, and we will add a feature to account for the effects of ASR performance. We are also considering using collected data for direct supervised or off-policy reinforcement learning of SSE strategies.

Finally, we aim to extend our domain both in terms of interactive capabilities (e.g., handling communication problems, social obligations management, turn-taking) and task domain (e.g., handling more than the current maximum of 2 users, group orders, orders with multiple items). In order to make the (PO)MDP model more scalable and thus keeping the learning algorithms tractable, we also aim to incorporate techniques such as value function approximation into our model.

Acknowledgments

The research leading to these results has received funding from the European Union's Seventh Framework Programme (FP7/2007–2013) under grant agreement no. 270435, JAMES: Joint Action for Multimodal Embodied Social Systems, `http://james-project.eu/`. Thanks to Ingmar Kessler for help in running the user experiment.

References

Dan Bohus and Eric Horvitz. 2009. Learning to predict engagement with a spoken dialog system in open-world settings. In *Proceedings SIGdial*, London, UK.

Dan Bohus and Eric Horvitz. 2011. Multiparty turn taking in situated dialog: Study, lessons, and directions. In *Proceedings SIGdial*, Portland, OR.

A. Brooks, J. Gray, G. Hoffman, A. Lockerd, H. Lee, and C. Breazeal. 2012. Robot's play: Interactive games with sociable machines. *Computers in Entertainment*, 2(3).

H. Bunt, J. Alexandersson, J. Carletta, J.-W. Choe, A.C. Fang, K. Hasida, K. Lee, V. Petukhova, A. Popescu-Belis, L. Romary, C. Soria, and D. Traum. 2010. Towards an ISO standard for dialogue act annotation. In *Proceedings LREC*, Valletta, Malta.

Paul R. Cohen. 1995. *Empirical Methods for Artificial Intelligence*. MIT Press, Boston.

Heriberto Cuayáhuitl and Ivana Kruijff-Korbayová. 2012. An interactive humanoid robot exhibiting flexible sub-dialogues. In *Proceedings NAACL HLT*, Montreal, Canada.

H. Cuayáhuitl, I. Kruijff-Korbayová, and N. Dethlefs. 2012. Hierarchical dialogue policy learning using flexible state transitions and linear function approximation. In *Proceedings COLING*, Mumbai, India.

Juan Fasola and Maja J. Mataric. 2013. A socially assistive robot exercise coach for the elderly. *Journal of Human Robot Interaction*, 2(3). To appear.

Mary Ellen Foster, Andre Gaschler, Manuel Giuliani, Amy Isard, Maria Pateraki, and Ronald P. A. Petrick. 2012. Two people walk into a bar: Dynamic multi-party social interaction with a robot agent. In *Proceedings ICMI*, Santa Monica, CA.

Mary Ellen Foster. 2013. How can I help you? Comparing engagement classification strategies for a robot bartender. Submitted.

K. Huth, S. Loth, and J.P. De Ruiter. 2012. Insights from the bar: A model of interaction. In *Proceedings of Formal and Computational Approaches to Multimodal Communication*.

Simon Keizer, Mary Ellen Foster, Zhuoran Wang, and Oliver Lemon. 2013. Machine learning of social states and skills for multi-party human-robot interaction. Submitted.

David Klotz, Johannes Wienke, Julia Peltason, Britta Wrede, Sebastian Wrede, Vasil Khalidov, and Jean-Marc Odobez. 2011. Engagement-based multiparty dialog with a humanoid robot. In *Proceedings SIGdial*, Portland, OR.

Oliver Lemon and Olivier Pietquin, editors. 2012. *Data-driven Methods for Adaptive Spoken Dialogue Systems: Computational Learning for Conversational Interfaces*. Springer.

Pierre Lison. 2011. Multi-policy dialogue management. In *Proceedings SIGdial*, Portland, OR.

Maria Pateraki, Markos Sigalas, Georgios Chliveros, and Panos Trahanias. 2013. Visual human-robot communication in social settings. In *the Workshop on Semantics, Identification and Control of Robot-Human-Environment Interaction, held within the IEEE International Conference on Robotics and Automation (ICRA)*.

Ronald P. A. Petrick and Mary Ellen Foster. 2013. Planning for social interaction in a robot bartender domain. In *Proceedings ICAPS*, Rome, Italy.

Ronald P. A. Petrick, Mary Ellen Foster, and Amy Isard. 2012. Social state recognition and knowledge-level planning for human-robot interaction in a bartender domain. In *AAAI 2012 Workshop on Grounding Language for Physical Systems*, Toronto, ON, Canada, July.

Verena Rieser and Oliver Lemon. 2011. *Reinforcement Learning for Adaptive Dialogue Systems*. Springer.

R. Stiefelhagen, H. Ekenel, C. Fügen, P. Gieselmann, H. Holzapfel, F. Kraft, K. Nickel, M. Voit, and A. Waibel. 2007. Enabling multimodal human-robot interaction for the Karlsruhe humanoid robot. *IEEE Transactions on Robotics*, 23(5):840–851.

Richard S. Sutton and Andrew G. Barto. 1998. *Reinforcement Learning: An Introduction*. MIT Press.

L. Pfeifer Vardoulakis, L. Ring, B. Barry, C. Sidner, and T. Bickmore. 2012. Designing relational agents as long term social companions for older adults. In *Proceedings IVA*, Santa Cruz, CA.

Marilyn Walker, Candace Kamm, and Diane Litman. 2000. Towards developing general models of usability with PARADISE. *Natural Language Engineering*, 6(3–4):363–377.

Steve Young, Milica Gašić, Simon Keizer, François Mairesse, Blaise Thomson, and Kai Yu. 2010. The Hidden Information State model: a practical framework for POMDP based spoken dialogue management. *Computer Speech and Language*, 24(2):150–174.

Steve Young, M. Gašić, B. Thomson, and J. Williams. 2013. POMDP-based statistical spoken dialogue systems: a review. *Proceedings of the IEEE*. To appear.

Appendix A: Example session with two guests ordering a drink

Timestamp	Level 1 MDP		Level 2 MDP		Description
	State features	Action	State features	Action	
13:28:45:966	0 1 0 0 0 0 0 0	0	-	-	A1 visible, but not close to bar; no response generated yet.
13:28:48:029	1 2 0 0 0 0 0 0	2	-	-	A1 not close to bar and seeking attention: BT acknowledges this and engages with A1.
13:28:53:680	3 2 0 0 1 2 0 0	4	-	-	A2 visible, close to the bar, and seeking attention; BT is already engaged with A1 and therefore asks A2 to wait.
13:28:55:715	3 2 0 0 1 2 0 1	3	0 0 0	1	BT continues his interaction with A1 and asks for their order.
13:28:56:928	3 2 0 0 1 2 0 1	3	0 6 0	0	BT continues with A1 and waits for them to order.
13:28:56:928	3 2 0 0 1 2 0 1	3	0 6 0	0	Same as above: BT still waiting for A1's order.
...					Due to repeated ASR failures, this state action pair is encountered several times.
13:29:52:066	3 2 0 0 1 2 0 1	3	0 1 0	2	A1's has now been successfully recognised; BT serves the ordered drink to A1.
13:30:12:013	3 2 1 0 1 2 0 1	5	-	-	A2 still seeking attention; BT can now acknowledge this and engage with A1.
13:30:13:307	1 2 1 0 3 2 0 1	6	0 0 0	1	BT continues with A2 and asks for their order.
13:30:14:475	1 2 1 0 3 2 0 0	6	0 6 0	0	BT continues with A2 and waits for them to order
13:30:17:737	1 2 1 0 3 2 0 0	6	0 1 0	2	A2's recognised; BT serves ordered drink to A2.
13:30:37:623	1 2 1 0 3 2 1 0	0	-	-	Both A1 and A2 have been served; BT does nothing
13:30:41:440	1 2 1 0 3 2 1 0	0	-	-	Same as above.
...					

Table 6: SSE-MDP trajectory for one session from the evaluation data, showing the states and response actions taken for both MDPs. The states are represented via their value indices, corresponding to Tables 1 and 3; the action indices similarly correspond to the actions in Tables 2 and 4. In the descriptions, A1 and A2 refer to the first and second user detected; BT refers to the bartender.

Evaluation of Speech Dialog Strategies for Internet Applications in the Car

Hansjörg Hofmann
Ute Ehrlich
André Berton
Daimler AG / Ulm, Germany,
hansjoerg.hofmann@daimler.com

Angela Mahr
Rafael Math
Christian Müller
DFKI / Saarbrücken, Germany
angela.mahr@dfki.de

Abstract

Due to the mobile Internet revolution, people tend to browse the Web while driving their car which puts the driver's safety at risk. Therefore, an intuitive and non-distractive in-car speech interface to the Web needs to be developed. Before developing a new speech dialog system in a new domain developers have to examine what the user's preferred interaction style is in order to use such a system. This paper reports from a very recent driving simulation study and its preliminary results which are conducted in order to compare different speech dialog strategies. The use of command-based and conversational SDS prototypes while driving is evaluated on usability and driving performance. Different GUIs are designed in order to support the respective dialog strategy the most and to evaluate the effect of the GUI on usability and driver distraction. The preliminary results show that the conversational speech dialog performs more efficient than the command-based dialog. However, the conversational dialog distracts more from driving than the command-based. Furthermore, the results indicate that an SDS supported by a GUI is more efficient and better accepted by the user than without GUI.

1 Introduction

The pervasive use of smartphones in daily situations impacts the automotive environment. In order to stay "always connected" people tend to use their smartphone's Internet functions manually while driving. However, using a smartphone manually while driving, distracts the driver and endangers the driver's safety. According to Governors Highway Safety Association (2011) 25% of U.S. car crashes are related to drivers using their cellphones while driving. Therefore, the development of an intuitive and non-distractive in-car speech interface to the Web is essential in order to increase driver safety (Peissner et al., 2011).

Before developing a new speech dialog system (SDS) in a new domain developers have to examine how users would interact with such a system. An Internet user study by Hofmann et al. (2012a) in which the subjects had to solve Internet tasks orally, revealed that concerning communicational (e.g. sending an Email) and transactional tasks (e.g. booking a hotel) conversational and command-based speaking styles were used with equal frequency. Because of the equal frequency of occurrence you have to examine which speech dialog strategy - the command-based or the conversational - is the most suitable for these tasks.

First studies on the evaluation of dialog strategies have been conducted by Devillers and Bonneau-Maynard (1998) who compare two SDS allowing the user to retrieve touristic information. One dialog strategy guides the user via system suggestions, the other does not. The evaluated dialog strategies comprise the fundamental ideas the command-based and conversational dialog strategy consist of. By applying qualitative and quantitative criteria they conclude that user guidance is suitable for novices and appreciated by all kinds of users. However, there was no GUI involved and the speech interaction was performed as primary task. Considering the driving use case other results may be achieved since the primary task is driving. Furthermore, the use of these SDS among advanced users needs to be investigated.

In the TALK project, Mutschler et al. (2007) compared a command-based speech dialog to a conversational dialog where the driver had to control the in-car mp3-player by speech while driving. The same graphical user interface (GUI) was used for both dialog strategies. Although the conversational dialog was more efficient the command-based dialog was more appreciated by the subjects. According to Mutschler et al. the high error rate of the conversational strategy was the reason for the higher acceptance of the command-based dialog. There were no significant differences in the driving performance revealed when using the different SDS.

The speech recognizer quality has improved enormously within the last five years. Therefore, the weak speech recognition performance of Mutschler et al.'s conversational dialog may be nowadays less significant. Furthermore, the use of the same GUI for different dialog strategies could have additionally influenced the result. The GUI should be adapted to the particular dialog strategy in order to benefit from the advantages of the respective strategy the most and to allow for a comparison of optimal systems.

This paper reports from a very recent driving simulation study and its preliminary results which are conducted in order to compare different speech dialog strategies. The use of command-based and conversational SDS prototypes while driving is evaluated on usability and driving performance. The systems have been developed for German and allows users to perform a hotel booking by speech. Different GUIs are designed in order to support the respective dialog strategy the most and to evaluate the effect of the GUI on usability and driver distraction. The experiments have been conducted at DFKI, Saarbrücken using the OpenDS[1] driving simulation. The research work is performed within the scope of the EU FP7 funding project GetHomeSafe[2].

The remainder of the paper is structured as follows: In Section 2, the developed SDS prototypes are briefly described. Section 3 presents the experimental setup and its results and finally, conclusions are drawn.

2 SDS Prototype Concepts

The chosen use case for the design of the SDS concepts is booking a hotel by speech while driving since it covers many different subdialog types (parameter input, list presentation and browsing, etc.). For this purpose, the online hotel booking service HRS[3] has been used as data provider for the SDS.

Each SDS prototype concept offers the same functionality: First, the user has to input his search parameter to retrieve a list of hotels. The user can browse the list and ask for detailed information about a certain hotel. If the hotel matches his needs he is able to book the hotel. In addition, the user can change the search parameters.

In the following, the different speech dialog strategies and the corresponding GUI designs are briefly decribed. A detailed description of the human-machine interface (HMI) concepts can be found in Hofmann et al. (2012b).

2.1 Speech Dialog Strategy Design

SDS Prototypes for German language have been developed including the following SDS features: In order to speak to the system the driver has to press a Push-To-Activate (PTA) button. Furthermore, the driver is able to interrupt the system while prompting the user ("barge-in"). When designing the different dialog strategies we particularly focused our attention on the dialog initiative, the possibility to enter multiple input parameters and the acoustic feedback.

2.1.1 Command-based Speech Dialog Strategy

The dialog behavior of the command-based dialog strategy corresponds to the voice-control which can be found in current state-of-the-art in-car SDS. By calling explicit speech commands the speech dialog is initiated and the requested information is delivered or the demanded task is executed. There are several synonyms available for each command. By using implicit feedback in the voice prompts the driver is informed about what the system has understood. After the first command the user is guided by the system and executes the steps which are suggested and displayed by the system. The GUI supports the speech dialog by showing the "speakable" commands as widgets on the screen (see Section 2.2). A sample dialog is illustrated in the following:

Driver: *Book a hotel.*
System: *Where would you like to book a hotel?*
Driver: *In Berlin.*
System: *When do you want to arrive in Berlin?*
Driver: *Tomorrow.*
System: *How long would you like to stay in Berlin?*
Driver: *Until the day after tomorrow.*

[1]http://www.opends.eu/
[2]http://www.gethomesafe-fp7.eu
[3]http://www.hrs.com

2.1.2 Conversational Speech Dialog Strategy

In the conversational dialog strategy the dialog initiative switches during the speech interaction. The driver is able to speak whole sentences where multiple parameters can be set within one single utterance. Thereby, the dialog can be more natural, flexible and efficient. The driver is informed about what the system has understood by using implicit feedback. The GUI does not present the "speakable" commands on the screen. In order to indicate the possible functions icons are displayed (see Section 2.2). A sample dialog is presented in the the following:

Driver:	*I would like to book a hotel in Berlin.*
System:	*When do you arrive in Berlin?*
Driver:	*I'll arrive tomorrow and leave the day after tomorrow.*

As illustrated in the example the driver can already indicate some input parameters when addressing the system for the first time. The system verifies which input parameters are missing in order to send a hotel request. The system prompts the user and collects the missing information. Although the system asks for only one parameter, the user is able to give more or other information than requested.

2.2 GUI Design

The different GUIs have been designed in order to support the speech dialog strategies and to evaluate the effect of the GUI on usability and driving performance. The different GUIs have been customized corresponding to the dialog strategies only as much as necessary since an objective comparison is targeted. When designing the screens we followed the international standardized AAM-Guidelines (Driver Focus-Telematics Working Group, 2002).

2.2.1 Command-based GUI Design

In the command-based dialog strategy the driver uses commands to speak to the system. In order to give the driver an understanding of the "speakable" commands, the speech dialog is supported by the GUI. For that reason the currently possible speech commands are displayed on the screen at all times which may lead to a high visual distraction. Hence, in automotive terms the command-based speech dialog strategy is also called "speak-what-you-see" strategy.

Figure 1(a) illustrates the main screen of the hotel booking application at the beginning of the hotel booking dialog. Here, the first input parameter "destination" ("Ziel" in German) is requested by the system. Afterwards the user is guided step-by-step by the system. When the driver has given the requested information, a new widget appears on the screen and the system asks the driver for the corresponding input.

2.2.2 Conversational GUI Design

In the conversational dialog strategy the driver can speak freely and does not have to use certain commands. There is no need to give the driver a visual feedback of the currently "speakable" commands whereby the visual distraction may be lowered. For that reason, the content on the head unit screen does not have to indicate the possible options to proceed with the speech dialog. The subfunction line which was used to indicate the available commands is replaced by only few symbols which resemble the current GUI state. Figure 1(b) shows the form filling main screen at the beginning of the speech interaction where the user is already able to input several parameters at once.

2.2.3 Without GUI

We also investigated the need for a visual feedback, why the two speech dialog strategies are also evaluated "without GUI". In this case, without GUI means that no content information is displayed on the screen. However, a visual feedback which indicates if the user is allowed to talk is presented in the top bar of the screen (see Figure 1(c)).

3 Evaluation

3.1 Method

3.1.1 Participants

The experiment was conducted at DFKI, Saarbrücken. In total, 24 German participants (mainly students) participated in the experiment. All participants received a monetary expense allowance and possessed a valid driver's license. Due to missing data recordings during the experiment data of 1 participant had to be excluded from the analyses. The remaining participants comprised 9 male and 14 female subjects and the average age was 26 years (standard deviation (SD) = 4,1). 56,5% of the participants were driving their car at least once a day. 56,5% had little to no experience with speech-controlled devices.

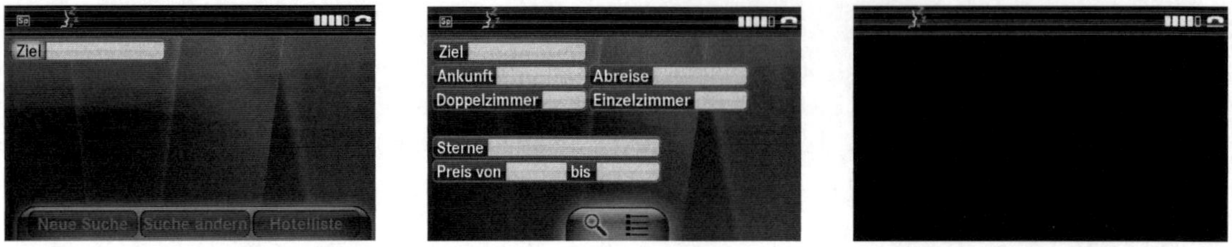

(a) Command-based GUI (b) Conversational GUI (c) "without" GUI

Figure 1: Main Screens at the Beginning of the Interaction.

3.1.2 Experimental Design

Four different HMI concept variants were evaluated in a 2x2 (speech dialog strategy: command-based vs. conversational, GUI: with vs. without) design. The Command-based and Conversational GUI were only used with the corresponding dialog strategy. The 4 HMI concepts were the following:

- Command-based speech dialog ("Comm")
  - with GUI ("CommGUI") and
  - without GUI ("CommNoGUI")
- Conversational speech dialog ("Conv")
  - with GUI ("ConvGUI") and
  - without GUI ("ConvNoGUI")

Each participant encountered all four conditions ("within-design"). For each condition, two tasks had to be accomplished. We investigated the participants speech dialog performance and influences on driving performance while using the SDS.

3.1.3 Materials

Speech Dialog Prototypes: In the experiment, the speech dialog prototypes described in Section 2 have been used. In order to explain the functionality and the control of the SDS prototypes to the user, instruction videos for each speech dialog strategy were presented. By presenting tutorial videos, we ensured that each participant was given identical instructions.

During the experiment, participants had to solve several tasks: They had to book a certain hotel according to given search parameters. The tasks were verbalized as little stories which contained the necessary parameters in a memorable manner. A sample task in English is presented below:

> *Imagine, you and your colleague are on the way to Cologne for a two-day meeting right now. You need two single rooms for these two nights which you have not booked, yet. Your appointment takes place in the city center of Cologne, where you would like to spend your night. Please look for a matching hotel for those nights.*

In total, participants had to perform 16 tasks. Four tasks were used as sample tasks to familiarize participants with the respective speech dialog strategy after showing the instruction video. The remaining eight tasks were used for the data collection.

Questionnaires: During the experiment different questionnaires were used:

- Preliminary Interview: In a preliminary questionnaire we collected demographical information (age, gender, etc.) about the participants. Furthermore, we surveyed driving habits, experience with speech-controlled devices, and hotel booking habits.
- SASSI questionnaire (Hone and Graham, 2001): The SASSI questionnaire covering 6 dimensions consists of 34 questions and is widely used to measure subjective usability evaluation of SDS.
- DALI questionnaire (Pauzie, 2008): The DALI questionnaire covers 6 dimensions in order to evaluate the user's cognitive load. The applied questionnaire consisted of 7 questions covering each dimension and an additional question addressing the manual demand.
- Final Interview: This questionnaire was designed to allow for a direct comparison of the respective SDS prototypes at the end of the experiment. Each participant had to rate the different SDS on a scale from 1 - 10 regarding several subjective measures. For each of the six SASSI dimensions, one question was asked. Additionally, we asked questions to directly compare cognitive load and to get information about the participants' personal preference of interaction style with the system at different sub dialogs.

Driving Simulation Setup: The experiment was conducted in the driving simulator at DFKI's "future lab" (see Figure 2). The participants were sitting on the driver's seat in a car which was placed in front of a canvas onto which the driving simulation was projected. The participants controlled the driving simulation by the car steering wheel and pedals. During the experiment the examiner was sitting on the passenger seat.

Figure 2: DFKI Driving Simulator Setup.

Previous driving simulation studies employ the standard Lane Change Test (LCT) by Mattes (2003). However, this driving task does not continuously mentally demand the user and thus, does not reflect the real cognitive load while driving. Furthermore, LCT is based on single tracks which limits the recordings to a certain time. We employed the ConTRe (Continuous Tracking and Reaction) task as part of the OpenDS[1] driving simulation software which complements the de-facto standard LCT including higher sensitivity and a more flexible driving task without restart interruptions. The steering task for lateral control resembles a continuous follow drive which will help to receive more detailed results about the two diverse dialog strategies. Furthermore, mental demand is addressed explicitly by employing an additional reaction task implemented as longitudinal control. A detailed description of the ConTRe task can be found in Mahr et al. (2012).

In the experiment, after giving the participant the hotel booking task instructions, the experimenter started the driving simulation. When the participant has crossed the start sign in the simulation he had to begin the speech dialog. When the hotel booking was completed, the experimenter stopped the driving simulation. Thereby, driving performance was only recorded during the speech dialog.

3.1.4 Procedure

In the experiment, 4 conditions were evaluated: The conversational speech dialog (with and without GUI) and the command-based speech dialog (with and without GUI). We did not randomize all four conditions, because the participants might have been confused if the speech dialog styles vary too often. Therefore, we decided to employ dialog styles blockwise (see Figure 3). In one block, only one speech dialog variant with the two GUI conditions was tested. The order of the two blocks was counterbalanced between participants to control for learning and order effects. Thereby, half of the participants were first introduced to the command-based dialog, whereas the other half of the participants started with the conversational dialog. Furthermore, the order of GUI conditions within one block was balanced between participants. In each of the four conditions, the participants had to perform two tasks. The order of the tasks was the same for all participants regardless of the system condition. Hence, all tasks were encountered in all dialog and GUI combinations. When the second task was finished, participants had to fill out the SASSI and the DALI questionnaire for each condition.

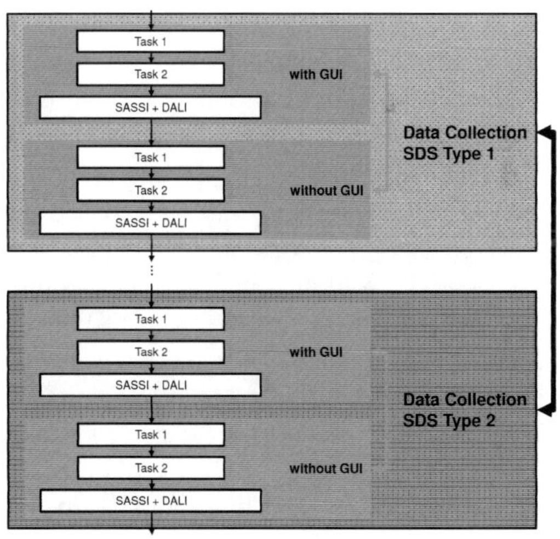

Figure 3: Experiment Structure.

The overall procedure of the experiment is illustrated in Figure 4. At the beginning of the experiment, participants had to fill out the preliminary questionnaire. Afterwards they had the possibility to get to know the driving simulation in a test drive lasting at least 4 minutes. After the test drive, the participants completed a 4 minutes baseline drive and had to fill out the DALI questionnaire afterwards to assess driving performance without secondary task. Next, the participants were shown the video of their first speech dialog variant and became familiar with the SDS by performing the 4 explorative tasks. Subsequently, participants performed the first SDS condition (SDS Type 1) both with and without GUI. After testing SDS Type 1, SDS Type 2 was introduced by presenting its instruction video and again the explorative tasks were performed. Participants performed the second SDS condition (SDS Type 2) also with and without GUI. Finally, participants completed a second baseline drive and filled out the final questionnaire.

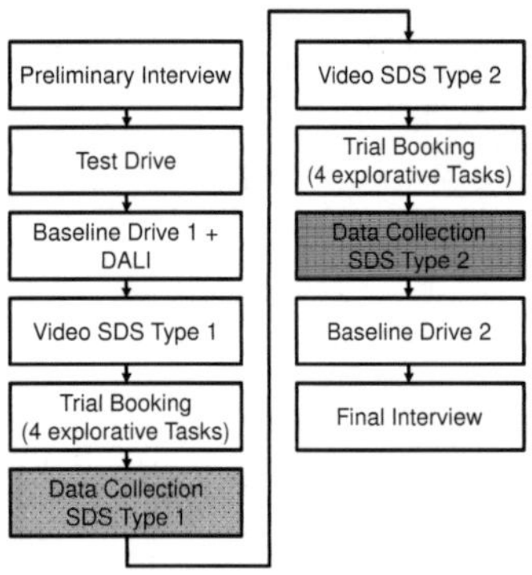

Figure 4: Overall Procedure of the Experiment.

3.1.5 Dependent Variables

In the experiment, we collected several types of data to evaluate the speech dialog and the driving performance data. During speech interaction the SDS produces log files, which contain the link to the recorded audio file of the spoken user utterance, the speech recognizer result, the interpretation of the natural language understanding (NLU) module, and the text-to-speech (TTS) output. Based on the log file, the whole speech dialog can be reconstructed. The driving simulation OpenDS also produces log files at runtime, which contain the steering wheel deviation for lateral control and the reaction times for longitudinal control for each recorded time frame. During the experiment, the examiner was observing the test procedure in order to take notes on task success. Based on the collected data, the measures illustrated in Table 1 were computed in order to evaluate the speech dialog and the driving performance. A detailed description and definition of the measures can be found in (Möller, 2005).

In this preliminary analysis, due to time constraints, only the first block of each participant could be transcribed and analyzed. In this report,

	Measure	Data Source
Speech Dialog Performance Measures	TS	Observations
	NoT	SDS logs
	DD	SDS logs
	CER	SDS logs
	Subjective Usability Assessment	SASSI, Final Interview
Driving Performance Measures	MDev	OpenDS logs
	Subjective Assessment of Cognitive Load	DALI, Final Interview

Table 1: Evaluation Measures of the Experiment.

we focus on the SDS performance. Based on the observations the task success (TS) of each speech dialog is assessed. The speech dialog logs are used to compute the Number of Turns (NoT) and the dialog duration (DD) of each dialog. We assess the concept error rate (CER) of each user utterance within a dialog instead of the word error rate (WER) since this value is crucial to a successful speech dialog. A subjective usability assessment is achieved by employing the SASSI questionnaire. Based on the OpenDS logs we compute the mean deviation (MDev) of the steering wheel. In the next step, the reaction time, the DALI questionnaire and the final interview are analyzed.

Overall, we expect better usability evaluation for the conversational dialog conditions compared with the command-based condition. The participants will accept the conversational dialog better than the command-based dialog because if reflects the human-human communication. Furthermore, we expect the conversational dialog to distract less than the command-based dialog because it is easier to control. Generally, a visual feedback makes it more comfortable to interact with an SDS. Therefore, we expect the participants to accept the SDS with GUI better than without GUI. However, concerning the influence of the GUI on the driving performance, we expect the GUI to cause more driver distraction due to the glances onto the GUI screen.

3.2 Results

In the following, the preliminary results concerning SDS quality and driving performance are presented. In total, 48 command-based dialogs and 44 conversational dialogs were transcribed and analyzed. First, the results of the speech dialog evaluation are described, followed by the results of the driving performance evaluation. When comparing the two speech dialog strategies ("Comm" vs. "Conv") dependent t-tests for paired examples have been applied. Concerning the comparison of the 4 GUI conditions ("CommGUI" vs. "CommNoGUI", "ConvGUI" vs. "ConvNoGUI") the repeated measures anova test was applied. For each comparison, a significance level α =0,05 was assumed.

3.2.1 Speech Dialog

In this Section, first, the results of the speech dialog performance measures are presented, followed by the results of the questionnaires.

Task Success: In the first block of each experiment, each participant had to solve 4 tasks while data was recorded. Each of the 92 dialogs were finished with a hotel booking. If the participant booked a hotel, which did not match the task requirements the task was annotated as failed. Figure 5 shows the percentage of solved tasks for both speech dialog strategies (left) and additionally split according to the two GUI conditions (right). Using the command-based SDS prototype, participants were able to solve 95,8% of the tasks. 93,8% of the tasks could be solved when using the conversational prototype. Participants solved tasks more effective when using the command-based prototype with GUI than without GUI. In contrast, the participants solved more tasks successfully when using the conversational prototype without GUI than with GUI. However, none of the differences was found to be significant.

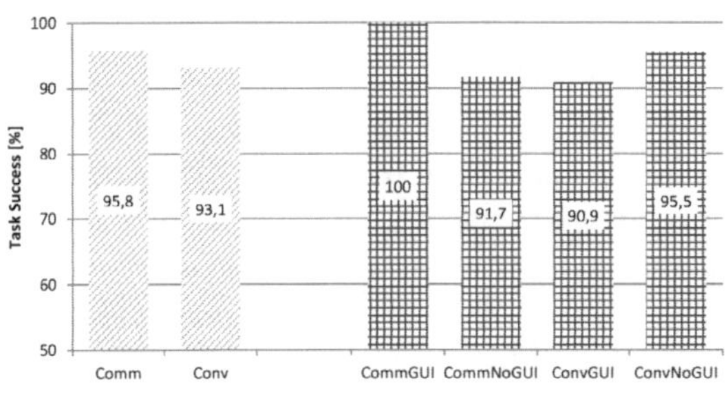

Figure 5: Overall TS rates.

Number of Turns: Figure 6 presents the average NoT. The high number of turns is due to the list browsing the user has to perform in order to find the matching hotel. Using the conversational SDS prototype, significantly fewer dialog turns were needed than using the command-based SDS prototype (p=0,047). The conditions without GUI needed less turns than the conditions with GUI. However, no significant differences were found when comparing the conditions with GUI with the conditions without GUI.

Dialog Duration: In Figure 7 the average DD is illustrated. The dialogs of the conversational

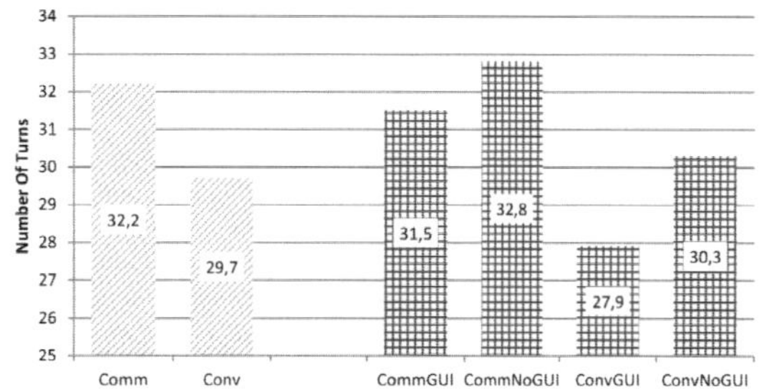

Figure 6: Average NoT per speech dialog.

speech dialogs were significantly shorter than the command-based speech dialogs (p=0,003). Comparing the GUI conditions within one speech dialog strategy, it seems that participants using the conversational speech dialog needed less time to accomplish a task when they could use the GUI. However, there was no significant difference revealed. Concerning the GUI conditions of the command-based dialog, no significant differences could be found, too.

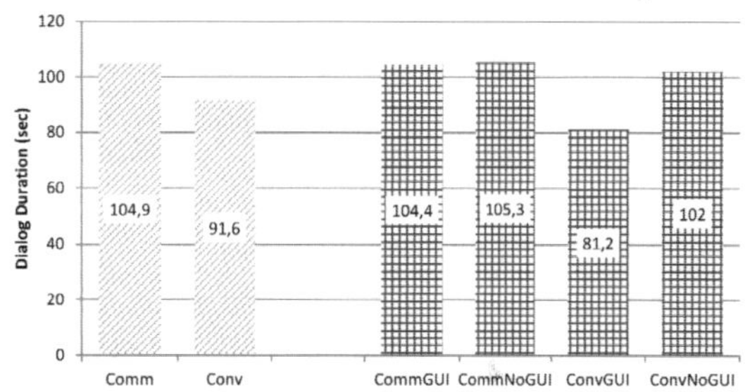

Figure 7: Average DD per speech dialog.

Concept Error Rate: The average CER per dialog is significantly smaller in the command-based speech dialog compared to the conversational speech dialog strategy (p=0,02) (see Figure 8). When comparing the GUI conditions within one speech dialog strategy, it seems that less concept errors occurred when the participants used the SDS prototypes supported by a GUI. However, no significant differences were found.

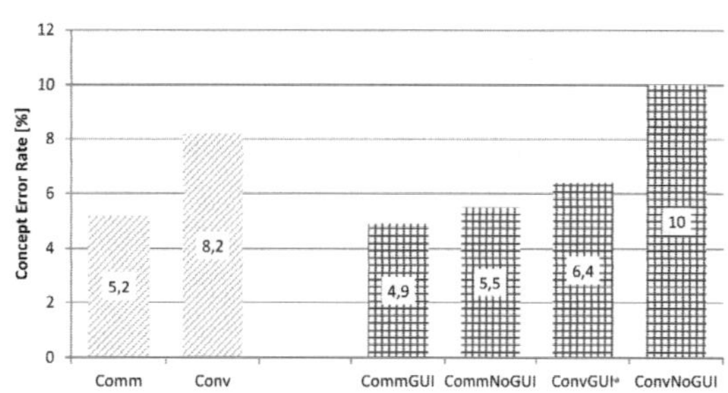

Figure 8: Average CER per speech dialog.

SASSI: The overall result of the SASSI questionnaire is illustrated in Figure 9. All SDS achieve a positive usability assessment. The conversational dialog is slightly better accepted by the user. It seems that the users accept the SDS supported by a GUI better than without a GUI. However, for none of the comparisons significant differences were found.

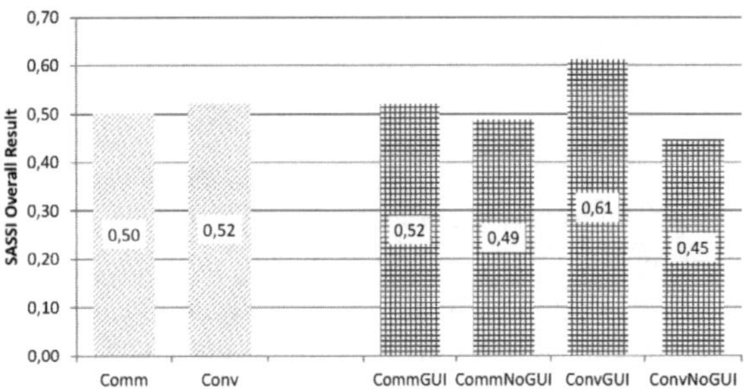

Figure 9: Overall SASSI result per speech dialog.

3.2.2 Driving Performance

In this Section a preliminary driving performance result is presented.

Mean Deviation: Figure 10 shows the MDev of the baseline drive (left), both speech dialog strategies (middle) and additionally split according to the two GUI conditions (right). The MDev of the baseline drive is 0,1. The MDev was significantly smaller when the participants used the command-based speech dialog (p=0,01) while driving compared to the conversational dialog. No significant differences were found when comparing the conditions with GUI with the conditions without GUI.

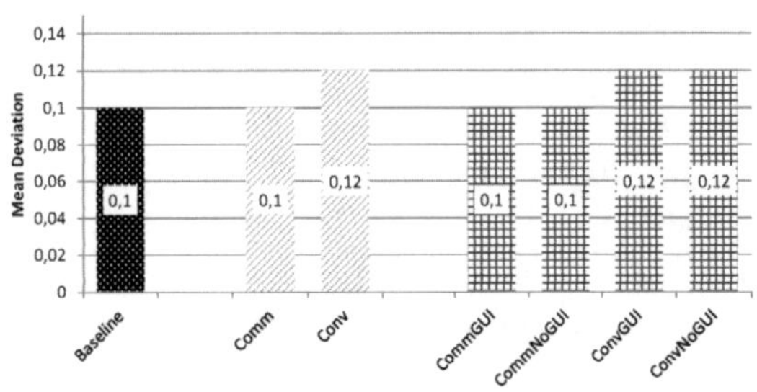

Figure 10: Average MDev per speech dialog.

3.3 Discussion

The preliminary results show that the participants were able to successfully finish the tasks with both SDS prototype variants. All SDS prototypes achieved a positive subjective usability assessment. Although the CER is higher when using the conversational dialog, it performs more efficient than the command-based dialog which is due to the possibility to input multiple parameters at once. The MDev of the baseline drive is as high as when using the command-based speech dialog while driving. Usually, one would expect a better driving performance when performing no secondary task. However, the ConTRe task is a quite difficult task since it continuously mentally demands the user. Therefore, the MDev is relatively high when only the driving task is performed. The conversational speech dialog distracts more from driving than the command-based dialog. Using the command-based dialog, the user is guided by the system step-by-step, which makes it easier to use. The mental demand when using the command-based SDS might be lower and therefore, this dialog strategy might be less distractive.

Concerning the comparison of the GUI conditions the results indicate that the conditions with GUI are more user-friendly than the conditions without GUI. However, we did not find any significant differences, yet, since the data set is too small when comparing the GUI conditions. When the whole data set of the experiment is analyzed further significances might be revealed.

4 Conclusions

This paper reports from a very recent driving simulation study and its preliminary results which are conducted in order to compare different speech dialog strategies. The use of command-based and conversational SDS prototypes while driving is evaluated on usability and driving performance. Different GUIs are designed in order to support the respective dialog strategy the most and to evaluate the effect of the GUI on usability and driver distraction. The preliminary results show that the conversational speech dialog performs more efficient than the command-based dialog. However, the conversational dialog distracts more from driving than the command-based. Furthermore, the results indicate that an SDS supported by a GUI is more efficient and better accepted by the user than without GUI.

In the next step, the data set will be analyzed on all mentioned usability and driving performance measures. The different subdialog types of each dialog will be investigated in detail on dialog performance and speaking styles. Furthermore, crosslinks between subdialogs and the driving performance measures are analyzed.

References

L. Devillers and H. Bonneau-Maynard. 1998. Evaluation of dialog strategies for a tourist information retrieval system. In *Proc. ICSLP*, pages 1187–1190.

Driver Focus-Telematics Working Group. 2002. Statement of principles, criteria and verification procedures on driver interactions with advanced in-vehicle information and communication systems. *Alliance of Automotive Manufacturers*.

Governors Highway Safety Association. 2011. Distracted driving: What research shows and what states can do. Technical report, U.S. Department of Transportation.

H. Hofmann, U. Ehrlich, A. Berton, and W. Minker. 2012a. Speech interaction with the internet - a user study. In *Proceedings of Intelligent Environments*, Guanajuato, Mexico, June.

H. Hofmann, Anna Silberstein, U. Ehrlich, A. Berton, and A. Mahr. 2012b. Development of speech-based in-car hmi concepts for information exchange internet apps. In *Proceedings of International Workshop on Spoken Dialogue Systems*, Paris, France, December.

K. S. Hone and R. Graham. 2001. Subjective assessment of speech-system interface usability. In *Proceedings of Eurospeech*.

Angela Mahr, Michael Feld, Mohammad Mehdi Moniri, and Rafael Math. 2012. The ConTRe (continuous tracking and reaction) task: A flexible approach for assessing driver cognitive workload with high sensitivity. In *Adjunct Proceedings of the 4th International Conference on Automotive User Interfaces and Interactive Vehicular Applications*, pages 88–91, Portsmouth, United States.

Stefan Mattes. 2003. The lane-change-task as a tool for driver distraction evaluation. *Proceedings of IGfA*, pages 1–30.

Sebastian Möller. 2005. Parameters describing the interaction with spoken dialogue systems. ITU-T Recommendation Supplement 24 to P-Series, International Telecommunication Union, Geneva, Switzerland, October. Based on ITU-T Contr. COM 12-17 (2009).

Hartmut Mutschler, Frank Steffens, and Andreas Korthauer. 2007. Final report on multimodal experiments - part 1: Evaluation of the sammie system. d6.4. talk public deliverables. Technical report.

Annie Pauzie. 2008. Evaluating driver mental workload using the driving activity load index (DALI). In *Proceedings of European Conference on Human Interface Design for Intelligent Transport Systems*, pages 67–77.

Matthias Peissner, Vanessa Doebler, and Florian Metze. 2011. Can voice interaction help reducing the level of distraction and prevent accidents? meta-study on driver distraction and voice interaction. Technical report, Fraunhofer-Institute for Industrial Engineering (IAO) and Carnegie Mellon University.

Predicting Tasks in Goal-Oriented Spoken Dialog Systems using Semantic Knowledge Bases

Aasish Pappu and Alexander I. Rudnicky
Language Technologies Institute
Carnegie Mellon University
{aasish, air}@cs.cmu.edu

Abstract

Goal-oriented dialog agents are expected to recognize user-intentions from an utterance and execute appropriate tasks. Typically, such systems use a semantic parser to solve this problem. However, semantic parsers could fail if user utterances contain out-of-grammar words/phrases or if the semantics of uttered phrases did not match the parser's expectations. In this work, we have explored a more robust method of task prediction. We define task prediction as a classification problem, rather than "parsing" and use semantic contexts to improve classification accuracy. Our classifier uses semantic smoothing kernels that can encode information from knowledge bases such as Wordnet, NELL and Freebase.com. Our experiments on two spoken language corpora show that augmenting semantic information from these knowledge bases gives about 30% absolute improvement in task prediction over a parser-based method. Our approach thus helps make a dialog agent more robust to user input and helps reduce number of turns required to detected intended tasks.

1 Introduction

Spoken dialog agents are designed with particular tasks in mind. These agents could provide information or make reservations, or other such tasks. Many dialog agents often can perform multiple tasks: think of a customer service kiosk system at a bank. The system has to decide which task it has to perform by talking to its user. This problem of identifying what to do based on what a user has said is called task prediction.

Task prediction is typically framed as a parsing problem: A grammar is written to semantically parse the input utterance from users, and these semantic labels in combination are used to decide what the intended task is. However, this method is less robust to errors in user-input. A dialog system consists of a pipeline of cascaded modules, such as speech recognition, parsing, dialog management. Any errors made by these modules propogate and accumulate through the pipeline. Bohus and Rudnicky (2005) have shown that this cascade of errors, coupled with users employing out-of-grammar phrases results in many "non-understanding" and "misunderstanding" errors.

There have been other approaches to perform dialog task prediction. Gorin et al. (1997) has proposed a salience-phrase detection technique that maps phrases to their corresponding tasks. Chu-Carroll and Carpenter (1999) casted the task detection as an information retrieval — detect tasks by measuring the distance between the query vector and representative text for each task. Bui (2003) and Blaylock and Allen (2006) have cast it as a hierarchical sequence labeling problem using Hidden Markov Models (HMM). More recently, (Bangalore and Stent, 2009) built an incremental parser that gradually determines the task based on the incoming dialog utterances. (Chen and Mooney, 2010) have developed a route instructions frame parser to determine the task in the context of a mobile dialog robot. These approaches mainly use local features such as dialog context, speech features and grammar-based-semantic features to determine the task. However grammar-based-semantic features would be insufficient if an utterance uses semantically similar phrases that are not in the system's domain or semantics. If the system could explore semantic information beyond the scope of its local knowledge and use external knowledge sources then they will help improve the task prediction.

(Cristianini et al., 2002) (Wang and Domeniconi, 2008) (Moschitti, 2009) found that open-domain semantic knowledge resources are useful for text classification problems. Their success in limited data scenario is an attractive prospect, since most dialog agents operate in scarce training data scenarios. (Bloehdorn et al., 2006) has proposed a semantic smoothing kernel based approach for text classification. The intuition behind their approach is that terms (particularly content words) of two similar sentences or documents share superconcepts (e.g., hypernyms) in a knowledge base. Semantic Similarity between two terms can be computed using different metrics (Pedersen et al., 2004) based on resources like WordNet.

Open domain resources such as world-wide-web, had been used in the context of speech recognition. (Misu and Kawahara, 2006) and (Creutz et al., 2009) used web-texts to improve the language models for speech recognition in a target domain. They have used a dialog corpus in order to query relevant web-texts to build the target domain models. Although (Araki, 2012) did not conduct empirical experiments, yet they have presented an interesting architecture that exploits an open-domain resource like Freebase.com to build spoken dialog systems.

In this work, we have framed the task prediction problem as a classification problem. We use the user's utterances to extract lexical semantic features and classify it into being one of the many tasks the system was designed to perform. We harness the power of semantic knowledge bases by bootstraping an utterance with semantic concepts related to the tokens in the utterance. The semantic distance/similarity between concepts in the knowledge base is incorporated into the model using a kernel. We show that our approach improves the task prediction accuracy over a grammar-based approach on two spoken corpora (1) Navagati (Pappu and Rudnicky, 2012): a corpus of spoken route instructions, and (2) Roomline (Bohus, 2003): a corpus of spoken dialog sessions in room-reservation domain.

This paper is organized as following: Section 2 describes the problem of dialog task prediction and the standard grammar based approach to predict the dialog task. Then in Section 3, we describe the open-domain knowledge resources that were used in our approach and their advantages/disadvantages. We will discuss our semantic kernel based approach in the Section 4. We report our experiment results on task prediction in Section 5. In Section 6, we will analyze the errors that occur in our approach, followed by concluding remarks and possible directions to this work.

2 Parser based Dialog Task Prediction

In a dialog system, there are two functions of a semantic grammar — encode linguistic constructs used during the interactions and represent the domain knowledge in-terms of concepts and their instances. Table 1 illustrates the tasks and the concepts used in a navigation domain grammar. The linguistic constructions help the parser to segment an utterance into meaningful chunks. The domain knowledge helps in labeling the tokens/phrases with concepts. The parser uses the labeled tokens and the chunked form of the utterance, to classify the utterance into one of the tasks.

Table 1: Tasks and Concepts in Grammar

Tasks	Examples
Imperative	GoToPlace, Turn, etc
Advisory Instructions	You_Will_See_Location
Grounding Instructions	You_are_at_Location
Concepts	**Examples**
Locations	buildings, other landmarks
Adjectives-of-Locations	large, open, black, small etc.
Pathways	hallway, corridor, bridge, etc.
LiftingDevice	elevator, staircase, etc.
Spatial Relations	behind, above, on left, etc.
Numbers	turn-angles, distance, etc.
Ordinals	first, second, etc. floor numbers

The dialog agent uses the root node of a parser output as the task. Figure 1 illustrates a semantic parser output for a fictitious utterance in the navigation domain. The dialog manager would consider the utterance as an "Imperative" for this example.

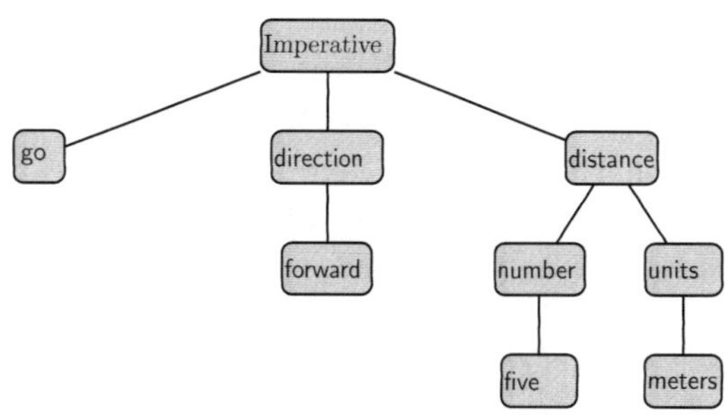

Figure 1: Illustration of Semantic Parse Tree used in a Dialog System

2.1 Grammar: A Knowledge Resource

Grammar is a very useful resource for a dialog system because it could potentially represent an expert's view of the domain. Since knowledge engineering requires time and effort, very few dialog systems can afford to have grammars that are expert-crafted and robust to various artefacts of spoken language. This becomes a major challenge for real world dialog systems. If the system's grammar or the domain knowledge does not conform to its users and their utterances, the parser will fail to produce a correct parse, if the parse is incorrect and/or the concept labeling is incorrect. Lack of comprehensive semantic knowledge is the cause of this problem. An open-domain knowledge base like Wordnet (Miller, 1995), Freebase (Bollacker et al., 2008) or NELL (Carlson et al., 2010) contains comprehensive information about concepts and their relationships present in the world. If used appropriately, open-domain knowledge resources can help compensate for incomplete semantic knowledge of the system.

3 Open-Domain Semantic Knowledge Bases

Like grammars, open-domain knowledge resources contain concepts, instances and relations. The purpose of these resources is to organize common sense and factoid information known to the mankind in a machine-understandable form. These resources, if filtered appropriately, contain valuable domain-specific information for a dialog agent. To this end, we propose to use three knowledge resources along with the domain grammar for the task prediction. A brief overview of each of the knowledge resources is given below:

3.1 Wordnet: Expert Knowledge Base

Wordnet (Miller, 1995) is an online lexical database of words and their semantics curated by language experts. It organizes the words and their morphological variants in a hierarchical fashion. Every word has at least one synset i.e., sense and a synset has definite meaning and a gloss to illustrate the usage. Synsets are connected through relationships such as hypernyms, hyponyms, meronyms, antonyms etc. Each synset can be considered as an instance and their parent synsets as concepts. Although Wordnet contains several (120,000) word forms, some of our domain-specific word forms (e.g., locations in a navigation domain) will not be present. Therefore, we would like to use other open-domain knowledge bases to augment the agent's knowledge.

3.2 Freebase: Community Knowledge Base

Freebase.com (Bollacker et al., 2008) is a collaboratively evolving knowledge base with the effort of volunteers. It organizes the facts based on types/concepts along with several predicates/properties and their values for each fact. The types are arranged in a hierarchy and the hierarchy is rooted at "domain". Freebase facts are constantly updated by the volunteers. Therefore, it is a good resource to help bootstrap the domain knowledge of a dialog agent.

3.3 NELL: Automated Knowledge Base

Never-Ending Language Learner(NELL) (Carlson et al., 2010) is a program that learns and organizes the facts from the web in an unsupervised fashion. NELL is on the other end of the knowledge base spectrum which is not curated either by experts or by volunteers. NELL uses a two-step approach to learn new facts: (1) extract information from the text using pattern-based, semi-structured relation extractors (2) improve the learning for next iteration based on the evidence from previous iteration. Every belief/fact in its knowledge base has concepts, source urls, extraction patterns, predicate, the surface forms of the facts and a confidence score for the belief. Although the facts could be noisy in comparison to ones in other knowledge bases, NELL continually adds and improves the facts without much human effort.

4 Semantic Kernel based Dialog Task Prediction

We would like to use this apriori knowledge about the world and the domain to help us predict the dialog task. The task prediction problem can be treated as a classification problem. Classification algorithms typically use bag-of-words representation that converts a document or sentence into a vector with terms as components of the vector. This representation produces very good results in scenarios with sufficient training data. However in a limited training data or extreme sparseness scenario such as ours, (Siolas and d'Alché Buc, 2000) has shown that Semantic Smoothing Kernel technique is a promising approach. The major advantage of this approach is that they can incorporate apriori knowledge from existing knowledge bases. The semantic dependencies between terms, dependencies between concepts and instances, can be encoded in these kernels. The semantic kernels can be easily plugged into a kernel based classifier help us predict the task from the goal-oriented dialog utterances.

In our experiments, we used an implementation of Semantic Kernel from (Bloehdorn et al., 2006) and plugged it into a Support Vector Machine (SVM) classifier (SVM^{light}) (Joachims, 1999). As a part of experimental setup, we will describe the details of how did we extract the semantic dependencies from each knowledge base and encoded them into the kernel.

5 Experiments

Our goal is to improve the task prediction for a given spoken dialog utterance by providing additional semantic context to the utterance with the help of relevant semantic concepts from the semantic knowledge bases. The baseline approach would use the Phoenix parser's output to determine the intended task for an utterance. From our experiments, we show that our knowledge-driven approach will improve upon the baseline performance on two corpora (1) Navagati Corpus: a navigation directions corpus (2) Roomline Corpus: a room reservation dialog corpus.

5.1 Setup

We have divided each corpus into training and testing datasets. We train our task classification models on the manual transcriptions of the training data and evaluated the models on the ASR output of the testing data. Both Navagati and Roomline corpora came with manually annotated task labels and manual transcriptions for the utterances. We filtered out the non-task utterances such as "yes", "no" and other clarifications from the Roomline corpus. We obtained the ASR output for the Navagati corpus by running the test utterances through PocketSphinx (Huggins-Daines et al., 2006). The Roomline corpus already had the ASR output for the utterances. Table 2 illustrates some of the statistics for each corpus.

Our baseline model for the task detection is the Phoenix (Ward, 1991) parser output, which is the default method used in the Ravenclaw/Olympus dialog systems (Bohus et al., 2007). For the Navagati Corpus we have obtained the parser output using the grammar and method described in (Pappu and Rudnicky, 2012). For the Roomline corpus, we extracted the parser output from the session logs from the the corpus distribution.

Corpus-Stats	**Navagati**	**RoomLine**
Tasks	4	7
Words	503	498
Word-Error-rate	46.3%	25.6%
Task Utts	934	1891[1]
Task Training-Utts	654	1324
Task Testing-Utts	280	567
Tasks		
	N1. Meta	R1. NeedRoom
	N2. Advisory	R2. ChooseRoom
	N3. Imperative	R3. QueryFeatures
	N4. Grounding	R4. ListRooms
		R5. Identification
		R6. CancelReservation
		R7. RejectRooms

Table 2: Corpus Statistics

5.1.1 Semantic Facts to Semantic Kernel

The semantic kernel takes a term proximity matrix as an input, then produces a positive semidefinite matrix which can be used inside the kernel function. In our case, we build a term proximity matrix for the words in the recognition vocabulary. (Bloehdorn et al., 2006) found that using the term-concept pairs in the proximity matrix is more meaningful following the intuition that terms that share more number of concepts are similar as opposed to terms that share fewer concepts. We have used following measures to compute the proximity value P and some of them are specific to respective knowledge bases:

- `gra`: No weighting for term-concept pairs in the Grammar, i.e.,
  $P = 1$, for all concepts c_i of t, $P = 0$ otherwise.

- `fb`: Weighting using normalized Freebase.com relevance score, i.e.,

$$P = \frac{fbscore(t, c_i) - fbscore(t, c_{min})}{fbscore(t, c_{max}) - fbscore(t, c_{min})} \quad (1)$$

- `nell`: Weighting for the NELL term-concept pairs using the probability for a belief i.e.,

$$P = nellprob(t, c_i) \quad (2)$$

  , for all concepts c_i of t, $P = 0$ otherwise.

[1] Originally has 10356 utts; filtered out non-task utts.

- `wnpath`: Weighting for the term-concept pairs in the Wordnet based on the shortest path, i.e.,

$$P = wn_{PATH}(t, c_i) \quad (3)$$

for all concepts c_i of t, $P = 0$ otherwise.

- `wnlch`: Weighting for the term-concept pairs in the Wordnet based on the Leacock-Chodorow Similiarity, i.e.,

$$P = wn_{LCH}(t, c_i) \quad (4)$$

for all concepts c_i of t, $P = 0$ otherwise.

- `wnwup`: Weighting for the term-concept pairs in the Wordnet based on the Wu-Palmer Similarity, i.e.,

$$P = wn_{WUP}(t, c_i) \quad (5)$$

for all concepts c_i of t, $P = 0$ otherwise.

- `wnres`: Weighting for the term-concept pairs in the Wordnet based on the Resnik Similarity using Information Content, i.e.,

$$P = wn_{RES}(t, c_i) \quad (6)$$

for all concepts c_i of t, $P = 0$ otherwise.

To create a grammar-based proximity matrix, we extracted the concept-token pairs from the parser output on the reference transcriptions in both corpora. In order to create a wordnet-based proximity matrix, we retrieve the hypernyms for the corresponding from Wordnet using the Wordnet 3.0 database [2]. For the freebase concept-token pairs, we query tokens for a list of types with the help of the MQL query interface[3] to the freebase. To retrieve beliefs from NELL we downloaded a tsv formatted database called every-belief-in-the-KB[4] and then queried for facts using unix `grep` command.

5.2 Results

Our objective is to evalute the effect of augmented semantic features on the task detection. As noted earlier, we divided both corpora into training and testing datasets. We build our models on the manual transcriptions from the training data and evaluate on the ASR hypotheses of the testing data. For the Navagati corpus, we use the same training-testing split that we used in our previous work because the grammar was developed based on the training data. For the Roomline corpus, we randomly sample 30% of the testing data from the entire corpus.

Our first semantic-kernel based model SEM-GRA uses the domain grammar as a "knowledge base". This is a two step process: (1) we extract the concept-token pairs from the parse output of the training data. (2) Then, assign a uniform proximity score (1.0) for all pairs of words that appear under a particular concept otherwise 0.0 (`gra` as mentioned in the previous section). We augment the grammar concepts to the utterances in the datasets, learn SEM-GRA model and classify the test-hypotheses. For all our models we use a fixed $C = 0.07$ value (soft-margin parameter) for the SVM classifiers. This model achieved highest performance at this value during a parameter-sweep. SEM-GRA model outperformed the parser-baseline on both datasets (see Table 3). It clearly takes advantage of the domain knowledge encoded in the form of semantic-relatedness between concepts and token pairs.

What if a dialog system does not have grammar to begin with? We use the same two step process to build semantic-kernel based models using one open-domain knowledge base at a time. We built Wordnet based models (SEM-WNWUP, SEM-WNPATH, SEM-WNLCH, SEM-WNRES) using different proximity measures described in the previous section. From Table 3 SEM-WNRES model, one that uses information content performs the best among all wordnet based models. In order to compute the information content we used the pair-wise mutual information scores available for brown-corpus.dat in the NLTK (Bird et al., 2009) distribution. Other path based scores were also computed using NLTK API for Wordnet.

We observed that our wordnet-based models capture relatedness between most-common nouns (e.g., room numbers) and their concepts but not for some of the less-common ones (e.g., location names). To compensate this imbalance, we use larger knowledge resources freebase.com and NELL. First we searched for the facts in each of these knowledge bases using every token in the vocabulary of both corpora. We pick the top concept for each token based on the score provided by the respective search interfaces. In freebase we have

[2] http://www.princeton.edu/wordnet/download/
[3] https://www.googleapis.com/freebase/v1/search
[4] http://rtw.ml.cmu.edu/rtw/resources

Table 3: F1 (in %) comparison of parse baseline against semantic-kernel models with their corresponding similarity metrics

Corpus	baseline	SEMGRA	SEMWNWUP	SEMWNPATH	SEMWNLCH	SEMWNRES	SEMFBASE	SEMNELL
Navagati	40.1	65.8	67.1	67.7	66.4	**69**	68.7	66.2
Roomline	54.3	79.7	77.3	79.5	79.6	**80.6**	83.3	81.1

about 100 concepts that are relevant to the vocabulary and in the NELL model we have about 250 concepts that are relevant to the vocabulary in each of the corpora. The models based on NELL (SEM-NELL) and Freebase (SEM-FBASE) capture relatedness between less-common nouns and their concepts. We can see that both of these models perform comparable to the domain grammar model SEM-GRA which also captures the relatedness between less-common nouns and their concepts. We believe that both freebase and NELL has a superior performance because of wider-range of concept coverage and non-uniform proximity measures used in the semantic kernel, which gives a better judgement of relatedness than a uniform measure used in the SEM-GRA model.

Since we observed that an individual model is good at capturing a particular aspect of an utterance, we extended the individual semantic models by combining the proximity matrices from each of them and augmenting their semantic concepts to the training and testing datasets. We built four combined models as shown in Table 4 by varying the wordnet's proximity metric to identify which one of them works best in combination with other semantic metrics. The `wnres` metric performs the best both in standalone and combination settings. (Bloehdorn et al., 2006) also found that `wnres` particularly performs well for lower values of the soft-margin parameter in their experiments.

Table 4: F1-Score (in %): Models with semantics combined from different KBs (ALL-KB)

Model	Navagati	Roomline
GRA+WNWUP+FBASE+NELL	70.8	82.2
GRA+WNPATH+FBASE+NELL	70.1	81.4
GRA+WNLCH+FBASE+NELL	70.8	81.3
GRA+WNRES+FBASE+NELL	**73.4**	**83.7**

6 Discussion

We have built a model that exploits different semantic knowledge bases and predicts the task on both corpora with high accuracy. But how is it affected by factors like misrecognition and context ambiguity?

6.1 Influence of Recognition Errors

When the recognition is bad, it is obvious that the accuracy would go down. We would like to know which of these knowledge resources can augment useful semantics despite misrecognitions. Table 2 shows that WER on the Navagati corpus is about 46% and the Roomline corpus is about 25%. We compared the F1-score of different models on utterances for different ranges of WER as shown in the Figure 2 on the Navagati Corpus. We notice that the model built using all knowledge bases is more robust even at higher WER. We did similar analysis on the Roomline corpus and did not notice any differences across models due to relatively lower WER (25.6%).

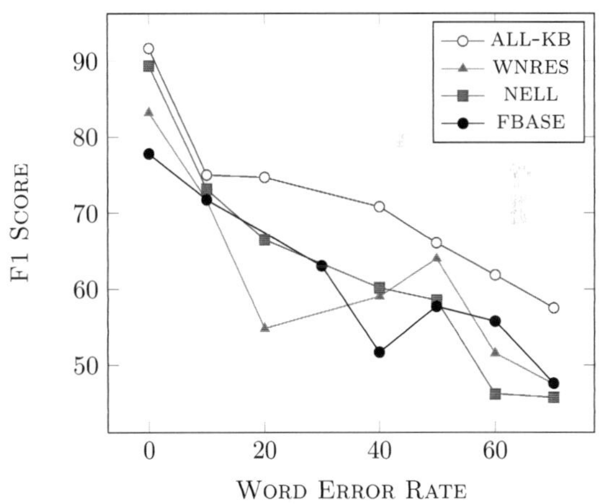

Figure 2: Word Error Rate vs F1-Score for KB-based Models on Navagati Corpus

6.2 Confusion among Tasks

We found that a particular pair of tasks are more confusing than others. Here we present an analysis of such confusion pairs for both corpora for different classification models. Table 5 and Table 6 show the pairs of tasks that are most confused in the experiments. The ALL-KB model (a combination of all knowledge bases) has least number of

Table 5: Most confusable pairs of tasks in Navagati Corpus for KB based classification models (See Table 2 for task labels)

KBType	ALL-KB		SEM-WNRES		SEM-NELL		SEM-FBASE		
ActualTask	N2	N4	N2	N4	N2	N4	N1	N2	N4
Predicted	N3	N1	N3	N3	N3	N3	N3	N3	N3
ConfusionPerTask	10.5%	27.7%	26.3%	33.3%	26.3%	38.8%	22.2%	28.9%	44.4%

Table 6: Most confusable pairs of tasks in Roomline Corpus for KB based classification models (See Table 2 for task labels)

KBType	ALL-KB	SEM-WNRES		SEM-NELL		SEM-FBASE			
ActualTask	R4	R4	R6	R4	R6	R3	R4	R5	R6
Predicted	R3	R5	R5	R1	R1	R1	R3	R1	R1
ConfusionPerTask	36.6%	48.7%	44.4%	25.6%	44.5%	32.5%	23%	53.4%	55.5%

confusion pairs among all the models. This is due to more relevant concepts are augmented to an utterance compared to fewer relevant concepts that augmented while using individual models.

We inspected the confused tasks by examining the feature vectors of misclassified examples. While using the ALL-KB model 10% of the utterances from N2 (Advisory) were confused for N3 (Imperative) because of phrases like "your left", "your right". These phrases were often associated with N3 utterances. To recovery from such ambiguities, the agent could ask a clarification question e.g., "are we talking about going there or find it on the way?" to resolve the differences between these tasks. The system could not only get clarification but also bootstrap the original utterance of the user with the clarification to gather additional context to retrain the task detection models. The individual models were also confused about N2 and N3 tasks, where we could use similar clarification strategies to improve the task prediction. 27% of the N4 (grounding about current robot's position) utterances were confused for N1 (meta comments about the robot's rounavigation route) because these utterances shared more number of freebase concepts with the N1 model. The system could resolve such utterances by asking a clarification question "are we talking about the current position?". Individual models i.e., SEM-WNRES, SEM-FBASE and SEM-NELL suffered mostly from the lack of concepts capturing semantics related to all types of entities (e.g., most common nouns, less common entities etc.,) found in an utterance.

We examined the confusion pairs in the Roomline corpus and observed that R4 (ListRooms) and R3 (Queries) tasks were most confused in the ALL-KB model. On closer inspection, we found that R4 utterances are about listing the rooms that are retrieved by the system. Whereas, R3 utterances are about asking whether a room has a facility (e.g., projector availability). In the ambiguous utterances, often the R4 utterances were about filtering the list of rooms by a facility type.

7 Conclusion

We proposed framing the dialog task prediction problem as a classification problem. We used an SVM classifier with semantic smoothing kernels that incorporate information from external knowledge bases such as Wordnet, NELL, Freebase. Our method shows good improvements over a parser-based baseline. Our analysis also shows that our proposed method makes task prediction be more robust to moderate recognition errors.

We presented an analysis on task ambiguity and found that these models can confuse one task for another. We believe that this analysis highlights the need for dialog based clarification strategies that cannot only help the system for that instance but also help the system improve its task prediction accuracy in future dialog sessions.

8 Future Work

This work stands as a platform to make a spoken dialog system learn relevant semantic information from external knowledge sources. We would like to extend this paradigm to let the system acquire more information through dialog with a user. The system could elicit new references to a known semantic concept. For example, a navigation agent knows a task called "GoToRestaurant" but the user-utterance had the word "diner" and it was not seen in the context of "restaurant". The agent somewhat predicts this utterance is related to "GoToRestaurant" using the approach described in this paper. It could ask the user an elicitation question: "You used diner in the context of a restaurant, is diner really a restaurant?". The answer to this question will help the system gradually understand what parts of an open-domain knowledge base can be added into its own domain knowledge base. We believe that the holistic approach of learning from automated processes and learning through dialog, will help the dialog systems get better interaction by interaction.

References

Masahiro Araki. 2012. Rapid development process of spoken dialogue systems using collaboratively constructed semantic resources. In *Proceedings of the 13th Annual Meeting of the Special Interest Group on Discourse and Dialogue*, pages 70–73, Seoul, South Korea, July. Association for Computational Linguistics.

Srinivas Bangalore and Amanda J Stent. 2009. Incremental parsing models for dialog task structure. In *Proceedings of the 12th Conference of the European Chapter of the Association for Computational Linguistics*, pages 94–102. Association for Computational Linguistics.

Steven Bird, Ewan Klein, and Edward Loper. 2009. *Natural language processing with Python*. O'Reilly Media.

Nate Blaylock and James Allen. 2006. Hierarchical instantiated goal recognition. In *Proceedings of the AAAI Workshop on Modeling Others from Observations*.

Stephan Bloehdorn, Roberto Basili, Marco Cammisa, and Alessandro Moschitti. 2006. Semantic kernels for text classification based on topological measures of feature similarity. In *Data Mining, 2006. ICDM'06. Sixth International Conference on*, pages 808–812. IEEE.

Dan Bohus and Alexander I Rudnicky. 2005. Sorry, I didn't catch that!-an investigation of non-understanding errors and recovery strategies. In *6th SIGdial Workshop on Discourse and Dialogue*.

Dan Bohus, Antoine Raux, Thomas K Harris, Maxine Eskenazi, and Alexander I Rudnicky. 2007. Olympus: an open-source framework for conversational spoken language interface research. In *Proceedings of the workshop on bridging the gap Academic and industrial research in dialog technologies*, number April, pages 32–39. Association for Computational Linguistics.

Dan Bohus. 2003. Roomline. `http://www.cs.cmu.edu/~dbohus/RoomLine`.

Kurt Bollacker, Colin Evans, Praveen Paritosh, Tim Sturge, and Jamie Taylor. 2008. Freebase: a collaboratively created graph database for structuring human knowledge. *SIGMOD 08 Proceedings of the 2008 ACM SIGMOD international conference on Management of data*, pages 1247–1249.

Hung H Bui. 2003. A general model for online probabilistic plan recognition. In *International Joint Conference on Artificial Intelligence*, volume 18, pages 1309–1318. Citeseer.

Andrew Carlson, Justin Betteridge, Bryan Kisiel, Burr Settles, Estevam R Hruschka Jr., and Tom M Mitchell. 2010. Toward an Architecture for Never-Ending Language Learning. *Artificial Intelligence*, 2(4):1306–1313.

D.L. Chen and R.J. Mooney. 2010. Learning to interpret natural language navigation instructions from observations. *Journal of Artificial Intelligence Research*, 37:397–435.

Jennifer Chu-Carroll and Bob Carpenter. 1999. Vector-based natural language call routing. *Computational linguistics*, 25(3):361–388.

Mathias Creutz, Sami Virpioja, and Anna Kovaleva. 2009. Web augmentation of language models for continuous speech recognition of sms text messages. In *Proceedings of the 12th Conference of the European Chapter of the Association for Computational Linguistics*, pages 157–165. Association for Computational Linguistics.

Nello Cristianini, John Shawe-Taylor, and Huma Lodhi. 2002. Latent semantic kernels. *Journal of Intelligent Information Systems*, 18(2):127–152.

Allen L Gorin, Giuseppe Riccardi, and Jeremy H Wright. 1997. How may i help you? *Speech communication*, 23(1-2):113–127.

D. Huggins-Daines, M. Kumar, A. Chan, A.W. Black, M. Ravishankar, and A.I. Rudnicky. 2006. Pocketsphinx: A free, real-time continuous speech recognition system for hand-held devices. In *ICASSP*, volume 1. IEEE.

Thorsten Joachims. 1999. Making large-scale support vector machine learning practical. In *Advances in kernel methods*, pages 169–184. MIT Press.

George A Miller. 1995. WordNet: a lexical database for English. *Communications of the ACM*, 38(11):39–41.

Teruhisa Misu and Tatsuya Kawahara. 2006. A bootstrapping approach for developing language model of new spoken dialogue systems by selecting web texts. In *Proc. Interspeech*, pages 9–12.

Alessandro Moschitti. 2009. Syntactic and semantic kernels for short text pair categorization. In *Proceedings of the 12th Conference of the European Chapter of the ACL (EACL 2009)*, pages 576–584.

Aasish Pappu and Alexander I Rudnicky. 2012. The Structure and Generality of Spoken Route Instructions. *Proceedings of the 13th Annual Meeting of the Special Interest Group on Discourse and Dialogue*, pages 99–107.

Ted Pedersen, Siddharth Patwardhan, and Jason Michelizzi. 2004. WordNet:: Similarity: measuring the relatedness of concepts. In *Demonstration Papers at HLT-NAACL 2004*, pages 38–41. Association for Computational Linguistics.

Georges Siolas and Florence d'Alché Buc. 2000. Support vector machines based on a semantic kernel for text categorization. In *Neural Networks, 2000. IJCNN 2000, Proceedings of the IEEE-INNS-ENNS International Joint Conference*, volume 5, pages 205–209. IEEE.

Pu Wang and Carlotta Domeniconi. 2008. Building semantic kernels for text classification using wikipedia. In *Proceeding of the 14th ACM SIGKDD international conference on Knowledge discovery and data mining*, pages 713–721. ACM.

W. Ward. 1991. Understanding spontaneous speech: the phoenix system. In *ICASSP*. IEEE.

Surface Text based Dialogue Models for Virtual Humans

Sudeep Gandhe and **David Traum**
USC Institute for Creative Technologies,
12015 Waterfront Drive, Playa Vista, CA 90094, USA
srgandhe@gmail.com, traum@ict.usc.edu

Abstract

We present virtual human dialogue models which primarily operate on the surface text level and can be extended to incorporate additional information state annotations such as topics or results from simpler models. We compare these models with previously proposed models as well as two human-level upper baselines. The models are evaluated by collecting appropriateness judgments from human judges for responses generated for a set of fixed dialogue contexts. Our results show that the best performing models achieve close to human-level performance and require only surface text dialogue transcripts to train.

1 Introduction

Virtual Humans (VH) are autonomous agents who can play the role of humans in simulations (Rickel and Johnson, 1999; Traum et al., 2005). For these simulations to be convincing these agents must have the ability to communicate with humans and other agents using natural language. Like other dialogue system types, different architectures have been proposed for virtual human dialogue systems. These architectures can afford different features and require different sets of resources. E.g., an information state based architecture such as the one used in SASO-ST (Traum et al., 2005) can model detailed understanding of the task at hand and progression of dialogue, but at the cost of requiring resources such as information state update rules and an annotated corpus or grammar to be able to map surface text to dialogue acts.

For some virtual human dialogue genres such as simple question-answering or some negotiation domains, a simple model of dialogue progression would suffice. In such a case we can build dialogue models that primarily operate on a surface text level. These models only require surface text dialogue transcripts as a resource, and don't require expensive manual update rules, grammars, or even extensive corpus annotation.

In this paper, we describe the construction and evaluation of several models for engaging in dialogue by *selecting* an utterance that has been seen previously in a corpus. We include one model that has been used for this task previously (Gandhe and Traum, 2007b), an adaptation of a model that has been used in a similar manner, though on hand-authored data sets, rather than data sets extracted automatically from a corpus (Leuski and Traum, 2008), as well as a new set of models, using perceptrons on surface text features as well as more abstract information state annotations such as topics. We also tackle the question of evaluating such dialogue models manually as well as automatically, starting with systematically analyzing various decisions involved in the evaluation process. We situate our work with respect to previous evaluation methods.

2 Related Work

The task of a dialogue model is to formulate an utterance given a dialogue context. There are two approaches towards formulating an utterance: *Generation*, where a response is compositionally created from elements of the information state, including the context of previous utterances, and *Selection*, where a response is chosen from previously seen set of responses. In (Gandhe and Traum, 2010), we examined the theoretical potential for the selection approach, looking at a wide variety of domains, and evaluating based on similarity between the actual utterance and the best match in the previously seen corpus. We saw a wide variance in scores across domains, both as to the similarity scores and improvement of scores as more data is considered. For task-oriented planning domains, such as Monroe (Stent, 2000) and

TRAINS (Heeman and Allen, 1994), as well as open conversation in Switchboard (Godfrey et al., 1992), the performance was very low. On the other hand, for more limited domains such as simple question-answering (Leuski et al., 2006) or role-play negotiation in a scenario, the performance was high, with METEOR scores averaging over 0.8.

One possible selection criterion is to assume that the most appropriate response is the most probable response according to a model trained on human-human dialogues. More formally, let there be a dialogue $\langle u_1, u_2, \ldots, u_{t-1}, u_t, \ldots, u_T \rangle$, where utterance u_t appears in $context_t = \langle u_1, u_2, \ldots, u_{t-1} \rangle$. If we have a dialogue model P estimated from the training corpus then the formulated response u_q for some unseen $context_q$ is given by,

$$u_t = \underset{i}{\text{argmax}}\ P(u_i|context_t) \qquad \forall u_i \in U_{possible}$$

where $U_{possible}$ is a set of all possible response utterances. Ideally we would like to estimate a probability distribution P, but since it's hard to estimate and we only need *argmax* for this application, we approximate P with a ranking function. We can compare previous work within this framework.

In our previous work (Gandhe and Traum, 2007a), we used context similarity as the ranking function P (see section 3.1 for details). This model is trained from in-domain surface text dialogue transcripts. Leuski et al. (2006) model P as cross-lingual relevance, where the task of selecting an appropriate response is seen as cross-lingual information retrieval where the response utterance u_t is the relevant document and the $context_t$ is treated as a query from different language. This model has been applied to simple question answering where context is the previous utterance and the training data is manually annotated question-answer pairs. DeVault et al. (2011) have proposed to use a multi-class classification model (such as maximum entropy) for estimating P. Their method restricts the set $U_{possible}$ to a set of canonical utterances which represent distinct dialogue acts. This allows for a limited number of classes ($|U_{possible}|$) and also maximizes the number of distinct contexts seen per utterance. This model is also trained from manually annotated utterance-context pairs and can additionally use manually created utterance paraphrases.

Apart from the models discussed above which have been mainly applied to dialogue domains situated in a story context, there has been some work in surface text based dialogue models for open domains. Ritter et al. (2011) use information retrieval based and statistical machine translation (SMT) based approaches towards predicting the next response in Twitter conversations. Also Chatbots typically use surface text based processing such as string transformations (e.g., AIML rules (Wallace, 2003)). Such rules can also be learned from a dialogue corpus (Abu Shawar and Atwell, 2005). Systems employing SMT or string transformation rules are formulating a response by *Generation* approach and it can be frequently ungrammatical or incoherent, unlike the selection approach which will always pick something that someone has once said (even though it might be inappropriate in the current context).

3 Dialogue Models

3.1 Nearest Context

In previous work (Gandhe and Traum, 2007a), we modeled P as,

$$P(u_i|context_q) \approx Sim(context_i, context_q)$$

where $context_i$ is the context in which utterance u_i was seen in training corpus and Sim is context similarity in a customized vector-space model. The model restricts the set of possible response utterances ($U_{possible}$) to the set of utterances observed in the training data (U_{train}). The context is approximated using the previous two utterances (one from each speaker). This model does not use the contents of the utterance u_i itself.

3.2 Cross-lingual Relevance Model

Leuski et al. (2006) model P as a cross-lingual relevance model. This model takes into account the content of the utterance u_i as well as the content of the context. It does not impose any restriction on $U_{possible}$, but in practice it is restricted to the set of utterances in the training data. The model allows the context to be composed of multiple fields, each with its own weight. This allows us to extend the model where the context is approximated by the previous two utterances. The weights need to be learned using a held-out development set, which presents a challenge in the case of multiple fields (possible if we add more information state annotations), modest amounts of training data and non-availability of an automatic and reliable estimate of the model's performance. Here, for the first time, we apply this model to automatically extracted pairs of utterance-context and evaluate it. For our model we used the implementation that is available as a part of NPCEditor (Leuski and Traum, 2011) and manually set the field weights corresponding to the two previous utterances to be equal (0.5).

3.3 Perceptron

As discussed earlier, the task of selecting the most appropriate response can be viewed as multi-class classification. But there are a couple of issues. First, since we operate at the surface text level, each unique response utterance will be labeled as a separate class. The number of classes is the number of unique utterances seen in the training set, which is relatively large. As the training data grows, the number of classes will increase. Second, there are very few examples (on average a single example) per class. We need a classifier that can overcome these issues.

The perceptron algorithm and its variants – voted perceptron and averaged perceptron are well known classification models (Freund and Schapire, 1999). They have been extended for use in various natural language processing tasks such as part-of-speech tagging (Collins, 2002), parsing (Collins, 2004) and discriminative language modeling (Roark et al., 2007). Here we use the averaged perceptron model for mapping from dialogue context to an appropriate response utterance.

Collins (2002) outlines the following four components of a perceptron model:

- The training data. In our case it is a set of automatically extracted utterance-context pairs $\{\ldots, \langle u_i, context_i\rangle, \ldots\}$
- A function $\text{GEN}(context)$ that enumerates a set of all possible outputs (response utterances) for any possible input (dialogue context)
- A feature extraction function $\Phi : \langle u, context\rangle \rightarrow \mathbb{R}^d$ that is defined over all possible pairings of response utterances and dialogue contexts. d is the total number of possible features.
- A parameter vector $\bar{\alpha} \in \mathbb{R}^d$

Using such a perceptron model, the most appropriate response utterance (u_t) for the given dialogue context ($context_t$) is given by,

$$u_q = \operatorname*{argmax}_{u_i \in \text{GEN}(context)} \Phi(u_i, context_q) \cdot \bar{\alpha}$$

Algorithm 1 Perceptron Training Algorithm

Initialize: $t \leftarrow 0$; $\bar{\alpha}_0 \leftarrow 0$
for $iter = 1$ to *MAX_ITER* **do**
  for $i = 1$ to N **do**
    $r_i \leftarrow \operatorname*{argmax}_{u \in \text{GEN}(context_i)} \Phi(u, context_i) \cdot \bar{\alpha}_t$
    if $r_i \neq u_i$ **then**
      $\bar{\alpha}_{t+1} \leftarrow \bar{\alpha}_t + \Phi(u_i, context_i) - \Phi(r_i, context_i)$
    else
      $\bar{\alpha}_{t+1} \leftarrow \bar{\alpha}_t$
    end if
    $t \leftarrow t + 1$
  end for
end for
return $\bar{\alpha} \leftarrow (\sum_t \bar{\alpha}_t)/(MAX\_ITER \times N)$

The parameter vector $\bar{\alpha}$ is trained using the training algorithm described in Algorithm 1. The algorithm goes through the training data one instance at a time. For every training instance, it computes the best response utterance (r_i) for the context based on its current estimate of the parameter vector $\bar{\alpha}_t$. The algorithm changes the parameter vector only if it makes an error ($r_i \neq u_i$). The update drives the parameter vector away from the error (r_i) and towards the correct output (u_i). The final parameter vector $\bar{\alpha}$ is an average of all the intermediate $\bar{\alpha}_t$ values. The averaging of parameter vectors avoids overfitting.

The feature extraction function Φ can list any arbitrary features from the pair $\langle u, context\rangle$. We consider information state annotations (IS_t) along with the surface text corresponding to the previous two turns. The features could also include scores computed from other models, such as those presented in sections 3.1 and 3.2. Figure 1 illustrates an example context and utterance, and several features. We examine several sets of features, Surface text based features (Φ_S), Retrieval model based features (Φ_R), and Topic based features (Φ_T).

Surface text based features (Φ_S) are the features extracted from the surface text of the previous utterances in the dialogue context ($context_j$) and the response utterance (u_i). $\Phi_{S(d)}(u_x, u_y)$ extracts surface text features from two utterances – a response utterance (u_x) and an utterance (u_y) from the context that is (d) utterances away. There are four types of features we extract:

- $common\_term(d, w)$ features indicate the number of times a word w appears in both the utterances. The total number of possible features is $O(|V|)$ and we select a small subset of words ($Selected\_common(d)$) from the vocabulary.
- The $common\_term\_count(d)$ feature indicates the number of words that appear in both utterances.
- The $unique\_common\_term\_count(d)$ feature indicates the number of unique words that appear in both utterances.
- $cross\_term(d, w_x, w_y)$ features indicate the number of times the word w_x appears in the utterance u_x and the word w_y appears in the utterance u_y. The total possible number of such cross features is very large ($O(|V|^2)$), where $|V|$ is the utterance vocabulary size. In order to keep the training tractable and avoid overfitting, we select a small subset of cross_features ($Selected\_cross(d)$) from all possible features.

In this model, we perform feature selection by selecting the subsets $Selected\_cross(d)$ and $Selected\_common(d)$. The training algorithm requires evaluating the feature extraction (Φ_S) function for all possible pairings of response utterances and contexts. One simple feature selection criterion is to allow the features only appearing in *true pairings* of response utterance and context (i.e. features from $\Phi_S(\langle u_i, context_j\rangle)\ \forall i = j$). The subset $Selected\_common(d)$ for $common\_term$ features is selected by extracting features from only such *true pairings*.

For selecting $cross\_term(d, w_x, w_y)$ features we use only *true pairings* but we need to reduce this subset even further. We impose additional constraints based on the collection frequency of lexical events such as, $cf(w_x) > threshold_x$, $cf(w_y) > threshold_y$, $cf(\langle w_x, w_y\rangle) > threshold_{xy}$. Further reduction in size of the selected subset of $cross\_term$ features is achieved by ranking the features using a suitable ranking function and choosing the top n features. In this model, we rank the $cross\_term$ features based on pointwise mutual-information $pmi(\langle w_x, w_y\rangle)$ given by,

$$\log \frac{p(\langle w_x, w_y\rangle)}{p(w_x)p(w_y)} = \log \frac{\left(\frac{\#\langle w_x, w_y\rangle}{\#\langle\cdot,\cdot\rangle}\right)}{\left(\frac{\#\langle w_x,\cdot\rangle}{\#\langle\cdot,\cdot\rangle}\right)\cdot\left(\frac{\#\langle\cdot, w_y\rangle}{\#\langle\cdot,\cdot\rangle}\right)}$$

Summing up, $\Phi_{S(d)}(u_x, u_y) =$

$$\begin{aligned} &\{cross\_term(d, w_x, w_y) : w_x \in u_x \wedge \\ &\quad w_y \in u_y \wedge \langle w_x, w_y\rangle \in Selected\_cross(d)\} \\ \cup\ &\{common\_term(d, w) : w \in u_x \wedge w \in u_y \wedge \\ &\quad w \in Selected\_common(d)\} \\ \cup\ &\{common\_term\_count(d)\} \\ \cup\ &\{unique\_common\_term\_count(d)\} \end{aligned}$$

Retrieval model based features (Φ_R) are the scores computed in a fashion similar to the *Nearest Context* model. $Sim(u_x, u_y)$ is a cosine similarity function for tf-idf weighted vector space representations of utterances and $Sim(context_a, context_b)$ is the same function from *Nearest Context* model. We define three features,

- $retrieval\_score = \max_{k=1}^{|\mathcal{L}|} Sim(context_j, context_k) \cdot Sim(u_i, u_k)$
- $context\_sim@best\_utt\_match = Sim(context_j, context_b)$ where, $b = \operatorname{argmax}_{k=1}^{|\mathcal{L}|} Sim(u_i, u_k)$
- $utt\_sim@best\_context\_match = Sim(u_i, u_b)$ where, $b = \operatorname{argmax}_{k=1}^{|\mathcal{L}|} Sim(context_j, context_k)$

$$\begin{aligned} \Phi_R(\langle u_i, context_j\rangle) = \{&retrieval\_score, \\ &context\_sim@best\_utt\_match, \\ &utt\_sim@best\_context\_match\} \end{aligned}$$

Topic based feature (Φ_T) tracks the topic similarity between the topic of the dialogue context and the response utterance. A topic is marked as mentioned if a set of keywords triggering that topic have been previously mentioned in the dialogue. Each information state (IS) consists of a topic signature which can be viewed as a boolean vector representing mentions of topics.

$$\Phi_T(\langle u_i, context_j\rangle) = \{topic\_similarity\}$$
$$topic\_similarity = cosine(IS_i, IS_j)$$

where, IS_i is the topic and is part of $context_i$ which is the context associated with the utterance u_i.

The perceptron model presented here allows novel combinations of resources such as combining surface text transcripts with information state annotations for tracking topics in the conversation. As compared to the generative cross-lingual relevance model approach, the perceptron model is a discriminative model. It is also a parametric model and the inference requires linear time with respect to the size of candidate utterances ($|\text{GEN}(context)|$) and the number of features ($|\bar{\alpha}|$). Although, computing some of the features themselves (e.g., Φ_R features) requires linear time with

⋮

$context_j$	$[u_{j(-2)}]$	**Doctor**	you are the threat i need protection from you
	$[u_{j(-1)}]$	**Captain**	no no you do you do not need protection from me i am here to help you uh what i would like to do is move your your clinic to a safer location and uh give you money and medicine to help build it
$utterance$	$[u_i]$	**Doctor**	i have no way of moving

$$\Phi_S(\langle u_i, context_j \rangle) = \{ \; cross\_term(-2, \text{"moving"}, \text{"need"}) = 1,$$
$$common\_term(-2, \text{"i"}) = 1,$$
$$common\_term\_count(-2) = 1, unique\_common\_term\_count(-2) = 1,$$
$$cross\_term(-1, \text{"moving"}, \text{"give"}) = 1,$$
$$common\_term(-1, \text{"i"}) = 1, common\_term(-1, \text{"no"}) = 1,$$
$$common\_term\_count(-1) = 2, unique\_common\_term\_count(-1) = 2,$$
$$retrieval\_score = 0.198, context\_sim@best\_utt\_match = 0.198,$$
$$utt\_sim@best\_context\_match = 0,$$
$$topic\_similarity = 0.667 \; \}$$

Figure 1: Features extracted from a context ($context_j$) and a response utterance (u_i)

respect to the size of the training data. The perceptron model can rank an arbitrary set of utterances given a dialogue context. But some of the features (e.g., $topic\_similarity$) require that the utterance $u_i(u_i \in |\text{GEN}(context)|)$ be associated with a known context ($context_i$). For all our models we use $\text{GEN}(context) = U_{train}$.

We have implemented three different variants of the perceptron model based on the choice of features used. ***Perceptron(surface)*** model uses only surface text features ($\Phi = \Phi_S$). The other two models are ***Perceptron(surface+retrieval)*** where $\Phi = \Phi_S \cup \Phi_R$ and ***Perceptron(surface+retrieval+topic)*** where $\Phi = \Phi_S \cup \Phi_R \cup \Phi_T$.

Figure 2 shows a schematic representation of these models along with the set of resources being used by each model. The figure also shows the relationships between these models. The arrows point from a less informative model to a more informative model and the annotations on these arrows indicate the additional information used.

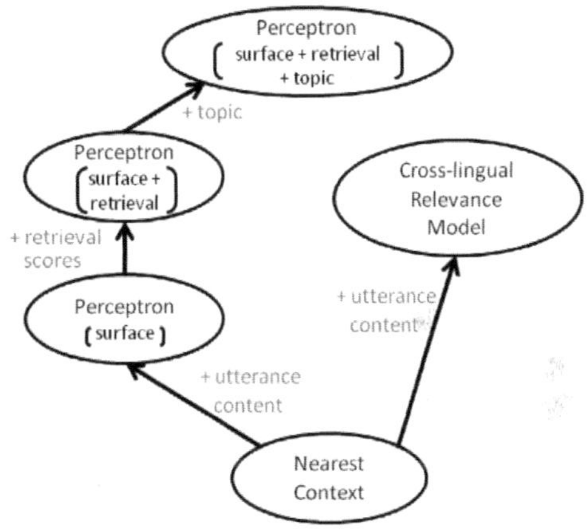

Figure 2: A schematic representation of implemented unsupervised dialogue models and the relationships between the information used by their ranking functions.

4 Evaluation

For the experiments reported in this paper, we used the human-human spoken dialogue corpus collected for the project SASO-ST (Traum et al., 2005). In this scenario, the trainee acts as an Army Captain negotiating with a simulated doctor to convince him to move his clinic to another location. The corpus is a collection of 23 roleplay dialogues and 13 WoZ dialogues lasting an average of 40 turns (a total of $\approx$ 1400 turns and $\approx$ 30k words).

We perform a *Static Context* evaluation (Gandhe, 2013). In *Static Context* evaluation, all the dialogue models being evaluated receive the same set of contexts as input. These dialogue contexts are extracted from actual in-domain human-human dialogues and are not affected by the dialogue model being evaluated. For every turn whose role is to be played by the system, we predict the most appropriate response in place of that turn given the dialogue context.

Since the goal for virtual humans is to be as human-like as possible, a suitable evaluation metric is how appropriate or human-like the responses are for a given dialogue context. The evaluation reported here employs human judges. We set up a simple subjective 5-point likert scale for rating appropriateness – 1 being a very inappropriate non-sensical response and 5 being a perfectly appropriate response.

We built five dialogue models to play the role of the doctor in SASO-ST domain, viz.: *Nearest Context* (section 3.1), *Cross-lingual Relevance Model* (section 3.2) and three *perceptron* models (section 3.3) with different feature sets. These dialogue models are evaluated using 5 in-domain human-human dialogues from the training data (2 roleplay and 3 WoZ dialogues, referred to as test dialogues). A dialogue model is trained in a leave-one-out fashion where the training data consists of all dialogues except the one test dialogue that is being evaluated. A dialogue model trained in this fashion is then used to predict the most appropriate response for every context that appears in the test dialogue. This process is repeated for each test dialogue and for each dialogue model being evaluated. In this evaluation setting, the actual response utterance found in the original human-human dialogue may not belong to the set of utterances being ranked by the dialogue model. We also compare these five dialogue models with two human-level upper baselines. Figure 4 in the appendix shows some examples of utterances returned by a couple of the models.

4.1 Human-level Upper Baselines

In order to establish an upper baseline for human-level performance for the evaluation task, we conducted a wizard data collection. We asked human volunteers (wizards) to perform a similar task to that performed by the dialogue models being evaluated. The wizard is presented with a set of utterances (U_{train}) and is asked to select a subset from these that will be appropriate as a response for the presented dialogue context. Compared to this, the task of the dialogue model is to select a single most appropriate response for the given context.

DeVault et al. (2011) carried out a similar wizard data collection but at the dialogue act level, where wizards were asked to select only one response dialogue act for each dialogue context. Their findings suggest that there are several valid response dialogue acts for a dialogue context. A specific dialogue act can be realized in several ways at the surface text level. For these reasons we believe that for a given dialogue context there are often several appropriate response utterances at the surface text level. In our setting the dialogue models work at the surface text level and hence the wizards were asked to select a subset of surface text utterances that would be appropriate responses. Each wizard was asked to select several (ideally between five and ten, but always at least one) appropriate responses for each dialogue context. Four wizards participated in this data collection with each wizard selecting responses for the contexts from the same five human-human test dialogues. The set of utterances to chose from (U_{train}) for every test dialogue was built in the same leave-one-out fashion as used for evaluating the implemented dialogue models.

There are a total of 89 dialogue contexts where the next turn belongs to *doctor*. As expected, wizards frequently chose multiple utterances as appropriate responses (mean = 7.80, min = 1, max = 25).

This data collected from wizards is used to build two human-level upper-baseline models for the task of selecting a response utterance given a dialogue context:

Wizard Max Voted model returns the response which gets the maximum number of votes from the four wizards. Ties are broken randomly.

Wizard Random model returns a random utterance from the list of all utterances marked as appropriate by one of the wizards.

4.2 Comparative Evaluation of Models

We performed a static context evaluation using four judges for the above-mentioned two human-level baselines (*Wizard Random* and *Wizard Max Voted*) and five dialogue models (*Nearest Context*, *Cross-lingual Relevance Model* and three *perceptron* models), as described in section 3.3. We tune the parameters used for the perceptron models based on the automatic evaluation metric, *Weak Agreement* (DeVault et al., 2011). According to this evaluation metric a response utterance is judged as perfectly appropriate (a score of 5) if any of the wizards chose this response utterance for given context and inappropriate (a score of 0) otherwise. The *Perceptron(surface)* model was trained using 30 iterations, the *Perceptron(surface+retrieval)* using 20 iterations, and the *Perceptron(surface+retrieval+topic)* was trained using 25 iterations. For all perceptron models we used $threshold_x = threshold_y = threshold_{xy} = 3$.

For a comparative evaluation of dialogue models, we need an evaluation setup where judges could see the complete dialogue context along with the response utterances generated by the dialogue models to be evaluated. In this setup, we show all the response utterances next to each other for easy comparison and we do not show the actual response utterance that was encountered in the original human-human dialogue. We built a web interface for collecting appropriateness ratings that addresses the above requirements. Figure 3 shows the web interface used by the four judges to evaluate the appropriateness of response utterances for given dialogue context. The appropriateness was rated on the same scale of 1 to 5. The original human-human dialogue (roleplay or WoZ) is shown on the left hand side and the response utterances from different dialogue models are shown on the right hand side. In cases where different dialogue models produce the same surface text response only one candidate surface text is shown to judge. Once the judge has rated all the candidate responses they can proceed to the next dialogue context. This setting allows for comparative evaluation of different dialogue models. The presentation order of responses from different dialogue models is randomized. Two of the judges also performed the role of the wizards in our wizard data collection as outlined in section 4.1, but the wizard data collection and the evaluation tasks were separated by a period of over 3 months.

Table 1 shows the results of our comparative evaluation for each judge and averaged over all judges. We also computed inter-rater agreement for individual ratings for all response utterances using Krippendorff's α (Krippendorff, 2004). There were a total of $n = 397$ distinct response utterances that were judged by the evaluators. The Krippendorff's α for all four judges was 0.425 and it ranges from 0.359 to 0.495 for different subsets of judges. The value of α indicates that the inter-rater agreement is substantially above chance ($\alpha > 0$), but indicates a fair amount of disagreement, indicating that judging appropriateness is a hard task even for human judges. Although there is low inter-rater agreement at the individual response utterance level there is high agreement at the dialogue model level. Pearson's correlation between the average appropriateness for different dialogue models ranges from 0.928 to 0.995 for different pairs of judges.

We performed a paired Wilcoxon test to check for statistically significant differences in different dialogue models. *Wizard Max Voted* is significantly more appropriate than all other models ($p < 0.001$). *Wizard Random* is significantly more appropriate than *Cross-lingual Relevance Model* ($p < 0.05$) and significantly more appropriate than the three perceptron models as well as *Nearest Context* model ($p < 0.001$). *Cross-lingual Relevance Model* is significantly more appropriate than *Nearest Context* ($p < 0.01$). All other differences are not statistically significant at the 5 percent level.

We found that adding topic annotations did not help. This is in contrast with previous observation (Gandhe and Traum, 2007b), where topic information helped when evaluation was performed in *Dynamic Context* setting. In *Dynamic Context* setting, the dialogue model is used in an online fashion where the response utterances it generates become part of the dialogue contexts with respect to which the subsequent responses are predicted and evaluated. The topic information ensures systematic progression of dialogue. But for static context evaluation such help is not required as the dialogue contexts are extracted from human human dialogues and are fixed.

5 Conclusion

In this paper we introduced dialogue models that can be trained simply from in-domain surface text dialogue transcripts. Some of these models also allow for incorporating additional information state features such as topics or results of simpler models. We have evaluated the appropriateness of responses and have compared these models with two human-level baselines. Evaluating response appropriateness is highly subjective as

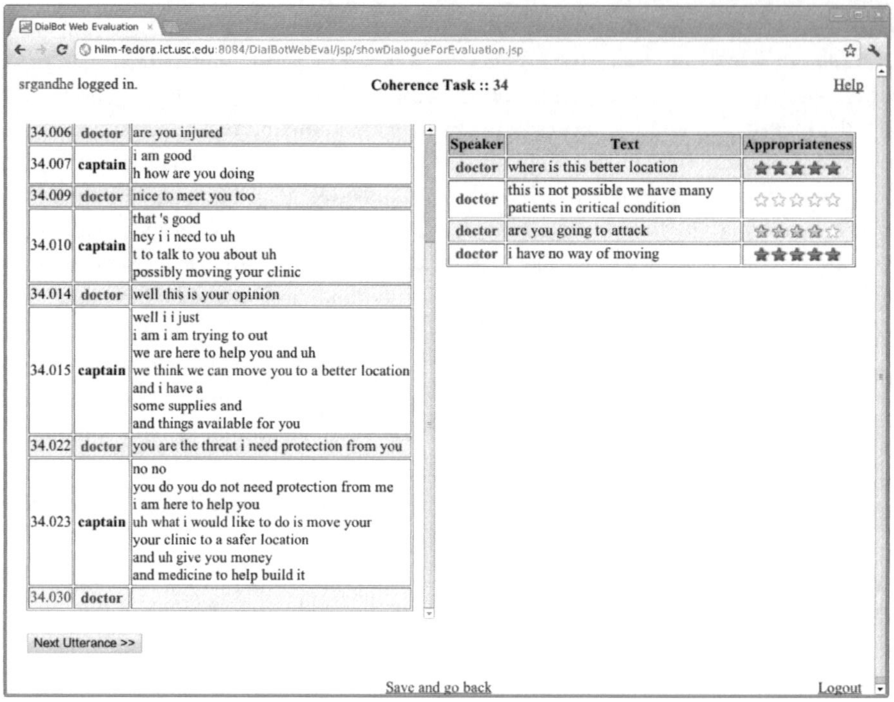

Figure 3: Screenshot of the user interface for static context comparative evaluation of dialogue models

Model	#Utts	Avg. appropriateness				Appropriateness (All judges)	
		Judge 1	Judge 2	Judge 3	Judge 4	Avg	stddev
Nearest Context	89	4.12	3.98	3.40	3.53	3.76	1.491
Perceptron(surface)	89	3.97	4.11	3.51	3.62	3.80	1.445
Perceptron (surface+retrieval)	89	4.26	4.12	3.51	3.72	3.90	1.414
Perceptron (surface+retrieval+topic)	89	4.21	4.09	3.51	3.57	3.85	1.433
Cross-lingual Relevance Model	89	4.28	4.31	3.70	3.91	4.05	1.314
Wizard Random	89	4.55	4.55	4.03	4.16	4.32	1.153
Wizard Max Voted	89	4.76	4.84	4.40	4.52	4.63	0.806

Table 1: Offline comparative evaluation of dialogue models.

can be seen from the fact that utterances which receive more wizard votes (*Wizad Max Voted*) receive significantly higher appropriateness ratings than those which receive fewer votes (*Wizard Random*). The performance of best performing dialogue models are close to human-level baselines. In future we plan to use larger datasets which should be easy, since no additional annotations are required for training these dialogue models.

Acknowledgments

The effort described here has been sponsored by the U.S. Army. Any opinions, content or information presented does not necessarily reflect the position or the policy of the United States Government, and no official endorsement should be inferred.

References

Bayan Abu Shawar and Eric Atwell. 2005. Using corpora in machine-learning chatbot systems. *International Journal of Corpus Linguistics*, 10:489–516.

Michael Collins. 2002. Discriminative training methods for hidden markov models: theory and experiments with perceptron algorithms. In *Proceedings of the ACL-02 conference on Empirical methods in natural language processing - Volume 10*, EMNLP '02, pages 1–8, Stroudsburg, PA, USA. Association for Computational Linguistics.

Michael Collins, 2004. *Parameter estimation for statistical parsing models: theory and practice of distribution-free methods*, pages 19–55. Kluwer Academic Publishers, Norwell, MA, USA.

David DeVault, Anton Leuski, and Kenji Sagae. 2011. Toward learning and evaluation of dialogue policies with text examples. In *Proceedings of the SIGDIAL 2011 Conference*, pages 39–48, Portland, Oregon, June. Association for Computational Linguistics.

Yoav Freund and Robert E. Schapire. 1999. Large margin classification using the perceptron algorithm. *Mach. Learn.*, 37:277–296, December.

Sudeep Gandhe and David Traum. 2007a. Creating spoken dialogue characters from corpora without annotations. In *Proceedings of Interspeech-07.*

Sudeep Gandhe and David Traum. 2007b. First steps towards dialogue modeling from an un-annotated human-human corpus. In *5th Workshop on knowledge and reasoning in practical dialogue systems*, Hyderabad, India.

Sudeep Gandhe and David Traum. 2010. I've said it before, and i'll say it again: an empirical investigation of the upper bound of the selection approach to dialogue. In *Proceedings of the 11th Annual Meeting of the Special Interest Group on Discourse and Dialogue*, SIGDIAL '10, pages 245–248, Stroudsburg, PA, USA. Association for Computational Linguistics.

Sudeep Gandhe. 2013. *Rapid prototyping and evaluation of dialogue systems for virtual humans.* Ph.D. thesis, University of Southern California.

J. J. Godfrey, E. C. Holliman, and J. McDaniel. 1992. Switchboard: Telephone speech corpus for research and development. In *Proc. of ICASSP-92*, pages 517–520.

P. A. Heeman and J. Allen. 1994. The TRAINS 93 dialogues. TRAINS Technical Note 94-2, Department of Computer Science, University of Rochester.

Klaus Krippendorff. 2004. *Content Analysis, An Introduction to Its Methodology 2nd Edition.* Sage Publications.

Anton Leuski and David Traum. 2008. A statistical approach for text processing in virtual humans. In *Proccedings of 26th Army Science Conference.*

Anton Leuski and David Traum. 2011. Npceditor: Creating virtual human dialogue using information retrieval techniques. *AI Magazine*, 32(2):42–56.

Anton Leuski, Ronakkumar Patel, David Traum, and Brandon Kennedy. 2006. Building effective question answering characters. In *Proceedings of the 7th SIGdial Workshop on Discourse and Dialogue*, pages 18–27, Sydney, Australia, July. Association for Computational Linguistics.

Jeff Rickel and W. Lewis Johnson. 1999. Virtual humans for team training in virtual reality. In *Proceedings of the Ninth International Conference on Artificial Intelligence in Education*, pages 578–585. IOS Press.

Alan Ritter, Colin Cherry, and William B. Dolan. 2011. Data-driven response generation in social media. In *Proceedings of the Conference on Empirical Methods in Natural Language Processing*, EMNLP '11, pages 583–593, Stroudsburg, PA, USA. Association for Computational Linguistics.

Brian Roark, Murat Saraclar, and Michael Collins. 2007. Discriminative n-gram language modeling. *Comput. Speech Lang.*, 21:373–392, April.

A. J. Stent. 2000. The monroe corpus. Technical Report 728, Computer Science Dept. University of Rochester.

David Traum, William Swartout, Jonathan Gratch, and Stacy Marsella. 2005. Virtual humans for non-team interaction training. In *AAMAS-05 Workshop on Creating Bonds with Humanoids*, July.

Richard Wallace. 2003. *AIML Overview.* ALICE A. I. Foundation.

	Original Human-Human Dialogue	Model response
Captain	hello how are you doing sir	
Doctor	what do you want i have patients waiting for me	hello what can i do for you mr
Captain	sir i come by to offer you some assistance ah on behalf of my commander ah we want to try to support you in this hospital and ah improving the health and welfare of the civilians that you have under your care	
Doctor	well this is your opinion	i see captain is this a is this a suggestion from your commander
Captain	i am sorry sir could you say again	
Doctor	well this is your opinion	you are the threat i need protection from you

(a) *Perceptron(surface)*

	Original Human-Human Dialogue	Model response
Captain	hello doctor perez	
Doctor	hello	hello what was your name captain dezois very nice to meet you i am sorry but i am very busy today so i only have a limited amount of time what can i help you with
Captain	i am captain xx	
Doctor	so do you need help	ok what do you want i have patients waiting for me
Captain	yes i have a very urgent matter to discuss with you	
Doctor	are you injured	pl please captain i i am sorry to cut you off but i really must uh go i was in the middle of examining a patient

(b) *Cross-lingual Relevance Model*

Figure 4: Example interaction for the dialogue models in static context setting. The second column shows the original human-human dialogue and the third column shows the dialogue model's response for the corresponding system turn.

Speech Reduction, Intensity, and F0 Shape are Cues to Turn-Taking

Oliver Niebuhr
Dept. of General Linguistics
University of Kiel
Kiel, Germany
niebuhr@isfas.uni-kiel.de

Karin Görs
Dept. of General Linguistics
University of Kiel
Kiel, Germany
kgoers@arcor.de

Evelin Graupe
Dept. of General Linguistics
University of Kiel
Kiel, Germany
evelin_graupe@yahoo.de

Abstract

Based on German production data from the 'Kiel Corpus of Spontaneous Speech', we conducted two perception experiments, using an innovative interactive task in which participants gave real oral responses to resynthesized question stimuli. Differences in the time interval between stimulus question and response show that segmental reduction, intensity level, and the shape of the phrase-final rise all function as cues to turn-taking in conversation. Thus, the phonetics of turn-taking goes beyond the traditional triad of duration, voice quality, and F0 level.

1 Introduction

1.1 Empirical background

Signalling turn-taking intentions is essential for successful speech communication. Accordingly, it was shown for all well-described languages that turn holding and yielding cues are robustly encoded in complex redundant bundles of morphosyntactic and/or phonetic patterns. The phonetic patterns primarily rely on prosody, taking a considerable part of its functional load. Compared with turn holding, turn yielding is typically signalled phrase-finally by extensive terminal falling or high rising F0 movements, deviation from modal phonation – mostly in the direction of creak phonation – and increasing final lengthening from penultimate to ultimate syllables. These differences seem to be used in the same way across many languages, and not least for this reason their validity is beyond doubt (e.g., Duncan, 1972; Beattie, 1981; Lehiste, 1982; Kohler, 1983; Nakatani et al., 1995; Ogden, 2001; Fon, 2002; Kohler, 2004; Peters, 2006; Vaissière & Michaud 2006; Gravano, 2009; Fon et al., 2011).

However, leaving aside gaze and gesture patterns (cf. Kendon, 1995; Taboada, 2006), a growing body of evidence from production studies suggests that the phonetics of turn-taking is still richer and goes beyond the traditional triad of voice quality, duration, and the level or direction of F0 patterns. Turn holding or yielding also seems to include the fourth prosodic dimension, i.e. *intensity*, as well as details in the *shape* of phrase-final rises and the degree of phrase-final *segmental reduction*.

For example, phrase-final voiceless plosives in English are realized either fully pronounced and with strong post-aspiration, or in reduced forms that lack post-aspiration and are (partly) replaced by glottalization, cf. "got" [ɡʷɒtʰ] vs. [ɡʷɒ̰ʔᵗ], and "cap" [k̟ʰæpʰ] vs. [k̟ʰæʔp̚]. The difference between the unreduced and reduced forms was for a long time claimed to be a matter of free variation, until it was revealed in corpus analyses of different varieties of English that reduced forms were produced turn-medially whereas unreduced forms occurred almost exceptionally at the end of a speaker's turn (Local et al., 1986; Docherty et al., 1997; Local & Walker, 2012).

More recently, it was additionally found for English and French in independent analyses of spontaneous speech corpora that the intensity levels of phrase-final syllables differ depending on whether the syllables occur turn-medially or turn-finally (Gravano & Hirschberg, 2009; Clemens & Dieckhaus, 2009; Raux, 2008; Friedberg, 2011). The difference was the same in both languages: "*speakers tend to lower their voices when approaching turn boundaries, whereas they reach turn-internal pauses with a higher intensity*" (Gravano & Hirschberg, 2009:256).

Furthermore, Dombrowski & Niebuhr (2005) showed on the basis of one of the largest corpora of Standard Northern German – the Kiel Corpus of Spontaneous Speech – that it is not only the range of phrase-final intonation movements that distinguishes turn-internal from turn-final boundaries. At least in the case of rises, it also matters whether the shape of the rise is concave (slow rise followed by fast rise) or convex (fast rise followed by slow rise). Convex rises occurred predominantly turn-medially, whereas concave rises were used by speakers almost invariably at the end of a turn. A similar distribution of rise shapes was found by Asu (2006) for discourse markers in spontaneous dialogues of Estonian.

1.2 Question and aim

The three groups of cross-linguistic findings on reduction levels, intensity levels and rise shapes have in common that their perceptual relevance for turn-taking has never been tested as yet. That is, do listeners actually interpret phrase-final differences in (i) the degree of segmental reduction, (ii) the intensity level, and (iii) the shape of F0 rises as signals of turn-holding and/or turn-yielding? Providing a first answer to this question is the main aim of the present paper.

Clayards et al. (2007) showed that the more systematically acoustic cues are used in speech production the more likely they are exploited by listeners. Given the distinct production findings for (i)-(iii) and their consistency across languages or language varieties, it was already expectable that the answer to our question would be 'yes'; and, indeed our results met our expectation. Yet, empirical testing was indispensable.

1.3 Research subject

Our study was based on a single language variety: Standard Northern German. However, in view of the strong cross-linguistic parallels in the phonetics of turn-taking (cf. 1.1), it is reasonable to assume that our results will also be applicable to many other languages.

In order to test the effects of intensity differences and particularly of reduction differences on the perception of turn-internal and turn-final boundaries, we used the most frequent sonorous word-final syllable in German: <-en#>. It always occurs unstressed and is phonologically represented as a sequence of schwa and alveolar nasal /ən/. However, next to its corresponding canonical pronunciation as [ən] (or rather [ɪ̞n]), the word-final <-en#> syllable is known to undergo different reduction processes. The two most important processes are /ə/ elision, which leaves a syllabic nasal, and assimilation of the syllabic nasal to the place of articulation of the preceding consonant. For example, "lieben" (to love) can be realized as [ˈliːbən], [ˈliːbn̩], or [ˈliːbm̩]. Likewise, possible pronunciations of "sagen" (to say) are [ˈzaːgən], [ˈzaːgn̩], and [ˈzaːgŋ̍].

However, prior to conducting any perception experiments, we first had to confirm that the differences in the turn-internal vs. turn-final reduction and intensity levels found for English and French (cf. 1.1) do occur as well in Standard Northern German (the differences in rise shape are already known for Standard Northern German and thus need not be replicated). Therefore, our perception experiments were preceded by an analysis of the Kiel Corpus of Spontaneous Speech. This analysis is detailed below.

2 Corpus analysis

2.1 Analysis method

The Kiel Corpus of Spontaneous Speech includes 117 dialogues which add up to more than four hours of Standard Northern German speech from 52 male or female interlocutors (Kohler, 1996). The corpus is completely annotated, segmentally and prosodically. The segmental annotations are made such that they specify reduction processes like assimilation, elision, lenition, and "articulatory prosodies" in terms of deviations from the canonical forms of the spoken words (articulatory prosodies preserve the "phonetic essence" of segmentally elided words or syllables in the form of suprasegmental sound qualities and are thus an important cue to word identification in reduced speech, Kohler & Niebuhr 2011). Furthermore, the structure of the corpus in combination with the prosodic annotation allows a differential search for phrase and turn boundaries.

On this basis, we conducted an annotation-based analysis of unstressed word-final <-en#> syllables in turn-final and turn-internal position. The turn-internal tokens were further subdivided into phrase-final and phrase-internal syllables. The latter phrase-internal syllables were not directly relevant for our research question but still included for the sake of completeness. Our corpus query yielded a total of 17,023 word-final <-en#> syllables. The majority of the syllables, viz. 11,329 tokens, occurred in phrase- and turn-internal position. For the phrase-final but turn-internal position, we found 4,090 <-en#> syllables. The phrase- and turn-final position was represented by 1,604 tokens. The information about whether the <-en#> syllables were subject of reduction processes, and if so, whether degree of reduction differed across the three syntactic-prosodic positions was derived from the segmental annotation. We focussed on the two main reduction processes exemplified in 1.3: /ə/ elision and, if the /ə/ is absent, additional progressive place assimilation of the syllabic nasal /n/ towards [m] or [ŋ].

In a subsequent step, we took random sub-samples of 50 <-en#> syllables from each of the three syntactic-prosodic positions and analyzed their intensity levels manually in Adobe Audition. Measurements were taken in terms of mean acoustic energy (in dB). As mixing syllables with and without schwa could have biased our intensity measurements, all three sub-samples only contained syllabic [n̩] nasals. The results of our reduction and intensity analyses are presented in the following section.

2.2 Results of the production data

To put it in a nutshell, analyzing the segmental annotation of the Kiel Corpus clearly showed: The more finally a <-en#> syllable was produced the lower was its degree of segmental reduction. This fact is illustrated in Figures 1(a)-(b). While virtually no <-en#> syllable in turn-medial *and* phrase-medial position was realized with a [ə] or a similar vocoid sound before the nasal, about 7% of the <-en#> syllables in turn-medial *but* phrase-*final* position showed such a vocoid section (Fig.1a). The amount of schwas or similar vocoids increased above 10% for those <-en#> syllables that occurred phrase-finally *and* turn-finally. Among the <-en#> syllables that were realized without /ə/, the frequency of place assimilation of the syllabic /n/ decreased from almost 80% in phrase-medial and turn-medial position, through about 66% in turn-medial *but* phrase-*final* position, to only about 20% in phrase-final *and* turn-final position (Fig.1b).

Although these figures speak for themselves, we also assessed their statistical significance by means of a χ^2 test. The test was based on the absolute number of /ə/ and /n/ occurrences in the 3x2 conditions of Figures 1(a)-(b). The test statistics corroborate that reduction becomes significantly stronger under increasing finality (χ^2=373.554, *df*=2, p<0.001).

A similar tripartite picture emerged for the intensity measurements. The intensity level in the random sub-samples of 3x50 <-en#> syllables (realized as syllabic nasals) decreased successively by on average about 3.5-6.2 dB (for female speakers less than for male speakers) from phrase- and turn-medial tokens to tokens which are both phrase-final *and* turn-final. That is, the softest <-en#> syllables occurred immediately before a turn transition. A one-way ANOVA showed that the intensity decrease across the three finality conditions was highly significant (F[2,147]=45.941, p<0.001).

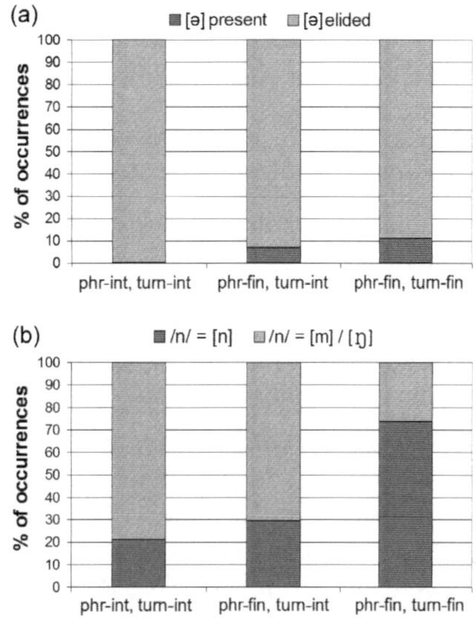

Figure 1: Degree of reduction of <-en#> syllables in terms of (a) /ə/ elision and (b) place assimilation of /n/ by the preceding consonant (when /ə/ is absent). The <-en#> syllables occurred in phrase- and turn-internal position (left), in turn-internal but phrase-final position (middle), or in phrase- and turn-final position (right).

2.3 Conclusion from the production data

Three conclusions can be drawn from the results of our corpus analysis. First, the degree of reduction of sound segments in Standard Northern German – represented by <-en#> syllables – differs substantially depending on whether they coincide with phrase boundaries or turn boundaries. The degree of reduction is lower at turn-final than at turn-internal boundaries. Second, also the intensity levels before different types of syntactic-prosodic boundaries show clear differences. However, while the degree of segmental reduction *de*creases from phrase-internal through phrase-final to turn-final boundaries, the degree of intensity reduction *in*creases by on average up to 100%. Third, the findings for Standard Northern German, particularly the direction of changes from phrase-*final* but turn-*internal* to phrase- *and* turn-final boundaries, are qualitatively consistent with those that have been found before for spontaneous dialogues in English and French.

After having confirmed that Standard Northern German resembles English and French with regard to the production of reduction and intensity differences at turn-internal and turn-final boundaries, we continued with conducting two perception experiments. They were based on question stimuli, whose ends were varied in a binary fashion with respect to <-en#> reduction, intensity level and the shape of the final F0 rise.

3 Perception experiment 1: reduction and rise shape

3.1 Stimulus generation

When it comes to testing the perceptual relevance of phonetic details for turn yielding or holding, internal/ecological validity is a big issue. We addressed this issue by developing an interactive experimental design in which the participants gave real verbal responses to the stimuli. Our target stimuli were syntactically marked questions, whose last constituent was concluded by a target word. As there were 16 different questions, we had 16 different target words. All of them were similarly frequent verbal infinitives of two or three syllables, and with lexical stress and a rising nuclear pitch accent (L+H*) on the penultimate syllable. The pitch-accent rise was complemented by a high boundary tone (H-%), and hence the rise continued across the final syllable until the end of the utterance. The final syllable was <-en#>. Two target-word examples have already been given in 1.3; further examples are “fliegen” (to fly), “liegen” (to lie), “kramen” (to fish sth out), and “fragen” (to question). In half (i.e. eight) of the target words, <-en#> was preceded by a labial consonant (/m,b/). The other half had a velar consonant (/ŋ,g/) before the <-en#> syllable. Moreover, the target words were balanced with respect to vowel quantity and height of the stressed vowel (/i(:)/ or /a(:)/).

The target questions were embedded in context frames, i.e. they were preceded by 1-2 introductory statements and followed by an alternative question starting with “oder” (or). For example, “Ich hab Anjas Freund letztens Hand in Hand mit einer anderen durch die Stadt laufen sehen. Meinst Du, ich soll Ihr das sagen ? – oder soll ich mich da lieber raus halten?“ (I saw Anja‘s boyfriend yesterday wandering hand in hand through the streets with another girl. Do you think I should tell her? – or should I rather butt out?). The crucial point is that the alternative question is optional. It may or may not be there so that the target question could equally be turn-internal or turn-final. In order to validate this positional ambiguity, we ran a pretest with 12 participants and orthographic representations of our target questions. The pretest confirmed that none of the target questions had a semantic bias towards occurring in turn-internal or turn-final position (i.e. with/without an alternative question).

The 16 sequences of preparatory statement(s), target question and alternative question were produced by a phonetically trained female speaker (KG) with unreduced, canonically pronounced <-en#> syllables ([ən]) at the end of the target words. The sequences were digitally recorded and constituted our first set of 16 base stimuli. Then, KG produced the same 16 sequences again, but this time the <-en#> syllables were highly reduced to either [m̩] or [ŋ̍]. The latter segments were used to create a second set of 16 base stimuli by taking the stimuli of the first set and replacing (with Adobe Audition) their fully pronounced [ən] syllables with the corresponding highly reduced nasal. In this way, we ended up with two sets 16 base stimuli. The stimuli in each set were phonetically absolutely identical except for the <-en#> syllables, which were either fully pronounced or highly reduced.

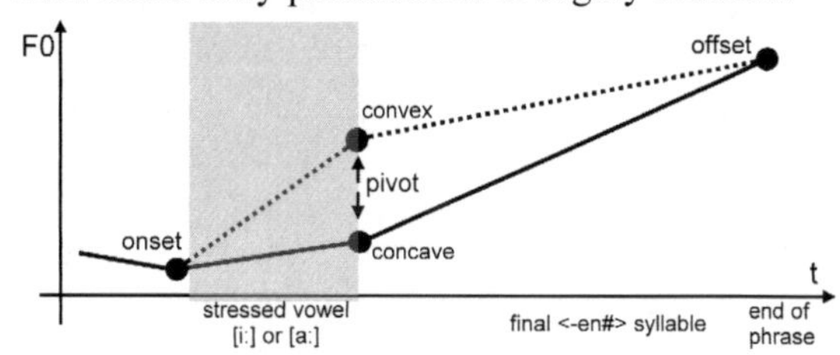

Figure 2: Shape manipulation of the nuclear F0 rise L+H* H-% at the end of the target questions, yielding 32 questions with convex and 32 questions with concave rises.

Before proceeding with the next step, we checked our base stimulus endings for confounding turn-taking factors. First, there were no deviations from modal phonation in the target syllables. Second, final lengthening was also controlled insofar as the fully pronounced and highly reduced target syllables showed no systematic duration differences. Moreover, all duration differences were below the just noticeable difference of 20% (cf. Klatt 1976), which corresponds to about 40 ms in the case of our target syllables.

All 32 base stimuli were then subjected to a PSOLA manipulation in PRAAT, in which we firstly set the pause between target and alternative question to exactly 1.5 seconds. For reasons that will be explained in 3.2, this interval is at the upper limit of turn-internal pauses in dialogues and thus suitable to raise the reasonable suspicion that no alternative question would follow (e.g., Edlund & Heldner, 2005). Finally, we replaced the naturally produced F0 patterns at the end of the 32 target questions (all of them were more or less linear rises) by clearly convex and concave rises of the same overall range, as is illustrated in Figure 2. The rises were stylized at rise onset, pivot, and rise offset. They set in right before the stressed vowel; the pivot was located at the end of the stressed vowel.

The PSOLA manipulations resulted in 64 resynthesized stimuli. Another 64 stimuli were created by cutting off the alternative questions from the 64 resynthesized stimuli.

3.2 Subjects and procedure

Twenty native speakers of Standard Northern German participated in the perception experiment (14 females, 6 males, 20-30 years old). All participants were undergraduate students of Empirical Linguistics at the University of Kiel.

The participants sat in a sound-treated room and put on a headset. Then, they were instructed that they would be presented with 64 stimuli, each of which would end in a question. Their task would be to conceive themselves in a dialogue situation and to respond to the questions of their female dialogue partner with short, plain answers ('yes/no', 'don't know', 'we'll see' and the like) as soon as they would think that they were given the floor. However, if they answered too early, i.e. before their dialogue partner's turn had ended, their answer would count as a failure. On the other hand, if they did not respond within 1.5 seconds after their dialogue partner's turn had ended (indicated by a bleep), then their answer would count as a failure, too. At the end of the experiment, that participant who gave the most valid answers in the shortest average response time would win a prize (a 50 € voucher).

The crucial point in this procedure was that the participants did not know when the target question was turn-internal or turn-final, i.e. when it was followed by an additional alternative question, as this variable was randomly distributed across the 64 stimuli. In this way, we avoided that the participants were able to learn artificial turn yielding or holding cues during the experiment by correlating the phonetic variation at the end of the target questions with the occurrence of alternative questions. Furthermore, informal pretests showed that the dichotomous forces of the competitive task – i.e. the risk of premature vs. overdue responses – were effective in making participants focus on the stimuli and exploiting given acoustic cues.

Prior to the actual experimental session, which took about 20 min, the participants received a practice session with 12 stimuli that were randomly selected for each participant. The 64 stimuli of the subsequent experimental session were also played in individually randomized orders.

The entire experimental sessions of all participants were recorded via their headsets. Recordings were made with Audacity in the form of digital stereo files with separate channels for stimuli and responses. On this basis, we measured the response times, i.e. the time intervals from the end of the target question to the first response signal of the participant (which included smacks). This response-time measure (in ms) served as dependent variable. Response-time measurements were made manually in Audacity. Figure 3 displays an example. If the relevant first response came too late (e.g., after an alternative question had begun) or not at all, response time measurements were capped at 1.5 seconds.

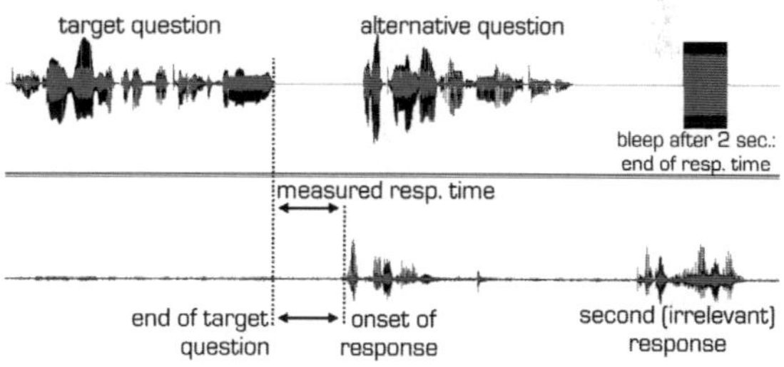

Figure 3: Audacity screenshot showing an example of a response-time measurement; top: stimulus channel, bottom: response channel.

3.3 Hypotheses of Experiment 1

Assuming that participants would respond more readily/reluctantly when they perceived turn-yielding/-holding cues in the target questions of their virtual female dialogue partner, we hypothesized that response times would be shorter (i) for target questions ending in concave than in convex rises and (ii) for target questions ending in unreduced [ən] syllables rather than in the reduced syllabic nasals [m̩] or [ŋ̍].

Although we used target questions with different wordings (that included the target words), a pretest showed that none of these wordings created a semantic bias towards a turn-internal or turn-final interpretation (cf. 3.1). Thus, we expected no effect of the variable Question Wording on response times. The same was true for the target-word internal variable Segmental Context (<-en#> preceded by a labial or velar consonant).

3.4 Results of Experiment 1

The results of the first perception experiment are depicted in Figure 4 in terms of response times per stimulus condition, averaged across all 20 participants. For the statistical analysis, we used a four-way repeated-measures ANOVA (n=20) based on the fixed factors Reduction (2 levels), Rise Shape (2 levels), Segmental Context (2 levels), and Question Wording (8 levels). The ANOVA yielded three significant main effects on the dependent variable Response Time (in ms). The main effects concerned Reduction ($F_{[1,19]}$= 57.716, p<0.001, η_p^2= 0.752), Rise Shape ($F_{[1,19]}$= 63.462, p<0.001, η_p^2= 0.770), and Segmental Context ($F_{[1,19]}$= 10.991, p<0.001, η_p^2= 0.366). The factor Question Wording was not significant, neither was any of the interactions. Insofar, our results allow a straightforward analysis. As is shown in Figure 4, response times were significantly shorter …

- when the target questions ended in the unreduced [ən] syllables rather than in the reduced syllables [m̩] or [ŋ̍];
- when the rising intonation at the end of the target questions had a concave rather than a convex shape, i.e. when the F0 rise started shallowly across the initial, accented syllable of the utterance-final verb and continued steeply until the end of the utterance (cf. Fig.2);
- when the final <-en#> syllable was preceded by a labial rather than a velar plosive or nasal.

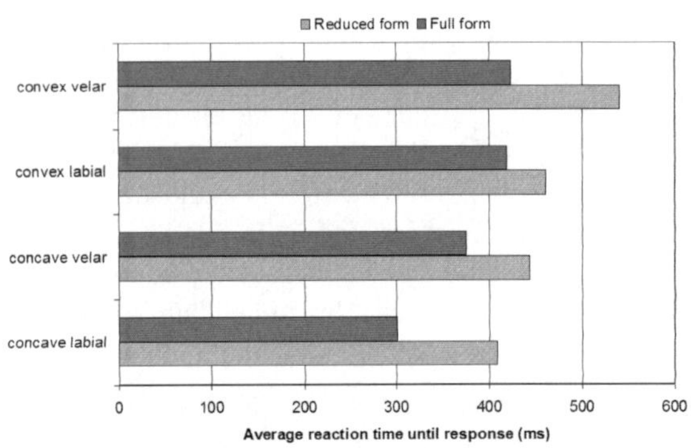

Figure 4: Results of Experiment 1 in terms of average response times (in ms) per stimulus condition; each bar n=20.

3.5 Conclusions from Experiment 1

Our hypotheses concerning the effects of rise shape and the degree of (question-)final reduction on the participants' response times were confirmed. Participants responded slowest after target questions that ended in a convex final rise across a widely reduced <-en#> syllable, and they responded fastest after target questions that ended in a concave final rise across an unreduced <-en#> syllable. The latter target questions caused response times of only 300-400 ms, which is exactly in the order of magnitude of successful – i.e. intended and correctly interpreted – turn transitions in German (Weilhammer & Rabold, 2003). This fact lends further support to our main conclusion: Rise shape and degree of reduction, which were both found to vary utterance-finally on the part of speech production, also function as cues to turn-yielding and/or turn-holding on the part of speech perception.

Moreover, as expected on the basis of our semantic pretest, Question Wording had no effect on response times. However, we found an unexpected response-time effect of Segmental Context, i.e. the place of articulation of the consonant that preceded the <-en#> syllables. We have no clear explanation for this finding as yet. It could be an experimental artefact caused by different frequencies of occurrence of our 'labial' and 'velar' target words. Such frequency differences, even if they are small, could be associated with different reduction baselines. These baselines could have then interacted differently with the turn-taking interpretation of our Reduction variable. Alternatively, the effect of Segmental Context could be due to a difference in intrinsic intensity, which is slightly higher for velar than for labial consonants. This difference also applied to the final nasal /n/ when it was assimilated to [m̩] or [ŋ̍]. That a lower/higher intensity level towards the end of utterances can basically be interpreted as a turn-yielding and/or turn-holding cue will be shown in the following Experiment 2.

4 Perception experiment 2: reduction and intensity level

Although Experiment 2 primarily tested, if and how utterance-final intensity variation affected the listeners' response times, it was additionally used to investigate the reduction effect of Experiment 1 in more detail. In Experiment 1, we contrasted widely reduced <-en#> syllables ([m̩], [ŋ̍]) with their maximally unreduced counterpart [ən], being aware of the fact that [ən] is a rare realization of <-en#>, cf. Figure 1(a). Now, in Experiment 2, we turned to the much more frequent, but also perceptually much more subtle reduction difference in <-en#> syllables: assimilated and non-assimilated syllabic nasals.

4.1 Hypotheses of Experiment 2

Our hypotheses were that response times would be shorter (i) for target questions ending in low rather than in high intensity levels and (ii) for target questions ending in less reduced (non-assimilated) [n̩] rather than in reduced (assimilated) [m̩] or [ŋ̍]. In addition, we expect to replicate the secondary findings of Experiment 1: There should be no systematic effect of Question Wording; and, concerning the Segmental Context, there should be faster response times for the group of target words with 'labial' consonants.

4.2 Method of Experiment 2

The method was the same as in Experiment 1, except for three points.

First, we performed a second round of recordings in which we attenuated the reduction difference at the end of the target questions from [ən] vs. [m̩]/[ŋ̍] to [n̩] vs. [m̩]/[ŋ̍]. That is, all <-en#> syllables were realized as syllabic nasals so that the reduction difference became only a matter of presence vs. absence of place assimilation by the preceding labial or velar consonant. The pause between target and alternative question in the stimuli was again set to 1.5 seconds by inserting or cutting out silence.

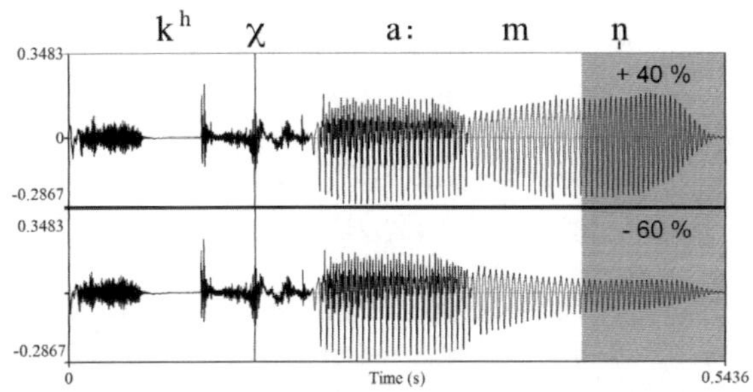

Figure 5: Intensity contrast (loud: +40%, top vs. soft: -60%, bottom) created for Experiment 2, exemplified by "kramen" (to fish sth. out).

Second, instead of the difference in rise shape (all target questions of Experiment 2 ended in a similarly concave rise), we created a difference in the intensity level of the <-en#> syllable. More specifically, the naturally produced intensity pattern of each syllabic nasal [n̩], [m̩] or [ŋ̍] (which typically featured a small intensity increase towards the center of the sound segment, followed by a steep intensity decrease until the end of the target question) was expanded by 40% for the "loud" condition and abated by 60% for the "soft" condition. So, the resulting pairs of stimuli showed a clearly perceivable intensity contrast – "loud" vs. "soft" – in the amount of 100% or 6 dB at the end of the target questions. The intensity manipulation was conducted with Adobe Audition. An example of two waveforms of the question-final target word "kramen" (to fish sth. out, without place assimilation of /n/) is presented in Figure 5.

Third, Experiment 2 was run with a different group of 20 native speakers of Standard Northern German (15 females, 5 males, 23-38 years old).

4.3 Results of Experiment 2

We used again a four-way repeated-measures ANOVA for analyzing our response-time measurements. The fixed factors were the same as in Experiment 1, except that the former factor Rise Shape was substituted by the factor Intensity Decrease. The results of the ANOVA are restricted to three significant main effects that concerned the fixed factors Reduction ($F_{[1,19]}$= 324.653, $p<0.001$, η_p^2= 0.945), Intensity Decrease ($F_{[1,19]}$= 460.355, $p<0.001$, η_p^2= 0.96), and Segmental Context ($F_{[1,19]}$= 72.091, $p<0.001$, η_p^2= 0.791).

As can be seen in Figure 6, the effect of Reduction is due to the fact that participants responded more quickly in the less reduced [n̩] condition than in the reduced [m̩] or [ŋ̍] conditions. Furthermore, responses came faster when the degree of intensity reduction at the end of the target question was stronger, i.e. when target questions ended softer rather than louder. Finally, response times were shorter when the syllabic nasal at the end of the target question was labial rather than velar and/or preceded by a labial rather than a velar consonant.

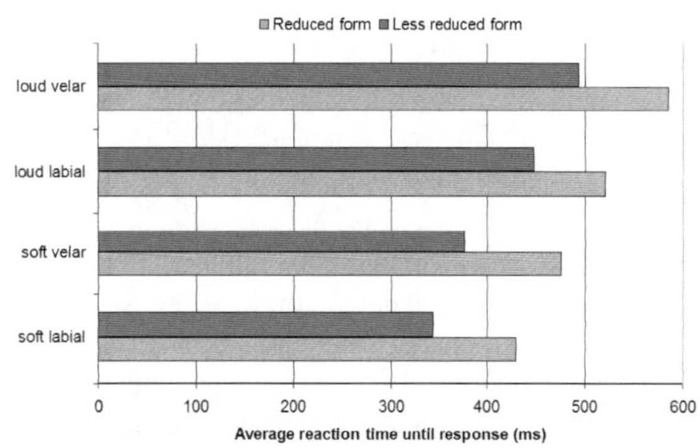

Figure 6: Results of Experiment 2 in terms of average response times (in ms) per stimulus condition; each bar n=20.

4.4 Conclusions from Experiment 2

All hypotheses in 4.1 were supported by Experiment 2 The effect of Reduction means that our participants detected the subtle phonetic difference between non-assimilated and assimilated question-final /n/, and their reaction to this subtle difference was consistent with that of Experiment 1: Participants respond readily when the target question ended less reduced, and/or they hesitated to respond after those target questions whose final <-en#> syllables were more strongly reduced. So, Experiment 2 provided additional evidence for our conclusion that stronger segmental reduction functions as a cue to turn-holding and/or that weaker segmental reduction functions as a cue to turn-yielding.

The intensity level of the final <-en#> syllables had a separate effect. That louder ending questions delayed the participants' response times suggests that a high utterance-final intensity level has a turn-holding function. Additionally (or alternatively), the immediate responses after soft ending questions indicate that the lower utterance-final intensity level is a cue to turn-yielding. Like for the segmental effects above, the intensity effects fit in well with the real use and distribution of intensity differences in spontaneous dialogues, cf. 1.1.

If we view the loud vs. soft contrast in terms of a low vs. high degree of reduction, then we can see that intensity reduction and segmental reduction played opposite roles in turn-taking. Stronger reduction at the segmental level pointed in the direction of turn-holding, whereas stronger intensity reduction pointed in the direction of turn-yielding. This fact leads to the conclusion that turn-taking cues are no indexical cues insofar as they cannot be uniformly projected onto changes in the speaker's effort.

Furthermore, Experiment 2 also replicated the Segmental-Context effect of Experiment 1. Assuming – in accord with previous studies and informal measurements in our stimuli – that the labial condition was associated with an overall lower intensity level in the target words than the velar condition (e.g., due to longer closure durations, less intense releases, and closed lips during nasal production), then the unexpected Segmental-Context effect becomes understandable as an additional reflection of the role of intensity in turn-taking. That is, as has been anticipated in 3.5, the intrinsically higher intensity in our velar target words created a bias towards turn-holding, and/or the intrinsically less intense labial target words created a bias towards turn-yielding.

Finally, a comparison of Figures 4 and 6 shows that the response times yielded by Experiment 2 were overall longer than those of Experiment 1. This general bias should not be over interpreted as it is probably just due to the fact that Experiment 2 was performed in the evening, whereas Experiment 1 took place in the morning.

5 General discussion

It is known for a long time that turn yielding and holding rely on complex form-function systems. So far, these systems have been typically associated with the prosodic triplet of duration, voice quality, and F0 level. Together they create bundles of perceptually salient phrase-final patterns that involve the direction and range of intonation movements, final lengthening, and non-modal voice qualities (typically glottalization).

More recently, analyses of spontaneous dialogues suggested that the bundles of final turn yielding and holding cues are still richer and include also comparatively subtle differences in the degree of segmental reduction, the intensity level, and the shape of intonation movements, especially of rises. Our study enhanced this production evidence and confirmed for Standard Northern German that listeners do in fact pick up on these additional phrase-final differences and interpret them – in parallel to their use in production – as cues to turn yielding and/or holding.

The question that we raised in 1.2 can thus be answered affirmatively; and this means that our study laid the ground for a broader scope in the phonetics of turn-taking. In particular, as is demonstrated by the turn-taking effects of segmental elision and assimilation, this broader scope has to span the traditionally separated segmental and prosodic layers of the speech signal. That is, like for prominence, intonation, and many other form-function systems, the phonetics of turn-taking is not merely a matter of prosody.

Moreover, our findings stress that understanding speech communication includes having a constant eye on phonetic detail. Every phonetic detail should initially be considered functional rather than prejudging it as epiphenomenal or random variation.

Previous studies, some of which are cited in 1.1, have shown that the production and perception of turn yielding and holding exhibit strong similarities across many – even unrelated – languages. For this reason, we assume that our findings are of general cross-linguistic significance. Testing this assumption will be the obvious next step. The corresponding perception experiments should use the same innovative task as the present study. Although this task is complex, its interactive concept proved to yield clear results while ensuring a high level of ecological validity.

References

E.L. Asu. 2006. Rising intonation in Estonian: an analysis of map task dialogues and spontaneous conversations. *Proc. Phonetic Symposium 2006, Helsinki, Finland*: 1-9.

W.G. Beattie. 1981. The regulation of speaker turns in face-to-face conversation: Some implications for conversation in sound-only communication channels. *Semiotica*, 34: 55-70.

M. Clayards, R.N. Aslin, M.K. Tanenhaus, and R.A. Jacobs. 2007. Within category phonetic variability affects perceptual uncertainty. *Proc. 16th International Congress of Phonetic Sciences, Saarbrücken, Germany:* 701-704.

C. Clemens and C. Diekhaus. 2009. Prosodic turn-yielding Cues with and without optical Feedback. *Proc. SIGDIAL 2009: the 10th Annual Meeting of the Special Interest Group in Discourse and Dialogue, London, UK*: 107–110.

G.J. Docherty, J. Milroy, L. Milroy, and D. Walshaw. 1997. Descriptive adequacy in phonology: A variationist perspective. *J. of Linguistics*, 33: 275-310.

E. Dombrowski and O. Niebuhr. 2005. Acoustic patterns and communicative functions of phrase-final rises in German: activating and restricting contours. *Phonetica,* 62: 176-195.

S. Duncan, Jr.. 1972. Some signals and rules for taking speaking turns in conversations. *Journal of Personality and Social Psychology*, 23: 283-292.

J. Edlund and M. Heldner. 2005. Exploring prosody in interaction control. *Phonetica*, 62: 215-226.

J.-Y. Fon. 2002. *A cross-linguistic study on syntactic and discourse boundary cues in spontaneous speech*. PhD thesis, Ohio State University, USA.

J.-Y. Fon, K. Johnson, and S. Chen. 2011. Durational Patterning at Syntactic and Discourse Boundaries in Mandarin Spontaneous Speech. *Language and Speech*, 54: 5-32.

H. Friedberg. 2011. Turn-taking cues in a human tutoring cirpus. *Proc. Association for Computational Linguistics, Portland, USA*: 94-98.

A. Gravano. 2009. *Turn-taking and affirmative cue words in task-oriented dialogue*. PhD thesis, Columbia University, USA.

A. Gravano and J. Hirschberg. 2009. Turn yielding cues in task-oriented dialogue. *Proc. SIGDIAL 2009: the 10th Annual Meeting of the Special Interest Group on Discourse and Dialogue, London, UK:* 253-261.

A. Kendon. 1995. Gestures as illocutionary and discourse structure markers in Southern Italian conversation. *Journal of Pragmatics,* 23: 247-279.

K.J. Kohler. 1983. Prosodic boundary signals in German. *Phonetica*, 40: 89–134.

K.J. Kohler. 1996. Labelled data bank of spoken Standard German: The Kiel Corpus of Spontaneous Speech. *Proc. 4th International Conference on Spoken Language Processing, Philadelphia, USA*: 1938-1941.

K.J. Kohler. 2004. Categorical speech perception revisited. *Proc. of the Conference From Sound to Sense: 50+ years of discoveries in speech communication, MIT, Cambridge, USA*: 1-6.

K.J. Kohler and O. Niebuhr. 2011. On the role of articulatory prosodies in German message decoding. *Phonetica,* 68: 1-31.

D. H. Klatt. 1976. Linguistic uses of segmental duration in English: Acoustic and perceptual evidence. *Journal of the Acoustical Society of America 59*: 1208-21.

I. Lehiste. 1982. Some phonetic characteristics of discourse. *Studia Linguistica*, 36: 117-130

J. Local, J. Kelly, and W.H. Wells. 1986. Towards a phonology of conversation: Turn-taking in Tyneside English. *Journal of Linguistics*, 22: 411–437.

J. Local and. G. Walker. 2012. How phonetic features project more talk. *Journal of the International Phonetic Association*, 42: 255-281.

C.H. Nakatani, J. Hirschberg, and B.J. Grosz. 1995. Discourse structure in spoken language: Studies on speech corpora. *Proc. AAAI Spring Symposium on Empirical Methods in Discourse Interpretation and Generation, Palo Alto, USA*: 1-7.

R.A. Ogden. 2001. Turn transition, creak and glottal stop in Finnish talk-in-interaction. *Journal of the International Phonetic Association*, 31: 139–152.

B. Peters. 2006. *Form und Funktion prosodischer Grenzen im Gespräch*. PhD thesis, Christian-Albrechts-Universität zu Kiel, Germany.

A. Raux. 2008. *Flexible turn-taking for spoken dialog systems*. PhD thesis, Carnegie Mellon University, Pittsburgh, USA.

M. Taboada. 2006. Spontaneous and non-spontaneous turn taking. *Pragmatics*, 16: 329-360.

J. Vaissière, J. and A. Michaud. 2006. Prosodic constituents in French: a data-driven approach. In I. Fónagy, Y. Kawaguchi, T. Moriguchi (eds), *Prosody and syntax* (pp. 47-64). Amsterdam: John Benjamins.

K. Weilhammer and S. Rabold. 2003. Durational aspects in turn taking. *Proc. 15th International Congress of Phonetic Sciences, Barcelona, Spain* : 931–934.

Gesture Semantics Reconstruction Based on Motion Capturing and Complex Event Processing: a Circular Shape Example

Thies Pfeiffer, Florian Hofmann
Artificial Intelligence Group
Faculty of Technology
Bielefeld University, Germany
(tpfeiffe|fhofmann)
@techfak.uni-bielefeld.de

Florian Hahn, Hannes Rieser, Insa Röpke
Collaborative Research Center
"Alignment in Communication" (CRC 673)
Bielefeld University, Germany
(fhahn2|hannes.rieser|iroepke)
@uni-bielefeld.de

Abstract

A fundamental problem in manual based gesture semantics reconstruction is the specification of preferred semantic concepts for gesture trajectories. This issue is complicated by problems human raters have annotating fast-paced three dimensional trajectories. Based on a detailed example of a gesticulated circular trajectory, we present a data-driven approach that covers parts of the semantic reconstruction by making use of motion capturing (mocap) technology. In our FA^{3}ME framework we use a complex event processing approach to analyse and annotate multi-modal events. This framework provides grounds for a detailed description of how to get at the semantic concept of circularity observed in the data.

1 Introduction

Focussing on iconic gestures, we discuss the benefit of motion capturing (mocap) technology for the reconstruction of gesture meaning and speech meaning: A fundamental problem is the specification of semantic concepts for gesture trajectories, e.g., for describing circular movements or shapes. We start with demonstrating the limitations of our manual based annotation. Then we discuss two strategies of how to deal with these, pragmatic inference *vs.* low level annotation based on mocap technology yielding a more precise semantics. We then argue that the second strategy is to be preferred to the inferential one.

The annotation of mocap data can be realised semi-automatically by our FA^{3}ME framework for the analysis and annotation of multimodal events, which we use to record multi-modal corpora. For mocap we use the tracking system ART DTrack2 (advanced realtime tracking GmbH, 2013), but the framework is not restricted to this technical set-up. In cooperation with others (e.g., (Kousidis et al., 2012)), we also have used products from Vicon Motion Systems (2013) and the Microsoft Kinect (Microsoft, 2013). Pfeiffer (2013) presents an overview on mocap technology for documenting multi-modal studies.

We thus provide details about the way gestures are analysed with FA^{3}ME and about the procedure to reconstruct the gesture meaning for the circular movement in our chosen example. We conclude with a discussion of how these low-level reconstructions can be integrated into the reconstruction of speech and gesture meaning.

2 From Linguistic Annotation to MoCap

In this section we describe our methodology for the reconstruction of gesture meaning, speech meaning and its interfacing, illustrated by an example. We then show a shortcoming of our corpus-based annotation and discuss two possible solutions to amend it, pragmatic inference *vs.* semantics based on mocap technology. The technology described in Section 3 will in the end enable us to get the preferred reconstruction of gesture semantics.

The reconstruction of the gesture meaning and its fusion with speech meaning to get a multimodal proposition works as follows: On the speech side we start with a manual transcription, upon which we craft a context free syntax analysis followed by a formal semantics. On the gesture side we build an AVM-based representation of the gesture resting on manual annotation.[1] Taking the gesture as a sign with independent meaning (Rieser, 2010), this representation provides the basis for the formal gesture semantics. In the next

[1]We do not use an explicit gesture model, which would go against our descriptive intentions. The range of admissible gestures is fixed by annotation manuals and investigations in gesture typology.

Figure 1: Our example: a circular gesture (left: video still) to describe the path around the pond (right).

step, the gesture meaning and the speech meaning are fused into an interface (Röpke et al., 2013). Every step in these procedures is infested by underspecification which, however, we do not deal with here. These are, for instance, the selection of annotation predicates, the attribution of logical form to gestures and the speech analysis.

In our example, we focus on two gesture parameters, the movement feature of the gesture and the representation technique used. It originates from the systematically annotated corpus, called SaGA, the Bielefeld Speech-and-Gesture Alignment-corpus (Lücking et al., 2012). It consists of 25 dialogues of dyads conversing about a "bus ride" through a Virtual Reality town. One participant of each dyad, the so-called Route-Giver (RG), has done this ride and describes the route and the sights passed to the other participant, the so-called Follower (FO). The taped conversations are annotated in a fine-grained way.

In the example, the RG describes a route section around a pond to the FO. While uttering "Du gehst drei Viertel rum/You walk three quarters around", she produces the gesture depicted in Figure 1. Intuitively, the gesture conveys a circularity information not expressed in the verbal meaning. In order to explicate the relation of speech and gesture meaning, we use our methodology as described above. To anticipate, we get a clear contribution of the speech meaning which is restricted by the gesture meaning conveying the roundness information. The first step is to provide a syntactical analysis which you can see in Figure 2.[2]

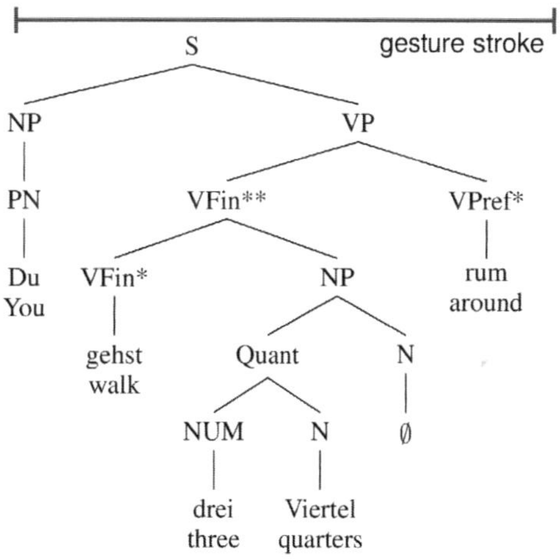

Figure 2: Syntax analysis

The speech representation is inspired by a Montague-Parsons-Reichenbach event ontology, and uses type-logic notions. Ignoring the embedding in an indirect speech act[3], the speech semantics represents an AGENT (the FO) who is engaged in a WALK-AROUND event e related to some path F, and a THEME relating the WALK-AROUND event e with the path F.

$$\exists e y \mathrm{F}\ 3/4x(\textsc{walk-around}(e) \wedge \mathrm{AGENT}(e, \mathrm{FO}) \wedge \mathrm{THEME}(e, x) \wedge \mathrm{F}(x, y)) \quad (1)$$

The gesture semantics is obtained using the annotated gesture features. The relevant features are the movement of the wrist (Path_of_Wrist) and the Representation_Technique used.

Path_of_Wrist	ARC<ARC< ARC<ARC
Representation_Technique	Drawing

[4]

Interpreting the values ARC<ARC< ARC<ARC and Drawing, respectively, the calculated gesture semantics represents a bent trajectory consisting of four segments:

[2]The gesture stroke extends over the whole utterance. Verb phrases can feature so-called "sentence brackets". Here, due to a sentence bracket, the finite verb stem "gehst" is separated from its prefix ("rum"). Together they embrace the German *Mittelfeld*, here "drei Viertel". Observe the N-ellipsis "∅" in the NP. The prefix and the finite verb stem cannot be fully interpreted on their own and are therefore marked with an asterisk.

[3]We have treated the function of speech-gesture ensembles in dialogue acts and dialogues elsewhere (Rieser and Poesio (2009), Rieser (2011), Hahn and Rieser (2011), Lüecking et al. (2012)).

[4]This is a shortened version of the full gesture-AVM. Features like hand shape etc. are ignored. See Rieser (2010) for other annotation predicates.

$$\exists x y_1 y_2 y_3 y_4(\text{TRAJECTORY}_0(x) \wedge \text{BENT}(y_1) \wedge \text{BENT}(y_2) \wedge \text{BENT}(y_3) \wedge \text{BENT}(y_4) \wedge y_1 < y_2 < y_3 < y_4 \wedge \text{SEGMENT}(y_1, x) \wedge \text{SEGMENT}(y_2, x) \wedge \text{SEGMENT}(y_3, x) \wedge \text{SEGMENT}(y_4, x)). \quad (2)$$

The paraphrase is: There exists a TRAJECTORY$_0$ x which consists of four BENT SEGMENTS y_1, y_2, y_3, y_4. We abbreviate this formula to:

$$\exists x_1(\text{TRAJECTORY}_1(x_1)) \quad (3)$$

In more mundane verbiage: There is a particular TRAJECTORY$_1$ x_1. In a speech-gesture interface[5] (Rieser, 2010) both formulae are extended by adding a parameter in order to compositionally combine them:

$$\lambda Y.\exists ey\text{F } 3/4x \ (\text{WALK-AROUND}(e) \wedge \text{AGENT}(e, \text{FO}) \wedge \text{THEME}(e, x) \wedge \text{F}(x, y) \wedge \text{Y}(y)) \quad (4)$$

We read this as: There is a WALK-AROUND event e the AGENT of which is FO related to a three quarters (path) F. This maps x onto y which is in turn equipped with property Y.

$$\lambda z.\exists x_1(\text{TRAJECTORY}_1(x_1) \ \wedge \ x_1 = z) \quad (5)$$

This means "There is a TRAJECTORY$_1$ x_1 identical with an arbitrary z". The extensions (4) and (5) are based on the intuition that the preferred reading is a modification of the (path) F by the gesture.

Taking the gesture representation as an argument for the speech representation, we finally get a simplified multi-modal interface formula. The resulting proposition represents an AGENT (FO) who is engaged in a WALK-AROUND event e and a THEME that now is specified as being related to a bent trajectory of four arcs due to formula (2):

$$\exists ey\, 3/4x \ \exists \text{F}(\text{WALK-AROUND}(e) \wedge \text{AGENT}(e, \text{FO}) \wedge \text{THEME}(e, x) \wedge \text{F}(x, y) \wedge \text{TRAJECTORY}_1(y)) \quad (6)$$

We take this to mean "There is an AGENT FO's WALK-AROUND event e related to a three quarters (path) F having a TRAJECTORY$_1$ y".

As a result, the set of models in which the orginal speech proposition is true is restricted to the set of models that contain a bent trajectory standing in relation to the (path) F. But this restriction is too weak. Intuitively, the gesture conveys the meaning of a horizontal circular trajectory and not just four bent arcs. To see the shortcoming, note that the set of models also includes models which include a path having four bends that do not form a circular trajectory.

We envisage two methods to get the appropriate circularity intuition: pragmatic enrichment and an improvement of our gesture datum to capture the additional information conveyed in the gesture: By pragmatic enrichment, on the one hand, horizontal orientation and circularity of the gesture trajectory are inferred using abduction or defaults. However, the drawback of working with defaults or abduction rules is that we would have to set up too many of them depending on the various shapes and functions of bent trajectories.

On the other hand, the datum can be improved to yield a circularly shaped trajectory instead of the weaker one consisting of four bent arcs. Our motion capture data supports the second method: The motion capture data allows us to compute the complete trajectory drawn in the gesture space. This will be the basis for producing a mapping from gesture parameters to qualitative relations which we need in the truth conditions. In the end, we achieve a circular trajectory that is defined as one approximating a circle, see Section 4.3.

In this mapping procedure resides an underspecification, which is treated by fixing a threshold for the application of qualitative predicates through raters' decisions. This threshold value will be used in giving truth conditions for, e.g., (11), especially for determining APPROXIMATE.

We prefer the second method since it captures our hypothesis that the gesture as a sign conveys the meaning *circular trajectory*. The gain of the automated annotation *via* mocap which we will see subsequently is an improvement of our original gesture datum to a more empirically founded one. As a consequence, the set of models that satisfy our multi-modal proposition can be specified. This is also the reason for explicitly focussing on gesture semantics in this paper.

3 FA^{3}ME - Automatic Annotation as Complex Event Processing

The creation of FA^{3}ME, our *Framework for the Automatic Annotation and Augmentation of Multi-*

[5]How our model deals with interfacing speech meaning and gesture meaning has been elaborated in a series of papers (see footnote 3). We are well aware of the work on gesture-speech integration by Lascarides and colleagues which we deal with in a paper on interfaces (Rieser (2013)).

modal Events, is *inter alia* motivated by our key insight from previous studies that human raters have extreme difficulties when annotating 3D gesture poses and trajectories. This is especially true when they only have a restricted view on the recorded gestures. A typical example is the restriction to a fixed number of different camera angles from which the gestures have been recorded. In previous work (Pfeiffer, 2011), we proposed a solution for the restricted camera perspectives based on mocap data: Our Interactive Augmented Data Explorer (IADE) allowed human raters to immerse into the recorded data via virtual reality technology. Using a 3D projection in a CAVE (Cruz-Neira et al., 1992), the raters were enabled to move freely around and through the recorded mocap data, including a 3D reconstruction of the experimental setting. This interactive 3D visualisation supported an advanced annotation process and improved the quality of the annotations but at high costs. Since then, we only know of Kipp (2010) who makes mocap data visible for annotators by presenting feature graphs in his annotation tool Anvil in a desktop-based setting. In later work, Nguyen and Kipp (2010) also support a 3D model of the speaker, but this needed to be handcrafted by human annotators. A more holistic approach for gesture visualizations are the Gesture Space Volumes Pfeiffer (2011), which summarize gesture trajectories over longer timespans or multiple speakers.

The IADE system also allowed us to add visual augmentations during the playback of the recorded data. These augmentations were based on the events from the mocap data, but aggregated several events to higher-level representations. In a study on pointing gestures (Lücking et al., 2013), we could test different hypotheses about the construction of the direction of pointing by adding visual pointing rays shooting in a 3D reconstruction of the original real world setting. This allowed us to asses the accuracy of pointing at a very high level in a data-driven manner and derive a new model for the direction of pointing (Pfeiffer, 2011).

3.1 Principles in FA^{3}ME

In the FA^{3}ME project, we iteratively refine our methods for analysing multi-modal events. As a central concept, FA^{3}ME considers any recorded datum as a *first-level multi-modal event* (see Figure 3, left). This can be a time-stamped frame from a video camera, an audio sample, 6-degree-of-freedom matrices from a mocap system or gaze information from an eye-tracking system (e.g., see Kousidis et al. (2012)).

A distinctive factor of FA^{3}ME is that we consider annotations as *second-level multi-modal events*. That is, recorded and annotated data share the same representation. Annotations can be added by both, human raters and classification algorithms (the event rules in Figure 3, middle). Annotations can themselves be target of annotations. This allows us, for example, to create automatic classifiers that rely on recorded data and manual annotations (e.g., the first yellow event in Figure 3 depends on first-level events above and the blue second-level event to the right). This is helpful when classifiers for complex events are not (yet) available. If, for instance, no automatic classifiers for the stroke of a gesture exists, these annotations can be made by human raters. Once this is done, the automatic classifiers can describe the movements during the meaningful phases by analysing the trajectories of the mocap data.

Third-level multi-modal events are augmentations or extrapolations of the data. They might represent hypotheses, such as in the example of different pointing rays given above.

3.2 Complex Event Processing

In FA^{3}ME, we consider the analysis of multi-modal events as a *complex event processing* (CEP) problem. CEP is an area of computer science dedicated to the timely detection, analysis, aggregation and processing of events (Luckham, 2002). In the past years, CEP has gained an increased attention especially in the analysis of business relevant processes where large amount of data, e.g., share prices, with high update rates are analysed. This has fostered many interesting tools and frameworks for the analysis of structured events (Arasu et al., 2004a; EsperTech, 2013; Gedik et al., 2008; StreamBase, 2013). Hirte et al. (2012) apply CEP to a motion tracking stream from a Microsoft Kinect for real-time interaction, but we know of no uses of CEP for the processing of multi-modal event streams for linguistic analysis.

Dedicated query languages have been developed by several CEP frameworks which allow us to specify our event aggregations descriptively at a high level of abstraction (Arasu et al., 2004b;

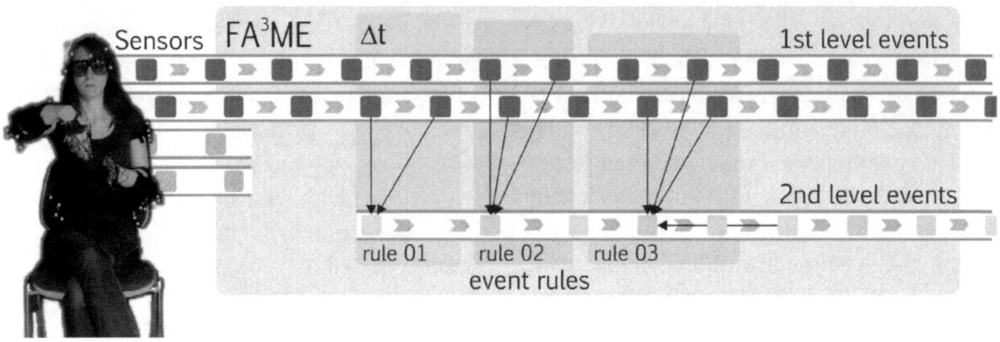

Figure 3: In FA^{3}ME, incoming multi-modal events are handled by a complex event processing framework that matches and aggregates events based on time windows to compose 2nd level multi-modal events. All multi-modal events can then be mapped to tiers in an annotation tool.

Gedik et al., 2008). The framework we use for FA^{3}ME is Esper (EsperTech, 2013), which provides a SQL-like query language. As a central extension of SQL, CEP query languages introduce the concept of event streams and time windows as a basis for aggregation (see Figure 3).

The CEP approach of FA^{3}ME allows us to create second- and third-level multi-modal events on-the-fly. We can thus provide near real-time annotations of sensor events. However, we have to consider the latencies introduced by sensors or computations and back-date events accordingly.

As a practical result, once we have specified our annotation descriptions formally in the language of CEP, these descriptions can be used to create classifiers that operate both on pre-recorded multimodal corpora and on real-time data. This makes CEP interesting for projects where research in Linguistics and Human-Computer Interaction meet.

4 From MoCap to Linguistic Models

In this section, we will now address the problem of annotating the circular trajectory. In order to get the preferred semantics we yet cannot rely exclusively on the automatic annotation. We need the qualitative predicate "phase" to identify the meaningful part of the gesture (the stroke). Additionally, the qualitative predicate "representation technique" is required to select the relevant mocap trackers. For instance, the representation technique "drawing" selects the marker of the tip of the index finger. We thus require a hybrid model of manual and automatic annotations. In the following, we will focus on the automatic annotation.

First of all, when using mocap to record data, a frame of reference has to be specified as a basis for all coordinate systems. We chose a person-centered frame of reference anchored in the solar plexus (see Figure 4). The coronal plane is defined by the solar plexus and the two shoulders. The transverse plane is also defined by the solar plexus, perpendicular to the coronal plane with a normal-vector from solar plexus to the point ST (see Figure 4) between the two shoulders.

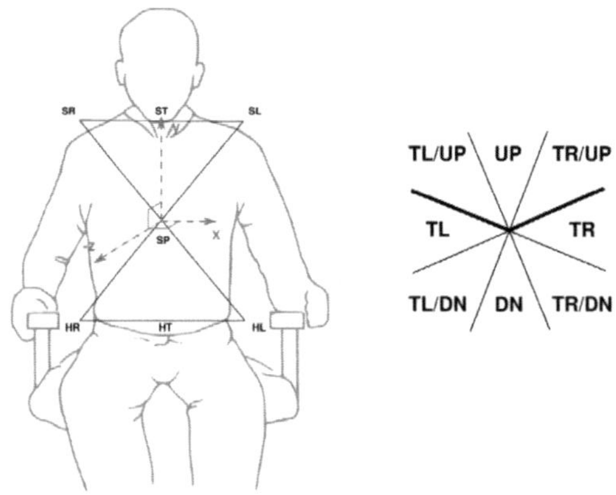

Figure 4: The coordinate system of the speaker (left). The orientations of the palms are classified into eight main directions (right).

4.1 Basic Automatic Gesture Annotations

The analysis of mocap data allows us to create basic annotations that we use in our corpora on-the-fly. This speeds up the annotation process and lets human raters focus on more complex aspects. One basic annotation that can be achieved automatically is the classification of the position of gesturing hands according to the gesture space model of McNeill (1992). As his annotation schema (see Figure 5, right) is tailored for the annotation of

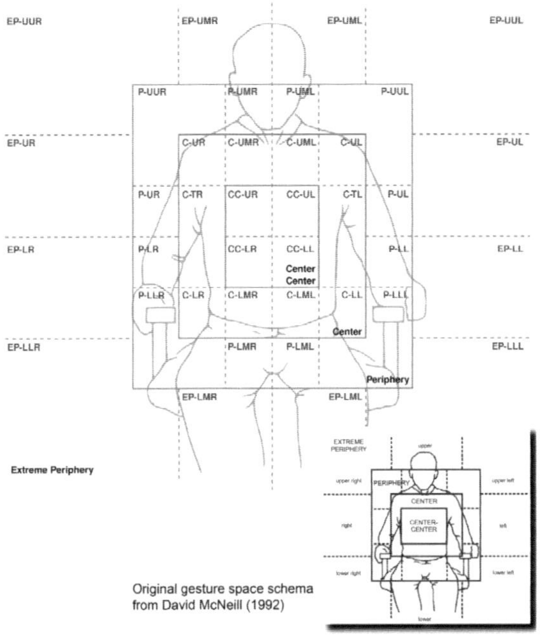

Figure 5: Our extended gesture space categorisation (upper left) is based on the work of McNeill (lower right).

video frames, we extended this model to support mocap as well (see Figure 5, left). The important point is that the areas of our schema are derived from certain markers attached to the observed participant. The upper right corner of the area C-UR (Center-Upper Right), for example, is linked to the marker for the right shoulder. Our schema thus scales directly with the size of the participant. Besides this, the sub-millimeter resolution of the mocap system also allows us to have a more detailed structure of the center area. The schema is also oriented according to the current coronal plane of the participant and not, e.g., according to the perspective of the camera.

A second example is the classification of the orientation of the hand, which is classified according to the scheme depicted in Figure 4, right. This classification is made relative to the transversal plane of the speaker's body.

4.2 Example: The Circular Trajectory

For the detection and classification of gestures drawing shapes two types of multi-modal events are required. First, multi-modal events generated by the mocap system for the hand. These events contain matrices describing the position and orientation of the back of the hand. Second, multi-modal events that mark the gesture stroke (one event for the start and one for the end) have to be generated, either by hand or automatically. At the moment, we rely on our manual annotations for the existing SaGA corpus.

We realise the annotation of circular trajectories in two steps. First, we reduce the trajectory provided by the mocap system to two dimensions. Second, we determine how closely the 2D trajectory approximates a circle.

Projection of the 3D Trajectory

The classifier for circles collects all events for the hand that happened between the two events for the stroke. As noted above, these events represent the position and orientation of the hand in 3D-space. There are several alternatives to reduce these three dimensions to two for classifying a circle (a 3D Object matching a 2D circle would be a sphere, a circular trajectory through all 3 dimensions a spiral). The principal approach is to reduce the dimensions by projecting the events on a 2D plane.

$$\exists xy\,(\text{TRAJECTORY}(x) \land \text{PROJECTION-OF}(x,y) \land \text{TRAJECTORY2D}(y)) \quad (7)$$

Which plane to chose depends on the choice made for the annotation (e.g., global for the corpus) and thus on the context. For the description of gestures in dialogue there are several plausible alternatives. First, the movements could be projected onto one of the three body planes (sagittal plane, coronal plane, transversal plane). In our context, the transversal plane is suitable, as we are dealing with descriptions of routes, which in our corpus are made either with respect to the body of the speaker or with respect to the plane of an imaginary map, both extend parallel to the floor. Figure 6 (upper left) shows the circular movement in the transversal plane. A different perspective is presented in Figure 6 (right). There the perspective of a bystander is chosen. This kind of perspective can be useful for describing what the recipient of a dialogue act perceives, e.g., to explain misunderstandings. For this purpose, the gesture could also be annotated twice, once from the speaker's and once from the recipient's perspective.

At this point we want to emphasise that position and orientation of the planes do not have to be static. They can be linked to the reference points provided by the mocap system. Thus when the speaker turns her body, the sagittal, coronal and

<< click here for video >>

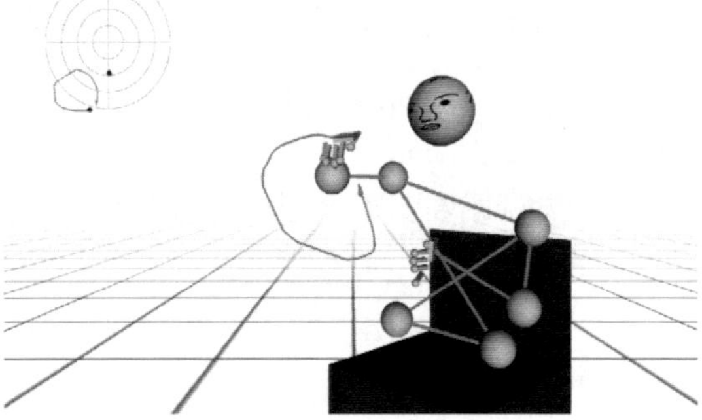

Figure 6: The circle-like gesture from our example can be visualised based on the mocap data. The right side shows the visualisation from the perspective of an interlocutor, the visualisation in the upper left corner is a projection of the movement on the transversal plane of the speaker.

transversal planes will move accordingly and the gestures are always interpreted according to the current orientation.

The plane used for projection can also be derived from the gesture itself. Using principal component analysis, the two main axes used by the gesture can be identified. These axes can then have arbitrary orientations. This could be a useful approach whenever 3D objects are described and the correct position and orientation of the ideal circle has to be derived from the gesture.

Circle Detection

Once the gesture trajectory has been projected onto a 2D plane, the resulting coordinates are classified. For this, several sketch-recognition algorithms have been proposed (e.g., (Alvarado and Davis, 2004; Rubine, 1991)). These algorithms have been designed for sketch-based interfaces (such as tablets or digitisers), either for recognising commands or for prettifying hand-drawn diagrams. However, once the 3D trajectory has been mapped to 2D, they can also be applied to natural gestures. The individual sketch-recognition algorithms differ in the way they are approaching the classification problem. Many algorithms follow a feature-based approach in which the primitives to be recognised are described by a set of features (such as aspect ratio or ratio of covered area) (Rubine, 1991). This approach is especially suited, when new primitives are to be learned by example. An alternative approach is the model-based approach in which the primitives to be recognised are described based on geometric models (Alvarado and Davis, 2004; Hammond and Davis, 2006). Some hybrid approaches also exist (Paulson et al., 2008). The model-based approaches are in line with our declarative approach to modelling, and are thus our preferred way for classifying shapes.

In our case, the projected 2D trajectory of the gesture is thus classified by a model-based sketch-recognition algorithm, which classifies the input into one of several shape classes (circle, rectangle, ...) with a corresponding member function $\text{ISSHAPE}(y, \text{CIRCLE}) \in [0 \ldots 1]$. By this, we can satisfy a subformula $\text{APPROXIMATES}(y, z) \wedge \text{CIRCLE}(z)$ by pre-setting a certain threshold. The threshold has to be chosen by the annotators, e.g., by rating positive and negative examples, as it may vary between participants and express the sloppiness of their gestures.

4.3 From MoCap to a Revision of Semantics

The result of the FA^{3}ME reconstruction of our gesture example can be expressed as follows:

$$\begin{aligned}&\exists xyz\ (\text{TRAJECTORY}(x)\\ &\wedge \text{PROJECTION-OF}(x, y) \wedge \text{TRAJECTORY2D}(y)\\ &\wedge \text{APPROXIMATES}(y, z) \wedge \text{CIRCLE}(z)) \quad (8)\end{aligned}$$

So we have: There is a projection of TRAJECTORY x, TRAJECTORY2D y, which is approximating a circle. We can now provide a description of the domain which can satisfy formula (8). Consequently, formula (8) is enhanced by definition (9).

$$\begin{aligned}&\text{CIRCULAR\_TRAJECTORY}(x) =_{\text{DEF}}\\ &\exists yz(\text{TRAJECTORY}_2(x) \wedge \text{PROJECTION-OF}(x, y) \wedge\\ &\text{APPROXIMATES}(y, z) \wedge \text{circle}(z)) \quad (9)\end{aligned}$$

This definition reads as "a CIRCULAR TRAJECTORY x is a TRAJECTORY_2 which has a PROJECTION y that approximates some circle z".

The formula (9) substitutes the TRAJECTORY_1 notion. The improved multi-modal meaning is (10):

$$\begin{aligned}&\exists ey\, 3/4x\ \exists \text{F}(\text{WALK-AROUND}(e) \wedge\\ &\text{AGENT}(e, \text{FO}) \wedge \text{THEME}(e, x) \wedge \text{F}(x, y)\\ &\wedge \text{CIRCULAR\_TRAJECTORY}(y)) \quad (10)\end{aligned}$$

Interfacing the new gesture representation with the speech representation captures our intuition that the gesture reduces the original set of models to a set including a circular-shaped trajectory.

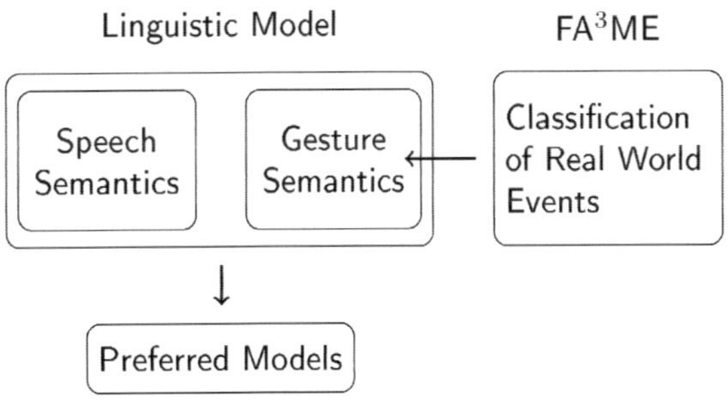

Figure 7: Specification of gesture semantics due to results of classification in FA^{3}ME. Simulation data feed into the gesture semantics which interfaces with the speech semantics.

The division of labour between linguistic semantics and FA^{3}ME technology regarding the semantic reconstruction is represented in Figure 7.

By way of explanation: We have the multi-modal semantics integrating speech semantics and gesture semantics accomplished *via* λ-calculus techniques as shown in Section 2. As also explained there, it alone would be too weak to delimit the models preferred with respect to the gesture indicating roundness. Therefore FA^{3}ME technology leading to a definition of CIRCULAR_TRAJECTORY is used which reduces the set of models to the preferred ones assuming a threshold n for the gestures closeness of fit to a circle. Thus, the relation between some gesture parameters and qualitative relations like *circular* can be considered as a mapping, producing values in the range $[0 \ldots 1]$. Still, it could happen that formula (8) cannot be satisfied in the preferred models. As a consequence, the multi-modal meaning would then fall short of satisfaction.

5 Conclusion

During our work on the interface between speech and gesture meaning our previous annotations turned out to be insufficient to support the semantics of concepts such as CIRCULAR_TRAJECTORY. This concept is a representative of many others that for human annotators are difficult to rate with the rigidity required for the symbolic level of semantics. Scientific visualisations, such as depicted in Figure 6, can be created to support the human raters. However, there is still the problem of perspective distortions three dimensional gestures are subject to when viewed from different angles and in particular when viewed on a 2D screen. It is also difficult to follow the complete trajectory of such gestures over time. Thus, one and the same gesture can be rated differently depending on the rater, while an algorithm with a defined threshold is not subject to these problems.

The presented hybrid approach based on qualitative human annotations, mocap and our FA^{3}ME framework is able to classify the particular 2D trajectories we are interested in following a three-step process: After the human annotator identified the phase and selected relevant trackers, the dimensions are reduced to two and a rigid model-based sketch-recognition algorithm is used to classify the trajectories. This classification is repeatable, consistent and independent of perspective. A first comparison of the manually annotated data and the automatic annotations revealed a high match. All differences between the annotations can be explained by restrictions of the video data which yielded a lower precision in the human annotations specifying the slant of the hand. Thus, the main issues we had with the results of human raters have been addressed, however a more formal evaluation on a large corpus remains to be done. What also remains is a specification of membership functions for each kind of gesture trajectories of interest (e.g., circular, rectangular, etc.). For this, a formal specification of what we commonly mean by, for instance, CIRCULAR, RECTANGULAR etc. is required.

The automated annotation *via* mocap improves our original gesture datum to capture the circularity-information conveyed in the gesture. We have a better understanding of the gesture meaning adopted *vis-à-vis* the datum considered. As it turns out, resorting to pragmatic inference cannot be avoided entirely, but we will exclude a lot of unwarranted readings which the manual-based logical formulae would *still* allow by using the approximation provided by body tracking methods. Not presented here is the way third-level multi-modal events are generated by re-simulating the data in a 3D world model to generate context events, e.g., to support pragmatics.

Acknowledgments

This work has been funded by the Deutsche Forschungsgemeinschaft (DFG) in the Collaborative Research Center 673, *Alignment in Communication*. We are grateful to three reviewers whose arguments we took up in this version.

References

[advanced realtime tracking GmbH2013] A.R.T. advanced realtime tracking GmbH. 2013. Homepage. Retrieved May 2013 from `http://www.ar-tracking.de`.

[Alvarado and Davis2004] Christine Alvarado and Randall Davis. 2004. SketchREAD: a multi-domain sketch recognition engine. In *Proceedings of the 17th annual ACM symposium on User interface software and technology*, UIST '04, pages 23–32, New York, NY, USA. ACM.

[Arasu et al.2004a] Arvind Arasu, Brian Babcock, Shivnath Babu, John Cieslewicz, Mayur Datar, Keith Ito, Rajeev Motwani, Utkarsh Srivastava, and Jennifer Widom. 2004a. Stream: The stanford data stream management system. Technical report, Stanford InfoLab.

[Arasu et al.2004b] Arvind Arasu, Shivnath Babu, and Jennifer Widom. 2004b. CQL: A language for continuous queries over streams and relations. In *Database Programming Languages*, pages 1–19. Springer.

[Cruz-Neira et al.1992] Carolina Cruz-Neira, Daniel J. Sandin, Thomas A. DeFanti, Robert V. Kenyon, and John C. Hart. 1992. The cave: audio visual experience automatic virtual environment. *Communications fo the ACM 35 (2)*, 35(6):64–72.

[EsperTech2013] EsperTech. 2013. Homepage of Esper. Retrieved May 2013 from `http://esper.codehaus.org/`.

[Gedik et al.2008] Bugra Gedik, Henrique Andrade, Kun-Lung Wu, Philip S Yu, and Myungcheol Doo. 2008. SPADE: The System S Declarative Stream Processing Engine. In *Proceedings of the 2008 ACM SIGMOD international conference on Management of data*, pages 1123–1134. ACM.

[Hahn and Rieser2011] Florian Hahn and Hannes Rieser. 2011. Gestures supporting dialogue structure and interaction in the Bielefeld speech and gesture alignment corpus (SaGA). In *Proceedings of SEMdial 2011, Los Angelogue, 15th Workshop on the Semantics and Pragmatics of Dialogue*, pages 182–183, Los Angeles, California.

[Hammond and Davis2006] Tracy Hammond and Randall Davis. 2006. LADDER: A language to describe drawing, display, and editing in sketch recognition. In *ACM SIGGRAPH 2006 Courses*, page 27. ACM.

[Hirte et al.2012] Steffen Hirte, Andreas Seifert, Stephan Baumann, Daniel Klan, and Kai-Uwe Sattler. 2012. Data3 – a kinect interface for OLAP using complex event processing. *Data Engineering, International Conference on*, 0:1297–1300.

[Kipp2010] Michael Kipp. 2010. Multimedia annotation, querying and analysis in anvil. *Multimedia information extraction*, 19.

[Kousidis et al.2012] Spyridon Kousidis, Thies Pfeiffer, Zofia Malisz, Petra Wagner, and David Schlangen. 2012. Evaluating a minimally invasive laboratory architecture for recording multimodal conversational data. In *Proceedings of the Interdisciplinary Workshop on Feedback Behaviors in Dialog, INTERSPEECH2012 Satellite Workshop*, pages 39–42.

[Luckham2002] David Luckham. 2002. *The Power of Events: An Introduction to Complex Event Processing in Distributed Enterprise Systems*. Addison-Wesley Professional.

[Lücking et al.2012] Andy Lücking, Kirsten Bergman, Florian Hahn, Stefan Kopp, and Hannes Rieser. 2012. Data-based analysis of speech and gesture: the Bielefeld Speech and Gesture Alignment corpus (SaGA) and its applications. *Journal on Multimodal User Interfaces*, -:1–14.

[Lücking et al.2013] Andy Lücking, Thies Pfeiffer, and Hannes Rieser. 2013. Pointing and reference reconsidered. *International Journal of Corpus Linguistics*. to appear.

[McNeill1992] David McNeill. 1992. *Hand and Mind: What Gestures Reveal about Thought*. University of Chicago Press, Chicago.

[Microsoft2013] Microsoft. 2013. Homepage of KINECT for Windows. Retrieved May 2013 from `http://www.microsoft.com/en-us/kinectforwindows/develop/`.

[Nguyen and Kipp2010] Quan Nguyen and Michael Kipp. 2010. Annotation of human gesture using 3d skeleton controls. In *Proceedings of the 7th International Conference on Language Resources and Evaluation*. ELDA.

[Paulson et al.2008] Brandon Paulson, Pankaj Rajan, Pedro Davalos, Ricardo Gutierrez-Osuna, and Tracy Hammond. 2008. What!?! no Rubine features?: using geometric-based features to produce normalized confidence values for sketch recognition. In *HCC Workshop: Sketch Tools for Diagramming*, pages 57–63.

[Pfeiffer2011] Thies Pfeiffer. 2011. *Understanding Multimodal Deixis with Gaze and Gesture in Conversational Interfaces*. Berichte aus der Informatik. Shaker Verlag, Aachen, Germany, December.

[Pfeiffer2013] Thies Pfeiffer. 2013. Documentation with motion capture. In Cornelia Müller, Alan Cienki, Ellen Fricke, Silva H. Ladewig, David McNeill, and Sedinha Teendorf, editors, *Body-Language-Communication: An International Handbook on Multimodality in Human Interaction*, Handbooks of Linguistics and Communication Science. Mouton de Gruyter, Berlin, New York. to appear.

[Rieser and Poesio2009] Hannes Rieser and M. Poesio. 2009. Interactive Gesture in Dialogue: a PTT Model. In P. Healey, R. Pieraccini, D. Byron, S. Yound, and M. Purver, editors, *Proceedings of the SIGDIAL 2009 Conference*, pages 87–96.

[Rieser2010] Hannes Rieser. 2010. On factoring out a gesture typology from the Bielefeld Speech-And-Gesture-Alignment corpus (SAGA). In Stefan Kopp and Ipke Wachsmuth, editors, *Proceedings of GW 2009: Gesture in Embodied Communication and Human-Computer Interaction*, pages 47–60, Berlin/Heidelberg. Springer.

[Rieser2011] Hannes Rieser. 2011. Gestures indicating dialogue structure. In *Proceedings of SEMdial 2011, Los Angelogue, 15th Workshop on the Semantics and Pragmatics of Dialogue*, pages 9–18, Los Angeles, California.

[Rieser2013] Hannes Rieser. 2013. Speech-gesture Interfaces. An Overview. In Heike Wiese and Malte Zimmermann, editors, *Proceedings of 35th Annual Conference of the German Linguistic Society (DGfS), March 12-15 2013 in Potsdam*, pages 282–283.

[Röpke et al.2013] Insa Röpke, Florian Hahn, and Hannes Rieser. 2013. Interface Constructions for Gestures Accompanying Verb Phrases. In Heike Wiese and Malte Zimmermann, editors, *Proceedings of 35th Annual Conference of the German Linguistic Society (DGfS), March 12-15 2013 in Potsdam*, pages 295–296.

[Rubine1991] Dean Rubine. 1991. Specifying gestures by example. In *Proceedings of the 18th annual conference on Computer graphics and interactive techniques*, SIGGRAPH '91, pages 329–337, New York, NY, USA. ACM.

[StreamBase2013] StreamBase. 2013. Homepage of StreamBase. Retrieved May 2013 from `http://www.streambase.com/`.

[Vicon Motion Systems2013] Vicon Motion Systems. 2013. Homepage. Retrieved May 2013 from `http://www.vicon.com`.

Open-ended, Extensible System Utterances Are Preferred, Even If They Require Filled Pauses

Timo Baumann
Universität Hamburg
Department of Informatics
Germany
baumann@informatik.uni-hamburg.de

David Schlangen
University of Bielefeld
Faculty of Linguistics and Literary Studies
Germany
david.schlangen@uni-bielefeld.de

Abstract

In many environments (e. g. sports commentary), situations incrementally unfold over time and often the future appearance of a relevant event can be predicted, but not in all its details or precise timing. We have built a simulation framework that uses our incremental speech synthesis component to assemble in a timely manner complex commentary utterances. In our evaluation, the resulting output is preferred over that from a baseline system that uses a simpler commenting strategy. Even in cases where the incremental system *overcommits* temporally and requires a filled pause to wait for the upcoming event, the system is preferred over the baseline.

1 Introduction

In spontaneous speech, speakers often commit *temporally*, e. g. by starting utterances that they do not yet know how to complete (Clark, 1996), putting time pressure on them for the generation of a completion. While this may be for planning and efficiency reasons, it also enables them to start commenting on events for which the outcome is not yet known. For example when a ball is flying towards the goal, but it is uncertain yet whether it will hit, in sports commentary.

To accommodate this *incremental* behaviour, human speakers plan their utterances just somewhat ahead, typically in chunks of major phrases (Levelt, 1989), and remain flexible to change or abandon the original plan, or to hesitate, e. g. to adapt their timing. This flexibility is in contrast to speech output in spoken dialogue systems (SDSs) which typically generate, synthesize and deliver speech in units of full utterances that cannot be changed while ongoing, apart from being aborted or interrupted (Edlund, 2008).

Recently, incremental speech synthesis (iSS) has been presented (Dutoit et al., 2011; Baumann and Schlangen, 2012b) which allows to start partial utterances that are then smoothly extended during verbalization. Incremental spoken output for dialogue systems has been shown to improve naturalness (Buschmeier et al., 2012) and Skantze and Hjalmarsson (2010) have used filled pauses to hold a turn. Dethlefs et al. (2012) present an incremental NLG strategy to reduce the need for filled pauses in interactions.

We investigate the impact of incremental spoken output in a *highly dynamic* environment, that is, where the rate of external events is high enough to allow only few utterances to finish as planned. As an example, we choose an otherwise simple commentary domain, where incremental output enables the system to combine multiple events into one complex commenting utterance that takes into account predictions about upcoming events. If the system overcommits to the timing of future events, it autonomously uses a filled pause until more material becomes available.

2 Related Work

A paradigmatic example of a domain that uses open-ended utterances is sports commentary, which has received some attention in the NLG community. For example, Chen and Mooney (2008) present a system that learns from hand-annotated data what to comment on. However, attention seems to have been placed more on truthfulness of the content, as, judging from videos provided on their website,[1] the formulations that are produced are rather monotonic ("`pink7 dribbles towards the goal. pink7 shoots for the goal. pink7 passes to...`"). More importantly, the delivery of a produced utterance does not seem to be temporally tied to the occurrence of the event.

[1] http://www.cs.utexas.edu/users/ml/clamp/sportscasting

Figure 1: The map shown in the *CarChase* domain, including the car on one of its itineraries (red; another in blue). At the depicted moment we can assume that the car will take a turn, but do not know whether left or right.

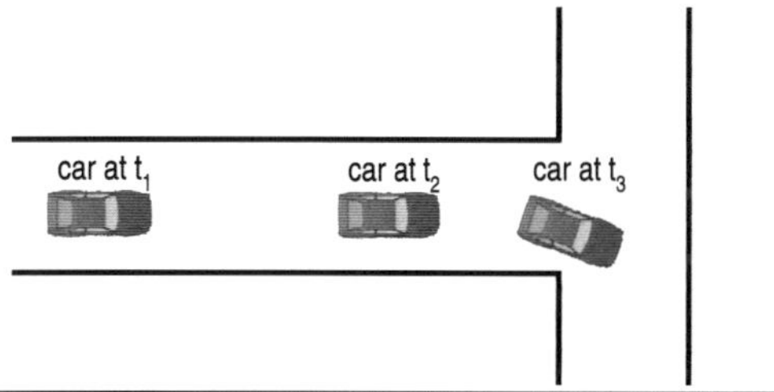

time	event description	ongoing utterance (already realized part in **bold**, newly appended continuation in *italic*)
t_1	car on Main Street	**The** car drives along Main Street.
t_2	car will likely turn	...**drives along Main Street** *and then turns* ‹hes›
t_3	car turns right	...**drives along Main Street and the**n turns *right.*

Figure 2: Example of incremental utterance production as a car drives along a street and turns. The ongoing utterance is extended as events unfold.

Repeatedly, utterances are synthesized long after the fact that they describe which sometimes has become obsolete at that point (for example, a goal is scored while the system still talks about a pass).

Lohmann et al. (2011) describe another domain that can be called highly dynamic: a system that adds spoken assistance to tactile maps for the visually impaired. In their settings, users can move around on a computer representation of a map with a hand-held haptic force-feedback device. Users are given spoken advice about the currently traversed streets' names, the relation of streets to each other, and to other map objects in the user's vicinity. Such exploratory moves by users can become rather quick, which in the system they describe can lead to output that comes late, referring to a position that has long been left.

3 A Highly Dynamic Commenting Domain

Our example domain combines properties of the sports commentary and map exploration domains mentioned above: the *CarChase* domain depicted in Figure 1. In the domain, a car drives around streets on the map and a commentator (supposed to be observing the scene from above) comments on where it is driving and what turns it is taking.

The car's itinerary in our domain simulator is scripted from a configuration file which assigns target positions for the car at different points in time and from which the motion and rotation of the car is animated. The speed of the car is set so that the event density is high enough that the setting cannot be described by simply producing one utterance per event – in other words: the domain is highly dynamic.

4 A Strategy for Incremental Commentary

We distinguish three types of events in the domain: *identification* (ID) events trigger the system to name the street the car is on, *turn* events fire when the car is taking a turn. Finally, *turn-prep* events fire when it is obvious that the car will turn but the direction of the turn remains open. These three event types are shown in Figure 2 at time t_1 (ID), t_2 (turn-prep), and t_3 (turn).

As can be seen in the example in Figure 2, the *turn-prep* event enables a system that is able to incrementally update its ongoing utterance to continue speaking about the anticipated future ("and then turns") without knowing the direction of the turn. This allows an incremental system to output efficient utterances that fluently combine multiple events and avoid repetition. Furthermore, *turn-prep* events enable the system to output the direction of the turn (the most important information) very shortly after the fact.

A non-incremental system, in contrast, must output individual utterances for every event and utterances can only start after the fact. Furthermore, a non-incremental system cannot extend ongoing utterances, rendering *turn-prep* events useless.

5 Implemented System

The system used for the experiment reported below uses an early version of incremental speech synthesis as implemented in INPROTK (Baumann and Schlangen, 2012c), a toolkit for incremental spoken dialogue processing based on the IU model (Schlangen and Skantze, 2009). The system allows to extend ongoing utterances, enabling the incremental commenting strategy outlined above.

In addition, we implemented a capability to synthesize a hesitation if no more content is specified, and to continue as soon as content becomes available. (Thus, in contrast to (Skantze and Hjalmarsson, 2010), hesitations do not consume additional time.) By using hesitations, the system gracefully accommodates temporal *over-commitment* (i. e. the obligation to produce a continuation that is not fulfilled in time) which may occur, e. g. when the car drives slower than anticipated and a turn's direction is not yet known when the system needs it.

In the preliminary version of iSS used for the experiments, no prosodic integration of continuations takes place, resulting in prosodic discontinuities; see (Baumann and Schlangen, 2012a) for a detailed assessment of prosodic integration in iSS.

As we focus on the merit of iSS in this work, we did not implement a scene analysis/event detection nor a NLG component for the task.[2] Instead, the commentary is scripted from the same configuration file that controls the car's motion on the board. iSS events lag behind slightly, ensuring that visual analysis would be possible, and event/text correspondence is close, matching NLG capabilities.

6 Experiment

To evaluate the incremental system, we compared it to a non-incremental baseline system which is unable to alter speech incrementally and hence cannot smoothly extend ongoing partial utterances. Instead, the baseline system always produces full utterances, one per event. To ensure the temporal proximity of delivery with the causing event in the baseline system, utterances can be marked as optional (in which case they are skipped if the system is still outputting a previous utterance), or non-optional (in which case an ongoing utterance is aborted in favour of the new utterance). All 'turn' events in the domain were marked as optional, all street ID events as non-optional.

We devised 4 different configurations (including the itineraries shown in Figure 1), and the timing of events was varied (by having the car go at different speeds, or by delaying some events), resulting in 9 scenarios; in 3 of these, the incremental system generated one or more hesitations. Both systems' output for the 9 scenarios was recorded with a screen-recorder, resulting in 18 videos that were played in random order to 9 participants (university students not involved in the research). Participants were told that various versions of commentary-generating systems generated the commentary based on the running picture in the videos and were then asked to rate each video on a five-point Likert scale with regards to how natural (similar to a human) the spoken commentary was (a) formulated, and (b) pronounced. In total, this resulted in 81 paired samples for each question.[3]

The assumption (and rationale for the second question) was that the incremental system's formulations would result in higher formulation ratings, while we hoped the acoustic and prosodic artefacts resulting from the coarsely implemented incremental synthesis would not significantly hurt pronunciation ratings. In order to not draw the subjects' attention towards incremental aspects, no question regarding the timeliness of the commentary was asked for explicitly.

7 Results

The mean ratings for both formulation quality and pronunciation quality for the incremental and baseline systems is shown in Figure 3. The median differences in the ratings of the two conditions is 2 points on the Likert scale for question (a) and 0 points for question (b) (means of 1.66 and 0.51, respectively), favouring the incremental system. The sign test shows that the advantage of the incremental system is clearly significant for questions (a) (68+/9=/4-; $p < .0001$) and (b) (38+/30=/13-; $p < .0007$)[4].

Thus, it is safe to say that the production strategies enabled by incremental speech synthesis (i. e. starting to speak before all evidence is known and extending the utterance as information becomes available) allows for formulations in the spoken commentary that are favoured by human listeners.

Incremental behaviour in the 3 scenarios that required hesitations was rated significantly worse than in those scenarios without hesitations for both questions (t-tests, $p < .001$ (a) and $p < .01$ (b)). This

[2] However, Lohmann et al. (2012) present an incremental NLG strategy for a similar task.

[3] The experiment was conducted in one language (German) only, but we believe our results to carry over to other languages. Specifically, we assume that most or all languages cater for commenting, and believe that human commenters universally use their ability to integrate events late in the utterance. However, practices of commenting may work differently (and differently well) among languages.

[4] We also conducted a non-paired t-test for question (b), as the different formulations of the systems might have effects on pronunciation quality; this test was also significant ($p < .0012$).

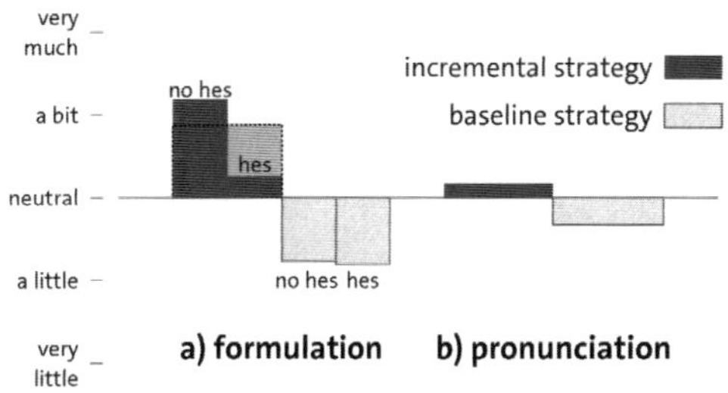

Figure 3: Mean ratings of formulation and pronunciation for the incremental and baseline systems; the formulation rating differs for utterances with and without hesitations in the incremental system.

is a clear indication that a system should try to avoid over-commitment, as users do not accept hesitations as inevitable (given that there was simply no evidence yet where the car would turn, for example). However, even in those scenarios that require filled pauses, the incremental commentary's formulation is rated as significantly better than the baseline system's (sign test, 18+/5=/4-; p<.005) while there is no effect on pronunciation in these cases.

8 Discussion & Outlook

The results indicate a clear user preference for open-ended, extensible utterances that grow as events unfold. Furthermore, this preference is stronger than the negative impact of filled pauses that are needed to cover temporal over-commitment, and despite the poor quality of filled pauses in the current system, which we plan to improve in the future.

Similarly to spoken commentary in dynamic domains, conversational speech requires revisions and reactions to events such as listener feedback, or the absence thereof (Clark, 1996). Thus, we believe that our results, as well as iSS in general, also apply to a broad range of conversational SDS tasks.

Finally, synthesis quality appears to be less important than interaction *adequacy*: we found no difference in rating of perceptual quality ('pronunciation') between the variants, even though in isolation iSS sounded noticeably worse in the prototype. This result calls for interactive adequacy as an optimization target over (isolated) perception ratings for speech synthesis, and also challenges the use of canned speech in conversational SDSs, which does not adapt to the interaction.

Acknowledgements The first author would like to thank Wolfgang Menzel for fruitful discussions on the topic, and permanent encouragement.

References

Timo Baumann and David Schlangen. 2012a. Evaluating prosodic processing for incremental speech synthesis. In *Procs. of Interspeech*, Portland, USA.

Timo Baumann and David Schlangen. 2012b. INPRO_iSS: A component for just-in-time incremental speech synthesis. In *Proceedings of ACL System Demonstrations*, Jeju, Korea.

Timo Baumann and David Schlangen. 2012c. The INPROTK 2012 release. In *Proceedings of SDCTD*, Montréal, Canada.

Hendrik Buschmeier, Timo Baumann, Benjamin Dorsch, Stefan Kopp, and David Schlangen. 2012. Combining incremental language generation and incremental speech synthesis for adaptive information presentation. In *Procs. of SigDial*, pages 295–303, Seoul, Korea.

David L. Chen and Raymond J. Mooney. 2008. Learning to sportscast: A test of grounded language acquisition. In *Proceedings of 25th Int. Conference on Machine Learning (ICML)*, Helsinki, Finland.

Herbert H. Clark. 1996. *Using Language*. Cambridge University Press.

Nina Dethlefs, Helen Hastie, Verena Rieser, and Oliver Lemon. 2012. Optimising incremental generation for spoken dialogue systems: Reducing the need for fillers. In *Procs. of the Seventh Int. Natural Language Generation Conf.*, pages 49–58, Utica, USA.

Thierry Dutoit, Maria Astrinaki, Onur Babacan, Nicolas d'Alessandro, and Benjamin Picart. 2011. pHTS for Max/MSP: A Streaming Architecture for Statistical Parametric Speech Synthesis. Technical Report 1, numediart Research Program on Digital Art Technologies.

Jens Edlund. 2008. Incremental speech synthesis. In *Second Swedish Language Technology Conference*, pages 53–54, Stockholm, Sweden. System Demo.

William J.M. Levelt. 1989. *Speaking: From Intention to Articulation*. MIT Press.

Kris Lohmann, Carola Eschenbach, and Christopher Habel. 2011. Linking spatial haptic perception to linguistic representations: assisting utterances for tactile-map explorations. In *Spatial information theory*, pages 328–349, Berlin, Heidelberg. Springer.

Kris Lohmann, Ole Eichhorn, and Timo Baumann. 2012. Generating situated assisting utterances to facilitate tactile-map understanding: A prototype system. In *Procs. of SLPAT 2012*, Montréal, Canada.

David Schlangen and Gabriel Skantze. 2009. A General, Abstract Model of Incremental Dialogue Processing. In *Procs. of the EACL*, Athens, Greece.

Gabriel Skantze and Anna Hjalmarsson. 2010. Towards incremental speech generation in dialogue systems. In *Procs. of SigDial*, pages 1–8, Tokyo, Japan.

A Four-Participant Group Facilitation Framework for Conversational Robots

Yoichi Matsuyama, Iwao Akiba, Akihiro Saito, Tetsunori Kobayashi
Department of Computer Science, Waseda University
27 Waseda, Shunjuku-ku, Tokyo, Japan
{matsuyama,akiba,saito}@pcl.cs.waseda.ac.jp
koba@waseda.jp

Abstract

In this paper, we propose a framework for conversational robots that facilitates four-participant groups. In three-participant conversations, the minimum unit for multiparty conversations, social imbalance, in which a participant is left behind in the current conversation, sometimes occurs. In such scenarios, a conversational robot has the potential to facilitate situations as the fourth participant. Consequently, we present model procedures for obtaining conversational initiatives in incremental steps to engage such four-participant conversations. During the procedures, a facilitator must be aware of both the presence of dominant participants leading the current conversation and the status of any participant that is left behind. We model and optimize these situations and procedures as a partially observable Markov decision process. The results of experiments conducted to evaluate the proposed procedures show evidence of their acceptability and feeling of groupness.

1 Introduction

We present a framework for conversational robots that facilitates four-participant groups with proper procedures for obtaining initiatives. Figure 1 (a) depicts a two-participant conversation. In such situations, conversational contexts including floor exchanges are commonly grounded between two interlocutors. Many dialogue systems have dealt with such two-participant situations (Raux and Eskenazi, 2009) (Chao and Thomaz, 2012). However, in three-participant conversations, as is shown in Figure 1(b), which is the minimum unit for multiparty conversation, floor exchanges cannot always be identified among the participants. Clark presented the participation structure model (Clark, 1996), drawing on Goffman's work (Goffman, 1981). In such three-participant situations, interactions between two dominant participants out of the three primarily occur (between participant A and B) and the other participant, who cannot properly get the floor to speak for a long while (cannot be promoted to be either a speaker or an addressee) tends to get left behind, even though all of them are "ratified participants" considered by the current speaker.

In terms of engagement among conversational participants, Martin et al., (Martin and White, 2005) proposed the appraisal theory that encompasses three subcategories, namely *Attitude*, *Engagement*, and *Graduation*. *Attitude* deals with expressions of affect, judgement, and appreciation. *Engagement* focuses on language use by which speakers negotiate an interpersonal space for their positions and the strategies which they uses to either acknowledge, ignore, or curtail other voices or points of view. *Graduation* focuses on the resources by which sparkers regulate the impact of these resources. Sidner et al., defined engagement as "the process by which two (or more) participants establish, maintain and end their perceived connection during interactions they jointly undertake" (Sidner et al., 2004). Based on these previous studies, we define engagement as the process establishing connections among participants using dialogue actions so that they can represent their own positions properly. So, the three-participant model dictates the need for one more participant who helps the participant who is left behind to engage him/her in the conversation. Conversational robots have the potential to participate in such conversations as the fourth participant, as illustrated in Figure 1 (c-1). Figure 1 (c-2) gives an example of the participants' speech activities in a certain duration. In this example, participant C's activity is relatively smaller than that of the others, and so he/she is likely to get left behind in the current conversational situation for a number of reasons. When a robot steps into the situation to coordinate, there should be proper procedures in place to obtain initiatives to control conversational contexts and to give it back to the others. If a robot naively starts to approach a participant who is left behind just after a left-behind situation is detected, it could break the current conversation. In order to coordinate situations, a facilitator (robot) must take the following procedural steps: (1) Be aware of both the presence of dominant participants leading the current conversation and the status of a participant who is left behind, (2) Obtain the initiative to control the situation and wait for approval from the others, either explicitly or implicitly, and (3) Give the floor to a suitable participant.

Research on specially situated facilitation agents in

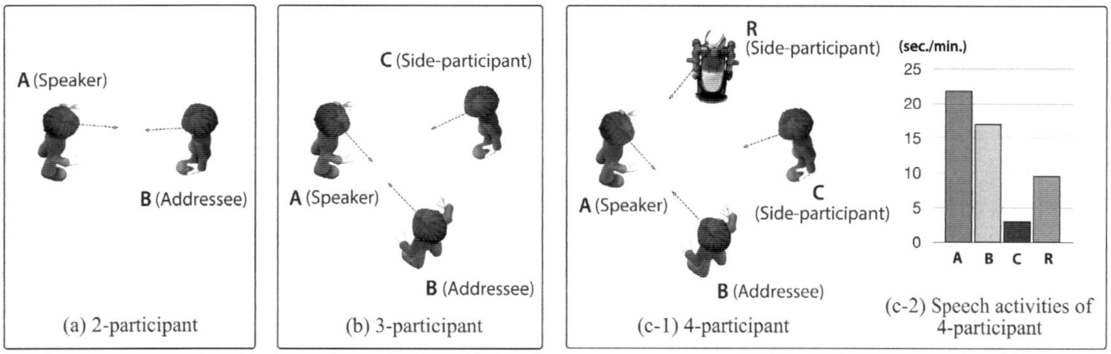

Figure 1: Types of conversations according to number of participants (dashed arrows represent their gazes): (a) Two-participant conversation model, which conventional dialogue systems have focused on. (b) Three-participant conversation model, the minimum unit for a multiparty conversation. In such multiparty conversations, social imbalance occasionally occurs. (c-1) Four-participant conversation, with a robot that regulates the imbalance situation, and (c-2) chart showing the unequal speech activities of the participants. In this case, participant C appears to have less opportunity to take the floor to speak, hence, the robot is expected to help him.

multiparty conversations has been conducted by various researchers. Matsusaka et al. pioneered the act of a physical robot participating in multiparty conversations (Matsusaka et al., 2003). We previously developed a multiparty quiz-game type facilitation system for elderly care (Matsuyama et al., 2008) and reported on the effectiveness of the existence of a robot (Matsuyama et al., 2010). Dosaka et al. developed a thought-evoking dialogue system for multiparty conversations with a quiz game task (Dohsaka et al., 2009). They reported that the existence of agents and empathic expressions are effective for user satisfaction and increase the number of user utterances. Bohus modeled engagement in multiparty conversations along Sinder's definition, namely open world dialogue (Bohus and Horvitz, 2009). In terms of facilitation, Benne et al. (Benne and Sheats, 1948) and Bales (Bales, 1950) pioneered investigations into small group dynamics, including functional facilitation roles. Kumar et al. designed a dialogue action selection model based on Bales's Socio-Emotional Interaction Categories for text-based character agents (Kumar et al., 2011).

In this paper, we propose a framework of procedural facilitation process to increase the total engagement of a group, with caring about side-effects of behaviors at the same time. The situations and procedures are modeled and optimized as a partially observable Markov decision process (POMDP), which is suitable for real-world sequential decision processes, including dialogue systems (Williams and Young, 2007). We begin by reviewing facilitation of small groups, and summarize requirement specifications for facilitation robots in the next section. In Section 3, we first describe representations of small group situations and procedures for maintaining small groups, then we discuss how to model them as POMDP. In Section 4, we give an overview of the architecture of our proposed system. We then discuss two experiments conducted to verify the efficacy of the small group maintenance procedures. Finally, we summarize our work and conclude this paper.

2 Facilitating Small Groups

2.1 Maintaining Small Groups

Benne et al. analyzed functional roles in small groups to understand the activities of individuals in small groups (Benne and Sheats, 1948). They categorized functional roles in small groups into three classes: *Group task roles*, *Group building and maintenance roles*, and *Individual roles*. The *Group task roles* are defined as "related to the task which the group is deciding to undertake or has undertaken." Those roles address concerns about the facilitation and coordination activities for task accomplishment. The *Group building and maintenance roles* are defined as "oriented toward the functioning of the group as a group." They contribute to social structures and interpersonal relations. Finally, the *Individual roles* are directed toward the individual satisfaction of each participant's individual needs. They deal with individual goals that are not relevant either to the group task or to group maintenance. Drawing on Benne's work, Bales proposed interaction process analysis (IPA), a framework for the classification of individual behavior in a two-dimensional role space consisting of a *Task area* and a *Socio-emotional area* (Bales, 1950). The roles related to the *Task area* concern behavioral manifestations that impact the management and solution of problems that a group is addressing. Examples of task-oriented activities include initiating the floor, giving information, and providing suggestions regarding a task. The roles related to the *Socio-emotional area* affect the interpersonal relationships either by supporting, enforcing, or weakening them. For instance, complementing another person to increase group cohesion and mutual trust among members is one example of positive socio-emotional behavior. Benne's typology of functional roles is evaluated as valuable with remarkable accuracy. In this paper, we employ Benne's *Group building and maintenance roles*,[1] which are related to Bales's *Socio-emotional area*, in order to arrange the following three abstract functional roles of group maintenance:

1. **Topic Maintenance Role**: Maintaining for conflict, ideas, and topics. This person mediates the difference between other members, attempts to reconcile disagreements, and relieves tension in conflict situations. This role inherits *Compromiser*, *Harmonizer*, and *Standard setter*.

2. **Floor Maintenance Role**: Maintaining the chance for the floor in the group in a direct/indirect way. This person encourages or asks questions of the person who is not or could not get engaged in conversations, and attempts to keep the communication channel open. This role inherits *Gatekeeper*, *Expediter*, and *Encourager*.

3. **Observation Role**: Overlooking the conversation situation by finding appropriate topics, observing the motivations and moods of the participants, and comprehending the relations between participants in conversations. This person follows the conversation and comments and interprets the group's internal process. This role inherits *Observer and commentator* and *Encourager*.

2.2 Procedures for Small Group Maintenance

In order that a participant who wants to claim an initiative (we call this participant a "claimant") is transferred an initiative by the participant leading the current conversation (we call this participant a "leader"), the claimant must take procedural steps. First, the claimant must participate in the current dominant conversation the leader is leading, try to claim an initiative, and then wait for either explicit or implicit approval from the leader. Let us take the example shown in Figure 2. In the figure, participants A and B are primarily leading the current conversation. Participant C cannot get the floor to speak, and so the robot desires to give the floor to C. If the robot speaks to C directly, without being aware of A and B, the conversation might be broken, or separated into two (A-B and C-Robot), at best. In order not to break the situation, the robot should participate in the dominant conversation between A and B first, and set the stage such that the robot is approved to initiate the next situation. In this paper, we define such a state in which a person is participating in a dominant conversation as a "*Engaged*" state, and the opposite state as "*Unengaged*". Thus, in Clark's participation structure, speaker and addressee are automatically *Engaged* participants. Side-participants are divided into *Engaged* and *Unengaged* participants based on their situations. In this paper, we assume that an *Unengaged* participant needs to respond to a *Engaged* participant's adjacency pair part to be engaged. Adjacency pairs are minimal units of conversation that are composed of two utterances by several speakers (Schegloff and Sacks, 1973). The speaking of the first utterance (the first part) provokes a responding utterance (the second part), and sometimes a third response (the third part). Understanding adjacency pairs is, therefore, essential to detecting cut-in timing.

[1] Benne's *Group building and maintenance roles* are *Compromiser, Harmonizer, Standard setter, Gatekeeper and expediter, Encourager, Observer and commentator*, and *Follower*.

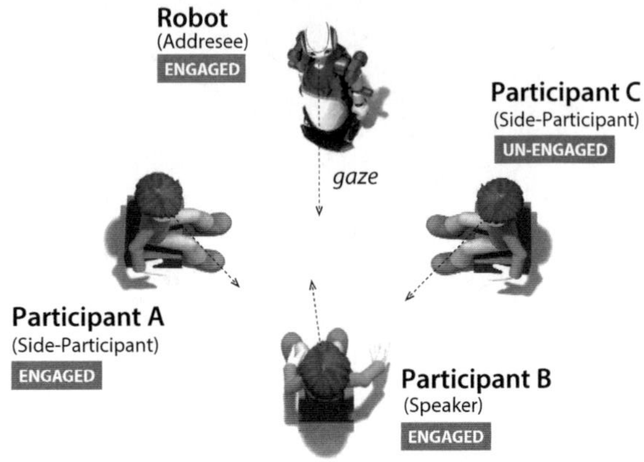

Figure 2: Four-participant conversational group. Four participants, including a robot, are talking about a certain topic. Participants A and B are leading the conversation, and mainly keep the floor. The robot also engages with A and B in line with the topic. C is an *unengaged* participant, who does not have many chances to take the floor for a while. The dashed arrows indicate the direction they are facing, assuming their gazes.

On the basis of our discussion above, we define the following constraints for both *Engaged* and *Unengaged* participants when they address and shift current topics:

1. **Constraint of addressing**: An unengaged participant must not address the other unengaged participants directly.

2. **Constraint of topic shifting**: An engaged participant must not shift the current topic when he/she addresses the other unengaged participants.

The relationship between subjective and objective participants that are permitted to approach in the two constraints are shown in Tables 1 and 2. In the following sections, we describe a computational model that has the group maintenance functions discussed above.

3 Procedure Optimization

3.1 Representation of Engagement State

We assume only one speaker and one addressee exist at each time-step and one or two side-participants may

Table 1: Permission relationship between subjective and objective participants for the constraint of addressing. "Engaged" means a participant is assigned as a speaker or an addressee or a side-participant, who engages with the conversational group. "Unengaged" means a participant is assigned as an unengaged side-participant.

Subject \ Objective	Engaged	Unengaged
Engaged	permitted	permitted
Unengaged	permitted	NOT permitted

Table 2: Permission relationship for permission between subjective and objective participants in the constraint of topic shifting.

Subject \ Objective	Engaged	Unengaged
Engaged	permitted	NOT permitted
Unengaged	NOT permitted	NOT permitted

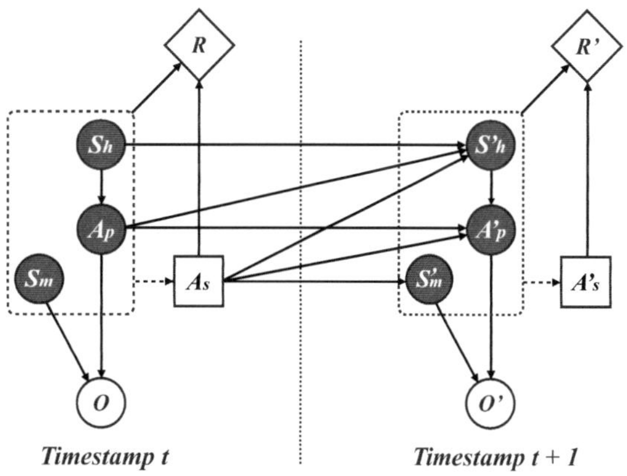

Figure 3: Influence diagram representation of the POMDP model. Circles represent random variables, squares represent decision nodes, and diamonds represent utility nodes. Shaded circles indicate random variables, while unshaded circles represent observed variables. Solid directed arcs indicate casual effect, while dashed directed arcs indicate that a distribution is used.

exist in four-participant conversations. We define side-participants as having two states: "*Engaged*" and "*Unengaged*". In the scenario shown in Figure 2, participant C may not be able to take the floor for a while. The situation probably resolves itself when the current topic is shifted. Hence, we define the depth of side-participant $Depth_{SPT}$ as the duration that a participant is assigned while the same topic continues, which represents the level of engagement.

$$Depth_{SPT_i} = Duration_{SPT_i} / Duration_{topic_j} \quad (1)$$

$$UnengagedSPT = \begin{cases} SPT_i & \text{if } Depth_{SPT_i} > Threshold \\ none & \text{otherwise} \end{cases} \quad (2)$$

The suffix i represents a participant's ID.

We also define an *Un-Engaged* participant's motivation to speak on the current topic. Thus, this state affects decision-making about topic maintenance. The amount of motivation of a participant is calculated as a linear sum of speech activities, smiling duration, and nodding duration. Further, the motivations in our current model are heuristically assumed to be binary variables.

$$Motivation_i = \begin{cases} 1 & \text{if } MotivAmount_i > Threshold \\ 0 & \text{otherwise} \end{cases} \quad (3)$$

3.2 Procedure Optimization using POMDP

To optimize the procedures discussed above, we model the task as a partially observable Markov decision process (POMDP) (Williams and Young, 2007). Formally, a POMDP is defined as a tuple $\beta = \{S, A, T, R, O, Z, \gamma, b_0\}$, where S is a set of states describing the agent's world, A is a set of actions that the agent may take, T defines a transition probability $P(s'|s,a)$, R defines the expected reward $r(s,a)$, O is a set of observations the agent can receive about the world, and Z defines an observation probability, $P(o'|s',a)$, γ is a geometric discount factor $0 < \gamma < 1$, and b_0 is an initial belief state $b_0(s)$. At each time-step, the belief state distribution b is updated as follows:

$$b'(s') = \gamma \cdot P(o'|s',a) \sum_s P(s'|s,a) b(s) \quad (4)$$

In this paper, we assume S can be factored into three components: the participants' engagement states S_e, the participants' motivation states S_m, and the participants' actions A_p. Hence, the factored POMDP state S is defined as

$$s = (s_e, s_m, a_p) \quad (5)$$

and the belief state b becomes

$$b = b(s_e, s_m, a_p) \quad (6)$$

To compute the transition function and observation function, a few intuitive assumptions are made:

$$\begin{aligned} P(s'|s,a) =& P(s'_e, s'_m, a'_p | s_e, s_m, a_p, a_s) \\ =& P(s'_e | s_h, s_m, a_p, a_s) \cdot \\ & P(s'_m | s'_e, s_h, s_m, a_p, a_s) \cdot \\ & P(a'_p | s'_m, s'_e, s_e, s_m, a_p, a_s) \end{aligned} \quad (7)$$

Figure 3 shows the influence diagram depiction of our proposed model. We assume conditional independence as follows: The first term in (7), which we call the *participants' engagement model* T_{S_e}, indicates how the robot engages in the current dominant conversation at each time-step. We assume that the participants' engagement state at each time-step depends only on the previous engagement state, the participants' action, and the system action. In this paper, the *participants' engagement model* only contains the robot's engagement states because it is sufficient for the obtaining initiatives procedures . Table 3 shows the states of engagement.

$$T_{S_e} = P(s'_e|s_e, a_p, a_s) \quad (8)$$

In this paper, the probabilities of (8) were handcrafted, based on the consideration in Section 2.2 and our experiences. When the engagement state is the *Un-Engaged* state and the robot is asked by a current speaker, the state should be changed to the *Pre-Engaged* state, where the robot is awaiting the speaker's approval for the *Engaged* state. We assume that any dialogue acts from the speaker addressing the robot in the *Pre-Engaged* are approvals. Otherwise, the state will be back to the *Un-Engaged*. The *Engaged* state gradually goes down to the *Un-Engaged* state in time-steps unless the robot selects any dialogue acts.

We call the second term the *participants' motivation model* T_{S_m}. It indicates how an *Un-Engaged* participant has the motivation to take the floor at each time-step. This state implies that the participant who is left behind (target person) has a motivation to speak on the current topic. Thus, this state affects decision-making about topic shift. We assume that a participant's motivation at each time-step depends only on the previous system action. The motivations are defined as an unengaged participant's ID and a binary (true/false) variable, which is calculated by (3) .

$$T_{S_m} = P(s'_m|a_s) \quad (9)$$

We call the third term the *participants' action model* T_{A_p}. It indicates what actions the participants are likely to take at each time-step. We assume the participants' actions at each time-step depends on the previous participant's action, the previous system action, and the current robot's engagement state. As shown in Table 5, participants' actions include adjacency pair types. Understanding adjacency pairs is essential to detecting cut-in timing. In this paper, we recognize the adjacency pairs only by keyword matching using the results of speech recognition.

$$T_{A_p} = P(a'_p|s'_h, a_p, a_s) \quad (10)$$

The transition probabilities of adjacency pair types are based on a corpus we collected. We recorded two four-participant conversational groups (all participants were human subjects), where they were talked about movies. The total duration was around 60 minutes. Each utterance is segmented automatically by our speech recognition. After the recording, adjacency pair types were manually annotated for all speech segments.

We define the observation probability Z as follows:

$$Z = P(o'|s', a) = P(o'|s'_m, a'_p, a_s) \quad (11)$$

Table 3: Engagement states S_e

Engagement states	Meaning
Un-Engaged	The robot is not engaging with the current conversation.
Pre-Engaged	The robot is waiting for approval to engage with the current conversation.
Engaged	The robot is engaging with the current conversation.

Table 4: Motivation states S_m

Motivation states	Meaning
Motivated	The participant who is left behind has a motivation to speak on the current topic (interested in the current topic).
Not-Motivated	The participant who is left behind does not have any motivation to speak (not interested in the current topic).

Given the definitions above, the belief state can be updated at each time-step by substituting (8), (9), and (10) into (4).

$$b'(s'_m, a'_p) = \gamma \cdot \underbrace{P(o'|s'_m, a'_p, a_s)}_{\text{observation model}} \cdot \underbrace{P(s'_m|a_s)}_{\text{motivation model}} \cdot \underbrace{P(a'_p|s'_e, a_p, a_s)}_{\text{participants' action model}} \cdot \sum_{s_h} \underbrace{P(s'_e|s_e, a_p, a_s)}_{\text{engagement model}} \cdot b(s_m, a_p) \quad (12)$$

Table 6 shows the system actions. The system has seven actions available.

On the basis of the consideration of the constraints in Section 2.2, the reward measure includes components for both the appropriateness and inappropriateness of the robot's behaviors.

As an optimization algorithm, we employed the heuristic search value iteration (HSVI) algorithm proposed by Smith et al., which is one of point-based algorithms (Smith and Simmons, 2012).

4 System Architecture

Based on the studies on small group maintenance, we propose an architecture for conversational robots that has the capability to facilitate small groups, as shown in Figure 4. The framework primarily comprises Situation Analysis, Dialogue Management, and Sentence Generation processes.

4.1 Situation Analysis and Dialogue Management

Each time the system detects an endpoint of speech from the automatic speech recognition (ASR) module, it interprets the current situation. The Situation Analysis process includes participation roles recognition, adjacency pair part recognition, and question analysis.

Participation roles including a speaker, an addressee, and side-participants are recognized by the results of voice activity detection (VAD) and face directions recognition. The face directions are captured by depth-RGB cameras (Microsoft Kinect). In this paper, we use a hand-crafted role classifier. The speaker classification accuracy is 75.1% and the addressee classifi-

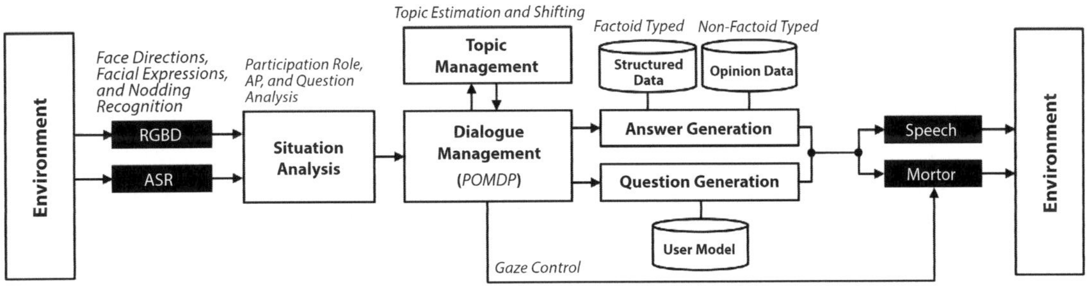

Figure 4: The architecture of the system primarily comprises the Situation Analysis, the Dialogue Management, and the Sentence Generation processes. The Situation Analysis process receives sensory information from RGBD cameras (Microsoft Kinect) and speech recognizers for each participant. The Dialogue Management process is described in Section 3. The Answer Generation process has the capability of doing additional phrasing with the robot's own opinions.

Table 5: Participants' actions A_p

Participants' actions	Meaning
first-part	A participant made an adjacency part (question)
second-part	A participant made a second adjacency part (answer)
third-part	A participant made a third adjacency part
other	A participant asked or answered the other participant
call	A participant called the robot's name

Table 6: System actions A_s

System actions	Meaning
answer	Answering the current speaker's question
question-new-topic	Asking someone a question related to a new topic
question-current-topic	Asking someone a question related to the current topic
trivia	Giving a trivia
simple-reaction	Reacting simply
nod	Nodding to the current speaker
none	Doing nothing

cation accuracy is 67.2% Adjacency pairs are recognized by the results of the participation role recognion and speech recognition. We use a hand-crafted adjacency pairs classifier. The classification accuracy is around 60%, which mostly depends on the classification accuracy of addressing for a robot. In the question analysis process, a speech utterance is interpreted with question types (5W1H interrogatives: e.g., "who," "what," "how," etc.) and predicate (verbs and adjectives). Questions are classified into two categories: Factoid type questions and Non-factoid type questions.

In the Dialogue Management process, a dialog action is selected based on abstracted conversational situation to maintain a small group, which we described in Section 3.

4.2 Sentence Generation

The Sentence Generation process consists of two components: Answer Generation and Question Generation. Based on the results of the Question Analysis process, answers are classified into two types: Factoid type answers and Non-factoid type answers (opinions). Factoid answers are generated from a structured database. In this research, we use Semantic Web technologies. After analyzing a question, it is interpreted as a SPARQL query, a resource description framework (RDF) format query language to search RDF databases. We use DBpedia as an RDF database[2].

The opinion (non-factoid type answers) generation process refers opinion data automatically collected from a large amount of reviews in the Web. The opinion generation consists of four process: document collection, opinion extraction, sentence style conversion, and sentence ranking. As an example task, we collected review documents from the Yahoo! Japan Movie site [3].

The opinion extraction consists of two processes: extraction of evaluative expressions and classification of their sentiment polarities (positive/negative). We eliminate opinions with negative sentiments because the system is expected to talk about positive contents in our conversational task. Nakagawa et al. (Nakagawa et al., 2008) used both a subjective evaluative dictionary (Higashiyama et al., 2008) and an evaluative noun dictionary (Kobayashi et al., 2007). We use an evaluative word dictionary we prepare based on their works. In order to extract evaluative expressions which can appear at any position in a sentence, we use the IOB encoding method, which has been commonly used for extent-identification tasks (Breck et al., 2007). Using IOB, each word is tagged as either (B)eginning an entity, being (I)n an entity, or being (O)utside of an entity. Based on the proposed method by Nakagawa et al, we use linear-chain conditional random fields (CRF) for the IBO encoding.

In order to preserve consistency of system's character, sentence styles are converted based on a hand-craft rule we prepare. After Japanese morphological analysis, punctuation marks and particular symbols and are eliminated. Then the last morpheme is converted.

We propose three ranking algorithms in terms of length and novelty: *Short*, *Standard* and *Diverse*. The *Short* is short length first algorithm. In this algorithm,

[2]http://ja.dbpedia.org/

[3]http://movies.yahoo.co.jp

at first, top 30% of sentences by TF-IDF score, which consists of seven to ten morphemes, are extracted. We assume top 30% of candidates is reasonably associated with a current topic. For the *Standard* and *Diverse* algorithms, at first, top 30% of sentences by TF-IDF score, which consists of fifteen to twenty morphemes, are extracted. The *Standard* algorithm is expected to contain substantial opinions or reasons, which can appeal to users about a certain topic. In this algorithm, the list is sorted by adjective term frequency. The *Diverse* algorithm is expected to express opinions or reasons with novel styles, which can be unpredictable or sometimes serendipitous to users about a certain topic. In this algorithm, the list is sorted in the inverse order by adjective term frequency.

4.3 Question Generation and User Model

The Question Generation module has two main functions: giving someone the floor and collecting users' preferences and experiences for the User Model.

The User Model is preferred for topic maintenance. A preferred new topic is decided using cosine similarity of TF-IDF scores. The topic scores ($TopicScore$) of all topics are calculated based on cosine similarities of the current topic ($CurrentTopic$), a user's topic preferences of all topics ($PreferenceTopic$), and experiences ($ExperienceTopic$) between the $CurrentTopic$ and each $Topic$.

$$\begin{aligned} TopicScore_i = {} & \alpha \cos(Topic_i \cdot CurrentTopic) \\ & + \beta\left(\sum_m \cos(Topic_i \cdot PreferenceTopic_m)\right) \\ & + \gamma\left(\sum_n \cos(Topic_i \cdot ExperienceTopic_m)\right) \end{aligned} \tag{13}$$

4.4 Experimental Platform

For our experimental platform, we used the multimodal conversation robot "SCHEMA([ʃe:ma])," (Matsuyama et al., 2009) shown in Figure 2. SCHEMA is approximately 1.2[m] in height, which is the same as the level of the eyes of an adult male sitting down in a chair. It has 10 degrees of freedom for right-left eyebrows, eyelids, right-left eyes (roll and pitch) and neck (pitch and yaw). It can express anxiousness and surprise using its eyelids and control its gaze using eyes, neck, and autonomous turret. In addition, it has six degrees of freedom for each arm, which can express gestures. One degree of freedom is assigned to the mouth to indicate explicitly whether the robot is speaking or not. A computer is inside the belly to control the robot's actions, and an external computer sends commands to execute various behaviors though a WiFi network. All modules, including the ASRs and a speech synthesizer are connected to each other though a middleware called the Message-Oriented NEtworked-robot Architecture (MONEA), which we earlier produced (Nakano et al., 2006).

5 Experiments

We designed the following two experiments to evaluate the appropriateness and feeling of groupness of our proposed procedures for multiparty conversations (**experiment 1**), and the appropriateness of timing for initiating procedures (**experiment 2**). In order to cancel the effects of recognition errors, we prepared video recordings of four-participant situations (Human participant A, B, C, and a robot), just like 2. We created the following three conditions, all of which are optimized as POMDP. All subjects were native Japanese speakers recruited from Waseda University campus. They were first given a brief description of the purpose and the procedure of the conversation. They were instructed that A and B have a friendly relationship with each other, C is coming in for the first time and is feeling nervous, therefore, C is left behind in the conversation, and a robot is trying to maximize the total engagement of this situation. We also explained "a engaged situation" meant "a situation in which all participant are given their opportunities to speak something fairly."

5.1 Experiment 1: Appropriateness and Groupness by Usage of Procedures

A total of 35 subjects (23 males and 12 females) participated in this experiment. The ages of the subjects ranged between 20 and 25 years with an average age of 20.5 years. After they watched the videos, they were asked to complete questionnaires about their feeling of groupness ("For which condition did you feel a sense of groupness?") and free-form questionnaires. The following four conditions were videotaped, and the video edited at around 30 s. All videos contained the same topic ("*Princess Mononoke*"). The spatial arrangement was the same as shown in Figure 2.

Condition 1: Without procedures (without topic shifting). A robot directly asks a participant left behind without procedures claiming an initiative. As is shown in Figure 8, just after a sequence of interactions between A and B, which is segmented by a third adjacency pair part, a robot directly asks C. The topic is still maintained ("*Princess Mononoke*").

Condition 2: With procedures (without topic shifting). A robot directly asks a participant left behind with a procedure. As is shown in Figure 9, Just after a sequence of interactions between A and B, a robot asks A with the first pair part and waits for A's response (the second part). Then it finishes the interaction with A, and asks C to give a floor. In this case, topic is still maintained the current one ("*Princess Mononoke*").

Condition 3: Without procedures + topic shifting. In #6 question of Condition 1 (Figure 8), a robot initiates a new topic ("*From Up On Poppy Hill*") instead.

Condition 4: With procedures + topic shifting. In #7 question of Condition 2 (Figure 9), a robot initiates a new topic ("*From Up On Poppy Hill*") instead.

After watching the movies, they were requested to answer Likert 7-scaled questionnaires about (a) **appro-**

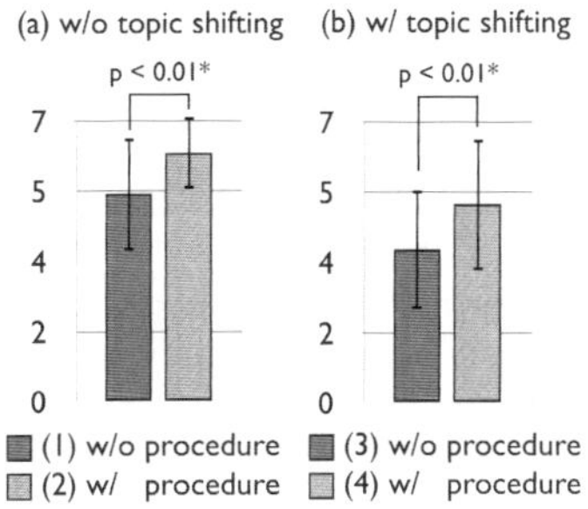

Figure 5: Result of experiment 1-a

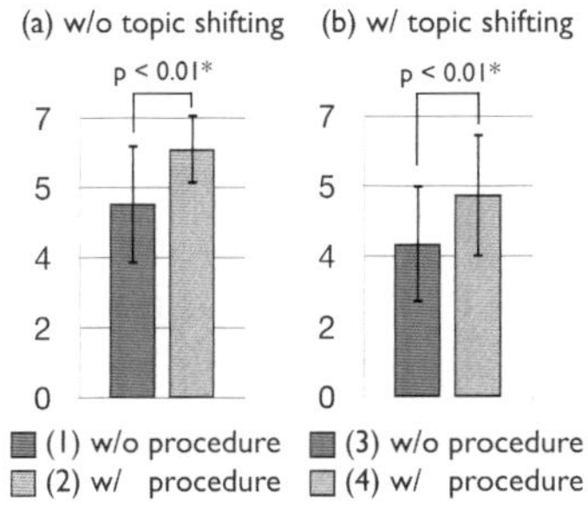

Figure 6: Result of experiment 1-b

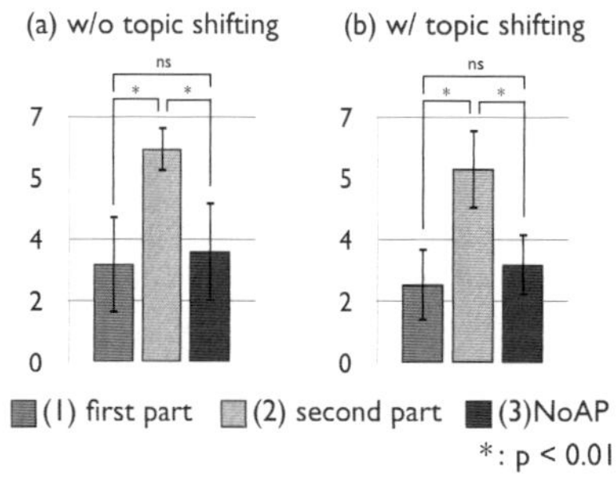

Figure 7: Result of experiment 2

priateness of procedures, (b) **Feeling of groupness**.

5.2 Experiment 2: Appropriateness of Timing of Initiating Procedures

A total of 32 subjects (21 males and 11 females) participated in this experiment. The ages of the subjects ranged between 20 and 25 years with an average age of 20.5 years. After they watched the videos, they were asked to complete questionnaires about the timing of the initiating procedures ("Which video did you feel was the most appropriate?"). The following three conditions were videotaped, and edited at around 30 s. All videos contained the same topic ("*Princess Mononoke*"). The spatial arrangement was the same as shown in Figure 2. We created three conditions:

Condition 1 (first part): Initiating a procedure just after the first adjacent pair part.

Condition 2 (second part): Initiating a procedure just after the second adjacent pair part.

Condition 3 (No AP): Out of consideration of adjacency pairs.

In conditions 1 and 2, the robot initiated its procedures just after the first and second parts, respectively. In condition 3, the robot initiated its procedure in the middle of the adjacency pairs, which is intended to show that the robot does not care about adjacency pairs. We did not consider the timings of the third part of the adjacency pair because we had already examined the appropriateness of the timing of the third part in experiment 1. After watching the movies, they were requested to answer Likert 7-scaled questionnaires about the robot's **appropriateness of behavior**.

5.3 Results and Discussions

Figure 5 shows usages of procedures are appropriate to approach a participant left behind either with or without topic shifting. The t-test result shows a significant difference between condition 1 and 2, as well as between 3 and 4 ($p < 0.01$). Figure 6 shows usages of procedures generate feelings of groupness. The t-test result also shows a significant difference between condition 1 and 2, as well as between 3 and 4 ($p < 0.01$).

Figure 7 (a) shows initiating procedures without topic shifting in timings of just after the second pair parts is more appropriate than other conditions. The result of an analysis of variance (ANOVA) shows significant differences among conditions ($F[2,26] = 34.46$, $p < 0.01$). The result of multiple comparisons with the Tukey HSD method shows a significant difference between condition 1 and 2, as well as between 2 and 3 ($p < 0.01$). Figure 7 (b) shows initiating procedures with topic shifting in timings of just after the second pair parts is more appropriate than other conditions. The result of an analysis of variance (ANOVA) shows significant differences among conditions ($F[2,26] = 42.52$, $p < 0.01$). The result of multiple comparisons with the Tukey HSD method shows a significant difference between condition 1 and 2, as well as between 2 and 3 ($p < 0.01$).

From these results, usages of procedures obtaining initiatives before approaching a participant left behind showed evidences of acceptability as a participant's behaviors, and feeling of groupness in a group. As for timings, initiating the procedures just after the second or third adjacency pair parts is felt more appropriate than the first pairs by participants.

6 Conclusions

We proposed a framework for conversational robots facilitating four-participant groups. Based on a representation of conversational situations, we presented a model of procedures obtaining conversational initiatives in incremental steps to maximize total engagement of such four-participant conversations. These situations and procedures were modeled and optimized as a partially observable Markov decision process. As the results of two experiments, usages of procedures obtaining initiatives showed evidences of acceptability as a participant's behaviors, and feeling of groupness. As for timings, initiating the procedures just after the second or third adjacency pair parts is felt more appropriate than the first pairs by participants.

7 Acknowledgements

This research was supported by the Grant-in-Aid for scientific research WAKATE-B (23700239). TOSHIBA corporation provided the speech synthesizer customized for our spoken dialogue system.

References

Robert F Bales. 1950. Interaction process analysis. *Cambridge, Mass.*

Kenneth D Benne and Paul Sheats. 1948. Functional roles of group members. *Journal of social issues*, 4(2):41–49.

Dan Bohus and Eric Horvitz. 2009. Models for multiparty engagement in open-world dialog. In *Proceedings of the SIGDIAL 2009 Conference: The 10th Annual Meeting of the Special Interest Group on Discourse and Dialogue*, pages 225–234. Association for Computational Linguistics.

Eric Breck, Yejin Choi, and Claire Cardie. 2007. Identifying expressions of opinion in context. In *Proceedings of the 20th international joint conference on Artifical intelligence*, pages 2683–2688. Morgan Kaufmann Publishers Inc.

Crystal Chao and Andrea Lockerd Thomaz. 2012. Timing in multimodal turn-taking interactions: Control and analysis using timed petri nets. *Journal of Human-Robot Interaction*, 1(1).

Herbert H Clark. 1996. *Using language*, volume 4. Cambridge University Press Cambridge.

Kohji Dohsaka, Ryota Asai, Ryuichiro Higashinaka, Yasuhiro Minami, and Eisaku Maeda. 2009. Effects of conversational agents on human communication in thought-evoking multi-party dialogues. In *Proceedings of the SIGDIAL 2009 Conference: The 10th Annual Meeting of the Special Interest Group on Discourse and Dialogue*, pages 217–224. Association for Computational Linguistics.

Erving Goffman. 1981. *Forms of talk*. University of Pennsylvania Press.

Masahiko Higashiyama, Kentaro Inui, and Yuji Matsumoto. 2008. Acquiring noun polarity knowledge using selectional preferences. In *Proceedings of the 14th Annual Meeting of the Association for Natural Language Processing*, pages 584–587.

Nozomi Kobayashi, Kentaro Inui, and Yuji Matsumoto. 2007. Opinion mining from web documents: Extraction and structurization. *Information and Media Technologies*, 2(1):326–337.

Rohit Kumar, Jack L Beuth, and Carolyn P Rosé. 2011. Conversational strategies that support idea generation productivity. In *in Groups, 9 th Intl. Conf. on Computer Supported Collaborative Learning, Hong Kong 160 and Rosé, 2010a) Rohit Kumar, Carolyn P. Rosé, 2010, Conversational Tutors with Rich Interactive Behaviors that support Collaborative Learning, Workshop on Opportunity*. Citeseer.

James R Martin and Peter RR White. 2005. *The language of evaluation*. Palgrave Macmillan Basingstoke and New York.

Yosuke Matsusaka, Tojo Tsuyoshi, and Tetsunori Kobayashi. 2003. Conversation robot participating in group conversation. *IEICE transactions on information and systems*, 86(1):26–36.

Yoichi Matsuyama, Hikaru Taniyama, Shinya Fujie, and Tetsunori Kobayashi. 2008. Designing communication activation system in group communication. In *Humanoid Robots, 2008. Humanoids 2008. 8th IEEE-RAS International Conference on*, pages 629–634. IEEE.

Yoichi Matsuyama, Kosuke Hosoya, Hikaru Taniyama, Hiroki Tsuboi, Shinya Fujie, and Tetsunori Kobayashi. 2009. Schema: multi-party interaction-oriented humanoid robot. In *ACM SIGGRAPH ASIA 2009 Art Gallery & Emerging Technologies: Adaptation*, pages 82–82. ACM.

Yoichi Matsuyama, Shinya Fujie, Hikaru Taniyama, and Tetsunori Kobayashi. 2010. Psychological evaluation of a group communication activation robot in a party game. In *Eleventh Annual Conference of the International Speech Communication Association*.

Tetsuji Nakagawa, Takuya Kawada, Kentaro Inui, and Sadao Kurohashi. 2008. Extracting subjective and objective evaluative expressions from the web. In *Universal Communication, 2008. ISUC'08. Second International Symposium on*, pages 251–258. IEEE.

Teppei Nakano, Shinya Fujie, and Tetsunori Kobayashi. 2006. Monea: message-oriented networked-robot architecture. In *Robotics and Automation, 2006. ICRA 2006. Proceedings 2006 IEEE International Conference on*, pages 194–199. IEEE.

Antoine Raux and Maxine Eskenazi. 2009. A finite-state turn-taking model for spoken dialog systems. In *Proceedings of Human Language Technologies: The 2009 Annual Conference of the North American Chapter of the Association for Computational Linguistics*, pages 629–637. Association for Computational Linguistics.

Emanuel A Schegloff and Harvey Sacks. 1973. Opening up closings. *Semiotica*, 8(4):289–327.

Candace L Sidner, Cory D Kidd, Christopher Lee, and Neal Lesh. 2004. Where to look: a study of human-robot engagement. In *Proceedings of the 9th international conference on Intelligent user interfaces*, pages 78–84. ACM.

Trey Smith and Reid Simmons. 2012. Point-based pomdp algorithms: Improved analysis and implementation. *arXiv preprint arXiv:1207.1412*.

Jason Williams and Steve Young. 2007. Partially observable markov decision processes for spoken dialog systems. *Computer Speech & Language*, 21(2):393–422.

#	SPK → ADD	AP	Sentences
1	A→B	First	Have you ever watched "Princess Mononoke"?
2	B→A	Second	Yes, I have
3	A→B	First	Oh, you have?
4	B→A	Second	Yeah.
5	A→B	Third	I see
6	R→C	First	**Have you ever watched "Princess Mononoke"?**
7	C→R	Second	Yes, I have

Figure 8: Transcript of condition 1 (experiment 2)

#	SPK → ADD	AP	Sentences
1	A→B	1st	Have you ever watched "Princess Mononoke"?
2	B→A	Second	Yes, I have
3	A→B	Third	I see.
4	R→A	First	**It is one of my favorite movies among Ghibri's**
5	A→B	Second	Really?
6	B→A	Third	Yes.
7	R→C	First	**Have you ever watched "Princess Mononoke"?**
8	C→R	Second	Yes, I have

Figure 9: Transcript of condition 2 (experiment 2)

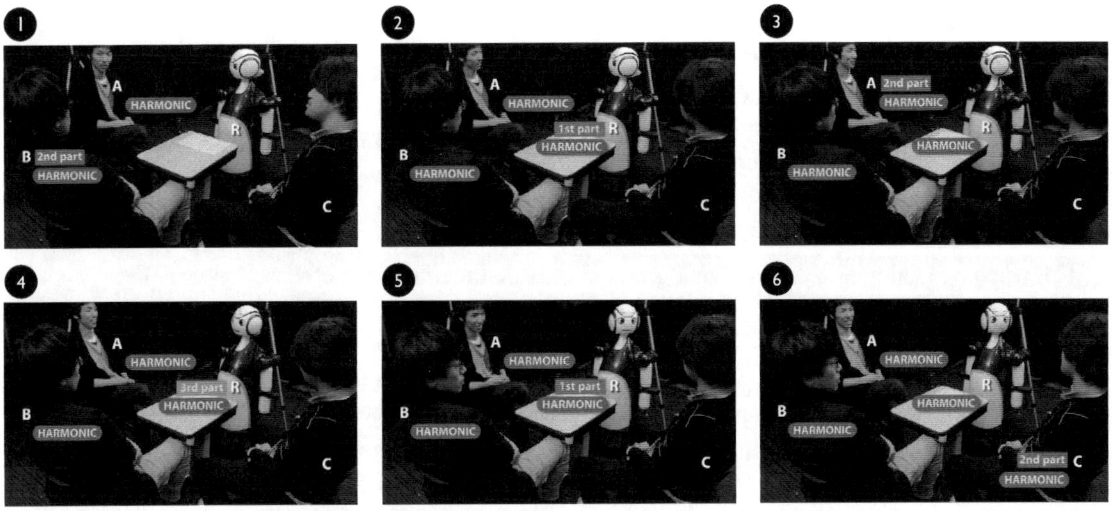

#	SPK → ADD	AP	S_e	Sentences	Scene
				(Topic: "007 Skyfall")	
1	A→B	1st	*Un*	Let's talk about the "Skyfall."	
2	A→B	1st	*Un*	Have you ever seen the latest one?	
3	B→A	2nd	*Un*	Well, I've not seen that.	1
4	A→B	3rd	*Un*	Oh, really.	
5	R→A	1st	*Pre*	Well, I like the Bond Girl.	2
6	A→R	2nd	*Pre*	I see.	2
7	R→A	1st	*Pre*	I think that movie is good because of the setting of the "old age" for the 44-year old James Bond.	2
8	A→R	2nd	*H*	Uh-huh.	3
				(R is approved to obtain an initiative)	
9	R→A	3rd	*H*	Yes.	4
10	R→C	1st	*H*	Have you ever seen the "Skyfall"?	5
11	C→R	2nd	*H*	No, I haven't.	6
12	A→C	1st	*H*	Oh, you haven't seen it?	
13	C→A	2nd	*H*	I never seen that before.	

Figure 10: Interaction scenes. The "AP" signifies adjacency pair types. At **#4**, the system recognized A's adjacency third part and then generated a spontaneous opinion addressed to A (#5) as the first part. At that point, the system assumed the state of engagement (S_e) had changed from *Un-Engaged* to *Pre-Engaged*. After the system observed A's second part at **#8**, it assumed it at gotten approval to obtain an initiative to control the context (*Engaged*). At **#10**, the robot asked C a question in order to give him the floor.

Tacit Contracts for Wheelchairs

Daniel Couto Vale
SFB/TR8 Spatial Cognition
University of Bremen
danielvale@uni-bremen.de

Vivien Mast
SFB/TR8 Spatial Cognition
University of Bremen
viv@tzi.de

Abstract

In this paper, we propose a novel approach to infer dialogue acts using the notion of *tacit contracts*. We describe the interpersonal linguistic features that our analysis grammar can identify in uttered texts and present an inference procedure that strictly separates the semantic and pragmatic steps of utterance understanding, thereby meeting a higher degree of modularity, a prerequisite for extending robot functionality.

Keywords: Dialogue System; Dialogue Act; Attitude; Stance

1 Introduction

John is reading "Merlin", when the door bell rings. He cannot walk, but his intelligent wheelchair Rolland is nearby. He says: "Rolland, I need to open the door. Can you take me there?" Rolland responds "Sure, I'm coming!", comes to him, waits for him to sit comfortably, and then says "Let's go!" before driving him to the door side where John is able to reach the door handle.

So seamless are the interactions in our Wizard-of-Oz experiment (Anastasiou et al., 2012; Vale and Mast, 2012b) yet so difficult for an intelligent wheelchair. How is it to know that "I need to open the door" and "Can you take me there?" should not be understood separately as a statement and a question but together as a command to move towards the door for enabling the user to open it?

Each utterance is an action that affects the interactive situation. Not only does it construe events, but it also constitutes exchanges between interactants such as stating the speaker's need of performing an action and asking about the listener's capability of providing a service.

All speaking robots need some method of coping with this dual character of situated utterances. A frequent approach is Dialogue Act Detection, a family of statistical methods trained on human-annotated corpora (Allen and Core, 1997; Jurafsky et al., 1997; Jurafsky et al., 1997; Jekat et al., 1995). An alternative approach is Plan Recognition, which consists of using a planner having linguistic meaning and a domain model as inputs. We depart from this tradition by proposing a contractual approach in which semantic and pragmatic aspects of understanding are symbolically explored in separate steps of inference.

The main rationale for not pursuing the detection of dialogue acts as patterns in the uttered text is that the intended effect of an utterance is not to be found in the wording (Marcu, 1997); and the rationale for not taking construed events directly as plan steps is that the functional roles of interactants in cooperative work are decisive for interpreting attitudes.

In this paper, we present an automatic semantic analysis of the interpersonal features of linguistic units and propose a compatible three-step procedure consisting of transformation, contextualization and inference to enable an intelligent wheelchair to understand implied dialogue acts.

In the following two sections, we describe prior approaches to understanding interpersonal meaning and discuss their relevance for our approach. Then we introduce a classification of interpersonal linguistic features and explain how we re-express these implicit features of language explicitly in a standardised format. Finally, we describe the procedure used by the pragmatic module of our wheelchair in order to contextualise utterance meaning and infer implied dialogue acts.

2 Dialogue Act Detection

Dialogue act detection is the most frequently used approach for dealing with the interpersonal aspect of dialogue. In this section, we review two frameworks for dialogue act detection: the annotation standard DAMSL (Allen and Core, 1997) and the dialogue act component of the successful application Verbmobil (Jekat et al., 1995).

2.1 DAMSL and Derivates

The tagging system of Dialogue Act Markup in Several Layers (DAMSL) is a tag system for speaker's intention. It uses binary decision trees for tagging utterances with up to four attributes (layers) of the speaker's intention: communicative status, information level, backward- and forward-looking functions. DAMSL has been thoroughly tested for annotation (Core and Allen, 1997; Jurafsky et al., 1997; Ivanovic, 2005; Stolcke et al., 2000) with inter-annotator agreement reaching approx. 70-85%. Recent attempts to automatise DAMSL dialogue act detection using statistical methods (Core, 1997; Rosset and Lamel, 2004; Rangarajan Sridhar et al., 2007; Rosset et al., 2008; Rangarajan Sridhar et al., 2009) reach similar accuracy.

However, high accuracy scores need to be relativized, as precision and recall may be very low for most tags— Rangarajan Sridhar et al. (2009) report <1% for all but the two most frequent tags. Moreover, agreement rates tell nothing about the severity of mistagging for application usage.

The second and most compromising issue lies in the annotation scheme itself. Context-dependent decision trees turn utterance tagging into guess work, since utterances map differently to world models in different situations. For instance, there is danger "of annotators confusing surface form with [contextual] speaker intent, for instance labelling an *info-request* in the form of a statement as an *other-statement*" (Stent, 2000).

The third issue concerns applicability. The DAMSL research community has built annotated corpora and automated dialogue act detection. Only lately, there has been research on automatic learning of dialogue act flow patterns on large manually annotated corpora of dialogue. Whether these dialogue act flows will be usable in real applied systems is yet to be determined.

2.2 Verbmobil

A different approach to Dialogue Act Detection is followed by Verbmobil, a successful applied dialogue system for travel booking. It uses 55 types of dialogue act, tailored to the particular application domain of travel booking, e.g. *Request-Suggest-Duration*. Classification of utterances is achieved by detecting keywords and syntactic patterns in the word sequence of the utterance and matching them against keyword and pattern lists which are typical for each dialogue act type. Ambiguity is solved by using a context-based preference order learnt from a large annotated corpus.

This approach works with a caveat: embedding domain content like stay duration in dialogue act types may cause an explosion of categories for less restricted domains and, while easily recognisable, such tailored categories are domain specific. Therefore, they are not reusable when creating an application for a new domain.

2.3 Detection Trade-Off

In short, we argue that statistical methods of dialogue act detection do not scale. This approach always leads to a trade-off between suboptimal inter-annotator agreement as in DAMSL or lack of reusability as in Verbmobil.

The reason for this trade-off is that two issues of different natures are tackled at the same time: semantics and pragmatics. The lack of a stratified linguistic theory with semantic and pragmatic steps behind these classifications is the cause of a bad fit between categories and grammatical structure in the case of DAMSL. This shortcoming can be partially overcome through the usage of tailored categories at the expense of large annotated training corpora and a low reusability.

Tailoring is particularly expensive when experimental data is not easily obtainable as for human-wheelchair interaction. Therefore we need a different approach that separates text analysis from utterance contextualisation (see Section 4).

3 Belief-Desire-Intention Approach

The formal theory of rational interaction (FTRI) is a plan-based approach to dialogue management that divides user mental representations into beliefs, desires and intentions (BDI). The dialogue manager keeps track of which planned tasks are feasible for, assigned to and/or completed by particular agents (Sadek, 1992; Sadek, 1994; Sadek et al., 1996; Sadek et al., 1997). Logical inferences are made with respect to interactant's mental states in order to plan the next verbal action of the dialogue system. The interpersonal features of the linguistic model are very simple. User utterances are classified into one of 3 categories of syntactic patterns (directive, interrogative, or affirmative), and are used in combination with spotted verbs in order to determine the beliefs, desires, and intentions of the user. Lists of implications are used in order to infer actions from certain combinations of intentions and beliefs. An example for such an implication is: If a user *u* intends (*I*) to have an action *a DONE*, *u* intends (*I*) her/his utterance to have the same rational effect *RE* as performing *a* by her/himself; in other words, by informing the system about her or his intention to have a task performed, the user delegates the performance of this task to the system. The formal theory of rational interaction along with similar theories have received strong criticism. They lack a formalization of linguistic meaning (structural meaning) capable of encapsulating the richness and flexibility of linguistic systems. Moreover, "[BDI p]lan-based approaches [to dialogue management] are also criticised as being more opaque, especially given the large amount of procedural processing and lack of a well-founded semantics for plan-related operations" (Traum et al., 1999). Improving upon BDI plan-based approaches, Traum's work takes into account dialogue acts (Traum and Hinkelman, 1992) and obligations (Traum and Allen, 1994). Reflecting Traum et al.'s critique of the BDI approach, the present work can be understood as a step towards the theoretical conceptualization of some of BDI's opaque operations within an information-state approach to dialogue management.

4 Contract-Supported Interaction

Our work is supported by automatic functional text analysis (parsing) with Combinatory Categorial Grammar (CCG) (Steedman and Baldridge, 2011) using Systemic Functional Theory (Halliday and Matthiessen, 2004). This enables us to detect personal stances and attitude automatically in the syntactic structure of the utterance (see Section 4.1). Based on these detected concepts, we generate a standardised typed feature structure, which captures the commonalities of different utterance types with respect to the implied expectations from the addressee. Rather than hypothesizing about the user's mental states, we are able to base our interpretation solely on what is linguistically expressed as required from the addressee. Our usage of inference is somewhat similar to the one proposed by FTRI; however, with the formalised concept of tacit contracts—further formalizing the update operations in the dialogue system of Matheson et al. (2000)., we gain situational flexibility which is of great value, because tacit contracts are not universally valid, but depend on the roles of the interactants in a given situation.

4.1 Interpersonal Upper Model

On the semantic level, we adopt the most comprehensive linguistic description of the interpersonal component of human languages, which is found in the Systemic Functional Grammar of English (Halliday and Matthiessen, 2004). We created an ontology of linguistic units, the *Interpersonal Upper Model*, covering all interpersonal features of Systemic Functional Theory with minor adjustments and extensions. Using this classification of linguistic units, we implemented a Combinatory Categorial Grammar for German to parse a corpus collected in a Wizard-of-Oz experiment where users gave commands to an intelligent wheelchair in order to perform simple domestic tasks like washing their hands or opening the door (Anastasiou et al., 2012; Vale and Mast, 2012b; Vale and Mast, 2012a).

For an intelligent wheelchair to understand the utterances of the user, first it must cope with the various ways in which interpersonal meaning is expressed in language. For example, by uttering either of the clauses "I want you to leave." or "Leave!", the speaker commands the addressee to perform the action of leaving. Although they share this interpersonal function, the first makes the command explicit by referring to the requirer and performer of the service while the second leaves it implicit in the structure of the clause.

Halliday and Matthiessen (2004) call such expression pairs, where different wordings represent the same interpersonal meaning, interpersonally *agnate expressions*. In their work, *grammatical metaphor* is defined as the process whereby concepts which are usually implicit in the structure of clauses are re-expressed with more explicit referential representations.

It must be noted that this analysis relies strictly on utterance semantics, i.e. the information that can be gained from automatically analyzing the utterance alone, without relying on linguistic or situational context. By relying on parsing rather than string-level methods such as POS-tagging, keyword spotting and statistical utterance classification, we have the advantage of retaining the rich information contained in the structure of the utterance. For our approach, we rely on parsing with Categorial Combinatory Grammar (CCG) (Steedman and Baldridge, 2011) based on Systemic Functional Theory. This methodology provides us with a systematic, theory-based way of retrieving features of the linguistic structure of an utterance that are relevant for human-computer interaction. When parsing with a functional grammar, syntactic units are classified according to their function. Therefore, the segmentation of the utterance into constituents is based on the compositionality of semantic units.

In the remainder of this section, we will explain in detail the two main characters of interpersonal meaning, *attitude* and *stance* and how they are recognised in linguistic structure. In the following section, we will proceed to demonstrate how we turn the concept of grammatical metaphors into a method for representing interpersonal linguistic features explicitly in a standardised manner.

4.1.1 Attitude

Attitudes (or direct speech acts) specify the kind of thing negotiated: a mercative attitude indicates an exchange of goods ("A beer, please!"), an imperative attitude an exchange of services ("Please take me to the kitchen!"), and a declarative attitude an exchange of information ("Is the door closed?"). They also specify the orientation of the exchange between the interactants: whether the speaker is offering something to the addressee ("Your beer!" – offertive attitude) or demanding something from them ("A beer please!" – mandative).

By classifying attitudes in these two dimensions, we have a clear separation of exchange orientation (speaker to addressee or vice-versa) and exchange stock (good, service, or information). The combination of these options yielding six different attitudes[1], as shown in Table 1.

Table 1: Orientation $\times$ Stock $\rightarrow$ Attitude

	Orientation × Stock	Attitude
demand info	mandative × declarative	interrogative
offer info	offertive × declarative	affirmative
demand service	mandative × imperative	directive
offer service	offertive × imperative	preemptive
demand good	mandative × mercative	questive
offer good	offertive × mercative	donative

[1]The full ontology contains more distinctions that are ignored here for the sake of brevity.

As Example (1) shows, a mercative attitude (exchange of goods) is usually expressed by noun groups with modifiers such as "please". There is no constituent for Process nor Subject. Imperative attitudes (exchange of services) are usually expressed by predicates, that is, they have no Subject constituent as shown in Example (2). Finally, declarative attitudes (exchange of information) are usually expressed by full predications [2], as in Examples (3) and (4).

(1) "A beer, please!" (mercative)
(2) "Please take me to the kitchen!" (imperative)
(3) "The door is closed." (declarative)
(4) "Is the door closed?" (declarative)

Because there is a mapping between the syntactic level of an utterance structure and the kind of stock being exchanged (goods, services or information), we can automatically detect which attitude each utterance has.

4.1.2 Stance

Stance (or modality) "construe[s] the region of cognitive uncertainty that lies between 'yes' and 'no'" (Halliday and Matthiessen, 2004). There are two primary kinds of stance: *control* determines whether someone wants something (inclination, e.g. "is keen to", "wants") or is wanted for something (regulation, e.g. "is supposed to", "must"), and *conviction* determines how likely something is (likelihood, e.g. "it's likely to rain", "it's definitely not going to rain"), or how often it occurs (usuality, e.g. "It often rains in summer.", "it never rains in the desert."). Because Systemic Functional Theory works by delimiting semantically classified syntactic units based on possible semantic oppositions, combinatory categorial parsing of expressions is straight forward.

4.2 Grammatical Metaphor

As discussed in the previous section, attitude has an orientation from the speaker to the addressee or vice versa (offering or demanding). The service requirer and/or provider are not explicitly mentioned, but determined by the syntactic structure used and the roles of the interactants in the dialogue, speaker and addressee. Halliday and Matthiessen (2004) call this *interpersonal orientation* . Stance provides a linguistic tool to explicitly express the source and target of orientation, detaching them from the interactional situation.

[2]i.e. association between a subject and a predicate

For instance, "Leave!" is a service demand with an *interpersonal orientation* from the addressee to the speaker. If one rephrases this with "must" as in "you must leave." or "he must leave.", one obtains a *personal stance*, that is, an orientation from the speaker to the provider of the service which is explicitly expressed by a reference such as "you" or "he". By rephrasing the utterance again with "require" as in "you are required by me" or "you are required by law", one obtains an *impersonal stance*, that is, both requirer and service performer are referred to explicitly and not assumed from the orientation of the linguistic exchange.

It is possible to express the same interpersonal meaning with an *impersonal orientation* as with an *interpersonal orientation*. For example, "You are required by me to leave.", just like "Leave!", takes the speaker as the requirer and the addressee as the performer of the required action of leaving, therefore these two expressions are *agnate*, making the first a grammatical metaphor of the second.

Table 2: Possible orientations.

Interpers.	Personal	Impersonal
leave	you must leave he must leave	you are required by me to leave he is required by me to leave you are required by law to leave he is required by law to leave

4.2.1 Addressee-centered perspective

Each attitude brings about a *required response* from the addressee: offertive attitudes, by offering a stock, pose a requirement to receive this stock and mandative attitudes, by demanding a stock, pose a requirement to give one. These required responses can be expressed explicitly in more metaphorical agnate expressions. For example, the attitude of offering goods (offertive $\times$ mercative $\rightarrow$ donative) is represented by the process "take" in agnate expressions with the addressee as the subject as in "Take some cookies.". Table 3 shows the mapping of all 6 main attitudes onto their corresponding requirements from the addressee.

With mappings from the less metaphorical expressions to more metaphorical ones, the wheelchair can construe a standardised semantic representation to work with. This explicitation method enables us to capture the semantic commonalities of a broad variety of different linguistic expressions. Examples (5) and (6) show two different utterances whose standardised representations are highly similar. Example (5) is an information offer, re-expressed as a requirement to know a given information. Agnately, Example (6) is a service demand, re-expressed as a requirement to perform the service of *being aware* of the same information, a particular way of knowing it[3].

Table 3: Mapping of attitudes onto requirements from the addressee

Attitude	Required Reaction	Process
donative	receive goods	take
questive	give goods	hand
preemptive	receive services	assign
directive	give services	perform
affirmative	receive information	know
interrogative	give information	say

(5) "it's snowing"

LINGUISTIC MEANING:

```
Speaker offers to Addressee information that
    it's snowing
```

ADDRESSEE-CENTERED MEANING:

```
Speaker requires Addressee
    to know that
        it's snowing
```

(6) "be aware that it's snowing"

LINGUISTIC MEANING:

```
Speaker demands from Addressee service
    of being aware that
        it's snowing
```

ADDRESSEE-CENTERED MEANING:

```
Speaker requires Addressee
    to perform
        being aware that
            it's snowing
Speaker requires Addressee
    to be aware that
        it's snowing
```

The standardised semantic representation has the advantage that the wheelchair needs to treat requirements in only the most explicit representation when deciding which action it is expected to perform. In the following section, we will explain the concept of *tacit contracts*, and how they are used by our *interpersonal calculus* in order to extract the dialogue act from the user utterance as represented by the addressee-centered semantic representation and the situation model.

4.3 Tacit Contracts

While the addressee-centered semantic treatment enables an intelligent wheelchair to deal with utterances such as (7) and the more metaphorical (8) in a standardised manner independent of the situation, there is a further step of processing needed

[3]As performing an action is the same as acting, in Example (6), "requiring to perform being aware" can be simplified to "requiring to be aware".

in order to deal with the full scope of utterances collected in our usability experiment.

(7) "Take me to the kitchen."

(8) "I want you to take me to the kitchen."

(9) "I must go to the kitchen."

For instance, the wheelchair needs to understand that utterance (9) is, in the dialogue situation, not only an offering of information of a need of the user, but a more polite variant to Examples (7) and (8) (Vale and Mast, 2012a). The meaning the speaker intends to convey goes beyond *what is said*. Grice (1975) called this kind of pragmatic inference *conversational implicature*. They arise from the the understanding of a set of *conversational maxims* which humans can be expected to observe in conversation in combination with features of the interactional situation in which it is uttered. In contrast, *conventional implicatures* arise from the meaning of the uttered sentence and the *maxims of communication*, without any influence from the interactional situation. Récanati (1991) improved the Gricean model of maxims, but for theoretical reasons accepted no linguistic formalism, which makes his model impossible to apply in intelligent wheelchair design.

Relevance Theory (Sperber and Wilson, 1995; Carston, 1998) further develops the concept of inference in a cognitive paradigm by replacing maxims of communication with a balance between the cognitive effort needed to make an inference and its positive cognitive effect under the principle of relevance. Like Récanati, they establish the *linguistic meaning* as the boundary between semantics and pragmatics and divide the inferential process into the two subprocesses *enrichment* (resulting in the *explicatum*) and *deduction* (resulting in the *implicatum*).

As the main aim of this theory is to explain human cognition and not to design artificial intelligence, it is not directly translatable into a method for automation in applied robotics. One problem for automation is the assumption that interactants access and use all kinds of information, as needed. The inherently open nature of this theory makes its operationalization as a general framework impossible. In addition, assessing the *relevance* and cognitive effort of every item of information and process of reasoning makes it computationally too complex for practical applications. Moreover, Relevance Theory is not backed by a grammatical theory, and therefore lacks a comprehensive set of interpersonal linguistic features such as attitudes and stances.

In our approach, we follow the principle of separating meaning into linguistic meaning, explicatum, and implicatum, as proposed by Relevance Theory. Instead of the general effort-effect balance, we propose the concept of *tacit contracts* which operate on the pragmatic deduction step of communication in the Relevance Theory framework. Tacit contracts also differ from Grice's system of conversational maxims, which is not specific enough to distinguish which inferences are expected from particular individuals in their current functional roles.

Rather than general maxims of communication, tacit contracts are specific agreements entered into by two or more parties that establish obligations between those parties. These contracts determine the services that a party is required to perform in given situations. Therefore they determine the services that the speaker can expect from the addressee when he or she causes these situations to happen. For example, a contract such as "your wish is my command" only applies to interactants occupying a given role in the interaction, such as caregiver, waiter, etc., and only for a given set of actions that correspond to this role. If Karl is sitting in a café and says to the waiter "I would like steak for the main course.", the waiter would treat this wish as a command to serve the desired food, because bringing food is part of his tacit contract as a waiter. If Karl were to state "I would like to have your hat.", the waiter would not consider this a command, but a statement, because, although he would be capable to do so, providing the hat is not part of his contract as a waiter.

Politeness, in this perspective, is a manner of obtaining a stock whereby a speaker replaces his or her requirement for an addressee to give out a stock with an exchange of information about the current situation. The new information triggers a tacit contract which then enables the addressee to infer the contractual requirement for the current situation in a separate step of deduction.

4.3.1 Interactional Situation

For inferring implicata it is also important to differentiate two types of *businesses*: *stocks* and *issues*. For instance, in the afore-mentioned table-attending situation, let's suppose Karl had said the same utterance to his friend Hanna "I would like steak for the main course. Because Hanna cannot give a steak to Karl, the business of this interaction, providing a steak, is an issue and not a stock—they cannot exchange it, but only talk about it. The difference to the hat example above is that the waiter can provide his hat, but is not required to do so by any applicable contract, whereas Hanna may want to provide the steak, but is not able to[4].

By classifying businesses into stocks and issues, it is possible to trim down the inferential process further to avoid undesired implicatures. For instance, a wheelchair should treat the following two utterances differently: 1. "I would like to go to the kitchen" and 2. "I would like to open the door". Taking someone to the kitchen is a stock in this interaction—a service that the wheelchair can perform and that the user can assign to it. Opening the door, on the other hand, is not in the range of the wheelchair's capabilities and therefore an issue.

In the following subsection, we will explain how contracts and business kinds are used in the inferential calculus for generating an implicatum out of the explicatum. Then we will proceed to present the specific contracts relevant for the interaction with an intelligent wheelchair.

4.3.2 Contractual Calculus

Reference resolution and all other situational attachments of meaning are dealt with in the enriching step of the inferential process. Example (10) shows the enrichment of an utterance in the wheelchair scenario.

(10)"I would like to go to the kitchen"

ADDRESSEE-CENTERED MEANING:

```
Speaker requires Addressee
    to know that
        Speaker would like
            to go to the kitchen
```

EXPLICATUM:

```
JOHN requires ROLLAND
    to know that
        JOHN is keen
            to go to KITCHEN#1
```

After enrichment, the contractual phase is entered. Contracts may be triggered by a requirement towards the wheelchair to say or know. This is then re-interpreted as a polite requirement to give or receive goods, services, or information depending on the contract.

The process for selecting applicable tacit contracts is the following: once a declarative requirement has been detected, the system checks

Table 4: Surrogation

User: "I need to go to the kitchen."

I	need	to go	to the kitchen
Subject	Finite	–	–
Actor	–	Process	Destination
Medium	–	–	–

Wheelchair: "Ok, I'll take you there."

I	'll	take	**you**	there
Subject	Finite	–	–	–
Actor	–	Process	Action-Goal	Destination
Agent	–	–	**Medium**	–

whether the speaker is the *requirer* and the addressee the *provider* of the impersonal stance. If so, for each known contract, it is determined whether the contract applies for the given requirer and provider in their current functional roles. For each applicable contract, the contract script is performed, as will be shown in the following section.

4.3.3 Wheelchair Contracts

Here we present the contracts needed for understanding the utterances that occurred in our wheelchair-usage corpus. All user utterances in the corpus, except for three cases, can be understood appropriately with the given contracts.

Surrogation is the contract whereby a statement by the speaker of their inclination or obligation to perform an action is interpreted as a demand of a service. For example, if the user puts a bottle on the intelligent wheelchair and tells it "I need to take this bottle to Hannah", the wheelchair should treat this as a command to take the bottle to Hannah, assuming she is close by (similar to the implication in FTRI discussed in section 3).

For a non-affecting action such as "going", the entity that undergoes change as a result of the action (the *Medium*) is the *Actor*. In an affecting action such as "put", on the other hand, the *Medium* is the *Action-Goal* or action target—the thing being put. If a person states that they need to perform an action, the wheelchair needs to perform a service in which it is the *Actor* and which imposes the same result on the *Medium*. As Table 4 shows, this entails substituting a non-affecting action ("go") with an affecting action ("take").

Example (11) shows the performance of a contractual implicature in the deductive process.

(11)"I need to go to the kitchen"

EXPLICATUM:

```
JOHN requires ROLLAND
    to know that
```

[4]Notice that this reasoning constraint is similar to the Feasibility predicate of FTRI.

```
JOHN is required
        to go to the kitchen
IMPLICATUM:
JOHN politely requires ROLLAND
    to take JOHN to the kitchen
```

Supply is a contract whereby *requiring X to say whether X will do* should be interpreted as *requiring X to do.*

Need gleaning is a contract whereby the addressee is required to interpret a question about the availability of a stock as a statement of its need by the speaker. This contract is used together with Surrogation to create polite commands. Example (12) shows the inference of first applying the contract *need gleaning*, interpreting a *requiring X to say whether X can do Y* as a *requiring X to know that Y needs to be done*, and then applying the contract *surrogation*, as described above.

(12)"Can you take me to the kitchen?"

```
EXPLICATUM:
JOHN requires ROLLAND
    to say whether
        ROLLAND can
            take JOHN to the kitchen
IMPLICATUM: NEED GLEANING
JOHN politely requires ROLLAND
    to know that
        JOHN needs
            to be taken to the kitchen
IMPLICATUM: SURROGATION
JOHN requires ROLLAND very politely
    to take JOHN to the kitchen
```

Support is a contract whereby the statement of the speaker's inclination or obligation to perform an action is understood as a command to offer the stock that serves to fulfill the preconditions for performing his or her intended or required action. As Example (13) shows, *requiring X to know that Y is keen to* is interpreted as *requiring X to perform an action that enables Y to.*

(13)"I'd like to open the door!"

```
EXPLICATUM:
JOHN requires ROLLAND
    to know that
        JOHN is keen
            to open the door
IMPLICATUM: SUPPORT
JOHN politely requires ROLLAND
    to take JOHN to a place
        where JOHN can open the door
```

This contract is dependent on the classification of entities by affordances and usage preconditions. A wheelchair can only decide where to take the user who says "I would like to do a mouth wash", if it knows that doing a mouth wash requires the user to be at a certain position in front of a wash basin.

In addition, in order to distinguish whether to apply the contract *support* or the contract *surrogate*, the distinction between *stock* and *issue* is central. If the desired action of the speaker is a *stock*, i.e. a service that can be performed by the wheelchair, the contract *surrogate* should be applied. If it is an *issue*, the contract *support* should be applied instead.

5 Discussion and Outlook

We have presented the main linguistic features of our Enactment Upper Model and shown how to infer dialogue acts by using tacit contracts. With this procedure, we are able to determine automatically which actions the wheelchair is expected to do for most utterances of our corpus. From a theoretical point of view, we proposed a method of deducing implicata by applying contractual scripts that combine a linguistic and a philosophical approach with the strict purpose of automation and, in specific, of controlling an intelligent wheelchair. In doing so, we fill the gap between a linguist's set of lexicogrammatical features with requiring force and a philosopher's set of axioms from which it can be deduced whether the user made a request.

On a robot design perspective, we have spared the text analysis component from creating specific speech acts for a number of clause structures such as "can you..." and "will you..." and so on, which would otherwise be necessary, and spared the dialogue manager from managing a large number of user's dialogue-related intentions and from dealing with the otherwise present ambiguity of contextually interpretable utterances such as "I need to open the door". In addition, our approach enables adjustment for new wheelchair functionality without rewriting the whole text analysis component and allows for an easy addition of new tacit contracts with corresponding scripts.

The approach presented in this paper provides a principled way for inferring dialogue acts that uses the structural information present in the clause and therefore enables high accuracy and reusability both on the semantic and on the pragmatic level. In order to gain a full understanding of the scalability of this approach, further investigation of applicable contracts in different application domains is necessary.

Acknowledgments

We gratefully acknowledge the support of the Deutsche Forschungsgemeinschaft (DFG) through the Collaborative Research Center SFB/TR8 Spatial Cognition. We also thank Dimitra Anastasiou for collaboration in designing and conducting the experiment.

References

James F. Allen and Mark G. Core. 1997. Draft of DAMSL: Dialog Act Markup in Several Layers. retrieved from: http://www.cs.rochester.edu/research/speech/damsl/RevisedManual/, July 16th 2013.

Dimitra Anastasiou, Cui Jian, and Desislava Zhekova. 2012. Speech and Gesture Interaction in an Ambient Assisted Living Lab. In *SMIAE '12 Proceedings of the 1st Workshop on Speech and Multimodal Interaction in Assistive Environments*, pages 18–27, Jeju, Republic of Korea. Association for Computational Linguistics.

Robyn Carston. 1998. The Semantics/Pragmatics Distinction: A View from Relevance Theory. *UCL Working Papers in Linguistics*, 10:303–329.

Mark G. Core and James F. Allen. 1997. Coding Dialogs with the DAMSL Annotation Scheme. Technical report.

Mark G. Core. 1997. Analyzing and Predicting Patterns of DAMSL Utterance Tags. In *Working notes AAAI spring symposium on applying machine learning to discourse processing*, pages 18–24.

Herbert P. Grice. 1975. Logic and Conversation. *Syntax and Semantics 3: Speech arts*, pages 41–58.

Michael A. K. Halliday and Christian M. I. M. Matthiessen. 2004. *Introduction to Systemic Functional Grammar*. Arnold, London, 3 edition.

Edward Ivanovic. 2005. Dialogue Act Tagging for Instant Messaging Chat Sessions. In *Proceedings of the ACL Student Research Workshop*, pages 79–84, Stroudsburg, PA, USA. Association for Computational Linguistics.

Susanne Jekat, Alexandra Klein, Elisabeth Maier, Ilona Maleck, Marion Mast, and J. Joachim Quantz. 1995. Dialogue Acts in VERBMOBIL. Technical report.

Daniel Jurafsky, Elizabeth Shriberg, and Debra Biasca. 1997. Switchboard SWBD-DAMSL Shallow-Discourse-Function Annotation Coders Manual, August.

Daniel Marcu. 1997. Perlocutions: The Achilles' Heel of Speech Act Theory. *Journal of Pragmatics*.

Colin Matheson, Massimo Poesio, and David Traum. 2000. Modelling Grounding and Discourse Obligations Using Update Rules. In *Proceedings of the 1st North American chapter of the Association for Computational Linguistics conference*, pages 1–8. Association for Computational Linguistics.

Vivek K. Rangarajan Sridhar, Srinivas Bangalore, and Shrikanth Narayanan. 2007. Exploiting Prosodic Features for Dialog Act Tagging in a Discriminative Modeling Framework. In *Proceedings of InterSpeech*, pages 150–153, Antwerp, Belgium.

Vivek K. Rangarajan Sridhar, Srinivas Bangalore, and Shrikanth Narayanan. 2009. Combining Lexical, Syntactic and Prosodic Cues for Improved Online Dialog Act Tagging. *Computer Speech & Language*, 23(4):407–422.

François Récanati. 1991. The Pragmatics of What is Said. In Steven Davis, editor, *Pragmatics: a reader*, pages 97–120. Oxford University Press, New York.

Sophie Rosset and Lori Lamel. 2004. Automatic Detection of Dialog Acts Based on Multi-level Information. In *in ICSLP, Jeju Island*, pages 540–543.

Sophie Rosset, Delphine Tribout, and Lori Lamel. 2008. Multi-level information and automatic dialog act detection in human-human spoken dialogs. *Speech Communication*, 50(1):1–13.

M. David Sadek, A. Ferrieux, A. Cozannet, Philippe Bretier, Franck Panaget, and J. Simonin. 1996. Effective Human-Computer Cooperative Spoken Dialogue: the AGS Demonstrator. In *Spoken Language, 1996. ICSLP 96. Proceedings., Fourth International Conference on*, pages 546–549 vol.1.

M. David Sadek, Philippe Bretier, and Franck Panaget. 1997. ARTIMIS: Natural Dialogue Meets Rational Agency. In *in Proceedings of IJCAI-97*, pages 1030–1035. Morgan Kaufmann.

M. David Sadek. 1992. A Study in the Logic of Intention. In *Proceedings of the 3rd International Conference on Principles of Knowledge Representation and Reasoning (KR'92). Cambridge, MA, October 25-29, 1992*, pages 462–473. Morgan Kaufmann.

M. David Sadek. 1994. Communication Theory = Rationality Principles + Communicative Act Models. In *In: Proc. of AAAI 94 Workshop on Planning for Interagent Comm.*

Dan Sperber and Deirdre Wilson. 1995. *Relevance*. Communication and Cognition. Wiley-Blackwell.

Mark Steedman and Jason Baldridge. 2011. Combinatory Categorial Grammar.

Amanda J. Stent. 2000. The Monroe Corpus. Technical report.

Andreas Stolcke, Noah Coccaro, Rebecca Bates, Paul Taylor, Carol Van Ess-Dykema, Klaus Ries, Elizabeth Shriberg, Daniel Jurafsky, Rachel Martin, and Marie Meteer. 2000. Dialogue Act Modeling for Automatic Tagging and Recognition of Conversational Speech. *Computational Linguistics*, 26(3):339–373.

David R. Traum and James F. Allen. 1994. Discourse Obligations in Dialogue Processing. In *Proceedings of the 32nd annual meeting on Association for Computational Linguistics*, pages 1–8. Association for Computational Linguistics.

David R. Traum and Elizabeth A. Hinkelman. 1992. Conversation Acts in Task-oriented Spoken Dialogue. *Computational intelligence*, 8(3):575–599.

David Traum, Johan Bos, Robin Cooper, Staffan Larsson, Ian Lewin, Colin Matheson, and Massimo Poesio. 1999. A Model of Dialogue Moves and Information State Revision. Technical report.

Daniel Couto Vale and Vivien Mast. 2012a. Key Interpersonal Communication Skills for Wheelchairs. In *CogInfoCom '12 Proceedings of the 3rd IEEE International Conference on Cognitive Infocommunications*, pages 421–426, Kosice, Slovakia. IEEE.

Daniel Couto Vale and Vivien Mast. 2012b. Using Foot-Syllable Grammars to Customize Speech Recognizers for Dialogue Systems. In *TSD '12 Lecture Notes in Artificial Intelligence vol. 7499*, Brno, Czech Republic. Springer.

Laughter and Topic Transition in Multiparty Conversation

Emer Gilmartin, Francesca Bonin, Carl Vogel, Nick Campbell
Trinity College Dublin
{gilmare, boninf, vogel, nick}@tcd.ie

Abstract

This study explores laughter distribution around topic changes in multiparty conversations. The distribution of shared and solo laughter around topic changes was examined in corpora containing two types of spoken interaction; meetings and informal conversation. Shared laughter was significantly more frequent in the 15 seconds leading up to topic change in the informal conversations. A sample of informal conversations was then analysed by hand to gain further insight into links between laughter and topic change.

1 Introduction

Human spoken interaction comprises a bundle of signals and cues, together and separately providing information relevant to the topic or task at hand, and serving to build or maintain social bonds. Dialogue is multifunctional, serving social as well as information transfer goals. Laughter is predominantly social rather than a solo activity, is universally present in humans, part of the 'universal human vocabulary', innate, instinctual, and inherited from primate ancestors (Provine, 2004; Glenn, 2003). In conversation, it predominantly punctuates rather than interrupts speech. Accounts of laughter's role range from response to humour to a social cohesion or bonding mechanism used since our primate days. It has been suggested that laughter is often a co-operative mechanism which can provide clues to dialogue structure (Holt, 2011). Herein, we investigate the relevance of laughter to topic change by analysing two corpora of conversational speech in terms of temporal distribution of laughter, first through statistical analysis of laughter and topic change distribution, then by manual study of an hour of spontaneous conversation.

2 Laughter and Topic Change

Conversation analysis has highlighted connections between laughter and topic change; many conversations in the Holt corpus of mostly two person telephone dialogues include laughter at topic closings (Holt, 2010). Laughter has been linked to topic closure in situations where one participant produces jokes or laughs, thus inviting others to join in, with this invitation open to refusal if interlocutors continue speaking on the topic at hand (Jefferson, 1979). Holt (2010) suggests that laughter may arise at topic changes because turns consisting only of laughter are backwards looking, not adding to the last topic, and thus constituting a signal that the current topic has been exhausted and that the conversation is at a topic change relevant point. We hypothesise that these laughter turns form a 'buffer' allowing participants a reassuring moment of social bonding. In a meeting, there is a set agenda, a chairperson, and protocols for moving from topic to topic. In social dialogue, the goal is to pass time together, and topics are not lined up ready for use. Aversion to potentially embarrassing silence may be more pertinent in informal conversation; thus laughter preceding topic change may be more likely in informal dialogue.

Although there is much mention of laughter in conversation analysis, it is difficult to find quantitative data on its distribution in spoken interaction. Previous work (Bonin et al., 2012b) established that laughter, particularly shared laughter, is less likely to occur in the first quarter of a topic than in the final quarter, and that this distinction is greater in social conversation. In this work we test the hypothesis that laughter should be frequently found before rather than simply around topic changes. We examine the frequency of laughter within a range of distances from either side of a topic change, to investigate if there is a period of higher laughter frequency independent of topic length. We are also interested in exploring whether the turns leading to topic change follow the observations on topic change sequences and laughter distribution in two party conversations in the literature. If there are identifiable sequences involving laughter leading to topic change, knowledge of their architecture will aid in creating algorithms for discourse recognition and segmentation in multiparty conversation.

The notion of topic in discourse has been studied extensively but a concise definition is difficult to find. Topic has been described at sentence level (Lambrecht, 1996), at discourse level (Van Dijk, 1981); as a manifestation of speakers intentions (Passonneau and Litman, 1997), and as coherent segments of discourse about the same thing (Van Dijk, 1996). Here, we consider topic at discourse level as a chunk of coherent content.

3 Corpora

We analysed two datasets to cover free natural interaction and more structured meetings.

3.1 Topic annotation in TableTalk and AMI

Both TableTalk and AMI have topic annotations freely available. TableTalk topics were annotated manually by two labellers at a single level; AMI annotations include top-level or core topics whose content reflects the main meeting structure, and subtopics for small digressions inside the core topics. Here we use the core topic segmentation which is more in line with the TableTalk annotation.

3.2 TableTalk

The TableTalk corpus contains multimodal recordings of free flowing natural conversations among five participants, recorded at the Advanced Telecommunication Research Labs in Japan (Campbell, 2009). In order to collect as natural data as possible, neither topics of discussion nor activities were restricted in advance. Three sessions were recorded over three consecutive days in an informal setting over coffee, by three female (Australian, Finnish, and Japanese) and two male (Belgian and British) participants (Jokinen, 2009). The conversations are fully transcribed and segmented for topic, and also annotated for affective state of participants and for gesture and postural communicative functions using MUMIN (Allwood et al., 2007). Table-talk has been analyzed in terms of engagement and laughter (Bonin et al., 2012a) and lexical accommodation (Vogel and Behan, 2012). Our analyses used transcripts of the entire corpus: about 3h 30, 31523 tokens and 5980 turns. Laughter was transcribed in intervals on the speech transcription tier as @w, (unless inserted as part of a longer utterance). The total number of laughs is 713. Shared laughter was automatically annotated as described in §4.

3.3 AMI

The AMI (Augmented Multi-party Interaction) Meeting Corpus is a multimodal data set of 100 hours of meeting recordings (McCowan et al., 2005). The corpus contains real and scenario-driven meetings. We base our analysis on the scenario based meetings, with a total of 717,239 tokens. Each meeting has four participants, and the same subjects meet over four different sessions to discuss a design project. The sessions correspond to four different project steps (Project kick-off meeting, Functional Design, Conceptual Design and Detailed Design). Each participant is given a role to play (project manager, marketing expert, industrial designer and user interface designer) and keeps this role until the end of the scenario. Conversations are all in English, with 91 native speakers and 96 non-native speakers participating. There are 11,277 instances of laughter, annotated in the transcripts as vocal-sounds/laugh. About 25% of these laughs are annotated with start time only.

4 Analytical methodologies

4.1 Automated and manual analyses

Both corpora were also analysed automatically, and a one-hour sample of the TableTalk corpus was analysed on a case-by-case basis to investigate if laughter around topic change did indeed follow the patterns proposed in the literature.

For the initial stages of ongoing manual analysis

to gain more insight into the mechanisms underlying laughter and topic change, a one-hour stretch of conversation from the second day of the TableTalk was selected for study. The mechanism outlined by Holt, based on Jefferson's work on laughter and Schegloff's topic final sequences (Schegloff, 2007), hinges on whether a laughter invitation is taken up an interlocutor in two party dialogue. If it is, then one or more laughter turns ensue and the likelihood of topic change is high. The opposite occurs when the interlocutor does not take up the invitation but rather continues with further talk on the topic, averting topic change. We were interested in observing if this phenomenon occurred in multiparty conversation, and if subsequent topic change was dependent on how many of the group took up the invitation to laugh. As analysis of the two corpora showed higher likelihood of laughter before topic change in more informal conversation, we chose to examine a sample of TableTalk for preliminary study.

This sample contained 1834 utterances, 36 T-event or topic change instants, and 329 laughs among the five participants, of which 76 were solo while the remainder contributed to a total of 68 shared laugh events, all of which were manually annotated on separate laughter tiers. For each instance of laughter, we also annotated the number of participants who laughed and the distance from the laughter to the next topic commencement.

4.2 Temporal definitions and measurement

We use an algorithm resulting from earlier work to annotate shared and solo laughter. The algorithm was motivated by the observation that in both corpora laughter was sometimes annotated with start time only, and also that laughter in response to the same stimulus should be considered shared laughter. These two factors taken together allow us to recover shared laughter that may be missed if we simply count overlapping laughs of distinct speakers. The algorithm defines shared laughter as: (a) overlapping laughs of distinct speakers; or (b) consecutive laughs of distinct speakers within distance ϵ. We calculate ϵ using the probability distribution that successive laughs with observation of start time only are part of a shared laugh event, trained on a subset of overlapping laughs from the corpora.

Topic changes (T-events) are the annotated time points where topic shifts in conversation. We counted the frequency of laughter, shared laughter, and solo laughter into 5-second bins at T-event minus multiples of 5 seconds (T-5, T-10, T-15, T-20) in order to look at the laughter trend near topic termination. A meaningful threshold emerges (T-15 seconds) where a change in the laughter trend is visible. Hence we counted the frequency of laughter between T-15 and T, and T and T+15.

5 Results

5.1 Automated processing

We counted the frequency of laughter, shared laughter, and solo laughter in 5-second bins at T- event time T minus multiples of 5 seconds (T-5, T-10, T-15, T-20). Fig. 1 shows the mean frequency of laughs per bin in TableTalk. While in AMI the distribution over the bins does not show significant trends, in TableTalk, we noticed a significant change at T-15.[1] Hence we take T-15 as a rational threshold marking some change in the laughter distribution before a topic boundary in informal chat.

Then we analyzed the frequency of laughter between T-15 and T (we call this segment *wt*) and T+15 (*wb*). As shown in Fig. 2, we notice a significant difference in the amount of both shared and solo laughter between topic terminations (*wt*) and topic beginnings (*wb*). In particular topic terminations show a higher frequency of laughter than topic beginnings. The result holds in AMI and in TableTalk.

5.2 Manual processing

The first observation from the manual analysis is that the shared/solo laugh ratio is heavily skewed towards shared laughter (253 laughs were shared vs 79 solo). Laughs were combined into laugh events according to the number of participants involved. The length of laugh events was significantly shorter for one-person laugh events than for shared laughter, see Fig. 3. Distance to next topic change and number of

[1]The laughter counts in the bins for each of T-5, T-10 and T-15 are significantly greater than random samples of 5 sec. conversation slices (Wilcox directed test, $p < 0.002$); the counts for T-20 are not significantly greater than random slices. Further, the counts for T-20 are significantly less than those in each of T-15 ($p < 0.02$), T-10 ($p < 0.02$) and T-5 ($p < 0.005$), while the pairwise differences among T-15, T-10 and T-5 are not signficant. We conclude that T-15 contains an inflection point.

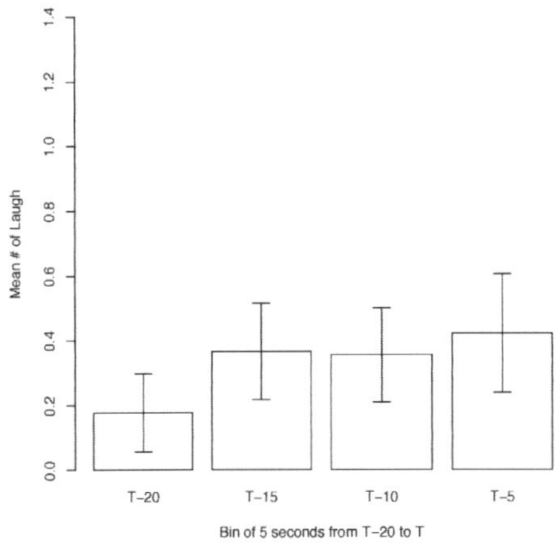

Figure 1: Frequency of laughter in TableTalk between T-20 and T in 5-second bins. Bars represent the mean laugh count per bin

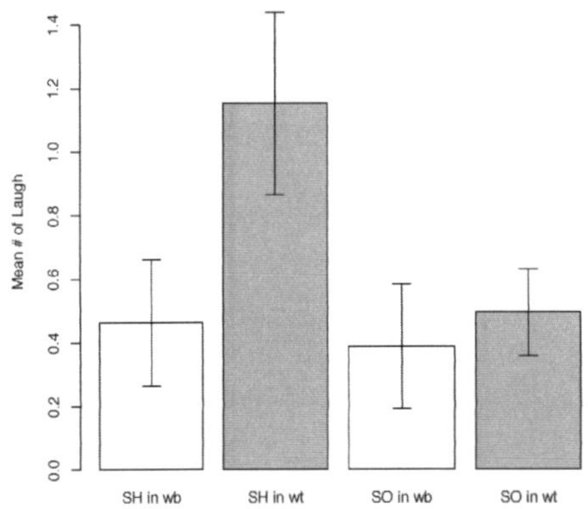

Figure 2: Shared (sh) and Solo (so) laughs in topic termination (wt) and topic beginning segments (wb)-TableTalk

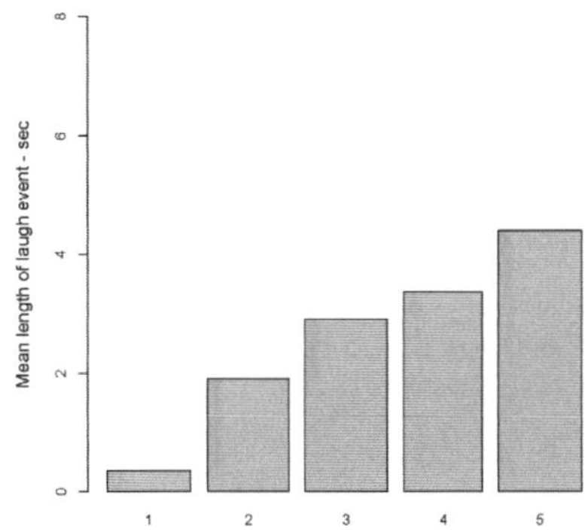

Figure 3: Laughter event length by number of laughers.

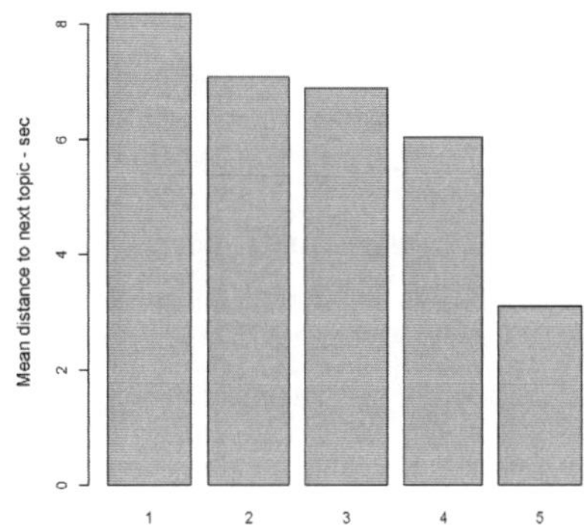

Figure 4: Distance to next topic by number of laughers.

laughers in a laugh event, seen in Fig. 4, showed significant negative correlation ($p < 0.05$).

6 Discussion and Conclusion

Our results indicate a likelihood of shared laugher appearing in the final 15 seconds before a new topic commences. This is in line with the literature which reports laughter at topic transition relevant places, and thus before a topic change. We have also seen that the number of people sharing laughter is related to reducing distance from the laughter to the next topic change, and that laugh events are longer as more participants join in. Models of a complexity adequate to predict human behaviour require exhaustively detailed analysis of stretches of conversation in addition to broad statistical analysis. Our combination of approaches has proven fruitful. Several observations from the preliminary close examination of the TableTalk data provide fruit for further research. Many of the short solo laughs may be seen as responses to one's own or another participant's content, while stronger solo laughs may tend to invite longer and stronger laughter from others, leading to topic change possibilities. An acoustic analysis of the laughter will investigate this. We also observed that shared laughter among several participants which did not result in topic change were frequently interpretable as attempts to draw an ongoing topic to a close. This merits investigation to see whether these laugh events can be considered topic transition relevant places. Analysis of speaker changes and turn retrieval in and around these laughter events is underway to model these events.

Acknowledgments

This work is supported by the Innovation Bursary of Trinity College Dublin, the Speech Communication Lab at TCD, and by the SFI FastNet project 09/IN.1/1263. We are grateful to the anonymous reviewers for helpful feedback.

References

Jens Allwood, Loredana Cerrato, Kristiina Jokinen, Costanza Navarretta, and Patrizia Paggio. 2007. The mumin coding scheme for the annotation of feedback, turn management and sequencing phenomena. *Language Resources and Evaluation*, 41(3-4):273–287.

Francesca Bonin, Ronald Böck, and Nick Campbell. 2012a. How do we react to context? annotation of individual and group engagement in a video corpus. In *SocialCom/PASSAT*, pages 899–903.

Francesca Bonin, Nick Campbell, and Carl Vogel. 2012b. Laughter and topic changes: Temporal distribution and information flow. In *Cognitive Infocommunications (CogInfoCom), 2012 IEEE 3rd International Conference on*, pages 53–58.

Nick Campbell. 2009. An audio-visual approach to measuring discourse synchrony in multimodal conversation data. In *Proceedings of Interspeech 2009*.

P. Glenn. 2003. *Laughter in Interaction*. Studies in Interactional Sociolinguistics. Cambridge University Press.

Elizabeth Holt. 2010. The last laugh: Shared laughter and topic termination. *Journal of Pragmatics*, 42:1513–1525.

Elizabeth Holt. 2011. On the nature of 'laughables' : laughter as a response to overdone figurative phrases. *Pragmatics*, 21(3):393–410, September.

Gail Jefferson. 1979. A technique for inviting laughter and its subsequent acceptance/declination. In G Psathas, editor, *Everyday language: Studies in ethnomethodology.*, pages 79–96. Irvington Publishers: New York,NY.

Kristiina Jokinen. 2009. Gaze and gesture activity in communication. In Constantine Stephanidis, editor, *Universal Access in Human-Computer Interaction. Intelligent and Ubiquitous Interaction Environments*, volume 5615 of *Lecture Notes in Computer Science*, pages 537–546. Springer Berlin / Heidelberg.

K. Lambrecht. 1996. *Information Structure and Sentence Form: Topic, Focus, and the Mental Representations of Discourse Referents*. Cambridge Studies in Linguistics. Cambridge University Press.

I. McCowan, G. Lathoud, M. Lincoln, A. Lisowska, W. Post, D. Reidsma, and P. Wellner. 2005. The ami meeting corpus. In *In: Proceedings Measuring Behavior 2005, 5th International Conference on Methods and Techniques in Behavioral Research. L.P.J.J. Noldus, F. Grieco, L.W.S. Loijens and P.H. Zimmerman (Eds.), Wageningen: Noldus Information Technology*.

Rebecca J. Passonneau and Diane J. Litman. 1997. Discourse segmentation by human and automated means. *Computational Linguistics*, 23(1):103–139.

Robert R. Provine. 2004. Laughing, tickling, and the evolution of speech and self. *Current Directions in Psychological Science*, 13(6):215–218.

E.A. Schegloff. 2007. *Sequence Organization in Interaction: Volume 1: A Primer in Conversation Analysis*. Cambridge University Press.

Teun A. Van Dijk, 1981. *Sentence Topic versus Discourse Topic*, pages 177–194. Mouton.

Teun A. Van Dijk. 1996. Discourse, power and access. In Carmen Rosa Caldas-Coulthard and Malcolm Coulthard, editors, *Texts and Practices, Readings in Critical Discourse Analysis*, pages 84–104. Routledge.

Carl Vogel and Lydia Behan. 2012. Measuring synchrony in dialog transcripts. In Anna Esposito, Antonietta M. Esposito, Alessandro Vinciarelli, Rüdiger Hoffmann, and Vincent C. Müller, editors, *Behavioural Cognitive Systems*, pages 73–88. Springer, LNCS 7403.

IMHO: An Exploratory Study of Hedging in Web Forums

Liliana Mamani Sanchez
Trinity College Dublin
mamanisl@scss.tcd.ie

Carl Vogel
Trinity College Dublin
vogel@tcd.ie

Abstract

We explore hedging in web forum conversations, which is interestingly different to hedging in academic articles, the main focus of recent automatic approaches to hedge detection. One of our main results is that forum posts using hedges are more likely to get high ratings of their usefulness. We also make a case for focusing annotation efforts on hedges that take the form of first-person epistemic phrases.

1 Introduction

Computational linguistics research in hedging, use of linguistic expressions whose contribution to sentence meaning is a modulation of the accuracy of the content they embed, and speculation detection has been done intensively in the domain of scholarly texts. The interest created in this domain has expanded to some extent to other domains such as news and reviews. Automatic processing of speculation requires at some stage the annotation of words or phrases conveying uncertainty (Vincze et al., 2008). More complex endeavours imply the annotation of various elements of context involved in the expression of hedging (Rubin et al., 2005; Wiebe et al., 2005).

In web forums where users' contributions play a vital role in the forum dynamics, such as mutual support forums that are part of the ecosystem of technology company supports for users, exploring the features that make a contributor outstanding is relevant.[1] A user shows a distinctive behavior by writing useful posts that help other users in the problem that first motivated their participation in the forum. This paper emerges from our interest in finding features that predict which contributors will be most appreciated.

Many lexical and grammatical devices aid hedging (expressions such as epistemics verbs, modals, adjectives, etc. name but a few) as do non-lexical devices such as conditionals. We deem singular first person epistemic phrases as hedges that can help to identify the subject of a hedging event. We analyze the correlation between the use of epistemic phrases (vs. other types of hedges) and the probability of posts containing these hedges of being considered useful by the forum community. We also explore whether epistemic phrases constitute a distinctive feature that support user classifications. In §2, we described the function of hedges according to a hedging classification framework and in relation to the domain of web forums. Then §3 describes the profiling work done and discusses the main findings. We conclude in §4.

2 Functions of hedging

The research by Hyland (1998) is one of the broadest studies about hedging functions in scientific articles, and which makes use of categories that have strong relationship, at face value, to the likelihood that the reader of hedged material will find the material sufficiently useful or sufficiently well expressed to prompt the reader to rate highly the message containing the material, whether with an explicit facility to record kudos or otherwise. Hyland proposed a poly-pragmatic classification of hedges based on their indicating function: reader-oriented, writer-oriented, attribute and reliability. Briefly, attribute and reliability hedges both relate to the accuracy of the message conveyed. Attribute hedges relate to the conformity of the described situation with encyclopedic expectations (1), while reliability hedges relate to the level of certainty of the speaker about the propositional content (2). In a different dimension, reader ori-

[1]Throughout, we use "web forum" to refer to such ecosystems: we speculate that their informal nature makes our observations generalize to other sorts of web forum in which solutions to problems are not the focal point; even general discussion forums can be witnessed to trigger community weighting of contributions.

ented hedges are composed with the concern that the "reader" accept the truth of the embedded content (3), thereby presupposing the "writer's" commitment to the content, while writer oriented hedges disclaim commitment to the content (4).

(1) **Protypical** mammals are land-dwellers.

(2) **Probably,** respected ancient Greeks thought whales to be fish.

(3) **I think** that if you reboot, the changes will take effect.

(4) **Based on** what you've said, you seem right.

Applying this classification scheme not to scholarly prose but to web forums, it seems likely that readers in technical forums would prefer the accuracy of attribute hedges (1) over the relative uncertainty of reliability hedges (2), and that the reader oriented hedges (3) supply comfort in the implication of both the quality of the embedded claims and the absence of arrogance. This research is attempting to test these hypotheses by assessing the relationship between the likelihood of posts receiving kudos and the quantity of hedges in these categories that the posts contain.

Unfortunately, answering the question is complex, because it is not in all cases obvious whether a linguistic expression contains a hedge or what function the hedges serve when they do exist. Therefore, we attempt a partial answer to the question by examining those hedge expressions which can be processed with some reliability using automated means. Consider the taxonomy of linguistic expressions in Fig. 1. The boxed regions of this taxonomy are amenable to automatic processing. Further, epistemic hedges with first-person singular subjects relate strongly to reader oriented hedges (3) in Hyland's taxonomy. The non-phrasal hedges are heterogeneous in function.

Figure 1: A taxonomy of linguistic expressions.

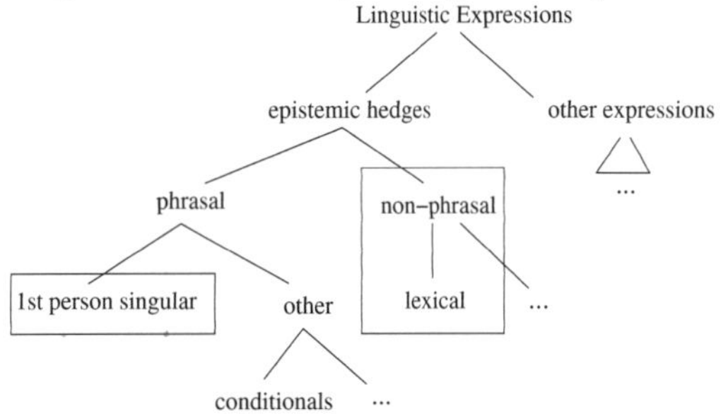

We do not claim this separation of hedging markers can fully account for pragmatic and semantic analysis of hedging in web forums, but we are confident this classification supports reliable annotation for quantificational assessment of certainty and hedging in this informal domain. We base our profiling experiments (§3) on this functional separation of hedging markers.

3 Profiling posts by hedging

3.1 Description of the forum dataset

The dataset we used created out of a forum that is part of customer support services provided by a software vendor company. Although we were not able to confirm the forum demographics, we can infer they are mostly American English speakers as the forum was set up first for USA customers. Some other features are best described by Vogel and Mamani Sanchez (2013). Our dataset is composed of 172,253 posts that yield a total of 1,044,263 sentences. This dataset has been intensively "cleaned", as originally it presented a great variety of non-linguistic items such as HTML codes for URLS, emoticons, IP addresses, etc. These elements were replaced by wild-cards and also user names have been anonymised, although some non-language content may remain.

A forum user can give a post "kudos" if he/she finds it useful or relevant to the topic being addressed in a forum conversation.[2] We counted the number of kudos given to each post. There are four user categories in the forum: {employee, guru, notranked, ranked}.[3] A poster's rank depends, among other factors, on the number of posts they make and their aggregate kudos.

3.2 Epistemic phrases versus other hedges

We created two lexicons, one composed by first person singular epistemic phrases and one by non-phrasal hedges. Initially, a set of epistemic phrases where taken from Kärkkäinen (2010): {I think, I don't know, I know, etc.} and from Wierzbicka (2006). The non-phrasal hedge lexicon was created from words conveying at least some degree of uncertainty: {appear, seem, sometimes, suggest, unclear, think, etc.}, taken from Rubin (2006). Additional hedges were included after the pilot

[2]A user may accord kudos for any reason at all, in fact.

[3]In the forum we studied, there are actually many ranks, with guru as the pinnacle for a non-employee; we grouped the non-guru ranked posters together.

annotation. The lexicons are composed by 76 and 109 items, respectively. There are many other hedge instances that are not included in these lexicons but our experiment restricts to these items. Epistemic phrases include acronyms such as "IMHO", "IMO" and "AFAIK" that we deem meet functions described in §2.

A pilot manual annotation of hedges was conducted on in order to verify the viability of automatic annotation. Our automatic annotation procedure performs a sentence by sentence matching and tagging of both kinds of hedging. The procedure uses a maximal matching strategy to tag hedges, e.g. if "I would suggest" is found, this is tagged and not "suggest". This automatic tagging procedure does not account for distinctions between epistemic and deontic readings of hedges, nor between speculative or non-speculative uses of non-phrasal hedges. 107,134 posts contain at least one hedge: 34,301 posts contain at least one epistemic phrase; 101,086, at least one non-phrasal hedge; 28,253, at least one of each.

3.3 Methods of analysis

In §3.1 we showed there are two ways to characterize a post: 1) By its writer category and 2) by the number of times it gets accorded *kudos*. We devise a third characterisation by exploring epistemic phrases and non-phrasal hedge usage in individual posts as a whole, tracking use of both types of hedge in each post. We devised three discretization functions (DF) for assigning a label to each post depending on the type of hedges contained within. The DFs take two parameters, each one representing either the relative or binarized frequency non-phrasal hedges and epistemic phrases ($nphr$ or $epphr$). DF1 relies on the occurrence of either type of hedge; a post is of a mixed nature if it has at least one of each hedge type. DF2 is based on a majority decision depending on the hedge type that governs the post and only assigns the label `hedgmixed` when both types of hedges appear in the same magnitude. DF3 expands DF1 and DF2 by evaluating whether either majority or only one type of hedge is found, e.g. we wanted to explore the fact that even when non-phrasal hedges domain one post, an epistemic phrase is contained as well, in contrast to when only non-phrasal hedges occur in a post.

DF1		$epphr$==0	$epphr$>0
	$nphr$ ==0	nohedges	epphrasal
	$nphr$ >0	nonphrasal	hedgmixed

DF2		
	$nphr$=0 & $epphr$=0	nohedges
	$nphr > epphr$	nonphrasal
	$nphr < epphr$	epphrasal
	$nphr = epphr$	hedgmixed

DF3		$epphr$=0	$epphr$>0	
	$nphr$=0	nohedges	epphronly	
	$nphr$>0	nonphronly	$nphr > epphr$	nonphrmostly
			$nphr < epphr$	epphrmostly
			$nphr = epphr$	hedgmixed

We computed four measures for each post based on these functions, $m1$ is calculated by using $DF1$ having raw frequencies of hedges as parameters, $m2$ and $m3$ result from applying $DF3$ and $DF2$ respectively to frequencies of hedge type averaged by the corresponding lexicon size, and $m4$ is calculated from $DF3$ over hedge frequencies averaged by post word count. Other measures are also possible, but these seemed most intuitive.

We were interested in the extent that hedge-based post categories correlate with a post's kudos and with a post's user category as tests of hypothesis outlined in §2. We want to know which correlations hold regardless of the choice of intuitive measure and which are measure dependent.

3.4 Results and discussion

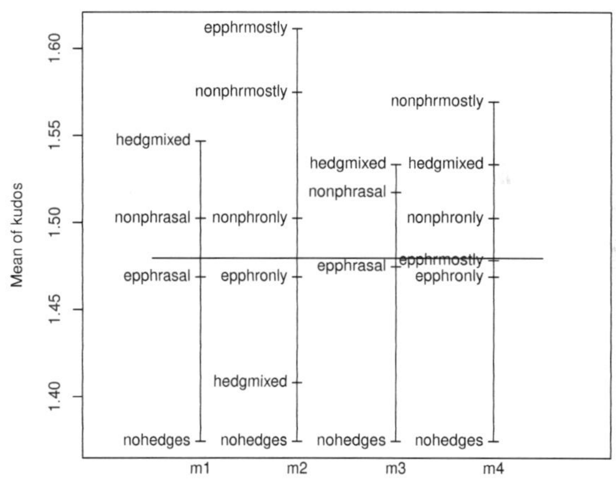

Figure 2: Design plot with the mean of kudos of each kind of post per each measure.

In Fig. 2, we show how the different hedge-based classifications of posts ($m1$, $m2$, $m3$, $m4$) relate to the average kudo counts for posts. Each measure is shown in an individual scale.[4] The horizontal line represents the average of kudos for all posts so we can observe which categories are above/below the mean. Comparison and contrast

[4]For this comparison, we dropped extreme outliers in the number of kudos and hedges, and we calculated these measures only in posts that had at least one kudo attribution.

of the relationship between categorisation of posts with each m^i and mean kudos is interesting. For example, when epistemic phrases dominate a post (`epphrmostly`), there is the greatest mean of kudos visible with the measure $m2$. The second highest positive effect is of non-phrasal hedges dominating a post (`nonphrmostly`) in $m2$ and $m4$. The next strongest effect occurs when both of hedges types appear in a post (`hedgmixed` in $m1$ and $m3$) and when they have about the same average density ($m4$), followed by when non-phrasal hedges appear exclusively in a post. While there is no consensus across the different scales that epistemic phrase-dominated posts are the most likely to obtain kudos, still their occurrence has a positive effect in the average of kudos obtained. There is low probability of kudos when only epistemic phrases appear and the lowest probability when no hedge occurs.[5] Thus, we argue that the four measures are jointly and individually useful.

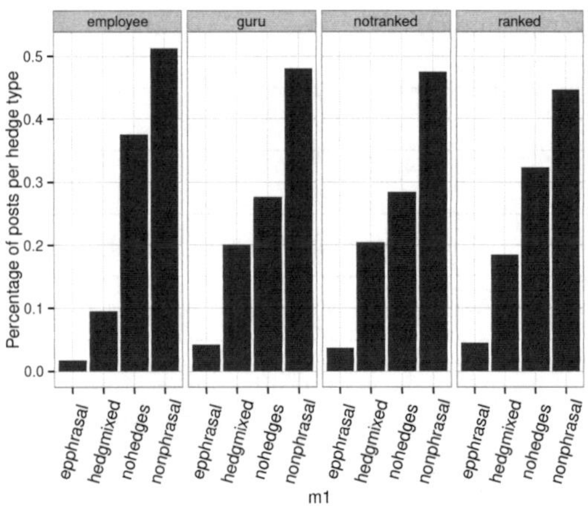

Figure 3: Percentages of $m1$-hedge types in each user category.

The relationship between hedge use and user category is depicted (for $m1$) in Fig. 3. While for all four user roles, epistemic phrases are exclusively present in the lowest percentage of posts, their contribution is shown in posts with mixed hedge types. Posts with only non-phrasal hedges are the most frequent across all user categories. We had predicted no significance in this respect since non-phrasal hedges could map into any of Hyland's functions, however our intuition was wrong as there is a significant difference ($p<0.05$) in the proportions of posts per hedge type category when making comparisons across user categories one to one. Only when comparing proportions of hedge type posts by gurus and notranked users is there no significant difference in `hedgmixed`, `nonphrasal` and `nohedges` posts.[6] Employees and ranked users have the highest rates of use of mixed hedges. Ranked and guru posts have the highest ratios of exclusively epistemic phrase hedges, meeting expectations. Employees have the lowest ratio of user of epistemic phrases on their own, this presumably since they frequently write posts on behalf of the company so they are least likely to make subjective comments: their posts have the lowest percentage of use of "I" and "my".

These two approaches to assessing associations between different classifications of forum posts reveal that posts using hedges are the most likely to be accorded kudos and that guru and ranked users are the most frequent users of epistemic phrases in general. This lends support to the view that first person singular epistemic phrases, the epitome of reader-oriented hedges, are predictive of coarse grained rank in the forum.

4 Conclusions and future work

We have found that the hedges used contribute to the probability of a post getting high ratings. Posts with no hedges are the ones awarded least kudos. We have still to test the correlation between epistemic phrases and other types of hedges when they both are found in a single post. We think that automatic methods should focus in first person epistemic phrases as they show writer's stance at the same time as softening their commitment or anticipating reader's response. Following the annotation described here, manual annotation work is under way, where epistemic phrases and non-phrasal hedges constitute two distinct categories. Our ongoing work seeks other ways to measure the contribution of these categories to reader expression of appreciation of posts and whether hedge usage creates natural user categorizations. We also study other types of web forum dialogue to explore whether hedging follows similar trends.

[5]The contribution of epistemic phrases to the likelihood of kudos could be due to other factors such as the use of first person in general. We profiled the use of pronouns "I" and "my" and we found a negative correlation between frequency of these pronouns and the number of kudos per post. There is a small but not significant correlation restricting to those posts with non-zero kudos.

[6]A two-sample test of proportions was used to test the significance of differences between amounts of hedge type posts for each category.

Acknowledgements

This research is supported by the Trinity College Research Scholarship Program and the Science Foundation Ireland (Grant 07/CE/I1142) as part of the Centre for Next Generation Localisation (www.cngl.ie) at Trinity College Dublin. This paper has benefited from input from the anonymous reviewers and from Ron Artstein.

References

Ken Hyland. 1998. *Hedging in Scientific Research Articles*. Pragmatics & beyond. John Benjamins Publishing Company.

Elise Kärkkäinen. 2010. Position and scope of epistemic phrases in planned and unplanned american english. In *New approaches to hedging*, pages 207–241. Elsevier, Amsterdam.

Victoria Rubin, Elizabeth Liddy, and N. Kando. 2005. Certainty identification in texts: Categorization model and manual tagging results. In James G. Shanahan, Yan Qu, and Janyce Wiebe, editors, *Computing Attitude and Affect in Text*. Springer.

Victoria L. Rubin. 2006. *Identifying Certainty in Texts*. Ph.D. thesis, Syracuse University, Syracuse, NY.

Veronika Vincze, Gyorgy Szarvas, Richard Farkas, Gyorgy Mora, and Janos Csirik. 2008. The BioScope corpus: biomedical texts annotated for uncertainty, negation and their scopes. *BMC Bioinformatics*, 9(Suppl 11).

Carl Vogel and Liliana Mamani Sanchez. 2013. Epistemic signals and emoticons affect kudos. *Cognitive Infocommunications (CogInfoCom), 2012 IEEE 3rd International Conference on*, pages 517–522.

Janyce Wiebe, Theresa Wilson, and Claire Cardie. 2005. Annotating expressions of opinions and emotions in language ANN. *Language Resources and Evaluation*, 39(2/3):164–210.

A. Wierzbicka. 2006. *English: meaning and culture*. Oxford University Press, USA.

Impact of ASR N-Best Information on Bayesian Dialogue Act Recognition

Heriberto Cuayáhuitl, Nina Dethlefs, Helen Hastie, Oliver Lemon
School of Mathematical and Computer Sciences,
Heriot-Watt University, Edinburgh, UK
{h.cuayahuitl,n.s.dethlefs,h.hastie,o.lemon}@hw.ac.uk

Abstract

A challenge in dialogue act recognition is the mapping from noisy user inputs to dialogue acts. In this paper we describe an approach for re-ranking dialogue act hypotheses based on Bayesian classifiers that incorporate dialogue history and Automatic Speech Recognition (ASR) N-best information. We report results based on the Let's Go dialogue corpora that show (1) that including ASR N-best information results in improved dialogue act recognition performance (+7% accuracy), and (2) that competitive results can be obtained from as early as the first system dialogue act, reducing the need to wait for subsequent system dialogue acts.

1 Introduction

The primary challenge of a Dialogue Act Recogniser (DAR) is to find the correct mapping between a noisy user input and its true dialogue act. In standard "slot-filling" dialogue systems a dialogue act is generally represented as *DialogueActType(attribute-value pairs)*, see Section 3. While a substantial body of research has investigated different types of models and methods for dialogue act recognition in spoken dialogue systems (see Section 2), here we focus on re-ranking the outputs of an existing DAR for evaluation purposes. In practice the re-ranker should be part of the DAR itself. We propose to use multiple Bayesian classifiers to re-rank an initial set of dialogue act hypotheses based on information from the dialogue history as well as ASR N-best lists. In particular the latter type of information helps us to learn mappings between dialogue acts and common mis-recognitions. We present experimental results based on the Let's Go dialogue corpora which indicate that re-ranking hypotheses using ASR N-best information can lead to improved recognition. In addition, we compare the recognition accuracy over time and find that high accuracy can be obtained with as little context as one system dialogue act, so that there is often no need to take a larger context into account.

2 Related Work

Approaches to dialogue act recognition from spoken input have explored a wide range of methods. (Stolcke et al., 2000) use HMMs for dialogue modelling, where sequences of observations correspond to sequences of dialogue act types. They also explore the performance with decision trees and neural networks and report their highest accuracy at 65% on the Switchboard corpus. (Zimmermann et al., 2005) also use HMMs in a joint segmentation and classification model. (Grau et al., 2004) use a combination of Naive Bayes and n-grams with different smoothing methods. Their best models achieve an accuracy of 66% on English Switchboard data and 89% on a Spanish corpus. (Sridhar et al., 2009; Wright et al., 1999) both use a maximum entropy classifier with n-grams to classify dialogue acts using prosodic features. (Sridhar et al., 2009) report an accuracy of up to 74% on Switchboard data and (Wright et al., 1999) report an accuracy of 69% on the DCIEM Maptask Corpus. (Bohus and Rudnicky, 2006) maintain an N-best list of slot values using logistic regression. (Surendran and Levow, 2006) use a combination of linear support vector machines (SVMs) and HMMs. They report an accuracy of 65.5% on the HCRC MapTask corpus and conclude that SVMs are well suited for sparse text and dense acoustic features. (Gambäck et al., 2011) use SVMs within an active learning framework. They show that while passive learning achieves an accuracy of 77.8% on Switchboard data, the active learner achieves up to 80.7%. (Henderson et al., 2012) use SVMs for dialogue act recognition from ASR word confusion networks.

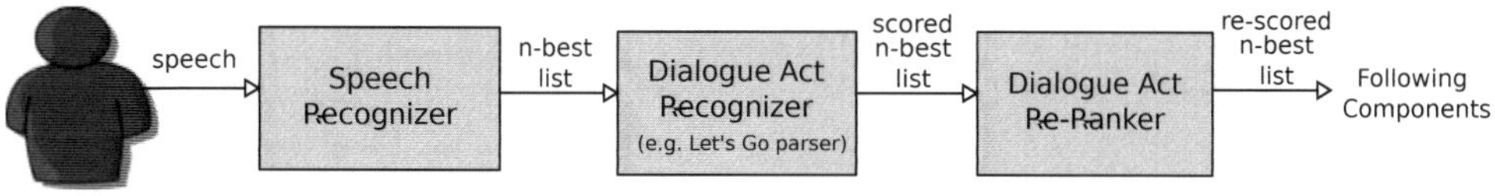

Figure 1: *Pipeline architecture for dialogue act recognition and re-ranking component. Here, the input is a list of dialogue acts with confidence scores, and the output is the same list of dialogue acts but with recomputed confidence scores. A dialogue act is represented as DialogueActType(attribute-value pairs).*

Several authors have presented evidence in favour of Bayesian methods. (Keizer and op den Akker, 2007) have shown that Bayesian DARs can outperform baseline classifiers such as decision trees. More generally, (Ng and Jordan, 2001) show that generative classifiers (e.g. Naive Bayes) reach their asymptotic error faster than discriminative ones. As a consequence, generative classifiers are less data intensive than discriminative ones.

In addition, several authors have investigated dialogue belief tracking. While our approach is related to belief tracking, we focus here on spoken language understanding under uncertainty rather than estimating user goals. (Williams, 2007; Thomson et al., 2008) use approximate inference to improve the scalability of Bayes nets for belief tracking and (Lison, 2012) presents work on improving their scalability through abstraction. (Mehta et al., 2010) model user intentions through the use of probabilistic ontology trees.

Bayes nets have also been applied to other dialogue-related tasks, such as surface realisation within dialogue (Dethlefs and Cuayáhuitl, 2011) or multi-modal dialogue act recognition (Cuayáhuitl and Kruijff-Korbayová, 2011). In the following, we will explore a dialogue act recognition technique based on multiple Bayesian classifiers and show that re-ranking with ASR N-best information can improve recognition performance.

3 Re-Ranking Dialogue Acts Using Multiple Bayesian Networks

Figure 1 shows an illustration of our dialogue act re-ranker within a pipeline architecture. Here, processing begins with the user's speech being interpreted by a speech recogniser, which produces a first N-best list of hypotheses. These hypotheses are subsequently passed on and interpreted by a dialogue act recogniser, which in our case is represented by the Let's Go parser. The parser produces a first set of dialogue act hypotheses, based on which our re-ranker becomes active. A full dialogue act in our scenario consists of three elements: dialogue act types, attributes (or slots), and slot values. An example dialogue act is *inform(from=Pittsburgh Downtown)*. The dialogue act re-ranker thus receives a list of hypotheses in the specified form (triples) from its preceding module (a DAR or in our case the Let's Go parser) and its task is to generate confidence scores that approximate true label (i.e. the dialogue act really spoken by a user) as closely as possible.

We address this task by using multiple Bayesian classifiers: one for classifying a dialogue act type, one for classifying a set of slots, and the rest for classifying slot values. The use of multiple classifiers is beneficial for scalability purposes; for example, assuming 10 dialogue act types, 10 slots, 10 values per slot, and no other dialogue context results in a joint distribution of 10^{11} parameters. Since a typical dialogue system is required to model even larger joint distributions, our adopted approach is to factorize them into multiple independent Bayesian networks (with combined outputs). A multiple classifier system is a powerful solution to complex classification problems involving a large set of inputs and outputs. This approach not only decreases training time but has also been shown to increase the performance of classification (Tax et al., 2000).

A Bayesian Network (BN) models a joint probability distribution over a set of random variables and their dependencies, see (Bishop, 2006) for an introduction to BNs. Our motivation for using multiple BNs is to incorporate a fairly rich dialogue context in terms of what the system and user said at lexical and semantic levels. In contrast, using a single BN for all slots with rich dialogue context faces scalability issues, especially for slots with large numbers of domain values, and is therefore not an attractive option. We denote our set of Bayesian classifiers as $\lambda = \{\lambda^{dat}, \lambda^{att}, ..., \lambda^{val(i)}\}$, where BN λ^{dat} is used to rank dialogue act types, BN λ^{att} is used to rank attributes, and the other BNs ($\lambda^{val(i)}$) are used to rank values for each slot i. The score of a user dialogue act ($< d, a, v >$) is computed as:

$$P(d, a, v) = \frac{1}{Z} \prod P(d|pa_d)P(a|pa_a)P(v|pa_v),$$

where d is a dialogue act type, a is an attribute (or slot), v is a slot value, pa_x is a parent random variable, and Z is a normalising constant. This implies that the score of a dialogue act is the product of probabilities of dialogue act type and slot-value pairs. For dialogue acts including multiple slot-value pairs, the product above can be extended accordingly. The best and highest ranked hypothesis (from space $\mathcal{H}$) can be obtained according to:

$$< d, a, v >^* = \arg \max_{<d,a,v> \in \mathcal{H}} P(d, a, v).$$

In the following, we describe our experimental setting. Here, the structure and parameters of our classifiers will be estimated from a corpus of spoken dialogues, and we will use the equations above for re-ranking user dialogue acts. Finally, we report results comparing Bayesian classifiers that make use of ASR N-best information and dialogue context against Bayesian classifiers that make predictions based on the dialogue context alone.

4 Experiments and Results

4.1 Data

Our experiments are based on the Let's Go corpus (Raux et al., 2005). Let's Go contains recorded interactions between a spoken dialogue system and human users who make enquiries about the bus schedule in Pittsburgh. Dialogues are driven by system-initiative and query the user sequentially for five slots: *an optional bus route, a departure place, a destination, a desired travel date,* and *a desired travel time*. Each slot needs to be explicitly (or implicity) confirmed by the user. Our analyses are based on a subset of this data set containing 779 dialogues with 7275 turns, collected in the Summer of 2010. From these dialogues, we used 70% for training our classifiers and the rest for testing (with 100 random splits). Briefly, this data set contains 12 system dialogue act types[1], 11 user dialogue act types[2], and 5 main slots with variations[3]. The number of slot values ranges between

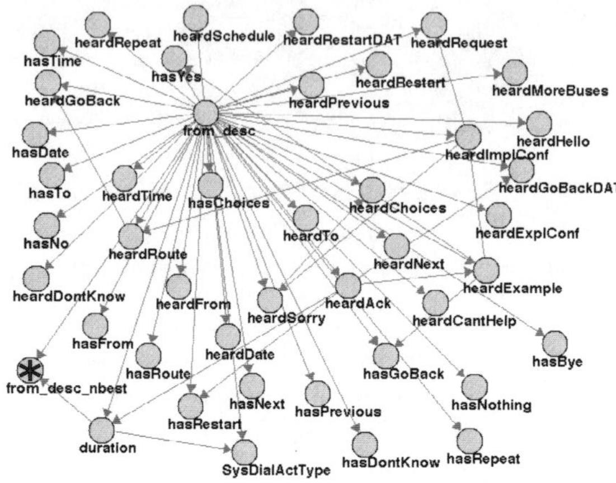

Figure 2: *Bayesian network for probabilistic reasoning of locations (variable "from_desc"), which incorporates ASR N-best information in the variable "from_desc_nbest" and dialogue history information in the remaining random variables.*

10^2 and 10^3 so that the combination of all possible dialogue act types, attributes and values leads to large amounts of triplets. While the majority of user inputs contain one user dialogue act, the average number of system dialogue acts per turn is 4.2. Note that for the user dialogue act types, we also model *silence* explicitly. This is often not considered in dialogue act recognisers: since the ASR will always try to recognise something out of any input (even background noise), typical dialogue act recognisers will then try to map the ASR output onto a semantic interpretation.

4.2 Bayesian Networks

We trained our Bayesian networks in a supervised learning manner and used 43 discrete features (or random variables) plus a class label (also discrete). The feature set is described by three main subsets: **25** system-utterance-level binary features[4] derived from the system dialogue act(s) in the last turn; **17** user-utterance-level binary features[5] derived from (a) what the user heard prior to the current turn, or (b) what keywords the system recognised in its

[1] ack, cant help, example, expl_conf, go back, hello, impl_conf, more buses, request, restart, schedule, sorry.

[2] affirm, bye, go back, inform, negate, next bus, prevbus, repeat, restart, silence, tellchoices.

[3] date.absday, date.abmonth, date.day, date.relweek, from, route, time.ampm, time.arriveleave, time.hour, time.minute, time.rel, to.

[4] System utterance features: heardAck, heardCantHelp, heardExample, heardExplConf, heardGoBackDAT, heardHello, heardImplConf, heardMoreBuses, heardRequest, heardRestartDAT, heardSchedule, heardSorry, heardDate, heardFrom, heardRoute, heardTime, heardTo, heardNext, heardPrevious, heardGoBack, heardChoices, heardRestart, heardRepeat, heardDontKnow, lastSystemDialActType.

[5] User utterance features: hasRoute, hasFrom, hasTo, hasDate, hasTime, hasYes, hasNo, hasNext, hasPrevious, hasGoBack, hasChoices, hasRestart, hasRepeat, hasDontKnow, hasBye, hasNothing, duration in secs. (values=0,1,2,3,4,>5).

list of speech recognition hypotheses; and **1** word-level non-binary feature (*_nbest) corresponding to the slot values in the ASR N-best lists.

Figure 2 shows the Bayes net corresponding to the classifier used to rank location names. The random variable *from_desc* is the class label, the random variable *from_desc_nbest* (marked with an asterisk) incorporates slot values from the ASR N-best lists, and the remaining variables model dialogue history context. The structure of our Bayesian classifiers were derived from the K2 algorithm[6], and their parameters were derived from maximum likelihood estimation. In addition, we performed probabilistic inference using the Junction tree algorithm[7]. Based on these data and tools, we trained 14 Bayesian classifiers: one for scoring dialogue act types, one for scoring attributes (slots), and the rest for scoring slot values.

4.3 Experimental Results

We compared 7 different dialogue act recognisers in terms of classification accuracy. The comparison was made against gold standard data from a human-labelled corpus. (Semi-Random) is a recogniser choosing a random dialogue act from the Let's Go N-best parsing hypotheses. (Inc_i) is our proposed approach considering a context of i system dialogue acts, and (Ceiling) is a recogniser choosing the correct dialogue act from the Let's Go N-best parsing hypotheses. The latter was used as a gold standard from manual annotations, which reflects the proportion of correct labels in the N-best parsing hypotheses.

We also assessed the impact of ASR N-best information on probabilistic inference. To this end, we compared Bayes nets with a focus on the random variable "*_nbest", which in one case contains induced distributions from data and in the other case contains an equal distribution of slot values. Our hypothesis is that the former setting will lead to better performance.

Figure 3 shows the classification accuracy of our dialogue act recognisers. The first point to notice is that the incorporation of ASR N-best information makes an important difference. The performance of recogniser IncK (K being the number of system dialogue acts) is 66.9% without ASR N-best information and 73.9% with ASR N-best information (the difference is significant[8] at

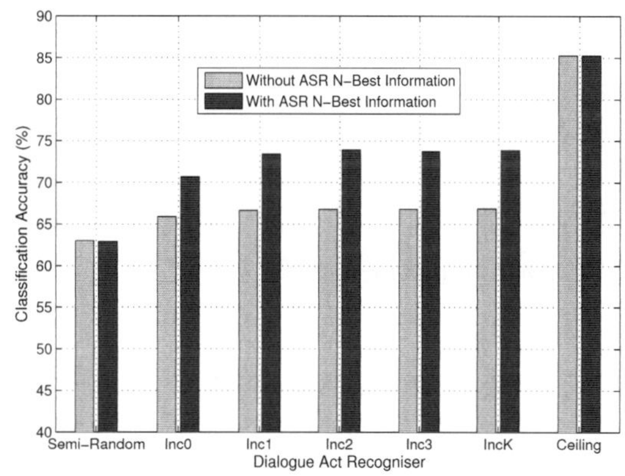

Figure 3: *Bayesian dialogue act recognisers showing the impact of ASR N-best information.*

$p < 0.05$). The latter represents a substantial improvement over the semi-random baseline (62.9%) and Lets Go dialogue act recognizer (69%), both significant at $p < 0.05$. A second point to notice is that the differences between Inc_i ($\forall$ i>0) recognisers were not significant. We can say that the use of one system dialogue act as context is as competitive as using a larger set of system dialogue acts. This suggests that dialogue act recognition carried out at early stages (e.g. after the first dialogue act) in an utterance does not degrade recognition performance. The effect is possibly domain-specific and generalisations remain to be investigated.

Generally, we were able to observe that more than half of the errors made by the Bayesian classifiers were due to noise in the environment and caused by the users themselves, which interfered with ASR results. Detecting when users do not convey dialogue acts to the system is therefore still a standing challenge for dialogue act recognition.

5 Conclusion and Future Work

We have described a re-ranking approach for user dialogue act recognition. Multiple Bayesian classifiers are used to rank dialogue acts from a set of dialogue history features and ASR N-best information. Applying our approach to the Let's Go data we found the following: (1) that including ASR N-best information results in improved dialogue act recognition performance; and (2) that competitive results can be obtained from as early as the first system dialogue act, reducing the need to include subsequent ones.

Future work includes: (a) a comparison of our

[6] www.cs.waikato.ac.nz/ml/weka/

[7] www.cs.cmu.edu/~javabayes/Home/

[8] Based on a two-sided Wilcoxon Signed-Rank test.

Bayesian classifiers with other probabilistic models and forms of training (for example by using semi-supervised learning), (b) training dialogue act recognisers in different (multi-modal and multi-task) domains, and (c) dealing with random variables that contain very large domain values.

6 Acknowledgements

This research was funded by the EC FP7 programme under grant agreement no. 287615 (PARLANCE) and no. 270019 (SPACEBOOK).

Sample Re-Ranked User Inputs

User input: "forty six d"

N-Best List of Dialogue Acts	Let's Go Score	Bayesian Score
inform(route=46a)	3.33E-4	1.9236763E-6
inform(route=46b)	1.0E-6	1.5243509E-16
inform(route=46d)	0.096107	**7.030841E-4**
inform(route=46k)	**0.843685**	4.9941495E-10
silence()	NA	0

User input: "um jefferson hills to mckeesport"

N-Best List of Dialogue Acts	Let's Go Score	Bayesian Score
inform(from=mill street)	7.8E-4	3.5998527E-16
inform(from=mission street)	0.015577	3.5998527E-16
inform(from=osceola street)	0.0037	3.5998527E-16
inform(from=robinson township)	0.007292	3.5998527E-16
inform(from=sheraden station)	0.001815	3.1346254E-8
inform(from=brushton)	2.45E-4	3.5998527E-16
inform(from=jefferson)	0.128727	**0.0054255757**
inform(from=mckeesport)	**0.31030**	2.6209198E-4
silence()	NA	0

References

[Bishop2006] Christopher M. Bishop. 2006. *Pattern Recognition and Machine Learning (Information Science and Statistics)*. Springer-Verlag New York, Inc., Secaucus, NJ, USA.

[Bohus and Rudnicky2006] D. Bohus and A. Rudnicky. 2006. A k hypotheses + other" belief updating model. In *AAAI Workshop on Statistical and Empirical Approaches to Spoken Dialogue Systems*.

[Cuayáhuitl and Kruijff-Korbayová2011] H. Cuayáhuitl and I. Kruijff-Korbayová. 2011. Learning human-robot dialogue policies combining speech and visual beliefs. In *IWSDS*, pages 133–140.

[Dethlefs and Cuayáhuitl2011] Nina Dethlefs and Heriberto Cuayáhuitl. 2011.. Combining Hierarchical Reinforcement Learning and Bayesian Networks for Natural Language Generation in Situated Dialogue. In *ENLG*, Nancy, France.

[Gambäck et al.2011] Björn Gambäck, Fredrik Olsson, and Oscar Täckström. 2011. Active Learning for Dialogue Act Classification. In *INTERSPEECH*, pages 1329–1332.

[Grau et al.2004] Sergio Grau, Emilio Sanchis, Maria Jose Castro, and David Vilar. 2004. Dialogue Act Classification Using a Bayesian Approach. In *SPECOM*.

[Henderson et al.2012] Matthew Henderson, Milica Gasic, Blaise Thomson, Pirros Tsiakoulis, Kai Yu, and Steve Young. 2012. Discriminative spoken language understanding using word confusion networks. In *SLT*, pages 176–181.

[Keizer and op den Akker2007] Simon Keizer and Rieks op den Akker. 2007. Dialogue Act Recognition Under Uncertainty Using Bayesian Networks. *Natural Language Engineering*, 13(4):287–316.

[Lison2012] Pierre Lison. 2012. Probabilistic dialogue models with prior domain knowledge. In *SIGDIAL Conference*, pages 179–188.

[Mehta et al.2010] Neville Mehta, Rakesh Gupta, Antoine Raux, Deepak Ramachandran, and Stefan Krawczyk. 2010. Probabilistic ontology trees for belief tracking in dialog systems. In *SIGDIAL Conference*, pages 37–46.

[Ng and Jordan2001] Andrew Y. Ng and Michael I. Jordan. 2001. On discriminative vs. generative classifiers: A comparison of logistic regression and naive bayes. In *NIPS*, pages 841–848.

[Raux et al.2005] Antoine Raux, Brian Langner, Dan Bohus, Alan W. Black, and Maxine Eskenazi. 2005. Let's go public! Taking a Spoken Dialog System to the Real World. In *INTERSPEECH*, pages 885–888.

[Sridhar et al.2009] Vivek Kumar Rangarajan Sridhar, Srinivas Bangalore, and Shrikanth Narayanan. 2009. Combining Lexical, Syntactic and Prosodic Cues for Improved Online Dialog Act Tagging. *Computer Speech & Language*, 23(4):407–422.

[Stolcke et al.2000] Andreas Stolcke, Klaus Ries, Noah Coccaro, Elizabeth Shriberg, Rebecca A. Bates, Daniel Jurafsky, Paul Taylor, Rachel Martin, Carol Van Ess-Dykema, and Marie Meteer. 2000. Dialog Act Modeling for Automatic Tagging and Recognition of Conversational Speech. *Computational Linguistics*, 26(3):339–373.

[Surendran and Levow2006] Dinoj Surendran and Gina-Anne Levow. 2006. Dialog Act Tagging with Support Vector Machines and Hidden Markov Models. In *INTERSPEECH*.

[Tax et al.2000] David M. Tax, Martijn van Breukelen, Robert P. Duin, and Josef Kittler. 2000. Combining multiple classifiers by averaging or by multiplying? *Pattern Recognition*, 33(9):1475–1485, September.

[Thomson et al.2008] Blaise Thomson, Jost Schatzmann, and Steve Young. 2008. Bayesian update of dialogue state for robust dialogue systems. In *ICASSP*, pages 4937–4940.

[Williams2007] Jason D. Williams. 2007. Using particle filters to track dialogue state. In *ASRU*, pages 502–507.

[Wright et al.1999] H. Wright, Massimo Poesio, and Stephen Isard. 1999. Using high level dialogue information for dialogue act recognition using prosodic features. In *Proceedings of an ESCA Tutorial and Research Workshop on Dialogue and Prosody*, pages 139–143, Eindhoven, The Netherlands.

[Zimmermann et al.2005] Matthias Zimmermann, Yang Liu, Elizabeth Shriberg, and Andreas Stolcke. 2005. Toward Joint Segmentation and Classification of Dialog Acts in Multiparty Meetings. In *MLMI*, pages 187–193.

Investigating speaker gaze and pointing behaviour in human-computer interaction with the *mint.tools* collection

Spyros Kousidis **Casey Kennington** **David Schlangen**
Dialogue Systems Group / CITEC / SFB 673
Bielefeld University
spyros.kousidis@uni-bielefeld.de

Abstract

Can speaker gaze and speaker arm movements be used as a practical information source for naturalistic conversational human–computer interfaces? To investigate this question, we recorded (with eye tracking and motion capture) a corpus of interactions with a (wizarded) system. In this paper, we describe the recording, analysis infrastructure that we built for such studies, and analysis we performed on these data. We find that with some initial calibration, a "minimally invasive", stationary camera-based setting provides data of sufficient quality to support interaction.

1 Introduction

The availability of sensors such as Microsoft Kinect and (almost) affordable eye trackers bring new methods of naturalistic human-computer interaction within reach. Studying the possibilities of such methods requires building infrastructure for recording and analysing such data (Kousidis et al., 2012a). We present such an infrastructure—the *mint.tools* collection (see also (Kousidis et al., 2012b))[1]—and present results of a study we performed on whether speaker gaze and speaker arm movements can be turned into an information source for an interactive system.

2 The *mint.tools* Collection

The *mint.tools* collection comprises tools (and adaptations to existing tools) for recording and analysis of multimodal data. The recording architecture (Figure 1) is highly modular: each information source (sensor) runs on its own dedicated workstation and transmits its data via the local area network. In the setup described in this paper, we

[1]Available at http://dsg-bielefeld.de/mint/.

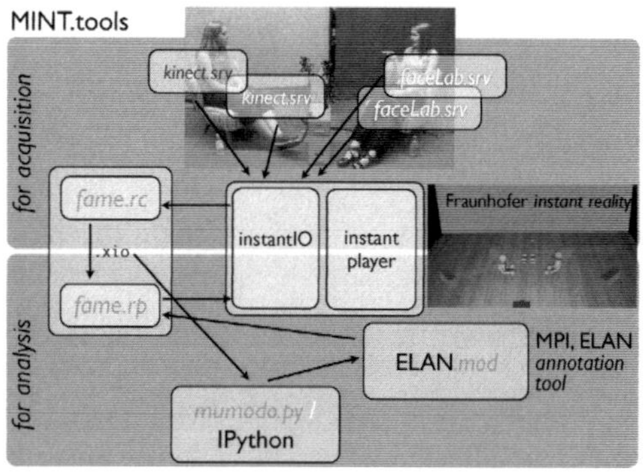

Figure 1: Overview of components of *mint.tools*; our contributions denoted by italics font. Top middle shows example lab setup; middle right shows corresponding VR scene, visualising motion capture and tracking of head posture, eye and gaze

perform motion capture via Microsoft Kinect and head, eye and gaze tracking via Seeingmachines Facelab 5.[2] We have developed specialised plugins that connect these sensors to the central component in our architecture, *Instantreality*.[3] This is a VR environment we use for monitoring the recording process by visualising a reconstructed 3D scene in real-time. A logging component simultaneously streams the timestamped and integrated sensor data to disk, ensuring that all data are synchronised. The data format is a shallow XML representation of timed, typed events.

The tracking equipment used in this setting is camera-based, providing for a minimally invasive setting, as subjects are not required to wear any equipment or tracking markers. In addition to the tracking sensors, video and audio are recorded us-

[2]http://www.microsoft.com/en-us/kinectforwindows/, http://www.seeingmachines.com/product/facelab/, respectively

[3]Built by IGD Fraunhofer, http://www.instantreality.org

ing one HD camera. The AV channel is synchronised with the stream data from the sensors by means of a timecode in view of the camera.

Representative of the high modularity and flexibility of the *mint.tools* architecture is the ease with which components can be added. For the setting described here, a GUI was created which connects to the VR environment as an additional sensor, transmitting all of its state updates, which then are synchronously logged together with all other stream data from the trackers. This allows us to recreate the full scene (subject behaviour and the stimuli they received) in the virtual reality environment, for later inspection (see below Figure 6).

The analysis part of the *mint.tools* collection comprises a package for the Python programming language (described below) and a version of the ELAN annotation tool (Lausberg and Sloetjes, 2009), which we modified to control the replay of the virtual reality scene; this makes it possible to view video, annotations and the 3D reconstruction at the same time and in synchronisation.

Sensors are represented as nodes in a node-tree within the 3D environment. The values of data fields in these nodes are continuously updated as new data is received from the network. Using more than one sensor of the same type means simply another instantiation of that node type within the tree. In this way, our architecture facilitates tracking many people or complex setups where many sensors are required to cover an area.

3 Procedure / The TAKE Corpus

Our experiment is a Wizard-of-Oz scenario in which subjects (7 in total) were situated in front of a 40" screen displaying random Pentomino boards (Fernández et al., 2007). Each board configuration had exactly 15 Pentomino pieces of various colours and shapes, divided in four grids located near the four corners of the screen (see Figure 3 below). At the beginning of the session, a head and gaze model were created for the subject within the FaceLab software. Next, the subjects were asked to point (with their arm stretched) at the four corners and the center of the screen (with each hand), to calibrate to their pointing characteristics.

In the main task, subjects were asked to (silently) choose a piece and instruct the "system" to select it, using speech and/or pointing gestures. A wizard then selected the indicated piece, causing it to be highlighted. Upon approval by the subject, the wizard registered the result and a new board was created. We denote the time-span from the creation of a board to the acknowledgement by the subject that the correct piece was selected an *episode*. The wizard had the option to not immediately highlight the indicated piece, in order to elicit a more detailed description of the piece or a pointing gesture. What we were interested in learning from these data was whether speaker gaze and arm movements could be turned into signals that can support a model of situated language understanding. We focus here on the signal processing and analysis that was required; the model is described in (Kennington et al., 2013).

4 Analysis and Results

We perform the analyses described in this section using the analysis tools in the *mint.tools* collection, *mumodo.py*. This is a python package we have developed that interfaces our recorded stream data with powerful, freely available, scientific computing tools written in the Python programming language.[4] *mumodo.py* facilitates importing streamed data into user-friendly, easily manageable structures such as *dataframes* (tables with extended database functionality), or compatible formats such as Praat TextGrids (Boersma and Weenink, 2013) and ELAN tiers. In addition, *mumodo.py* can remote-control playback in ELAN and Instant Reality for the purpose of data viewing and annotation.

4.1 Gaze

Our post-processing and analysis of the gaze data focuses primarily on the detection of eye fixations in order to determine the pentomino pieces that the subjects look at while speaking. This knowledge is interesting from a reference resolution point of view. Although Koller et al (2012) explored listener gaze in that context, it is known that gaze patterns differ in interactions, depending on whether one speaks or listens (Jokinen et al., 2009).

Facelab provides a mapping between a person's gaze vector and the screen, which yields an intersection point in pixel coordinates. However, due to limitations to the accuracy of the calibration procedure and noise in the data, it is pos-

[4] Especially IPython and Pandas, as collected for example in `https://www.enthought.com/products/epd/`. Example of finished analyses using this package can be found at `http://dsg-bielefeld.de/mint/mintgaze.html`

sible that the gaze vector does not intersect the model of the screen when the subject is looking at pieces near screen corners. For this reason, we first perform offline linear interpolation, artificially extending the screen by 200 pixels in each direction, by means of linear regression of the x, y components of the gaze vector with the x, y pixel coordinates, respectively ($R^2 > 0.95$ in all cases). Figure 2 shows the probability density function of intersection points before (left) and after this process (right), for one of the subjects. We see on the right plot that many intersection points fall outside the viewable screen area, denoted by the shaded rectangle.

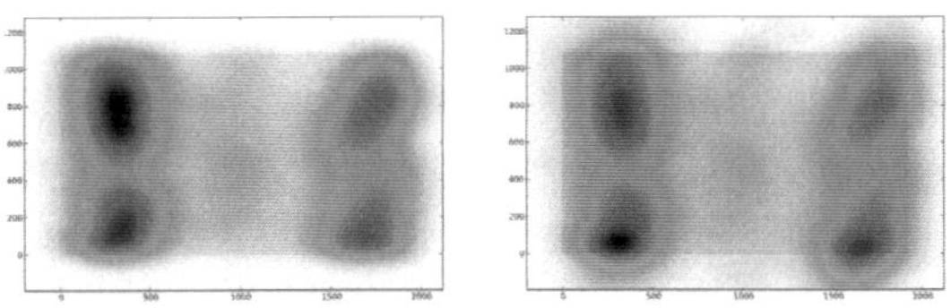

Figure 2: Probability density function of gaze intersections on screen before (left) and after interpolating for points 200 pixels around screen edges (right). Shaded rectangle shows screen size

In order to detect the eye fixations, we use two common algorithms, namely the I-DT and velocity algorithms, as described in (Nyström and Holmqvist, 2010). The I-DT algorithm requires the points to lie within a pre-defined "dispersion" area (see Figure 3), while the velocity algorithm requires the velocity to remain below a threshold. In both algorithms, a *minimum fixation time* threshold is also used, while a fixation centroid is calculated as the midpoint of all points in a fixation. Increasing the minimum fixation time threshold and decreasing the dispersion area or velocity (depending on the algorithm) results in fewer fixations being detected.

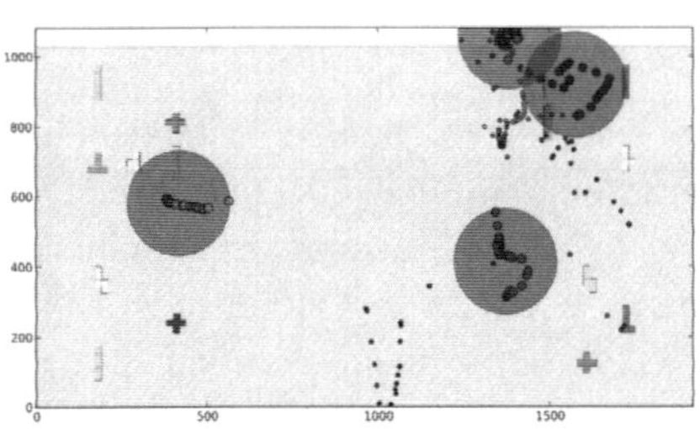

Figure 3: Fixation detection using the I-DT algorithm, circles show the dispersion radius threshold

Gaze fixations can be combined with information on the pentomino board in order to determine which piece is being looked at. To do this, we calculate the euclidean distance between each piece and the fixation centroid, and assign the piece a probability of being gazed at, which is inversely proportional to its distance from the centroid.

Figure 4 illustrates the gazing behaviour of the subjects during 1051 episodes: After an initial rapid scan of the whole screen (typically before they start speaking), subjects fixate on the piece they are going to describe (the "gold piece"). This is denoted by the rising number of fixations on the gold piece between seconds 5–10. At the same time, the *average rank* of the gold piece is higher (i.e. closer to 1, hence lower in the plot). Subsequently, the average rank drops as subjects tend to casually look around the screen for possible distractors (i.e. pieces that are identical or similar to the gold piece).

We conclude from this analysis that, especially around the onset of the utterance, gaze can provide a useful signal about intended referents.

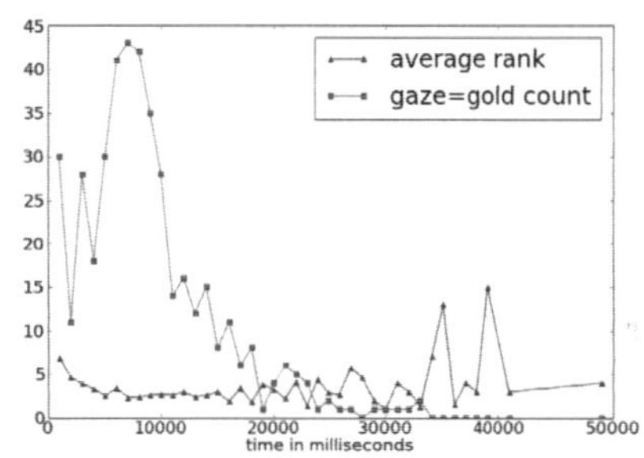

Figure 4: Average Rank and Counts over time (all episodes)

4.2 Pointing Gestures

We detect pointing gestures during which the arm is stretched from Kinect data (3D coordinates of 20 body joints) using two different methods. The first is based on the distance of the *hand* joint from the body (Sumi et al., 2010). We define the body as a plane, using the coordinates of the two *shoulders*, *shoulder-center* and *head* joints, and use a threshold beyond which a movement is considered a possible pointing gesture.

The second detection method uses the idea that, while the arm is stretched, the vectors defined by the *hand* and *elbow*, and *hand* and *shoulder* joints, respectively, should be parallel, i.e. have a dot product close to 1 (vectors are first normalised).

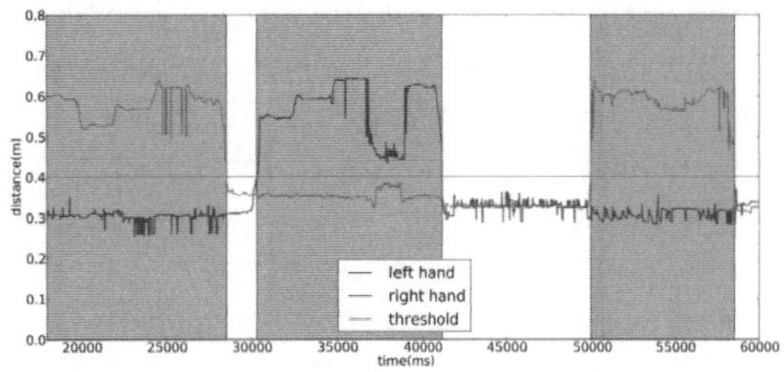

Figure 5: detection of pointing thresholds by distance of left(blue) or right(green) hand from body

In reality, the arm is never strictly a straight line, hence a threshold (0.95-0.98) is set, depending on the subject. The result of this process is an annotation tier of pointing gestures (for each hand), similar to the one shown in Figure 5. To make pointing gesture detection more robust, we only consider gestures identified by *both* methods, i.e. the intersection of the two annotation tiers.

Further, we want to map the pointing gestures to locations on the screen. Following a methodology similar to Pfeiffer (2010), we define two methods of determing pointing direction: (a) the extension of the arm, i.e. the shoulder-hand vector, and (b) the hand-head vector, which represents the subjective point-of-view (looking through the tip of one's finger). Figure 6 shows both vectors: depending on the subject and the target point, we have found that both of these vectors perform equally well, by considering the gaze intersection point (green dot on screen) and assuming that subjects are looking where they are pointing.

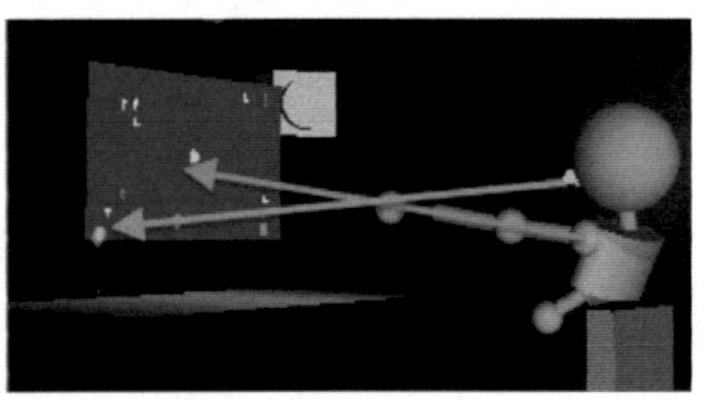

Figure 6: Hand-to-head and hand-to-shoulder pointing vectors

In order to map the pointing gestures to actual locations on the screen, we use the calibration points acquired at the beginning of the session, and plot their intersections to the screen plane, which we compute analytically, as we already have a spatial model of both the vector in question (Kinect data) and the screen location (Instantreality model).

Based on the pointing gestures we have detected, we look at the pointing behaviour of participants as a function of the presence of distractors. This knowledge can be used in designing system responses in a multimodal interactive enviroment or in training models to expect pointing gestures depending on the state of the scene. Figure 7 shows the result from 868 episodes (a subset that satisfies minor technical constraints). Overall, the subjects pointed in 60% of all episodes. Pieces on the board may share any of three properties: shape, colour, and location (being in the same corner on the screen). The left plot shows that subjects do not point more than normal when only one property is shared, regardless of how many such distractors are present, while they point increasingly more when pieces that share two or all three properties exist. The plot on the right shows that subjects point more when the number of same colour pieces increases (regardless of position and shape) and even more when identical pieces occur anywhere on the board. Interestingly, shape by itself does not appear to be considered a distractor by the subjects.

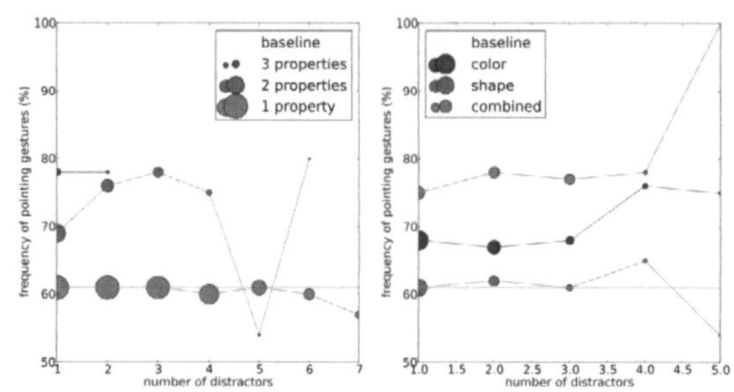

Figure 7: Frequency of pointing gestures as a function of the presence of distractors. Dot size denotes the confidence of each point, based on sample size

5 Conclusions

We have presented a detailed account of analysis procedures on multimodal data acquired from experiments in situated human-computer interaction. These analyses have been facilitated by *mint.tools*, our collection of software components for multimodal data acquisition, annotation and analysis and put to use in (Kennington et al., 2013). We will continue to further improve our approach for manageable and easily reproducible analysis.

References

Paul Boersma and David Weenink. 2013. Praat: doing phonetics by computer (version 5.3.48)[computer program]. retrieved may 1, 2013.

Raquel Fernández, Andrea Corradini, David Schlangen, and Manfred Stede. 2007. Towards Reducing and Managing Uncertainty in Spoken Dialogue Systems. In *Proceedings of the 7th International Workshop on Computational Semantics (IWCS'07)*, pages 1–3.

Kristiina Jokinen, Masafumi Nishida, and Seiichi Yamamoto. 2009. Eye-gaze experiments for conversation monitoring. In *Proceedings of the 3rd International Universal Communication Symposium*, pages 303–308. ACM.

Casey Kennington, Spyros Kousidis, and David Schlangen. 2013. Interpreting situated dialogue utterances: an update model that uses speech, gaze, and gesture information. In *Proceedings of SIGdial 2013*.

Alexander Koller, Maria Staudte, Konstantina Garoufi, and Matthew Crocker. 2012. Enhancing referential success by tracking hearer gaze. In *Proceedings of the 13th Annual Meeting of the Special Interest Group on Discourse and Dialogue*, pages 30–39. Association for Computational Linguistics.

Spyros Kousidis, Thies Pfeiffer, Zofia Malisz, Petra Wagner, and David Schlangen. 2012a. Evaluating a minimally invasive laboratory architecture for recording multimodal conversational data. In *Proc. of the Interdisciplinary Workshop on Feedback Behaviours in Dialogue*.

Spyros Kousidis, Thies Pfeiffer, and David Schlangen. 2012b. Mint.tools: Tools and adaptors supporting acquisition, annotation and analysis of multimodal corpora. In *to appear in Proc. of Interspeech 2013*.

Hedda Lausberg and Han Sloetjes. 2009. Coding gestural behavior with the neuroges-elan system. *Behavior research methods*, 41(3):841–849.

Marcus Nyström and Kenneth Holmqvist. 2010. An adaptive algorithm for fixation, saccade, and glissade detection in eyetracking data. *Behavior research methods*, 42(1):188–204.

Thies Pfeiffer. 2010. *Understanding multimodal deixis with gaze and gesture in conversational interfaces*. Ph.D. thesis, Bielefeld University, Technical Faculty.

Yasuyuki Sumi, Masaharu Yano, and Toyoaki Nishida. 2010. Analysis environment of conversational structure with nonverbal multimodal data. In *International Conference on Multimodal Interfaces and the Workshop on Machine Learning for Multimodal Interaction*, page 44. ACM.

In-Context Evaluation of Unsupervised Dialogue Act Models for Tutorial Dialogue

Aysu Ezen-Can
Department of Computer Science
North Carolina State University
Raleigh, North Carolina 27695
aezen@ncsu.edu

Kristy Elizabeth Boyer
Department of Computer Science
North Carolina State University
Raleigh, North Carolina 27695
keboyer@ncsu.edu

Abstract

Unsupervised dialogue act modeling holds great promise for decreasing the development time to build dialogue systems. Work to date has utilized manual annotation or a synthetic task to evaluate unsupervised dialogue act models, but each of these evaluation approaches has substantial limitations. This paper presents an in-context evaluation framework for an unsupervised dialogue act model within tutorial dialogue. The clusters generated by the model are mapped to tutor responses by a handcrafted policy, which is applied to unseen test data and evaluated by human judges. The results suggest that in-context evaluation may better reflect the performance of a model than comparing against manual dialogue act labels.

1 Introduction

A central focus within the dialogue systems research community is developing techniques for rapidly constructing dialogue systems. One technique that has proven highly promising is to take a corpus-based approach to dialogue system authoring, for example by bootstrapping policy learning (Henderson, Lemon, & Georgila, 2008; Williams & Young, 2003), predicting what a human agent would do (Bangalore, Di Fabbrizio, & Stent, 2008), or learning supervised dialogue act models (Stolcke et al., 2000). Traditionally, these corpus-based approaches require some amount of manual annotation prior to learning the dialogue models. In many cases, this manual annotation is a problematic bottleneck for system development.

For tutorial dialogue systems, which aim to support students in acquiring skills or knowledge, heavy manual annotation is often required for learning models that classify student utterances with respect to dialogue acts (Forbes-Riley & Litman, 2005; Serafin & Di Eugenio, 2004), questioning strategies (Becker, Palmer, Vuuren, & Ward, 2012), or information sharing (Mayfield, Adamson, & Rosé, 2012)

For dialogue act modeling in particular, recent work has demonstrated the great promise of unsupervised approaches, which are learned without the use of manual labels (Crook, Granell, & Pulman, 2009; Ezen-Can & Boyer, 2013; Ritter, Cherry, & Dolan, 2010). However, because gold standard labels are not a part of model learning, how to best evaluate unsupervised models represents a significant open research question (Vlachos, 2011).

Most quantitative evaluations of unsupervised dialogue act models have relied on agreement with manual dialogue act annotations, though these annotations were not used in model learning (Crook et al., 2009; Rus, Moldovan, Niraula, & Graesser, 2012; Ezen-Can & Boyer, 2013). Relying on manually tagged dialogue act labels to evaluate an unsupervised model has two major drawbacks: it does not fully avoid the manual annotation bottleneck, and it imposes a hand-authored criterion onto a fully data-driven model, which may be unnecessarily limiting. Distinctions made by an unsupervised model may be useful within a dialogue system, even if these categories are different from the distinctions made within a hand-authored dialogue act tagset.

This paper presents a novel evaluation framework for unsupervised dialogue act classification of user utterances within tutorial dialogue. Instead of attempting to evaluate the model intrinsically, we evaluate its performance on an external task: triggering an appropriate utterance via a simple dialogue policy. This evaluation, which does not require an end-to-end dialogue system, judges the model in the simulated context of the target task. The results demonstrate that this in-context evaluation may be equally useful as comparing against gold standard dialogue act labels, while substantially reducing the time required for human annotation.

2 Related Work

Perhaps the earliest unsupervised approach for dialogue act modeling investigated hidden Markov models with a bag-of-words approach in a meeting scheduling domain (Woszczyna & Waibel, 1994), using perplexity with respect to manual labels for evaluating the number of hidden states. Dirichlet process clustering has been investigated for dialogue act classification in the train fares and scheduling domain (Crook et al., 2009), evaluating on intra-cluster similarity and inter-cluster similarity along with error rates with respect to manual labels. Another Bayesian approach utilized hidden Markov models and topic modeling to classify Twitter posts (Ritter et al., 2010). Notably, Ritter et al. utilize an utterance ordering task, rather than manual labels, for quantitative evaluation. Most recently, standard *k*-means and EM clustering algorithms were used for dialogue act clustering on an educational corpus, and the model's accuracy was again evaluated with respect to manual labels (Rus et al., 2012). The current paper builds on these prior findings by applying a recently developed clustering framework and proposing a novel in-context evaluation scheme that can be used regardless of the unsupervised dialogue act modeling technique underlying it.

3 Dialogue Act Clustering

We consider an unsupervised dialogue act classification model on a corpus of human-human student and tutor dialogues centered on a computer programming task within a textual dialogue environment (Boyer et al., 2009). There are 1,525 student utterances and 3,332 tutor utterances in the corpus. This paper focuses on dialogue act classification for student utterances, since in a tutorial dialogue system the tutor dialogue acts are system-generated.

The corpus was manually labeled in prior work with nine dialogue acts tailored to capture phenomena of interest within tutorial dialogue: general *Question*, *Evaluation Question* (request specific feedback on the task), *Statement*, *Positive Feedback*, *Lukewarm Feedback*, *Negative Feedback*, *Grounding*, *Greeting,* and *Extra-domain* (utterances that are off topic). The Kappa for agreement on these manual tags was 0.76. These tags will be used within the present work to compare the in-context performance of the unsupervised policy with a manual-tag policy, but the tags are not used to learn or tune the unsupervised model.

The unsupervised dialogue act model evaluated here is based on a recently developed approach that adapts the query-likelihood technique from information retrieval to rank utterances similar to each target utterance (Ezen-Can & Boyer, 2013). Each utterance within the training set is queried against all other utterances within the training set using bigram features.

Vectors encode the resulting utterance similarity, and these vectors are provided to a *k*-means clustering algorithm to partition the utterances into dialogue acts. Our recent work (Ezen-Can & Boyer, 2013) evaluated query-likelihood dialogue act clustering against two other approaches with respect to classifying manual labels, and the query-likelihood approach outperformed *k*-means clustering using leading tokens (Rus et al., 2012) and Dirichlet process clustering (Crook et al., 2009). In the current work we add to the feature vectors the first level of the parse tree as provided by the Stanford parser (Klein & Manning, 2003).

The number of clusters was selected based on sum of squared errors (SSE). As with many parameterized models, model fit tends to increase with more parameters, but there are important tradeoffs in computation time and risk of overfitting. In experiments, *k*=number of clusters ranged from 2 to 24. 21 clusters were chosen, corresponding to the rightmost "knee" within the SSE graph (see Appendix).[1]

4 Evaluation Framework

Evaluating unsupervised dialogue act clusters presents numerous challenges. In prior evaluations of query-likelihood clustering, we computed accuracy with respect to the manually applied dialogue act tags described earlier, demonstrating 41.64% accuracy for a model with 8 clusters, compared to 34.90% accuracy for the Rus et al.

[1] Selecting the number of clusters is a subjective decision. Nonparametric techniques, such as variations on Dirichlet process clustering, hold promise for addressing this limitation in the future.

(2012) *k*-means approach and 24.48% accuracy for Dirichlet process clustering (Crook et al., 2009) on our corpus. However, the goal of the current work is to substantially reduce the human tagging required to evaluate the model. We also aim to test the hypothesis that comparing against manual labels under-represents the utility of the unsupervised model. That is, a dialogue policy built on the unsupervised model could perform better than the relatively low classification accuracy for manual tags would suggest. Our evaluation will explore this hypothesis.

In order to achieve these goals, we first trained an unsupervised dialogue act model on 75% of the corpus using the query-likelihood approach described in Section 3. The resulting model has 21 clusters. Then, we handcrafted a dialogue policy for tutor responses by qualitatively examining each cluster of training data and creating one tutor response for each cluster. Some clusters and their corresponding tutor utterances are depicted in Figure 1. This policy was applied by classifying unseen utterances from a held-out test set (25% of the corpus) using the learned model (Figure 2). The result of this process is that for each student utterance from the test set, a tutor response is generated based on the policy. This process resulted in 373 student utterances, one for each utterance in the 25% testing set, each paired with a corresponding tutor response generated by the hand-authored policy.

The evaluation goal is to determine whether the responses made by this policy are reasonable, which will represent the utility of the unsupervised dialogue act model for its intended use within a dialogue manager. We used human judges to rate the output of the policy. Thirty student utterances and tutor responses were randomly selected from the available utterances generated by the test set. An example set of utterances and policies can be seen in the Appendix. These items were placed in a survey that asked the reader to rate the extent to which each tutor response makes sense given the student utterance. (One item was inadvertently omitted from the survey, resulting in 29 items that were evaluated by the judges and that will be analyzed here.) To avoid bias introduced by the ordering of items, they were presented in a different randomized order for each of the seven judges who completed the survey. (29 items from a comparison condition using manual tags were also randomly interleaved into the survey, as described later in this section.) Judges used a rating scale from 1 to 4 (1=*makes no sense*, 2=*makes a little sense*, 3=*makes a lot of sense,* and 4=*makes perfect sense*). Since the models only used the current student utterance, the dialogue history was also not shown to the human raters.

Across the seven judges, the average rating of the tutor responses selected by the unsupervised policy was 2.35. We also collapsed the ratings into *positive* (≥2.5 average across seven judges) and *negative* (<2.5 average). With this binary categorization, 44.8% of the time tutor responses generated by the unsupervised policy were rated positively. It is important to note that no information other than dialogue act was considered for generating the tutor responses; the tutor utterances were relatively content-free and based only on the dialogue act categorization given by the unsupervised model.

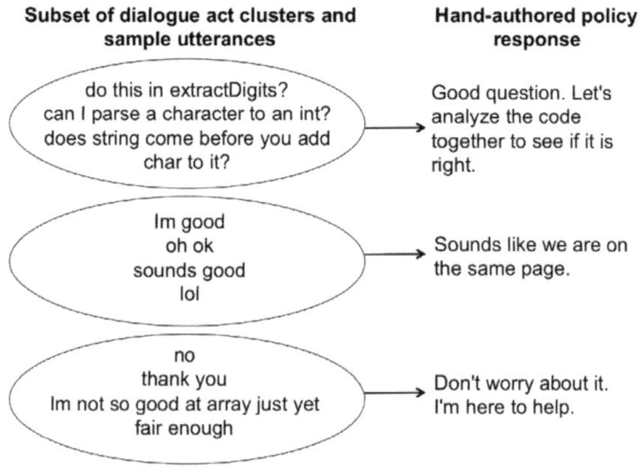

Figure 1: Clusters from unsupervised dialogue act modeling and corresponding dialogue policy (typographical errors originated in corpus)

For comparison, we also constructed a handcrafted dialogue policy using the manual dialogue act labels and applied this policy to the same utterances as were used to evaluate the unsupervised model. These pairs of student utterances and tutor responses were interleaved randomly on the same survey provided to seven human judges. The same tutor responses as in the unsupervised policy were used whenever possible for this manual-tag policy. The tutor responses generated from the manual-tag policy received an average score of 2.22, slightly lower than the average of 2.35 for tutor responses generated by the unsupervised policy. The binary positive-negative split for these ratings reveals that 31% were rated positively (≥2.5 average), compared to 44.8% for the unsupervised policy.

Direct comparisons between the unsupervised policy and the manual-tag policy must be interpreted with caution, in part because the unsupervised policy was more granular (based on 21 clusters) than the manual-tag policy (based on 9 tags) and also because it can be difficult to ensure that the two policies were of equal quality. On the other hand, the unsupervised policy utilized no manual labels and was applied to an unseen test set, while the manual-tag policy was based on reliable tags applied to the actual utterances from the testing set.

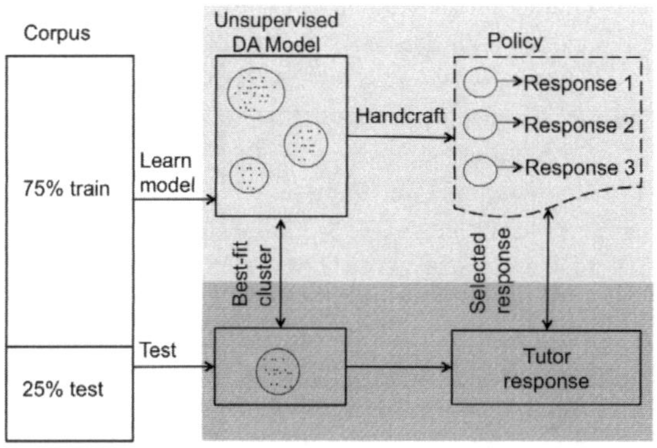

Figure 2: Evaluation framework structure

Finally, we evaluated the extent to which the 4-category rating scheme was reliable across judges. The weighted Kappa (Cohen, 1968), used for ordinal scales because it penalizes disagreements less if they are closer together, was 0.30 averaged across all pairs of judges, indicating *fair* agreement (Landis & Koch, 2013). For the collapsed binary ratings, average pairwise ordinary Kappa was 0.36.

5 Discussion

It was hypothesized that evaluating an unsupervised dialogue act model against manual labels may be an inappropriately strict metric, requiring the model to conform to the criteria used by humans to handcraft the manual tagset. Indeed, the accuracy of the unsupervised dialogue act model presented here with 21 clusters was 30.4% for identifying manual labels (arrived at by assigning the majority class tag to each unsupervised cluster after clustering was complete). The majority class baseline (most frequent student dialogue act tag) was *Evaluation Question* with a relative frequency of 25.87%, so on accuracy for identifying manual labels, the unsupervised model improved modestly over baseline. In contrast, when this unsupervised model was used to select a tutor response within a dialogue policy, the response was judged positively 44.8% of the time by human judges. Moreover, recall that the tutor responses were content free and took only the dialogue act label into account (no information state or topic). Therefore, it is meaningful to consider what percent of the time the responses were rated as making some sense (receiving a 2, 3, or 4 rating average across the human judges). By this criterion, 65.5% of tutor responses selected by the unsupervised policy were rated as sensible.

Finally, this evaluation approach demonstrates promise for alleviating the bottleneck of manual annotation for dialogue act models. Each item within the current evaluation survey required approximately 15 seconds to judge, using untrained human judges, for a total of approximately 1 hour of effort across *all seven* judges. The time required for handcrafting policies was relatively small, approximately 1 hour. In contrast, the dialogue act annotation scheme required approximately 35 seconds per utterance (amortizing substantial up-front training time for each annotator) when applied as part of previous work, for a total of approximately 50 hours per annotator.

6 Conclusion

Unsupervised dialogue act modeling holds great promise for decreasing development time of dialogue systems. We have presented an unsupervised dialogue act model and an evaluation framework to judge the utility of the unsupervised model within a dialogue management task. The results demonstrate that in-context evaluation of an unsupervised dialogue act model, rather than accuracy against manual labels, may better reflect the usefulness of the model for dialogue management. Furthermore, this evaluation technique may greatly reduce the time required by human judges to evaluate the model.

One of the most promising directions for future work involves devising unsupervised dialogue act models that leverage a richer representation in order to perform better. These rich features may include dialogue history, adjacency pair information, and topic modeling. Additionally, it is important for the community to evaluate unsupervised dialogue models in the full context of deployed systems.

Acknowledgments. This material is based upon work supported by the National Science Foundation under Grants DRL-1007962 and CNS-1042468. Any opinions, findings, conclusions, or recommendations expressed in this report are those of the authors and do not necessarily represent the views of the National Science Foundation.

References

Bangalore, S., Di Fabbrizio, G., & Stent, A. (2008). Learning the Structure of Task-Driven Human-Human Dialogs. *IEEE Transactions on Audio, Speech and Language Processing*, *16*(7), 1249–1259.

Becker, L., Palmer, M., Vuuren, S. Van, & Ward, W. (2012). Learning to Tutor Like a Tutor: Ranking Questions in Context. *Proceedings of the International Conference on Intelligent Tutoring Systems*, 368–378.

Boyer, K. E., Philips, R., Ha, E. Y., Wallis, M. D., Vouk, M. A., & Lester, J. C. (2009). Modeling Dialogue Structure with Adjacency Pair Analysis and Hidden Markov Models. *Proceedings of NAACL HLT*, 49–52.

Cohen, J. (1968). Weighted kappa: Nominal scale agreement provision for scaled disagreement or partial credit. *Psychological Bulletin*, *70*(4), 213-220.

Crook, N., Granell, R., & Pulman, S. (2009). Unsupervised Classification of Dialogue Acts Using a Dirichlet Process Mixture Model. *Proceedings of SIGDIAL,* 341–348.

Ezen-Can, A., & Boyer, K. E. (2013). Unsupervised Classification of Student Dialogue Acts With Query-likelihood Clustering. *International Conference on Educational Data Mining*, 20–27.

Forbes-Riley, K., & Litman, D. J. (2005). Using Bigrams to Identify Relationships Between Student Certainness States and Tutor Responses in a Spoken Dialogue Corpus. *Proceedings of SIGDIAL*, 87–96.

Henderson, J., Lemon, O., & Georgila, K. (2008). Hybrid Reinforcement / Supervised Learning of Dialogue Policies from Fixed Data Sets. *Computational Linguistics, 34(4),* 487-511.

Klein, D., & Manning, C. D. (2003). Accurate Unlexicalized Parsing. *Proceedings of ACL*, 423–430.

Landis, J. R., & Koch, G. G. (1994). The Measurement of Observer Agreement for Categorical Data Data for Categorical of Observer Agreement The Measurement. *International Biometric Society*, *33*(1), 159–174.

Mayfield, E., Adamson, D., & Rosé, C. P. (2012). Hierarchical Conversation Structure Prediction in Multi-Party Chat. *Proceedings of SIGDIAL*, 60–69.

Ritter, A., Cherry, C., & Dolan, B. (2010). Unsupervised Modeling of Twitter Conversations. *Proceedings of NAACL HLT*, 172–180.

Rus, V., Moldovan, C., Niraula, N., & Graesser, A. C. (2012). Automated Discovery of Speech Act Categories in Educational Games. *Proceedings of the International Conference on Educational Data Mining,* 25-32.

Serafin, R., & Di Eugenio, B. (2004). FLSA : Extending Latent Semantic Analysis with features for dialogue act classification. *Proceedings of ACL,* 692–699.

Stolcke, A., Ries, K., Coccaro, N., Shriberg, E., Bates, R., Jurafsky, D., Taylor, P., et al. (2000). Dialogue Act Modeling for Automatic Tagging and Recognition of Conversational Speech. *Computational Linguistics*, *26*(3), 339–373.

Vlachos, A. (2011). Evaluating unsupervised learning for natural language processing tasks. *Proceedings of EMNLP*, 35–42.

Williams, J. D., & Young, S. (2003). Using Wizard-of-Oz simulations to bootstrap Reinforcement-Learning- based dialog management systems. *Proceedings of SIGDIAL*, 135–139.

Woszczyna, M., & Waibel, A. (1994). Inferring linguistic structure in spoken language. *Proceedings of ICSLP,* 847-850.

Appendix

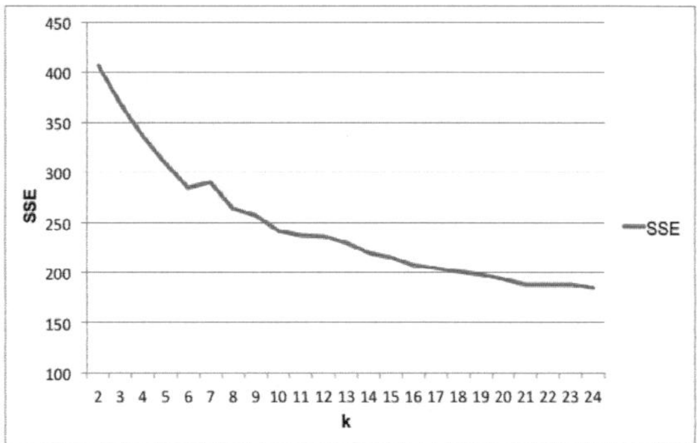

Figure 3: Sum of squared errors graph

Table 1: Example student utterances and tutor responses

Student Utterance	Tutor Response (Unsupervised Policy)	Tutor Response (Manual-Tag Policy)
I'm trying to think, heh	Don't worry about it. I'm here to help.	That part is tricky.
how can I pull values out of an array or can I reference them with code like zipDigits[1]?	Great question. Let's look at the task decription together to see if it can help.	Good question. Let's analyze the code together to see if it is right.
thanks for the reminder	I'm here to help!	Great, seems like we agreed.
does that mean I should declare it at the top of the code?	Maybe you should try it out.	Good question. Let's analyze the code together to see if it is right.

Spoken Dialog Systems for Automated Survey Interviewing

Michael Johnston[1], Patrick Ehlen[2], Frederick G. Conrad[3], Michael F. Schober[4], Christopher Antoun[3], Stefanie Fail[4], Andrew Hupp[3], Lucas Vickers[4], Huiying Yan[3], Chan Zhang[3]
AT&T Labs Research, Florham Park, NJ, USA[1], AT&T, San Francisco, CA, USA[2]
Survey Research Center, University of Michigan, Ann Arbor, USA[3]
The New School, New York, NY, USA[4]
johnston@research.att.com, ehlen@research.att.com, fconrad@umich.edu, schober@newschool.edu, antoun@umich.edu, stefaniefail@gmail.com, ahupp@umich.edu, lucasvickers@gmail.com, yanhuier@umich.edu, chanzh@umich.edu

Abstract

We explore the plausibility of using automated spoken dialog systems (SDS) for administering survey interviews. Because the goals of a survey dialog system differ from more traditional information-seeking and transactional applications, different measures of task accuracy and success may be warranted. We report a large-scale experimental evaluation of an SDS that administered survey interviews with questions drawn from government and social scientific surveys. We compare two dialog confirmation strategies: (1) a traditional strategy of explicit confirmation on low-confidence recognition; and (2) no confirmation. With explicit confirmation, the small percentage of residual errors had little to no impact on survey data measurement. Even without confirmation, while there are significantly more errors, impact on the substantive conclusions of the survey is still very limited.

1 Introduction

Survey interviews play a critical role in the operation of government and commerce. Large-scale social scientific surveys provide key indicators of the success or failure of economic and social policies, driving critical policy and funding decisions. Market research surveys are key in evaluating products and services for business.

Survey interviews are typically conducted either via telephone or face-to-face by skilled human interviewers. But ongoing changes in communication technology threaten the viability of these methods. As people migrate from landline telephony to mobile-only (Ehlen and Ehlen 2007) and Voice-over-IP (Fuchs 2008) as primary modes of communication, they undermine the effectiveness of traditional survey sampling techniques that rely on random selection of numbers within a dial code. Telephone respondents were once reachable at a fixed geographic location in a largely predictable conversational environment. Now they are increasingly mobile, and more apt to prefer asynchronous communication. Thus it is imperative to understand how these changing behaviors affect survey results.

The work described here is part of a larger research project (see Schober et al. 2012; Conrad et al. 2013) that investigates the viability of four different modes for administering a survey interview over a smartphone: automated voice, human voice, automated SMS text, and human SMS text. Here we focus specifically on the automated voice mode and explore the use of a spoken dialog system for survey administration.

Spoken dialog systems are widely used in telephony applications such as customer service, information access, and transaction fulfillment. They are also now common in virtual assistant applications for smartphones and mobile devices. But survey designers seeking automation have mostly eschewed spoken dialog in favor of textual web surveys or touchtone DTMF response systems. A preliminary comparison of spoken dialog and touchtone survey systems is available in Bloom (2008), and Stent et al. (2007) offer an evaluation of a spoken dialog system for academic course ratings. The work presented here describes the first large-scale investigation into spoken dialog technology as a viable means of administering the kinds of surveys that produce official statistics and social scientific data.

Survey interview designers should be interested in using spoken dialog systems for several reasons. The most obvious reason is to curtail the error and bias that human interviewers are known to introduce to survey results data. Decades of research and investment led to "standardized interviewing techniques" to reduce this error (Fowler and Mangione 1990), and limit a survey interviewer's ability to offer help or clarification in ways that might affect results. Automated dialog systems can be thought of as the ultimate in standardization, as they can be designed to provide exactly the same interaction possibilities to all respondents. In effect, everyone can be interviewed by the same "interviewer." Or, if survey designers want to allow clarification in an interview, an automated spoken dialog system can ensure that the same possibilities are available to all respondents (Schober and Conrad 1997).

Unlike systems that use human interviewers, there is marginal additional cost per interview after the initial investment of building a system. This offers significant potential for cost savings in large cross-sectional samples or repeated panel surveys, such as the U.S. Current Population Survey or the American Community Survey. Repeated data collection allows refinement and retraining of speech models to improve performance. Spoken dialog system surveys can be administered on demand at any time of day, allowing a better fit with respondents' circumstances and schedules. Compared to asynchronous text-based interviews like web or paper-and-pencil surveys, spoken dialog systems can capture richer verbal paradata (Couper 2009) or process data like pauses, disfluencies and prosody (Ehlen et al. 2007). Finally, survey tasks fit nicely within the limitations of current recognition and dialog technology, since they tend to have a purposefully structured and controlled interaction flow and generally require only a limited number of responses to each question.

While spoken dialog systems have the potential to remove data error that is introduced by variation in human interviewer behaviors, they also introduce risks to survey data quality due to speech recognition and understanding error. Numerous strategies for mitigating error have been explored in research on dialog systems (Bohus and Rudnicky 2005, Litman et al. 2006). One approach is to use either an explicit or implicit confirmation of the user's input. Following previous research showing that explicit confirmation is less confusing for users (Shin et al. 2002), we adopt an explicit confirmation strategy, which is also more in keeping with standardized interview techniques.

The effects of speech recognition and understanding errors may be different in a survey dialog system than in most current spoken dialog applications. One consideration is speaker initiative, and the stake of the user in the interaction. In systems for customer service, information access, or transactions, the user generally initiates contact with the system and seeks to accomplish a task where the system's recognition accuracy will affect success of the user's own goal. But in a survey dialog, the system initiates contact, and most respondents do not have a stake in whether the designers of the survey system succeed at collecting high quality data from them.

This is a key point where a survey interviewing system might differ from traditional SDS: From the survey researchers' perspective, the critical question is not whether individual users achieve some goal, but rather the extent to which individual errors in system recognition and understanding affect the distribution of responses across the population sample, affecting the quality of the estimates produced. If recognition errors do not affect the substantive conclusions based on the survey data, then survey researchers should be able to tolerate the imprecision of recognition error. This situation makes survey system evaluation rather different from how one would expect to evaluate the task success of a traditional SDS, like a customer service system.

In Section 2, we characterize the content of the survey items, describe the dialog strategy, and provide examples of interaction. Section 3 describes the technical architecture of the survey dialog system. We provide experimental evaluation in Section 4, and conclusions in Section 5.

2 Survey interview dialogs

After an initial question assessing whether the respondent is in an environment where it is safe for them to talk, our system administers a series of 32 questions drawn from major U.S. social surveys, including the Behavioral Risk Factor Surveillance System (BRFSS), National Survey of Drug Use and Health (NSDUH), General Social Survey (GSS), and the Pew Internet and American Life Project. The sample transcribed dialogs in Appendix 1 illustrate various features of interaction with the system. Question types include Yes/No, categorical (where users pick from a specified set of response options), and numerical questions. Some categorical items are grouped into battery questions with the same response options for all the items.

The system supports explicit requests to repeat the question or ask for help, and mimics a "standardized interviewing" style of interaction that trained interviewers would use to repeat or clarify a question when the answer is rejected or requires confirmation. Thresholds set on acoustic and language confidence scores are used to decide whether to reject, explicitly confirm, or accept a response. The final question in the dialog in Appendix A ("Thinking about ...") illustrates the importance of confirmation in ensuring the correct survey response is recorded. In this case, the system misrecognized "None" for "Nine," but this was caught by the explicit confirmation prompt. Two terms are introduced in the final example that we will return to in the evaluation. *First hypothesis* indicates the speech recognition and semantic result produced by the system the first time the question is asked. *Last hypothesis* indicates the speech recognition and semantic result that the system produced the last time the question was asked within the segment.

3 System Architecture

The survey dialog system is directly integrated with a custom-built survey data case collection management system (PAMSS). When a survey case is administered, the case management system makes an HTTP request to a voice gateway, which initiates a call to the respondent. When the respondent answers, it bridges the call to a spoken dialog system running within the AT&T Watson[SM] speech platform. The system uses prerecorded prompts for survey questions and reprompts. Confirmations for numeric responses combine prompts with TTS output.

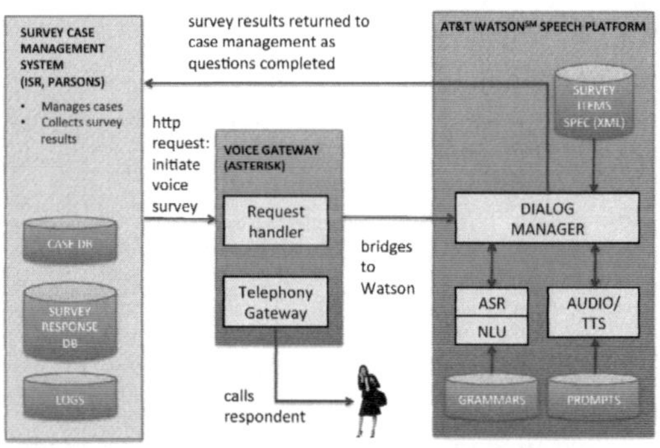

Figure 1: Survey Dialog System Architecture

Users' spoken inputs are recognized using state-specific grammars for each question. Data were not initially available for training statistical models, so SRGS (Hunt and McGlashan 2004) grammars were built for each answer. These were tuned in an initial pilot phase. The grammars included standard responses for the question, along with common paraphrases and framing words from the question. In the Watson platform, a dialog manager (built in Python) is integrated with ASR and TTS engines. Questions to be administered are represented in a declarative format in a survey item specification along with references to the appropriate prompts and grammars. The dialog manager interprets this specification to administer the survey and control the interaction flow. As the user responds to questions, the answers are posted back to the survey case management system.

4 Experimental Evaluation

We evaluated the survey dialog system as part of the first phase of a larger experiment comparing different survey interaction modes (Schober et al. 2012). In this phase, 642 subjects were recruited from Craigslist, Facebook, Google Ads, and Amazon Mechanical Turk. A web-based screener application verified respondents to be over 21 and collected their zip code. Of these, 158 respondents were randomly assigned to the automated voice condition. A $20 iTunes gift card was given as an incentive after completion of a post-interview web questionnaire. This included multiple-choice questions examining user satisfaction with their experience. In total there were 8,228 spoken inputs over the 158 respondent dialogs. These responses were transcribed, coded, and annotated for semantic content.

The questions we sought to answer were: What is the performance of a spoken dialog system on a typical survey task? What impact does speech recognition and concept error have on overall survey estimates? Does an automated survey system benefit from implementing a traditional confirmation strategy, where responses with low confidence scores are verified with confirmation dialog? We also examine the impact of dialog length and confirmation prompts on a qualitative measure of user satisfaction.

4.1 ASR and concept accuracy

We evaluated overall word, sentence, and concept accuracy for all 8,228 spoken utterances to the system, shown in the first row of Table 1.

Accuracy:	Word	Sentence	Concept
All	80%	78.2%	90.3%
First	81.2%	78%	88.9%
Last	88.5%	85.4%	**95.6%**

Table 1: System Performance

An input is "concept accurate" if the semantic value assigned by the system exactly matches that assigned by the annotator. *First* shows the performance on the first response made by a user to each question before any confirmation dialog. *Last* shows performance on the last time each question was asked. Concept accuracy on *last* responses is 95.6%, showing that the confirmation strategy resulted in a 60% relative reduction in error compared to the first response.

4.2 Impact of Errors on Survey Estimates

Recognition error is undoubtedly a key factor in overall user experience. But unlike dialog systems for information access, search, and transactions, the most important factor in a survey dialog system is the impact of errors on the quality of the estimates derived from the survey. To examine the impact of the residual 4.4% concept error on overall survey error, we compared answer distributions derived from the system hypothesis for the last response versus the annotation of the last response using paired t-tests.

For the 18 categorical questions, we conducted t-tests comparing the counts for each response option of each question. For all 18 questions (a total of 77 response categories) none of the differences were statistically significant ($p<0.05$). For the 14 numerical questions, for only one ("Number of times shopping in a grocery store in the last month") did the interpretations differ significantly (Annotated: 7.8 times, Hypothesis: 7.6 times, $p=0.04$).[1] This is strong evidence that speech recognition errors in this system did not have a major effect on survey estimates.

How much survey error would have occurred without the dialog strategy? To test this, we compared the annotated last response to the system hypothesis for the first response, simulating an interaction without confirmation dialog, and thus lower recognition accuracy—see Table 1 (This is not a perfect simulation, as we have no independent evidence on whether the first or final response is true). There would indeed have been more survey error without dialog, although the overall level was still surprisingly low. For the 18 categorical questions, 14 of the 77 response categories show significant differences ($p<0.05$). For the 14 numerical questions, two showed significant differences.

4.3 User Satisfaction

One of the post-interview questionnaire items provided a qualitative measure of user satisfaction: "*Overall, how satisfied were you with the interview?*" The results were: *Very satisfied* (47.3%), *Somewhat satisfied* (41.8%), *Somewhat dissatisfied* (7.1%), and *Very dissatisfied* (0.6%). We examined the impact of various dialog features that seemed on intuitive grounds plausibly connected with satisfaction: average number of turns per question, average number of clarification prompts per session, and average number of no input response prompts. We conducted a series of logistic regressions with one variable controlled at a time to see the extent to which each of these features affected satisfaction. A Chi-squared test was used to measure significance. All three features were significant predictors when comparing *Somewhat/Very Dissatisfied* to *Very/Somewhat satisfied* (Table 2).

Feature	Odds ratio	SE	p
# turns per Q	10.411	0.787	0.003
# clarifications	1.043	0.033	0.024
# no input	2.001	0.176	<0.001

Table 2: User satisfaction regression

5 Conclusion

Our results demonstrate the viability of conducting survey interviews of the sort from which important national statistics are derived with spoken dialog systems. In our system, the speech recognition errors (with an overall concept recognition rate of 95.6%) did not substantially affect the error of the survey estimates; for only one of 32 questions was there a significant difference in the survey estimate determined by the automated spoken dialog system compared to the annotated result. Of course, we don't know whether these results generalize to dialog systems with other features, different questions, or different respondents; much remains to be learned.

Nonetheless, our results provide some guidance for improving respondent satisfaction and minimizing survey error in future development of survey dialog systems. For example, for numerical questions, which generally involve larger numbers of response options, recognition errors may be reduced by adopting the strategy of asking the respondent to select among categories representing ranges (e.g. "none", "1 to 5 times", "6 to 10 times"). Recognition performance could be improved by tuning confirmation strategies, e.g. applying a tighter confidence threshold for numerical vs. categorical questions. In a broad scale application of a repeated spoken dialog survey, greater amounts of data could be available for training statistical models for the responses, for improved recognition accuracy and further reduced concept error. Finally, it is worth exploring the trade-offs for survey error and respondent satisfaction between adding potentially frustrating confirmation dialog and accepting lower-confidence recognition for subsequent human annotation and processing.

[1] If we treat the two interpretations as independent samples, the response distributions did not differ significantly at all.

Acknowledgments: NSF #SES-1025645 and SES-1026225 to Conrad and Schober.

References

Jonathan Bloom. 2008. The Speech IVR as a Survey Interviewing Methodology. In Conrad and Schober (eds.), Envisioning the Survey Interview of the Future. Wiley, New York.

Dan Bohus and Alex Rudnicky. 2005. Sorry, I didn't Catch That: An Investigation of Non-Understanding Errors and Recovery Strategies. Proceedings of SIGdial-2005, Lisbon, Portugal.

Frederick G. Conrad, Michael F. Schober, Chan Zhang, Huiying Yan, Lucas Vickers, Michael Johnston, Andrew L. Hupp, Lloyd Hemingway, Stefanie Fail, Patrick Ehlen, and Chris Antoun. 2013. Mode Choice on an iPhone Increases Survey Data Quality. 68th Annual Conference of the American Association for Public Opinion Research (AAPOR), Boston, MA.

Mick P. Couper, 2009. The Role of Paradata in Measuring and Reducing Measurement Error in Surveys. NCRM Network for Methodological Innovation 2009: The Use of Paradata in UK Social Surveys.

John Ehlen and Patrick Ehlen. 2007. Cellular-Only Substitution in the United States as Lifestyle Adoption. Public Opinion Quarterly: Special Issue Vol 71 (5), pp. 717-733.

Patrick Ehlen, Michael Schober, and Frederick G. Conrad. 2007. Modeling Speech Disfluency to Predict Conceptual Misalignment in Speech Survey Interfaces. Discourse Processes 44:3, pp. 245–265.

Floyd J. Fowler and Thomas W. Mangione 1990. Standardized Survey Interviewing; Minimizing Interviewer Related Error. Sage Publications, CA.

Marek Fuchs, 2008. Mobile Web Surveys: A Preliminary Discussion of Methodological Implications. In Conrad and Schober (eds.), Envisioning the Survey Interview of the Future. Wiley, New York.

Andrew Hunt and Scott McGlashan. 2004. Speech Recognition Grammar Specification Version 1.0. W3C Recommendation 16 March 2004. http://www.w3.org/TR/speech-grammar/.

Diane Litman, Julia Hirschberg, and M. G. J. Swerts. 2006. Characterizing and Predicting Corrections in Spoken Dialogue Systems. Computational Linguistics 32:3, pp. 417-438.

Michael F. Schober and Frederick G. Conrad. 1997. Does conversational interviewing reduce survey measurement error? Public Opinion Quarterly, 61, pp. 576-602.

Michael F. Schober, Frederick G. Conrad, Chris Antoun, Carroll, Patrick Ehlen, Stefanie Fail, Andrew L. Hupp, Michael Johnston, Courtney Kellner, Kelly Nichols, Leif Percifield, Lucas Vickers, Huiying Yan, and Chan Zhang. 2012. Disclosure and Quality of Answers in Text and Voice Interviews on iPhones. 67th Annual Conference of the American Association for Public Opinion Research (AAPOR) Orlando, FL.

Jongho Shin, Shrikanth Narayanan, Laurie Gerber, Abe Kazemzadeh, and Dani Byrd. 2002. Analysis of User Behavior under Error Conditions in Spoken Dialogs. Proceedings of ICSLP-2002.

Amanda Stent, Svetlana Stenchikova, and Matthew Marge. 2006. Dialog systems for surveys: The Rate-a-Course system. Proceedings of the IEEE/ACL 2006 Workshop on Spoken Language Technology. pp. 210-213.

Appendix – Sample Survey Dialogs

I: Have you smoked at least 100 cigarettes in your entire life? Yes or no.
R: No
I: Thanks

I: Now I'd like to ask you some questions specific to your diet. For the next group of questions, I'll ask you how much you favor or oppose engaging in certain behaviors. After I say the behavior, please say one of the following: strongly favor, somewhat favor, neither favor nor oppose, somewhat oppose or strongly oppose. The first behavior...avoiding fast food.
R: Strongly oppose
I: You said strongly oppose, right?
R: Yes
I: Got it
I: The next behavior: Maintaining a healthy diet
R: Repeat
I: The next behavior: Maintaining a healthy diet
R: Strongly agree
I: Sorry, I didn't hear you. When thinking about 'maintaining a healthy diet', please say one of the following: strongly favor, somewhat favor, neither favor nor oppose, somewhat oppose or strongly oppose.
R: Somewhat favor
I: You said somewhat favor, right?
R: Yes
I: Thanks
. . .
I: Thinking about the time since your eighteenth birthday (including the recent past that you've already told us about), how many male partners have you had sex with?
R: None (*First hypothesis*: "Nine")
I: I think you said '9'. Is that right? Yes or No.
R: No
I: Thinking about the time since your eighteenth birthday (including the recent past that you've already told us about), how many male partners have you had sex with?
R: Zero (*Last hypothesis*: "Zero")
I: Thanks

Open-domain Utterance Generation for Conversational Dialogue Systems using Web-scale Dependency Structures

Hiroaki Sugiyama*, **Toyomi Meguro***, **Ryuichiro Higashinaka****, **Yasuhiro Minami***
*NTT Communication Science Laboratories
2-4, Hikari-dai, Seika-cho, Souraku-gun, Kyoto, Japan
**NTT Media Intelligence Laboratories
1-1, Hikari-no-Oka, Yokosuka-shi, Kanagawa, Japan
{sugiyama.hiroaki,meguro.toyomi,higashinaka.ryuichiro,minami.yasuhiro}@lab.ntt.co.jp

Abstract

Even though open-domain conversational dialogue systems are required in many fields, their development is complicated because of the flexibility and variety of user utterances. To address this flexibility, previous research on conversational dialogue systems has selected system utterances from web articles based on surface cohesion and shallow semantic coherence; however, the generated utterances sometimes contain irrelevant sentences with respect to the input user utterance. We propose a template-based approach that fills templates with the most salient words in a user utterance and with related words that are extracted using web-scale dependency structures gathered from Twitter. Our open-domain conversational dialogue system outperforms retrieval-based conventional systems in chat experiments.

1 Introduction

The need for open-domain conversational dialogue systems continues to grow. Such systems are beginning to be actively investigated from their social and entertainment aspects (Shibata et al., 2009; Ritter et al., 2011; Wong et al., 2012); conversational dialogues also have potential for therapy purposes and for evoking a user's unconscious requests in task-oriented dialogues (Bickmore and Cassell, 2001). However, developing open-domain conversational dialogue systems is difficult, since the huge variety of user utterances makes it harder to build knowledge resources for generating appropriate system responses. To address this issue, previous research has selected system utterances from web articles or microblogs on the basis of surface cohesion and shallow semantic coherence (Shibata et al., 2009; Jafarpour and Burges, 2010; Wong et al., 2012); however, the selected utterances sometimes contain sentences irrelevant to the user utterance since they originally appeared in a different context.

To satisfy both web-scale topic coverage and suppression of irrelevant sentences, we propose a template-based approach that fills templates with words related to the topic of the user utterance and with words related to the topic-words. This approach enables us to generate a wide range of system responses when we properly extract related words. To obtain words related to topic-words, we analyzed the dependency structures of a huge number of sentences posted to such microblogs as Twitter, where a large number and variety of sentences are posted daily. This way, we can generate a variety of appropriate system responses despite wide variation in user utterances.

We develop a conversational dialogue system that generates system utterances with our proposed utterance generation approach and examine its effectiveness by chat experiments with real users.

2 Related Work

To generate system utterances for conversational dialogue systems, Ritter et al. (2011) proposed a statistical machine translation-based approach that considers source-reply tweet pairs as a bilingual corpus. They compared the following three approaches: IR-status, which retrieves reply tweets whose associated source tweets most resemble the user utterance (Jafarpour and Burges, 2010); IR-response, which retrieves reply tweets that are the most similar to the user utterance; and their proposed SMT-based approach, named MT-chat. They reported that MT-chat outperformed the other approaches and that IR-response was superior to IR-status. However, these approaches used only the words, and not the structures, of user utterances to generate system utterances.

Yoshino et al. (2011) proposed a QA system that answers questions about current events by retrieving, from news articles, descriptions containing similar dependency structures as those of the user's questions. Although this retrieval-based approach is effective for answering the user's factual questions, it is insufficient to generate subjective utterances for conversational dialogue systems since such systems are required to introduce new topics or to respond with opinions related to user utterances.

3 Open-domain Utterance Generation

Open-domain conversational dialogue systems should be able to respond to any user utterance on any topic. To achieve this, we adopt a template-based approach that estimates the topic of the user utterance, extracts words related to the topic-words, and fills templates with these words. The template-based approach resembles previous rule-based approaches, but these dialogue systems had difficulty achieving coverage for template fillers. In contrast, our approach utilizes the dependency structures of sentences gathered from microblogs that have a wide range of topics, in order to extract the related words used in template-filling. The dependency parser we use is a state-of-the-art Japanese dependency parser that uses Conditional Random Fields trained on text and blog posts, and performs cascaded chunking until all dependencies are found. This parser achieved 84.59% dependency accuracy on a corpus of Japanese blog posts (Imamura et al., 2007).

Microblog posts do not typically contain formulaic utterances such as greetings or back-channels. Therefore, in addition to the template-filling approach, we adopt dialogue act based utterance generation for the formulaic uttenances. Figure 1 illustrates the whole architecture of our system.

3.1 Topic-word-driven Template-based Utterance Generation

Our topic-word-driven template-based approach consists of the following three steps: topic estimation, related word extraction, and template-filling utterance generation.

3.1.1 Topic Estimation

We identify three types of potential topic in an input user utterance: proper nouns, common nouns, and predicates (verbs, adjectives, adjectival verbs, and verbal nouns).

Proper Nouns We take the last proper noun that appears in the user's utterance as a potential topic. Since general Japanese morphological analyzers cannot capture recent proper nouns, we complement the proper noun dictionary entries with Wikipedia entries[1].

Common Nouns To identify potential topics from common nouns, we calculate the inverse document frequency (IDF) of each common noun (all nouns except for proper, time-related, and verbal ones) in the user's utterance. We use a corpus of microblog posts and treat each post as a document. We adopt the word with the highest IDF as a potential topic.

[1]https://github.com/nabokov/mecab-dic-overdrive

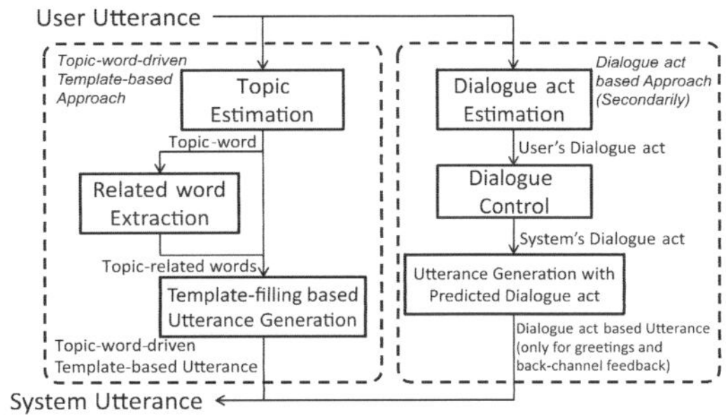

Figure 1: System Architecture

Predicates We take the predicate that composes a dependency in the highest layer of the dependency structure as a potential topic. For example, we adopt "ask", but not "walk" from the utterance "I asked the man walking on the street".

3.1.2 Related word Extraction

To obtain topic-related words, a thesaurus or topic model such as Latent Dirichlet Allocation are the most popular approaches (Blei et al., 2003). However, these approaches return semantically similar words to input query words, which do not effectively introduce new information into the system utterances. Therefore, we count the dependencies between words in a huge number of sentences gathered from microblogs, and utilize the most frequently dependent words. This approach enables us to extract adjectives related to proper noun topics; for example, the adjectives *beautiful, good, clear, white,* and *huge* are extracted for Mt. Fuji. Since microblogs contain a huge number of subjective posts, we expect the extracted words to be subjective and suitable for conversational dialogue systems. In this work, we extract adjectives for proper and common nouns, and nouns and their case frames for predicates. Examples of extracted words are shown in Table 2.

3.1.3 Template-filling Utterance Generation

We generate two types of system utterances using manually defined templates: subjective sentences with proper nouns and common nouns; and questions with predicates and their case frames.

Noun-driven Subjective Sentence Generation We generate system utterances using the proper and common nouns and their related adjectives. Here, we adopt different templates for each word type; proper nouns have explicit meanings, so adjectives related to them are easily suited for any dialogue context. By contrast, since common nouns are used in various contexts in microblogs, adjectives related to common nouns may not fit the dialogue context. Thus, we use "suki" ("like" in English), or "nigate" ("don't like" in English) in the templates based on the proportion of positive/negative adjectives in the set of related words for a common noun topic. Table 3 shows representative examples for each type. If the system generates subjective utterances as the system's own impression of the dialogue topic, the user will expect the system to justify or explain its opinion; however, our system cannot answer that kind of question. Thus, we define the templates using hedges such as "I hear that..." to avoid such questions. The number of templates for proper nouns is eight, and for common nouns is four for each polarity.

Predicate-driven Question Sentence Generation We generate question sentences using predicates and their related nouns and case frames. To elicit user utterances on a particular topic, we generate How/What/Where/When types of questions as shown in Table 3. To select a question word, we use the predicate types and the classes of the related nouns. If the predicate type is adjective or adjectival noun, we select "how" for the question word. If the predicate type is verbal noun or verb and *location* class words appear in the related noun phrase, we select "where" for the question word; the *time* class induces the question word "when". When no proper noun is found in the topic-word, we select "what". The number of templates for proper nouns is three for each interrogative type.

3.2 Dialogue act based Utterance Generation

Our approach has difficulty generating appropriate responses to formulaic utterances such as greetings and back-channels. To address this weakness, we adopt dialogue act based utterance generation for these types of utterance. A dialogue act is an abstract expression of a speaker's intention (Stolcke et al., 2000); we used the 33 dialogue acts defined in Meguro et al. (2010).

Our dialogue act based approach estimates the next dialogue act that the system should output based on the user's utterance, and generates a system utterance based on the system's predicted dialogue act if the dialogue act is greetings, sympathy, non-sympathy, filler, or confirmation.

3.2.1 User's Dialogue act Estimation

We collected 1,259 conversational dialogues from 47 human subjects and labeled each sentence of the collected data using the 33 dialogue acts. 67,801 dialogue acts are contained in the corpus.

We estimated the 33 dialogue acts from user utterances using a logistic regression model and adopted 1- and 2-gram words and 3- and 4-gram characters as model features. We trained our model using 1,000 dialogues and evaluated it using 259 dialogues. The estimation accuracy was about 61%, whereas the human annotation agreement rate was about 59%.

3.2.2 Dialogue control Model and Utterance Generation with Predicted Dialogue act

We developed a dialogue control model that estimates the system's next dialogue act based on the user's dialogue act. The model features are the user's current dialogue act vector, the system's last dialogue act vector, and the user's last dialogue act vector. Each dialogue act vector consists of a 33-dimensional binary vector space. We used the dialogue corpus described above to train and evaluate our model, which we trained with 1,000 dialogues and evaluated using 259 dialogues. The estimation accuracy was 31%, whereas the dialogue act annotation agreement rate between humans is 60%. We exploited the fact that formulaic utterances can pre-define corresponding utterances regardless of the context. Table 4 shows example generated sentences for each dialogue act.

4 Experiment

4.1 Experiment Setting

We recruited ten native Japanese-speaking participants in their 20's and 30's (two males and eight females) from outside of the authors' organization, who have experience using chat systems (not bots). Each participant chatted with the following systems, provided subjective evaluation scores for each system for each of the eight criteria shown in Table 1 (2)-(10) using 7-point Likert scales, and at the end ranked all the systems. We examined the effectiveness of our proposed approach by comparison with the following six systems.

We built the following proposed systems with about 150 M posts gathered from Twitter (excluding posts that contain "@", "RT", "http" and brackets, and posts that don't contain any dependency pairs). At the beginning of a dialogue or the end of a conversation topic when the topic-based approach didn't generate system utterances, the proposed approaches generated questions such as "What is your favorite movie?" to introduce the next conversation topic. These questions were gathered from utterances in the self-introduction phase (about the five initial utterances) of each dialogue in our dialogue corpus. We manually selected 109 questions that have no context from 179 questions gathered from our corpus, and chose a question at random to generate each topic-inductive question.

Proposed-All This approach used all found topics: proper and common nouns, and predicates. This approach is expected to be well-balanced since it generates both content-focused utterances and general WH-type questions.

Proposed-Nouns This approach used only proper and common nouns, not predicates.

Proposed-Predicates This approach used only predicates, not proper nor common nouns.

Retrieval-Self This approach resembles the IR-response method in Ritter et al. (2011). This approach chose the most similar posts to the user ut-

	Prop.-All	Prop.-Noun	Prop.-Pred.	Ret.-self	Ret.-reply	Human
(1) Number of superior prefs. vs. Prop.-All	-	4	3	0**	2*	9**
(2) Naturalness of dialogue flow	4.0	3.1**	3.5	2.2**	3.5	6.5**
(3) Grammatical correctness	4.0	3.7	4.4	4.1	3.9	6.4**
(4) Dialogue usefulness	3.7	2.9**	3.9	2.7**	3.5	6.1**
(5) Ease of considering next utterance	3.5	3.4	4.4**	2.4**	3.3	5.7**
(6) Variety of system utterances	4.3	4.0	4.2	2.9**	4.0	5.5
(7) User motivation	4.5	4.0*	4.7	3.7*	4.6	5.6**
(8) System motivation that the user feels	4.7	4.1*	4.3	3.5**	4.5	5.7*
(9) Desire to chat again	3.7	2.8**	3.3	2.0**	3.1	5.7**
(10) Averaged score of all evaluation items	4.05	3.50**	4.08	2.93**	3.8*	5.9**

Table 1: System preferences and evaluation scores on 7-point Likert scale (*: $p<.1$, **: $p<.05$)

terance from source posts using the Lucene[2] information retrieval library, which is an IDF-weighted vector-space similarity. We built about 55 M source-reply post pairs from Twitter.

Retrieval-Reply This approach is the same as the IR-status method in Ritter et al. (2011). It chooses a reply post whose associated source posts most resemble the user's utterance.

Human As an upper-bound of these systems, the user chats with a human using the same chat interface used by the other systems.

Each dialogue took place over four minutes and was conducted through a text chat interface, and the orders of presentation of systems to participants was randomized. Since the humans have to type their utterances and the systems can generate utterances much faster than typing, we set the transition of the system utterances to about ten seconds to avoid different response intervals between the systems and the humans. Table 5 shows a dialogue example.

4.2 Results and Discussion

Table 1 shows that Proposed-All is ranked the highest of all the automatic systems (1), and achieves the best average evaluation scores (2)-(10). Statistical analyses were performed using the Binomial test for (1) and Welch's t test for (2) to (10). Proposed-All was ranked higher than the retrieval-based approaches (10 of 10 participants ranked Proposed-All higher than Retrieval-Self, and 8 participants ranked Proposed-All higher than Retrieval-Reply), but none of our three proposed approaches was ranked significantly higher than the others.

The evaluation scores also demonstrate the characteristics of each approach. Proposed-Nouns shows significantly low scores in dialogue flow (2), dialogue usefulness (4), and system motivation (9). Since this approach is overly affected by the nouns in the user utterances, users didn't feel that the system was actually thinking. Proposed-Predicates shows a high score in ease of thinking about the next utterance (5) since it generates WH-type questions for which users can easily produce answer utterances.

[2]http://lucene.apache.org

For conventional retrieval-based approaches, contrary to Ritter et al. (2011), Retrieval-Self shows significantly lower scores in almost all the evaluation items, and Retrieval-Reply shows scores close to Proposed-All. These results reflect the retrieved corpus size, which is 40 times larger than that of Ritter et al. (2011). When the retrieval performance improves, Retrieval-Self returns posts that are too similar to user utterances, while Retrieval-Reply can find appropriate source posts. Retrieval-Reply shows almost the same scores as Proposed-All for each single evaluation metric, but Retrieval-Reply is inferior to Proposed-All in the averaged evaluation items (10). This is a reason why Retrieval-Reply is also inferior in (1).

None of the systems approached human performance. The users thought that the systems were not able to respond to user utterances that referred to the system itself, like personal questions; and that the systems didn't understand user utterances since the systems sometimes generate a question that contains different but semantically similar words to those used by the user, due to the lack of thesaurus knowledge.

5 Conclusions

We proposed a novel open-domain utterance generation approach for a conversational dialogue system that generates system utterances using templates populated with topics and related words extracted from a huge number of dependency structures. Our chat experiments demonstrated that our template-based approach generated system utterances preferred over those produced with retrieval-based approaches, and that WH-type questions make it easy for users to produce their next utterance. Our work also indicated that template-based utterance generation, which is considered a legacy approach, has potential when the template-filling resource is huge. Future work includes improving the data-driven topic selection in the proposed approach, the aggregation of words with web-scale class structures like Tamagawa et al. (2012), response generation for utterances that describe the systems themselves, and exploitation of information about the user to generate system utterances.

References

Timothy Bickmore and Justine Cassell. 2001. Relational Agents: A Model and Implementation of Building User Trust. In *Proceedings of the SIGCHI Conference on Human Factors in Computing Systems*, pages 396–403.

David M. Blei, Andrew Y. Ng, and Michael I. Jordan. 2003. Latent Dirichlet Allocation. *Journal of Machine Learning Research*, 3:993–1022.

Kenji Imamura, Genichiro Kikui, and Norihito Yasuda. 2007. Japanese Dependency Parsing Using Sequential Labeling for Semi-Spoken Language. In *Proceedings of the 45th Annual Meeting of the ACL on Interactive Poster and Demonstration Sessions*, pages 225–228.

Sina Jafarpour and Christopher J.C. Burges. 2010. Filter, Rank, and Transfer the Knowledge: Learning to Chat. Technical Report MSR-TR-2010-93, Microsoft.

Toyomi Meguro, Ryuichiro Higashinaka, Yasuhiro Minami, and Kohji Dohsaka. 2010. Controlling Listening-oriented Dialogue using Partially Observable Markov Decision Processes. In *Proceedings of the 23rd International Conference on Computational Linguistics*, pages 761–769.

Alan Ritter, Colin Cherry, and William.B. Dolan. 2011. Data-Driven Response Generation in Social Media. In *Proceedings of the 2011 Conference on Empirical Methods in Natural Language Processing*, pages 583–593.

Masahiro Shibata, Tomomi Nishiguchi, and Yoichi Tomiura. 2009. Dialog System for Open-Ended Conversation Using Web Documents. *Informatica*, 33:277–284.

Andreas Stolcke, Klaus Ries, Noah Coccaro, Elizabeth Shriberg, Rebecca Bates, Daniel Jurafsky, Paul Taylor, Rachel Martin, Carol Van Ess-Dykema, and Marie Meteer. 2000. Dialogue Act Modeling for Automatic Tagging and Recognition of Conversational Speech. *Computational Linguistics*, 26(3):339–373.

Susumu Tamagawa, Takeshi Morita, and Takahira Yamaguchi. 2012. Extracting Property Semantics from Japanese Wikipedia. In *Proceedings of the 8th international conference on Active Media Technology*, pages 357–368.

Wilson Wong, Lawrence Cavedon, John Thangarajah, and Lin Padgham. 2012. Strategies for Mixed-Initiative Conversation Management using Question-Answer Pairs. In *Proceedings of the 24th International Conference on Computational Linguistics*, pages 2821–2834.

Koichiro Yoshino, Shinsuke Mori, and Tatsuya Kawahara. 2011. Spoken Dialogue System based on Information Extraction using Similarity of Predicate Argument Structures. In *Proceedings of the 12th Annual Meeting of the Special Interest Group on Discourse and Dialogue*, pages 59–66.

Appendix

Topic-word	Extracted topic-related words
Mt.Fuji	beautiful, good, clear, white, huge (adj)
Bread	delicious, good, like, cute (adj)
Eat	I (“ga”: subject-case), rice (“wo”: target-case) together (“ni”: “with”,“ to”)

Table 2: Extracted topic-related words (translated by authors)

Word type	Template example
Proper nouns	I hear that [Noun] is [adj], isn't it? [Noun] ha [adj] deshitakke? (JP)
General nouns	Actually, I am weak in [Noun]... [Noun] ha chotto nigate desu... (JP)
Adjectives and adjectival nouns	How does it [Noun]? douiu huuni [Noun] nndesuka? (JP)
Verbs and verbal nouns	Where do you [Verb]? doko de [Verb] nndesuka? (JP)

Table 3: Templates for topic types (translated by authors)

Dialogue act	Example
Greetings	Hello.
Sympathy	Good./ Nice.
Non-sympathy	Not so good..
Filler	Uh.
Confirmation	Really?/Oh, [Noun].

Table 4: Generated utterances for dialogue acts (translated by authors)

Speaker	Utterance
User	Hello.
System	Hello. Do you like movies?
User	I like movies.
System	Good. I think movie is fun, isn't it?
User	I like reading more than going to the movies.
System	Reading is also good.
User	I borrow books from my local library.
System	Nice. I hear that libraries are quiet.
User	Yes, they usually are. I used to study, write reports, and read books.

Table 5: Dialogues between user and Proposed-All (translated by authors)

Evaluating State Representations for Reinforcement Learning of Turn-Taking Policies in Tutorial Dialogue

Christopher M. Mitchell **Kristy Elizabeth Boyer** **James C. Lester**
Department of Computer Science
North Carolina State University
Raleigh, NC, USA
{cmmitch2, keboyer, lester}@ncsu.edu

Abstract

Learning and improving natural turn-taking behaviors for dialogue systems is a topic of growing importance. In task-oriented dialogue where the user can engage in task actions in parallel with dialogue, unrestricted turn taking may be particularly important for dialogue success. This paper presents a novel Markov Decision Process (MDP) representation of dialogue with unrestricted turn taking and a parallel task stream in order to automatically learn effective turn-taking policies for a tutorial dialogue system from a corpus. It also presents and evaluates an approach to automatically selecting features for an MDP state representation of this dialogue. The results suggest that the MDP formulation and the feature selection framework hold promise for learning effective turn-taking policies in task-oriented dialogue systems.

1 Introduction

Determining when to make a dialogue move is a topic of growing importance in dialogue systems. While systems historically relied on explicit turn-taking cues, more recent work has focused on learning and improving on natural turn-taking behaviors (Raux and Eskenazi 2012; Selfridge et al. 2012). For tutorial dialogue in particular, effectively timing system moves can substantially impact the success of the dialogue. For example, failing to provide helpful feedback to a student who is confused may lead to decreased learning (Shute 2008) or to disengagement (Forbes-Riley and Litman 2012), while providing tutorial feedback or interventions at inappropriate times could also have a negative impact on the outcome of the dialogue (D'Mello et al. 2010).

Reinforcement Learning (RL) is a widely used approach to constructing effective dialogue policies using either MDPs or POMDPs (Williams and Young 2007). To date, RL has been applied to learn the most effective dialogue move to make, but has not been applied to learning the timings of these moves, although the related concept of when to release a turn has been explored (English and Heeman 2005). The domain of tutorial dialogue poses an additional modeling challenge: the dialogue is task-oriented, but unlike many task-oriented dialogues in which all information is communicated via dialogue, students solve problems within a separate task stream which conveys essential information for dialogue management decisions.

This paper addresses dialogue with both unrestricted turn taking and a parallel task stream with a novel Markov Decision Process representation. Because turn boundaries are not clearly defined or enforced, we apply RL to the problem of *when* to make a dialogue move, rather than *what type* of dialogue move to make. In order to determine which criteria are most relevant to making this decision, the approach utilizes a feature selection approach based on a new *Separation Ratio* metric and compares the selected features against an existing approach based on expected cumulative reward (Chi et al. 2011). Finally, the resulting feature spaces are evaluated with simulated users acquired in a supervised fashion from held-out portions of the corpus. The results inform the development of turn-taking policies in task-oriented dialogue systems.

2 Corpus

The corpus used for this work was collected during 2011 and 2012 as part of the JavaTutor tutorial dialogue project. It consists of 66 textual dialogues between human tutors and students, with an average of 90 tutor dialogue moves and 36 student dialogue moves. Each pair interacted for through a computer-mediated interface to complete introductory computer programming tasks. Students edited their computer programs within a parallel task stream also collected as part of the corpus (see Appendix A). Tutors viewed the task actions synchronously through the interface. The success of each dialogue was measured by learning gain between pretest and posttest. Overall the dialogues were effective; the average learning gain was 42.3% (statistically > 0; $p < .0001$). The substantial variation in learning gains (*min*=-28.6%; *max*= 100%) will be leveraged within the MDP reward structure.

3 MDP Representation

A Markov Decision Process (MDP) models a system in which a policy can be learned to maximize reward (Sutton and Barto 1998). It consists of a set of states S, a set of actions A representing possible actions by an agent, a set of transition probabilities indicating how likely it is for the model to transition to each state $s' \in S$ from each state $s \in S$ when the agent performs each action $a \in A$ in state s, and a reward function R that maps real values onto transitions and/or states, thus signifying their utility.

Previous applications of RL to dialogue systems, using both MDPs and POMDPs, have dealt with the decision of *what type* of dialogue move to make (Chi et al. 2011; Williams and Young 2007). These systems make this decision either at predetermined decision points (Tetreault and Litman 2008), following the trigger of a silence threshold (Raux and Eskenazi 2012), or when the system determines it has enough information to advance the dialogue (Selfridge et al. 2012). For the JavaTutor corpus, however, the tutor could choose to make a move at any time. Rather than applying handcrafted rules to determine decision points, we apply RL to learn *when* to make a dialogue move in order to maximize the success of the dialogue. For this MDP, the action set is defined as $A = \{TutorMove, NoMove\}$.

The states for the MDP consist of combinations of features representing the current state of the session. The possible features available for selection are described in Table 1, and are all automatically extracted from system logs. The *Task Trajectory* and *Edit Distance* features are based on computing a token-level edit distance from a student's program with respect to that student's final correct solution. This distance measures a student's progress over the course of a dialogue while avoiding the need to manually annotate the task stream. In a deployed system, this edit distance can be estimated by comparing to previously acquired solutions from other students.

Feature	Description	Values
Current Action	The current action being taken by the student	• TASK • STUDENTDIAL • NOACTION
Task Trajectory	The effect of the last task action on the edit distance to the final task solution	• CLOSER • FARTHER • NOCHANGE
Last Action	Last turn taken by either interlocutor	• TUTORDIAL • STUDENTDIAL • TASK
Number of Tutor Moves	Number of tutor turns taken thus far in the dialogue	• LOW (< 30) • MID (30-59) • HIGH (> 60)
Edit Distance	The edit distance to the final solution	• LOW (< 20) • MID (20-49) • HIGH (> 50)
Elapsed Idle Time	The number of seconds since the last student action	• LOW (< 7) • MID (7-15) • HIGH (> 15)

Table 1. Features available to be selected

Tutor moves are encoded as MDP actions, while student actions are encoded as transitions to a new state with a *NoMove* tutor action. To account for the possibility that both interlocutors could construct messages simultaneously or that dialogue and task actions could happen at the same time, the following protocol was applied: if a tutor was making a dialogue move (*i.e.*, typing a message), the state transition accompanying a student action was made after the tutor move was complete, and the student move was associated with that *TutorMove* action.

Another important consideration for this representation was how to segment the task stream into discrete actions. Through empirical investigation the timeout threshold of 1.5 seconds was selected as a balance between large numbers of successive task events or very few, most of which overlapped with tutor turns.

There were three additional states in the MDP: the *Initial* state and two final states, *FinalHigh* and *FinalLow*, occurring only at the end of a dialogue and providing rewards of +100 and −100, respectively. A median split on student learning gains was used to assign each dialogue to either the *FinalHigh* state or *FinalLow* state.

4 Feature Selection

While retaining all six features would allow for a rich state representation, it would also lead to issues with sparsity (Singh et al. 2002). In fact, nearly 90% of states averaged less than one visit per dialogue when using all six features, leading to inadequate coverage of the state space on which to build reliable MDP policies. This section compares two methods used to select features from among the six available.

The first approach is based on the *Expected Cumulative Reward* (ECR) in the initial state, a metric previously used to evaluate state representations for a tutorial dialogue system using RL (Chi et al. 2011; Tetreault and Litman 2008). A higher initial-state ECR indicates a higher probability of achieving a favorable outcome when following a reward-maximizing policy. Maximizing ECR has also been the focus of other feature selection approaches for RL (Misu and Kashioka 2012, Li et al. 2009).

While initial-state ECR provides a measure of the likelihood of a favorable outcome, it does not address how well a particular state representation captures key decision points. That is, it does not directly represent the extent to which each decision along the path to a successful outcome contributed to that outcome, or whether the second-best decision in a particular state would have been equally useful. In order to measure this difference, we introduce the *Separation Ratio* (SR), which represents how much better a particular policy is compared to its alternatives. SR for a state is calculated by taking the absolute difference between the estimated values of two actions in that state and dividing by the mean of the two values. SR for a policy is the mean of the SRs across all states.

An SR near zero for a state indicates that the decision to take one action over another in that state is likely to have little effect on the final outcome of the dialogue. On the other hand, a high SR indicates a crucial decision point, where taking an off-policy action leads to a much lower probability of a successful outcome. The intuition behind this metric is that a state representation that supports policies with high SR highlights features that are useful in executing an effective turn-taking policy, while a state representation that produces policies with low SR fails to capture this information.

Using these two metrics, we evaluated the utility of each of the six features. Starting with two empty state representations, one for each metric, a greedy algorithm added one feature at a time to each. That is, at each step for each metric, the feature was added that led to the highest value on the metric when combined with the features already chosen. For each of the two metrics, we built a state representation and used it as the basis for an MDP. This MDP was then trained with policy iteration (Sutton and Barto 1998), and the two state representations that led to the highest value on each metric were carried over to the next iteration. The goal here is to evaluate the relative utility of each feature, so we continued adding features until they were exhausted, leading to a full ordering of features for each condition (Table 2).

Iteration	Initial-State ECR Feature Ordering	Mean SR Feature Ordering
1	Last Action	Number of Tutor Moves
2	Task Trajectory	Edit Distance
3	Current Action	Last Action
4	Elapsed Idle Time	Current Action
5	Number of Tutor Moves	Elapsed Idle Time
6	Edit Distance	Task Trajectory

Table 2. Feature selection using Expected Cumulative Reward (ECR) and Separation Ratio (SR)

Given the orderings in Table 2, the next step in building a RL system is to decide which iteration of the feature spaces to use. That is, how does a system designer determine when to stop adding features? Previous work (Chi et al. 2011; Tetreault and Litman 2008) viewed an absolute increase in the value of initial-state ECR as a signal for the quality of a newly added feature. So, one could say that feature addition should stop if initial-state ECR does not increase between iterations. In the current analysis, however, this would result in termination at the second iteration for the mean SR ordering and termination at the first iteration for the initial-state ECR ordering. These undesirably early terminations most likely occur because the first features selected in both orderings represent tutor actions: a tutor can always choose to make a move, thus setting the *Last Action* feature to TUTORDIAL, and a tutor has direct control over the value of *Number of Tutor Moves*. This control of features leads to deterministic control of state if the context provided by student-driven features is absent. This can allow a policy to remain in the state that maximizes the transition probability to the end state, thus increasing ECR for all states due to deterministic transitions. Therefore, a different type of stopping criterion is required.

A stopping criterion must balance two competing goals. On the one hand, the size of the state space must be limited to avoid issues with sparsity, as state-action pairs that are not well explored during training might not be assigned values proportional to their expected rewards in a deployed system. On the other hand, a feature space that is too small may not sufficiently represent the possible states of the world, and might fail to capture the criteria most relevant to making decisions. These competing goals of compactness and descriptive power must both be considered when choosing an appropriate feature space for a RL model.

In an attempt to balance these goals, we propose a stopping criterion based on the ratio of states that are sparse states. A sparse state is defined as any state that occurs less than once per dialogue on average. A sharp increase in sparse states was observed between the third and fourth iterations for both metrics (15% to 56% for ECR and 26% to 47% for SR), so feature addition stopped at the third iteration. This resulted in only one of the three selected features being shared among the two conditions: the *Last Action* made by either person (Table 2). In addition, both feature sets include a feature related to the task progress of the student: *Task Trajectory* for ECR and *Edit Distance* for SR. The next section reports on an experiment to evaluate these two feature spaces.

5 Evaluation

A series of simulated dialogues was used to evaluate the two resulting feature spaces via the policies derived using them. These simulations were based on five-fold cross-validation, as in prior work (Henderson et al. 2008), with policies trained on four of the five folds and simulated users learned from the remaining fold.

As noted above, the rewards in the MDP were based on student learning gain, but learning gain (like user satisfaction in other dialogue domains) is not directly observable during the dialogues. However, we found that students in the high learning gain group had fewer *non-zero* task actions (actions that changed the edit distance to the final task solution) than students in the low learning gain group ($p < 0.05$). Therefore, number of non-zero task actions is used as a measure of dialogue success, with lower numbers being better. We derived the average change in edit distance on each state transition from the testing folds, and defined that a simulated dialogue would end when the edit distance reached zero (*i.e.*, the student arrived at the correct solution).

Table 3 shows the results of running 5,000 simulations in each fold for both the learned policy and for an anti-policy where each decision was reversed. The anti-policy is included to provide a point of comparison for the policies learned in each feature space, and offers insight into the quality of the learned policies, similar to the inverse policies learned in prior work (Chi et al. 2011). The table shows that the learned policies in the ECR feature space had slightly better results overall (lower number of non-zero task actions), while the SR feature space had larger separation between the learned policies and anti-policies. These results suggest that feature selection based on SR was able to identify important decision criteria with only a minor decrease in reward compared to ECR.

Feature Space	Policy	Average non-zero task action count
ECR	Learned policy	43.2
	Anti-policy	49.6
SR	Learned policy	47.3
	Anti-policy	97.4

Table 3. Results of simulated dialogues (lower non-zero task action count is better)

6 Conclusion

Modeling unrestricted turn taking within an RL framework, particularly for task-oriented dialogue with both a dialogue and a parallel task stream, presents numerous challenges. This paper has presented a novel representation of such dialogue with a tutoring domain, and has presented and evaluated a feature selection method based on a new *Separation Ratio* metric, which can inform the development of turn-taking policies in dialogue systems. Future work includes a more fine-grained analysis of the timing of dialogue moves as well as an evaluation of these results in a deployed system.

Acknowledgements

This work is supported in part by the National Science Foundation through Grants DRL-1007962 and CNS-1042468. Any opinions, findings, conclusions, or recommendations expressed in this report are those of the participants, and do not necessarily represent the official views, opinions, or policy of the National Science Foundation.

References

Chi, M., VanLehn, K., Litman, D., and Jordan, P. (2011). An Evaluation of Pedagogical Tutorial Tactics for a Natural Language Tutoring System: a Reinforcement Learning Approach. *International Journal of Artificial Intelligence in Education*, 21(1), 83–113.

D'Mello, S.K., Olney, A., and Person, N. (2010). Mining Collaborative Patterns in Tutorial Dialogues. *Journal of Educational Data Mining*, 2(1), 1–37.

English, M.S. and Heeman, P.A. (2005). Learning Mixed Initiative Dialog Strategies By Using Reinforcement Learning On Both Conversants. In *Proceedings of the Conference on Human Language Technology and Empirical Methods in Natural Language Processing*, 1011–1018.

Forbes-Riley, K. and Litman, D.J. (2012). Adapting to Multiple Affective States in Spoken Dialogue. In *Proceedings of the 13th Annual SIGDIAL Meeting on Discourse and Dialogue*, 217–226.

Henderson, J., Lemon, O., and Georgila, K. (2008). Hybrid Reinforcement/Supervised Learning of Dialogue Policies from Fixed Data Sets. *Computational Linguistics*, 34(4), 487–511.

Li, L., Williams, J. D., and Balakrishnan, S. (2009). Reinforcement Learning for Dialog Management Using Least-Squares Policy Iteration and Fast Feature Selection. In *Proceedings of the Conference of the International Speech Communication* Association. 2475–2478.

Misu, T., and Kashioka, H. (2012). Simultaneous Feature Selection and Parameter Optimization for Training of Dialog Policy by Reinforcement Learning. In *Proceedings of the IEEE Workshop on Spoken Language Technology*, 1–6.

Raux, A. and Eskenazi, M. (2012). Optimizing the Turn-Taking Behavior of Task-Oriented Spoken Dialog Systems. *Transactions on Speech and Language Processing*, 9(1), 1–23.

Selfridge, E.O., Arizmendi, I., Heeman, P.A., and Williams, J.D. (2012). Integrating Incremental Speech Recognition and POMDP-based Dialogue Systems. In *Proceedings of the 13th Annual SIGDIAL Meeting on Discourse and Dialogue*, 275–279.

Shute, V.J. (2008). Focus on Formative Feedback. *Review of Educational Research*, 78(1), 153–189.

Singh, S., Litman, D., Kearns, M., and Walker, M. (2002). Optimizing Dialogue Management with Reinforcement Learning: Experiments with the NJFun System. *Journal of Artificial Intelligence Research*, 16, 105–133.

Sutton, R. and Barto, A. (1998). *Reinforcement Learning*. MIT Press, Cambridge, MA, 1998.

Tetreault, J.R. and Litman, D.J. (2008). A Reinforcement Learning Approach to Evaluating State Representations in Spoken Dialogue Systems. *Speech Communication*, 50(8), 683–696.

Williams, J.D. and Young, S. (2007). Partially Observable Markov Decision Processes for Spoken Dialog Systems. *Computer Speech & Language*, 21(2), 393–422.

Appendix A. Corpus excerpt

1. *Student begins declaring a String variable.*
2. *Student starts typing a message.*
3. **Student message:** Could I type in String The Adventure Quest; ? or would I need to put in quotes or something?
4. *Student resumes working on task.*
5. *Tutor starts typing a message.*
6. **Tutor message:** TheAdventureQuest is fine
7. *Student declares variable called* `The Adven-ture Quest` *(Incorrect Java syntax)*
8. *Tutor starts typing a message.*
9. *Student catches mistake and renames variable to* `TheAdventureQuest`
10. **Tutor message:** *Can't have spaces :)*
11. *Tutor starts typing a message*
12. **Tutor message:** Good job

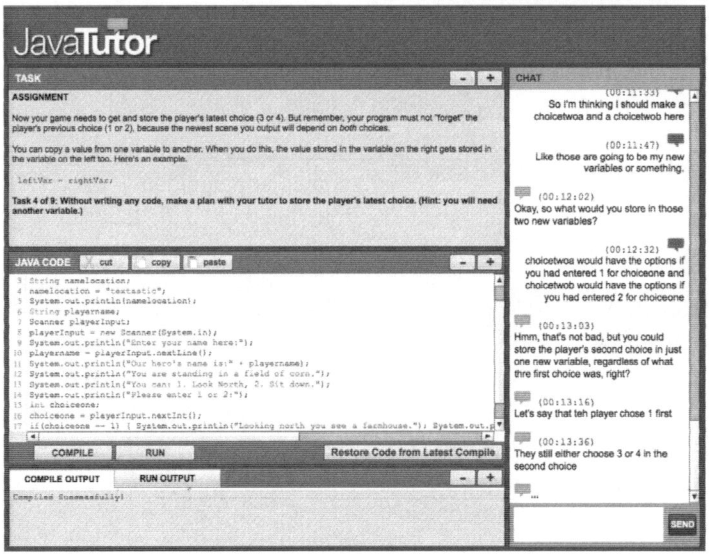

Appendix B. Dialogue interface

A Semi-supervised Approach for Natural Language Call Routing

Tatiana Gasanova
Institute of Communications Engineering, Ulm University, Germany
tatiana.gasanova@uni-ulm.de

Eugene Zhukov
Institute of Computer Science and Telecommunications, Siberian State Aerospace University, Russia
zhukov.krsk@gmail.com

Roman Sergienko
Institute of Computer Science and Telecommunications, Siberian State Aerospace University, Russia
romaserg@list.ru

Eugene Semenkin
Institute of Computer Science and Telecommunications, Siberian State Aerospace University, Russia
eugenesemenkin@yandex.com

Wolfgang Minker
Institute of Communications Engineering, Ulm University, Germany
wolfgang.minker@uni-ulm.de

Abstract

Natural Language call routing remains a complex and challenging research area in machine intelligence and language understanding. This paper is in the area of classifying user utterances into different categories. The focus is on design of algorithm that combines supervised and unsupervised learning models in order to improve classification quality. We have shown that the proposed approach is able to outperform existing methods on a large dataset and do not require morphological and stop-word filtering. In this paper we present a new formula for term relevance estimation, which is a modification of fuzzy rules relevance estimation for fuzzy classifier. Using this formula and only 300 frequent words for each class, we achieve an accuracy rate of 85.55% on the database excluding the "garbage" class (it includes utterances that cannot be assigned to any useful class or that can be assigned to more than one class). Dividing the "garbage" class into the set of subclasses by agglomerative hierarchical clustering we achieve about 9% improvement of accuracy rate on the whole database.

1 Introduction

Natural language call routing can be treated as an instance of topic categorization of documents (where the collection of labeled documents is used for training and the problem is to classify the remaining set of unlabeled test documents) but it also has some differences. For instance, in document classification there are much more terms in one object than in single utterance from call routing task, where even one-word utterances are common.

A number of works have recently been published on natural language call classification. B. Carpenter, J. Chu-Carroll, C.-H. Lee and H.-K. Kuo proposed approaches using a vector-based information retrieval technique, the algorithms designed by A. L. Gorin, G. Riccardi, and J. H. Wright use a probabilistic model with salient phrases. R. E. Schapire and Y. Singer focused on a boosting-based system for text categorization.

The most similar work has been done by A. Albalate, D. Suendermann, R. Pieraccini, A. Suchindranath, S. Rhinow, J. Liscombe, K. Dayanidhi, and W. Minker. They have worked on the data with the same structure: the focus was on the problem of big part of non-labeled data and only few labeled utterances for each class, methods of matching the obtained clusters and the given classes have also been considered; they provided the comparison of several classification methods that are able to perform on the large scale data.

The information retrieval approach for call routing is based on the training of the routing matrix, which is formed by statistics of appearances of words and phrases in a training set (usually after morphological and stop-word filtering). The new caller request is represented as a feature vector and is routed to the most similar destination vector. The most commonly used similarity criterion is the cosine similarity. The performance of systems, based on this approach, often depends on the quality of the destination vectors.

In this paper we propose a new term relevance estimation approach based on fuzzy rules relevance for fuzzy classifier (H. Ishibuchi, T. Nakashima, and T. Murata., 1999) to improve routing accuracy. We have also used a decision rule different from the cosine similarity. We assign relevancies to every destination (class), calculate the sums of relevancies of words from the current utterance and choose the destination with the highest sum.

The database for training and performance evaluation consists of about 300.000 user utterances recorded from caller interactions with commercial automated agents. The utterances were manually transcribed and classified into 20 classes (call reasons), such as *appointments*, *operator*, *bill*, *internet*, *phone* or *video*. Calls that cannot be routed certainly to one reason of the list are classified to class *_TE_NOMATCH.*

A significant part of the database (about 27%) consists of utterances from the "garbage" class (*_TE_NOMATCH*). Our proposed approach decomposes the routing task into two steps. On the first step we divide the "garbage" class into the set of subclasses by one of the clustering algorithms and on the second step we define the call reason considering the "garbage" subclasses as separate classes. We apply genetic algorithms with the whole numbers alphabet, vector quantization network and hierarchical agglomerative clustering in order to divide "garbage" class into subclasses. The reason to perform such a clustering is due to simplify the detection of the class with non-uniform structure.

Our approach uses the concept of salient phrases: for each call reason (class) only 300 words with the highest term relevancies are chosen. It allows us to eliminate the need for the stop and ignore word filtering. The algorithms are implemented in C++.

As a baseline for results comparison we have tested some popular classifiers from RapidMiner, which we have applied to the whole database and the database with decomposition.

This paper is organized as follows: In Section II, we describe the problem and how we perform the preprocessing. Section III describes in detail the way of the term relevance calculating and the possible rules of choosing the call class. In Section IV we present the clustering algorithms which we apply to simplify the "garbage" class detection. Section V reports on the experimental results. Finally, we provide concluding remarks in Section VI.

2 Problem Description and Data Preprocessing

The data for testing and evaluation consists of about 300.000 user utterances recorded from caller interactions with commercial automated agents. Utterances from this database are manually labeled by experts and divided into 20 classes (*_TE_NOMATCH, appointments, operator, bill, internet, phone* etc). Class *_TE_NOMATCH* includes utterances that cannot be put into another class or can be put into more than one class. The database is also unbalanced, some classes include much more utterances than others (the largest class *_TE_NOMATCH* includes 6790 utterances and the smallest one consists of only 48 utterances).

The initial database has been preprocessed to be a binary matrix with rows representing utterances and columns representing the words from the vocabulary. An element from this binary matrix, aij, equals to 1 if in utterance i the word j appears and equals to 0 if it does not appear.

Utterance duplicates were removed. The preprocessed database consisting of 24458 utterances was divided into train (22020 utterances, 90,032%) and test set (2438 utterances, 9,968%) such that the percentage of classes remained the same in both sets. The size of the dictionary of the whole database is 3464 words, 3294 words appear in training set, 1124 words appear in test set, 170 words which appear only in test set and do not appear in training set (unknown words), 33 utterances consisted of only unknown words, and 160 utterances included at least one unknown word.

3 Term Relevance Estimation

For each term we assign a real number term relevance that depends on the frequency in utterances. Term relevance is calculated using a modified formula of fuzzy rules relevance estimation for fuzzy classifier. Membership function has been replaced by word frequency in the current class. The details of the procedure are:

Let L be the number of classes; n_i is the number of utterances of the $_i$th class; N_{ij} is the number of

jth word occurrence in all utterances of the ith class; $T_{ji}=N_{ji}/n_i$ is the relative frequency of jth word occurrence in the ith class.
$R_j=max_i\ T_{ji}$, $S_j=arg(max_i\ T_{ji})$ is the number of class which we assign to jth word;
The term relevance, C_j, is given by

$$C_j = \frac{1}{\sum_{i=1}^{L} T_{ji}} (R_j - \frac{1}{L-1} \sum_{\substack{i=1 \\ i \neq S_j}}^{L} T_{ji}).$$

C_j is higher if the word occurs often in few classes than if it appears in many classes.
The learning phase consists of counting the C values for each term, it means that this algorithm uses the statistical information obtained from train set. We have tested several different decision rules defined in Table 1.

	Decision rules	
RC	$A_i = \sum_{j:S_j=i} R_j C_j$	For each class i we calculate A_i
RC max	$A_i = \sum_{j:S_j=i} \max R_j C_j$	Then we find the number of class which achieves maximum of A_i
C	$A_i = \sum_{j:S_j=i} C_j$	
C with limit	$A_i = \sum_{\substack{j:S_j=i \\ C_j>const}} C_j$	
R	$A_i = \sum_{j:S_j=i} R_j$	$winner = \arg(\max_i A_i)$

Table 1. Decision Rules

The best obtained accuracies is achieved with the decision rule C, where the destination is chosen that has the highest sum of word relevancies from the current utterance. In Table 2 we show the obtained results on the whole database and database without "garbage" class.

	Train	Test
With class "garbage"	0,614	0,551
Without class "garbage"	0,887	0,855

Table 2. Performance of the new TRE approach

4 Clustering methods

After the analysis of the performances of standard classification algorithms on the given database, we can conclude that there exists one specific class (class *_TE_NOMATCH*) where all standard techniques perform worse. Due to the non-uniform structure of the "garbage" class it is difficult to detect the whole class by the proposed procedure. If we apply this procedure directly we achieve only 55% of accuracy rate on the test data (61% on the train data). We suggest to divide the "garbage" class into the set of subclasses using one of the clustering methods and then recount the values of C_j taking into account that there are 19 well defined classes and that the set of the "garbage" subclasses can be consider as separate classes.
In this paper the following clustering methods are used: a genetic algorithm with integers, vector quantization networks trained by a genetic algorithm, hierarchical agglomerative clustering with different metrics.

4.1 Genetic Algorithm

The train set accuracy is used as a fitness function. Each individual is the sequence of nonnegative integer numbers (each number corresponds to the number of "garbage" subclass). The length of this sequence is the number of utterances from train set which belong to the "garbage" class.
We apply this genetic algorithm to find directly the optimal clustering using different numbers of clusters and we can conclude that with increasing the clusters number (in the "garbage" class) we get better classification accuracy on the whole database. We have used the following parameters of GA: population size = 50, number of generation = 50, weak mutation, tournament selection, uniform crossover, averaged by 50 runs. Applying this method we achieve about 7% improvement of accuracy rate on train data and about 5% on test data.

4.2 Vector Quantization Network

We have also implemented vector quantization network. For a given number of subclasses we search for the set of code vectors (the number of code vectors is equal to the number of subclasses). These code vectors are optimized using genetic algorithm where as a fitness function we use the classification quality on the train set. Each code vector corresponds to a certain "garbage" subclass. The object belongs to the subclass if the distance between it and the corresponding code vector is smaller than the distances between the object and all other code vectors. Applying this algorithm to the given database we obtain results similar to the results of the genetic algorithm.

4.3 Hierarchical Agglomerative Clustering

In this work we consider hierarchical agglomerative binary clustering where we set each utterance to one subclass and then we consequently group classes into pairs until there is only one class containing all utterances or until we achieve a certain number of classes. The performance of hierarchical clustering algorithms depends on the metric (the way to calculate the distance between objects) and the criterion for clusters union. In this work we use Hamming metric and Ward criterion (J. Ward. 1963).

5 Experimental results

The approach described above has been applied on the preprocessed corpus which has been provided by Speech Cycle company. We propose that only terms with highest value of RC (product of R and C) are contributed to the total sum. We have investigated the dependence of the new TRE approach on the frequent words number (Figure 1). The best accuracy rate was obtained with more than 300 frequent words. By using only limited set of words we eliminated the need of stop and ignore words filtering. This also shows that the method works better if utterance includes terms with high C values. This approach requires informative well-defined classes and enough data for statistical model.

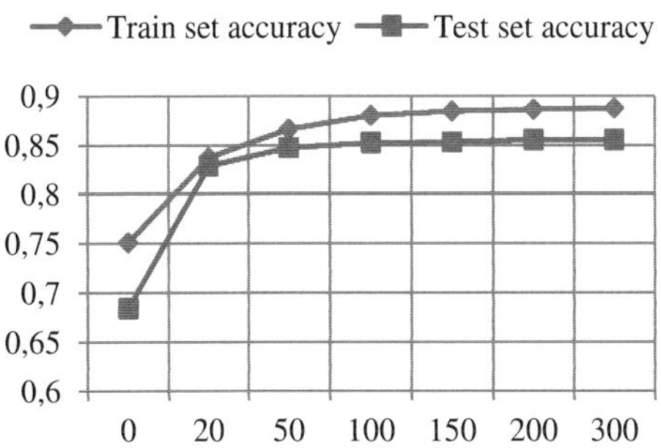

Figure 1. New TRE approach with different numbers of frequent words (x-axis: number of frequent words; y-axis: accuracy)

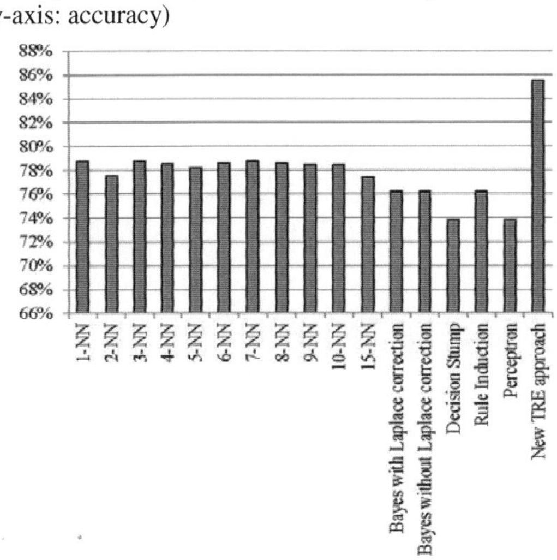

Figure 2. Overall accuracy

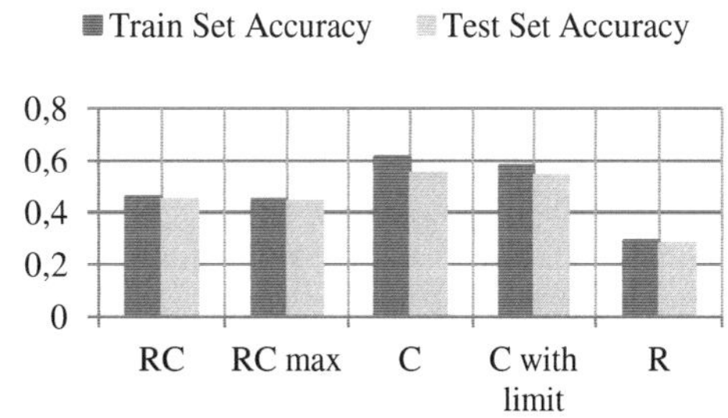

Figure 3. Comparison of decision rules (x-axis: decision rule; y-axis: accuracy)

We have tested standard classification algorithms (k-nearest neighbors algorithms, Bayes classifiers, Decision Stump, Rule Induction, perceptron) and the proposed approach on the database with "garbage" class and on the database without it (Figure 2). The proposed algorithm outperforms all other methods with has an accuracy rate of 85.55%. Figure 3 provides accuracies of different decision rules. Applying the proposed formula to the whole database we obtain 61% and 55% of classification quality on train and test data. We should also mention that the common tf.idf approach gives us on the given data 45% and 38% of accuracy rate on the train and test data. The proposed approach performs significantly better on this kind of data.

Using the agglomerative hierarchical clustering we achieve about 9% improvement. The best classification quality is obtained with 35 subclasses on the train data (68.7%) and 45 subclasses on the test data (63.9%). Clustering into 35 subclasses gives 63.7% of accuracy rate on the test data.

6 Conclusion

This paper reported on call classification experiments on large corpora using a new term relevance estimation approach. We propose to split the classification task into two steps: 1) clustering of the "garbage" class in order to simplify its detection; 2) further classification into meaningful classes and the set of "garbage" subclasses. The performance of the proposed algorithm is compared to several standard classification algorithms on the database without the "garbage" class and found to outperform them with the accuracy rate of 85.55%.

Dividing the "garbage" class into the set of subclasses by genetic algorithm and vector quantization network we obtain about 5% improvement of accuracy rate and by agglomerative hierarchical clustering we achieve about 9% improvement of accuracy rate on the whole database.

References

A. Albalate, D. Suendermann, R. Pieraccini, and W. Minker. 2009. *Mathematical Analysis of Evolution, Information, and Complexity*, Wiley, Hoboken, USA.

A. Albalate, D. Suendermann D., and W. Minker. 2011. *International Journal on Artificial Intelligence Tools*, 20(5).

A. Albalate, A. Suchindranath, D. Suendermann, and W. Minker. 2010. *Proc. of the Interspeech 2010, 11th Annual Conference of the International Speech Communication Association*, Makuhari, Japan.

A. Albalate, S. Rhinow, and D. Suendermann. 2010. *Proc. of the ICAART 2010, 2nd International Conference on Agents and Artificial Intelligence*, Valencia, Spain.

A.L. Gorin, G. Riccardi, and J. H. Wright. 1997. *Speech Commun.*, vol. 23, pp. 113–127.

B. Carpenter and J. Chu-Carroll. 1998. *Proc. ICSLP-98*, pp. 2059–2062.

C.-H. Lee, B. Carpenter, W. Chou, J. Chu-Carroll, W. Reichl, A. Saad, and Q. Zhou. 2000. *Speech Commun.*, vol. 31, no. 4, pp. 309–320.

D. Suendermann, J. Liscombe, K. Dayanidhi, and R. Pieraccini. 2009. *Proc. of the SIGDIAL 2009*, London, UK.

H. Ishibuchi, T. Nakashima, and T. Murata. 1999. *Trans. on Systems, Man, and Cybernetics*, vol. 29, pp. 601-618.

H.-K. Kuo and C.-H. Lee. 2000. *Proc. of ICSLP'00.*

J. Chu-Carroll and B. Carpenter. 1999. *Comput. Linguist.*, vol. 25, no. 3, pp. 361- 388.

J. Ward. 1963. *Journal of the American Statistical Association*, 58 (301): 236-244.

J. H. Wright, A. L. Gorin, and G. Riccardi. 1997. *Proc. Eurospeech-97*, pp. 1419–1422.

K. Evanini, D. Suendermann, and R. Pieraccini. 2007. *Proc. of the ASRU 2007*, Kyoto, Japan.

R. E. Schapire and Y. Singer. 2000. *Mach. Learn.*, vol. 39, no. 2/3, pp. 135–168.

Counseling Dialog System with 5W1H Extraction

Sangdo Han, Kyusong Lee, Donghyeon Lee, Gary Geunbae Lee
Department of Computer Science and Engineering, POSTECH, South Korea
{hansd,kyusonglee,semko,gblee}@postech.ac.kr

Abstract

In this paper, we introduce our counseling dialog system. Our system interacts with users by recognizing what the users say, predicting the context, and following the users' feelings. For this interaction, our system follows three basic counseling techniques: paraphrasing, asking open questions, and reflecting feelings. To follow counseling techniques, we extracted 5W1H information and user emotions from user utterances, and we generated system utterances while using the counseling techniques. We used the conditional random field algorithm to extract 5W1H information, and constructed our counseling algorithm using a dialog strategy that was based on counseling techniques. A total of 16 adults tested our system and rated it with a higher score as an interactive communicator compared with the baseline system.

1 Introduction

Over the past 45 years, suicide rates have increased by 60% worldwide.[1] To prevent suicide, suicide people need to counsel with counselors. However, counseling with a human counselor requires a substantial cost, and in addition, there is a location restriction. Developing a counseling dialog system could be an effective solution to address this problem because the system has no limitations with respect to time and location.

In this study, we present a counseling dialog system. The system interacts with users by recognizing what the users say, predicting the context, and following the users' feelings. We used three counseling techniques for our system, to interact with the users. The system performs paraphrasing, asks open questions, and reflects feelings.

Paraphrasing is a technique that paraphrases user utterances. For example, when a user utterance is "My dog picked up the ball", then it could be paraphrased by "Oh, your dog picked up the ball". The technique of asking open questions is to ask some questions to the user, to obtain more information. For example, when a user says "I played computer games", then the counselor could say "When did you play?" or "Where did you play?". Finally, reflecting a feeling is a similar technique to paraphrasing, but it includes emotional comments. For example, when a user says "My dog died. I'm so sad", then the counselor could say, "Oh, your dog died. You look depressed." or "You look so sad".

In our approach, we extract 5W1H (who, what, when, where, why, how) information and four basic emotions (happy, afraid, sad, and angry) from user utterances. We generate system utterances using 5W1H information and basic emotions.

2 Counseling Techniques

Counselors show empathy with clients by listening and understanding them. Clients feel comfortable by a counselor's attention. Counselors listen, ask questions, answer questions, and concentrate on clients. Attention and empathy is important for counseling. Counselors show interest and care about the clients' emotions. Our counseling dialog system also focused on attending and empathy.

Many counseling techniques are used in counseling. Basic attending, self-expression, and micro-training skills are introduced in Theron et al. (2008). Basic attending and self-expression skills are about non-verbal behavior, such as tone of voice and eye contact. Micro-training skills are the basic verbal counseling techniques that are learned for counseling beginners: open and closed questions, minimal encouragement, paraphrasing, reflection of feelings and summarization.

1 http://www.who.int/mental_health/prevention/suicide/suicideprevent/en/

We chose three micro-training skills to attend and show empathy with clients. These skills are open questions, paraphrasing, and reflection of feelings because they are basic techniques to show emphasize effectively.

3 Related Work

The SEMAINE project aims to build a Sensitive Artificial Listeners (SAL) – conversational agents that are designed to interact with a human user through robust recognition and the generation of non-verbal behavior (Schröder et al., 2008). This system detects user emotions by multimodal sensors (camera, microphone). A virtual face in this system shows facial expressions based on user emotions, and it encourages the user to speak by reacting and asking questions. These techniques could show empathy with users. However, it has limited verbal skills because SEMAINE does not have language understanding module. In our research, our system follows user utterances and generates system utterances based on user's 5W1H.

4 Data Collection

We generated 4,284 utterances by using fifty-three 5W1H information sets and four basic emotions (Figure 1). Each utterance could be generated by using part of the 5W1H information and four emotions.

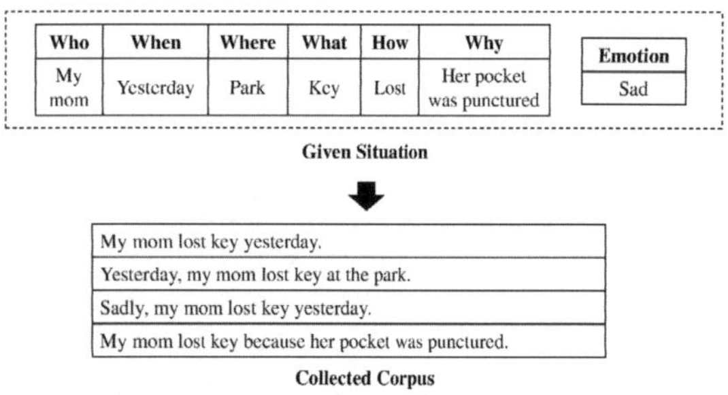

Figure 1. Counseling Corpus Collecting Process

We tagged each 5W1H element in each utterance and the user intention for each utterance (Table 1). The system's actions were labeled by following counseling strategies which will be discussed in section 5.3.

Tagged Corpus	User Intention	System Action
<who>My mom</who> <how>lost</how> <what>a key</what> <when>yesterday</when>.	Inform_5W1H	Ask_Open_Question
<when>Yesterday</when>, <who>my mom</who> <how>lost</how> <what>a key</what> at the <where>park</where>.	Inform_5W1H	Paraphrase
<who>My mom</who> <how>lost</how> <what>a key</what> <when>yesterday</when>. I'm so sad.	Inform_5W1H_ Emotion	Reflect_Feeling
I'm so sad.	Inform_Emotion	Reflect_Feeling
Thank you.	Thank	Welcome
Good bye.	Bye	Bye

Table 1. Corpus Tagging Examples

User intentions we defined can be separated in two groups: 'counseling' and 'others'. Utterances in 'counseling' group include 5W1H information or emotional information. Utterances which do not including them are in 'others' group. Greetings, thanks, and farewells are included (Table 2).

Counseling group	Others group
Inform_5W1H, Inform_emotion, Inform_5W1H_emotion, ...	Thank, Bye, Greeting, Agree, Disagree, ...

Table 2. Two Separated Groups of User Intentions.

5 Method

5.1 Architecture

Our system architecture is given in graph 2. When a user inputs a sentence, a natural language understanding (NLU) module understands the main action (the user's intention) and extracts the 5W1H entities from the user's utterance. The emotion detection module detects the user's emotions using the emotional keyword dictionary. The dialog management module decides the system's action from the main action and the 5W1H information from the trained module from the example dialog corpus. The natural language generation (NLG) module generates the system utterance using a system utterance template. We can generate the system utterance by replacing 5W1H slots with entities.

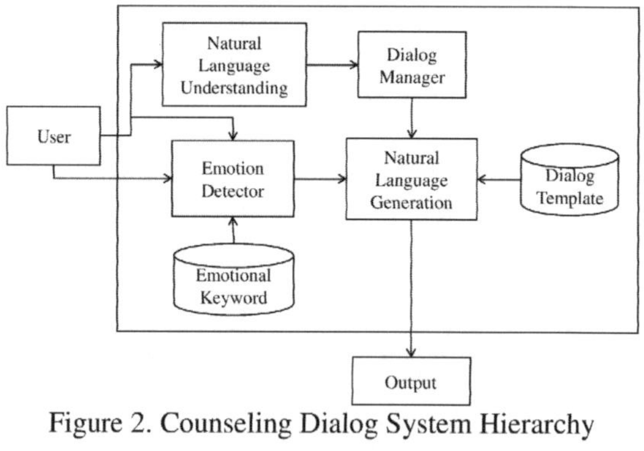

Figure 2. Counseling Dialog System Hierarchy

5.2 Natural Language Understanding

In our approach, the NLU module understands the user utterance by classifying the main action and the 5W1H entities from the user utterance. To classify user intention, we used maximum entropy model (Ratnaparkhi, 1998) trained on a linguistically motivated features. We used a lexical word features for the utterance model. The lexical word features are lexical trigrams using previous, current, and next lexical words. To extract 5W1H entities, we used a conditional random field (CRF) model (Laffery et al., 2001). We also used lexical word features (lexical trigrams) to train model.

5.3 Dialog Management with Counseling Strategy

When we extract 5W1H information or user emotions, the dialog management module keeps them in the emotion slot or in the six 5W1H slots. This slot information is discussed in a dialog.

The dialog management module decides the system's action by the main action, the 5W1H entities, and the user's emotions. Dialog management follows the rules in figure 3, which is our dialog strategy for the counseling system. In figure 3, 'Counseling group?' node finds users intentions included in 'others group' (rejection or thanks could be included). The 'User Emotion Detection' node figures out whether the user utterance is to include emotional keywords or whether the user emotion is already known by the discourse. The '6 slot empty' node checks whether the user utterance includes at least one of the 5W1H elements or whether the 5W1H entity is already known. The '6 slot full' node decides whether the user utterance with a discourse has all six 5W1H entries. From this strategy, we can notice that we cannot reflect a user's feeling without the user's emotion. We cannot ask open questions when all of the 5W1H slots are filled.

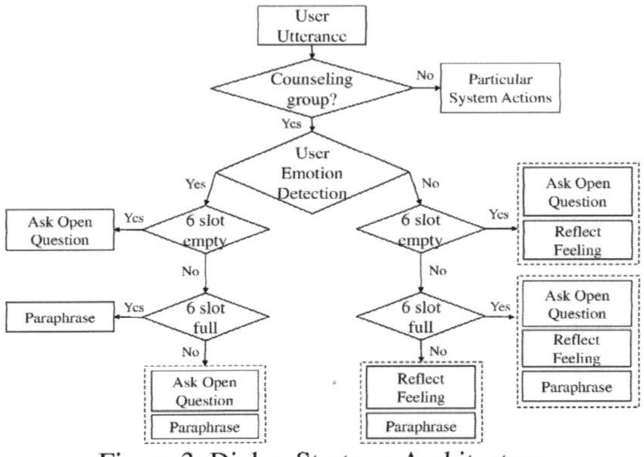

Figure 3. Dialog Strategy Architecture

5.4 Emotion Detection

The emotion detection module decides the user's emotion with respect to the four basic emotions. To detect the user's emotions, we find emotional keywords in the user's utterances. If any emotional keyword appears in a user utterance, we decide that the user's emotion which includes that keyword. For this approach, we made a dictionary of emotional keywords for each basic emotion. The dictionary has approximately 15 emotional keywords for each basic emotion (Table 3).

Emotion	Keywords
Happy	happy, joy, glad, pleasure, ...
Sad	sad, depress, grief, sorrow, ...
Angry	anger, rage, indignation, wrath, ...
Afraid	afraid, fear, terror, dread, ...

Table 3. Emotional Keywords for Emotions

5.5 Natural Language Generation

The NLG module generates the system's utterances by selecting an utterance template from the template database. There are various system templates for each system action, for the 5W1H slot entities, and for the user's emotions (Figure 4). When the system template is chosen, we can generate system utterances by replacing the 5W1H slot with a 5W1H discourse. 'O' means we should have the entity, 'X' means we do not have the entity, and '*' means we do not care whether we have the entity or not.

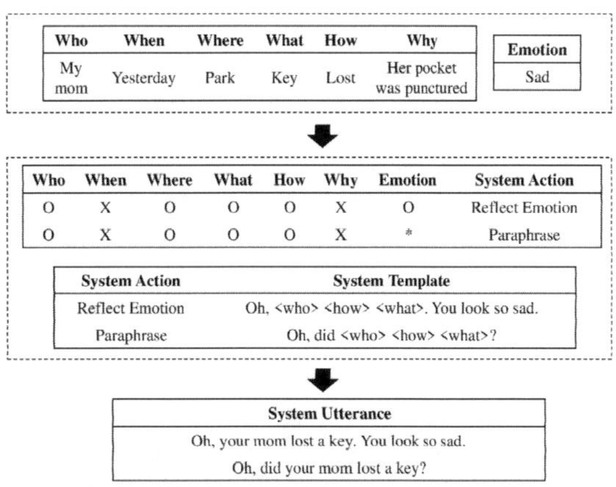

Figure 4. System Utterance Generation

Our overall counseling dialog example is shown in (Table 4).

User	My mom lost a key yesterday.
System	Oh, where did you mom lost a key?
User	At the park.
System	Your mom lost a key at the park, right?
User	Yes, that's right. I'm so sad.
System	You look so sad. Cheer up.
User	Thank you.
System	My pleasure.

Table 4. Counseling Dialog Example

6 Experiment

We measured how systems show empathy with users. Our baseline system is a Korean chat-oriented dialog system (Kim et al., 2012). The chat-oriented dialog system shows empathy by understanding user utterances and making a conversation. In our experiment, 7 basic situations are given for each person. Situations are explained by 5W1H, and users generated various utterances using that information. Each person generated approximately 100 utterances during 30 minutes and made estimates for each system. We recruited 16 volunteers to use our system and to estimate its effectiveness. Each user checked 17 questions from 1 to 10. The questions ask users how does each system understand the user utterance, is it appropriate for counseling, and does it satisfy the users (Table 5).

Question	Chat-Oriented	Counseling
1-1. The system used counseling techniques: paraphrasing, open question, reflect feeling.	3.50	7.06
1-2. The system knows my emotion.	3.44	6.88
1-3. There was no break in the conversation.	2.63	6.88
1-4. The system acts like a counselor.	2.88	6.69
1-5. The system shows empathy with me.	4.69	7.31
1-6. I feel the system understands me.	2.56	6.50
2-1. The system understands what I said.	2.88	6.81
2-2. The system understands 5W1H information.	4.13	7.44
2-3. System utterances are appropriate.	2.75	6.94
2-4. System utterances have no problem.	3.50	5.50
3-1. I could speak about various situations.	4.31	6.38
3-2. I had a casual conversation.	4.75	6.88
3-3. Scenarios look expandable.	5.50	7.63
4-1. I satisfied overall conversation.	3.10	6.56
4-2. I satisfied overall counseling.	2.38	6.56
4-3. The system looks appropriate as a counselor.	2.50	6.38
4-4. I'll recommend the system as a counselor to my friends.	2.31	5.38
Mean	3.40	6.69
Standard Deviation	0.96	0.59

Table 5. Experiment Results

Questions 1-1 to 1-6 ask users how each system is appropriate as a counselor. Counseling system rated 6.89 for mean. Questions 2-1 to 2-4 are about users' utterances understandability. In these questions, counseling system rated 6.67 on the average. Questions 3-1 to 3-3 show how various dialogs covered. Our system got 6.96 for mean. Finally, questions 4-1 to 4-4 are about overall satisfaction. These questions rated 6.22 for mean. Our p-value through t-test was $3.77*10^{-11}$.

Counseling system got higher score than chat-oriented system because users felt empathy better with our system than baseline system. As a counselor, counseling system is much better than chat-oriented system. Our baseline system was not appropriate as a counselor because it rated 3.39 for average. However, our system scored over 6.5 overall. It means our system is valuable as a counselor.

7 Conclusion

In this study, we introduced counseling techniques that we used to implement counseling dialog system. The experimental results showed that our system shows empathy with users. Although the results of this study bring us a step closer to implementing counseling dialog system, the results are only valid with 5W1H information in Korean. Our future works are to improve our counseling dialog system using new NLU module which extracts 5W1H information from more general utterances, with new emotion detection method, and with more counseling techniques.

Acknowledgments

This research was supported by the Basic Science Research Program through the National Research Foundation of Korea(NRF) funded by the Ministry of Education, Science and Technology(2012-0008835).

This research was supported by the MSIP(Ministry of Science, ICT&Future Planning), Korea, under the ITRC(Information Technology Research Center) support program supervised by the NIPA(National IT Industry Promotion Agency) (NIPA-2013-H0301-13-3002)

References

Kim, Y., Noh, H., & Lee, G. G. (2012). Dialog management on chatting system based on lexico-syntactic patterns and named entity types. *Proceedings of Spring Conference of Korean Society of Speech Sciences,* 41-42, Seoul, Korea.

Lafferty, J., McCallum, A., & Pereira, F. (2001). Conditional random fields: Probabilistic models for segmenting and labeling sequence data. *Proceedings of the 18th International Conference on Machine Learning*, 282-289.

Ratnaparkhi, A. (1998). Maximum entropy models for natural language ambiguity resolution. *Computer and Information Science,* University of Pennsylvania, Philadelphia, USA.

Schröder, M., Cowie, R., Heylen, D., Pantic, M., Pelachaud, C., & Shuller, B. (2008). Towards responsive sensitive artificial listeners. *Workshop on Human-Computer Conversation*, Bellagio, Italy.

Theron, M. J. (2008). A manual for basic relational skills training in psychotherapy. *Masters of Arts in Clinical Psychology,* University of South Africa, South Africa.

Integration and test environment for an in-vehicle dialogue system in the SIMSI project

Staffan Larsson, Sebastian Berlin
University of Gothenburg
Box 200
SE-405 30 Gothenburg
Sweden
sl@ling.gu.se
sebastian.berlin@gu.se

Anders Eliasson
Mecel AB
Box 140 44
SE-400 20 Gothenburg
Sweden
anders.eliasson@mecel.se

Fredrik Kronlid
Talkamatic AB
Första långgatan 18
SE-413 28 Gothenburg
Sweden
fredrik@talkamatic.se

Abstract

The goal of the SIMSI (Safe In-vehicle Multimodal Speech Interaction) project is threefold. Firstly, to integrate a dialogue system for menu-based dialogue with a GUI-driven in-vehicle infotainment system. Secondly, to further improve the integrated system with respect to driver distraction, thus making the system safer to use while driving. Thirdly, to verify that the resulting system decreases visual distraction and cognitive load during interaction. This demo paper describes the integration of the two existing systems, and the test environment designed to enable evaluation of the system.

1 Background

1.1 Driver distraction and safety

Driver distraction is one common cause of accidents, and is often caused by the driver interacting with technologies such as mobile phones, media players or navigation systems. The so-called 100-car study (Neale et al., 2005) revealed that secondary task distraction is the largest cause of driver inattention, and that the handling of wireless devices is the most common secondary task. The goal of SIMSI is to design systems which enable safe interaction with technologies in vehicles, by reducing the cognitive load imposed by the interaction and minimizing head-down time.

1.2 The Talkamatic Dialogue Manager

Based on Larsson (2002) and later work, Talkamatic AB has developed the Talkamatic Dialogue Manager (TDM) with the goal of being the most competent and usable dialogue manager on the market, both from the perspective of the user and from the perspective of the HMI developer. TDM provides a general interaction model founded in human interaction patterns, resulting in a high degree of naturalness and flexibility which increases usability. Also, TDM reduces complexity for developers and users, helping them to reach their goals faster and at a lower cost.

A major problem with the current state-of-the-art in-vehicle spoken dialogue systems is that they are either too simplistic to be useful to the end user, or alternatively that they are fairly sophisticated but unmanageable for the manufacturer due to the size and complexity of the implementation. TDM offers sophisticated multi-modal interaction management solutions which allow for easy modification and development, allowing interaction designers to easily explore new solutions and reducing overhead for new dialogue applications in terms of code and development man-hours.

TDM deals with several interaction patterns which are basic to human-human linguistic interaction, and offers truly integrated multimodality which allows user to freely switch between (or combine) modalities. All these solutions are domain-independent which means that they need not be implemented in each application. Using Talkamatic technology, dialogue behaviour can be altered without touching application properties, and application properties can be updated without touching the dialogue logic. This makes testing of different dialogue strategies, prompts etc. considerably quicker and easier than when using regular state-machine-based dialogue systems.

In addition, as the dialogue strategy is separated from the application logic, development time for new dialogue applications can be significantly reduced. Furthermore, the developer designing the application does not need to be a dialogue expert as the dialogue design is built into the dialogue manager.

1.3 Integrated multimodality in TDM

There are reasons to believe that multi-modal interaction is more efficient and less distracting than uni-modal interaction (Oviatt et al., 2004). TDM supports multi-modal interaction where voice output and input (VUI) is combined with a traditional menu-based GUI with graphical output and haptic input. In cases where a GUI already exists, TDM can replace the GUI-internal interaction engine, thus adding speech while keeping the original GUI design. All system output is realized both verbally and graphically, and the user can switch freely between uni-modal (voice or screen/keys) and multi-modal interaction.

To facilitate the browsing of lists (a well known interaction problem for dialogue systems), Talkamatic has developed its Voice-Cursor technology[1] (Larsson et al., 2011). It allows a user to browse a list in a multi-modal dialogue system without looking at a screen and without being exposed to large chunks of readout information.

A crucial property of TDM's integrated multimodality is the fact that it enables the driver of a vehicle to carry out all interactions without ever looking at the screen, either by speaking to the system, by providing haptic input, or by combining the two. We are not aware of any current multimodal in-vehicle dialogue system offering this capability. Additional information is available at `www.talkamatic.se`.

1.4 Mecel Populus

While TDM offers full menu-based multimodal interaction, the GUI itself is fairly basic and does not match the state of the art when it comes to graphical design. By contrast, Mecel Populus is an commercial-grade HMI (Human Machine Interface) with professionally designed visual output. The Mecel Populus suite is a complete tool chain for designing, developing and deploying user interfaces for distributed embedded systems. It minimizes the time and cost of producing eye-catching, full-featured HMIs.

The Mecel Populus concept has several unique features compared to traditional HMI development. These features, when combined, remove the barriers that traditionally exist between the people working with requirements, system engineering, HMI design and implementation. An HMI is created and verified in Mecel Populus Editor without having to write any software. The HMI is then downloaded to the target environment where Mecel Populus Engine executes it. Mecel Populus has been designed for the automotive industry to deliver high performance user interfaces with a short time-to-market and to enable efficient software life cycle management. Additional information is available at `www.mecel.se/products`.

[1] Patent Pending

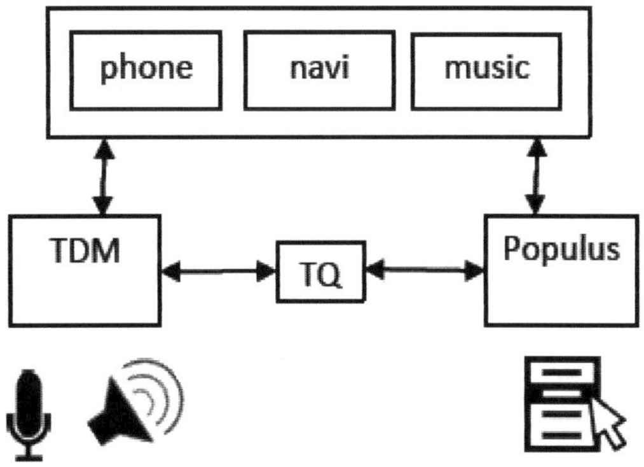

Figure 1: SIMSI system overview

2 System integration

The goal of this part of SIMSI is to provide a project-specific integration of TDM and the Mecel Populus platform. In this way, we establish a commercial-grade HMI for experiments and demonstrations. At the same time, the integration of TDM and Populus increases the commercial potential of both platforms, since it integrates a state-of-the-art HMI tool without voice capabilities and a dialogue manager with limited graphical capabilities.

The major problem in integrating Populus and TDM is that both systems keep track of the current state of the interaction and manage transitions between states resulting from user or system actions. Hence, there is a need to keep the systems in sync at all times. This is managed by a Transition Queue (TQ) module which keeps a lock which can be grabbed by either system at any time, unless it has already been grabbed by the other system. The systems then enter into a master-slave relation where the master is the system which owns the lock. The master tells the slave how the interaction state is to be updated, and the slave only waits for messages from the master until the lock has been returned to the TQ.

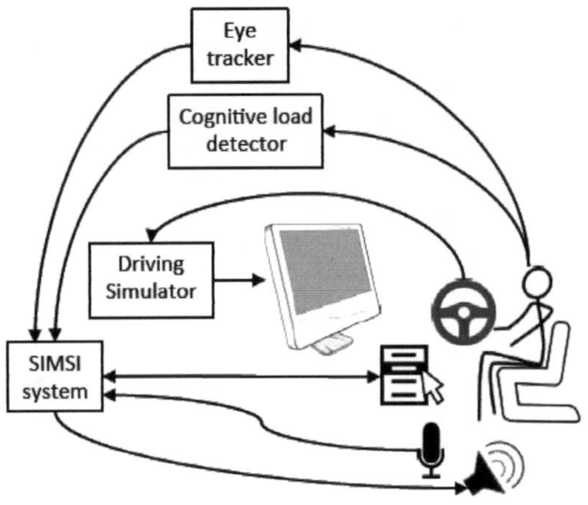

Figure 2: SIMSI test environment overview

Figure 3: SIMSI test environment in action

3 Test environment

The purpose of this part of the project is to conduct ecologically valid test of the applications, and to begin and continue an iterative development cycle of testing - evaluation - development. We want to find the best interaction solutions in cases where it is not intuitively clear what is best. This involves implementing variants of a behaviour, testing them on naive users, collecting data from these interactions, and establishing statistically significant results based on the collected data.

The test environment consists of two parts, apart from the dialogue system: a driving simulator (SCANeR from Octal) and an eye tracker (Smart Eye Pro from Smarteye). In later tests we will also include instruments for measuring cognitive load.

In our setup we have three monitors, giving the user a wide field of view. We also have a gaming steering wheel, including pedals, gear lever and a driver's seat. These are used mainly to control the driving simulator, but there are also a number of buttons on the steering wheel which are used to browse the menus in the HMI and as Push-to-talk (PTT). An Android tablet (Asus Eee Pad Transformer TF101) showing the HMI GUI is placed in front of the user, trying to match the position of a display in a car. Both TDM and Populus run on the same desktop computer as the driving simulator, and a Populus Android app runs on the tablet. The app allows the user to select items by tapping them, as well as scrolling in lists in normal smart phone fashion. The eye tracker runs on a separate desktop computer, as it requires a substantial amount of processing power.

Studio software that comes with the driving simulator is used to design and run scenarios. The scenarios govern how autonomous traffic should behave and events, such as weather change and the state of traffic signals. The simulator logs data for the environment and each vehicle. Data like lane deviation (where in the lane the vehicle is) and how the user handles instruments, e.g. steering wheel and pedals, can be used to measure cognitive load. At a later stage this kind of data can also be used to trigger behaviour in the dialogue system.

The eye tracker uses three cameras to track the user's eyes and head at 60 Hz. The cameras are spaced to give good tracking in the middle of the scene, where you typically look when you're driving, and at the same time capture head movement to the side. As we are interested in when the user is looking at the tablet, we placed one of the cameras specifically to improve eye tracking in this area.

References

Staffan Larsson, Alexander Berman, and Jessica Villing. 2011. Adding a speech cursor to a multimodal dialogue system. In *INTERSPEECH 2011, 12th Annual Conference of the International Speech Communication Association, Florence, Italy, 2011*, pages 3319–3320.

Staffan Larsson. 2002. *Issue-based Dialogue Management.* Ph.D. thesis, Göteborg University.

Vicki L. Neale, Thomas A. Dingus, Sheila G. Klauer, Jeremy Sudweeks, and Michael Goodman. 2005. An overview of the 100-car naturalistic study and findings.

Sharon L. Oviatt, Rachel Coulston, and Rebecca Lunsford. 2004. When do we interact multimodally?: cognitive load and multimodal communication patterns. In *ICMI*, pages 129–136.

Weakly and Strongly Constrained Dialogues for Language Learning

Claire Gardent
CNRS/LORIA, Nancy
claire.gardent@loria.fr

Alejandra Lorenzo
Université de Lorraine
LORIA, Nancy
alejandra.lorenzo@loria.fr

Laura Perez-Beltrachini
KRDB Research Centre
FUB, Bolzano
laura.perez@loria.fr

Lina Rojas-Barahona
Université de Lorraine
LORIA, Nancy
lina.rojas@loria.fr

Abstract

We present two dialogue systems for language learning which both restrict the dialog to a specific domain thereby promoting robustness and the learning of a given vocabulary. The systems vary in how much they constrain the learner's answer : one system places no other constrain on the learner than that provided by the restricted domain and the dialog context ; the other provides the learner with an exercise whose solution is the expected answer. The first system uses supervised learning for simulating a human tutor whilst the second one uses natural language generation techniques to produce grammar exercises which guide the learner toward the expected answer.

1 Introduction

Work on dialog based tutors for language learning includes both chatbot systems which maintain a free flowing dialog with the learner (Shawar and Atwell, 2007; Jia, 2004) and form-focused dialog systems which restrict the learner answer e.g., by providing her with an answer template to be filled in for the dialog to continue (Wilske and Wolska, 2011). While the former encourages language practice with a virtual tutor and requires a good knowledge of the language, the latter focuses on linguistic forms and usually covers a more restricted lexical field thereby being more amenable to less advanced learners.

In these notes, we describe a dialog architecture which (i) supports both free-flowing and form-focused man/machine dialog ; and (ii) ensures that in both cases, dialogs are restricted to a specific lexical field. The free-flowing dialog system uses supervised classification techniques to predict the system dialog move based on the learner's input and does not explicitely constrain the learner's answer. In contrast, the dialog system for intermediate learners provides an exercise which the learner must solve to construct her answer.

To restrict the dialog to a specific domain and to improve system robustness, we make use of a finite-state automaton (FSA) describing the range of permissible interactions within a given domain. This FSA serves to guide the collection of human-human interactions necessary to train the classifier ; to verify and if necessary to adjust the system's predicted answer ; and to support the generation of the exercise provided in the form-focused dialog engine.

2 Finite State Automaton and Domain Representation

To support focused dialog and promote robustness, we make use of the FSA depicted in Figure 2. This FSA models a generic sequence of (System Question, Learner Answer, System Reaction) turns instantiating 4 main question/answer patterns and two possible system reactions.

The system question systematically formulates a question which explicitly lists a set of possible answers.

The learner's answer is then classified into four main types. It selects one of the proposed answers ; it chooses another alternative not mentioned in the system's question ; it indicates that the learner does not know the correct answer or does not understand the question ; or it meets neither of these categories.

Finally, for each answer, the system can continue the dialogue by making a "confirmation" which is used to reassure the learner in the free dialogue system and to provide some feedback in the guided dialogue system ; or just by "informing" to the learner of the correct answer before getting into the next question.

Given a specific domain, this generic FSA is

```
>S:Welcome to my house!, I'm the cat. Do you want
to play with me?   || ask(ready)
>L:Ok.      || answer(ready)
>S:Great! How are you doing? || ask(health)
>L: I'm doing very well, thanks!
|| answer(health, pref-option)
>S: Awesome!  || confirm(health,pref-option)
>S: Come! I want to show you the kitchen!
|| inform(health)
>S:In the kitchen we prepare lunch. I prepare
soup very often. Do you prefer soup or salad?
|| ask(pref-meal)
>L:I prefer salad.
|| answer(pref-meal,pref-option)
>S:So do I! || confirm(pref-meal,pref-option)
>S:I also love cheese. || inform(pref-meal)
>S:Where do we usually keep the cheese?
|| ask(cheese where)
>L:In the fridge || answer(cheese where,pref-option)
>S:You are right || confirm(cheese where,pref-option)
>S:In the fridge || inform(cheese where)
...
>S:Thanks for this little chat! See you soon
|| quit
```

FIGURE 1 – Example of a dialog (translated from French to English)

instantiated differently for each question/answer pair making up a dialog. In particular, in the current demonstration system, it is instantiated to model a dialog situated in the kitchen of a virtual world. Figure 1 shows an example dialog.

3 Situated Dialogues for language learning

Our dialog systems for language learning are integrated in a serious game called I-FLEG (Interactive French Learning Game, (Amoia et al., 2012)) in which the learner can trigger grammar exercices and interactive dialog sessions by clicking on the objects present in the virtual world.

IFLEG integrates the two dialog systems for language learning mentioned above namely, a "free answer dialog system" where the learner answer is guided only by the preceding dialog exchanges ; and a "guided dialog system" which restricts the set of permissible answers by providing the learner with an exercise whose solution provides a possible answer given the current dialog context.

3.1 Data collection

To provide the training data necessary to train the free dialog system, we conducted a Wizard-of-Oz experiment where language learners were invited to engage in a conversation with the wizard, a French tutor. In these experiments, we followed the methodology and used the tools for data collection and annotation presented in (Rojas-Barahona et al., 2012a). Given an FSA specifiying a set of 5 questions the learner had to answer, the wizard guided the learner through the dialog using this FSA. The resulting corpus consists of 52 dialogues and 1906 sentences.

3.2 Free answer Dialogue System

The free answer dialogue system simulates the behavior of the wizard tutor by means of a Logistic-Regression classifier, the FSA and a generation-by-selection algorithm. The system first uses the FSA to determine the next question to be asked. Then for each question, the Logistic-Regression classifier is used to map the learner answer to a system dialog act. At this stage, the FSA is used again, in two different ways. First, it is used to ensure that the predicted system dialog act is consistent with the states in the FSA. In case of a mismatch, a valid dialog act is selected in the current context. In particular, unpredicted "preferred options" and "do not know" learner answers are detected using keyword spotting methods. If the classifier prediction conflicts with the prediction made by key word spotting, it is ignored and the FSA transition is prefereed.

Second, since the system has several consecutive turns, and given that the classifier only predicts the next one, the FSA is used to determine the following system dialog acts sequence. For instance, if the predicted next system dialog act was "confirm", according to the FSA the following system dialog act is "inform" and then eiher the next question encoded in the FSA or "quit".

Training the simulator To train the classifier, we labeled each learner sentence with the dialog act caracterising the next system act. The features used for trainig included *context features* (namely, the four previous system dialogue acts) and the set of *content words* present in the learner turns after filtering using tf*idf (Rojas Barahona et al., 2012b). Given the learner input and the current dialog context, the classifier predicts the next system move.

Generation by Selection Given the system move predicted by the dialog manager, the system turn is produced by randomly selecting from the training corpus an utterance annotated with that dialog move.

3.3 Guided dialogue system

Unlike the free answer dialogue, the guided dialogue strongly constrains the learner answer by suggesting it in the form of a grammar exercise.

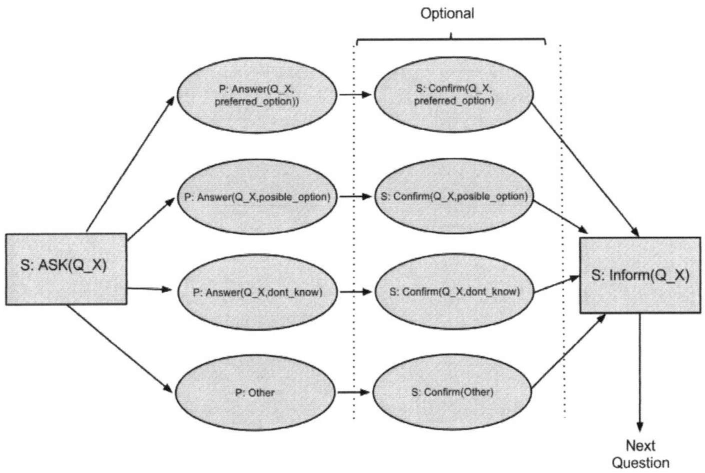

FIGURE 2 – Finite-state automata that defines the different states in the dialog for each question Q_X. S defines the system, and P the learner.

In the guided dialogue system, the dialogue paths contained in the training corpus are used to decide on the next dialogue move. In a first step, learner's moves are labelled with the meaning representation associated to them by the grammar underlying the natural language generator used to produce IFLEG grammar exercises. Given a sequence S/L contained in the training corpus with S, a system turn and L the corresponding learner's turn, the system then constructs the exercise providing the learner's answer using the methodology described in (Perez-Beltrachini et al., 2012). First, a sentence is generated from the meaning representation of the learner answer. Next, the linguistic information (syntactic tree, morpho-syntactic information, lemmas) associated by the generator with the generated sentence is used to build a shuffle, a fill-in-the-blank or a transformation exercise. Here is an example interaction produced by the system :

S : Vous préférez la soupe ou le fromage ? (*Do you prefer soup or salad ?*)
Please answer using the following words : { je, adorer, le, soupe }

This dialogue setting has several benefits. The dialogue script provides a rich context for each generated exercise item, learners are exposed to example communicative interactions, and the system can provide feedback by comparing the answer entered by the learner against the expected one.

4 Sample Dialogue

In this demo, the user will be able to interact with both dialogue systems, situated in the kitchen of a virtual world, and where the tutor prompts the learner with questions about meals, drinks, and various kitchen related activities such as floor cleaning and food preferences.

References

M. Amoia, T. Brétaudière, A. Denis, C. Gardent, and L. Perez-Beltrachini. 2012. A Serious Game for Second Language Acquisition in a Virtual Environment. *Journal on Systemics, Cybernetics and Informatics (JSCI)*, 10(1) :24–34.

J. Jia. 2004. The study of the application of a web-based chatbot system on the teaching of foreign languages. In *Society for Information Technology & Teacher Education International Conference*, volume 2004, pages 1201–1207.

L. Perez-Beltrachini, C. Gardent, and G. Kruszewski. 2012. Generating Grammar Exercises. In *NAACL-HLT 7th Workshop on Innovative Use of NLP for Building Educational Applications*, Montreal, Canada, June.

L. M. Rojas-Barahona, A. Lorenzo, and C. Gardent. 2012a. Building and exploiting a corpus of dialog interactions between french speaking virtual and human agents. In *Proceedings of the 8th International Conference on Language Resources and Evaluation*.

L. M. Rojas Barahona, A. Lorenzo, and C. Gardent. 2012b. An end-to-end evaluation of two situated dialog systems. In *Proceedings of the 13th Annual Meeting of the Special Interest Group on Discourse and Dialogue*, pages 10–19, Seoul, South Korea, July. ACL.

B. Abu Shawar and E. Atwell. 2007. Chatbots : are they really useful ? In *LDV Forum*, volume 22, pages 29–49.

S. Wilske and M. Wolska. 2011. Meaning versus form in computer-assisted task-based language learning : A case study on the german dative. *JLCL*, 26(1) :23–37.

Open-Domain Information Access with Talking Robots

Kristiina Jokinen and Graham Wilcock
University of Tartu, Estonia and University of Helsinki, Finland
kjokinen@ut.ee, graham.wilcock@helsinki.fi

Abstract

The demo shows Wikipedia-based open-domain information access dialogues with a talking humanoid robot. The robot uses face-tracking, nodding and gesturing to support interaction management and the presentation of information to the partner.

1 Introduction

The demo shows open-domain information access dialogues with the WikiTalk system on a Nao humanoid robot (Jokinen and Wilcock, 2012b). An annotated video of the demo can be seen at https://docs.google.com/file/d/0B-D1kVqPMlKdOEcyS25nMWpjUG8.

The WikiTalk system can be viewed from two complementary perspectives: as a spoken dialogue system or as a question-answering (QA) system.

Viewed as a spoken dialogue system, WikiTalk supports constructive interaction for talking about interesting topics (Jokinen and Wilcock, 2012a). However, using Wikipedia as its knowledge source instead of a finite database means that WikiTalk is completely open-domain. This is a significant breakthrough compared with traditional closed-domain spoken dialogue systems.

Viewed as a QA system, WikiTalk provides Wikipedia-based open-domain knowledge access (Wilcock, 2012). However, by using sentences and paragraphs from Wikipedia, the system is able to talk about the topic in a conversational manner, thus differing from a traditional QA system.

The Nao robot prototype version of WikiTalk was implemented by Csapo et al. (2012) during eNTERFACE 2012, the 8th International Summer Workshop on Multimodal Interfaces at Supélec in Metz (Figure 1). The humanoid robot uses face-tracking, nodding and gesturing to support interaction management and the presentation of new information to the partner (Han et al., 2012; Meena et al., 2012).

Figure 1: Working with the Nao humanoid robot.

2 Outline of the system

At the heart of the system (Figure 2) is a conversation manager based on a finite state machine. However, the states are not based on the domain-specific tasks and utterences for a fixed domain. In WikiTalk, the states function at a more abstract dialogue management level dealing for example with topic initiation, topic continuation, and topic switching. Further details of this approach are given by Wilcock (2012).

The finite state machine also has extensions that store various parameters of past interactions and influence the functionality of the state machine. The conversation manager communicates with a Wikipedia manager to obtain information from Wikipedia, and a Nao manager to map its states onto the actions of the robot.

To enable the robot to react to various events while getting information from Wikipedia, the Nao manager registers events and alerts the appropriate components of the system when anything of interest occurs either on the inside or the outside of the system. Figure 2 shows three examples of

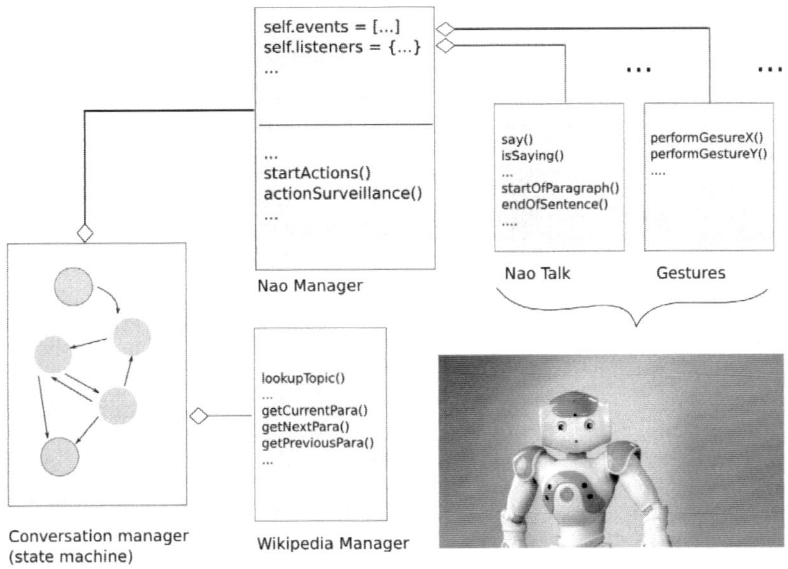

Figure 2: The system architecture, from (Csapo et al., 2012).

event handling within the Nao Talk module which drives the robot's speech functionality. The functions `isSaying()`, `startOfParagraph()`, and `endOfSentence()` are called periodically by the Nao manager, and return True whenever the robot is talking, reaches the start of a paragraph, or finishes a sentence, respectively. Whenever such events occur, the Nao manager can trigger appropriate reactions, for example, through the Gestures module which drives the robot's nodding and gesturing functionalities.

The history of the user's interactions is stored in a statistics dictionary in the conversation manager. Using a set of simple heuristics, it is possible to create more interesting dialogues by ensuring that the robot does not give the same instructions to the user in the same way over and over again, and by varying the level of sophistication in terms of the functionalities that are introduced to the user by the robot. For example, at first the robot gives simple instructions, allowing the user to practice and understand the basic functionalities of the system. For more advanced users, the system suggests new kinds of use cases which may not have previously been known to the user.

A corpus of videos of user trials with the system (Figure 3) was collected at the eNTERFACE 2012 workshop. The user trials and user questionnaires were used for system evaluation, which is reported by Anastasiou et al. (2013).

3 Outline of the demo

The demo is deliberately live, unscripted, and improvised. However, it typically starts with the robot in a sitting position. The robot stands up and greets the user, then asks what topic the user wants to hear about. The robot suggests some of its own favourite topics.

When the user selects a topic, the system gets information about the topic from Wikipedia and divides it into chunks suitable for spoken dialogue contributions. The system then manages the spoken presentation of the chunks according to the user's reactions. If the user asks for more, or otherwise shows interest in the topic, the system continues with the next chunk.

Crucially, the system makes smooth topic shifts by following the hyperlinks in Wikipedia whenever the user repeats the name of one of the links. For example, if the system is talking about Shakespeare and says "Shakespeare was born in Stratford-upon-Avon", the user can say "Stratford-upon-Avon?" and the system smoothly switches topics and starts talking about Stratford-upon-Avon using the Wikipedia information about this new topic.

The user can ask for any chunk to be repeated, or go back to the previous chunk. The user can also interrupt the current chunk and ask to skip to another chunk on the same topic.

Figure 3: Testing spoken interaction with Nao.

The user can interrupt the robot at any time by touching the top of the robot's head. The robot stops talking and explicitly acknowledges the interruption by saying "Oh sorry!" and waiting for the user's input. The user can then tell it to continue, to go back, to skip to another chunk, or to switch to a new topic.

The dialogue is open-domain and typically wanders freely from topic to topic by smooth topic shifts following the links in Wikipedia. However, if the user wants to jump to an entirely unrelated topic, an awkward topic shift can be made by saying the command "Alphabet!" and spelling the first few letters of the new topic using a spelling alphabet (Alpha, Bravo, Charlie, etc.).

As well as talking about topics selected by the user, the robot can take the initiative by suggesting potentially interesting new topics. One way to do this is by using the "Did you know ...?" sections from Wikipedia that are new every day.

The demo ends when the user tells the robot to stop. The robot thanks the user and sits down.

4 Previous demos

The system was first demonstrated in July 2012 at the 8th International Summer Workshop on Multimodal Interfaces (eNTERFACE 2012) in Metz.

An annotated video of this demo can be seen at `https://docs.google.com/file/d/0B-D1kVqPMlKdOEcyS25nMWpjUG8`.

The system was also demonstrated at the 3rd IEEE International Conference on Cognitive Infocommunications (CogInfoCom 2012).

Acknowledgements

We thank Adam Csapo, Emer Gilmartin, Jonathan Grizou, Frank Han, Raveesh Meena and Dimitra Anastasiou for their collaboration, both on the Nao WikiTalk implementation and on the user evaluations conducted at eNTERFACE 2012.

We also thank Supélec and especially Professor Olivier Pietquin for providing the Nao robots both for the eNTERFACE 2012 workshop and for the SIGDIAL-2013 demo.

References

Dimitra Anastasiou, Kristiina Jokinen, and Graham Wilcock. 2013. Evaluation of WikiTalk - user studies of human-robot interaction. In *Proceedings of 15th International Conference on Human-Computer Interaction (HCII 2013)*, Las Vegas, USA.

Adam Csapo, Emer Gilmartin, Jonathan Grizou, JingGuang Han, Raveesh Meena, Dimitra Anastasiou, Kristiina Jokinen, and Graham Wilcock. 2012. Multimodal conversational interaction with a humanoid robot. In *Proceedings of 3rd IEEE International Conference on Cognitive Infocommunications (CogInfoCom 2012)*, pages 667–672, Kosice.

JingGuang Han, Nick Campbell, Kristiina Jokinen, and Graham Wilcock. 2012. Investigating the use of non-verbal cues in human-robot interaction with a Nao robot. In *Proceedings of 3rd IEEE International Conference on Cognitive Infocommunications (CogInfoCom 2012)*, pages 679–683, Kosice.

Kristiina Jokinen and Graham Wilcock. 2012a. Constructive interaction for talking about interesting topics. In *Proceedings of Eighth International Conference on Language Resources and Evaluation (LREC 2012)*, Istanbul.

Kristiina Jokinen and Graham Wilcock. 2012b. Multimodal open-domain conversations with the Nao robot. In *Fourth International Workshop on Spoken Dialogue Systems (IWSDS 2012)*, Paris.

Raveesh Meena, Kristiina Jokinen, and Graham Wilcock. 2012. Integration of gestures and speech in human-robot interaction. In *Proceedings of 3rd IEEE International Conference on Cognitive Infocommunications (CogInfoCom 2012)*, pages 673–678, Kosice.

Graham Wilcock. 2012. WikiTalk: A spoken Wikipedia-based open-domain knowledge access system. In *Proceedings of the COLING 2012 Workshop on Question Answering for Complex Domains*, pages 57–69, Mumbai.

Demonstration of the Emote Wizard of Oz Interface for Empathic Robotic Tutors

Shweta Bhargava[1], Srinivasan Janarthanam[1], Helen Hastie[1], Amol Deshmukh[1], Ruth Aylett[1], Lee Corrigan[2], Ginevra Castellano [2]
[1]School of Mathematical and Computer Sciences, Heriot-Watt University, Edinburgh
[2]School of Electronic, Electrical and Computer Engineering, University of Birmingham
sb426,sc445,h.hastie,a.deshmukh,r.s.aylett@hw.ac.uk,
ljc228,g.castellano@bham.ac.uk

Abstract

We present a Wizard of Oz (WoZ) environment that was designed to build an artificial embodied intelligent tutoring system (ITS) that is capable of empathic conversations with school pupils aged between 10-13. We describe the components and the data that we plan to collect using the environment.

1 Introduction

We present a Wizard of Oz (WoZ) environment that was built as a part of the EC FP7 EMOTE project[1]. The objective of this work is to collect multimodal interaction data to build an artificial embodied intelligent tutoring system (ITS) that is capable of empathic conversations with school pupils aged between 10-13. Specifically, the EMOTE (EMbOdied-perceptive Tutors for Empathy-based learning) project aims to design and evaluate a new generation of robotic tutors that have perceptive and expressive capabilities to engage in empathic interactions with learners in schools and home environments. The project will carry out interdisciplinary research on affect recognition, learner models, adaptive behaviour and embodiment for human-robot interaction in learning environments, grounded in psychological theories of emotion in social interaction and pedagogical models for learning facilitation. An overview of the project can be found in (Deshmukh et al., 2013).

Wizard of Oz is an effective technique in Human Computer Interaction (HCI) studies where an interactive agent, which is not yet fully autonomous, is remotely controlled by a human wizard. However the participants who are interacting with the agent are not told that the agent is being remotely controlled. The wizard may be tasked to control one or many parts of the agent such as speech recognition and understanding, affect recognition, dialogue management, utterance and gesture generation and so on. Studies have shown that users "go easy" on computers during interaction and therefore interaction with "wizarded" system are at the level of complexity that can be learned and emulated (Pearson et al., 2006).

The WoZ environment presented in this paper will be used to collect data to inform the algorithms for affect recognition and empathic dialogue management. The WoZ environment is designed to collect data on how human tutors aided with a robotic interface adapt to learners' emotions and cognitive states in tutorial tasks. In this study, the wizard plays the same role as that of affect recognition and dialogue management modules in the actual final system.

2 Previous work

Wizard-of-Oz (WoZ) frameworks have been used in several studies since (Fraser and Gilbert, 1991) in order to collect human-computer dialogue data to help design dialogue systems. WoZ systems have been used to collect data to learn (e.g. (Strauss et al., 2007)) and evaluate dialogue management policies (e.g. (Cuayáhuitl and Kruijff-Korbayova, 2012)).

3 The EMOTE Wizard of Oz environment

The WoZ environment consists of the wizard's desk, the interactive touch table, sensors, and the robotic embodiment as shown in Figure 1. The

[1]http://emote-project.eu/

wizard will be seated in a different room away from the learner.

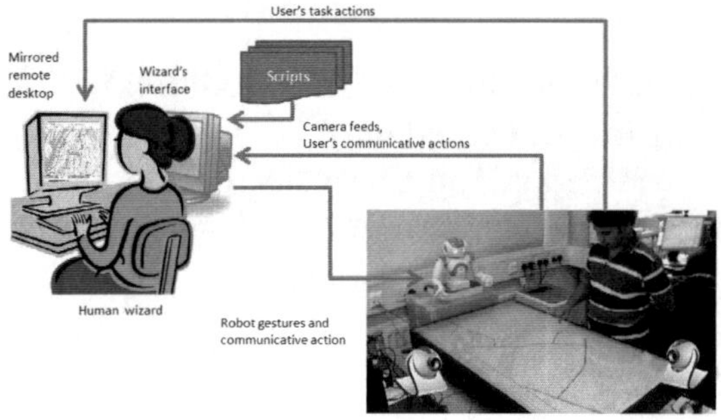

Figure 1: Wizard of Oz environment

3.1 Wizard's desk

The wizard's desk consists of two display screens. The touch table display at the user end will be mirrored on to one of the displays at the wizard's desk using which the wizard can observe the learner's activities related to the educational application. Another display will contain the Wizard Interface, a software application that allows the wizard to interact with the learner (see Figure 2). The Wizard Interface consists of four panels: task control, information, learner response and operations. In the `task control panel`, the wizard will be able to choose a task plan for the learner and access the tool and curriculum scripts (XML file). The tool script contains information on how to use the tools that are at the disposal of the learner. For instance, to create a marker on the map, one has to click on the appropriate tool and click on the map and so on. The curriculum script contains information on the skills that the learner needs to exercise or develop during his interaction with the system. For instance, in order to identify the right direction, the system will present the mneumonic phrase "**N**aughty **E**lephants **S**quirt **W**ater" in various forms such as a hint, question, pumping move, etc. to provide support to the learner. The `information panel` contains the video feed from two cameras (see Section 3.4). This will allow the wizard to determine the affective state of the learner. The learner's response to the agent's utterances (such as answering questions in the curriculum scripts) will also be displayed in the `learner response panel`. Finally, the `operations panel` provides options for the Wizard to respond to the learner based on the tools and curriculum scripts. These responses are either customised or predefined. The customised responses facilitate the wizard to execute robot movements on lower level (individual head, arm movements) and predefined responses contain a list for combined predefined speech, sound and behaviours.

Figure 2: Wizard's Interface

3.2 Touch table

The interactive touch table is a 55 inch Multitaction table capable of sensing multiple touch events simultaneously. The educational application is displayed on the table surface. A map based application has been developed to teach learners basic and advanced map reading skills (see Figure 3). The touch interface allows the learner to use touch to click, drag and zoom the map. The application has two panels of GUI objects such as buttons and text boxes namely, the tools panel and the interaction panel. The tools panel consists of tools that the learner can use to manipulate the map, while using the interaction panel the learner can interact with the tutor. Some of the tools that are currently available are to get grid references for a position on the map, dropping markers on the map, change map types, etc. For instance, if the tutor asks a yes/no question, the learner can respond by pressing the yes or the no button. The learner can answer the tutor's questions by typing into the text box in the interaction panel.

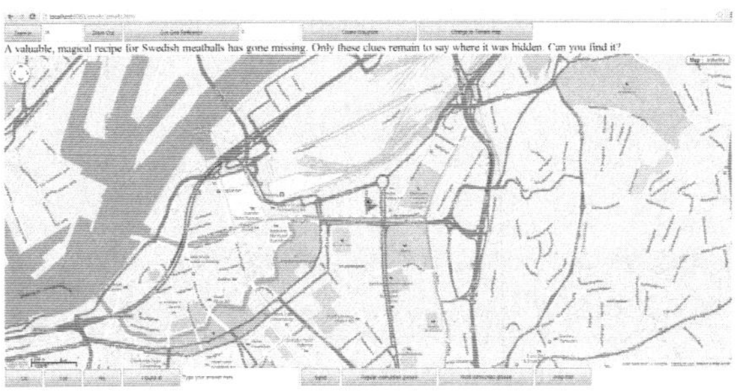

Figure 3: Map reading skills application

3.3 Robotic embodiment

The robotic embodiment is a Nao robot (torso version) that sits on the side of the touch table. It is capable of head, arm and body gestures in addition to synthesised speech. The robot receives the text and gestures selected by the wizard through the Wizard Interface. Tutor's utterances will be synthesized into speech using the in-built text to speech (TTS) engine while the gestures are realised using appropriate head, arm and body motions. To increase naturalness, the robot will also have idle movement in-between wizard selections.

3.4 Sensors

The environment has an array of sensors such as two video cameras and a Kinect sensor. A Kinect sensor and a video camera are placed in front the learner. Another camera is placed in front of the robot (as shown in Figure 1).

4 Data collection

In this section, we discuss the data that we aim to collect using the WoZ environment. We intend to collect these data during experiments where human tutors play the wizard's role and the learners from in the 10-13 year age-range will play the role of learners. The task for the learner is to carry out an expedition using the map application that he or she is provided with. In order to solve the steps of the expedition, the learner will have to exercise his/her map reading skills. Map reading skills such as compass directions, contour lines, grid lines, etc. will have to be exercised using appropriate map tools provided in the application. The tutor's role is to observe the learner responses (both verbal and physical) and respond to them appropriately using the interaction panel in the Wizard Interface application.

Simultaneous video feeds from two cameras and the Kinect sensor will be recorded during the tutor-learner interaction. These data will be further used for affect recognition tasks based on learner's head, arm and body gestures. The interaction between the tutor and the learner in terms of tutor dialogue actions, utterances and learner responses in terms of button presses will also be logged.

5 Demo

We propose to demonstrate the WoZ environment set up using two laptops: learner desktop with the map application and another with the wizard's interface. The learner desktop will also display a simulated Nao robot. We will also exhibit the logs that we collect from the pilot studies with a Geogrphy teacher acting as the wizard tutor and school pupils as tutees.

Acknowledgements

This work was partially supported by the European Commission (EC) and was funded by the EU FP7 ICT-317923 project EMOTE. The authors are solely responsible for the content of this publication. It does not represent the opinion of the EC, and the EC is not responsible for any use that might be made of data appearing therein.

References

H. Cuayáhuitl and I Kruijff-Korbayova. 2012. An Interactive Humanoid Robot Exhibiting Flexible Sub-Dialogues. In *Proceedings of the NAACL-HTL, Montreal, Canada.*

A. Deshmukh, G. Castellano, A. Kappas, W. Barendregt, F. Nabais, A. Paiva, T. Ribeiro, I. Leite, and R. Aylett. 2013. Towards empathic artificial tutors. In *Proceedings of the 8th ACM/IEEE international conference on Human-robot interaction.*

N. Fraser and G. N. Gilbert. 1991. Simulating speech systems. *Computer Speech and Language*, 5:81–99.

J. Pearson, J. Hu, H. P. Branigan, M. J. Pickering, and C. Nass. 2006. Adaptive language behavior in HCI: how expectations and beliefs about a system affect users' word choice. In *Proceedings of the SIGCHI conference on Human Factors in computing systems, Montral.*

P. M. Strauss, H. Hoffmann, and S. Scherer. 2007. Evaluation and user acceptance of a dialogue system using Wizard-of-Oz recordings. In *Proceedings of 3rd IET International Conference on Intelligent Environments.*

The Map Task Dialogue System: A Test-bed for Modelling Human-Like Dialogue

Raveesh Meena **Gabriel Skantze** **Joakim Gustafson**
KTH Speech, Music and Hearing
Stockholm, Sweden
raveesh@csc.kth.se, gabriel@speech.kth.se, jocke@speech.kth.se

Abstract

The demonstrator presents a test-bed for collecting data on human–computer dialogue: a fully automated dialogue system that can perform Map Task with a user. In a first step, we have used the test-bed to collect human–computer Map Task dialogue data, and have trained various data-driven models on it for detecting feedback response locations in the user's speech. One of the trained models has been tested in user interactions and was perceived better in comparison to a system using a random model. The demonstrator will exhibit three versions of the Map Task dialogue system—each using a different trained data-driven model of *Response Location Detection*.

1 Introduction

A common procedure in modelling human-like dialogue systems is to collect data on human–human dialogue and then train models that predict the behaviour of the interlocutors. However, we think that it might be problematic to use a corpus of human–human dialogue as a basis for implementing dialogue system components. One problem is the interactive nature of the task. If the system produces a slightly different behaviour than what was found in the original data, this would likely result in a different behaviour in the interlocutor. Another problem is that humans are likely to behave differently towards a system as compared to another human (even if a more human-like behaviour is being modelled). Yet another problem is that much dialogue behaviour is optional and therefore makes the actual behaviour hard to use as a gold standard.

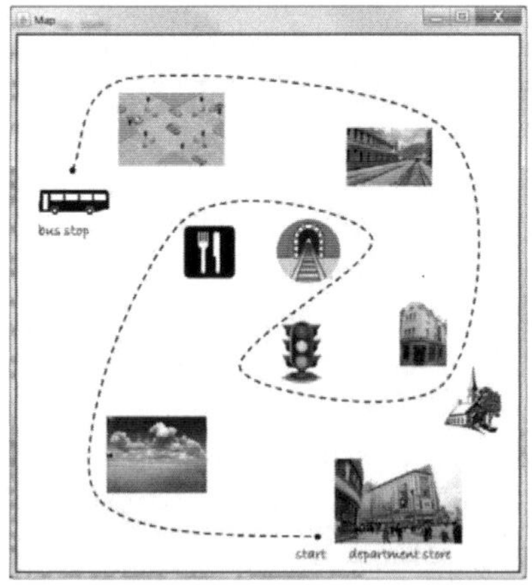

Figure 1: The Map Task system user interface

To improve current systems, we need both a better understanding of the phenomena of human interaction, better computational models and better data to build these models. An alternative approach that has proven to be useful is to train models on human–computer dialogue data collected through *Wizard-of-Oz* studies (Dahlbäck et al., 1993). However, the methodology might be hard to use when the issue under investigation is time-critical behaviour such as back-channels.

A third alternative is to use a *boot-strapping* procedure, where more and more advanced (or human-like) versions of the system are built iteratively. After each iteration, users interact with the system and data is collected. This data is then used to train/improve data-driven models of interaction in the system. A problem here, however, is how to build the first iteration of the system, since many components, e.g., Automatic Speech Recognition (ASR), need some data to be useful at all.

In this demonstration we present a test-bed for collecting data on time-critical human–computer dialogue phenomena: a fully automated dialogue system that can perform the Map Task with a user (Skantze, 2012). In a first step, following the boot-strapping procedure, we collected human–computer Map Task dialogue data using this test-bed and then trained various data-driven models on this data for detecting feedback response locations in user's speech. A trained model has been implemented and evaluated in interaction with users—in the same environment used for collecting the data (Meena et al., in press). The demonstrator will exhibit three versions of the Map Task dialogue system—each using a different trained data-driven model of *Response Location Detection* (RLD).

2 The Map Task Dialogue System

Map Task is a common experimental paradigm for studying human–human dialogue. In our setup, the user (the information *giver*) is given the task of describing a route on a map to the system (the information *follower*). The choice of Map Task is motivated partly because the system may allow the user to keep the initiative during the whole dialogue, and thus only produce responses that are not intended to take the initiative, most often some kind of feedback. Thus, the system might be described as an *attentive listener*.

The basic components of the system can be seen in Figure 2. Dashed lines indicate components that were not part of the first iteration of the system (used for data collection), but which have been used in the second iteration of the system that uses a model trained on the collected data. To make the human–computer Map Task dialogue feasible without any full speech understanding we have implemented a trick: the user is presented with a map on a screen (see Figure 1) and instructed to move the mouse cursor along the route as it is being described. The user is told that this is for logging purposes, but the real reason for this is that the system tracks the mouse position and thus knows what the user is currently talking about. It is thereby possible to produce a coherent system behaviour without any speech recognition at all, only basic speech detection. This often results in a very realistic interaction[1].

The system uses a simple energy-based speech detector to chunk the user's speech into inter-pausal units (IPUs), that is, periods of speech that contain no sequence of silence longer than 200 ms. Such a short threshold allows the system to give backchannels (seemingly) while the user is speaking or take the turn with barely any gap. The end of an IPU is a candidate for the RLD model to identify whether it is a Response Location (RL).

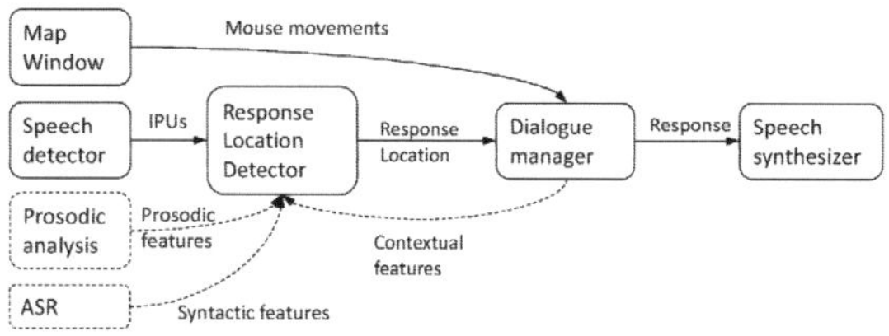

Figure 2: The basic components of the system.

Each time the RLD detects a RL, the dialogue manager produces a response, depending on the current state of the dialogue and the position of the mouse cursor. Table 1 shows an example Map Task dialogue illustrating the different types of responses the system could produce. The dialogue manager always starts with an Introduction and ends with an Ending, once the mouse cursor has reached the destination. Between these, it selects from the other responses (Reprise Fragment, Clarification and Backchannel), partly randomly, but also depending on the length of the last user turn (longer turn triggers Repeat or Restart) and the current mouse location (e.g., a Guess if mouse hovers over the same area for some time).

Table 1: An example Map Task dialogue between a user (U) and system (S) [*User utterances with ASR error(s) are indicated with a* *]

S	Introduction	Could you help me to find my way to the bus stop?
U		start from the department store
S	Backchannel	yeah
U		and eh
S	Guess	Should I start by going west?
U		yeah do that
U		then you will get to a meadow and when you get to the meadow **you get to a meadow until you get to the meadow*
S	Repeat	Eh, could you repeat that?
U		you go straight and you see a meadow on your right side
S	Clarification Request	A green field?
U		ehm yeah a field
S	Backchannel	mhm
U		pass the meadow and turn right so you are going north **the meadow and turn right to your going north*
S	Backchannel	okay
U		you get to a restaurant

[1] An example video can be seen at http://www.youtube.com/watch?v=MzL-B9pVbOE.

S	Reprise Fragment	A restaurant
U		then you have to turn right and that will take you to **you have turned right and at will take you turn*
S	Restart	Eh, I think I lost you at the restaurant, could you take that again?
...		
U		at the junction go south and then you will get to the bus stop
S	Ending	Okay, thanks a lot.

3 Data-driven models of RLD

Using the system described in the previous section a corpus of 50 human–computer Map Task dialogue was collected and used to train a data-driven model of RLD. Since we didn't have a sophisticated model of RLD during the first iteration a naïve model was used. This model would wait for a random period between 0 and 800 ms after an IPU ended. If no new IPUs were initiated during this period, a RL was detected. Each IPU in the corpus was then manually labelled as either Hold (a response would be inappropriate) or Respond (a response is expected) type. On this data various models were trained on online extractable features—covering syntax, context and prosody. Table 2 illustrates the performance of the various models. Going a step further, model #6 was deployed in the Map Task dialogue system (with an ASR component) and evaluated in user interactions. The result suggests that the trained model provide for smooth turn-transitions in contrast to the Random model (Meena et al., in press).

Table 2: Performance of various models of RLD [*NB: Naïve Bayes; SVM: Support Vector Machine; Models with * will be exhibited in the demonstration*]

#	RLD model	% accuracy (on ASR results)
1*	Random	50.79% majority class baseline
2	Prosody	64.5% (SVM learner)
3	Context	64.8% (SVM learner)
4*	Prosody + Context	69.1% (SVM learner)
5	Syntax	81.1% (NB learner)
6*	Syntax + Prosody + Context	82.0 % (NB learner)

4 Future applications

The Map Task test-bed presented here has the potential for modelling other human-like conversational behaviour in dialogue systems:

Clarification strategies: by deploying explicit (*did you mean turn right?*) and implicit (a reprise such as *turn right*) or elliptical (*'right?'*) clarification forms in the *grounding* process one could investigate the efficiency and effectively of these human-like clarification strategies.

User utterance completion: It has been suggested that completion of user utterances by a dialogue system would result in human-like conversational interactions. However, completing user's utterance at every opportunity may not be the best strategy (DeVault et al., 2009). The presented system could be used to explore when it is appropriate to do so. We have observed in our data that the system dialogue acts Guess (cf. Table 1) and Reprise often helped the dialogue proceed further – by completing user utterances – when the user had difficulty describing a landmark on a route.

Visual cues: the system could be integrated in a robotic head, such as Furhat (Al Moubayed et al., 2013), and visual cues from the user could be used for improving the current model of RLD. This could be used further to explore the use of extra-linguistic system behaviours, such as head nods and facial gestures, as feedback responses.

Acknowledgement

This work is supported by the Swedish research council (VR) project *Incremental processing in multimodal conversational systems* (2011-6237)

References

Al Moubayed, S., Skantze, G., & Beskow, J. (2013). The Furhat Back-Projected Humanoid Head - Lip reading, Gaze and Multiparty Interaction. *International Journal of Humanoid Robotics, 10*(1).

Dahlbäck, N., Jönsson, A., & Ahrenberg, L. (1993). Wizard of Oz studies – why and how. In *Proceedings from the 1993 International Workshop on Intelligent User Interfaces* (pp. 193-200).

DeVault, D., Sagae, K., & Traum, D. (2009). Can I Finish? Learning When to Respond to Incremental Interpretation Results in Interactive Dialogue. In *Proceedings of SIGdial* (pp. 11-20). London, UK.

Meena, R., Skantze, G., & Gustafson, J. (in press). A Data-driven Model for Timing Feedback in a Map Task Dialogue System. To be published in *14th Annual Meeting of the Special Interest Group on Discourse and Dialogue - SIGdial*. Metz, France.

Skantze, G. (2012). A Testbed for Examining the Timing of Feedback using a Map Task. In *Proceedings of the Interdisciplinary Workshop on Feedback Behaviors in Dialog*. Portland, OR.

A Robotic Agent in a Virtual Environment that Performs Situated Incremental Understanding of Navigational Utterances

Takashi Yamauchi
Seikei University
3-3-1 Kichijoji-Kitamachi
Musashino, Tokyo, Japan
dm126222@cc.seikei.ac.jp

Mikio Nakano
Honda Research Institute
Japan Co., Ltd.
8-1 Honcho, Wako
Wako, Saitama, Japan
nakano@jp.honda-ri.com

Kotaro Funakoshi
Honda Research Institute
Japan Co., Ltd.
8-1 Honcho, Wako
Wako, Saitama, Japan
funakoshi@jp.honda-ri.com

Abstract

We demonstrate a robotic agent in a 3D virtual environment that understands human navigational instructions. Such an agent needs to select actions based on not only instructions but also situations. It is also expected to immediately react to the instructions. Our agent incrementally understands spoken instructions and immediately controls a mobile robot based on the incremental understanding results and situation information such as the locations of obstacles and moving history. It can be used as an experimental system for collecting human-robot interactions in dynamically changing situations.

1 Introduction

Movable robots are ones that can execute tasks by moving around. If such robots can understand spoken language navigational instructions, they will become more useful and will be widely used. However, spoken language instructions are sometimes ambiguous in that their meanings differ depending on the situations such as robot and obstacle locations, so it is not always easy to make them understand spoken language instructions. Moreover, when they receive instructions while they are moving and they understand instructions only after they finish, accurate understanding is not easy since the situation may change during the instruction utterances.

Although there have been several pieces of work on robots that receive linguistic navigational instructions (Marge and Rudnicky, 2010; Tellex et al., 2011), they try to understand instructions before moving and they do not deal with instructions when situations dynamically change.

We will demonstrate a 3D virtual robotic system that understands spoken language navigational instructions in a situation-dependent way. It incrementally understands instructions so that it can understand them based on the situation at that point in time when the instructions are made.

2 A Mobile Robot in a 3D Virtual Environment

We use a robotic system that works in a virtual environment built on top of SIROS (Raux, 2010), which was originally developed for collecting dialogues between two participants who are engaging in an online video game. As an example, a convenience store environment was developed and a corpus of interaction was collected (Raux and Nakano, 2010). One of the participants, the operator, controls a (simulated) humanoid robot whose role is to answer all customer requests. The other participant plays the role of a remote manager who sees the whole store but can only interact with the operator through speech. The operator has the robot view (whose field of view and depth are limited to simulate a robot's vision) and the manager has a birds-eye view of the store (Figure 1). Customers randomly visit the store and make requests at various locations. The manager guides the operator towards customers needing attention. The operator then answers the customer's requests and gets points for each satisfied request.

Using the virtual environment described above, we have developed a system that operates the robot according to the human manager's instructions. Currently we deal with only navigational instructions for moving the robot to a customer.

Figure 2 depicts the architecture for our system. We use Sphinx-4 (Lamere et al., 2003) for speech recognition. Its acoustic model is trained on the Wall Street Journal Corpus and its trigram language model was trained on 1,616 sentences in the human-human dialogue corpus described above. Its vocabulary size is 275 words. We use Festival (Black et al., 2001) for speech synthesis.

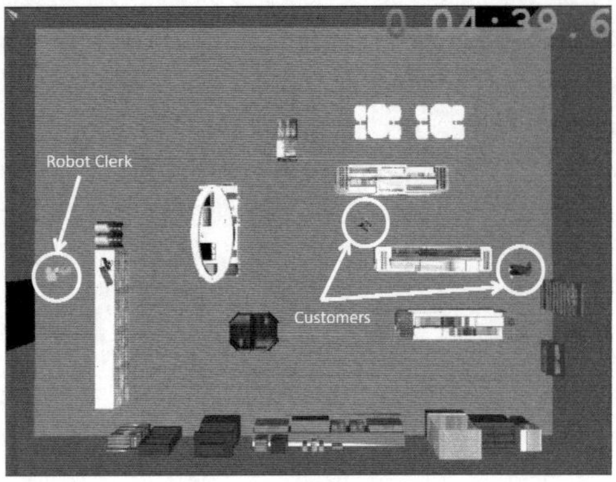

Figure 1: The manager's view of the convenience store.

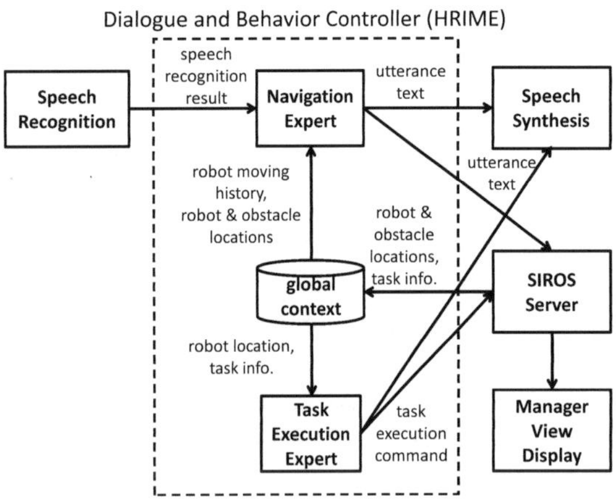

Figure 2: System architecture.

We use HRIME (HRI Intelligence Platform based on Multiple Experts) (Nakano et al., 2008) for dialogue and behavior control. In an HRIME application, experts, which are modules dedicated to specific tasks, are activated at appropriate times and perform tasks. The navigation expert is activated when the system receives a navigational instruction. There are seven semantic categories of instructions; they are *turn-right*, *turn-left*, *go-forward*, *go-back*, *repeat-the-previous-action*, *do-the-opposite-action-of-the-previous-one*, and *stop*. Utterances that do not fall into any of these are ignored. We assume that there are rules that match linguistic patterns and those semantic categories. For example, "right" corresponds to *turn-right*, and "more" corresponds to *repeat-the-previous-action*. The navigation expert sends the SIROS server navigation commands based on the recognized semantic categories. Those commands move the robot in the same way as a human operator operates the robot using the keyboard, and the results are shown on the display the manager is watching. When the robot starts moving and it cannot move because of an obstacle, it reports it to the manager by sending its utterance to the speech synthesizer.

When the robot has approached a customer who is requesting help, the task is automatically performed by the task execution expert.

The global context in the dialogue and behavior controller stores information on the environment which is obtained from the SIROS server, and it can be used by the experts. As in the same way in the human-human interaction, it holds information only on customers and obstacles close to the robot so that restricted robot vision can be simulated.

3 Situated Incremental Understanding

Sometimes manager utterances last without pauses like "right, right, more right, stop", and the situation changes during the utterances because the robot and the customers can move. So our system employs incremental speech recognition and moves the robot if a navigational instruction pattern is found in the incremental output. To obtain incremental speech recognition outputs, we employed InproTK (Baumann et al., 2010), which is an extension to Sphinx-4. It enables the system to receive tentative results every 10ms, which is a hypothesis for the interval from the beginning of speech to the point in time.

However, since incremental outputs are sometimes unstable and the instructions are ambiguous in that the amount of movement is not specified, not only incremental speech recognition outputs but also obstacle locations and moving history is used to determine the navigation commands.

In our system, the robot navigation expert receives incremental recognition results and if it finds a navigational instruction pattern, it consults the situation information in the global context, and issues a navigation command based on several situation-dependent understanding rules that are manually written. Below are examples.

- If there is an obstacle in the direction that the recognized instruction indicates, ignore the recognized instruction. For example, when "go forward" is recognized but there is an obstacle ahead, it is guessed that the recognition result was an error.

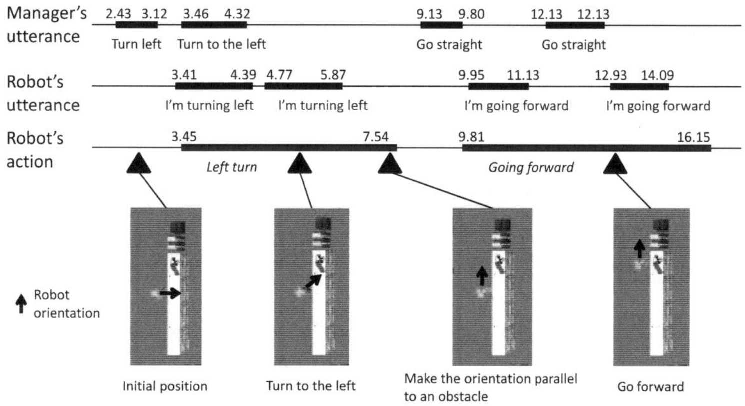

Figure 3: Interaction example.

- When rotating, adjust the degree of rotation so that the resulting orientation becomes parallel to obstacles such as a display shelf. This enables the robot to smoothly go down the aisles.

Figure 3 shows an example interaction. In the demonstration, we will show how the robot moves according to the spoken instructions by a human looking at the manager display. We will compare our system with its non-incremental version and a version that does not use situation-dependent understanding rules to show how incremental situated understanding is effective.

4 Future Work

We are using this system for collecting a corpus of human-robot interaction in dynamically changing situations so that we can analyze how humans make utterances in such situations. Future work includes to make the system understand more complicated utterances such as "turn a little bit to the left". We are also planning to work on automatically learning the situation-dependent action selection rules from such a corpus (Vogel and Jurafsky, 2010) to navigate the robot more smoothly.

Acknowledgments

We thank Antoine Raux and Shun Sato for their contribution to building the previous versions of this system. Thanks also go to Timo Baumann Okko Buß, and David Schlangen for making their InproTK available.

References

Timo Baumann, Okko Buß, and David Schlangen. 2010. InproTK in Action: Open-Source Software for Building German-Speaking Incremental Spoken Dialogue Systems. In *Proc. of ESSV.*

Alan Black, Paul Taylor, Richard Caley, Rob Clark, Korin Richmond, Simon King, Volker Strom, and Heiga Zen. 2001. The Festival Speech Synthesis System, Version 1.4.2. *Unpublished document available via http://www. cstr. ed. ac. uk/projects/festival. html.*

Paul Lamere, Philip Kwok, William Walker, Evandro Gouvea, Rita Singh, Bhiksha Raj, and Peter Wolf. 2003. Design of the CMU Sphinx-4 decoder. In *Proc. of Eurospeech-2003.*

Matthew Marge and Alexander I. Rudnicky. 2010. Comparing spoken language route instructions for robots across environment representations. In *Proc. of SIGDIAL-10.*

Mikio Nakano, Kotaro Funakoshi, Yuji Hasegawa, and Hiroshi Tsujino. 2008. A framework for building conversational agents based on a multi-expert model. In *Proc. of SIGDIAL-08*, pages 88–91.

Antoine Raux and Mikio Nakano. 2010. The dynamics of action corrections in situated interaction. In *Proc. of SIGDIAL-10*, pages 165–174.

Antoine Raux. 2010. SIROS: A framework for human-robot interaction research in virtual worlds. In *Proc. of the AAAI 2010 Fall Symposium on Dialog with Robots.*

Stefanie Tellex, Thomas Kollar, Steven Dickerson, Matthew R. Walter, Ashis Gopal Banerjee, Seth Teller, and Nicholas Roy. 2011. Understanding natural language commands for robotic navigation and mobile manipulation. In *Proc. of AAAI-2011.*

Adam Vogel and Dan Jurafsky. 2010. Learning to follow navigational directions. In *Proc. of ACL-2010*, pages 806–814.

Roundtable: An Online Framework for Building Web-based Conversational Agents

Eric Forbell and **Nicolai Kalisch** and **Fabrizio Morbini**
and **Kelly Christoffersen**
and **Kenji Sagae** and **David Traum** and **Albert A. Rizzo**
Institute for Creative Technologies
University of Southern California
Los Angeles, CA 90094, USA
{lastname}@ict.usc.edu

Abstract

We present an online system that provides a complete web-based sandbox for creating, testing and publishing embodied conversational agents. The tool, called Roundtable, empowers many different types of authors and varying team sizes to create flexible interactions by automating many editing workflows while limiting complexity and hiding architectural concerns. Finished characters can be published directly to web servers, enabling highly interactive applications.

1 Introduction

To support the creation of a virtual guide system called SimCoach (Rizzo et al, 2011) designed to help military service personnel and their families understand behavioral healthcare issues and learn about support resources, a core virtual human architecture that included a new dialogue management approach was developed (Morbini et al., 2012b). SimCoach is an embodied, conversational virtual human guide delivered via the web and is supported by a flexible information state dialogue manager called FLoReS designed to support mixed initiative dialogue with conversational systems. Morbini et al. (2012a) provide a detailed description of the dialogue manager.

Although FLoReS supports a wide variety of virtual human character behaviors, these must be specified in dialogue policies that must be authored manually. Initially, authoring for this dialogue manager required coding of policies using a custom programming language. Therefore significant training for content authors was necessary, as well as substantial support from dialogue system developers in managing resources such as training data for the language understanding system. To improve the accessibility of the system to non-technical subject matter experts and other creative staff, it became clear that additional tools were necessary. In this demonstration, we present Roundtable: a web-based authoring environment for virtual human characters that is designed for use by subject matter experts who are qualified for content authoring in targeted domains, but who may not possess technical skills in programming or experience in dialogue system design.

2 Supporting rapid authoring of dialogue agents for the web

Roundtable is a complete web-based authoring system enabling the end-to-end creation, validation, testing and web publishing of virtual human characters using the SimCoach virtual human architecture. The system provides features that empower many types of authors, team sizes and makeups. The system allows an author to select from a set of preconfigured 3D character models, model the dialogue policy through behavior templates and more direct subdialogue editing, train and test the natural language understanding component, render animation performances associated with character behaviors and utterances, and test both text-based and fully animated interactions. Finally, the complete character dataset can be exported and deployed to a live, highly available server environment, where interaction data can be monitored and periodically collected for analysis and refinement, all from within the same browser environment (Figure 1). The entire system, from authoring to end-user interaction with the virtual human character, is web-based and requires only a current web browser for content authors and end users.

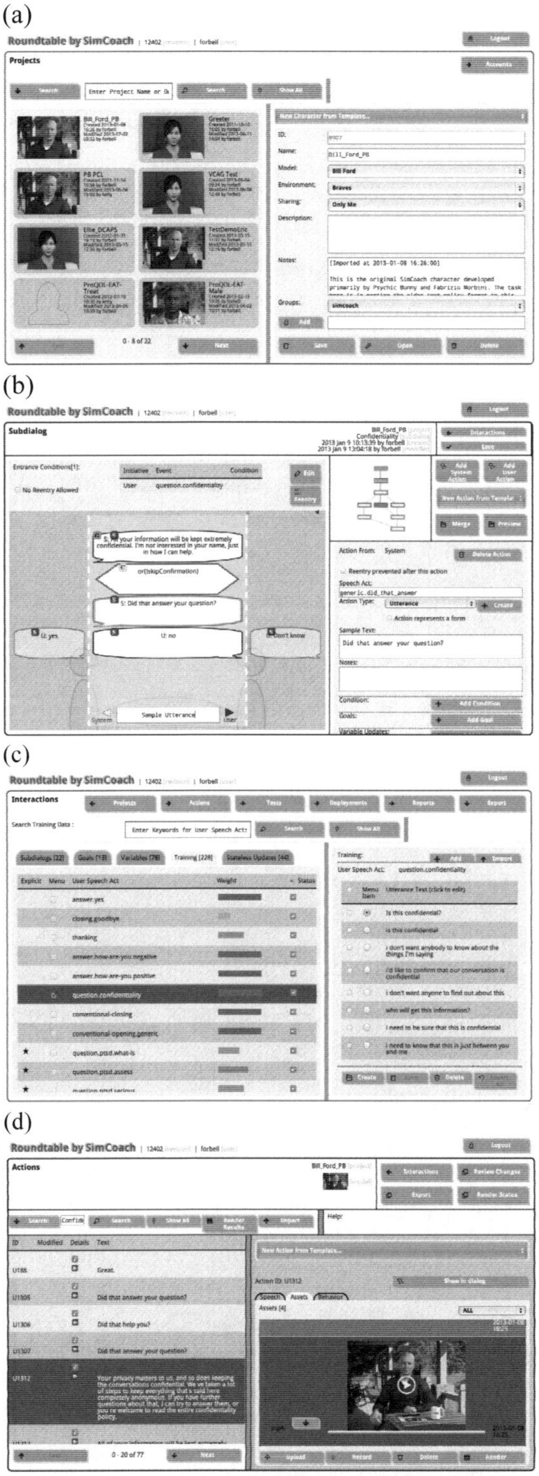

Figure 1: Selected modules from the Roundtable character authoring system (a) character project browser; (b) dialogue policy editor; (c) training data manager (d) action and animation asset manager

At the core of the authoring application is an object-oriented information model and set of management systems that span the following roles:

- **Dialogue content management**, responsible for persistence, search, validation and retrieval operations of all dialogue elements including subdialogue networks; information state variables and effects; goals and effects; and dialogue action annotations that provide the mapping to the action database.
- **Training data management,** concerned with managing training items for a data-driven natural language understanding module, as well as providing support for running regressions when updating the training set.
- **Action management**, provides data operations for managing potentially large sets of virtual human performance-related assets, including utterance text, speech audio when not system-generated, annotated nonverbal behavior schedules, as well as non-performance actions which include web-hosted videos, digested web articles, or any arbitrary HTML effect.
- **Deployment management**, enabling rapid deployment of locally tested characters to highly available web servers as well as review and data warehousing functions for both analytic and refinement purposes.

The information model is implemented in a relational database that fully specifies, relates and allows inquiry and validation of authored information. Additionally, a complete web application programming interface (API) powers the Roundtable application, providing a transactional framework for data operations as well as user privilege enforcement, but which also allows application expansion.

The information model also serves to decouple the authoring representation from the data structures necessary to drive dialogue behavior at runtime. Prior to realizing an authored character in the FLoReS engine, project dialogue data elements are exported into the format expected by the runtime target, a process that we expect to expand in the future to support different dialogue managers and language understanding configurations.

Figure 2: The interactive virtual human character published to the web, accessible by current browsers.

3 Demo script

This demonstration will show how to build a simple conversational virtual human character using Roundtable, from acquiring an account (http://authoring.simcoach.org, free for academic research) to obtaining the URL for the newly created character, and all of the steps in between. The workflow to build a character is as follows:

1. In the project module (Figure 1a) we create a new character by providing a unique name and selecting an existing 3D character model.
2. Opening the newly created project brings up the interaction module (Figure 1b) where we choose from a list of available subdialogue templates that can be used for common dialogue behaviors (question-answer, greeting, etc.). The provided *Greeting* and *Goodbye* templates are used to define the character's conversational behavior when initiating and ending an interaction, respectively. Invoking the *Question-Answer* template, we can quickly define how the character will respond to a specific question or statement. Each template requires a name and sample text for any user or system utterance.
3. Following the template-based subdialogue generation, we create training data for the natural language understanding component by providing possible user utterances associated with each user dialogue act in the templates used (Figure 1c).
4. The last task is to refine system utterances, which are generated automatically during the step of policy authoring, and generate animation data. From the action module, we can search and inspect all system actions. For any system action, with a single button click, we can synthesize audio and render animations (Figure 1d).
5. Finally, we navigate to the test module, compile our character project, and are then able to chat with the new character to ensure expected behavior. At this point, the character is ready to be deployed, with its unique URL, and is immediately accessible on the web (Figure 2).

4 Conclusion

We described the Roundtable online authoring framework that has been designed to support non-expert users in rapidly creating embodied, conversational virtual characters of varying complexities. The tool, being web-based, requires zero configuration to get started and authored virtual characters can be deployed to Internet-facing web servers immediately, expanding the reach of many dialogue-driven applications.

Acknowledgments

The effort described here has been sponsored by the U.S. Army. Any opinions, content or information presented does not necessarily reflect the position or the policy of the United States Government, and no official endorsement should be inferred.

References

A. Rizzo, B. Lange, J.G. Buckwalter, E. Forbell, J. Kim, K. Sagae, J. Williams, B.O. Rothbaum, J. Difede, G. Reger, T. Parsons, and P. Kenny. An intelligent virtual human system for providing healthcare information and support. In J.D. Westwood et al., editor, Technology and Informatics. IOS Press, 2011.

Fabrizio Morbini, David Devault, Kenji Sagae, Jillian Gerten, Angela Nazarian and David Traum FLoReS: A Forward Looking, Reward Seeking, Dialogue Manager in proceedings of International Workshop on Spoken Dialog Systems (IWSDS-2012), Ermenonville, France, November 2012b.

Fabrizio Morbini, Eric Forbell, David DeVault, Kenji Sagae, David Traum and Albert Rizzo. A Mixed-Initiative Conversational Dialogue System for Healthcare. Demonstration in SIGdial 2012, the 13th Annual SIGdial meeting on Discourse and Dialogue, Seoul, South Korea, 2012a.

A Data-driven Model for Timing Feedback in a Map Task Dialogue System

Raveesh Meena **Gabriel Skantze** **Joakim Gustafson**
KTH Speech, Music and Hearing
Stockholm, Sweden
raveesh@csc.kth.se, gabriel@speech.kth.se, jocke@speech.kth.se

Abstract

We present a data-driven model for detecting suitable response locations in the user's speech. The model has been trained on human–machine dialogue data and implemented and tested in a spoken dialogue system that can perform the Map Task with users. To our knowledge, this is the first example of a dialogue system that uses automatically extracted syntactic, prosodic and contextual features for online detection of response locations. A subjective evaluation of the dialogue system suggests that interactions with a system using our trained model were perceived significantly better than those with a system using a model that made decisions at random.

1 Introduction

Traditionally, dialogue systems have rested on a very simple model for turn-taking, where the system uses a fixed silence threshold to detect the end of the user's utterance, after which the system responds. However, this model does not capture human-human dialogue very accurately; sometimes a speaker just hesitates and no turn-change is intended, sometimes the turn changes after barely any silence (Sacks et al., 1974). Therefore, such models can result in systems that interrupt the user or are perceived as unresponsive. Related to the problem of turn-taking is that of *backchannels* (Yngve, 1970). Backchannel feedback – short acknowledgements such as *uh-huh* or *mm-hm* – are used by human interlocutors to signal continued attention to the speaker, without claiming the floor. If a dialogue system should be able to manage smooth turn-taking and back-channelling, it must be able to first identify suitable locations in the user's speech to do so.

Duncan (1972) found that human interlocutors continuously monitor several cues, such as content, syntax, intonation, paralanguage, and body motion, in parallel to manage turn-taking. Similar observations have been made in various other studies investigating the turn-taking and back-channelling phenomena in human conversations. Ward (1996) has suggested that a low pitch region is a good cue that backchannel feedback is appropriate. On the other hand, Koiso et al. (1998) have argued that both syntactic and prosodic features make significant contributions in identifying turn-taking and back-channelling relevant places. Cathcart et al. (2003) have shown that syntax in combination with pause duration is a strong predictor for backchannel *continuers*. Gravano & Hirschberg (2009) observed that the likelihood of occurrence of a backchannel increases with the number of syntactic and prosodic cues conjointly displayed by the speaker.

However, there is a general lack of studies on how such models could be used online in dialogue systems and to what extent that would improve the interaction. There are two main problems in doing so. First, the data used in the studies mentioned above are from human–human dialogue and it is not obvious to what extent the models derived from such data transfers to human–machine dialogue. Second, many of the features used were manually extracted. This is especially true for the transcription of utterances, but several studies also rely on manually annotated prosodic features.

In this paper, we present a data-driven model of what we call *Response Location Detection* (RLD), which is fully online. Thus, it only relies on automatically extractable features—covering syntax, prosody and context. The model has been trained on human–machine dialogue data and has been implemented in a dialogue system that is in turn evaluated with users. The setting is that of a Map Task, where the user describes the route and the system may respond with for example acknowledgements and clarification requests.

2 Background

Two influential theories that have examined the turn-taking mechanism in human conversations are the signal-based mechanism of Duncan (1972) and the rule-based mechanism proposed by Sacks (1974). According to Duncan, "the turn-taking mechanism is mediated through signals composed of clear-cut behavioural cues, considered to be perceived as discrete". Duncan identified six discrete behavioural cues that a speaker may use to signal the intent to yield the turn. These behavioural cues are: (i) any deviation from the sustained intermediate pitch level; (ii) drawl on the final syllable of a terminal clause; (iii) termination of any hand gesticulation or the relaxation of tensed hand position—during a turn; (iv) a stereotyped expression with *trailing off* effect; (v) a drop in pitch and/or loudness; and (vi) completion of a grammatical clause. According to the rule-based mechanism of Sacks (1974) turn-taking is regulated by applying rules (e.g. "one party at a time") at Transition-Relevance Places (TRPs)—possible completion points of basic units of turns, in order to minimize gaps and overlaps. The basic units of turns (or turn-constructional units) include sentential, clausal, phrasal, and lexical constructions.

Duncan (1972) also suggested that speakers may display behavioural cues either singly or together, and when displayed together they may occur either simultaneously or in tight sequence. In his analysis, he found that the likelihood that a listener attempts to take the turn is higher when the cues are conjointly displayed across the various modalities.

While these theories have offered a function-based account of turn-taking, another line of research has delved into corpora-based techniques to build models for detecting turn-transition and feedback relevant places in speaker utterances.

Ward (1996) suggested that a 110 millisecond (ms) region of low pitch is a fairly good predictor for back-channel feedback in casual conversational interactions. He also argued that more obvious factors, such as utterance end, rising intonation, and specific lexical items, account for less than they seem to. He contended that prosody alone is sometimes enough to tell you what to say and when to say.

In their analysis of turn-taking and backchannels based on prosodic and syntactic features, in Japanese Map Task dialogs, Koiso et al. (1998) observed that some part-of-speech (POS) features are strong syntactic cues for turn-change, and some others are strongly associated with no turn-change. Using manually extracted prosodic features for their analysis, they observed that falling and rising F0 patterns are related to changes of turn, and flat, flat-fall and rise-fall patterns are indications of the speaker continuing to speak. Extending their analysis to backchannels, they asserted that syntactic features, such as filled pauses, alone might be sufficient to discriminate when back-channelling is inappropriate, whereas presence of backchannels is always preceded by certain prosodic patterns.

Cathcart et al. (2003) presented a shallow model for predicting the location of backchannel *continuers* in the HCRC Map Task Corpus (Anderson et al., 1991). They explored features such as POS, word count in the preceding speaker turn, and silence pause duration in their models. A model based on silence pause only inserted a backchannel in every speaker pause longer than 900 ms and performed better than a word model that predicted a backchannel every seventh word. A tri-gram POS model predicted that nouns and pronouns before a pause are the two most important cues for predicting backchannel continuers. The combination of the tri-gram POS model and pause duration model offered a five-fold improvement over the others.

Gravano & Hirschberg (2009) investigated whether backchannel-inviting cues differ from turn-yielding cues. They examined a number of acoustic features and lexical cues in the speaker utterances preceding smooth turn-changes, backchannels, and holds. They have identified six measureable events that are strong predictors of a backchannel at the end of an *inter-pausal unit*: (i) a final rising intonation; (ii) a higher intensity level; (iii) a higher pitch level; (iv) a final POS bi-gram equal to 'DT NN', 'JJ NN', or 'NN NN'; (v) lower values of noise-to-harmonic ratios; and (vi) a longer IPU duration. They also observed that the likelihood of a backchannel increases in quadratic fashion with the number of cues conjointly displayed by the speaker.

When it comes to using these features for making turn-taking decisions in dialogue systems, there is however, very little related work. One notable exception is Raux & Eskenazi (2008) who presented an algorithm for dynamically setting *endpointing* silence thresholds based on features from discourse, semantics, prosody, timing, and speaker characteristics. The model was also applied and evaluated in the Let's Go dialogue system for bus timetable information. However, that model only predicted the endpointing threshold based on the previous interaction up to the last system utterance, it did not base the decision on the current user utterance to which the system response is to be made.

In this paper, we train a model for online Response Location Detection that makes a decision whether to respond at every point where a very short silence (200 ms) is detected. The model is trained on human–machine dialogue data taken from a first set of interactions with a system that used a very naïve policy for Response Location Detection. The trained model is then applied to the same system, which has allowed us to evaluate the model online in interaction with users.

3 A Map Task dialogue system

In a previous study, we presented a fully automated spoken dialogue system that can perform the Map Task with a user (Skantze, 2012). Map Task is a common experimental paradigm for studying human-human dialogue, where one subject (the information *giver*) is given the task of describing a route on a map to another subject (the information *follower*). In our case, the user acts as the giver and the system as the follower. The choice of Map Task is motivated partly because the system may allow the user to keep the initiative during the whole dialogue, and thus only produce responses that are not intended to take the initiative, most often some kind of feedback. Thus, the system might be described as an *attentive listener*.

Implementing a Map Task dialogue system with full speech understanding would indeed be a challenging task, given the state-of-the-art in automatic recognition of conversational speech. In order to make the task feasible, we have implemented a trick: the user is presented with a map on a screen (see Figure 1) and instructed to move the mouse cursor along the route as it is being described. The user is told that this is for logging purposes, but the real reason for this is that the system tracks the mouse position and thus knows what the user is currently talking about. It is thereby possible to produce a coherent system behaviour without any speech recognition at all, only basic speech detection. This often results in a very realistic interaction, as compared to what users are typically used to when interacting with dialogue systems—in our experiments, several users first thought that there was a hidden operator behind it[1].

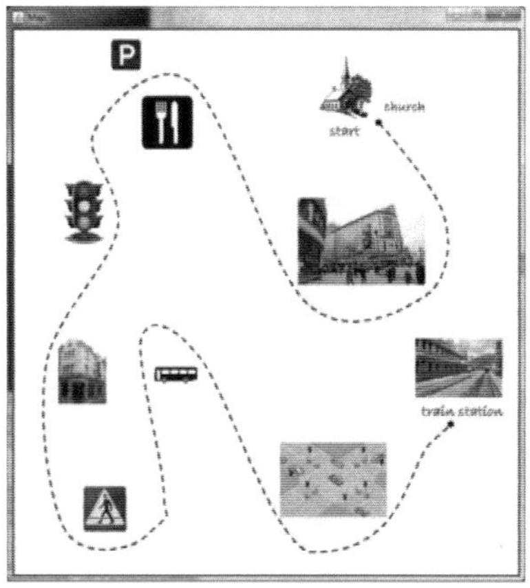

Figure 1: The user interface, showing the map.

The basic components of the system can be seen in Figure 2. Dashed lines indicate components that were not part of the first iteration of the system (used for data collection), but which have been used in the model presented and evaluated here. The system uses a simple energy-based speech detector to chunk the user's speech into inter-pausal units (IPUs), that is, periods of speech that contain no sequence of silence longer than 200 ms. Such a short threshold allows the system to give backchannels (seemingly) while the user is speaking or take the turn with barely any gap. Similar to Gravano & Hirschberg (2009) and Koiso et al. (1998), we define the end of an IPU as a candidate for the Response Location Detection model to identify as a Response Location (RL). We use the term *turn* to refer to a sequence of IPUs which do not have any responses between them.

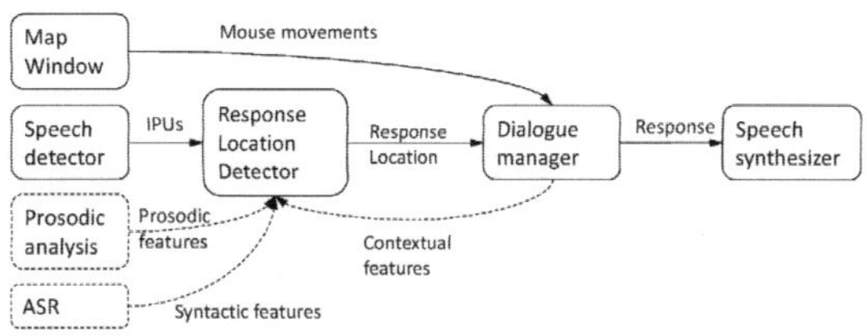

Figure 2: The basic components of the system.

[1] An example video can be seen at http://www.youtube.com/watch?v=MzL-B9pVbOE.

Each time the RLD model detected a RL, the dialogue manager produced a Response, depending on the current state of the dialogue and the position of the mouse cursor. Table 1 shows the different types of responses the system could produce. The dialogue manager always started with an Introduction and ended with an Ending, once the mouse cursor had reached the destination. Between these, it selected from the other responses, partly randomly, but also depending on the length of the last user turn and the current mouse location. Longer turns often led to Restart or Repetition Requests, thus discouraging longer sequences of speech that did not invite the system to respond. If the system detected that the mouse had been at the same place over a longer time, it pushed the task forward by making a Guess response. We also wanted to explore other kinds of feedback than just backchannels, and therefore added short Reprise Fragments and Clarification Requests (see for example Skantze (2007) for a discussion on these).

Table 1: Different responses from the system

Introduction	"Could you help me to find my way to the train station?"
Backchannel	"Yeah", "Mhm", "Okay", "Uhu"
Reprise Fragment	"A station, yeah"
Clarification Request	"A station?"
Restart	"Eh, I think I lost you at the hotel, how should I continue from there?"
Repetition Request	"Sorry, could you take that again?"
Guess	"Should I continue above the church?"
Ending	"Okay, thanks a lot."

A naïve version of the system was used to collect data. Since we initially did not have any sophisticated model of RLD, it was simply set to wait for a random period between 0 and 800 ms after an IPU ended. If no new IPUs were initiated during this period, a RL was detected, resulting in random response delays between 200 and 1000 ms. Ten subjects participated in the data collection. Each subject did 5 consecutive tasks on 5 different maps, resulting in a total of 50 dialogues.

Each IPU in the corpus was manually annotated into three categories: Hold (a response would be inappropriate), Respond (a response is expected) and Optional (a response would not be inappropriate, but it is perfectly fine not to respond). Two human-annotators labelled the corpus separately. For all the three categories the kappa score was 0.68, which is substantial agreement (Landis & Koch, 1977). Since only 2.1% of all the IPUs in the corpus were identified for category Optional, we excluded them from the corpus and focused on the Respond and Hold categories only. The data-set contains 2272 IPUs in total; the majority of which belong to the class Respond (50.79%), which we take as our majority class baseline. Since the two annotators agreed on 87.20% of the cases, this can be regarded as an approximate upper limit for the performance expected from a model trained on this data.

In (Skantze, 2012), we used this collected data to build an offline model of RLD that was trained on prosodic and contextual features. In this paper, we extend this work in three ways. First, we bring in Automatic Speech Recognition (ASR) for adding syntactic features to the model. Second, the model is implemented as a module in the dialogue system so that it can extract the prosodic features online. Third, we evaluate the performance of our RLD model against a baseline system that makes a random choice, in a dialogue system interacting with users.

In contrast to some related work (e.g. Koiso et al., 1998), we do not discriminate between locations for backchannels and turn-changes. Instead, we propose a general model for response location detection. The reason for this is that the system mostly plays the role of an attentive listener that produces utterances that are not intended to take the initiative or claim the floor, but only to provide different types of feedback (cf. Table 1). Thus, suitable response locations will be where the user invites the system to give feedback, regardless of whether the feedback is simply an acknowledgement that encourages the system to continue, or a clarification request. Moreover, it is not clear whether the acknowledgements the system produces in this domain should really be classified as backchannels, since they do not only signal continued attention, but also that some action has been performed (cf. Clark, 1996). Indeed, none of the annotators felt the need to mark relevant response locations within IPUs.

4 A data-driven model for response location detection

The human–machine Map Task corpus described in the previous section was used for training a new model of RLD. We describe below how we extracted prosodic, syntactic and contextual features from the IPUs. We test the contribution of these feature categories—individually as well as in combination, in classifying a given IPU as either Respond or Hold type. For this we explore the Naïve Bayes (NB) and Support Vector Machine (SVM) algorithms in the WEKA toolkit (Hall et al., 2009). All results presented here are based on 10-fold cross-validation.

4.1 Prosodic features

Pitch and intensity (sampled at 10 ms) for each IPU were extracted using ESPS in Wavesurfer/Snack (Sjölander & Beskow, 2000). The values were transformed to log scale and z-normalized for each user. The final 200 ms voiced region was then identified for each IPU. For this region, the **mean pitch**, **slope of the pitch** (using linear regression)—in combination with the **correlation coefficient *r*** for the regression line, were used as features. In addition to these, we also used the **duration** of the voiced region as a feature. The last 500 ms of each IPU were used to obtain the **mean intensity** (also z-normalised). Table 2 illustrates the power of prosodic features, individually as well as collectively (last row), in classifying an IPU as either Respond or Hold type. Except for mean intensity all other features individually provide an improvement over the baseline. The best accuracy, 64.5%, was obtained by the SVM algorithm using all the prosodic features. This should be compared against the baseline of 50.79%.

Table 2: Percentage accuracy of prosodic features in detecting response locations

	Algorithm	
Feature(s)	**NB**	**SVM**
Mean pitch	60.3	62.7
Pitch slope	59.0	57.8
Duration	58.1	55.6
Mean intensity	50.3	52.2
Prosody (all combined)	63.3	**64.5**

4.2 Syntactic features

As lexico-syntactic features, we use the **word form** and **part-of-speech tag** of the last two words in an IPU. All the IPUs in the Map Task corpus were manually transcribed. To obtain the part-of-speech tag we used the LBJ toolkit (Rizzolo & Roth, 2010). Column three in Table 3 illustrates the discriminatory power of syntactic features—extracted from the manual transcription of the IPUs. Using the last two words and their POS tags, the Naïve Bayes learner achieves the best accuracy of 83.6% (cf. row 7). While POS tag is a generic feature that would enable the model to generalize, using word form as a feature has the advantage that some words, such as *yeah*, are strong cues for predicting the Respond class, whereas pause fillers, such as *ehm*, are strong predictors of the Hold class.

Table 3: Percentage accuracy of syntactic features in detecting response locations

		Manual transcriptions		ASR results	
#	**Feature(s)**	**NB**	**SVM**	**NB**	**SVM**
1	Last word (Lw)	82.5	83.9	80.8	80.9
2	Last word part-of-speech (Lw-POS)	79.4	79.5	74.5	74.6
3	Second last word (2ndLw)	68.1	67.7	67.1	67.0
4	Second last word Part-of-speech (2ndLw-POS)	66.9	66.5	65.8	66.1
5	Lw + 2ndLw	82.3	81.5	80.8	80.6
6	Lw-POS + 2ndLw-POS	80.3	80.5	75.4	74.87
7	Lw + 2ndLw + Lw-POS + 2ndLw-POS	**83.6**	81.7	79.7	79.7
8	Last word dictionary (Lw-Dict)	83.4	83.4	78.0	78.0
9	Lw-Dict + 2ndLw-Dict	81.2	82.6	76.1	77.7
10	Lw + 2ndLw + Lw-Conf + 2ndLw-Conf	82.3	81.5	**81.1**	80.5

An RLD model for online predictions requires that the syntactic features are extracted from the output of a speech recogniser. Since speech recognition is prone to errors, an RLD model trained on manual transcriptions alone would not be robust when making predictions in noisy data. Therefore we train our RLD model on actual speech recognised results. To achieve this, we did an 80-20 split of the Map Task corpus into training and test sets respectively. The transcriptions of IPUs in the training set were used to train the language model of the Nuance 9 ASR system. The audio recordings of the IPUs in the test set were then recognised by the trained ASR system. After performing five iterations of splitting, training and testing, we had obtained the speech recognised results for all the IPUs in the Map Task corpus. The mean word error rate for the five iterations was 17.22% (*SD* = 3.8%).

Column four in Table 3 illustrates the corresponding performances of the RLD model trained on syntactic features extracted from the best speech recognized hypotheses for the IPUs. With the introduction of a word error rate of 17.22%, the performances of all the models using only POS tag feature decline. The performances are bound to decline further with increase in ASR errors. This is because the POS tagger itself uses the left context to make POS tag predictions. With the introduction of errors in the left context, the tagger's accuracy is affected, which in turn affects the accuracy of the RLD models. However, this decline is not significant for models that use word form as a feature. This suggests that using context independent lexico-syntactic features would still offer better performance for an online model of RLD. We therefore also created a word class **dictionary**, which generalises the words into domain-specific classes in a simple way (much like a class-based n-gram model)**.** Row 9 in Table 3 illustrates that using a dictionary instead of POS tag (cf. row 6) improves the performance of the online model. We have also explored the use of word-level **confidence scores (Conf)** from the ASR as another feature that could be used to reinforce a learning algorithm's confidence in trusting the recognised words (cf. row 10 in Table 3).

The best accuracy, 81.1%, for the *online* model of RLD is achieved by the Naïve Bayes algorithm using the features word form and confidence score, for last two words in an IPU.

4.3 Contextual features

We have explored three discourse context features: **turn** and **IPU length** (in words and seconds) and **last system dialogue act**. Dialogue act history information have been shown to be vital for predicting a listener response when the speaker has just responded to the listener's clarification request (Koiso et al. (1998); Cathcart et al. 2003; Gravano & Hirschberg (2009); Skantze, 2012). To verify if this rule holds in our corpus, we extracted turn length and dialogue act labels for the IPUs, and trained a J48 decision tree learner. The decision tree achieved an accuracy of 65.7%. One of the rules learned by the decision tree is: *if the last system dialogue act is Clarification or Guess (cf. Table 1), and the turn word count is less than equal to 1, then Respond.* In other words, if the system had previously sought a clarification, and the user has responded with a yes/no utterance, then a system response is expected. A more general rule in the decision tree suggests that: *if the last system dialogue act was a Restart or Repetition Request, and if the turn word count is more than 4 then Respond otherwise Hold.* In other words, the system should wait until it gets some *amount* of information from the user.

Table 4 illustrates the power of these contextual features in discriminating IPUs, using the NB and the SVM algorithms. All the features individually provide improvement over the baseline of 50.79%. The best accuracy, 64.8%, is achieved by the SVM learner using the features *last system dialogue act* and *turn word count.*

Table 4: Percentage accuracy of contextual features in detecting response locations

	Manual transcriptions		ASR results	
Features	**NB**	**SVM**	**NB**	**SVM**
Last system dialogue act	54.1	54.1	54.1	54.1
Turn word count	61.8	61.9	61.5	62.9
Turn length in seconds	58.4	58.8	58.4	58.8
IPU word count	58.4	58.2	58.1	59.3
IPU length in seconds	57.3	61.2	57.3	61.2
Last system dialogue act + Turn word count	59.9	**64.5**	60.4	**64.8**

4.4 Combined model

Table 5 illustrates the performances of the RLD model using various feature category combinations. It could be argued that the discriminatory power of prosodic and contextual feature categories is comparable. A model combining prosodic and contextual features offers an improvement over their individual performances. Using the three feature categories in combination, the Naïve Bayes learner provided the best accuracy: 84.6% (on transcriptions) and 82.0% (on ASR output). These figures are significantly better than the majority class baseline of 50.79% and approach the expected upper limit of 87.20% on the performance.

Table 5: Percentage accuracy of combined models

	Manual transcriptions		ASR results	
Feature categories	**NB**	**SVM**	**NB**	**SVM**
Prosody	63.3	64.5	63.3	64.5
Context	59.9	64.5	60.4	64.8
Syntax	82.3	81.5	81.1	80.5
Prosody + Context	67.7	70.2	67.5	69.1
Prosody + Context + Syntax	**84.6**	77.2	**82.0**	77.1

Table 6 illustrates that the Naïve Bayes model for Response Location Detection trained on combined syntactic, prosodic and contextual features, offers better precision (fraction of correct decisions in all model decisions) and recall (fraction of all relevant decisions correctly made) in comparison to the SVM model.

Table 6: Precision and Recall scores of the NB and the SVM learners trained on combined prosodic, contextual and syntactic features.

Prediction class	Precision (in %)		Recall (in %)	
	NB	SVM	NB	SVM
Respond	81.0	73.0	87.0	84.0
Hold	85.0	81.0	78.0	68.0

5 User evaluation

In order to evaluate the usefulness of the combined model, we have performed a user evaluation where we test the trained model in the Map Task dialogue system that was used to collect the corpus (cf. section 3). A version of the dialogue system was created that uses a Random model, which makes a random choice between Respond and Hold. The Random model thus approximates our majority class baseline (50.79% for Respond). Another version of the system used the Trained model – our data-driven model – to make the decision. For both models, if the decision was a Hold, the system waited 1.5 seconds and then responded anyway if no more speech was detected from the user.

We hypothesize that since the Random model makes random choices, it is likely to produce false-positive responses (resulting in overlap in interaction) as well as false-negative responses (resulting in gap/delayed response) in equal proportion. The Trained model on the other hand would produce fewer overlaps and gaps.

In order to evaluate the models, 8 subjects (2 female, 6 male) were asked to perform the Map Task with the two systems. Each subject performed five dialogues (which included 1 trial and 2 tests) with each version of the system. This resulted in 16 test dialogues each for the two systems. The trial session was used to allow the users to familiarize themselves with the dialogue system. Also, the audio recording of the users' speech from this session was used to normalize the user pitch and intensity for the online prosodic extraction. The order in which the systems and maps were presented to the subjects was varied over the subjects to avoid any ordering effect in the analysis.

The 32 dialogues from the user evaluation were, on average, 1.7 min long (*SD* = 0.5 min). The duration of the interactions with the Random and the Trained model were not significantly different. A total of 557 IPUs were classified by the Random model whereas the Trained model classified 544 IPUs. While the Trained model classified 57.7% of the IPUs as Respond type the Random model classified only 48.29% of the total IPUs as Respond type, suggesting that the Random model was somewhat quieter.

It turned out that it was very hard for the subjects to perform the Map Task and at the same time make a valid subjective comparison between the two versions of the system, as we had initially intended. Therefore, we instead conducted another subjective evaluation to compare the two systems. We asked subjects to listen to the interactions and press a key whenever a system response was either lacking or inappropriate. The subjects were asked not to consider *how* the system actually responded, only evaluate the timing of the response.

Eight users participated in this subjective judgment task. Although five of these were from the same set of users who had performed the Map Task, none of them got to judge their own interactions. The judges listened to the Map Task interactions in the same order as the users had interacted, including the trial session. Whereas it had been hard for the subjects who participated in the dialogues to characterize the two versions of the system, almost all of the judges could clearly tell the two versions apart. They stated that the Trained system provided for a smooth flow of dialogue. The timing of the IPUs was aligned with the timing of the judges' key-presses in order to measure the numbers of IPUs that had been given inappropriate response decisions. The results show that for the Random model, 26.75% of the RLD decisions were perceived as inappropriate, whereas only 11.39% of the RLD decisions for the Trained model were perceived inappropriate. A two-tailed two-sample t-test for difference in mean of the fraction of inappropriate instances (key-press count divided by IPU count) for Random and Trained model show a clear significant difference ($t = 4.66$, $dF = 30$, $p < 0.001$).

We have not yet analysed whether judges penalized false-positives or false-negatives to a larger extent, this is left to future work. However, some judges informed us that they did not penalize delayed response (false-negative), as the system eventually responded after a delay. In the context of a system trying to follow a route description, such delays could sometimes be expected and wouldn't be unnatural. For other types of interactions (such as story-telling), such delays may on the other hand be perceived as unresponsive. Thus, the balance between false-positives and false-negatives might need to be tuned depending on the topic of the conversation.

6 Conclusion

We have presented a data-driven model for detecting response locations in the user's speech. The model has been trained on human–machine dialogue data and has been integrated and tested in a spoken dialogue system that can perform the Map Task with users. To our knowledge, this is the first example of a dialogue system that uses automatically extracted syntactic, prosodic and contextual features for making *online* detection of response locations. The models presented in earlier works have used only prosody (Ward, 1996), or combinations of syntax and prosody (Koiso et al., 1998), syntax and context (Cathcart et al., 2003), prosody and context (Skantze, 2012), or prosody, context and semantics (Raux & Eskenazi (2008). Furthermore, we have evaluated the usefulness of our model by performing a user evaluation of a dialogue system interacting with users. None of the earlier models have been tested in user evaluations.

The significant improvement of the model gained by adding lexico-syntactic features such as word form and part-of-speech tag corroborates with earlier observations about the contribution of syntax in predicting response location (Koiso et al., 1998; Cathcart et al., 2003; Gravano & Hirschberg, 2009). While POS tag alone is a strong generic feature for making predictions in offline models its contribution to decision making in online models is reduced due to speech recognition errors. This is because the POS tagger itself uses the left context to make predictions, and is not typically trained to handle noisy input. We have shown that using only the word form or a dictionary offers a better performance despite speech recognition errors. However, this of course results in a more domain-dependent model.

Koiso et al., (1998), have shown that prosodic features contribute almost as strongly to response location prediction as the syntactic features. We do not find such results with our model. This difference could be partly attributed to inter-speaker variation in the human–machine Map Task corpus used for training the models. All the users who participated in the corpus collection were non-native speakers of English. Also, our algorithm for extracting prosodic features is not as powerful as the manual extraction scheme used in (Koiso et al., 1998). Although prosodic and contextual features do not seem to improve the performance very much when syntactic features are available, they are clearly useful when no ASR is available (70.2% as compared to the baseline of 50.79%).

The subjective evaluation indicates that the interactions with a system using our trained model were perceived as smoother (more accurate responses) as compared to a system using a model that makes a random choice between Respond and Hold.

7 Future work

Coordination problems in turn-transition and responsiveness have been identified as important short-comings of turn-taking models in current dialogue systems (Ward et al., 2005). In continuation of the current evaluation exercise, we would next evaluate our Trained model—on an objective scale, in terms of its responsiveness and smoothness in turn-taking and back-channels. An objective measure is the proportion of judge key-presses coinciding with false-positive and false-negative model decisions. We argue that in comparison to the Random model our Trained model produces (i) fewer instances of false-negatives (gap/delayed response) and therefore has a faster response time, and (ii) fewer instances of false-positives (overlap) and thus provides for smooth turn-transitions.

We have so far explored syntactic, prosodic and contextual features for predicting response location. An immediate extension to our model would be to bring semantic features in the model. In Meena et al. (2012) we have presented a data-driven method for semantic interpretation of verbal route descriptions into *conceptual route graphs*—a semantic representation that captures the semantics of the way human structure information in route descriptions. Another possible extension is to situate the interaction in a face-to-face Map Task between a human and a robot and add features from other modalities such as gaze.

In a future version of the system, we do not only want to determine *when* to give responses but also *what* to respond. In order to do this, the system will need to extract the semantic concepts of the route directions (as described above) and utilize the confidence scores from the spoken language understanding component in order to select between different forms of clarification requests and acknowledgements.

Acknowledgments

This work is supported by the Swedish research council (VR) project *Incremental processing in multimodal conversational systems* (2011-6237).

References

Anderson, A., Bader, M., Bard, E., Boyle, E., Doherty, G., Garrod, S., Isard, S., Kowtko, J., McAllister, J., Miller, J., Sotillo, C., Thompson, H., & Weinert, R. (1991). The HCRC Map Task corpus. *Language and Speech, 34*(4), 351-366.

Cathcart, N., Carletta, J., & Klein, E. (2003). A shallow model of backchannel continuers in spoken dialogue. In *10th Conference of the European Chapter of the Association for Computational Linguistics*. Budapest.

Clark, H. H. (1996). *Using language*. Cambridge, UK: Cambridge University Press.

Duncan, S. (1972). Some Signals and Rules for Taking Speaking Turns in Conversations. *Journal of Personality and Social Psychology, 23*(2), 283-292.

Gravano, A., & Hirschberg, J. (2009). Backchannel-inviting cues in task-oriented dialogue. In *Proceedings of Interspeech 2009* (pp. 1019-1022). Brighton, U.K.

Hall, M., Frank, E., Holmes, G., Pfahringer, B., Reutemann, P., & Witten, I. H. (2009). The WEKA Data Mining Software: An Update. *SIGKDD Explorations, 11*(1).

Koiso, H., Horiuchi, Y., Tutiya, S., Ichikawa, A., & Den, Y. (1998). An analysis of turn-taking and backchannels based on prosodic and syntactic features in Japanese Map Task dialogs. *Language and Speech, 41*, 295-321.

Landis, J., & Koch, G. (1977). The measurement of observer agreement for categorical data. *Biometrics, 33*(1), 159-174.

Meena, R., Skantze, G., & Gustafson, J. (2012). A Data-driven Approach to Understanding Spoken Route Directions in Human-Robot Dialogue. In *Proceedings of Interspeech*. Portland, OR, US.

Raux, A., & Eskenazi, M. (2008). Optimizing endpointing thresholds using dialogue features in a spoken dialogue system. In *Proceedings of SIGdial 2008*. Columbus, OH, USA.

Rizzolo, N., & Roth, D. (2010). Learning Based Java for Rapid Development of NLP Systems. *Language Resources and Evaluation*.

Sacks, H., Schegloff, E., & Jefferson, G. (1974). A simplest systematics for the organization of turn-taking for conversation. *Language, 50*, 696-735.

Sjölander, K., & Beskow, J. (2000). WaveSurfer - an open source speech tool. In Yuan, B., Huang, T., & Tang, X. (Eds.), *Proceedings of ICSLP 2000, 6th Intl Conf on Spoken Language Processing* (pp. 464-467). Beijing.

Skantze, G. (2007). *Error Handling in Spoken Dialogue Systems - Managing Uncertainty, Grounding and Miscommunication*. Doctoral dissertation, KTH, Department of Speech, Music and Hearing.

Skantze, G. (2012). A Testbed for Examining the Timing of Feedback using a Map Task. In *Proceedings of the Interdisciplinary Workshop on Feedback Behaviors in Dialog*. Portland, OR.

Ward, N., Rivera, A., Ward, K., & Novick, D. (2005). Root causes of lost time and user stress in a simple dialog system. In *Proceedings of Interspeech 2005*. Lisbon, Portugal.

Ward, N. (1996). Using prosodic clues to decide when to produce backchannel utterances. In *Proceedings of the fourth International Conference on Spoken Language Processing* (pp. 1728-1731). Philadelphia, USA.

Yngve, V. H. (1970). On getting a word in edgewise. In *Papers from the sixth regional meeting of the Chicago Linguistic Society* (pp. 567-578). Chicago.

Continuously Predicting and Processing Barge-in During a Live Spoken Dialogue Task

Ethan O. Selfridge†, Iker Arizmendi‡, Peter A. Heeman†, and Jason D. Williams[1]

† Center for Spoken Language Understanding, Oregon Health & Science University, Portland, OR, USA
‡AT&T Labs – Research, Shannon Laboratory, Florham Park, NJ, USA
[1]Microsoft Research, Redmond, WA, USA
selfridg@ohsu.edu

Abstract

Barge-in enables the user to provide input during system speech, facilitating a more natural and efficient interaction. Standard methods generally focus on single-stage barge-in detection, applying the dialogue policy irrespective of the barge-in context. Unfortunately, this approach performs poorly when used in challenging environments. We propose and evaluate a barge-in processing method that uses a prediction strategy to continuously decide whether to pause, continue, or resume the prompt. This model has greater task success and efficiency than the standard approach when evaluated in a public spoken dialogue system.

Index Terms: spoken dialogue systems, barge-in

1 Introduction

Spoken dialogue systems (SDS) communicate with users with spoken natural language; the optimal SDS being effective, efficient, and natural. Allowing input during system speech, known as *barge-in*, is one approach that designers use to improve system performance. In the ideal use case, the system detects user speech, switches off the prompt, and then responds to the user's utterance. Dialogue efficiency improves, as the system receives information prior to completing its prompt, and the interaction becomes more natural, as the system demonstrates more human-like turn-taking behavior. However, barge-in poses a number of new challenges; the system must now recognize and process input during its prompt that may *not* be well-formed system directed speech. This is a difficult task and standard barge-in approaches often stop the prompt for input that will not be understood, subsequently initiating a clarification sub-dialogue ("I'm sorry, I didn't get that. You can say...etc."). This non-understood barge-in (NUBI) could be from environmental noise, non-system directed speech, poorly-formed system directed speech, legitimate speech recognition difficulties (such as acoustic model mismatch), or any combination thereof.

This paper proposes and evaluates a barge-in processing method that focuses on handling NUBIs. Our Prediction-based Barge-in Response (PBR) model continuously predicts interpretation success by applying adaptive thresholds to incremental recognition results. In our view, *predicting* whether the recognition will be understood has far more utility than detecting whether the barge-in is truly system directed speech as, for many domains, we feel only understandable input has more discourse importance than system speech. If the input is predicted to be understood, the prompt is paused. If it is predicted or found to be NUBI, the prompt is resumed. Using this method, the system may resume speaking before recognition is complete and will never initiate a clarifying sub-dialogue in response to a NUBI. The PBR model was implemented in a public Lets Go! statistical dialogue system (Raux et al., 2005), and we compare it with a system using standard barge-in methods. We find the PBR model has a significantly better task success rate and efficiency.

Table 1 illustrates the NUBI responses produced by the standard barge-in (Baseline) and PBR models. After both prompts are paused, the standard method initiates a clarifying sub-dialogue whereas PBR resumes the prompt.

We first provide background on Incremental Speech Recognition and describe the relevant related work on barge-in. We then detail the Prediction-based Barge-in Response model's operation and motivation before presenting a whole-call and component-wise analysis of the PBR

[1]Work done while at AT&T Labs - Research

Table 1: *System response to Non-Understood Barge-In (NUBI)*

Baseline	Ok, sixty one <*NUBI*> Sorry, say a bus route like twenty eight x
PBR	Ok, sixty one <*NUBI*> sixty one c. Where are you leaving from?

model. The paper concludes with a discussion of our findings and implications for future SDS.

2 Background and Related Work

Incremental Speech Recognition: Incremental Speech Recognition (ISR) provides the real-time information critical to the PBR model's continuous predictions. ISR produces partial recognition results ("partials") until input ceases and the "final" recognition result is produced following some silence. As partials have a tendency to be revised as more audio is processed, stability measures are used to predict whether a given partial hypothesis will be present in the final recognition result (McGraw and Gruenstein, 2012; Selfridge et al., 2011). Here, we use Lattice-Aware ISR, which produces partials after a Voice Activity Detector (VAD) indicates speech and limits them to be a complete language model specified phrase or have guaranteed stability (Selfridge et al., 2011).

Barge-In: Using the standard barge-in model, the system stops the prompt if barge-in is detected and applies the dialogue logic to the final recognition result. This approach assumes that the barge-in context should not influence the dialogue policy, and most previous work on barge-in has focused on detection: distinguishing system directed speech from other environmental sounds. Currently, these methods are either based on a VAD (e.g. (Ström and Seneff, 2000)), ISR hypotheses (Raux, 2008), or some combination (Rose and Kim, 2003). Both approaches can lead to detection errors: background speech will trigger the VAD, and partial hypotheses are unreliable (Baumann et al., 2009). To minimize this, many systems only enable barge-in at certain points in the dialogue.

One challenge with the standard barge-in model is that detection errors can initiate a clarifying sub-dialogue to non-system directed input, as it is unlikely that this input will be understood (Raux, 2008). Since this false barge-in, which in most cases is background speech (e.g. the television), is highly indicative of poor recognition performance overall, the system's errant clarifying response can only further degrade user experience.

Strom and Seneff (2000) provide, to our knowledge, the only mature work that proposed deviating from the dialogue policy when responding to a barge-in recognition. Instead of initiating a clarifying sub-dialogue, the system produced a filled-pause disfluency ('umm') and resumed the prompt at the phrase boundary closest to the prompt's suspension point. However, this model only operated at the final recognition level (as opposed the incremental level) and, unfortunately, they provide no evaluation of their approach. An explicit comparison between the approaches described here and the PBR model is found in Section 3.5.

3 Prediction-based Barge-in Response

The PBR model is characterized by three high-level states: State 1 (Speaking Prediction), whose goal is to pause the prompt if stability scores predict understanding; State 2 (Silent Prediction), whose goal is to resume the prompt if stability scores and the incremental recognition rate predict non-understanding; and State 3 (Completion), which operates on the final recognition result, and resumes the prompt unless the recognition is understood and the new speech act will advance the dialogue. Here, we define "advancing the dialogue" to be any speech act that does not start a clarifying sub-dialogue indicating a NUBI. Transitions between State 1 and 2 are governed by adaptive thresholds — repeated resumptions suggest the user is in a noisy environment, so each resumption increases the threshold required to advance from State 1 to State 2 and decreases the threshold required to advance from State 2 to State 1. A high-level comparison of the standard model and our approach is shown in Figure 1; a complete PBR state diagram is provided in the Appendix.

3.1 State 1: Speaking Prediction

In State 1, Speaking Prediction, the system is both speaking and performing ISR. The system scores each partial for stability, predicting the probability that it will remain "stable" – i.e., will not be later revised – using a logistic regression model (Selfridge et al., 2011). This model uses a number of features related to the recognizer's generic confidence score, the word confusion network, and lattice characteristics. Table 2 shows partial results

Table 2: *Background noise and User Speech ISR*

Background Noise		User Utterance	
Partial	Stab. Scr.	Partial	Stab. Scr.
one	0.134	six	0.396
two	0.193	sixty	0.542
six	0.127	fifty one	0.428
two	0.078	sixty one a	0.491

and stability scores for two example inputs: background noise on the left, and the user saying "sixty one a" on the right.

State 1 relies on the internal threshold parameter, T_1. If a partial's stability score falls below T_1, control remains in State 1 and the partial result is discarded. If a stability score meets T_1, the prompt is paused and control transitions to State 2. T_1 is initially set to 0 and is adapted as the dialogue progresses. The adaptation procedure is described below in Section 3.4. If a *final* recognition result is received, control transitions directly to State 3. Transitioning from State 1 to State 2 is only allowed during the middle 80% of the prompt; otherwise only transitions to State 3 are allowed.[1]

3.2 State 2: Silent Prediction

Upon entering State 2, Silent Prediction, the prompt is paused and a timer is started. State 2 requires continuous evidence (at least every T_2 ms) that the ISR is recognizing valid speech and each time a partial result that meets T_1 is received, the timer is reset. If the timer reaches the time threshold T_2, the prompt is resumed and control returns to State 1. T_2 is initially set at 1.0 seconds and is adapted as the dialogue progresses. Final recognition results trigger a transition to State 3.

The resumption prompt is constructed using the temporal position of the VAD specified speech start to find the percentage of the prompt that was played up to that point. This percentage is then reduced by 10% and used to create the resumption prompt by finding the word that is closest to, but not beyond, the modified percentage. White space characters and punctuation are used to determine word boundaries for text-to-speech prompts, whereas automatically generated word-alignments are used for pre-recorded prompts.

[1]We hypothesized that people will rarely respond to the current prompt during the first 10% of prompt time as overlaps at the beginning of utterances are commonly initiative conflicts (Yang and Heeman, 2010). Users may produce early-onset utterances during the last 10% that should not stop the prompt as it is not an "intentional" barge-in.

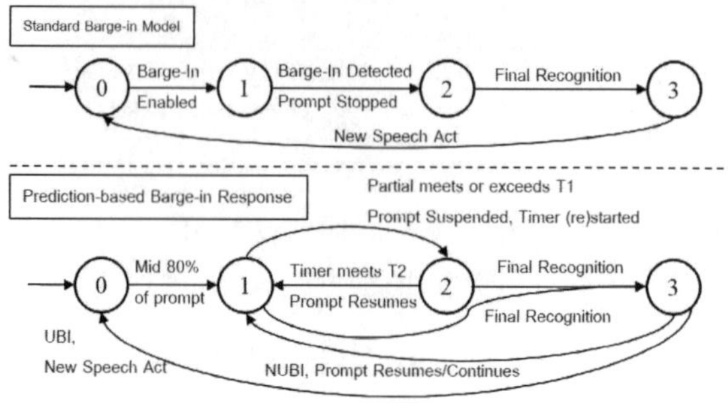

Figure 1: *The Standard Barge-in and PBR Models*

3.3 State 3: Completion

State 3, Completion, is entered when a final recognition result is received and determines whether the current dialogue policy will advance the dialogue or not. Here, the PBR model relies on the ability of the dialogue manager (DM) to produce a speculative action without transitioning to the next dialogue state. If the new action will not advance the dialogue, it is discarded and the recognition is NUBI. However, if it *will* advance the dialogue then it is classified as an Understood Barge-In (UBI). In the NUBI case, the system either continues speaking or resumes the current prompt (transitioning to State 1). In the UBI case, the system initiates the new speech act after playing a short reaction sound and the DM transitions to the next dialogue state. This reaction sound precedes *all* speech acts outside the barge-in context but is *not* used for resumption or timeout prompts. Note that by depending solely on the new speech act, our model does not require access to the DM's internal understanding or confidence scoring components.

3.4 Threshold adjustments

States 1 and 2 contain parameters T_1 and T_2 that are adapted to the user's environment. T_1 is the stability threshold used in State 1 and State 2 that controls how stable an utterance must be before the prompt should be paused. In quiet environments — where only the user's speech produces partial results — a low threshold is desirable as it enables near-immediate pauses in the prompt. Conversely, noisy environments yield many spurious partials that (in general) have much lower stability scores, so a higher threshold is advantageous. T_2 is the timing threshold used to resume the prompt *during* recognition in State 2. In quiet environments, a higher threshold reduces the chance that the system will resume its prompt during a well-formed user speech. In noisy environ-

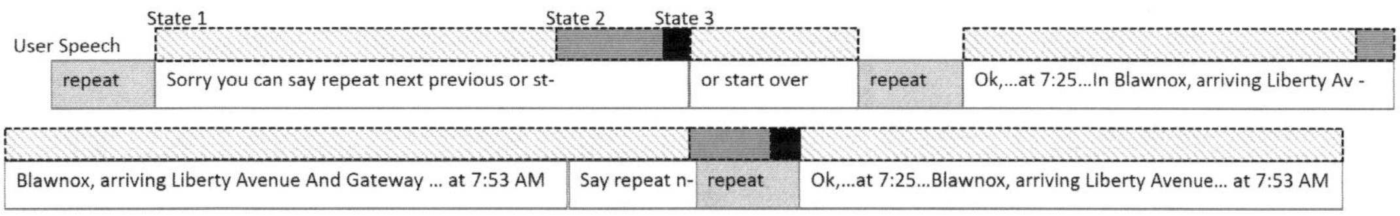

Figure 2: *Example dialogue fragment of PBR Model*

ments, a lower threshold allows the system to resume quickly as the NUBI likelihood is greater.

Both T_1 and T_2 are dependent on the number of system resumptions, as we view the action of resuming the prompt as an indication that the threshold is not correct. With every resumption, the parameter R is incremented by 1 and, to account for changing environments, R is decremented by 0.2 for every full prompt that is not *paused* until it reaches 0. Using R, T_1 is computed by $T_1 = 0.17 \cdot R$, and T_2 by $T_2 = argmax(0.1, 1 - (0.1 \cdot R))$.[2]

3.5 Method Discussion

The motivation behind the PBR model is both theoretical and practical. According to Selfridge and Heeman (2010), turn-taking is best viewed as a collaborative process where the turn assignment should be determined by the importance of the utterance. During barge-in, the system is speaking and so should only yield the turn if the user's speech is more important than its own. For many domains, we view non-understood input as less important than the system's prompt and so, in this case, the system should not release the turn by stopping the prompt and initiating a clarifying subdialogue. On the practical side, there is a high likelihood that non-advancing input is not system directed, to which the system should neither consume, in terms of belief state updating, nor respond to, in terms of asking for clarification. In the rare case of non-understood system directed speech, the user can easily repeat their utterance. Here, we note that in the event that the user is backchanneling, the PBR model will behave correctly and not release the turn.

The PBR approach differs from standard barge-in approaches in several respects. First, standard barge-in stops the prompt (i.e., transitions from State 1 to State 2) if either the VAD or the partial hypothesis suggests that there is speech; our approach — using acoustic, language model, and lattice features — predicts whether the input is likely to contain an interpretable recognition result. Second, standard barge-in uses a static threshold; our approach uses dynamic thresholds that adapt to the user's acoustic environment. Parameter adjustments are straightforward since our method automatically classifies each barge-in as NUBI or UBI. In practice, the prompt will be paused incorrectly only a few times in a noisy environment, after which the adaptive thresholds will prevent incorrect pauses at the expense of being less responsive to true user speech. If the noise level decreases, the thresholds will become more sensitive again, enabling swifter responses. Finally, with the exception of Strom and Seneff, standard approaches always discard the prompt; our approach can resume the prompt if recognition is not understood or is proceeding poorly, enabling the system to resume speaking before recognition is complete. Moreover, resumption yields a natural user experience as it often creates a repetition disfluency ("Ok, sixty - sixty one c"), which are rarely noticed by the listener (Martin and Strange, 1968).

An example dialogue fragment is shown in Figure 2, with the state transitions shown above. Note the transition from State 2 to State 1, which is the system resuming speech *during* recognition. This recognition stream, produced by non-system directed user speech, does not end until the user says "repeat" for the last time.

4 Evaluation Results

The PBR model was evaluated during the Spoken Dialog Challenge 2012-2013 in a live Lets Go! bus information task. In this task, the public can access bus schedule information during off hours in Pittsburgh, PA via a telephonic interaction with a dialogue system (Raux et al., 2005). The task can be divided into five sub-tasks: route, origin, destination, date/time, and bus schedules. The last sub-task, bus schedules, provides information to the user whereas the first four gather information. We entered two systems using the same POMDP-based DM (Williams, 2012). The first system, the "Baseline", used the standard barge-in model with VAD barge-in detection and barge-in disabled in

[2]The threshold update values were determined empirically by the authors.

Figure 3: *Estimated success rate for the PBR and Baseline systems. Stars indicate p<0.018 with χ^2 test.*

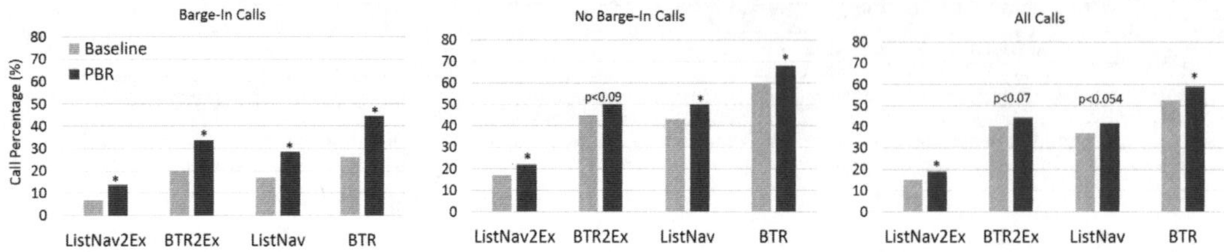

a small number of dialogue states that appeared problematic during initial testing. The second system used the PBR model with an Incremental Interaction Manager (Selfridge et al., 2012) to produce speculative actions in State 3. The public called both systems during the final weeks of 2011 and the start of 2012. The DM applied a logistic regression based confidence measure to determine whether the recognition was understood. Both systems used the AT&T WATSON^{SM} speech recognizer (Goffin et al., 2005) with the same sub-task specific rule-based language models and standard echo cancellation techniques. The beam width was set to maximize accuracy while still running faster than real-time. The PBR system used a WATSON modification to output lattice-aware partial results.

Call and barge-in statistics are shown in Table 3. Here, we define (potential) barge-in (somewhat imprecisely) as a full recognition that at some point overlaps with the system prompt, as determined by the call logs. We show the calls with barge-in *before* the bus schedule sub-task was reached (BI-BS) and the calls with barge-in during any point of the call (BI All). Since the Baseline system only enabled barge-in at specific points in the dialogue, it has fewer instances of barge-in (Total Barge-In) and fewer barge-in calls. Regretfully, due to logging issues with the PBR system, recognition specific metrics such as Word Error Rate and true/false barge-in rates are unavailable.

4.1 Estimated Success Rate

We begin by comparing the success rate and efficiency between the Baseline and PBR systems.

Table 3: *Baseline and PBR call/barge-in statistics.*

	Baseline	PBR
Total Calls	1027	892
BI-BS	228 (23%)	345 (39%)
BI All	281 (27%)	483 (54%)
Total Barge-In	829	1388

tems. Since task success can be quite difficult to measure, we use four increasingly stringent task success definitions: Bus Times Reached (BTR), where success is achieved if the call reaches the bus schedule sub-task; List Navigation (List Nav.), where success is achieved if the user says ''next", "previous", or "repeat" — the intuition being that if the user attempted to navigate the bus schedule sub-task they were somewhat satisfied with the system's performance so far; and Immediate Exit (BTR2Ex and ListNav2Ex), which further constrains both of the previous definitions to only calls that finish directly after the initial visit to the bus times sub-task. Success rate for the definitions were automatically computed (not manually labeled). Figure 3 shows the success rate of the PBR and Baseline systems for all four definitions of success. It shows, from left to right, Barge-In, No Barge-In (NBI), and All calls. Here we restrict barge-in calls to those where barge-in occurred prior to the bus schedule task being reached.

For the calls with barge-in, a χ^2 test finds significant differences between the PBR and Baseline for all four task success definitions. However, we also found significant differences in the NBI calls. This was surprising since, when barge-in is not triggered, both systems are ostensibly the same. We speculate this could be due to the Baseline's barge-in enabling strategy: an environment that triggers barge-in in the Baseline would always trigger barge-in in the PBR model, whereas the converse is *not* true as the Baseline only enabled barge-in in *some* of the states. This means that there is a potential mismatch when separating the calls based on barge-in, and so the fairest comparison is using *All* the calls. This is shown on the far right of Figure 3. We find that, while the effect is not as large, there are significant differences in the success rate for the PBR model for the most and least stringent success definition, and very strong trends for the middle two definitions ($p < 0.07$ for BTR2Ex and $p < 0.054$ for List Nav.). Taken as a whole, we feel this offers compelling evidence

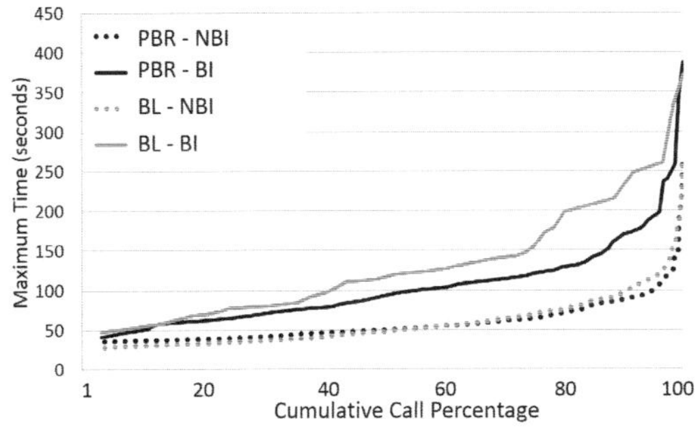

Figure 4: *Seconds from beginning of dialogue to reaching the Bus Schedule Information sub-task*

that the PBR method is more effective: i.e. yields higher task completion.

Next, we turn our attention to task efficiency. For this, we report the amount of clock time from the beginning of the call to when the Bus Schedule sub-task was reached. Calls that do not reach this sub-task are obviously excluded, and PBR times are adjusted for the reaction sound (explained in Section 3.3). Task efficiency is reported by cumulative percentage in Figure 4. We find that, while the NBI call times are nearly identical for both systems, the PBR barge-in calls are much faster than the Baseline calls. Here, we do not feel the previously described mismatch is particularly problematic as all the calls reached the goal state and the NBI are nearly identical. In fact, as more NUBI should actually *reduce* efficiency, the potential mismatch only strengthens the result.

Taken together, these results provide substantial evidence that the PBR model is more effective and more efficient than the Baseline. In order to explain PBR's performance, we explore the effect of prediction and resumption in isolation.

4.2 State 1: Speaking Prediction

State 1 is responsible for pausing the prompt, the goal being to pause the prompt for UBI input and not to pause the prompt for NUBI input. The prompt is paused if a partial's stability score meets or exceeds the T_1 threshold. We evaluate the efficacy of State 1 and T_1 by analyzing the statistics of NUBI/UBI input and Paused/Not Paused (hereafter *Continued*) prompts. Since resuming the prompt during recognition affects the recognition outcome, we restrict our analysis to recognitions that do not transition from State 2 back to State 1. For comparison we show the overall UBI/NUBI percentages for the Baseline and PBR systems. This represents the recognition distribution for the live Baseline VAD detection and off-line speculation for the PBR model. Recall PBR *does* have VAD activation preceding partial results and so the off-line PBR VAD shows how the model *would* have behaved if it only used the VAD for detection, as the Baseline does.

Table 4: *Evaluation of T_1, off-line PBR, and Baseline VAD. For T_1 we respectively ('-' split) show the UBI/NUBI % that are Paused/Continued, the Paused/Continued % that are UBI/NUBI, and the percentage over all recognitions*

	T_1 (%)		VAD (%)	
	Paused	Continued	PBR	BL
UBI	72-40-26	28-29-10	36	54
NUBI	61-60-39	39-71-25	64	46

Table 4 provides a number of percentages, with three micro-columns separated by dashes ('-') for T_1. The first micro-column shows the percentage of UBI/NUBI that either Paused or Continued the prompt (sums to 100 horizontally). The second micro-column shows the percentage of Paused/Continued that are UBI/NUBI (sums to 100 vertically). The third micro-column shows the percentage of each combination (e.g. UBI and Paused) over all the barge-in recognitions. The VAD columns show the percentage of UBI/NUBI that (would) pause the prompt.

We first look at UBI/NUBI percentage that are Paused/Continued (first micro-column): We find that 72% of UBI are paused and 28% are Continued versus 61% of NUBI that are Paused with 39% Continued. We now look at the Paused/Continued percentage that are UBI/NUBI (second micro-column): We find that 40% of Paused are UBI and 60% are NUBI, whereas 29% of Continued are UBI and 71% are NUBI. So, while T_1 suspends the prompt for the majority of NUBI (not desirable, though expected since T_1 starts at 0), it has high precision when continuing the prompt. This reduces the number of times that the prompt is paused erroneously for NUBI while minimizing incorrect (UBI) continues. This is clearly shown by considering all of the recognitions (third micro-column). We find that PBR erroneously paused the prompt for 39% of recognitions, as opposed to 64% for the off-line PBR and 46% for the Baseline. This came at the cost of reducing the number of correct (UBI) pauses to 26% from 36% (off-line PBR) and 54% (Baseline VAD).

The results show that the T_1 threshold had

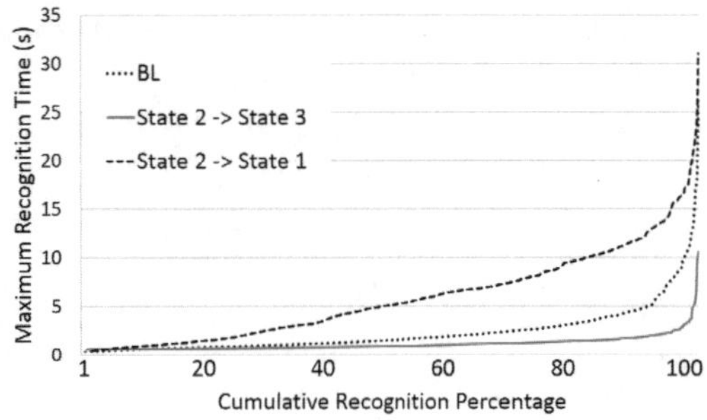

Figure 5: *Secs from Speech Start to Final Result*

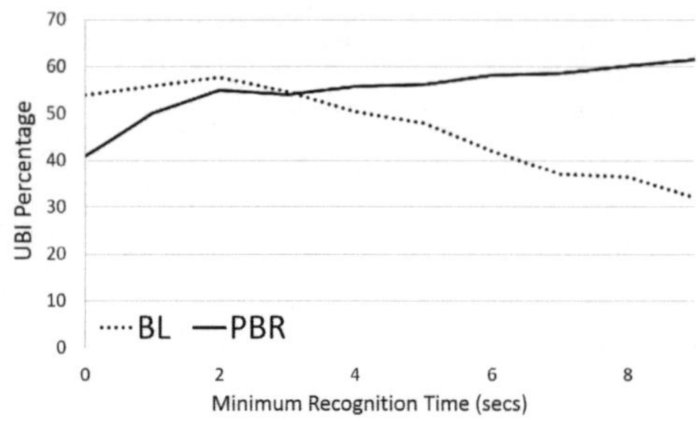

Figure 6: *UBI % by minimum recognition time*

modest success at discriminating UBI and NUBI; while continuing the prompt had quite a high precision for NUBI, the recall was substantially lower. We note that, since erroneous pauses lead to resumptions and erroneous continues still lead to a new speech act, there is minimal cost to these errors. Furthermore, in our view, reducing the percentage of recognitions that pause and resume the prompt is more critical as these needlessly disrupt the prompt. In this, T_1 is clearly effective, reducing the percentage from 64% to 39%.

4.3 State 2: Silent Prediction

State 2 governs whether the prompt will remain paused or be resumed *during* incremental recognition. This decision depends on the time parameter T_2, which should trigger resumptions for NUBIs. Since the act of resuming the prompt during recognition changes the outcome of the recognition, it is impossible to evaluate how well T_2 discriminated recognition results. However, we *can* evaluate the effect of that resumption by comparing UBI percentages between the PBR and Baseline systems. We first present evidence that T_2 is most active during longer recognitions, and then show that longer Baseline recognitions have a lower UBI percentage than longer PBR recognitions specifically because of T_2 resumptions. "Recognitions" refer to speech recognition results, with "longer" or "shorter" referring to the clock time between speech detection and the final recognition result.

We first report the PBR and Baseline response and recognition time. We separate the PBR barge-in recognitions into two groups: State 2→State 3, where the system *never* transitions from State 2 to State 1, and State 2→State 1, where the system resumes the prompt *during* recognition, transitioning from State 2 to State 1. The cumulative percentages of the time from speech detection to final recognition are shown in Figure 5. We find that the State 2→State 3 recognitions are far faster than the Baseline recognitions, which in turn are far faster than the State 2→State 1 recognitions. The difference between PBR and Baseline recognitions implies that T_2 has greater activation during longer recognitions. Given this, the overall barge-in response time for PBR should be faster than the Baseline (as the PBR system is resuming where the Baseline is silent). Indeed this is the case: the PBR system's overall mean/median response time is 1.58/1.53 seconds whereas Baseline has a mean/median response time of 2.61/1.8 seconds.

The goal of T_2 is for the system to resume when recognition is proceeding poorly, and we have shown that it is primarily being activated during longer recognitions. If T_2 is functioning properly, recognition length should be inversely related to recognition performance, and longer recognitions should be less likely to be understood. Furthermore, if T_2 resumption improves the user's experience then longer PBR recognitions should perform better than Baseline recognitions of comparable length. Figure 6 presents the UBI percentage by the minimum time for recognitions that reach State 2. We find that, when all recognitions are accounted for (0 second minimum), the Baseline has a higher rate of UBI. However, as recognition time increases the Baseline UBI percentage decreases (suggesting successful T_2 functioning) whereas the PBR UBI percentage actually increases. Since longer PBR recognitions are dominated by T_2 resumptions, we speculate this improvement is driven by users repeating or initiating new speech that leads to understanding success, as the PBR system is responding where the Baseline system is silent.

4.4 Resumption

The PBR model relies on resumption to recover from poor recognitions, either produced in State 2 or State 3. Instead of a resumption, the Baseline

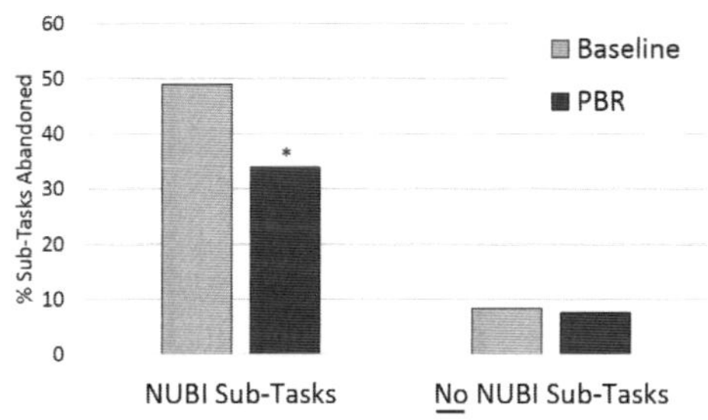

Figure 7: *Sub-Task Abandonment Rate. NUBI is different at* $p < 0.003$

system initiates a clarifying sub-dialogue when a barge-in recognition is not understood. We compare these two behaviors using the call abandonment rate — the user hangs-up — of sub-tasks with and without NUBI. Here, we exclude the Bus Schedule sub-task as it is the goal state.

Figure 7 shows the call abandonment rate for sub-tasks that either have or do not have NUBI. We find that there is a significant difference in abandoned calls for NUBI sub-tasks between the two systems (33% vs 48%, $p < 0.003$ using a χ^2 test), but that there is no difference for the calls that do not have NUBI (7.6% vs 8.4%). This result shows that prompt resumption is viewed far more favorably by users than initiating a clarifying sub-dialogue.

5 Discussion and Conclusion

The above results offer strong evidence that the PBR model increases task success and efficiency, and we found that all three states contribute to the improved performance by creating a more robust, responsive, and natural interaction. T_1 prediction in State 1 reduced the number of spurious prompt suspensions, T_2 prediction in State 2 led to improved understanding performance, and prompt resumption (States 2 and 3) reduced the number of abandoned calls.

An important feature of the Prediction-based Barge-in Response model is that, while it leverages incremental speech processing for barge-in processing, it does not require an incremental dialogue manager to drive its behavior. Since the model is also domain independent and does not require access to internal dialogue manager components, it can easily be incorporated into any existing dialogue system. However, one limitation of the current model is that the prediction thresholds are hand-crafted. We also believe that substantial improvements can be made by explicitly attempting to predict eventual understanding instead of using the stability score and partial production rate as a proxy. Furthermore, the PBR model does not distinguish between the causes of the non-understanding, specifically whether the input contained in-domain user speech, out-of-domain user speech, or background noise. This case is specifically applicable in domains where system and user speech are in the same channel, such as interacting via speaker phone. In this context, the system *should* be able to initiate a clarifying sub-dialogue and release the turn, as the system must be more sensitive to the shared acoustic environment and so its current prompt may be less important than the user's non-understood utterance.

The results challenge a potential assumption regarding barge-in: that barge-in indicates greater user pro-activity and engagement with the task. One of the striking findings was that dialogues with barge-in are slower and less successful than dialogues without barge-in. This suggests that, for current systems, dialogues with barge-in are more indicative of environmental difficulty than user pro-activity. The superior performance of the PBR model, which is explicitly resistant to non-system directed speech, implies that dominant barge-in models will have increasingly limited utility as spoken dialogue systems become more prevalent and are used in increasingly difficult environments. Furthermore, within the context of overall dialogue systems, the PBR model's performance emphasizes the importance of continuous processing for future systems.

This paper has proposed and evaluated the Prediction-based Barge-in Response model. This model's behavior is driven by continuously predicting whether a barge-in recognition will be understood successfully, and combines incremental speech processing techniques with a prompt resumption procedure. Using a live dialogue task with real users, we evaluated this model against the standard barge-in model and found that it led to improved performance in both task success and efficiency.

Acknowledgments

Many thanks to Vincent Goffin for help with this work, and to the anonymous reviewers for their insightful comments and critique. We acknowledge funding from the NSF under grant IIS-0713698.

References

T. Baumann, M. Atterer, and D. Schlangen. 2009. Assessing and improving the performance of speech recognition for incremental systems. In *Proc. NAACL: HLT*, pages 380–388. Association for Computational Linguistics.

V. Goffin, C. Allauzen, E. Bocchieri, D. Hakkani-Tur, A. Ljolje, S. Parthasarathy, M. Rahim, G. Riccardi, and M. Saraclar. 2005. The AT&T WATSON speech recognizer. In *Proceedings of ICASSP*, pages 1033–1036.

James G Martin and Winifred Strange. 1968. The perception of hesitation in spontaneous speech. *Perception & Psychophysics*, 3(6):427–438.

Ian McGraw and Alexander Gruenstein. 2012. Estimating word-stability during incremental speech recognition. In *in Proc. of Interspeech 2012*.

A. Raux, B. Langner, D. Bohus, A.W. Black, and M. Eskenazi. 2005. Lets go public! taking a spoken dialog system to the real world. In *in Proc. of Interspeech 2005*.

A. Raux. 2008. *Flexible Turn-Taking for Spoken Dialog Systems*. Ph.D. thesis, CMU.

Richard C Rose and Hong Kook Kim. 2003. A hybrid barge-in procedure for more reliable turn-taking in human-machine dialog systems. In *Automatic Speech Recognition and Understanding, 2003. ASRU'03. 2003 IEEE Workshop on*, pages 198–203. IEEE.

E.O. Selfridge and P.A. Heeman. 2010. Importance-Driven Turn-Bidding for spoken dialogue systems. In *Proc. of ACL 2010*, pages 177–185. Association for Computational Linguistics.

E.O. Selfridge, I. Arizmendi, P.A. Heeman, and J.D. Williams. 2011. Stability and accuracy in incremental speech recognition. In *Proceedings of the SIGdial 2011*.

E.O. Selfridge, I. Arizmendi, P.A. Heeman, and J.D. Williams. 2012. Integrating incremental speech recognition and pomdp-based dialogue systems. In *Proceedings of the SIGdial 2012*.

Nikko Ström and Stephanie Seneff. 2000. Intelligent barge-in in conversational systems. *Procedings of ICSLP*.

Jason D Williams. 2012. A critical analysis of two statistical spoken dialog systems in public use. In *Spoken Language Technology Workshop (SLT), 2012 IEEE*, pages 55–60. IEEE.

Fan Yang and Peter A. Heeman. 2010. Initiative conflicts in task-oriented dialogue". *Computer Speech Language*, 24(2):175 – 189.

A Appendix

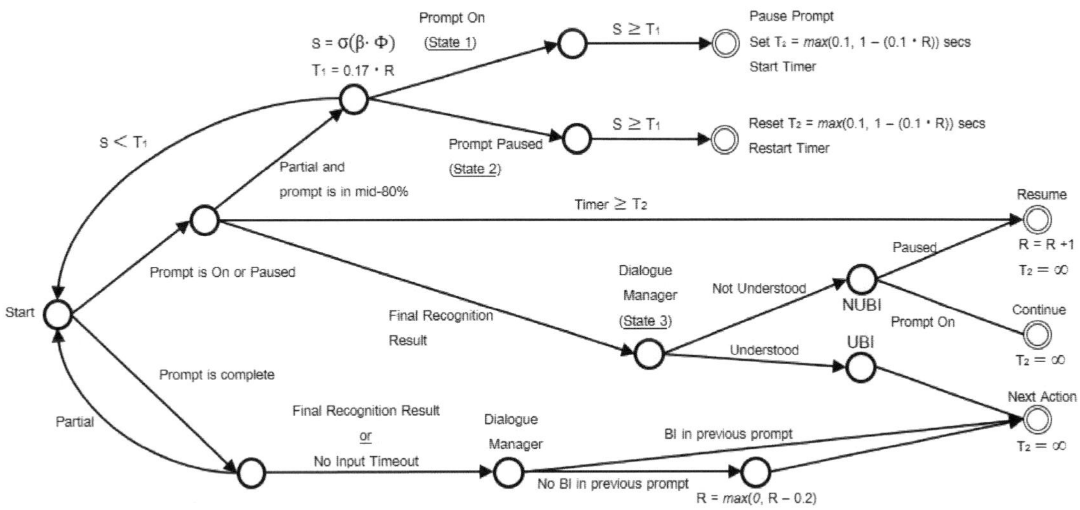

This diagram represents the possible operating positions the Prediction-based Barge-in Response model can be in. If the prompt is complete, the PBR model applies the dialogue policy to the final recognition result and initiates the on-policy speech act. If the prompt was finished without being paused it decrements R. In the latter case (barge-in), it operates using the three states as described in Section 2. When a partial is recognized the Stability Score is computed and compared to the T_1 threshold parameter. If the score is below T_1 the partial is discarded. Otherwise, if the model is in State 1 (the prompt is on) the prompt is paused, a timer is started, and control transitions to State 2. If the model is in State 2 the timer is restarted. After transitioning to State 2, control only returns to State 1 if the timer exceeds T_2. At this time, the prompt is resumed and the resumption parameter R is incremented. Control immediately transitions to State 3 if a final recognition result is received. The result is evaluated by the dialogue manager, and the new speech act is returned. If the speech act indicates the recognition was not understood successfully, the system either resumes (if in State 1) or continues (if in State 2). In the case of resumption, R is incremented. If the new speech act indicates understanding success, the new speech is immediately produced.

Which ASR should I choose for my dialogue system?

Fabrizio Morbini, Kartik Audhkhasi, Kenji Sagae, Ron Artstein, Doğan Can, Panayiotis Georgiou, Shri Narayanan, Anton Leuski and David Traum
University of Southern California
Los Angeles, California, USA
{morbini,sagae,artstein,leuski,traum}@ict.usc.edu
{audhkhas,dogancan}@usc.edu {georgiou,shri}@sipi.usc.edu

Abstract

We present an analysis of several publicly available automatic speech recognizers (ASRs) in terms of their suitability for use in different types of dialogue systems. We focus in particular on cloud based ASRs that recently have become available to the community. We include features of ASR systems and desiderata and requirements for different dialogue systems, taking into account the dialogue genre, type of user, and other features. We then present speech recognition results for six different dialogue systems. The most interesting result is that different ASR systems perform best on the data sets. We also show that there is an improvement over a previous generation of recognizers on some of these data sets. We also investigate language understanding (NLU) on the ASR output, and explore the relationship between ASR and NLU performance.

1 Introduction

Dialogue system developers who are not also speech recognition experts are in a better position than ever before in terms of the ease of integrating existing speech recognizers in their systems. While there have been commercial solutions and toolkits for a number of years, there were a number of problems in getting these systems to work. For example, early toolkits relied on specific machine hardware, software, and firmware to function properly, often had a difficult installation process, and moreover often didn't work well for complex dialogue domains, or challenging acoustic environments. Fortunately the situation has greatly improved in recent years. Now there are a number of easy to use solutions, including open-source systems (like PocketSphinx), as well as cloud-based approaches.

While this increased choice of quality recognizers is of great benefit to dialogue system developers, it also creates a dilemma – which recognizer to use? Unfortunately, the answer is not simple – it depends on a number of issues, including the type of dialogue domain, availability and amount of training data, availability of internet connectivity for the runtime system, and speed of response needed. In this paper we assess several freely available speech recognition engines, and examine their suitability and performance in several dialogue systems. Here we extend the work done in Yao et al. (2010) focusing in particular on cloud based freely available ASR systems. We include 2 local ASRs for reference, one of which was also used in the earlier work for easy comparison.

2 Speech Recognizer Features and Engines

The following are some of the major criteria for selection of a speech recognizer.

Customization Some of the available speech recognizers allow the users to tune the recognizer to the environment it will operate in, by providing a specialized **lexicon**, trained **language models** or **acoustic models**. Customization is especially important for dialogue systems whose input contains specialized vocabulary (see section 4).

Output options A basic recognizer will output a string of text, representing its best hypothesis about the transcription of the speech input. Some recognizers offer additional outputs which are useful for dialogue systems: ranked **n-best hypotheses** allow later processing to use context for disambiguation, and **incremental results** allow the system to react while the user is still speaking.

Performance characteristics Dialogue systems differ in their requirements for **response speed**; a

System	Customization	Output options		Open Source	Performance	
		N-best	Incremental		Speed	Installation
Pocketsphinx	Full	Yes	Yes	Yes	realtime	Local
Apple	No	No[a]	No	No	network	Cloud
Google	No	Yes	Yes[b]	No	network	Cloud
AT&T	Partial[c]	Yes	No	No	network	Cloud
Otosense-Kaldi	Full	Yes	No	Yes[d]	variable[e]	Local

[a]Single output annotated with alternative hypotheses. [b]Only for web-delivered applications in a Google Chrome browser. [c]Custom language models. [d]Release scheduled for Fall 2013. [e]User controls trade-off between speed and output quality.

Table 1: Speech recognizer features important for use in dialogue systems

speech recognizer that **runs locally** can help by avoiding network latencies.

Output quality Typically, a dialogue system would want the best **recognition accuracy** possible given the constraints. Ultimately, dialogue systems want the output that would yield the best performance for **Natural Language Understanding** and other downstream processes. As a rule, better speech recognition leads to better language understanding, though this is not necessarily the case for specific applications (see section 5).

We evaluated 5 freely available speech recognizers. Their features are summarized in Table 1. We did not include the MIT WAMI toolkit[1] as we are focused on speech services that can directly be used by stand alone applications as opposed to web delivered ones. We did not include commercial recognizers such as Nuance, because licensing terms can be difficult for research institutions, and in particular, disallow publishing benchmarks.

Pocketsphinx is a version of the CMU Sphinx ASR system optimized to run also on embedded systems (Huggins-Daines et al., 2006). Pocketsphinx is fast, runs locally, and requires relatively modest computational resources. It provides n-best lists and lattices, and supports incremental output. It also provides a voice activity detection functionality for continuous ASR. This ASR is fully customizable and trainable, but users are expected to provide language models suitable for their applications. A few acoustic models are provided, and can be adapted using the CMUSphinx tools.[2]

Apple Dictation is the OS level feature in both MacOSX and iOS.[3] It is integrated into the text input system pipeline so a user can replace her keyboard with a microphone for entering text in any application. Dictation is often associated with the Siri personal assistant feature of iOS. While it is likely that Dictation and Siri share the same ASR technology, Dictation only does speech recognition. Apple states that Dictation learns the characteristics of the user's voice and adapts to her accent (Apple Inc, 2012). Dictation requires an internet connection to send recorded user speech to Apple's servers and receive ASR results. Processing starts as soon as the user starts speaking so the delay of getting the recognition results after the user finishes speaking is minimal.

To integrate Dictation into a dialogue system, a system designer needs to include any system defined text input control into her application and use the control APIs to observe text changes. The user would need to press a key when starting to speak and push the key again once she is done speaking. The ASR result is a text string annotated with alternative interpretations of individual words or phrases in the text. There is an API for extracting those interpretations from the result. While the Dictation feature is reasonably fast and easy to integrate, dialogue system developers have no control over the ASR process, which must be treated as a black box. Apple dictation is limited in that no customization is possible, no partial recognition results are provided, and there is an unspecified limit on the number of utterances dictated for a period of time, which is not a problem for interaction between a single user and a dialogue system, but may be an issue in dialogue systems that support multiple concurrent users.

[1]http://wami.csail.mit.edu/
[2]http://cmusphinx.sourceforge.net/wiki/tutorialadapt

[3]Dictation was introduced in iOS 5.0 and MacOSX 10.8.

Google Speech API provides support for the HTML 5 speech input feature.[4] It is a cloud based service in which a user submits audio data using an HTML POST request and receives as reply the ASR output in the form of an n-best list. The audio data is limited to roughly 10 seconds in length, longer clips are rejected and return no ASR results. The user can (1) customize the number of hypotheses returned by the ASR, (2) specify which language the audio file contains and (3) enable a filter to remove profanities from the output text. As is the case with Apple Dictation, ASR must be treated as a black box, and no task customization is possible for dialogue system developers. Users cannot specify or provide custom language models or acoustic models. The service returns only the final hypothesis, there is no incremental output.[5] In addition, results for the same inputs may change unpredictably, since Google may update or otherwise change its service and models, and models may be adapted using specific audio data supplied by users. In our experiments, we observed accuracy improvements when submitting the same audio files over repeated trials over two weeks.

AT&T Watson is the ASR engine available through the AT&T Speech Mashup service.[6] It is a cloud based service that can be accessed through HTML POST requests, like the Google Speech API. AT&T Watson is designed to support the demands of online spoken dialogue systems, and can be customized with data specific to a dialogue system. Additionally, in our tests we did not observe any limitation in the maximum length of the input audio data. However, AT&T does not provide a default general-purpose language model, and application-specific models must be built within the Speech Mashup service using user-provided text data. The acoustic model must be selected from a list provided by the AT&T service, and acoustic models can be further customized within the Speech Mashup service. The ASR returns an n-best list of hypotheses but does not provide incremental output.

Otosense-Kaldi Another ASR we employed was the Kaldi-based OtoSense-Kaldi engine developed at SAIL.[7] OtoSense-Kaldi[8] is an on-line, multi-threaded architecture based on the Kaldi toolkit (Povey et al., 2011) that allows for dynamically configurable and distributed ASR.

3 Dialogue Systems, Users, and Data

All spoken dialogue systems are similar in some respects, in that there is speech by a user (or users) that needs to be recognized, and this speech is punctuated by speech from the system. Moreover, the speech is not fully independent, but utterances are connected to other utterances, e.g. answers to questions, or clarifications. There are, however many ways in which systems can differ, that have implications for which speech recognizers are most appropriate. Some of the dimensions to consider are:

Type of microphone(s) One of the biggest impacts on ASR is the acoustic environment. Will the audio be clean, coming from a close-talking head or lapel-mounted microphone, or will it need to be picked up from a broader directional microphone or microphone array?

Number of speakers/microphones Will there be one designated microphone per person, or will speaker identification need to be performed? Will audio from the system confuse the ASR?

Push to talk or continuous speech Will the user clearly identify the start and end of speech, or will the system need to detect speech acoustically?

Type of Users Will there be designated long-term users, where user-training or system model adaptation is feasible, or will there be many unknown users, where training is not feasible? See also section 3.1 for more on user types.

Genre What kinds of things will people be saying to the system? Is it mostly commands or short answers to questions, or more open-ended conversation? See section 3.2 for more on genre issues.

Training Data Is within-domain training data available, and if so how much?

3.1 Types of Users

The type of user is important for the overall design of the system and has implications for

[4]https://www.google.com/speech-api/v1/recognize

[5]The demo page shows continuous speech understanding with incremental results but requires Google Chrome to run and is specific to web delivered applications: http://www.google.com/intl/en/chrome/demos/speech.html

[6]https://service.research.att.com/smm

[7]http://sail.usc.edu

[8]OtoSense-Kaldi will be released (BSD license) in 2013.

ASR performance as well. One important aspect is the broad physical differences among speakers, such as male vs female, adult vs child (e.g. Bell and Gustafson, 2003), or language proficiency/accent, that will have implications for the acoustics of what is said, and ASR results. Other aspects of users have implications for what will be said, and how successful the interface may be, overall. Many (e.g. Hassel and Hagen, 2006; Jokinen and Kanto, 2004) have looked at the differences between novice and expert users. Ai et al. (2007a) also points out a difference between real users and recruited subjects. Real users also come in many different flavors, depending on their purposes. E.g. are they interacting with the system for fun, to do a specific task that they need to get done, to learn something (specific or general), or with some other purpose in mind?

We considered the following classes of users, ordered from easiest to hardest to get to acceptable performance and robustness levels:

Demonstrators are generally the easiest for a system to understand – a demonstrator is trained in use of the system, knows what can and can't be said, is motivated toward success, and is generally interested in showing off the most impressive/successful aspects of the system to an audience rather than using it for its own sake.

Trained/Expert Users are similar to demonstrators, but use the system to achieve specific results rather than just to show off its capabilities. This means that users may be forced down lines that are not ideal for the system, if these are necessary to accomplish the task.

Motivated Users do not have the training of expert users, and may say many things that the system can not handle as opposed to equivalent expressions that could be handled. However motivated users do want the system to succeed, and in general are willing to do whatever they think is necessary to improve system performance. Unlike expert users, motivated users might be incorrect about what will help the system (e.g. hyperarticulation in response to system misunderstanding).

Casual Users are interested in finding out what the system can do, but do not have particular motivations to help or hinder the system. Casual Users may also leave in the middle of an interaction, if it is not engaging enough.

Red Teams are out to test or "break" the system, or show it as not-competent, and may try to do things the system can't understand or react well to, even when an alternative formulation is known to work.

3.2 Types of Dialogue System Genres

Dialogue Genres can be distinguished along many lines, e.g. the number and relationship of participants, specific conversational rules, purposes of the participants, etc. We distinguish here four genres of dialogue system that have been in use at the Institute for Creative Technologies and that we have available corpora for (there are many other types of dialogue genres, including tutoring, casual conversation, interviewing,...). Each genre has implications for the internal representations and system architectures needed to engage in that genre of dialogue.

Simple Question-answering This genre involves strong user-initiative and weak global dialogue coherence. The user can ask any question to the system at any time, and the system should respond, with an appropriate answer if able, or with some other reply indicating either inability or unwillingness to provide the answer. This genre allows modeling dialogue at a surface-text level (Gandhe, 2013), without internal semantic representations of the input, and where the result of "understanding" input is the system's expected output. The NCPEditor[9] (Leuski and Traum, 2011) is a toolkit that provides an authoring environment, classification, and dialogue capability for simple question-answering characters. The SGT Blackwell, SGT Star, and Twins systems described below are all systems in this genre.

Advanced Question-answering This genre is similar to the simple question-answering characters, in that the main task of the user is to elicit information from the system character. The difference is that there is more long-range and intermediate dialogue coherence, in that questions can be answered several utterances after they have been asked, there can be intervening sub-dialogues, and characters sometimes take the initiative to pursue their own goals rather than just responding to the user. Because of the requirements for somewhat deeper understanding, and relation of input to con-

[9]Available free for academic research purposes from https://confluence.ict.usc.edu/display/VHTK/Home

text and character goals and policies, there is a need of at least a shallow semantic representation and representation of the dialogue information state, and the character must distinguish understanding of the input from the character output (since the latter will depend on the dialogue policy and information state, not just the understanding of input). The tactical questioning architecture (Gandhe et al., 2009)[10] provides authoring and run-time support for advanced question-answering characters, and has been used to build over a dozen characters for purposes such as training tactical questioning, training culture, and psychology experiments (Gandhe et al., 2011). The Amani character described below is in this genre.

Slot-filling Probably the most common type of dialogue system (at least in the research community) is slot-filling. Here the dialogue is fairly structured, with an initial greeting phase, then one or more tasks, which all start with the user selecting the task, and the system taking over initiative to "fill" and possibly confirm the needed slots, before retrieving some information from a database, or performing a simple service.[11] This genre also requires a semantic representation, at least of the slots and acceptable values. Generally, the set of possible values is large enough, that some form of NLG is needed (at least template filling), rather than authoring of all full sentences. There are a number of toolkits and development frameworks that are well suited to slot-filling systems, e.g. Ravenclaw (Bohus and Rudnicky, 2003) or Trindikit (Larsson and Traum, 2000). The Radiobots system, described below is in this genre.

Negotiation and Planning In this genre, the system is more of an equal partner with the user, than a servant, as in the slot-filling systems. The system must not merely understand user requests, but must also evaluate whether they meet the system goals, what the consequences and preconditions of requests are, and whether there are better alternatives. For this kind of inference, a more detailed semantic representation is required than just filling in slots. While we are not aware of publicly available software that makes this kind of system easy to construct, there have been several built using an information-state approach, or the soar cognitive architecture. The TRIPS system (Allen et al., 2001) also has many similarities.

[10]Soon to be released as part of the virtual human toolkit.

[11]Mixed-initiative versions of this genre exist, where the user can also provide unsolicited information, which reduces the number of system queries needed.

3.3 ICT Dialogue Systems Tested

We tested the recognizers described in section 2 on data sets collected from six different dialogue domains. Five are the same ones tested in Yao et al. (2010), to which we added the Twins set. Details on the size of the training and development sets may be found in Yao et al. (2010), here we report only the numbers relevant to the Twins domain and to the NLU analysis, which are not in Yao et al. (2010).

SGT Blackwell was created as a virtual human technology demonstration for the 2004 Army Science Conference. This is a question-answering character, with no internal semantic representation and the primary NLU task merged with Dialogue management as selecting the best response.

The original users were ICT demonstrators. However, there were also some experiments with recruited participants (Leuski et al., 2006a; Leuski et al., 2006b). Later SGT Blackwell became a part of the "best design in America" triennial at the Cooper-Hewitt Museum in New York City, and the data set here is from visitors to the museum, who are mostly casual users, but range from expert to red-team. Users spoke into a mounted directional microphone (see Robinson et al., 2008 for more details).

SGT STAR (Artstein et al., 2009a) is a question-answering character similar to SGT Blackwell, although designed to talk about Army careers rather than general knowledge. The users are Army personnel who went to job fairs and visited schools in the mobile Army adventure vans, speaking using headset microphones, and performing for an audience. The users are somewhere between demonstrators and expert users. They are speaking to SGT STAR for the benefit of an audience, but their primary purpose is to convey information to the audience in a memorable way (through dialogue with SGT STAR) rather than to show off the highlights of the character.

The Twins are two life-size virtual characters who serve as guides at the Museum of Science in Boston (Swartout et al., 2010). The characters promote interest in Science, Technology, Engineering and Mathematics (STEM) in children between the ages of 7 and 14. They are question-answering characters, but unlike SGTs Blackwell and Star, the response is a whole dialogue sequence, potentially involving interchange from both characters, rather than a single character turn.

There are two types of users for the Twins: demonstrators, who are museum staff members, using head-mounted microphones, and museum visitors, who use a Shure 522 table-top mounted microphone (Traum et al., 2012). More on analysis of the museum data can be found in (Aggarwal et al., 2012). We also investigated speech recognition and NLU performance in this domain in Morbini et al. (2012).

This dataset contains 14K audio files each annotated with one of the 168 possible response sequences. The division in training development and test is the same used in Morbini et al. (2012) (10K for training, the rest equally divided between development and test).

Amani (Artstein et al., 2009b; Artstein et al., 2011) is an advanced question-answering character used as a prototype for systems meant to train soldiers to perform tactical questioning. The users are in between real users and test subjects: they were cadets at the U.S. Military Academy in April 2009, who interacted with Amani as a university course exercise on negotiation techniques. They used head-mounted microphones to talk with Amani.

This dataset comprises of 1.8K audio files each annotated with one of the 105 possible NLU semantic classes.

Radiobots (Roque et al., 2006) is a training prototype that responds to military calls for artillery fire in a virtual reality urban combat environment. This is a domain in the slot-filling genre, where there is a preferred protocol for the order in which information is provided and confirmed. Users are generally trainees, learning how to do calls for fire, they are motivated users with some training. The semantic processing involved tagging each word with the dialogue act and parameter that it was associated with (Ai et al., 2007b).

This data set was collected during the development of the system in 2006 at Fort Sill, Oklahoma, during two evaluation sessions from recruited volunteer trainees who performed calls for specific missions (Robinson et al., 2006). These subjects used head-mounted microphones rather than the ASTI simulated radios from later data collection.

SASO-EN (Traum et al., 2008) is a negotiation training prototype in which two virtual characters negotiate with a human "trainee" about moving a medical clinic. The genre is negotiation and planning, where the human participant must try to form a coalition, and the characters reason about utilities of different proposals, as well as causes and effects. The output of NLU is a frame representation including both semantic elements, like thematic argument structure, and pragmatic elements, such as addressee and referring expressions. Further contextual interpretation is performed by each of the virtual characters to match the (possibly partial) representation to actions and states in their task model, resolve other referring expressions, and determine a full set of dialogue acts (Traum, 2003). Speech was collected at the USC Institute for Creative Technologies (ICT) during 2006–2009, mostly from visitors and new hires, who acted as test subjects.

This dataset has 4K audio files each annotated with one of the 117 different NLU semantic classes.

4 ASR Performance

We tested each of the Datasets described in Section 3.3 with some of the recognizers described in Section 2. All recognizers were tested on the Amani, SASO-EN, and Twins domains, and we also tested a natural language understanding component on these data sets (Section 5). For SGT Blackwell, SGT STAR, and Radiobots, we report the performance on the same development set used in Yao et al. (2010). For Amani and SASO-EN (where we also report the NLU performance), we run a 10-fold cross-validation in which 9 folds where used to train the NLU and ASR language model and the 10th was used for testing. For the Twins dialogue system, we used the same partition into training, development and testing reported in Morbini et al. (2012) and the results reported here are from the development set. Due to differences in training/testing regimens, performance of systems are only comparable within each domain.

Table 2 summarizes the performance of the various ASR engines on the evaluation data sets. Performance is measured as Word Error Rate and was obtained using the NIST SCLITE tool.[12]

Note that only Otosense-Kaldi in the Twins domain had adapted acoustic models. In the remain-

[12]http://www.itl.nist.gov/iad/mig/tools/

Speech recognizer	Evaluation data set					
	Amani	Radiobots	SASO-EN	SGT Blackwell	SGT Star	Twins
Pocketsphinx	39.7	**11.8**	28.4	51	28.6	81
Apple	28	—	30.9	—	—	29
AT&T	29	12.1	**16.3**	27.3	**21.7**	28.8
Google	**23.8**	36.3	20	**18**	26	20.6
Otosense-Kaldi	33.7	—	22.1	—	—	**18.7**

Table 2: Word Error Rates (%) for the various dialogue systems and ASR systems tested.

ing cases only the language model was adapted. Looking at the results on the development set reported in Yao et al. (2010), we have improvements in 3 out of 5 domains: Amani (−11.8% Google), SASO-EN (−11.7% AT&T) and SGT Blackwell (−13% Google). In Radiobots and SGT Star the performance achieved with just language model adaptation, when permitted, is worse: +4.8% and +1.7% respectively.

We find that there is no single best performing speech recognizer: results vary greatly between the evaluation test sets. In 4 of the 6 datasets overall, and 2 of the 3 datatests tested with Otosense-Kaldi, the best performer is a cloud-based service (Google or AT&T). There are two datasets for which a local, fully customizable recognizer performs better than the cloud-based services. Radiobots, consisting of military calls for artillery fire, has a fairly limited and very specialized vocabulary, and indeed the two recognizers with custom language models (Pocketsphinx and AT&T) perform much better than the non-customizable recognizer (Google).

The Twins dataset is unique in that for the Otosense-Kaldi system we custom-trained acoustic and language models, while standard WSJ acoustic models and adapted language models were used for the other dialogue systems. In both cases the models were triphone based with a Linear Discriminant Analysis (LDA) front end, and Maximum Likelihood Linear Transformation (MLLT) and Maximum Mutual Information (MMI) training. This reflects on the very good performance in the Twins domain, decent performance on the SASO-EN domain (reasonable mismatch of WSJ and SASO-EN) and very degraded performance in Amani (highly mismatched Amani and WSJ domains). The observed degradation in performance is accentuated by the MMI discriminative training on the mismatched-WSJ data. As with PocketSphinx and Watson, and unlike with Apple Dictation and Google Speech API, with Kaldi we fully control experimental conditions and can guarantee no contamination of the train-test data.

In summary, our evaluation shows that customizable recognizers are useful when the expected speech is highly specialized, or when substantial resources are available for tuning the recognizer.

5 NLU Accuracy & Relation between ASR and NLU

While the different genres of system have different types of output for NLU: response text, dialogue act and parameter tags, speech acts, or semantic frames, many of them can be coerced into a selection task, in which the NLU selects the right output from a set of possible outputs. This allows any multiclass classification algorithm to be used for NLU. A possible drawback is that for some inputs, the right output might not be available in the set considered by the training data, even if it might easily be constructed from known parts using a generative approach.

A second issue is that even though we can cast the problem as multi-class classification, classification accuracy is not always the most appropriate metric of NLU quality. For question-answering characters, getting an appropriate and relevant reply is more important than picking the exact reply selected by a human domain designer or annotator: there might be multiple good answers, or even the best available answer might not be very good. For that reason, the question-answering characters allow an "off-topic" answer and Error-return plots (Artstein, 2011) might be necessary to choose an optimal threshold. For the SASO-EN system, slot-filler metrics such as precision, recall, and f-score are more appropriate than frame accuracy, because some frames may have many slots in common and few that are different (e.g. just a different addressee). Nonetheless, we begin our analysis within this common framework. For simplicity, we start with just three domains: Twins, Amani, and SASO-EN. SGT STAR and Blackwell are very similar to Twins in terms of NLU. Radiobots is more challenging to coerce to multiclass classification.

Conventional wisdom in the speech and language processing community is that performance of ASR and NLU are closely tied: improved speech recognition leads to better language understanding, while deficiencies in speech recognition cause difficulty in understanding. This conventional wisdom is borne out by decades of experience with speech and dialogue systems, though we are not aware of attempts to systematically demonstrate it. The present study shows that the expected relation between speech recognition and language understanding holds for the systems we tested.

Accepted assumptions about the relation between speech recognition and language understanding have been repeatedly challenged. Direct challenges are typically limited to specific applications. Wang et al. (2003) show that for a slot-filling NLU, ASR can be specifically tuned to recognize those words that are relevant to the slot-filling task, resulting in improved understanding despite a decrease in performance on overall word recognition. However, Boros et al. (1996) found that when not optimizing the ASR for the specific slot filling task there is a nearly linear correlation between word accuracy and NLU accuracy. Alshawi (2003) and Huang and Cox (2006) show that in call-routing applications the word level can be dispensed with altogether and calls routed based on phonetic information alone without noticeable loss in performance. These challenges suggest that the speech-language divide is not as clean as the theory suggests.

To investigate the relation between ASR and NLU, we ran each ASR output from each of the 5 recognizers through an understanding component to obtain an NLU output (each dataset had a separate NLU component, which was held constant for all speech recognizers). ASR and NLU performance are conventionally measured on scales of opposite polarity: better performance shows up as lower word error rates but higher NLU accuracies. For the correlations we invert the conventional ASR scale and use word accuracy, so that higher numbers signify better performance on both scales.[13]

Figure 1 shows the results obtained in the 3 dialogue systems by the various ASR systems. The figures plot ASR performance against NLU performance; NLU results on manual transcriptions are included for comparison. There are too few data points for the correlations between ASR and NLU performance to be significant, but the trends are positive, as expected.

Our experiments lend supporting evidence to the claim that in general, ASR performance is positively linked to NLU performance (special cases notwithstanding). The 3 datasets exhibit positive correlations between speech recognition and language understanding performance. Thus, we claim that the basis of the conventional wisdom is sound: speech recognition directly affects language understanding. This conclusion holds when the speech recognizer has been optimized to produce the most accurate transcript, rather than for a specific NLU.

6 Conclusion and Future Work

We have extended here the ASR system evaluation published in Yao et al. (2010) including some new cloud based ASR services that achieve very good performance showing an improvement of around 12%. We also showed that ASR and NLU performance are correlated.

One possible avenue of future work is to extract importance weights for each word from the learnt NLU models and use these weights to try to explain those cases that diverge from the correlation between ASR and NLU performance. This may also give us a better measure than WER for assessing ASR performance in dialogue systems. Another avenue of future work involves examining different types of NLU engines, and different metrics for the different dialogue system genres, which, again, may lead to a more relevant assessment of ASR performance.

Acknowledgments

The effort described here has been sponsored by the U.S. Army. Any opinions, content or information presented does not necessarily reflect the posi-

[13]We define "accuracy" as 1 minus WER, so this number can in principle dip below zero if there are more errors than words.

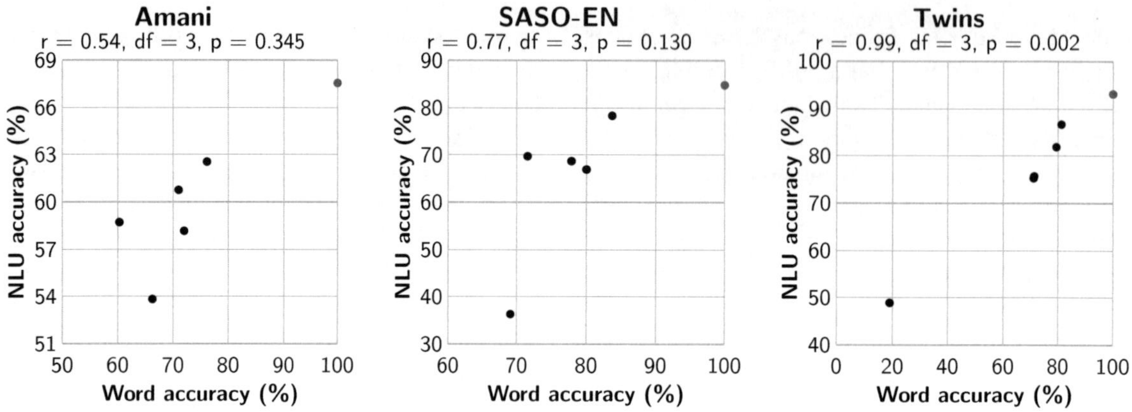

Figure 1: Relation between ASR and NLU performance (red dots are manual transcriptions)

tion or the policy of the United States Government, and no official endorsement should be inferred.

References

Priti Aggarwal, Ron Artstein, Jillian Gerten, Athanasios Katsamanis, Shrikanth Narayanan, Angela Nazarian, and David Traum. 2012. The Twins corpus of museum visitor questions. In *LREC-2012*, Istanbul, Turkey, May.

Hua Ai, Antoine Raux, Dan Bohus, Maxine Eskenazi, and Diane Litman. 2007a. Comparing spoken dialog corpora collected with recruited subjects versus real users. In *SIGdial 2007*.

Hua Ai, Antonio Roque, Anton Leuski, and David Traum. 2007b. Using information state to improve dialogue move identification in a spoken dialogue system. In *Proceedings of the 10th Interspeech Conference*, Antwerp, Belgium, August.

James F. Allen, George Ferguson, and Amanda Stent. 2001. An architecture for more realistic conversational systems. In *IUI*, pages 1–8.

Hiyan Alshawi. 2003. Effective utterance classification with unsupervised phonotactic models. In *HLT-NAACL 2003*, pages 1–7, Edmonton, Alberta, May.

Apple Inc. 2012. Mac basics: Dictation (Technote HT5449), November.

R. Artstein, S. Gandhe, J. Gerten, A. Leuski, and D. Traum. 2009a. Semi-formal evaluation of conversational characters. In O. Grumberg, M. Kaminski, S. Katz, and S. Wintner, editors, *Languages: From Formal to Natural. Essays Dedicated to Nissim Francez on the Occasion of His 65th Birthday*, volume 5533 of *Lecture Notes in Computer Science*, pages 22–35. Springer, Berlin.

Ron Artstein, Sudeep Gandhe, Michael Rushforth, and David R. Traum. 2009b. Viability of a simple dialogue act scheme for a tactical questioning dialogue system. In *DiaHolmia 2009: Proceedings of the 13th Workshop on the Semantics and Pragmatics of Dialogue*, page 43–50, Stockholm, Sweden, June.

Ron Artstein, Michael Rushforth, Sudeep Gandhe, David Traum, and MAJ Aram Donigian. 2011. Limits of simple dialogue acts for tactical questioning dialogues. In *7th IJCAI Workshop on Knowledge and Reasoning in Practical Dialogue Systems*, Barcelona, Spain, July.

Ron Artstein. 2011. Error return plots. In *12th SIGdial Workshop on Discourse and Dialogue*, Portland, OR, June.

Linda Bell and Joakim Gustafson. 2003. Child and adult speaker adaptation during error resolution in a publicly available spoken dialogue system. In *INTERSPEECH 2003*.

Dan Bohus and Alexander I. Rudnicky. 2003. Ravenclaw: dialog management using hierarchical task decomposition and an expectation agenda. In *INTERSPEECH 2003*.

M. Boros, W. Eckert, F. Gallwitz, G. Grz, G. Hanrieder, and H. Niemann. 1996. Towards understanding spontaneous speech: Word accuracy vs. concept accuracy. In *In Proceedings of (ICSLP 96)*, pages 1009–1012.

Sudeep Gandhe, Nicolle Whitman, David R. Traum, and Ron Artstein. 2009. An integrated authoring tool for tactical questioning dialogue systems. In *6th Workshop on Knowledge and Reasoning in Practical Dialogue Systems*, Pasadena, California, July.

Sudeep Gandhe, Michael Rushforth, Priti Aggarwal, and David R. Traum. 2011. Evaluation of an integrated authoring tool for building advanced question-answering characters. In *Proceedings of Interspeech-11*, Florence, Italy, 08/2011.

Sudeep Gandhe. 2013. *Rapid prototyping and evaluation of dialogue systems for virtual humans*. Ph.D. thesis, University of Southern California.

Liza Hassel and Eli Hagen. 2006. Adaptation of an automotive dialogue system to users' expertise and evaluation of the system. *Language Resources and Evaluation*, 40(1):67–85.

Quiang Huang and Stephen Cox. 2006. Task-independent call-routing. *Speech Communication*, 48(3–4):374–389.

D. Huggins-Daines, M. Kumar, A. Chan, A.W. Black, M. Ravishankar, and A.I. Rudnicky. 2006. Pocketsphinx: A free, real-time continuous speech recognition system for hand-held devices. In *Acoustics, Speech and Signal Processing, 2006. ICASSP 2006 Proceedings. 2006 IEEE International Conference on*, volume 1, pages I–I.

Kristiina Jokinen and Kari Kanto. 2004. User expertise modeling and adaptivity in a speech-based e-mail system. In Donia Scott, Walter Daelemans, and Marilyn A. Walker, editors, *ACL*, pages 87–94. ACL.

Staffan Larsson and David Traum. 2000. Information state and dialogue management in the TRINDI dialogue move engine toolkit. *Natural Language Engineering*, 6:323–340, September. Special Issue on Spoken Language Dialogue System Engineering.

Anton Leuski and David R. Traum. 2011. NPCEditor: Creating virtual human dialogue using information retrieval techniques. *AI Magazine*, 32:42–56.

Anton Leuski, Brandon Kennedy, Ronakkumar Patel, and David Traum. 2006a. Asking questions to limited domain virtual characters: How good does speech recognition have to be? In *25th Army Science Conference*.

Anton Leuski, Ronakkumar Patel, David Traum, and Brandon Kennedy. 2006b. Building effective question answering characters. In *Proceedings of the 7th SIGdial Workshop on Discourse and Dialogue*, pages 18–27.

Fabrizio Morbini, Kartik Audhkhasi, Ron Artstein, Maarten Van Segbroeck, Kenji Sagae, Panayiotis S. Georgiou, David R. Traum, and Shrikanth S. Narayanan. 2012. A reranking approach for recognition and classification of speech input in conversational dialogue systems. In *SLT*, pages 49–54. IEEE.

Daniel Povey, Arnab Ghoshal, Gilles Boulianne, Lukáš Burget, Ondřej Glembek, Nagendra Goel, Mirko Hannemann, Petr Motlíček, Yanmin Qian, Petr Schwarz, Jan Silovský, Georg Stemmer, and Karel Veselý. 2011. The Kaldi speech recognition toolkit. In *IEEE 2011 Workshop on Automatic Speech Recognition and Understanding*, December.

S.M. Robinson, A. Roque, A. Vaswani, D. Traum, C. Hernandez, and B. Millspaugh. 2006. Evaluation of a spoken dialogue system for virtual reality call for fire training. In *25th Army Science Conference*, Orlando, Florida, USA.

S. Robinson, D. Traum, M. Ittycheriah, and J. Henderer. 2008. What would you ask a conversational agent? Observations of human-agent dialogues in a museum setting. In *Proc. of Sixth International Conference on Language Resources and Evaluation (LREC)*, Marrakech, Morocco.

A. Roque, A. Leuski, V. Rangarajan, S. Robinson, A. Vaswani, S. Narayanan, and D. Traum. 2006. Radiobot-CFF: A spoken dialogue system for military training. In *Proc. of Interspeech*, Pittsburgh, Pennsylvania, USA.

W. Swartout, D. Traum, R. Artstein, D. Noren, P. Debevec, K. Bronnenkant, J. Williams, A. Leuski, S. Narayanan, D. Piepol, C. Lane, J. Morie, P. Aggarwal, M. Liewer, J. Chiang, J. Gerten, S. Chu, and K. White. 2010. Ada and Grace: Toward realistic and engaging virtual museum guides. In J. Allbeck, N. Badler, T. Bickmore, C. Pelachaud, and A. Safonova, editors, *Intelligent Virtual Agents: 10th International Conference, IVA 2010, Philadelphia, PA, USA, September 20–22, 2010 Proceedings*, volume 6356 of *Lecture Notes in Artificial Intelligence*, pages 286–300. Springer, Heidelberg.

David R. Traum, Stacy Marsella, Jonathan Gratch, Jina Lee, and Arno Hartholt. 2008. Multi-party, multi-issue, multi-strategy negotiation for multi-modal virtual agents. In *IVA*, pages 117–130.

David Traum, Priti Aggarwal, Ron Artstein, Susan Foutz, Jillian Gerten, Athanasios Katsamanis, Anton Leuski, Dan Noren, and William Swartout. 2012. Ada and grace: Direct interaction with museum visitors. In *The 12th International Conference on Intelligent Virtual Agents (IVA)*, Santa Cruz, CA, September.

David Traum. 2003. Semantics and pragmatics of questions and answers for dialogue agents. In *proceedings of the International Workshop on Computational Semantics*, pages 380–394.

Ye-Yi Wang, A. Acero, and C. Chelba. 2003. Is word error rate a good indicator for spoken language understanding accuracy. In *IEEE Workshop on Automatic Speech Recognition and Understanding (ASRU '03)*, pages 577–582.

Xuchen Yao, Pravin Bhutada, Kallirroi Georgila, Kenji Sagae, Ron Artstein, and David R. Traum. 2010. Practical evaluation of speech recognizers for virtual human dialogue systems. In Nicoletta Calzolari, Khalid Choukri, Bente Maegaard, Joseph Mariani, Jan Odijk, Stelios Piperidis, Mike Rosner, and Daniel Tapias, editors, *LREC*. European Language Resources Association.

The Dialog State Tracking Challenge

Jason Williams[1], **Antoine Raux**[2]*, **Deepak Ramachandran**[3]*, **and Alan Black**[4]
[1]Microsoft Research, Redmond, WA, USA [2]Lenovo Corporation, Santa Clara, CA, USA
[3]Nuance Communications, Mountain View, CA, USA [4]Carnegie Mellon University, Pittsburgh, PA, USA
jason.williams@microsoft.com araux@lenovo.com deepak.ramachandran@nuance.com awb@cmu.edu

Abstract

In a spoken dialog system, *dialog state tracking* deduces information about the user's goal as the dialog progresses, synthesizing evidence such as dialog acts over multiple turns with external data sources. Recent approaches have been shown to overcome ASR and SLU errors in some applications. However, there are currently no common testbeds or evaluation measures for this task, hampering progress. The *dialog state tracking challenge* seeks to address this by providing a heterogeneous corpus of 15K human-computer dialogs in a standard format, along with a suite of 11 evaluation metrics. The challenge received a total of 27 entries from 9 research groups. The results show that the suite of performance metrics cluster into 4 natural groups. Moreover, the dialog systems that benefit most from dialog state tracking are those with less discriminative speech recognition confidence scores. Finally, generalization is a key problem: in 2 of the 4 test sets, fewer than half of the entries out-performed simple baselines.

1 Overview and motivation

Spoken dialog systems interact with users via natural language to help them achieve a goal. As the interaction progresses, the dialog manager maintains a representation of the state of the dialog in a process called *dialog state tracking* (DST). For example, in a bus schedule information system, the dialog state might indicate the user's desired bus route, origin, and destination. Dialog state tracking is difficult because automatic speech recognition (ASR) and spoken language understanding (SLU) errors are common, and can cause the system to misunderstand the user's needs. At the same time, state tracking is crucial because the system relies on the estimated dialog state to choose actions – for example, which bus schedule information to present to the user.

Most commercial systems use hand-crafted heuristics for state tracking, selecting the SLU result with the highest confidence score, and discarding alternatives. In contrast, statistical approaches compute scores for many *hypotheses* for the dialog state (Figure 1). By exploiting correlations between turns and information from external data sources – such as maps, bus timetables, or models of past dialogs – statistical approaches can overcome some SLU errors.

Numerous techniques for dialog state tracking have been proposed, including heuristic scores (Higashinaka et al., 2003), Bayesian networks (Paek and Horvitz, 2000; Williams and Young, 2007), kernel density estimators (Ma et al., 2012), and discriminative models (Bohus and Rudnicky, 2006). Techniques have been fielded which scale to realistically sized dialog problems and operate in real time (Young et al., 2010; Thomson and Young, 2010; Williams, 2010; Mehta et al., 2010). In end-to-end dialog systems, dialog state tracking has been shown to improve overall system performance (Young et al., 2010; Thomson and Young, 2010).

Despite this progress, direct comparisons between methods have not been possible because past studies use different domains and system components, for speech recognition, spoken language understanding, dialog control, etc. Moreover, there is little agreement on how to evaluate dialog state tracking. Together these issues limit progress in this research area.

The Dialog State Tracking Challenge (DSTC) provides a first common testbed and evaluation

*Most of the work for the challenge was performed when the second and third authors were with Honda Research Institute, Mountain View, CA, USA

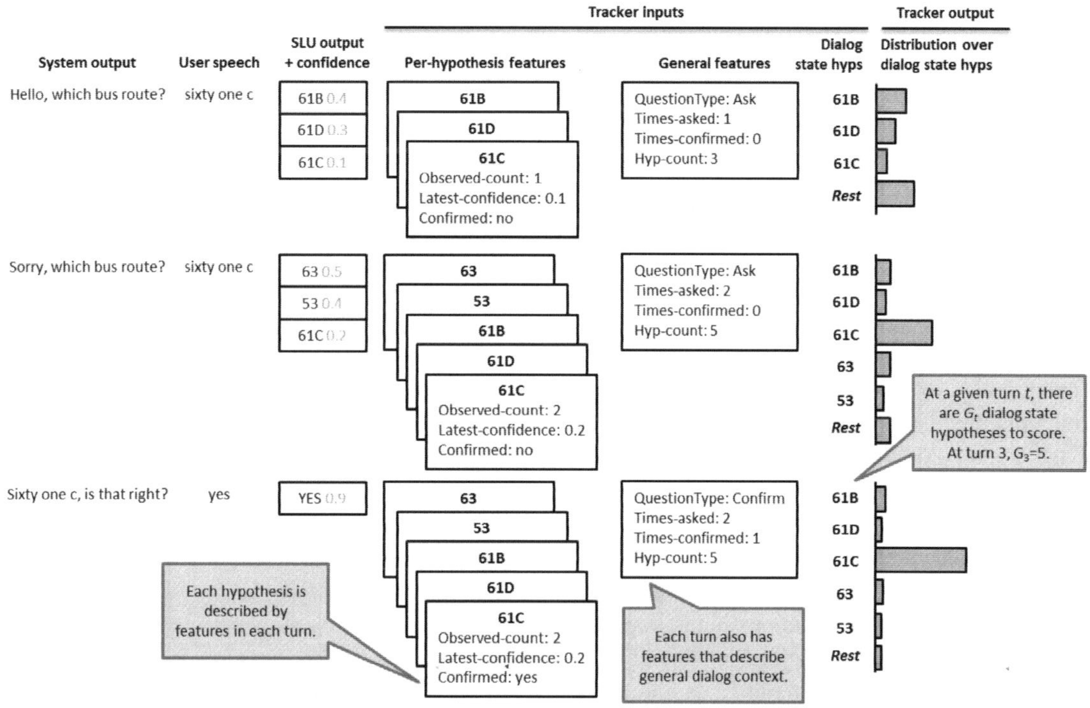

Figure 1: Overview of dialog state tracking. In this example, the dialog state contains the user's desired bus route. At each turn t, the system produces a spoken output. The user's spoken response is processed to extract a set of spoken language understanding (SLU) results, each with a *local* confidence score. A set of N_t dialog state hypotheses is formed by considering all SLU results observed so far, including the current turn and all previous turns. Here, $N_1 = 3$ and $N_2 = 5$. The dialog state tracker uses features of the dialog context to produce a distribution over all N_t hypotheses and the meta-hypothesis that none of them are correct.

suite for dialog state tracking. The DSTC organizers made available a public, heterogeneous corpus of over 15K transcribed and labeled human-computer dialogs. Nine teams entered the challenge, anonymously submitting a total of 27 dialog state trackers.

This paper serves two roles. First, sections 2 and 3 provide an overview of the challenge, data, and evaluation metrics, all of which will remain publicly available to the community (DST, 2013). Second, this paper summarizes the results of the challenge, with an emphasis on gaining new insights into the dialog state tracking problem, in Section 4. Section 5 briefly concludes.

2 Challenge overview

2.1 Problem statement

First, we define the dialog state tracking problem. A dialog state tracker takes as input all of the observable elements up to time t in a dialog, including all of the results from the automatic speech recognition (ASR) and spoken language understanding (SLU) components, and external knowledge sources such as bus timetable databases and models of past dialogs. It also takes as input a set of N_t possible dialog state hypotheses, where a hypothesis is an assignment of values to slots in the system. The tracker outputs a probability distribution over the set of N_t hypotheses, and the meta-hypothesis REST which indicates that none of them are correct. The goal is to assign probability 1.0 to the correct state, and 0.0 to other states. Note that the set of dialog states is *given*. Also note that N_t varies with t – typically as the dialog progresses and more concepts are discussed, the number of candidate hypotheses increases. An example is given in Figure 1.

In this challenge, dialog states are generated in the usual way, by enumerating all slots values that have appeared in the SLU N-best lists or system output up until the current turn. While this approach precludes a tracker assigning a score to an

SLU value that has *not* been observed, the cardinality of the slots is generally large, so the likelihood of a tracker correctly guessing a slot value which hasn't been observed anywhere in the input or output is vanishingly small.

2.2 Challenge design

The dialog state tracking challenge studies this problem as a *corpus-based task* – i.e., dialog state trackers are trained and tested on a *static corpus of dialogs*, recorded from systems using a variety of state tracking models and dialog managers. The challenge task is to *re-run* state tracking on these dialogs – i.e., to take as input the runtime system logs including the SLU results and system output, and to output scores for dialog states formed from the runtime SLU results. This corpus-based design was chosen because it allows different trackers to be evaluated on the same data, and because a corpus-based task has a much lower barrier to entry for research groups than building an end-to-end dialog system.

In practice of course, a state tracker will be used in an end-to-end dialog system, and will drive action selection, thereby affecting the distribution of the dialog data the tracker experiences. In other words, it is known in advance that the distribution in the training data and live data will be mismatched, although the nature and extent of the mis-match are not known. Hence, unlike much of supervised learning research, drawing train and test data from the same distribution in offline experiments may overstate performance. So in the DSTC, train/test mis-match was explicitly created by choosing test data to be from different dialog systems.

2.3 Source data and challenge corpora

The DSTC uses data from the public deployment of several systems in the Spoken Dialog Challenge (SDC) (Black et al., 2010), provided by the Dialog Research Center at Carnegie Mellon University. In the SDC, telephone calls from real passengers of the Port Authority of Allegheny County, who runs city buses in Pittsburgh, were forwarded to dialog systems built by different research groups. The goal was to provide bus riders with bus timetable information. For example, a caller might want to find out the time of the next bus leaving from Downtown to the airport.

The SDC received dialog systems from three different research groups, here called Groups A, B, and C. Each group used its own ASR, SLU, and dialog manager. The dialog strategies across groups varied considerably: for example, Groups A and C used a mixed-initiative design, where the system could recognize any concept at any turn, but Group B used a directed design, where the system asked for concepts sequentially and could only recognize the concept being queried. Groups trialled different system variants over a period of almost 3 years. These variants differed in acoustic and language models, confidence scoring model, state tracking method and parameters, number of supported bus routes, user population, and presence of minor bugs. Example dialogs from each group are shown in the Appendix.

The dialog data was partitioned into 5 training corpora and 4 testing corpora (Table 1). The partioning was intended to explore different types of mis-match between the training and test data. Specifically, the dialog system in TRAIN1A, TRAIN1B, TRAIN1C, TRAIN2, and TEST1 are all very similar, so TEST1 tests the case where there is a large amount of similar data. TEST2 uses the same ASR and SLU but a different dialog controller, so tests the case where there is a large amount of somewhat similar data. TEST3 is very similar to TRAIN3 and tests the case where there is a small amount of similar data. TEST4 uses a completely different dialog system to any of the training data.

2.4 Data preparation

The dialog system log data from all three groups was converted to a common format, which described SLU results and system output using a uniform set of dialog acts. For example, the system speech *East Pittsburgh Bus Schedules. Say a bus route, like 28X, or say I'm not sure.* was represented as *hello(), request(route), example(route=28x), example(route=dontknow)*. The user ASR hypothesis *the next 61c from oakland to mckeesport transportation center* was represented as *inform(time.rel=next), inform(route=61c), inform(from.neighborhood=oakland), inform(to.desc="mckeesport transportation center")*. In this domain there were a total of 9 slots: the bus route, date, time, and three components each for the origin and destination, corresponding to streets, neighborhoods, and points-of-interest like universities. For complete details see (Williams et al., 2012).

	TRAIN					TEST			
	1A	1B	1C	2	3	1	2	3	4
Group	A	A	A	A	B	A	A	B	C
Year(s)	2009	2009	2009	2010	2010	2011	2012	2011-2	2010
Dialogs	1013	1117	9502	643	688	715	750	1020	438
Turns/Dialog	14.7	13.3	14.5	14.5	12.6	14.1	14.5	13.0	10.9
Sys acts/turn	4.0	3.8	3.8	4.0	8.4	2.8	3.2	8.2	4.6
Av N-best len	21.7	22.3	21.9	22.4	2.9	21.2	20.5	5.0	3.2
Acts/N-best hyp	2.2	2.2	2.2	2.3	1.0	2.1	2.0	1.0	1.6
Slots/turn	44.0	46.5	45.6	49.0	2.1	41.4	36.9	4.3	3.5
Transcribed?	yes	yes	yes	yes	yes	yes	yes	yes	yes
Labelled?	yes	no	no	yes	yes	yes	yes	yes	yes
1-best WER	42.9%	41.1%	42.1%	58.2%	40.5%	57.9%	62.1%	48.1%	55.6%
1-best SLU Prec.	0.356	-	-	0.303	0.560	0.252	0.275	0.470	0.334
1-best SLU Recall	0.522	-	-	0.388	0.650	0.362	0.393	0.515	0.376
N-best SLU Recall	0.577	-	-	0.485	0.738	0.456	0.492	0.634	0.413

Table 1: Summary of the datasets. One turn includes a system output *and* a user response. *Slots* are named entity types such as bus route, origin neighborhood, date, time, etc. N-best SLU Recall indicates the fraction of concepts which appear anywhere on the SLU N-best list.

Group B and C systems produced N-best lists of ASR and SLU output, which were included in the log files. Group A systems produced only 1-best lists, so for Group A systems, recognition was *re-run* with the Pocketsphinx speech recognizer (Huggins-Daines et al., 2006) with N-best output enabled, and the results were included in the log files.

Some information in the raw system logs was specific to a group. For example, Group B's logs included information about word confusion networks, but other groups did not. All of this information was included in a "system specific" section of the log files. Group A logs contained about 40 system-specific name/value pairs per turn, and Group B about 600 system-specific name/value pairs per turn. Group C logs contained no system specific data.

3 Labeling and evaluation design

The output of a dialog state tracker is a probability distribution over a set of given dialog state hypotheses, plus the REST meta-hypothesis. To evaluate this output, a label is needed for each dialog state hypothesis indicating its *correctness*.

In this task-oriented domain, we note that the user enters the call with a specific goal in mind. Further, when goal changes do occur, they are usually explicitly marked: since all of the systems first collect slot values, and then provide bus timetables, if the user wishes to change their goal, they need to start over from the beginning. These "start over" transitions are obvious in the logs. This structure allows the correctness of each dialog state to be equated to the correctness of the SLU items it contains. As a result, in the DSTC we labeled the correctness of SLU hypotheses in each turn, and then assumed these labels remain valid until either the call ends, or until a "start over" event. Thus to produce the labels, the labeling task followed was to assign a correctness value to every SLU hypothesis on the N-best list, given a transcript of the words actually spoken in the dialog up to the current turn.

To accomplish this, first all user speech was transcribed. The TRAIN1 datasets had been transcribed using crowd-sourcing in a prior project (Parent and Eskenazi, 2010); the remainder were transcribed by professionals. Then each SLU hypothesis was labled as correct or incorrect. When a transcription exactly and unambiguously matched a recognized slot value, such as the bus route "sixty one c", labels were assigned automatically. The remainder were assigned using crowd-sourcing, where three workers were shown the true words spoken and the recognized concept, and asked to indicate if the recognized concept was correct – *even if it did not match the recognized words exactly.* Workers were also shown dialog history, which helps decipher the user's meaning when their speech was ambiguous. If the 3 workers were not unanimous in their labels (about 4% of all turns), the item was labeled manually by the organizers. The REST meta-hypothesis was not explicitly labeled; rather, it was deemed to be correct if none of the prior SLU results were labeled as correct.

In this challenge, state tracking performance was measured on each of the 9 slots separately, and also on a *joint* dialog state consisting of all the slots. So at each turn in the dialog, a tracker output 10 scored lists: one for each slot, plus a 10th list where each dialog state contains values from all slots. Scores were constrained to be in the range $[0, 1]$ and to sum to 1.

To evaluate tracker output, at each turn, each hypothesis (including REST) on each of the 10 lists was labeled as correct or incorrect by looking up its corresponding SLU label(s). The scores and labels over all of the dialogs were then compiled to compute 11 metrics. **Accuracy** measures the percent of turns where the top-ranked hypothesis is correct. This indicates the correctness of the item with the maximum score. **L2** measures the L^2 distance between the vector of scores, and a vector of zeros with 1 in the position of the correct hypothesis. This indicates the quality of all scores, when the scores as viewed as probabilities.

AvgP measures the mean score of the first correct hypothesis. This indicates the quality of the score assigned to the correct hypothesis, ignoring the distribution of scores to incorrect hypotheses. **MRR** measures the mean reciprocal rank of the first correct hypothesis. This indicates the quality of the ordering the scores produces (without necessarily treating the scores as probabilities).

The remaining measures relate to receiver-operating characteristic (ROC) curves, which measure the discrimination of the score for the highest-ranked state hypothesis. Two versions of ROC are computed – V1 and V2. V1 computes correct-accepts (CA), false-accepts (FA), and false-rejects (FR) as fractions of *all* utterances, so for example

$$CA.V1(s) = \frac{\#CA(s)}{N} \tag{1}$$

where $\#CA(s)$ indicates the number of correctly accepted states when only those states with score $\geq s$ are accepted, and N is the total number of states in the sample. The V1 metrics are a

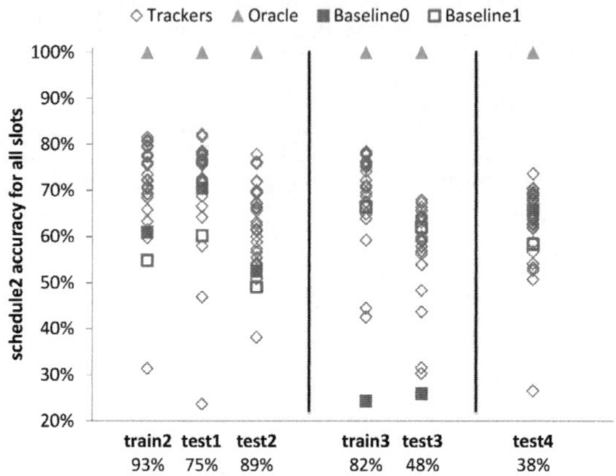

Figure 2: Schedule2 accuracy averaged over slots for every tracker on every dataset. Percentages under the datasets indicate the percent of the trackers which exceeded the performance of both baselines.

useful indication of overall performance because they combine discrimination and overall accuracy – i.e., the maximum $CA.V1(s)$ value is equal to accuracy computed above.

V2 considers fractions of *correctly classified utterances*, so for example

$$CA.V2(s) = \frac{\#CA(s)}{\#CA(0)}. \tag{2}$$

The V2 metrics are useful because they measure the discrimination of the scoring independently of accuracy – i.e., the maximum value of $CA.V2(s)$ is always 1, regardless of accuracy.

From these ROC statistics, several metrics are computed. **ROC.V1.EER** computes $FA.V1(s)$ where $FA.V1(s) = FR.V1(s)$. The metrics **ROC.V1.CA05**, **ROC.V1.CA10**, and **ROC.V1.CA20** compute $CA.V1(s)$ when $FA.V1(s) = 0.05, 0.10$, and 0.20 respectively. **ROC.V2.CA05**, **ROC.V2.CA10**, and **ROC.V2.CA20** do the same using the V2 versions.

Apart from *what* to measure, there is currently no standard that specifies *when* to measure – i.e., which turns to include when computing each metric. So for this challenge, a set of 3 *schedules* were used. **schedule1** includes every turn. **schedule2** include turns where the target slot is either present on the SLU N-best list, or where the target slot is included in a system confirmation action – i.e., where there is some observable new information

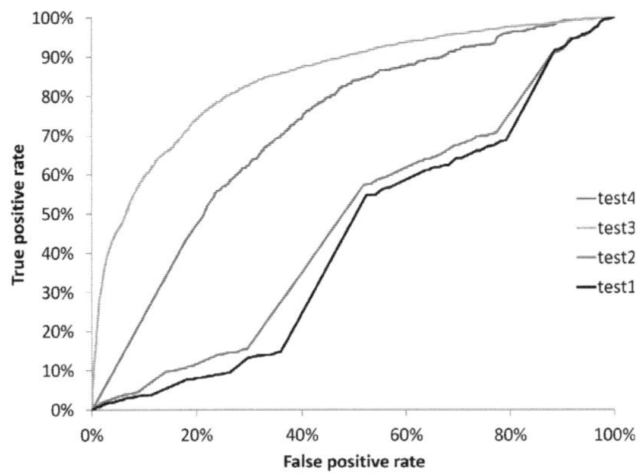

Figure 3: Receiver operating characteristc (ROC) curve for SLU confidence scores of the 1-best hypothesis in the test datasets. The SLU confidence score in TEST3 is most discriminative; TEST1 and TEST2 are the least discriminative.

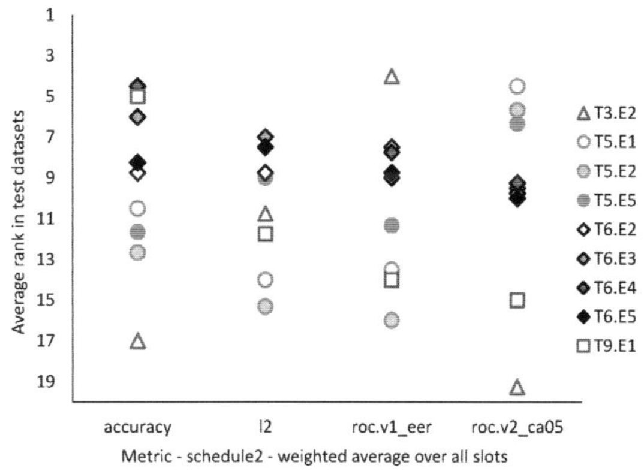

Figure 4: Average rank of top-performing trackers for the four metrics identified in Figure 6. Ranking was done using the given metric, schedule2, and the weighted average of all slots. $Tn.Em$ indicates team n, entry m.

about the target slot. **schedule3** includes only the last turn of a dialog.

In sum, for each tracker, one measurement is reported for each test set (4), schedule (3), and metric (11) for each of the 9 slots, the "joint" slot, and a weighted average of the individual slots (11), for a total of $4 \cdot 3 \cdot 11 \cdot 11 = 1452$ measurements per tracker. In addition, each tracker reported average latency per turn – this ranged from 10ms to 1s.

3.1 Baseline trackers

For comparisons, two simple baselines were implemented. The first (Baseline0) is a majority class baseline that always guesses REST with score 1. The second (Baseline1) follows simple rules which are commonly used in spoken dialog systems. It maintains a single hypothesis for each slot. Its value is the SLU 1-best with the highest confidence score observed so far, with score equal to that SLU item's confidence score.

4 Results and discussion

Logistically, the training data and labels, bus timetable database, scoring scripts, and baseline system were publicly released in late December 2012. The test data (without labels) was released on 22 March 2013, and teams were given a week to run their trackers and send results back to the organizers for evaluation. After the evaluation, the test labels were published. Each team could enter up to 5 trackers. For the evaluation, teams were asked to process the test dialogs online – i.e., to make a single pass over the data, as if the tracker were being run in deployment. Participation was open to researchers at any institution, including the organizers and advisory board. To encourage participation, the organizers agreed not to identify participants in publications, and there was no requirement to disclose how trackers were implemented.

9 teams entered the DSTC, submitting a total of 27 trackers. The raw output and all 1452 measurements for each tracker (and the 2 baselines) are available from the DSTC homepage (DST, 2013).

4.1 Analysis of trackers and datasets

We begin by looking at one illustrative metric, schedule2 accuracy averaged over slots, which measures the accuracy of the top dialog hypothesis for every slot when it either appears on the SLU N-best list or is confirmed by the system.[1] Results in Figure 2 show two key trends. First, relative to the baselines, performance on the test data is markedly lower than the training data. Comparing TRAIN2 to TEST1/TEST2 and TRAIN3 to TEST3, the relative gain over the baselines is much lower on test data. Moreover, only 38% of trackers performed better than a simple majority-class baseline on TEST4, for which there was no matched training data. These findings suggests that generalization is an important open issues for dialog state trackers.

Second, Figure 2 indicates that the gains made

[1]Results using the joint dialog state are broadly similar, and are omitted for space.

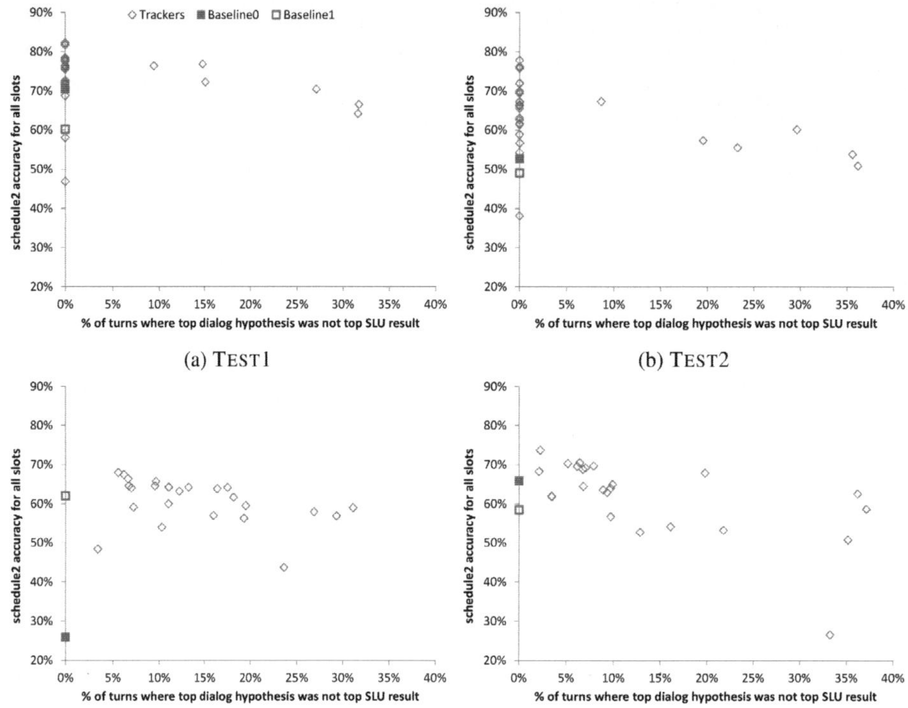

(a) TEST1 (b) TEST2 (c) TEST3 (d) TEST4

Figure 5: Percent of highest-scored dialog state hypotheses which did not appear in the top-ranked SLU position vs. schedule2 accuracy over all slots. Trackers – including those with the highest accuracy – for TEST1 and TEST2 rarely assigned the highest score to an SLU hypothesis other than the top. All trackers for TEST3 and TEST4 assigned the highest score to an SLU hypothesis other than the top in a non-trivial percent of turns.

by the trackers over the baselines are larger for Group A systems (TEST1 and TEST2) than for Group B (TEST3) and C (TEST4) systems. Whereas the baselines consider only the top SLU hypothesis, statistical trackers can make use of the entire N-best list, increasing recall – compare the 1-best and N-best SLU recall rates in Table 1. However, Group A trackers almost never assigned the highest score to an item below the top position in the SLU N-best list. Rather, the larger gains for Group A systems seem due to the relatively poor discrimination of Group A's SLU confidence score (Figure 3): whereas the trackers use a multitude of features to assign scores, the baselines rely entirely on the SLU confidence for their scores, so undiscriminative SLU confidence measures hamper baseline performance.

4.2 Analysis of metrics

This challenge makes it possible to study the empirical differences among the evaluation metrics. Intuitively, if the purpose of a metric is to *order* a set of trackers from best to worst, then 2 metrics are similar if they yield a similar ordering over trackers. Specifically, for every metric m, we have a value $x(m, d, s, t)$ where d is the dataset, and s is the evaluation schedule, and t is the tracker. We define $r(m, d, s, t)$ as the *rank* of tracker t when ordered using metric m, dataset d and evaluation schedule s. Using these ranks, we compute Kendall's Tau for every d, s, and *pair* of metrics m_1 and m_2 (Kendall, 1938). We then compute the average Kendall's Tau for m_1 and m_2 by averaging over all d and s.[2]

Results are in Figure 6. Here we see 4 natural clusters emerge: a cluster for **correctness** with Accuracy, MRR, and the ROC.V1.CA measures; a cluster for **probability quality** with L2 and Average score; and two clusters for **score discrimination** – one with ROC.V1.EER and the other with the three ROC.V2 metrics. This finding suggest

[2] A similar analysis over schedules showed that the differences in ranking for different schedules were smaller than for metrics.

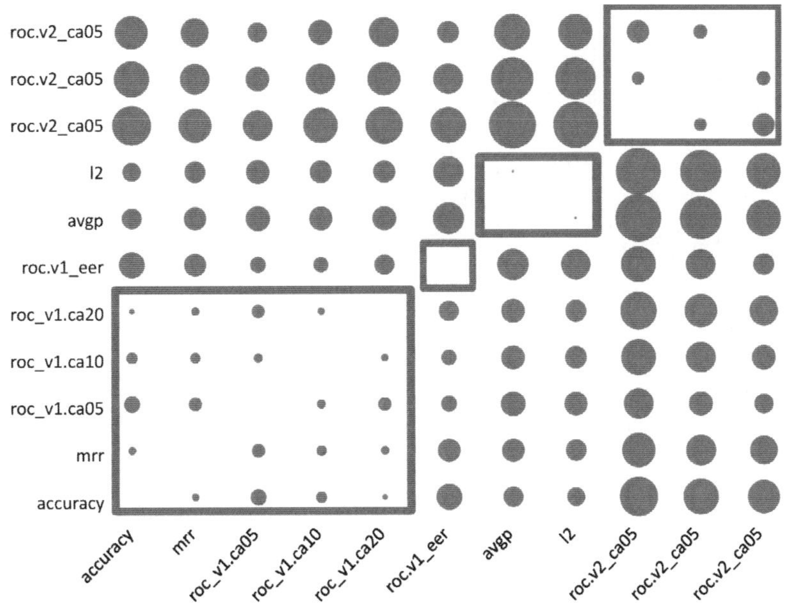

Figure 6: Average divergence between rank orderings produced by different metrics. The size of a circle at (x, y) is given by $1 - \tau$, where τ is the average Kendall's Tau computed on the rank orderings produced by methods x and y. Larger circles indicate dissimilar rankings; smaller circles indicate similar rankings; missing circles indicate identical rankings. The red boxes indicate groups of metrics that yield similar rankings.

that measuring one metric from each cluster will contain nearly the same information as all 9 metrics. For example, one might report only Accuracy, L2, ROC.V1.EER, and ROC.V2.CA5.

Using these 4 metrics, we rank-ordered each tracker, using schedule2 and a weighted average of all slots. We then computed the average rank across the 4 test sets. Finally we selected the set of trackers with the top three average ranks for each metric. Results in Figure 4 emphasize that different trackers are tuned for different performance measures, and the optimal tracking algorithm depends crucially on the target performance measure.

5 Conclusion

The dialog state tracking challenge has provided the first common testbed for this task. The data, evaluation tools, and baselines will continue to be freely available to the research community (DST, 2013). The details of the trackers themselves will be published at SIGDIAL 2013.

The results of the challenge show that the suite of performance metrics cluster into 4 natural groups. We also find that larger gains over conventional rule-based baselines are present in dialog systems where the speech recognition confidence score has poor discrimination. Finally, we observe substantial limitations on generalization: in mismatched conditions, around half of the trackers entered did not exceed the performance of two simple baselines.

In future work, it should be verified that improvements in dialog state tracking lead to improvements in end-to-end dialog performance (e.g., task completion, user satisfaction, etc.). In addition, it would be interesting to study dialogs where goal changes are more common.

Acknowledgements

The organizers thank the advisory board for their valuable input on the design of the challenge: Daniel Boies, Paul Crook, Maxine Eskenazi, Milica Gasic, Dilek Hakkani-Tur, Helen Hastie, Kee-Eung Kim, Ian Lane, Sungjin Lee, Teruhisa Misu, Olivier Pietquin, Joelle Pineau, Blaise Thomson, David Traum, and Luke Zettlemoyer. The organizers also thank Ian Lane for his support for transcription, and Microsoft and Honda Research Institute USA for funding the challenge. Finally, we thank the participants for making the challenge successful.

References

AW Black, S Burger, B Langner, G Parent, and M Eskenazi. 2010. Spoken dialog challenge 2010. In *Proc SLT, Berkeley*.

D Bohus and AI Rudnicky. 2006. A 'K hypotheses + other' belief updating model. In *Proc AAAI Workshop on Statistical and Empirical Approaches for Spoken Dialogue Systems, Boston*.

2013. Dialog State Tracking Challenge Homepage. `http://research.microsoft.com/events/dstc/`.

H Higashinaka, M Nakano, and K Aikawa. 2003. Corpus-based discourse understanding in spoken dialogue systems. In *Proc ACL, Sapporo*.

D Huggins-Daines, M Kumar, A Chan, A W Black, M Ravishankar, and A I Rudnicky. 2006. PocketSphinx: A Free, Real-Time Continuous Speech Recognition System for Hand-Held Devices. In *Proc ICASSP, Toulouse*.

M Kendall. 1938. A new measure of rank correlation. *Biometrika*, 30(1-2):81–89.

Y Ma, A Raux, D Ramachandran, and R Gupta. 2012. Landmark-based location belief tracking in a spoken dialog system. In *Proc SigDial, Seoul*.

N Mehta, R Gupta, A Raux, D Ramachandran, and S Krawczyk. 2010. Probabilistic ontology trees for belief tracking in dialog systems. In *Proc SigDial, Tokyo*.

T Paek and E Horvitz. 2000. Conversation as action under uncertainty. In *Proc UAI, Stanford*, pages 455–464.

G Parent and M Eskenazi. 2010. Toward Better Crowdsourced Transcription: Transcription of a Year of the Let's Go Bus Information System Data. In *Proc SLT, Berkeley*.

B Thomson and SJ Young. 2010. Bayesian update of dialogue state: A POMDP framework for spoken dialogue systems. *Computer Speech and Language*, 24(4):562–588.

JD Williams and SJ Young. 2007. Partially observable Markov decision processes for spoken dialog systems. *Computer Speech and Language*, 21(2):393–422.

JD Williams, A Raux, D Ramachandran, and AW Black. 2012. Dialog state tracking challenge handbook. Technical report, Microsoft Research.

JD Williams. 2010. Incremental partition recombination for efficient tracking of multiple dialogue states. In *Proc. of ICASSP*.

SJ Young, M Gašić, S Keizer, F Mairesse, J Schatzmann, B Thomson, and K Yu. 2010. The hidden information state model: a practical framework for POMDP-based spoken dialogue management. *Computer Speech and Language*, 24(2):150–174.

Appendix 1: Sample dialog excerpts

Below are transcripts of calls in the DSTC corpus. The user's side shows utterances as transcribed by human annotators.

Group A

SYS: Welcome to the CMU Let's Go bus information system. To get help at any time, just say Help or press zero. What can I do for you?
USR: *61c evening hours*
SYS: For example, you can say, when is the next 28X from DOWNTOWN to THE AIRPORT? or I'd like to go from MCKEESPORT to HOMESTEAD tomorrow at 10 a.m.
USR: *i'd like to go [noise]*
SYS: Where are you leaving from?
USR: *from Kennywood tomorrow at 6:30 PM*
SYS: Leaving from MCKEE. Is this correct?
USR: *yes*
SYS: Okay What is your destination?
USR: *downtown*
SYS: Going to DOWNTOWN. Is this correct?
USR: *yes*
SYS: Right When do you want to travel?
USR: *6:30 PM*
SYS: Leaving at 6 30 p.m.. Is this correct?
USR: *[noise] yes*
SYS: Alright Hold on. I'll look that up. There is a 71D leaving FIFTH AVENUE AT DARRAGH MCKEE at 6 40 p.m.. It will arrive at FIFTH AVENUE AT MARKET at 6 58 p.m.. To get more information about buses related to this trip, you can say, when is the next bus, or, when is the previous bus. To ask about a different trip, you can say, start a new query. If you are finished, you can say goodbye.
USR: *start a new query*
SYS: Okay, let's start from the beginning.
USR: ...

Group B

SYS: East Pittsburgh Bus Schedules. Say a bus route, like 28X, or say I'm not sure.
USR: *61A*
SYS: Okay, 61A. To change, say go back. Where are you leaving from?
USR: *Downtown*
SYS: Okay, downtown. You can always say go back. And where are you going to?
USR: *East Pittsburgh East Pittsburgh*
SYS: Pittsburgh. Is that right?

USR: *No*
SYS: Oh, sorry, where are you going to?
USR: *East Pittsburgh*
SYS: Okay, East Pittsburgh. Do you want times for the next few buses? Say yes or no.
USR: *Yes*
SYS: Ok, the next few buses. To change, say go back. At 7:45 PM today, there is a 61 A, from Fifth Avenue And Market Street, Downtown, arriving Dynamo Alley And Beech Avenue, In East Pittsburgh, at 8:42 PM. Say repeat, next, previous, or start over.

Group C

SYS: Welcome to the Lets Go! bus information system for Pittsburgh. Where would you like to leave from?
USR: *[noise]*
SYS: Where do you wanna leave from?
USR: *[noise] um I'm leaving from Forbes avenue and Murray avenue*
SYS: I'm sorry but I do not know any stops in the moon neighborhood. The routes I currently cover are the following: 28X, 54C, 56U, 61A, 61B, 61C, 61D and 64.
USR: *um I need the scheduling information for the 61D*
SYS: Where would you like to leave from?
USR: *Forbes and Murray*
SYS: Where do you wanna go?
USR: *Greenfield*
SYS: When are you going to take that bus?
USR: *61D*
SYS: When are you going to take that bus?
USR: *61D*
SYS: When would you like to travel? Say next bus for the the next bus .
USR: *next bus*
SYS: The next bus from forbes avenue at murray to greenfield is the 61D, leaving at 8 43 p.m. . It arrives at murray avenue at loretta at 8 52 p.m. . You may now say. next bus, previous bus, restart, or goodbye.
USR: *[noise] good-bye*
SYS: Thank you goodbye

Appendix 2: Example log fragment

Following is a log from a call in TRAIN3. Some elements have been omitted for space. Logs are formatted in JavaScript Object Notation (JSON).


```
{
 "session-id": "dt-201007221854-4808D",
 "turns": [ {
  "input": {
   "asr-hyps": [
    { "asr-hyp": "sixty one b",
      "score": 0.834314,
    },
    ...
   ],
   "slu-hyps": [
    { "slu-hyp": [
      {"act": "inform",
       "slots": [["route", "61b"]]},
     ],
     "score": 0.834314,
    },
    ...
   ],
   "audio-file": "002.raw",
   "start-time": 7.504
   },
   "output": {
    "start-time": 0.078,
    "transcript": "East Pittsburgh Bus
      Schedules. Say a bus route, like
      28X, or say I'm not sure.",
    "dialog-acts": [
     { "act": "hello",
       "slots": [] },
     { "act": "request",
       "slots": [["route",null]] },
     { "act": "example",
       "slots": [["route","28x"]] },
     { "act": "example",
       "slots": [["route","dontknow"]] }
    ],
   }
   "system-specific": {
    "wcn": {
     "best_path_score": 0.9965,
     "best_path": {
      "word": ["sixty","one","b"],
      "prob": [ 1.0,1.0,0.9965 ],
     }
     "network": [ ... ]
    },
    "nbest": [
     {
      "normSpeechLhood": -152.654,
      "lastSpeechFrame": 266,
      "numFrames": 354,
      "udelta": -3.0280,
      "speechLikelihood": -15876.0,
     },
     ...
    ],
    ...
   },
  },
  ...
 ]
}
```

Recipe For Building Robust Spoken Dialog State Trackers: Dialog State Tracking Challenge System Description

Sungjin Lee
Language Technologies Institute,
Carnegie Mellon University,
Pittsburgh, Pennsylvania, USA
sungjin.lee@cs.cmu.edu

Maxine Eskenazi
Language Technologies Institute,
Carnegie Mellon University,
Pittsburgh, Pennsylvania, USA
max@cs.cmu.edu

Abstract

For robust spoken conversational interaction, many dialog state tracking algorithms have been developed. Few studies, however, have reported the strengths and weaknesses of each method. The *Dialog State Tracking Challenge* (DSTC) is designed to address this issue by comparing various methods on the same domain. In this paper, we present a set of techniques that build a robust dialog state tracker with high performance: wide-coverage and well-calibrated data selection, feature-rich discriminative model design, generalization improvement techniques and unsupervised prior adaptation. The DSTC results show that the proposed method is superior to other systems on average on both the development and test datasets.

1 Introduction

Even though we have recently seen an explosive growth of interest in speech-enabled applications, there are still many problems to overcome in order to provide users with practical and profitable services. One of the long-standing problems which may often frustrate users is *Automatic Speech Recognition* (ASR) error. Due to ASR error, it is barely possible to directly observe what the user said and finally figure out the true user goal. The aim of dialog state tracking is, therefore, to accurately estimate the true dialog state from erroneous observations as a dialog unfolds.

In order to achieve this goal, many dialog state tracking algorithms have been developed. Few studies, however, have reported the strengths and weaknesses of each method. The *Dialog State Tracking Challenge*[1] (DSTC) was organized to advance state-of-the-art technologies for dialog state tracking by allowing for reliable comparisons between different approaches using the same datasets. Unlike other machine learning-based empirical tasks, DSTC is also carefully designed to take into consideration diverse realistic mismatches. For instance, there are test datasets that were collected by systems using different speech recognizers, spoken language understanding (SLU) modules, and dialog managers. Also there are test datasets that were produced by similar systems but deployed at a different time (1 year later) with extended coverage. Since such mismatches between training and test data may often happen in real deployment, it is important to build a tracker which constantly shows high performance across all test datasets despite various mismatches.

The aim of this paper is to describe a set of techniques used to build a robust tracker with high performance: wide-coverage and well-calibrated data selection, feature-rich discriminative model design, generalization improvement techniques and unsupervised prior adaptation. Our challenge systems are basically various combinations of those techniques. The DSTC results demonstrate the effectiveness of each technique.

This paper is structured as follows. Section 2 describes the challenge setup. Section 3 elaborates on our proposed approaches. Section 4 briefly describes previous research and other systems that participated in DSTC. Section 5 presents and discusses the results. Finally, Section 6 concludes with a brief summary and suggestions for future research.

[1] http://research.microsoft.com/en-us/events/dstc/

2 Dialog State Tracking Challenge

This section describes the task for DSTC and datasets provided for training and test. Most part of this section is borrowed from the DSTC manual[2].

2.1 Task Description

DSTC data is taken from several different spoken dialog systems which all provided bus schedule information for Pittsburgh, Pennsylvania, USA as part of the *Spoken Dialog Challenge* (Black et al., 2011). There are 9 slots which are evaluated: *route*, *from.desc*, *from.neighborhood*, *from.monument*, *to.desc*, *to.neighborhood*, *to.monument*, *date*, and *time*. Since both marginal and joint representations of dialog states are important for deciding dialog actions, the challenge takes into consideration both. Each joint representation is an assignment of values to all slots. Thus there are 9 marginal outputs and 1 joint output in total, which are all evaluated separately.

The dialog tracker receives SLU N-best hypotheses for each user turn, each with a confidence score. In general, there are a large number of values for each slot, and the coverage of N-best hypotheses is good, thus the challenge confines consideration of goals to slots and values that have been observed in an SLU output. By exploiting this aspect, the task of a dialog state tracker is to generate a set of observed slot and value pairs, with a score between 0 and 1. The sum of all scores is restricted to sum to 1.0. Thus 1.0 – total score is defined as the score of a special value *None* that indicates the user's goal has not yet been appeared on any SLU output.

2.2 Datasets

The data is divided into 2 training sets and 4 test sets (Table 1). For standardized development sets, each training set is split in half. Participants were asked to report results on the second half of each set. The data from group A in train2, and test1 was collected using essentially the same dialog system. Only a few updates were made to reflect changes to the bus schedule. The data in test2 was collected using a different version of group A's dialog manager. The data from group B in train3 and test3 were collected using essentially the same dialog system; the main difference is that test3 covers more bus routes. Test4 tests the condition when training and testing using totally different dialog systems, and when there is no same-system training data available.

Dataset	Source	Calls	Time period
train2	Group A	678	Summer 2010
train3	Group B	779	Summer 2010
test1	Group A	765	Winter 2011-12
test2	Group A	983	Winter 2011-12
test3	Group B	1037	Winter 2011-12
test4	Group C	451	Summer 2010

Table 1: Dataset description.

2.3 Metrics

There are a variety of aspects of tracker performance that were measured: accuracy, mean reciprocal rank (MRR), ROC curves, Average score[3], and Brier score[4]. There are three schedules for determining which turns to include in each evaluation.

- Schedule 1: Include all turns.
- Schedule 2: Include a turn for a given concept only if that concept either appears on the SLU N-Best list in that turn, or if the system's action references that concept in that turn.
- Schedule 3: Include only the turn before the system starts over from the beginning, and the last turn of the dialog.

3 Recipe for Building a Robust Tracker

In this section, we present several ingredients for building a robust state tracker that come into play at various levels of the development process: from data selection to model adaptation.

3.1 Wide-Coverage and Well-Calibrated Data Selection

The first step to create a robust dialog state tracker is the use of data which covers diverse system dialog actions and user inputs with well-calibrated confidence scores. Since dialog policies can be varying according to how a dialog proceeds, it is crucial to arrange a training dialog corpus with well-balanced dialog actions. For example, group A datasets barely have implicit confirmation and heavily rely on explicit confirmation, while group B datasets have both types of confirmation. Thus a model trained on group A datasets cannot exploit implicit

[2] http://research.microsoft.com/apps/pubs/?id=169024

[3] the average score assigned to the correct item

[4] the L2 norm between the vector of scores output by dialog state tracker and a vector with 1 in the position of the correct item, and 0 elsewhere

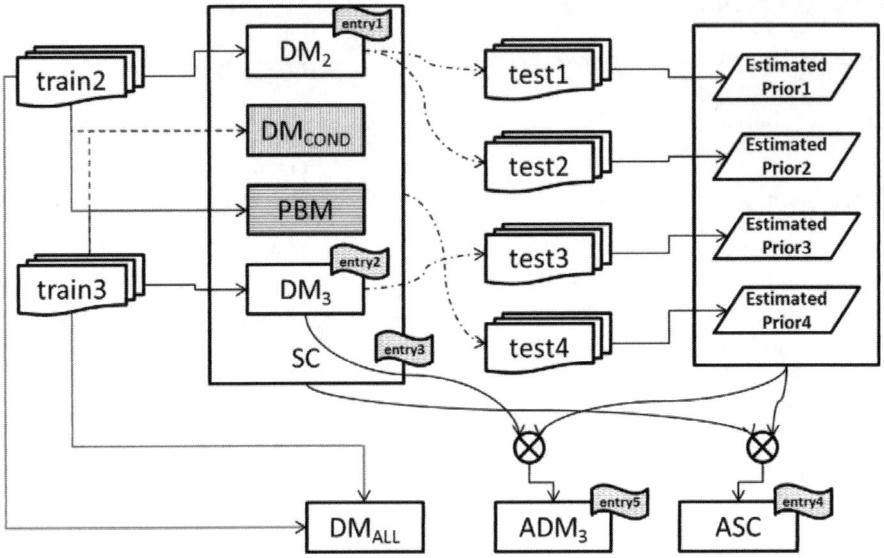

Figure 1: Diagram showing the relation between datasets and models. Each team could have up to five systems entered. Our challenge entries are tagged by their entry numbers. More detailed descriptions about each model are provided in Section 3.

confirmation when applied to group B datasets, whereas a model trained on group B datasets can be applied to group A datasets without much loss.

Another important aspect of the data is how well user inputs are calibrated. If the confidence score is well-calibrated, confirmation can be skipped in the case of a hypothesis with a high confidence. On the contrary, if the quality of the confidence score is very poor, a successful dialog will only be possible via heavy use of confirmation. Thus a model trained on a well-calibrated dataset is likely to perform well on the poorly-calibrated dataset because of backup confirmation. Whereas, a model trained on the poorly-calibrated dataset will not perform well on the well-calibrated dataset due to the mismatch of the confidence score as well as the scarceness of confirmation information. The group A datasets have been shown to be poorly calibrated (Lee and Eskenazi, 2012); this is also shown in Fig. 2. Group B datasets are relatively well-calibrated, however.

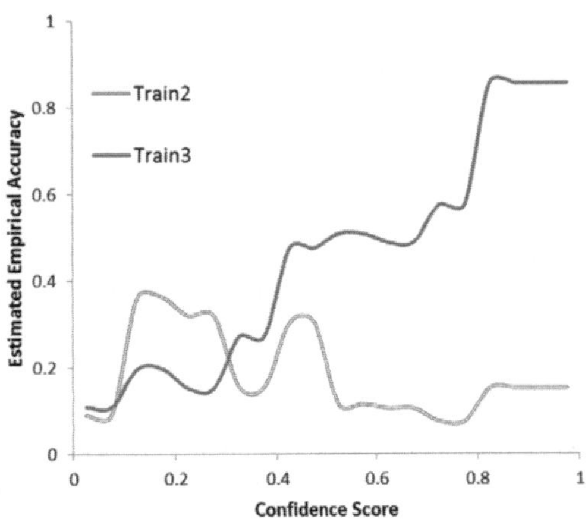

Figure 2: Estimated empirical accuracy of confidence score for *from* slot. Ideally calibrated confidence score should be directly proportional to empirical accuracy.

The importance of wide coverage and well-calibrated data can be observed by examining the results of entry1 and entry2 (Fig. 1) which are trained on group A and B datasets, respectively.

3.2 Feature-Rich Discriminative Model Design

Most previous approaches are based on generative temporal modeling where the current dialog state is estimated using a few features such as the current system action and N-best hypotheses with corresponding confidence scores given the estimated dialog state at the previous turn (Gasic and Young, 2011; Lee and Eskenazi, 2012; Raux and Ma, 2011; Thomson and Young, 2010; Williams, 2010; Young et al., 2010). However, several fundamental questions have been raised recently about the formulation of the dialog state update as a generative temporal model: limitation in modeling correlations between observations in different time slices; and the insensitive discrimination between true and false dialog states (Williams, 2012).

In fact, such limitations can be improved by adopting a discriminative approach, which enables the incorporation of a rich set of features without worrying about their interdependence (Sutton and McCallum, 2006). For example, a hypothesis that repeats with low confidence scores is likely to be a manifestation of ASR error correlations between observations in different time slices. Thus, the highest confidence score that a hypothesis has attained so far could be a useful feature in preventing repeated incorrect hypotheses from defeating the correct hypothesis (which had a higher score but was only seen once). Another useful feature could be the distribution of confidence scores that a hypothesis has attained thus far, since it may not have the same effect as having a single observation with the total score due to the potential nonlinearity of confidence scores. There are many other potentially useful features. The entire list of features used for the challenge system is found in Appendix A.

In addition to the role of rich features in performance enhancement, the incorporation of rich features is also important for robust state tracking. If the tracker estimates the true state by considering various aspects of observations and prior knowledge, then the influence of differences in certain factors between datasets can be mitigated by many other factors that are retained relatively unchanged between datasets.

For the challenge system, we employed a *Maximum Entropy* (MaxEnt) model which is one of most powerful undirected graphical models. Unlike previous work using MaxEnt (Bohus and Rudnicky, 2006) where the model is limited to maintain only the top K-best hypotheses, we amended MaxEnt to allow for the entire set of observed hypotheses to be incorporated; Several feature functions which differ only by output labels were aggregated into one common feature function so that they can share common parameters and gather their statistics together (Appendix A). This modification is also crucial for robust estimation of the model parameters since some slots such as *from* and *to* can have about 10^4 values but most of them are not seen in the training corpus.

The effectiveness of feature-rich discriminative modeling can be observed by comparing the results of DM_{ALL} and PBM (Fig. 1) which are discriminative and generative models, respectively.

Note that interesting relational constraints, e.g. whether or not departure and arrival places are valid on a route, can be incorporated by adopting a structured model such as *Conditional Random Field* (CRF). But CRF was not used for the challenge since the bus information that was provided is not compatible with every dataset. The effectiveness of a structured model has been investigated in a separate publication (Lee, 2013).

3.3 Generalization Improvement Techniques

Even though the incorporation of a set of rich features helps overcome the weaknesses of previous approaches, it also implies a risk of overfitting training datasets due to its increased capacity of function class. Overfitting is a serious hazard especially for test datasets that are severely dissimilar to training datasets. As noted above, since the test datasets of the challenge are intentionally arranged to have various mismatches, it is crucial that we prevent a model from overfitting training datasets. In the rest of this section, we describe various ways of controlling the capacity of a model.

The most obvious method to control the capacity is to penalize larger weights proportional to the squared values of the weights or the absolute values of the weights. We employ the *Orthant-wise Limited-memory Quasi Newton* optimizer (Andrew and Gao, 2007) for L1 regularization. The weights for L1 regularization were set to be 10 and 3 for the prior features and the other features, respectively. These values were chosen through cross-validation over several values rather than doing a thorough search.

A second method, which is often convenient, is to start with small weights and then stop the learning before it has time to overfit provided that it finds the true regularities before it finds the spurious regularities that are related to specific training datasets. It could be hard, however, to decide when to stop. A typical technique is to keep learning until the performance on the validation set gets worse and then stop training and go back to the best point. For the challenge systems, we applied a simpler method that is to stop the training if the average objective function change over the course of 10 previous iterations is less than 0.1, which is usually set to a much smaller number such as 10^{-4}.

In general, prediction errors can be decomposed into two main subcomponents, i.e., error due to bias and variance (Hastie et. al, 2009). It is also known that there is a tradeoff between bias and variance. If a model is flexible enough to fit the given data, errors due to bias will decrease while errors due to variance will increase. The methods stated above try to achieve less error by decreasing errors due to variance. However we cannot avoid increasing errors due to bias in this way. Thus we need a method to alleviate the tradeoff between bias and variance.

System combination is one powerful way to reduce variance without raising bias. If we average models that have different forms and make different mistakes, the average will do better than the individual models. This effect is largest when the models make very different predictions from one another. We could make the models different by simply employing different machine learning algorithms as well as by training them on different subsets of the training data.

The challenge system, entry3, consists of three discriminative models and one generative model (Fig. 1). Entry1 and entry2 were trained on different training datasets to make them produce different predictions. DM_{ALL} is a discriminative model trained on both train2 and train3. Also, DM_{ALL} differs from other discriminative models in the way that it was trained: the parameters associated with the features which are computable without grounding action information (features (1), (5), (8), (9) and (10) in Appendix A) are trained first and then the other features are learned given the former parameters. The idea behind this training method is to encourage the model to put more weight on dialog policy invariant features. The final component PBM is the *AT&T Statistical Dialog Toolkit*[5] which is one of the state-of-the-art generative model-based systems. We modified it to process implicit confirmation and incorporate the prior distribution which was estimated on the training corpus. The prior distribution was smoothed by an approximate *Good-Turing* estimation on the fly when the system encounters an unseen value at run time. The improvement from system combination is verified by the results of entry3.

3.4 Unsupervised Prior Adaptation

While a prior is a highly effective type of information for dialog state tracking, it is also able to hamper the performance when incorrectly estimated. Thus it is worthwhile to investigate adapting the prior to the test datasets. Since a dialog state tracker is meant to estimate the posterior probabilities over hypotheses, we can extract estimated labels from test datasets by setting an appropriate threshold, taking the hypotheses with a greater probability than the threshold as labels. By combining the predictive prior from test datasets and the prior from training datasets, we adapted entry2 and entry3 in an unsupervised way to produce entry5 and entry4, respectively (Fig. 1). For each test dataset, we used different thresholds: 0.95 for test1, test2 and test3, and 0.85 for test4.

4 Related Work

Since the *Partially Observable Markov Decision Process* (POMDP) framework has offered a well-founded theory for both state tracking and decision making, most earlier studies adopted generative temporal models, the typical way to formulate belief state updates for POMDP-based systems (Williams and Young, 2007). Several approximate methods have also emerged to tackle the vast complexity of representing and maintaining belief states, e.g., partition-based approaches (Gasic and Young, 2011; Lee and Eskenazi, 2012; Williams, 2010; Young et al., 2010) and Bayesian network (BN)-based methods (Raux and Ma, 2011; Thomson and Young, 2010). A drawback of the previous generative models is that it is hard to incorporate a rich set of observation features, which are often partly dependent on one another. Moreover, the quality of the confidence score will be critical to all generative models proposed so far, since they do not usually try to handle potential nonlinearity in confidence scores.

As far as discriminative models are concerned, the MaxEnt model has been applied (Bohus and Rudnicky, 2006). But the model is restricted to maintaining only the top K-best hypotheses, where K is a predefined parameter, resulting in potential degradation of performance and difficulties in extending it to structured models.

Finally, there is a wide range of systems that participated in *Dialog State Tracking Challenge* 2013: from rule-based systems to fairly complex statistical methods such as *Deep Neural Networks*. Since we have not only traditional generative models such as *Dynamic Bayesian Network* and partition-based approaches, but also newly-proposed discriminative approaches such as log-linear models, *Support Vector Machines* and *Deep Neural Networks*, the analysis of the challenge results is expected to reveal valuable lessons and future research directions.

[5] http://www2.research.att.com/sw/tools/asdt/

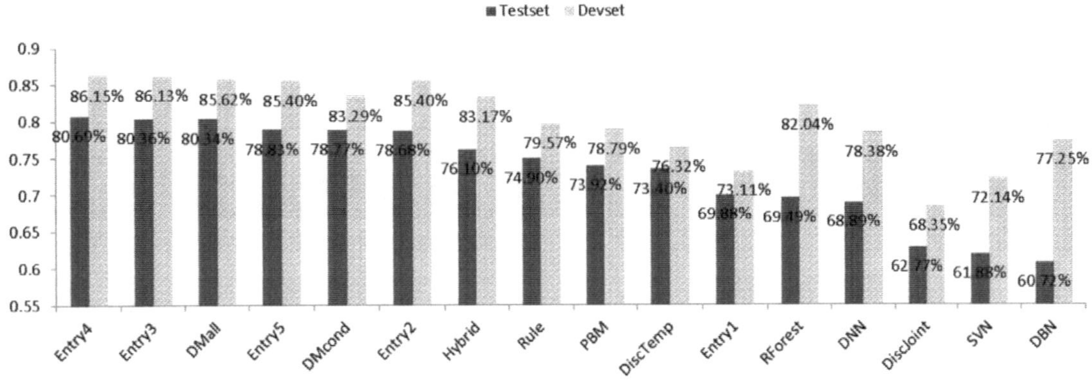

(a) *All* slot: a weighted average accuracy across all slots

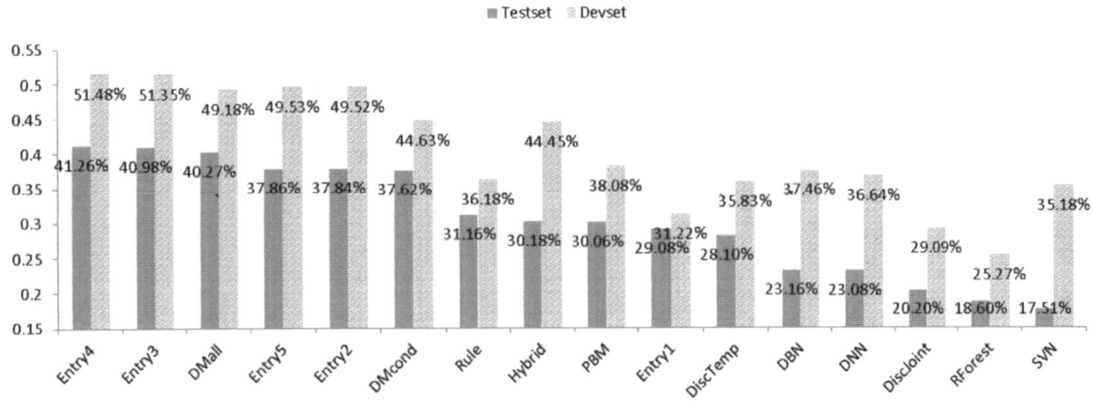

(b) *Joint* slot

Figure 3: Accuracy measured at schedule 3 averaged over the test and development datasets. Models which do not appear in Fig. 1 are the best system of each team except for us. Rule denotes a rule-based system, Hybrid a hybrid system of discriminative and generative approaches, DiscTemp a discriminative temporal model, RForest a random forest model, DNN a deep neural network model, DiscJoint a discriminative model which deals with slots jointly, SVM a support vector machine model, and DBN a dynamic Bayesian network mode.

5 Results and Discussion

The official results of the challenge are publicly available and our team is team6. As mentioned in Section 2.3, there are a variety of aspects of tracker performance that were measured on different schedules. Since prediction accuracy at the end of a dialog directly translates to the success of the entire task, we first show the average accuracy across all test datasets measured at schedule 3 in Fig. 3. The average accuracy at schedule 3 also well represents how robust a state tracker is since the test datasets are widely distributed in the dimensions of dialog policies, dialog length and the quality of user input and confidence score.

First of all, we note that our 4 entries (entries2-5) took the top positions in both the *All* and *Joint* categories. Entry4, which showed the best performance, outperformed the best entry from other teams by 4.59% (entry2 of team9) and 10.1% (entry2 of team2). Specificially, the large improvement in *Joint* implies that our model performs evenly well for all slots and is more robust to the traits of each slot.

Furthermore, from the results we can verify the effectiveness of each technique for achieving robustness. Given the large gap between the performance of entry1 and of entry2, it is clearly shown that a model trained on a wide-coverage and well-calibrated dialog corpus can be applicable to a broad range of test datasets without much loss. Even though entry2 was trained on only 344 dialogs (the first half of train3), it already surpasses most of competing models.

The utility of a feature-rich discriminative model is demonstrated by the fact that DM_{ALL} greatly outperformed PBM. We also note that just using a discriminative model does not guarantee improved performance since many discriminative systems that participated in the challenge underperformed some of the entries that were based on generative modeling or rules. This result implies that devising effective features is central to performance.

In addition, this result also points to the necessity of controlling the capacity of a model. While our models constantly show good performance both on development sets and test sets, the performance of the other models significantly dropped off. In fact, this explains why Hybrid and Rule systems switch their positions in the *Joint* slot. Moreover, many other systems in the graph tail seem to be severely overfitted, resulting in poor performance on test datasets despite relatively good performance on development datasets. As expected, system combination gives rise to better accuracy without loss of robustness; entry3 clearly outperforms each of its components, i.e. entry1, entry2, DM_{COND} and PBM, on both development and test datasets.

Finally, the improvement observed when using unsupervised prior adaptation is also shown to be positive but its effect size is not significant: entry5 vs. entry2 and entry4 vs. entry3. Given that the way in which we have adapted the model is fairly primitive, we believe that there is much room to refine the unsupervised adaptation method.

MRR measures the average of 1/R, where R is the rank of the first correct hypothesis. MRR at schedule 3 measures the quality of the final ranking which may be most important to a multi-modal interface that can display results to the user. Even though the results are not displayed due to space limitations, the results for MRR are very similar to those for accuracy. Our 4 entries (entries2-5) still take the top positions.

The ROC curves assess the discrimination of the top hypothesis' score. The better discrimination at schedule 2 may be helpful for reducing unnecessary confirmations for values with sufficiently high belief. Also, the better discrimination at schedule 3 may enable a model to adapt to test data in an unsupervised manner by allowing us to set a proper threshold to produce predictive labels. The ROC curves of our systems again showed the highest levels of discrimination.

6 Conclusion

In this paper, we presented a set of techniques to build a robust dialog state tracker without losing performance: wide-coverage and well-calibrated data selection, feature-rich discriminative model design, generalization improvement techniques and unsupervised prior adaptation. The results in terms of various metrics show that the proposed method is truly useful for building a tracker prominently robust not only to mismatches between training and test datasets but also to the traits of different slots. Since we used relatively simple features for this work, there is much room to boost performance through feature engineering. Also, more thorough search for regularization weights can give additional performance gain. Moreover, one can extend the present discriminative model presented here to a structured version which can improve performance further by allowing relational constraints to be incorporated (Lee, 2013). Finally, we believe that once a more detailed and thorough investigation of the challenge results has been carried out, we will be able to take the best of each system and combine them to generate a much better dialog state tracker.

Acknowledgments

This work was funded by NSF grant IIS0914927. The opinions expressed in this paper do not necessarily reflect those of NSF.

References

G. Andrew and J. Gao, 2007. Scalable training of L1-regularized log-linear models. In Proceedings of ICML.

A. Black et al., 2011. Spoken dialog challenge 2010: Comparison of live and control test results. In Proceedings of SIGDIAL.

D. Bohus and A. Rudnicky, 2006. A K hypotheses + other belief updating model. In Proceedings of AAAI Workshop on Statistical and Empirical Approaches for Spoken Dialogue Systems.

M. Gasic and S. Young, 2011. Effective handling of dialogue state in the hidden information state POMDP-based dialogue manager. ACM Transactions on Speech and Language Processing, 7(3).

T. Hastie, R. Tibshirani, and J. Friedman, 2009. The Elements of Statistical Learning: Data Mining, Inference, and Prediction (2nd edition). Springer.

S. Lee and M. Eskenazi, 2012. Exploiting Machine-Transcribed Dialog Corpus to Improve Multiple Dialog States Tracking Methods. In Proceedings of SIGDIAL, 2012.

S. Lee, 2013. Structured Discriminative Model For Dialog State Tracking. Submitted to SIGDIAL, 2013.

A. Raux, B. Langner, D. Bohus, A. W Black, and M. Eskenazi, 2005. Let's Go Public! Taking a Spoken Dialog System to the Real World. In Proceedings of Interspeech.

A. Raux and Y. Ma, 2011. Efficient Probabilistic Tracking of User Goal and Dialog History for Spoken Dialog Systems. In Proceedings of Interspeech.

C. Sutton and A. McCallum, 2006. An Introduction to Conditional Random Fields for Relational Learning. Introduction to Statistical Relational Learning. Cambridge: MIT Press.

B. Thomson and S. Young, 2010. Bayesian update of dialogue state: A POMDP framework for spoken dialogue systems. Computer Speech & Language, 24(4):562-588.

B. Thomson, F. Jurccek, M. Gasic, S. Keizer, F. Mairesse, K. Yu, S. Young, 2010a. Parameter learning for POMDP spoken dialogue models. In Proceedings of SLT.

J. Williams and S. Young, 2007. Partially observable Markov decision processes for spoken dialog systems. Computer Speech & Language, 21(2):393-422.

J. Williams, 2010. Incremental partition recombination for efficient tracking of multiple dialog states. In Proceedings of ICASSP.

J. Williams, 2011. An Empirical Evaluation of a Statistical Dialog System in Public Use, In Proceedings of SIGDIAL.

J. Williams, 2012. A Critical Analysis of Two Statistical Spoken Dialog Systems in Public Use. In Proceedings of SLT.

S. Young, M. Gasic, S. Keizer, F. Mairesse, J. Schatzmann, B. Thomson and K. Yu, 2010. The Hidden Information State Model: a practical framework for POMDP-based spoken dialogue management. Computer Speech and Language, 24(2):150–174.

Appendix A. Feature Functions

Feature functions are playing a central role to the performance of discriminative models. We describe the feature functions that we used for the challenge system in the following. To facilitate readers' understanding an example of feature extraction is illustrated in Fig. 4.

One of the most fundamental features for dialog state tracking should exploit the confidence scores assigned to an informed hypothesis. The simplest form could be direct use of confidence scores. But often pre-trained confidence measures fail to match the empirical distribution of a given dialog domain (Lee and Eskenazi, 2012; Thomson et al. 2010). Also the distribution of confidence scores that a hypothesis has attained so far may not have the same effect as the total score of the confidence scores (e.g., in Fig. 4, two observations for 61C with confidence score 0.3 vs. 0.6 which is the sum of the scores). Thus we create a feature function that divides the range of confidence scores into bins and returns the frequency of observations that fall into the corresponding bin:

$$inform_k(y, \boldsymbol{x}_1^t) = \begin{cases} y \neq \text{'None'}, & bin\_freq(k, CS_{inf}(y, \boldsymbol{x}_1^t)) \\ otherwise, & 0 \end{cases} \quad (1)$$

where $CS_{inf}(\cdot)$ returns the set of confidence scores whose action informs y in the sequence of observations $\boldsymbol{x}_1^t$. $bin\_freq(k,\cdot)$ computes the frequency of observations that fall into the kth bin.

There are two types of grounding actions which are popular in spoken dialog systems, i.e., implicit and explicit confirmation. To leverage affirmative or negative responses, the following feature functions are introduced in a similar fashion as the $inform$ feature function:

$$affirm_k(y, \boldsymbol{x}_1^t) = \begin{cases} y \neq \text{'None'}, & bin\_freq(k, CS_{aff}(y, \boldsymbol{x}_1^t)) \\ otherwise, & 0 \end{cases} \quad (2)$$

$$negate_k(y, \boldsymbol{x}_1^t) = \begin{cases} y \neq \text{'None'}, & bin\_freq(k, CS_{neg}(y, \boldsymbol{x}_1^t)) \\ otherwise, & 0 \end{cases} \quad (3)$$

where $CS_{aff}(\cdot)$ / $CS_{neg}(\cdot)$ returns the set of confidence scores whose associated action affirms / negates y in the sequence of observations $\boldsymbol{x}_1^t$.

$$impl\_affirm(y, \boldsymbol{x}_1^t) = \begin{cases} y \neq \text{'None'}, & I_{impl\_aff}(y, \boldsymbol{x}_1^t) \\ otherwise, & 0 \end{cases} \quad (4)$$

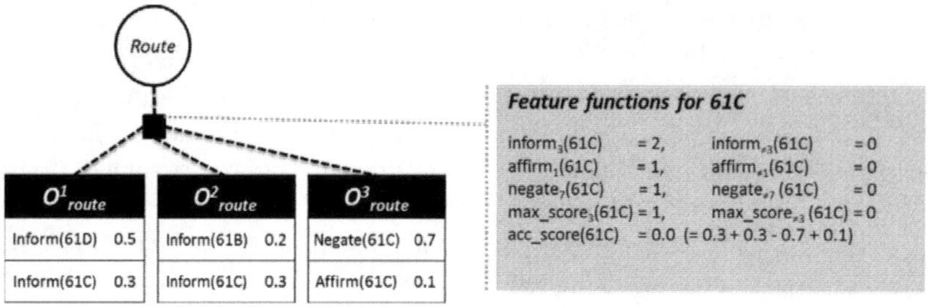

Figure 4: A simplified example of feature extraction for the route concept. It shows the values that each feature will have when three consecutive user inputs are given.

where $I_{impl\_aff}(\cdot)$ indicates whether or not the user has negated the system's implicit confirmation in the sequence of observations $\boldsymbol{x}_1^t$.

One of interesting feature functions is the so-called baseline feature which exploits the output of a baseline system. The following feature function emulates the output of the baseline system which always selects the top ASR hypothesis for the entire dialog:

$$max\_score_k(y, \boldsymbol{x}_1^t) = \begin{cases} y \neq 'None', & bin(k, MAX\_CS_{inf}(y, \boldsymbol{x}_1^t)) \\ otherwise, & 0 \end{cases} \quad (5)$$

where $MAX\_CS_{inf}(\cdot)$ returns the maximum confidence score whose action informs y in the sequence of observations $\boldsymbol{x}_1^t$. $bin(k,\cdot)$ indicates whether or not the maximum score falls into the kth bin.

Yet another feature function of this kind is the accumulated score which adds up all confidence scores associated with *inform* and *affirm* and subtracts the ones with *negation*:

$$acc\_score(y, \boldsymbol{x}_1^t) = \begin{cases} y \neq 'None', & \sum CS_{inf}(y, \boldsymbol{x}_1^t) \\ & +\sum CS_{aff}(y, \boldsymbol{x}_1^t) \\ & -\sum CS_{neg}(y, \boldsymbol{x}_1^t) \\ otherwise, & 0 \end{cases} \quad (6)$$

Since we have a partition-based tracker, it is also possible to take advantage of its output:

$$pbm\_score(y, \boldsymbol{x}_1^t) = \begin{cases} y \neq 'None', & PBM(y, \boldsymbol{x}_1^t) \\ otherwise, & 0 \end{cases} \quad (7)$$

where $PBM(\cdot)$ returns the posterior probability of a hypothesis estimated by the partition-based tracker. Note that such feature functions as $ax\_score(\cdot)$, $acc\_score(\cdot)$ and $PBM(\cdot)$ are not independent of the others defined previously, which may cause generative models to produce deficient probability distributions.

It is known that prior information can boost the performance (Williams, 2012) if the prior is well-estimated. One of advantages of generative models is that they provide a natural mechanism to incorporate a prior. Discriminative models also can exploit a prior by introducing additional feature functions:

$$prior_k(y, \boldsymbol{x}_1^t) = \begin{cases} y \neq 'None', & bin(k, prior\_frac(y)) \\ otherwise, & 0 \end{cases} \quad (8)$$

where $prior\_frac(y)$ returns the fraction of occurrences of y in the set of true labels.

If the system cannot process a certain user request, it is highly likely that the user change his/her goal. The following feature function is designed to take care of such cases:

$$canthelp(y, \boldsymbol{x}_1^t) = \begin{cases} y \neq 'None', & I_{ooc}(y) \\ otherwise, & 0 \end{cases} \quad (9)$$

where $I_{ooc}(\cdot)$ indicates whether or not y is out-of-coverage.

As with other log-linear models, we also have feature functions for bias:

$$bias(y, \boldsymbol{x}_1^t) = 1$$
$$bias_{none}(y, \boldsymbol{x}_1^t) = \begin{cases} y = 'None', & 1 \\ otherwise, & 0 \end{cases} \quad (10)$$

Note that we have an additional bias term for *None* to estimate an appropriate weight for it. Here, *None* is a special value to indicate that the true hypothesis has not yet appeared in the ASR N-best lists. Since there are generally a large number of values for each concept, the probability of the true hypothesis will be very small unless the true hypothesis appears on the N-best lists. Thus we can make inferences on the model very quickly by focusing only on the observed hypotheses at the cost of little performance degradation.

A Simple and Generic Belief Tracking Mechanism for the Dialog State Tracking Challenge: On the believability of observed information

Zhuoran Wang and **Oliver Lemon**
Interaction Lab, MACS, Heriot-Watt University
Edinburgh, EH14 4AS, United Kingdom
{zhuoran.wang; o.lemon}@hw.ac.uk

Abstract

This paper presents a generic dialogue state tracker that maintains beliefs over user goals based on a few simple domain-independent rules, using basic probability operations. The rules apply to observed system actions and partially observable user acts, without using any knowledge obtained from external resources (i.e. without requiring training data). The core insight is to maximise the amount of information directly gainable from an error-prone dialogue itself, so as to better lower-bound one's expectations on the performance of more advanced statistical techniques for the task. The proposed method is evaluated in the Dialog State Tracking Challenge, where it achieves comparable performance in hypothesis accuracy to machine learning based systems. Consequently, with respect to different scenarios for the belief tracking problem, the potential superiority and weakness of machine learning approaches in general are investigated.

1 Introduction

Spoken dialogue system (SDS) can be modelled as a decision process, in which one of the main problems researchers try to overcome is the uncertainty in tracking dialogue states due to error-prone outputs from automatic speech recognition (ASR) and spoken language understanding (SLU) components (Williams, 2012). Recent advances in SDS have demonstrated that maintaining a distribution over a set of possible (hidden) dialogue states and optimising dialogue policies with respect to long term expected rewards can significantly improve the interaction performance (Roy et al., 2000; Williams and Young, 2007a). Such methods are usually developed under a partially observable Markov decision process (POMDP) framework (Young et al., 2010; Thomson and Young, 2010; Williams, 2010), where the distribution over dialogue states is called a 'belief' and is modelled as a posterior updated every turn given an observation. Furthermore, instead of simply taking the most probable (or highest confidence score) hypothesis of the user act as in 'traditional' handcrafted systems, the observation here may consist of an n-best list of the SLU hypotheses (dialogue acts) with (normalised) confidence scores. See (Henderson and Lemon, 2008; Williams and Young, 2007b; Thomson et al., 2010; Young et al., 2013) for more details of POMDP-based SDS.

It is understandable that beliefs more accurately estimating the true dialogue states will ease the tuning of dialogue policies, and hence can result in better overall system performance. The accuracy of belief tracking has been studied in depth by Williams (2012) based on two SDS in public use. Here the effects of several mechanisms are analysed, which can alter the 'most-believed' dialogue state hypothesis (computed using a generative POMDP model) from the one derived directly from an observed top SLU hypothesis. Williams's work comprehensively explores how and why a machine learning approach (more specifically the generative model proposed in (Williams, 2010)) functions in comparison with a naive baseline. However, we target a missing intermediate analysis in this work: how much information one can gain purely from the SLU n-best lists (and the corresponding confidence scores), without any prior knowledge either being externally learned (using data-driven methods) or designed (based on domain-specific strategies), but beyond only considering the top SLU hypotheses. We explain this idea in greater detail as follows.

Firstly, we can view the belief update procedure in previous models as re-constructing the hidden dialogue states (or user goals) based on the previous belief, a current observation (normally an SLU n-best list), and some prior knowledge. The prior knowledge can be observation probabilities given a hidden state, the previous system action and/or dialogue histories (Young et al., 2010; Thomson and Young, 2010; Williams, 2010), or probabilistic domain-specific ontologies (Mehta et al., 2010), where the probabilities can be either trained on a collection of dialogue examples or manually assigned by human experts. In such models, a common strategy is to use the confidence scores in the observed n-best list as immediate information substituted into the model for belief computation, which implies that the performance of such belief tracking methods to a large extent depends on the reliability of the confidence scores. On the other hand, since the confidence scores may reflect the probabilities of the occurrences of corresponding user acts (SLU hypotheses), a belief can also be maintained based on basic probability operations on those events (as introduced in this paper). Such a belief will advance the estimation obtained from top SLU hypotheses only, and can serve as a baseline to justify how much further improvement is actually contributed by the use of prior knowledge. Note that the fundamental method in this paper relies on the assumption that confidence scores carry some useful information, and their informativeness will affect the performance of the proposed method as will be seen in our experiments (Section 5).

Therefore, this paper presents a generic belief tracker that maintains beliefs over user goals only using information directly observable from the dialogue itself, including SLU n-best list confidence scores and user and system behaviours, such as a user not disconfirming an implicit confirmation of the system, or the system explicitly rejecting a query (since no matching item exists), etc. The belief update is based on simple probability operations and a few very general domain-independent rules. The proposed method was evaluated in the Dialog State Tracking Challenge (DSTC) (Williams et al., 2013). A systematic analysis is then conducted to investigate the extent to which machine learning can advance this naive strategy. Moreover, the results show the performance of the proposed method to be comparable to other machine learning based approaches, which, in consideration of the simplicity of its implementation, suggests that another practical use of the proposed method could be as a module in an initial system installation to collect training data for machine learning techniques, in addition to functioning as a baseline for further analysing them.

The remainder of this paper is organised as follows. Section 2 reviews some basic mathematical background, based on which Section 3 introduces the proposed belief tracker. Section 4 briefly describes the DSTC task. The evaluation results and detailed analysis are illustrated in Section 5. Finally, we further discuss in Section 6 and conclude in Section 7.

2 Basic Mathematics

We first review some basic mathematics, which provide the fundamental principles for our belief tracker. Let $P(X)$ denote the probability of the occurrence of an event X, then the probability of X not occurring is simply $P(\neg X) = 1 - P(X)$. Accordingly, if X occurs at a time with probability $P_1(X)$, and at a second time, it occurs with probability $P_2(X)$ independently of the first time, then the overall probability of its occurrence is $P(X) = 1 - P_1(\neg X)P_2(\neg X) = 1 - (1 - P_1(X))(1 - P_2(X))$. To generalise, we can say that in a sequence of k independent events, if the probability of X occurring at the ith time is $P_i(X)$, the overall probability of X having occurred at least once among the k chances is $P(X) = 1 - \prod_{i=1}^{k} P_i(\neg X) = 1 - \prod_{i=1}^{k}(1 - P_i(X))$. This quantity can also be computed recursively as:

$$P^t(X) = 1 - (1 - P^{t-1}(X))(1 - P_t(X)) \quad (1)$$

where $P^t(X)$ denotes the value of $P(X)$ after t event occurring chances, and we let $P^0(X) = 0$.

Now we consider another situation. Let A be a binary random variable. Suppose that we know the prior probability of A being true is $Pr(A)$. If there is a chance where with probability $P(B)$ we will observe an event B independent of A, and we assume that if B happens, we must set A to false, then after this, the probability of A still being true will become $P(A = \text{true}) = Pr(A) * P(\neg B) = Pr(A)(1 - P(B))$.

3 A Generic Belief Tracker

In this section, we will take the semantics defined in the bus information systems of DSTC as examples to explain our belief tracker. Without losing generality, the principle applies to other domains and/or semantic representations. The SDS we are interested in here is a turn-based slot-filling task. In each turn, the system executes an action and receives an observation. The observation is an SLU n-best list, in which each element could be either a dialogue act without taking any slot-value arguments (e.g. `affirm()` or `negate()`) or an act presenting one or more slot-value pairs (e.g. `deny(route=64a)` or `inform(date.day=today, time.ampm=am)`), and normalised confidence scores are assigned to those dialogue act hypotheses. In addition, we follow a commonly used assumption that the user's goal does not change during a dialogue unless an explicit `restart` action is performed.

3.1 Tracking Marginal Beliefs

Since a confidence score reflects the probability of the corresponding dialogue act occurring in the current turn, we can apply the probability operations described in Section 2 plus some 'common sense' rules to track the marginal probability of a certain goal being stated by the user during a dialogue trajectory, which is then used to construct our beliefs over user goals. Concretely, we start from an initial belief b_0 with zero probabilities for all the slot-value hypotheses and track the beliefs over individual slot-value pairs as follows.

3.1.1 Splitting-Merging Hypotheses

Firstly, in each turn, we split those dialogue acts with more than one slot-value pairs into single slot-value statements and merge those identical statements among the n-best list by summing over their confidence scores, to yield marginal confidence scores for individual slot-value representations. For example, an n-best list observation:

```
inform(date.day=today, time.ampm=am) 0.7
              inform(date.day=today) 0.3
```

after the splitting-merging procedure will become:

```
inform(date.day=today)    1
 inform(time.ampm=am)     0.7
```

3.1.2 Applying Rules

Let $P_t(u, s, v)$ denote the marginal confidence score for a user dialogue act $u(s = v)$ at turn t. Then the belief $b_t(s, v)$ for the slot-value pair (s, v) is updated as:

- **Rule 1:** If u = `inform`, then $b_t(s, v) = 1 - (1 - b_{t-1}(s, v))(1 - P_t(u, s, v))$.
- **Rule 2:** If u = `deny`, then $b_t(s, v) = b_{t-1}(s, v)(1 - P_t(u, s, v))$.

In addition, motivated by some strategies commonly used in rule-based systems (Bohus and Rudnicky, 2005), we consider the effects of certain system actions on the beliefs as well. Let $a(h)$ be one of the system actions performed in turn t, where h stands for a set of n slot-value arguments taken by a, i.e. $h = \{(s_1, v_1), \ldots, (s_n, v_n)\}$. We check:

- **Rule 3:** If a is an implicit or explicit confirmation action (denoted by `impl-conf` and `expl-conf`, respectively) and an `affirm` or `negate` user act u is observed with confidence score $P_t(u)$:
  - **Rule 3.1:** If u = `affirm`, then $b_t(s_i, v_i) = 1 - (1 - b_{t-1}(s_i, v_i))(1 - P_t(u)), \forall(s_i, v_i) \in h$.
  - **Rule 3.2:** If u = `negate`, then $b_t(s_i, v_i) = b_{t-1}(s_i, v_i)(1 - P_t(u)), \forall(s_i, v_i) \in h$.
- **Rule 4:** Otherwise, if a is an `impl-conf` action, and there are no `affirm`/`negate` user acts observed, and no information presented in a is re-informed or denied in the current turn, then we take all $(s_i, v_i) \in h$ as being affirmed by the user with probability 1.

However, note that, the marginal probabilities $b(s, v)$ computed using the above rules do not necessarily yield valid beliefs, because sometimes we may have $\sum_v b(s, v) > 1$ for a given slot s. When this occurs, a reasonable solution is to seek a multinomial vector $\bar{b}(s, \cdot)$ that minimises the symmetrised Kullback-Leibler (KL) divergence between $b(s, \cdot)$ and itself. It can be checked that solving such an optimisation problem is actually equivalent to simply normalising $b(s, \cdot)$, for which the proof is omitted here but can be found in Appendix B.

Finally, we consider an extra fact that normally a user will not insist on a goal if he/she has been notified by the system that it is impossible to satisfy. (In the DSTC case, such notifications correspond to those `canthelp.*` system actions.) Therefore, we have:

- **Rule 5:** If the system has explicitly disabled a hypothesis h, we will block the generation of any hypotheses containing h in the belief tracking procedure, until the dialogue finishes.

Note here, if h is a marginal hypothesis, eliminating it from our marginal belief will result in joint hypotheses (see Section 3.2) containing h also being blocked, but if h is a joint representation, we will only block the generation of those joint hypothesis containing h, without affecting any marginal belief.

3.2 Constructing Joint Representations

Beliefs over joint hypotheses can then be constructed by probabilistic disjunctions of those marginal representations. For example, given two marginal hypotheses (s_1, v_1) and (s_2, v_2) $(s_1 \neq s_2)$ with beliefs $b(s_1, v_1)$ and $b(s_2, v_2)$ respectively, one can compute the beliefs of their joint representations as:

$$b^{\text{joint}}(s_1 = v_1, s_2 = v_2) = b(s_1, v_1)b(s_2, v_2)$$
$$b^{\text{joint}}(s_1 = v_1, s_2 = \texttt{null}) = b(s_1, v_1)b(s_2, \texttt{null})$$
$$b^{\text{joint}}(s_1 = \texttt{null}, s_2 = v_2) = b(s_1, \texttt{null})b(s_2, v_2)$$

where `null` represents that none of the current hypotheses for the corresponding slot is correct, i.e. $b(s, \texttt{null})$ stands for the belief that the information for slot s has never been presented by the user, and can be computed as $b(s, \texttt{null}) = 1 - \sum_v b(s, v)$.

3.3 Limitations

The insight of the proposed approach is to explore the upper limit of the observability one can expect from an error-prone dialogue itself. Nevertheless, this method has two obvious deficiencies. Firstly, the dialogue acts in an SLU n-best list are assumed to be independent events, hence error correlations cannot be handled in this method (which is also a common drawback of most existing models as discussed by Williams (2012)). Modelling error correlations requires statistics on a certain amount of data, which implies a potential space of improvement left for machine learning techniques. Secondly, the model is designed to be biased on the accuracy of marginal beliefs rather than that of joint beliefs. The beliefs for joint hypotheses in this method can only lower-bound the true probability, as the observable dependencies among some slot-value pairs are eliminated by the splitting-merging and rejoining procedures described above. For example, in the worst case, a multi-slot SLU hypothesis `inform`$(s_1 = v_1, s_2 = v_2)$ with a confidence score $p < 1$ may yield two marginal beliefs $b(s_1, v_1) = p$ and $b(s_2, v_2) = p$,[1] then the re-constructed joint hypothesis will have its belief $b^{\text{joint}}(s_1 = v_1, s_2 = v_2) = p^2$, which is exponentially reduced compared to the originally observed confidence score. However, the priority between the marginal hypotheses and the joint representations to a greater extent depends on the action selection strategy employed by the system.

4 Description of DSTC

DSTC (Williams et al., 2013) is a public evaluation of belief tracking (a.k.a. dialogue state tracking) models based on the data collected from different dialogue systems that provide bus timetables for Pittsburgh, Pennsylvania, USA. The dialogue systems here were fielded by three anonymised groups (denoted as Group A, B, and C).

There are 4 training sets (`train1a`, `train1b`, `train2` and `train3`) and 4 test sets (`test1...4`) provided, where all the data logs are transcribed and labelled, except `train1b` which is transcribed but not labelled (and contains a much larger number of dialogues than others). It is known in advance to participants that `test1` was collected using the same dialogue system from Group A as `train1*` and `train2`, `test2` was collected using a different version of Group A's dialogue manager but is to a certain extent similar to the previous ones, `train3` and `test3` were collected using the same dialogue system from Group B (but the training set for this scenario is relatively smaller than that for `test1`), and `test4` was collected using Group C's system totally different from any of the training sets.

The evaluation is based on several different metrics[2], but considering the nature of our system, we will mainly focus on the hypothesis accuracy, i.e.

[1]The worst case happens when (s_1, v_1) and (s_2, v_2) are stated for the first time in the dialogue and cannot merge with any other marginal hypotheses in the current turn, as their marginal beliefs will remain p without being either propagated by the belief update rules, or increased by the merging procedure.

[2]Detailed descriptions of these metrics can be found in the DSTC handbook at `http://research.microsoft.com/en-us/events/dstc/`

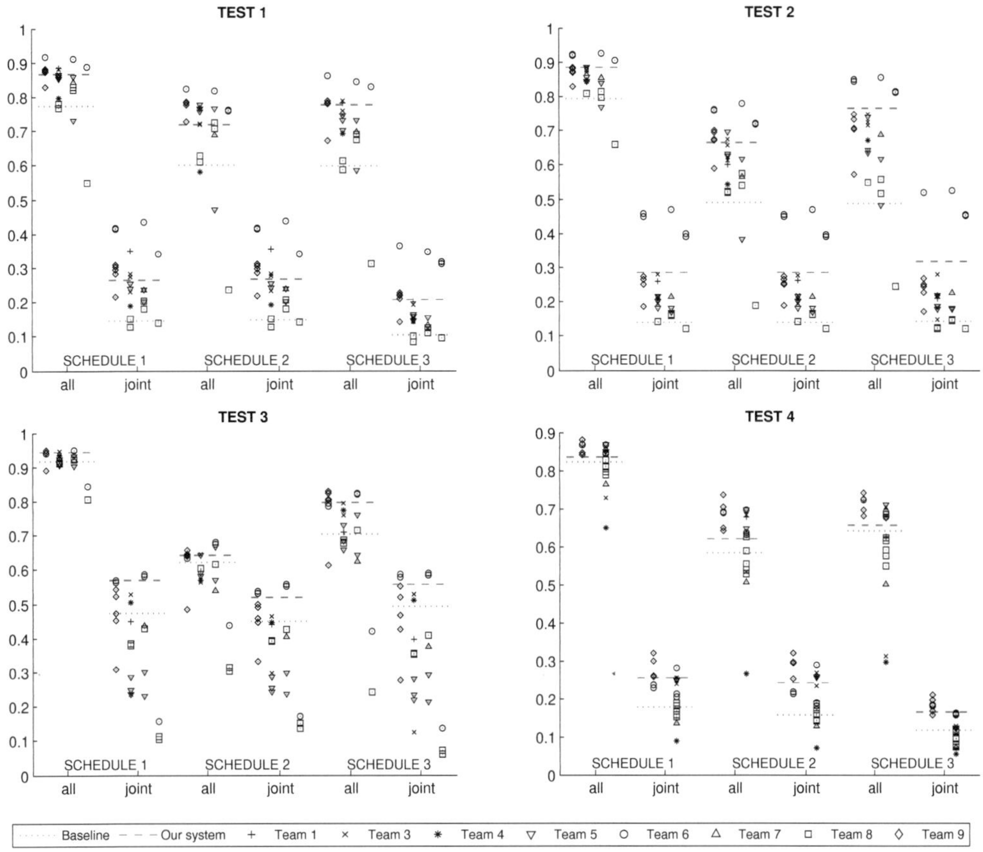

Figure 1: Hypothesis accuracy on the four test sets: the columns in each `schedule`, from left to right, stand for the *ensemble*, *mixed-domain*, *in-domain* and *out-of-domain* system groups, except for `test4` where the last three groups are merged into the right-hand side column.

percentage of turns in which the tracker's 1-best hypothesis is correct, but with the receiver operating characteristic (ROC) performance briefly discussed as well. In addition, there are 3 'schedules' for determining which turns to include when measuring a metric: `schedule 1` – including all turns, `schedule 2` – including a turn for a given concept only if that concept either appears on the SLU n-best list in that turn, or if the system action references that concept in that turn, and `schedule 3` – including only the turn before the `restart` system action (if there is one), and the last turn of the dialogue.

5 Evaluation and Analysis

The method proposed in this paper corresponds to `Team 2, Entry 1` in the DSTC submissions. In the following analysis, we will compare it with the 26 machine learning models submitted by the other 8 anonymised participant teams plus a baseline system (`Team 0, Entry 1`) that only considers the top SLU result.

Each team can submit up to 5 systems, whilst the systems from a same team may differ from each other in either the statistical model or the training data selection (or both of them). There is a brief description of each system available after the challenge. For the convenience of analysis and illustration, on each test set we categorise these systems into the following groups: *in-domain* – systems trained only using the data sets which are similar (including the 'to-some-extent-similar' ones) to the particular test set, *out-of-domain* – systems trained on the data sets which are totally different from the particular test set, *mixed-domain* – systems trained on a mixture of the *in-domain* and *out-of-domain* data, and *ensemble* – systems combining multiple models to generate their final output. (The *ensemble* systems here are all trained on the *mixed-domain* data.) Note that,

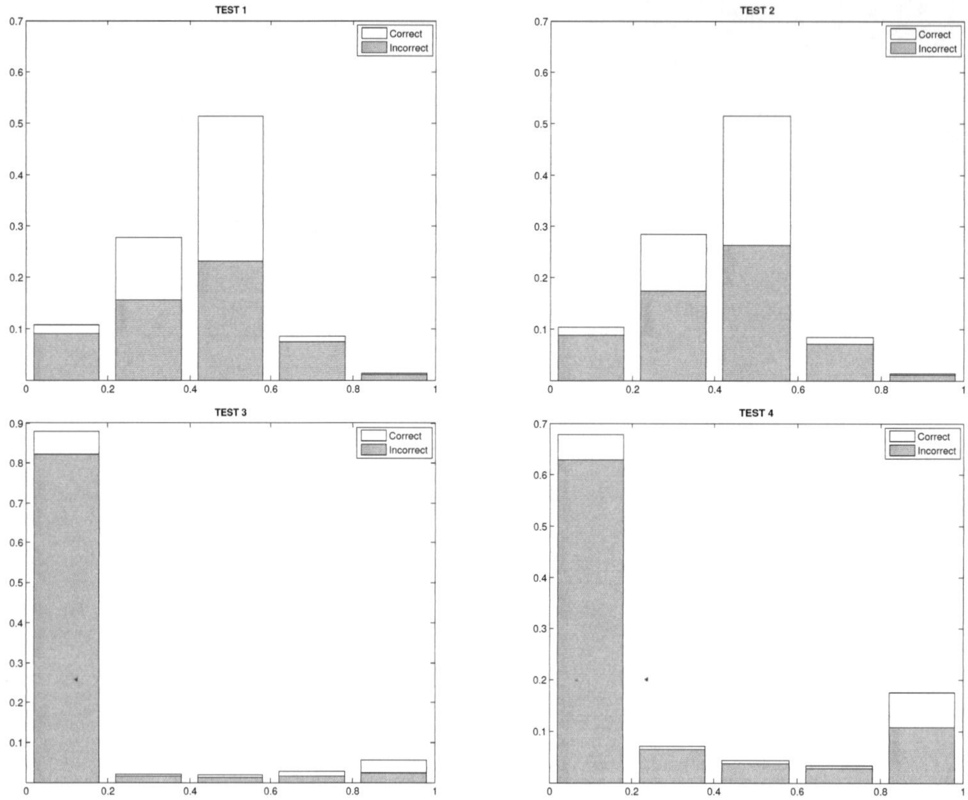

Figure 2: Distributions of SLU confidence scores on the four test sets: The x-axis stands for the confidence score interval, and the y-axis stands for the occurrence rate.

for `test4` there are no *in-domain* data available, so all those *non-ensemble* systems are merged into one group. Detailed system categorisation on each test set can be found in Appendix A.

5.1 Hypothesis Accuracy

We plot the hypothesis accuracy of our method (red dashed line) on the 4 test sets in comparison with the baseline system (blue dotted line) and other systems in Figure 1, where different markers are used to identify the systems from different teams. Here we use the overall accuracy of the marginal hypotheses (`all`) and the accuracy of the joint hypotheses (`joint`) to sketch the general performance of the systems, without looking into the result for each individual slot.

It can be seen that the proposed method produces more accurate marginal and joint hypotheses than the baseline on all the test sets and in all the `schedules`. Moreover, generally speaking, further improvement can be achieved by properly designed machine learning techniques. For example, some systems from `Team 6`, especially their *in-domain* and *ensemble* ones, almost consistently outperform our approach (as well as most of the models from the other teams) in all the above tasks. In addition, the following detailed trends can be found.

Firstly, and surprisingly, our method tends to be more competitive when measured using `schedule 1` and `schedule 3` than using `schedule 2`. As `schedule 2` is supposed to measure system performance on the concepts that are in focus, and to prevent a belief tracker receiving credit for new guesses about those concepts not in focus, the results disagree with our original expectation of the proposed method. A possible explanation here is that some machine learning models tend to give a better belief estimation when a concept is in focus, however their correct top hypotheses might more easily be replaced by other incorrect ones when the focus on the concepts in those correct hypotheses are lost (possibly due to improperly assigned correlations among the concepts). In this sense, our method is more robust, as the beliefs will not change if their corresponding concepts are not in focus.

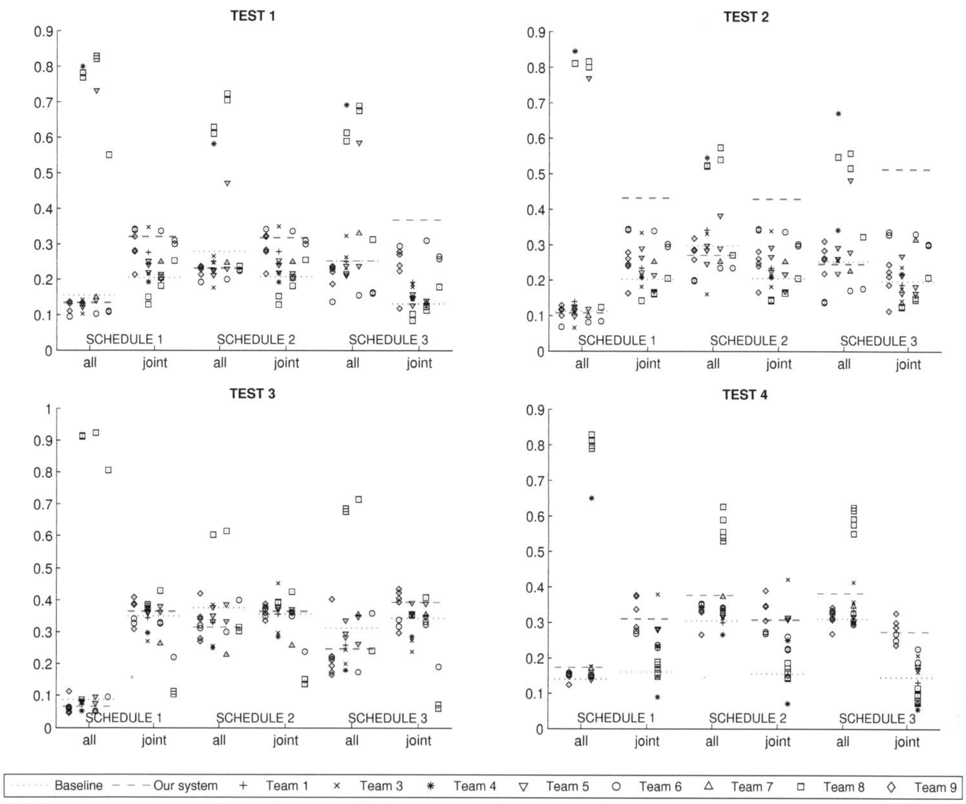

Figure 3: ROC equal error rate on the four test sets: The columns in each `schedule`, from left to right, stand for the *ensemble*, *mixed-domain*, *in-domain* and *out-of-domain* system groups, except for `test4` where the last three groups are merged into the right-hand side column.

Secondly, the proposed method had been supposed to be more preferable when there are no (or not sufficient amount of) *in-domain* training data available for those statistical methods. Initial evidence to support this point of view can be observed from the results on `test1`, `test2` and `test3`. More concretely, when the test data distribution becomes less identical to the training data distribution on `test2`, out system outperforms most of the other systems except those from `Team 6` (and a few others in the `schedule 2/all` task only), compared to its middle-level performance on `test1`. Similarly, on `test3` when the amount of available *in-domain* training data is small, our approach gives more accurate beliefs than most of the others with only a few exceptions in each scenario, even if extra *out-of-domain* data are used to enlarge the training set for many systems. However, the results on `test4` entirely contradicts the previous trend, where a significant number of machine learning techniques perform better than our domain-independent rules without using any *in-domain* training data at all. We analyse such results in detail as follows.

To explain the unexpected outcome on `test4`, our first concern is the influence of Rule 4, which is relatively 'stronger' and more artificial than the other rules. Hence, for the four test sets, we compute the percentage of dialogues where a `impl-conf` system action occurs. The statistics show that the occurrence rates of the implicit confirmation system actions in `test1...4` are 0.01, 0, 0.94 and 0.67, respectively. This means that the two very extreme cases happen in `test3` and `test2` (the situation in `test1` is very similar to `test2`), and the result for `test4` is roughly right in the middle of them, which suggests that Rule 4 will not be the main factor to affect our performance on `test4`. Therefore, we further look into the distributions of the SLU confidence scores across these different test sets. A normalised histogram of the confidence scores for correct and incorrect SLU hypotheses observed in each test set is plotted in Figure 2. Here we only consider the SLU hypotheses that will actually contribute during our belief tracking processes, i.e. only the `inform`, `deny`, `affirm` and `negate` user dialogue acts. It can be found that the dialogue system used to collect the data in `test4` tends to produce significantly more 'very confident' SLU hypotheses (those with confidence scores greater than 0.8) than the dialogue systems used for collecting the other test sets, where, however, a considerable proportion of its highly confident hypotheses are incorrect. In such a case, our system would be less capable in revising those incorrect hypotheses with high confidence scores than many machine learning techniques, since it to a greater extent relies on the confidence scores to update the beliefs. This finding indicates that statistical approaches will be helpful when observed information is less reliable.

5.2 Discussions on the ROC Performance

Besides the hypothesis accuracy, another important issue will be the ability of the beliefs to discriminate between correct and incorrect hypotheses. Williams (2012) suggests that a metric to measure such performance of a system is the ROC curve. Note that, in the DSTC task, most of the systems from the other teams are based on discriminative models (except two systems, a simple generative model from `Team 3` and a deep neural network method from `Team 1`), which are optimised specifically for discrimination. Unsurprisingly, our approach becomes much less competitive when evaluated based on the ROC curve metrics, as illustrated in Figure 3 using the ROC equal error rate (EER) for the `all` and `joint` scenarios. (ERR stands for the intersection of the ROC curve with the diagonal, i.e. where the false accept rate equals the false reject rate. The smaller the ERR value, the better a system's performance is.) However, our argument on this point is that since an optimised POMDP policy is not a linear classifier but has a manifold decision surface (Cassandra, 1998), the ROC curves may not be able to accurately reflect the influence of beliefs on a system's decision quality, for which further investigations will be needed in our future work.

6 Further Discussions

In this paper, we made the rules for our belief tracker as generic as possible, in order to ensure the generality of the proposed mechanism. However, in practice, it is extendable by using more detailed rules to address additional phenomena if those phenomena are deterministically identifiable in a particular system. For example, when the system confirms a joint hypothesis $(s_1 = v_1, s_2 = v_2)$ and the user negates it and only re-informs one of the two slot-values (e.g. `inform(`$s_1 = v_1'$`)`), one may consider that it is more reasonable to only degrade the belief on $s_1 = v_1$ instead of reducing the beliefs on both $s_1 = v_1$ and $s_2 = v_2$ synchronously as we currently do in Rule 3.2. However, the applicability of this strategy will depend on whether it is possible to effectively determine such a compact user intention from an observed SLU n-best list without ambiguities.

7 Conclusions

This paper introduces a simple rule-based belief tracker for dialogue systems, which can maintain beliefs over both marginal and joint representations of user goals using only the information observed within the dialogue itself (i.e. without needing training data). Based on its performance in the DSTC task, potential advantages and disadvantages of machine learning techniques are analysed. The analysis here is more focused on general performance of those statistical approaches, where our concerns include the similarity of distributions between the training and test data, the adequacy of available training corpus, as well as the SLU confidence score distributions. Model-specific features for different machine learning systems are not addressed at this stage. Considering its competitiveness and simplicity of implementation, we suggest that the proposed method can serve either as a reasonable baseline for future research on dialogue state tracking problems, or a module in an initial system installation to collect training data for those machine learning techniques.

Acknowledgments

The research leading to these results was supported by the EC FP7 projects JAMES (ref. 270435) and Spacebook (ref. 270019). We thank Jason D. Williams for fruitful comments on an earlier version of this paper. We also acknowledge helpful discussions with Simon Keizer and Heriberto Cuayáhuitl.

References

Dan Bohus and Alexander I. Rudnicky. 2005. Constructing accurate beliefs in spoken dialog systems. In *Proceedings of the IEEE Workshop on Automatic Speech Recognition and Understanding*, pages 272–277.

Anthony R. Cassandra. 1998. *Exact and Approximate Algorithms for Partially Observable Markov Decision Processes*. Ph.D. thesis, Brown University, Providence, RI, USA.

James Henderson and Oliver Lemon. 2008. Mixture model POMDPs for efficient handling of uncertainty in dialogue management. In *Proceedings of the 46th Annual Meeting of the Association for Computational Linguistics on Human Language Technologies: Short Papers*, pages 73–76.

Neville Mehta, Rakesh Gupta, Antoine Raux, Deepak Ramachandran, and Stefan Krawczyk. 2010. Probabilistic ontology trees for belief tracking in dialog systems. In *Proceedings of the 11th Annual Meeting of the Special Interest Group on Discourse and Dialogue*, pages 37–46.

Nicholas Roy, Joelle Pineau, and Sebastian Thrun. 2000. Spoken dialogue management using probabilistic reasoning. In *Proceedings of the 38th Annual Meeting on Association for Computational Linguistics*, pages 93–100.

Blaise Thomson and Steve Young. 2010. Bayesian update of dialogue state: A POMDP framework for spoken dialogue systems. *Computer Speech and Language*, 24(4):562–588.

Blaise Thomson, Filip Jurčíček, Milica Gašić, Simon Keizer, Francois Mairesse, Kai Yu, and Steve Young. 2010. Parameter learning for POMDP spoken dialogue models. In *Proceedings of IEEE Workshop on Spoken Language Technology*.

Jason D. Williams and Steve Young. 2007a. Partially observable Markov decision processes for spoken dialog systems. *Computer Speech and Language*, 21(2):393–422.

Jason D. Williams and Steve Young. 2007b. Scaling POMDPs for spoken dialog management. *IEEE Transactions on Audio, Speech, and Language Processing*, 15(7):2116–2129.

Jason D. Williams, Antoine Raux, Deepak Ramachandran, and Alan W. Black. 2013. The Dialog State Tracking Challenge. In *Proceedings of the 14th Annual Meeting of the Special Interest Group on Discourse and Dialogue*.

Jason D. Williams. 2010. Incremental partition recombination for efficient tracking of multiple dialog states. In *Proceedings of the IEEE International Conference on Acoustics, Speech, and Signal Processing*, pages 5382–5385.

Jason D. Williams. 2012. Challenges and opportunities for state tracking in statistical spoken dialog systems: Results from two public deployments. *IEEE Journal of Selected Topics in Signal Processing*, 6(8):959–970.

Steve Young, Milica Gašić, Simon Keizer, Francois Mairesse, Jost Schatzmann, Blaise Thomson, and Kai Yu. 2010. The Hidden Information State model: a practical framework for POMDP-based spoken dialogue management. *Computer Speech and Language*, 24(2):150–174.

Steve Young, Milica Gašić, Blaise Thomson, and Jason D. Williams. 2013. POMDP-based statistical spoken dialog systems: A review. *Proceedings of the IEEE*, 101(5):1160–1179.

A System Categorisation

Table 1 shows detailed categorisation of the systems submitted to DSTC, where `TiEj` stands for `Team i,Entry j`.

<table>
<tr><td colspan="3">ensemble</td></tr>
<tr><td colspan="3">T6E3, T6E4, T9E1, T9E2, T9E3
T9E4, T9E5</td></tr>
<tr><td colspan="3">mixed-domain</td><td rowspan="8">non-ensemble for test4</td></tr>
<tr><td colspan="3">T1E1, T3E1, T3E2, T3E3, T4E1
T5E2, T5E4, T5E5, T8E4, T8E5</td></tr>
<tr><td colspan="3">in-domain</td></tr>
<tr><td>test1
test2</td><td>T6E1, T8E1, T8E2</td><td rowspan="2">T5E1
T5E3
T7E1</td></tr>
<tr><td>test3</td><td>T6E2, T6E5, T8E3</td></tr>
<tr><td colspan="3">out-of-domain</td></tr>
<tr><td>test1
test2</td><td colspan="2">T6E2, T6E5, T8E3</td></tr>
<tr><td>test3</td><td colspan="2">T6E1, T8E1, T8E2</td></tr>
</table>

Table 1: Categorisation of the systems submitted to DSTC.

B Symmetrised KL-divergence Minimisation

We prove the following proposition to support our discussions in the end of Section 3.1.

Proposition 1 *Let $p \in \mathbb{R}^N$ be an arbitrary N-dimensional non-negative vector (i.e. $p \geq 0$). Let $\bar{p} = \frac{p}{\|p\|_1}$, where $\|\cdot\|_1$ stands for the ℓ_1-norm of a vector. Then $\bar{p}$ is the solution of the optimisation problem. $\min_{q \geq 0, \|q\|_1 = 1} D_{\mathrm{SKL}}(p\|q)$, where $D_{\mathrm{SKL}}(p\|q)$ denotes the symmetrised KL-divergence between p and q, defined as:*

$$\begin{aligned} D_{\mathrm{SKL}}(p\|q) &= D_{\mathrm{KL}}(p\|q) + D_{\mathrm{KL}}(q\|p) \qquad (2) \\ &= \sum_i p_i \log \frac{p_i}{q_i} + \sum_i q_i \log \frac{q_i}{p_i} \end{aligned}$$

and p_i and q_i denote the ith element in p and q respectively.

Proof Let $q^* = \arg\min_{q \geq 0, \|q\|_1 = 1} D_{\text{SKL}}(p\|q)$. Firstly, using the facts that $\lim_{x \to 0} x \log \frac{x}{y} \to 0$ and $\lim_{x \to 0} y \log \frac{y}{x} \to +\infty, \forall y > 0$, one can easily prove that if $p_i = 0$ then $q_i^* = 0$, and $p_i \neq 0$ then $q_i^* \neq 0$, because otherwise the objective value of Eq. (2) will become unbounded.

Therefore, we only consider the case $p > 0$ and $q > 0$. By substituting $p_i = \bar{p}_i \|p\|_1$ into Eq. (2), we obtain:

$$
\begin{aligned}
D_{\text{SKL}}(p\|q) &= \|p\|_1 \sum_i \bar{p}_i \log \frac{\|p\|_1 \bar{p}_i}{q_i} \\
&\quad + \sum_i q_i \log \frac{q_i}{\|p\|_1 \bar{p}_i} \\
&= \|p\|_1 \left(\sum_i \bar{p}_i \log \frac{\bar{p}_i}{q_i} + \sum_i \bar{p}_i \log \|p\|_1 \right) \\
&\quad + \sum_i q_i \log \frac{q_i}{\bar{p}_i} - \sum_i q_i \log \|p\|_1 \\
&= \|p\|_1 \sum_i \bar{p}_i \log \frac{\bar{p}_i}{q_i} + \sum_i q_i \log \frac{q_i}{\bar{p}_i} \\
&\quad + (\|p\|_1 - 1) \log \|p\|_1 \\
&= \|p\|_1 D_{\text{KL}}(\bar{p}\|q) + D_{\text{KL}}(q\|\bar{p}) \\
&\quad + (\|p\|_1 - 1) \log \|p\|_1 \\
&\geq (\|p\|_1 - 1) \log \|p\|_1
\end{aligned}
$$

where we use the facts that $\sum_i \bar{p}_i = 1$, $\sum_i q_i = 1$, $D_{\text{KL}}(\bar{p}\|q) \geq 0$ and $D_{\text{KL}}(q\|\bar{p}) \geq 0$, since $\bar{p}$ and q are valid distributions. It can be found that the minimum $(\|p\|_1 - 1) \log \|p\|_1$ is only achievable when $D_{\text{KL}}(\bar{p}\|q) = 0$ and $D_{\text{KL}}(q\|\bar{p}) = 0$, i.e. $q = \bar{p}$, which proves Proposition 1. ∎

Multi-domain learning and generalization in dialog state tracking

Jason D. Williams
Microsoft Research, Redmond, WA, USA
jason.williams@microsoft.com

Abstract

Statistical approaches to dialog state tracking synthesize information across multiple turns in the dialog, overcoming some speech recognition errors. When training a dialog state tracker, there is typically only a *small* corpus of well-matched dialog data available. However, often there is a large corpus of *mis-matched* but related data – perhaps pertaining to different semantic concepts, or from a different dialog system. It would be desirable to use this related dialog data to supplement the small corpus of well-matched dialog data. This paper addresses this task as *multi-domain learning*, presenting 3 methods which synthesize data from different slots and different dialog systems. Since deploying a new dialog state tracker often changes the resulting dialogs in ways that are difficult to predict, we study how well each method *generalizes* to unseen distributions of dialog data. Our main result is the finding that a simple method for multi-domain learning substantially improves performance in highly mis-matched conditions.

1 Introduction

Spoken dialog systems interact with users via natural language to help them achieve a goal. As the interaction progresses, the dialog manager maintains a representation of the state of the dialog in a process called *dialog state tracking*. For example, in a bus schedule information system, the dialog state might indicate the user's desired bus route, origin, and destination. Dialog state tracking is difficult because errors in automatic speech recognition (ASR) and spoken language understanding (SLU) are common, and can cause the system to misunderstand the user's needs. At the same time, state tracking is crucial because the system relies on the estimated dialog state to choose actions – for example, which bus schedule information to present to the user.

Most commercial systems use hand-crafted rules for state tracking, selecting the SLU result with the highest confidence score observed so far, and discarding alternatives. In contrast, statistical approaches compute a posterior *distribution* over many *hypotheses* for the dialog state, and in general these have been shown to be superior (Horvitz and Paek, 1999; Williams and Young, 2007; Young et al., 2009; Thomson and Young, 2010; Bohus and Rudnicky, 2006; Metallinou et al., 2013).

Unfortunately, when training a dialog state tracker, there is rarely a large corpus of *matched* data available. For example, a pilot version of the system may be fielded in a controlled environment to collect a small initial corpus. Yet there is often a large quantity of *mis-matched* dialog data available. For example, dialog data might be available from another dialog system – such as an earlier version with a different recognizer, dialog controller, and user population – or from a related task – such as searching for restaurants instead of hotels.

In this paper, we tackle the general problem of **how to make use of disparate sources of data** when training a dialog state tracker. For example, should a tracker for each slot be trained on small sets of slot-specific data, or should data from all slots be combined somehow? Can dialog data from another system be used to build effective tracker for a new system for which no data (yet) exists? Once data from the new system is available, is the old data still useful?

These inter-related questions can be formalized as **multi-domain learning** and **generalization**. Multi-domain learning (**MDL**) refers to the task of building a model – here, a state tracker – for a target domain using training data from both the target domain and a different but related domain. Generalization refers to the ability of a model to perform well in a domain unlike that seen in any of the training data. Both multi-domain learning and generalization are active research topics in the machine learning community, with broad applications. (Joshi et al., 2012) provides a comparison of popular methods on several (non-dialog) tasks, including sentiment classification in on-line product reviews.

In dialog state tracking, there are a variety of properties that could be cast as a "domain". In this paper, we explore two obvious domains: different *dialog systems*, and different *slots*, where slots are informational sub-units of the dialog state, such as the origin, bus route, and departure time in a bus timetables spoken dialog system. We apply several methods for MDL across varied dialog systems, slots, and combinations of both. MDL is attractive for dialog state tracking because the distribution across slots and systems is related but *not identical*. For example, the ranges of speech recognition confidence scores for two slots such as bus route and date may be different, or one system may use confirmations much more often than another. Despite these differences, there are useful patterns: regardless of the slot or system, higher confidence scores and responses of "yes" to confirmations provide more certainty. The hope is that MDL can provide a principled way of using all available data to maximize accuracy.

An important problem in dialog state tracking is that deploying a new tracker into production will produce a new distribution of dialog data that may be unlike data observed at training time in ways that are difficult to predict. As a result, it is important to test the *generalization* of dialog state tracking models on data that differs from the training distribution. In this paper, we evaluate each of the MDL approaches on multiple held-out datasets, ranging from well-matched to very mis-matched – i.e., dialog data from the same dialog system, a modified version of the dialog system, and a completely different dialog system.

We show that dialog data from multiple existing systems can be used to build good state trackers for a completely new system, and that a simple form of MDL improves generalization substantially. We also find that, if well-matched data from that new system is available, the effect (positive or negative) of MDL is slight. Since in practice the level of mis-match can be difficult to predict, this suggests that training with (a particular form of) MDL is the safest approach.

This paper is organized as follows. Section 2 describes the algorithm used for state tracking and the dialog data employed. Section 3 then introduces methods for multi-domain learning. Section 4 presents results and Section 5 briefly concludes.

2 Preliminaries

We begin by describing the core model used for dialog state tracking, and the source data. Both of these will be important for the development of the multi-domain learning methods in Section 3.

2.1 Dialog state tracking model

There are two dominant approaches to statistical methods for dialog state tracking. *Generative* approaches use generative models that capture how the SLU results are generated from hidden dialog states (Horvitz and Paek, 1999; Williams and Young, 2007; Young et al., 2009; Thomson and Young, 2010). In contrast, *discriminative* approaches use conditional models, trained in a discriminative fashion to directly estimate the distribution over a set of state hypotheses based on a large set of informative features (Bohus and Rudnicky, 2006). Previous work has found that discriminative approaches yield better performance (Metallinou et al., 2013), so we base our experiments on a discriminative model.

We will assume that each dialog state hypothesis is described by a feature vector $\mathbf{x}$, consisting of $|\mathbf{x}| = X$ features. For example, a feature might be the confidence score of the most recent recognition result corresponding to the hypothesis. Features can also be included which describe the current dialog context, such as how many times the target slot has been requested or confirmed. At a turn in a dialog with index i, there are $N_{(i)}$ dialog state hypotheses, each described by X features. We denote the concatenation of all $N_{(i)}$ feature vectors as $\mathbf{X}_{(i)}$, which has size $XN_{(i)}$.

The dialog state tracking task is to take as input the complete feature vector $\mathbf{X}_{(i)}$, and output a distribution over the $N_{(i)}$ hypotheses, plus an additional meta-hypothesis REST that indicates that none of the hypotheses is correct. For training, labels $y_{(i)}$ indicate which of the $N_{(i)}$ hypotheses is correct, or else if none of them is correct. By con-

	Feats/hyp				
Group	$\|\mathbf{X}\|$	$\|\mathbf{X}^*\|$	Corpus	Dialogs	Mismatch to training data
A	90	54	TRAIN2	643	None – same distribution
			TEST1	715	Low
			TEST2	750	Medium
B	90	316	TRAIN3	1020	None – same distribution
			TEST3	438	Low
C	90	0	TEST4		High

Table 1: Corpora used in this paper. $|\mathbf{X}|$ denotes the number of *common* features, and $|\mathbf{X}^*|$ denotes the number of *system-specific* features. The data in systems TEST1 and TEST3 has low mis-match to the training data because they use very similar dialog managers as in TRAIN2 and TRAIN3, respectively. The system in corpus TEST2 used a different dialog manager from TRAIN2, but the same set of system actions, speech recognizer, and TTS, resulting in a medium level of mis-match. The system in corpus TEST4 was completely different from any system in the training data. On average there were approximately 13 system turns and 13 user turns per dialog across all corpora. The TRAIN* corpora are used for training, and the TEST* corpora are used for testing. Complete details of the corpora are given in (Williams et al., 2013).

struction the hypotheses are disjoint; with the addition of the REST meta-hypothesis, exactly one hypothesis is correct by construction. After the dialog state tracker has output its distribution, this distribution is passed to a separate, downstream process that chooses what action to take next (e.g., how to respond to the user).

Note that the dialog state tracker is not predicting the *contents* of the dialog state hypotheses: the dialog state hypotheses' contents and features are given by some external process – for example, simply enumerating all SLU values observed so far in the dialog. Rather, the task is to predict a probability distribution over the hypotheses, where the probability assigned to a hypothesis indicates the probability that it is correct.

In our previous work, we developed a discriminatively-trained maximum-entropy model for dialog state tracking (Metallinou et al., 2013). The model estimates a single weight for each feature in $\mathbf{x}$; to keep learning tractable, these weights are shared across all state hypotheses being scored. The model includes L1 and L2 regularization. This model was found to out-perform generative models, rule-based approaches typically used in industry, and competing discriminative approaches. The complete details are given in (Metallinou et al., 2013) and are not crucial to this paper, because the multi-domain learning approaches used here will not modify the learning algorithm, but rather modify the *features*, as described below.

2.2 Dialog data

We use dialog data and evaluation methods from the Dialog State Tracking Challenge (Williams et al., 2013; Williams et al., 2012). This data comes from public deployments of dialog systems which provide bus schedule information for Pittsburgh, USA. Three different research groups – denoted Groups A, B, and C – provided dialog systems. Each group used completely different systems, composed of different speech recognizers, acoustic and language models, language understanding, dialog design, and text-to-speech. The differences between systems from different groups was substantial: for example, Group A and C systems allowed users to provide any information at any time, whereas Group B systems followed a highly directed flow, separately collecting each slot. In addition, Groups A and B fielded several versions of their systems over a multi-year period – these versions differed in various ways, such as acoustic models, confidence scoring model, state tracking method and parameters, number of supported bus routes, presence of minor bugs, and user population. Differences across versions and groups yielded differences in overall performance and distributions in the data (Black et al., 2011; Williams, 2012). Following the dialog state tracking challenge, we use these differences to test the ability of dialog state tracking methods to generalize to new, unseen distributions of dialog data. Table 1 lists the groups, datasets, and the relative match/mis-match between training and test data.

In this data, there are 9 slots: the bus route, date, time, and three components each for the origin and destination, roughly corresponding to streets, neighborhoods, and points-of-interest like universities. In this paper we will build trackers that operate on slots independently – i.e., at each turn, a total of 9 trackers will each output a ranked list of dialog state hypotheses for its slot.[1] The state hypotheses consist of all of the values for that slot observed so far in the dialog – either in an SLU result or output by the system – plus the meta-hypothesis REST that represents the case that none of the observed values is correct.

Each dialog state hypothesis is described by a set of features extracted from the dialog data. The Dialog State Tracking Challenge provides data from all systems in a standard format, from which we extracted 90 features per dialog state hypothesis. We refer to these as *common features*, because they are available for all systems. We denote the concatenation of all common features for all hypotheses at a given turn as $\mathbf{X}_A$, $\mathbf{X}_B$, or $\mathbf{X}_C$, subscripted based on the system from which they were extracted. In addition, the challenge data includes system-specific information. From the Group A and B logs we extracted 54 and 316 *system-specific* features per hypothesis, respectively. We denote the concatenation of all system-specific features for all hypotheses at a given turn as $\mathbf{X}^*_A$ or $\mathbf{X}^*_B$, subscripted based on the system from which they were extracted. Group C logs provided no additional system-specific information. Examples of features are provided in the Appendix.

3 Multi-domain learning methods

3.1 Models for multi-domain learning

In multi-domain learning (MDL), data instances are of the form $(\mathbf{X}_{(i)}, y_{(i)}, d_{(i)})$, where $\mathbf{X}_{(i)}$ are features for instance i, $y_{(i)}$ is the label for instance i, and $d_{(i)}$ is the *domain* of instance i, where there are a total of D domains. The goal is to build a good model for $P_d(y|\mathbf{X})$ – i.e., to predict the label of an instance given its features *and* domain. A baseline model uses only data from domain d to train $P_d(y|\mathbf{X})$; MDL tackles the problem of how to build models that use data from all domains to improve on this baseline. In this paper, we consider the fully-supervised case, where all of the training data has been labeled.

We explore four ways of constructing models. First, in the **IND** baseline model, we build D separate models using only data from a single domain. Next, in the **POOL** model, the data from all domains is simply pooled together into one large corpus; the single model trained on this corpus is used in all domains. Each feature vector is augmented to include an indicator of the domain $d_{(i)}$ from which it originated, as this has been found to confer much of the benefit of more complex MDL algorithms (Joshi et al., 2012). The POOL model can be viewed as the simplest form of MDL.

Next, the **MDL1** model employs a simple but powerful method for MDL developed by (Daume III, 2007). For each data instance, a *synthetic feature vector* is formed with $D + 1$ blocks of size $|\mathbf{X}|$. Each block is set to all zeros, except for block $d_{(i)}$ and block $D + 1$ which are both set to $\mathbf{X}_{(i)}$. For example, with $D = 3$ domains, the synthetic feature vector for $\mathbf{X}_{(i)}$ from domain 1 would be $\langle \mathbf{X}_{(i)}, \mathbf{0}, \mathbf{0}, \mathbf{X}_{(i)} \rangle$, and for $\mathbf{X}_{(j)}$ from domain 2 would be $\langle \mathbf{0}, \mathbf{X}_{(j)}, \mathbf{0}, \mathbf{X}_{(j)} \rangle$, where $\mathbf{0}$ is a vector of zeros of size $|\mathbf{X}|$. This synthetic corpus is then used to train a single model which is used in any domain.

This approach has been found to be successful on a variety of machine learning tasks, including several NLP tasks (Daume III, 2007). To explain the intuition, consider a single feature component of $\mathbf{X}$, $\mathbf{X}[k]$, which appears $D + 1$ times in the synthetic feature vectors. For model estimation, assume a standard loss function with a term that penalizes classification errors, and a regularization term that penalizes non-zero feature weights. Intuitively, if an individual scalar feature $\mathbf{X}[k]$ behaves *differently* in the domains, the classifier will prefer the per-domain copies, and assign a zero weight to the final copy, reducing the error term of the loss function, at the expense of a small increase in the regularization term. On the other hand, if an individual scalar feature $\mathbf{X}[k]$ behaves *similarly* across domains, the model will prefer to assign a single non-zero weight to the final copy and zeros to the per-domain copies, as this will reduce the regularization term in the loss function. In other words, the classifier will prefer the shared copy when doing so has little impact to accuracy – i.e., the classifier chooses on a feature-by-feature basis when to keep domains separate, and when to pool do-

[1] For simplicity, in this paper we do not consider *joint* state hypotheses, which include more than one slot.

Method	Target Slot	Synthetic feature vector encoding for data from: Slot 1	Slot 2	···	Slot 9
SLOTIND	1	$\mathbf{X}_1$	not used	···	not used
	2	not used	$\mathbf{X}_2$	···	not used
	...	...	...	...	...
	9	not used	not used	···	$\mathbf{X}_9$
SLOTPOOL	all	$\mathbf{X}_1$	$\mathbf{X}_2$	···	$\mathbf{X}_3$
SLOTMDL1	all	$\mathbf{X}_1, \mathbf{0}, \ldots, \mathbf{0}, \mathbf{X}_1$	$\mathbf{0}, \mathbf{X}_2, \ldots, \mathbf{0}, \mathbf{X}_2$	···	$\mathbf{0}, \mathbf{0}, \ldots, \mathbf{X}_9, \mathbf{X}_9$
SLOTMDL2	1	$\mathbf{X}_1, \mathbf{0}, \mathbf{X}_1$	$\mathbf{0}, \mathbf{X}_2, \mathbf{X}_2$	···	$\mathbf{0}, \mathbf{X}_9, \mathbf{X}_9$
	2	$\mathbf{0}, \mathbf{X}_1, \mathbf{X}_1$	$\mathbf{X}_2, \mathbf{0}, \mathbf{X}_2$	···	$\mathbf{0}, \mathbf{X}_9, \mathbf{X}_9$
	...	...	...	...	...
	9	$\mathbf{0}, \mathbf{X}_1, \mathbf{X}_1$	$\mathbf{0}, \mathbf{X}_2, \mathbf{X}_2$	···	$\mathbf{X}_9, \mathbf{0}, \mathbf{X}_9$

Table 2: Synthetic features constructed for each multi-domain learning method applied to *slots*. Here, the subscript on $\mathbf{X}$ indicates the *slot* it describes.

mains.

When the number of domains D is large, MDL1 can produce large, sparse synthetic feature vectors, confounding training. **MDL2** addresses this by constructing D separate models; in model d, data from all domains *except* d is pooled into one meta-domain. Then the procedure in MDL1 is followed. For example, for model $d = 1$, instances $\mathbf{X}_{(i)}$ from domain $d_{(i)} = 1$ is represented as $\langle \mathbf{X}_{(i)}, \mathbf{0}, \mathbf{X}_{(i)} \rangle$; data from *all other domains* $d_{(i)} \neq 1$ is represented as $\langle \mathbf{0}, \mathbf{X}_{(i)}, \mathbf{X}_{(i)} \rangle$. This synthetic data is then used to train a model for domain 1.

3.2 Application to dialog state tracking

In this study, we consider two orthogonal dimensions of domain – *systems* and *slots* – and combinations of the two.

Multi-domain learning across *slots* means building a tracker for one slot using dialog data pertaining to that slot, plus data pertaining to other slots. In the experiments below, this is done by treating each of the 9 slots as a domain and applying each of the four MDL methods above. Table 2 specifies the precise form of the synthetic feature vectors for each method.

Multi-domain learning across *systems* means building a tracker for one dialog system using dialog data collected with that system, plus data from other dialog systems. Each of the two corpora in the training data – TRAIN2 from Group A and TRAIN3 from Group B – is treated as a domain. Since only the *common* features are shared across domains (i.e., systems), model complexity can be reduced by building different models depending on the target group – the group the model will be tested on – and including system-specific features only for the target group. For example, when a model will be trained on data from Groups A and B, then tested on data from Group A, we include common features from A and B but system-specific features from only A. Table 3 specifies the precise form of the synthetic feature vectors for each method. Also, when MDL is applied across systems, there are only 2 sources of training data, so MDL2 is identical to MDL1 (and thus isn't shown in the results).

Applying multi-domain learning to both systems and slots is done by composing the two feature synthesis steps. This process is simple but can increase the size of synthetic feature vectors by up to an order of magnitude.

3.3 Evaluation method

In the experiments below, we train dialog state trackers that output a scored list of dialog state hypotheses *for each slot* at each turn in the dialog. For evaluation, we measure the fraction of output lists where the top dialog state hypothesis is correct. A dialog state hypothesis is correct if it corresponds to a slot value which has been recognized correctly. The dialog state tracker may include the meta-hypothesis REST among its hypotheses – this meta-hypothesis is labeled as correct if no correct values have yet been recognized for this slot.

Since most turns contain no information about most slots, we limit evaluation to turns where new information for a slot appears either in the speech recognition output, or in the system output. For

Method	Target group	Synthetic feature vector encoding for data from: Group A	Group B
SYSTEMIND	A	$\mathbf{X}_A, \mathbf{X}_A^*$	not used
	B	not used	$\mathbf{X}_B, \mathbf{X}_B^*$
SYSTEMIND-A	C	$\mathbf{X}_A$	not used
SYSTEMIND-B	C	not used	$\mathbf{X}_B$
SYSTEMPOOL	A	$\mathbf{X}_A, \mathbf{X}_A^*$	$\mathbf{X}_B, \mathbf{0}$
	B	$\mathbf{X}_A, \mathbf{0}$	$\mathbf{X}_B, \mathbf{X}_B^*$
	C	$\mathbf{X}_A$	$\mathbf{X}_B$
SYSTEMMDL	A	$\mathbf{X}_A, \mathbf{X}_A^*, \mathbf{0}, \mathbf{X}_A$	$\mathbf{0}, \mathbf{0}, \mathbf{X}_B, \mathbf{X}_B$
	B	$\mathbf{0}, \mathbf{0}, \mathbf{X}_A, \mathbf{X}_A$	$\mathbf{X}_B, \mathbf{X}_B^*, \mathbf{0}, \mathbf{X}_B$

Table 3: Synthetic features constructed for each multi-domain learning method applied to *systems*. Here, the subscript on $\mathbf{X}$ indicates the *system* it originated from. Asterisk super-scripts indicate system-specific features, which are only included for the group the tracker will be tested on (i.e., the *target group*).

example, in turn i, if a system confirms a bus route, and a date appears in the speech recognition output, both of these slots in turn i will be included when computing average accuracy. If the time slot appears in neither the system output nor anywhere in the speech recognition output of turn i, then the time slot in turn i is excluded when computing average accuracy. The accuracy computation itself was done by the scoring tool from the Dialog State Tracking Challenge, using the *schedule2* accuracy metric for *all* slots (Williams et al., 2013; Williams et al., 2012).

For comparison, we also report performance of a simple rule-based tracker. For each slot, this tracker scans over all values recognized so far in the dialog, and returns the value which has been recognized with the highest *local* SLU confidence score.

4 Results

We first evaluated performance of multi-domain learning in isolation, *excluding* the effects of generalization. To do this, we divided TRAIN2 and TRAIN3 in half, using the first halves for training and the second halves for testing. This experiment gives an indication of the performance of multi-domain learning if conditions in deployment match the training data.

Results are shown in Figure 1a-1b. Here, the effects of multi-domain learning across systems and slots is rather small, and inconsistent. For example, pooling slot data yields best performance on TRAIN3, and worst performance in TRAIN2. Applying MDL across systems yields best performance for TRAIN3, but not for TRAIN2. Overall, when training and test data are very well-matched, MDL has little effect.

Of course, in practice, training and test data will *not* be well-matched, so we next evaluated performance of multi-domain learning *including* the effects of generalization. Here we trained using the complete TRAIN2 and TRAIN3 corpora, and tested on TEST1, TEST2, TEST3, and TEST4.

Results are shown in Figures 1c-1f. The dominant trend is that, at high levels of mis-match as in TEST3 and TEST4, simply pooling together all available data yields a large increase in accuracy compared to all other methods. The majority of the increase is due to pooling across slots, though pooling across systems yields a small additional gain. This result echos past work, where pooling data is often competitive with more sophisticated methods for multi-domain learning (Joshi et al., 2012).

In our case, one possible reason for this result is that simply pooling the data introduces a sort of regularization: note that the models with SLOTPOOL and SYSTEMPOOL have the highest ratio of training data to model parameters. The MDL methods also use all the data, but via their larger synthetic feature vectors, they increase the number of model parameters. The smaller model capacity of the POOL models limit the ability to completely fit the training data. This limitation can be a liability for matched conditions – see for example Figure 1a – but may help the model to generalize

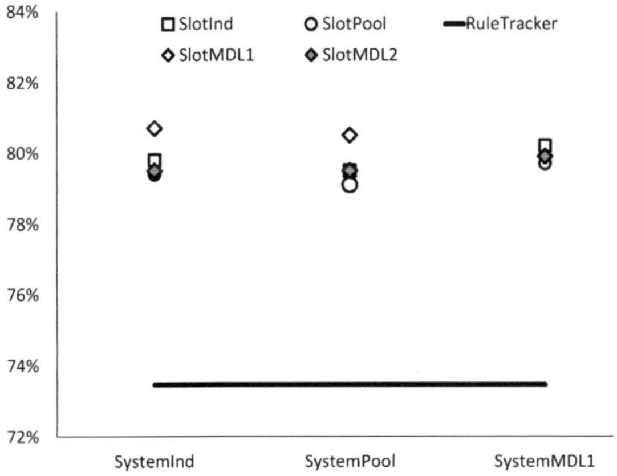

(a) Evaluation on TRAIN2 (Group A), in which there is *minimal* mis-match between the training and test data.

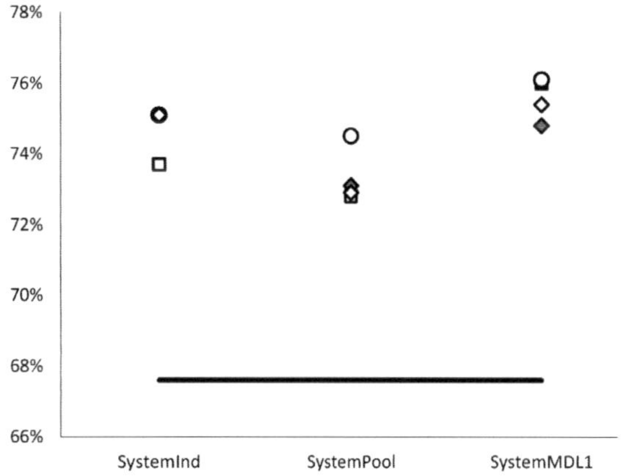

(b) Evaluation on TRAIN3 (Group B), in which there is *minimal* mis-match between the training and test data.

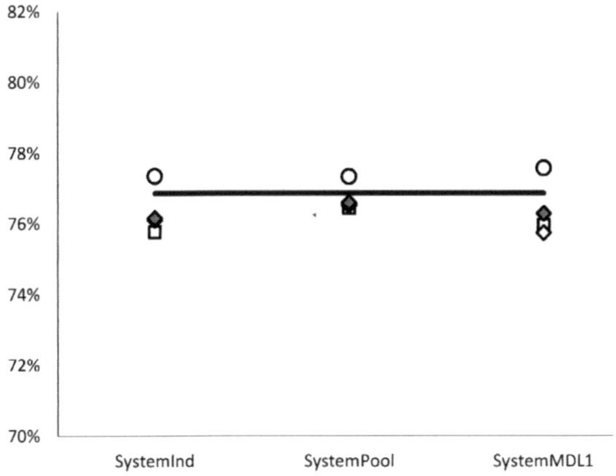

(c) Evaluation on TEST1 (Group A), in which there is *low* mis-match between the training and test data.

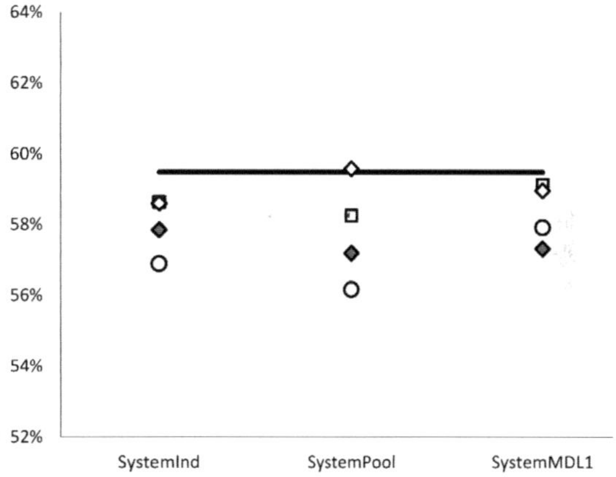

(d) Evaluation on TEST3 (Group B), in which there is *low* mis-match between the training and test data.

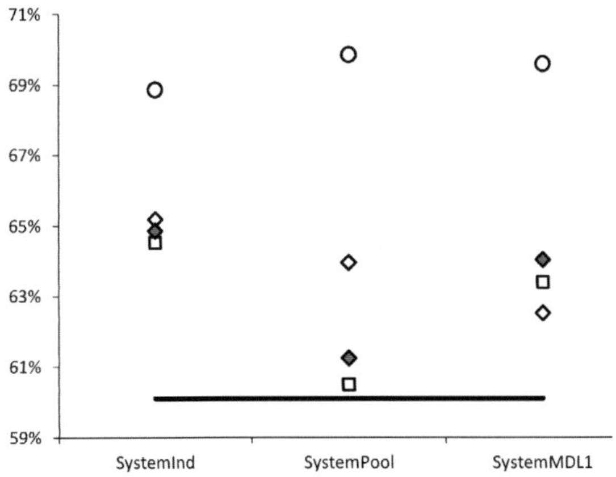

(e) Evaluation on TEST2 (Group A), in which there is *medium* mis-match between the training and test data.

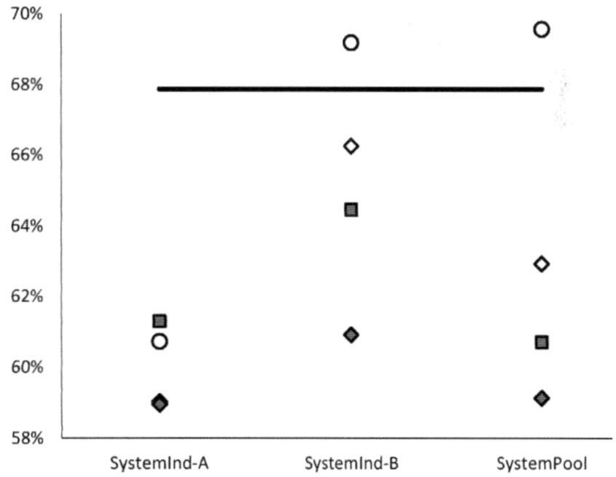

(f) Evaluation on TEST4 (Group C), in which there is *high* mis-match between all of the training data and test data.

Figure 1: Average accuracy of different approaches to multi-domain learning in dialog state tracking. Squares show SLOTIND, circles SLOTPOOL, unshaded diamonds SLOTMDL1, and shaded diamonds SLOTMDL2. The solid line shows performance of a simple rule-based tracker, which is not trained on data. In all plots, the vertical axis is shown on the same scale for comparability (12% from bottom to top), and indicates average accuracy of the top dialog state (c.f., Section 3.3). In panels 1a and 1b, training is done on the first halves of TRAIN2 and TRAIN3, and testing on the second halves. In the other panels, training uses all of TRAIN2 and TRAIN3. In panel 1f, the categories for TEST4 – for which there is no in-domain data – are different than the other panels.

in mis-matched conditions.

5 Conclusion

This paper has examined multi-domain learning and generalization in dialog state tracking. Two dimensions of domain have been studied – learning across slots and learning across systems – and three simple methods for multi-domain learning have been studied. By using corpora of real dialogs from the Dialog State Tracking Challenge, generalization has been studied through varying levels of mis-match between training and test data.

The results show that simply pooling together data yields large benefits in highly mis-matched conditions and has little effect in well-matched conditions. In practice of course, the level of mismatch a new tracker will produce is difficult to predict. So the safest strategy seems to be to always pool together all available data.

There are a variety of issues to examine in future work. First, the MDL methods used in this study were chosen for their simplicity and versatility: by augmenting features, no changes were required to the learning method. There exist other methods of MDL which *do* modify the learning, and in some cases yield better performance. It would be interesting to test them next, perhaps including methods that can construct deeper representations than the maximum entropy model used here.

More broadly, this study has been limited to *supervised* multi-domain learning, in which *labeled* data from multiple domains is available at training time. It would clearly be desirable to develop a method for *unsupervised* adaptation, in which the model is adjusted as the *unlabeled* test data is experienced.

For now, the contribution of this study is to provide at least an initial recommendation to practitioners on how to best make use of disparate sources of dialog data when building a statistical dialog state tracker.

Acknowledgements

Thanks to Dan Bohus for making his machine learning software available.

References

Alan W Black, Susanne Burger, Alistair Conkie, Helen Hastie, Simon Keizer, Oliver Lemon, Nicolas Merigaud, Gabriel Parent, Gabriel Schubiner, Blaise Thomson, Jason D. Williams, Kai Yu, Steve Young, and Maxine Eskenazi. 2011. Spoken dialog challenge 2010: Comparison of live and control test results. In *Proc SIGdial Workshop on Discourse and Dialogue, Portland, Oregon*.

Dan Bohus and Alex Rudnicky. 2006. A 'K hypotheses + other' belief updating model. In *Proc American Association for Artificial Intelligence (AAAI) Workshop on Statistical and Empirical Approaches for Spoken Dialogue Systems, Boston*.

Hal Daume III. 2007. Frustratingly easy domain adaptation. In *Proceedings of the 45th Annual Meeting of the Association of Computational Linguistics*, pages 256–263, Prague, Czech Republic, June. Association for Computational Linguistics.

Eric Horvitz and Tim Paek. 1999. A computational architecture for conversation. In *Proc 7th International Conference on User Modeling (UM), Banff, Canada*, pages 201–210.

Mahesh Joshi, Mark Dredze, William W Cohen, and Carolyn Rose. 2012. Multi-domain learning: When do domains matter? In *Proc Joint Conference on Empirical Methods in Natural Language Processing and Computational Natural Language Learning, Jeju, Korea*.

Angeliki Metallinou, Dan Bohus, and Jason D. Williams. 2013. Discriminative state tracking for spoken dialog systems. In *Proc Association for Computational Linguistics, Sofia*.

Blaise Thomson and Steve Young. 2010. Bayesian update of dialogue state: A POMDP framework for spoken dialogue systems. *Computer Speech and Language*, 24(4):562–588.

Jason D Williams and Steve Young. 2007. Partially observable Markov decision processes for spoken dialog systems. *Computer Speech and Language*, 21(2):393–422.

Jason D Williams, Antoine Raux, Deepak Ramachandran, and Alan W Black. 2012. Dialog state tracking challenge handbook. Technical report, Microsoft Research.

Jason D. Williams, Antoine Raux, Deepak Ramachandran, and Alan Black. 2013. The dialog state tracking challenge. In *Submitted to SigDial 2013*.

Jason D. Williams. 2012. Challenges and opportunities for state tracking in statistical spoken dialog systems: Results from two public deployments. *IEEE Journal of Selected Topics in Signal Processing, Special Issue on Advances in Spoken Dialogue Systems and Mobile Interface*, 6(8):959–970.

Steve Young, Milica Gašić, Simon Keizer, François Mairesse, Jost Schatzmann, Blaise Thomson, and Kai Yu. 2009. The hidden information state model: a practical framework for POMDP-based spoken dialogue management. *Computer Speech and Language*, 24(2):150–174.

Appendix

Example *common features* extracted for all systems
Number of times slot value has been observed in any previous speech recognition result
Whether the most recent speech recognition result includes this slot value
The highest rank on the speech recognition N-best list that this slot value has been observed
The number of times this slot has been requested by the system
Whether the system requested this slot in the current turn
The number of items on the current speech recognition N-best list
Whether confirmation for this slot has been attempted
If confirmation for this slot has been attempted, whether the user was recognized as saying "yes"
The fraction of recognitions of this slot value in the training set which were correct
The fraction of dialogs in the training set in which the user requested this slot value
Example *system-specific features* extracted for Group A systems
Acoustic model score
Average word confidence score
Whether barge-in was triggered
Decoder score
Language model score
Maximum and minimum confidence score of any word
Estimated speaking rate
Estimated speaker gender (male/female)
Example *system-specific features* extracted for Group B systems
Score of best path through the word confusion network
Lowest score of any word on the best path through the word confusion network
Number of speech frames found
Decoder cost
Garbage model likelihood
Noise model likelihood
Average difference in decoder cost, per frame, between the best path and any path through the lattice
Whether barge-in was triggered

Table 4: Examples of features used for dialog state tracking. Group C logs provided no system-specific information.

Structured Discriminative Model For Dialog State Tracking

Sungjin Lee
Language Technologies Institute,
Carnegie Mellon University,
Pittsburgh, Pennsylvania, USA
sungjin.lee@cs.cmu.edu

Abstract

Many dialog state tracking algorithms have been limited to generative modeling due to the influence of the Partially Observable Markov Decision Process framework. Recent analyses, however, raised fundamental questions on the effectiveness of the generative formulation. In this paper, we present a structured discriminative model for dialog state tracking as an alternative. Unlike generative models, the proposed method affords the incorporation of features without having to consider dependencies between observations. It also provides a flexible mechanism for imposing relational constraints. To verify the effectiveness of the proposed method, we applied it to the Let's Go domain (Raux et al., 2005). The results show that the proposed model is superior to the baseline and generative model-based systems in accuracy, discrimination, and robustness to mismatches between training and test datasets.

1 Introduction

With the recent remarkable growth of speech-enabled applications, dialog state tracking has become a critical component not only for typical telephone-based spoken dialog systems but also for multi-modal dialog systems on mobile devices and in automobiles. With present *Automatic Speech Recognition* (ASR) and *Spoken Language Understanding* errors, it is impossible to directly observe the true user goal and action. It is crucial, therefore, to accurately estimate the true dialog state from erroneous observations as a dialog unfolds.

Since the *Partially Observable Markov Decision Process* (POMDP) framework has offered a well-founded theory for both state tracking and decision making, most earlier studies adopted generative temporal models, the typical way to formulate belief state updates for POMDP-based systems (Williams and Young, 2007). Several approximate methods have also emerged to tackle the vast complexity of representing and maintaining belief states, e.g., partition-based approaches (Gasic and Young, 2011; Lee and Eskenazi, 2012a; Williams, 2010; Young et al., 2010) and Bayesian network (BN)-based methods (Raux and Ma, 2011; Thomson and Young, 2010).

To verify the effectiveness of these techniques, some were deployed in a real user system for the Spoken Dialog Challenge (Black et al., 2010). The results demonstrated that the use of statistical approaches helps estimate the true dialog state and achieves increased robustness to ASR errors (Thomson et al., 2010b; Lee and Eskenazi 2012b; Williams, 2011; Williams, 2012). However, further analysis also raised several fundamental questions about the formulation of the belief update as a generative temporal model: limitation in modeling correlations between observations in different time slices; and the insensitive discrimination between true and false dialog states (Williams, 2012). There are more potential downsides of generative models, which will be discussed in detail in Section 2.

On the other hand, natural language processing, computer vision and other machine learning research areas have increasingly profited from discriminative approaches. Discriminative approaches directly model the class posteriors, allowing them to incorporate a rich set of features without worrying about their dependencies on one another. This could result in a deficient probability distribution with generative models (Sutton and McCallum, 2006).

The aim of this paper is to describe a first attempt to adopt a structured discriminative model for dialog state tracking. To handle nonlinearity of confidence score and variable cardinality of the possible values of output variables, the traditional approaches applied to other tasks have been modified.

To verify the effectiveness of the proposed method, we applied it to the Let's Go[1] domain (Raux et al., 2005). The proposed model was compared with its unstructured version without relational constraints, the baseline system which always takes the top ASR hypothesis in the entire dialog, and finally the AT&T Statistical Dialog Toolkit[2] (ASDT) which is one of the state-of-the-art generative model-based systems.

This paper is structured as follows. Section 2 describes previous research and the novelty of our approach. Section 3 elaborates on our proposed structured discriminative approach. Section 4 explains the experimental setup. Section 5 presents and discusses the results. Finally, Section 6 concludes with a brief summary and suggestions for future research.

2 Background and Related Work

A statistical dialog system needs to update its dialog state when taking the action a_s and observing o. Since the POMDP framework assumes the Markovian property between states, updating a belief state involves only the previous belief state, the system action, and the current observation:

$$b'(s') = k \cdot P(o'|s') \sum_{s \in S} P(s'|s, a_s) b(s) \quad (1)$$

where $b(\cdot)$ denotes the probability distribution over states s, $P(o|s)$ the likelihood of o given the state s, $P(s'|s, a_s)$ the state transition probability, and k is a normalizing constant.

In practice, however, belief state updates (Equation 1) in many domains are often computationally intractable due to the tremendously large size of the belief state space. In order to reduce the complexity of the belief states, the following belief state factorization has been commonly applied to the belief update procedure (Williams et al., 2005):

$$b'(g', a'_u, h') \propto \quad (2)$$

$$\underbrace{P(o'|a'_u)}_{observation\ model} \cdot \underbrace{P(a'_u|g', a'_s)}_{user\ action\ model} \cdot$$

$$\sum_h \underbrace{P(h'|h, a'_u, a'_s)}_{history\ model} \cdot \sum_g \underbrace{P(g'|g, a'_s)}_{goal\ model} \cdot$$

$$\sum_{a_u} b(g, a_u, h)$$

where g, h, a_u, represents the user goal, the dialog history, and the user action, respectively.

Partition-based approaches (Gasic and Young, 2011; Lee and Eskenazi, 2012; Williams, 2010; Young et al., 2010) attempt to group user goals into a small number of partitions and split a partition only when this distinction is required by observations. This property endows it with the high scalability that is suitable for fairly complex domains. In partition-based approaches, the *goal model* in Equation 2 is further approximated as follows:

$$\sum_g P(g'|g, a'_s) = \sum_p P(p'|p) \quad (3)$$

where p is a partition from the current turn. One of the flaws of the partition-based approaches is that when one defines a partition to be a Cartesian product of subsets of possible values of multiple concepts, it will be difficult to adopt sophisticated prior distributions over partitions. That may lead to either employing very simple priors such as uniform distribution or maintaining partition structures separately for each concept. This is one of the main reasons that the previous partition-based approaches could not incorporate probabilistic or soft relational constraints into the models.

To allow for relational constraints and alleviate the complexity problem at the same time, *Dynamic Bayesian Networks* (DBN) with more detailed structures for the user goal have also been developed (Thomson and Young, 2010). Nevertheless, there is still a limitation on the types of constraints they can afford. Since DBN is a directed network, it is not quite suitable for specifying undirected constraints. For example, in the Let's Go domain, users can say the same name for the arrival place as the departure place if they are distracted, missing the prompt for the arrival place and so repeating themselves with the departure place. It is also possible for some place names with similar pronunciations to be recognized as the same (e.g. *Forbes* and *Forward*). The system can, in this

[1] In this task, users call the spoken dialog system to

[2] http://www2.research.att.com/sw/tools/asdt/

case, use the constraint that the departure and arrival places may not be identical.

Another drawback of both approaches is that it is hard to incorporate a rich set of observation features, which are often partly dependent on each other. One can create a feature which reflects ASR error correlations between observations in different time slices. For example, a hypothesis that repeats with low confidence scores is likely to be a manifestation of ASR error correlations. Thus, the highest confidence score that a hypothesis has attained so far could be a useful feature in preventing repeated incorrect hypotheses from defeating the correct hypothesis (which had a higher score but was only seen once). Another useful feature could be the distribution of confidence scores that a hypothesis has attained thus far, since it may not have the same effect as having a single observation with the total score due to the potential nonlinearity of confidence scores. There are many other potentially useful features. The entire list of features is found in Section 3.2.

Dynamic Probabilistic Ontology Trees (Raux and Ma, 2011) is another method based upon DBN which does not impose explicit temporal structures. Since it does not impose temporal structures, it is more flexible in considering multiple observations together. However, it is still difficult to capture co-dependent features, which are exemplified above, without introducing probabilistic deficiency due to its generative foundation (Appendix E). Moreover, the quality of the confidence score will be critical to all generative models up to that point since they do not usually try to handle potential nonlinearity in confidence scores.

As far as discriminative models are concerned, the *Maximum Entropy* (MaxEnt) model has been applied (Bohus and Rudnicky, 2006). But the model is limited to a set of separate models for each concept, not incorporating relational dependencies. Also, it is restricted to maintain only top K-best hypotheses where K is a predefined parameter, resulting in potential degradation of performance and difficulties in extending it to structured models. In Section 3, our structured discriminative model is described. It is designed to take into consideration the aforementioned limitations of generative models and the previous discriminative approach.

3 Structured Discriminative Model

Unlike generative models, discriminative models directly model the class posterior given the observations. *Maximum Entropy* is one of most powerful undirected graphical models (Appendix A). But for some tasks that predict structured outputs, e.g. a dialog state, MaxEnt becomes impractical as the number of possible outputs astronomically grows. For example, in the Lets Go domain, the size of possible joint output configurations is around 10^{17}. To address this problem, *Conditional Random Field* (CRF) was introduced which allows dependencies between output variables to be incorporated into the statistical model (Appendix B).

3.1 Model Structure for Dialog State Tracking

We now describe our model structure for dialog state tracking in detail using the Let's Go domain as a running example. The graphical representation of the model is shown in Fig. 1. The global output nodes for each concept (clear nodes in Fig. 1) are unlike other temporal models, where a set of output nodes are newly introduced for each time slice. Instead, as a dialog proceeds, a set of new observations $\boldsymbol{o}_*^t$ (shaded nodes in Fig. 1) are continuously attached to the model structure and the feature

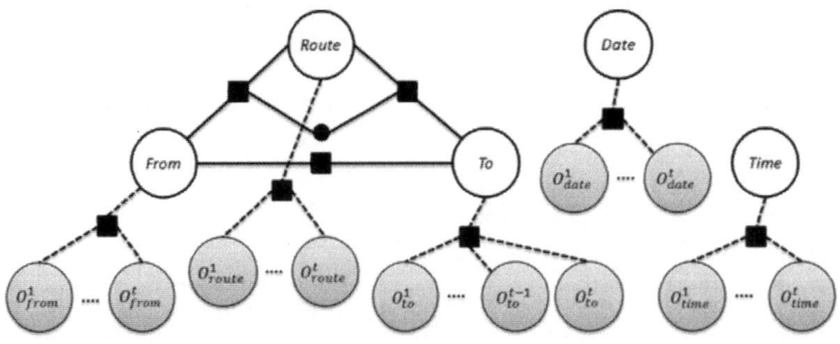

Figure 1: Factor graph representing the structured discriminative model in the Let's Go domain. The shaded nodes show observed random variables. The smaller solid node is the deterministic parameters and explicitly represents parameter sharing between two associated factors.

functions are responsible for producing fixed length feature vectors. The sequence of observations includes not only ASR N-best lists but also system actions from the beginning of the dialog to the current time slice t. Any output node can be freely connected to any other to impose desirable constraints between them whether or not the connections form a loop (solid lines in Fig. 1).

In practice, models rely extensively on parameter tying, e.g., transition parameters in a *Hidden Markov Model*. One specific example of relational constraints and parameter tying naturally arises in the Let's Go domain: the feature function which indicates whether a place is valid on a given route could use the same weights for both departure and arrival places (the solid node and the associated factor nodes in Fig. 1). Parameter tying is also implicitly taking place. This is crucial for robust estimation of the model parameters in spite of data sparseness. Some concepts such as *from* and *to* can have about 10^4 values but most of them are not seen in the training corpus. Thus we aggregate several feature functions which differ only by output labels into one common feature function so that they can gather their statistics together. For example, we can aggregate the observation feature functions (dotted lines in Fig. 1) associated with each output label except for *None* (Section 3.2). Here, *None* is a special value to indicate that the true hypothesis has not yet appeared in the ASR N-best lists. Since there are generally a large number of values for each concept, the probability of the true hypothesis will be very small unless the true hypothesis appears on the N-best lists. Thus we can make inferences on the model very quickly by focusing only on the observed hypotheses at the cost of little performance degradation. Additionally, the feature function aggregation allows for the entire observed hypotheses to be incorporated without being limited to only the pre-defined number of hypotheses.

3.2 Model Features

In this section, we describe the model features which are central to the performance of discriminative models. Features can be broadly split into observation features and relational features. To facilitate readers' understanding an example of feature extraction is illustrated in Fig. 2.

One of the most fundamental features for dialog state tracking should exploit the confidence scores assigned to an informed hypothesis. The simplest form could be direct use of confidence scores. But often pre-trained confidence measures fail to match the empirical distribution of a given dialog domain (Lee and Eskenazi, 2012; Thomson et al. 2010a). Also the distribution of confidence scores that a hypothesis has attained so far may not have the same effect as the total score of the confidence scores (e.g., in Fig. 2, two observations for 61C with confidence score 0.3 vs. 0.6 which is the sum of the scores). Thus we create a feature function that divides the range of confidence scores into bins and returns the frequency of observations that fall into the corresponding bin:

$$inform_k(y, \boldsymbol{x}_1^t) = \begin{cases} y \neq 'None', & bin\_freq(k, CS_{inf}(y, \boldsymbol{x}_1^t)) \\ otherwise, & 0 \end{cases} \quad (4)$$

where $CS_{inf}(\cdot)$ returns the set of confidence scores whose action informs y in the sequence of observations $\boldsymbol{x}_1^t$. $bin\_freq(k,\cdot)$ computes the frequency of observations that fall into the kth bin.

There are two types of grounding actions which are popular in spoken dialog systems, i.e., implicit and explicit confirmation. To leverage affirmative or negative responses to such system acts, the following feature functions are introduced in a similar fashion as the $inform$ feature function:

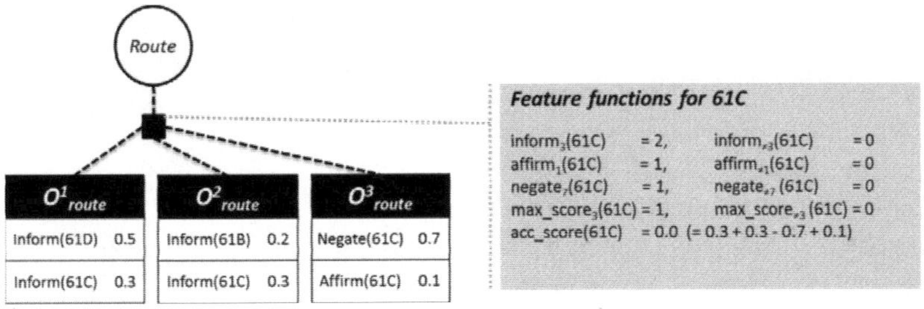

Figure 2: A simplified example of feature extraction for the route concept. It shows the values that each feature will have when three consecutive user inputs are given.

$$affirm_k(y, \boldsymbol{x}_1^t) = \begin{cases} y \neq 'None', & bin\_freq(k, CS_{aff}(y, \boldsymbol{x}_1^t)) \\ otherwise, & 0 \end{cases} \quad (5)$$

$$negate_k(y, \boldsymbol{x}_1^t) = \begin{cases} y \neq 'None', & bin\_freq(k, CS_{neg}(y, \boldsymbol{x}_1^t)) \\ otherwise, & 0 \end{cases} \quad (6)$$

where $CS_{aff}(\cdot)$ / $CS_{neg}(\cdot)$ returns the set of confidence scores whose associated action affirms / negates y in the sequence of observations $\boldsymbol{x}_1^t$.

$$impl\_affirm(y, \boldsymbol{x}_1^t) = \begin{cases} y \neq 'None', & I_{impl\_aff}(y, \boldsymbol{x}_1^t) \\ otherwise, & 0 \end{cases} \quad (7)$$

where $I_{impl\_aff}(\cdot)$ indicates whether or not the user has negated the system's implicit confirmation in the sequence of observations $\boldsymbol{x}_1^t$.

Another interesting feature function is the so-called baseline feature which exploits the output of a baseline system. The following feature function emulates the output of the baseline system which always selects the top ASR hypothesis for the entire dialog:

$$max\_score_k(y, \boldsymbol{x}_1^t) = \begin{cases} y \neq 'None', & bin(k, MAX\_CS_{inf}(y, \boldsymbol{x}_1^t)) \\ otherwise, & 0 \end{cases} \quad (8)$$

where $MAX\_CS_{inf}(\cdot)$ returns the maximum confidence score whose action informs y in the sequence of observations $\boldsymbol{x}_1^t$. $bin(k,\cdot)$ indicates whether or not the maximum score falls into the kth bin.

Yet another feature function of this kind is the accumulated score which adds up all confidence scores associated with *inform* and *affirm* and subtracts the ones with *negation*:

$$acc\_score(y, \boldsymbol{x}_1^t) = \begin{cases} y \neq 'None', & \sum CS_{inf}(y, \boldsymbol{x}_1^t) \\ & +\sum CS_{aff}(y, \boldsymbol{x}_1^t) \\ & -\sum CS_{neg}(y, \boldsymbol{x}_1^t) \\ otherwise, & 0 \end{cases} \quad (9)$$

Note that such feature functions as $max\_score(\cdot)$ and $acc\_score(\cdot)$ are not independent of the others defined previously, which may cause generative models to produce deficient probability distributions (Appendix E).

It is known that prior information can boost the performance (Williams, 2012) if the prior is well-estimated. One of advantages of generative models is that they provide a natural mechanism to incorporate a prior. Discriminative models also can exploit a prior by introducing additional feature functions:

$$prior_k(y, \boldsymbol{x}_1^t) = \begin{cases} y \neq 'None', & bin(k, prior\_frac(y)) \\ otherwise, & 0 \end{cases} \quad (10)$$

where $prior\_frac(y)$ returns the fraction of occurrences of y in the set of true labels.

If the system cannot process a certain user request, it is highly likely that the user change his/her goal. The following feature function is designed to take care of such cases:

$$canthelp(y, \boldsymbol{x}_1^t) = \begin{cases} y \neq 'None', & I_{ooc}(y) \\ otherwise, & 0 \end{cases} \quad (11)$$

where $I_{ooc}(\cdot)$ indicates whether or not y is out-of-coverage.

As with other log-linear models, we also have feature functions for bias:

$$bias(y, \boldsymbol{x}_1^t) = 1$$
$$bias_{none}(y, \boldsymbol{x}_1^t) = \begin{cases} y = 'None', & 1 \\ otherwise, & 0 \end{cases} \quad (12)$$

Note that we have an additional bias term for *None* to estimate an appropriate weight for it.

Regarding relational constraints, we have created two feature functions. To reflect the presumption that it is likely for the true hypothesis for the place concepts (i.e. *from* and *to*) to be valid on the true hypothesis for the *route* concept, we have:

$$place\_in\_route(p, r) = \begin{cases} p \neq 'None', & valid(p, r) \\ otherwise, & 0 \end{cases} \quad (13)$$

where $valid(p, r)$ indicates whether or not the place p is valid on the route r. Another feature function considers the situation where the same place name for both departure and arrival places is given:

$$has\_same\_places(p_f, p_t) = \begin{cases} both\ p_f, p_t \neq ' None' and\ p_f = p_t, & 1 \\ otherwise, & 0 \end{cases} \quad (14)$$

3.3 Inference & Parameter Estimation

One of the common grounding actions of spoken dialog systems is to ask a confirmation question about hypotheses which do not have sufficient marginal beliefs. This makes marginal inference to be one of the fundamental reasoning tools for dialog state tracking. In treelike graphs, exact marginal probabilities are efficiently computable by using the *Junction Tree* algorithm (Lauritzen and Spiegelhalter, 1988) but in general it is intractable on structured models with loops.

Since it is highly likely to have loopy structures in various domains (e.g. Fig. 1), we need to adopt approximate inference algorithms instead. Note that CRF (Equation 16) is an instance of the exponential family. For the exponential family, it is known that the exact inference can be formulated as an optimization problem (Wainwright and Jordan, 2008). The variational formulation opens the door to various approximate inference methods. Among many possible approximations, we adopt the *Tree Reweighted Belief Propagation* (TRBP) method which convexifies the optimization problem that it guarantees finding the global solution (Appendix C).

On the other hand, joint inference also becomes important for either selecting a hypothesis to confirm or determining the final joint configuration when there exist strong relational dependencies between concepts. Moreover, we would like to find not just the best configuration but rather the top M configurations. Since the number of concept nodes is generally moderate, we approximate the inference by searching for the top M configurations only within the Cartesian product of the top K hypotheses of each concept. For domains with a large number of concepts, one can use more advanced methods, e.g., *Best Max-Marginal First* (Yanover and Weiss, 2004) and *Spanning Tree Inequalities and Partitioning for Enumerating Solutions* (Fromer and Globerson, 2009).

The goal of parameter estimation is to minimize the empirical risk. In this paper, we adopt the negative of the conditional log likelihood (Appendix D). Given the partial derivative (Equation 26), we employ the *Orthant-wise Limited-memory Quasi Newton* optimizer (Andrew and Gao, 2007) for L1 regularization to avoid model overfitting.

4 Experimental Setup

In order to evaluate the proposed method, two variants of the proposed method (discriminative model (DM) and structured discriminative model (SDM)) were compared with the baseline system, which always takes the top ASR hypothesis for

	Route	From	To	Date	Time	Joint
Training	378	334	309	33	30	378
Test	379	331	305	54	50	379

(a) Dataset A

	Route	From	To	Date	Time	Joint
Training	94	403	353	18	217	227
Test	99	425	376	18	214	229

(b) Dataset B

Table 1: Counts for each concept represent the number of dialogs which have non-empty utterances for that concept. *From* and *To* concepts add up the counts for their sub-concepts. *Joint* denotes the joint configuration of all concepts.

the entire dialog and outputs the joint configuration using the highest average score, and the ASDT system as being the state-of-the-art partition-based model (PBM). To train and evaluate the models, two datasets from the Spoken Dialog Challenge 2010 are used: a) AT&T system (Williams, 2011), b) Cambridge system (Thomson et. al, 2010b).

For discriminative models, we used 10 bins for the feature functions that need to discretize their inputs (Section 3.2). Parameter tying for relational constraints was applied to dataset A but not to dataset B. To make sure that TRBP produces an upper bound on the original entropy, the constants ρ_c were set to be $2/3$ for SDM and 1 for DM (Appendix C). Also the weights for L1 regularization were set to be 10 and 2.5 for the prior features and the other features, respectively. These values were chosen through cross-validation over several values rather than doing a thorough search. For the ASDT system, we modified it to process implicit confirmation and incorporate the prior distribution which was estimated on the training corpus. The prior distribution was smoothed by approximate Good-Turing estimation on the fly when the system encounters an unseen value at run time.

Two aspects of tracker performance were measured at the end of each dialog, i.e. Accuracy and Receiver Operating Characteristic (ROC). Accuracy measures the percent of dialogs where the tracker's top hypothesis is correct. ROC assesses the discrimination of the top hypothesis's score. Note that we considered *None* as being correct if there is no ASR hypothesis corresponding to the transcription. If all turns are evaluated regardless of context, concepts which appear earlier in the dialog will be measured more times than concepts later in the dialog. In order to make comparisons across concepts fair, concepts are only measured when

N-best	All (%)				Joint			
	Baseline	PBM	DM	SDM	Baseline	PBM	DM	SDM
1-best	74.80	77.93	83.65	83.74	53.56	54.62	60.16	60.69
3-best	74.80	84.00	88.83	89.10	53.56	64.38	70.18	70.98
5-best	74.80	84.54	89.54	89.81	53.56	65.70	72.30	73.09
All	74.80	84.81	89.81	**90.26**	53.56	65.96	73.09	**74.67**

(a) Dataset A

N-best	All				Joint			
	Baseline	PBM	DM	SDM	Baseline	PBM	DM	SDM
1-best	65.46	68.73	78.00	**80.12**	11.35	12.23	26.20	**30.13**
3-best	65.46	68.02	78.00	79.51	11.35	11.35	27.51	28.82
5-best	65.46	67.40	77.92	79.15	11.35	11.79	24.89	25.76
All	65.46	66.61	78.00	79.24	11.35	11.79	24.89	25.76

(b) Dataset B

Table 2: Accuracy of the comparative models. The best performaces across the models are marked in bold. *All* means a weighted average accuracy across all concepts.

they are in focus. It does not, however, allow for a tracker to receive score for new estimations about concepts that are not in focus. In addition, dialogs with more turns will have a greater effect than dialogs with fewer turns. Therefore we only measure concepts which appear in the dialog at the last turn of the dialog before restart. The statistics of the training and test datasets are summarized in Table 1.

5 Results and Discussion

The results indicate that discriminative methods outperform the baseline and generative method by a large performance gap for both dataset A and B (Table 2). Also, SDM exceeds DM, demonstrating the effectiveness of using relational constraints. Furthermore, the performance of SDM surpasses that of the best system in the *Dialog State Tracking Challenge*[3] (Lee and Eskenazi, 2013). Even though the generative model underperforms discriminative models, it is also shown that dialog state tracking methods in general are effective in improving robustness to ASR errors. Another noteworthy result is that the gains for *Joint* by using discriminative models are much larger than those for *All*. Estimating joint configurations correctly is crucial to eventually satisfy the user's request. This result implies that the proposed model performs evenly well for all concepts and is more robust to the traits of each concept. For example, PBM works relatively poorly for *To* on dataset A. What makes *To* different is that the quality of the ASR hypotheses of the training data is much better than that of test data: the baseline accuracy on the training data is 84.79% while 77.05% on the test data. Even though PBM suffers this mismatch, the discriminative models are doing well without significant differences, implying that the discriminative models achieve robustness by considering not just the confidence score but also several features together.

Since there has been no clear evidence that the use of N-best ASR hypotheses is helpful for dialog state tracking (Williams, 2012), we also report accuracies while varying the number of N-best hypotheses. The results show that the use of N-bests helps boost accuracy across all models on dataset A. However, interestingly it hampers the performance in the case of dataset B. It demonstrates that the utility of N-bests depends on various factors, e.g., the quality of N-bests and dialog policies. The system which yielded dataset A employs implicit and explicit confirmation much more frequently than the system which produced dataset B does. The proposed model trained on dataset A without confirmation features incorporated actually showed a slight degradation in accuracy when using more than 3-bests. This result indicates that we need to take into consideration the type of dialog strategy to determine how many hypotheses to use. Thus, it can be conceivable to dynamically change the range of N-bests according to how a dialog proceeds. That allows the system to reduce processing time when a dialog goes well.

[3] http://research.microsoft.com/en-us/events/dstc/

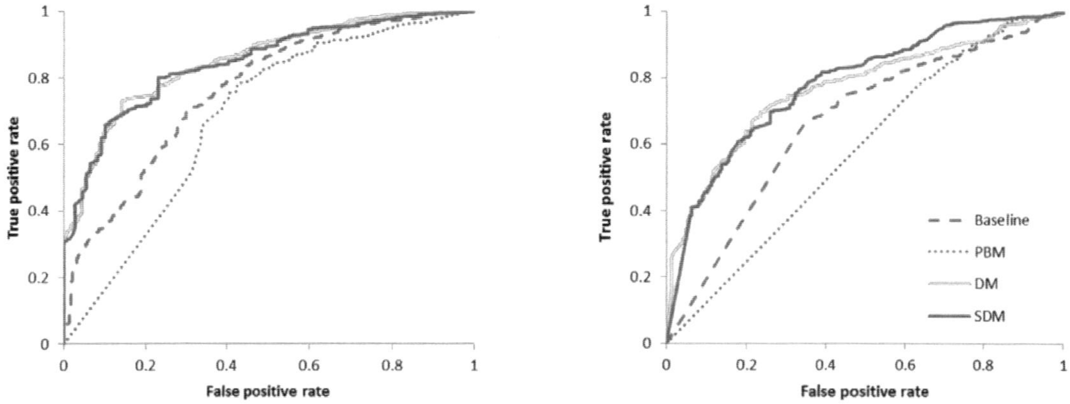

(a) Dataset A (b) Dataset B

Figure 3: Weighted average ROC curves across all concepts

The ROC curves assess the discrimination of the top hypothesis' score (Fig. 3). Note that the discriminative models are far better than PBM on both dataset A and B. In fact, PBM turns out to be even worse than the baseline. The better discrimination can give rise to additional values of a tracker. For example, it can reduce unnecessary confirmations for values with sufficiently high belief. Also, it enables a model to adapt to test data in an unsupervised manner by allowing us to set a proper threshold to produce predictive labels.

6 Conclusion

In this paper, we presented the first attempt, to our knowledge, to create a structured discriminative model for dialog state tracking. Unlike generative models, the proposed method allows for the incorporation of various features without worrying about dependencies between observations. It also provides a flexible mechanism to impose relational constraints. The results show that the discriminative models are superior to the generative model in accuracy, discrimination, and robustness to mismatches between training and test datasets. Since we used relatively simple features for this work, there is much room to boost performance through feature engineering. Also, more thorough search for regularization weights can give additional performance gain. Moreover, one can apply different loss functions, e.g., hinge loss to obtain structured support vector machine. In order to further confirm if the performance improvement by the proposed method can be translated to the enhancement of the overall spoken dialog system, we need to deploy and assess it with real users.

Acknowledgments

This work was funded by NSF grant IIS0914927. The opinions expressed in this paper do not necessarily reflect those of NSF. The author would like to thank Maxine Eskenazi for helpful comments and discussion.

References

G. Andrew and J. Gao, 2007. Scalable training of L1-regularized log-linear models. In Proceedings of ICML.

A. Black et al., 2011. Spoken dialog challenge 2010: Comparison of live and control test results. In Proceedings of SIGDIAL.

D. Bohus and A. Rudnicky, 2006. A K hypotheses + other belief updating model. In Proceedings of AAAI Workshop on Statistical and Empirical Approaches for Spoken Dialogue Systems.

M. Fromer and A. Globerson, 2009. An LP View of the M-best MAP problem. Advances in Neural Information Processing Systems, 22:567-575.

M. Gasic and S. Young, 2011. Effective handling of dialogue state in the hidden information state POMDP-based dialogue manager. ACM Transactions on Speech and Language Processing, 7(3).

S. Lauritzen and D. J. Spiegelhalter, 1988. Local Computation and Probabilities on Graphical Structures and their Applications to Expert Systems. Journal of Royal Statistical Society, 50(2):157–224.

S. Lee and M. Eskenazi, 2012a. Exploiting Machine-Transcribed Dialog Corpus to Improve Multiple Dialog States Tracking Methods. In Proceedings of SIGDIAL, 2012.

S. Lee and M. Eskenazi, 2012b. POMDP-based Let's Go System for Spoken Dialog Challenge. In Proceedings of SLT.

S. Lee and M. Eskenazi, 2013. Recipe For Building Robust Spoken Dialog State Trackers: Dialog State Tracking Challenge System Description. Submitted to SIGDIAL, 2013.

A. Raux, B. Langner, D. Bohus, A. W Black, and M. Eskenazi, 2005. Let's Go Public! Taking a Spoken Dialog System to the Real World. In Proceedings of Interspeech.

A. Raux and Y. Ma, 2011. Efficient Probabilistic Tracking of User Goal and Dialog History for Spoken Dialog Systems. In Proceedings of Interspeech.

C. Sutton and A. McCallum, 2006. An Introduction to Conditional Random Fields for Relational Learning. Introduction to Statistical Relational Learning. Cambridge: MIT Press.

B. Thomson and S. Young, 2010. Bayesian update of dialogue state: A POMDP framework for spoken dialogue systems. Computer Speech & Language, 24(4):562-588.

B. Thomson, F. Jurccek, M. Gasic, S. Keizer, F. Mairesse, K. Yu, S. Young, 2010a. Parameter learning for POMDP spoken dialogue models. In Proceedings of SLT.

B. Thomson, K. Yu, S. Keizer, M. Gasic, F. Jurcicek, F. Mairesse, S. Young, 2010b. Bayesian dialogue system for the Let's Go spoken dialogue challenge. In Proceedings of SLT.

M. Wainwright and M. Jordan, 2008. Graphical Models, Exponential Families, and Variational Inference. Foundations and Trends in Machine Learning, 1(1-2):1–305.

J. Williams and S. Young, 2007. Partially observable Markov decision processes for spoken dialog systems. Computer Speech & Language, 21(2):393-422.

J. Williams, 2010. Incremental partition recombination for efficient tracking of multiple dialog states. In Proceedings of ICASSP.

J. Williams, 2011. An Empirical Evaluation of a Statistical Dialog System in Public Use, In Proceedings of SIGDIAL.

J. Williams, 2012. A Critical Analysis of Two Statistical Spoken Dialog Systems in Public Use. In Proceedings of SLT.

C. Yanover and Y. Weiss, 2004. Finding the M Most Probable Configurations Using Loopy Belief Propagation. In Advances in Neural Information Processing Systems 16. MIT Press.

S. Young, M. Gasic, S. Keizer, F. Mairesse, J. Schatzmann, B. Thomson and K. Yu, 2010. The Hidden Information State Model: a practical framework for POMDP-based spoken dialogue management. Computer Speech and Language, 24(2):150–174.

Appendix A. Maximum Entropy

Maximum Entropy directly models the class posterior given the observations:

$$P(y|\boldsymbol{x}) = \frac{1}{Z(\boldsymbol{x})} \exp(\boldsymbol{\lambda}^T \boldsymbol{f}(y, \boldsymbol{x})) \qquad (15)$$

where $Z(\boldsymbol{x})$ is a normalization function, $\boldsymbol{\lambda}$ the model parameters, and $\boldsymbol{f}(y, \boldsymbol{x})$ the vector of feature functions which are key to performance.

Appendix B. Conditional Random Field

Let G be a factor graph over outputs $\boldsymbol{Y}$. Then, if the distribution $P(\boldsymbol{y}|\boldsymbol{x})$ factorizes according to G and $F = \{\Psi_A\}$ is the set of factors in G, the conditional distribution can be written as:

$$P(\boldsymbol{y}|\boldsymbol{x}) = \frac{1}{Z(\boldsymbol{x})} \prod_{\Psi_A \in G} \exp(\boldsymbol{\lambda}_A^T \boldsymbol{f}(\boldsymbol{y}_A, \boldsymbol{x}_A)) \qquad (16)$$

In practice, models rely extensively on parameter tying. To formalize this, let the factors of G be partitioned to $\mathcal{C} = \{C_1, C_2, \dots, C_P\}$, where each C_p is a clique template whose parameters are tied. Each clique template is a set of factors which has an associated vector of feature functions $\boldsymbol{f}_p(\boldsymbol{x}_p, \boldsymbol{y}_p)$ and parameters $\boldsymbol{\lambda}_p$. From these it follows (Sutton and McCallum, 2006):

$$P(\boldsymbol{y}|\boldsymbol{x}) = \frac{1}{Z(\boldsymbol{x})} \prod_{C_p \in \mathcal{C}} \prod_{\Psi_c \in C_p} \exp(\boldsymbol{\lambda}_p^T \boldsymbol{f}(\boldsymbol{y}_c, \boldsymbol{x}_c)) \qquad (17)$$

where the normalizing function is:

$$Z(\boldsymbol{x}) = \sum_{\boldsymbol{y}} \prod_{C_p \in \mathcal{C}} \prod_{\Psi_c \in C_p} \exp(\boldsymbol{\lambda}_p^T \boldsymbol{f}(\boldsymbol{y}_c, \boldsymbol{x}_c)) \qquad (18)$$

Appendix C. Tree-reweighted Belief Propagation

Unlike treelike graphs, computing exact marginal probabilities is in general intractable on structured models with loops. Therefore, we need to adopt approximate inference algorithms instead. Note that CRF (Equation 16) is an instance of exponential family:

$$P(\boldsymbol{y}; \boldsymbol{\theta}) = \exp(\boldsymbol{\theta}^T \boldsymbol{\phi}(\boldsymbol{y}) - A(\boldsymbol{\theta})) \qquad (19)$$

where $\boldsymbol{\theta}$ is a function of the observations $\boldsymbol{x}$ and the parameters $\boldsymbol{\lambda}$ above, $\boldsymbol{\phi}(\cdot)$ a vector of sufficient statistics consisting of indicator functions for each configuration of each clique and each variable, and $A(\boldsymbol{\theta})$ is the log-partition function $\log \sum_x \exp(\boldsymbol{\theta}^T \boldsymbol{\phi}(\boldsymbol{y}))$. For exponential family, it is known that the exact inference can be formulated as an optimization problem (Wainwright and Jordan, 2008):

$$A(\boldsymbol{\theta}) = \max_{\boldsymbol{\mu} \in \mathcal{M}} \boldsymbol{\theta}^T \boldsymbol{\mu} + H(\boldsymbol{\mu}) \tag{20}$$

where $\mathcal{M} = \{\boldsymbol{\mu}' | \exists \boldsymbol{\theta}, \boldsymbol{\mu}' = \boldsymbol{\mu}(\boldsymbol{\theta})\}$ is the marginal polytope, $\boldsymbol{\mu}(\boldsymbol{\theta})$ is the mapping from parameters to marginals, and $H(\boldsymbol{\mu})$ is the entropy. Applying Danskin's theorem to Equation 20 yields:

$$\boldsymbol{\mu}(\boldsymbol{\theta}) = \frac{dA}{d\boldsymbol{\theta}} = \operatorname*{argmax}_{\boldsymbol{\mu} \in \mathcal{M}} \boldsymbol{\theta}^T \boldsymbol{\mu} + H(\boldsymbol{\mu}) \tag{21}$$

Thus both the partition function (Equation 20) and marginals (Equation 21) can be computed at once. The variational formulation opens the door to various approximate inference methods: to derive a tractable algorithm, one approximates the log-partition function $\tilde{A}(\boldsymbol{\theta})$ by using a simpler feasible region of $\boldsymbol{\mu}$ and a tractable $H(\boldsymbol{\mu})$. Then the approximate marginals are taken as the exact gradient of $\tilde{A}$. Among many possible approximations, we adopt the *Tree Reweighted Belief Propagation* (TRBP) method which convexifies the optimization problem that it guarantees finding the global solution. TRBP takes the local polytope as a relaxation of the marginal polytope:

$$\mathcal{L} = \{\boldsymbol{\mu} | \sum_{\boldsymbol{y}_{c \setminus i}} \boldsymbol{\mu}(\boldsymbol{y}_c) = \boldsymbol{\mu}(y_i), \sum_{y_i} \boldsymbol{\mu}(y_i) = 1\} \tag{22}$$

where c and i index each clique and output variable, respectively. TRBP approximates the entropy as follows:

$$H(\boldsymbol{\mu}) = \sum_i H(\boldsymbol{\mu}_i) - \sum_c \rho_c \cdot I(\boldsymbol{\mu}_c) \tag{23}$$

where $I(\cdot)$ denotes the mutual information and the constants ρ_c need to be selected so that they generate an upper bound on the original entropy.

Appendix D. Parameter Estimation For Conditional Random Field

The goal of parameter estimation is to minimize the empirical risk:

$$R(\boldsymbol{\lambda}) = \sum_n L(\boldsymbol{\lambda}, \boldsymbol{y}_n, \boldsymbol{x}_n) \tag{24}$$

where there is summation over all training examples. The loss function $L(\boldsymbol{\lambda}, \boldsymbol{y}_n, \boldsymbol{x}_n)$ quantifies the difference between the true and estimated outputs. In this paper, we adopt the negative of the conditional log likelihood:

$$\ell(\boldsymbol{\lambda}) = \sum_{C_p \in \mathcal{C}} \sum_{\Psi_c \in C_p} \boldsymbol{\lambda}_p^T \boldsymbol{f}(\boldsymbol{y}_c, \boldsymbol{x}_c) + \log Z(\boldsymbol{x}) \tag{25}$$

The partial derivative of the log likelihood with respect to a vector of parameters $\boldsymbol{\lambda}_p$ associated with a clique template C_p is:

$$\begin{aligned} \frac{\partial \ell}{\partial \boldsymbol{\lambda}_p} = & \sum_{\Psi_c \in C_p} \boldsymbol{f}_p(\boldsymbol{y}_c, \boldsymbol{x}_c) \\ & - \sum_{\Psi_c \in C_p} \sum_{\boldsymbol{y}'_c} \boldsymbol{f}_p(\boldsymbol{y}'_c, \boldsymbol{x}_c) P(\boldsymbol{y}'_c | \boldsymbol{x}_c) \end{aligned} \tag{26}$$

Appendix E. Probabilistic Deficiency

To include interdependent features in a generative model, we have two choices: enhance the model to represent dependencies among the inputs, or make independence assumptions. The first approach is often difficult to do while retaining tractability. For example, it is hard to model the dependence between $inform_k$, $affirm_k$, $negate_k$, max_score_k, and acc_score. On the other hand, the second approach can hurt performance by resulting in poor probability estimates. Let's consider the joint probability $p(x_1, \cdots, x_n, y)$ which the generative approach is based on. Because of the independence assumption, the joint probability can be written as $p(y)p(x_1|y) \cdots p(x_n|y)$. For example, let's assume that we observe two hypotheses 61D and 61B with confidence score 0.6 and 0.2, respectively. Then the conditional probabilities can be written as:

$$\begin{aligned} & p(inform_6 = 1, acc\_score = 0.6 | 61\text{D}) \\ & \quad = p(inform_6 = 1 | 61\text{D}) \cdot \\ & \quad p(acc\_score = 0.6 | 61\text{D}) \end{aligned}$$

$$\begin{aligned} & p(inform_2 = 1, acc\_score = 0.2 | 61\text{B}) \\ & \quad = p(inform_2 = 1 | 61\text{B}) \cdot \\ & \quad p(acc\_score = 0.2 | 61\text{B}) \end{aligned}$$

Since $inform_k = 1$ and $acc\_score = 0.k$ have a strong correlation, their probability estimates should also be positively correlated. To simplify the discussion, now suppose 61B and 61D are equiprobable, $p(61\text{D}) = p(61\text{B})$ and have similar conditional probabilities:

$$\begin{aligned} & p(inform_k = 1 | 61\text{D}) \sim p(inform_k = 1 | 61\text{B}) \\ & p(acc\_score = 0.k | 61\text{D}) \sim \\ & \qquad p(acc\_score = 0.k | 61\text{B}) \end{aligned}$$

Then, multiplying those conditional probabilities, $p(inform_k = 1 | y) \cdot p(acc\_score = 0.k | y)$, will increase or decrease the confidence of the classifier too much, even though no new evidence has been added.

Comparison of Bayesian Discriminative and Generative Models for Dialogue State Tracking

Lukáš Žilka, David Marek, Matěj Korvas, Filip Jurčíček
Charles University in Prague
Faculty of Mathematics and Physics
Malostranské náměstí 25
118 00 Praha, Czech Republic
lukas@zilka.me, david@marek.me,
korvas@ufal.mff.cuni.cz, jurcicek@ufal.mff.cuni.cz

Abstract

In this paper, we describe two dialogue state tracking models competing in the 2012 Dialogue State Tracking Challenge (DSTC). First, we detail a novel discriminative dialogue state tracker which directly estimates slot-level beliefs using deterministic state transition probability distribution. Second, we present a generative model employing a simple dependency structure to achieve fast inference. The models are evaluated on the DSTC data, and both significantly outperform the baseline DSTC tracker.

1 Introduction

The core component of virtually any dialogue system is a dialogue state tracker. Its purpose is to monitor dialogue progress and provide compact representation of the past user input and system output in the form of a dialogue state. In previous works on this topics, Williams (2007) used particle filters to perform inference in a complex Bayesian network modelling the dialogue state, Williams (2008) presented a generative tracker and showed how to train an observation model from transcribed data, Young et al. (2010) grouped indistinguishable dialogue states into partitions and consequently performed dialogue state tracking on these partitions instead of the individual states, Thomson and Young (2010) used a dynamic Bayesian network to represent the dialogue model in an approximate form, and Mehta et al. (2010) used probabilistic ontology trees.

In this paper, we describe two probabilistic dialogue state trackers: (1) a *discriminative dialogue state tracker* (DT) – a model using a simple deterministic state transition probability, resulting in significant computational savings, and (2), a *generative dialogue state tracker* (GT) – a model using simple conditional dependency structure with tied and handcrafted model parameters. Both trackers were evaluated in the DSTC. The aim of the DSTC was to provide a common testbed for different dialogue state tracking methods and to evaluate these methods in a unified way. Because of limited space, the interested reader is referred to Williams et al. (2013) for information about the data and evaluation metrics used in the challenge.

This paper is structured as follows. The deterministic and generative trackers are detailed in Section 2 and the presented models are evaluated on the DSTC data in Section 3. Section 4 discusses the obtained results, and Section 5 concludes the paper.

2 Bayesian Dialogue State Tracking

The goal of dialogue state tracking is to monitor progress in the dialogue and provide a compact representation of the dialogue history in the form of a dialogue state. Because of the uncertainty in the user input, statistical dialogue systems maintain a probability distribution over all dialogue states called the *belief state* and every turn, as the dialogue progresses, updates this distribution in the light of the new observations in a process called *belief monitoring*.

Since the true observations are hidden, the belief state depends on the past and current observation probabilities, $p(\mathbf{o}_1), \ldots, p(\mathbf{o}_t)$, and system actions, $a_0, \ldots, a_{t-1}$, which are referred to as the observed history: $h_t = \{a_0, p(\mathbf{o}_1), \ldots, a_{t-1}, p(\mathbf{o}_t)\}$. If the system is Markovian, the belief state b_t depends only on the previous belief state b_{t-1}, the observation distribution $p(\mathbf{o}_t)$, and the last system action a_{t-1}. There are two ways to derive the belief state update using the Bayes theorem, resulting either in discriminative or generative probabilistic models.

The discriminative update can be represented as

follows:

$$b_t = b(\mathbf{s}_t|h_t) = \sum_{\mathbf{s}_{t-1},\mathbf{o}_t} p(\mathbf{s}_t|a_{t-1},\mathbf{s}_{t-1},\mathbf{o}_t)b(\mathbf{s}_{t-1}|h_{t-1})p(\mathbf{o}_t) \quad (1)$$

where the probability $p(\mathbf{s}_t|a_{t-1},\mathbf{s}_{t-1},\mathbf{o}_t)$ represents the discriminative dialogue model. By further factorisation of (1), we can derive the generative update formula:

$$b_t \propto \sum_{\mathbf{s}_{t-1},\mathbf{o}_t} p(\mathbf{s}_t|a_{t-1},\mathbf{s}_{t-1})p(\mathbf{o}_t|\mathbf{s}_t)\cdot \cdot\, b(\mathbf{s}_{t-1}|h_{t-1})p(\mathbf{o}_t) \quad (2)$$

where the transition probability $p(\mathbf{s}_t|a_{t-1},\mathbf{s}_{t-1})$ and the observation probability $p(\mathbf{o}_t|\mathbf{s}_t)$ represent the generative dialogue model.

In our approach, we define the dialogue state as a vector $\mathbf{s} = [s^1,\ldots,s^N]$ where s^i are values for slots in the dialogue domain, e.g. *to.desc* or *from.monument*. The observations are factored similarly to $\mathbf{o} = [o^1,\ldots,o^N]$, where o^i are individual slot-level observations, e. g. *inform(to.desc = downtown)* $\Leftrightarrow o^{to.desc} = downtown$. The probability of the slot-level observations $p(o^i)$ can be easily obtained by marginalising the observation probability $p(\mathbf{o})$. Because of limited space, only the processing of the *inform* dialogue acts is described in detail.

In the next two sections, we present the discriminative and generative models of belief update employed in the DSTC challenge by using the factorisation of the full belief state into independent factors to obtain computationally efficient updates.

2.1 Discriminative Belief Update

In this work, the belief state b_t is defined as a product of marginal probabilities of the individual slots, $b(\mathbf{s}_t) = \prod_i b(s^i_t)$, where s^i_t is the i-th slot at the turn t and the slot belief $b(s^i_t)$ is a probability distribution over all values for the slot i. To keep the notation uncluttered, the slot index, i, will be omitted in the following text. To further simplify the belief updates, similarly to the full belief monitoring represented by (1), the slot belief depends only on the previous slot belief b_{t-1}, the observation distribution $p(o_t)$, and the last system action a_{t-1}. This results in update rules for individual slots s as follows:

$$b(s_t) = \sum_{s_{t-1},o_t} p(s_t|a_{t-1},s_{t-1},o_t)b(s_{t-1})p(o_t) \quad (3)$$

where the conditional probability distribution $p(s_t|a_{t-1},s_{t-1},o_t)$ represents the slot-level dialogue model.

There are two aspects which have to be taken into account when we consider the presented belief update: (1) the computational complexity and (2) the parameters of the dialogue model. First, the complexity of the belief update is given by the number of slot values and observations because the sum must be evaluated for all their combinations. This suggests that even this update may be computationally too expensive for slots where observations have a large number of values. Second, the slot-level dialogue model describes probabilistically how the value of a slot changes according to the context and the observations. Parameters of this conditional distribution would ideally be estimated from annotated data. Because of data sparsity, however, such estimates tend to be rather poor and either they must be smoothed or the parameters must be tied. To overcome this problem, we decided to set the parameters manually on the basis of two simple assumptions leading to very computationally efficient updates. First, we assume that our dialogue model should completely trust what the user says. Second, we assume that the user goal does not change when the user is silent. For example, if the user says: "I want to go downtown", $o^{to.desc}_t = downtown$, then the state should be $s^{to.desc}_t = downtown$; and when the user says nothing in the next turn, $o^{to.desc}_{t+1} = \odot$ (where the symbol $\odot$ is a special slot value representing that the user was silent), the state remains $s^{to.desc}_{t+1} = downtown$. This is captured by the following definition of the slot-level dialogue model:

$$p(s_t|a_{t-1},s_{t-1},o_t) = \begin{cases} 1 & (s_t = o_t \wedge o_t \neq \odot)\vee \\ & (s_t = s_{t-1} \wedge o_t = \odot) \\ 0 & otherwise \end{cases} \quad (4)$$

When (4) is substituted into (3), the belief update greatly simplifies and appears into the following form:

$$b(s_t) = \begin{cases} s_t = \odot: & p(s_{t-1} = \odot)p(o_t = \odot) \\ s_t \neq \odot: & p(o_t = s_t) \\ & + p(o_t = \odot)p(s_{t-1} = s_t) \end{cases} \quad (5)$$

Note that this model effectively accumulates probability from multiple hypotheses and from multiple turns. For example, its ability to "remember" the belief from the previous turn is proportional to the probability mass assigned to the SLU hypothesis that the user was silent about the slot in question. In the special case when the user is silent with probability 1.0, the current belief is equal to the previous belief.

This belief update is very computationally efficient. First, instead of summing over all combinations of the slot and observation values (3), the belief can be computed by means of a simple formula (5). Second, if the user does not mention a particular slot value during the dialogue, this value will always have a probability of zero. Therefore, only the probability for values suggested by the SLU component has to be maintained.

2.2 Generative model for belief update

Similarly to the discriminative belief update, the generative model relies on factorisation of the full belief state into a product of marginal slot beliefs and a simple dependency structure where a slot belief depends only on the previous slot belief, the slot observation distribution $p(o_t^i)$, and the last system action a_{t-1}. The dialogue model $p(s_t|a_{t-1}, s_{t-1}, o_t)$ is further factored, however, into the transition model $p(s_t|a_{t-1}, s_{t-1})$ and the observation model $p(o_t|s_t)$ as given in (2).

The transition model describes the probability that the user will change his/her goal, given the previous goal and the last system action. For example, if the system asks the user about a specific slot, then it is reasonable to have a larger probability of this slot changing its value. As noted for the discriminative model, estimation of the dialogue model parameters requires a large amount of data, which was not available in the challenge. Therefore, we used parameter tying as described by Thomson and Young (2010), and set the tied parameters manually:

$$p(s_t|a_{t-1}, s_{t-1}) = \begin{cases} \theta_t & \text{if } s_t = s_{t-1} \\ \frac{1-\theta_t}{|values|-1} & \text{otherwise} \end{cases} \quad (6)$$

where θ_t describes the probability of a slot value staying the same and $|values|$ denotes the number of values for the slot. In other words, the probability θ_t sets a tradeoff between the system's ability to remember everything that was said in the past and accepting new information from the user. If θ_t is too high, the system will put a strong emphasis on the previous states and will largely ignore what the user is saying. When testing different values of θ_t on heldout data, we observed that if they are selected reasonably, the overall performance of the system does not change much. Therefore, the θ_t value was fixed at 0.8 for all slots and all datasets.

The observation model $p(o_t|s_t)$ describes the dependency between the observed values and the slot values. Similarly to the transition model, parameters of the observation probability distribution were tied and set manually:

$$p(o_t|s_t) = \begin{cases} \theta_o & \text{if } o_t = s_t \\ \frac{1-\theta_o}{|values|-1} & \text{otherwise.} \end{cases} \quad (7)$$

where θ_o defines the probability of the agreement between the observation and the slot value. The probability of agreement describes how the model is robust to noise and systematic errors in SLU. When θ_o is set high, the model assumes that the SLU component makes perfect predictions, and therefore the SLU output must agree with the slot values. Based on manual tuning on held-out data, θ_o was set to 0.8.

Inference in the presented model is performed with Loopy Belief Propagation (LBP) (Pearl, 1988). LBP is an approximate message passing inference algorithm for Bayesian networks (BN). LBP can be computationally intensive if there are nodes with many parents in the network. Therefore, as previously described, our model uses a simple dependency structure where slots depend only on the same slot from the previous turn, and slot-level observations depend on the corresponding slot from the same turn. To make the inference even more efficient, one can take advantage of the tied observation and transition probabilities. We group all unobserved values in the nodes of BN together and maintain only a probability for the group as a whole, as suggested by Thomson and Young (2010).

3 Evaluation

The discriminative (DT) and generative dialogue (GT) trackers described in Sections 2.1 and 2.2 were evaluated on the DSTC data.

The input of DT and GT were the SLU n-best lists either with original probabilities or the scores mapped into the probability space. The trackers were evaluated on both live and batch data. The metrics were computed with Schedule 1 (see Williams et al. (2013)). In addition, we include into the evaluation the DSTC baseline tracker. The results on the live and batch data are shown in Table 1 in the Appendix. Please note that the results for GT differ from the results submitted for DSTC. Only after the submission deadline, did we find that some of the parameters in the transition model were set incorrectly. After the setting was fixed, the results improved.

The results show that the DT consistently outperforms the baseline tracker and the DT achieves comparable or better results than the GT. The DT clearly provides better estimates of the dialogue states because of the incorporation of the context and the processing of multiple hypotheses. To assess the statistical significance of the accuracy metric, 95% confidence scores for all measurements were computed. Overall, the confidence intervals were between 0.1% and 0.4% on the individual tests. On this basis, all differences larger than 1.0% can be considered statistically significant.

The GT outperforms the baseline tracker on all but the batch data. Manual inspection of the results revealed that the generative model is very sensitive to the probabilities assigned to the observations. For the batch data, presumably due to the score normalisation, the probabilities of hypotheses in the n-best lists were very similar to each other. As a result, the generative model had difficulties discriminating between the observed values.

In comparison with all trackers submitted for DSTC, the DT achieves second-best accuracy among the submitted trackers and the GT is among the average trackers. For more details see Table 2 in the Appendix, where the average scores were computed from the accuracy and the Brier score on test sets 1, 2, 3, and 4.

Regarding the Brier score, the results show that the DT outperforms the baseline tracker and estimates the belief state as well as the best tracker in the DSTC. This can prove especially important when the tracker is used within a complete dialogue system where the policy decisions do not depend on the best dialogue state but on the belief state.

4 Discussion

The presented discriminative and generative models differ in two main areas: (1) how they incorporate observations into the belief state and (2) computational efficiency.

(1) Both the DT and GT models can accumulate information from multiple hypotheses and from multiple turns. The GT, however, tends to "forget" the dialogue history because the generative model indiscriminately distributes some of the probability mass from a slot value that was not recently mentioned to all other slot values each turn. This behaviour (see Table 3 for an example) is not easy to control because "forgetting" is a consequence of the model being able to represent the dynamics of a user changing his/her goal. The DT does not have this problem because the change in the goal is directly conditioned on the observations. If the user is silent, then the DT "copies" the past belief state and no probability in the belief state is distributed as described in (5).

(2) The DT tracker is significantly faster compared with the GT tracker while offering comparable or better performance. The slot level belief update in the discriminative model has a complexity of $O(n)$ whereas in the generative model it has a complexity of $O(n^2)$, where n is the number of values in the slot. When tested on a regular personal computer, the DT processed all four DSTC test sets, 4254 dialogues in total, in 2.5 minutes whereas the GT tracker needed 51 minutes. Therefore, the DT tracker is about 20 times more computationally efficient on the DSTC data. Although GT achieved performance allowing real-time use (it needed 0.1 seconds per turn) in the Let's Go domain, for more complex applications the GT could simply be too slow. In this case, the proposed discriminative tracker offers a very interesting alternative.

5 Conclusion

This paper described two dialogue state tracking models submitted for the DSTC challenge: (1) the discriminative tracker and (2) the generative tracker. The discriminative tracker is based on a conceptually very simple dialogue model with deterministic transition probability. Interestingly, this discriminative model gives performance comparable to the more complex generative tracker; yet it is significantly more computationally efficient. An extended description of this work can be found in the technical report (Žilka et al., 2013).

Acknowledgements

This research was partly funded by the Ministry of Education, Youth and Sports of the Czech Republic under the grant agreement LK11221 and core research funding of Charles University in Prague. The authors would like to thank Ondřej Dušek and Ondřej Plátek for useful comments.

A Comparison of the BT, DT, and GT trackers

live data	metric	BT	DT	GT
test1	accuracy	0.77	**0.88**	**0.88**
	Brier score	0.29	**0.21**	**0.21**
test2	accuracy	0.79	**0.89**	0.85
	Brier score	0.27	**0.20**	0.23
test3	accuracy	0.92	**0.94**	0.93
	Brier score	0.14	**0.11**	0.16
test4	accuracy	0.82	0.86	**0.87**
	Brier score	0.24	0.21	**0.20**
ALL	accuracy	0.83	**0.89**	0.88
	Brier score	0.24	**0.18**	0.20
batch data	metric	BT	DT	GT
test1	accuracy	0.75	**0.88**	0.74
	Brier score	0.35	**0.27**	0.39
test2	accuracy	0.79	**0.88**	0.77
	Brier score	0.30	**0.26**	0.33
ALL	accuracy	0.77	**0.88**	0.76
	Brier score	0.32	**0.27**	0.36

Table 1: Accuracy of the trackers on the live and batch test sets, where BT stands for the DSTC baseline tracker, DT denotes the discriminative tracker, and GT denotes the generative tracker. ALL denotes the average scores over the live and batch test sets.

B Comparison with the DSTC trackers

team/system	accuracy	Brier score
BT - C	0.81	0.27
BT	0.83	0.24
DT	0.89	**0.18**
GT	0.88	0.20
team1	0.88	0.23
team2	0.88	0.21
team4	0.81	0.28
team5	0.88	0.21
team6	**0.91**	**0.18**
team7	0.85	0.23
team8	0.83	0.24
team9	0.89	0.20

Table 2: Accuracy of the trackers submitted for the DSTC, where BT - C denotes the DSTC baseline tracker without removing the systematically erroneous SLU hypotheses, BT denotes the DSTC baseline tracker, DT denotes the discriminative tracker, GT denotes the generative tracker, and team* denote the best trackers submitted by other teams. The scores are averaged scores obtained on the four DSTC test sets.

C The problem of "forgetting" of the observed values in the GT tracker

#	P	SLU hyp.	slot value	GS	DS
1	1.0	centre	centre	0.8	1.0
	0.0	null	null	0.2	0.0
2	1.0	null	centre	0.68	1.0
			null	0.32	0.0
3	1.0	null	centre	0.608	1.0
			null	0.392	0.0

Table 3: Example of three turns in which the generative system "forgets" the observed value. # denotes the turn number, P denotes the probability of the observation, SLU hyp. denotes the observed hypothesis, GS denotes the belief of the generative system, and DS denotes the belief of the discriminative system.

References

Neville Mehta, Rakesh Gupta, Antoine Raux, Deepak Ramachandran, and Stefan Krawczyk. 2010. Probabilistic ontology trees for belief tracking in dialog systems. In *Proceedings of SigDial*, pages 37–46. Association for Computational Linguistics.

Judea Pearl. 1988. *Probabilistic reasoning in intelligent systems: networks of plausible inference*. Morgan Kaufmann Publishers Inc., San Francisco, CA, USA.

Blaise Thomson and Steve Young. 2010. Bayesian update of dialogue state: A POMDP framework for spoken dialogue systems. *Computer Speech and Language*, 24(4):562–588.

Jason D. Williams, Antoine Raux, Deepak Ramachandran, and Alan W. Black. 2013. The Dialog State Tracking Challenge. In *Proceedings of SigDial*, Metz, France.

Jason D. Williams. 2007. Using particle filters to track dialogue state. In *IEEE Workshop on Automatic Speech Recognition & Understanding, 2007. ASRU*, pages 502–507. IEEE.

Jason D. Williams. 2008. Exploiting the ASR N-best by tracking multiple dialog state hypotheses. *Proc ICSLP, Brisbane*.

Steve Young, Milica Gašić, Simon Keizer, Francois Mairesse, Jost Schatzmann, Blaise Thomson, and Kai Yu. 2010. The Hidden Information State Model: a practical framework for POMDP-based spoken dialogue management. *Computer Speech and Language*, 24(2):150–174.

Lukáš Žilka, David Marek, Matěj Korvas, and Filip Jurčíček. 2013. Bayesian Discriminative and Generative Models used in the 2012 Dialogue State Tracking Challenge. Technical report, Faculty of Mathematics and Physics, Charles University in Prague, July.

Dialog State Tracking using Conditional Random Fields

Hang Ren, Weiqun Xu, Yan Zhang,Yonghong Yan
The Key Laboratory of Speech Acoustics and Content Understanding
Institute of Acoustics, Chinese Academy of Sciences
21 North 4th Ring West Road, Beijing, China, 100190
{renhang, xuweiqun, zhangyan, yanyonghong}@hccl.ioa.ac.cn

Abstract

This paper presents our approach to dialog state tracking for the Dialog State Tracking Challenge task. In our approach we use discriminative general structured conditional random fields, instead of traditional generative directed graphic models, to incorporate arbitrary overlapping features. Our approach outperforms the simple 1-best tracking approach.

1 Introduction

Spoken dialog systems have been widely developed in recent years. However, when dialogs are conducted in noisy environments or the utterance itself is noisy, it is difficult for machines to correctly recognize or understand user utterances. In this paper we present a novel dialog state tracking method, which directly models the joint probability of hypotheses on N-best lists. Experiments are then conducted on the DSTC shared corpus, which provides a common dataset and an evaluation framework

The remainder of this paper is organized as follows. Section 2 reviews relevant studies in dialog state tracking. Section 3 introduces our new approach and presents the model and features we used in detail. Section 4 describes experiment settings and gives the result. Section 5 concludes this paper with a discussion for possible future directions.

2 Previous Work

For the task of dialog state tracking, previous research focused on dynamic Bayesian models (DBN)(Young et al., 2013). User goal, dialog history and other variables are modeled in a graphical model. Usually, Markov assumptions are made and in each turn the dialog state is dependent on the ASR outputs and the dialog state of the previous turn. Dependency on other features, such as system action, dialog history could be assumed as long as their likelihood is modeled. For a POMDP-based dialog model, the state update rule is as follows:

$$b_{t+1}(s_{t+1}) = \eta P(o_{t+1}|s_{t+1}, a_t) \sum_{s_t} P(s_{t+1}|s_t, a_t) b_t(s_t) \quad (1)$$

where $b_t(s_t)$ is the belief state at time t, o_{t+1} is the observation at time $t+1$, a_t is the machine action. Thus the dialog states are estimated incrementally turn by turn.

Since each node has hundreds, or even thousands, of possible assignments, approximation is necessary to make efficient computation possible. In POMDP-based dialog systems, two common approaches are adopted (Young et al., 2013), i.e., N-best approximation and domain factorization.

In the N-best approach, the probability distribution of user goals are approximated using N-best list. The hidden information state (HIS) model (Young et al., 2010) makes a further simplification that similar user goals are grouped into a single entity called *partition*, inside which all user goals are assigned the same probabilities. The Bayesian update of dialog state (BUDS) model (Thomson and Young, 2010) is a representative of the second approach and adopts a different approximation strategy, where each node is further divided into sub-nodes for different domain concepts and independence assumptions of sub-nodes across concepts are made. Recent studies have suggested that a discriminative model may yield better performance than a generative one (Bohus and Rudnicky, 2006). In a discriminative model, the *emission* part of the state update rule is modeled discriminatively. Possible flawed assumptions in a completely generative models could be mitigated in this way, such as the approximation of observation probability using SLU scores (Williams, 2012a; Williams, 2012b).

3 Proposed Method

3.1 Discriminative State Tracking Model

Most previous methods model the distribution of user goals for each turn explicitly, which can lead to high computation cost. In our work, the joint probability of all items on the N-best lists from SLU is modeled directly and the state tracking result is generated at a post-processing stage. Thus the state tracking problem is converted into a labeling task as is shown in equation 2, which involves modeling the joint probability of the N-best hypotheses.

$$b_t(s_t) = P(H_{1,1}, H_{1,2}, ..., H_{t,m-1}, H_{t,m}) \quad (2)$$

where $H_{t,m}$ is a binary variable indicating the truthfulness of the m-th hypothesis at turn t.

For each turn, the model takes into account all the slots on the N-best lists from the first turn up to the current one, and those slots predicted to be true are added to the dialog state. The graphical model is illustrated in figure 1. To predict dialog state at turn t, the N-best items from turn 1 to t are all considered. Hypotheses assigned true labels are included in the dialog state. Compared to the DBN approach, the dialog states are built 'jointly'. This approach is reasonable because what the tracker generates is just some combinations of all N-best lists in a session, and there is no point guessing beyond SLU outputs. We leverage general structured Conditional Random Fields (CRFs) to model the probabilities of the N-best items, where *factors* are used to strengthen local dependency. Since CRF is a discriminative model, arbitrary overlapping features can be added, which is commonly considered as an advantage over generative models.

3.2 Conditional Random Fields

CRF is first introduced to address the problem of *label bias* in sequence prediction (Lafferty et al., 2001). Linear-chain CRFs are widely used to solve common sequence labeling problem in natural language processing. General structured CRF has also been reported to be successful in various tasks (Sutton and McCallum, 2012).

In general structured CRF, *factor templates* are utilized to specify both model structure and *parameter tying* (Sutton and McCallum, 2012). Factors are partitioned into a series of templates, and factors inside each template share the same parameters.

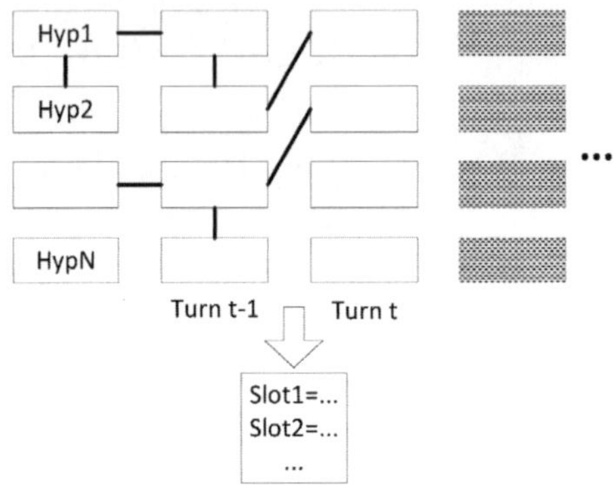

Figure 1: Dialog state update using CRFs, where the 8 rectangles above denote N-best hypotheses for each turn, and the box below represents the dialog state up to the current turn. Connections between rectangles denote 'Label-Label' factors. 'Label-Observation' factors are not shown for simplicity.

$$p(\mathbf{y}|\mathbf{x}) = \frac{1}{Z(\mathbf{x})} \prod_{C_p \in \mathcal{C}} \prod_{\Psi_c \in C_p} \Psi_c(\mathbf{x_c}, \mathbf{y_c}; \theta_p), \quad (3)$$

where $\mathcal{C}$ is the set of factor templates and $\mathbf{x}, \mathbf{y}$ are inputs and labels respectively. Template factors are written as

$$\Psi_c(\mathbf{x_c}, \mathbf{y_c}; \theta_p) = \exp \sum_{k=1}^{K(p)} \theta_{pk} f_{pk}(\mathbf{x_c}, \mathbf{y_c}) \quad (4)$$

and $Z(\mathbf{x})$ is the normalizing function

$$Z(\mathbf{x}) = \sum_{\mathbf{y}} \prod_{C_p \in \mathcal{C}} \prod_{\Psi_c \in C_p} \Psi_c(\mathbf{x_c}, \mathbf{y_c}; \theta_p) \quad (5)$$

In the experiment we use Factorie[1] to define and train the model.

3.3 Model Structure and Features

In the model, slots in every N-best item up to the current turn are represented as binary variables. For simplification of data structure, each slot in a single N-best item is extracted and represented using different label variables, with the same *rank* indicating their

[1]Available from `https://github.com/factorie/factorie`.

original places in the N-best list. For example, the item `slots: [from: Pittsburgh, data: Tuesday], score: 0.85, rank: 2`, is converted to two slots: `slots: [from: Pittsburgh], score: 0.85, rank: 2` and `slots: [date: Tuesday], score: 0.85, rank: 2`. *Label-label* connections are specified using factor templates between slot pairs, and *Label-observation* templates are used to add slot-wise features. Without label-label connection the model is reduced to a maximum entropy model, and with more connections added, the graph tends to have loopy structures.

Two classes of feature sets (templates) in the experiment are defined as follows.

(1) Label-Label factor templates are used to strengthen the bond between certain slots.

Pairwise-slots of the same rank This template is built for pairs of slots in a turn with the same rank to *bind* their boolean assignment. To avoid creating too many loops and make inference efficient, the factors are added in such an order that the slots involved in a single turn are linked in a linear way.

Pairwise-slots with identical value Slots with identical value may appear in the N-best list for multiple times. Besides, user can mention the same slot in different turns, making these slots more reliable. Similar ordering mechanism is utilized to avoid redundant loops.

(2) Label-observation templates are used to add features for the identification of the truthfulness of slots.

SLU score and rank of slot The score generated by the ASR and SLU components is a direct indicator of the correctness degree of slots. However, a slot's true *reliability* is not necessarily linear with its score. The relationship is quite different for various ASR and SLU algorithms, and scores produced by some ASR are not valid probabilities. As we adopt a data-driven approach, we are able to learn this relationship from data. In addition to the SLU score, the slot rank is also added to the feature set.

Dialog history (grounding information) In most spoken dialog systems, explicit and implicit groundings are adapted to indicate the correctness of the system belief. This information is useful to determine the correctness of slots. The grounding information includes grounding type (implicit or explicit grounding), user reply (negation or confirmation) and corresponding SLU scores.

Count of slots with identical value As previously mentioned, slots with identical values can appear several times and slots with more frequent occurrences are more likely to be correct.

Domain-specific features Slots for some domain concepts often have values with specific forms. For example, in the DSTC data sets, the route slots are usually filled with values like '61d', '35b', and SLU often generates noisy outputs like '6d', '3d'. Thus the lexical form is a very useful feature.

Baseline Tracker The simple and fast 1-best tracking algorithm is used as the baseline tracker and exhibits a satisfying performance. Thus the tracking result is added as an additional feature. This indicates the possibility of combining tracking outputs from different algorithms in this discriminative model, which may improve the overall tracking performance.

4 Experiment

4.1 Task and Data

The Dialog State Tracking Challenge (DSTC)[2] aims at evaluating dialog state tracking algorithms on shared real-user dialog corpus. In each dialog session, ASR and SLU results are annotated, making it possible to conduct direct comparison among various algorithms. For further details, please refer to the DSTC handbook (Williams et al., 2013b).

4.2 Corpus Preprocessing

The ASR and SLU components can generate many noisy hypotheses which are completely wrong, rendering the dialog corpus seriously imbalanced at the level of slots (there are more wrong slots than true slots). We use resampling to prevent

[2]http://research.microsoft.com/en-us/events/dstc/

the model from biasing towards making negative judgements. Before training, the total number of correct slots in a set is counted, and equal number of wrong slots are sampled from the subset of all the wrong slots. These chosen negative slots plus all the positive slots together constitute the effective slot set for model training, with remaining slots fixed to their true value and regarded as observed variables. To make full use of the dialog corpus, this process is repeated for eight times, producing a bigger and balanced corpus.

4.3 Model Training

In the training phase, the log-likelihood function is optimized using the LBFGS method with L2-regularization. Loopy belief propagation is used as the inference routine. It can be shown that for factor graphs without loops, the marginal probabilities produced by loopy belief propagation are exact. Model selection is done according to the log-likelihood on the development set.

4.4 Predicting and Tracking

For each dialog session, the predicted slot labels are mapped to tracking results. To produce a N-best list of tracking results, the top N configurations of slots and corresponding probability scores are generated. Gibbs sampling is adopted. The sampling is repeated for 1000 times in each corpus, after each sampling the configuration of slots is mapped to certain tracking state. More efficient inference routines, such as M-best belief propagation (Yanover and Weiss, 2004), could be utilized, which would be suitable for practical real-time application.

4.5 Results

After tracker outputs are generated based on the sampling results, they are scored using evaluation tools provided by the DSTC organizers. Several metrics are evaluated, including precisions, ROC performance, etc. Individual and joint slots are scored respectively. And different schedules are used, which indicats the turns included for evaluation. Partial results are shown in table 1. A systematic analysis by the organizers is in the DSTC overview paper (Williams et al., 2013a). The complete challenge results can be found on DSTC website. On the test sets of test1, test2 and test3, the CRF-based model achieves better performance than the simple baseline in most metrics. However, on test4, the performance degrades seriously when there is a mismatch between training data and test data, since test4 is produced by a different group and does not match the training set. It shows that the CRF-based model is very flexible and is able to learn the properties of ASR and SLU, thus adapting to a specific system. But it has a tendency of overfitting .

	Test1		**Test4**	
Metric	CRF	BASE	CRF	BASE
ACC	**0.987**	0.983	0.960	**0.986**
L2	**0.020**	0.021	0.046	**0.017**
MRR	**0.990**	0.988	0.980	**0.990**
CA05	**0.987**	0.983	0.960	**0.986**
EER	**0.015**	0.983	0.021	**0.012**

Table 1: Results of slot 'Date' on Test1 and Test4 (schedule1 is used). The tracker used on Test4 is trained on Test3. Details of the metrics can be found in DSTC handbook(Williams et al., 2013b)

5 Conclusions and Future Directions

We proposed a CRF-based discriminative approach for dialog state tracking. Preliminary results show that it achieves better performance than the 1-best baseline tracker in most metrics when the training set and testing set match. This indicates the feasibility of our approach which directly models joint probabilities of the N-best items.

In the future, we will focus on the following possible directions to improve the performance. Firstly, we will enrich the feature set and add more domain-related features. Secondly, interactions of slots between dialog turns are not well modeled currently. This problem can be alleviated by tuning graph structures, which deservers further studies. Moreover, it is challenging to use online training methods, so that the performance could be improved incrementally when more training samples are available.

6 Acknowledgments

This work is partially supported by the National Natural Science Foundation of China (Nos. 10925419, 90920302, 61072124, 11074275, 11161140319, 91120001), the Strategic Priority Research Program of the Chinese Academy of Sciences (Grant Nos. XDA06030100, XDA06030500), the National 863 Program (No. 2012AA012503) and the CAS Priority Deployment Project (No. KGZD-EW-103-2).

References

Dan Bohus and Alex Rudnicky. 2006. A "k hypotheses + other" belief updating model. In *Proceedings of the 2006 AAAI Workshop on Statistical and Empirical Approaches for Spoken Dialogue Systems*, pages 13–18, Menlo Park, California. The AAAI Press.

John Lafferty, Andrew Mccallum, and Fernando Pereira. 2001. Conditional random fields: Probabilistic models for segmenting and labeling sequence data. In *Proc. 18th International Conf. on Machine Learning*, pages 282–289. Morgan Kaufmann, San Francisco, CA.

Charles A. Sutton and Andrew McCallum. 2012. An introduction to conditional random fields. *Foundations and Trends in Machine Learning*, 4(4):267–373.

Blaise Thomson and Steve Young. 2010. Bayesian update of dialogue state: A POMDP framework for spoken dialogue systems. *Computer Speech and Language*, 24(4):562–588.

Jason D. Williams, Antoine Raux, Deepak Ramachandran, and Alan Black. 2013a. The dialog state tracking challenge. In *Proceedings of the 14th SIGdial workshop on Discourse and Dialogue*.

Jason D. Williams, Antoine Raux, Deepak Ramachandran, and Alan Black. 2013b. Dialog state tracking challenge handbook. Available from `http://research.microsoft.com/apps/pubs/?id=169024`.

Jason D. Williams. 2012a. Challenges and opportunities for state tracking in statistical spoken dialog systems: Results from two public deployments. *Selected Topics in Signal Processing, IEEE Journal of*, 6(8):959 –970.

Jason D. Williams. 2012b. A critical analysis of two statistical spoken dialog systems in public use. In *SLT*, pages 55–60. IEEE.

Chen Yanover and Yair Weiss. 2004. Finding the m most probable configurations using loopy belief propagation. *Advances in Neural Information Processing Systems*, 16:289–296.

Steve Young, Milica Gašić, Simon Keizer, François Mairesse, Jost Schatzmann, Blaise Thomson, and Kai Yu. 2010. The hidden information state model: A practical framework for POMDP-based spoken dialogue management. *Computer Speech and Language*, 24(2):150–174.

Steve Young, Milica Gašić, Blaise Thomson, and Jason D. Williams. 2013. POMDP-based statistical spoken dialog systems: A review. *Proceedings of the IEEE*, 101(5):1160–1179.

Engineering Statistical Dialog State Trackers: A Case Study on DSTC

Daejoong Kim, Jaedeug Choi, Kee-Eung Kim
Department of Computer Science, KAIST
South Korea
{djkim, jdchoi, kekim}@ai.kaist.ac.kr

Jungsu Lee, Jinho Sohn
LG Electronics
South Korea
{jungsu.lee, jinho.sohn}@lge.com

Abstract

We describe our experience with engineering the dialog state tracker for the first Dialog State Tracking Challenge (DSTC). Dialog trackers are one of the essential components of dialog systems which are used to infer the true user goal from the speech processing results. We explain the main parts of our tracker: the observation model, the belief refinement model, and the belief transformation model. We also report experimental results on a number of approaches to the models, and compare the overall performance of our tracker to other submitted trackers. An extended version of this paper is available as a technical report (Kim et al., 2013).

1 Introduction

In spoken dialog systems (SDSs), one of the main challenges is to identify the user goal from her utterances. The significance of accurately identifying the user goal, referred to as *dialog state tracking*, has emerged from the need for SDSs to be robust to inevitable errors in the spoken language understanding (SLU).

A number of studies have been conducted to track the dialog state through multiple dialog turns using a probabilistic framework, treating SLU results as noisy observations and maintaining probability distribution (*i.e.*, belief) on user goals (Bohus and Rudnicky, 2006; Mehta et al., 2010; Roy et al., 2000; Williams and Young, 2007; Thomson and Young, 2010; Kim et al., 2011).

In this paper, we share our experience and lessons learned from developing the dialog state tracker that participated in the first Dialog State Tracking Challenge (DSTC) (Williams et al., 2013). Our tracker is based on the belief update in the POMDP framework (Kaelbling et al., 1998), particularly the hidden information state (HIS) model (Young et al., 2010) and the partition recombination method (Williams, 2010).

2 Dialog State Tracking

Our tracker mainly follows the belief update in HIS-POMDP (Young et al., 2010). The SDS executes system action a, and the user with goal g responds to the system with utterance u. The SLU processes the utterance and generates the result as an N-best list $\boldsymbol{o} = [\langle \tilde{u}_1, f_1 \rangle, \ldots, \langle \tilde{u}_N, f_N \rangle]$ of the hypothesized user utterance $\tilde{u}_i$ and its associated confidence score f_i. Because the SLU is not perfect, the system maintains a probability distribution over user goals, called a *belief*. In addition, the system groups user goals into equivalence classes and assigns a single probability for each equivalence class since the number of user goals is often too large to perform individual belief updates for all possible user goals. The equivalence classes are called partitions and denoted as ψ. Hence, given the current belief b, system action a, and recognized N-best list $\boldsymbol{o}$, the dialog state tracker updates the belief b' over partitions as follows:

$$b'(\psi') \propto \sum_{u} \Pr(\boldsymbol{o}|u) \Pr(u|\psi', a) \Pr(\psi'|\psi) b(\psi) \quad (1)$$

where $\Pr(\boldsymbol{o}|u)$ is the observation model, $\Pr(u|\psi, a)$ is the user utterance model, $\Pr(\psi'|\psi)$ is the belief refinement model.

2.1 Observation Model

The observation model $\Pr(\boldsymbol{o}|u)$ is the probability that the SLU produces the N-best list $\boldsymbol{o}$ when the user utterance is u. We experimented with the following three models for the observation model.

Confidence score model: as in HIS-POMDP, this model assumes that the confidence score f_i obtained from the SLU is exactly the probability of generating the hypothesized user utterance $\tilde{u}_i$. Hence, $f_i = \Pr(\tilde{u}_i, f_i|u)$.

Histogram model: this model estimates a function that maps the confidence score to the probability of correctness. We constructed a histogram of confidence scores from the training datasets to obtain the empirical probability $\Pr(cor(f_i))$ of whether the entry associated with confidence score f_i is a correct hypothesis or not.

Generative model: this model is a simplified version of a generative model in (Williams, 2008) that only uses confidence score: $\Pr(\tilde{u}_i, f_i|u) = \Pr(cor(i))\Pr(f_i|cor(i))$ where $\Pr(cor(i))$ is the probability of the i-th entry being a correct hypothesis and $\Pr(f_i|cor(i))$ is the probability of the i-th entry having confidence score f_i when it is a correct hypothesis.

2.2 User Utterance Model

The user utterance model $\Pr(u|\psi, a)$ indicates how the user responds to the system action a when the user goal is in ψ. We adopted the HIS-POMDP user utterance model, consisting of a bigram model and an item model. The details are described in (Kim et al., 2013).

2.3 Belief Refinement Model

Given the SLU result $\tilde{u}_i$ and the system action a, the partition ψ is split into ψ'_i with probability $\Pr(\psi'_i|\psi)$ and $\psi - \psi'_i$ with probability $\Pr(\psi - \psi'_i|\psi)$. The belief refinement model $\Pr(\psi'_i|\psi)$ can be seen as the proportion of the belief that is carried from ψ to ψ'_i. This probability can be defined by the following models:

Empirical model: we count $n(\psi)$ from the training datasets, which is the number of user goals that are consistent with partition ψ. The probability is then modeled as $\Pr(\psi'_i|\psi) = \frac{n(\psi'_i)}{n(\psi)}$ if $n(\psi) > 0$ and $\Pr(\psi'_i|\psi) = 0$ otherwise.

Word-match model: this model extends the empirical model by using the domain knowledge when the SLU result $\tilde{u}_i$ does not appear in the training datasets. We calculated how many words $w \in W$ in the user utterance $\tilde{u}_i$ were included in a bus timetable $\mathcal{D}$. The model is thus defined as $\Pr(\psi'_i|\psi) = \frac{n(\psi'_i)}{n(\psi)}$ if $n(\psi'_i) > 0$ and $\Pr(\psi'_i|\psi) = \frac{\alpha}{|W|}\sum_{w \in W}\delta(w \in \mathcal{D})$ otherwise. δ is the indicator function ($\delta(x) = 1$ if x holds and $\delta(x) = 0$ otherwise) and α is the parameter estimated via cross-validation.

Mixture model: this model mixes the empirical model with a uniform probability, defined as $\Pr(\psi'_i|\psi) = \epsilon\frac{1}{n_G} + (1-\epsilon)\frac{n(\psi'_i)}{n(\psi)}$ if $n(\psi'_i) > 0$ and $\Pr(\psi'_i|\psi) = \frac{1}{n_G}$ otherwise. n_G is the number of all possible user goals which is treated as the parameter of the model and found via cross-validation, together with the mixing parameter $\epsilon \in [0, 1]$.

2.4 Belief Transformation Model

The belief update described above produces the M-best hypotheses of user goals $[\langle\tilde{g}_1, b(\tilde{g}_1)\rangle, \ldots, \langle\tilde{g}_M, b(\tilde{g}_M)\rangle]$ in each dialog turn, which consists of M most likely user goal hypotheses $\tilde{g}_i$ and their associated beliefs $b(\tilde{g}_i)$. The last hypothesis $\tilde{g}_M$ is reserved as the null hypothesis $\varnothing$ with the belief $b(\varnothing) = 1 - \sum_{i=1}^{M-1} b(\tilde{g}_i)$, which represents that the user goal is not known up to the current dialog turn.

One of the problems with the belief update is that the null hypothesis often remains as the most probable hypothesis even when the SLU result contains the correct user utterance with a high confidence score. This is because an atomic hypothesis has a very small prior probability.

To overcome this problem, we added a post-processing step which transforms each belief $b(h_i)$ to the final confidence score s_i.

Threshold model: this model ensures that the top hypothesis has confidence score θ when a belief of the hypothesis is greater than a threshold δ. The final output list is $[\langle h^*, s^*\rangle, \langle\varnothing, 1-s^*\rangle]$ where $h^* = \text{argmax}_{h\in\{\tilde{g}_1,\ldots,\tilde{g}_{M-1}\}} b(h)$ and

$$s^* = \begin{cases} \theta, & \text{if } b(h^*) > \delta \\ b(h^*), & \text{otherwise.} \end{cases} \quad (2)$$

Full-list regression model: this model estimates the probability that each hypothesis is correct via casting the task as regression. The model uses two logistic regression functions $F_\varnothing$ and F_h. $F_\varnothing$ predicts the probability of correctness for the null hypothesis $\varnothing$ using the single input feature $\phi_\varnothing = b(\varnothing)$. Likewise, F_h predicts the probability of correctness for non-null hypotheses h_i using the input feature $\phi_i = b(h_i)$. The model generates the final output list $[\langle h_1, s_1\rangle, \ldots, \langle h_{M-1}, s_{M-1}\rangle, \langle\varnothing, s_M\rangle]$ where $h_i = \tilde{g}_i$ and

$$s_i = \begin{cases} \frac{F_\varnothing(\phi_i)}{\sum_{j=1}^{M-1} F_h(\phi_j) + F_\varnothing(\phi_\varnothing)}, & \text{if } i = M \\ \frac{F_h(\phi_i)}{\sum_{j=1}^{M-1} F_h(\phi_j) + F_\varnothing(\phi_\varnothing)}, & \text{otherwise.} \end{cases} \quad (3)$$

Rank regression model: this model works in a similar way as in the full-link regression model, except that it uses a single logistic regression function F_r for both the non-null and null hypotheses, and takes the rank value of the hypotheses as an additional input feature. The final output list is $[\langle h_1, s_1\rangle, \ldots, \langle h_{M-1}, s_{M-1}\rangle, \langle \varnothing, s_M\rangle]$ where $h_i = \tilde{g}_i$ and

$$s_i = \frac{F_r(\phi_i)}{\sum_{j=1}^{M} F_r(\phi_j)}. \quad (4)$$

3 Experimental Setup

In the experiments, we used three labeled training datasets (train1a, train2, train3) and three test datasets (test1, test2, test3) used in DSTC. There was an additional test dataset (test4), which we decided not to include in the experiments since we found that a significant number of labels were missing or incorrect.

. We measured the tracker performance according to the following evaluation metrics used in DSTC[1]: **accuracy (acc)** measures the rate of the most likely hypothesis h_1 being correct, **average score (avgp)** measures the average of scores assigned to the correct hypotheses, **l2 norm** measures the Euclidean distance between the vector of scores from the tracker and the binary vector with 1 in the position of the correct hypotheses, and 0 elsewhere, **mean reciprocal rank (mrr)** measures the average of $1/R$, where R is the minimum rank of the correct hypothesis, **ROC equal error rate (eer)** is the sum of false accept (FA) and false reject (FR) rates when FA rate=FR rate, and **ROC.**$\{$**v1,v2**$\}$**.**P measures correct accept (CA) rate when there are at most $P\%$ false accept (FA) rate[2].

4 Results and Analyses

Since there are multiple slots to track in the dialog domain, we report the average performance over the "marginal" slots including the "joint" slot that assigns the values to all slots.

4.1 Observation Model

Tbl. 1 shows the cross-validation results of the three observation models. In train1a and train2, no model had a clear advantage to others, whereas in train3, the confidence score model outperformed others. Further analyses revealed that the confidence scores from the SLU results were not sufficiently indicative of the SLU accuracy in train1a and train2. The histogram and the generative models are expected to perform at least as well as the confidence score model in train3, but they didn't in the experiments. We suspect that this is due to the naive binning strategy we used to model the probability distribution.

Table 1: Evaluation of observation models.

	Train1a			Train2			Train3		
	Conf	Hist	Gen	Conf	Hist	Gen	Conf	Hist	Gen
accuracy	0.81	0.82	**0.82**	0.84	**0.86**	0.85	**0.90**	0.89	0.88
avgp	0.77	0.78	**0.78**	0.81	**0.82**	0.82	**0.81**	0.79	0.77
l2	0.31	0.30	**0.30**	0.26	**0.25**	0.25	**0.25**	0.27	0.30
mrr	0.87	0.87	**0.88**	0.89	**0.89**	0.89	**0.94**	0.93	0.92
roc.v1.05	0.69	**0.70**	0.70	0.73	0.74	**0.74**	**0.82**	0.80	0.79
roc.v1.10	0.74	0.75	**0.75**	0.78	0.80	**0.80**	**0.87**	0.85	0.83
roc.v1.20	0.78	0.79	**0.79**	0.83	0.84	**0.84**	**0.89**	0.87	0.85
roc.v1.eer	0.14	**0.14**	0.14	**0.12**	0.13	0.13	**0.10**	0.11	0.12
roc.v2.05	**0.34**	0.34	0.34	**0.24**	0.15	0.23	0.52	**0.54**	0.52
roc.v2.10	**0.54**	0.46	0.46	**0.33**	0.26	0.25	**0.71**	0.67	0.70
roc.v2.20	**0.70**	0.70	0.69	**0.43**	0.41	0.41	**0.83**	0.78	0.80

Table 2: Evaluation of belief refinement models.

	Train1a			Train2			Train3		
	Emp	Word	Mix	Emp	Word	Mix	Emp	Word	Mix
accuracy	0.75	0.77	**0.81**	0.80	0.84	**0.84**	0.71	0.88	**0.90**
avgp	0.75	0.76	**0.77**	0.78	0.80	**0.81**	0.68	0.80	**0.81**
l2	0.34	0.34	**0.31**	0.31	0.27	**0.26**	0.42	0.26	**0.25**
mrr	0.83	0.85	**0.87**	0.86	0.89	**0.89**	0.82	0.93	**0.94**
roc.v1.05	0.66	0.68	**0.69**	0.64	0.68	**0.73**	0.58	0.78	**0.82**
roc.v1.10	0.69	0.71	**0.74**	0.73	0.78	**0.78**	0.65	0.83	**0.87**
roc.v1.20	0.73	0.74	**0.78**	0.77	0.82	**0.83**	0.68	0.86	**0.89**
roc.v1.eer	0.22	**0.13**	0.14	0.13	0.13	**0.12**	0.13	0.11	**0.10**
roc.v2.05	0.34	0.24	**0.34**	**0.30**	0.24	0.24	**0.61**	0.51	0.52
roc.v2.10	0.47	0.38	**0.54**	**0.42**	0.26	0.33	0.64	0.67	**0.71**
roc.v2.20	**0.72**	0.60	0.70	**0.56**	0.37	0.43	0.72	0.77	**0.83**

4.2 Belief Refinement Model

As shown in Tbl. 2, the mixture model outperformed others throughout the metrics. It even outperforms the word-match model which tries to leverage the domain knowledge to handle novel user goals. This implies that, unless the domain knowledge is used properly, simply taking the mixture with the uniform distribution yields a sufficient level of performance.

4.3 Belief Transformation Model

Tbl. 3 summarizes the performances of the belief transformation models. All three models outperformed the pure belief update, although not shown

[1]http://research.microsoft.com/apps/pubs/?id=169024

[2]There are two types of ROC measured in DSTC depending on how CA and FA rates are calculated. The detailed discussion is provided in the longer version of the paper (Kim et al., 2013).

Table 3: Evaluation of belief transform models.

	Train1a			Train2			Train3		
	Thre	Full	Rank	Thre	Full	Rank	Thre	Full	Rank
accuracy	0.81	**0.81**	0.81	0.83	0.84	**0.85**	0.89	**0.90**	0.90
avgp	**0.80**	0.77	0.77	**0.82**	0.81	0.81	**0.85**	0.81	0.78
l2	**0.28**	0.31	0.32	**0.25**	0.26	0.26	**0.22**	0.25	0.28
mrr	0.84	**0.87**	0.87	0.86	0.89	**0.89**	0.91	**0.94**	0.92
roc.v1.05	0.66	0.69	**0.69**	0.65	**0.73**	0.72	0.45	**0.82**	0.80
roc.v1.10	0.71	0.74	**0.75**	0.69	0.78	**0.79**	0.68	**0.87**	0.86
roc.v1.20	0.71	0.78	**0.78**	0.74	0.83	**0.83**	0.79	**0.89**	0.89
roc.v1.eer	0.18	0.14	**0.14**	0.21	0.12	**0.12**	0.49	0.10	**0.09**
roc.v2.05	0.22	**0.34**	0.34	0.20	0.24	**0.24**	0.42	**0.52**	0.48
roc.v2.10	0.41	**0.54**	0.52	0.22	**0.33**	0.33	0.42	**0.71**	0.56
roc.v2.20	0.64	0.70	**0.71**	0.30	0.43	**0.49**	0.43	**0.83**	0.75

in the table. The full-list and the rank regression models show a similar level of performance improvement. This is a naturally expected result since they use regression to convert the beliefs to final confidence scores, as an attempt to compensate for the errors incurred by approximations and assumptions made in the observation and belief refinement models.

4.4 DSTC Result

In order to compare our tracker with others participated in DSTC, we chose tracker4[3] as the most effective one among our 5 submitted trackers since it achieved the top scores in the largest number of evaluation metrics. In the same way, we selected tracker2 for team3, tracker3 for team6, tracker3 for team8, and tracker1 for the rest of the teams. The results of each team are presented in Tbl. 4. The baseline tracker is included as a reference, which simply outputs the hypothesis with the largest SLU confidence score in the N-best list.

Compared to other teams, our tracker showed strong performance in acc, avgp, l2 and mrr. A detailed discussion on the results is provided in the longer version of the paper (Kim et al., 2013).

Table 4: Results of the trackers. The bold face denotes top 3 scores in each evaluation metric. T9 is our tracker.

	Base	T1	T2	T3	T4	T5	T6	T7	T8	T9
Test 1										
accuracy	0.71	**0.83**	0.81	0.81	0.74	0.80	**0.87**	0.78	0.51	**0.82**
avgp	0.73	0.77	0.77	**0.81**	0.74	0.79	**0.82**	0.76	0.49	**0.79**
l2	0.38	0.32	0.32	**0.27**	0.37	0.30	**0.25**	0.34	0.72	**0.29**
mrr	0.80	**0.88**	0.86	0.85	0.81	0.85	**0.90**	0.84	0.59	**0.88**
roc.v1.05	0.62	**0.72**	0.67	0.60	0.20	0.71	**0.76**	0.65	0.20	**0.72**
roc.v1.10	0.63	**0.78**	0.75	**0.77**	0.29	0.75	**0.82**	0.70	0.33	0.76
roc.v1.20	0.67	**0.82**	0.79	0.79	0.53	0.78	**0.85**	0.76	0.35	**0.79**
roc.v1.eer	0.24	**0.13**	0.25	0.24	0.74	**0.12**	**0.12**	0.15	0.52	0.14
roc.v2.05	**0.49**	**0.64**	0.01	0.02	0.00	**0.55**	0.16	0.19	0.04	0.26
roc.v2.10	**0.69**	**0.71**	0.14	0.03	0.00	**0.68**	0.39	0.35	0.05	0.47
roc.v2.20	**0.71**	**0.80**	0.48	0.29	0.00	**0.74**	0.59	0.58	0.27	0.62
Test 2										
accuracy	0.55	0.65	**0.71**	0.68	0.63	0.62	**0.79**	0.65	0.34	**0.71**
avgp	0.57	0.55	0.63	**0.68**	0.63	0.62	**0.71**	0.65	0.29	**0.65**
l2	0.60	0.63	0.50	**0.45**	0.52	0.54	**0.39**	0.49	1.00	**0.48**
mrr	0.65	0.72	**0.79**	0.76	0.71	0.72	**0.84**	0.74	0.46	**0.80**
roc.v1.05	0.43	0.49	**0.52**	0.45	0.16	0.48	**0.66**	0.48	0.04	**0.49**
roc.v1.10	0.45	0.54	**0.57**	**0.63**	0.16	0.51	**0.71**	0.54	0.11	0.57
roc.v1.20	0.48	0.59	**0.64**	**0.64**	0.27	0.54	**0.76**	0.60	0.26	0.63
roc.v1.eer	0.19	0.20	0.39	**0.14**	0.63	0.21	**0.16**	**0.19**	0.36	0.22
roc.v2.05	**0.43**	**0.52**	0.24	0.27	0.00	0.40	**0.46**	0.41	0.05	0.38
roc.v2.10	0.47	**0.60**	0.40	0.37	0.00	**0.62**	**0.53**	0.47	0.17	0.41
roc.v2.20	0.50	**0.70**	0.48	0.56	0.00	**0.70**	**0.62**	0.55	0.44	0.47
Test 3										
accuracy	0.79	0.79	**0.84**	0.82	0.82	0.78	**0.84**	0.79	0.79	**0.85**
avgp	0.75	0.72	0.76	**0.79**	**0.78**	0.70	0.75	0.75	**0.76**	0.74
l2	0.35	0.37	0.32	**0.29**	**0.30**	0.40	0.33	0.34	**0.32**	0.34
mrr	0.83	0.85	**0.88**	0.85	0.85	0.83	**0.89**	0.84	0.80	**0.89**
roc.v1.05	0.56	0.65	0.68	**0.72**	**0.70**	0.62	0.69	0.70	0.33	**0.74**
roc.v1.10	0.66	0.70	**0.77**	**0.77**	0.76	0.69	0.76	0.74	0.47	**0.78**
roc.v1.20	0.74	0.76	**0.82**	0.80	0.80	0.74	**0.81**	0.77	0.61	**0.82**
roc.v1.eer	0.19	0.16	0.15	0.27	**0.12**	0.17	0.15	**0.12**	0.34	**0.13**
roc.v2.05	0.56	**0.62**	0.34	0.28	0.21	**0.62**	**0.61**	0.14	0.00	0.56
roc.v2.10	0.59	**0.71**	0.48	0.37	0.52	0.66	**0.66**	0.42	0.00	**0.67**
roc.v2.20	0.66	0.78	0.73	0.52	**0.82**	0.71	0.78	**0.87**	0.00	**0.79**

5 Conclusion

In this paper, we described our experience with engineering a statistical dialog state tracker while participating in DSTC. Our engineering effort was focused on improving three important models in the tracker: the observation, the belief refinement, and the belief transformation models. Using standard statistical techniques, we were able to produce a tracker that performed competitively among the participants.

As for the future work, we plan to refine the user utterance model for improving the performance of the tracker since there are a number of user utterances that are not handled by the current model. We also plan to re-evaluate our tracker with properly handling the joint slot, since the current tracker constructs models independently for each marginal slot and then combines the results by simply multiplying the predicted scores.

Acknowledgement

This work was supported by NRF of Korea (Grant# 2012-007881), and MKE/KEIT of Korea (IT R&D Program Contract# 10041678)

[3]The tracker4 used the confidence score model, the mixture model and the rank regression model.

References

Dan Bohus and Alex Rudnicky. 2006. A "k hypotheses + other" belief updating model. In *Proceedings of the AAAI Workshop on Statistical and Empirical Approaches for Spoken Dialogue Systems.*

Leslie Pack Kaelbling, Michael L. Littman, and Anthony R. Cassandra. 1998. Planning and acting in partially observable stochastic domains. *Artificial Intelligence*, 101(1–2):99–134.

Dongho Kim, Jin Hyung Kim, and Kee-Eung Kim. 2011. Robust performance evaluation of POMDP-based dialogue systems. *IEEE Transactions on Audio, Speech, and Language Processing*, 19(4):1029–1040.

Daejoong Kim, Jaedeug Choi, Kee-Eung Kim, Jungsu Lee, and Jinho Sohn. 2013. Engineering statistical dialog state trackers:a case study on DSTC. Technical Report CS-TR-2013-379, Department of Computer Science, KAIST.

Neville Mehta, Rakesh Gupta, Antoine Raux, Deepak Ramachandran, and Stefan Krawczyk. 2010. Probabilistic ontology trees for belief tracking in dialog systems. In *Proceedings of the 11th Annual Meeting of the Special Interest Group on Discourse and Dialogue (SIGDIAL)*, pages 37–46.

Nicholas Roy, Joelle Pineau, and Sebastian Thrun. 2000. Spoken dialogue management using probabilistic reasoning. In *Proceedings of the 38th Annual Meeting on Association for Computational Linguistics (ACL)*, pages 93–100.

Blaise Thomson and Steve Young. 2010. Bayesian update of dialogue state: A POMDP framework for spoken dialogue systems. *Computer Speech and Language*, 24(4):562–588.

Jason D. Williams and Steve Young. 2007. Partially observable Markov decision processes for spoken dialog systems. *Computer Speech and Language*, 21(2):393–422.

Jason Williams, Antoine Raux, Deepak Ramachandran, and Alan Black. 2013. The dialog state tracking challenge. In *Proceedings of the 14th Annual Meeting of the Special Interest Group on Discourse and Dialogue (SIGDIAL).*

Jason D. Williams. 2008. Exploiting the ASR N-best by tracking multiple dialog state hypotheses. In *Proceedings of the 9th Annual Conference of the International Speech Communication Association (INTERSPEECH)*, pages 191–194.

Jason D. Williams. 2010. Incremental partition recombination for efficient tracking of multiple dialog states. In *Proceedings of the IEEE International Conference on Acoustics Speech and Signal Processing (ICASSP)*, pages 5382–5385.

Steve Young, Milica Gašić, Simon Keizer, François Mairesse, Jost Schatzmann, Blaise Thomson, and Kai Yu. 2010. The hidden information state model: A practical framework for POMDP-based spoken dialogue management. *Computer Speech and Language*, 24(2):150–174.

Deep Neural Network Approach for the Dialog State Tracking Challenge

Matthew Henderson, Blaise Thomson and Steve Young
Department of Engineering,
University of Cambridge, U.K.
{mh521, brmt2, sjy}@eng.cam.ac.uk

Abstract

While belief tracking is known to be important in allowing statistical dialog systems to manage dialogs in a highly robust manner, until recently little attention has been given to analysing the behaviour of belief tracking techniques. The Dialogue State Tracking Challenge has allowed for such an analysis, comparing multiple belief tracking approaches on a shared task. Recent success in using deep learning for speech research motivates the Deep Neural Network approach presented here. The model parameters can be learnt by directly maximising the likelihood of the training data. The paper explores some aspects of the training, and the resulting tracker is found to perform competitively, particularly on a corpus of dialogs from a system not found in the training.

1 Introduction

Statistical dialog systems, in maintaining a distribution over multiple hypotheses of the true dialog state, are able to behave in a robust manner when faced with noisy conditions and ambiguity. Such systems rely on probabilistic tracking of dialog state, with improvements in the tracking quality being important in the system-wide performance in a dialog system (see e.g. Young et al. (2009)).

This paper presents a Deep Neural Network (DNN) approach for dialog state tracking which has been evaluated in the context of the Dialog State Tracking Challenge (DSTC) (Williams, 2012a; Williams et al., 2013)[1].

Using Deep Neural Networks allows for the modelling of complex interactions between arbitrary features of the dialog. This paper shows improvements in using deep networks over networks with fewer hidden layers. Recent developments in speech research have shown promising results using deep learning, motivating its use in the context of dialog (Hinton et al., 2012; Li et al., 2013).

This paper presents a technique which solves the task of outputting a sequence of probability distributions over an arbitrary number of possible values using a single neural network, by learning tied weights and using a form of sliding window. As the classification task is not split into multiple sub-tasks for a given slot, the log-likelihood of the tracker on training data can be directly maximised using gradient ascent techniques.

The domain of the DSTC is bus route information in the city of Pittsburgh, but the presented technique is easily transferable to new domains, with the learned models in fact being domain independent. No domain specific knowledge is used, and the classifier learned does not require knowledge of the set of possible values. The tracker performed highly competitively in the 'test4' dataset, which consists of data from a dialog system not seen in training. This suggests the model is capable of capturing the important aspects of dialog in a robust manner without overtuning to the specifics of a particular system.

Most attention in the dialog state belief tracking literature has been given to generative Bayesian network models (Paek and Horvitz, 2000; Thomson and Young, 2010). Few trackers have been published using discriminative classifiers, a notable exception being Bohus and Rudnicky (2006). An analysis by Williams (2012b) demonstrates how such generative models can in fact degrade belief tracking performance relative to a simple baseline. The successful use of discriminative models for belief tracking has recently been alluded to by Williams (2012a) and Li et al. (2013), and was a prominent theme in the results of the DSTC.

[1] More information on the DSTC is available at
http://research.microsoft.com/en-us/events/dstc/

2 The Dialog State Tracking Challenge

This section describes the domain and methodology of the Dialog State Tracking Challenge (DSTC). The Challenge uses data collected during the course of the Spoken Dialog Challenge (Black et al., 2011), in which participants implemented dialog systems to provide bus route information in the city of Pittsburgh. This provides a large corpus of real phonecalls from members of the public with real information needs.

Set	Number of calls	Notes
train1a	1013	Labelled training data
train1b&c	10619	Same dialog system as train1a, but unlabelled
train2	678	Similar to train1*
train3	779	Different participant to other train sets
test1	765	Very similar to train1* and train2
test2	983	Somewhat similar to train1* and train2
test3	1037	Very similar to train3
test4	451	System not found in any training set

Table 1: Summary of datasets in the DSTC

Table 1 summarises the data provided in the challenge. Labelled training sets provide labels for the caller's true goal in each dialog for 5 slots; route, from, to, date and time.

Participants in the DSTC were asked to report the results of their tracker on the four test sets in the form of a probability distribution over each slot for each turn. Performance was determined using a basket of metrics designed to capture different aspects of tracker behaviour Williams et al. (2013). These are discussed further in Section 4.

The DNN approach described here is referred to in the results of the DSTC as 'team1/entry1'.

3 Model

For a given slot s at turn t in a dialog, let $S_{t,\,s}$ denote the set of possible values for s which have occurred as hypotheses in the SLU for turns $\leq t$. A tracker must report a probability distribution over $S_{t,\,s} \cup \{\text{other}\}$ representing its belief of the user's true goal for the slot s. The probability of 'other' represents the probability that the user's true goal is yet to appear as an SLU hypothesis.

A neural network structure is defined which gives a discrete distribution over the $|S_{t,\,s}|+1$ values, taking the turns $\leq t$ as input.

Figure 1 illustrates the structure used in this approach. Feature functions $f_i\,(t,\,v)$ for $i = 1 \ldots M$ are defined which extract information about the value v from the SLU hypotheses and machine actions at turn t. A simple example would be $f_{\text{SLU}}\,(t,\,v)$, the SLU score that $s{=}v$ was informed at turn t. A list of the feature functions actually used in the trial is given in Section 3.1. For notational convenience, feature functions at negative t are defined to be zero:
$\forall i\, \forall v, t' < 0 \Rightarrow f_i\,(t',\,v) = 0$.

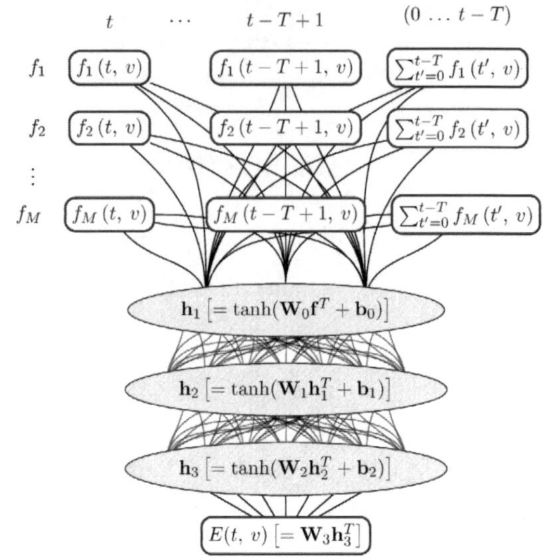

Figure 1: The Neural Network structure for computing $E\,(t,\,v) \in \mathbb{R}$ for each possible value v in the set $S_{t,\,s}$. The vector $\mathbf{f}$ is a concatenation of all the input nodes.

The input layer for a given value v is fixed in size by choosing a window size T, such that the feature functions are summed for turns $\leq t - T$. The input layer therefore consists of $(T \times M)$ input nodes set to $f_i\,(t',\,v)$ for $t' = t{-}T{+}1 \ldots t$ and $i = 1 \ldots M$, and M nodes set to $\sum_{t'=0}^{t-T} f_i\,(t',\,v)$ for $i = 1 \ldots M$.

A feed-forward structure of hidden layers is chosen, which reduces to a single node denoted $E\,(t,\,v)$. Each hidden layer introduces a weight matrix $\mathbf{W}_i$ and a bias vector $\mathbf{b}_i$ as parameters, which are independent of v but possibly trained separately for each s. The equations for each layer in the network are given in Figure 1.

The final distribution from the tracker is:

$$\begin{aligned} \mathbb{P}\,(s = v) &= {}^{e^{E(t,\,v)}}\!/_Z \\ \mathbb{P}\,(s \notin S_{t,\,s}) &= {}^{e^B}\!/_Z \\ Z &= e^B + \sum_{v' \in S_{t,\,s}} e^{E(t,\,v')} \end{aligned}$$

where B is a new parameter of the network, independent of v and possibly trained separately for each slot s.

3.1 Feature Functions

As explained above, a feature function is a function $f(t, v)$ which (for a given dialog) returns a real number representing some aspect of the turn t with respect to a possible value v. A turn consists of a machine action and the subsequent Spoken Language Understanding (SLU) results. The functions explored in this paper are listed below:

1. **SLU score**; the score assigned by the SLU to the user asserting $s{=}v$.
2. **Rank score**; $1/r$ where r is the rank of $s{=}v$ in the SLU n-best list, or 0 if it is not on the list.
3. **Affirm score**; SLU score for an `affirm` action if the system just confirmed $s{=}v$.
4. **Negate score**; as previous but with `negate`.
5. **Go back score**; the score assigned by the SLU to a `goback` action matching $s{=}v$.
6. **Implicit score**; $1-$ the score given in the SLU to a contradictory action if the system just implicitly confirmed $s{=}v$, otherwise 0.
7. **User act type**; a feature function for each possible user act type, giving the total score of the user act type in the SLU. Independent of s & v.
8. **Machine act type**; a feature function for each possible machine act type, giving the total number of machine acts with the type in the turn. Independent of s & v.
9. **Cant help**; 1 if the system just said that it cannot provide information on $s{=}v$, otherwise 0.
10. **Slot confirmed**; 1 if $s{=}v'$ was just confirmed by the system for some v', otherwise 0.
11. **Slot requested**; 1 if the value of s was just requested by the system, otherwise 0.
12. **Slot informed**; 1 if the system just gave information on a set of bus routes which included a specific value of s, otherwise 0.

4 Training

The derivatives of the training data likelihood with respect to all the parameters of the model can be computed using back propagation, i.e. the chain rule. Stochastic Gradient Descent with mini-batches is used to optimise the parameters by descending the negative log-likelihood in the direction of the derivatives (Bottou, 1991). Termination is triggered when performance on a held-out development set stops improving.

Each turn t and slot s in a dialog for which $|S_{t,s}| > 0$ provides a non-zero summand to the total log-likelihood of the training data. These instances may be split up by slot to train a separate network for each slot. Alternatively the data can be combined to learn a slot independent model. The best approach found was to train a slot independent model for a few epochs, and then switch to training one model per slot (see Section 4.4).

This section presents experiments varying the training of the model. In each case the parameters are trained using all of the labelled training sets. The results are reported for test4 since this system is not found in the training data. They are therefore unbiassed and avoid overtuning problems.

The ROC curves, accuracy, Mean Reciprocal Rank (MRR) and l2 norm of the tracker across all slots are reported here. (A full definition of the metrics is found in Williams et al. (2013).) These are computed throughout using statistics at every turn t where $|S_{t,s}| > 0$ (referred to as 'schedule 2' in the terminology of the challenge.) Table 2 and Figure 3 in Appendix A show these metrics. The 'Baseline' system ('team0/entry1' in the challenge), considers only the top SLU hypothesis so far, and assigns the SLU confidence score as the tracker probability. It does not therefore incorporate any belief tracking.

4.1 Window Size

The window size, T, was varied from 2 to 20. T must be selected so that it is large enough to capture enough of the sequence of the dialog, whilst ensuring sufficient data to train the weights connecting the inputs from the earlier turns. The results suggest that $T = 10$ is a good compromise.

4.2 Feature Set

The features enumerated in Section 3.1 were split into 4 sets. $F_1 = \{1\}$ includes only the SLU scores; $F_2 = \{1, ..., 6\}$ includes feature functions which depend on the user act and the value; $F_3 = \{1, ..., 8\}$ also includes the user act and machine act types; and finally $F_4 = \{1, ..., 12\}$ includes functions which depend on the system act and the value. The results clearly show that adding more and more features in this manner monotonically increases the performance of the tracker.

4.3 Structure

Some candidate structures of the hidden layers $(h_1, h_2, ...)$ were evaluated, including having no hidden layers at all, which gives a logistic regression model. In Table 2 the structure is represented as a list giving the size of each hidden layer in turn.

Three layers in a funnelling [20, 10, 2] configuration is found to outperform the other structures. The l2 norm is highly affected by the use of deeper network structure, suggesting it is most useful in tweaking the calibration of the confidence scores.

	ROC	Acc.	MRR	l2
Baseline				
	⊖	0.5841	0.7574	0.5728
Window Size				
$T = 2$	●	0.6679	0.8044	0.5405
5	△	0.6875	0.8191	**0.5164**
10	▲	**0.6922**	**0.8207**	0.5331
15	◇	0.6718	0.8107	0.5352
20	◆	0.6817	0.8190	0.5174
Feature Set				
F_1	●	0.5495	0.7364	0.6838
F_2	△	0.6585	0.7954	0.6631
F_3	▲	0.6823	0.8134	0.5525
F_4	⟠	**0.6922**	**0.8207**	**0.5331**
Structure				
[]	●	0.6751	0.8074	0.5658
[50]	△	0.6679	0.8046	0.5450
[20]	▲	0.6656	0.8060	0.5394
[50, 10]	⟠	0.6645	0.8045	0.5404
[20, 2]	◆	0.6543	0.7952	0.5514
[20, 10, 2]	⬠	**0.6922**	**0.8207**	**0.5331**
Initialisation				
Separate	●	0.6907	0.8206	0.5472
Single Model	△	0.6779	0.8111	0.5570
Shared Init.	▲	**0.6922**	**0.8207**	**0.5331**

Table 2: Results for variant trackers described in Section 4. By default, we train using the shared initialisation training method with $T = 10$, all the features enumerated in Section 3.1, and 3 hidden layers of size 20, 10 and 2.

4.4 Initialisation

The three methods of training alluded to in Section 4 were evaluated; training a model for each slot without sharing data between slots (*Separate*); training a single slot independent model (*Single Model*); and training for a few epochs a slot independent model, then using this to initialise the training of separate models (*Shared Initialisation*).

The method of shared initialisation appears to be the most effective, scoring the best on accuracy, MRR and l2. Training in this manner is particularly beneficial for slots which are under represented in the training data, as it initiates the parameters to sensible values before going on to specialise to that particular slot.

5 Performance in the DSTC

A DNN tracker was trained for entry in the DSTC. Training used T=10, the full feature set, a [20, 10, 2] hidden structure and the shared initialisation training method. Other parameters such as the learning rate and regularisation coefficient were tweaked by analysing performance on a held out subset of the training data. All the labelled training data available was used. The tracker is labelled as 'team1/entry1' in the DSTC.

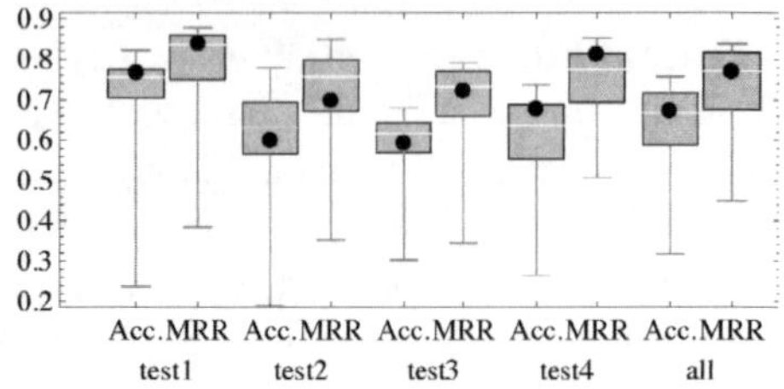

Figure 2: Accuracy and MRR of the 28 entries in the DSTC for all slots. Boxplots show minimum, maximum, quartiles and the median. Dark dot is location of the entry presented in this paper (DNN system).

The DNN approach performed competitively in the challenge. Figure 2 summarises the performance of the approach relative to all 28 entries in the DSTC. The results are less competitive in test2 and test3 but very strong in test1 and test4.

The performance in test4, dialogs with an unseen system, was probably the best because the chosen feature functions forced the learning of a general model which was not able to exploit the specifics of particular ASR+SLU configurations. Features which depend on the identity of the slot-values would have allowed better performance in test2 and test3, allowing the model to learn different behaviours for each value and learn typical confusions. It would also have been possible to exploit the *system-specific* data available in the challenge, such as more detailed confidence metrics from the ASR.

For a full comparison across the entries in the DSTC, see Williams et al. (2013). In making comparisons it should be noted that this team did not alter the training for different test sets, and submitted only one entry.

6 Conclusion

This paper has presented a discriminative approach for tracking the state of a dialog which takes advantage of deep learning. While simple Gradient Ascent training was tweaked in this paper using the 'Shared Initialisation' scheme, a possible promising future direction would be to further experiment with more recent methods for training deep structures e.g. initialising the networks layer by layer (Hinton et al., 2006).

Richer feature representations of the dialog contribute strongly to the performance of the model. The feature set presented is applicable across a broad range of slot-filling dialog domains, suggesting the possibility of using the models across domains without domain-specific training data.

A ROC Curves

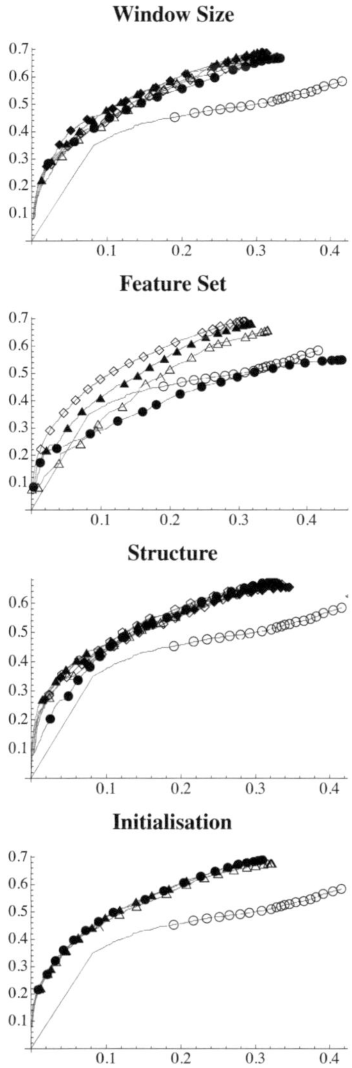

Figure 3: ROC (Receiver Operating Characteristic) Curves x-axis and y-axis are false acceptance and true acceptance respectively. Lines are annotated as per Table 2.

Acknowledgments

The authors would like to thank the organisers of the DSTC. The principal author was funded by a studentship from the EPSRC.

References

Alan W. Black, Susanne Burger, Alistair Conkie, Helen Wright Hastie, Simon Keizer, Oliver Lemon, Nicolas Merigaud, Gabriel Parent, Gabriel Schubiner, Blaise Thomson, Jason D. Williams, Kai Yu, Steve Young, and Maxine Eskenazi. 2011. Spoken dialog challenge 2010: Comparison of live and control test results. In *SigDIAL*.

Dan Bohus and Alex Rudnicky. 2006. A K-hypotheses+ Other Belief Updating Model. *Proc. of the AAAI Workshop on Statistical and Empirical Methods in Spoken Dialogue Systems*.

Léon Bottou. 1991. Stochastic gradient learning in neural networks. In *Proceedings of Neuro-Nîmes 91*, Nîmes, France. EC2.

Geoffrey Hinton, Simon Osindero, and Yee-Whye Teh. 2006. A Fast Learning Algorithm for Deep Belief Nets. *Neural computation*.

Geoffrey Hinton, Li Deng, Dong Yu, George Dahl, Abdel-rahman Mohamed, Navdeep Jaitly, Andrew Senior, Vincent Vanhoucke, Patrick Nguyen, Tara Sainath, and Brian Kingsbury. 2012. Deep neural networks for acoustic modeling in speech recognition. *Signal Processing Magazine*.

Deng Li, Jinyu Li, Jui-Ting Huang, Kaisheng Yao, Dong Yu, Frank Seide, Michael L Seltzer, Geoff Zweig, Xiaodong He, Jason D. Williams, Yifan Gong, and Alex Acero. 2013. Recent Advances in Deep Learning for Speech Research at Microsoft. In *ICASSP*.

Tim Paek and Eric Horvitz. 2000. Conversation as action under uncertainty. In *The Sixteenth Conference on Uncertainty in Artificial Intelligence*. Morgan Kaufmann.

Blaise Thomson and Steve Young. 2010. Bayesian update of dialogue state: A POMDP framework for spoken dialogue systems. *Computer Speech & Language*.

Jason D. Williams, Antoine Raux, Deepak Ramachandran, and Alan W. Black. 2013. The Dialogue State Tracking Challenge. In *SigDIAL*.

Jason D. Williams. 2012a. A belief tracking challenge task for spoken dialog systems. In *NAACL HLT 2012 Workshop on Future directions and needs in the Spoken Dialog Community: Tools and Data*. Association for Computational Linguistics.

Jason D. Williams. 2012b. Challenges and opportunities for state tracking in statistical spoken dialog systems: Results from two public deployments. *J. Sel. Topics Signal Processing*, 6(8):959–970.

Steve Young, Milica Gašić, Simon Keizer, François Mairesse, Jost Schatzmann, Blaise Thomson, and Kai Yu. 2009. The Hidden Information State model: A practical framework for POMDP-based spoken dialogue management. *Computer Speech & Language*.